MANAGEMENT INFORMATION SYSTEMS

MANAGING THE DIGITAL FIRM

D1216599

MANAGEMENT INFORMATION SYSTEMS

MANAGING THE DIGITAL FIRM

Eighth Edition

KENNETH C. LAUDON

New York University

JANE P. LAUDON

Azimuth Information Systems

PEARSON
Education

Credits and acknowledgments borrowed from other sources and reproduced, with permission, in this textbook appear on the appropriate page within the text.

Microsoft and Windows are registered trademarks of the Microsoft Corporation in the U.S.A. and other countries. Microsoft screen shots and icons reprinted with permission from the Microsoft Corporation. This book is not sponsored or endorsed by or affiliated with the Microsoft Corporation.

Copyright © 2004 by Pearson Education, Inc.
This edition is published by arrangement with Pearson Education, Inc.

This book is sold subject to the condition that it shall not, by way of trade or otherwise, be lent, resold, hired out, or otherwise circulated without the publisher's prior written consent in any form of binding or cover other than that in which it is published and without a similar condition including this condition being imposed on the subsequent purchaser and without limiting the rights under copyright reserved above, no part of this publication may be reproduced, stored in or introduced into a retrieval system, or transmitted in any form or by any means (electronic, mechanical, photocopying, recording or otherwise), without the prior written permission of both the copyright owner and the above-mentioned publisher of this book.

ISBN 81-297-0203-7

First Indian Reprint, 2004

This edition is manufactured in India and is authorized for sale only in India, Bangladesh, Pakistan, Nepal, Sri Lanka and the Maldives.

Published by Pearson Education (Singapore) Pte. Ltd., Indian Branch, 482 F.I.E. Patparganj, Delhi 110 092, India.

Printed in India by Baba Barkha Nath Printer.

FOR
ERICA AND ELISABETH

ABOUT THE AUTHORS

Kenneth C. Laudon is a Professor of Information Systems at New York University's Stern School of Business. He holds a B.A. in Economics from Stanford and a Ph.D. from Columbia University. He has authored twelve books dealing with electronic commerce, information systems, organizations, and society. Professor Laudon has also written over forty articles concerned with the social, organizational, and management impacts of information systems, privacy, ethics, and multimedia technology.

Professor Laudon's current research is on the planning and management of large-scale information systems and multimedia information technology. He has received grants from the National Science Foundation to study the evolution of national information systems at the Social Security Administration, the IRS, and the FBI. A part of this research is concerned with computer-related organizational and occupational changes in large organizations, changes in management ideology, changes in public policy, and understanding productivity change in the knowledge sector.

Ken Laudon has testified as an expert before the United States Congress. He has been a researcher and consultant to the Office of Technology Assessment (United States Congress) and to the Office of the President, several executive branch agencies, and Congressional Committees. Professor Laudon also acts as an in-house educator for several consulting firms and as a consultant on systems planning and strategy to several Fortune 500 firms. Ken has worked with the Concours Group to provide advice to firms developing enterprise systems.

At NYU's Stern School of Business, Professor Laudon teaches courses on Managing the Digital Firm, Information Technology and Corporate Strategy, and Electronic Commerce and Digital Markets. Ken Laudon's hobby is sailing and he is a veteran Newport to Bermuda Race captain.

Jane Price Laudon is a management consultant in the information systems area and the author of seven books. Her special interests include systems analysis, data management, MIS auditing, software evaluation, and teaching business professionals how to design and use information systems.

Jane received her Ph.D. from Columbia University, her M.A. from Harvard University, and her B.A. from Barnard College. She has taught at Columbia University and the New York University Graduate School of Business. She maintains a lifelong interest in Oriental languages and civilizations.

The Laudons have two daughters, Erica and Elisabeth.

Management Information Systems: Managing the Digital Firm reflects a deep understanding of MIS research and teaching as well as practical experience designing and building real-world systems.

BRIEF CONTENTS

CONTENTS

PREFACE

Management Information Systems: Managing the Digital Firm, Eighth Edition, is based on the premise that information systems knowledge is essential for creating competitive firms, managing global corporations, adding business value, and providing useful products and services to customers. This book provides an introduction to management information systems (MIS) that undergraduate and MBA students will find vital to their professional success.

DIGITAL INTEGRATION OF THE ENTERPRISE: THE EMERGING DIGITAL FIRM

The growth of the Internet, the globalization of trade, and the rise of information economies have recast the role of information systems (IS) in business and management. Internet technology is supplying the foundation for new business models, new business processes, and new ways of distributing knowledge. The wave of dot-com failures has not deterred companies from using Internet technology to drive their businesses. Companies are relying on Internet and networking technology to conduct more of their work electronically, seamlessly linking factories, offices, and sales forces around the globe. Leading-edge firms, such as Cisco Systems, Dell Computer, and Procter & Gamble, are extending these networks to suppliers, customers, and other groups outside the organization so they can react instantly to customer demands and market shifts. Cisco Systems corporate managers can use information systems to "virtually close" their books at any time, generating consolidated financial statements based on up-to-the-minute figures on orders, discounts, revenue, product margins, and staffing expenses. Executives can constantly analyze performance at all levels of the organization. This digital integration both within the firm and without, from the warehouse to the executive suite, from suppliers to customers, is changing how we organize and manage a business firm. Ultimately, these changes are leading to fully digital firms where all internal business processes and relationships with customers and suppliers are digitally enabled. In digital firms, information to support business decisions is available any time and anywhere in the organization. Accordingly, we have changed the subtitle of this text to *Managing the Digital Firm.*

NEW TO THE EIGHTH EDITION

This edition more fully explores the digital integration of the firm and the use of Internet technology to digitally enable business processes for electronic business and electronic commerce. It pays special attention to new applications and technologies that improve firms' relationships with customers and create additional value through closer collaboration with suppliers and other business partners. It also calls attention to the need to demonstrate the business value of information systems in the organization. The following features and content reflect this new direction.

EXPANDED COVERAGE OF ENTERPRISE APPLICATIONS FOR DIGITAL INTEGRATION

Systems for supply chain management, customer relationship management, and knowledge management, along with enterprise systems are the major enterprise applications that firms today are using to achieve digital integration. This edition more fully explores how companies are using enterprise applications to coordinate activities, decisions, and knowledge across the enterprise and to create value networks with customers and suppliers.

▌ Chapters 1 and 2 introduce the four enterprise applications.

▌ Chapter 2 provides detailed discussions of enterprise systems and systems for supply chain management and customer relationship management.

∎ Chapter 10 provides an expanded discussion of knowledge management systems.

∎ Other chapters of the text include additional discussion of enterprise applications. For example, Chapter 13 contains a section on the difficulties of implementing enterprise applications; Chapter 3 discusses value webs; Chapter 4 discusses how the Internet can be used for supply chain management; Chapter 11 details decision-support and executive support applications for customer relationship management, supply chain management, and enterprise-wide decision making; and Chapter 14 addresses the security issues raised by enterprise applications.

∎ Every chapter contains a "Window On" box or a case study devoted to enterprise applications, digital integration, or Internet technology.

∎ Chapters 6, 9, and 12 expand coverage of the information technology infrastructure for digital integration, including Web services, XML, enterprise application integration software, and Internet tools and services.

NEW FOCUS ON THE BUSINESS VALUE OF INFORMATION SYSTEMS.

New material in Chapter 1 alerts students to the need to demonstrate how information systems contribute to better management decisions and higher firm profitability. Chapter 13 ("Understanding the Business Value of Systems and Managing Change") has been reworked to incorporate the most up-to-date research in the MIS field on how to measure the business value of information systems.

Chapter 6 discusses the total cost of ownership of information technology assets and the question of whether firms should rent hardware, software, and other technologies from technology service providers or own them. Case studies, "Window On" boxes, and projects ask students to analyze how the systems that are being discussed provide value to the firm.

MORE ATTENTION TO FUNCTIONAL BUSINESS APPLICATIONS

The Make IT Your Business icon helps students identify functional business applications of chapter concepts. Students can immediately see how chapter material relates to business careers.

A new Make IT Your Business section concluding every chapter shows how the topics in each chapter specifically relate to the major functional areas of business: finance and accounting, human resources, manufacturing and production, and sales and marketing. This section also directs students to pages in the chapter on which functional business examples can be found. To further aid students in identifying these functional applications, icons are positioned adjacent to functional business examples in chapter opening vignettes, "Window On" boxes, chapter-ending cases, and in the body of the chapter itself.

MORE ACTIVE HANDS-ON LEARNING PROJECTS AND PROBLEM SOLVING

This edition is more problem-solving–and project-oriented than earlier editions. It includes new active hands-on learning projects that help students make text concepts more meaningful.

New Running Case for Real-World Problem Solving

We have added a new Running Case to this edition to provide students with additional opportunities for real-world problem solving. Students learn about a simulated company called Dirt Bikes USA where they can apply problem-solving skills to an ongoing real-world business scenario. Each chapter contains a project requiring students to use application software, Web tools, or analytical skills to solve a problem that Dirt Bikes USA has encountered. Examples of Running Case projects include:

▌ Analyzing Dirt Bikes' supply chain

▌ Identifying opportunities for knowledge management at Dirt Bikes

▌ Analyzing the return on investment for a new employee training system for Dirt Bikes

▌ Performing a competitive analysis for Dirt Bikes

▌ Redesigning Dirt Bikes' database for customer relationship management

The Running Case is briefly described in the Tools for Interactive Learning section. The complete Running Case project and any required files are on the Laudon Web site <www.prenhall.com/laudon> and the Laudon Multimedia CD-ROM.

New Improved Hands-On Application Software Exercises

Each chapter features more challenging hands-on Application Software Exercises where students can solve problems using spreadsheet, database, Web page development, or electronic presentation software. Some of these exercises require students to use these application software tools in conjunction with Web activities. The exercises have been redesigned so that they require more critical thinking than the exercises in previous editions and so that they are more relevant to the topics in each chapter. The new Application Software Exercises include business problems such as the following:

▌ Improving supply chain management (Chapter 2)

▌ Analyzing a dot-com business (Chapter 4)

▌ Designing a customer database for auto sales (Chapter 12)

▌ Capital budgeting for information technology investments (Chapter 13)

The Application Exercises are included in each chapter and on the Laudon Web site along with the required data files and complete instructions.

New E-Business Projects

New e-business projects have been added to the Tools for Interactive Learning sections concluding each chapter. Students can engage in e-business projects (such as redesigning business processes for supply chain management) as well as e-commerce projects at the Laudon Web site.

NEW LEADING-EDGE TOPICS

In addition to new coverage of enterprise applications and the business value of systems that we have already described, this edition includes up-to-date treatment of topics such as

▌ Web services (Chapter 12)

▌ Wi-Fi wireless networks (Chapter 8) and Wi-Fi security issues (Chapter 14)

▌ Utility computing model (Chapter 6)

▌ Peer-to-peer and grid computing (Chapter 6)

▌ Object-oriented modeling (Chapter 12) and Unified Modeling Language (UML) (Chapter 14)

▌ Business intelligence (Chapter 11)

▌ Collaborative commerce (Chapters 2 and 4)

▌ New Internet business models and private exchanges (Chapter 4)

INCREASED ATTENTION TO ETHICS AND PRIVACY

The chapter on ethics has been moved to an earlier part in the text to reflect its new importance. Chapter 5 provides a fresh, new look at ethical and social issues in the digital firm. E-commerce has made privacy and intellectual property protection among the most pressing ethical and social issues today—issues that managers and business professionals cannot afford to ignore.

NEW MANAGER'S TOOLKIT WITH HOW-TO CHECKLISTS FOR MANAGERS

Each chapter contains a MIS in Action: Manager's Toolkit section with a checklist to help students use chapter concepts to deal with specific business problems, such as how to integrate the Wireless Web into business strategy, how to benefit from customer relationship management, or how to develop a disaster recovery plan. Students will find these sections useful guides when they work on projects for the course and in their future jobs.

MORE APPLIED CHAPTER OBJECTIVES

We have redesigned the chapter learning objectives to make them more "student friendly." The objectives now list questions that each chapter answers in language that both IS professionals and general business managers can easily understand and each chapter summary shows how the chapter answers those questions. Examples of these new objectives are:

How can Internet technology support e-business and supply chain management?

What computer processing and storage capability does our organization need to handle its information and business transactions?

How should we manage our firm's hardware and software assets?

Students can see clearly how they can use this knowledge in their jobs.

BOOK OVERVIEW

Part One is concerned with the organizational foundations of systems, their strategic role, and the organizational and management changes driving electronic business and the emerging digital firm. It provides an extensive introduction to real-world systems, focusing on their relationships to organizations, management, business processes, and important ethical and social issues.

Part Two provides the technical foundation for understanding information systems. It describes the hardware, software, data storage, and telecommunications technologies that comprise the organization's information technology infrastructure. Part II concludes by describing how all of these information technologies work together with the Internet to create a new infrastructure for the digital integration of the enterprise.

Part Three describes the role of information systems in capturing and distributing organizational knowledge and in enhancing management decision making across the enterprise. It shows how knowledge management, work group collaboration, and individual and group decision making are supported by knowledge work, group collaboration, artificial intelligence, decision support, and executive support systems.

Part Four focuses on the process of building systems in organizations. It describes how companies use new information systems to redesign their organizations and business processes and the role of new technologies such as Web services for rapid application development and digital integration. Managers must understand the business value of systems and manage system-related change.

Part Five details issues in managing information systems, including international information systems. It details technologies, policies, and procedures that must be in place to assure quality, security, and control. Numerous examples are drawn from multinational systems and global business environments. Applications of Internet technology are integrated throughout the text and the entire learning package.

Chapter Outline

Each chapter contains the following:

- A detailed outline to provide an overview
- An opening vignette describing a real-world organization to establish the theme and importance of the chapter
- A diagram analyzing the opening vignette in terms of the management, organization, and technology model used throughout the text
- A series of chapter learning objectives in an easy-to-understand language for students
- Management Challenges related to the chapter theme
- A Manager's Toolkit with checklists to help students apply chapter concepts to specific business problems
- Marginal glosses of key terms in the text
- An Internet Connection icon directing students to related material on the Internet
- Make IT Your Business icons and discussions directing students to portions of the chapter dealing with functional business applications of chapter concepts
- A Management Wrap-Up tying together the key management, organization, and technology issues for the chapter, with questions for discussion
- A chapter summary keyed to the learning objectives
- A list of key terms that students can use to review concepts
- Review questions for students to test their comprehension of chapter material
- An Application Software Exercise requiring students to use application software tools to develop solutions to real-world business problems based on chapter concepts
- A group project to develop teamwork and presentation skills
- A Tools for Interactive Learning section showing specifically how the chapter can be integrated with the Laudon Web site and CD-ROM edition of the text
- A chapter-ending case study illustrating important themes

Companion Web Site
(WWW.PRENHALL.COM/LAUDON)

The text is accompanied by a Companion Web site that brings students a rich Web experience. The Laudon Web site <www.prenhall.com/laudon> provides a wide array of capabilities for interactive learning and management problem solving that have been carefully prepared for use with the text. They include the following.

Electronic Commerce and Electronic Business Projects

On the Laudon Web site are Web-based Electronic Commerce and Electronic Business Projects for each chapter. Students can use interactive software at various company Web sites and other Web tools to solve specific business problems related to chapter concepts. These projects encourage critical thinking skills as students explore business resources on the Internet and take learning MIS on the Internet to the next level.

Students are presented with a problem to develop a savings and asset allocation plan for college tuition and retirement. To obtain the information required for the solution, they can input data online and use the interactive software at this Web site to perform the required calculations or analysis.

Student responses to questions are automatically graded and can be e-mailed to the instructor.

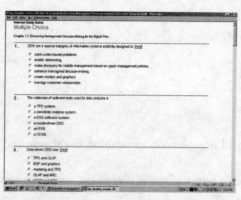

INTERACTIVE STUDY GUIDE

Each chapter of the text features an Interactive Study Guide to help students review skills and test their mastery of chapter concepts with a series of multiple-choice, true—false, and essay questions.

RUNNING CASE

The complete Running Case for each chapter and any files required by the chapter project are displayed on the Laudon Web site.

INTERNET CONNECTIONS

Internet Connections noted by marginal icons in the chapter direct students to exercises and projects on the Laudon Web site that are related to organizations and concepts in the chapter.

MANAGEMENT DECISION PROBLEMS

A Management Decision Problem for each chapter can be found on the Laudon Web site. Management Decision Problems provide opportunities to apply chapter concepts to additional real-world, management decision-making scenarios. These problems can be used for practical group learning or individual learning both in and outside of the classroom. The problems require students to make decisions based on real-world MIS issues such as the following:

- Analyzing enterprise process integration (Chapter 2)
- Monitoring how much time employees spend on the Web (Chapter 5)
- Creating company-wide data standards (Chapter 7)

ADDITIONAL CASE STUDIES

The Web site contains additional case studies with hyperlinks to the Web sites of the organizations discussed.

INTERNATIONAL RESOURCES

Links to Web sites of non-U.S. companies are provided for users interested in international material.

UNIQUE FEATURES OF THIS TEXT FOR THE STUDENT

Management Information Systems: Managing the Digital Firm, Eighth Edition, has many unique features designed to create an active, dynamic learning environment.

A special diagram accompanying each chapter-opening vignette graphically illustrates how management, organization, and technology elements work together to create an information system solution to the business challenges discussed in the vignette.

INTEGRATED FRAMEWORK FOR DESCRIBING AND ANALYZING INFORMATION SYSTEMS

An integrated framework portrays information systems as being composed of management, organization, and technology elements. This framework is used throughout the text to describe and analyze information systems and information system problems.

REAL-WORLD EXAMPLES

Real-world examples drawn from business and public organizations are used throughout the text to illustrate text concepts. More than 100 companies in the United States and nearly 100 organizations in Canada, Europe, Australia, Asia, Latin America, and the Middle East are discussed.

Each chapter opens with a vignette illustrating the themes of the chapter and showing how a real-world organization meets a business challenge using information systems. Each chapter also contains two "Window On" boxes (Window on Management, Window on Organizations, or Window on Technology) that present real-world examples illustrating the management, organization, and technology issues in the chapter. Each "Window On" box concludes with a section called "To Think About" containing questions for students to consider in applying chapter concepts to management problem solving. The themes for each box are as follows:

Window on Management

Management problems raised by systems and their solution; management strategies and plans; careers and experiences of managers using systems.

Window on Technology

Hardware, software, telecommunications, data storage, standards, and systems-building methodologies.

Window on Organizations

Activities of private and public organizations using information systems; experiences of people working with systems.

MANAGEMENT WRAP-UP OVERVIEWS OF KEY ISSUES

Management Wrap-Up sections at the end of each chapter summarize key issues using the authors' management, organization, and technology framework for analyzing information systems.

MANAGEMENT WRAP-UP

Managers need to carefully review their strategy and business models to determine how to maximize the benefits of Internet technology. Managers should anticipate making organizational changes to take advantage of this technology, including new business processes, new relationships with the firm's value partners and customers, and even new business designs. Determining how and where to digitally enable the enterprise with Internet technology is a key management decision.

The Internet can dramatically reduce transaction and agency costs and is fueling new business models. By using the Internet and other networks for electronic commerce, organizations can exchange purchase and sale transactions directly with customers and suppliers, eliminating inefficient intermediaries. Organizational processes can be streamlined by using the Internet and intranets to make communication and coordination more efficient. To take advantage of these opportunities, organizational processes must be redesigned.

Internet technology has created a universal computing platform that has become the primary infrastructure for electronic commerce, electronic business, and the emerging digital firm. Web-based applications integrating voice, data, video, and audio are providing new products, services, and tools for communicating with employees and customers. Intranets enable companies to make information flow between disparate systems, business processes, and parts of the organization.

For Discussion:
1. How does the Internet change consumer and supplier relationships?
2. The Internet may not make corporations obsolete, but they will have to change their business models. Do you agree? Why or why not?

The Management Wrap-Up provides a quick overview of the key issues in each chapter, reinforcing the authors' management, organization, and technology framework.

A TRULY INTERNATIONAL PERSPECTIVE

A full chapter (Chapter 15) is devoted to managing international information systems. All chapters of the text are illustrated with real-world examples from nearly 100 corporations in Canada, Europe, Asia, Latin America, Africa, Australia, and the Middle East. Each chapter contains at least one "Window On" box, case study, or opening vignette drawn from a non-U.S. firm, and often more. The text concludes with four major international case studies contributed by leading MIS experts in Canada, Europe, and Hong Kong: V. Joseph Compeau and Professor Deborah Compeau, University of Western Ontario (Canada); Gerhard Schwabe, University of Zurich (Switzerland); Donald A. Marchand and Katarina Paddack, International Institute for Management Development (Switzerland); and Ali Farhoomand, Dennis Kira, Amir Hoosain, and Shamza Khan, The University of Hong Kong (Hong Kong).

PEDAGOGY TO PROMOTE ACTIVE LEARNING AND MANAGEMENT PROBLEM SOLVING

In addition to the Running Case, Web projects and hands-on Application Exercises, *Management Information Systems: Managing the Digital Firm, Eighth Edition,* contains many other features that encourage students to learn actively and to engage in management problem solving.

Comprehensive Projects

A longer comprehensive project concludes each major part of the text. These five projects require students to apply text concepts to demanding problems that they might encounter as firms become more digitally integrated and Internet enabled. The projects include the following:

- Analyzing business processes for an enterprise system (Part I Project)
- Creating a new Internet business (Part II Project)
- Designing an enterprise information portal (Part III Project)
- Redesigning business processes (Part IV Project)
- Analyzing the total cost of ownership (TCO) for a Web Site (Part V Project)

Case Studies

Each chapter concludes with a case study based on a real-world organization. These cases help students synthesize chapter concepts and apply this new knowledge to concrete problems and scenarios. Major international case studies and electronic case studies at the Laudon Web site <www.prenhall.com/laudon> provide additional opportunities for management problem solving.

Management Challenges Section

Each chapter begins with several challenges relating to the chapter topic that managers are likely to encounter. These challenges are multifaceted and sometimes pose dilemmas. They make excellent springboards for class discussion. Some of the Management Challenges include finding the right Internet business model, overcoming the organizational obstacles to building a database environment, and measuring system costs and benefits when they are difficult to quantify.

Group Projects

At the end of each chapter is a group project that encourages students to develop teamwork and oral and written presentation skills. The group projects have been enhanced to make more use of the Internet. For instance, students might be asked to work in small groups to evaluate the Web sites of two competing businesses or to develop a corporate ethics code on privacy that considers e-mail privacy and the monitoring of employees using networks.

TOOLS FOR INTERACTIVE LEARNING: TECHNOLOGY INTEGRATED WITH CONTENT

An interactive CD-ROM multimedia version of the text is available with the text. In addition to the full text and bullet text summaries by chapter, the CD-ROM features audio/video overviews explaining key concepts, online quizzes, hyperlinks to the exercises on the Laudon Web site, the complete Running Case with required files, technology updates, and more. Students can use the CD-ROM edition as an interactive supplement or as an alternative to the traditional text.

The Tools for Interactive Learning section concluding each chapter shows students how they can extend their knowledge of each chapter with projects and exercises on the Laudon Web site and the CD-ROM multimedia edition.

Students can reinforce and extend their knowledge of chapter concepts using the glossaries and other interactive resources in the CD-ROM edition.

TOOLS FOR INTERACTIVE LEARNING

■ **INTERNET CONNECTION**

The Internet Connection for this chapter will take you to several Web sites where you can complete an exercise to evaluate several virtual storefront businesses.

■ **INTERACTIVE STUDY GUIDE**

You can use the Interactive Study Guide to test your knowledge of the topics in this chapter and get instant feedback where you need more practice.

■ **RUNNING CASE**

The Running Case provides an opportunity for you to develop an e-commerce strategy and Web site for Dirt Bikes USA. You can find a complete description of this project on the Laudon Web site for Chapter 4 and on the Multimedia Edition CD-ROM.

■ **ELECTRONIC COMMERCE PROJECT**

At the Laudon Web site for Chapter 4, you will find an Electronic Commerce project where you can build an electronic commerce storefront.

■ **MANAGEMENT DECISION PROBLEM**

At the Laudon Web site for Chapter 4, you will find an Management Decision Problem on measuring the effectiveness of Web advertising.

■ **CD-ROM**

If you use the Multimedia Edition CD-ROM with this chapter, you can find an audio overview of the major themes of this chapter, a video clip on Danka Office Imaging's Web-based business, and bullet text summarizing the key points of the chapter.

Students and instructors can see at a glance exactly how the Internet Connections, Electronic Business and Electronic Commerce Projects, and Running Case can be used to enhance student learning for each chapter. Students can also see immediately how the chapter can be used in conjunction with the optional CD-ROM edition.

INSTRUCTIONAL SUPPORT MATERIALS

INSTRUCTOR'S RESOURCE CD-ROM (0-13-101503-6)

Most of the support materials described in the following section are conveniently available for adopters of the Instructor's Resource CD-ROM. The CD includes the Instructor's Resource Manual, Test Item File, Windows PH Test Manager, PowerPoint slides, and the helpful lecture tool "Image Library."

IMAGE LIBRARY (ON INSTRUCTOR'S RESOURCE CD-ROM)

The Image Library is an impressive resource to help instructors create vibrant lecture presentations. Almost every figure and photo in the text is provided and organized by chapter for convenience. These images and lecture notes can be easily imported into Microsoft PowerPoint to create new presentations or to add to existing ones.

INSTRUCTOR'S MANUAL (ON INSTRUCTOR'S RESOURCE CD-ROM)

The Instructor's Manual, by Dr. M. Lisa Miller of the University of Central Oklahoma, not only features answers to review, discussion, case study, and group project questions but also an in-depth lecture outline, teaching objectives, key terms, and teaching suggestions. This supplement can be downloaded from the secure faculty section of the Laudon Web site <www.prenhall.com/laudon> and is also available on the Instructor's Resource CD-ROM.

TEST ITEM FILE (ON INSTRUCTOR'S RESOURCE CD-ROM)

The Test Item File, by Professor Betty Spaulding, is a comprehensive collection of true–false, multiple-choice, fill-in-the-blank, and essay questions. The questions are rated by difficulty level and the answers are referenced by section. An electronic version of the Test Item File is available as the Windows PH Test Manager on the Instructor's Resource CD-ROM.

POWERPOINT SLIDES (ON WEB AND INSTRUCTOR'S RESOURCE CD-ROM)

Electronic color slides were created by Azimuth Interactive, Inc., and are available in Microsoft PowerPoint 2000. The slides illuminate and build on key concepts in the text. Both students and faculty can download the PowerPoint slides from the Web site, and they are also provided on the Instructor's Resource CD-ROM.

VIDEOS

Prentice Hall MIS Video, Volume 1 (0-13-027199-3)

The first video in the Prentice Hall MIS Video Library includes custom clips created exclusively for Prentice Hall featuring real companies, such as Andersen Consulting, Lands' End, Lotus Development Corporation, Oracle Corporation, and Pillsbury Company.

Prentice Hall MIS Video, Volume 2 (0-13-101500-1)

Video clips are provided to adopters to enhance class discussion and projects. These clips highlight real-world corporations and organizations and illustrate key concepts found in the text.

WEB SITE

The *Eighth Edition* is supported by an excellent Web site at <www.prenhall.com/laudon> that truly reinforces and enhances text material with the complete Running Case, Electronic Commerce and Electronic Business Projects, hands-on Application Exercises, Management Decision Problems, Internet Exercises, an Interactive Study Guide, international resources, additional case studies, and PowerPoint slides. The Web site also features a secure password-protected faculty area from which instructors can download the Instructor's Manual, and suggested answers to the Running Case, Internet Connections, and Electronic Business and Electronic Commerce Projects. The site has an improved online syllabus tool to help professors add their own personal syllabi to the site in minutes. Please see the complete description discussed earlier in the preface.

ONLINE COURSE

WebCT www.prenhall.com/webct

Gold Level Customer Support, available exclusively to adopters of Prentice Hall courses, is provided free of charge on adoption and provides priority assistance, training discounts, and dedicated technical support.

BlackBoard www.prenhall.com/blackboard

Prentice Hall's abundant online content, combined with Blackboard's popular tools and interface, result in robust Web-based courses that are easy to implement, manage, and use—taking your courses to new heights in student interaction and learning.

CourseCompass www.prenhall.com/coursecompass

CourseCompass is a dynamic, interactive, online course management tool powered exclusively for Pearson Education by Blackboard. This exciting product allows you to teach market-leading Pearson Education content in an easy-to-use customizable format.

TUTORIAL SOFTWARE

For instructors seeking application software support to use with this text, Prentice Hall is pleased to offer the PH Train IT CD-ROM and the Web-delivered PH Train & Assess IT for Office 2000 and XP. These exciting tutorial and assessment products are fully certified up to the expert level of the Microsoft Office User Specialist (MOUS) Certification Program. These items are not available as stand-alone items but can be packaged with the *Eighth Edition* at an additional charge. Please go to <www.prenhall.com/phit> for an online demonstration of these products or contact your local Prentice Hall representative for more details.

PACKAGING OPTIONS

With *MIS Cases: Decision Making with Application Software,* by M. Lisa Miller, students will prepare to make management level decisions with the most complete and interactive management information systems casebook on the market! This casebook contains 20 cases rated on a 1 to 5 level of difficulty. The reader will be required to use spreadsheets, databases, and Web page development tools to find solutions to the problems in the cases. Tutorials on these tools are included at <www.prenhall.com/miller> to ensure success. Many cases will ask the reader to prepare written and oral presentations of their solutions, just as if the reader was making these decisions at an actual firm. The casebook can be packaged with the *Eighth Edition* text at an additional charge.

What a difference a year or two makes! MIS graduates, for the first time in many years, are having to battle for employment. Using real data and recent research, Fran Quittel, noted career columnist for *Computerworld,* identifies the best entry-level jobs and career paths for 2002–2003 in *The Prentice Hall IT Career Guide.* She also provides strategies on how to network, intern, and interview. Filled with current and pragmatic advice, this guide can benefit the brand new IT job seeker! This guide is available free of charge when packaged with *Management Information Systems: Managing the Digital Firm, Eighth Edition.*

For more details on these items or for additional packaging options, please contact your local Prentice Hall representative.

SOFTWARE CASES

A series of optional management software cases, *Solve it! Management Problem Solving with PC Software,* has been developed to support the text. *Solve it!* consists of 10 spreadsheet cases, 10 database cases, and 6 Internet projects drawn from real-world businesses, plus a data disk with the files associated with the cases. The cases are graduated in difficulty. The casebook contains complete tutorial documentation showing how to use spreadsheet, database, and Web browser software to solve the problems. A new version of *Solve it!* with all new cases is published every year. *Solve it!* must be adopted for an entire class. It can be purchased directly from the supplier, Azimuth Interactive Corporation, 23 North Division Street, Peekskill, New York, 10566 (telephone: 800-416-6786 extension 14; Web site: <www.mysolveit.com>.

ACKNOWLEDGMENTS

The production of any book involves valued contributions from a number of persons. We would like to thank all of our editors for encouragement, insight, and strong support for many years. David Alexander is a truly outstanding editor who guided the development of this edition. We remain grateful to Natalie Anderson for her support of this project. We thank Sharon K. Turkovich, senior marketing manager, for her superb marketing work.

We praise Kyle Hannon for her role in managing this project and for her supervision of ancillary material preparation. Audri Anna Bazlen and Ann Imhof must be commended for production/manufacturing of this text under an extraordinarily ambitious schedule. We thank Shirley Webster for her energetic photo research work.

Our special thanks go to Barb Ellestad, M. Lisa Miller, and Betty Spaulding for their work on supporting materials.

We remain deeply indebted to Marshall R. Kaplan for his invaluable assistance in the preparation of the text. Jiri Rodovsky and Todd Traver provided additional suggestions for improvements.

The Stern School of Business at New York University and the Information Systems Department provided a very special learning environment—one in which we and others could rethink the field of MIS. Special thanks to Professors Vasant Dhar and Alex Tuzhilin for providing critical feedback and support where deserved. Professor William H. Starbuck of the Management Department at New York University provided valuable comments and insights in our joint graduate seminar on organization theory.

Professor Edward Stohr of Stevens Institute of Technology, Professors Al Croker and Michael Palley of Baruch College and New York University, and Professor Thomas J. Housel of the Naval Postgraduate School provided additional suggestions for improvement. We continue to remember the late Professor James Clifford of the Stern School as a wonderful friend and colleague who also made valuable recommendations for improving our discussion of files and databases.

One of our goals was to write a book that was authoritative, synthesized diverse views in the MIS literature, and helped define a common academic field. A large number of leading scholars in the field were contacted and assisted us in this effort. Reviewers and consultants for *Management Information Systems: Managing the Digital Firm, Eighth Edition,* are listed in the back endpapers of the book. We thank them for their contributions. Consultants for the *Eighth Edition* include Lynn Collen, St. Cloud State University; John Dalphin, SUNY Potsdam; Rassule Hadidi, University of Illinois at Springfield; Stephen Klein, Ramapo College; Cenk Kocas, Michigan State University; Susan K. Lippert, George Washington University; Ronald E. McGaughey, Arkansas Technical University; Roger McHaney, Kansas State University; Leonard Presby, William Patterson University; Mary E. Rasley, Lehigh Carbon Community College; Paula Ruby, Arkansas State University; and Pam Taylor, University of Tennessee at Chattanooga.

It is our hope that this group endeavor contributes to a shared vision and understanding of the MIS field.

—K.C.L.

—J.P.L.

PART I

ORGANIZATIONS, MANAGEMENT, AND THE NETWORKED ENTERPRISE

CHAPTER 1

MANAGING THE DIGITAL FIRM

As a manager, you'll need to know how information systems can make businesses more competitive, efficient, and profitable. After reading this chapter, you will be able to answer the following questions:

1. *What is the role of information systems in today's competitive business environment?*
2. *What exactly is an information system? What do managers need to know about information systems?*
3. *How are information systems transforming organizations and management?*
4. *How have the Internet and Internet technology transformed business?*
5. *What are the major management challenges to building and using information systems?*

Toyota's Grand Vision

Building only cars that customers order and building them in record time has been every auto maker's dream. Now, it appears that Toyota Motor Corporation is coming close to making that dream come true. In March 2002, Toyota signed an agreement to purchase $800 million to $1.2 billion in software, hardware, and services from France's Dassault Systems S.A. and IBM to link Toyota's 56 plants in 25 countries and its 1000-plus suppliers. This technology will enable Toyota to model every aspect of car production, including the automobile's look, the parts that make it run, the sequence in which components are assembled, and the design of the factory itself.

Dassault will supply Toyota with its 3D Product Lifecycle Management suite, which includes design collaboration, product-life-cycle management (PLM), and production-support applications. IBM will supply hardware, services, and additional software to link this system with other systems in the company. The new system will replace Toyota's own internally developed computer-aided design (CAD) and product-data management systems, which have been highly praised, but could not perform the functions Toyota needs to stay ahead of the curve in automobile manufacturing.

Dassault's design-collaboration software, called Catia, will enable Toyota's designers to collaborate with each other and with far-flung suppliers that are also design partners. They will be able to construct 3-D designs on the computer and

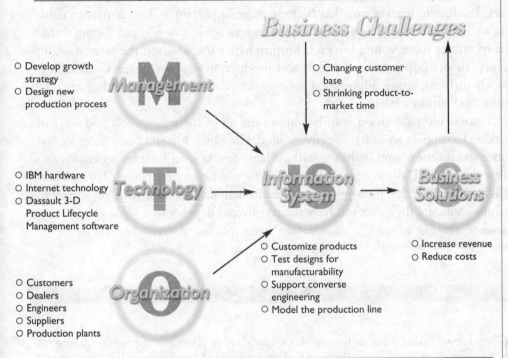

Business Challenges

- Develop growth strategy
- Design new production process

Management

- Changing customer base
- Shrinking product-to-market time

- IBM hardware
- Internet technology
- Dassault 3-D Product Lifecycle Management software

Technology

Information System

Business Solutions

- Customers
- Dealers
- Engineers
- Suppliers
- Production plants

Organization

- Customize products
- Test designs for manufacturability
- Support converse engineering
- Model the production line

- Increase revenue
- Reduce costs

then test these digital designs for "manufacturability"—determining whether the design of individual parts and assemblies of parts makes them easy to install as the car is being assembled. Toyota will be the first auto manufacturer to test designs for manufacturability on a global basis. Other manufacturers can only use such tools for isolated processes, such as testing the fit of precision parts in a critical assembly.

Toyota also plans to use the Catia tools for converse engineering: Instead of having engineers decide down to the last details of a car's design before sending a design prototype to production, many parts, such as alternators, that do not affect the car's styling will be created later in the process by production engineers. Rather than have concept and design drive manufacturing and other downstream processes, Toyota prefers using manufacturing efficiency to drive concept and design. Catia will also enable Toyota to reuse designs for parts, such as a hood. The car maker's engineers will be able to search a library of existing hood designs, use the software to change the shape and contours of a design, and automatically test the new design for manufacturability. Toyota can then use the hood's current supplier for the new part.

Dassault's production-support software, called Delmia, will let separate engineering teams use design and manufacturability data to create a plan that specifies the order in which parts are to be installed in a car as it moves down a production line. Toyota ultimately hopes to use that plan to digitally model the entire factory environment, specifying what's done at each step in the production process; which tools, supplies, and parts are required; the number of

3

people stationed at each assembly stop; and the tasks they will perform. Toyota has already started using Delmia to model the production line in a few of its plants.

Once the design, production plan, and factory-floor strategy fit together, Toyota can transmit the specifications for the new car model to its production and supply-chain management systems. Integration of digital design and digital manufacturing will enable Toyota to bring new models to market in 10 months instead of several years. Product-to-market time has become more important as Toyota tries to culti-vate a younger market. The average Toyota buyer's age is now 45, and Toyota would like to attract more young buyers who purchase cars based on the latest fashion trends. Toyota hopes its new design and production support systems will help it quickly turn marketing information about young consumers into cars that can take to the road within weeks.

Toyota's ultimate vision is to be able to use all of these new tools and ways of working to support an order-to-delivery model in which it could build a car to cus-tomer specifications and deliver it within days. Toyota used Internet technology to create the Dealer Daily system that links Toyota and Lexus dealers with Toyota's new design and production management system to help dealers work with customers to custom-configure their cars and have them delivered days later.

Sources: Steve Konicki, "Revving Up," *Information Week*, April 1, 2002, and "Toyota Paves the Road to Customization," *Information Week*, June 3, 2002.

The changes taking place at Toyota Motor Corporation exemplify the transformation of business firms throughout the world as they rebuild themselves as fully digital firms. Such digital firms use the Internet and networking technology to make data flow seamlessly among different parts of the organization; streamline the flow of work; and create electronic links with customers, suppliers, and other organizations.

All types of businesses, both large and small, are using information systems, networks, and Internet technology to conduct more of their business electronically, achieving new lev-els of efficiency, competitiveness, and profitability. This chapter starts our investigation of information systems and organizations by describing information systems from both techni-cal and behavioral perspectives and by surveying the changes they are bringing to organiza-tions and management.

1.1   WHY INFORMATION SYSTEMS?

Today it is widely recognized that information systems knowledge is essential for managers because most organizations need information systems to survive and prosper. Information systems can help companies extend their reach to faraway locations, offer new products and services, reshape jobs and work flows, and perhaps profoundly change the way they conduct business.

THE COMPETITIVE BUSINESS ENVIRONMENT AND THE EMERGING DIGITAL FIRM

Four powerful worldwide changes have altered the business environment. The first change is the emergence and strengthening of the global economy. The second change is the trans-formation of industrial economies and societies into knowledge- and information-based service economies. The third is the transformation of the business enterprise. The fourth is the emergence of the digital firm. These changes in the business environment and climate, summarized in Table 1-1, pose a number of new challenges to business firms and their management.

TABLE 1-1	THE CHANGING CONTEMPORARY BUSINESS ENVIRONMENT

Globalization	Transformation of the Enterprise
Management and control in a global marketplace	Flattening
Competition in world markets	Decentralization
Global work groups	Flexibility
Global delivery systems	Location independence
	Low transaction and coordination costs
Transformation of Industrial Economies	Empowerment
Knowledge- and information-based economies	Collaborative work and teamwork
New products and services	
Knowledge: a central productive and strategic asset	**Emergence of the Digital Firm**
Time-based competition	Digitally enabled relationships with customers, suppliers, and employees
Shorter product life	Core business processes accomplished via digital networks
Turbulent environment	Digital management of key corporate assets
Limited employee knowledge base	Rapid sensing and responding to environmental changes

Emergence of the Global Economy

A growing percentage of the American economy—and other advanced industrial economies in Europe and Asia—depends on imports and exports. Foreign trade, both exports and imports, accounts for more than 25 percent of the goods and services produced in the United States, and even more in countries such as Japan and Germany. Companies are also distributing core business functions in product design, manufacturing, finance, and customer support to locations in other countries where the work can be performed more cost effectively. The success of firms today and in the future depends on their ability to operate globally.

Today, information systems provide the communication and analytic power that firms need for conducting trade and managing businesses on a global scale. Controlling the far-flung global corporation—communicating with distributors and suppliers, operating 24 hours a day in different national environments, coordinating global work teams, and servicing local and international reporting needs—is a major business challenge that requires powerful information system responses.

Globalization and information technology also bring new threats to domestic business firms: Because of global communication and management systems, customers now can shop in a worldwide marketplace, obtaining price and quality information reliably 24 hours a day. To become competitive participants in international markets, firms need powerful information and communication systems.

Transformation of Industrial Economies

The United States, Japan, Germany, and other major industrial powers are being transformed from industrial economies to knowledge- and information-based service economies, whereas manufacturing has been moving to low-wage countries. In a knowledge- and information-based economy, knowledge and information are key ingredients in creating wealth.

The knowledge and information revolution began at the turn of the twentieth century and has gradually accelerated. By 1976, the number of U.S. white-collar workers employed in offices surpassed the number of farm workers, service workers, and blue-collar workers employed in manufacturing (see Figure 1-1). Today, most people no longer work on farms or in factories but instead are found in sales, education, healthcare, banks, insurance firms, and law firms; they also provide business services like copying, computer programming, or making deliveries. These jobs primarily involve working with, distributing, or creating new knowledge and information. In fact, knowledge and information work now accounts for a

Figure 1-1 The growth of the information economy. Since the beginning of the twentieth century, the United States has experienced a steady decline in the number of farm workers and blue-collar workers who are employed in factories. At the same time, the country is experiencing a rise in the number of white-collar workers who produce economic value by using knowledge and information.
Sources: U.S. Department of Commerce, Bureau of the Census, *Statistical Abstract of the United States, 2001,* Table 593; and *Historical Statistics of the United States, Colonial Times to 1970,* Vol. 1, Series D, pp. 182–232.

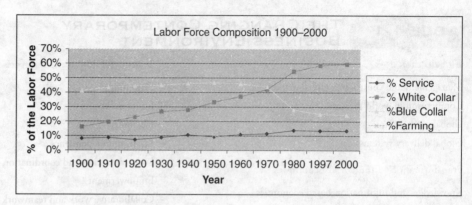

knowledge- and information-intense products

Products that require a great deal of learning and knowledge to produce.

digital firm

Organization where nearly all significant business processes and relationships with customers, suppliers, and employees are digitally enabled, and key corporate assets are managed through digital means.

significant 60 percent of the American gross national product and nearly 55 percent of the labor force.

Knowledge and information are becoming the foundation for many new services and products. **Knowledge- and information-intense products** such as computer games require a great deal of knowledge to produce. Entire new information-based services have sprung up, such as Lexis, Dow Jones News Service, and America Online. These fields are employing millions of people. Knowledge is used more intensively in the production of traditional products as well. In the automobile industry, as shown in the chapter-opening description of Toyota, both design and production now rely heavily on knowledge and information technology.

In a knowledge- and information-based economy, information technology and systems take on great importance. Knowledge-based products and services of great economic value, such as credit cards, overnight package delivery, and worldwide reservation systems, are based on new information technologies. Information technology constitutes more than 70 percent of the invested capital in service industries such as finance, insurance, and real estate.

Across all industries, information and the technology that delivers it have become critical, strategic assets for business firms and their managers (Leonard-Barton, 1995). Information systems are needed to optimize the flow of information and knowledge within the organization and to help management maximize the firm's knowledge resources. Because employees' productivity depends on the quality of the systems serving them, management decisions about information technology are critically important to the firm's prosperity and survival.

Transformation of the Business Enterprise

There has been a transformation in the possibilities for organizing and managing the business enterprise. Some firms have begun to take advantage of these new possibilities.

The traditional business firm was—and still is—a hierarchical, centralized, structured arrangement of specialists that typically relied on a fixed set of standard operating procedures to deliver a mass-produced product (or service). The new style of business firm is a flattened (less hierarchical), decentralized, flexible arrangement of generalists who rely on nearly instant information to deliver mass-customized products and services uniquely suited to specific markets or customers.

The traditional management group relied—and still relies—on formal plans, a rigid division of labor, and formal rules. The new manager relies on informal commitments and networks to establish goals (rather than formal planning), a flexible arrangement of teams and individuals working in task forces, and a customer orientation to achieve coordination among employees. The new manager appeals to the knowledge, learning, and decision making of individual employees to ensure proper operation of the firm. Once again, information technology makes this style of management possible.

The Emerging Digital Firm

Intensive use of information technology in business firms since the mid-1990s, coupled with equally significant organizational redesign, has created the conditions for a new phenomenon in industrial society—the fully digital firm. The **digital firm** can be defined along several dimensions. A digital firm is one where nearly all of the organization's *significant business relationships* with customers, suppliers, and employees are digitally enabled and mediated.

Core business processes are accomplished through digital networks spanning the entire organization or linking multiple organizations. **Business processes** refer to the unique manner in which work is organized, coordinated, and focused to produce a valuable product or service. Developing a new product, generating and fulfilling an order, or hiring an employee are examples of business processes, and the way organizations accomplish their business processes can be a source of competitive strength. (A detailed discussion of business processes can be found in Chapter 2.) *Key corporate assets*—intellectual property, core competencies, and financial and human assets—are managed through digital means. In a digital firm, any piece of information required to support key business decisions is available at anytime and anywhere in the firm. Digital firms *sense and respond* to their environments far more rapidly than traditional firms, giving them more flexibility to survive in turbulent times. Digital firms offer extraordinary opportunities for more global organization and management. By digitally enabling and streamlining their work, digital firms have the potential to achieve unprecedented levels of profitability and competitiveness.

Digital firms are distinguished from traditional firms by their near total reliance on a set of information technologies to organize and manage. For managers of digital firms, information technology is not simply a useful handmaiden, an enabler, but rather it is the core of the business and a primary management tool.

There are four major systems that help define the digital firm and that we describe in detail throughout the book. **Supply chain management systems** seek to automate the relationship between suppliers and the firm to optimize the planning, sourcing, manufacturing, and delivery of products and services. **Customer relationship management systems** attempt to develop a coherent, integrated view of all the relationships a firm maintains with its customers. **Enterprise systems** create an integrated enterprise-wide information system to coordinate key internal processes of the firm, integrating data from manufacturing and distribution, sales, finance, and human resources. Finally, **knowledge management systems** seek to create, capture, store, and disseminate firm expertise and knowledge. Collectively, these four systems represent the areas where corporations are digitally integrating their information flows and making major information system investments. You will learn more about these systems in subsequent chapters, and they receive special attention in Chapters 2 and 10.

A few firms, such as Cisco Systems or Dell Computer Corporation, are close to becoming fully digital firms, using the Internet to drive every aspect of their business. In most other companies, a fully digital firm is still more vision than reality but this vision is driving them toward digital integration. Despite the recent decline in technology investments and Internet-only dot-com businesses, firms are continuing to invest heavily in information systems that integrate internal business processes and build closer links with suppliers and customers.

business processes
The unique ways in which organizations coordinate and organize work activities, information, and knowledge to produce a product or service.

supply chain management systems
Information systems that automate the relationship between a firm and its suppliers in order to optimize the planning, sourcing, manufacturing, and delivery of products and services.

customer relationship management systems
Information systems for creating a coherent integrated view of all of the relationships a firm maintains with its customers

enterprise systems
Integrated enterprise-wide information systems that coordinate key internal processes of the firm, integrating data from manufacturing and distribution, finance, sales, and human resources.

knowledge management systems
Systems that support the creation, capture, storage, and dissemination of firm expertise and knowledge.

Toyota Motor Corporation is using new software tools and Internet technology to drive its processes for designing and manufacturing automobiles and to integrate them with customers and suppliers. The company is moving toward a digital firm organization.

information system

Interrelated components working together to collect, process, store, and disseminate information to support decision making, coordination, control, analysis, and visualization in an organization.

information

Data that have been shaped into a form that is meaningful and useful to human beings.

data

Streams of raw facts representing events occurring in organizations or the physical environment before they have been organized and arranged into a form that people can understand and use.

input

The capture or collection of raw data from within the organization or from its external environment for processing in an information system.

processing

The conversion, manipulation, and analysis of raw input into a form that is more meaningful to humans.

Toyota Motor Corporation, described in the chapter-opening vignette, is moving toward a digital firm organization as it electronically integrates its key business processes with customers and suppliers.

WHAT IS AN INFORMATION SYSTEM?

An **information system** can be defined technically as a set of interrelated components that collect (or retrieve), process, store, and distribute information to support decision making and control in an organization. In addition to supporting decision making, coordination, and control, information systems may also help managers and workers analyze problems, visualize complex subjects, and create new products.

Information systems contain information about significant people, places, and things within the organization or in the environment surrounding it. By **information** we mean data that have been shaped into a form that is meaningful and useful to human beings. **Data,** in contrast, are streams of raw facts representing events occurring in organizations or the physical environment before they have been organized and arranged into a form that people can understand and use.

A brief example contrasting information to data may prove useful. Supermarket checkout counters ring up millions of pieces of data, such as product identification numbers or the cost of each item sold. Such pieces of data can be totaled and analyzed to provide meaningful information such as the total number of bottles of dish detergent sold at a particular store, which brands of dish detergent were selling the most rapidly at that store or sales territory, or the total amount spent on that brand of dish detergent at that store or sales region (see Figure 1-2).

Three activities in an information system produce the information that organizations need to make decisions, control operations, analyze problems, and create new products or services. These activities are input, processing, and output (see Figure 1-3). **Input** captures or collects raw data from within the organization or from its external environment. **Processing** converts this raw input into a more meaningful form. **Output** transfers the processed information to the people who will use it or to the activities for which it will be used. Information systems also require **feedback,** which is output that is returned to appropriate members of the organization to help them evaluate or correct the input stage.

In Toyota Motor Corporation's system for transmitting designs to production, the raw input would most likely consist of the part identification number, the part description, the cost of the part, the identification number and name of the part supplier, and perhaps a graphic rep-

331 Brite Dish Soap 1.29		
863 BL Hill Coffee 4.69		Sales Region: Northwest
173 Meow Cat .79		Store: Superstore #122
331 Brite Dish Soap 1.29		
663 Cntry Ham 3.29		
524 Fiery Mustard 1.49		
113 Ginger Root .85		
331 Brite Dish Soap 1.29		

ITEM NO.	DESCRIPTION	UNITS SOLD
331	Brite Dish Soap	7156

YTD SALES
$ 9,231.24

Data   **Information**

Figure 1-2   Data and information. Raw data from a supermarket checkout counter can be processed and organized in order to produce meaningful information such as the total unit sales of dish detergent or the total sales revenue from dish detergent for a specific store or sales territory.

ENVIRONMENT

Suppliers   Customers

ORGANIZATION

INFORMATION SYSTEM

| Input | Processing
Classify
Arrange
Calculate | Output |

Feedback

Regulatory   Stockholders   Competitors
Agencies

Figure 1-3 Functions of an information system. An information system contains information about an organization and its surrounding environment. Three basic activities—input, processing, and output—produce the information organizations need. Feedback is output returned to appropriate people or activities in the organization to evaluate and refine the input. Environmental factors such as customers, suppliers, competitors, stockholders, and regulatory agencies interact with the organization and its information systems.

resentation of that component. A computer stores these data and processes them by analyzing how a part's shape and size might change if engineers changed a few specifications, the impact of using that part on the cost of producing a car, and whether it would be easy to assemble in Toyota cars. The system would display graphics showing changes made to the part designs and reports indicating the cost and manufacturability of these parts, which become the system outputs. The system thus provides meaningful information, such as what parts are supplied by what manufacturers, the cost of these parts, what designs could be reused, and whether a specific part would fit well in a Toyota car.

Our interest in this book is in formal, organizational **computer-based information systems (CBIS)** like those designed and used by Toyota Motor Corporation and its customers, suppliers, and employees. **Formal systems** rest on accepted and fixed definitions of data and procedures for collecting, storing, processing, disseminating, and using these data. The formal systems we describe in this text are structured; that is, they operate in conformity with predefined rules that are relatively fixed and not easily changed. For instance, Toyota's systems would require a unique number for identifying each part, a description of that part, the identification of the part supplier, and the cost of the part.

Informal information systems (such as office gossip networks) rely, by contrast, on unstated rules of behavior. There is no agreement on what is information, or on how it will be stored and processed. Such informal systems are essential for the life of an organization, but an analysis of their qualities is beyond the scope of this text.

Formal information systems can be either computer-based or manual. Manual systems use paper-and-pencil technology. These manual systems serve important needs, but they too are not the subject of this text. Computer-based information systems, in contrast, rely on computer hardware and software technology to process and disseminate information. From this point on, when we use the term *information systems,* we are referring to computer-based information systems—formal organizational systems that rely on computer technology. The Window on Technology describes some of the typical technologies used in computer-based information systems today.

Although computer-based information systems use computer technology to process raw data into meaningful information, there is a sharp distinction between a computer and a computer program on the one hand, and an information system on the other. Electronic computers and related software programs are the technical foundation, the tools and materials, of modern information systems. Computers provide the equipment for storing and processing information. Computer programs, or software, are sets of operating instructions that direct and control computer processing. Knowing how computers and computer programs work is important in designing solutions to organizational problems,

output
The distribution of processed information to the people who will use it or to the activities for which it will be used.

feedback
Output that is returned to the appropriate members of the organization to help them evaluate or correct input.

computer-based information systems (CBIS)
Information systems that rely on computer hardware and software for processing and disseminating information.

formal system
System resting on accepted and fixed definitions of data and procedures, operating with predefined rules.

UPS COMPETES GLOBALLY WITH INFORMATION TECHNOLOGY

United Parcel Service, the world's largest air and ground package-distribution company, started out in 1907 in a closet-size basement office. Jim Casey and Claude Ryan—two teenagers from Seattle with two bicycles and one phone—promised the "best service and lowest rates." UPS has used this formula successfully for more than 90 years.

Today UPS delivers more than 13.6 million parcels and documents each day to the United States and to more than 200 other countries and territories. The firm has been able to maintain its leadership in small-package delivery services in the face of stiff competition from FedEx and Airborne Express by investing heavily in advanced information technology. During the past decade, UPS has poured more than $1 billion a year into technology and systems to boost customer service while keeping costs low and streamlining its overall operations.

Using a handheld computer called a Delivery Information Acquisition Device (DIAD), UPS drivers automatically capture customers' signatures along with pickup, delivery, and time-card information. The drivers then place the DIAD into their truck's vehicle adapter, an information-transmitting device that is connected to the cellular telephone network. (Drivers may also transmit and receive information using an internal radio in the DIAD.) Package tracking information is then transmitted to UPS's computer network for storage and processing in UPS's main computers in Mahwah, New Jersey, and Alpharetta, Georgia. From there, the information can be accessed worldwide to provide proof of delivery to the customer or respond to customer queries.

Through its automated package tracking system, UPS can monitor packages throughout the delivery process. At various points along the route from sender to receiver, a barcode device scans shipping information on the package label; the information is then fed into the central computer. Customer service representatives can check the status of any package from desktop computers linked to the central computers and are able to respond immediately to inquiries from customers.

UPS customers can also access this information from the company's Web site using their own computers or wireless devices such as pagers and cell phones.

Anyone with a package to ship can access the UPS Web site to track packages, check delivery routes, calculate shipping rates, determine time in transit, and schedule a pickup. Businesses anywhere can use the Web site to arrange UPS shipments and bill the shipments to the company's UPS account number or to a credit card. The data collected at the UPS Web site are transmitted to the UPS central computer and then back to the customer after processing. UPS also provides tools that enable customers such Cisco Systems to embed UPS functions, such as tracking and cost calculations into their own Web sites so that they can track shipments without visiting the UPS site.

UPS recently created a UPS Supply Chain Solutions division that provides a complete bundle of standardized services to subscribing companies at a fraction of what it would cost to build their own systems and infrastructure. These services include supply chain design and management, freight forwarding, customs brokerage, mail services, multimodal transportation, and financial services in addition to logistics services.

To Think About: What are the inputs, processing, and outputs of UPS's package tracking system? What technologies are used? How are these technologies related to UPS's business strategy? How do they provide value for the company? What would happen if these technologies were not available?

Sources: Dave Clarke Mora, "UPS CEO Mike Eskew, Thinking at the Speed of Business," *Profit,* May 2002; "Eskew: UPS Targeting Supply Chain," *JoC Online,* May 7, 2002; "UPS Logistics Interview with Tim Geiken, UPS Vice President of E-Commerce Marketing," *eyefortransport,* March 22, 2002, www.eyefortransport. com; Brent Adams, "UPS Logistics Provides Variety of Services at Local Center," *Business First,* April 19, 2002; Samuel Greengard, "United Parcel Service: Ahead of Time," *IQ Magazine,* May/June 2001; and Rick Brooks, "Got Mail?" *Wall Street Journal,* June 22, 2001; and Rick Brooks, "Outside the Box," *Wall Street Journal E-Commerce section,* February 12, 2001.

TECHNOLOGY

but computers are only part of an information system. A house is an appropriate analogy. Houses are built with hammers, nails, and wood, but these do not make a house. The architecture, design, setting, landscaping, and all of the decisions that lead to the creation of these features are part of the house and are crucial for solving the problem of putting a roof over one's head. Computers and programs are the hammer, nails, and lumber of CBIS, but alone they cannot produce the information a particular organization needs. To understand information systems, one must understand the problems they are designed to solve, their architectural and design elements, and the organizational processes that lead to these solutions.

A BUSINESS PERSPECTIVE ON INFORMATION SYSTEMS

Businesses are not in the business of processing information for its own sake. Instead they process information in order to improve organizational performance and produce profits.

From a business perspective, an information system is an important instrument for creating value for the organization. There are many ways in which information systems can contribute to firm value, including increasing the firm's return on its investments (accounting ROI), enhancing the company's strategic position, or increasing the market value of the firm's stock. (More detail on alternative ways to measure the business value of information systems can be found in Chapters 3 and 13). Information processing activities support management decision making, enhance the execution of business processes *and as a result* increase business value. For example, the information system for analyzing supermarket checkout data illustrated in Figure 1-2 can increase firm profitability by helping managers make better decisions about which products to stock and promote in retail supermarkets.

Using a handheld computer called a Delivery Information Acquisition Device (DIAD), UPS drivers automatically capture customers' signatures along with pickup, delivery and time-card information. UPS information systems use these data to track packages while they are being transported.

Every business has an *information value chain*, illustrated in Figure 1-4, in which raw information is systematically acquired, and then transformed through various stages that add value to that information. Immediately we can see then that the value of an information system to a business, as well as the decision to invest in any new information system, is in large part determined by the extent to which the system will lead to better management decisions, more efficient business processes, and higher firm profitability. Although there are other reasons why systems are built, their primary purpose is to contribute to corporate value.

The business perspective calls attention to the organizational and managerial nature of information systems. An information system also represents an organizational and

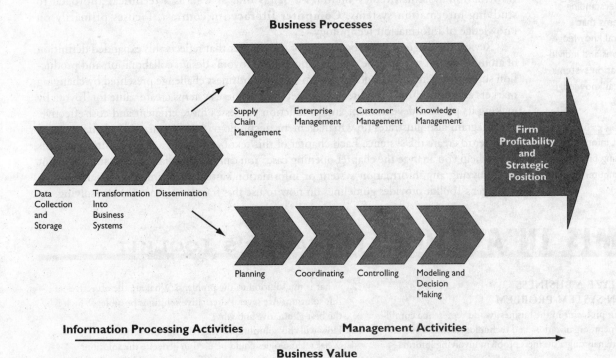

Business Processes

Data Collection and Storage → Transformation Into Business Systems → Dissemination

Supply Chain Management · Enterprise Management · Customer Management · Knowledge Management

Planning · Coordinating · Controlling · Modeling and Decision Making

Firm Profitability and Strategic Position

Information Processing Activities   **Management Activities**

Business Value

Figure 1.4 The business information value chain. From a business perspective, information systems are part of a series of value-adding activities for acquiring, transforming, and distributing information that managers can use to improve decision making, enhance organizational performance, and ultimately increase firm profitability.

Figure 1-5 Information systems are more than computers. Using information systems effectively requires an understanding of the organization, management, and information technology shaping the systems. All information systems can be described as organizational and management solutions to challenges posed by the environment that will help create value for the firm.

management solution, based on information technology, to a challenge posed by the environment. To fully understand information systems, a manager must understand the broader organization, management, and information technology dimensions of systems (see Figure 1-5) and their power to provide solutions to challenges and problems in the business environment. We refer to this broader understanding of information systems, which encompasses an understanding of the management and organizational dimensions of systems as well as the technical dimensions of systems as **information systems literacy.** Information systems literacy includes a behavioral as well as a technical approach to studying information systems. **Computer literacy,** in contrast, focuses primarily on knowledge of information technology.

Review the diagram at the beginning of the chapter that reflects this expanded definition of an information system. The diagram shows how Toyota's design collaboration and production support systems and its dealer system solve the business challenge presented by changing markets and diminishing product-to-market cycles. These systems create value for Toyota by making its product development and production processes more efficient and cost-effective. The diagram also illustrates how management, technology, and organization elements work together to create the systems. Each chapter of this text begins with a diagram similar to this one to help you analyze the chapter opening case. You can use this diagram as a starting point for analyzing any information system or information system problem you encounter. The Manager's Toolkit provides guidelines on how to use this framework for problem solving.

information systems literacy
Broad-based understanding of information systems that includes behavioral knowledge about organizations and individuals using information systems as well as technical knowledge about computers.

computer literacy
Knowledge about information technology, focusing on understanding how computer-based technologies work.

MIS IN ACTION: MANAGER'S TOOLKIT

HOW TO ANALYZE A BUSINESS INFORMATION SYSTEM PROBLEM

Information system problems in the business world represent a combination of management, organization, and technology issues. Here is a six-step process for analyzing a business problem involving information systems.

1. Identify the problem. What kind of problem is it? Is it a management problem, an organizational problem, a technology problem, or a combination of these? What are the management, organization, and technology issues that contributed to the problem?

2. What is the solution to the problem? What are the objectives of this solution? Are several alternative solutions possible? Which is the best alternative and why?

3. How will this solution provide value for the firm?

4. What technologies could be used to generate the solution?

5. What changes to organizational processes will be required by the solution?

6. What management policy will be required to implement the solution?

TABLE 1-2   MAJOR BUSINESS FUNCTIONS

Function	Purpose
Sales and marketing	Selling the organization's products and services
Manufacturing and production	Producing products and services
Finance	Managing the organization's financial assets (cash, stocks, bonds, etc.)
Accounting	Maintaining the organization's financial records (receipts, disbursements, paychecks, etc.); accounting for the flow of funds
Human resources	Attracting, developing, and maintaining the organization's labor force; maintaining employee records

Organizations

Information systems are an integral part of organizations. Indeed, for some companies, such as credit reporting firms, without an information system, there would be no business. The key elements of an organization are its people, structure, operating procedures, politics, and culture. We introduce these components of organizations here and describe them in greater detail in Chapter 3. Organizations are composed of different levels and specialties. Their structures reveal a clear-cut division of labor. Experts are employed and trained for different functions, The major **business functions,** or specialized tasks performed by business organizations, consist of sales and marketing, manufacturing, finance, accounting, and human resources (see Table 1-2).

Chapter 2 provides more detail on these business functions and the ways in which they are supported by information systems. Each chapter of this text now concludes with a *Make IT Your Business* section showing how chapter topics relate to each of these functional areas. The section also provides page numbers in each chapter where these functional examples can be found. Icons placed next to these functional business examples in the chapter-opening vignettes, Window On boxes, chapter ending case studies, and in the body of the chapters will help you identify them.

An organization coordinates work through a structured hierarchy and formal, standard operating procedures. The hierarchy arranges people in a pyramid structure of rising authority and responsibility. The upper levels of the hierarchy consist of managerial, professional, and technical employees, whereas the lower levels consist of operational personnel.

Standard operating procedures (SOPs) are formal rules that have been developed over a long time for accomplishing tasks. These rules guide employees in a variety of procedures, from writing an invoice to responding to customer complaints. Most procedures are formalized and written down, but others are informal work practices, such as a requirement to return telephone calls from co-workers or customers that are not formally documented. The firm's business processes, which we defined earlier, are based on its standard operating procedures and many business processes and SOPs are incorporated into information systems, such as how to pay a supplier or how to correct an erroneous bill.

Organizations require many different kinds of skills and people. In addition to managers, **knowledge workers** (such as engineers, architects, or scientists) design products or services and create new knowledge and **data workers** (such as secretaries, bookkeepers, or clerks) process the organization's paperwork. **Production or service workers** (such as machinists, assemblers, or packers) actually produce the organization's products or services.

Each organization has a unique culture, or fundamental set of assumptions, values, and ways of doing things, that has been accepted by most of its members. Parts of an organization's culture can always be found embedded in its information systems. For instance, the United Parcel Service's concern with placing service to the customer first is an aspect of its organizational culture that can be found in the company's package tracking systems.

Different levels and specialties in an organization create different interests and points of view. These views often conflict. Conflict is the basis for organizational politics. Information systems come out of this cauldron of differing perspectives, conflicts, compromises, and

---

business functions

Specialized tasks performed in a business organization, including manufacturing and production, sales and marketing, finance, accounting, and human resources.

standard operating procedures (SOPs)

Formal rules for accomplishing tasks that have been developed to cope with expected situations.

knowledge workers

People such as engineers or architects who design products or services and create knowledge for the organization.

data workers

People such as secretaries or bookkeepers who process the organization's paperwork.

production or service workers

People who actually produce the products or services of the organization.

agreements that are a natural part of all organizations. In Chapter 3 we examine these features of organizations in greater detail.

Management

Management's job is to make sense out of the many situations faced by organizations, make decisions, and formulate action plans to solve organizational problems. Managers perceive business challenges in the environment, they set the organizational strategy for responding and allocate the human and financial resources to achieve the strategy and coordinate the work. Throughout, they must exercise responsible leadership. The business information systems described in this book reflect the hopes, dreams, and realities of real-world managers.

But managers must do more than manage what already exists. They must also create new products and services and even re-create the organization from time to time. A substantial part of management responsibility is creative work driven by new knowledge and information. Information technology can play a powerful role in redirecting and redesigning the organization. Chapter 3 describes managers' activities and management decision making in detail.

It is important to note that managerial roles and decisions vary at different levels of the organization. **Senior managers** make long-range strategic decisions about what products and services to produce. **Middle managers** carry out the programs and plans of senior management. **Operational managers** are responsible for monitoring the firm's daily activities. All levels of management are expected to be creative, to develop novel solutions to a broad range of problems. Each level of management has different information needs and information system requirements.

Technology

Information technology is one of many tools managers use to cope with change. **Computer hardware** is the physical equipment used for input, processing, and output activities in an information system. It consists of the following: the computer processing unit; various input, output, and storage devices; and physical media to link these devices together. Chapter 6 describes computer hardware in greater detail.

Computer software consists of the detailed preprogrammed instructions that control and coordinate the computer hardware components in an information system. Chapter 6 explains the importance of computer software in information systems.

Storage technology includes both the physical media for storing data, such as magnetic or optical disk or tape, and the software governing the organization of data on these physical media. More detail on physical storage media can be found in Chapter 6, whereas Chapter 7 covers data organization and access methods.

Communications technology, consisting of both physical devices and software, links the various pieces of hardware and transfers data from one physical location to another. Computers and communications equipment can be connected in networks for sharing voice, data, images, sound, or even video. A **network** links two or more computers to share data or resources such as a printer. Chapters 8 and 9 provide more details on communications and networking technology and issues.

All of these technologies represent resources that can be shared throughout the organization and constitute the firm's **information technology (IT) infrastructure.** The IT infrastructure provides the foundation or platform on which the firm can build its specific information systems. Each organization must carefully design and manage its information technology infrastructure so that it has the set of technology services it needs for the work it wants to accomplish with information systems. Chapters 6 through 9 of this text examine each major technology component of information technology infrastructure and show how they all work together to create the technology platform for the organization.

Let us return to UPS's package tracking system in the Window on Technology and identify the organization, management, and technology elements. The organization element anchors the package tracking system in UPS's sales and production functions (the main product of UPS is a service—package delivery). It specifies the required procedures for identifying packages with both sender and recipient information, taking inventory, tracking the packages en route, and providing package status reports for UPS customers and customer

---

senior managers
People occupying the topmost hierarchy in an organization who are responsible for making long-range decisions.

middle managers
People in the middle of the organizational hierarchy who are responsible for carrying out the plans and goals of senior management.

operational managers
People who monitor the day-to-day activities of the organization.

computer hardware
Physical equipment used for input, processing, and output activities in an information system.

computer software
Detailed, preprogrammed instructions that control and coordinate the work of computer hardware components in an information system.

storage technology
Physical media and software governing the storage and organization of data for use in an information system.

communications technology
Physical devices and software that link various computer hardware components and transfer data from one physical location to another.

network
The linking of two or more computers to share data or resources, such as a printer.

information technology (IT) infrastructure
Computer hardware, software, data and storage technology, and networks providing a portfolio of shared information technology resources for the organization.

service representatives. The system must also provide information to satisfy the needs of managers and workers. UPS drivers need to be trained in both package pickup and delivery procedures and in how to use the package tracking system so that they can work efficiently and effectively. UPS customers may need some training to use UPS in-house package tracking software or the UPS Web site. UPS's management is responsible for monitoring service levels and costs and for promoting the company's strategy of combining low-cost and superior service. Management decided to use automation to increase the ease of sending a package via UPS and of checking its delivery status, thereby reducing delivery costs and increasing sales revenues. The technology supporting this system consists of handheld computers, barcode scanners, wired and wireless communications networks, desktop computers, UPS's central computer, storage technology for the package delivery data, UPS in-house package tracking software, and software to access the World Wide Web. The result is an information system solution to the business challenge of providing a high level of service with low prices in the face of mounting competition.

1.2 CONTEMPORARY APPROACHES TO INFORMATION SYSTEMS

Multiple perspectives on information systems show that the study of information systems is a multidisciplinary field. No single theory or perspective dominates. Figure 1-6 illustrates the major disciplines that contribute problems, issues, and solutions in the study of information systems. In general, the field can be divided into technical and behavioral approaches. Information systems are sociotechnical systems. Though they are composed of machines, devices, and "hard" physical technology, they require substantial social, organizational, and intellectual investments to make them work properly.

TECHNICAL APPROACH

The technical approach to information systems emphasizes mathematically based models to study information systems, as well as the physical technology and formal capabilities of these systems. The disciplines that contribute to the technical approach are computer science, management science, and operations research. Computer science is concerned with establishing theories of computability, methods of computation, and methods of efficient data storage and access. Management science emphasizes the development of models for decision-making and management practices. Operations research focuses on mathematical techniques for optimizing selected parameters of organizations such as transportation, inventory control, and transaction costs.

BEHAVIORAL APPROACH

An important part of the information systems field is concerned with behavioral issues that arise in the development and long-term maintenance of information systems. Issues such as

Figure 1-6 Contemporary approaches to information systems. The study of information systems deals with issues and insights contributed from technical and behavioral disciplines.

strategic business integration, design, implementation, utilization, and management cannot be explored usefully with the models used in the technical approach. Other behavioral disciplines contribute important concepts and methods. For instance, sociologists study information systems with an eye toward how groups and organizations shape the development of systems and also how systems affect individuals, groups, and organizations. Psychologists study information systems with an interest in how human decision makers perceive and use formal information. Economists study information systems with an interest in what impact systems have on control and cost structures within the firm and within markets.

The behavioral approach does not ignore technology. Indeed, information systems technology is often the stimulus for a behavioral problem or issue. But the focus of this approach is generally not on technical solutions. Instead it concentrates on changes in attitudes, management and organizational policy, and behavior.

APPROACH OF THIS TEXT: SOCIOTECHNICAL SYSTEMS

management information systems (MIS)

The study of information systems focusing on their use in business and management.

The study of **management information systems (MIS)** arose in the 1970s to focus on computer-based information systems aimed at managers (Davis and Olson, 1985). MIS combines the theoretical work of computer science, management science, and operations research with a practical orientation toward developing system solutions to real-world problems and managing information technology resources. It also pays attention to behavioral issues surrounding the development, use, and impact of information systems raised by sociology, economics, and psychology. The study of information systems has just started to influence other disciplines (Baskerville and Myers, 2002) through concepts such as the information processing view of the firm.

Our experience as academics and practitioners leads us to believe that no single perspective effectively captures the reality of information systems. Problems with systems—and their solutions—are rarely all technical or all behavioral. Our best advice to students is to understand the perspectives of all disciplines. Indeed, the challenge and excitement of the information systems field is that it requires an appreciation and tolerance of many different approaches.

Adopting a sociotechnical systems perspective helps to avoid a purely technological approach to information systems. For instance, the fact that information technology is rapidly declining in cost and growing in power does not necessarily or easily translate into productivity enhancement or bottom-line profits.

In this book, we stress the need to optimize the system's performance as a whole. Both the technical and behavioral components need attention. This means that technology must be changed and designed in such a way as to fit organizational and individual needs. At times, the technology may have to be "de-optimized" to accomplish this fit. Organizations and individuals must also be changed through training, learning, and planned organizational change in order to allow the technology to operate and prosper (see, for example, Liker et al., 1987). People and organizations change to take advantage of new information technology. Figure 1-7 illustrates this process of mutual adjustment in a sociotechnical system.

Figure 1-7 A sociotechnical perspective on information systems. In a sociotechnical perspective, the performance of a system is optimized when both the technology and the organization mutually adjust to one another until a satisfactory fit is obtained.

1.3 TOWARD THE DIGITAL FIRM: THE NEW ROLE OF INFORMATION SYSTEMS IN ORGANIZATIONS

Managers cannot ignore information systems because they play such a critical role in contemporary organizations. Today's systems directly affect how managers decide, plan, and manage their employees; and, they increasingly shape what, where, when, and how products are produced. Therefore, responsibility for systems cannot be delegated to technical decision makers.

THE WIDENING SCOPE OF INFORMATION SYSTEMS

Figure 1-8 illustrates the new relationship between organizations and information systems. There is a growing interdependence between business strategy, rules, and procedures on the one hand, and information systems software, hardware, databases, and telecommunications on the other. A change in any of these components often requires changes in other components. This relationship becomes critical when management plans for the future. What a business would like to do in five years often depends on what its systems will be able to do. Increasing market share, becoming the high-quality or low-cost producer, developing new products, and increasing employee productivity depend more and more on the kinds and quality of information systems in the organization.

A second change in the relationship between information systems and organizations results from the growing reach and scope of system projects and applications. Building and managing systems today involves a much larger part of the organization than it did in the past. As firms become more like "digital firms," the system enterprise extends to customers, vendors, and even industry competitors (see Figure 1-9). Where early systems produced largely technical changes that affected only a few people in the firm, contemporary systems have been bringing about managerial changes (who has what information about whom, when, and how often) and institutional "core" changes (what products and services are produced, under what conditions, and by whom). As companies move toward digital firm organizations, nearly all the firm's managers and employees—as well as customers and vendors—participate in a variety of firm systems, tied together by a digital information web. For instance, what a customer does on a firm's Web site can trigger an employee to make an on-the-spot pricing decision or alert a firm's suppliers of potential "stockout" situations.

THE NETWORK REVOLUTION AND THE INTERNET

One reason information systems play such a large role in organizations and affect so many people is the soaring power and declining cost of computer technology. Computing power,

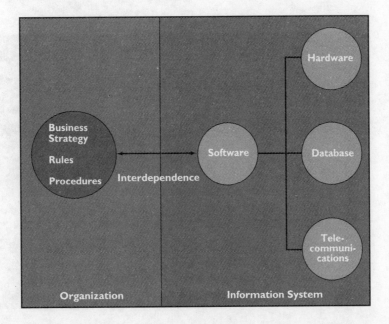

Figure 1-8 The interdependence between organizations and information systems. In contemporary systems there is a growing interdependence between organizational business strategy, rules, and procedures and the organization's information systems. Changes in strategy, rules, and procedures increasingly require changes in hardware, software, databases, and telecommunications. Existing systems can act as a constraint on organizations. Often, what the organization would like to do depends on what its systems will permit it to do.

Figure 1-9 The widening scope of information systems. Over time, information systems have come to play a larger role in the life of organizations. Early systems brought about largely technical changes that were relatively easy to accomplish. Later systems affected managerial control and behavior and subsequently "core" institutional activities. In the digital firm era, information systems extend far beyond the boundaries of the firm to encompass vendors, customers, and even competitors.

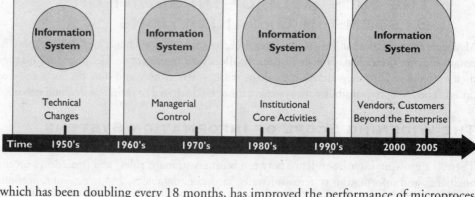

Internet

International network of networks that is a collection of hundreds of thousands of private and public networks.

which has been doubling every 18 months, has improved the performance of microprocessors over 25,000 times since their invention 30 years ago. With powerful, easy-to-use software, the computer can crunch numbers, analyze vast pools of data, or simulate complex physical and logical processes with animated drawings, sounds, and even tactile feedback.

The soaring power of computer technology has spawned powerful communication networks that organizations can use to access vast storehouses of information from around the world and to coordinate activities across space and time. These networks are transforming the shape and form of business enterprises, creating the foundation for the digital firm.

The world's largest and most widely used network is the **Internet.** The Internet is an international network of networks that are both commercial and publicly owned. The Internet connects hundreds of thousands of different networks from more than 200 countries around the world. Nearly 600 million people working in science, education, government, and business use the Internet to exchange information or perform business transactions with other organizations around the globe.

The Internet is extremely elastic. If networks are added or removed or failures occur in parts of the system, the rest of the Internet continues to operate. Through special communication and technology standards, any computer can communicate with virtually any other computer linked to the Internet using ordinary telephone lines. Companies and private individuals can use the Internet to exchange business transactions, text messages, graphic images, and even video and sound, whether they are located next door or on the other side of the globe. Table 1-3 describes some of the Internet's capabilities.

The Internet is creating a new "universal" technology platform on which to build all sorts of new products, services, strategies, and organizations. It is reshaping the way information systems are being used in business and daily life. By eliminating many technical, geographic, and cost barriers obstructing the global flow of information, the Internet is inspiring

The Internet. This global network of networks provides a highly flexible platform for information sharing. Digital information can be distributed at almost no cost to millions of people throughout the world.

Function	Description
Communicate and collaborate	Send electronic mail messages; transmit documents and data; participate in electronic conferences
Access information	Search for documents, databases, and library card catalogs; read electronic brochures, manuals, books, and advertisements
Participate in discussions	Join interactive discussion groups; conduct voice transmission
Supply information	Transfer computer files of text, computer programs, graphics, animations, sound, or videos
Find entertainment	Play interactive video games; view short video clips; listen to sound and music clips; read illustrated and even animated magazines and books
Exchange business transactions	Advertise, sell, and purchase goods and services

TABLE 1-3

WHAT YOU CAN DO ON THE INTERNET

new uses of information systems and new business models. The Internet provides the primary technology platform for the digital firm.

Because it offers so many new possibilities for doing business, the Internet capability known as the **World Wide Web** is of special interest to organizations and managers. The World Wide Web is a system with universally accepted standards for storing, retrieving, formatting, and displaying information in a networked environment. Information is stored and displayed as electronic "pages" that can contain text, graphics, animations, sound, and video. These Web pages can be linked electronically to other Web pages, regardless of where they are located, and viewed by any type of computer. By clicking on highlighted words or buttons on a Web page, you can link to related pages to find additional information, software programs, or still more links to other points on the Web. The Web can serve as the foundation for new kinds of information systems such as those described in the Window on boxes and chapter-opening vignette.

All of the Web pages maintained by an organization or individual are called a **Web site.** Businesses are creating Web sites with stylish typography, colorful graphics, push-button interactivity, and often sound and video to disseminate product information widely, to "broadcast" advertising and messages to customers, to collect electronic orders and customer data, and, increasingly, to coordinate far-flung sales forces and organizations on a global scale.

In Chapters 4 and 9 we describe the Web and other Internet capabilities in greater detail. We also discuss relevant features of Internet technology throughout the text because it affects so many aspects of information systems in organizations.

World Wide Web
A system with universally accepted standards for storing, retrieving, formatting, and displaying information in a networked environment.

Web site
All of the World Wide Web pages maintained by an organization or an individual.

NEW OPTIONS FOR ORGANIZATIONAL DESIGN: THE DIGITAL FIRM AND THE COLLABORATIVE ENTERPRISE

The explosive growth in computing power and networks, including the Internet, is turning organizations into networked enterprises, allowing information to be instantly distributed within and beyond the organization. Companies can use this information to improve their internal business processes and to coordinate these business processes with those of other organizations. These new technologies for connectivity and collaboration can be used to redesign and reshape organizations, transforming their structure, scope of operations, reporting and control mechanisms, work practices, work flows, products, and services. The ultimate end product of these new ways of conducting business electronically is the digital firm.

Flattening Organizations and the Changing Management Process

Large, bureaucratic organizations, which primarily developed before the computer age, are often inefficient, slow to change, and less competitive than newly created organizations. Some of these large organizations have downsized, reducing the number of employees and the number of levels in their organizational hierarchies. For example, when Eastman Chemical Co. split off from Kodak in 1994 it had $3.3 billion in revenue and 24,000 full-time employees. By 2000, it generated $5 billion in revenue with only 17,000 employees (*InformationWeek*, 2000).

In digital firms, hierarchy and organizational levels do not disappear. But digital firms develop "optimal hierarchies" that balance the decision-making load across an organization, resulting in flatter organizations. Flatter organizations have fewer levels of management, with lower-level employees being given greater decision-making authority (see Figure 1-10). Those employees are empowered to make more decisions than in the past, they no longer work standard nine-to-five hours, and they no longer necessarily work in an office. Moreover, such employees may be scattered geographically, sometimes working half a world away from the manager.

These changes mean that the management span of control has also been broadened, allowing high-level managers to manage and control more workers spread over greater distances. Many companies have eliminated thousands of middle managers as a result of these changes. AT&T, IBM, and GM are only a few of the organizations that have eliminated more than 30,000 middle managers in one fell swoop.

Information technology is also recasting the management process by providing powerful new tools for more precise planning, forecasting, and monitoring. For instance, it is now possible for managers to obtain information on organizational performance down to the level of specific transactions from just about anywhere in the organization at any time. Product managers at Frito-Lay Corporation, the world's largest manufacturer of salty snack foods, can know within hours precisely how many bags of Fritos have sold on any street in America at its customers' stores, how much they sold for, and what the competition's sales volumes and prices are.

Separating Work from Location

Communications technology has eliminated distance as a factor for many types of work in many situations. Salespersons can spend more time in the field with customers and have more up-to-

Figure 1-10 Flattening organizations. Information systems can reduce the number of levels in an organization by providing managers with information to supervise larger numbers of workers and by giving lower-level employees more decision-making authority.

A traditional hierarchical organization with many levels of management

An organization that has been "flattened" by removing layers of management

date information with them while carrying much less paper. Many employees can work remotely from their homes or cars, and companies can reserve space at smaller central offices for meeting clients or other employees. Collaborative teamwork across thousands of miles has become a reality as designers work on a new product together even if they are located on different continents. Lockheed Martin Aeronautics developed a real-time system for collaborative product design and engineering based on the Internet, which it uses to coordinate tasks with its partners such as BAE and Northrup Grumman. Engineers from all three companies work jointly on designs over the Internet. Previously, the company and its partners worked separately on designs, hammering out design differences in lengthy face-to-face meetings. A drawing that once took 400 hours now takes 125 and the design phase of projects has been cut in half (Konicki, 2001).

Reorganizing Work Flows

Information systems have been progressively replacing manual work procedures with automated work procedures, work flows, and work processes. Electronic work flows have reduced the cost of operations in many companies by displacing paper and the manual routines that accompany it. Improved work flow management has enabled many corporations not only to cut costs significantly but also to improve customer service at the same time. For instance, insurance companies can reduce processing of applications for new insurance from weeks to days (see Figure 1-11).

Redesigned work flows can have a profound impact on organizational efficiency and can even lead to new organizational structures, products, and services. We discuss the impact of restructured work flows on organizational design in greater detail in Chapters 3 and 12.

Increasing Flexibility of Organizations

Companies can use communications technology to organize in more flexible ways, increasing their ability to sense and respond to changes in the marketplace and to take advantage of new opportunities. Information systems can give both large and small organizations additional flexibility to overcome some of the limitations posed by their size. Table 1-4 describes some of the ways in which information technology can help small companies act "big" and help big companies act "small." Small organizations can use information systems to acquire some of the muscle and reach of larger organizations. They can perform coordinating activities, such as processing bids or keeping track of inventory, and many manufacturing tasks with very few managers, clerks, or production workers.

Large organizations can use information technology to achieve some of the agility and responsiveness of small organizations. One aspect of this phenomenon is **mass customization,** the ability to offer individually tailored products or services on a large scale. Information systems can make the production process more flexible so that products can be tailored to each customer's unique set of requirements (Zipkin, 2001). Software and computer networks can be used to link the plant floor tightly with orders, design, and purchasing and to finely control production machines so products can be turned out in greater variety and easily customized with no added cost for small production runs. For example, Levi

mass customization

The capacity to offer individually tailored products or services on a large scale.

Figure 1-11   Redesigned work flow for insurance underwriting. An application requiring 33 days in a paper system would only take 5 days using computers, networks, and a streamlined work flow.

TABLE 1-4 **HOW INFORMATION TECHNOLOGY INCREASES ORGANIZATIONAL FLEXIBILITY**

Small Companies

Desktop machines, inexpensive computer-aided design (CAD) software, and computer-controlled machine tools provide the precision, speed, and quality of giant manufacturers.

Information immediately accessed by telephone and communications links eliminates the need for research staff and business libraries.

Managers can easily obtain the information they need to manage large numbers of employees in widely scattered locations.

Large Companies

Custom manufacturing systems allow large factories to offer customized products in small quantities.

Massive databases of customer purchasing records can be analyzed so that large companies can know their customers' needs and preferences as easily as local merchants.

Information can be easily distributed down the ranks of the organization to empower lower-level employees and work groups to solve problems.

Strauss has equipped its stores with an option called Original Spin, which allows customers to design jeans to their own specifications, rather than picking the jeans off the rack. Customers enter their measurements into a personal computer, which then transmits the customer's specifications over a network to Levi's plants. The company is able to produce the custom jeans on the same lines that manufacture its standard items. There are almost no extra production costs because the process does not require additional warehousing, production overruns, and inventories. Lands' End has implemented a similar system for customizing chino slacks and jeans that allows customers to enter their measurements over its Web site.

A related trend is micromarketing, in which information systems can help companies pinpoint tiny target markets for these finely customized products and services—as small as individualized "markets of one." We discuss micromarketing in more detail in Chapters 2, 3 and 11.

Redefining Organizational Boundaries: New Avenues for Collaboration

A key feature of the emerging digital firm is the ability to conduct business across firm boundaries almost as efficiently and effectively as it can conduct business within the firm. Networked information systems allow companies to coordinate with other organizations across great distances. Transactions such as payments and purchase orders can be exchanged electronically among different companies, thereby reducing the cost of obtaining products and services from outside the firm. Organizations can also share business data, catalogs, or mail messages through networks. These networked information systems can create new efficiencies and new relationships between an organization, its customers, and suppliers, redefining organizational boundaries.

The chapter-opening vignette described how the Toyota Motor Corporation is networked to its suppliers, including the Dana Corporation of Toledo Ohio, a tier-one supplier of chassis, engines, and other major automotive components. Through this electronic link, the Dana Corporation monitors Toyota production and ships components exactly when needed (McDougall, 2001). Toyota and Dana have thus become linked business partners with mutually shared responsibilities.

interorganizational systems
Information systems that automate the flow of information across organizational boundaries and link a company to its customers, distributors, or suppliers.

The information system linking Toyota to its supplier is called an interorganizational information system. Systems linking a company to its customers, distributors, or suppliers are termed **interorganizational systems** because they automate the flow of information across organizational boundaries. Digital firms use interorganizational systems to link with suppliers, customers, and sometimes even competitors, to create and distribute new products and services without being limited by traditional organizational boundaries or physical locations. For example, Cisco Systems does not manufacture the networking products it sells; it uses other companies, such as Flextronics, for this purpose. Cisco uses the Internet to transmit orders to Flextronics and to monitor the status of orders as they are being shipped. (More detail on Flextronics can be found in the Chapter 3 opening vignette.)

Many of these interorganizational systems are increasingly based on Web technology and providing more intense sharing of knowledge, resources, and business processes than in the past. Firms are using these systems to work jointly with suppliers and other business partners on product design and development and on the scheduling and flow of work in manufacturing, procurement, and distribution. These new levels of interfirm collaboration and coordination can lead to higher levels of efficiency, value to customers, and ultimately significant competitive advantage.

THE DIGITAL FIRM: ELECTRONIC COMMERCE, ELECTRONIC BUSINESS, AND NEW DIGITAL RELATIONSHIPS

The changes we have just described represent new ways of conducting business electronically both inside and outside the firm that can ultimately result in the creation of digital firms. Increasingly, the Internet is providing the underlying technology for these changes. The Internet can link thousands of organizations into a single network, creating the foundation for a vast digital marketplace. A **digital market** is an information system that links together many buyers and sellers to exchange information, products, services, and payments. Through computers and networks, these systems function like electronic intermediaries, with lowered costs for typical marketplace transactions, such as matching buyers and sellers, establishing prices, ordering goods, and paying bills (Bakos, 1998). Buyers and sellers can complete purchase and sale transactions digitally, regardless of their location.

A vast array of goods and services are being advertised, bought, and exchanged worldwide using the Internet as a global marketplace. Companies are furiously creating eye-catching electronic brochures, advertisements, product manuals, and order forms on the World Wide Web. All kinds of products and services are available on the Web, including fresh flowers, books, real estate, musical recordings, electronics, and steaks. Even electronic financial trading has arrived on the Web for stocks, bonds, mutual funds, and other financial instruments. The Window on Organizations describes another type of Web-based financial service, Internet-only banking.

Increasingly the Web is being used for business-to-business transactions as well. For example, airlines can use the Boeing Corporation's Web site to order parts electronically and check the status of their orders. Altranet Energy Technologies of Houston operates an online marketplace called altranet.com where many different energy industry suppliers and buyers can meet any time of day or night to trade natural gas, liquids, and electricity in a spot market for immediate delivery. Participants can select their trading partners, confirm transactions, and obtain credit and insurance.

The global availability of the Internet for the exchange of transactions between buyers and sellers has fueled the growth of electronic commerce. **Electronic commerce,** also known

digital market
A marketplace that is created by computer and communication technologies that link many buyers and sellers.

electronic commerce (e-commerce)
The process of buying and selling goods and services electronically involving transactions using the Internet, networks, and other digital technologies.

Smile.com is an Internet-only bank where customers can view their accounts and perform banking transactions any hour of the day or night. A wide array of banking and financial services are available on the Web.

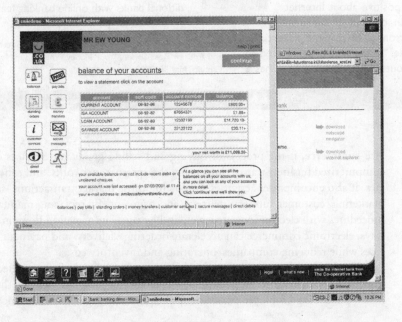

WHY ARE INTERNET-ONLY BANKS SMILING IN THE UNITED KINGDOM?

Despite the recent collapse of many dot-coms, some Internet businesses are starting to catch on. Internet banking appears to be taking a foothold in the United Kingdom. Four Internet-only banks have collectively captured 5 percent of the total U.K. banking market.

What can these online-only banks offer their customers? Perhaps their most important benefit is that customers use the Web to bank at any hour of the day or night, including weekends and holidays—a service that no physical bricks-and-mortar bank can offer. Customers can also view their current records, determine if a particular check has cleared yet, apply for new or additional credit, pay bills (at no cost to them, not even postage), and communicate with the bank—ask questions and receive answers, often within 24 hours. With those services, customers can control their own banking, for example, by avoiding overdrafts. Also, the banks' costs are usually much lower, enabling the online banks to lower customer costs and pay higher interest rates. Smile, an Internet-only British bank, says its costs are only 10 percent of the costs of a competing bricks-and-mortar bank, and Smile puts much of its savings into higher interest rates for customer checking and savings accounts.

On the other hand, online-only banks have their shortcomings. Banking at a physical bank enables customers to make deposits directly, cash checks, withdraw cash, and even talk with bankers face-to-face. Today some online-only banks are allowing their customers to use ATMs to withdraw cash, and in some cases the bank eats the normal charges when one bank's customer uses another bank's ATM machine. Deposits are normally only made by mail, a drawback for some. Moreover, when customers bank with online-only banks the customers cannot talk with their bankers face-to-face, a personal touch that many bank customers desire. And some transactions, such as mortgages, are complex and working with live bankers is considered a necessity by many.

Nonetheless many still feel positive about Internet banking. "I feel much more in control of my own finances," says Annabelle Watson, a 26-year-old advertising executive and customer of Smile. "In the past I felt dictated to by my own bank," she points out. She claims her bank has a

user-friendly Web site that gives customers the impression they are dealing with an attentive 24-hour bank manager. Smile.com has added a do-it-yourself area to its Web site that contains savings and budget calculators and other tools and it is considering giving clients access to their accounts through wireless phones.

Bricks-and-mortar banks have their problems too. Customers appreciate and now often need online banking because of its ease and the ability of customers to bank on their own schedule. In response many traditional banks have added online Internet banking features so they can offer the best of both worlds. However, their costs quite naturally remain higher than online-only banks because of their bricks-and-mortar side. Other traditional banks have started online-only bank subsidiaries, including Cooperative Bank PLC, a well-established British bank that is the founder and parent of Smile.

Internet-only banks have faced very tough times in the United States. For example, one of the largest such banks, Wingspan, was recently absorbed by its parent Bank One Corp. The question is, can they survive? Bob Head, the CEO of Smile, is positive about the future of his company. "We believe Internet banking will become the norm for millions of people in the future, and Smile will be successful in the long term because it offers so much more [than traditional banking]." If Smile can keep attracting new customers and improve service while established U.K. banks are shifting more of their service to the Internet, they may indeed become a dot-com success story.

To Think About: Do you think Internet-only banking will survive? Why or why not? What are the organizational and technical problems Internet-only banks face? What are the organizational and technical problems traditional banks with online banking features face?

Source: Susannah Rodgers, "Keep on Smiling," *Wall Street Journal,* April 15, 2002; and Andrew Ross Sorkin, "Your Money Where Your Modem Is," *New York Times* Circuits, May 30, 2002.

ORGANIZATIONS

as **e-commerce,** is the process of buying and selling goods and services electronically with computerized business transactions using the Internet, networks, and other digital technologies. It also encompasses activities supporting those market transactions, such as advertising, marketing, customer support, delivery, and payment. By replacing manual and paper-based procedures with electronic alternatives, and by using information flows in new and dynamic ways, electronic commerce can accelerate ordering, delivery, and payment for goods and services while reducing companies' operating and inventory costs.

The Internet has emerged as the primary technology platform for electronic commerce. Equally important, Internet technology is facilitating management of the rest of the business—publishing employee personnel policies, reviewing account balances and production

Visitors to the Travelocity.com Web site can find information on airlines, hotels, and vacation packages and they can make airline and hotel reservations online. The Internet is fueling the growth of electronic commerce.

plans, scheduling plant repairs and maintenance, and revising design documents. Companies are taking advantage of the connectivity and ease of use of Internet technology to create internal corporate networks called **intranets** that are based on Internet technology. The number of these private intranets for organizational communication, collaboration, and coordination is soaring.

The chapter-opening vignette described how Toyota Motor Corporation is allowing its dealers to access portions of its private intranet to help them coordinate customer orders with production and design activities. Private intranets extended to authorized users outside the organization are called **extranets,** and firms use such networks to coordinate their activities with other firms for making purchases, collaborating on design, and other interorganizational work. Chapters 4 and 9 provide more detail on intranet and extranet applications and technology.

It is these broader uses of Internet technology, along with e-commerce, that are driving the move toward digital firms. In this text, we use the term **electronic business,** or **e-business** to describe the use of Internet and digital technology to execute all of the business processes in the enterprise. E-business includes e-commerce as well as processes for the internal management of the firm and for coordination with suppliers and other business partners.

Figure 1-12 illustrates a digital firm making intensive use of Internet and digital technology for electronic business. Information can flow seamlessly among different parts of the company and between the company and external entities—its customers, suppliers, and business partners. Organizations will move toward this digital firm vision as they use the Internet, intranets, and extranets to digitally enable their internal business processes and their interorganizational relationships.

E-business can fundamentally change the way organizations perform their work. To use the Internet and other digital technologies successfully for e-business, e-commerce, and the creation of digital firms, organizations may have to redefine their business models, reinvent business processes, change corporate cultures, and create much closer relationships with customers and suppliers. We treat these issues in greater detail in following chapters.

intranet

An internal network based on Internet and World Wide Web technology and standards.

extranet

Private intranet that is accessible to authorized outsiders.

electronic business (e-business)

The use of Internet and digital technology to execute all the business processes in the enterprise. Includes e-commerce as well as processes for the internal management of the firm and for coordination with suppliers and other business partners.

1.4 LEARNING TO USE INFORMATION SYSTEMS: NEW OPPORTUNITIES WITH TECHNOLOGY

Although information systems are creating many exciting opportunities for both businesses and individuals, they are also a source of new problems, issues, and challenges for managers. In this course, you will learn about both the challenges and opportunities information systems pose, and you will be able to use information technology to enrich your learning experience.

Figure I-12 Electronic business and electronic commerce in the emerging digital firm. Companies can use the Internet, intranets, and extranets for e-commerce transactions with customers and suppliers, for managing internal business processes, and for coordinating with suppliers and other business partners. E-business includes e-commerce as well as the management and coordination of the enterprise.

THE EMERGING DIGITAL FIRM
ELECTRONIC BUSINESS

Electronic Commerce

Factories
• Just-in-time production
• Continuous inventory replenishment
• Production planning

Customers
• On-line marketing
• On-line sales
• Built-to-order products
• Customer service
• Sales force automation

Remote offices and work groups
• Communicate plans and policies
• Group collaboration
• Electronic communication
• Scheduling

Suppliers
• Procurement
• Supply chain management

Business partners
• Joint design
• Outsourcing

THE CHALLENGE OF INFORMATION SYSTEMS: KEY MANAGEMENT ISSUES

Although information technology is advancing at a blinding pace, there is nothing easy or mechanical about building and using information systems. There are five key challenges confronting managers:

1. **The Strategic Business Challenge: Realizing the Digital Firm: How can businesses use information technology to become competitive, effective, and digitally enabled?** Creating a digital firm and obtaining benefits is a long and difficult journey for most organizations. Despite heavy information technology investments, many organizations are not realizing significant business value from their systems, nor are they becoming digitally enabled. The power of computer hardware and software has grown much more rapidly than the ability of organizations to apply and use this technology. To fully benefit from information technology, realize genuine productivity, and take advantage of digital firm capabilities, many organizations actually need to be redesigned. They will have to make fundamental changes in organizational behavior, develop new business models, and eliminate the inefficiencies of outmoded organizational structures. If organizations merely automate what they are doing today, they are largely missing the potential of information technology.

2. **The Globalization Challenge: How can firms understand the business and system requirements of a global economic environment?** The rapid growth in international trade and the emergence of a global economy call for information systems that can support both producing and selling goods in many different countries. In the past, each regional office of a multinational corporation focused on solving its own unique information problems. Given language, cultural, and political differences among countries, this focus frequently resulted in chaos and the failure of central

management controls. To develop integrated, multinational, information systems, businesses must develop global hardware, software, and communications standards; create cross-cultural accounting and reporting structures (Roche, 1992); and design transnational business processes.

3. **The Information Architecture and Infrastructure Challenge: How can organizations develop an information architecture and information technology infrastructure that can support their goals when business conditions and technologies are changing so rapidly?** Many companies are saddled with expensive and unwieldy information technology platforms that cannot adapt to innovation and change. Their information systems are so complex and brittle that they act as constraints on business strategy and execution. Meeting new business and technology challenges may require redesigning the organization and building a new information architecture and information technology (IT) infrastructure.

Information architecture is the particular form that information technology takes in an organization to achieve selected goals or functions. It is a design for the firm's key business application systems and the specific ways that they are used by each organization. Because managers and employees directly interact with these systems, it is critical for organizational success that the information architecture meet business requirements now and in the future.

It is difficult—if not impossible—to represent the complexity of contemporary information architecture and IT infrastructure in a single diagram as firms move toward digital firm organizations. Figure 1-13 nevertheless attempts to illustrate the major elements of information architecture found in today's emerging digital firms. Figure 1-13 depicts the firm's major vertical business application systems for each of the major functional areas of the business, including sales and marketing, manufacturing, finance, accounting, and human resources. These systems were among the first

information architecture
The particular design that information technology takes in a specific organization to achieve selected goals or functions.

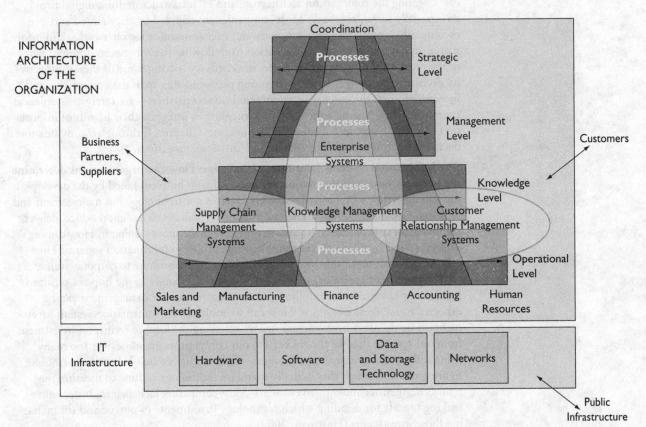

Figure 1-13 Information architecture and information technology infrastructure. Today's managers must know how to arrange and coordinate the various computer technologies and business system applications to meet the information needs of each level of the organization, and the needs of the organization as a whole.

built in most organizations. The figure also depicts major horizontal systems automating business processes that cross functional and hierarchical boundaries. These systems are typically built after major functional systems are in place. Finally, this figure depicts major contemporary IT investments in enterprise, supply chain management, customer relationship management, and knowledge management systems—key waypoints on the journey towards a truly digital firm. These contemporary systems extend outwards to suppliers and customers, and inwards to employee knowledge and expertise, supporting firm-wide processes that span across all organizational units.

The firm's IT infrastructure provides the technology platform for this architecture. Computer hardware, software, data and storage technology, networks, and human resources required to operate the equipment constitute the shared IT resources of the firm and are available to all of its applications. Contemporary IT infrastructures are linked to public infrastructures such as the Internet. Although this technology platform is typically operated by technical personnel, general management must decide how to allocate the resources it has assigned to hardware, software, data storage, and telecommunications networks to make sound information technology investments (Weill and Broadbent, 1997 and 1998).

Typical questions regarding information architecture and IT infrastructure facing today's managers include the following: Should the corporate sales data and function be distributed to each corporate remote site, or should they be centralized at headquarters? Should the organization build systems to connect the entire enterprise or maintain separate islands of applications? Should the organization extend its infrastructure outside its boundaries to link to customers or suppliers? There is no one right answer to each of these questions (see Allen and Boynton, 1991). Moreover, business needs are constantly changing, which requires the IT architecture to be reassessed continually (Feeny and Willcocks, 1998).

Creating the information architecture and IT infrastructure for a digital firm is an especially formidable task. Most companies are crippled by fragmented and incompatible computer hardware, software, telecommunications networks, and information systems that prevent information from flowing freely between different parts of the organization. Although Internet standards are solving some of these connectivity problems, creating data and computing platforms that span the enterprise—and, increasingly, link the enterprise to external business partners—are rarely as seamless as promised. Many organizations are still struggling to integrate their islands of information and technology into a coherent architecture. Chapters 6 through 9 provide more detail on information architecture and IT infrastructure issues.

4. **The Information Systems Investment Challenge: How can organizations determine the business value of information systems?** A major problem raised by the development of powerful, inexpensive computers involves not technology but management and organizations. It's one thing to use information technology to design, produce, deliver, and maintain new products. It's another thing to make money doing it. How can organizations obtain a sizable payoff from their investment in information systems? How can management make sure that information systems contribute to corporate value?

Engineering massive organizational and system changes in the hope of positioning a firm strategically is complicated and expensive. Senior management can be expected to ask these questions: How can we evaluate our information system investments as we do other investments? Are we receiving the kind of return on investment from our systems that we should be? Do our competitors get more? Far too many firms still cannot answer these questions. Their executives are likely to have trouble figuring out how much they actually spend on technology or how to measure the returns on their technology investments. Most companies lack a clearcut decision-making process for deciding which technology investments to pursue and for managing those investments (Hartman, 2002).

5. **The Responsibility and Control Challenge: How can organizations ensure that their information systems are used in an ethically and socially responsible manner?** How can we design information systems that people can control and understand? Although information systems have provided enormous benefits and efficien-

TABLE 1-5   POSITIVE AND NEGATIVE IMPACTS OF INFORMATION SYSTEMS

Benefit of Information System	Negative Impact
Information systems can perform calculations or process paperwork much faster than people.	By automating activities that were previously performed by people, information systems may eliminate jobs.
Information systems can help companies learn more about the purchase patterns and preferences of their customers.	Information systems may allow organizations to collect personal details about people that violate their privacy.
Information systems provide new efficiencies through services such as automated teller machines (ATMs), telephone systems, or computer-controlled airplanes and air terminals.	Information systems are used in so many aspects of everyday life that system outages can cause shutdowns of businesses or transportation services, paralyzing communities.
Information systems have made possible new medical advances in surgery, radiology, and patient monitoring.	Heavy users of information systems may suffer repetitive stress injury, technostress, and other health problems.
The Internet distributes information instantly to millions of people across the world.	The Internet can be used to distribute illegal copies of software, books, articles, and other intellectual property.

cies, they have also created new problems and challenges of which managers should be aware. Table 1-5 describes some of these problems and challenges.

Many chapters of this text describe scenarios that raise these ethical issues, and Chapter 5 is devoted entirely to this topic. A major management challenge is to make informed decisions that are sensitive to the negative consequences of information systems as well to the positive ones.

Managers will also be faced with ongoing problems of security and control. Information systems are so essential to business, government, and daily life that organizations must take special steps to ensure that they are accurate, reliable, and secure. A firm invites disaster if it uses systems that don't work as intended, that don't deliver information in a form that people can interpret correctly and use, or that have control rooms where controls don't work or where instruments give false signals. Information systems must be designed so that they function as intended and so that humans can control the process.

Managers will need to ask: Can we apply high quality assurance standards to our information systems, as well as to our products and services? Can we build information systems that respect people's rights of privacy while still pursuing our organization's goals? Should information systems monitor employees? What do we do when an information system designed to increase efficiency and productivity eliminates people's jobs?

This text is designed to provide future managers with the knowledge and understanding required to deal with these challenges. To further this objective, each succeeding chapter begins with a Management Challenges box that outlines the key issues of which managers should be aware.

INTEGRATING TEXT WITH TECHNOLOGY: NEW OPPORTUNITIES FOR LEARNING

In addition to the changes in business and management that we have just described, we believe that information technology creates new opportunities for learning that can make the MIS course more meaningful and exciting. We have provided a Web site and an interactive multimedia CD-ROM for integrating the text with leading-edge technology.

As you read each chapter of the text, you can visit the Prentice Hall Laudon Web site (www.prenhall.com/laudon) and use the Internet for interactive learning and management problem solving. The Internet Connection icon in the chapter directs you to Web sites for which we have provided additional exercises and projects related to the concepts and organizations described in that particular chapter. For each chapter, you will also find an Electronic Commerce or Electronic Business project where you can use Web research and interactive software at various company Web sites to solve specific problems. A graded online Interactive Study Guide contains questions to help you review what you have learned and test your mastery of chapter concepts. The Web site for each chapter includes a Management Decision Problem with a real world decision-making scenario for you to analyze. You can also use the Laudon Web site to find links to additional online case studies, international resources, and technology updates.

New to this edition is a Running Case study based on a simulated company that allows students to learn about a specific business and develop information system solutions for that business. Each chapter of the text contains a Running Case scenario and project where students can apply their analytical skills and chapter concepts. Some of these projects require extensive use of the Web or spreadsheet and database software. A complete description of each Running Case project and required data files can be found on the Laudon Web site and on the Laudon interactive multimedia CD-ROM.

The interactive CD-ROM multimedia version of the text features audio/video overviews explaining key concepts, bullet text summaries of key points in each chapter, full-color graphics and photos, Web links to the companion Web site, interactive quizzes, Dynamic Blackboard, a hyperlinked digital glossary, and the complete Running Case, along with any files or materials required by each Running Case project. You can use the CD-ROM as an interactive study guide or as an alternative to the traditional text.

Application software exercises require students to use spreadsheet, database, Web browser, and other application software in hands-on projects related to chapter concepts. They have been redesigned for this edition to make them more challenging and relevant to chapter topics. Students can apply the application software skills they have learned in other courses to real-world business problems. You can find these exercises following the Review Questions at the end of each chapter and both the exercises and their data files on the Laudon Web site.

Longer, comprehensive projects conclude each major section of the text. These projects require students to apply what they have learned to more demanding problems, such as analyzing enterprise system requirements, developing an Internet business model, designing a corporate knowledge intranet, redesigning business processes, and calculating the Total Cost of Ownership (TCO) of a Web site. Some of these projects require use of the Web.

 You will find a Tools for Interactive Learning section with this icon toward the end of every chapter to show how you can use the Web and interactive multimedia to enrich your learning experience.

MAKE **IT** YOUR BUSINESS

FINANCE AND ACCOUNTING
The Internet has created vast electronic marketplaces for the purchase and sale of stocks, bonds, and other financial products. Online trading and management of investment accounts is also available. Financial systems, some of the first to computerize, are based today on high-speed computers and networks. Financial and accounting information can be obtained instantly from internal computer systems and can flow instantly across entire organizations. Financial information can also be obtained immediately on the Internet. You can find examples of finance and accounting applications on page 24.

HUMAN RESOURCES
Human resources record keeping is now largely computer based, allowing companies to instantly track their employee resources. Networked communication systems and the Internet make it much easier for managers to communicate with many employees simultaneously, and manage distant task forces and worker teams. Work can be separated from location and managed from afar.

MANUFACTURING AND PRODUCTION
Internet and network technology have enhanced the precision and flexibility of the manufacturing and production function in both large and small companies. Large manufacturers can use software and networks for mass customization, whereas small manufacturers can use desktop computers with computer-aided design software and computer-controlled machines to output products with the precision and speed of larger firms. Companies can also use these technologies to work collaboratively with other companies and coordinate their production processes more tightly with those of suppliers and distributors. You can find examples of manufacturing and production applications on pages 2–4, 10, and 34–35.

SALES AND MARKETING
The Internet and the Web have opened up a powerful new sales and marketing channel to retail consumers and to other businesses. Companies can use the Internet for advertising, customer support, and even some forms of product testing, with customers ordering products and services over the Web from their desktop computers. The ubiquity of the Internet makes it possible for small businesses to sell their wares in many areas of the globe without a physical sales force or front offices. You can find examples of sales and marketing applications on pages 2–4 and 34–35.

MANAGEMENT WRAP-UP

Managers are problem solvers who are responsible for analyzing the many challenges confronting organizations and for developing strategies and action plans. Information systems are one of their tools, delivering the information required for solutions. Information systems both reflect management decisions and serve as instruments for changing the management process.

Information systems are rooted in organizations, an outcome of organizational structure, culture, politics, work flows, and standard operating procedures. They are instruments for organizational change and value creation, making it possible to recast these organizational elements into new business models and redraw organizational boundaries. Advances in information systems are accelerating the trend toward globalized, knowledge-driven economies and flattened, flexible, decentralized organizations that can coordinate with other organizations across great distances.

A network revolution is under way. Information systems technology is no longer limited to computers but consists of an array of technologies that enable computers to be networked together to exchange information across great distances and organizational boundaries. The Internet provides global connectivity and a flexible platform for the seamless flow of information across the enterprise and between the firm and its customers and suppliers.

For Discussion

1. Information systems are too important to be left to computer specialists. Do you agree? Why or why not?

2. As computers become faster and cheaper and the Internet becomes more widely used, most of the problems we have with information systems will disappear. Do you agree? Why or why not?

SUMMARY

1. *What is the role of information systems in today's competitive business environment?* Information systems have become essential for helping organizations deal with changes in global economies and the business enterprise. Information systems provide firms with communication and analytic tools for conducting trade and managing businesses on a global scale. Information systems are the foundation of new knowledge-based products and services in knowledge economies and help firms manage their knowledge assets. Information systems make it possible for businesses to adopt flatter, more decentralized structures and more flexible arrangements of employees and management. Organizations are trying to become more competitive and efficient by transforming themselves into digital firms where nearly all core business processes and relationships with customers, suppliers, and employees are digitally enabled.

2. *What exactly is an information system? What do managers need to know about information systems?* The purpose of an information system is to collect, store, and disseminate information from an organization's environment and internal operations to support organizational functions and decision making, communication, coordination, control, analysis, and visualization. Information systems transform raw data into useful information through three basic activities: input, processing, and output. From a business perspective, an information system represents an organizational and management

solution based on information technology to a challenge posed by the environment. The information system is part of a series of value-adding activities for acquiring, transforming, and distributing information that managers can use to improve decision making, enhance organizational performance, and, ultimately, increase firm profitability.

Information systems literacy requires an understanding of the organizational and management dimensions of information systems as well as the technical dimensions addressed by computer literacy. Information systems literacy draws on both technical and behavioral approaches to studying information systems. Both perspectives can be combined into a sociotechnical approach to systems.

3. *How are information systems transforming organizations and management?* The kinds of systems built today are very important for the organization's overall performance, especially in today's highly globalized and information-based economy. Information systems are driving both daily operations and organizational strategy. Powerful computers, software, and networks, including the Internet, have helped organizations become more flexible, eliminate layers of management, separate work from location, coordinate with suppliers and customers, and restructure work flows, giving new powers to both line workers and management. Information technology provides managers with tools for more precise planning, forecasting, and monitoring of the

business. To maximize the advantages of information technology, there is a much greater need to plan the organization's information architecture and information technology (IT) infrastructure.

4. *How have the Internet and Internet technology transformed business?* The Internet provides the primary technology infrastructure for electronic commerce, electronic business, and the emerging digital firm. The Internet and other networks have made it possible for businesses to replace manual and paper-based processes with the electronic flows of information. In electronic commerce (e-commerce), businesses can exchange electronic purchase and sale transactions with each other and with individual customers. Electronic business (e-business) uses Internet and other digital technology for organizational communication and

coordination, collaboration with business partners, and the management of the firm as well as for electronic commerce transactions. Digital firms use Internet technology intensively to manage their internal processes and relationships with customers, suppliers, and other external entities.

5. *What are the major management challenges to building and using information systems?* There are five key management challenges in building and using information systems: (1) designing systems that are competitive and efficient; (2) understanding the system requirements of a global business environment; (3) creating an information architecture and IT infrastructure that support the organization's goals; (4) determining the business value of information systems; and (5) designing systems that people can control, understand, and use in a socially and ethically responsible manner.

KEY TERMS

Business functions, 13

Business processes, 7

Communications technology, 14

Computer-based information systems (CBIS), 9

Computer hardware, 14

Computer literacy, 12

Computer software, 14

Customer relationship management systems, 7

Data, 8

Data workers, 13

Digital firm, 6

Digital market, 23

Electronic business (e-business), 25

Electronic commerce (e-commerce), 23

Enterprise systems, 7

Extranet, 25

Feedback, 8

Formal system, 9

Information, 8

Information architecture, 27

Information system, 8

Information systems literacy, 12

Information technology (IT) infrastructure, 14

Input, 8

Internet, 18

Interorganizational systems, 22

Intranet, 25

Knowledge- and information-intense products, 6

Knowledge management systems, 7

Knowledge workers, 13

Management information systems (MIS), 16

Mass customization, 21

Middle managers, 14

Network, 14

Operational managers, 14

Output, 8

Processing, 8

Production or service workers, 13

Senior managers, 14

Standard operating procedures (SOPs), 13

Storage technology, 14

Supply chain management systems, 7

Web site, 19

World Wide Web, 19

REVIEW QUESTIONS

1. Why are information systems essential in business today? Describe four trends in the global business environment that have made information systems so important.

2. Describe the capabilities of a digital firm. Why are digital firms so powerful? What are the four principal systems driving the movement toward digital firms?

3. What is an information system? Distinguish between a computer, a computer program, and an information system. What is the difference between data and information?

4. What activities convert raw data to usable information in information systems? What is their relationship to feedback?

5. What are the functions of an information system from a business perspective? What role do they play in the business information value chain?

6. What is information systems literacy? How does it differ from computer literacy?

7. What are the organization, management, and technology dimensions of information systems?

8. Distinguish between a behavioral and a technical approach to information systems in terms of the questions asked and the answers provided. What major disciplines contribute to an understanding of information systems?

9. What is the relationship between an organization and its information systems? How has this relationship changed over time?

10. What are the Internet and the World Wide Web? How have they changed the role played by information systems in organizations?

11. Describe some of the major changes that information systems are bringing to organizations.

12. How are information systems changing the management process?

13. What is the relationship between the network revolution, the digital firm, electronic commerce, and electronic business?

14. What are interorganizational systems? Why are they becoming more important? How has Internet and Web technology affected these systems?

15. What do we mean by information architecture and information technology infrastructure? Why are they important concerns for managers?

16. What are the key management challenges involved in building, operating, and maintaining information systems today?

APPLICATION SOFTWARE EXERCISE

DATABASE EXERCISE: ADDING VALUE TO INFORMATION FOR MANAGEMENT DECISION MAKING

Effective information systems add value to data to create meaningful information for management decisions that improve business performance. At the Laudon Web site for Chapter 1 you can find a Store and Regional Sales Database with raw data on weekly store sales of computer equipment in various sales regions. The database includes fields for store identification number, sales region number, item number, item description, unit price, units sold, and the weekly sales period when the sales were made. Develop some reports and queries to make this information more useful for management. Modify the database table, if necessary, to provide all of the information you require. Here are some questions you might consider:

A. Which are the best performing stores and sales regions?
B. What are the best selling products?
C. Which stores and sales regions are strongest in which products?
D. What are the strongest and weakest selling periods? For which stores? Which sales regions? Which products?
E. How can your company improve sales in the weakest store and sales region? (Answers will vary.)

GROUP PROJECT

In a group with three or four classmates, find a description in a computer or business magazine of an information system used by an organization. Look for information about the company on the Web to gain further insight into the company and prepare a brief description of the business. Describe the system you have selected in terms of its inputs, processes, and outputs, and in terms of its organization, management, and technology features and the importance of the system to the company. If possible, use electronic presentation software to present your analysis to the class.

TOOLS FOR INTERACTIVE LEARNING

■ INTERNET CONNECTION

The Internet Connection for this chapter will take you to the United Parcel Service Web site, where you can complete an exercise to evaluate how UPS uses the Web and other information technology in its daily operations.

■ INTERACTIVE STUDY GUIDE

You can use the Interactive Study Guide to test your knowledge of the topics in this chapter, and get instant feedback where you need more practice.

■ RUNNING CASE

The Running Case provides an opportunity for you to learn about Dirt Bikes USA and to analyze the management, organization, and technology dimensions of its business. You can use spreadsheet software to assess the firm's financial position. You can find a complete description of this project on the Laudon Web site for Chapter 1 and on the Multimedia Edition CD-ROM.

■ ELECTRONIC COMMERCE PROJECT

At the Laudon Web site for Chapter 1, you will find an Electronic Commerce project that will use the interactive software at the UPS Web site to help a company calculate and budget for its shipping costs.

■ MANAGEMENT DECISION PROBLEM

At the Laudon Web site for Chapter 1, you will find a Management Decision Problem on planning a new Internet business.

■ CD-ROM

If you use the Multimedia Edition CD-ROM with this chapter, you will find a video clip illustrating FedEx's package tracking system, an audio overview of the major themes of this chapter, and bullet text summarizing the key points of the chapter.

CASE STUDY—*ShopKo and Pamida: Systems Triumph or Tragedy?*

ShopKo, a general merchandise retail chain headquartered in Green Bay, Wisconsin, has about 140 stores in 15 states and had sales of $3.5 billion in 2001. Traditionally companies that sell apparel have four product cycles a year, one for each of the seasons. However such companies now face serious competition from companies like Gap that now operate on rapidly changing product cycles, often bringing in new product lines every two to four weeks. One of the growing problems ShopKo had to address was what to do with the excess (or overstocked) merchandise when a cycle ends.

At the end of a season (or cycle), companies have faced two problems. One is the need to empty its shelves in time for the arrival of the new cycle products (bathing suits do not sell well in the winter while fur coats are not in demand in the summer). The other problem is getting rid of the overstocked items at the highest possible price in an attempt to minimize losses in revenue. Traditionally the method ShopKo (and most other clothing retailers) used to determine clearance prices for overstocked items was to set each product price based upon clearance prices of similar products in past years. On average it found it needed to lower prices four times to clear the overstock at the end of a cycle, selling as much at each price as possible before lowering the price again. However, it always faced the calendar in addition to the customers' willingness to purchase at each price. Mike Martin, ShopKo's director of business alignment and planning, explains, "The first few markdowns buyers tend to take are very conservative. So they [Shopko] end up taking too many markdowns to clear [merchandise] out."

This markdown strategy proved to be costly as the number of cycles per year increased. The clearance price for each item was the same in every store throughout the entire chain. However, specific items were more popular and sold better in some stores than in others. Also, traditionally markdown timing was always the same for all stores, and yet seasonal changes can differ from store to store based on local geography and culture. The result was that the company could have set higher markdown prices in stores where the demand was higher or the cycle lasted a little longer. Moreover, a clothing markdown usually means a manual price change on each clothing item, and the staff time required to change the prices can be very costly. Four markdowns per item is very expensive.

ShopKo had made substantial information systems investments and one was a system to help the company optimize prices during markdowns. ShopKo implemented Markdown Optimizer from Spotlight Solutions in Mason, Ohio, which helps companies price leftovers so that the products will sell faster and with a better profit at each store. The software enables companies to price a product according to season, geography (specific store location), local tastes, and past demand, by analyzing historical pricing and sales data. It is proving very useful in helping stores get rid of the leftovers in time to make space for incoming products of the next cycle. This type of computer system is similar to the yield management software developed by the airlines. This software determines the best prices for airline seats at any given time. The goal is to fill the plane at the best total price possible.

ShopKo's CIO, Paul Burrows expressed his understanding that "The more you sell during the first markdown, the fewer you have left even if you have to take a second markdown." ShopKo's weekly sales data are stored in a merchandise data repository, and its computer system automatically feeds the data into Markdown Optimizer. Each piece of data contains the specific store, item number, and date for each item sold. Markdown Optimizer automatically stores the previous recommendation for each item in each individual store so that it can evaluate past results and then produce recommendations for the closeout of the current cycle. In 2001, ShopKo ran a pilot on the new product and the results were excellent. For the leftovers the pilot showed a 25 percent increase in its gross margin from previous years, while its payroll costs fell by 24 percent and the percentage of unsold goods at the end of each cycle fell from seven percent to two percent. Burrows was most pleased, claiming that a 15 percent increase would mean a $15 million growth in net profit.

In 1999, ShopKo purchased Pamida, a general merchandise retail chain focused on small towns such as Crete, Nebraska, (25 miles southwest of Lincoln, population 6000+) and Belle Fourche, South Dakota (Butte County, population about 4,000). With headquarters in Omaha, Nebraska, Pamida's slogan is "Bringing smaller communities what they want." ShopKo's aim in purchasing Pamida was to increase its presence in the small towns where competition from retailing powerhouses such as Wal-Mart and Target was not as strong. Pamida was the only major retail store in most of these small towns, and its strategy was to compete by maintaining a high in-stock rate rather than by becoming the lowest price competitor. Pamida relies on information systems to execute that strategy, and its SEC filing stated, "Pamida's information technology strategy is aimed at providing the customer with . . . merchandise which is always available as advertised." When ShopKo purchased Pamida, the chain had a total of about 180 stores, although that number increased to 229 stores in 16 states when ShopKo purchased the P.M. Place chain of 49 small town Midwestern stores in May 2000 and merged it into Pamida.

Despite its strategy, Pamida had too many out-of-stock items. To make matters worse, many key products were in warehouses even though they were not on store shelves. In addition, the company's gross margin was too low and falling. ShopKo wanted to expand the number of Pamida stores in small towns. Pamida's solution was to consolidate its five warehouses into three and modernize its inventory management systems to increase stores' ability to keep their shelves stocked. The plan execution began early in 2000 with the Lebanon (Indiana) Distribution Center Project to convert the Lebanon distribution center servicing 107 of Pamida's 229 stores, to a full-service warehouse. The concept was to transform the warehouse from a flow-through facility (where goods arrive at the warehouse and are immediately shipped to the stores) to a full-service distribution center (where inventory is stored so that it can be shipped to the stores immediately when needed). The warehouse was expanded from 200,000 square feet to 418,000 square feet, but the warehousing software was neither updated nor replaced.

Initially, the new inventory management system created serious bottlenecks in Pamida warehouses, causing Pamida's earnings to decline in the first nine months of 2001 and its corporate parent ShopKo to lose $6.7 million in overall revenue. Pamida's old warehouse management information system came from Catalyst International, and the company had never updated the software, which was several versions behind. According to Dan Trew, Catalyst's vice president of product strategy, "We have made significant enhancements in the configurability of the product, things we couldn't do when Pamida was [originally installing] its system," and so the system was out-of-date and inadequate. The software made it difficult to lay out and run a full-service center in the most logical and efficient manner. "It's not real flexible so the processes at the distribution center had to conform to the system," said Pamida's CIO Dan Nicklen. Newer versions of warehouse management software can handle full-service distribution centers much more easily.

Nicklen said Pamida's warehouse management software was not updated when the rest of the warehouse was modernized because the software had been working fine under the old distribution system. Pamida had the support of ShopKo's management in making technology investments to become more effective, but chose to continue using the old warehouse software. Instead, Pamida focused on a three-year program to replace all of its major large computer systems and software, including new merchandising software from Retek Information Systems.

The product supply shortage became even more serious as the 2000 holiday season approached. The estimated loss in sales for the 107 stores served by the Lebanon distribution center was $5 million, lagging 5 percent behind sales for the remaining 122 stores in the chain. Shareholders filed several class-action lawsuits, charging that management had not revealed the seriousness of the distribution center problems, partly to keep its stock prices up until November 2000, when it could no longer hide the problem. The quarterly report released that month showed gross margins of 20.8 cents in that quarter versus 26.3 cents previously.

Pamida partly blamed the problem on the previous owners, "Our resources were stretched thin," said Nicklen. "Under our previous owners we were always under funded." But there were also other problems. Certainly Pamida management turnover contributed, with the CEO, Steve Fishman, leaving in July 1999, and a new CEO arriving early in 2000. ShopKo also had a major management turnover when CEO William Podany resigned as chairman in May 2001. Moreover, the task of merging P.M. Place with Pamida in the spring of 2000 placed a heavy burden on the company.

Pamida eventually turned around its distribution center and it became fully functional by the end of 2001. ShopKo now feels confident enough in Pamida's new distribution system that it is closing a smaller warehouse in Missouri to consolidate distribution at its Indiana and Nebraska centers.

Sources: Carolyn Abate, "Going Once, Going Twice... Sold!" *Smart Business*, May 1, 2002; Edward Cone, "Pamida's Distribution Debacle," *Baseline*, January 1, 2002; Meridith Levinson, "Everything Must Go," *CIO*, May 1, 2002; Meridith Levinson, "They Know What You'll Buy Next Summer (*They Hope*)" *CIO*, May 1, 2002; and Bob Tedeschi, "The Price is Right," *Smart Business*, May 1, 2002.

CASE STUDY QUESTIONS

1. Evaluate the role of information systems in the way ShopKo and Pamida run their business. How important are they?

2. Evaluate the importance of Pamida's distribution center consolidation project for both Pamida and ShopKo. What management, organization and technology factors prevented Pamida's new distribution center from working successfully?

3. Are ShopKo and Pamida using information systems effectively? Why or why not? How much value do their systems provide to the business?

4. If you were the CEO of ShopKo, how would you have addressed the problem? If you were the CEO of Pamida when it was purchased by ShopKo, would you have recognized the problem? Explain. How would you have solved the problem?

5. What management challenges does this case study illustrate? Explain your answer.

2

CHAPTER

INFORMATION SYSTEMS IN THE ENTERPRISE

objectives

As a manager, you will need to understand the role of the various types of information systems in organizations. After completing this chapter, you will be able to answer the following questions:

1. *What are the major types of systems in a business? What roles do they play?*

2. *How do information systems support the major business functions: sales and marketing, manufacturing and production, finance and accounting, and human resources?*

3. *Why should managers pay attention to business processes? Why do firms need to integrate their business processes?*

4. *What are the benefits and challenges of using enterprise systems?*

5. *What are the benefits of using information systems to support supply chain management and collaborative commerce?*

6. *What are the business benefits of using information systems for customer relationship management and knowledge management?*

Fast-Track Fashions at Zara

In the fast-paced world of fashion retailing, nothing is as important as time to market, not even advertising or labor costs. No company knows that better than Zara, a worldwide women's apparel chain headquartered in La Coruna, Spain, that is now part of the Inditex global retail conglomerate. For decades, apparel companies have farmed out their production to low-wage countries, hoping to benefit from lower labor costs. Zara decided against this because its management believed that the ability to respond quickly to shifts in customer tastes would prove much more efficient and profitable than outsourcing to low-cost contract manufacturers. As Jose Maria Castellano, Inditex CEO, put it succinctly: "The fashion world is in constant flux and is driven not by supply but by customer demand."

By meticulously coordinating the entire production process, Zara can react much more quickly than its competitors to percolating fashion trends. Zara has what many believe is the world's most responsive supply chain. About half the items it sells are made in its own factories; the rest are outsourced. Zara restocks its stores twice a week, delivering both reordered items and completely new

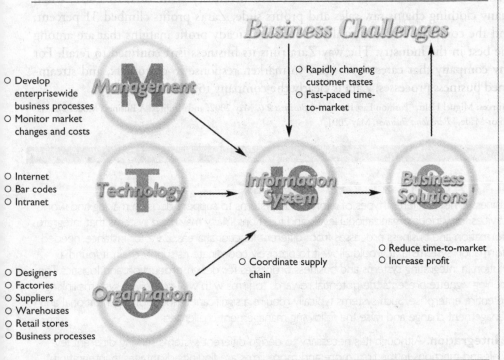

styles. Rival apparel chains, in contrast, only receive new designs once or twice a season. Zara's prolific design department likewise outstrips the competition by churning out more than 10,000 fresh new designs each year. No competitor comes close. "It's like you walk into a new store every two weeks," observes Tracy Mullin, president and CEO of the National Retail Federation.

Every working day, the manager of a Zara store reports exactly what has been sold to corporate headquarters via the Internet. This information is quickly relayed to the Zara's design department, which can create or alter products in a matter of days. Zara's 200 designers draw the latest fashion ideas on their computers and send them over Zara's intranet to Zara's nearby factories. Within days, the new garments are cut, dyed, stitched, and pressed. In just 3 weeks the clothes will be hanging in Zara stores all over the world. Zara's time to market is 12 times faster than rivals such as the Gap.

Zara maintains a gigantic 9 million square foot warehouse in La Coruna that is connected to 14 of its factories through a maze of tunnels, each with a rail hanging from its ceiling. Along these rails, cables transport bunches of clothes on hangers or in suspended racks into the warehouse. Each bundle is supported by a metal bar with a series of tabs coded to indicate exactly where in the warehouse that bundle should be placed. There, the merchandise is sorted, rerouted, and resorted until it gets to the staging area of the distribution center. Every Zara store has its own staging area here to assemble its orders. As soon as a store's order is complete, it is carted directly to a loading dock, and packed with other stores' shipments, in order of delivery. Deliveries to European stores are placed on trucks; shipments outside Europe are sent by plane. The vast majority of items are only in the warehouse a few hours and Zara constantly fine-tunes the size and sequence of deliveries to maintain that tight schedule.

Zara's manufacturing costs run 15 to 20 percent higher than those of rivals, but they are more than offset by the advantages of split-second time to market. By responding so quickly to customer tastes, Zara almost never needs to correct merchandise blunders or stage across-the-board inventory write offs. In 2001, when many clothing chains saw sales and profits slide, Zara's profits climbed 31 percent, and the company has historically maintained steady profit margins that are among the best in the industry. The way Zara runs its business isn't confined to retail. For any company that cares about time to market, response to customers, and streamlined business processes, Zara is clearly the company to watch.

Sources: Miguel Helft, "Fashion Fast Forward," *Business 2.0*, May 2002; and "Inditex: A Business Model That Is Tailor-Made," *Barcelona Business*, May 2001.

MANAGEMENT CHALLENGES

Businesses need different types of information systems to support decision making and work activities for various organizational levels and functions. Many may need systems that integrate information and business processes from different functional areas. Zara, for instance, needed information systems that would allow it to precisely coordinate its supply chain. It found a solution in integrating systems and business processes for design, production, and logistics. The opening vignette presents the potential rewards to firms with well-conceived systems linking the entire enterprise. Such systems typically require a significant amount of organizational and management change and raise the following management challenges:

1. **Integration.** Although it is necessary to design different systems serving different levels and functions in the firm, more and more firms are finding advantages in integrating systems. However, integrating systems for different organizational levels and functions to freely exchange information can be technologically difficult and costly. Managers need to determine what level of system integration is required and how much it is worth in dollars.

2. **Enlarging the scope of management thinking.** Most managers are trained to manage a product line, a division, or an office. They are rarely trained to optimize the performance of the organization as a whole and often are not given the means to do so. But enterprise systems and industrial networks require managers to take a much larger view of their own behavior, including other products, divisions, departments, and even outside business firms. Investments in enterprise systems are huge, they must be developed over long periods of time, and they must be guided by a shared vision of the objectives.

In this chapter we examine the role of the various types of information systems in organizations. First, we look at ways of classifying information systems based on the organizational level they support. Next, we look at systems in terms of the organizational function they serve. We show how systems can support business processes for the major business functions and processes that span more than one function. We then examine enterprise applications—enterprise systems, supply chain management systems, customer relationship management systems, and knowledge management systems—which enable organizations to integrate information from multiple functions and business processes across entire firms and even entire industries.

2.1 MAJOR TYPES OF SYSTEMS IN ORGANIZATIONS

Because there are different interests, specialties, and levels in an organization, there are different kinds of systems. No single system can provide all the information an organization needs. Figure 2-1 illustrates one way to depict the kinds of systems found in an organization.

KIND OF INFORMATION SYSTEM

Strategic Level

Management Level

Knowledge Level

Operational Level

GROUPS SERVED

Senior Managers

Middle Managers

Knowledge and Data Workers

Operational Managers

FUNCTIONAL AREAS   Sales and Marketing   Manufacturing   Finance   Accounting   Human Resources

Figure 2-1 Types of information systems. Organizations can be divided into strategic, management, knowledge, and operational levels and into five major functional areas: sales and marketing, manufacturing, finance, accounting, and human resources. Information systems serve each of these levels and functions.

In the illustration, the organization is divided into strategic, management, knowledge, and operational levels and then is further divided into functional areas such as sales and marketing, manufacturing, finance, accounting, and human resources. Systems are built to serve these different organizational interests (Anthony, 1965).

DIFFERENT KINDS OF SYSTEMS

Four main types of information systems serve different organizational levels: operational-level systems, knowledge-level systems, management-level systems, and strategic-level systems. **Operational-level systems** support operational managers by keeping track of the elementary activities and transactions of the organization, such as sales, receipts, cash deposits, payroll, credit decisions, and the flow of materials in a factory. The principal purpose of systems at this level is to answer routine questions and to track the flow of transactions through the organization. How many parts are in inventory? What happened to Mr. Williams's payment? To answer these kinds of questions, information generally must be easily available, current, and accurate. Examples of operational-level systems include a system to record bank deposits from automatic teller machines or one that tracks the number of hours worked each day by employees on a factory floor.

Knowledge-level systems support the organization's knowledge and data workers. The purpose of knowledge-level systems is to help the business firm integrate new knowledge into the business and to help the organization control the flow of paperwork. Knowledge-level systems, especially in the form of workstations and office systems, are among the fastest-growing applications in business today.

Management-level systems serve the monitoring, controlling, decision-making, and administrative activities of middle managers. The principal question addressed by such systems is: Are things working well? Management-level systems typically provide periodic reports rather than instant information on operations. An example is a relocation control system that reports on the total moving, house-hunting, and home financing costs for employees in all company divisions, noting wherever actual costs exceed budgets.

Some management-level systems support nonroutine decision making (Keen and Morton, 1978). They tend to focus on less-structured decisions for which information requirements are not always clear. These systems often answer "what-if" questions: What would be the impact on production schedules if we were to double sales in the month of December? What would happen to our return on investment if a factory schedule were delayed for six months? Answers to these questions frequently require new data from outside the organization, as well as data from inside that cannot be easily drawn from existing operational-level systems.

operational-level systems
Information systems that monitor the elementary activities and transactions of the organization.

knowledge-level systems
Information systems that support knowledge and data workers in an organization.

management-level systems
Information systems that support the monitoring, controlling, decision-making, and administrative activities of middle managers.

strategic-level systems
Information systems that support the long-range planning activities of senior management.

Strategic-level systems help senior management tackle and address strategic issues and long-term trends, both in the firm and in the external environment. Their principal concern is matching changes in the external environment with existing organizational capability. What will employment levels be in five years? What are the long-term industry cost trends, and where does our firm fit in? What products should we be making in five years?

Information systems also serve the major business functions, such as sales and marketing, manufacturing, finance, accounting, and human resources. A typical organization has operational-, management-, knowledge-, and strategic-level systems for each functional area. For example, the sales function generally has a sales system on the operational level to record daily sales figures and to process orders. A knowledge-level system designs promotional displays for the firm's products. A management-level system tracks monthly sales figures by sales territory and reports on territories where sales exceed or fall below anticipated levels. A system to forecast sales trends over a five-year period serves the strategic level. We first describe the specific categories of systems serving each organizational level and their value to the organization. Then we show how organizations use these systems for each major business function.

SIX MAJOR TYPES OF SYSTEMS

Figure 2-2 shows the specific types of information systems that correspond to each organizational level. The organization has executive support systems (ESS) at the strategic level, management information systems (MIS) and decision-support systems (DSS) at the management level, knowledge work systems (KWS) and office systems at the knowledge level, and transaction processing systems (TPS) at the operational level. Systems at each level in turn are specialized to serve each of the major functional areas. Thus, the typical systems found in organizations are designed to assist workers or managers at each level and in the functions of sales and marketing, manufacturing, finance, accounting, and human resources.

Table 2-1 summarizes the features of the six types of information systems. It should be noted that each of the different systems might have components that are used by organiza-

Figure 2-2 The six major types of information systems. This figure provides examples of TPS, office systems, KWS, DSS, MIS, and ESS, showing the level of the organization and business function that each supports.

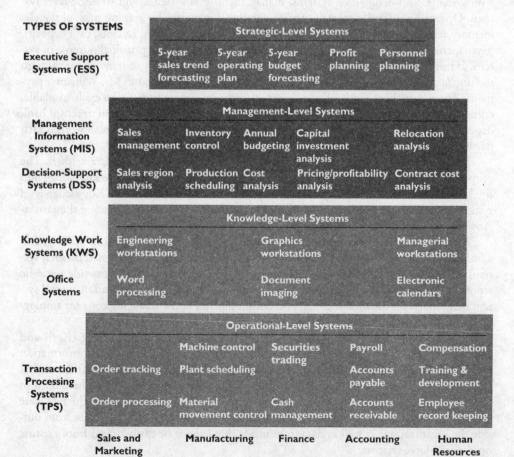

TABLE 2-1	CHARACTERISTICS OF INFORMATION PROCESSING SYSTEMS			
Type of System	Information Inputs	Processing	Information Outputs	Users
ESS	Aggregate data; external, internal	Graphics; simulations; interactive	Projections; responses to queries	Senior managers
DSS	Low-volume data or massive databases optimized for data analysis; analytic models and data analysis tools	Interactive; simulations; analysis	Special reports; decision analyses; responses to queries	Professionals; staff managers
MIS	Summary transaction data; high-volume data; simple models	Routine reports; simple models; low-level analysis	Summary and exception reports	Middle managers
KWS	Design specifications; knowledge base	Modeling; simulations	Models; graphics	Professionals; technical staff
Office systems	Documents; schedules	Document management; scheduling; communication	Documents; schedules; mail	Clerical workers
TPS	Transactions; events	Sorting; listing; merging; updating	Detailed reports; lists; summaries	Operations personnel; supervisors

tional levels and groups other than their main constituencies. A secretary may find information on an MIS, or a middle manager may need to extract data from a TPS.

Transaction Processing Systems

Transaction processing systems (TPS) are the basic business systems that serve the operational level of the organization. A transaction processing system is a computerized system that performs and records the daily routine transactions necessary to conduct business. Examples are sales order entry, hotel reservation systems, payroll, employee record keeping, and shipping.

At the operational level, tasks, resources, and goals are predefined and highly structured. The decision to grant credit to a customer, for instance, is made by a lower-level supervisor according to predefined criteria. All that must be determined is whether the customer meets the criteria.

Figure 2-3 depicts a payroll TPS, which is a typical accounting transaction processing system found in most firms. A payroll system keeps track of the money paid to employees. The master file is composed of discrete pieces of information (such as a name, address, or employee number) called data elements. Data are keyed into the system, updating the data elements. The elements on the master file are combined in different ways to make up reports of interest to management and government agencies and to send paychecks to employees. These TPS can generate other report combinations of existing data elements.

Other typical TPS applications are identified in Figure 2-4. The figure shows that there are five functional categories of TPS: sales/marketing, manufacturing/production, finance/accounting, human resources, and other types of TPS that are unique to a particular industry. The UPS package tracking system described in Chapter 1 is an example of a manufacturing TPS. UPS sells package delivery services; the TPS system keeps track of all of its package shipment transactions.

Transaction processing systems are often so central to a business that TPS failure for a few hours can spell a firm's demise and perhaps other firms linked to it. Imagine what would happen to UPS if its package tracking system were not working! What would the airlines do without their computerized reservation systems?

Managers need TPS to monitor the status of internal operations and the firm's relations with the external environment. TPS are also major producers of information for the other types of systems. (For example, the payroll system illustrated here, along with other accounting

transaction processing systems (TPS)

Computerized systems that perform and record the daily routine transactions necessary to conduct the business; they serve the organization's operational level.

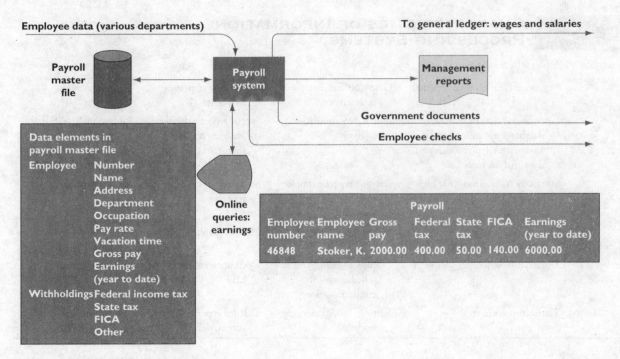

Figure 2-3 A symbolic representation for a payroll TPS.

TPS, supplies data to the company's general ledger system, which is responsible for maintaining records of the firm's income and expenses and for producing reports such as income statements and balance sheets.)

Knowledge Work and Office Systems

Knowledge work systems (KWS) and **office systems** serve the information needs at the knowledge level of the organization. Knowledge work systems aid knowledge workers,

knowledge work systems (KWS)

Information systems that aid knowledge workers in the creation and integration of new knowledge in the organization.

TYPE OF TPS SYSTEM				
Sales/ marketing systems	**Manufacturing/ production systems**	**Finance/ accounting systems**	**Human resources systems**	**Other types (e.g., university)**
Major functions of system				
Sales management	Scheduling	Budgeting	Personnel records	Admissions
Market research	Purchasing	General ledger	Benefits	Grade records
Promotion	Shipping/receiving	Billing	Compensation	Course records
Pricing	Engineering	Cost accounting	Labor relations	Alumni
New products	Operations		Training	
Major application systems				
Sales order information system	Machine control systems	General ledger	Payroll	Registration system
Market research system	Purchase order systems	Accounts receivable/payable	Employee records	Student transcript system
Sales commission system	Quality control systems	Funds management systems	Benefit systems	Curriculum class control systems
			Career path systems	Alumni benefactor system

Figure 2-4 Typical applications of TPS. There are five functional categories of TPS: sales/marketing, manufacturing/production, finance/accounting, human resources, and other types of systems specific to a particular industry. Within each of these major functions are subfunctions. For each of these subfunctions (e.g., sales management) there is a major application system.

whereas office systems primarily aid data workers (although they are also used extensively by knowledge workers).

As first discussed in Chapter 1, *knowledge workers* are people who hold formal university degrees and who are often members of recognized professions such as engineers, doctors, lawyers, and scientists. Their jobs consist primarily of creating new information and knowledge. KWS, such as scientific or engineering design workstations, promote the creation of new knowledge and ensure that new knowledge and technical expertise are properly integrated into the business. *Data workers* typically have less formal advanced educational degrees and tend to process rather than create information. They consist primarily of secretaries, bookkeepers, filing clerks, or managers whose jobs are principally to use, manipulate, or disseminate information. Office systems are information technology applications designed to increase data workers' productivity by supporting the coordinating and communicating activities of the typical office. Office systems coordinate diverse information workers, geographic units, and functional areas: The systems communicate with customers, suppliers, and other organizations outside the firm and serve as clearinghouses for information and knowledge flows.

Typical office systems handle and manage documents through word processing, desktop publishing, document imaging, and digital filing; scheduling through electronic calendars; and communication through electronic mail, voice mail, or videoconferencing. **Word processing** refers to the software and hardware technology that creates, edits, formats, stores, and prints documents (see Chapter 6). Word processing systems represent the single most common application of information technology to office work, in part because producing documents is what offices are all about. **Desktop publishing** produces professional publishing-quality documents by combining output from word processing software with design elements, graphics, and special layout features. Companies are now starting to publish documents in the form of Web pages for easier access and distribution. We describe Web publishing in more detail in Chapter 10.

Document imaging systems are another widely used knowledge application. Document imaging systems convert paper documents and images into digital form so that they can be stored and accessed by the computer.

Management Information Systems

In Chapter 1, we defined management information systems as the study of information systems in business and management. The term *management information systems (MIS)* also designates a specific category of information systems serving management-level functions. **Management information systems (MIS)** serve the management level of the organization, providing managers with reports and, in some cases, with online access to the organization's current performance and historical records. Typically, they are oriented almost exclusively to

office systems
Computer systems, such as word processing, electronic mail systems, and scheduling systems, that are designed to increase the productivity of data workers in the office.

word processing
Office system technology that facilitates the creation of documents through computerized text editing, formatting, storing, and printing.

desktop publishing
Technology that produces professional-quality documents combining output from word processors with design, graphics, and special layout features.

document imaging systems
Systems that convert paper documents and images into digital form so that they can be stored and accessed by the computer.

management information systems (MIS)
Information systems at the management level of an organization that serve the functions of planning, controlling, and decision making by providing routine summary and exception reports.

Desktop publishing software enables users to control all aspects of the design and layout process for professional-looking documents.

Figure 2-5 How management information systems obtain their data from the organization's TPS. In the system illustrated by this diagram, three TPS supply summarized transaction data at the end of the time period to the MIS reporting system. Managers gain access to the organizational data through the MIS, which provides them with the appropriate reports.

internal, not environmental or external, events. MIS primarily serve the functions of planning, controlling, and decision making at the management level. Generally, they depend on underlying transaction processing systems for their data.

MIS summarize and report on the company's basic operations. The basic transaction data from TPS are compressed and are usually presented in long reports that are produced on a regular schedule. Figure 2-5 shows how a typical MIS transforms transaction level data from inventory, production, and accounting into MIS files that are used to provide managers with reports. Figure 2-6 shows a sample report from this system.

MIS usually serve managers interested in weekly, monthly, and yearly results—not day-to-day activities. MIS generally provide answers to routine questions that have been specified in advance and have a predefined procedure for answering them. For instance, MIS reports might list the total pounds of lettuce used this quarter by a fast-food chain or, as illustrated in Figure 2-6, compare total annual sales figures for specific products to planned targets.

Figure 2-6 A sample report that might be produced by the MIS in Figure 2-5.

Consolidated Consumer Products Corporation
Sales by Product and Sales Region: 2003

PRODUCT CODE	PRODUCT DESCRIPTION	SALES REGION	ACTUAL SALES	PLANNED	ACTUAL VS. PLANNED
4469	Carpet Cleaner	Northeast	4,066,700	4,800,000	0.85
		South	3,778,112	3,750,000	1.01
		Midwest	4,867,001	4,600,000	1.06
		West	4,003,440	4,400,000	0.91
		TOTAL	16,715,253	17,550,000	0.95
5674	Room Freshener	Northeast	3,676,700	3,900,000	0.94
		South	5,608,112	4,700,000	1.19
		Midwest	4,711,001	4,200,000	1.12
		West	4,563,440	4,900,000	0.93
		TOTAL	18,559,253	17,700,000	1.05

These systems are generally not flexible and have little analytical capability. Most MIS use simple routines such as summaries and comparisons, as opposed to sophisticated mathematical models or statistical techniques.

Decision-Support Systems

Decision-support systems (DSS) also serve the management level of the organization. DSS help managers make decisions that are unique, rapidly changing, and not easily specified in advance. They address problems where the procedure for arriving at a solution may not be fully predefined in advance. Although DSS use internal information from TPS and MIS, they often bring in information from external sources, such as current stock prices or product prices of competitors.

Clearly, by design, DSS have more analytical power than other systems. They are built explicitly with a variety of models to analyze data, or they condense large amounts of data into a form in which they can be analyzed by decision makers. DSS are designed so that users can work with them directly; these systems explicitly include user-friendly software. DSS are interactive; the user can change assumptions, ask new questions, and include new data.

An interesting, small, but powerful DSS is the voyage-estimating system of a subsidiary of a large American metals company that exists primarily to carry bulk cargoes of coal, oil, ores, and finished products for its parent company. The firm owns some vessels, charters others, and bids for shipping contracts in the open market to carry general cargo. A voyage-estimating system calculates financial and technical voyage details. Financial calculations include ship/time costs (fuel, labor, capital), freight rates for various types of cargo, and port expenses. Technical details include a myriad of factors such as ship cargo capacity, speed, port distances, fuel and water consumption, and loading patterns (location of cargo for different ports). The system can answer questions such as the following: Given a customer delivery schedule and an offered freight rate, which vessel should be assigned at what rate to maximize profits? What is the optimum speed at which a particular vessel can maximize its profit and still meet its delivery schedule? What is the optimal loading pattern for a ship bound for the U.S. West Coast from Malaysia? Figure 2-7 illustrates the DSS built for this company. The system operates on a powerful desktop personal computer, providing a system of menus that makes it easy for users to enter data or obtain information. We describe other types of DSS in Chapter 11.

Executive Support Systems

Senior managers use **executive support systems (ESS)** to make decisions. ESS serve the strategic level of the organization. They address nonroutine decisions requiring judgment, evaluation, and insight because there is no agreed-on procedure for arriving at a solution. ESS create a generalized computing and communications environment rather than providing any fixed application or specific capability. ESS are designed to incorporate data about external events such as new tax laws or competitors, but they also draw summarized information from internal MIS and DSS. They filter, compress, and track critical data, emphasizing the reduction of time and effort required to obtain information useful to executives. ESS

decision-support systems (DSS)
Information systems at the organization's management level that combine data and sophisticated analytical models or data analysis tools to support semistructured and unstructured decision making.

executive support systems (ESS)
Information systems at the organization's strategic level designed to address unstructured decision making through advanced graphics and communications.

Figure 2-7 Voyage-estimating decision-support system. This DSS operates on a powerful PC. It is used daily by managers who must develop bids on shipping contracts.

Figure 2-8 Model of a typical executive support system. This system pools data from diverse internal and external sources and makes them available to executives in an easy-to-use form.

employ the most advanced graphics software and can deliver graphs and data from many sources immediately to a senior executive's office or to a boardroom.

Unlike the other types of information systems, ESS are not designed primarily to solve specific problems. Instead, ESS provide a generalized computing and telecommunications capacity that can be applied to a changing array of problems. Although many DSS are designed to be highly analytical, ESS tend to make less use of analytical models.

Questions ESS assist in answering include the following: What business should we be in? What are the competitors doing? What new acquisitions would protect us from cyclical business swings? Which units should we sell to raise cash for acquisitions (Rockart and Treacy, 1982)? Figure 2-8 illustrates a model of an ESS. It consists of workstations with menus, interactive graphics, and communications capabilities that can access historical and competitive data from internal corporate systems and external databases such as Dow Jones News/Retrieval or the Gallup Poll. Because ESS are designed to be used by senior managers who may have little direct contact or experience with computer-based information systems, they incorporate easy-to-use graphic interfaces. More details on leading-edge applications of DSS and ESS can be found in Chapter 11.

RELATIONSHIP OF SYSTEMS TO ONE ANOTHER

Figure 2-9 illustrates how the systems serving different levels in the organization are related to one another. TPS are typically a major source of data for other systems, whereas ESS are

Figure 2-9 Interrelationships among systems. The various types of systems in the organization have interdependencies. TPS are major producers of information that is required by the other systems, which, in turn, produce information for other systems. These different types of systems are only loosely coupled in most organizations.

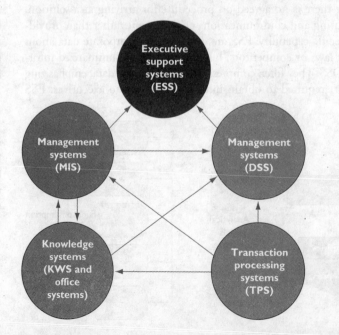

primarily a recipient of data from lower-level systems. The other types of systems may exchange data with each other as well. Data may also be exchanged among systems serving different functional areas. For example, an order captured by a sales system may be transmitted to a manufacturing system as a transaction for producing or delivering the product specified in the order or to a MIS for financial reporting.

It is definitely advantageous to have some measure of integration among these systems so that information can flow easily between different parts of the organization. But integration costs money, and integrating many different systems is extremely time consuming and complex. Each organization must weigh its needs for integrating systems against the difficulties of mounting a large-scale systems integration effort. The discussion of enterprise systems in Section 2.3 treats this issue in greater detail.

2.2 SYSTEMS FROM A FUNCTIONAL PERSPECTIVE

Information systems can be classified by the specific organizational function they serve as well as by organizational level. We now describe typical information systems that support each of the major business functions and provide examples of functional applications for each organizational level.

SALES AND MARKETING SYSTEMS

The sales and marketing function is responsible for selling the organization's product or service. Marketing is concerned with identifying the customers for the firm's products or services, determining what they need or want, planning and developing products and services to meet their needs, and advertising and promoting these products and services. Sales is concerned with contacting customers, selling the products and services, taking orders, and following up on sales. **Sales and marketing information systems** support these activities.

Table 2-2 shows that information systems are used in sales and marketing in a number of ways. At the strategic level, sales and marketing systems monitor trends affecting new products and sales opportunities, support planning for new products and services, and monitor the performance of competitors. At the management level, sales and marketing systems support market research, advertising and promotional campaigns, and pricing decisions. They analyze sales performance and the performance of the sales staff. Knowledge-level sales and marketing systems support marketing analysis workstations. At the operational level, sales and marketing systems assist in locating and contacting prospective customers, tracking sales, processing orders, and providing customer service support.

Review Figure 2-6. It shows the output of a typical sales information system at the management level. The system consolidates data about each item sold (such as the product code, product description, and amount sold) for further management analysis. Company managers examine these sales data to monitor sales activity and buying trends.

sales and marketing information systems
Systems that help the firm identify customers for the firm's products or services, develop products and services to meet customers' needs, promote these products and services, sell the products and services, and provide ongoing customer support.

ᴼTABLE 2-2 EXAMPLES OF SALES AND MARKETING INFORMATION SYSTEMS

System	Description	Organizational Level
Order processing	Enter, process, and track orders	Operational
Market analysis	Identify customers and markets using data on demographics, markets, consumer behavior, and trends	Knowledge
Pricing analysis	Determine prices for products and services	Management
Sales trend forecasting	Prepare 5-year sales forecasts	Strategic

TABLE 2-3	EXAMPLES OF MANUFACTURING AND PRODUCTION INFORMATION SYSTEMS	
System	Description	Organizational Level
Machine control	Control the actions of machines and equipment	Operational
Computer-aided design (CAD)	Design new products using the computer	Knowledge
Production planning	Decide when and how many products should be produced	Management
Facilities location	Decide where to locate new production facilities	Strategic

MANUFACTURING AND PRODUCTION SYSTEMS

The manufacturing and production function is responsible for actually producing the firm's goods and services. Manufacturing and production systems deal with the planning, development, and maintenance of production facilities; the establishment of production goals; the acquisition, storage, and availability of production materials; and the scheduling of equipment, facilities, materials, and labor required to fashion finished products. **Manufacturing and production information systems** support these activities.

manufacturing and production information systems

Systems that deal with the planning, development, and production of products and services, and with controlling the flow of production.

Table 2-3 shows some typical manufacturing and production information systems arranged by organizational level. Strategic-level manufacturing systems deal with the firm's long-term manufacturing goals, such as where to locate new plants or whether to invest in new manufacturing technology. At the management level, manufacturing and production systems analyze and monitor manufacturing and production costs and resources. Knowledge manufacturing and production systems create and distribute design knowledge or expertise to drive the production process, and operational manufacturing and production systems deal with the status of production tasks.

Most manufacturing and production systems use some sort of inventory system, as illustrated in Figure 2-10. Data about each item in inventory, such as the number of units depleted because of a shipment or purchase or the number of units replenished by reordering or returns, are either scanned or keyed into the system. The inventory master file contains basic data about each item, including the unique identification code for each item, the description of the item, the number of units on hand, the number of units on order, and the reorder point (the number of units in inventory that triggers a decision to reorder to prevent a stockout). Companies can estimate the number of items to reorder or

Information systems can guide the action of machines and equipment to help firms monitor and control the manufacturing process.

Shipment and order data

Inventory master file

Data elements in inventory master file:

Item code
Description
Units on hand
Units on order
Reorder point

Online queries

Inventory Status Report Report Date: 1/14/2003			
Item Code	Description	Units on Hand	Units on Order
6361	Fan belt	10,211	0
4466	Power cord	55,710	88,660
9313	Condenser	663	10,200
8808	Paint sprayer	11,242	0

Figure 2-10 Overview of an inventory system. This system provides information about the number of items available in inventory to support manufacturing and production activities.

they can use a formula for calculating the least expensive quantity to reorder called the *economic order quantity*. The system produces reports such as the number of each item available in inventory, the number of units of each item to reorder, or items in inventory that must be replenished.

FINANCE AND ACCOUNTING SYSTEMS

The finance function is responsible for managing the firm's financial assets, such as cash, stocks, bonds, and other investments in order to maximize the return on these financial assets. The finance function is also in charge of managing the capitalization of the firm (finding new financial assets in stocks, bonds, or other forms of debt). In order to determine whether the firm is getting the best return on its investments, the finance function must obtain a considerable amount of information from sources external to the firm.

The accounting function is responsible for maintaining and managing the firm's financial records—receipts, disbursements, depreciation, payroll—to account for the flow of funds in a firm. Finance and accounting share related problems—how to keep track of a firm's financial assets and fund flows. They provide answers to questions such as these: What is the current inventory of financial assets? What records exist for disbursements, receipts, payroll, and other fund flows?

Table 2-4 shows some of the typical **finance and accounting information systems** found in large organizations. Strategic-level systems for the finance and accounting function establish long-term investment goals for the firm and provide long-range forecasts of the firm's financial performance. At the management level, information systems help managers oversee and control the firm's financial resources. Knowledge systems support finance and accounting by providing analytical tools and workstations for designing the right mix of investments to maximize returns for the firm. Operational systems in finance and accounting track the flow of funds in the firm through transactions such as paychecks, payments to vendors, securities reports, and receipts.

Review Figure 2-3, which illustrates a payroll system, a typical accounting TPS found in all businesses with employees.

finance and accounting information systems
Systems that keep track of the firm's financial assets and fund flows.

TABLE 2-4	EXAMPLES OF FINANCE AND ACCOUNTING INFORMATION SYSTEMS

System	Description	Organizational Level
Accounts receivable	Track money owed the firm	Operational
Portfolio analysis	Design the firm's portfolio of investments	Knowledge
Budgeting	Prepare short-term budgets	Management
Profit planning	Plan long-term profits	Strategic

TABLE 2-5	EXAMPLES OF HUMAN RESOURCES INFORMATION SYSTEMS	
System	Description	Organizational Level
Training and development	Track employee training, skills, and performance appraisals	Operational
Career pathing	Design career paths for employees	Knowledge
Compensation analysis	Monitor the range and distribution of employee wages, salaries, and benefits	Management
Human resources planning	Plan the long-term labor force needs of the organization	Strategic

HUMAN RESOURCES SYSTEMS

human resources information systems

Systems that maintain employee records; track employee skills, job performance, and training; and support planning for employee compensation and career development.

The human resources function is responsible for attracting, developing, and maintaining the firm's work force. **Human resources information systems** support activities such as identifying potential employees, maintaining complete records on existing employees, and creating programs to develop employees' talents and skills.

Strategic-level human resources systems identify the manpower requirements (skills, educational level, types of positions, number of positions, and cost) for meeting the firm's long-term business plans. At the management level, human resources systems help managers monitor and analyze the recruitment, allocation, and compensation of employees. Knowledge systems for human resources support analysis activities related to job design, training, and the modeling of employee career paths and reporting relationships. Human resources operational systems track the recruitment and placement of the firm's employees (see Table 2-5).

Figure 2-11 illustrates a typical human resources TPS for employee record keeping. It maintains basic employee data, such as the employee's name, age, sex, marital status, address, educational background, salary, job title, date of hire, and date of termination. The system can produce a variety of reports, such as lists of newly hired employees, employees who are terminated or on leaves of absence, employees classified by job type or educational level, or employee job performance evaluations. Such systems are typically designed to provide data that can satisfy federal and state record keeping requirements for Equal Employment Opportunity (EEO) and other purposes.

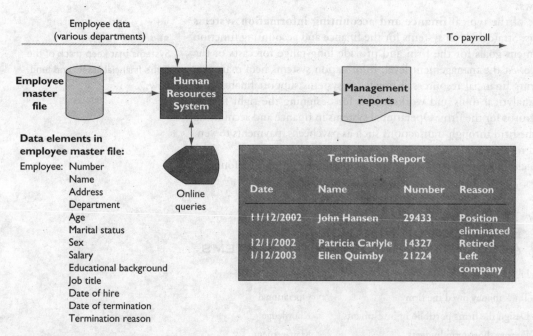

Figure 2-11   An employee record keeping system. This system maintains data on the firm's employees to support the human resources function.

2.3 ENTERPRISE APPLICATIONS: ENTERPRISE SYSTEMS AND SYSTEMS FOR SUPPLY CHAIN MANAGEMENT, CUSTOMER RELATIONSHIP MANAGEMENT, AND KNOWLEDGE MANAGEMENT

Electronic commerce, electronic business, and intensifying global competition are forcing firms to focus on speed to market, improving customer service, and more efficient execution. The flow of information and work needs to be orchestrated so that the organization can perform like a well-oiled machine. These changes require powerful new systems that can integrate information from many different functional areas and organizational units and coordinate firm activities with those of suppliers and other business partners.

In previous sections of this chapter you learned that there are many specialized types of systems found in organizations serving different business functions and organizational levels. Many of these systems were built in isolation from each other and consequently could not automatically exchange information. Information needed to support decision making was often "stuck" in these specialized systems. Manufacturing units might not know exactly how many and what types of items to produce because their systems could not easily obtain information from systems that processed customer orders. Managers planning American business units could not easily share information with Asian offices or European offices because each had built their own set of systems. In this environment, operating a "global firm" or even a highly coordinated enterprise within a single country becomes nearly impossible.

One solution is to build a separate "middleware" software bridge to each of these specialized systems to link them all together (see Chapter 6). This is both an expensive and unsatisfactory solution. Another solution, now more common, is to build or buy entirely new **enterprise applications** that can coordinate activities, decisions, and knowledge across many different functions, levels, and business units in a firm. Chapter 1 introduced the principal digital firm applications used for this purpose: enterprise systems, supply chain management systems, customer relationship management systems, and knowledge management systems. Each of these enterprise applications integrates a related set of functions and business processes to enhance the performance of the organization as a whole.

Generally these more contemporary systems take advantage of corporate intranets and Web technologies that enable the efficient transfer of information within the firm and to partner firms. These systems are inherently cross-level, cross-functional and business process oriented. Review Figure 1-13 in Chapter 1, which shows that the architecture for these enterprise applications encompasses processes spanning the entire organization and in some cases, extending beyond the organization to customers, suppliers, and other key business partners.

enterprise applications
Systems that can coordinate activities, decisions, and knowledge across many different functions, levels, and business units in a firm. Include enterprise systems, supply chain management systems, customer relationship management systems, and knowledge management systems.

INTEGRATING FUNCTIONS AND BUSINESS PROCESSES

The new digital firm business environment and the deployment of enterprise applications requires companies to think more strategically about their business processes, which we introduced in Chapter 1. *Business processes* refer to the manner in which work is organized, coordinated, and focused to produce a valuable product or service. Business processes are concrete work flows of material, information, and knowledge—sets of activities. Business processes also refer to the unique ways in which organizations coordinate work, information, and knowledge, and the ways in which management chooses to coordinate work. A company's business processes can be a source of competitive strength if they enable the company to innovate better or to execute better than its rivals. Business processes can also be a liability if they are based on outdated ways of working that impede organizational responsiveness and efficiency.

Some business processes support the major functional areas of the firm, others are cross-functional. Table 2-6 describes some typical business processes for each of the functional areas.

Many business processes are cross-functional, transcending the boundaries between sales, marketing, manufacturing, and research and development. These cross-functional processes cut across the traditional organizational structure, grouping employees from different functional specialties to complete a piece of work. For example, the order fulfillment

TABLE 2-6	EXAMPLES OF FUNCTIONAL BUSINESS PROCESSES

Functional Area	Business Process
Manufacturing and production	Assembling the product
	Checking for quality
	Producing bills of materials
Sales and marketing	Identifying customers
	Making customers aware of the product
	Selling the product
Finance and accounting	Paying creditors
	Creating financial statements
	Managing cash accounts
Human resources	Hiring employees
	Evaluating employees' job performance
	Enrolling employees in benefits plans

process at many companies requires cooperation among the sales function (receiving the order, entering the order), the accounting function (credit checking and billing for the order), and the manufacturing function (assembling and shipping the order). Figure 2-12 illustrates how this cross-functional process might work. Information systems support these cross-functional processes as well as processes for the separate business functions.

Today's firms are finding that they can become more flexible and productive by coordinating their business processes more closely and in some cases integrating these processes so they focus more on efficient management of resources and customer service. Enterprise applications are designed to support organization-wide process coordination and integration. Enterprise systems create an integrated organization-wide platform to coordinate key internal processes of the firm. Information systems for supply chain management (SCM) and customer relationship management (CRM) can help coordinate processes for managing the firm's relationship with its suppliers and customers. Knowledge management systems enable organizations to better manage processes for capturing and applying knowledge and expertise.

ENTERPRISE SYSTEMS

Enterprise systems, which we introduced in Chapter 1, provide a technology platform where organizations can integrate and coordinate their major internal business processes. They address the problem of organizational inefficiencies created by isolated islands of information, business processes, and technology. A large organization typically has many different

Figure 2-12 The order fulfillment process. Generating and fulfilling an order is a multistep process involving activities performed by the sales, manufacturing and production, and accounting functions.

Figure 2-13 Traditional view of systems. In most organizations, separate systems built over a long period of time support discrete business processes and discrete business functions. The organization's systems rarely included vendors and customers.

kinds of information systems that support different functions, organizational levels, and business processes. Most of these systems are built around different functions; business units and business processes that do not "talk" to each other. Managers might have a hard time assembling the data they need for a comprehensive, overall picture of the organization's operations. For instance, sales personnel might not be able to tell at the time they place an order whether the items that were ordered were in inventory; customers could not track their orders; and manufacturing could not communicate easily with finance to plan for new production. This fragmentation of data in hundreds of separate systems could thus have a negative impact on organizational efficiency and business performance. Figure 2-13 illustrates the traditional arrangement of information systems.

Enterprise systems, also known as enterprise resource planning (ERP) systems solve this problem by providing a single information system for organization-wide coordination of key business processes. Enterprise software models and automates many business processes, such as filling an order or scheduling a shipment, with the goal of integrating information across the company and eliminating complex, expensive links between computer systems in different areas of the business. Information that was previously fragmented in different systems can seamlessly flow throughout the firm so that it can be shared by business processes in manufacturing, accounting, human resources, and other areas of the firm. Discrete business processes from sales, production, finance, and logistics can be integrated into company-wide business processes that flow across organizational levels and functions. An enterprise-wide technical platform serves all processes and levels. Figure 2-14 illustrates how enterprise systems work.

The enterprise system collects data from various key business processes (see Table 2-7) and stores the data in a single comprehensive data repository where they can be used by other

Figure 2-14 Enterprise systems. Enterprise systems can integrate the key business processes of an entire firm into a single software system that allows information to flow seamlessly throughout the organization. These systems focus primarily on internal processes but may include transactions with customers and vendors.

TABLE 2-7	BUSINESS PROCESSES SUPPORTED BY ENTERPRISE SYSTEMS

Manufacturing processes, including inventory management, purchasing, shipping, production planning, production scheduling, material requirements planning, and plant and equipment maintenance

Financial and accounting processes, including accounts payable, accounts receivable, cash management and forecasting, product-cost accounting, cost-center accounting, asset accounting, general ledger, and financial reporting

Sales and marketing processes, including order processing, pricing, shipping, billing, sales management, and sales planning

Human resource processes, including personnel administration, time accounting, payroll, personnel planning and development, benefits accounting, applicant tracking, and travel expense reporting

parts of the business. Managers emerge with more precise and timely information for coordinating the daily operations of the business and a firmwide view of business processes and information flows.

For instance, when a sales representative in Brussels enters a customer order, the data flow automatically to others in the company who need to see them. The factory in Hong Kong receives the order and begins production. The warehouse checks its progress on-line and schedules the shipment date. The warehouse can check its stock of parts and replenish whatever the factory has depleted. The enterprise system stores production information, where it can be accessed by customer service representatives to track the progress of the order through every step of the manufacturing process. Updated sales and production data automatically flow to the accounting department. The system transmits information for calculating the salesperson's commission to the payroll department. The system also automatically recalculates the company's balance sheets, accounts receivable and payable ledgers, cost-center accounts, and available cash. Corporate headquarters in London can view up-to-the-minute data on sales, inventory, and production at every step of the process, as well as updated sales and production forecasts and calculations of product cost and availability.

Enterprise systems have been primarily oriented toward helping companies manage their internal manufacturing, financial, and human resource processes and were not originally designed to support major processes encompassing entities outside the firm. However, enterprise software vendors are starting to enhance their products so that firms can link their enterprise systems with systems of vendors, suppliers, manufacturers, distributors, and retailers or link their enterprise systems to systems for supply chain management and customer relationship management.

Benefits and Challenges of Enterprise Systems

Enterprise systems promise to integrate the diverse business processes of a firm into a single, integrated information architecture, but they also present major challenges.

Benefits of Enterprise Systems   Enterprise systems promise to greatly change four dimensions of business: firm structure, management process, technology platform, and business capability. Companies can use enterprise systems to support organizational structures that were not previously possible or to create a more disciplined organizational culture. For example, they might use enterprise systems to integrate the corporation across geographic or business unit boundaries or to create a more uniform organizational culture in which everyone uses similar processes and information. An enterprise-enabled organization does business the same way worldwide, with cross-functional coordination and information flowing freely across business functions.

Information supplied by an enterprise system is structured around cross-functional business processes, and it can improve management reporting and decision making. For example, an enterprise system might help management more easily determine which products are most or least profitable. An enterprise system could potentially supply management with better data about business processes and overall organizational performance.

Enterprise systems promise to provide firms with a single, unified, and all-encompassing information system technology platform that houses data on all the key business processes.

The data have common, standardized definitions and formats that are accepted by the entire organization. You will learn more about the importance of standardizing organizational data in Chapter 7.

Enterprise systems can also help create the foundation for a customer or demand-driven organization. By integrating discrete business processes in sales, production, finance, and logistics, the entire organization can respond more efficiently to customer requests for products or information, forecast new products, and build and deliver them as demand requires. Manufacturing has better information to produce only what customers have ordered, procure exactly the right amount of components or raw materials to fill actual orders, stage production, and minimize the time that components or finished products are in inventory.

Challenges of Enterprise Systems   Although enterprise systems can improve organizational coordination, efficiency, and decision making, they have proven very difficult and costly to build. They require not only large technology investments but also fundamental changes in the way the business operates. Companies will need to rework their business processes to make information flow smoothly between them. Employees will have to take on new job functions and responsibilities. Many barriers must be overcome before the benefits of enterprise systems can be realized (Robey, Ross, and Boudreau, 2002). Organizations that don't understand how much change will be required or that are unable to make this change will have problems implementing enterprise systems or they may not be able to achieve a higher level of functional and business process integration.

Enterprise systems require complex pieces of software and large investments of time, money, and expertise. (A typical enterprise system installation costs $15 million and may run over $100 million for very large companies implementing full-function systems across many divisions. [Hitt, Wu, and Zhou, 2002; O'Leary, 2000]) Enterprise software is deeply intertwined with corporate business processes. It might take a large company three to five years to fully implement all of the organizational and technology changes required by an enterprise system. Because enterprise systems are integrated, it is difficult to make a change in only one part of the business without affecting other parts as well. There is the prospect that the new enterprise systems could eventually prove as brittle and hard to change as the old systems they replaced, binding firms to outdated business processes and systems.

Companies may also fail to achieve strategic benefits from enterprise systems if integrating business processes using the generic models provided by standard ERP software prevents the firm from using unique business processes that had been sources of advantage over competitors. Enterprise systems promote centralized organizational coordination and decision making, which may not be the best way for some firms to operate. There are companies that clearly do not need the level of integration provided by enterprise systems (Davenport, 2000 and 1998). Chapter 13 provides more detail on the organizational and technical challenges to enterprise system implementation.

SUPPLY CHAIN MANAGEMENT
AND COLLABORATIVE COMMERCE

Supply chain management systems are more outward-facing, focusing on helping the firm manage its relationship with suppliers. **Supply chain management** is the close linkage and coordination of activities involved in buying, making, and moving a product. It integrates supplier, manufacturer, distributor, and customer logistics processes to reduce time, redundant effort, and inventory costs. The **supply chain** is a network of organizations and business processes for procuring materials, transforming raw materials into intermediate and finished products, and distributing the finished products to customers. It links suppliers, manufacturing plants, distribution centers, conveyances, retail outlets, people, and information through processes such as procurement, inventory control, distribution, and delivery to supply goods and services from source through consumption. Materials, information, and payments flow through the supply chain in both directions. Goods start out as raw materials and move through logistics and production systems until they reach customers. The supply chain includes **reverse logistics** in which returned items flow in the reverse direction from the buyer back to the seller.

Figure 2-15 provides a simplified illustration of a supply chain. The *upstream* portion of the supply chain includes the organization's suppliers and their suppliers and the processes for

supply chain management
Close linkage and coordination of activities involved in buying, making and moving a product.

supply chain
Network of organizations and business processes for procuring materials, transforming raw materials into intermediate and finished products, and distributing the finished products to customers.

reverse logistics
The return of items from buyers to sellers in a supply chain.

Figure 2-15   A supply chain. This figure illustrates the major entities in the supply chain and the flow of information upstream and downstream to coordinate the activities involved in buying, making, and moving a product. Suppliers transform raw materials into intermediate products or components, and then manufacturers turn them into finished products. The products are shipped to distribution centers and from there to retailers and customers.

managing relationships with them. The *downstream* portion consists of the organizations and processes for distributing and delivering products to the final customers. The manufacturer also manages internal supply chain processes for transforming the materials, components, and services furnished by suppliers into finished goods and for managing materials and inventory.

The supply chain illustrated in Figure 2-15 has been simplified. Most supply chains, especially those for large manufacturers such as automakers, are multitiered, with many thousands of primary, secondary, and tertiary suppliers. DaimlerChrysler, for instance, has over 20,000 suppliers of parts, packaging, and technology. Its primary suppliers are its principal suppliers, which furnish chassis, engines, and other major automotive components. These suppliers have their own suppliers (secondary suppliers), who in turn may have their own set of suppliers (tertiary suppliers). To manage the supply chain, a company tries to eliminate redundant steps, delays, and the amount of resources tied up along the way.

Companies that skillfully manage their supply chains get the right amount of their products from their source to their point of consumption with the least amount of time and the lowest cost. Information systems make supply chain management more efficient by helping companies coordinate, schedule, and control procurement, production, inventory management, and delivery of products and services. Supply chain management systems can be built using intranets, extranets, or special supply chain management software. Table 2-8 describes how companies can benefit from using information systems for supply chain management.

Inefficiencies in the supply chain, such as parts shortages, underutilized plant capacity, excessive finished goods inventory, or runaway transportation costs, are caused by inaccurate or untimely information. For example, manufacturers may keep too many parts in inventory because they don't know exactly when they will receive their next shipment from their suppliers. Suppliers may order too few raw materials because they don't have precise information on demand. These supply chain inefficiencies can waste as much as 25 percent of a company's operating costs.

One recurring problem in supply chain management is the **bullwhip effect,** in which information about the demand for a product gets distorted as it passes from one entity to the next across the supply chain (Lee, Padmanabhan, and Wang, 1997). A slight rise in demand

bullwhip effect

Large fluctuations in inventories along the supply chain resulting from small unanticipated fluctuations in demand.

TABLE 2-8	**HOW INFORMATION SYSTEMS CAN FACILITATE SUPPLY CHAIN MANAGEMENT**

Information Systems Can Help Participants in the Supply Chain

Decide when and what to produce, store, and move

Rapidly communicate orders

Track the status of orders

Check inventory availability and monitor inventory levels

Reduce inventory, transportation, and warehousing costs

Track shipments

Plan production based on actual customer demand

Rapidly communicate changes in product design

---

for an item might cause different members in the supply chain—distributors, manufacturers, suppliers, suppliers' suppliers, and suppliers' suppliers' suppliers—to stockpile inventory so each has enough "just in case." These changes will ripple throughout the supply chain, magnifying what started out as a small change from planned orders, creating excess inventory, production, warehousing, and shipping costs. If all members of the supply chain could share dynamic information about inventory levels, schedules, forecasts, and shipments they would have a more precise idea of how to adjust their sourcing, manufacturing, and distribution plans.

Supply chain management uses systems for supply chain planning (SCP) and supply chain execution (SCE). *Supply chain planning systems* enable the firm to generate demand forecasts for a product and to develop sourcing and manufacturing plans for that product. *Supply chain execution systems* manage the flow of products through distribution centers and warehouses to ensure that products are delivered to the right locations in the most efficient manner. Table 2-9 provides more details on supply chain planning and execution systems.

Collaborative Commerce

Successful supply chain management requires an atmosphere of trust where all the members of the supply chain agree to cooperate and to honor the commitments they have made to each other (Welty and Becerra-Fernandez, 2001). They must be able to work together

J.D. Edwards Supply Chain Management software includes capabilities for production scheduling that can calculate the quantity of each item in production that is needed to meet customer demand and send alerts to suppliers to ship more items when inventory is running too low. This demand Gantt chart shows which customer orders are affected by a missed delivery so that alternative suppliers can be located.

TABLE 2-9	SUPPLY CHAIN PLANNING AND EXECUTION SYSTEMS

Capabilities of Supply Chain Planning Systems

Order planning: Select an order fulfillment plan that best meets the desired level of service to the customer given existing transportation and manufacturing constraints.

Advanced scheduling and manufacturing planning: Provide detailed coordination of scheduling based on analysis of changing factors such as customer orders, equipment outages, or supply interruptions. Scheduling modules create job schedules for the manufacturing process and supplier logistics.

Demand planning: Generate demand forecasts from all business units using statistical tools and business forecasting techniques.

Distribution planning: Create operating plans for logistics managers for order fulfillment, based on input from demand and manufacturing planning modules.

Transportation planning: Track and analyze inbound and outbound movement of materials and products to ensure that materials and finished goods are delivered at the right time and place at the minimum cost.

Capabilities of Supply Chain Execution Systems

Order commitments: Allow vendors to quote accurate delivery dates to customers by providing more real-time detailed information on the status of orders from availability of raw materials and inventory to production and shipment status.

Final Production: Organize and schedule final subassemblies required to make each final product.

Replenishment: Coordinate component replenishment work so that warehouses remain stocked with the minimum amount of inventory in the pipeline.

Distribution management: Coordinate the process of transporting goods from the manufacturer to distribution centers to the final customer. Provide online customer access to shipment and delivery data.

Reverse distribution: Track the shipment and accounting for returned goods or remanufactured products.

on the same goal and to redesign some of their business processes so that they can coordinate their activities more easily. In some industries, companies have extended their supply chain management systems to collaborate more closely with customers, suppliers, and other firms in their industry. This is a much broader mission than traditional supply chain management systems, which focused primarily on managing the flow of transactions among organizations. It focuses on using shared systems and business processes to optimize the value of relationships.

Companies are relying on these new collaborative relationships to further improve their planning, production, and distribution of goods and services. The use of digital technologies to enable multiple organizations to collaboratively design, develop, build, move, and manage products through their lifecycles is called **collaborative commerce.** Firms can integrate their systems with those of their supply chain partners to coordinate demand forecasting, resource planning, production planning, replenishment, shipping, and warehousing. They can work jointly with suppliers on product design and marketing. Customers can provide feedback for marketers to use to improve product design, support, and service. Equipped with appropriate software tools, they can actually help companies design and develop some types of products. For example, LIS Logic Corp. and VLSI Technology provide customers with tools for designing their own specialized computer chips. GE Plastics provides its customers with Web-based tools to help them design better plastic products (Thomke and von Hippel, 2002). A firm engaged in collaborative commerce with its suppliers and customers can achieve new levels of efficiency in reducing product design cycles, minimizing excess inventory, forecasting demand, and keeping partners and customers informed (see Figure 2-16).

One of the most difficult aspects of supply chain management is accurately forecasting demand. If the information going into a demand forecasting system is flawed, or if the fore-

collaborative commerce
The use of digital technologies to enable multiple organizations to collaboratively design, develop, build, and manage products through their lifecycles.

Engineers
• Design documents

Suppliers
• Replenishment
• Price schedules

Manufacturing
• Bills of material
• Demand forecasts
• Order status

Firm Extranet or Private Network

Customers
• Orders
• Product modification requests

Sales and Marketing
• Marketing coordination

Figure 2-16 Collaborative commerce. Collaborative commerce is a set of digitally enabled collaborative interactions between an enterprise and its business partners and customers. Data and processes that were once considered internal can be shared by the collaborative community.

casters do not properly interpret the data, demand forecasts will be off target. Companies are trying to address this problem by working together with their business partners on **collaborative planning, forecasting, and replenishment (CPFR).** Companies can collaborate with suppliers and buyers to formulate demand forecasts, develop production plans, and coordinate shipping, warehousing, and stocking activities to ensure that retail and wholesale shelf space is replenished with the right quantities of the right goods.

Another important area of collaboration is joint marketing coordination and product design. Manufacturers can coordinate their internal design and marketing activities with engineers and design companies as well as with their supply chain partners. By involving their suppliers in product design and marketing, manufacturing firms can ensure that the goods produced actually fulfill the claims of marketers. Marketers can channel customer feedback directly to product designers at the firm and its suppliers.

The Window on Management shows how some companies are engaging in collaborative commerce for this purpose. Collaborative commerce makes "closed loop marketing," in which customer feedback drives marketing and production, much closer to realization. Table 2-10 illustrates collaborative commerce applications for other important business processes.

Industrial Networks for Interoganizational Business Processes

Internet technology is making this level of collaboration possible by providing a platform where systems from different companies can seamlessly exchange information. Web enabled networks for the coordination of transorganizational business processes provide an infrastructure for collaborative commerce activities. Such networks can be termed **private industrial networks,** and they permit firms and their business partners to share product design and development, marketing, inventory, production scheduling, and unstructured communications such as transmission of graphics, e-mail, and CAD drawings. Many of these networks are "owned" and managed by large companies who use them to coordinate purchases, orders, and other activities with their suppliers, distributors, and selected business partners.

For instance, Procter & Gamble (P&G), the world's largest consumer goods company, developed an integrated industry-wide system to coordinate grocery store point-of-sale systems with grocery store warehouses, shippers, its own manufacturing facilities, and its suppliers of raw materials. This single industry-spanning system effectively allows P&G to monitor the movement of all its products from raw materials to customer purchase. P&G uses data collected from point-of-sale terminals to trigger shipments to retailers of items that customers have purchased and that need restocking. Electronic

collaborative planning, forecasting, and replenishment (CPFR)
Firms collaborating with their suppliers and buyers to formulate demand forecasts, develop production plans, and coordinate shipping, warehousing, and stocking activities.

private industrial networks
Web-enabled networks linking systems of multiple firms in an industry for the coordination of transorganizational business processes.

| TABLE 2-10 | HOW BUSINESSES ARE ENGAGING IN COLLABORATIVE COMMERCE |

Business Process	Collaborative Commerce Activities
Product design and development: Companies can work jointly with customers and business partners on designing new products or modifying existing products	Extranet enables customers of Cummins Inc. to access updates on their engine orders. Truck manufacturers can view early prototypes for Cummins' line of engines and ask for modifications. Real-time design collaboration tools let Cummins engineers work with customers' engineers via the Web. A customer council reviews all significant updates to the Cummins site.
Service and support: Companies can share information about service, support, and troubleshooting	American Axle and Manufacturing, which produces automobile driveline systems, chassis components, and forged products, uses the Web to share photos of defective parts that stall its assembly line with suppliers, discuss the problem, and solve it on the spot.
Supply chain coordination: Companies can work closely with suppliers and contract manufacturers, reducing inventory	Hewlett Packard Laserjet Imaging Systems uses a Web-based workgroup collaboration system to share information with its contract manufacturers, distribution centers, and resellers. The application extracts parts plans entered in HP's ERP system and forwards them to a shared electronic workspace where the plans can be accessed by suppliers. Suppliers can adjust their plans so that their inventory and HP's are coordinated with each other.
Logistics: Companies can reduce logistics costs by coordinating their deliveries to share transportation and shipping facilities	General Mills, Kellogg, Land O' Lakes, and Monsanto use a common system based on Internet technology to share their excess shipping capacity. The system uses a private network to coordinate underutilized shipping capacity of container trucks and railroad cars to reduce participating companies' logistics costs.
Sales support and training: Companies and their distributors can share technical information, conduct training, and provide technical support information	Group Dekko consists of 12 independently operated manufacturing companies that produce components such as wire harnesses, molded plastic parts, metal stamping for automobiles, and office furniture. The Group uses a common shared data repository where partner firms share documents about quality standards, graphics, engineering drawings, material bills, pricing, and routing information.
Channel management: Companies and their distributors can collaborate on pricing and share sales leads	Compaq Computer Asia/Pacific uses the Partners Online Web-based system to coordinate pricing with its Asian distributors, where prices are often negotiable. Distributors can enter the pricing requirements of bids to customers into the system so that they can be routed to the salesperson in charge of the account and to the finance department for approval or rejection.

links to suppliers enable P&G to order materials from its own suppliers when its inventories are low. The system helps P&G reduce its inventory by allowing the company to produce products as they are demanded by retailers. P&G is implementing an Ultimate Supply System that uses Internet technology to link retailers and suppliers to its private corporate intranet. By having retailers and suppliers integrate their systems with P&G's systems, P&G hopes to reduce product cycle time by half, inventory costs by $4.5 billion, and systems costs by $5 billion.

Similarly, Safeway U.K. has electronic links to suppliers where it can share information about forecasts, shelf space, and inventory in its supermarkets so suppliers can track demand for their products, adjust production, and adjust the timing and size of deliveries. The suppliers can download Safeway's information into their enterprise systems or production planning systems. Suppliers send Safeway information about product availability, production capacity, and inventory levels.

Although private industrial networks are primarily used today to coordinate the activities of a single firm and its business partners, some can encompass an entire industry, coordinating the business processes for the key players in that industry, including suppliers, transporters, production firms, distributors, and retailers. For example, the OASIS system Web sites link U.S. electrical utility companies in regional power pool groups to sell their surplus power to wholesalers and to locate the transmission facilities for moving the power between its source and the customers.

A few industrial networks have been built to support collaboration among firms in multiple industries. General Mills, Kellogg, Land O' Lakes, and Monsanto now use a shared Internet system to share their excess shipping capacity. The system uses a private network to

THE JOY OF COLLABORATION

When Johnson Controls won a contract to supply the dashboard controls, overhead computer console, interior lights, and seats for DaimlerChrysler's 2002 Jeep Liberty, it was a big step up for this auto supplier. Johnson had moved from being a top-tier supplier to an elite components integrator responsible for engineering and manufacturing a complete section of a vehicle based on the automaker's specifications. Johnson used online design collaboration and product development software to coordinate with DaimlerChrysler as they worked on the design together.

Johnson used both its own and DaimlerChrysler's Web-based design collaboration systems to design the part of the Liberty interior that's closest to the driver, including the steering wheel, pedals, instrument panels, heating and air conditioning, air bags, trim, and related interior wiring. DaimlerChrysler designers and engineers worked closely with Johnson Controls as it developed the look, feel, and behavior of the driver's controls. Johnson Controls then took over management of engineering all components, working with its own network of 35 major suppliers and dozens of smaller ones using MatrixOne design collaboration and product development software tools to help engineer and build the actual parts.

In the past, DaimlerChrysler had to communicate with suppliers via fax or face-to-face meetings. Using collaborative systems has cut the time to communicate design changes to suppliers and receive revised designs by 60 to 90 percent. When one design partner makes a change in an engineering plan, the system immediately informs all of the people inside and outside the company impacted by this change. Companies such as DaimlerChrysler can create new products more quickly while handing off more responsibility for the design and production to suppliers. DaimlerChrysler has decided to use the collaborative system for designing all its vehicles for the 2004 model year.

The efficiencies of design collaboration are being realized by companies in many other types of businesses, including elec-

tronics, medical equipment and pharmaceuticals, and aerospace. Lockheed Martin Aeronautics Co. is working with more than 80 suppliers in 187 locations to design and build components for the Joint Strike Fighter supersonic stealth fighter aircraft for the U.S. Defense Department. A system of 90 Web software tools will let Lockheed and its partners such as Northrup Grumman and BAE systems share designs, track the exchange of documents, and make changes. Lockheed and its partners can each assign their best designers and engineers to a particular part of the project and have all of them work together on the design over the Internet. This system has reduced the time to produce a drawing from 400 hours to 125 and will let Defense Department and Lockheed project managers track daily progress in real time.

The Internet-based tools will also make it easier for suppliers to link their production and inventory systems with Lockheed. Lockheed used to have 25 or 30 project managers telephone suppliers each day to get production deadline updates. The collaboration system gives Lockheed visibility into suppliers' inventories and production schedules, automatically alerting the appropriate manager if a supplier is having problems meeting inventory deadlines. This collaboration is expected to expedite delivery of the new planes and it represents an enormous computing feat.

To Think About: How has online collaboration changed the way companies design and build automobiles and airplanes? What are its management benefits? What management, organization, and technology issues would have to be addressed when building an online collaboration system for product design and development?

Sources: Steve Konicki, "Groupthink Gets Smart," *InformationWeek*, January 14, 2002; and Faith Keenan and Spencer E. Ante, "The New Teamwork," *BusinessWeek*, February 18, 2002.

MANAGEMENT

coordinate underutilized shipping capacity of container trucks and railroad cars to reduce participating members' logistics costs.

CUSTOMER RELATIONSHIP MANAGEMENT (CRM)

Instead of treating customers as exploitable sources of income, businesses are now viewing them as long-term assets to be nurtured through customer relationship management. *Customer relationship management (CRM),* which we introduced in Chapter 1, focuses on managing all of the ways that a firm deals with its existing and potential new customers. CRM is both a business and technology discipline that uses information systems to integrate all of the business processes surrounding the firm's interactions with its customers in sales,

Siebel Systems provides an integrated suite of customer relationship management applications to help organizations implement customer-driven best practices across their sales, marketing, and customer service. Illustrated here are capabilities for tracking the responses to sales campaigns across all customer contact points: direct mail, telephone, e-mail, the Web, and face-to-face interactions.

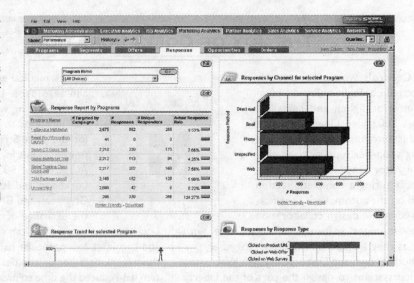

marketing, and service. The ideal CRM system provides end-to-end customer care from receipt of an order through product delivery.

In the past, a firm's processes for sales, service, and marketing were highly compartmentalized and did not share much essential customer information. Some information on a specific customer might be stored and organized in terms of that person's account with the company. Other pieces of information about the same customer might be organized by products that were purchased. There was no way to consolidate all of this information to provide a unified view of a customer across the company. CRM tools try to solve this problem by integrating the firm's customer-related processes and consolidating customer information from multiple channels—retail stores, telephone, e-mail, wireless devices, or the Web—so that the firm can present one coherent face to the customer (see Figure 2-17).

Good CRM systems consolidate customer data from multiple sources and provide analytical tools for answering questions such as: What is the value of a particular customer to the firm over his or her lifetime? Who are our most loyal customers? (It costs six times more to sell to a new customer than to an existing customer [Kalakota and Robinson, 2001].) Who

Sales
  Telephone sales
  Web sales
  Field sales
  Retail sales

Marketing
  Campaign data
  Content
  Data analysis

Customer Service
  Call center data
  Web self-service data
  Field service data
  Wireless data

• **Unified view of customers**
• **Consistent message to customers**
• **End-to-end customer care**
• **Long-term customer relationships**
• **Identification of best customers**

Figure 2-17 Customer relationship management (CRM). Customer relationship management applies technology to look at customers from a multifaceted perspective. CRM uses a set of integrated applications to address all aspects of the customer relationship, including customer service, sales, and marketing.

CUSTOMER RELATIONSHIP MANAGEMENT: A BOON FOR FINANCIAL SERVICES

Competition in the financial services industry is more intense than ever, with banks, brokerage firms, and insurance companies vying for each other's business. To survive, financial service firms need to find better ways of serving their customers—and profiting from them. Meriwest Credit Union, the former IBM San Jose Employees Federal Credit Union, found itself facing a new competitive environment when it reorganized in 1998 from a federally-chartered employee credit union to a state-chartered credit union. Meriwest had already expanded beyond IBM to become the employee credit union for about 350 companies, but with the change to a community charter, Meriwest could pitch its services to more than 6 million people in the San Francisco Bay area who could also be served by traditional banks. Meriwest also needed to increase the number of deposit dollars per customer and loans to its longstanding customers.

The systems Meriwest had been using were not up to the job. Customer service representatives spent excessive amounts of time switching between multiple systems in order to respond to customer inquiries about savings and checking account balances, loans, mortgages, and credit card bills. Even after all the systems had been polled for this information, service representatives were still left with an incomplete picture of what type of customer they were dealing with because these systems could not easily assemble historical data about each customer's activity.

In 1999, Meriwest implemented Siebel Systems' customer relationship management software to both consolidate customer account information and make it more meaningful. The new customer relationship management system pulled together data from 11 different systems into a common view of the customer that could be used to offer more services. For example,

the CRM system would enable Meriwest to identify customers with high balances who might be interested in a certificate of deposit or customers with college age children or retirement planning needs that the credit union could service. Customer relationship management, combined with stepped-up advertising and representative training is paying off. At the end of 2001, deposits were up 27 percent over the 1998 level, and loans per customer were up 46 percent.

The insurance industry is also turning to customer relationship management to more effectively market new and existing services in competition with other financial services companies. MetLife implemented DWL Customer software to consolidate customer data from all of its existing legacy information systems. Any of MetLife's 40 lines of business will be able to update and view customer files and sell other products of interest to specific customers. Australia's P&C Direct is trying to ensure that every business unit has a current and consistent view of a customer's data. The company created a data repository that marks all customer records with census data and lifestyle codes so that the sales department can better target customers for cross-selling. For example, the marketing representatives could view all the products a customer has purchased so that, for example, they could sell life insurance policies to customers with health insurance policies.

To Think About: How have customer relationship management systems changed how organizations can service their customers? How have the organizations described here obtained value from CRM systems?

Sources: David F. Carr, "Cozying Up to the Customer," *Baseline,* June 2002; and Jennifer Maselli, "Insurers Look to CRM for Profits," *InformationWeek,* May 6, 2002.

ORGANIZATIONS

are our most profitable customers? (Typically 80 to 90 percent of a firm's profits are generated by 10 to 20 percent of its customers.) What do these profitable customers want to buy? Firms can then use the answers to acquire new customers, provide better service and support, customize their offerings more precisely to customer preferences, and provide ongoing value to retain profitable customers. Chapters 3, 4, 9, and 11 provide additional details on customer relationship management applications and technologies. The Window on Organizations shows how some financial services companies have benefited from customer relationship management.

Investing in CRM software alone won't automatically produce better information about customers, and many customer relationship management systems fall short of their objectives. These systems require changes in sales, marketing, and customer service processes to encourage sharing of customer information; support from top management; and a very clear idea of the benefits that could be obtained from consolidating customer data (Ebner et. al., 2002; Goodhue, Wixom, and Watson, 2002). Chapter 13 provides more detail on the challenges of implementing successful CRM systems and the Manager's Toolkit describes some of the customer data issues that managers must address.

MIS IN ACTION: MANAGER'S TOOLKIT

HOW TO BENEFIT FROM CUSTOMER RELATIONSHIP MANAGEMENT

When setting up CRM systems, managers need to have a clear understanding of the business questions concerning customers that the system should answer. Here are some key questions to ask when gathering customer information:

Customer status: Is the firm interested in formation about existing customers, new customers, or both?

Customer value: What is the customer's value to the business? Why is this customer important?

Channels: What channel or channels did the customer use to interact with the company? Were these interactions over the telephone, via e-mail, through the corporate Web site, or through company sales representatives or retail stores? Which channel or channels are the most important?

Nature of interaction: Why did the customer interact with the company? Was it to purchase an item, to secure customer service, or to return merchandise? What is the intended outcome for this interaction?

Metrics: How can the company measure the value of its interaction with the customer? Can it be measured in terms of cost savings, increased revenue, or higher levels of customer satisfaction?

KNOWLEDGE MANAGEMENT SYSTEMS IN THE ENTERPRISE

The value of a firm's products and services is based not only on its physical resources but also on intangible knowledge assets. Some firms can perform better than others because they have better knowledge about how to create, produce, and deliver products and services. This firm knowledge is difficult to imitate, unique, and can be leveraged into long-term strategic benefit. *Knowledge management systems*, which we introduced in Chapter 1, collect all relevant knowledge and experience in the firm and make it available wherever and whenever it is needed to support business processes and management decisions. They also link the firm to external sources of knowledge.

Knowledge management systems (KMS) support processes for discovering and codifying knowledge, sharing knowledge, and distributing knowledge, as well as processes for creating new knowledge and integrating it into the organization. This chapter has already described several kinds of systems used in knowledge management, office systems for the distribution of knowledge and information and knowledge work systems to facilitate knowledge creation. Other knowledge management applications help companies map sources of knowledge, create corporate knowledge directories of employees with special areas of expertise, identify and share best practices, and codify the knowledge of experts so that it can be embedded in information systems and used by other members of the organization. Knowledge management systems also include tools for knowledge discovery that enable the organization to recognize patterns and important relationships in large pools of data. Table 2-11 provides examples of knowledge management systems and Chapters 10 and 11 describe these knowledge management applications in detail.

TABLE 2-11	KNOWLEDGE MANAGEMENT SYSTEMS IN THE ORGANIZATION
Organizational Process	**Role of Knowledge Management Systems**
Creating knowledge	Knowledge work systems provide knowledge workers with graphics, analytical, communication, and document management tools as well as access to internal and external sources of data to help them generate new ideas.
Discovering and codifying knowledge	Artificial intelligence systems can elicit and incorporate expertise from human experts or find patterns and relationships in vast quantities of data. DSS analyzing large databases can also be used for knowledge discovery.
Sharing knowledge	Group collaboration systems can help employees access and work simultaneously on the same document from many different locations and coordinate their activities.
Distributing knowledge	Office systems and communication tools can distribute documents and other forms of information among information and knowledge workers and link offices to other business units inside and outside the firm.

Make IT Your Business

FINANCE AND ACCOUNTING

Finance and accounting systems help firms keep track of their assets and fund flows. They can help firms maximize returns on their financial assets and investments and maintain financial records. Enterprise systems can integrate financial information with production and sales information so that the impact of sales and manufacturing transactions can be immediately reflected on the firm's balance sheets, accounts receivable and payable ledgers, and reports of cash flows. Management can use enterprise systems to obtain up-to-the-minute reports of the firm's overall financial performance. You can find examples of finance and accounting applications on page 63.

HUMAN RESOURCES

Human resources systems help businesses develop staffing requirements; identify potential new employees; maintain employee records; track employee training, skills, and job performance; and help managers develop appropriate plans for employee compensation and career development. Enterprise systems can help businesses coordinate their staffing levels with sales and production activities and financial resources.

MANUFACTURING AND PRODUCTION

Manufacturing and production systems solve problems related to the planning, development, and delivery of products and services, and con-

trol the flow of production. Supply chain management (SCM) systems provide information to coordinate sourcing and procurement, production scheduling, order fulfillment, inventory management, product development, warehousing, and customer service. When these processes are coordinated among supply chain members, goods can move smoothly and on time from suppliers to manufacturers to customers. Collaborative commerce can promote further supply chain and product development efficiencies by facilitating collaborative interactions between the firm and its suppliers, customers, and other business partners. Knowledge management systems provide tools and information to help engineers, designers, and product development staff innovate and design new products. You can find examples of manufacturing and production applications on pages 36–38, 59–61, and 68–71.

SALES AND MARKETING

Information systems help businesses promote products, contact customers, track sales, and provide ongoing service and support. They can also be used to analyze the performance of the firm's sales staff. Today, customer relationship management (CRM) systems are especially useful for consolidating customer data from different sources so that the firm can coordinate its interactions with customers and provide better long-term customer relationships. You can find examples of sales and marketing applications on pages 36–38, 59–61, 63, and 68–71.

MANAGEMENT WRAP-UP

Enterprise applications require management to take a firmwide view of business processes and information flows. Managers need to determine which business processes should be integrated, the short- and long-term benefits of this integration, and the appropriate level of financial and organizational resources to support this integration.

There are many types of information systems in an organization that support different organizational levels, functions, and business processes. Some of these systems, including the enterprise applications (enterprise systems, supply chain management, customer relationship management, and knowledge management), span more than one function or business process and may be tied to the business processes of other organizations. Systems integrating information from different business functions, business processes, and organizations often require extensive organizational change.

Information systems that support firm- or industry-wide information flows and business processes require major technology investments and planning. Firms must have an information technology (IT) infrastructure that can support firm- or industry-wide computing.

For Discussion

1. Supply chain management is less about managing the physical movement of goods and more about managing information. Discuss the implications of this statement.

2. Adopting an enterprise system is a key business decision as well as a technology decision. Do you agree? Why or why not? Who should make this decision?

SUMMARY

1. *What are the major types of systems in a business? What role do they play?* There are six major types of information systems in contemporary organizations. Operational-level systems are transaction processing systems (TPS), such as payroll or order processing, that track the flow of the daily routine transactions that are necessary to conduct business. Knowledge-level systems support clerical, managerial, and professional workers. They consist of office systems for increasing data workers' productivity and knowledge work systems for enhancing knowledge workers' productivity. Management-level systems (MIS and DSS) provide the management control level with reports and access to the organization's current performance and historical records. Most MIS reports condense information from TPS and are not highly analytical. Decision-support systems (DSS) support management decisions when these decisions are unique, rapidly changing, and not specified easily in advance. They have more advanced analytical models and data analysis capabilities than MIS and often draw on information from external as well as internal sources. Executive support systems (ESS) support the strategic level by providing a generalized computing and communications environment to assist senior management's decision making. They have limited analytical capabilities but can draw on sophisticated graphics software and many sources of internal and external information.

    The various types of systems in the organization exchange data with one another. TPS are a major source of data for other systems, especially MIS and DSS. ESS primarily receive data from lower-level systems.

2. *How do information systems support the major business functions: sales and marketing, manufacturing and production, finance and accounting, and human resources?* At each level of the organization there are information systems supporting the major functional areas of the business. Sales and marketing systems help the firm identify customers for the firm's products or services, develop products and services to meet customers' needs, promote the products and services, sell the products and services, and provide ongoing customer support. Manufacturing and production systems deal with the planning, development, and production of products and services, and controlling the flow of production. Finance and accounting systems keep track of the firm's financial assets and fund flows. Human resources systems maintain employee records; track employee skills, job performance, and training; and support planning for employee compensation and career development.

3. *Why should managers pay attention to business processes? Why do firms need to integrate their business processes?* Business processes refer to the manner in which work is organized, coordinated, and focused to produce a valuable product or service. Business processes are concrete work flows of material, information, and knowledge. They also represent unique ways in which organizations coordinate work, information, and knowledge, and the ways in which management chooses to coordinate work. Managers need to pay attention to business processes because they determine how well the organization can execute, and thus are a potential source of strategic success or failure. Although each of the major business functions has its own set of business processes, many other business processes are cross-functional, such as fulfilling an order. Information systems can help organizations achieve great efficiencies by automating parts of these processes or by helping organizations rethink and streamline them. Firms can become more flexible and efficient by coordinating their business processes more closely, and, in some cases, integrating these processes so they are more focused on efficient management of resources and customer service. Enterprise applications such as enterprise systems, supply chain management systems, customer relationship management systems, and knowledge management systems are designed to support organization-wide process coordination and integration.

4. *What are the benefits and challenges of using enterprise systems?* Enterprise systems create an integrated organization-wide platform to coordinate key internal processes of the firm. Enterprise systems integrate the key business processes in sales, production, finance, logistics, and human resources into a single software system so that information can flow throughout the organization, improving coordination, efficiency, and decision making. Enterprise systems can help create a more uniform organization in which everyone uses similar processes and information, and measures their work in terms of organization-wide performance standards. The coordination of sales, production, finance, and logistics processes provided by enterprise systems helps organizations respond more rapidly to customer demands.

    Enterprise systems are very difficult to implement successfully. They require extensive organizational change, use complicated technologies, and require large up-front costs for long-term benefits that are difficult to quantify. Once implemented, enterprise systems are very difficult to change. Management vision and foresight is required to take a firm and industry-wide view of problems and to find solutions that realize strategic value from the investment.

5. *What are the benefits of using information systems to support supply chain management and collaborative commerce?* Information systems for supply chain management can help coordinate processes for managing the firm's relationship with its customers. Supply chain management is the close linkage of activities involved in buying, making, and

moving products. Information systems make supply chain management more efficient by helping companies coordinate, schedule, and control procurement, production, inventory management, and delivery of products and services to customers.

Collaborative commerce relies on digital technologies to enable multiple organizations to collaboratively design, develop, build, move, and manage products through their lifecycles. A firm engaged in collaborative commerce with its suppliers and customers can achieve new efficiencies by reducing product design cycles, minimizing excess inventory, forecasting demand, and keeping partners and customers informed. Private industrial networks are Web-enabled networks that support collaborative commerce activities by providing an infrastructure for transorganizational business processes and information flows.

6. *What are the business benefits of using information systems for customer relationship management and knowledge management?* Customer relationship management (CRM) uses information systems to coordinate all of the business processes surrounding the firm's interactions with its customers. CRM systems consolidate customer information from multiple sources—telephone, e-mail, wireless devices, traditional sales and marketing systems, or the Web—so that the firm can obtain a unified view of a customer. CRM systems help businesses identify profitable customers and opportunities for improving customer service. Knowledge management systems enable firms to optimize the creation, sharing, and distribution of knowledge to improve business processes and management decisions.

KEY TERMS

Bullwhip effect, 56

Collaborative commerce, 58

Collaborative planning, forecasting, and replenishment (CPFR), 58

Decision-support systems (DSS), 45

Desktop publishing, 43

Document imaging systems, 43

Enterprise applications, 51

Executive support systems (ESS), 45

Finance and accounting information systems, 49

Human resources information systems, 50

Knowledge-level systems, 39

Knowledge work systems (KWS), 42

Management information systems (MIS), 43

Management-level systems, 39

Manufacturing and production information systems, 48

Office systems, 42

Operational-level systems, 39

Private industrial networks, 59

Reverse logistics, 55

Sales and marketing information systems, 47

Strategic-level systems, 40

Supply chain, 55

Supply chain management, 55

Transaction processing systems (TPS), 41

Word processing, 43

REVIEW QUESTIONS

1. Identify and describe the four levels of the organizational hierarchy. What types of information systems serve each level?

2. List and briefly describe the major types of systems in organizations.

3. What are the five types of TPS in business organizations? What functions do they perform? Give examples of each.

4. Describe the functions performed by knowledge work and office systems and some typical applications of each.

5. What are the characteristics of MIS? How do MIS differ from TPS? From DSS?

6. What are the characteristics of DSS? How do they differ from those of ESS?

7. Describe the relationship between TPS, office systems, KWS, MIS, DSS, and ESS.

8. List and describe the information systems serving each of the major functional areas of a business.

9. What is a business process? Give two examples of processes for functional areas of the business and one example of a cross-functional process.

10. Why are organizations trying to integrate their business processes? What are the four key enterprise applications for organization-wide process integration?

11. What are enterprise systems? How do they change the way an organization works?

12. What are the benefits and challenges of implementing enterprise systems?

13. What is supply chain management? What activities does it comprise? Why is it so important to businesses? How do information systems facilitate supply chain management?

14. What is collaborative commerce? How can organizations benefit from it?

15. How can organizations benefit from participating in private industrial networks?

16. What is customer relationship management? Why is it so important to businesses? How do information systems facilitate customer relationship management?

17. What is the role of knowledge management systems in the enterprise? What organizational processes are supported by knowledge management applications?

APPLICATION SOFTWARE EXERCISE

SPREADSHEET EXERCISE: IMPROVING SUPPLY CHAIN MANAGEMENT

You run a company that manufactures aircraft components. You have many competitors who are trying to offer lower prices and better service to customers and you are trying to determine if you can benefit from better supply chain management. At the Laudon Web site for Chapter 2 you can find a spreadsheet file that contains a list of all of the items that your firm has ordered from its suppliers over the past three months. The fields on the spreadsheet file include vendor name, vendor identification number, the purchaser's order number, item identification number and item description (for each item ordered from the vendor), the cost per item, number of units of the item ordered, the

total cost of each order, the vendors' accounts payable terms, promised shipping date, promised transit time, and actual arrival date for each order.

Prepare a recommendation of how you can use the data in this spreadsheet database to improve your supply chain management. You may wish to look at ways to identify preferred suppliers or other ways of improving the movement and production of your products. Some criteria you might consider include the supplier's track record for on-time deliveries, suppliers offering the best accounts payable terms, and suppliers offering lower pricing when the same item can be provided by multiple suppliers. Use your spreadsheet software to prepare reports and, if appropriate, graphs to support your recommendations.

GROUP PROJECT

With a group of three or four other students, select a business using an industrial network for supply chain management. Use the Web, newspapers, journals, and computer or business magazines to find out more about that organization and its use of

information technology and links to other organizations. If possible, use presentation software to present your findings to the class.

TOOLS FOR INTERACTIVE LEARNING

■ INTERNET CONNECTION

The Internet Connection for this chapter will take you to a series of Web sites where you can complete an exercise to evaluate supply chain management software.

■ INTERACTIVE STUDY GUIDE

You can use the Interactive Study Guide to test your knowledge of the topics in this chapter and get instant feedback when you need more practice.

■ RUNNING CASE

The Running Case provides an opportunity for you to analyze Dirt Bikes USA's supply chain and identify opportunities for improving supply chain management. You can find a complete description of this project on the Laudon Web site for Chapter 2 and on the Multimedia Edition CD-ROM.

■ ELECTRONIC BUSINESS PROJECT

At the Laudon Web site for Chapter 2 you will find an Electronic Business project for logistics planning.

■ MANAGEMENT DECISION PROBLEM

At the Laudon Web site for Chapter 2 you will find a Management Decision Problem requiring you to analyze enterprise process integration and its impact on production planning.

■ CD-ROM

If you use the Multimedia Edition CD-ROM with this chapter, you can find an audio overview of the major themes of this chapter, a video clip illustrating Lands' End's information systems, and bullet text summarizing the key points of the chapter.

CASE STUDY—*Can Information Systems Save U.S. Steel?*

In capacity U.S. Steel (USS) is the 10th largest integrated steel manufacturer in the world and the largest in the United States. Headquartered in Pittsburgh, Pennsylvania, it can produce about 14 million tons annually. The world's largest steel maker, Europe's Arcelor, produces more than 40 million tons annually, while South Korea's POSCO, the second largest, produces about 30 million tons. In fiscal 2001 USS's total revenue was $6.38 billion, with a net loss of $218 million. Its information

technology budget was about 1.1 percent or $70 million, a very low number for that industry. Its third largest customer is the Ford Motor Company, an automobile manufacturer that requires an immense amount of steel.

In 1996, Ford viewed USS as the worst in performance amongst its leading suppliers, and it threatened to turn elsewhere for its steel supplies despite their 70-year relationship. "We were in danger of losing Ford's business," explained Gene Trudell, USS's Cheif Information Officer. "It was that serious."

Ford's biggest complaint, among many, was that it was not notified when its steel shipments would arrive, leaving Ford unable to operate efficiently. To USS, Ford's threat was a wakeup call causing it to examine its whole production cycle.

USS identified a number of challenges beyond its notification system. It knew it needed to lower production costs, including its cost per ton of steel and the number of hours per person required to produce a ton, as well as the costly size of its steel inventory. It had to return to profitability, and to accomplish that it needed to increase its share of the high-end steel market. Internally it needed to centralize management of the various USS businesses and factories and their information technology infrastructures, which in 1996 were locally controlled.

USS's major problems were reflected in its order-taking process. Orders were often manual, very imprecise, and filled with errors. Moreover, once an order arrived, USS was unable to track it during processing. Processing began when one of its four plants transformed the raw materials into steel coils, which were then sent to USS's processors to be turned into finished products. USS has over 120 processors (35 to 40 of which work on Ford products). A single piece of steel might be processed by up to five different processors as they treat, shape, and finish the products. The reason for the complexities is that these orders require blending and shaping of the materials, including manipulating such characteristics as heat and tensile strength. USS was unable to follow each order as it was processed and delivered.

One problem was that each processor had its own tracking and order systems, and each assigned its own inventory codes, making tracking impossible for USS. In addition, each processor communicated its processing data to USS over a dialup system. When the data arrived, they then had to be manually translated into a format that could be used by USS's own system before the information could be sent to the customer. This translation took about 90 minutes per message. It was a very expensive and inefficient system, and it left USS's customers without enough information for their own production planning. USS did send advanced shipping notices (ASNs) to customers notifying them of the arrival time, but the ASNs often arrived after the steel, too late to benefit the customers. Late shipments made customers such as Ford more inefficient. Some Ford plants are only 20 minutes away from the processors. If a truckload of steel arrived without an ASN, Ford employees would have to record the delivery information manually, a process requiring excess labor while increasing errors. The tracking system's inadequacies also created forecasting and inventory problems, forcing the company to hold too much inventory, which in turn raised USS's costs even higher. It needed to modernize its order taking, tracking, and inventory systems.

USS moved rapidly to solve these problems. One objective was to enable customers to enter orders electronically so that they would be accurate. Using the Web, customers now can specify the product, quantity, price, composition, size, thickness, and even delivery date for their orders. To achieve all of this, the system had to handle information on production limitations such as metallurgical rules and production capabilities. It even had to calculate cost and delivery date. All of this had to be done rapidly so the customer knew cost and dates

immediately after entering the order. USS even connected DecisionExpress software from LiveCapital to speed up credit authorization, enabling USS to reduce uncollectible debts while approving most orders.

To track orders, USS developed an event-driven system that recorded each step in processing an order, automatically triggering the next step when the current step was finished, including the steps performed by the external processors. The new system even triggered ASNs and the delivery of the order. One benefit was that USS was able to handle processor messages in 12 minutes rather than 90. Both USS and the customers knew exactly where the supplies were and how the processing was proceeding. USS now found that when customer orders and ASNs were correct, its customers were more likely to give the steel company repeat orders. "You need a way to differentiate your business," said Tom Zielinsky, senior director of IT strategy at competitor Weirton Steel, "and I think you can do that with repeatability of customer orders." David Sherwin, USS director of order fulfillment, agreed, saying, "Everyone was producing the same steel; how to fulfill orders would be different."

All of this required very complex software, much of it home grown. In addition to information about price, quantity, and delivery date, an order must capture information on each steel product's composition, size, and thickness. USS used order fulfillment and data management software supplied by the Oracle Corporation, a product configuration system from Concentra, plus its own software for capturing very complex business rules and procedures for handling the intricate mix of product specifications and prices for customers. The business rules "required thousands of hours of interviews and logic revisions," because "much of the knowledge was resident in the minds of our metallurgical engineers," explained Trudell. When the system was completed, USS's need to revise orders dropped by two-thirds while greatly reducing order-taking staff time.

USS replaced its order fulfillment system with i2 Technologies' Factory Planner forecasting software, which the programmers connected to their order system. They also connected three homegrown systems, including iTrac, which tracks orders as they go to processors or customers and an automatic order generation system for repeat customers called MIGS (Mechanical Item Generation System). MIGS reduced inventory by improving the forecasting of demand for finished goods at the customer's location. When MIGS was first used, it reduced inventories from 33,500 to 24,000 tons. The system has been upgraded and is now called MOGS (Mechanical Order Generation System).

While in 2000, $946 million inventory was needed to support $6.1 billion in revenue, in 2001 only $870 million was required for $6.4 billion in revenue. U.S. Steel now keeps only 20 days of inventory on hand to meet demand, while it required 33 days of inventory on hand in 2000.

Overall, this whole system, known as continuous flow manufacturing, made the company the vanguard of the industry. According to Michael Shanahan, a consultant to USS from the Boston Consulting Group, the sweep of these order tracking and inventory systems for a continuous flow manufacturing business such as steel is "astonishing." These systems can go from the shop, through U.S. Steel's own production facilities and third-party service centers to the customer, managing the entire supply chain through a single integrated system.

Once USS started deriving benefits from its new supply chain management system, its management concluded that the system could provide a new source of profits. It could be adapted to serve smaller companies who bought USS products through service centers and could be sold to other steel and non-steel companies. In 2001, USS created Straightline Source, a new division that sells steel products directly to smaller customers such as the Pate Company, a $5 million metal roofing products manufacturer, bypassing service center intermediaries. Straightline was set up like an independent company so that it could compete for the steel service center business (which sold steel to small companies) without alienating the 15 percent of USS's business that already came through other service centers. In essence the smaller customers could place their orders directly to USS through Straightline. Straightline gave customers the ability to know when their orders would be delivered as soon as they were placed, a source of competitive advantage over service centers. The software manages customer inventories, handles shipping to the customers, and includes order fulfillment and supply chain management. Registered customers can check the status of their order any time.

Straightline added other features that would be difficult for conventional service centers to match, such as online credit checking and order aggregation. For order aggregation, Straightline implemented software called SmartTrim from Strategic Systems International, which combines similar orders and routes them through its processors in chains that minimize waste and scrap. USS found that reducing apparently insignificant amounts of waste saves the company millions of dollars each year. Straightline uses LiveCapital's DecisionExpress software for online authorization of credit, helping customers speed up their steel purchases while reducing USS's uncollectible debts. The combined power of all of Straightline's information systems makes it possible for Straightline to take into account everything that will affect the price of an order when pricing a product for a customer. While traditional service centers might take several days to develop price quotes, Straightline can quote competitive prices in seconds. Many service centers are angered that USS is competing against them.

USS created a subsidiary called USS Engineers and Consultants (now called UEC Technologies) in 1969 to generate additional revenue from the technology and services USS developed in-house. UEC's principal products are an order-fulfillment system for businesses in the metals, glass, and pulp and paper industries; a set of supply chain software toolsets jointly marketed with i2 Technologies that can help other steel companies manage their suppliers; and a tool to help companies set up an extranet for customers to place orders, check status, exchange electronic contract documents, and provide shipping information. To maintain USS's competitive edge, UEC sells technology that is one generation behind what USS actually uses. According to UEC President Chris Navetta, the venture has been highly profitable.

· USS has continued to upgrade itself. One example is Mon Valley Works, one of its four plants, which is located on the Monongahela River valley 10 miles south of Pittsburgh. It was originally built in 1875 and upgraded several times since, the last project occurring from 1998 to 2000. This was a $36 million project that replaced the computer controls and the mechanical equipment, including, for example, its laser sensors that are central to current steel making. The plant's output had been boosted from 270 tons per hour to 335 tons per hour. It had needed 9,300 steel workers to tend the blast furnaces and presses, but that number has been reduced to only 2,100 in this half-mile long plant. In 2001, the U.S. Department of Energy's Office of Industrial Technologies named Mon Valley Works the "Plant of the Year."

Has U.S. Steel's use of information technology solved its problems? The company has become very efficient, as shown by the time it takes to produce a ton of steel. USS requires about three person hours for one ton while in Germany it is 4 hours (a 33 percent increase), Japan 4.5 hours, and POSCO 4.8 hours (a 63 percent increase). Although countries like India need 34 person hours, their hourly labor rate is much lower. However "Everybody has access to the same technology [referring to both information technology and advanced equipment]," says Richard Fruehan, a Carnegie Mellon University professor of metallurgy, and "These can be purchased." And still, USS's labor costs remain high—$66 per ton higher than POSCO's. In fact, USS estimates it lost $57 per ton in the fourth quarter of 2001. Many observers claim that one reason is that USS spends $40 per ton for retiree health care costs and has only about 130,000 employees supporting over 600,000 retirees and their dependents. However, Thomas Usher, USS's chairman, claims its pension liabilities are well-funded. Ikenson says USS is quite efficient but is simply not large enough to equal its foreign competitors. According to Daniel Ikenson, the senior trade analyst at the Cato Institute, a conservative Washington, D.C., think tank, "U.S. Steel's biggest problem is it doesn't have the same economies of scale that its foreign competitors have."

In addition, in July 2001, when the Straightline system was completed, the United States was in a recession, prices had fallen to all-time lows, and USS was experiencing its worst losses in ten years. USS pushed for an industry bailout, and President George W. Bush did grant a 30 percent tariff on flat-rolled steel in March 2002 despite his strong commitment to free trade. Many analysts believe the tariff solves nothing but only delays the inevitable consolidation. Analysts also point out that worldwide the steel industry annually produces 200 million more tons of steel than the world consumes.

Another issue for USS is that Nucor and other innovative U.S. steel makers use scrap steel as inexpensive raw material, forcing USS to make higher-grade steel from coal and iron, the type of steel used in automobiles and skyscrapers. USS has stated it would like to combine with Bethlehem Steel, National Steel, and maybe even Weirton Steel, but only if the U.S. government takes over about $10 billion of their cost of benefits. These "mini-mills" oppose this because they are non-unionized and don't have the medical and pension expenses of the bigger companies. Dan Dimicco, Nucor's CEO, said that the U.S. Steel proposals are "nothing more than an attempt to get the government to help a couple of companies at the expense of the rest of the U.S. steel industry and the taxpayers."

Comparison with South Korea's POSCO might further help explain USS's problems. In the nineteenth and early twentieth centuries, U.S. steel companies located themselves near the sources of iron and coal. However half the cost of producing a $210 ton of steel today is for purchasing and shipping raw materials, while energy is 6 percent, labor 6 percent, and the remaining costs of 38 percent are for such factors as maintenance, information technology, and administration. Today companies locate themselves on Atlantic, Pacific, and Mediterranean coastlines to reduce their largest single cost.

In 1966, as South Korea was attempting to modernize and rise out of third world status, its government decided to establish a steel industry, even though it has almost no domestic iron or coal. It invested $296 million (U.S.), eventually named the company POSCO, and situated the factory at Pohang on its Pacific coastline to keep its costs low. Pohang has the harbor depth to handle the largest container ships. South Korea later built a second production facility nearby. It built very modern facilities, and then 18 years later upgraded them. In 1999, according to Sang-Boo Yoo, POSCO's chairman, the company undertook a $247 million project, named Process Innovation. Its purpose was to enable the company to use the Internet for all aspects of the company's activities, including booking and monitoring its fleet of 44 ships. In 2000, POSCO became the largest steel producer in the world, although it was surpassed in 2001 when Arcelor was created by merging three large European companies.

POSCO's costs are about $175–$180 per ton versus $240 a ton at USS and about $210 a ton at Arcelor. Its advantages are its seaport location and its late start, enabling it to start with more modern equipment and information technology. Frank Voelker, CEO of Alstom Power Conversion, who has worked on both POSCO and USS systems, says USS's are every bit as good as POSCO's and better than most of its competitors. But USS cannot do anything about its lack of a seaside location because of the high cost of moving its facilities. "I'd love to have a seaport paid for

by the government, just like POSCO," but it would cost too much, said Usher.

Sources: Mel Duvall, "U.S. Steel: Selling Tech—or Selling Out?" *Baseline*, June 18, 2002; John McCormick and Mel Duvall, "U.S. Steel Tries Tech Alchemy," *Baseline*, June 17, 2002; Mel Duvall, "U.S. Steel: Why the Red Ink?" *Baseline*, June 17, 2002; Mel Duvall, "POSCO: The Next Big Steel," *Baseline*, June 17, 2002; Kim S. Nash, "Enterprise Servers: HP's Alpha Division," *Baseline*, June 17, 2002; John McCormick, "At U.S. Steel, New Computers Revive Old Plant," *Baseline*, June 15, 2002; Sean Gallagher, "Gotcha! Managing Continuous Flow Manufacturing," *Baseline*, June 15, 2002; UEC Technologies, "USS Engineers & Consultants Is Now UEC Technologies," July 1, 2002; accessed September 5, 2002, <www.USS.com>; "Straightline E-Enabled Steel Distribution Service Optimized by Software from Strategic Systems," April 9, 2002 and Straightline corporate Web site, www. Straightline.com.

CASE STUDY QUESTIONS:

1. Summarize U.S. Steel's current competitive situation.

2. How are information systems related to the way U.S. Steel runs its business? What role is played by supply chain management systems? How do these systems provide value for USS?

3. What management, organization, and technology factors were responsible for USS's inability to compete with other steel manufacturers?

4. Describe how USS has responded to its global and American competition.

5. How helpful were information systems in addressing USS problems?

6. Evaluate the decision by USS to sell its software to other companies. Could it help or hinder USS? Explain your answer.

3 CHAPTER

INFORMATION SYSTEMS, ORGANIZATIONS, MANAGEMENT, AND STRATEGY

objectives

As a manager, you'll need to know how to use information systems strategically and how systems can help you make better decisions. After completing this chapter, you will be able to answer the following questions:

1. *What do managers need to know about organizations in order to build and use information systems successfully?*

2. *What impact do information systems have on organizations?*

3. *How do information systems support the activities of managers in organizations?*

4. *How can businesses use information systems for competitive advantage?*

5. *Why is it so difficult to build successful information systems, including systems that promote competitive advantage?*

Flextronics' Strategic Supply Chain

You may not have heard of Flextronics, but you probably use something they've made every day. Singapore-based Flextronics is a contract manufacturer that makes the innards of technology products such as cellphones, PCs, and Internet hardware for household names such as Cisco Systems, Dell Computers, and Ericsson mobile phones. In the fast-paced, hyper-competitive technology industry, profit margins for electronic manufacturing services, such as Flextronics, are razor-thin, amounting to no more than 3 to 5 percent. Yet during the past seven years Flextronics has been able to skyrocket from a tiny company into a multibillion-dollar global operation. How did Flextronics do it?

The answer lies in skillful supply chain management. Flextronics continually collects and analyzes its supply chain information to standardize and coordinate the work of its factories around the globe. The company built a low-cost manufacturing network in China, Singapore, Mexico, and other locations around the world. Flextronics facilities are built like campuses with water, sewer, computer lines, and buildings for suppliers so that they can be close to its factories. The campuses are standardized so that they look and perform the same way, regardless of their location. Flextronics thus can offer

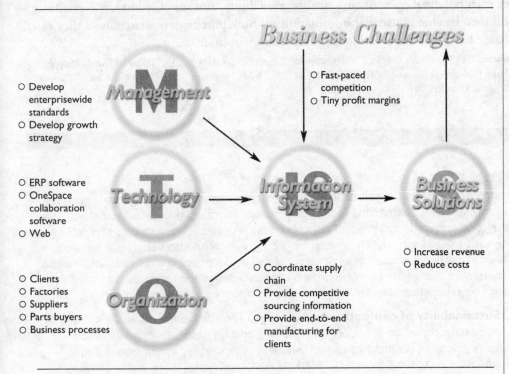

Business Challenges

- Fast-paced competition
- Tiny profit margins

Management
- Develop enterprisewide standards
- Develop growth strategy

Technology
- ERP software
- OneSpace collaboration software
- Web

Organization
- Clients
- Factories
- Suppliers
- Parts buyers
- Business processes

Information System
- Coordinate supply chain
- Provide competitive sourcing information
- Provide end-to-end manufacturing for clients

Business Solutions
- Increase revenue
- Reduce costs

inexpensive manufacturing facilities that are not too far away from its European and U.S clients.

Flextronics uses the same enterprise resource planning software in the same configuration in all of its factories so that it can standardize and coordinate their work more precisely. The same business processes for doing manufacturing work are thus replicated worldwide. Employees who access Flextronics' global information system can see data pulled together from practically every Flextronics factory on four continents. A parts buyer in Mexico can see what prices a Singapore parts buyer is obtaining for a specific component and use that information to get a price break from suppliers. When someone uses the system to place an order, the system displays a pop-up window that might show where he or she could get a better price on that same item and whether the component could be obtained from a Flextronics factory that overstocked on that item. Flextronics' 2000 design engineers can work jointly on design specifications from many different locations using OneSpace Web-based collaboration software.

Armed with such powerful software and well-designed business processes, Flextronics is now assuming responsibility for even larger portions of its clients' supply chains. About 85 to 90 percent of Flextronics' revenue comes from its traditional outsourced manufacturing work, where the company makes a part of a product for a client and then ships it to the client for assembly into the finished product. What Flextronics' new strategy will do is enable customers, such as Cisco Systems, to entrust the manufacturing process for entire products to Flextronics. Cisco will focus on product design and marketing and Flextronics will do the rest. Flextronics can also use its new end-to-end manufacturing capabilities for other clients as well. Ericsson, the Swedish cellphone manufacturer recently contracted to hand over its entire manufacturing process to Flextronics.

Flextronics would like to take over design work for customers as well. In the works is a Web-based product design system that extracts individual component information from a repository of product data and delivers it to designers so they can see each potential component's quality, availability, and supplier history. Flextronics will then be able to use that information for bulk purchases of materials so they can charge less for manufacturing and, hopefully, win more clients.

Sources: Tzyh Ng, "Inside the No. 1 Tech Outsourcer," *Business Week,* February 19, 2002; Mel Duvall, "Supply Chain: Forecasts on Demand," *CIO Insight,* May 15, 2002; and Christopher Koch, "Yank Your Chain," *Darwin Magazine,* October 2001.

MANAGEMENT CHALLENGES

Flextronics illustrates the interdependence of business environments, organizational culture, management strategy, and the development of information systems. Flextronics developed enterprise systems and global business processes in response to competitive pressures from its surrounding environment, but this systems effort could not succeed without a significant amount of organizational and management change. New information systems have changed the way Flextronics runs its business and makes management decisions. The experience of Flextronics raises the following management challenges:

1. **Sustainability of competitive advantage.** The competitive advantages strategic systems confer do not necessarily last long enough to ensure long-term profitability. Because competitors can retaliate and copy strategic systems, competitive advantage isn't always sustainable. Markets, customer expectations, and technology change; globalization has made these changes even more rapid and unpredictable (Eisenhardt, 2002). The Internet can make competitive advantage disappear very quickly as virtually all companies can use this technology (Porter, 2001; Yoffie and Cusumano, 1999). Classic strategic systems, such as American Airlines's SABRE computerized reservation system, Citibank's ATM system, and FedEx's package tracking system, benefited by being the first in their industries. Then rival systems emerged. Information systems alone cannot provide an enduring business advantage. Systems originally intended to be strategic frequently become tools for survival, required by every firm to stay in business, or they may inhibit organizations from making the strategic changes essentials for future success (Eardley, Avison, and Powell, 1997).

2. **Fitting technology to the organization (or vice-versa).** On the one hand, it is important to align information technology to the business plan, to the firm's business processes, and to senior management's strategic business plans. Information technology is, after all, supposed to be the servant of the organization. On the other hand, these business plans, processes, and management strategy all may be very outdated or incompatible with the envisioned technology. In such instances, managers will need to change the organization to fit the technology or to adjust both the organization and the technology to achieve an optimal "fit."

 This chapter explores the relationships between organizations, management, information systems, and business strategy. We introduce the features of organizations that you will need to understand when you design, build, and operate information systems. We also scrutinize the role of a manager and the management decision-making process, identifying areas where information systems can enhance managerial effectiveness. We conclude by examining the problems firms face from competition and the ways in which information systems can provide competitive advantage.

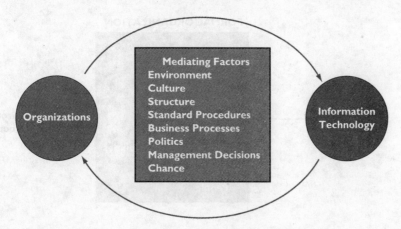

3.1 ORGANIZATIONS AND INFORMATION SYSTEMS

Information systems and organizations influence one another. Information systems must be aligned with the organization to provide information that important groups within the organization need. At the same time, the organization must be aware of and be open to the influences of information systems in order to benefit from new technologies.

The interaction between information technology and organizations is very complex and is influenced by a great many mediating factors, including the organization's structure, standard operating procedures, politics, culture, surrounding environment, and management decisions (see Figure 3-1). Managers must be aware that information systems can markedly alter life in the organization. They cannot successfully design new systems or understand existing systems without understanding organizations. Managers do decide what systems will be built, what they will do, how they will be implemented, and so forth. Sometimes, however, the outcomes are the result of pure chance and of both good and bad luck.

WHAT IS AN ORGANIZATION?

An **organization** is a stable, formal social structure that takes resources from the environment and processes them to produce outputs. This technical definition focuses on three elements of an organization. Capital and labor are primary production factors provided by the environment. The organization (the firm) transforms these inputs into products and services in a production function. The products and services are consumed by environments in return for supply inputs (see Figure 3-2). An organization is more stable than an informal group (such as a group of friends that meets every Friday for lunch) in terms of longevity and routineness. Organizations are formal legal entities with internal rules and procedures that must abide by laws. Organizations are also social structures because they are a collection of social elements, much as a machine has a structure—a particular arrangement of valves, cams, shafts, and other parts.

organization (technical definition)
A stable, formal, social structure that takes resources from the environment and processes them to produce outputs.

Figure 3-2 The technical microeconomic definition of the organization. In the microeconomic definition of organizations, capital and labor (the primary production factors provided by the environment) are transformed by the firm through the production process into products and services (outputs to the environment). The products and services are consumed by the environment, which supplies additional capital and labor as inputs in the feedback loop.

Figure 3-3 The behavioral view of organizations. The behavioral view of organizations emphasizes group relationships, values, and structures.

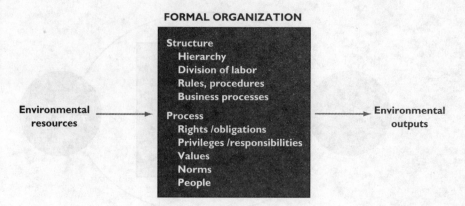

FORMAL ORGANIZATION

Structure
    Hierarchy
    Division of labor
    Rules, procedures
    Business processes
Process
    Rights /obligations
    Privileges /responsibilities
    Values
    Norms
    People

Environmental resources →

→ Environmental outputs

organization (behavioral definition)

A collection of rights, privileges, obligations, and responsibilities that are delicately balanced over a period of time through conflict and conflict resolution

This definition of organizations is powerful and simple, but it is not very descriptive or even predictive of real-world organizations. A more realistic behavioral definition of an **organization** is that it is a collection of rights, privileges, obligations, and responsibilities that are delicately balanced over a period of time through conflict and conflict resolution (see Figure 3-3). In this behavioral view of the firm, people who work in organizations develop customary ways of working; they gain attachments to existing relationships; and they make arrangements with subordinates and superiors about how work will be done, how much work will be done, and under what conditions. Most of these arrangements and feelings are not discussed in any formal rulebook.

How do these definitions of organizations relate to information system technology? A technical view of organizations encourages us to focus on the way inputs are combined into outputs when technology changes are introduced into the company. The firm is seen as infinitely malleable, with capital and labor substituting for each other quite easily. But the more realistic behavioral definition of an organization suggests that building new information systems or rebuilding old ones involves much more than a technical rearrangement of machines or workers—that some information systems change the organizational balance of rights, privileges, obligations, responsibilities, and feelings that have been established over a long period of time.

Technological change requires changes in who owns and controls information, who has the right to access and update that information, and who makes decisions about whom, when, and how. For instance, Flextronics is using enterprise systems to provide buyers with more information on parts purchases so that they can make better purchasing decisions. This more complex view forces us to look at the way work is designed and the procedures used to achieve outputs.

The technical and behavioral definitions of organizations are not contradictory. Indeed, they complement each other: The technical definition tells us how thousands of firms in competitive markets combine capital, labor, and information technology, whereas the behavioral model takes us inside the individual firm to see how that technology affects the organization's inner workings. Section 3.2 describes how each of these definitions of organizations can help explain the relationships between information systems and organizations.

Some features of organizations are common to all organizations; others distinguish one organization from another. Let us look first at the features common to all organizations.

COMMON FEATURES OF ORGANIZATIONS

You might not think that Apple Computer, United Airlines, and the Aspen, Colorado, Police Department have much in common, but they do. In some respects, all modern organizations are alike because they share the characteristics that are listed in Table 3-1. A German sociologist, Max Weber, was the first to describe these "ideal-typical" characteristics of organizations in 1911. He called organizations **bureaucracies** that have certain "structural" features.

According to Weber, all modern bureaucracies have a clear-cut division of labor and specialization. Organizations arrange specialists in a hierarchy of authority in which everyone is accountable to someone and authority is limited to specific actions. Authority and action are further limited by abstract rules or procedures (standard operating procedures, or SOPs) that

bureaucracy

Formal organization with a clear-cut division of labor, abstract rules and procedures, and impartial decision making that uses technical qualifications and professionalism as a basis for promoting employees.

TABLE 3-1	STRUCTURAL CHARACTERISTICS OF ALL ORGANIZATIONS

Clear division of labor
Hierarchy
Explicit rules and procedures
Impartial judgments
Technical qualifications for positions
Maximum organizational efficiency

are interpreted and applied to specific cases. These rules create a system of impartial and universal decision making; everyone is treated equally. Organizations try to hire and promote employees on the basis of technical qualifications and professionalism (not personal connections). The organization is devoted to the principle of efficiency: maximizing output using limited inputs.

According to Weber, bureaucracies are prevalent because they are the most efficient form of organization. Other scholars have supplemented Weber, identifying additional features of organizations. All organizations develop standard operating procedures, politics, and cultures.

Standard Operating Procedures

Organizations that survive over time become very efficient, producing a limited number of products and services by following standard routines. These standard routines become codified into reasonably precise rules, procedures, and practices called **standard operating procedures (SOPs)** that are developed to cope with virtually all expected situations. Some of these rules and procedures are written, formal procedures. Most are "rules of thumb" to be followed in select situations. Business processes are based on SOPs.

These standard operating procedures have a great deal to do with the efficiency that modern organizations attain. For instance, in the assembly of a car, managers and workers develop complex standard procedures to handle thousands of motions in a precise fashion, permitting the finished product to roll off the assembly line. Any change in SOPs requires an enormous organizational effort. Indeed, the organization may need to halt the entire production process before the old SOPs can be retired.

Difficulty in changing standard operating procedures is one reason Detroit automakers have been slow to adopt Japanese mass-production methods. For many years, U.S. automakers followed Henry Ford's mass-production principles. Ford believed that the cheapest way to build a car was to churn out the largest number of autos by having workers repeatedly perform a simple task. By contrast, Japanese automakers have emphasized "lean production" methods whereby a smaller number of workers, each performing several tasks, can produce cars with less inventory, less investment, and fewer mistakes. Workers have multiple job responsibilities and are encouraged to stop production in order to correct a problem.

Organizational Politics

People in organizations occupy different positions with different specialties, concerns, and perspectives. As a result, they naturally have divergent viewpoints about how resources, rewards, and punishments should be distributed. These differences matter to both managers and employees, and they result in political struggle, competition, and conflict within every organization. Political resistance is one of the great difficulties of bringing about organizational change—especially the development of new information systems. Virtually all information systems that bring about significant changes in goals, procedures, productivity, and personnel are politically charged and will elicit serious political opposition.

Organizational Culture

All organizations have bedrock, unassailable, unquestioned (by the members) assumptions that define their goals and products. **Organizational culture** is this set of fundamental assumptions about what products the organization should produce, how it should produce

standard operating procedures (SOPs)
Precise rules, procedures, and practices developed by organizations to cope with virtually all expected situations.

organizational culture
The set of fundamental assumptions about what products the organization should produce, how and where it should produce them, and for whom they should be produced.

TABLE 3-2   ORGANIZATIONAL STRUCTURES

Organizational Type	Description	Example
Entrepreneurial structure	Young, small firm in a fast-changing environment. It has a simple structure and is managed by an entrepreneur serving as its single chief executive officer.	Small start-up business
Machine bureaucracy	Large bureaucracy existing in a slowly changing environment, producing standard products. It is dominated by a centralized management team and centralized decision making.	Midsize manufacturing firm
Divisionalized bureaucracy	Combination of multiple machine bureaucracies, each producing a different product or service, all topped by one central headquarters.	Fortune 500 firms such as General Motors
Professional bureaucracy	Knowledge-based organization where goods and services depend on the expertise and knowledge of professionals. Dominated by department heads with weak centralized authority.	Law firms, school systems
Adhocracy	"Task force" organization that must respond to rapidly changing environments. Consists of large groups of specialists organized into short-lived multidisciplinary teams and has weak central management.	Consulting firms such as the Rand Corporation

them, where, and for whom. Generally, these cultural assumptions are taken totally for granted and are rarely publicly announced or spoken about (Schein, 1985).

You can see organizational culture at work by looking around your university or college. Some bedrock assumptions of university life are that professors know more than students, the reason students attend college is to learn, and classes follow a regular schedule. Organizational culture is a powerful unifying force that restrains political conflict and promotes common understanding, agreement on procedures, and common practices. If we all share the same basic cultural assumptions, then agreement on other matters is more likely.

At the same time, organizational culture is a powerful restraint on change, especially technological change. Most organizations will do almost anything to avoid making changes in basic assumptions. Any technological change that threatens commonly held cultural assumptions usually meets a great deal of resistance. However, there are times when the only sensible way for a firm to move forward is to employ a new technology that directly opposes an existing organizational culture. When this occurs, the technology is often stalled while the culture slowly adjusts.

UNIQUE FEATURES OF ORGANIZATIONS

Although all organizations do have common characteristics, no two organizations are identical. Organizations have different structures, goals, constituencies, leadership styles, tasks, and surrounding environments.

Different Organizational Types

One important way in which organizations differ is in their structure or shape. The differences among organizational structures are characterized in many ways. Mintzberg's classification, described in Table 3-2, identifies five basic kinds of organizations (Mintzberg, 1979).

Organizations and Environments

Organizations reside in environments from which they draw resources and to which they supply goods and services. Organizations and environments have a reciprocal relationship. On the one hand, organizations are open to, and dependent on, the social and physical environment that surrounds them. Without financial and human resources—people willing to

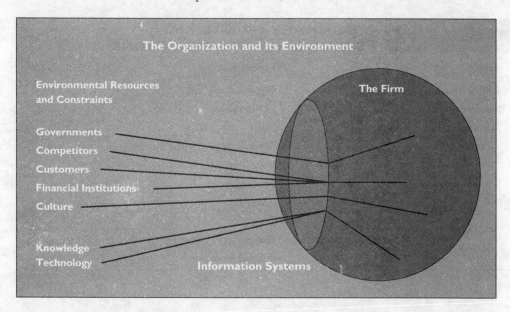

Figure 3-4 Environments and organizations have a reciprocal relationship. Environments shape what organizations can do, but organizations can influence their environments and decide to change environments altogether. Information technology plays a critical role in helping organizations perceive environmental change, and in helping organizations act on their environment.

work reliably and consistently for a set wage or revenue from customers—organizations could not exist. Organizations must respond to legislative and other requirements imposed by government, as well as the actions of customers and competitors. On the other hand, organizations can influence their environments. Organizations form alliances with others to influence the political process; they advertise to influence customer acceptance of their products.

Figure 3-4 shows that information systems play an important role in helping organizations perceive changes in their environments and also in helping organizations act on their environments. Information systems are key instruments for *environmental scanning*, helping managers identify external changes that might require an organizational response.

Environments generally change much faster than organizations. The main reasons for organizational failure are an inability to adapt to a rapidly changing environment and a lack of resources—particularly among young firms—to sustain even short periods of troubled times (Freeman et al., 1983). New technologies, new products, and changing public tastes and values (many of which result in new government regulations) put strains on any organization's culture, politics, and people. Most organizations do not cope well with large environmental shifts. The inertia built into an organization's standard operating procedures, the political conflict raised by changes to the existing order, and the threat to closely held cultural values typically inhibit organizations from making significant changes. It is not surprising that only 10 percent of the Fortune 500 companies in 1919 still exist today.

Other Differences Among Organizations

Organizations have different shapes or structures for many other reasons also. They differ in their ultimate goals and the types of power used to achieve them. Some organizations have coercive goals (e.g., prisons); others have utilitarian goals (e.g., businesses). Still others have normative goals (universities, religious groups). Organizations also serve different groups or have different constituencies, some primarily benefiting their members, others benefiting clients, stockholders, or the public. The nature of leadership differs greatly from one organization to another—some organizations may be more democratic or authoritarian than others. Another way organizations differ is by the tasks they perform and the technology they use. Some organizations perform primarily routine tasks that could be reduced to formal rules that require little judgment (such as manufacturing auto parts), whereas others (such as consulting firms) work primarily with nonroutine tasks.

As you can see in Table 3-3, the list of unique features of organizations is longer than the common features list. It stands to reason that information systems will have different impacts on different types of organizations. Different organizations in different circumstances will experience different effects from the same technology. The Window on Organizations shows, for

TABLE 3-3	A SUMMARY OF SALIENT FEATURES OF ORGANIZATIONS

Common Features	Unique Features
Formal structure	Organizational type
Standard operating procedures (SOPs)	Environments
Politics	Goals
Culture	Power
	Constituencies
	Function
	Leadership
	Tasks
	Technology
	Business processes

example, how unique environments, culture, and organizational characteristics have affected Internet use and electronic commerce in South Korea and the Middle East. Only by close analysis of a specific organization can a manager effectively design and manage information systems.

3.2 THE CHANGING ROLE OF INFORMATION SYSTEMS IN ORGANIZATIONS

Information systems have become integral, online, interactive tools deeply involved in the minute-to-minute operations and decision making of large organizations. We now describe the changing role of systems in organizations and how it has been shaped by the interaction of organizations and information technology.

INFORMATION TECHNOLOGY INFRASTRUCTURE AND INFORMATION TECHNOLOGY SERVICES

information systems department

The formal organizational unit that is responsible for the information systems function in the organization.

programmers

Highly trained technical specialists who write computer software instructions.

systems analysts

Specialists who translate business problems and requirements into information requirements and systems, acting as a liaison between the information systems department and the rest of the organization.

information systems managers

Leaders of the various specialists in the information systems department.

One way that organizations can influence how information technology will be used is through decisions about the technical and organizational configuration of systems. Previous chapters described the ever-widening role of information systems in organizations. Supporting this widening role have been changes in information technology (IT) infrastructure, which we defined in Chapter 1. Each organization determines exactly how its infrastructure will be configured. Chapters 6 through 9 detail the various technology alternatives that organizations can use to design their infrastructures.

Another way that organizations have affected information technology is through decisions about who will design, build, and maintain the organization's IT infrastructure. These decisions determine how information technology services will be delivered.

The formal organizational unit or function responsible for technology services is called the **information systems department.** The information systems department is responsible for maintaining the hardware, software, data storage, and networks that comprise the firm's IT infrastructure.

The information systems department consists of specialists, such as programmers, systems analysts, project leaders, and information systems managers (see Figure 3-5). **Programmers** are highly trained technical specialists who write the software instructions for the computer. **Systems analysts** constitute the principal liaison between the information systems groups and the rest of the organization. It is the systems analyst's job to translate business problems and requirements into information requirements and systems. **Information systems managers** are leaders of teams of programmers and analysts, project managers, physical facility managers, telecommunications managers, and heads of office system groups. They are also managers of computer operations and data entry staff. Also external specialists, such as hardware vendors and manufacturers, software firms, and consultants

E-COMMERCE, SOUTH KOREAN AND MIDDLE EASTERN STYLE

Why is e-commerce not spreading relatively equally throughout the world? In some countries its use is exploding, while in other countries, few people have turned to using the Internet despite its growing value and importance. Let us compare South Korea at one end of the spectrum with the Arab Middle Eastern countries at the other end.

E-commerce, including commerce using wireless mobile devices, is growing rapidly in South Korea, a country with only 11 million households. According to research firm eMarketer, Korean retail e-commerce revenue was $3.69 billion in 2001, and is expected to reach almost $16 billion in 2004. That research also predicts that in 2004 business-to-business e-commerce will rise to over $14 billion. To understand why the growth is so rapid, we need to examine the country's economic and cultural environment.

Part of the answer is that, per capita, South Korea has the highest online penetration in the world. Nearly half of the South Koreans use the Internet and about 95 percent of them are online at least once a week. In fact the country has a higher high-speed network penetration than any other country, and by 2001 over 59 percent of South Koreans were using mobile phones. South Korean Internet users spend twice as much time online as do people in the United States. One key factor is that the cost of these technologies is not too high for most Koreans. Another factor is that the government has played a major role in the growing commitment to these technologies. Several government organizations, such as its Ministry of Commerce, Industry, and Energy, its Fair Trade Commission, and its Ministry of Culture and Tourism are all working to advance use of these technologies.

One challenge for Korean e-commerce is that Korean citizens use the Internet mostly for communication and information. Only about 12.3 percent of them are shopping online. Their main problem is their fear that the Internet lacks security. (According to the Australian Institute of Criminology, approximately 5 percent to 10 percent of online transactions in Asia involve fraud.) To address this problem, the government has developed a highly secure digital-signature system, and it is also promoting the use of electronic money and credit cards.

Compare this with the Middle East. With an Arab population of about 270 million, only 4.22 million are online. Moreover, of the 20 most used sites in the Arab world, only Kunoozy.com is purely for e-commerce, and it ranks 19th in popularity. According to Stephane Jais, the Middle East and Africa sales manager for DoubleClick, the Internet advertising firm, "There aren't a lot of e-commerce sites in the Middle East." Moreover, she says the few commercial sites that do exist are small with only about 1,000 visitors daily. And most of their sales are for Arabs who are living abroad. Why the difference?

Cost is definitely the major reason. In 2000, for example, the gross domestic product (GDP) in Jordan was $3,500, while the average PC cost was about $2,500 and 30 hours of Internet usage per month cost about $1,400. In the same year only 2.2 Egyptians out of 100 owned a PC, while in Syria that number was only 1.43. In comparison, the per capita ownership in the United States is 58.5 per 100. Even the Internet cafes in the Middle East are few and small with only one or two computers in grocery store back rooms. These are mainly used for communication.

Online shopping is difficult for other reasons. Very few Middle Easterners have credit cards, although they are vital for online retail shopping. Moreover, tariffs are as high as 100 percent making foreign products too expensive. In addition, the common approach to shopping in that part of the world is haggling over price, a pleasure to many residents.

To Think About: What organizational factors describe why South Korea and the Arab Middle East have had such different experiences in adopting e-commerce? How would a company's management, organization, and technology have to change to either purchase or sell goods in South Korea or the Middle East?

Sources: David Rosenberg, "No Sale," *Wall Street Journal*, April 15, 2002; Mark Resch, "South Korea," *IQ Magazine*, January/February 2002; and Jessica Schneider Davis, "Safe Business in Asia," *IQ Magazine*, July/August 2002

ORGANIZATIONS

frequently participate in the day-to-day operations and long-term planning of information systems.

In many companies, the information systems department is headed by a **chief information officer (CIO).** The CIO is a senior management position that oversees the use of information technology in the firm.

End users are representatives of departments outside of the information systems group for whom applications are developed. These users are playing an increasingly large role in the design and development of information systems.

In the early years, the information systems group was composed mostly of programmers, who performed very highly specialized but limited technical functions. Today a growing proportion of staff members are systems analysts and network specialists, with the information

chief information officer (CIO)
Senior manager in charge of the information systems function in the firm.

end users
Representatives of departments outside the information systems group for whom applications are developed.

Figure 3-5 Information technology services. Many types of specialists and groups are responsible for the design and management of the organization's information technology (IT) infrastructure.

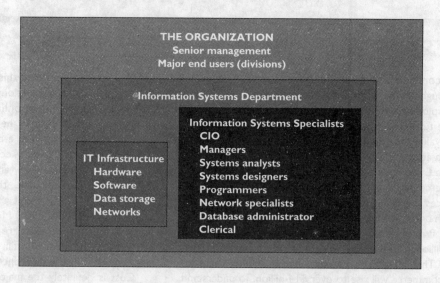

THE ORGANIZATION
Senior management
Major end users (divisions)

Information Systems Department

Information Systems Specialists
CIO
Managers
Systems analysts
Systems designers
Programmers
Network specialists
Database administrator
Clerical

IT Infrastructure
Hardware
Software
Data storage
Networks

systems department acting as a powerful change agent in the organization. The information systems department suggests new business strategies and new information-based products and services, and coordinates both the development of the technology and the planned changes in the organization.

In the past, firms generally built their own software and managed their own computing facilities. Today, many firms are turning to external vendors to provide these services (see Chapters 6, 9, and 12) and using their information systems departments to manage these service providers.

How Information Systems Affect Organizations

How have changes in information technology affected organizations? To find answers, we draw on research and theory based on both economic and behavioral approaches.

Economic Theories

From an economic standpoint, information system technology can be viewed as a factor of production that can be freely substituted for capital and labor. As the cost of information system technology falls, it is substituted for labor, which historically has been a rising cost. Hence, information technology should result in a decline in the number of middle managers and clerical workers as information technology substitutes for their labor.

Information technology also helps firms contract in size because it can reduce transaction costs—the costs incurred when a firm buys on the marketplace what it cannot make itself. According to **transaction cost theory,** firms and individuals seek to economize on transaction costs, much as they do on production costs. Using markets is expensive (Williamson, 1985; Coase, 1937) because of costs such as locating and communicating with distant suppliers, monitoring contract compliance, buying insurance, obtaining information on products, and so forth. Traditionally, firms have tried to reduce transaction costs by getting bigger, hiring more employees, or buying their own suppliers and distributors, as General Motors used to do.

Information technology, especially the use of networks, can help firms lower the cost of market participation (transaction costs), making it worthwhile for firms to contract with external suppliers instead of using internal sources. For example, by using computer links to external suppliers, the DaimlerChrysler Corporation can achieve economies by obtaining more than 70 percent of its parts from the outside. Information systems make it possible for companies such as Cisco Systems and Dell Computer to outsource their production to contract manufacturers such as Flextronics instead of making their products themselves. Figure 3-6 shows that as transaction costs decrease, firm size (the number of employees) should shrink because it becomes easier and cheaper for the firm to contract for the purchase of goods and services in the marketplace rather than to make the product or service itself. Firm size can stay constant or contract even if the company increases its revenues. (For example, General

transaction cost theory
Economic theory stating that firms grow larger because they can conduct marketplace transactions internally more cheaply than they can with external firms in the marketplace.

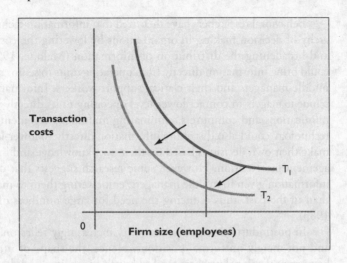

Figure 3-6 The transaction cost theory of the impact of information technology on the organization. Firms traditionally grew in size in order to reduce transaction costs. IT potentially reduces the costs for a given size, shifting the transaction cost curve inward, opening up the possibility of revenue growth without increasing size, or even revenue growth accompanied by shrinking size.

Electric reduced its workforce from about 400,000 people in the early 1980s to about 230,000 while increasing revenues 150 percent.)

Information technology also can reduce internal management costs. According to **agency theory,** the firm is viewed as a "nexus of contracts" among self-interested individuals rather than as a unified, profit-maximizing entity (Jensen and Meckling, 1976). A principal (owner) employs "agents" (employees) to perform work on his or her behalf. However, agents need constant supervision and management because otherwise they will tend to pursue their own interests rather than those of the owners. As firms grow in size and scope, agency costs or coordination costs rise, because owners must expend more and more effort supervising and managing employees.

Information technology, by reducing the costs of acquiring and analyzing information, permits organizations to reduce agency costs because it becomes easier for managers to oversee a greater number of employees. Figure 3-7 shows that by reducing overall management costs, information technology allows firms to increase revenues while shrinking the number of middle management and clerical workers. We have seen examples in earlier chapters where information technology expanded the power and scope of small organizations by allowing them to perform coordinating activities such as processing orders or keeping track of inventory with very few clerks and managers.

agency theory
Economic theory that views the firm as a nexus of contracts among self-interested individuals who must be supervised and managed.

Behavioral Theories

Although economic theories try to explain how large numbers of firms act in the marketplace, behavioral theories from sociology, psychology, and political science are more useful for describing the behavior of individual firms. Behavioral research has found little evidence that information systems automatically transform organizations, although the systems may be instrumental in accomplishing this goal once senior management decides to pursue this end.

Figure 3-7 The agency cost theory of the impact of information technology on the organization. As firms grow in size and complexity, traditionally they experience rising agency costs. IT shifts the agency cost curve down and to the right, allowing firms to increase size while lowering agency costs

Behavioral researchers have theorized that information technology could change the hierarchy of decision making in organizations by lowering the costs of information acquisition and broadening the distribution of information (Malone, 1997). Information technology could bring information directly from operating units to senior managers, thereby eliminating middle managers and their clerical support workers. Information technology could permit senior managers to contact lower-level operating units directly by using networked telecommunications and computers, eliminating middle management intermediaries. Information technology could also distribute information directly to lower-level workers, who could then make their own decisions based on their own knowledge and information without any management intervention. However, some research suggests that computerization increases the information given to middle managers, empowering them to make more important decisions than in the past, thus reducing the need for large numbers of lower-level workers (Shore, 1983).

In postindustrial societies, authority increasingly relies on knowledge and competence, and not merely on formal positions. Hence, the shape of organizations should "flatten," because professional workers tend to be self-managing; and decision making should become more decentralized as knowledge and information become more widespread throughout (Drucker, 1988). Information technology may encourage "task force" networked organizations in which groups of professionals come together—face-to-face or electronically—for short periods of time to accomplish a specific task (e.g., designing a new automobile); once the task is accomplished, the individuals join other task forces. More firms may operate as **virtual organizations** where work no longer is tied to geographic location. Virtual organizations use networks to link people, assets, and ideas. They can ally with suppliers, customers, and even sometimes competitors to create and distribute new products and services without being limited by traditional organizational boundaries or physical locations. For example, Calyx and Corolla is a networked virtual organization selling fresh flowers directly to customers, bypassing traditional florists. The firm takes orders via telephone or from its Web site and transmits them to grower farms, which ship them in FedEx vans directly to customers.

Who makes sure that self-managed teams do not head off in the wrong direction? Who decides which person works on what team and for how long? How can managers evaluate the performance of someone who is constantly rotating from team to team? How do people know where their careers are headed? New approaches for evaluating, organizing, and informing workers are required; and not all companies can make virtual work effective (Davenport and Pearlson, 1998).

No one knows the answers to these questions, and it is not clear that all modern organizations will undergo this transformation. General Motors, for example, may have many self-managed knowledge workers in certain divisions, but it still will have a manufacturing division structured as a large, traditional bureaucracy. In general, the shape of organizations historically changes with the business cycle and with the latest management fashions. When times are good and profits are high, firms hire large numbers of supervisory personnel; when times are tough, they let go many of these same people (Mintzberg, 1979).

Another behavioral approach views information systems as the outcome of political competition between organizational groups for influence over the organization's policies, procedures, and resources (Laudon, 1974; Keen, 1981; Kling, 1980; Laudon, 1986). Information systems inevitably become bound up in organizational politics because they influence access to a key resource—namely, information. Information systems can affect who does what to whom, when, where, and how in an organization. Because information systems potentially change an organization's structure, culture, politics, and work, there is often considerable resistance to them when they are introduced.

There are several ways to visualize organizational resistance. Leavitt (1965) used a diamond shape to illustrate the interrelated and mutually adjusting character of technology and organization (see Figure 3-8). Here, changes in technology are absorbed, deflected, and defeated by organizational task arrangements, structures, and people. In this model, the only way to bring about change is to change the technology, tasks, structure, and people simultaneously. Other authors have spoken about the need to "unfreeze" organizations before introducing an innovation, quickly implementing it, and "refreezing" or institutionalizing the change (Kolb, 1970; Alter and Ginzberg, 1978).

---

virtual organization

Organization using networks to link people, assets, and ideas to create and distribute products and services without being limited to traditional organizational boundaries or physical locations.

THE INTERNET AND ORGANIZATIONS

The Internet, especially the World Wide Web, is beginning to have an important impact on the relationships between firms and external entities, and even on the organization of business processes inside a firm. The Internet increases the accessibility, storage, and distribution of information and knowledge for organizations. In essence, the Internet is capable of dramatically lowering the transaction and agency costs facing most organizations. For instance, brokerage firms and banks in New York can now "deliver" their internal-operations procedures manuals to their employees at distant locations by posting them on their corporate Web sites, saving millions of dollars in distribution costs. A global sales force can receive nearly instant price product information updates via the Web or instructions from management via e-mail. Vendors of some large retailers can access retailers' internal Web sites directly for up-to-the-minute sales information and initiate replenishment orders instantly.

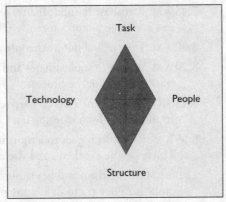

Figure 3-8 Organizational resistance and the mutually adjusting relationship between technology and the organization. Implementing information systems has consequences for task arrangements, structures, and people. According to this model, in order to implement change, all four components must be changed simultaneously.
Source: Leavitt, 1965

Businesses are rapidly rebuilding some of their core business processes based on Internet technology and making this technology a key component of their information technology (IT) infrastructures. If prior networking is any guide, one result will be simpler business processes, fewer employees, and much flatter organizations than in the past.

3.3   MANAGERS, DECISION MAKING, AND INFORMATION SYSTEMS

To determine how information systems can benefit managers, we must first examine what managers do and what information they need for decision making and other functions. We must also understand how decisions are made and what kinds of decisions can be supported by formal information systems.

THE ROLE OF MANAGERS IN ORGANIZATIONS

Managers play a key role in organizations. Their responsibilities range from making decisions, to writing reports, to attending meetings, to arranging birthday parties. We can better understand managerial functions and roles by examining classical and contemporary models of managerial behavior.

Classical Descriptions of Management

The **classical model of management,** which describes what managers do, was largely unquestioned for the more than 70 years since the 1920s. Henri Fayol and other early writers first described the five classical functions of managers as planning, organizing, coordinating, deciding, and controlling. This description of management activities dominated management thought for a long time, and it is still popular today.

classical model of management
Traditional description of management that focused on its formal functions of planning, organizing, coordinating, deciding, and controlling.

But these terms actually describe formal managerial functions and are unsatisfactory as a description of what managers actually do. The terms do not address what managers do when they plan, decide things, and control the work of others. We need a more fine-grained understanding of how managers actually behave.

Behavioral Models

Contemporary behavioral scientists have observed that managers do not behave as the classical model of management led us to believe. Kotter (1982), for example, describes the morning activities of the president of an investment management firm.

> 7:35 A.M. Richardson arrives at work, unpacks her briefcase, gets some coffee, and begins making a list of activities for the day.

7:45 A.M. Bradshaw (a subordinate) and Richardson converse about a number of topics and exchange pictures recently taken on summer vacations.

8:00 A.M. They talk about a schedule of priorities for the day.

8:20 A.M. Wilson (a subordinate) and Richardson talk about some personnel problems, cracking jokes in the process.

8:45 A.M. Richardson's secretary arrives, and they discuss her new apartment and arrangements for a meeting later in the morning.

8:55 A.M. Richardson goes to a morning meeting run by one of her subordinates. Thirty people are there, and Richardson reads during the meeting.

11:05 A.M. Richardson and her subordinates return to the office and discuss a difficult problem. They try to define the problem and outline possible alternatives. She lets the discussion roam away from and back to the topic again and again. Finally, they agree on a next step.

In this example, it is difficult to determine which activities constitute Richardson's planning, coordinating, and decision making. **Behavioral models** state that the actual behavior of managers appears to be less systematic, more informal, less reflective, more reactive, less well-organized, and much more frivolous than the classical model of management would indicate.

Observers find that managerial behavior actually has five attributes that differ greatly from the classical description: First, managers perform a great deal of work at an unrelenting pace—studies have found that managers engage in more than 600 different activities each day, with no break in their pace. Second, managerial activities are fragmented; most activities last for less than nine minutes, and only 10 percent of the activities exceed one hour in duration. Third, managers prefer speculation, hearsay, gossip—they want current, specific, and ad hoc information (printed information often will be too old). Fourth, they prefer oral forms of communication to written forms because oral media provide greater flexibility, require less effort, and bring a faster response. Fifth, managers give high priority to maintaining a diverse and complex web of contacts that acts as an informal information system and helps them execute their personal agendas and short- and long-term goals.

Analyzing managers' day-to-day behavior, Mintzberg found that it could be classified into 10 **managerial roles.** Managerial roles are expectations of the activities that managers should perform in an organization. Mintzberg found that these managerial roles fell into three categories: interpersonal, informational, and decisional.

behavioral models

Descriptions of management based on behavioral scientists' observations of what managers actually do in their jobs.

managerial roles

Expectations of the activities that managers should perform in an organization.

interpersonal roles

Mintzberg's classification for managerial roles where managers act as figureheads and leaders for the organization.

A corporate chief executive learns how to use a computer. Some senior managers lack computer knowledge or experience and require systems that are extremely easy to use.

Interpersonal Roles. Managers act as figureheads for the organization when they represent their companies to the outside world and perform symbolic duties such as giving out employee awards. Managers act as leaders, attempting to motivate, counsel, and support subordinates. Managers also act as liaisons between various organizational levels; within each of these levels, they serve as liaisons among the members of the management team. Managers provide time and favors, which they expect to be returned.

Informational Roles. Managers act as the nerve centers of their organization, receiving the most concrete, up-to-date information and redistributing it to those

TABLE 3-4	MANAGERIAL ROLES AND SUPPORTING INFORMATION SYSTEMS

Role	Behavior	Support Systems
Interpersonal Roles		
Figurehead		None exist
Leader	Interpersonal	None exist
Liaison		Electronic communication systems
Informational Roles		
Nerve center		Management information systems, ESS
Disseminator	Information-processing	Mail, office systems
Spokesperson		Office and professional systems, workstations
Decisional Roles		
Entrepreneur	Decision-making	None exist
Disturbance handler		None exist
Resource allocator		DSS systems
Negotiator		None exist

Source: Kenneth C. Laudon and Jane P. Laudon; and Mintzberg, 1971.

who need to be aware of it. Managers are therefore information disseminators and spokespersons for their organizations.

Decisional Roles. Managers make decisions. They act as entrepreneurs by initiating new kinds of activities; they handle disturbances arising in the organization; they allocate resources to staff members who need them; and they negotiate conflicts and mediate between conflicting groups in the organization.

Table 3-4, based on Mintzberg's role classifications, is one look at where systems can and cannot help managers. The table shows that information systems do not yet contribute to some important areas of management life. These areas will provide great opportunities for future systems efforts.

MANAGERS AND DECISION MAKING

Decision making is often a manager's most challenging role. Information systems have helped managers communicate and distribute information; however, they have provided only limited assistance for management decision making. Because decision making is an area that system designers have sought most of all to affect (with mixed success), we now turn our attention to this issue.

The Process of Decision Making

Decision making can be classified by organizational level, corresponding to the strategic, management, knowledge, and operational levels of the organization introduced in Chapter 2. **Strategic decision making** determines the long-term objectives, resources, and policies of the organization. Decision making for **management control** is principally concerned with how efficiently and effectively resources are used and how well operational units are performing. **Operational control** decision making determines how to carry out the specific tasks set forth by strategic and middle-management decision makers. **Knowledge-level decision making** deals with evaluating new ideas for products and services, ways to communicate new knowledge, and ways to distribute information throughout the organization.

Within each of these levels of decision making, researchers classify decisions as structured and unstructured. **Unstructured decisions** are those in which the decision maker must provide judgment, evaluation, and insights into the problem definition. Each of these

informational roles
Mintzberg's classification for managerial roles where managers act as the nerve centers of their organizations, receiving and disseminating critical information.

decisional roles
Mintzberg's classification for managerial roles where managers initiate activities, handle disturbances, allocate resources, and negotiate conflicts.

strategic decision making
Determining the long-term objectives, resources, and policies of an organization.

management control
Monitoring how efficiently and effectively resources are used and how well operational units are performing.

operational control
Deciding how to carry out specific tasks specified by upper and middle management, and establishing criteria for completion and resource allocation.

knowledge-level decision making
Evaluating new ideas for products, services, ways to communicate new knowledge, and ways to distribute information throughout the organization.

unstructured decisions
Nonroutine decisions in which the decision maker must provide judgment, evaluation, and insights into the problem definition; there is no agreed-on procedure for making such decisions.

Figure 3-9 Different kinds of information systems at the various organization levels support different types of decisions.

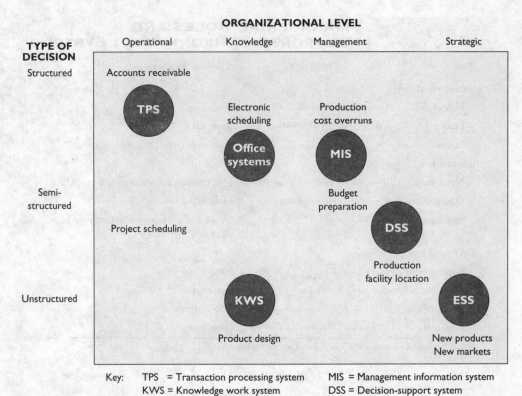

ORGANIZATIONAL LEVEL

Key: TPS = Transaction processing system   MIS = Management information system
        KWS = Knowledge work system   DSS = Decision-support system
                                                ESS = Executive support system

structured decisions

Decisions that are repetitive, routine, and have a definite procedure for handling them.

intelligence

The first of Simon's four stages of decision making, when the individual collects information to identify problems occurring in the organization.

design

Simon's second stage of decision making, when the individual conceives of possible alternative solutions to a problem.

choice

Simon's third stage of decision making, when the individual selects among the various solution alternatives.

implementation

Simon's final stage of decision making, when the individual puts the decision into effect and reports on the progress of the solution.

decisions is novel, important, and nonroutine, and there is no well-understood or agreed-on procedure for making them (Gorry and Scott-Morton, 1971). **Structured decisions,** by contrast, are repetitive and routine, and they involve a definite procedure for handling them so that they do not have to be treated each time as if they were new. Some decisions are semistructured; in such cases, only part of the problem has a clear-cut answer provided by an accepted procedure.

The grid shown in Figure 3-9 combines these two views of decision making. In general, operational control personnel face fairly well structured problems. In contrast, strategic planners tackle highly unstructured problems. Many of the problems knowledge workers encounter are fairly unstructured as well. Nevertheless, each level of the organization contains both structured and unstructured problems.

Stages of Decision Making

Making decisions consists of several different activities. Simon (1960) described four different stages in decision making: intelligence, design, choice, and implementation.

Intelligence consists of identifying and understanding the problems occurring in the organization—why the problem, where, and with what effects. Traditional MIS systems that deliver a wide variety of detailed information can help identify problems, especially if the systems report exceptions.

During solution **design,** the individual designs possible solutions to the problems. Smaller DSS systems are ideal in this stage of decision making because they operate on simple models, can be developed quickly, and can be operated with limited data.

Choice consists of choosing among solution alternatives. Here the decision maker might need a larger DSS system to develop more extensive data on a variety of alternatives and complex models or data analysis tools to account for all of the costs, consequences, and opportunities.

During solution **implementation,** when the decision is put into effect, managers can use a reporting system that delivers routine reports on the progress of a specific solution. Support systems can range from full-blown MIS systems to much smaller systems, as well as project-planning software operating on personal computers.

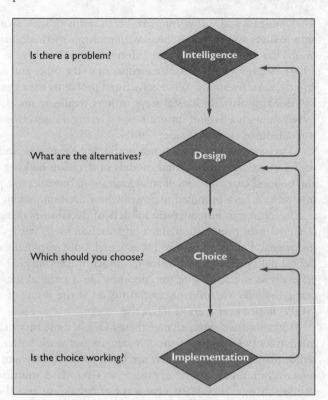

Figure 3-10 The decision-making process. Decisions are often arrived at after a series of iterations and evaluations at each stage in the process. The decision maker often must loop back through one or more of the stages before completing the process.

In general, the stages of decision making do not necessarily follow a linear path. Think again about the decision you made to attend a specific college. At any point in the decision-making process, you may have to loop back to a previous stage (see Figure 3-10). For instance, one can often come up with several designs but may not be certain about whether a specific design meets the requirements for the particular problem. This situation requires additional intelligence work. Alternatively, one can be in the process of implementing a decision, only to discover that it is not working. In such a case, one is forced to repeat the design or choice stage.

Models of Decision Making

A number of models attempt to describe how people make decisions. Some of these models focus on individual decision making, whereas others focus on decision making in groups.

Individual models of decision making assume that human beings are in some sense rational. The **rational model** of human behavior is built on the idea that people engage in basically consistent, rational, value-maximizing calculations. According to this model, an individual identifies goals, ranks all possible alternative actions by their contributions to those goals, and chooses the alternative that contributes most to those goals.

Critics of this model show that in fact people cannot specify all of the alternatives, and that most individuals do not have singular goals and so are unable to rank all alternatives and consequences. Many decisions are so complex that calculating the choice (even if done by computer) is virtually impossible. Instead of searching through all alternatives, people tend to choose the first available alternative that moves them toward their ultimate goal. In making policy decisions, people choose policies most like the previous policy (Lindblom, 1959). Finally, some scholars point out that decision making is a continuous process in which final decisions are always being modified.

Other research has found that humans differ in how they maximize their values and in the frames of reference they use to interpret information and make choices. Tversky and Kahneman showed that humans have built-in biases that can distort decision making. People can be manipulated into choosing alternatives that they might otherwise reject simply by changing the frame of reference (Tversky and Kahneman, 1981).

Cognitive style describes underlying personality dispositions toward the treatment of information, the selection of alternatives, and the evaluation of consequences. **Systematic decision makers** approach a problem by structuring it in terms of some formal method.

rational model
Model of human behavior based on the belief that people, organizations, and nations engage in basically consistent, value-maximizing calculations.

cognitive style
Underlying personality dispositions toward the treatment of information, selection of alternatives, and evaluation of consequences.

systematic decision makers
Cognitive style that describes people who approach a problem by structuring it in terms of some formal method.

intuitive decision makers

Cognitive style that describes people who approach a problem with multiple methods in an unstructured manner, using trial and error to find a solution.

organizational models of decision making

Models of decision making that take into account the structural and political characteristics of an organization.

bureaucratic models of decision making

Models of decision making where decisions are shaped by the organization's standard operating procedures (SOPs).

political models of decision making

Models of decision making where decisions result from competition and bargaining among the organization's interest groups and key leaders.

"garbage can" model

Model of decision making that states that organizations are not rational and that decisions are solutions that become attached to problems for accidental reasons.

They evaluate and gather information in terms of their structured method. **Intuitive decision makers** approach a problem with multiple methods, using trial and error to find a solution. They tend not to structure information gathering or evaluation (McKenney and Keen, 1974). Neither style is considered superior to the other and each may be advantageous in certain decision situations. While structured problems with clear-cut issues can be best handled by "thinking first" in logical steps, others requiring novel, creative solutions may be best solved through a flash of intuition or by trying out several courses of action and seeing what works (Mintzberg and Westley, 2001).

Decision making often is not performed by a single individual but by entire groups or organizations. **Organizational models of decision making** take into account the structural and political characteristics of an organization. Bureaucratic, political, and even "garbage can" models have been proposed to describe how decision making takes place in organizations.

According to **bureaucratic models of decision making** an organization's most important goal is the preservation of the organization itself. The reduction of uncertainty is another major goal. Policy tends to be incremental, only marginally different from the past, because radical policy departures involve too much uncertainty. These models depict organizations generally as not "choosing" or "deciding" in a rational sense. Rather, according to bureaucratic models, whatever organizations do is the result of standard operating procedures (SOPs) honed over years of active use.

Organizations rarely change these SOPs because they may have to change personnel and incur risks (who knows if the new techniques work better than the old ones?). Although senior management and leaders are hired to coordinate and lead the organization, they are effectively trapped by the organization's standard solutions. Some organizations do, of course, change; they learn new ways of behaving; and they can be led. But all of these changes require a long time. Look around and you will find many organizations doing pretty much what they did 10, 20, or even 30 years ago.

In **political models of decision making,** what an organization does is a result of political bargains struck among key leaders and interest groups. Organizations do not come up with "solutions" that are "chosen" to solve some "problem." They come up with compromises that reflect the conflicts, the major stakeholders, the diverse interests, the unequal power, and the confusion that constitute politics.

A theory of decision making, called the **"garbage can" model,** states that organizations are not rational. Decision making is largely accidental and is the product of a stream of solutions, problems, and situations that are randomly associated. This model could explain why organizations sometimes apply the wrong solutions to the wrong problems. The Exxon Corporation's delayed response to the 1989 Alaska oil spill is an example. Within an hour after the Exxon tanker Valdez ran aground in Alaska's Prince William Sound on March 29, 1989, workers were preparing emergency equipment; however, the aid was not dispatched. Instead of sending out emergency crews, the Alyeska Pipeline Service Company (which was responsible for initially responding to oil spill emergencies) sent the crews home. The first full emergency crew did not arrive at the spill site until at least 14 hours after the shipwreck, by which time the oil had spread beyond effective control. Yet enough equipment and personnel had been available to respond effectively. Much of the 10 million gallons of oil fouling the Alaska shoreline in the worst tanker spill in American history could have been confined had Alyeska acted more decisively.

IMPLICATIONS FOR THE DESIGN AND UNDERSTANDING OF INFORMATION SYSTEMS

In order to deliver genuine benefits, information systems must be built with a clear understanding of the organization in which they will reside and of exactly how they can contribute to managerial decision making. In our experience, the central organizational factors to consider when planning a new system are

- The environment in which the organization must function.
- The structure of the organization: hierarchy, specialization, and standard operating procedures.
- The organization's culture and politics.

- The type of organization and its style of leadership.

- The principal interest groups affected by the system and the attitudes of workers who will be using the system.

- The kinds of tasks, decisions, and business processes that the information system is designed to assist.

Systems should be built to support both group and organizational decision making. Information systems builders should design systems that have the following characteristics:

- They are flexible and provide many options for handling data and evaluating information.

- They are capable of supporting a variety of styles, skills, and knowledge as well as keeping track of many alternatives and consequences.

- They are sensitive to the organization's bureaucratic and political requirements.

3.4 INFORMATION SYSTEMS AND BUSINESS STRATEGY

Certain types of information systems have become especially critical to firms' long-term prosperity and survival. Such systems, which are powerful tools for staying ahead of the competition, are called *strategic information systems*.

WHAT IS A STRATEGIC INFORMATION SYSTEM?

Strategic information systems change the goals, operations, products, services, or environmental relationships of organizations to help them gain an edge over competitors. Systems that have these effects may even change the business of organizations. For instance, Cardinal Health transformed its core business from distributing pharmaceuticals to hosting information systems for hospital pharmacies, providing hospital pharmacy management services, and designing and producing customized packaging for drugs. Hanover Compressor, which started out renting equipment to move natural gas through production and distribution pipelines, used information systems to take over the management and maintenance of customers' pipeline monitoring systems (Slywotzky and Wise, 2002).

Strategic information systems should be distinguished from strategic-level systems for senior managers that focus on long-term, decision-making problems. Strategic information systems can be used at all organizational levels and are more far-reaching and deep rooted than the other kinds of systems we have described. Strategic information systems profoundly alter the way a firm conducts its business or the very business of the firm itself. As we will see, organizations may need to change their internal operations and relationships with customers and suppliers in order to take advantage of new information systems technology.

Traditional models of strategy are being modified to accommodate the impact of digital firms and new information flows. Before the emergence of the digital firm, business strategy emphasized competing head-to-head against other firms in the same marketplace. Today, the emphasis is increasingly on exploring, identifying, and occupying new market niches before competitors; understanding the customer value chain better; and learning faster and more deeply than competitors.

There is generally no single all-encompassing strategic system, but instead there are a number of systems operating at different levels of strategy—the business, the firm, and the industry level. For each level of business strategy, there are strategic uses of systems. And for each level of business strategy, there is an appropriate model used for analysis.

BUSINESS-LEVEL STRATEGY AND THE VALUE CHAIN MODEL

At the business level of strategy, the key question is, "How can we compete effectively in this particular market?" The market might be light bulbs, utility vehicles, or cable television. The most common generic strategies at this level are (1) to become the low-cost producer, (2) to differentiate your product or service, and/or (3) to change the scope of competition by either enlarging the market to include global markets or narrowing the market by focusing on small niches not

strategic information systems
Computer systems at any level of the organization that change goals, operations, products, services, or environmental relationships to help the organization gain a competitive advantage.

well served by your competitors. Digital firms provide new capabilities for supporting business-level strategy by managing the supply chain, building efficient customer "sense and response" systems, and participating in "value webs" to deliver new products and services to market.

Leveraging Technology in the Value Chain

At the business level the most common analytical tool is value chain analysis. The **value chain model** highlights specific activities in the business where competitive strategies can be best applied (Porter, 1985) and where information systems are most likely to have a strategic impact. The value chain model identifies specific, critical leverage points where a firm can use information technology most effectively to enhance its competitive position. Exactly where can it obtain the greatest benefit from strategic information systems—what specific activities can be used to create new products and services, enhance market penetration, lock in customers and suppliers, and lower operational costs? This model views the firm as a series or "chain" of basic activities that add a margin of value to a firm's products or services. These activities can be categorized as either primary activities or support activities.

 Primary activities are most directly related to the production and distribution of the firm's products and services that create value for the customer. Primary activities include inbound logistics, operations, outbound logistics, sales and marketing, and service. Inbound logistics include receiving and storing materials for distribution to production. Operations transforms inputs into finished products. Outbound logistics entail storing and distributing finished products. Sales and marketing includes promoting and selling the firm's products. The service activity includes maintenance and repair of the firm's goods and services. **Support activities** make the delivery of the primary activities possible and consist of organization infrastructure (administration and management), human resources (employee recruiting, hiring, and training), technology (improving products and the production process), and procurement (purchasing input).

 Organizations have competitive advantage when they provide more value to their customers or when they provide the same value to customers at a lower price. An information system could have a strategic impact if it helped the firm provide products or services at a lower cost than competitors or if it provided products and services at the same cost as competitors but with greater value. The activities that add the most value to products and services depend on the features of each particular firm.

 The firm's value chain can be linked to the value chains of its other partners, including suppliers, distributors, and customers. Figure 3-11 illustrates the activities of the firm value chain and the industry value chain, showing examples of strategic information systems that could be developed to make each of the value activities more cost effective. A firm can achieve a strategic advantage by providing value, not only through its internal value chain processes but also through powerful, efficient ties to industry value partners.

 Digitally enabled networks can be used not only to purchase supplies but also to closely coordinate production of many independent firms. For instance, the Italian casual wear company Benetton uses subcontractors and independent firms for labor-intensive production processes such as tailoring, finishing, and ironing while maintaining control of design, procurement, marketing, and distribution. Benetton uses computer networks to provide independent businesses and foreign production centers with production specifications so that they can efficiently produce the items needed by Benetton retail outlets (Camuffo, Romano and Vinelli, 2001).

 Internet technology has made it possible to extend the value chain so that it ties together all the firm's suppliers, business partners, and customers into a value web. A **value web** is a collection of independent firms who use information technology to coordinate their value chains to collectively produce a product or service for a market. It is more customer-driven and operates in less linear fashion than the traditional value chain. Figure 3-12 shows that this value web functions like a dynamic business ecosystem, synchronizing the business processes of customers, suppliers, and trading partners among different companies in an industry or related industries. These value webs are flexible and adaptive to changes in supply and demand. Relationships can be bundled or unbundled in response to changing market conditions. A company can use this value web to maintain long-standing relationships with many customers over long periods or to respond immediately to individual customer trans-

---

value chain model

Model that highlights the primary or support activities that add a margin of value to a firm's products or services where information systems can best be applied to achieve a competitive advantage.

primary activities

Activities most directly related to the production and distribution of a firm's products or services.

support activities

Activities that make the delivery of a firm's primary activities possible. Consist of the organization's infrastructure, human resources, technology, and procurement.

value web

Customer-driven network of independent firms who use information technology to coordinate their value chains to collectively produce a product or service for a market.

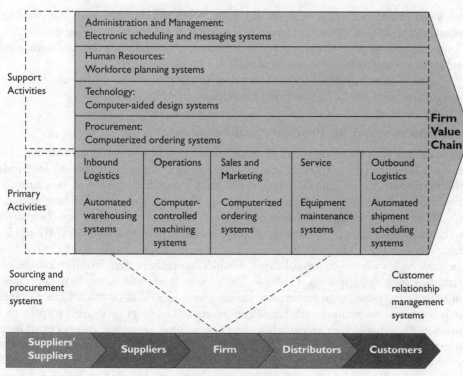

Figure 3-11 The firm value chain and the industry value chain. Illustrated are various examples of strategic information systems for the primary and support activities of a firm and of its value partners that would add a margin of value to a firm's products or services.

actions. Firms can accelerate time to market and to customers by optimizing their value web relationships to make quick decisions on who can deliver the required products or services at the right price and location.

Businesses should try to develop strategic information systems for both the internal value chain activities and the external value activities that add the most value. A strategic analysis might, for example, identify sales and marketing activities where information systems could provide the greatest boost. The analysis might recommend a system to reduce marketing costs by targeting marketing campaigns more efficiently or by providing information for developing products more finely attuned to a firm's target market. A series of systems, including some linked to systems of other value partners, might be required to create a strategic advantage.

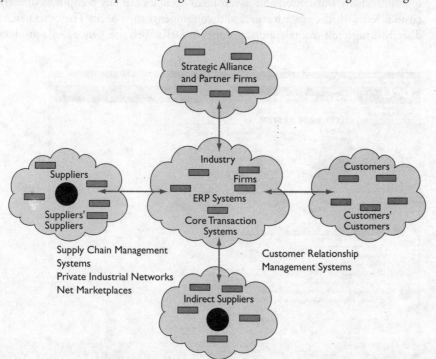

Figure 3-12 The value web. The value web is a networked business ecosystem that can synchronize the value chains of business partners within an industry to rapidly respond to changes in supply and demand.

Value chains and value webs are not static. From time to time they may have to be redesigned to keep pace with changes in the competitive landscape (Fine et. al., 2002). Companies may need to reorganize and reshape their structural, financial, and human assets and recast systems to tap new sources of value.

We now show how information technology at the business level helps the firm reduce costs, differentiate products, and serve new markets.

Information System Products and Services

Firms can use information systems to create unique new products and services that can be easily distinguished from those of competitors. Strategic information systems for **product differentiation** can prevent the competition from responding in kind so that firms with these differentiated products and services no longer have to compete on the basis of cost.

Many of these information technology–based products and services have been created by financial institutions. Citibank developed automatic teller machines (ATMs) and bank debit cards in 1977. Citibank became at one time the largest bank in the United States. Citibank ATMs were so successful that Citibank's competitors were forced to counterstrike with their own ATM systems. Citibank, Wells Fargo Bank, and others have continued to innovate by providing online electronic banking services so that customers can do most of their banking transactions with home computers linked to proprietary networks or the Internet. These banks have recently launched new account aggregation services that let customers view all of their accounts, including their credit cards, investments, online travel rewards, and even accounts from competing banks, from a single online source. Some companies such as NetBank have used the Web to set up "virtual banks" offering a full array of banking services without any physical branches. (Customers mail in their deposits and use designated ATMs to obtain cash.)

Computerized reservation systems such as American Airlines' SABRE system started out as a powerful source of product differentiation for the airline and travel industries. These traditional reservation systems are now being challenged by new travel services where consumers can make their own airline, hotel, and car reservations directly on the Web, bypassing travel agents and other intermediaries. The Window on Management describes how competitive strategy is changing in this industry.

Manufacturers and retailers are starting to use information systems to create products and services that are custom-tailored to fit the precise specifications of individual customers. Dell Computer Corporation sells directly to customers using assemble-to-order manufacturing. Individuals, businesses, and government agencies can buy computers directly from Dell, customized with the exact features and components they need. They can place their orders directly using a toll-free telephone number or Dell's Web site. Once Dell's production control

---

product differentiation

Competitive strategy for creating brand loyalty by developing new and unique products and services that are not easily duplicated by competitors.

At Dell Computer Corporation's Web site, customers can select the options they want and order their computer custom-built to these specifications. Dell's assemble-to-order system is a major source of competitive advantage.

DUELING TRAVEL SITES

Travel is a gigantic business, generating bookings worth $500 billion in 2001 in the United States alone. Travel agents have traditionally been paid by the providers, including airlines, hotels, and car rentals. This cost to providers has risen about 7 percent annually over the last decade, so that airlines pay $12 to $15 per ticket, and they are desperate to lower those costs. Now the Internet has made it simple for customers to bypass agents and handle travel transactions themselves. In 2001, about 10 percent of all travel reservations in the United States were made using the Internet and that share could eventually grow to 50 percent or more.

The struggle for the online travel business has taken a new twist with the entry of Henry Silverman of Cendant and Barry Diller of Expedia. They have different visions and different strategies on how to use Internet technology and information systems to build a profitable business.

Silverman built HFS, the precursor of Cendant, into a powerhouse with interests in lodging (such as Ramada, Travelodge, and Howard Johnson), timeshares (RCI's 60,000 units), and car rentals (Avis). In June 2001, he bought Galileo International, the second largest reservations booking system used by travel agents (after SABRE). Silverman's vision is to transform Galileo from a transaction system into one that could help airlines market their tickets better by using the existing network of travel agents to sell special packaged trips. Galileo could help airlines, hotels, car-rental companies, and tours assemble special deals that the system would broadcast to travel agents. (Cendant-owned or controlled brands could be emphasized in such promotions.) By expanding the use of Galileo, which receives a transaction fee for each reservation booked on the system, Cendant could expect an earnings growth of 10% from this part of its business.

To hedge his bets on the Internet, Silverman also developed his own online travel agency called Trip.com, which he inherited with Galileo, and purchased Cheap Tickets, a top-10 online travel site featuring bargain airline tickets. Silverman's vision includes personalizing these sites so that travelers could sort vacation destinations based on

cost, schedule, and even "personality" (sports, family, etc.).

Analysts caution that Silverman is backing the travel agents, which are looking more like "industry dinosaurs," and that Web travel sites such as Expedia, Orbitz, and Travelocity all have great head starts over Cendant. In addition to eliminating travel agent commissions, airlines are trying to cut the transaction fee they pay to reservation systems such as Galileo, which, they claim, use expensive and out-of-date technology. In 2001, Galileo's share of airline bookings fell to 26 percent, compared to 31 percent in 1998.

Barry Diller has been chairman of Paramount Pictures and a founder of the Fox Broadcasting TV network and the Home Shopping Network (HSN). Using HSN as a base, he obtained majority ownership of cable television and film studio companies, as well as Ticketmaster, Hotels.com (a hotel room broker), CitySearch.com, and Match.com (a dating service). Early in 2002, he purchased a controlling stake in Expedia, the number-one online travel site from Microsoft. Diller's vision is an online emporium where travelers will be able to fulfill all their travel needs. Diller believes he can use the Internet and other media to package travel in ways that traditional travel agencies and booking systems cannot. Moreover, he plans to use Expedia to create a 24-hour TV channel dedicated to selling travel packages based on his properties. Consumers will be able to book a flight, a hotel room, tickets to a game, obtain restaurant reservations, and even make a date all at the same time using his Web site or a toll-free telephone number.

To Think About: Describe the problems traditional and online travel agents face, and then describe the Cendant and Expedia strategies. Which of the two companies is most likely to succeed? Why?

Sources: Motoko Rich and Julia Angwin, "Two Tycoons Make Unlikely Bets on the Turbulent Travel Industry," *Wall Street Journal,* May 3, 2002; Saul Hansell, "For Cendant's Travel Business, Ride Is Bumpier than Expected," *New York Times,* July 8, 2002; and Motoko Rich, "Trip.com Starts Tough Trek to Top Spot in Online Travel," *Wall Street Journal,* April 29, 2002.

MANAGEMENT

receives an order, it directs an assembly plant to assemble the computer based on the configuration specified by the customer using components from an on-site warehouse. Chapter 1 describes other instances in which information technology is creating customized products and services while retaining the cost efficiencies of mass-production techniques. These assemble-to-order strategies require careful coordination of customer requirements with production and flexible processes throughout the firm's value chain (Holweg and Pil, 2001).

Systems to Focus on Market Niche

Businesses can create new market niches by identifying a specific target for a product or service that it can serve in a superior manner. Through **focused differentiation,** the firm can provide a specialized product or service for this narrow target market better than competitors.

focused differentiation
Competitive strategy for developing new market niches for specialized products or services where a business can compete in the target area better than its competitors.

An information system can give companies a competitive advantage by producing data for finely tuned sales and marketing techniques. Such systems treat existing information as a resource that the organization can "mine" to increase profitability and market penetration. Information systems enable companies to finely analyze customer buying patterns, tastes, and preferences so that they efficiently pitch advertising and marketing campaigns to smaller and smaller target markets.

The data come from a range of sources—credit card transactions, demographic data, purchase data from checkout counter scanners at supermarkets and retail stores, and data collected when people access and interact with Web sites. Sophisticated software tools can find patterns in these large pools of data and infer rules from them that can be used to guide decision making. Analysis of such data can drive one-to-one marketing where personal messages can be created based on individualized preferences.

For example, Sears Roebuck continually analyzes purchase data from its 60 million past and present credit card users to target appliance buyers, gardening enthusiasts, and mothers-to-be with special promotions. The company might mail customers who purchase a washer and dryer a maintenance contract and annual contract renewal forms. Yahoo.com captures and analyzes data generated when people visit its Web site. It uses this information to target users with personalized content and advertising geared to their interests, such as auto purchases or personal finance. The Canadian Imperial Bank of Commerce (CIBC) analyzes its customer account data to identify its most profitable customers so that it can offer them special services. The level of fine-grained customization provided by these data analysis systems parallels that for mass customization described in Chapter 1. More examples of customer data analysis can be found in Chapters 7 and 11.

The cost of acquiring a new customer has been estimated to be five times that of retaining an existing customer. By carefully examining transactions of customer purchases and activities, firms can identify profitable customers and win more of their business. Likewise, companies can use these data to identify nonprofitable customers. Companies that skillfully use customer data will focus on identifying their most valued customers and use data from a variety of sources to understand their needs (Reinartz and Kumar, 2002; Davenport, Harris, and Kohli, 2001; Clemons and Weber, 1994).

Supply Chain Management and Efficient Customer Response Systems

Digital firms have the capabilities to go far beyond traditional strategic systems for taking advantage of digital links with other organizations. A powerful business-level strategy available to digital firms involves linking the value chains of vendors and suppliers to the firm's value chain. Integration of value chains can be carried further by linking the customer's value chain to the firm's value chain in an "efficient customer response system." Firms using systems to link with customers and suppliers can reduce their inventory costs while responding rapidly to customer demands.

Wal-Mart's continuous inventory replenishment system uses sales data captured at the checkout counter to transmit orders to restock merchandise directly to its suppliers. The system enables Wal-Mart to keep costs low while fine-tuning its merchandise to meet customer demands.

By keeping prices low and shelves well stocked using a legendary inventory replenishment system, Wal-Mart has become the leading retail business in the United States. Wal-Mart's "continuous replenishment system" sends orders for new merchandise directly to suppliers as soon as consumers pay for their purchases at the cash register. Point-of-sale terminals record the bar code of each item passing the checkout counter and send a purchase transaction directly to a central computer at Wal-Mart headquarters. The computer collects the orders from all Wal-Mart stores and transmits them to suppliers. Suppliers can also access Wal-Mart's sales and inventory data using Web technology. Because the system can replenish inventory with lightning speed, Wal-Mart does not need to spend much money on maintaining large inventories of goods in its own warehouses. The system also allows Wal-Mart to adjust purchases of store items to meet customer demands. Competitors such as Sears have been spending 24.9 percent of sales on overhead. But by using systems to keep operating costs low, Wal-Mart pays only 16.6 percent of sales revenue for overhead. (Operating costs average 20.7 percent of sales in the retail industry.)

Wal-Mart's continuous replenishment system is an example of efficient supply chain management, which we introduced in Chapter 2. Supply chain management systems can not only lower inventory costs but they can also deliver the product or service more rapidly to the customer. Supply chain management can thus be used to create **efficient customer response systems** that respond to customer demands more efficiently. An efficient customer response system directly links consumer behavior back to distribution, production, and supply chains. Wal-Mart's continuous replenishment system provides such efficient customer response. Dell Computer Corporation's assemble-to-order system, described earlier, is another example of an efficient customer response system.

The convenience and ease of using these information systems raise **switching costs** (the cost of switching from one product to a competing product), which discourages customers from going to competitors. For example, Baxter Healthcare International's "stockless inventory" and ordering system uses supply chain management to create an efficient customer response system. Participating hospitals become unwilling to switch to another supplier because of the system's convenience and low cost. Baxter supplies nearly two-thirds of all products used by U.S. hospitals. Terminals tied to Baxter's own computers are installed in hospitals. When hospitals want to place an order, they do not need to call a salesperson or send a purchase order—they simply use a Baxter computer terminal on-site to order from the full Baxter supply catalog. The system generates shipping, billing, invoicing, and inventory information, and the hospital terminals provide customers with an estimated delivery date. With more than 80 distribution centers in the United States, Baxter can make daily deliveries of its products, often within hours of receiving an order.

Baxter delivery personnel no longer drop off their cartons at loading docks to be placed in hospital storerooms. Instead, they deliver orders directly to the hospital corridors, dropping them at nursing stations, operating rooms, and supply closets. This has created in effect a "stockless inventory," with Baxter serving as the hospitals' warehouse.

Figure 3-13 compares stockless inventory with the just-in-time supply method and traditional inventory practices. Whereas just-in-time supply allows customers to reduce

efficient customer response system

System that directly links consumer behavior back to distribution, production, and supply chains.

switching costs

The expense a customer or company incurs in lost time and resources when changing from one supplier or system to a competing supplier or system.

Figure 3-13 Stockless inventory compared to traditional and just-in-time supply methods. The just-in-time supply method reduces inventory requirements of the customer, whereas stockless inventory allows the customer to eliminate inventories entirely. Deliveries are made daily, sometimes directly to the departments that need the supplies.

their inventories by ordering only enough material for a few days' inventory, stockless inventory allows them to eliminate their inventories entirely. All inventory responsibilities shift to the distributor, who manages the supply flow. The stockless inventory is a powerful instrument for "locking in" customers, thus giving the supplier a decided competitive advantage. Information systems can also raise switching costs by making product support, service, and other interactions with customers more convenient and reliable (Vandenbosch and Dawar, 2002; Chen and Hitt, 2002).

Supply chain management and efficient customer response systems are two examples of how emerging digital firms can engage in business strategies not available to traditional firms. Both types of systems require network-based information technology infrastructure investment and software competence to make customer and supply chain data flow seamlessly among different organizations. Both types of strategies have greatly enhanced the efficiency of individual firms and the U.S. economy as a whole by moving toward a *demand-pull production system,* and away from the *traditional supply-push economic system* in which factories were managed on the basis of 12-month official plans rather than on near-instantaneous customer purchase information. Figure 3-14 illustrates the relationships between supply chain management, efficient customer response, and the various business-level strategies.

FIRM-LEVEL STRATEGY AND INFORMATION TECHNOLOGY

A business firm is typically a collection of businesses. Often, the firm is organized financially as a collection of strategic business units, and the returns to the firm are directly tied to strategic business unit performance. Information systems can improve the overall performance of these business units by promoting synergies and core competencies. The idea driving synergies is that when some units can be used as inputs to other units, or two organizations can pool markets and expertise, these relationships can lower costs and generate profits. Recent bank and financial firm mergers, such as the merger of J.P. Morgan and Co. and Chase Manhattan Corp., Wells Fargo and Norwest Corp., Deutsche Bank and Bankers Trust, and Citicorp and Travelers Insurance, occurred precisely for this purpose. One use of information technology in these synergy situations is to tie together the operations of disparate business units so that they can act as a whole. For example, Citigroup can cross-market both Citicorp and Travelers financial products to customers. Such systems would lower retailing costs, increase customer access to new financial products, and speed up the process of marketing new instruments.

Figure 3-14 Business-level strategy. Efficient customer response and supply chain management systems are often interrelated, helping firms "lock in" customers and suppliers while lowering operating costs. Other types of systems can be used to support product differentiation, focused differentiation, and low-cost producer strategies.

Enhancing Core Competencies

A second concept for firm-level strategy involves the notion of "core competency." The argument is that the performance of all business units can increase insofar as these business units develop, or create, a central core of competencies. A **core competency** is an activity at which a firm is a world-class leader. Core competencies may involve being the world's best miniature parts designer, the best package delivery service, or the best thin-film manufacturer. In general, a core competency relies on knowledge that is gained over many years of experience and a first-class research organization or simply key people who follow the literature and stay abreast of new external knowledge.

Any information system that encourages the sharing of knowledge across business units enhances competency. Such systems might encourage or enhance existing competencies and help employees become aware of new external knowledge; such systems might also help a business leverage existing competencies to related markets.

core competency
Activity at which a firm excels as a world-class leader.

INDUSTRY-LEVEL STRATEGY AND INFORMATION SYSTEMS: COMPETITIVE FORCES AND NETWORK ECONOMICS

Firms together comprise an industry, such as the automotive industry, telephone, television broadcasting, and forest products industries, to name a few. The key strategic question at this level of analysis is, "How and when should we compete with as opposed to cooperate with others in the industry?" Whereas most strategic analyses emphasize competition, a great deal of money can be made by cooperating with other firms in the same industry or firms in related industries. For instance, firms can cooperate to develop industry standards in a number of areas; they can cooperate by working together to build customer awareness, and by working collectively with suppliers to lower costs (Shapiro and Varian, 1999). The three principal concepts for analyzing strategy at the industry level are information partnerships, the competitive forces model, and network economics.

Information Partnerships

Firms can form information partnerships and even link their information systems to achieve unique synergies. In an **information partnership,** both companies can join forces without actually merging by sharing information (Konsynski and McFarlan, 1990). American Airlines has an arrangement with Citibank to award one mile in its frequent flier program for every dollar spent using Citibank credit cards. American benefits from increased customer loyalty, and Citibank gains new credit card subscribers and a highly creditworthy customer base for cross-marketing. Northwest Airlines has a similar arrangement with U.S. Bank. American and Northwest have also allied with MCI, awarding frequent flier miles for each dollar of long-distance billing.

Such partnerships help firms gain access to new customers, creating new opportunities for cross-selling and targeting products. Companies that have been traditional competitors may find such alliances to be mutually advantageous. Baxter Healthcare International offers its customers medical supplies from competitors and office supplies through its electronic ordering channel.

information partnership
Cooperative alliance formed between two or more corporations for the purpose of sharing information to gain strategic advantage.

The Competitive Forces Model

In Porter's **competitive forces model,** which is illustrated in Figure 3-15, a firm faces a number of external threats and opportunities: the threat of new entrants into its market, the pressure from substitute products or services, the bargaining power of customers, the bargaining power of suppliers, and the positioning of traditional industry competitors (Porter, 1985).

Competitive advantage can be achieved by enhancing the firm's ability to deal with customers, suppliers, substitute products and services, and new entrants to its market, which in turn may change the balance of power between a firm and other competitors in the industry in the firm's favor.

How can information systems be used to achieve strategic advantage at the industry level? By working with other firms, industry participants can use information technology to

competitive forces model
Model used to describe the interaction of external influences, specifically threats and opportunities, that affect an organization's strategy and ability to compete.

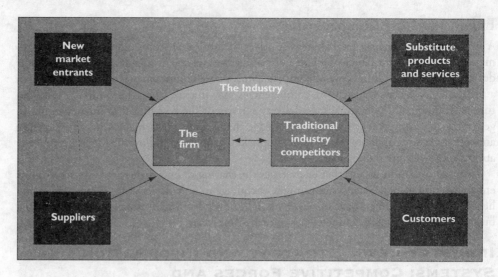

Figure 3-15 Porter's competitive forces model. There are various forces that affect an organization's ability to compete and therefore greatly influence a firm's business strategy. There are threats from new market entrants and from substitute products and services. Customers and suppliers wield bargaining power. Traditional competitors constantly adapt their strategies to maintain their market positioning.

develop industry-wide standards for exchanging information or business transactions electronically (see Chapters 6, 8, and 9), which force all market participants to subscribe to similar standards. Earlier we described how firms can benefit from value webs with complementary firms in the industry. Such efforts increase efficiency at the industry level as well as the business level—making product substitution less likely and perhaps raising entry costs—thus discouraging new entrants. Also, industry members can build industry-wide, IT-supported consortia, symposia, and communications networks to coordinate activities concerning government agencies, foreign competition, and competing industries.

An example of such industry-level cooperation can be found in Covisint, an electronic marketplace shared by the major automobile manufacturers for procurement of auto parts. Although General Motors, Ford, and DaimlerChrysler aggressively compete on such factors as design, service, quality, and price, they can raise the industry's productivity by working together to create an integrated supply chain. Covisint enables all manufacturers and suppliers to trade on a single Internet site, sparing manufacturers the cost of setting up their own Web-based marketplaces.

In the digital firm era, the competitive forces model needs modification. The traditional Porter model assumes a relatively static industry environment; relatively clear-cut industry boundaries; and a relatively stable set of suppliers, substitutes, and customers. Instead of participating in a single industry, today's firms are much more aware that they participate in "industry sets"— multiple related industries that consumers can choose from to obtain a product or service (see Figure 3-16). For instance, automobile companies compete against other automobile companies in the "auto industry," but they also compete against many other industries in the transportation industry "set," such as train, plane, and

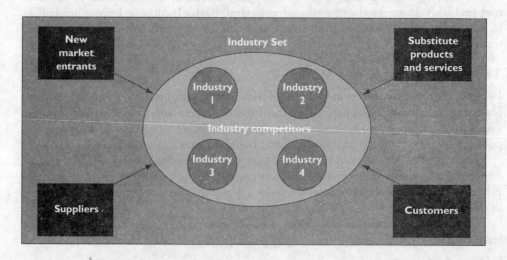

Figure 3-16 The new competitive forces model. The digital firm era requires a more dynamic view of the boundaries between firms, customers, and suppliers, with competition occurring among industry sets.

bus transportation companies. Success or failure for a single auto company may depend on the success or failure of various other industries. Colleges may think they are in competition with other traditional colleges, but in fact they are in competition with electronic distance learning universities, publishing companies who have created online college courses, and private training firms who offer technical certificates—all of whom are members of a much larger "education industry set." In the digital firm era, we can expect greater emphasis on building strategies to compete—and cooperate—with members of the firm's industry set.

Nevertheless, the competitive forces model remains a valid model for analyzing strategy, even considering the impact of the Internet. Internet technology has affected industry structure by providing technologies that make it easier for rivals to compete on price alone and for new competitors to enter the market. Profits have also been dampened because the Internet dramatically increases the information available to customers for comparison shopping, thus raising their bargaining power. Although the Internet can provide benefits, such as new channels to customers and new operating efficiencies, firms cannot achieve competitive advantage unless they have carefully integrated Internet initiatives into their overall strategy and operations. In the age of the Internet, the traditional competitive forces are still at work, but competitive rivalry has become much more intense (Porter, 2001).

Network Economics

A third strategic concept useful at the industry level is **network economics.** In traditional economics—the economics of factories and agriculture—production experiences diminishing returns. The more any given resource is applied to production, the lower the marginal gain in output, until a point is reached where the additional inputs produce no additional outputs. This is the law of diminishing returns, and it is the foundation for most of modern economics.

In some situations the law of diminishing returns does not work. For instance, in a network, the marginal costs of adding another participant are about zero, whereas the marginal gain can be much larger. The larger the number of subscribers in a telephone system, or the Internet, the greater the value to all participants. It's no more expensive to operate a television station with 1,000 subscribers than with 10 million subscribers. And the value of a community of people grows with size, whereas the cost of adding new members is inconsequential.

From this network economics perspective, information technology can be strategically useful. Internet sites can be used by firms to build "communities of users"—like-minded customers who want to share their experiences. This can build customer loyalty and enjoyment, and build unique ties to customers. EBay, the giant online auction site and iVillage, an online community for women, are examples. Both businesses are based on networks of millions of users and both companies have used the Web and Internet communication tools to build communities.

network economics

Model of strategic systems at the industry level based on the concept of a network where adding another participant entails zero marginal costs but can create much larger marginal gain.

USING SYSTEMS FOR COMPETITIVE ADVANTAGE: MANAGEMENT ISSUES

Strategic information systems often change the organization as well as its products, services, and operating procedures, driving the organization into new behavior patterns. Using technology for strategic benefit requires careful planning and management. Managers interested in using information systems for competitive advantage will need to perform a strategic systems analysis. The Manager's Toolkit describes some of the issues this analysis will have to address.

Managing Strategic Transitions

Adopting the kinds of strategic systems described in this chapter generally requires changes in business goals, relationships with customers and suppliers, internal operations, and information architecture. These sociotechnical changes, affecting both social and technical elements of the organization, can be considered **strategic transitions**—a movement between levels of sociotechnical systems.

strategic transitions

A movement from one level of sociotechnical system to another. Often required when adopting strategic systems that demand changes in the social and technical elements of an organization.

MIS IN ACTION: MANAGER'S TOOLKIT

IDENTIFYING OPPORTUNITIES FOR STRATEGIC INFORMATION SYSTEMS

Managers are expected to identify the types of systems that would provide a strategic advantage to their firms. Here are some key questions to ask:

1. Examine the structure of the industry to which the firm belongs.
   - What are some of the competitive forces at work in the industry? Are there new entrants to the industry? What is the relative power of suppliers, customers, and substitute products and services over prices?
   - Is the basis of competition quality, price, or brand?
   - What are the direction and nature of change within the industry? From where are the momentum and change coming?
   - How is the industry currently using information technology? Is the organization behind or ahead of the industry in its application of information systems?

2. Examine business, firm, and industry value chains.
   - How is the company creating value for the customer? Through lower prices and transaction costs or higher quality? Are there any places in the value chain where the business could create more value for customers and additional profit for the company?
   - Does the firm understand and manage its business processes using the best practices available? Is it taking maximum advantage of supply chain management, customer relationship management, and enterprise systems?
   - Does the firm leverage its core competencies?
   - Is the industry supply chain and customer base changing in ways that benefit or harm the firm?
   - Could the firm benefit from strategic partnerships and value webs?
   - Where in the value chain would information systems provide the greatest value to the firm?

Such changes often entail blurring of organizational boundaries, both external and internal. Suppliers and customers must become intimately linked and may share each other's responsibilities. For instance, in Baxter International's stockless inventory system, Baxter has assumed responsibility for managing its customers' inventories (Johnston and Vitale, 1988). Managers will need to devise new business processes for coordinating their firms' activities with those of customers, suppliers, and other organizations. The organizational change requirements surrounding new information systems are so important that they merit attention throughout this text. Chapters 12 and 13 examine organizational change issues in great detail.

MAKE IT YOUR BUSINESS

FINANCE AND ACCOUNTING

Information systems promote better management of the firm's assets and cash flows that can increase revenues and reduce operating costs, thereby enhancing its competitive position. Online systems provide more immediate tracking and identification of the firm's assets and the return on the firm's investments. The accounting function can monitor transaction flows and keep track of costs and revenues more precisely in real-time. Tracking and identifying changes in assets and fund flows that used to take weeks can now be accomplished in hours or days.

HUMAN RESOURCES

Information systems lower agency costs, enabling the firm to manage more employees with fewer resources. Networked systems also make it possible to create work groups outside traditional places of work. Employees from many different locations can use information systems to work together on virtual teams. Understanding human resource issues is essential for successful system implementation because people need to adjust to the organizational change created by introducing a new information system.

MANUFACTURING AND PRODUCTION

Information systems can be used to streamline manufacturing and production processes so that they require fewer steps and less human intervention. By taking advantage of more precise flows of information, firms can tighten coordination of production and distribution, lowering transaction and agency costs. You can find examples of manufacturing and production applications on pages 72–74 and 106–109.

SALES AND MARKETING

Information systems provide a rich new set of capabilities for fine-tuning sales and marketing that are often a source of competitive advantage. Systems can be used to analyze vast pools of data for highly targeted marketing campaigns, and they can also generate unique new products and services that the organization can sell. Efficient customer response systems can improve sales by tightly coordinating production and distribution with customer orders. You can find examples of sales and marketing applications on pages 81, 95, 96, and 106–109.

Information technology provides tools for managers to carry out both their traditional and newer roles, allowing them to monitor, plan, and forecast with more precision and speed than ever before and to respond more rapidly to the changing business environment. Finding ways to use information technology to achieve competitive advantage at the business, firm, and industry level is a key management responsibility. In addition to identifying the business processes, core competencies, and the relationships with others in the industry that can be enhanced with information technology, managers need to oversee the sociotechnical changes required to implement strategic systems.

Each organization has a unique constellation of information systems that result from its interaction with information technology. Contemporary information technology can lead to major organizational changes—and efficiencies—by reducing transaction and agency costs and can also be a source of competitive advantage. Developing meaningful strategic systems generally requires extensive changes in organizational structure, culture, and business processes that often encounter resistance.

Information technology offers new ways of organizing work and using information that can promote organizational survival and prosperity. Technology can be used to differentiate existing products, create new products and services, nurture core competencies, and reduce operational costs. Selecting an appropriate technology for the firm's competitive strategy is a key decision.

For Discussion

1. It has been said that there is no such thing as a sustainable strategic advantage. Do you agree? Why or why not?

2. It has been said that the advantage that leading-edge retailers such as Dell and Wal-Mart have over their competition isn't technology, it's their management. Do you agree? Why or why not?

SUMMARY

1. *What do managers need to know about organizations in order to build and use information systems successfully?* Managers need to understand certain essential features of organizations in order to build and use information systems successfully. All modern organizations are hierarchical, specialized, and impartial. They use explicit standard operating procedures to maximize efficiency. All organizations have their own cultures and politics arising from differences in interest groups. Organizations differ in goals, groups served, social roles, leadership styles, incentives, surrounding environments, and types of tasks performed. These differences create varying types of organizational structures and they also help explain differences in organizations' use of information systems.

2. *What impact do information systems have on organizations?* Information systems and the organizations in which they are used interact with and influence each other. The introduction of a new information system will affect organizational structure, goals, work design, values, competition

between interest groups, decision making, and day-to-day behavior. At the same time, information systems must be designed to serve the needs of important organizational groups and will be shaped by the organization's structure, tasks, goals, culture, politics, and management. Information technology can reduce transaction and agency costs, and such changes have been accentuated in organizations using the Internet. The information systems department is the formal organizational unit that is responsible for the organization's information systems function. Organizational characteristics and managerial decisions determine the role this group will actually play.

3. *How do information systems support the activities of managers in organizations?* There are several different models of what managers actually do in organizations that show how information systems can be used for managerial support. Early classical models of managerial activities stressed the functions of planning, organizing, coordinating, deciding, and controlling. Contemporary research looking at the actual

behavior of managers has found that managers' real activities are highly fragmented, variegated, and brief in duration, with managers moving rapidly and intensely from one issue to another. Managers spend considerable time pursuing personal agendas and goals, and contemporary managers shy away from making grand, sweeping policy decisions.

The nature and level of decision making are important factors in building information systems for managers. Decisions can be structured, semistructured, or unstructured, with structured decisions clustering at the operational level of the organization and unstructured decisions at the strategic planning level. Decision making can also take place at the individual or group level. Individual models of decision making assume that human beings can rationally choose alternatives and consequences based on the priority of their objectives and goals. Organizational models of decision making illustrate that real decision making in organizations takes place in arenas where many psychological, political, and bureaucratic forces are at work.

Information systems have been most helpful to managers by providing support for their roles in disseminating information, providing liaison between organizational levels, and allocating resources. However, some managerial roles cannot be supported by information systems, and information systems are less successful at supporting unstructured decisions.

4. *How can businesses use information systems for competitive advantage?* Businesses can use strategic information systems to gain an edge over competitors. Such systems change organizations' goals, business processes, products, services, or environmental relationships, driving them into new forms of behavior.

Information systems can be used to support strategy at the business, firm, and industry level. At the business level

of strategy, information systems can be used to help firms become the low-cost producers, differentiate products and services, or serve new markets. Information systems can also be used to "lock in" customers and suppliers using efficient customer response and supply chain management applications. Value chain analysis is useful at the business level to highlight specific activities in the business where information systems are most likely to have a strategic impact.

At the firm level, information systems can be used to achieve new efficiencies or to enhance services by tying together the operations of disparate business units so that they can function as a whole or promoting the sharing of knowledge across business units. At the industry level, systems can promote competitive advantage by facilitating cooperation with other firms in the industry, creating consortiums or communities for sharing information, exchanging transactions, or coordinating activities. The competitive forces model, information partnerships, and network economics are useful concepts for identifying strategic opportunities for systems at the industry level.

5. *Why is it so difficult to build successful information systems, including systems that promote competitive advantage?* Information systems are closely intertwined with an organization's structure, culture, and business processes. New systems disrupt established patterns of work and power relationships, so there is often considerable resistance to them when they are introduced.

Implementing strategic systems often requires extensive organizational change and a transition from one sociotechnical level to another. Such changes are called *strategic transitions* and are often difficult and painful to achieve. Moreover, not all strategic systems are profitable, and they can be expensive to build. Many strategic information systems are easily copied by other firms, so that strategic advantage is not always sustainable.

KEY TERMS

Agency theory, 83

Behavioral models, 86

Bureaucracy, 76

Bureaucratic model of decision making, 90

Chief information officer (CIO), 81

Choice, 88

Classical model of management, 85

Cognitive style, 88

Competitive forces model, 99

Core competency, 99

Decisional roles, 87

Design, 88

Efficient customer response system, 97

End users, 81

Focused differentiation, 95

"Garbage can" model, 90

Implementation, 88

Information partnership, 99

Information systems department, 80

Information systems managers, 80

Informational roles, 87

Intelligence, 88

Interpersonal roles, 86

Intuitive decision makers, 90

Knowledge-level decision making, 87

Management control, 87

Managerial roles, 86

Network economics, 101

Operational control, 87

Organization, 75

Organizational culture, 77

Organizational models of decision making, 90

Political models of decision making, 90

Primary activities, 92

Product differentiation, 94

Programmers, 80

Rational model, 88

Standard operating procedures (SOPs), 77

Strategic decision making, 87

Strategic information system, 00

Strategic transitions, 101

Structured decisions, 88

Support activities, 92

Switching costs, 97

Systematic decision makers, 88

Systems analysts, 80

Transaction cost theory, 82

Unstructured decisions, 87

Value chain model, 92

Value web, 92

Virtual organization, 84

REVIEW QUESTIONS

1. What is an organization? Compare the technical definition of organizations with the behavioral definition.

2. What features do all organizations have in common? In what ways can organizations differ?

3. How are information technology services delivered in organizations? Describe the role played by programmers, systems analysts, information systems managers, and the chief information officer (CIO).

4. Describe the major economic theories that help explain how information systems affect organizations.

5. Describe the major behavioral theories that help explain how information systems affect organizations.

6. Why is there considerable organizational resistance to the introduction of information systems?

7. Compare the descriptions of managerial behavior in the classical and behavioral models.

8. What specific managerial roles can information systems support? Where are information systems particularly strong in supporting managers, and where are they weak?

9. What are the four stages of decision making described by Simon?

10. Compare individual and organizational models of decision making.

11. What is the impact of the Internet on organizations and the process of management?

12. What is a strategic information system? What is the difference between a strategic information system and a strategic-level system?

13. Describe appropriate models for analyzing strategy at the business level, and the types of strategies and information systems that can be used to compete at this level.

14. Describe appropriate strategies for the firm level and how information systems can help companies compete at this level.

15. How can the competitive forces model, information partnerships, and network economics be used to identify strategies at the industry level?

16. How have the value chain and competitive forces models changed as a result of the Internet and the emergence of digital firms?

17. Why are strategic information systems difficult to build?

APPLICATION SOFTWARE EXERCISE

DATABASE EXERCISE: USING A DATABASE FOR STRATEGIC BUSINESS DEVELOPMENT

The Presidents' Inn is a small three-story hotel on the Atlantic Ocean in Cape May, NJ, a popular Northeastern U.S. resort. Ten rooms overlook side streets, ten rooms have bay windows that offer limited views of the ocean, and the remaining ten rooms in the front of the hotel face the ocean. Room rates are based on room choice, length of stay, and number of guests per room. Room rates are the same for one to four guests. Fifth and sixth guests must pay an additional $20 charge each per day. Guests staying for seven days or more receive a 10 percent discount on their daily room rates.

Business has grown steadily over the past 10 years. Now totally renovated, the hotel uses a romantic weekend package to attract couples, a vacation package to attract young families, and a weekday discount package to attract business travelers. The owners currently use a manual reservation and bookkeeping system, which has caused many problems. Sometimes two families have been booked in the same room at the same time. Management does not have immediate data about the hotel's daily operations and income.

Use the information provided in this description and in the database tables on the Laudon Web site for Chapter 3 to develop reports that would provide information to help management make the business more competitive and profitable. The database and related queries should be designed to make it easy to identify information, such as the average length of stay per room type, the average number of visitors per room type, and the base income per room (i.e., length of visit multiplied times the daily rate) during a specified period of time.

After identifying the above information, write a brief report describing what your database information tells you about your current business situation. For example, what is your strongest customer base? What specific business strategies might you pursue to increase room occupancy and revenue? How could the database be improved to provide better information for strategic decisions?

GROUP PROJECT

With a group of three or four students, select a company described in the *Wall Street Journal*, *Fortune*, *Forbes*, or another business publication. Visit the company's Web site to find out additional information about that company and to see how the firm is using the Web. On the basis of this information, analyze the business. Include a description of the organization's features, such as important business processes, culture, structure, and environment, as well as its business strategy. Suggest strategic information systems appropriate for that particular business, including those based on Internet technology, if appropriate. If possible, use electronic presentation software to present your findings to the class.

TOOLS FOR INTERACTIVE LEARNING

■ INTERNET CONNECTION

The Internet Connection for this chapter will take you to the NetBank Web site where you can see how one company used the Internet to create an entirely new type of business. You can complete an exercise for analyzing this Web site's capabilities and its strategic benefits.

■ INTERACTIVE STUDY GUIDE

You can use the Interactive Study Guide to test your knowledge of this chapter and get instant feedback where you need more practice.

■ RUNNING CASE

The Running Case provides an opportunity for you to use the Web to perform a competitive analysis for Dirt Bikes USA. You can find a complete description of this project on the Laudon Web site for Chapter 3 and on the Multimedia Edition CD-ROM.

■ ELECTRONIC COMMERCE PROJECT

At the Laudon Web site for Chapter 3, you will find an Electronic Commerce project on competitive auto pricing and sales on the Web.

■ MANAGEMENT DECISION PROBLEM

At the Laudon Web Site for Chapter 3, you will find a Management Decision Problem where you can analyze customer acquisition costs.

■ CD-ROM

If you use the Multimedia Edition CD-ROM with this chapter, you will find a video clip illustrating the role of information systems in Schneider National's organization, an audio overview of the major themes of this chapter, and bullet text summarizing the key points of the chapter.

CASE STUDY—*What Happened to Kmart?*

On January 22, 2002, Kmart filed for Chapter 11 bankruptcy protection. It was the largest retailer ever to do so and shocked many people. Kmart had made retail history when its founder, the Kresge "five and dime store" chain, invented the concept of the discount store. The first Kmart was established in Detroit in 1962, the same year Wal-Mart opened its first store in Rogers, Arkansas. By the end of 1963 Kmart had 63 stores converted from Kresge's.

In the following years, however, Wal-Mart expanded quickly by following a strategy of everyday low prices. Wal-Mart used information technology (IT) to track sales in all its stores and to replenish its fastest selling products. Wal-Mart demonstrated its willingness to spend needed funds on IT by installing registers with bar-code scanners in each store during the late 1970s and early 1980s, which fed the sales data into the back-end store computers. The result was Wal-Mart sales data were always current and store managers knew what was selling well and what was not. In time many orders were routed straight from the Wal-Mart store to the appropriate supplier, and the delivery went from that supplier directly to the store. Wal-Mart recently developed an extranet to work closely with key suppliers on problems such as how to increase sales on specific products. Many analysts believe Wal-Mart has the most sophisticated supply chain systems in the industry.

By 1983, with its cutting edge information systems, Wal-Mart was already spending only two cents per dollar getting goods to its stores while Kmart was spending five cents. From that differential alone, Wal-Mart could sell the same product at a price 3 percent lower than Kmart, an important saving to many shoppers. In 1990 Wal-Mart passed Kmart as the largest discount chain with annual sales of $32.6 billion for Kmart's $32.3 billion. Wal-Mart was well on its way to becoming the world's largest retailer. In December 2001, Target, Kmart's other

major competitor, passed Kmart as the second largest discount chain. Target had prospered by emphasizing its merchandising, distinguishing itself as a low-cost source of quality and style.

Kmart, in contrast, used a promotions-driven business model, drumming up business by advertising "blue-light" specials using circulars inserted into local newspapers. In an attempt to stay ahead of Wal-Mart, Kmart started investing $1 billion to modernize its information systems in 1987. According to David Carlson, then Kmart's CIO, the company developed capabilities to collect the necessary data, but it did not use them to forecast demand, relying instead on management's judgments. Carlson notes that Kmart's suppliers promoted as many of their products as they could sell rather than helping Kmart to focus on the better selling items, as was Wal-Mart's approach. Beginning in 1984, Kmart began diversifying its businesses by acquiring Waldenbooks, Payless Drugstores, Sports Authority, and OfficeMax. It also opened its first Super Kmart Center, a much larger store that now included groceries.

Kmart continued to lose ground to competitors while it gained the image of being old-fashioned, outdated, and frumpy. It had a reputation of being a run-down place to shop with an inferior selection of products. Many of its shelves were empty while its prices were too high. It was even considered to offer poor customer service and to not care about competition. By 1994, Kmart was on the verge of bankruptcy. It sold off its newer businesses to concentrate on its discount stores, and, in 1997, it inaugurated the very popular Martha Stewart product lines for the home. In 1999, Kmart began developing BlueLight.com, a Web site designed to sell a few items in order to draw customers to physical stores and to polish its image. In May 2000, watching its hemorrhaging continue, the company hired Charles Conaway, the former CVS drugstore chain president, as Kmart's chairman and CEO.

Conaway pledged to turn the company around within two years, and said his goal was to make Kmart the primary destination for mothers looking for low-priced clothing, housewares, and packaged food for their families. He announced plans to restructure Kmart to increase the productivity of Kmart stores, inventories, and information systems. He closed 72 stores, reducing staff by 5,000. He even announced Kmart would spend about $1.4 billion for IT over two years versus only $263 million during the previous two years. However, in August 2001, Kmart announced a second quarter loss of $22 million, and Conaway blamed pricing pressure, particularly from Wal-Mart. Kmart reduced prices on 30,000 of its 70,000 items and cut down on advertising circulars. Consumer habits are hard to change and Kmart sales took a big hit.

Sales at Wal-Mart and Target grew in 2001, while those at Kmart continued to decline. Conaway said he had not found a formula to distinguish his company from his competitors. Since Conaway had taken over, Kmart had increased the percentage of items in stock to 86 percent, compared to 73 percent two to three years earlier. In a conference with Wall Street analysts, Conaway said Kmart was "doing a phenomenal job of reinventing" its supply chain, which would be visible to all in a year's time.

Despite Kmart's continuing falling sales and rising losses Conaway again mandated price cuts, this time on 50,000 products. When Fleming Companies, now Kmart's sole grocery supplier, suspended shipments to Kmart because of Kmart's failure to meet its weekly payment of $78 million, the company realized it could no longer meet all of its financial obligations. Kmart had to declare Chapter 11 bankruptcy.

Kmart had clearly exhibited many problems. For instance, former Kmart CIO Dave Carlson said he had tried to unify Kmart's two separate computers in its distribution system, but he was turned down because the project was considered to be too expensive. When Conaway was first hired, he wanted to find new ways to bring customers into the stores, and so he cut back on Kmart's primary method of Sunday circulars but offered no clear alternative strategy. In 2000, central planners were still allocating 60 percent of Kmart's goods to specific stores. Conaway tried to address this problem, but by December 2001, 40 percent of its goods were still being allocated by central planning rather than by local stores. Also, Kmart continued to expand the variety of its products rather than focusing on fast selling items, as did Wal-Mart. Shipping was such a problem that in December 2000, being limited to only 900 trucks per day, Kmart was forced to choose between shipping toothpaste or Christmas trees. Warehousing was also an obvious problem since 15,000 truck-trailers were parked behind its stores holding excess inventory because they had no more storage space. Conaway did successfully eliminate this problem within a few months, thereby also reducing the "shrink" (stolen product) rate. Many analysts and observers, including Conaway, believed supply chain management was Kmart's most serious problem, particularly when compared to Wal-Mart. Kmart's promotions-driven business model created sharp spikes and drops in demand for products and has been much more difficult to support with supply chain management systems than everyday low pricing models such as Wal-Mart's. Indications of supply chain troubles were everywhere. Outdated technology at the distribution centers resulted in supplies often sitting on pallets for 24 or more

hours until they were recorded in the central tracking system. The shelves displaying popular products were often empty, and to reorder them from regional distribution centers, store merchandisers first had to hand sift through previous purchasing receipts. Kmart's inventory turnover rate was very low. In the year 2000, Kmart's was an anemic 3.6; while Wal-Mart's was 7.3, and Target's was 6.3. Gary Buzek, the president of IHL Consulting Group, estimated that Kmart could add $1.9 billion in profit just by matching its competitors' turnover rates.

Conaway moved ahead quickly. In July, he selected i2 Technologies of Dallas, Texas, to work with Kmart in a project to rebuild its supply-chain systems. I2 had been a highly successful vendor of supply-chain software, although principally for manufacturers, while Kmart's new software had to be designed for its retail business. The project was to improve Kmart's management of sales forecasting, inventory sourcing, logistics, and reporting. I2 planned to use the Kmart project to create templates for sale to the retail industry in general and then customize them specifically for Kmart. The project would also connect these new systems to appropriate in-store technology such as bar-code scanners at cash registers. It would also include micromerchandising, which enables individual stores to select their own merchandise according to the needs and demands of their local community. I2 claimed its software would track the ability of key suppliers to supply their products. It would also analyze Kmart's needs, and execute the required orders, schedule shipments, and record the delivery of products. I2 claimed its software would reduce excess inventory in stores and distribution centers, thus lowering costs, and enabling Kmart to lower prices. Sales would then grow and profits increase. Conaway stated Kmart's supply chain would become the best in the retail business, although Lora Cecere, a Gartner analyst, did question the ability of the project to succeed in such a giant, complex project.

Katrina Roche, i2's chief marketing officer, stated that "i2 excels at sales but its execution isn't always flawless." Supply-chain management software for manufacturing still accounted for 90 percent of i2's business, and it had only recent and limited experience in the retail sector. One major roadblock was that manufacturers use a relatively small number of stock-keeping units (SKUs) that must be handled by supply chain management software. Unfortunately, Kmart had over 70,000 SKUs in its 2,100 stores, meaning the system must deal with 147 million possible pairings, and this number is increased by inserting many distribution centers and time periods involved. The i2 software was simply not designed to handle such huge data sets. Yet advanced planning software is fundamental to supply chain management, and the problem could only be solved by Kmart purchasing more hardware; an expensive solution for a company facing Kmart's financial problems.

The i2 project was organized with a team of 500 working in an isolated location. It included over 100 personnel from Deloitte Consulting who were to customize i2's existing software, making it able to track the movement of goods to Kmart's more than 2,100 stores. Conaway announced that the first applications would go live in early 2001, followed by a "rapid, methodical rollout" of several dozen business releases with a total of 93 distinct improvements, all by August 2002.

In February 2001, several suppliers, including Pharmavite Corp. of Northridge, California, and Bell Sports Corp. of Irving, Texas, said they were seeing improved inventory management in the last three months. Also, Kmart announced a $200 million program to purchase and install new point-of-sale terminal cash registers from IBM to improve customer service with faster checkout technologies.

In June 2001, Kmart began installing new warehouse management software called PkMS, from Manhattan Associates. Its goal was to move products more quickly through Kmart's distribution centers to the stores, thereby cutting costs while getting the product on the shelves before it has been sold out. The software was installed at corporate headquarters and in all distribution centers. Using it, workers who pick, pack, and ship products to the stores use bar-code scanners to locate each item and to track the flow of the goods. A spokesperson said Kmart would save $15 million a year by increasing productivity and lowering labor costs. Management hoped it might also increase sales. The result was that Kmart could track 30 SKUs at the beginning of the third quarter (2001), 119,000 in late November, and 500,000 three months later. However, Buzek believed the information would be useless because management just didn't believe in the system. In September, the company announced a $148 million write-off of its previous warehouse management system because it was so extensively modified that it no longer could work well and cost too much to maintain. Observers and analysts claim the write-off included abandoning some of i2's software. Kmart also wrote off $65 million for two outdated distribution centers, replacing them with two newer ones purchased from Toys 'R' Us.

In December 2001, word came out that the i2 project had fallen way behind. John West, i2's chief technology officer until late in 2001, said the software worked, but the project had stalled because of Kmart's "operational issues." One member of the i2 users group said, "If the data's not right, it's not that it doesn't work; it's just that you won't get the answer you want." Interestingly, when i2 had problems with Nike, it also blamed its customer and not itself. According to Karen Peterson, a Gartner analyst, Kmart originally did not understand the complex difficulties of the project. Another observer, Jim Dion, president of Chicago retail consulting firm Dionco Inc., said that with the project's difficulty in connecting its point-of-sale and inventory systems to its distribution systems, Kmart was still sending many of its orders on paper. Also in December, Kmart indicated it was now trying to modernize 800 of its stores at a cost of around $1 billion, and that money was competing with funds needed to modernize its supply chain. During the Christmas 2001 selling period Kmart moved less product off its shelves than it had in 2000.

When Kmart was forced to declare bankruptcy, it did indicate some plans for survival. Conaway announced that the company would use Chapter 11 bankruptcy protection to break store leases in 284 stores in 40 states and then close them. In June 2002, Kmart changed the name of its Web site from BlueLight.com to Kmart.com to attract a younger audience and help focus on Kmart stores and sales promotions. (BlueLight had never become a profitable Web business.) Kmart.com will

also see an expanded variety of name brand products such as Pentax cameras and Disney apparel. Management believes Kmart.com also meshes better than BlueLight.com with the company's current "Stuff of Life" campaign, which is trying to position the chain as a family-friendly budget-minded store. Emphasizing exclusive brands such as Martha Stewart Everyday and Joe Boxer may help Kmart distinguish itself from its rivals. Conaway believes Kmart should be able to emerge from Chapter 11 in 2003.

The question is, will Kmart truly be able to bounce back? What will it take to keep going? The company still doesn't have a low enough cost structure to compete with Wal-Mart's low prices, nor does it have the trendy image of Target. What can Kmart do to become the shopping destination of choice?

Sources: Mitchell Pacelle and Amy Merrick, "Kmart Gets Pressure from Two Investors to Hurry a Rebound," *Wall Street Journal*, September 12, 2002; Jenny Strasburg, "Kmart Turns Off <BlueLight.Com>," *San Francisco Chronicle*, June 20, 2002; Amy Merrick, "Kmart Renames Its Web Site, Turned Off by BlueLight.com," *Wall Street Journal*, June 20, 2002; Michael Levy and Dhruv Grewal, "So Long, Kmart Shoppers," *Wall Street Journal*, January 28, 2002; Constance L. Hays, "Kmart to Close 284 Stores; 22,000 Jobs will be Cut," *New York Times*, March 9, 2002; Kim Girard, "Kmart: SCM Gone Wrong," *Baseline*, January 23, 2002, <www.baselinemag.com>; "Kmart Corporation to Close 284 Under-Performing Stores Based on Financial Objectives Review," Kmart Corporation, March 8, 2002; Carol Sliwa, "IT No Bargain for Troubled Kmart," *itworld.ca*, March 1, 2002; Carol Sliwa, "IT Difficulties Help Take Kmart Down," *ComputerWorld*, January 28, 2002; Steve Konicki, "Now in Bankruptcy, Kmart Struggled with Supply Chain," *InformationWeek*, January 28, 2002, <www.informationweek.com>; Carol Sliwa, "Beyond IT: Business Strategy Was a Problem, Too," *ComputerWorld*, January 25, 2002; Peter Abell, "Kmart Declares Chapter 11," *AMR Research*, January 23, 2002, <www.amrresearch.com>; Edward Cone, "Commentary: Blame Enough to Go Around at Kmart," *Baseline*, January 23, 2002, <www.baselinemag.com>; "Kmart Files Chapter 11," *ABCNEWS.com*, November 22, 2002, <www.abcnews.go.com>; Stephanie Strom and Leslie Kaufman, "Kmart is on Verge of Filing a Claim for Bankruptcy," *New York Times*, January 22, 2002; David F. Carr and Edward Cone, "Code Blue," *Baseline*, December 10, 2001, <www.baselinemag.com>; Ted Kemp, "Kmart Calls Supply Chain to Rescue," *InternetWeek*, December 7, 2001, <www.internetweek.com>; Constance L. Hays, "Slow Lane to Kmart's Recovery; Consumers Turn Frugal and Many Suppliers Discontent," *New York Times*, November 8, 2001; Constance L. Hays and Leslie Kaufman, "Some Suppliers Say Kmart Has Pressed for Deals," *New York Times*, October 25, 2001; Alorie Gilbert, "I2 Forecasts Slow Growth, Losses," *Information Week*, April 19, 2001; "Dog of the Day: I2 Technologies," *Forbes*, February 27, 2001; Jack McCarthy, "Managing through Reorganization," *InfoWorld*, July 20, 2001; Todd R. Weiss, "Kmart to Spend $270 Million on New Technology for its Stores," *ComputerWorld*, February 15, 2001; Marc L. Songini, "Pharmavite to Launch Collaborative System with Kmart," *ComputerWorld*, February 5, 2001; Chris Nolan, "Attention Kmart Shoppers," *Smart Business*, February 1, 2001.

CASE STUDY QUESTIONS:

1. Evaluate Kmart using the value chain and competitive forces models. What was Kmart's business model and business strategy?

2. What was the relationship of information systems to Kmart's business processes and business strategy? How well did its systems support its strategy?

3. What management, organization, and technology factors contributed to Kmart's problems?

4. How important was supply chain management in contributing to Kmart's problems? Evaluate Conaway's decision to use i2 software to improve Kmart's supply chain management.

5. Were those blaming software for the collapse of Kmart correct? Explain your answer.

6. It has been said that "Wal-Mart uses their IT strategically, and they fully integrate it into their operating model." Does this statement apply to Kmart? Explain your response.

7. List the problems Conaway faced when he took over Kmart, and then describe the short- and long-range policies you would have followed had you been in his place.

CHAPTER 4

THE DIGITAL FIRM: ELECTRONIC BUSINESS AND ELECTRONIC COMMERCE

As a manager, you'll want to know how your firm can benefit from conducting business electronically using Internet technology. After reading this chapter, you will be able to answer the following questions:

1. *How has Internet technology changed value propositions and business models?*

2. *What is electronic commerce? How has electronic commerce changed consumer retailing and business-to-business transactions?*

3. *What are the principal payment systems for electronic commerce?*

4. *How can Internet technology facilitate management and coordination of internal business processes and supply chain management?*

5. *What are the major managerial and organizational challenges posed by electronic business and electronic commerce?*

Telefonica S.A. Goes Digital

Telefonica S.A. is the leading provider of telecommunications services in the Spanish and Portuguese-speaking world, serving more than 500 million people. It is also the largest multinational company in Spain, with related telecommunications businesses in over 40 other countries.

Telefonica wants to become one of the top service providers in the world within the next four years, but reaching this goal won't be easy. Telecommunications deregulation in the European Union has removed Telefonica's near-monopolistic position, opening the marketplace to many new competitors, especially in the areas of services and long distance. Customers are demanding new services, such as high-capacity communication services, media, and the Internet, which can supplement telecommunications companies' traditional sources of revenue.

Telefonica thinks it can meet its objectives by moving both its internal and external business processes to the Web. In addition to improving its own efficiency and productivity, Telefonica hopes to leverage its expertise to help customers use Internet technology to change the way they work as well. The business processes that Telefonica is Internet-enabling span its entire value chain.

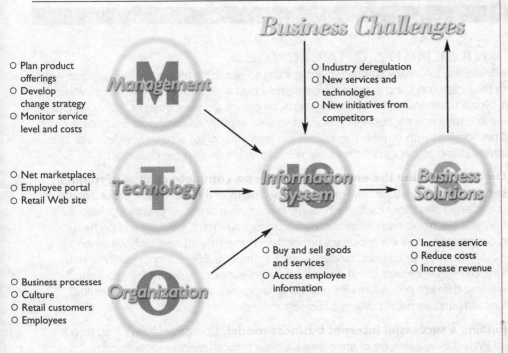

They include applications for on-line procurement and sales to customers as well as internal finance and human resources applications.

Telefonica and its partners have created a Net marketplace called Adquira to purchase indirect goods and services, including communications and office equipment, fixtures and fittings, travel, financial and insurance products, maintenance and repairs, and cleaning services. The Adquira platform offers three alternative technologies for businesses. Large companies can use an Internet procurement tool called Adquira Comprador to integrate procurement processes. Adquira Marketplace is an electronic Net marketplace where companies of any size can request bids for various products and make purchases. Adquira Subastas offers capabilities for buyers and suppliers to use complex auctions to buy and sell various goods and services.

Telefonica is 75 years old and had firmly established businesses processes. Cultural changes were required to make its electronic commerce and electronic business initiatives effective. People had to change the way they were doing their jobs and handled customer service. The company's CEO and top management communicated the importance of the Internet to the entire company, making it very clear that they fully backed the e-transformation process. Cisco Systems, which supplies much of Telefonica's networking and Internet technology, worked with Telefonica to identify the business processes where electronic commerce and electronic business could have the greatest impact.

Ideally, Telefonica would like to increase productivity by 25 percent in the next three to four years and has started to see results. Its eDomus employee information portal, with 27,000 page views per day, produced $20 million in savings the first year. The Telefonica Online Web site has also proved very successful as a new channel for selling products and services to customers.

Sources: Kay Watanabe, "Internet Transformation," *IQ Magazine*, July/August 2002; "Company Profiles: Adquira, Spain" <www.line56.com>, accessed July 20, 2002; and <www.telefonica.com> accessed July 20, 2002.

MANAGEMENT CHALLENGES

Like Telefonica S.A., many companies are starting to use the Internet to communicate with both their customers and suppliers, creating new digital electronic commerce networks that bypass traditional distribution channels. Companies are using Internet technology to streamline their internal business processes as well. Digitally enabling business processes and relationships with other organizations can help companies achieve new levels of competitiveness and efficiency, but they raise the following management challenges:

1. **Digitally enabling the enterprise requires a complete change of mindset.** Digital firms require new organizational designs and management processes. To use Internet and other digital technology for organizational coordination, collaboration, and electronic commerce successfully, companies must examine and perhaps redesign entire business processes rather than trying to graft new technology on existing business practices. Companies must consider a different organizational structure, changes in organizational culture, a different support structure for information systems, different procedures for managing employees and networked processing functions, and perhaps a different business strategy.

2. **Finding a successful Internet business model.** Companies have raced to put up Web sites in the hope of increasing earnings through electronic commerce. However, many electronic commerce sites have yet to turn a profit or to make a tangible difference in firms' sales and marketing efforts. Cost savings or access to new markets promised by the Web may not materialize. Companies need to think carefully about whether they can create a genuinely workable business model on the Internet and how the Internet relates to their overall business strategy. Internet technology alone is not a substitute for an effective business strategy (Rangan and Adner, 2001; Willcocks and Plant, 2001).

Internet technology is creating a universal technology platform for buying and selling goods and for driving important business processes inside the firm. It has inspired new ways of organizing and managing that are transforming businesses and the use of information systems in everyday life. In addition to bringing many new benefits and opportunities, electronic business and electronic commerce are creating new sets of management challenges. We describe these challenges so that organizations can understand the management, organization, and technology issues that must be addressed to benefit from digital integration.

4.1   ELECTRONIC BUSINESS, ELECTRONIC COMMERCE, AND THE EMERGING DIGITAL FIRM

Throughout this edition, we emphasize the benefits of integrating information across the enterprise, creating an information technology infrastructure in which information can flow seamlessly from one part of the organization to another and from the organization to its customers, suppliers, and business partners. The emerging digital firm requires this level of information integration, and companies increasingly depend on such an infrastructure today to remain efficient and competitive. Internet technology has emerged as the key enabling technology for this digital integration.

INTERNET TECHNOLOGY AND THE DIGITAL FIRM

For a number of years, companies used proprietary systems to integrate information from their internal systems and to link to their customers and trading partners. Such systems were expensive and based on technology standards that only a few could follow. The Internet is rapidly becoming the infrastructure of choice for electronic commerce because it offers businesses an even easier way to link with other businesses and individuals at a very low cost. It provides a universal and easy-to-use set of technologies and technology standards that can be adopted by all organizations, no matter what computer system or information technology platform the organizations are using.

Trading partners can directly communicate with each other, bypassing intermediaries and inefficient multilayered procedures. Web sites are available to consumers 24 hours a day. Some information-based products, such as software, music, and videos, can actually be physically distributed via the Internet. Vendors of other types of products and services can use the Internet to distribute the information surrounding their wares, such as product pricing, options, availability, and delivery time. The Internet can replace existing distribution channels or extend them, creating outlets for attracting and serving customers who otherwise would not patronize the company. For example, Web-based discount brokerages have attracted new customers who could not afford paying the high commissions and fees charged by conventional brokerage and financial services firms.

Companies can use Internet technology to radically reduce their transaction costs. Chapter 3 introduced the concept of transaction costs, which include the costs of searching for buyers and sellers, collecting information on products, negotiating terms, writing and enforcing contracts, and transporting merchandise. Information on buyers, sellers, and prices for many products is immediately available on the Web. For example, manually processing a single customer order can cost $15. Using a Web-based system, the cost drops to $.80 per transaction. Table 4-1 provides other examples of transaction cost reductions from the Internet or Internet technology. Handling transactions electronically can reduce transaction costs and delivery time for some goods, especially those that are purely digital (such as software, text products, images, or videos) because these products can be distributed over the Internet as electronic versions.

What's more, Internet technology is providing the infrastructure for running the entire business because its technology and technology standards can also be used to make information flow seamlessly from one part of the organization to another. Internet technology provides a much lower cost and easier to use alternative for coordination activities than proprietary networks. Managers can use e-mail and other Internet communication capabilities to oversee larger numbers of employees, to manage many tasks and subtasks in projects, and to coordinate the work of multiple teams working in different parts of the world. Internet standards can be used to link disparate systems, such as ordering and logistics tracking, which previously could not communicate with each other. The Internet also reduces other agency costs, such as the cost to coordinate activities of the firm with suppliers and other external business partners. The low-cost connectivity and universal standards provided by Internet technology are the driving force behind the explosion of electronic business and the emergence of the digital firm.

TABLE 4-1	HOW THE INTERNET REDUCES TRANSACTION COSTS	
Transaction	**Traditional**	**Internet**
Checking bank account balance	$1.08	$.13
Answering a customer question	$10–$45	Answering an e-mail query: $1–$5
		Web self service: $.10–$.20
Trading 100 shares of stock	$100	$9.95
Correcting an employee record	$128	$2.32
Processing an expense report	$36, 22 days	$4–$8, 72 hours
Sending an advertising brochure	$.75–$10.00	$0–$.25
Paying a bill	$2.22–$3.32	$.65–$1.10

NEW BUSINESS MODELS AND VALUE PROPOSITIONS

The Internet has introduced major changes in the way companies conduct business. It has created a dramatic drop in the cost of developing, sending, and storing information while making that information more widely available. Millions of people can exchange massive amounts of information directly, instantly, and for free.

In the past, information about products and services was usually tightly bundled with the physical value chain for those products and services. If a consumer wanted to find out about the features, price, and availability of a refrigerator or an automobile, for instance, that person had to visit a retail store that sold those products. The cost of comparison shopping was very high because people had to physically travel from store to store.

The Internet has changed that relationship. Once everyone is connected electronically, information about products and services can flow on its own directly and instantly to consumers. The traditional link between the flow of the product and the flow of product-related information can be broken. Information is not limited to traditional physical methods of delivery. Customers can find out about products on their own on the Web and buy directly from product suppliers instead of using intermediaries such as retail stores.

This unbundling of information from traditional value chain channels is having a disruptive effect on old business models and is creating new business models as well. A **business model** describes how the enterprise produces, delivers, and sells a product or service, showing how the enterprise delivers value to customers and how it creates wealth (Magretta, 2002). Some of the traditional channels for exchanging product information have become unnecessary or uneconomical, and business models based on the coupling of information with products and services may no longer be necessary.

For example in pre-Internet retailing days, people who wanted to purchase books had to go to a physical bookstore in order to learn what titles were available, the books' contents, and prices. The bookstore had a monopoly on this information. When Amazon.com opened as an online bookstore, it provided visitors to its Web site with a vast electronic catalog containing close to 3 million titles, along with tables of contents, reviews, and other information about those titles. People could order books directly from their desktop computers. Amazon.com was able to sell books at lower cost because it did not have to pay rent, employee salaries, warehousing, and other overhead to maintain physical retail bookstores. (Amazon had almost no inventory costs because it relied on book distributors to stock most of its books.) Traditional booksellers who maintained physical storefronts were threatened. Selling books and other goods directly to consumers on-line without using physical storefronts represents a new business model. Publishers are now challenging this business model by selling digital electronic books directly to consumers without any intermediaries at all.

Financial service business models underwent a similar revolution. In the past, people wishing to purchase stocks or bonds had to pay high commissions to full-service brokers such as Merrill Lynch. Individual investors relied on these firms both to execute their trading transactions and to provide them with investment information. It was difficult for individual investors to obtain stock quotes, charts, investment news, historical data, investment advice, and other financial information on their own. Such information can be found now in abundance on the Web, and investors can use financial Web sites to place their own trades directly for very small transaction fees. The unbundling of financial information from trading has sharply reduced the need for full-service retail brokers.

The Changing Economics of Information

The Internet and the Web have vastly increased the total amount and quality of information available to all market participants, consumers and merchants alike. Customers benefit from lower **search costs**—the effort to find suitable products and to find all the suppliers, prices, and delivery terms for a specific product anywhere in the world (Bakos, 1998). Merchants also benefit because they can use the same technology to find out much more about consumers and to provide more accurate and detailed information to target their marketing and sales efforts.

The Internet shrinks information asymmetry, making it easier for consumers to find out the variety of prices in a market and to discover the actual costs merchants pay for products. An **information asymmetry** exists when one party in a transaction has more information

---

business model

An abstraction of what an enterprise is and how the enterprise delivers a product or service, showing how the enterprise creates wealth.

search costs

The time and money spent locating a suitable product and determining the best price for that product.

information asymmetry

Situation where the relative bargaining power of two parties in a transaction is determined by one party in the transaction possessing more information essential to the transaction than the other party.

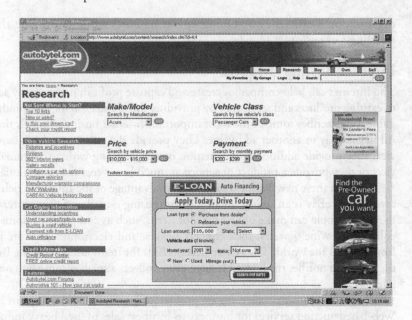

Visitors to Autobytel.com can research the price, availability, and features of most models of new and used cars and find the best prices and terms for auto purchases. The Internet can reduce search costs and information asymmetry.

that is important for the transaction than the other party. That information can determine their relative bargaining power. For example, until auto retailing sites appeared on the Web, there was a pronounced information asymmetry between auto dealers and customers. Only the auto dealers knew the manufacturers' prices, and it was difficult for consumers to shop around for the best price. Auto dealers' profit margins depended on this asymmetry of information. Now consumers have access to a legion of Web sites providing competitive pricing information, and the majority of auto buyers use the Internet to shop around for the best deal. Thus, the Web has reduced the information asymmetry surrounding an auto purchase. The Internet has also helped businesses seeking to purchase from other businesses reduce information asymmetries and locate better prices and terms.

Before the Internet, businesses had to make tradeoffs between the richness and reach of their information. **Richness** refers to the depth and detail of information—the amount of information the business can supply to the customer as well as information the business collects about the customer. **Reach** refers to how many people a business can connect with and how many products it can offer those people. Rich communication occurs, for example, when a sales representative meets with a customer, sharing information that is very specific to that interaction. Such an interaction is very expensive for a business because it can only take place with a small audience. Newspaper and television ads could reach millions of people quite inexpensively, but the information they provide is much more limited. It used to be prohibitively expensive for traditional businesses to have both richness and reach. Few, if any, companies could afford to provide highly detailed, customized information to a large mass audience. The Internet has transformed the richness and reach relationships (see Figure 4-1). Using the Internet and Web multimedia capabilities, companies can quickly and inexpensively provide detailed product information and detailed information specific to each customer to very large numbers of people simultaneously (Evans and Wurster, 2000).

New levels of richness and reach attainable

ENABLERS
• Explosion of connectivity
• Dissemination of standards

Reach

Richness

richness

Measurement of the depth and detail of information that a business can supply to the customer as well as information the business collects about the customer.

reach

Measurement of how many people a business can connect with and how many products it can offer those people.

Figure 4-1 The changing economics of information. In the past, companies have had to trade off between the richness and reach of their information. Internet connectivity and universal standards for information-sharing radically lower the cost of providing rich, detailed information to large numbers of people, reducing the tradeoff.
Reprinted by permission of Harvard Business School Press. From: *Blown to Bits: How the New Economics of Information Transforms Strategy* by Philip B. Evans and Thomas Wurster. Boston, MA, 2000, p. 31. Copyright © 2000 by the President of Fellows of Harvard College; all rights reserved.

Internet-enabled relationships between richness and reach are changing internal operations as well. Organizations can now exchange rich, detailed information among large numbers of people, making it easier for management to coordinate more jobs and tasks. In the past, management's span of control had to be much narrower because rich communication could only be channeled among a few people at a time using cumbersome manual paper-based processes. Digitally enabled business processes have become new sources of organizational efficiency, reducing operating costs while improving the accuracy and timeliness of customer service.

Internet Business Models

The Internet can help companies create and capture profit in new ways by adding extra value to existing products and services or by providing the foundation for new products and services. Table 4-2 describes some of the most important Internet business models that have emerged. All in one way or another add value: They provide the customer with a new product or service; they provide additional information or service along with a traditional product or service; or they provide a product or service at much lower cost than traditional means.

Some of these new business models take advantage of the Internet's rich communication capabilities. eBay is an online auction forum, using e-mail and other interactive features of the Web. People can make online bids for items, such as computer equipment, antiques and collectibles, wine, jewelry, rock-concert tickets, and electronics, that are posted by sellers from around the world. The system accepts bids for items entered on the Internet, evaluates the bids, and notifies the highest bidder. eBay collects a small commission on each listing and sale.

Business-to-business auctions are proliferating as well. GoIndustry, for instance, features Web-based auction services for business-to-business sales of used heavy industrial equipment and machinery. Online bidding, also known as **dynamic pricing,** is expected to grow rapidly because buyers and sellers can interact so easily through the Internet to determine what an item is worth at any particular moment.

dynamic pricing

Pricing of items based on real-time interactions between buyers and sellers that determine what an item is worth at any particular moment.

TABLE 4-2   INTERNET BUSINESS MODELS

Category	Description	Examples
Virtual storefront	Sells physical products directly to consumers or to individual businesses.	Amazon.com EPM.com
Information broker	Provides product, pricing, and availability information to individuals and businesses. Generates revenue from advertising or from directing buyers to sellers.	Edmunds.com Kbb.com, Insweb.com, ehealthinsurance.com IndustrialMall.com
Transaction broker	Saves users money and time by processing online sales transactions, generating a fee each time a transaction occurs. Also provides information on rates and terms.	E*TRADE.com Expedia.com
Online marketplace	Provides a digital environment where buyers and sellers can meet, search for products, display products, and establish prices for those products. Can provide online auctions or reverse auctions where buyers submit bids to multiple sellers to purchase at a buyer-specified price as well as negotiated or fixed pricing. Can serve consumers or B2B e-commerce, generating revenue from transaction fees.	eBay.com Priceline.com ChemConnect.com Pantellos.com
Content provider	Creates revenue by providing digital content, such as digital news, music, photos, or video, over the Web. The customer may pay to access the content, or revenue may be generated by selling advertising space.	WSJ.com CNN.com TheStreet.com Gettyimages.com MP3.com
Online service provider	Provides online service for individuals and businesses. Generates revenue from subscription or transaction fees, from advertising, or from collecting marketing information from users.	@Backup.com Xdrive.com Employease.com Salesforce.com
Virtual community	Provides online meeting place where people with similar interests can communicate and find useful information.	FortuneCity.com iVillage.com
Portal	Provides initial point of entry to the Web along with specialized content and other services.	Yahoo.com MSN.com StarMedia.com

The Internet has created online communities, where people with similar interests can exchange ideas from many different locations. Some of these virtual communities are providing the foundation for new businesses. Tripod, Geocities, and FortuneCity (which started out in Great Britain) provide communities for people wishing to communicate with others about arts, careers, health and fitness, sports, business, travel, and many other interests. Members can post their own personal Web pages, participate in online discussion groups, and join online "clubs" with other like-minded people. A major source of revenue for these communities is providing ways for corporate clients to target customers, including the placement of banner ads and pop-up ads on their Web sites. A **banner ad** is a graphic display on a Web page used for advertising. The banner is linked to the advertiser's Web site so that a person clicking on the banner will be transported to a Web page with more information about the advertiser. **Pop-up ads** work in the opposite manner. They automatically open up when a user accesses a specific Web site and the user must click on the ad to make it disappear.

Even traditional retailing businesses are enhancing their Web sites with chat, message boards, and community-building features as a means of encouraging customers to spend more time, return more frequently, and hopefully make more purchases on-line. Many retail Web sites have seen their sales increase after they added these features.

The Web's information resources are so vast and rich that special business models called **portals** have emerged to help individuals and organizations locate information more efficiently. A portal is a Web site or other service that provides an initial point of entry to the Web or to internal company data. Yahoo! is an example. It provides a directory of information on the Internet along with news, sports, weather, telephone directories, maps, games, shopping, e-mail, and other services. There are also specialized portals to help users with specific interests. For example, StarMedia is a portal customized for Latin American Internet users. (Companies are also building their own internal portals to provide employees with streamlined access to corporate information resources—see Chapter 10.)

Yahoo! and other portals and Web content sites often combine content and applications from many different sources and service providers. Other Internet business models use syndication as well to provide additional value. For example, E*TRADE, the discount Web trading site, purchases most of its content from outsiders sources such as Reuters (news), Bridge Information Systems (quotes), and BidCharts.com (charts). Online **syndicators** who aggregate content or applications from multiple sources, package them for distribution, and resell them to third-party Web sites have emerged as another variant of the online content provider business model (Werbach, 2000). The Web makes it much easier for companies to aggregate, repackage, and distribute information and information-based services.

Chapter 6 describes application service providers, such as Employease.com or Salesforce.com, that feature software that runs over the Web. They provide online services to

banner ad
A graphic display on a Web page used for advertising. The banner is linked to the advertiser's Web site so that a person clicking on it will be transported to the advertiser's Web site.

pop-up ad
Ad that opens automatically and does not disappear until the user clicks on it.

portal
Web site or other service that provides an initial point of entry to the Web or to internal company data.

syndicator
Business aggregating content or applications from multiple sources, packaging them for distribution, and reselling them to third-party Web sites.

iVillage is an Internet business based on an on-line community for women sharing similar interests, such as diet and fitness, parenting, pregnancy, home and garden, and food. The company generates revenue from advertising banners on its Web pages.

subscribing businesses. Other online service providers offer services to individual consumers, such as remote storage of data at Xdrive.com. Service providers generate revenue through subscription fees or from advertising.

Most of the business models described in Table 4-2 are called **pure-play** business models because they are based purely on the Internet. These firms did not have an existing bricks-and-mortar business when they designed their Internet business. However, many existing retail firms such as L. L. Bean, Office Depot, R.E.I., or the Wall Street Journal have developed Web sites as extensions of their traditional bricks-and-mortar businesses. Such businesses represent a hybrid **clicks-and-mortar** business model.

4.2   ELECTRONIC COMMERCE

Although most commercial transactions still take place through conventional channels, rising numbers of consumers and businesses are using the Internet for electronic commerce. Projections show that by 2006, total e-commerce spending by consumers and businesses could surpass $5 trillion.

CATEGORIES OF ELECTRONIC COMMERCE

There are many ways in which electronic commerce transactions can be classified. One is by looking at the nature of the participants in the electronic commerce transaction. The three major electronic commerce categories are business-to-consumer (B2C) e-commerce, business-to-business (B2B) e-commerce, and consumer-to-consumer (C2C) electronic commerce.

■ **Business-to-consumer (B2C) electronic commerce** involves retailing products and services to individual shoppers. Barnes&Noble.com, which sells books, software, and music to individual consumers, is an example of B2C e-commerce.

■ **Business-to-business (B2B) electronic commerce** involves sales of goods and services among businesses. Milpro.com, Milacron Inc.'s Web site for selling cutting tools, grinding wheels, and metal working fluids to more than 100,000 small machining businesses, is an example of B2B e-commerce.

■ **Consumer-to-consumer (C2C) electronic commerce** involves consumers selling directly to consumers. For example, eBay, the giant Web auction site, allows people to sell their goods to other consumers by auctioning the merchandise off to the highest bidder.

Another way of classifying electronic commerce transactions is in terms of the participants' physical connection to the Web. Until recently, almost all e-commerce transactions took place over wired networks. Now cell phones and other wireless handheld digital appliances are Internet enabled so that they can be used to send e-mail or access Web sites. Companies are rushing to offer new sets of Web-based products and services that can be accessed by these wireless devices. For example, in Britain, customers of Virgin Mobile can use their cell phones to browse Virgin's Web site and purchase compact disks, wine, TV sets, and washing machines. Subscribers to Japan's NTT DoCoMo Internet cell phone service can send and receive e-mail, tap into online news, purchase airplane tickets, trade stocks, and browse through restaurant guides, linking to Web sites that have been redesigned to fit on tiny screens. The use of handheld wireless devices for purchasing goods and services has been termed **mobile commerce** or **m-commerce.** Both business-to-business and business-to-consumer e-commerce transactions can take place using m-commerce technology. Chapter 9 discusses m-commerce and wireless Web technology in detail.

CUSTOMER-CENTERED RETAILING

Despite the many failures of dot-com retail companies since mid-2000, online retailing continues to grow at a brisk pace. The Internet provides companies with new channels of communication and interaction that can create closer yet more cost-effective relationships with customers in sales, marketing, and customer support. Companies can use the Web to provide

---

pure-play
Business models based purely on the Internet.

clicks-and-mortar
Business model where the Web site is an extension of a traditional bricks-and-mortar business.

business-to-consumer (B2C) electronic commerce
Electronic retailing of products and services directly to individual consumers.

business-to-business (B2B) electronic commerce
Electronic sales of goods and services among businesses.

consumer-to-consumer (C2C) electronic commerce
Consumers selling goods and services electronically to other consumers.

mobile commerce (m-commerce)
The use of wireless devices, such as cell phones or handheld digital information appliances, to conduct both business-to-consumer and business-to-business e-commerce transactions over the Internet.

ongoing information, service, and support, creating positive interactions with customers that can serve as the foundations for long-term relationships and repeat purchases.

Direct Sales over the Web

Manufacturers can sell their products and services directly to retail customers, bypassing intermediaries such as distributors or retail outlets. Eliminating intermediaries in the distribution channel can significantly lower purchase transaction costs. Operators of virtual storefronts, such as Amazon.com or EPM.com, do not have large expenditures for rent, sales staff, and the other operations associated with a traditional retail store. Airlines can sell tickets directly to passengers through their own Web sites or through travel sites such as Travelocity without paying commissions to travel agents.

To pay for all the steps in a traditional distribution channel, a product may have to be priced as high as 135 percent of its original cost to manufacture (Mougayar, 1998). Figure 4-2 illustrates how much savings can result from eliminating each of these layers in the distribution process. By selling directly to consumers or reducing the number of intermediaries, companies can achieve higher profits while charging lower prices. The removal of organizations or business process layers responsible for intermediary steps in a value chain is called **disintermediation.**

The Internet is accelerating disintermediation in some industries and creating opportunities for new types of intermediaries in others. In certain industries, distributors with warehouses of goods, or intermediaries such as real estate agents may be replaced by new "service hubs" specializing in helping Internet users reduce search costs, tailor offerings more precisely to their needs, obtain assurances about quality, handle product complexity, or preserve anonymity while conducting online transactions (Anderson and Anderson, 2002; Gallaugher, 2002; Hagel, III, and Singer, 1999). The information brokers listed in Table 4-2 are examples of one type of service where such intermediaries can provide value. The process of shifting the intermediary function in a value chain to a new source is called **reintermediation.**

Interactive Marketing and Personalization

Marketers can use the interactive features of Web pages to hold consumers' attention or to capture detailed information about their tastes and interests for one-to-one marketing (see Chapter 3). Web sites have become a bountiful source of detailed information about customer behavior, preferences, needs, and buying patterns that companies can use to tailor promotions, products, services, and pricing. Some customer information may be obtained by asking visitors to "register" online and provide information about themselves, but many

disintermediation
The removal of organizations or business process layers responsible for certain intermediary steps in a value chain.

reintermediation
The shifting of the intermediary role in a value chain to a new source.

Figure 4-2 The benefits of disintermediation to the consumer. The typical distribution channel has several intermediary layers, each of which adds to the final cost of a product, such as a sweater. Removing layers lowers the final cost to the consumer.

companies are also collecting customer information by using software tools that track the activities of Web site visitors. Companies can use special Web site auditing software capable of tracking the number of times visitors request Web pages, the Web pages of greatest interest to visitors after they have entered the sites, and the path visitors followed as they clicked from Web page to Web page. They can analyze this information about customer interests and behavior to develop more precise profiles of existing and potential customers.

For instance, TravelWeb, a Web site offering electronic information on more than 16,000 hotels in 138 countries and an online reservation capability, tracks the origin of each user and the screens and the Web page links he or she uses to learn about customer preferences. The Hyatt hotel chain found that Japanese users are most interested in the resort's golf facilities—valuable information in shaping market strategies and for developing hospitality-related products.

Communications and product offerings can be tailored precisely to individual customers. Firms can create unique personalized Web pages that display content or ads for products or services of special interest to each user, improving the customer's experience and creating additional value (see Figure 4-3). By using **Web personalization** technology to modify the Web pages presented to each customer, marketers can achieve the benefits of using individual salespeople at dramatically lower costs. Personalization can also help firms form lasting relationships with customers by providing individualized content, information, and services. Here are some examples:

Web personalization

The tailoring of Web content directly to a specific user.

- Amazon.com retains information on each customer's purchases. When a customer returns to the Amazon.com Web site, that person will be greeted with a Web page recommending books based on that person's purchase history or past purchases of other buyers with similar histories.

- American Airlines is using personalization to reduce its cost structure by encouraging customers to manage their frequent flyer accounts and purchase tickets through its Web site instead of from a travel agent. American Airlines can create individual "travel agencies" for its customers on the Web, informing them that if they take one more domestic flight this year, they can achieve platinum frequent flyer status next year. American expects to sell $500 million worth of tickets from its Web site.

- Dell Computer allows users to create their own personal "Dell sites," where Dell can offer them special prices and deals based on the information they provide about their interests

Figure 4-3 Web site personalization. Firms can create unique personalized Web pages that display content or ads for products or services of special interest to individual users, improving the customer experience and creating additional value.

Web sites can tailor their content to the specific interests of individual visitors. Bluefly.com personalizes its Web pages to display other items the visitor has viewed.

and computing requirements. Users can buy exactly what they want without having to call a representative, hunt down the products available, and try to work out deals.

Many other Web sites are using personalization technologies to deliver Web pages with content and banner ads geared to the specific interests of the visitor. Chapters 5, 9, and 11 describe additional technologies that gather the information on Web site visitors to make such personalized advertising and customer interaction possible. They also describe how companies are trying to combine Web visitor data with customer data from other sources such as off-line purchases, customer service records, or product registrations to create detailed profiles of individuals. Critics worry that companies gathering so much personal information on Web site visitors pose a threat to individual privacy, especially when much of this information is gathered without the customer's knowledge. Chapter 5 provides a detailed discussion of Web site privacy issues raised by these practices.

The cost of customer surveys and focus groups is very high. Learning how customers feel or what they think about one's products or services through visits to Web sites is much cheaper. Web sites providing product information also lower costs by shortening the sales cycle and reducing the amount of time sales staff must spend in customer education. The Web shifts more marketing and selling activities to the customer, because customers fill out their own online order forms. By using the Web to provide vendors with more precise information about their preferences and suggestions for improving products and services, customers are being transformed from passive buyers to active participants in creating value (Prahalad and Ramaswamy, 2000). The Window on Management shows how companies have benefited from using customers and customer communities on the Web to test and improve products and services.

M-Commerce and Next Generation Marketing

Within the next few years, the Web will be accessible from almost anywhere, as consumers turn to wireless telephones, handheld digital appliances, interactive television, or other information appliances to link to the Internet. Chapter 9 discusses m-commerce and new wireless Internet devices in greater detail. Travelers will be able to access the Internet in automobiles, airports, hotels, and train stations. Mobile commerce will provide businesses with additional channels for reaching customers and with new opportunities for personalization. Location tracking software in some of these devices will enable businesses to track users' movements and supply information, advertisements, and other services, such as local weather reports or directions to the nearest restaurant, while they are on the go. Instead of focusing on how to bring a customer to a Web site, marketing strategies will shift to finding ways of bringing the message directly to the customer at the point of need (Kenny and Marshall, 2000). Figure 4-4 illustrates how personalization can be extended via the ubiquitous Internet and m-commerce.

CUSTOMER COMMUNITIES BECOME PRODUCT DEVELOPMENT TOOLS

Customers are not merely buyers. Thanks to the Web, they have become powerful business tools for testing and improving products and services. Mercury Interactive of Sunnyvale, Calfornia, uses its online customer community to help it improve its software. Mercury recently released version 7.5 of LoadRunner, its testing and management software tool, which contained many improvements that were identified by Mercury's customers. Mercury's new approach was to establish online forums where its customers look to other customers, their peers, for solutions to their own problems. Customers post their problems, and their peers offer solutions where possible. In that way customers gain interim solutions to problems relatively quickly and users also have the pleasure of helping others. While Mercury employees also may offer help, software users who have already faced the issue are often the best source of solutions. Mercury's main role is to monitor its forum and to collect both software problems and possible solutions. Users have become such a valuable resource that when Mercury released v7.5, many LoadRunner users were delightfully surprised at the number and value of the improvements.

According to Bashier Said, a technical support manager for Mercury, its forums were founded in January 2001. One result was that in its first year, Mercury cut in half its expenditures for collecting information from customers while identifying more problems and solutions than they were able to in the past. Its site has 30,000 registered users of whom about 3,000 use their forums weekly. Sheryl Kingstone, a Yankee group analyst, said the result has been that "you can bring a product to market more quickly, and also give more pro-active service." One customer, Andrew L. Pollner, CEO of ALP International, a Bethesda, Maryland, consulting and training company, said "First and foremost, it means having a product that requires less customization for our

clients. That way, we can do it quicker and cheaper for them."

Other companies have benefited from this approach. Facing mounting competition, DirecTV Broadband was looking for ways to test and refine a new service for high-speed Internet access so that it could bring the service quickly to market. The company developed a prototype product called Connect & Protect, which would enable customers to link up to five computers to one high-speed Internet connection. A consulting firm called BetaSphere helped DirecTV recruit 60 customers for a one-month product trial. Customers ordered the product online, tested the online tool that sets up computers for networking, and called technical support. While these activities were taking place, BetaSphere software logged customer options and quickly relayed the results to DirecTV. According to David Allred, vice-president of DirecTV broadcast services, customers "basically broke in the product for us....They picked out any breakdowns, and we fixed the bugs." As a result of this rapid testing and improvement, Connect & Protect was able to go to market two months later, six months ahead of competitors, and had a product that worked very well the first time. Using customers had saved the company three to four months of research time, which would have been required had the service been tested the traditional way.

Think About: What are the management benefits of using customers for testing and market research? What value do online customer testing systems provide? What kinds of businesses can benefit from using the Web for this purpose?

Sources: Bob Tedeschi, "Using User Forums to Improve the Product," *New York Times,* February 11, 2002; Minda Zetlin and Bill Pfleging, "The Cult of Community," *Smart Business Magazine,* June 2002; and Theano Nikitas, "Your Customers Are Talking. Are You Listening?" *Smart Business Magazine,* February 2002.

MANAGEMENT

Customer Self-Service

The Web and other network technologies are inspiring new approaches to customer service and support. Many companies are using their Web sites and e-mail to answer customer questions or to provide customers with helpful information. The Web provides a medium through which customers can interact with the company, at the customers' convenience, and find information that previously required a human customer-support expert. Automated self-service or other Web-based responses to customer questions cost a fraction of the price of using a live customer service representative on the telephone.

Companies are realizing substantial cost savings from Web-based customer self-service applications. American, Northwest, and other major airlines have created Web sites where customers can review flight departure and arrival times, seating charts, and airport logistics; check frequent-flyer miles; and purchase tickets online. Yamaha Corporation of America has reduced customer calls concerning questions or problems by allowing customers to access technical solutions information from the service and support area of its Web site. If they can't

Target	Platform	When	Content and Service
Traveler	Computer-equipped car	Whenever car is moving	Provide maps, driving directions, weather reports, ads for nearby restaurants and hotels.
Parent	Cellphone	During school days	Notify about school-related closings: Hello, Caroline. Your children's school is closing early. Press 1 for closure reason. Press 2 for weather reports. Press 3 for traffic reports.
Stockbroker	Pager	During trading days. Notify if unusually high trading volume.	Summary portfolio analysis showing changes in positions for each holding.

Figure 4-4 Customer personalization with the ubiquitous Internet. Companies can use mobile wireless devices to deliver new value-added services directly to customers at any time and place, extending personalization and deepening their relationships.

find answers on their own, customers can send e-mail to a live technician. Chapter 1 described how customers of UPS can use its Web site to track shipments, calculate shipping costs, determine time in transit, and arrange for a package pickup. FedEx and other package delivery firms provide similar Web-based services.

New software products are even integrating the Web with customer call centers, where customer service problems have been traditionally handled over the telephone. A **call center** is an organizational department responsible for handling customer service issues by telephone and other channels. For example, visitors can click on a "push to talk" link on the Lands' End Web site that lets a user request a phone call. The user enters his or her telephone number and a call-center system directs a customer service representative to place a voice telephone call to the user's phone. Some systems also let the customer interact with a service representative on the Web while talking on the phone at the same time.

call center
An organizational department responsible for handling customer service issues by telephone and other channels.

BUSINESS-TO-BUSINESS ELECTRONIC COMMERCE: NEW EFFICIENCIES AND RELATIONSHIPS

For a number of years, companies have used proprietary systems for business-to-business (B2B) e-commerce. Now they are turning to the Web and Internet technology. By eliminating inefficient paper-based processes for locating suppliers, ordering supplies, or delivering goods, and by providing more opportunities for finding the lowest-priced products and services, business-to-business Web sites can save participants anywhere from 5 to 45 percent.

For business-to-business electronic commerce, companies can sell to other businesses using their own Web sites as electronic storefronts or they can execute purchase and sale transactions through private industrial networks or Net marketplaces. We introduced *private industrial networks* in Chapter 2. Private industrial networks focus on continuous business process coordination between companies for collaborative commerce and supply chain management. A private industrial network typically consists of a large firm using an extranet to link to its suppliers and other key business partners (see Figure 4-5). The network is owned by the buyer and it permits the firm and designated suppliers, distributors, and other business partners to share product design and development, marketing, production scheduling, inventory management, and unstructured communication, including graphics and e-mail. Another term for a private industrial network is a **private exchange.** Private exchanges are currently the fastest-growing type of B2B commerce.

private exchange
Another term for a private industrial network.

Figure 4-5 A private industrial network. A private industrial network, also known as a
private exchange, links a firm to
its suppliers, distributors, and
other key business partners for
efficient supply chain management and other collaborative
commerce activities.

Net marketplace

A single digital marketplace
based on Internet technology
linking many buyers to many
sellers.

Net marketplaces, which are sometimes called *e-hubs*, provide a single digital marketplace based on Internet technology for many different buyers and sellers (see Figure 4-6).
They are industry-owned or operate as independent intermediaries between buyers and sellers. Net marketplaces are more transaction-oriented (and less relationship-oriented) than private industrial networks, generating revenue from purchase and sale transactions and other
services provided to clients. Participants in Net marketplaces can establish prices through
online negotiations, auctions, or requests for quotations, or they can use fixed prices.

There are many different types of Net marketplaces and ways of classifying them. Some
Net marketplaces sell direct goods and some sell indirect goods. *Direct goods* are goods used
in a production process, such as sheet steel for auto body production. *Indirect goods* are all
other goods not directly involved in the production process, such as office supplies or products for maintenance and repair. Some Net marketplaces support contractual purchasing
based on long-term relationships with designated suppliers and others support short-term
spot purchasing, where goods are purchased based on immediate needs, often from many
different suppliers. Some Net marketplaces serve vertical markets for specific industries, such
as automobiles, telecommunications, or machine tools, while others serve horizontal markets
for goods and services that can be found in many different industries, such as office equipment or transportation.

W. W. Grainger serves the horizontal market for sourcing MRO (maintenance, repair,
and operations) products used in many different industries. Its Web site provides a single
source from which customers can make spot purchases of indirect goods from many different
suppliers. Grainger.com features on-line versions of Grainger's seven-pound paper catalog
plus access to parts and supplies from other sources and capabilities for electronic ordering
and payment. Most of this site is open to the public. Customers benefit from lower search
costs, lower transaction costs, wide selection, and lower prices, while Grainger earns revenue
by charging a markup on the products it distributes.

Ariba and CommerceOne are independently owned, third-party intermediaries that
bundle extensive e-commerce services with Net marketplaces for long-term contractual
purchasing of both indirect and direct goods. They provide both buyers and sellers with

Figure 4-6 A Net marketplace. Net marketplaces are
online marketplaces where multiple buyers can purchase from
multiple sellers.

ChemConnect.com is a Net marketplace for buyers and sellers of chemicals and plastics worldwide. Members can obtain up-to-date market information, negotiate prices, use tools to manage price and supply risk, and monitor fulfillment and shipment of orders.

software systems and services to run Net marketplaces, aggregating hundreds of catalogs into a single marketplace and customizing procurement and sales processes to work with their systems. For buyers, Ariba and CommerceOne automate sourcing, contract management, purchase orders, requisitions, business rules enforcement, and payment. For sellers, these Net marketplaces provide services for catalog creation and content management, order management, invoicing, and settlement. For example, FedEx uses Ariba's e-procurement system for $8 million in purchases. Employees use Ariba to order from more than 32 MRO suppliers and catalogs. The system automatically invokes FedEx's business rules for purchasing to route, review, and approve requisitions electronically. By using this Net marketplace, FedEx has reduced the cost of processing purchases by 75 percent and the prices paid for MRO supplies by 12 percent, and it has cut parts delivery time from an average of seven days to two days.

Covisint is an example of an industry-owned Net marketplace serving the vertical market for automobile manufacturing. It brings a small number of prechosen buyers in contact with thousands of preselected suppliers and provides value-added software services for procurement, transaction management, and payment. Industry-owned Net marketplaces focus on long-term contract purchasing relationships and on providing common networks and computing platforms for reducing supply chain inefficiencies. Buyer firms can benefit from competitive pricing among alternative suppliers, and suppliers can benefit by having stable long-term selling relationships with large firms. The ultimate goal of some industry-owned Net marketplaces is the unification of an entire industry supply chain. The Window on Organizations provides more detail on the challenges facing Covisint as it struggles to become a viable business model.

Exchanges are third-party Net marketplaces that can connect thousands of suppliers and buyers for spot purchasing. Many exchanges provide vertical markets for a single industry, such as food, electronics, or industrial equipment, and they primarily deal with direct inputs. For example, Altra Market Place operates an online exchange for spot purchases in the energy industry. Suppliers use the exchange to sell natural gas, liquids, and power to small utilities and energy distributors.

Exchanges proliferated during the early years of e-commerce, but many have failed. Suppliers were reluctant to participate because the exchanges encouraged competitive bidding that drove prices down and did not offer any long-term relationships with buyers or services to make lowering prices worthwhile. Many essential direct purchases are not conducted on a spot basis, requiring contracts and consideration of issues such as delivery timing, customization, and quality of products (Laudon, 2002; Wise and Morrison, 2000). The early exchanges primarily performed relatively simple transactions and could not handle these complexities as well as the more sophisticated B2B Net marketplaces we previously described (Andrew, Blackburn, and Sirkin, 2000).

exchange

Third-party Net marketplace that is primarily transaction oriented and that connects many buyers and suppliers for spot purchasing.

Covisint: The Vision and the Reality

When Covisint was first announced in early 2000 as a giant Net marketplace for the automotive industry, hopes ran high. General Motors, Ford, DaimlerChrysler, Renault, and Nissan, who helped found Covisint were counting on it to squeeze excess costs out of the process of purchasing auto parts and equipment. (The Big 3 U.S. automakers spend about $240 billion each year on direct and indirect supplies.) Lower prices would be achieved by requiring suppliers to bid for orders together over the Covisint Web site and by reducing the cost of each purchase order transaction from $100 to $10 or $20. Covisint includes an analysis tool to help the manufacturers weigh competing bids from suppliers using attributes such as quality, price, and delivery date. The automobile producers believed they could save billions every year, trimming costs by $1,200 to $3,000 per car. Even though these companies were rivals, they believed they could realize additional savings by sharing one common industry Net marketplace rather that bearing the costs of setting up their own procurement platforms. Covisint could also provide savings to suppliers by providing a low-cost point of entry for trading with manufacturers.

Eventually, Covisint would link automakers to the entire supply chain, providing online global communication for demand forecasting, capacity planning, and logistics that would make it possible build automobiles to order. Participating automobile manufacturers would be able to view their supply chains as components moved through the system, with purchase orders, supplier shipment dates, and production schedules displayed on the Covisint Web site. Covisint could help reduce the time it takes to develop a new automobile from 42 months to 12 to 18 months by providing collaborative software tools for car designers, engineers, parts manufacturers, and materials suppliers to share design documents and schedules.

That was the initial vision for Covisint. The reality has turned out to be less far-reaching. Auto industry suppliers have been reluctant to participate fully in Covisint. Many first-tier suppliers—the largest in the industry—have already built their own private networks to be used with the lower-tier suppliers who sell parts to them. The Tier 1 suppliers fear they could lose money and control over their own supply chains if Covisint becomes a single point of entry for transactions among all suppliers in the entire auto industry. Suppliers also worry that bidding for orders with competitors on an industry-wide exchange will turn their products into commodities, that they will lose the benefit of loyalty to their brands.

On June 28, 2002 Covisint announced it was scaling back operations and installing a new team of top managers. The restructuring eliminated Covisint's core supply chain management business, leaving Covisint with auctions and some procurement functions as its principal sources of revenue. Automakers will still be able to use Covisint to manage contracts with suppliers and to request proposals to build specific parts. Covisint will continue to target small suppliers who don't connect directly to automakers' private procurement networks.

To Think About: What are the strengths and weaknesses of Covisint's business model? How could it provide value to its users? Why has it been so difficult for Covisint to realize its original vision?

Sources: Anton Gonsalves and Steve Konicki, "Change at the Top for Covisint," *InformationWeek,* July 1, 2002; "English Resigns Covisint CEO Post as Auto-Parts Exchange Restructures," *Wall Street Journal,* June 28, 2002; Christopher Koch, "Motorcity Shakeup," *Darwin Magazine,* January 2002; Ruhan Memishi, "Covisint's Starts and Stops," *Internet World,* January 1, 2001; Bill Robinson," Covisint; Driving the Automotive Industry," *IQ Magazine,* January/February 2001; Richard Brown, "GM Spends $98 Billion Via Covisint," *Line56,* August 21, 2001; and Chuck Moozakis, "Big Auto Suppliers to Wield Tech Clout," *InternetWeek,* August 13, 2001.

ORGANIZATIONS

Electronic Commerce Payment Systems

electronic payment system
The use of digital technologies, such as credit cards, smart cards and Internet-based payment systems, to pay for products and services electronically.

digital credit card payment system
Secure services for credit card payments on the Internet that protect information transmitted among users, merchant sites, and processing banks.

Special **electronic payment systems** have been developed to handle ways of paying for goods electronically on the Internet. Electronic payment systems for the Internet include systems for credit card payments, digital cash, digital wallets, accumulated balance digital payment systems, stored value payment systems, peer-to-peer payment systems, electronic checks, and electronic billing presentment and payment systems.

Credit cards account for 95 percent of on-line payments in the United States and about 50 percent of all on-line transactions outside the United States. The more sophisticated electronic commerce software (see Chapter 9) has capabilities for processing credit card purchases on the Web. Businesses can also contract with services that extend the functionality of existing credit card payment systems. **Digital credit card payment systems** extend the functionality of credit cards so they can be used for online shopping payments. They make credit cards safer and more convenient for merchants and consumers by providing mechanisms for authenticating the purchaser's credit card to make sure it is valid and arranging for the bank that issued the credit card to deposit money for the amount of the purchase in the seller's bank account. Chapter 14 describes the technologies for secure credit card processing in more detail.

Digital wallets make paying for purchases over the Web more efficient by eliminating the need for shoppers to repeatedly enter their address and credit card information each time they buy something. A **digital wallet** securely stores credit card and owner identification information and provides that information at an electronic commerce site's "checkout counter." The electronic wallet enters the shopper's name, credit card number, and shipping information automatically when invoked to complete the purchase. Amazon.com's 1-Click shopping, which enables a consumer to automatically fill in shipping and credit card information by clicking one button, uses electronic wallet technology. Gator, Yahoo Wallet, and America Online's Quick Checkout are other digital wallet systems.

Micropayment systems have been developed for purchases of less than $10, such as downloads of individual articles or music clips, that would be too small for conventional credit card payments. Accumulated balance digital payment systems or stored value payment systems are useful for such purposes. **Accumulated balance digital payment systems** allow users to make micropayments and purchases on the Web, accumulating a debit balance that they must pay periodically on their credit card or telephone bills. Qpass, for instance, collects all of a consumer's tiny purchases for monthly billing on a credit card. The New York Times uses Qpass to bill consumers wishing to access articles from its Web site. Trivnet lets consumers charge small purchases to their monthly telephone bill.

Stored value payment systems enable consumers to make instant online payments to merchants and other individuals based on value stored in a digital account. Online value systems rely on the value stored in a consumer's bank, checking, or credit card account and some of these systems require the use of a digital wallet. Smart cards are another type of stored value system used for micropayments. A **smart card** is a plastic card the size of a credit card that stores digital information. The smart card can store health records, identification data, or telephone numbers, or it can serve as an "electronic purse" in place of cash. The Mondex and American Express Blue smart cards contain electronic cash and can be used to transfer funds to merchants in physical storefronts and to merchants on the Internet. Both are contact smart cards that require use of special card reading devices whenever the cards need to transfer cash to either an online or off-line merchant. (Internet users must attach a smart card reader to their PCs to use the card. To pay for a Web purchase, the user would swipe the smart card through the card reader.)

Digital cash (also known as electronic cash or e-cash) can also be used for micropayments or larger purchases. **Digital cash** is currency represented in electronic form that moves outside the normal network of money (paper currency, coins, checks, credit cards). Users are supplied with client software and can exchange money with another e-cash user over the Internet or with a retailer accepting e-cash. eCoin.net is an example of a digital cash service. In addition to facilitating micropayments, digital cash can be useful for people who don't have credit cards and wish to make Web purchases.

New Web-based **peer-to-peer payment systems** have sprung up to serve people who want to send money to vendors or individuals who are not set up to accept credit card payments. The party sending money uses his or her credit card to create an account with the designated payment at a Web site dedicated to peer-to-peer payments. The recipient "picks up" the payment by visiting the Web site and supplying information about where to send the payment (a bank account or a physical address.) PayPal has become a popular peer-to-peer payment system.

Digital checking payment systems, such as CHEXpedite and Western Union MoneyZap, extend the functionality of existing checking accounts so they can be used for online shopping payments. Digital checks are less expensive than credit cards and much faster than traditional paper-based checking. These checks are encrypted with a digital signature that can be verified and used for payments in electronic commerce. Electronic check systems are useful in business-to-business electronic commerce.

Electronic billing presentment and payment systems are used for paying routine monthly bills. They allow users to view their bills electronically and pay them through electronic fund transfers from bank or credit card accounts. These services support payment for online and physical store purchases of goods or services after the purchase has taken place. They notify

digital wallet
Software that stores credit card and owner identification information and provides these data automatically during electronic commerce purchase transactions.

micropayment
Payment for a very small sum of money, often less than $10.

accumulated balance digital payment systems
Systems enabling users to make micropayments and purchases on the Web, accumulating a debit balance on their credit card or telephone bills.

stored value payment systems
Systems enabling consumers to make instant online payments to merchants and other individuals based on value stored in a digital account.

smart card
A credit-card-size plastic card that stores digital information and that can be used for electronic payments in place of cash.

digital cash
Currency represented in electronic form that moves outside the normal network of money.

peer-to-peer payment system
Electronic payment system for people who want to send money to vendors or individuals who are not set up to accept credit card payments.

digital checking
Systems that extend the functionality of existing checking accounts so they can be used for online shopping payments.

electronic billing presentment and payment systems
Systems used for paying routine monthly bills that allow users to view their bills electronically and pay them through electronic funds transfers from banks or credit card accounts.

PayPal is a peer-to-peer payment system which enables users to pay anyone with an e-mail address or send a personal or group bill online.

purchasers about bills that are due, present the bills, and process the payments. Some of these services, such as CheckFree, consolidate subscribers' bills from various sources so that they can all be paid at one time. Table 4-3 summarizes the features of these payment systems.

The process of paying for products and services purchased on the Internet is complex and merits additional discussion. We discuss electronic commerce security in detail in Chapter 14. Figure 4-7 provides an overview of the key information flows in electronic commerce.

4.3 ELECTRONIC BUSINESS AND THE DIGITAL FIRM

Businesses are finding that some of the greatest benefits of Internet technology come from applications that lower agency and coordination costs. Although companies have used inter-

TABLE 4-3	EXAMPLES OF ELECTRONIC PAYMENT SYSTEMS FOR E-COMMERCE

Payment System	Description	Commercial Example
Digital credit card payment	Secure services for credit card payments on the Internet protect information transmitted among users, merchant sites, and processing banks	CyberSource IC Verify
Digital wallet	Software that stores credit card and other information to facilitate payment for goods on the Web	Gator AOL Quick Checkout
Accumulated balance payment system	Accumulates micropayment purchases as a debit balance that must be paid periodically on credit card or telephone bills	Qpass Trivnet
Stored value payment systems	Enables consumers to make instant payments to merchants based on value stored in a digital account	Mondex smart card American Express Blue smart card
Digital cash	Digital currency that can be used for micropayments or larger purchases	eCoin.net
Peer-to-peer payment systems	Sends money using the Web to individuals or vendors who are not set up to accept credit card payments	PayPal
Digital checking	Electronic check with a secure digital signature	Western Union MoneyZap CHEXpedite
Electronic billing presentment and payment	Supports electronic payment for online and physical store purchases of goods or services after the purchase has taken place	CheckFree

Figure 4-7 Electronic commerce information flows. Individuals can purchase goods and services electronically from online retailers, who in turn can use electronic commerce technologies to link directly to their suppliers or distributors. Electronic payment systems are used in both business-to-consumer and business-to-business electronic commerce.

nal networks for many years to manage and coordinate their business processes, intranets quickly are becoming the technology of choice for electronic business.

HOW INTRANETS SUPPORT ELECTRONIC BUSINESS

Intranets are inexpensive, scalable to expand or contract as needs change, and accessible from most computing platforms. Whereas most companies, particularly the larger ones, must support a multiplicity of computer platforms that cannot communicate with each other, intranets provide instant connectivity, uniting all computers into a single, virtually seamless, network system. Web software presents a uniform interface, which can be used to integrate many different processes and systems throughout the company. Companies can connect their intranets to internal company transaction systems, enabling employees to take actions central to a company's operations.

Intranets can help organizations create a richer, more responsive information environment. Internal corporate applications based on the Web page model can be made interactive using a variety of media, text, audio, and video. A principal use of intranets has been to create online repositories of information that can be updated as often as required. Product catalogs, employee handbooks, telephone directories, or benefits information can be revised immediately as changes occur. This "event-driven" publishing allows organizations to respond more rapidly to changing conditions than traditional paper-based publishing, which requires a rigid production schedule. Made available via intranets, documents always can be up-to-date, eliminating paper, printing, and distribution costs. For instance, Sun Healthcare, a chain of nursing and long-term care facilities headquartered in Albuquerque, New Mexico, saved $400,000 in printing and mailing costs when it put its corporate newsletter on an intranet. The newsletter is distributed to 69,000 employees in 49 states.

Conservative studies of returns on investment (ROIs) from intranets show ROIs of 23 to 85 percent, and some companies have reported ROIs of more than 1,000 percent. For example, the Mitre Corporation reported that its $7.9 million invested in the intranet collaboration environment described in the following section produced $62.1 million in reduced costs and increased productivity. Mitre also realized nonquantifiable benefits, such as higher quality and more innovative solutions for clients (Young, 2000). More information on the business value of intranets can be found in Chapter 13. Table 4-4 summarizes the organizational benefits of intranets.

INTRANETS AND GROUP COLLABORATION

Intranets provide a rich set of tools for creating collaborative environments in which members of an organization can exchange ideas, share information, and work together on common projects and assignments regardless of their physical location. For example, Noranda

TABLE 4-4	ORGANIZATIONAL BENEFITS OF INTRANETS

Connectivity: accessible from most computing platforms

Can be tied to internal corporate systems and core transaction databases

Can create interactive applications with text, audio, and video

Scalable to larger or smaller computing platforms as requirements change

Easy to use, universal Web interface

Low start-up costs

Richer, more responsive information environment

Reduced information distribution costs

Inc., a large Canadian mining company, uses an intranet to keep track of its mineral exploration research in a dozen offices in North and South America, Australia, and Europe.

Some companies are using intranets to create enterprise collaboration environments linking diverse groups, projects, and activities throughout the organization. For example, the Mitre Corporation, which conducts research and development work for the U.S. federal government, set up a collaborative environment called Mitre Information Infrastructure for sharing personnel, planning, and project information. This intranet includes a corporate directory with names, telephone numbers, and resumes of Mitre employees; a Lessons Learned Library with best practices and lessons learned from 10 years of Mitre projects; and capabilities for filing human resources reports, such as time sheets, service requests, and property inventory and tracking forms. Chapter 10 provides a detailed discussion of intranets in collaborative work.

INTRANET APPLICATIONS FOR ELECTRONIC BUSINESS

Intranets are springing up in all the major functional areas of businesses, allowing organizations to manage more business processes electronically. Figure 4-8 illustrates some of the intranet applications that have been developed for finance and accounting, human resources, sales and marketing, and manufacturing and production.

Finance and Accounting

Many organizations have extensive TPS that collect operational data on financial and accounting activities, but their traditional management reporting systems, such as general ledger systems and spreadsheets, often cannot bring this detailed information together for decision making and performance measurement. Intranets can be very valuable for finance and accounting because they can provide an integrated view of financial and accounting information on-line in an easy-to-use format. Table 4-5 provides some examples.

Figure 4-8 Functional applications of intranets. Intranet applications have been developed for each of the major functional areas of the business.

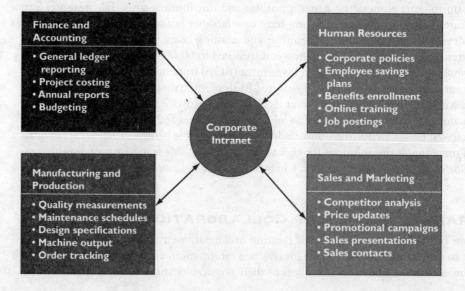

Finance and Accounting
- General ledger reporting
- Project costing
- Annual reports
- Budgeting

Human Resources
- Corporate policies
- Employee savings plans
- Benefits enrollment
- Online training
- Job postings

Corporate Intranet

Manufacturing and Production
- Quality measurements
- Maintenance schedules
- Design specifications
- Machine output
- Order tracking

Sales and Marketing
- Competitor analysis
- Price updates
- Promotional campaigns
- Sales presentations
- Sales contacts

TABLE 4-5	INTRANETS IN FINANCE AND ACCOUNTING
Organization	**Intranet Application**
J.P. Morgan Chase	Web-based system based on software from Hyperion Solutions manages how corporate units charge each other for services provided inside the corporation. Software consolidates information from a series of business and accounting systems and presents users with customizable pages that show the amounts their departments are being billed for services such as information processing or use of conference rooms. Users can compare actual bills with the amounts they budgeted and drill down to obtain additional information.
Cisco Systems	Sales and related financial data are updated three times daily and net income, margin, order, and expense numbers are made instantly available to managers over an intranet. The company can close its books within 24 hours after the end of each quarter.
British Standards Institution (BSI)	Web-based reporting system using software from Crystal Decisions allows the finance department to monitor un-invoiced income or outstanding debt each day.
Charles Schwab	SMART reporting and analysis application provides managers with a comprehensive view of Schwab's financial activities, including a risk-evaluation template that helps managers assess nine categories of risk. Schwab's intranet also delivers the FinWeb General Ledger reporting system online in an easy-to-digest format.

Human Resources

Principal responsibilities of human resources departments include keeping employees informed of company issues and providing information about employees' personnel records and benefits. Human resources can use intranets for online publishing of corporate policy manuals, job postings and internal job transfers, company telephone directories, and training classes. Employees can use an intranet to enroll in healthcare, employee savings, and other benefit plans if it is linked to the firm's human resources or benefits system, or to take online competency tests. Human resources departments can rapidly deliver information about upcoming events or company developments to employees using newsgroups or e-mail broadcasts. Table 4-6 lists examples of how intranets are used in the area of human resources.

Sales and Marketing

Earlier we described how the Internet and the Web can be used for selling to individual customers and to other businesses. Internet technology also can be applied to the internal management of the sales and marketing function. One of the most popular applications for corporate intranets is to oversee and coordinate the activities of the sales force. Sales staff can dial in for updates on pricing, promotions, rebates, or customers, or to obtain information about competitors. They can access presentations and sales documents and customize them for customers. Table 4-7 describes examples of these applications.

TABLE 4-6	INTRANETS IN HUMAN RESOURCES
Organization	**Intranet Application**
Henan Electric Power Transmission and Transformation Co. (China)	Company-wide intranet posts a centralized calendar of corporate events. When planning large meetings and events, employees can download standardized registration forms and process them online.
TransCanada Pipelines	Employees process their timesheets and expense reports, and manage their own health and pension benefits accounts using an intranet.
Medtronics	Employees use myMedtronic for self-service human resources administration tasks, such as changing addresses or employee payroll information or enrolling in benefit plans. Managers use myMedtronic to enter pay changes and promotions. A Life Event section provides information to guide employees through employee data and benefit changes that would have to be made if employees changed marital status or had a child.
E*TRADE	Uses Icarian Workforce software on the corporate intranet to automate the entire job applicant tracking process. The software automatically takes in applicant information from sources such as online headhunters and online job posting sites, tracking all applicants from requisition through interviewing. The data are integrated with the corporate human resources system.

Benefits.com enables human resources professionals to administer employee benefits programs and manage employee data over a corporate intranet.

Manufacturing and Production

In manufacturing, information-management issues are highly complex, involving massive inventories, capturing and integrating real-time production data flows, changing relationships with suppliers, and volatile costs. The manufacturing function typically uses multiple types of data, including graphics as well as text, which are scattered in many disparate systems. Manufacturing information is often very time sensitive and difficult to retrieve because files must be continuously updated. Developing intranets that integrate manufacturing data under a uniform user interface is more complicated than in other functional areas.

Despite these difficulties, companies are launching intranet applications for manufacturing. Intranets coordinating the flow of information between lathes, controllers, inventory systems, and other components of a production system can make manufacturing information more accessible to different parts of the organization, increasing precision and lowering costs. Table 4-8 describes some of these uses.

SUPPLY CHAIN MANAGEMENT AND COLLABORATIVE COMMERCE

Intranets can also be used to simplify and integrate business processes spanning more than one functional area. These cross-functional processes can be coordinated electronically, increasing organizational efficiency and responsiveness, and they can also be coordinated

TABLE 4-7   INTRANETS IN SALES AND MARKETING

Organization	Intranet Application
SwissAir	Marketing intranet provides reports, tools and design guidelines to help the company's marketing staff in 150 cities exchange minutes and presentations about upcoming marketing campaigns and develop themes and promotions.
American Express	Uses a Web-based sales management system by Salesnet to help its North American sales team (which sells gift checks and incentive cards to corporate clients) distribute and track qualified sales leads. More than 50 members of the sales team can access the system using wireless devices.
Yesmail.com	E-mail marketing company set up a sales intranet for sharing tools and documents about contacts, sales leads, and prospects, and used Web conferencing technologies to train remote sales staff. The application includes a methodology to measure the company's progress in different stages of the sales process.
Case Corp.	Supports sales and marketing teams with intranet collaboration tools for contact management, discussion forums, document management, and calendars. The intranet applications facilitate sharing of information on competitors, potential product-development, and research tasks, and include time-sensitive accountability to measure results.

TABLE 4-8	INTRANETS IN MANUFACTURING AND PRODUCTION

Organization	Intranet Application
Noranda Inc.	Intranet for its Magnola magnesium production facility in Quebec monitors plant operations remotely using a virtual control panel and video cameras.
Sony Corporation	Intranet delivers financial information to manufacturing personnel so that workers can monitor the production line's profit-and-loss performance and adapt performance accordingly. The intranet also provides data on quality measurements, such as defects and rejects, as well as maintenance and training schedules.
TransCanada Pipelines	Managers can schedule plant maintenance using an online system linked to procurement software that automatically secures needed parts from inventory or generates purchase orders.
Duke Power	Intranet provides online access to a computer-aided engineering tool for retrieving equipment designs and operating specifications that allows employees to view every important system in the plant at various levels of detail. Different subsets of systems can be formatted together to create a view of all the equipment in a particular room. Maintenance technicians, plant engineers, and operations personnel can use this tool with minimal training.
Rockwell International	Intranet improves process and quality of manufactured circuit boards and controllers by establishing home pages for its Milwaukee plant's computer-controlled machine tools that are updated every 60 seconds. Quality control managers can check the status of a machine by calling up its home page to learn how many pieces the machine output that day, what percentage of an order that output represents, and to what tolerances the machine is adhering.

with the business processes of other companies. Internet technology has proved especially useful for supply chain management and collaborative commerce.

Chapter 2 introduced the concept of supply chain management, which integrates procurement, production, and logistics processes to supply goods and services from their source to final delivery to the customer. In the pre-Internet environment, supply chain coordination was hampered by the difficulties of making information flow smoothly among many different kinds of systems servicing different parts of the supply chain, such as purchasing, materials management, manufacturing, and distribution. Enterprise systems could supply some of this integration for internal business processes, but such systems are difficult and costly to build.

Some of this integration can be supplied more inexpensively using Internet technology. Firms can use intranets to improve coordination among their internal supply chain processes, and they can use extranets to coordinate supply chain processes shared with their business partners. *Extranets*, which we introduced in Chapter 1, are private intranets extended to authorized users outside the company. Many of the private industrial networks discussed in this chapter and in Chapter 2, are based on extranets for streamlining supply chain management.

Using Internet technology, all members of the supply chain can instantly communicate with each other, using up-to-date information to adjust purchasing, logistics, manufacturing, packaging, and schedules. A manager can use a Web interface to tap into suppliers' systems to see if inventory and production capabilities match demand for the manufacturer's products. Business partners can use Web-based supply chain management tools to collaborate online on forecasts. Sales representatives can tap into suppliers' production schedules and logistics information to monitor customers' order status. As extended supply chains start sharing production, scheduling, inventory, forecasting, and logistics information online instead of by phone or fax, companies can respond more accurately to changing customer demand. Manufacturers can communicate up-to-the-minute information to suppliers so they can postpone their products' final configuration and delivery until the last moment. The low cost of providing this information with Web-based tools instead of costly proprietary systems encourages companies to share critical business information with a greater number of suppliers. Table 4-9 provides examples of Web-based supply chain management applications.

Logistics and fulfillment are receiving new attention in the quest for optimal supply chain management and successful e-commerce execution. As more and more companies embrace the Internet and e-commerce, they are reexamining how they move products to customers. Order fulfillment can be the most expensive—and sometimes the most critical—operation in electronic commerce. The Internet has introduced new ways of managing warehousing, shipping, and packaging based on access to supply chain information that can give companies an edge in

TABLE 4-9	EXAMPLES OF WEB-BASED SUPPLY CHAIN MANAGEMENT APPLICATIONS
Organization	**Supply Chain Management Application**
Celestica	Toronto-based electronics manufacturing services provider has an extranet for its 1,000 suppliers, which use it to pull production planning information from Celestica's supply chain systems. When Celestica gets demand forecast data from one of its large customers, suppliers can view the data through Celestica's corporate portal and let Celestica know how quickly they can deliver the required materials.
Acma Computers	Uses Datasweep Advantage Web-based supply chain management tool to track work orders for specific customers on-line, flag and manage product shortages, manage change orders, and monitor production and quality information throughout the product lifecycle. Increased on-time delivery of customer units from 78 to 96%.
Wesco Distribution Inc.	Distributor of electrical products and MRO supplies linked its logistics systems via Web technology with those of major suppliers. Salespeople can use the Web to directly accessed suppliers' finished-goods inventory systems to obtain availability and pricing information for customers.
Nabisco and Wegman's Food Markets	Created a joint Web-based forecast to maximize the profitability of shelf space for Nabisco Planter's products. The forecast initiated replenishment orders; refined the established forecasting–replenishment plan to drive sourcing, production, and transportation plans; and monitored execution against these plans. After this system was implemented Planters' sales increased by 54% while stock availability rose from 92.8 to 96.6%.
DaimlerChrysler Corporation	Supplier Partner Information Network (SPIN) allows 3,500 of DaimlerChrysler's 12,000 suppliers to access portions of its intranet, where they can get the most current data on design changes, parts shortages, packaging information, and invoice tracking. DaimlerChrysler can use the information from SPIN to reassign workers so that shortages do not hold up assembly lines. DaimlerChrysler believes SPIN has reduced the time to complete various business processes by 25 to 50%.

delivering goods and services at a reasonable cost. Companies can use information flows from the supply chain to postpone delivery decisions until they have the most up-to-date and complete information on what the customer wants so that products can be delivered in the most direct and cost-effective way (Lee and Whang, 2001).

Internet-based supply chain management applications are clearly changing the way businesses work internally and with each other. In addition to reducing costs, these supply chain management systems provide more responsive customer service, allowing the workings of the business to be driven more by customer demand. Earlier supply chain management systems were driven by production master schedules based on forecasts or best guesses of demand for products. With new flows of information made possible by Web-based tools, supply chain management can follow a demand-driven model.

Internet technology has given a great boost to collaborative product development that is more customer-driven as well. The development of a new product usually involves collaboration among different departments in a single firm and, increasingly, among several different organizations. Internet technology provides communication and collaboration tools to connect designers, engineers, marketing, and manufacturing employees. Companies can work internally or with their business partners more efficiently to bring products more rapidly to market, from their initial design and engineering to marketing and sales. Internet-based tools also help companies work with contract manufacturers to build these new products. Customer feedback from Web sites or online communities can be fed into product design.

Ultimately, the Internet could create a "digital logistics nervous system" throughout the supply chain. This system would permit simultaneous, multidirectional communication of information about participants' inventories, orders, and capacities, and works to optimize the activities of individual firms and groups of firms interacting in e-commerce marketplaces (see Figure 4-9). As more digital firms evolve, this future "digital logistics nervous system" will come closer to being realized.

4.4   MANAGEMENT CHALLENGES AND OPPORTUNITIES

Although digitally enabling the enterprise with Internet technology offers organizations a wealth of new opportunities and ways of doing business, it also presents managers with a series of challenges. Many new Internet business models have yet to prove enduring sources

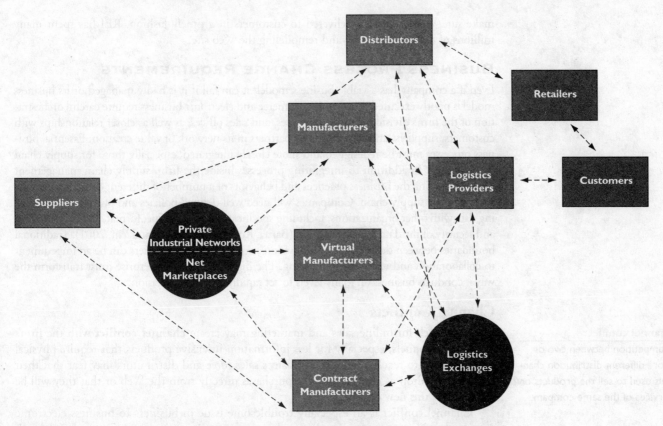

Figure 4-9   The future Internet-driven supply chain. The future Internet-driven supply chain operates like a digital logistics nervous system. It provides multidirectional communication among firms, networks of firms, and e-marketplaces so that entire networks of supply chain partners can immediately adjust inventories, orders, and capacities.

of profit. Web-enabling business processes for electronic commerce and electronic business requires far-reaching organizational change. The legal environment for electronic commerce has not yet solidified, and companies pursuing electronic commerce must be vigilant about establishing trust, security, and consumer privacy.

UNPROVEN BUSINESS MODELS

Not all companies make money on the Web. Hundreds of retail dot-com firms, including Kozmo.com, Webvan, Garden.com, Chinese Books Cyberstore, Productopia.com, and Pets.com, have closed their doors. Fleetscape.com, M-Xchange.com, Industrial Vortex.com, and other exchanges have shut down also. The consulting firm Booz Allen & Hamilton Inc. estimated there were 1734 online marketplaces in 2000 and only 407 are expected to remain by 2004 (Meehan, 2002). Dot-com stock prices collapsed after many of these companies failed to generate enough revenue to sustain their costly marketing campaigns, infrastructures, and staff salaries, losing money on every sale they made. Business models built around the Internet are new and largely unproven.

Doing business over the Internet is not necessarily more efficient or cost effective than traditional business methods. Virtual retailers may not need to pay for costly storefronts and retail workers, but they require heavy outlays for warehousing, customer service call centers, and customer acquisition. Challenges also confront businesses that are trying to use the Web to supplement or enhance a traditional business model. Businesses that are unclear about their online strategy—and its relationship to their overall business strategy—can waste thousands and even millions of dollars building and maintaining a Web site that fails to deliver the desired results (Pinker, Seidmann, and Foster, 2002). Even successful Web sites can incur very high costs. For example, Recreational Equipment Inc. (REI), the famous seller of outdoor gear, headquartered in Kent, Washington, has bricks-and-mortar retail stores, hefty catalog sales, and a profitable Web site that dominates its market. It has large payroll expenditures to pay for the skilled technical staff supporting the Web site and additional shipping expenses to make sure Web orders are delivered to customers in a timely fashion. REI has spent many millions of dollars upgrading and remodeling the Web site.

BUSINESS PROCESS CHANGE REQUIREMENTS

Even if a company has a viable business model, it can fail if it is badly managed or its business model is poorly executed. Electronic commerce and electronic business require careful orchestration of the firm's divisions, production sites, and sales offices, as well as closer relationships with customers, suppliers, and other business partners in its network of value creation. Essential business processes must be redesigned and more closely integrated, especially those for supply chain management. In addition to integrating processes inside the firm, supply chain management requires aligning the business practices and behaviors of a number of different companies participating in the supply chain. Companies will need well-defined policies and procedures for sharing data with other organizations, including specifications for the type, format, level of precision, and security of the data to be exchanged (Barua, Konana, Whinston, and Yin, 2001). Traditional boundaries between departments and divisions, companies and suppliers can be an impediment to collaboration and relationship building. The digitally enabled enterprise must transform the way it conducts business on many levels to act rapidly and with precision.

Channel Conflicts

channel conflict

Competition between two or more different distribution channels used to sell the products or services of the same company.

Using the Web for online sales and marketing may create **channel conflict** with the firm's traditional channels, especially for less information-intensive products that require physical intermediaries to reach buyers. A company's sales force and distributors may fear that their revenues will drop as customers make purchases directly from the Web or that they will be displaced by this new channel.

Channel conflict is an especially troublesome issue in business-to-business electronic commerce, where customers buy directly from manufacturers via the Web instead of through distributors or sales representatives. Milacron Inc. operates one of heavy industry's most extensive Web sites for selling machine tools to contract manufacturers. To minimize negative repercussions from channel conflict, Milacron is paying full commissions to its reps for on-line sales made in their territory, even if the sales reps do not personally work on the sale or meet the buyer. Other companies are devising other solutions, such as offering only a portion of their full product line on the Web. Using alternative channels created by the Internet requires very careful planning and management.

LEGAL ISSUES

Laws governing electronic commerce are still being written. Legislatures, courts, and international agreements are just starting to settle such questions as the legality and force of e-mail contracts, the role of electronic signatures, and the application of copyright laws to electronically copied documents. Moreover, the Internet is global, and it is used by individuals and organizations in hundreds of different countries. If a product were offered for sale in Thailand via a server in Singapore and the purchaser lived in Hungary, whose law would apply? The legal and regulatory environment for electronic commerce has not been fully established.

TRUST, SECURITY, AND PRIVACY

Electronic commerce cannot flourish unless there is an atmosphere of trust among buyers, sellers and other partners involved in online transactions. Since online relationships are more impersonal than those in "brick and mortar" commerce, many consumers remain hesitant to make purchases over the Web from unfamiliar vendors. Consumers also worry about the security and confidentiality of the credit card and other personal data that they supplied over the Internet (Bhattacherjee, 2002; McKnight, Choudhury, and Kacmar, 2002). The technological and institutional framework for e-commerce cannot yet dispel consumer perceptions of risk and uncertainty.

Internet-based systems are even more vulnerable to penetration by outsiders than private networks, because the Internet was designed to be open to everyone. Any information, including e-mail, passes through many computer systems on the Internet before it reaches its destination. It can be monitored, captured, and stored at any of these points along the route. Hackers, vandals, and computer criminals have exploited Internet weaknesses to break into computer systems, causing harm by stealing passwords, obtaining sensitive information, electronic eavesdropping, or "jamming"

MIS IN ACTION: MANAGER'S TOOLKIT

DIGITALLY ENABLING THE ENTERPRISE: TOP QUESTIONS TO ASK

Managers need to understand precisely how Internet technology will benefit their company and the challenges they face when implementing electronic commerce and electronic business applications. Here are some key questions to ask:

1. How much digital integration does our business need to remain competitive? How can the digital integration provided by Internet technology change our business model? Should we change our business model?

2. How can we measure the success of digitally enabling the enterprise? Will the benefits outweigh the costs?

3. How will business processes have to be changed to use Internet technology seriously for electronic commerce or electronic business? How much process integration is required?

4. How will we have to recast our relationships with customers, suppliers, and other business partners to take advantage of digitally enabled business processes?

5. Do we have the appropriate information technology infrastructure for digitally enabling our business? What technical skills and employee training will be required to use Internet technology? How can we integrate Internet applications with existing applications and data?

6. How can we make sure our intranet is secure from entry by outsiders? How secure is the electronic payment system we are using for electronic commerce?

7. Are we doing enough to protect the privacy of customers we reach electronically?

MAKE IT YOUR BUSINESS

FINANCE AND ACCOUNTING

Internet technology facilitates access to and integration of financial data from sources inside and outside the firm. Companies can use the Internet to obtain data on interest rates, market conditions, and other factors to help them monitor and plan their investments. Firms that have embarked on ambitious programs to integrate their systems can use corporate intranets to obtain company-wide views of their firm's financial performance. The Internet has also opened up new avenues for businesses to make and receive payments electronically and has provided the financial industry with new products and channels to customers.

HUMAN RESOURCES

Internet technology has led to efficiencies and cost savings in employee communication and training as well as the processing of basic human resources transactions. Many companies are installing self-service human resources (HR) systems on intranets to deliver HR-related services, such as enrolling in insurance and medical plans, maintaining employee savings plans, and applying for company jobs. Companies can realize productivity and publishing savings by using Web technology to deliver interactive employee training and human resources policy manuals and company directories. Human resources staff members can use intranets to access employee records from the firm's basic human resources transaction systems. You can find examples of human resources applications on pages 112 and 143.

MANUFACTURING AND PRODUCTION

Internet technology creates a common platform for communication and data exchange that can be used to integrate manufacturing and production data from disparate systems inside the firm and to coordinate manufacturing and production processes with those of suppliers and distributors. Internet technology can help companies bring products to market more quickly, optimize inventory management, and, in some cases, outsource most and even all of their production or order fulfillment. Public B2B commerce systems and private industrial networks can help reduce procurement costs and make other supply chain processes more efficient. You can find examples of manufacturing and production applications on pages 122, 126, and 141–143.

SALES AND MARKETING

Although the Internet may have not overwhelmed traditional retailing, it has spawned powerful new channels for reaching consumers and new digital products and services. A significant percentage of financial products and services, books, computers, music, video, and travel services are now purchased on the Web. Some of these products were actually created with Internet technology, such as online Web investing services and digital music.

The Internet has reduced consumer search costs and transaction costs, making it much easier to comparison shop and find the right combination of trust, fulfillment, customer service, and price to meet consumers' needs. Internet technologies can help differentiate products by using personalization, customization techniques, and community marketing techniques.

The Internet has broadened the scope of marketing communications by making it easier for firms to reach large numbers of people. The Internet has also increased the richness of marketing communications by combining text, video, and audio content into rich messages and providing capabilities for users to interactively control the experience. Personalized messages can be delivered at very low cost to individuals and groups. Finally, the Internet provides marketers with unparalleled, fine-grained, detailed real-time information about consumers as they transact on the Web. You can find examples of sales and marketing applications on pages 110–112, 120–123, and 141–143.

corporate Web sites to make them inaccessible. We explore Internet security, computer crime, and technology for secure electronic payments in greater detail in Chapters 5 and 14.

The Web provides an unprecedented ability to learn about and target customers. But the same capability can also undermine individual privacy. Companies collecting detailed customer information over the Web will need to balance their desire to profit from such information with the need to safeguard individual privacy.

Digitally enabling the enterprise with Internet technology requires careful management planning. The Manager's Toolkit lists some important questions managers should ask when exploring the use of the Internet for electronic commerce and electronic business.

MANAGEMENT WRAP-UP

Managers need to carefully review their strategy and business models to determine how to maximize the benefits of Internet technology. Managers should anticipate making organizational changes to take advantage of this technology, including new business processes, new relationships with the firm's value partners and customers, and even new business designs. Determining how and where to digitally enable the enterprise with Internet technology is a key management decision.

The Internet can dramatically reduce transaction and agency costs and is fueling new business models. By using the Internet and other networks for electronic commerce, organizations can exchange purchase and sale transactions directly with customers and suppliers, eliminating inefficient intermediaries. Organizational processes can be streamlined by using the Internet and intranets to make communication and coordination more efficient. To take advantage of these opportunities, organizational processes must be redesigned.

Internet technology has created a universal computing platform that has become the primary infrastructure for electronic business, electronic commerce, and the emerging digital firm. Web-based applications integrating voice, data, video, and audio are providing new products, services, and tools for communicating with employees and customers. Intranets enable companies to make information flow between disparate systems, business processes, and parts of the organization.

For Discussion:

1.   How does the Internet change consumer and supplier relationships?

2.   The Internet may not make corporations obsolete, but they will have to change their business models. Do you agree? Why or why not?

SUMMARY

1. *How has Internet technology changed value propositions and business models?* The Internet is rapidly becoming the infrastructure of choice for electronic commerce and electronic business because it provides a universal and easy-to-use set of technologies and technology standards that can be adopted by all organizations, no matter what computer system or information technology platform they are using. Internet technology provides a much lower cost and easier to use alternative for coordination activities than proprietary networks. Companies can use Internet technology to radically reduce their transaction costs.

The Internet radically reduces the cost of creating, sending, and storing information about products and services while making that information more widely available. Information is not limited to traditional physical methods of delivery. Customers can find out about products on their own on the Web and buy directly from product suppliers

instead of using intermediaries such as retail stores. This unbundling of information from traditional value chain channels is having a disruptive effect on old business models, and it is creating new business models as well. Some of the traditional channels for exchanging product information have become unnecessary or uneconomical, and business models based on the coupling of information with products and services may no longer be necessary.

The Internet shrinks information asymmetry and has transformed the relationship between information richness and reach. Using the Internet and Web multimedia capabilities, companies can quickly and inexpensively provide detailed product information and detailed information specific to each customer to very large numbers of people simultaneously. The Internet can help companies create and capture profit in new ways by adding extra value to existing products and services or by providing the foundation for new products and services. Many different business models for electronic commerce on the Internet have emerged, including virtual storefronts, information brokers, transaction brokers, online marketplaces, content providers, online service providers, virtual communities, and portals.

2. *What is electronic commerce? How has electronic commerce changed consumer retailing and business-to-business transactions?* Electronic commerce is the process of buying and selling goods electronically with computerized business transactions using the Internet or other digital network technology. It includes marketing, customer support, delivery, and payment. The three major types of electronic commerce are business-to-consumer (B2C), business-to-business (B2B), and consumer-to-consumer (C2C). Another way of classifying electronic commerce transactions is in terms of the participants' physical connection to the Web. Conventional e-commerce transactions, which take place over wired networks, can be distinguished from mobile commerce or m-commerce, the purchase of goods and services using handheld wireless devices.

The Internet provides a universally available set of technologies for electronic commerce that can be used to create new channels for marketing, sales, and customer support, and to eliminate intermediaries in buy and sell transactions. Interactive capabilities on the Web can be used to build closer relationships with customers in marketing and customer support. Firms can use various Web personalization technologies to deliver Web pages with content geared to the specific interests of each user, including technologies to deliver personalized information and ads through m-commerce channels. Companies can also reduce costs and improve customer service by using Web sites to provide helpful information as well as e-mail and even telephone access to customer service representatives.

B2B e-commerce generates efficiencies by enabling companies to electronically locate suppliers, solicit bids, place orders, and track shipments in transit. Businesses can use their own Web sites to sell to other businesses or use Net marketplaces or private industrial networks. Net marketplaces provide a single digital marketplace based on Internet technology for many buyers and sellers. Net marketplaces can be differentiated by whether they sell direct or indirect goods, support spot or long-term purchasing, or serve vertical or horizontal markets. Private industrial networks link a firm with its suppliers and other strategic business partners to develop highly efficient supply chains and to respond quickly to customer demands.

3. *What are the principal payment systems for electronic commerce?* The principal electronic payment systems for electronic commerce are credit card systems, digital wallets, accumulated balance digital payment systems, stored value systems, digital cash, peer-to-peer payment systems, electronic checks, and electronic billing presentment and payment systems. Accumulated balance systems, stored value systems (including smart cards), and digital cash are useful for small micropayments.

4. *How can Internet technology facilitate management and coordination of internal business processes and supply chain management?* Private, internal corporate networks called intranets can be created using Internet connectivity standards. Extranets are private intranets that are extended to selected organizations or individuals outside the firm. Intranets and extranets are forming the underpinnings of electronic business by providing a low-cost technology that can run on almost any computing platform. Organizations can use intranets to create collaboration environments for coordinating work and information sharing, and they can use intranets to make information flow between different functional areas of the firm. Intranets also provide a low-cost alternative for improving coordination among organizations' internal supply chain processes. Extranets can be used to coordinate supply chain processes shared with external organizations.

5. *What are the major managerial and organizational challenges posed by electronic business and electronic commerce?* Many new business models based on the Internet have not yet found proven ways to generate profits or reduce costs. Digitally enabling a firm for electronic commerce and electronic business requires far-reaching organizational change, including redesign of business processes; recasting relationships with customers, suppliers, and other business partners; and new roles for employees. Channel conflicts may erupt as the firm turns to the Internet as an alternative outlet for sales. Security, privacy, and legal issues pose additional electronic commerce challenges.

KEY TERMS

Accumulated balance digital payment system, 127

Banner ad, 117

Business model, 14

Business-to-business (B2B) electronic commerce, 118

Business-to-consumer (B2C) electronic commerce, 118

Call center, 123

Channel conflict, 136

Clicks-and-mortar, 118

Consumer-to-consumer (C2C) electronic commerce, 118

Digital cash, 127

Digital checking, 127

Digital credit card payment system, 126

Digital wallet, 127

Disintermediation, 119

Dynamic pricing, 116

Electronic billing presentment and payment systems, 127

Electronic payment system, 126

Exchange, 125

Information asymmetry, 114

Micropayment, 127

Mobile commerce (m-commerce), 118

Net marketplace, 124

Peer-to-peer payment system, 127

Pop-up ads, 117

Portal, 117

Private exchange, 123

Pure-play, 118

Reach, 115

Reintermediation, 119

Richness, 115

Search costs, 114

Smart card, 127

Stored value payment systems, 127

Syndicator, 117

Web personalization, 120

Review Questions

1. What are the advantages of using the Internet as the infrastructure for electronic commerce and electronic business?

2. How is the Internet changing the economics of information and business models?

3. Name and describe six Internet business models for electronic commerce. Distinguish between a pure-play Internet business model and a clicks-and-mortar business model.

4. Name and describe the various categories of electronic commerce.

5. How can the Internet facilitate sales and marketing to individual customers? Describe the role played by Web personalization.

6. How can the Internet help provide customer service?

7. How can Internet technology support business-to-business electronic commerce?

8. What are Net marketplaces? Why do they represent an important business model for B2B e-commerce? How do they differ from private industrial networks?

9. Name and describe the principal electronic payment systems used on the Internet.

10. Why are intranets so useful for electronic business?

11. How can intranets support organizational collaboration?

12. Describe the uses of intranets for electronic business in sales and marketing, human resources, finance and accounting, and manufacturing.

13. How can companies use Internet technology for supply chain management?

14. Describe the management challenges posed by electronic commerce and electronic business on the Internet.

15. What is channel conflict? Why is it becoming a growing problem in electronic commerce?

Application Software Exercise

SPREADSHEET EXERCISE: ANALYZING A DOT-COM BUSINESS

Pick one e-commerce company on the Internet such as Ashford.com, Buy.com, Yahoo.com or Priceline.com. Study the Web pages that describe the company and explain its purpose and structure. Look for articles at Web sites such as Bigcharts.com or Hoovers.com that comment upon the company. Then visit the Securities and Exchange Commission's Web site at <www.sec.gov> and access the company's 10-K forms showing income statements and balance sheets. Select only the sections of the 10-K form containing the desired portions of financial statements that you need to examine and download them into your spreadsheet. (Hint: When you find the page that lists specific forms, select the text version. Do not select the HTML version. The Laudon Web site for Chapter 4 provides more detailed instructions on how to download this 10-K data into a spreadsheet.) Create simplified spreadsheets of the company's balance sheets and income statements for the past three years.

Is the company a dot-com success, borderline business, or failure? What information is the basis of your decision? Why? When answering these questions, pay special attention to the company's three-year trends in revenues, costs of sales, gross margins, operating expenses, and net margins. The Laudon Web site provides definitions of these terms and how they are calculated. Prepare an overhead presentation (minimum of five slides), including appropriate spreadsheets or charts, and present your work to your professor and/or classmates. If the company is successful, what additional business strategies could it pursue to become even more successful? If the company is a borderline or failing business, what specific business strategies (if any) could make it more successful?

Group Project

Form a group with three or four of your classmates. Select two businesses that are competitors in the same industry and using their Web sites for electronic commerce. Visit their Web sites. You might compare, for example, the Web sites for virtual banking created by Citibank and Wells Fargo Bank, or the Internet trading Web sites of E*TRADE and Ameritrade. Prepare an evaluation of each business's Web site in terms of its functions, user friendliness, and how well it supports the company's business strategy. Which Web site does a better job? Why? Can you make some recommendations to improve these Web sites?

Tools for Interactive Learning

■ Internet Connection

The Internet Connection for this chapter will take you to several Web sites where you can complete an exercise to evaluate several virtual storefront businesses.

■ Interactive Study Guide

You can use the Interactive Study Guide to test your knowledge of the topics in this chapter and get instant feedback where you need more practice.

■ **RUNNING CASE**

The Running Case provides an opportunity for you to develop an e-commerce strategy and Web site for Dirt Bikes USA. You can find a complete description of this project on the Laudon Web site for Chapter 4 and on the Multimedia Edition CD-ROM.

■ **ELECTRONIC COMMERCE PROJECT**

At the Laudon Web site for Chapter 4, you will find an Electronic Commerce project where you can build an electronic commerce storefront.

■ **MANAGEMENT DECISION PROBLEM**

At the Laudon Web site for Chapter 4, you will find an Management Decision Problem on measuring the effectiveness of Web advertising.

■ **CD-ROM**

If you use the Multimedia Edition CD-ROM with this chapter, you can find an audio overview of the major themes of this chapter, a video clip on Danka Office Imaging's Web-based business, and bullet text summarizing the key points of the chapter.

CASE STUDY—*How Much Can the Internet Help GM?*

 General Motors (GM) is the world's largest automaker, with 386,000 employees in 50 countries. GM vehicle brands include Chevrolet, Pontiac, Buick, Cadillac, Saturn, and GMC Trucks. GM also has vehicle production relationships with Opel, Vauxhall, Subaru, and Alfa Romeo. Its nonvehicle ventures include Allison Transmission (manufacturer of medium and heavy-duty transmissions), GM Locomotives, and a 35 percent share of Hughes Electronics (producer of satellites and communications). GM's subsidiary, GM Acceptance Corp. (GMAC) is a major financing organization that specializes in financing GM vehicle purchases and home mortgages.

GM's auto sales have been declining, from about 60 percent of the U.S. vehicle market in the 1970s, to only 28 percent today. The company continues to face stiff competition from Ford, Daimler Chrysler, and the Japanese, all of which have lower production costs than GM—and reputations for cars with better styling and quality.

GM's sheer size has proved to be one of its greatest burdens. For 70 years, GM operated along the lines laid down by CEO Alfred Sloan, who rescued the firm from bankruptcy in the 1920s. Sloan separated the firm into five separate operating groups and divisions (Chevrolet, Pontiac, Oldsmobile—which is being phased out—Buick, and Cadillac). Each division functioned as a semiautonomous company with its own marketing operations. GM remained a far-flung vertically integrated corporation that at one time manufactured up to 70 percent of its own parts. This model of top-down control and decentralized execution had once been a powerful source of competitive advantage, enabling GM to build cars at lower cost than its rivals. Over time, however, it worked against the company. Domestic competitors such as Chrysler were able to make vehicles at lower costs because they could purchase their parts from outside vendors and bargain on pricing. GM was not able to move quickly to update its selection and styling, and the quality of its cars lagged behind Japanese and even U.S. rivals. It took GM more time and money than competitors to produce a car because the firm was saddled with a lumbering bureaucracy, inefficient production processes, and thousands of outdated "legacy" information systems that could not communicate with each other.

In February 2000, 47-year-old Rick Wagoner was appointed CEO of GM, replacing Jack Smith. At that time Wagoner stated four main goals for the corporation, including his intention to focus on innovative products and services and the development of e-business. Wagoner's management team believed that by intensively weaving Internet technology into all of its business processes, GM could become a smarter, leaner, faster company, more in tune with customers. It also hoped this technology would help GM reduce from 24 to 12 months the time to design, engineer, and manufacture a new vehicle, cutting up to 10 percent of the cost of making a vehicle by eliminating supply chain inefficiencies. Internet technology could be the catalyst for GM to reconstruct its entire value chain, transforming itself into a customer-focused business that provides many different electronic services to consumers, as well as cars.

In August 1999, GM had set up a new division called eGM headed by Mark Hogan specifically for this purpose. GM started dismantling eGM in late 2001, after the Internet bubble had burst. GM management claimed, however, that this change did not represent a retreat from e-business but was an acknowledgement e-business had been successfully integrated throughout the company and a separate business unit was no longer needed. Here are some of the areas where GM is continuing to rely on Internet technology.

Selling Vehicles Online

The role of dealers is fundamental to the sale of automobiles. In fact, the laws in most states make it extremely difficult for anyone other than licensed auto dealerships to sell new vehicles, thanks to the lobbying power of the National Auto Dealers Association (NADA). Dealers are vital to GM for several other reasons, including their close connection to their customers and to the automobile-purchasing public. "They understand what the online consumer is looking for," claims Scott McDonald, GM's director of e-sales. In addition, the dealers are essential because of their role in vehicle inventory. The process of making decisions about how many of which vehicles to produce requires a large inventory. The auto producers begin by making a guesstimate as to the number of each model to produce each year and in what color and with what options. The dealers in turn decide which of these vehicles they think they can sell and then make their purchases. Only then do customers begin to purchase, selecting from dealer inventories. To make the system work, the industry maintains about a two-month inventory of new vehicles. The value of GM's inventory is usually about $40 billion according to Hogan, making inventory costs very high. The dealer's role is crucial, because dealers hold most of this inventory and so assume much of the risk and expense of owning the vehicles.

GM has been experimenting with ways to sell vehicles online, although mostly with opposition from its dealers. They are concerned about GM trying to bypass them by selling vehicles online. GM does not actually sell vehicles directly online but provides Web sites with a range of services for both customers and dealers.

GMBuyPower.com, established in March 1999, is a Web site where visitors can browse for GM cars; search by color, options, and availability; and find a dealer in their area that stocks the car they want. The site indicates the cars those dealers have in inventory. Dealers involved in the BuyPower selling program are trained to work with customers who have done online car buying research and must surf every auto Web site that the customers could potentially have visited before landing at GM. This approach is proving highly successful. Since September 2001, GMBuyPower has generated more than 2000 leads to dealers per day and over 20 percent of those leads convert into auto purchases.

The GM Owner Center, launched in January 2002, stores maintenance records and manuals for current GM owners and also provides service reminders and tools for estimating vehicle value.

DealerWorld is a Web portal featuring applications such a VIN (vehicle identification number) lookup, which helps dealers determine which incentives a buyer qualifies for on a specific model.

GMAC SmartAuction is a Web site where GM dealers can bid for leased vehicles that were returned to dealers and are now owned by GM's finance arm GMAC (General Motors Acceptance Corporation.) This system is faster than live auctions and reduces the chances autos will be damaged while being transported to a physical auction site.

Building Vehicles to Order

One major weakness in the system of determining what to build is that if the manufacturers or the dealers guess wrong on total demand or on style, color, and other options, they must offer costly incentives to prod consumers to purchase these products. Auto producers are anxious to make cars that customers have actually ordered. "Build-to-order" has been around the auto industry for a long time, but only for very expensive cars, and it required a waiting period of two to three months before delivery. U.S. automakers have recently reduced wait time for ordered vehicles to six or seven weeks, and Toyota North America, the real leader, delivers a built-to-order vehicle in less than a month. Build-to-order would greatly reduce finished vehicle inventory costs as well as generate other production cost savings, potentially saving GM $20 billion per year.

Achieving this goal will require heavy reliance on GM's Internet infrastructure and extensive organizational change. The company will have to be able to take orders online, link its factories and suppliers online, change vehicle designs so they can be built more easily using modules, and greatly cut shipping times. Build-to-order requires producers to carry larger work-in-process inventories, a reversal of the 20-year trend of just-in-time component supply deliveries. According to James Mateyka, an automotive consultant at A. T. Kearney, "You would now need to hold, skillfully, inventories of certain kinds of parts [modules], such that you can be flexible enough to take a generically defined car, then at the last minute suddenly have a defined car."

In order to link factories to suppliers via cyberspace and reduce procurement and inventory costs, GM and other major auto manufacturers have established Covisint, a massive Net marketplace described in Section 4.2 of this chapter. GM spends $87 billion per year on raw materials and components and believes Covisint could cut the cost of producing each vehicle by perhaps $1,000 (estimates vary) as well as reduce the time from receiving a car order on-line to delivery from about 45 days to 10 days. Covisint is linked to GM's own private industrial network, called GMSupplyPower. This extranet gives suppliers access to the latest information on production scheduling, inventory, and the quality of their parts.

Online Services

Another information age venture GM has established is its wholly owned subsidiary, OnStar. It is a telematics system with onboard navigation, Internet, safety, and communications capabilities accessed through three buttons on the vehicle dashboard. A GPS (global positioning system) keeps the system constantly informed as to the location of the vehicle on the road. OnStar provides such services as emergency roadside assistance, stolen-vehicle tracking, and concierge support such as making dinner reservations.

OnStar Personal Calling enables drivers to make and receive hands-free calls with voice-activated phones. The OnStar Virtual Advisor service allows users to retrieve personal data on the Web, including e-mail, news, stock quotes, and traffic and road-condition reports within a given radius of the driver's location. Whether the hardware is standard or an option, any user of OnStar will pay an annual subscription fee ranging from $17 to $70 per month, depending on the services taken.

With OnStar, GM cars become a platform that generates a continuous stream of high-margin revenue from drivers downloading and paying by the minute for Internet, data, and telecommunications services. With 70 percent of wireless telephone minutes logged in vehicles, GM could eventually become the largest reseller of cellular minutes in the United States. The service already has close to 1 million subscribers. GM has licensed OnStar to Honda and Toyota, and it will also be providing them such services as roadside assistance as well.

OnStar has nearly 2 million subscribers but it is not yet profitable. Customers are balking at the monthly subscription fees and nearly half of OnStar subscribers don't renew their service after the first year. Since OnStar subsidizes some of the cost of its hardware installed in GM cars, getting customers to renew is critical.

Internal Uses

GM used to be hampered by thousands of incompatible systems that prevented it from streamlining and coordinating design and production. Since the early 1980s the company has tried to standardize and integrate these systems and this effort has accelerated under GM's current CIO Ralph Szygenda. One of GM's most effective uses of Internet technology has been to set up a collaborative engineering system that allows GM employees to share product design information. More than 16,000 designers and other workers use a Web-based product-life-cycle management system from Electronic Data Systems Corp. (EDS) called Teamcenter Engineer7 to share 3-D designs and keep track of parts and subassemblies. The system automatically updates the design data when changes are finalized so everyone can coordinate their work on the same design. Parts of the system have been extended to GM's parts suppliers who design the subsystems for GM cars. In the past, synchronizing design work among many different groups was a time-consuming manual process because GM lacked systems that could coordinate complex designs across its 14 engineering sites and external design partners. GM's new collaboration system has helped cut the time to complete a full mock-up of a car from 12 weeks to 2.

General Motors created an intranet portal called Socrates that enables users to search all of GM's internal sites from one starting point. Today 100,000 GM employees around the globe can access more than 500 internal GM sites through this portal. Employees can use Socrates to access their human resources information, participate in online training programs, and search through a repository of best practices. Socrates has capabilities for enabling employees to tailor the information they obtain to their own needs, making it easy for them to use. GM is even subsidizing the cost of home access for its employees because it wants to make the Internet a more integral part of their daily lives.

Two decades of restructuring and reorganization have brought about deep changes at GM, paring down the waste and overbloated bureaucracy. The company has slashed the time required to develop and produce a car from 48 to 18 months, eliminating $1 billion in engineering costs. It has also developed new online sales channels and sources of revenue. At the same time GM has made remarkable improvements in quality, with its quality ranking jumping to No. 3 behind Toyota Motor Corp and Honda Motor Corp. GM is becoming highly skilled in selling over the Internet. Can these efforts stop the decline in GM's market share? Foreign automakers are consolidating their grip on the U.S. auto market. Despite shedding tens of thousands of workers, chopping billions of dollars per year off of costs, and eliminating models, GM remains under heavy pressure to boost low profit margins.

GM's CIO Szygenda has said that "the [automobile production] company that links design, procurement and sales—and puts it all together electronically—wins." Will his words be borne out? Can GM use the Internet to transform its hidebound bureaucracy, and will this be enough to boost profits over the long run? GM remains burdened with very high fixed costs for pension and health care benefits. The company downsized so much that it must support 2.5 retirees for each active worker in the United States. In a business with narrow profit margins, such costs can be decisive. Ultimately, e-business won't mean very much if GM can't significantly increase its market share. GM has beefed up its design team and produced some of the most advanced designs in the automotive world, but this is still a weak spot. If GM has the greatest technology and technology services, but continues to be perceived as building uninspired vehicles, how much can e-business help?

Sources: Sean Gallagher, "Grand Test," *Baseline Magazine,* November, 2002; Steve Konicki, "Time Trials," *InformationWeek,* June 3, 2002; Derek Slater, "GM Proves E-Business Matters," *CIO Magazine,* April 1, 2002; Gregory L. White, "In-Car Internet Services Stall on Cost, Skeptical Customers," *Wall Street Journal,* April 9, 2002; Bob Tedeschi, "Going Online to Buy a Car," *New York Times,"* September 16, 2002; Faith Keenan and Spencer E. Ante, "The New Teamwork," *Business-Week,* February 18, 2002; Danny Hakim, "Is It G.M.'s Turn to Be the Favorite?" *New York Times,* March 3, 2002 and "What's Good for the Country Is Good for G.M.," *New York Times*, February 26, 2002; John Galvin, "Racing the Clock," *Smart Business Magazine,* May 2001; Antone Gonsalves, "IT's the Tiger in Their Tanks," *InformationWeek,* September 17, 2001; Jason Black, "Build Lasting Partnerships, " *Internet World*, August 1, 2001; Peter D. Henig, "The New Thin Client?" *Red Herring,* May 2001; Joseph B. White, Gregory L. White, and Horihiko Shirouzu, "Soon, the Big Three Won't Be, as Foreigners Make Inroads in U.S.," *Wall Street Journal*, August 13, 2001; Keith Bradsher, "G.M. Phaseout of Olds Is at Center of a Range of Cutbacks," *New York Times*, December 13, 2000; Dale Buss, "Custom Cars Stuck in Gridlock," *The Industry Standard,* October 16, 2000; Dale Buss, "The Race to Be Wired," *The Industry Standard*, September 4, 2000; Lee Copeland, "Automakers Put Workers Online," *Computerworld*, November 3, 2000; Lee Copeland, "General Motors' CIO Touts Corporate Benefits Portal," *Computerworld*, November 27, 2000; Lee Copeland, "GM Now Sells Web Technology, Not Just Cars," *Computerworld*, June, 5, 2000; Lee Copeland, "GM Shuts Doors on GMDriverSite.com," *Computerworld*, September 4, 2000; Sari Kalin, "Overdrive," *CIO Web Business Magazine*, July 1, 2000; Julia King and Lee Copeland, "GM Retools for E-Commerce That Goes Well Beyond Cars," *Computerworld*, April 17, 2000; Todd Lassa, "General Motors Is Making a Major Internet Play, and It's Put a Real 'Car Guy' Behind the Wheel. But Can He Drive an E-Business?" *Internet World*, March 1, 2000; Kathleen Melymuka, "GM Deal for Web-Based Dealership Software Falls Through," *Computerworld*, November 16, 2000; Robert L. Simison, "GM Retools to Sell Custom Cars Online," *Wall Street Journal*, February 22, 2000; Paul Strassmann, "GM's Info Gamble," *Computerworld*, June 5, 2000; Lauren Gibbons Paul, "The Biggest Gamble Yet," *CIO Magazine*, April 15, 2000; Todd Weiss, "GM to Begin Selling Oldsmobiles Online in Web-Site Pilot Program," *Computerworld*, September 19, 2000; Steve Ulfelder, "Internet Drag Race," *Computerworld*, March 6, 2000; Ken Yamada, "Shop Talk: Car Dealers, Customers Both Win on Web," *Red Herring*, September 26, 2000; Eric Young, "Stalled on the Digital Highway," *The Industry Standard*, September 4, 2000; and Jennifer Zaino, "OnStar Expands Services for Drivers," *InformationWeek*, November 14, 2000.

CASE STUDY QUESTIONS

1. Analyze GM using the competitive forces and value chain models.

2. Evaluate the current business strategy of GM in response to its competitive environment. What is the role of Internet technology in that strategy? How successful is that strategy?

3. Evaluate each of GM's e-commerce and e-business initiatives described in this case. How much value can they bring the company?

4. What management, organization, and technology issues do you think GM has had to face and will need to solve in implementing its Internet strategy?

5. How will GM have to redesign its business processes to be able to compete successfully and achieve a leading role in the new economy?

6. In GM's drive to sell cars online and to build-to-order, what are some of the problems that technology cannot address?

ETHICAL AND SOCIAL ISSUES IN THE DIGITAL FIRM

objectives

One of your managerial responsibilities is to make informed decisions that reflect an understanding of the ethical and social issues as well as the business issues surrounding the use of information systems. After reading this chapter, you will be able to answer the following questions:

1. *What ethical, social, and political issues are raised by information systems?*

2. *Are there specific principles for conduct that can be used to guide decisions about ethical dilemmas?*

3. *Why does contemporary information systems technology pose challenges to the protection of individual privacy and intellectual property?*

4. *How have information systems affected everyday life?*

5. *How can organizations develop corporate policies for ethical conduct?*

BT Cellnet Tests the Waters for Spamming

In the United Kingdom, using mobile phones for sending short text messages has skyrocketed, especially among teenagers and young adults. This is a demographic group that advertisers are anxious to reach. BT Cellnet, an operator of mobile phone services, is experimenting with using its text messaging service as a marketing channel. Mobile phone carriers maintain a great deal of demographic data from users when they sign up for their services, which marketers could use to target their advertisements more precisely to different age and income groups. On the whole, U.K. mobile service operators have been protective of their customers and aggressive about beaming unsolicited electronic messages to them. But the potential revenue stream from using these unsolicited messages, also known as *spam,* to market goods and services is so alluring that some carriers are quietly starting to test the waters.

Working with Enpocket, a spinoff of Engage, a U.S. enterprise marketing software firm, BT Cellnet started testing ads beamed as short text messages to its mobile phone users. One portion of its initial target group consisted of 3,000 customers who agreed beforehand to have advertising messages sent to them in exchange for a chance to win a 1000 U.K. pound (U.S. $1,400) prize. The other portion of the group consisted of 1000 customers who were beamed messages even though they didn't explicitly sign up for the program but were told how to stop the messages if they wished.

The use of spam in m-commerce has been criticized by privacy advocates and others concerned with ethical business practices. Many people resent being beamed electronic advertisements unless they have voluntarily signed up to receive them. The cost and "nuisance factor" for unsolicited mobile phone messages is much greater than for unsolicited postal mail. Unlike postal junk mail, the cost of electronic spam is generally borne by its recipients, who are charged for both sending and receiving short text messages. But one person's spam is another person's business model and some electronic pitches provide benefits. Alastair Tempest, director-general of the European Direct Marketing Association, points out that direct marketing is much more targeted than unsolicited spam and that a ban on spam would hamper "legitimate" marketing.

Sources: Brian McDonough, "BT Cellnet Tests the Water for Mobile Ads," *mBusiness*, February 2002; and Brandon Mitchener, "All Spam, All the Time, "*Wall Street Journal*, October 29, 2001.

MANAGEMENT CHALLENGES

Technology can be a double-edged sword. It can be the source of many benefits. One great achievement of contemporary computer systems is the ease with which digital information can be analyzed, transmitted, and shared among many people. But at the same time, this powerful capability creates new opportunities for breaking the law or taking benefits away from others. Balancing the convenience and privacy implications of using m-commerce technology to track consumers and send unsolicited e-mail is one of the compelling ethical issues raised by contemporary information systems. As you read this chapter, you should be aware of the following management challenges:

1. **Understanding the moral risks of new technology.** Rapid technological change means that the choices facing individuals also rapidly change, and the balance of risk and reward and the probabilities of apprehension for wrongful acts change as well. Protecting individual privacy has become a serious ethical issue precisely for this reason, in addition to other issues described in this chapter. In this environment it will be important for management to conduct an ethical and social impact analysis of new technologies. One might take each of the moral dimensions described in this chapter and briefly speculate on how a new technology will impact each dimension. There may not always be right answers for how to behave but there should be management awareness on the moral risks of new technology.

2. **Establishing corporate ethics policies that include information systems issues.** As managers you will be responsible for developing, enforcing, and explaining corporate ethics policies. Historically, corporate management has paid much more attention to financial integrity and personnel policies than to the information systems area. But from what you will know after reading this chapter, it is clear your corporation should have an ethics policy in the information systems area covering such issues as privacy, property, accountability, system quality, and quality of life. The challenge will be in educating non-IS managers to the need for these policies, as well as educating your workforce.

The Internet and electronic commerce have awakened new interest in the ethical and social impact of information systems. Internet and digital firm technologies that make it easier than ever to assemble, integrate, and distribute information have unleashed new concerns about appropriate use of customer information, the protection of personal privacy, and the protection of intellectual property. These issues have moved to the forefront of social and political debate in the United States and many other countries.

Although protecting personal privacy and intellectual property on the Internet are now in the spotlight, there are other pressing ethical issues raised by the widespread use of information systems. They include establishing accountability for the consequences of information systems, setting standards to safeguard system quality that protect the safety of the individual and society, and preserving values and institutions considered essential to the quality of life in an information society. This chapter describes these issues and suggests guidelines for dealing with these questions, with special attention to the ethical challenges posed by the Internet.

5.1 UNDERSTANDING ETHICAL AND SOCIAL ISSUES RELATED TO SYSTEMS

ethics

Principles of right and wrong that can be used by individuals acting as free moral agents to make choices to guide their behavior.

Ethics refers to the principles of right and wrong that individuals, acting as free moral agents, use to make choices to guide their behavior. Information technology and information systems raise new ethical questions for both individuals and societies because they create opportunities for intense social change, and thus threaten existing distributions of power, money, rights, and obligations. Like other technologies, such as steam engines, electricity, telephone, and radio, information technology can be used to achieve social progress, but it can also be used to commit crimes and threaten cherished social values. The development of information technology will produce benefits for many, and costs for others. When using information systems, it is essential to ask, what is the ethical and socially responsible course of action?

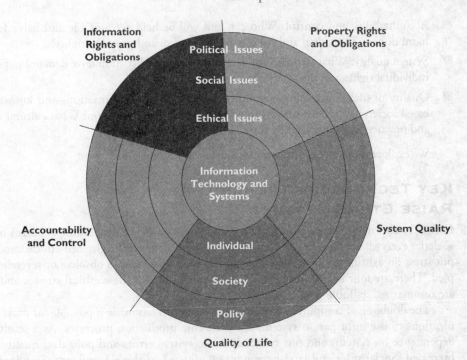

Information Rights and Obligations

Property Rights and Obligations

Political Issues

Social Issues

Ethical Issues

Information Technology and Systems

Accountability and Control

System Quality

Individual

Society

Polity

Quality of Life

Figure 5-1 The relationship between ethical, social, and political issues in an information society. The introduction of new information technology has a ripple effect, raising new ethical, social, and political issues that must be dealt with on the individual, social, and political levels. These issues have five moral dimensions: information rights and obligations, property rights and obligations, system quality, quality of life, and accountability and control.

A MODEL FOR THINKING ABOUT ETHICAL, SOCIAL, AND POLITICAL ISSUES

Ethical, social, and political issues are closely linked. The ethical dilemma you may face as a manager of information systems typically is reflected in social and political debate. One way to think about these relationships is given in Figure 5-1. Imagine society as a more or less calm pond on a summer day, a delicate ecosystem in partial equilibrium with individuals and with social and political institutions. Individuals know how to act in this pond because social institutions (family, education, organizations) have developed well-honed rules of behavior, and these are backed by laws developed in the political sector that prescribe behavior and promise sanctions for violations. Now toss a rock into the center of the pond. But imagine instead of a rock that the disturbing force is a powerful shock of new information technology and systems hitting a society more or less at rest. What happens? Ripples, of course.

Suddenly individual actors are confronted with new situations often not covered by the old rules. Social institutions cannot respond overnight to these ripples—it may take years to develop etiquette, expectations, social responsibility, "politically correct" attitudes, or approved rules. Political institutions also require time before developing new laws and often require the demonstration of real harm before they act. In the meantime, you may have to act. You may be forced to act in a legal "gray area."

We can use this model to illustrate the dynamics that connect ethical, social, and political issues. This model is also useful for identifying the main moral dimensions of the "information society," which cut across various levels of action—individual, social, and political.

MORAL DIMENSIONS OF THE INFORMATION AGE

The major ethical, social, and political issues raised by information systems include the following moral dimensions:

- Information rights and obligations: What **information rights** do individuals and organizations possess with respect to information about themselves? What can they protect? What obligations do individuals and organizations have concerning this information?

- Property rights: How will traditional intellectual property rights be protected in a digital society in which tracing and accounting for ownership is difficult, and ignoring such property rights is so easy?

information rights

The rights that individuals and organizations have with respect to information that pertains to themselves.

■ Accountability and control: Who can and will be held accountable and liable for the harm done to individual and collective information and property rights?

■ System quality: What standards of data and system quality should we demand to protect individual rights and the safety of society?

■ Quality of life: What values should be preserved in an information- and knowledge-based society? What institutions should we protect from violation? What cultural values and practices are supported by the new information technology?

We explore these moral dimensions in detail in Section 5.3.

KEY TECHNOLOGY TRENDS THAT RAISE ETHICAL ISSUES

Ethical issues long preceded information technology—they are the abiding concerns of free societies everywhere. Nevertheless, information technology has heightened ethical concerns, put stress on existing social arrangements, and made existing laws obsolete or severely crippled. There are four key technological trends responsible for these ethical stresses and they are summarized in Table 5-1.

The doubling of computing power every 18 months has made it possible for most organizations to use information systems for their core production processes. As a result, our dependence on systems and our vulnerability to system errors and poor data quality have increased. Social rules and laws have not yet adjusted to this dependence. Standards for ensuring the accuracy and reliability of information systems (see Chapter 14) are not universally accepted or enforced.

Advances in data storage techniques and rapidly declining storage costs have been responsible for the multiplying databases on individuals—employees, customers, and potential customers—maintained by private and public organizations. These advances in data storage have made the routine violation of individual privacy both cheap and effective. Already massive data storage systems are cheap enough for regional and even local retailing firms to use in identifying customers.

Advances in data analysis techniques for large pools of data are a third technological trend that heightens ethical concerns, because they enable companies to find out much detailed personal information about individuals. With contemporary information systems technology, companies can assemble and combine the myriad pieces of information stored on you by computers much more easily than in the past. Think of all the ways you generate computer information about yourself—credit card purchases, telephone calls, magazine subscriptions, video rentals, mail-order purchases, banking records, and local, state, and federal government records (including court and police records). Put together and mined properly, this information could reveal not only your credit information but also your driving habits, your tastes, your associations, and your political interests.

TABLE 5-1	TECHNOLOGY TRENDS THAT RAISE ETHICAL ISSUES	
Trend	**Impact**	
Computing power doubles every 18 months	More organizations depend on computer systems for critical operations	
Rapidly declining data storage costs	Organizations can easily maintain detailed databases on individuals	
Data analysis advances	Companies can analyze vast quantities of data gathered on individuals to develop detailed profiles of individual behavior	
Networking advances and the Internet	Copying data from one location to another and accessing personal data from remote locations are much easier.	

Companies with products to sell purchase relevant information from these sources to help them more finely target their marketing campaigns. Chapter 3 and 7 describe how companies can analyze large pools of data from multiple sources to rapidly identify buying patterns of customers and suggest individual responses. The use of computers to combine data from multiple sources and create electronic dossiers of detailed information on individuals is called **profiling.** For example, hundreds of Web sites allow DoubleClick <www.doubleclick. net>, an Internet advertising broker, to track the activities of their visitors in exchange for revenue from advertisements based on visitor information DoubleClick gathers. DoubleClick uses this information to create a profile of each online visitor, adding more detail to the profile as the visitor accesses an associated DoubleClick site. Over time DoubleClick can create a detailed dossier of a person's spending and computing habits on the Web that can be sold to companies to help them target their Web ads more precisely.

A new data analysis technology called **non-obvious relationship awareness (NORA)** has given both government and the private sector even more powerful profiling capabilities. NORA can take information about people from many disparate sources, such as employment applications, telephone records, customer listings, and "wanted" lists, and correlate relationships to find obscure hidden connections that might help identify criminals or terrorists (see Figure 5-2). NORA technology can scan data and extract information as the data are being generated so that it could, for example, instantly discover a man at an airline ticket counter who shares a phone number with a known terrorist before that person boards an airplane. The technology could prove a valuable tool for homeland security but does have privacy implications.

Last, advances in networking, including the Internet, promise to reduce greatly the costs of moving and accessing large quantities of data, and open the possibility of mining large pools of data remotely using small desktop machines, permitting an invasion of privacy on a scale and precision heretofore unimaginable.

The development of global digital-superhighway communication networks widely available to individuals and businesses poses many ethical and social concerns. Who will account for the flow of information over these networks? Will you be able to trace information collected

profiling

The use of computers to combine data from multiple sources and create electronic dossiers of detailed information on individuals.

non-obvious relationship awareness (NORA)

Technology that can find obscure hidden connections between people or other entities by analyzing information from many different sources to correlate relationships.

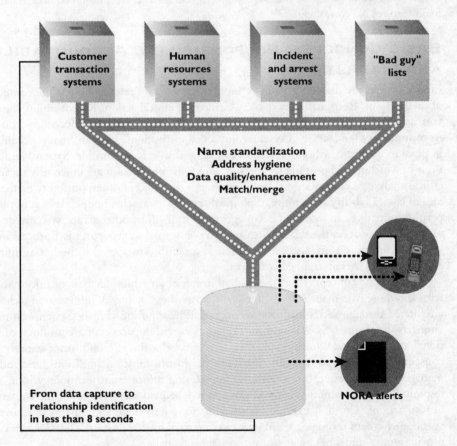

Figure 5-2 Non-Obvious Relationship Awareness (NORA). NORA technology can take information about people from disparate sources and find obscure, non-obvious relationships. It might discover, for example, that an applicant for a job at a casino shares a telephone number with a known criminal and issue an alert to the hiring manager.

Credit card purchases can make personal information available to market researchers, telephone marketers, and direct mail companies. Advances in information technology facilitate the invasion of privacy.

about you? What will these networks do to the traditional relationships between family, work, and leisure? How will traditional job designs be altered when millions of "employees" become subcontractors using mobile offices for which they themselves must pay?

In the next section we consider some ethical principles and analytical techniques for dealing with these kinds of ethical and social concerns.

5.2   ETHICS IN AN INFORMATION SOCIETY

Ethics is a concern of humans who have freedom of choice. Ethics is about individual choice: When faced with alternative courses of action, what is the correct moral choice? What are the main features of "ethical choice"?

BASIC CONCEPTS: RESPONSIBILITY, ACCOUNTABILITY, AND LIABILITY

responsibility

Accepting the potential costs, duties, and obligations for the decisions one makes.

accountability

The mechanisms for assessing responsibility for decisions made and actions taken.

liability

The existence of laws that permit individuals to recover the damages done to them by other actors, systems, or organizations.

due process

A process in which laws are well-known and understood and there is an ability to appeal to higher authorities to ensure that laws are applied correctly.

Ethical choices are decisions made by individuals who are responsible for the consequences of their actions. **Responsibility** is a key element of ethical action. Responsibility means that you accept the potential costs, duties, and obligations for the decisions you make. **Accountability** is a feature of systems and social institutions: It means that mechanisms are in place to determine who took responsible action, who is responsible. Systems and institutions in which it is impossible to find out who took what action are inherently incapable of ethical analysis or ethical action. Liability extends the concept of responsibility further to the area of laws. **Liability** is a feature of political systems in which a body of laws is in place that permits individuals to recover the damages done to them by other actors, systems, or organizations. **Due process** is a related feature of law-governed societies and is a process in which laws are known and understood and there is an ability to appeal to higher authorities to ensure that the laws are applied correctly.

These basic concepts form the underpinning of an ethical analysis of information systems and those who manage them. First, as discussed in Chapter 3, information technologies are filtered through social institutions, organizations, and individuals. Systems do not have "impacts" by themselves. Whatever information system impacts exist are products of institutional, organizational, and individual actions and behaviors. Second, responsibility for the consequences of technology falls clearly on the institutions, organizations, and individual managers who choose to use the technology. Using information technology in a "socially responsible" manner means that you can and will be held accountable for the consequences of your actions. Third, in an ethical political society, individuals and others can recover damages done to them through a set of laws characterized by due process. The Manager's Toolkit provides some guidelines for performing an ethical analysis.

MIS IN ACTION: MANAGER'S TOOLKIT

HOW TO CONDUCT AN ETHICAL ANALYSIS

When confronted with a situation that presents ethical issues, how should you analyze and reason about the situation? Here is a five-step process to guide your decision making:

1. *Identify and describe clearly the facts.* Find out who did what to whom, and where, when, and how. In many instances, you will be surprised at the errors in the initially reported facts, and often you will find that simply getting the facts straight helps define the solution. It also helps to get the opposing parties involved in an ethical dilemma to agree on the facts.

2. *Define the conflict or dilemma and identify the higher-order values involved.* Ethical, social, and political issues always reference higher values. The parties to a dispute all claim to be pursuing higher values (e.g., freedom, privacy, protection of property, and the free enterprise system). Typically, an ethical issue involves a dilemma: two diametrically opposed courses of action that support worthwhile values. For example, the chapter-opening vignette and the Window on Organizations

illustrate two competing values: the need for companies to use marketing to become more efficient and the need to protect individual privacy.

3. *Identify the stakeholders.* Every ethical, social, and political issue has stakeholders: players in the game who have an interest in the outcome, who have invested in the situation, and usually who have vocal opinions. Find out the identity of these groups and what they want. This will be useful later when designing a solution.

4. *Identify the options that you can reasonably take.* You may find that none of the options satisfy all the interests involved, but that some options do a better job than others. Sometimes arriving at a "good" or ethical solution may not always be a "balancing" of consequences to stakeholders.

5. *Identify the potential consequences of your options.* Some options may be ethically correct, but disastrous from other points of view. Other options may work in this one instance, but not in other similar instances. Always ask yourself, "What if I choose this option consistently over time?"

CANDIDATE ETHICAL PRINCIPLES

Once your analysis is complete, what ethical principles or rules should you use to make a decision? What higher-order values should inform your judgment? Although you are the only one who can decide which among many ethical principles you will follow, and how you will prioritize them, it is helpful to consider some ethical principles with deep roots in many cultures that have survived throughout recorded history.

1. Do unto others as you would have them do unto you (the Golden Rule). Putting yourself into the place of others, and thinking of yourself as the object of the decision, can help you think about "fairness" in decision making.

2. If an action is not right for everyone to take, then it is not right for anyone (**Immanuel Kant's Categorical Imperative**). Ask yourself, "If everyone did this, could the organization, or society, survive?"

3. If an action cannot be taken repeatedly, then it is not right to take at all (**Descartes' rule of change**). This is the slippery-slope rule: An action may bring about a small change now that is acceptable, but if repeated would bring unacceptable changes in the long run. In the vernacular, it might be stated as "once started down a slippery path you may not be able to stop."

4. Take the action that achieves the higher or greater value (**the Utilitarian Principle**). This rule assumes you can prioritize values in a rank order and understand the consequences of various courses of action.

5. Take the action that produces the least harm, or the least potential cost (**Risk Aversion Principle**). Some actions have extremely high failure costs of very low probability (e.g., building a nuclear generating facility in an urban area) or extremely high failure costs of moderate probability (speeding and automobile accidents). Avoid these high failure cost actions, paying greater attention obviously to high failure cost potential of moderate to high probability.

6. Assume that virtually all tangible and intangible objects are owned by someone else unless there is a specific declaration otherwise. (This is the **ethical "no free lunch" rule.**) If something someone else has created is useful to you, it has value, and you should assume the creator wants compensation for this work.

Although these ethical rules cannot be guides to action, actions that do not easily pass these rules deserve some very close attention and a great deal of caution. The appearance of unethical behavior may do as much harm to you and your company as actual unethical behavior.

Immanuel Kant's Categorical Imperative
A principle that states that if an action is not right for everyone to take it is not right for anyone.

Descartes' rule of change
A principle that states that if an action cannot be taken repeatedly, then it is not right to be taken at any time.

Utilitarian Principle
Principle that assumes one can put values in rank order and understand the consequences of various courses of action.

Risk Aversion Principle
Principle that one should take the action that produces the least harm or incurs the least cost.

ethical "no free lunch" rule
Assumption that all tangible and intangible objects are owned by someone else, unless there is a specific declaration otherwise, and that the creator wants compensation for this work.

PROFESSIONAL CODES OF CONDUCT

When groups of people claim to be professionals, they take on special rights and obligations because of their special claims to knowledge, wisdom, and respect. Professional codes of conduct are promulgated by associations of professionals such as the American Medical Association (AMA), the American Bar Association (ABA), the Association of Information Technology Professionals (AITP), and the Association of Computing Machinery (ACM). These professional groups take responsibility for the partial regulation of their professions by determining entrance qualifications and competence. Codes of ethics are promises by professions to regulate themselves in the general interest of society. For example, avoiding harm to others, honoring property rights (including intellectual property), and respecting privacy are among the General Moral Imperatives of the ACM's Code of Ethics and Professional Conduct (ACM, 1993).

SOME REAL-WORLD ETHICAL DILEMMAS

Information systems have created new ethical dilemmas in which one set of interests is pitted against another. For example, many of the large telephone companies in the United States are using information technology to reduce the sizes of their workforces. Voice recognition software reduces the need for human operators by allowing computers to recognize a customer's responses to a series of computerized questions.

Many companies monitor what their employees are doing on the Internet to prevent them from wasting company resources on nonbusiness activities. Computer Associates International fired at least 10 employees at its Herndon office in December 2000 for sending sexually explicit e-mail. Xerox Corporation fired 40 workers in 1999 for spending too much of their work time surfing the Web. Firms believe they have the right to monitor employee e-mail and Web use because they own the facilities, intend their use to be for business purposes only, and create the facility for a business purpose (see the Chapter 8 Window on Management).

In each instance, you can find competing values at work, with groups lined on either side of a debate. A company may argue, for example, that it has a right to use information systems to increase productivity and reduce the size of its workforce to lower costs and stay in business. Employees displaced by information systems may argue that employers have some responsibility for their welfare. Business owners might feel obligated to monitor employee e-mail and Internet use to minimize drains on productivity (Urbaczewski and Jessup, 2002). Employees might believe they should be able to use the Internet for short personal tasks in place of the telephone. A close analysis of the facts can sometimes produce compromised solutions that give each side "half a loaf." Try to apply some of the principles of ethical analysis described to each of these cases. What is the right thing to do?

SurfControl offers tools for tracking Web and e-mail activity and for filtering unauthorized e-mail and Web site content. The benefits of monitoring employee e-mail and Internet use should be balanced with the need to respect employee privacy.

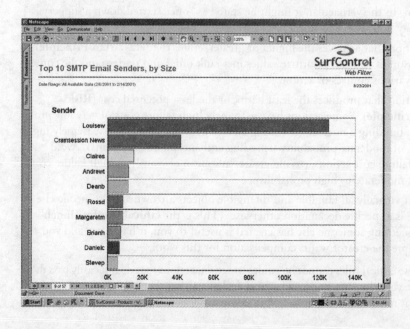

5.3 THE MORAL DIMENSIONS OF INFORMATION SYSTEMS

In this section, we take a closer look at the five moral dimensions of information systems first described in Figure 5-1. In each dimension we identify the ethical, social, and political levels of analysis and use real-world examples to illustrate the values involved, the stakeholders, and the options chosen.

INFORMATION RIGHTS: PRIVACY AND FREEDOM IN THE INTERNET AGE

Privacy is the claim of individuals to be left alone, free from surveillance or interference from other individuals or organizations, including the state. Claims to privacy are also involved at the workplace: Millions of employees are subject to electronic and other forms of high-tech surveillance (Ball, 2001). Information technology and systems threaten individual claims to privacy by making the invasion of privacy cheap, profitable, and effective.

The claim to privacy is protected in the U.S., Canadian, and German constitutions in a variety of different ways, and in other countries through various statutes. In the United States, the claim to privacy is protected primarily by the First Amendment guarantees of freedom of speech and association, Fourth Amendment protection against unreasonable search and seizure of one's personal documents or home, and the guarantee of due process. Table 5-2 describes the major U.S. federal statutes that set forth the conditions for handling information about individuals in such areas as credit reporting, education, financial records, newspaper records, and electronic communications. The Privacy Act of 1974 has been the most important of these laws, regulating the federal government's collection, use, and disclosure of information. At present, most U.S. federal privacy laws apply only to the federal government and regulate very few areas of the private sector.

Most American and European privacy law is based on a regime called Fair Information Practices (FIP) first set forth in a report written in 1973 by a federal government advisory committee (U.S. Department of Health, Education, and Welfare, 1973). **Fair Information Practices (FIP)** is a set of principles governing the collection and use of information about individuals. FIP principles are based on the notion of a "mutuality of interest" between the record holder and the individual. The individual has an interest in engaging in a transaction, and the record keeper—usually a business or government agency—requires information

privacy

The claim of individuals to be left alone, free from surveillance or interference from other individuals, organizations, or the state.

Fair Information Practices (FIP)

A set of principles originally set forth in 1973 that governs the collection and use of information about individuals and forms the basis of most U.S. and European privacy laws.

TABLE 5-2	FEDERAL PRIVACY LAWS IN THE UNITED STATES

General Federal Privacy Laws

Freedom of Information Act, 1966 as Amended (5 USC 552)

Privacy Act of 1974 as Amended (5 USC 552a)

Electronic Communications Privacy Act of 1986

Computer Matching and Privacy Protection Act of 1988

Computer Security Act of 1987

Federal Managers Financial Integrity Act of 1982

Privacy Laws Affecting Private Institutions

Fair Credit Reporting Act of 1970

Family Educational Rights and Privacy Act of 1974

Right to Financial Privacy Act of 1978

Privacy Protection Act of 1980

Cable Communications Policy Act of 1984

Electronic Communications Privacy Act of 1986

Video Privacy Protection Act of 1988

Children's Online Privacy Protection Act of 1998

TABLE 5-3	FEDERAL TRADE COMMISSION FAIR INFORMATION PRACTICE PRINCIPLES

1. *Notice/Awareness (core principle)*: Web sites must disclose their information practices before collecting data. Includes identification of collector, uses of data, other recipients of data, nature of collection (active/inactive), voluntary or required, consequences of refusal, and steps taken to protect confidentiality, integrity, and quality of the data.

2. *Choice/Consent (core principle)*. There must be a choice regime in place allowing consumers to choose how their information will be used for secondary purposes other than supporting the transaction, including internal use and transfer to third parties.

3. *Access/Participation:* Consumers should be able to review and contest the accuracy and completeness of data collected about them in a timely, inexpensive process.

4. *Security:* Data collectors must take responsible steps to assure that consumer information is accurate and secure from unauthorized use.

5. *Enforcement:* There must be in place a mechanism to enforce FIP principles. This can involve self-regulation, legislation giving consumers legal remedies for violations, or federal statutes and regulations.

about the individual to support the transaction. Once gathered, the individual maintains an interest in the record, and the record may not be used to support other activities without the individual's consent. In 1998 The Federal Trade Commission (FTC) restated and extended the original FIP to provide guidelines for protecting online privacy. Table 5-3 describes the FTC's Fair Information Practice Principles.

The FTC's FIP are being used as guidelines to drive changes in privacy legislation. In July 1998 the U.S. Congress passed the Children's Online Privacy Protection Act (COPPA), requiring Web sites to obtain parental permission before collecting information on children under the age of 13. (This law is in danger of being overturned.) The FTC has recommended additional legislation to protect online consumer privacy in advertising networks such as DoubleClick, which collect records of consumer Web activity to develop detailed profiles that are then used by other companies to target online ads. Other proposed e-commerce privacy legislation is focusing on protecting the online use of personal identification numbers such as social security numbers, limiting e-mail, and prohibiting the use of "spyware" programs that trace online user activities without the users' permission or knowledge.

Privacy protections have also been added to recent laws deregulating financial services and safeguarding the maintenance and transmission of health information about individuals. The Gramm-Leach-Bliley Act of 1999, which repeals earlier restrictions on affiliations among banks, securities firms, and insurance companies, includes some privacy protection for consumers of financial services. All financial institutions are required to disclose their policies and practices for protecting the privacy of non-public personal information and to allow customers to "opt-out" of information-sharing arrangements with non-affiliated third parties. The Health Insurance Portability and Accountability Act of 1996 (HIPAA) includes privacy protection regulations for medical records which were finalized on April 14, 2002. The law gives patients access to their personal medical records maintained by health care providers, hospitals, and health insurers and the right to authorize how protected information about themselves can be used or disclosed.

The European Directive on Data Protection

In Europe, privacy protection is much more stringent than in the United States. Unlike the United States, European countries do not allow businesses to use personally identifiable information without consumers' prior consent. On October 25, 1998, the European Commission's Directive on Data Protection came into effect, broadening privacy protection in the European Union (EU) nations. The directive requires companies to inform people when they collect information about them and disclose how it will be stored and used. Customers must provide their informed consent before any company can legally use data about them, and they have the right to access that information, correct it, and request that no further data be collected. **Informed consent** can be defined as consent given with knowledge of all the facts needed to make a rational decision. EU member nations must translate these principles into their own laws and cannot transfer personal data to countries such as the United States that don't have similar privacy protection regulations.

informed consent

Consent given with knowledge of all the facts needed to make a rational decision.

Working with the European Commission, the U.S. Department of Commerce developed a "safe harbor" framework for U.S. firms. U.S. businesses would be allowed to use personal data from EU countries if they develop privacy protection policies that meet EU standards. Enforcement would occur in the United States, using self-policing, regulation, and government enforcement of fair trade statutes.

Internet Challenges to Privacy

Internet technology has posed new challenges to the protection of individual privacy. Information sent over this vast network of networks may pass through many different computer systems before it reaches its final destination. Each of these systems is capable of monitoring, capturing, and storing communications that pass through it.

It is possible to record many online activities, including which online newsgroups or files a person has accessed, which Web sites and Web pages he or she has visited, and what items that person has inspected or purchased over the Web. Much of this monitoring and tracking of Web site visitors occurs in the background without the visitor's knowledge. Tools to monitor visits to the World Wide Web have become popular because they help organizations determine who is visiting their Web sites and how to better target their offerings. (Some firms also monitor the Internet usage of their employees to see how they are using company network resources.) Web retailers now have access to software that lets them watch the online shopping behavior of individuals and groups while they are visiting a Web site and making purchases. The commercial demand for this personal information is virtually insatiable.

Web sites can learn the identity of their visitors if the visitors voluntarily register at the site to purchase a product or service or to obtain a free service, such as information. Web sites can also capture information about visitors without their knowledge using "cookie" technology. **Cookies** are tiny files deposited on a computer hard drive when a user visits certain Web sites. Cookies identify the visitor's Web browser software and track visits to the Web site. When the visitor returns to a site that has deposited a cookie, the Web site software will search the visitor's computer, find the cookie, and "know" what that person has done in the past. It may also update the cookie, depending on the activity during the visit. In this way, the site can customize its contents for each visitor's interests. For example, if you purchase a book on the Amazon.com Web site and return later from the same browser, the site will welcome you by name and recommend other books of interest based on your past purchases. DoubleClick, introduced earlier in this chapter, uses cookies to build its dossiers with details of online purchases and to examine the behavior of Web site visitors. Figure 5-3 illustrates how cookies work.

Web sites using "cookie" technology cannot directly obtain visitors' names and addresses. However, if a person has registered at a site, that information can be combined with cookie data to identify the visitor. Web site owners can also combine the data they have gathered from "cookies" and other Web site monitoring tools with personal data from other sources such as off-line data collected from surveys or paper catalog purchases to develop very detailed profiles of their visitors.

The Internet is inspiring even more subtle and surreptitious tools for surveillance (Bennett, 2001). **Web bugs**

Cookies? I Didn't Order Any Cookies

Here is how a cookie works:

1. A user opens a Web browser and selects a Web site to visit.

2. The user's computer sends a request for information to the computer running the Web site.

3. The Web site computer, called a server, sends the information that allows the user's computer to display the Web site. It also sends a cookie —a data file that contains information like an encrypted user ID and information about when the user visited and what he did on the site.

4. The user's computer receives the cookie and places it in a file on the hard drive.

5. Whenever the user goes back to the Web site, the server running the site retrieves the cookie to help it identify the user.

Figure 5-3 How cookies can identify Web visitors. Cookies are written by a Web site on a visitor's hard drive. When the visitor returns to that Web site, the Web server requests the ID number from the cookie and uses it to access the data stored by that server on that visitor. The Web site can then use these data to display personalized information.

cookie

Tiny file deposited on a computer hard drive when an individual visits certain Web sites. Used to identify the visitor and track visits to the Web site.

Web bugs

Tiny graphic files embedded in e-mail messages and Web pages that are designed to monitor online Internet user behavior.

Cookies are tiny files deposited on a computer hard drive when users visit certain Web sites. Although cookies can provide valuable marketing information, the practice of collecting Web site visitor data raises worries about protecting individual privacy.

(sometimes called *invisible.GIFs* or *clear.GIFS*) are tiny graphic files embedded in e-mail messages and Web pages that are designed to monitor who is reading the e-mail message or Web page. They transmit information about the user and the page being viewed to a monitoring computer. Because Web bugs are very tiny, colorless, and virtually invisible, they can be difficult for unsophisticated Internet users to detect. Marketers use these Web bugs as another tool to monitor online behavior and can develop detailed consumer profiles by combining Web bug data with data from other sources.

The United States has allowed businesses to gather transaction information generated in the marketplace and then use that information for other marketing purposes without obtaining the informed consent of the individual whose information is being used. U.S. e-commerce sites are largely content to publish statements on their Web sites informing visitors about how their information will be used. Some have added *opt-out* selection boxes to these information policy statements. An **opt-out** model of informed consent permits the collection of personal information until the consumer specifically requests that the data not be collected. Privacy advocates would like to see wider use of an **opt-in** model of informed consent in which a business is prohibited from collecting any personal information unless the consumer specifically takes action to approve information collection and use.

The online industry has preferred self-regulation to privacy legislation for protecting consumers. In 1998 the online industry formed the Online Privacy Alliance to encourage self-regulation to develop a set of privacy guidelines for its members. The group is promoting the use of online "seals" such as that of TRUSTe, certifying Web sites adhering to certain privacy principles. Members of the advertising network industry, including DoubleClick, Adforce, Avenue A, and 24/7 Media, have created an additional industry association called the Network Advertising Initiative (NAI) to develop its own privacy policies to help consumers opt-out of advertising network programs and provide consumer redress from abuses. In general, however, most Internet businesses do little to protect the privacy of their customers and consumers do not do as much as they should to protect themselves (see the Window on Organizations).

Technical Solutions

In addition to legislation, new technologies are being developed to protect user privacy during interactions with Web sites. Many of these tools are used for encrypting e-mail, for making e-mail or Web surfing activities appear anonymous, or for preventing user computers from accepting "cookies." Table 5-4 describes some of these tools.

Interest is now growing in tools to help users determine the kind of personal data that can be extracted by Web sites. The Platform for Privacy Preferences, known as P3P

opt-out

Model of informed consent permitting the collection of personal information until the consumer specifically requests that the data not be collected.

opt-in

Model of informed consent prohibiting an organization from collecting any personal information unless the individual specifically takes action to approve information collection and use.

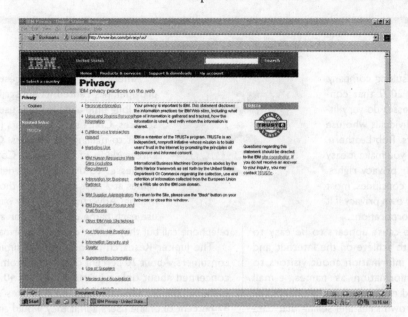

Web sites are starting to post their privacy policies for visitors to review. The TRUSTe seal designates Web sites that have agreed to adhere to TRUSTe's established privacy principles of disclosure, choice, access, and security.

enables automatic communication of privacy policies between an e-commerce site and its visitors. **P3P** provides a standard for communicating a Web site's privacy policy to Internet users and for comparing that policy to the user's preferences or to other standards such as the FTC's new FIP guidelines or the European Directive on Data Protection. Users can use P3P to select the level of privacy they wish to maintain when interacting with the Web site.

P3P

Industry standard designed to give users more control over personal information gathered on Web sites they visit. Stands for Platform for Privacy Preferences.

The P3P standard allows Web sites to publish privacy policies in a form that computers can understand. Once codified according to P3P rules, the privacy policy becomes part of the software for individual Web pages. Users of recent versions of Microsoft Internet Explorer Web browsing software can access and read the P3P site's privacy policy and a list of all cookies coming from the site. Internet Explorer lets users adjust their computers to screen out all cookies or let in selected cookies based on specific levels of privacy. For example, the "medium" level accepts cookies from "first-party" host sites that have opt-in or opt-out policies but rejects third-party cookies that use personally identifiable information without an opt-in policy.

However, P3P only works with Web sites of members of the World Wide Web Consortium who have translated their Web site privacy policies into P3P format. The technology will display cookies from Web sites that are not part of the consortium, but users won't be able to obtain sender information or privacy statements. Many users may also need to be educated about interpreting company privacy statements and P3P levels of privacy.

TABLE 5-4   PRIVACY PROTECTION TOOLS

Privacy Protection Function	Description	Example
Managing cookies	Block or limit cookies from being placed on the user's computer	Microsoft Internet Explorer 5 and 6 CookieCrusher
Blocking ads	Control ads that pop up based on user profiles and prevent ads from collecting or sending information	BHO Cop AdSubtract
Encrypting e-mail or data	Scramble e-mail or data so that they can't be read	Pretty Good Privacy (PGP)
Anonymizers	Allow users to surf the Web without being identified or to send anonymous e-mail	Anonymizer.com

PRIVACY FOR SALE

Window on
Organizations
MIS In Action

Jupiter Research, an online consulting company, published a report on June 3, 2002 that concluded that most Internet businesses do very little to protect the privacy of individuals who use the Net, nor do their customers. Rob Leathern, the author of the report, said, "If you make it easy for customers to exercise their privacy rights, they will do it." But, the report concludes, most customers will not protect their own privacy if it is difficult, and neither will the corporations.

For Internet companies, the cause appears to be easy to understand. Profits are difficult to achieve on the Internet, and so companies want to collect information about visitors to their sites, including such information as names, e-mail addresses, postal addresses, and even telephone numbers for the purpose of increasing their own sales and selling that data to other companies. Several studies have found that only 50 percent of the companies surveyed have privacy policies, even though most have Web sites. Of the companies that do post privacy polices on their Web sites, more than half do not monitor their sites to make sure they adhere to these policies.

Yahoo!, the giant Internet portal, is one of many examples. It has informed its registered users that it can send them e-mail advertisements and make telemarketing calls to them, even though some of them had previously chosen not to receive any marketing from Yahoo! Yahoo! claimed it had not loosened its privacy policy but only made it more explicit, and that it would focus primarily on selling its own services rather than those of its advertisers. "What Yahoo! has done is unconscionable," said Seth Godin, formerly Yahoo!'s vice president for direct marketing. He continued, "They would be better off sending offers to a million people who said they want to receive a coupon each day," rather than to 10 million, most of whom did not want to receive them. Mark Rotenberg, executive director of Electronic Privacy Information Center (EPIC), explained, "People thought they were going to get e-mail solicitations. They didn't expect that their dealings with Yahoo! would cause them to receive phone calls."

America Online, the largest Internet service provider, has rented its subscriber list to others for a long time and also calls users to promote its services. CNET's ZDNet rents (but does not sell) its list to mailing-list brokers. One such broker, Direct Media of Greenwich, Connecticut, enables businesses to use its list of nearly three million names at a cost of $125 per thousand for a single mailing. Advertisers typically pay for the right to use each name on the list for a single mailing or telephone call but they do not own the information outright.

The Jupiter Research report found a similar problem with consumers. About 70 percent of online customers claim they are concerned about online privacy, but only 40 percent say they even read the privacy statements on Web sites. At the same time, 82 percent of online users admit they would give personal information when shopping at new Web sites if they were offered a chance to win $100. Only one-third of one percent of Yahoo! users abandoned Yahoo! after it announced its new privacy policy. Several companies, such as Zero-Knowledge Systems and SafeWeb have offered products that enable users to surf the Web anonymously, but consumers have been reluctant to pay for such technologies. A few companies, such as Hewlett-Packard, install this software on the new computers they sell. Other companies also purchase the software so they can maintain privacy in their communications with their own remote employees. But consumers remain unwilling to purchase this software.

MAKE IT YOUR BUSINESS

To Think About: Apply the guidelines for ethical analysis to the failure to protect the privacy of individuals. Based upon this analysis, what legal or business steps do you think should be taken to better protect the privacy of customers using the Internet?

Sources: Bob Tedeschi, "Privacy Is Common Issue Online," *New York Times*, June 3, 2002; Saul Hansell, "Seeking Profits, Internet Companies Alter Privacy Policy," *New York Times*, April 11, 2002; "The Big Yahoo! Privacy Storm That Wasn't," *Wall Street Journal*, May 13, 2002; Rick Whiting, "Making Privacy Work," *Information-Week*, August 19, 2002; and Jane Black, "Faceless Snoopers Have the Upper Hand," *BusinessWeek* Online, June 5, 2002, <www.businessweek.com>.

ORGANIZATIONS

Ethical Issues

The ethical privacy issue in this information age is as follows: Under what conditions should I (you) invade the privacy of others? What legitimates intruding into others' lives through unobtrusive surveillance, through market research, or by whatever means? Do we have to inform people that we are eavesdropping? Do we have to inform people that we are using credit history information for employment screening purposes?

Social Issues

The social issue of privacy concerns the development of "expectations of privacy" or privacy norms, as well as public attitudes. In what areas of life should we as a society encourage peo-

Recent versions of Microsoft's Internet Explorer Web browsing software support the P3P system for establishing Web site visitor privacy preferences. Users can adjust P3P settings to the level of privacy protection they desire when accessing a Web site.

ple to think they are in "private territory" as opposed to public view? For instance, should we as a society encourage people to develop expectations of privacy when using electronic mail, cellular telephones, bulletin boards, the postal system, the workplace, or the street? Should expectations of privacy be extended to criminal conspirators?

Political Issues

The political issue of privacy concerns the development of statutes that govern the relations between record keepers and individuals. Should we permit the FBI to monitor e-mail at will in order to apprehend suspected criminals and terrorists (see the chapter ending case study). To what extent should e-commerce sites and other businesses be allowed to maintain personal data about individuals?

PROPERTY RIGHTS: INTELLECTUAL PROPERTY

Contemporary information systems have severely challenged existing laws and social practices that protect private intellectual property. **Intellectual property** is considered to be intangible property created by individuals or corporations. Information technology has made it difficult to protect intellectual property because computerized information can be so easily copied or distributed on networks. Intellectual property is subject to a variety of protections under three different legal traditions: trade secret, copyright, and patent law.

intellectual property
Intangible property created by individuals or corporations that is subject to protections under trade secret, copyright, and patent law.

Trade Secrets

Any intellectual work product—a formula, device, pattern, or compilation of data—used for a business purpose can be classified as a **trade secret,** provided it is not based on information in the public domain. Protections for trade secrets vary from state to state. In general, trade secret laws grant a monopoly on the ideas behind a work product, but it can be a very tenuous monopoly.

Software that contains novel or unique elements, procedures, or compilations can be included as a trade secret. Trade secret law protects the actual ideas in a work product, not only their manifestation. To make this claim, the creator or owner must take care to bind employees and customers with nondisclosure agreements and to prevent the secret from falling into the public domain.

The limitation of trade secret protection is that although virtually all software programs of any complexity contain unique elements of some sort, it is difficult to prevent the ideas in the work from falling into the public domain when the software is widely distributed.

trade secret
Any intellectual work or product used for a business purpose that can be classified as belonging to that business, provided it is not based on information in the public domain.

Copyright

copyright

A statutory grant that protects creators of intellectual property against copying by others for any purpose for a minimum of 70 years.

Copyright is a statutory grant that protects creators of intellectual property from having their work copied by others for any purpose during the life of the author plus an additional 70 years after the author's death (or 95 years for corporate copyright holders). Since the first Federal Copyright Act of 1790, and the creation of the Copyright Office to register copyrights and enforce copyright law, Congress has extended copyright protection to books, periodicals, lectures, dramas, musical compositions, maps, drawings, artwork of any kind, and motion pictures. The congressional intent behind copyright laws has been to encourage creativity and authorship by ensuring that creative people receive the financial and other benefits of their work. Most industrial nations have their own copyright laws, and there are several international conventions and bilateral agreements through which nations coordinate and enforce their laws.

In the mid-1960s the Copyright Office began registering software programs, and in 1980 Congress passed the Computer Software Copyright Act, which clearly provides protection for software program code and for copies of the original sold in commerce, and sets forth the rights of the purchaser to use the software while the creator retains legal title.

Copyright protection is clear-cut: It protects against copying of entire programs or their parts. Damages and relief are readily obtained for infringement. The drawback to copyright protection is that the underlying ideas behind a work are not protected, only their manifestation in a work. A competitor can use your software, understand how it works, and build new software that follows the same concepts without infringing on a copyright.

"Look and feel" copyright infringement lawsuits are precisely about the distinction between an idea and its expression. For instance, in the early 1990s Apple Computer sued Microsoft Corporation and Hewlett-Packard Inc. for infringement of the expression of Apple's Macintosh interface. Among other claims, Apple claimed that the defendants copied the expression of overlapping windows. The defendants counterclaimed that the idea of overlapping windows can only be expressed in a single way and, therefore, was not protectable under the "merger" doctrine of copyright law. When ideas and their expression merge, the expression cannot be copyrighted. In general, courts appear to be following the reasoning of a 1989 case—*Brown Bag Software* vs. *Symantec Corp.*—in which the court dissected the elements of software alleged to be infringing. The court found that similar concept, function, general functional features (e.g., drop-down menus), and colors are not protectable by copyright law (*Brown Bag* vs. *Symantec Corp.*, 1992).

Patents

patent

A legal document that grants the owner an exclusive monopoly on the ideas behind an invention for 20 years; designed to ensure that inventors of new machines or methods are rewarded for their labor while making widespread use of their inventions.

A **patent** grants the owner an exclusive monopoly on the ideas behind an invention for 20 years. The congressional intent behind patent law was to ensure that inventors of new machines, devices, or methods receive the full financial and other rewards of their labor and yet still make widespread use of the invention possible by providing detailed diagrams for those wishing to use the idea under license from the patent's owner. The granting of a patent is determined by the Patent Office and relies on court rulings.

The key concepts in patent law are originality, novelty, and invention. The Patent Office did not accept applications for software patents routinely until a 1981 Supreme Court decision that held that computer programs could be a part of a patentable process. Since that time hundreds of patents have been granted and thousands await consideration.

The strength of patent protection is that it grants a monopoly on the underlying concepts and ideas of software. The difficulty is passing stringent criteria of non-obviousness (e.g., the work must reflect some special understanding and contribution), originality, and novelty, as well as years of waiting to receive protection.

Challenges to Intellectual Property Rights

Contemporary information technologies, especially software, pose a severe challenge to existing intellectual property regimes and, therefore, create significant ethical, social, and political issues. Digital media differ from books, periodicals, and other media in terms of ease of replication; ease of transmission; ease of alteration; difficulty classifying a software work as a program, book, or even music; compactness—making theft easy; and difficulties in establishing uniqueness. In 2001, about 25 percent of business software programs in the United States were illegally copied and the global software piracy rate jumped from 37 percent in 2000 to 40 percent, costing the industry about $11 billion. Likewise, global sales of illegally copied music CDs jumped 50 percent in 2001 (Associated Press, 2002; Mariano, 2002).

The proliferation of electronic networks, including the Internet, has made it even more difficult to protect intellectual property. Before widespread use of networks, copies of software, books, magazine articles, or films had to be stored on physical media, such as paper, computer disks, or videotape, creating some hurdles to distribution. Using networks, information can be more widely reproduced and distributed.

The Internet was designed to transmit information freely around the world, including copyrighted information. With the World Wide Web in particular, one can easily copy and distribute virtually anything to thousands and even millions of people around the world, even if they are using different types of computer systems. Information can be illicitly copied from one place and distributed through other systems and networks even though these parties do not willingly participate in the infringement.

Individuals have been illegally copying and distributing digitized MP3 music files on the Internet. Napster provided software and services that enabled users to locate and share digital music files, including those protected by copyright. In July 2000, a federal district court in San Francisco ruled that Napster had to stop listing all copyrighted files without permission on its central index and the company was forced to declare bankruptcy. Major entertainment industry groups subsequently filed suit to block illegal file-sharing on other Web sites, such as Madster, Grokster, Kazaa, and Morpheus. However, other software and services for file trading over the Web, such as Gnutella, cannot be so easily regulated, so copyrighted music continues to be traded for free.

The manner in which information is obtained and presented on the Web further challenges intellectual property protections (Okerson, 1996). Web pages can be constructed from bits of text, graphics, sound, or video that may come from many different sources. Each item may belong to a different entity, creating complicated issues of ownership and compensation (see Figure 5-4). Web sites can also use a capability called **framing** to let one site

framing
Displaying content including the content of another Web site inside one's own Web site within a frame or a window

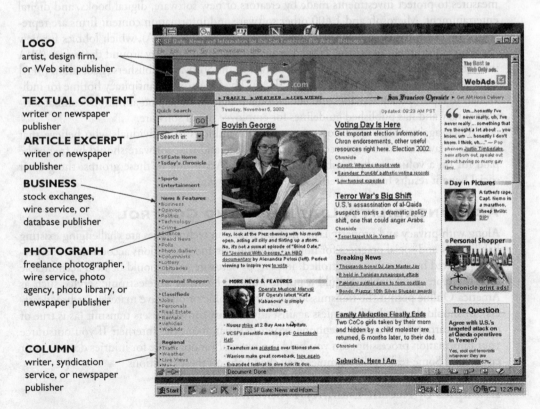

LOGO artist, design firm, or Web site publisher

TEXTUAL CONTENT writer or newspaper publisher

ARTICLE EXCERPT writer or newspaper publisher

BUSINESS stock exchanges, wire service, or database publisher

PHOTOGRAPH freelance photographer, wire service, photo agency, photo library, or newspaper publisher

COLUMN writer, syndication service, or newspaper publisher

Figure 5-4 Who Owns the Pieces? Anatomy of a Web page. Web pages are often constructed with elements from many different sources, clouding issues of ownership and intellectual property protection.

construct an on-screen border around content obtained by linking to another Web site. The first site's border and logo stay on screen, making the content of the new Web site appear to be "offered" by the previous Web site.

Mechanisms are being developed to sell and distribute books, articles, and other intellectual property on the Internet, and some copyright protection is being provided by the **Digital Millennium Copyright Act (DMCA)** of 1998. The DMCA implements a World Intellectual Property Organization treaty that makes it illegal to circumvent technology-based protections of copyrighted materials. Internet Service Providers (ISPs) are required to "take down" sites of copyright infringers that they are hosting once they are notified of the problem.

Digital Millennium Copyright Act (DMCA)
Adjusts copyright laws to the Internet age by making it illegal to make, distribute, or use devices that circumvent technology-based protections of copyrighted materials.

Ethical Issues

The central ethical issue concerns the protection of intellectual property such as software, digital books, digital music, or digitized video. Should I (you) copy for my own use a piece of software or other digital content material protected by trade secret, copyright, and/or patent law? Is there continued value in protecting intellectual property when it can be so easily copied and distributed over the Internet?

Social Issues

There are several property-related social issues raised by new information technology. Most experts agree that current intellectual property laws are breaking down in the information age. The vast majority of Americans report in surveys that they routinely violate some minor laws—everything from speeding to taking paper clips from work to copying books and software. The ease with which software and digital content can be copied contributes to making us a society of lawbreakers. These routine thefts threaten significantly to reduce the speed with which new information technologies can and will be introduced and, therefore, threaten further advances in productivity and social well-being.

Political Issues

The main property-related political issue concerns the creation of new property protection measures to protect investments made by creators of new software, digital books, and digital entertainment. Microsoft and 1,400 other software and information content firms are represented by the Software and Information Industry Association (SIIA), which lobbies for new laws and enforcement of existing laws to protect intellectual property around the world. (SIIA was formed on January 1, 1999, from the merger of the Software Publishers Association [SPA] and the Information Industry Association [IIA]). The SIIA runs an antipiracy hotline for individuals to report piracy activities and educational programs to help organizations combat software piracy and has published guidelines for employee use of software.

Allied against SIIA are a host of groups and millions of individuals who believe that antipiracy laws cannot be enforced in the digital age and that software should be free or be paid for on a voluntary basis (shareware software). According to these groups, the greater social benefit results from the free distribution of software.

ACCOUNTABILITY, LIABILITY, AND CONTROL

Along with privacy and property laws, new information technologies are challenging existing liability law and social practices for holding individuals and institutions accountable. If a person is injured by a machine controlled, in part, by software, who should be held accountable and, therefore, held liable? Should a public bulletin board or an electronic service such as America Online permit the transmission of pornographic or offensive material (as broadcasters), or should they be held harmless against any liability for what users transmit (as is true of common carriers such as the telephone system)? What about the Internet? If you outsource your information processing, can you hold the external vendor liable for injuries done to your customers? Some real-world examples may shed light on these questions.

Examples of Recent Liability Problems

On March 13, 1993, a blizzard hit the East Coast of the United States, knocking out an Electronic Data Systems Inc. (EDS) computer center in Clifton, New Jersey. The center operated 5,200 ATM machines in 12 different networks across the country involving more than 1 million cardholders. In the two weeks required to recover operations, EDS informed its customers to use alternative ATM networks operated by other banks or computer centers, and offered to cover more than $50 million in cash withdrawals. Because the alternative networks did not have access to the actual customer account balances, EDS was at substantial risk of fraud. Cash withdrawals were limited to $100 per day per customer to reduce the exposure. Most service was restored by March 26. Although EDS had a disaster-recovery plan, it did not have a dedicated backup facility. Who is liable for any economic harm caused to individuals or businesses that could not access their full account balances in this period (Joes, 1993)?

In April 1990, a computer system at Shell Pipeline Corporation failed to detect a human operator error. As a result, 93,000 barrels of crude oil were shipped to the wrong trader. The error cost $2 million because the trader sold oil that should not have been delivered to him. A court ruled later that Shell Pipeline was liable for the loss of the oil because the error was caused by a human operator who entered erroneous information into the system. Shell was held liable for not developing a system that would prevent the possibility of misdeliveries (King, 1992). Who would you have held liable—Shell Pipeline? The trader for not being more careful about deliveries? The human operator who made the error?

These cases point out the difficulties faced by information systems executives who ultimately are responsible for the harm done by systems developed by their staffs. In general, insofar as computer software is part of a machine, and the machine injures someone physically or economically, the producer of the software and the operator can be held liable for damages. Insofar as the software acts more like a book, storing and displaying information, courts have been reluctant to hold authors, publishers, and booksellers liable for contents (the exception being instances of fraud or defamation), and hence courts have been wary of holding software authors liable for "booklike" software.

In general, it is very difficult (if not impossible) to hold software producers liable for their software products when those products are considered like books, regardless of the physical or economic harm that results. Historically, print publishers, books, and periodicals have not been held liable because of fears that liability claims would interfere with First Amendment rights guaranteeing freedom of expression.

What about "software as service?" ATM machines are a service provided to bank customers. Should this service fail, customers will be inconvenienced and perhaps harmed economically if they cannot access their funds in a timely manner. Should liability protections be extended to software publishers and operators of defective financial, accounting, simulation, or marketing systems?

Software is very different from books. Software users may develop expectations of infallibility about software; software is less easily inspected than a book, and more difficult to compare with other software products for quality; software claims actually to perform a task rather than describe a task like a book; and people come to depend on services essentially based on software. Given the centrality of software to everyday life, the chances are excellent that liability law will extend its reach to include software even when it merely provides an information service.

Telephone systems have not been held liable for the messages transmitted because they are regulated "common carriers." In return for their right to provide telephone service, they must provide access to all, at reasonable rates, and achieve acceptable reliability. But broadcasters and cable television systems are subject to a wide variety of federal and local constraints on content and facilities. Organizations can be held liable for offensive content on their Web sites; and online services such as Microsoft Network (MSN) or America Online might be held liable for postings by their users.

Ethical Issues

The central liability-related ethical issue raised by new information technologies is whether individuals and organizations that create, produce, and sell systems (both hardware and software) are morally responsible for the consequences of their use (see Johnson and Mulvey, 1995). If so, under what conditions? What liabilities (and responsibilities) should the user assume, and what should the provider assume?

Social Issues

The central liability-related social issue concerns the expectations that society should allow to develop around service-providing information systems. Should individuals (and organizations) be encouraged to develop their own backup devices to cover likely or easily anticipated system failures, or should organizations be held strictly liable for system services they provide? If organizations are held strictly liable, what impact will this have on the development of new system services? Can society permit networks and bulletin boards to post libelous, inaccurate, and misleading information that will harm many persons? Or should information service companies become self-regulating, and self-censoring?

Political Issues

The leading liability-related political issue is the debate between information providers of all kinds (from software developers to network service providers), who want to be relieved of liability as much as possible (thereby maximizing their profits), and service users—individuals, organizations, and communities—who want organizations to be held responsible for providing high-quality system services (thereby maximizing the quality of service). Service providers argue they will withdraw from the marketplace if they are held liable, whereas service users argue that only by holding providers liable can they guarantee a high level of service and compensate injured parties. Should legislation impose liability or restrict liability on service providers? This fundamental cleavage is at the heart of numerous political and judicial conflicts.

SYSTEM QUALITY: DATA QUALITY AND SYSTEM ERRORS

The debate over liability and accountability for unintentional consequences of system use raises a related but independent moral dimension: What is an acceptable, technologically feasible level of system quality (see Chapter 14)? At what point should system managers say, "Stop testing, we've done all we can to perfect this software. Ship it!" Individuals and organizations may be held responsible for avoidable and foreseeable consequences, which they have a duty to perceive and correct. And the gray area is that some system errors are foreseeable and correctable only at very great expense, an expense so great that pursuing this level of perfection is not feasible economically—no one could afford the product. For example, although software companies try to debug their products before releasing them to the marketplace, they knowingly ship buggy products because the time and cost of fixing all minor errors would prevent these products from ever being released (Rigdon, 1995). What if the product was not offered on the marketplace, would social welfare as a whole not advance and perhaps even decline? Carrying this further, just what is the responsibility of a producer of computer services—should it withdraw the product that can never be perfect, warn the user, or forget about the risk (let the buyer beware)?

Three principal sources of poor system performance are software bugs and errors, hardware or facility failures caused by natural or other causes, and poor input data quality. Chapter 14 discusses why zero defects in software code of any complexity cannot be achieved and why the seriousness of remaining bugs cannot be estimated. Hence, there is a technological barrier to perfect software, and users must be aware of the potential for catastrophic failure. The software industry has not yet arrived at testing standards for producing software of acceptable but not perfect performance (Collins et al., 1994).

Although software bugs and facility catastrophe are likely to be widely reported in the press, by far the most common source of business system failure is data quality. Few companies routinely measure the quality of their data, but studies of individual organizations report data error rates ranging from 0.5 to 30 percent (Redman, 1998).

Ethical Issues

The central quality-related ethical issue that information systems raise is at what point should I (or you) release software or services for consumption by others? At what point can you conclude that your software or service achieves an economically and technologically adequate level of quality? What are you obliged to know about the quality of your software, its procedures for testing, and its operational characteristics?

Social Issues

The leading quality-related social issue once again deals with expectations: As a society, do we want to encourage people to believe that systems are infallible, that data errors are impossible? Do we instead want a society where people are openly skeptical and questioning of the output of machines, where people are at least informed of the risk? By heightening awareness of system failure, do we inhibit the development of all systems, which in the end contribute to social well-being?

Political Issues

The leading quality-related political issue concerns the laws of responsibility and accountability. Should Congress establish or direct the National Institute of Science and Technology (NIST) to develop quality standards (software, hardware, and data quality) and impose those standards on industry? Or should industry associations be encouraged to develop industrywide standards of quality? Or should Congress wait for the marketplace to punish poor system quality, recognizing that in some instances this will not work (e.g., if all retail grocers maintain poor quality systems, then customers have no alternatives)?

QUALITY OF LIFE: EQUITY, ACCESS, AND BOUNDARIES

The negative social costs of introducing information technologies and systems are beginning to mount along with the power of the technology. Many of these negative social consequences are not violations of individual rights, nor are they property crimes. Nevertheless, these negative consequences can be extremely harmful to individuals, societies, and political institutions. Computers and information technologies potentially can destroy valuable elements of our culture and society even while they bring us benefits. If there is a balance of good and bad consequences of using information systems, whom do we hold responsible for the bad consequences? Next, we briefly examine some of the negative social consequences of systems, considering individual, social, and political responses.

Balancing Power: Center Versus Periphery

An early fear of the computer age was that huge, centralized computers would concentrate power at corporate headquarters and in the nation's capital, resulting in a Big Brother society, as was suggested in George Orwell's novel, *1984.* The shift toward highly decentralized computing, coupled with an ideology of "empowerment" of thousands of workers, and the decentralization of decision making to lower organizational levels, have reduced fears of power centralization in institutions. Yet much of the "empowerment" described in popular business magazines is trivial. Lower-level employees may be empowered to make minor decisions, but the key policy decisions may be as centralized as in the past.

Rapidity of Change: Reduced Response Time to Competition

Information systems have helped to create much more efficient national and international markets. The now-more-efficient global marketplace has reduced the normal social buffers that permitted businesses many years to adjust to competition. "Time-based competition" has an ugly side: The business you work for may not have enough time to respond to global competitors and may be wiped out in a year, along with your job. We stand the risk of developing a "just-in-time society" with "just-in-time jobs" and "just-in-time" workplaces, families, and vacations.

Maintaining Boundaries: Family, Work, and Leisure

Parts of this book were produced on trains, planes, as well as on family "vacations" and what otherwise might have been "family" time. The danger of ubiquitous computing, telecommuting, nomad computing, and the "do anything anywhere" computing environment is that it might actually come true. If so, the traditional boundaries that separate work from family and just plain leisure will be weakened. Although authors have traditionally worked just about anywhere (typewriters have been portable for nearly a century), the advent of information systems, coupled with the growth of knowledge-work occupations, means that more and more people will be working when traditionally they would have been playing or communicating with family and friends. The "work umbrella" now extends far beyond the eight-hour day.

Although some people enjoy the convenience of working at home, the "do anything anywhere" computing environment can blur the traditional boundaries between work and family time.

Weakening these institutions poses clear-cut risks. Family and friends historically have provided powerful support mechanisms for individuals, and they act as balance points in a society by preserving "private life," providing a place for one to collect one's thoughts, think in ways contrary to one's employer, and dream.

Dependence and Vulnerability

Today, our businesses, governments, schools, and private associations, such as churches, are incredibly dependent on information systems and are, therefore, highly vulnerable if these systems should fail. With systems now as ubiquitous as the telephone system, it is startling to remember that there are no regulatory or standard-setting forces in place similar to telephone, electrical, radio, television, or other public-utility technologies. The absence of standards and the criticality of some system applications will probably call forth demands for national standards and perhaps regulatory oversight.

Computer Crime and Abuse

Many new technologies in the industrial era have created new opportunities for committing crime. Technologies, including computers, create new valuable items to steal, new ways to steal them, and new ways to harm others. **Computer crime** is the commission of illegal acts through the use of a computer or against a computer system. Computers or computer systems can be the object of the crime (destroying a company's computer center or a company's computer files), as well as the instrument of a crime (stealing computer lists by illegally gaining access to a computer system using a home computer). Simply accessing a computer system without authorization, or intent to do harm, even by accident, is now a federal crime. **Computer abuse** is the commission of acts involving a computer that may not be illegal but are considered unethical.

No one knows the magnitude of the computer crime problem—how many systems are invaded, how many people engage in the practice, or what is the total economic damage, but it is estimated to cost more than $1 billion in the United States alone. Many companies are reluctant to report computer crimes because they may involve employees. The most economically damaging kinds of computer crime are introducing viruses, theft of services, and disruption of computer systems. "Hackers" is the pejorative term for persons who use computers in illegal or abusive ways. Hacker attacks are on the rise, posing new threats to organizations linked to the Internet (see Chapter 14).

Computer viruses (see Chapter 14) have grown exponentially during the past decade. More than 20,000 viruses have been documented, many causing huge losses because of lost data or crippled computers. Although many firms now use antivirus software, the proliferation of computer networks will increase the probability of infections.

Following are some illustrative computer crimes:

computer crime

The commission of illegal acts through the use of a computer or against a computer system.

computer abuse

The commission of acts involving a computer that may not be illegal but are considered unethical.

- On January 17, 2002 Stewart Richardson, an online dealer in collectible figurines, with glowing reviews in his eBay feedback record, abruptly closed shop and left for parts unknown after withdrawing over $220,000 from his bank account. The money came from payments for items he auctioned off in early January. The people who had paid for these items never received them because many of these items never existed (Wingfield, 2002).

- Michael Whitt Ventimiglia, a former information technology worker at GTE Corporation, pled guilty to the charge of unintentionally damaging protected computers on May 15, 2000, at a Verizon Communications network support center in Tampa. Ventimiglia used his ability to gain access to GTE's secure computers and began to erase data on the computers, entering a command that prevented anyone from stopping the destruction. Ventimiglia's actions created more than $200,000 in damage (Sullivan, 2001).

■ An 11-member group of hackers, dubbed "The Phonemasters" by the FBI, gained access to telephone networks of companies including British Telecommunications, AT&T Corporation, MCI, Southwestern Bell, and Sprint. They were able to access credit-reporting databases belonging to Equifax and TRW Inc., as well as databases owned by LexisNexis and Dunn & Bradstreet information services. Members of the ring sold credit reports, criminal records, and other data they pilfered from the databases, causing $1.85 million in losses. The FBI apprehended group members Calvin Cantrell, Corey Lindsley, and John Bosanac, and they were sentenced to jail terms of two to four years in federal prison. Other members remain at large (Simons, 1999).

Traditionally, employees—insiders—have been the source of the most injurious computer crimes because they have the knowledge, access, and frequently a job-related motive to commit such crimes. However, the Internet's ease of use and accessibility have created new opportunities for computer crime and abuse by outsiders. Auction fraud is currently the most prevalent form of computer crime on the Internet.

Congress responded to the threat of computer crime in 1986 with the Computer Fraud and Abuse Act. This act makes it illegal to access a computer system without authorization. Most states have similar laws, and nations in Europe have similar legislation. Other existing legislation covering wiretapping, fraud, and conspiracy by any means, regardless of technology employed, has been dealing with computer crimes committed thus far.

One widespread form of abuse is **spamming,** in which organizations or individuals send out thousands and even hundreds of thousands of unsolicited e-mail and electronic messages. This practice has been growing because it only costs a few cents to send thousands of messages advertising one's wares to Internet users. Some state laws prohibit or restrict spamming, but it is largely unregulated. (The U.S. Congress is slowly considering legislation to outlaw false labeling of e-mail solicitations.) On May 30, 2002 the European Parliament passed a ban on unsolicited commercial messaging. Electronic marketing can only be targeted to people who have given prior consent. Table 5-5 describes other practices where the Internet has been used for illegal or malicious purposes.

spamming
The practice of sending unsolicited e-mail and other electronic communication.

TABLE 5-5	INTERNET CRIME AND ABUSE

Problem	Description
Spamming	Marketers send out unsolicited mass e-mail to recipients who have not requested this information.
Hacking	Hackers exploit weaknesses in Web site security to obtain access to proprietary data such as customer information and passwords. They may use "Trojan horses" posing as legitimate software to obtain information from the host computer.
Jamming	Jammers use software routines to tie up the computer hosting a Web site so that legitimate visitors can't access the site.
Malicious software	Cyber vandals use data flowing through the Internet to transmit computer viruses, which can disable computers that they "infect" (see Chapter 14).
Sniffing	Sniffing, a form of electronic eavesdropping, involves placing a piece of software to intercept information passing from a user to the computer hosting a Web site. This information can include credit card numbers and other confidential data.
Spoofing	Spoofers fraudulently misrepresent themselves as other organizations, setting up false Web sites where they can collect confidential information from unsuspecting visitors to the site.

Employment: Trickle-Down Technology and Reengineering Job Loss

Reengineering work (see Chapter 12) is typically hailed in the information systems community as a major benefit of new information technology. It is much less frequently noted that redesigning business processes could potentially cause millions of middle-level managers and clerical workers to lose their jobs. One economist has raised the possibility that we will create a society run by a small "high tech elite of corporate professionals. . .in a nation of the permanently unemployed" (Rifkin, 1993).

Other economists are much more sanguine about the potential job losses. They believe relieving bright, educated workers from reengineered jobs will result in these workers moving to better jobs in fast-growth industries. Left out of this equation are blue-collar workers, and older, less well educated middle managers. It is not clear that these groups can be retrained easily for high-quality (high-paying) jobs. Careful planning and sensitivity to employee needs can help companies redesign work to minimize job losses.

Equity and Access: Increasing Racial and Social Class Cleavages

Does everyone have an equal opportunity to participate in the digital age? Will the social, economic, and cultural gaps that exist in America and other societies be reduced by information systems technology? Or will the cleavages be increased, permitting the "better off" to become even better off relative to others?

These questions have not yet been fully answered because the impact of systems technology on various groups in society has not been thoroughly studied. What is known is that information, knowledge, computers, and access to these resources through educational institutions and public libraries are inequitably distributed along ethnic and social class lines, as are many other information resources. Several studies have found that certain ethnic and income groups in the United States are less likely to have computers or online Internet access even though computer ownership and Internet access have soared in the past five years. Higher-income families in each ethnic group are more likely to have home computers and Internet access than lower-income families in the same group (U.S. Department of Commerce, 1998; Rainie and Packel, 2001). A similar **digital divide** exists in U.S. schools, with schools in high-poverty areas much less likely to have computers, high-quality educational technology programs, or Internet access available for their students. Left uncorrected, the "digital divide" could lead to a society of information haves, computer literate and skilled, versus a large group of information have-nots, computer illiterate and unskilled.

Public interest groups want to narrow this "digital divide" by making digital information services—including the Internet—available to "virtually everyone" just as basic telephone service is now. The Window on Management describes how the Canadian province of Alberta is addressing this problem.

Health Risks: RSI, CVS, and Technostress

The most important occupational disease today is **repetitive stress injury (RSI).** RSI occurs when muscle groups are forced through repetitive actions often with high-impact loads (such as tennis) or tens of thousands of repetitions under low-impact loads (such as working at a computer keyboard).

The single largest source of RSI is computer keyboards. About 50 million Americans use computers at work. The most common kind of computer-related RSI is **carpal tunnel syndrome (CTS),** in which pressure on the median nerve through the wrist's bony structure, called a "carpal tunnel," produces pain. The pressure is caused by constant repetition of keystrokes: In a single shift, a word processor may perform 23,000 keystrokes. Symptoms of carpal tunnel syndrome include numbness, shooting pain, inability to grasp objects, and tingling. Millions of workers have been diagnosed with carpal tunnel syndrome.

RSI is avoidable. Designing workstations for a neutral wrist position (using a wrist rest to support the wrist), proper monitor stands, and footrests all contribute to proper posture and reduced RSI. New, ergonomically correct keyboards are also an option, although their effectiveness has yet to be clearly established. These measures should be backed by frequent

digital divide

Large disparities in access to computers and the Internet among different social groups and different locations.

repetitive stress injury (RSI)

Occupational disease that occurs when muscle groups are forced through repetitive actions with high-impact loads or thousands of repetitions with low-impact loads.

carpal tunnel syndrome (CTS)

Type of RSI in which pressure on the median nerve through the wrist's bony carpal tunnel structure produces pain.

ALBERTA NARROWS ITS DIGITAL DIVIDE

Internet access is increasing worldwide, but its cost can exacerbate cleavages between urban and rural areas as well as between different social classes and ethnic groups. The people in Canada's province of Alberta have seriously tried to address this problem.

Alberta is a province of immense size, almost as large as Texas in the United States. However, its population is relatively small and very spread out, with only 3 million people, or about 1/7 the population of Texas. Although the province has a flourishing technology industry, its economy depends heavily on agriculture, energy, and tourism. Alberta's digital divide is substantial, with most rural Alberta businesses having no access to high-speed Internet services. Until recently, those that did paid much higher prices than urban areas. Grant Chaney, chief technology officer for SuperNet, explained, "We were seeing a growing gap between urban Alberta and rural Alberta. We wanted to make sure that our own digital divide was being addressed." He added "Alberta has a pretty diverse geography and a lot of population in rural areas."

Making Internet access available to all homes in the rural areas with over 4,500 facilities in over 400 communities was clearly beyond the financial means of most residents. The rates were simply not competitive. For example the few rural-based businesses that used an Internet Service Provider (ISP) paid up to several thousand Canadian dollars per month. The Alberta government realized that all of its residents needed reliable, up-to-date information in their hospitals, libraries, schools, and government offices and that the only way to provide inexpensive and widespread access to this information would be through stable high-speed networks connected to the Internet.

Recognition of the problem led to the establishment of a project dubbed SuperNet. Alberta described its project's purpose this way. "Currently, only about 30 communities in Alberta have some access to affordable high-speed residential Internet services. Alberta SuperNet will give 422 communities that access at significantly lower rates than even slow-speed service, which may or may not be currently available."

Management decided it must offer rural access to SuperNet at prices that were very competitive with the Edmonton and Calgary urban areas. This meant that SuperNet must offer the rural ISPs access to the Internet at much lower rates than were currently available. Then the ISPs, in turn, would pass the savings on to their customers.

Aside from rural access, SuperNet has another positive financial result in that it gives business to the companies building and supplying the system. In addition to spurring economic activity, SuperNet is expected to promote better education and medical care. The rural areas would be able to access a comprehensive pharmaceutical information network, real-time health records transfer, and telemedicine applications. Specialists could use the network's video capabilities to help rural doctors diagnose patients with unfamiliar symptoms. Children in remote classrooms would be able to take classes that are unavailable at their local schools and learn from teachers in other parts of the province.

To Think About: Evaluate the SuperNet approach to narrowing the digital divide. Could this approach be used in other provinces, states, and countries? Explain your answer. Suggest other ways governments might help solve the digital inequity problem.

Sources: G Patrick Pawling, "The Alberta Connection: Government and Private Industry Are Working Together," *IQ Magazine,* January/February 2002; and "Alberta SuperNew," <http://www3.gov.ab.ca/innsci/supernet/inside.html>.

MANAGEMENT

rest breaks, rotation of employees to different jobs, and movement toward voice or scanner data entry.

RSI is not the only occupational illness computers cause. Back and neck pain, leg stress, and foot pain also result from poor ergonomic designs of workstations. **Computer vision syndrome (CVS)** refers to any eyestrain condition related to computer display screen use. Its symptoms, usually temporary, include headaches, blurred vision, and dry and irritated eyes.

The newest computer-related malady is **technostress,** which is stress induced by computer use. Its symptoms include aggravation, hostility toward humans, impatience, and fatigue. The problem according to experts is that humans working continuously with computers come to expect other humans and human institutions to behave like computers, providing instant response, attentiveness, and an absence of emotion. Computer-intense workers are aggravated when put on hold during phone calls and become incensed or alarmed when their PCs take a few seconds longer to perform a task. Technostress is thought to be

computer vision syndrome (CVS)

Eyestrain condition related to computer display screen use; symptoms include headaches, blurred vision, and dry and irritated eyes.

technostress

Stress induced by computer use; symptoms include aggravation, hostility toward humans, impatience, and enervation.

Repetitive stress injury (RSI) is the leading occupational disease today. The single largest cause of RSI is computer keyboard work.

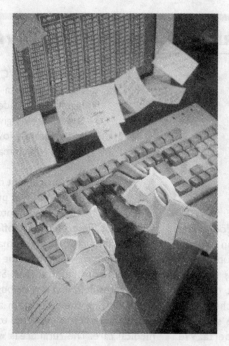

related to high levels of job turnover in the computer industry, high levels of early retirement from computer-intense occupations, and elevated levels of drug and alcohol abuse.

The incidence of technostress is not known but is thought to be in the millions in the United States and growing rapidly. Computer-related jobs now top the list of stressful occupations based on health statistics in several industrialized countries.

To date the role of radiation from computer display screens in occupational disease has not been proved. Video display terminals (VDTs) emit nonionizing electric and magnetic fields at low frequencies. These rays enter the body and have unknown effects on enzymes, molecules, chromosomes, and cell membranes. Long-term studies are investigating low-level electromagnetic fields and birth defects, stress, low birth weight, and other diseases. All manufacturers have reduced display screen emissions since the early 1980s, and European countries such as Sweden have adopted stiff radiation emission standards.

The computer has become a part of our lives—personally as well as socially, culturally, and politically. It is unlikely that the issues and our choices will become easier as information technology continues to transform our world. The growth of the Internet and the information economy suggests that all the ethical and social issues we have described will be heightened further as we move into the first digital century.

MANAGEMENT ACTIONS: A CORPORATE CODE OF ETHICS

Some corporations have developed far-reaching corporate IS codes of ethics, including FedEx, IBM, American Express, and Merck & Co. Most firms, however, have not developed these codes of ethics, leaving their employees in the dark about expected correct behavior. There is some dispute concerning a general code of ethics versus a specific information systems code of ethics. As managers, you should strive to develop an IS-specific set of ethical standards for each of the five moral dimensions:

- *Information rights and obligations.* A code should cover topics such as employee e-mail and Internet privacy, workplace monitoring, treatment of corporate information, and policies on customer information.

- *Property rights and obligations.* A code should cover topics such as software licenses, ownership of firm data and facilities, ownership of software created by employees on company hardware, and software copyrights. Specific guidelines for contractual relationships with third parties should be covered as well.

- *Accountability and control.* The code should specify a single individual responsible for all information systems, and reporting to this individual should be others who are responsible for individual rights, the protection of property rights, system quality, and quality of life (e.g., job design, ergonomics, employee satisfaction). Responsibilities for control of systems, audits, and management should be clearly defined. The potential liabilities of systems officers and the corporation should be detailed in a separate document.

- *System quality.* The code should describe the general levels of data quality and system error that can be tolerated with detailed specifications left to specific projects. The code should require that all systems attempt to estimate data quality and system error probabilities.

- *Quality of life.* The code should state that the purpose of systems is to improve the quality of life for customers and for employees by achieving high levels of product quality, customer service, employee satisfaction, and human dignity through proper ergonomics, job and work flow design, and human resource development.

MAKE **IT** YOUR BUSINESS

FINANCE AND ACCOUNTING

Poor data quality and software errors can have a devastating impact on the firm's financial and accounting systems because errors in these systems can easily lead to huge losses. Financial and accounting systems are prime targets for computer crime, as are the specialized financial systems of financial and banking institutions. One growing area of computer crime is securities fraud over the Internet.

HUMAN RESOURCES

Developing and enforcing a corporate ethics policy and procedures that balance the need to run the business responsibly and efficiently with the need to safeguard employee privacy, health, and well-being have become important responsibilities of the human resources function. Employees and their managers may need special training to sensitize them to the new ethical issues surrounding information systems, such as personal use of the Internet or corporate systems or copying digital material and software. You can find examples of human resources applications and issues on page 169.

MANUFACTURING AND PRODUCTION

Economic prosperity and the quality of daily life are highly dependent on the smooth and accurate flow of information among disparate manufacturing and production systems. Data quality problems and software errors in one system can affect the performance of other systems inside the firm and the performance of suppliers, distributors, and logistics services that depend on information from these systems.

SALES AND MARKETING

The Internet has provided powerful new ways of reaching customers and gathering information about them in order to provide more targeted marketing and products. Information about consumers' activities is marketing gold—and often a critical success factor—for companies doing business online. However, the customer information that's required to create a personalized Web experience raises serious privacy concerns, because contemporary information technology makes it so easy for businesses to monitor online behavior and assemble highly detailed profiles of individual consumers. You can find examples of sales and marketing applications on pages 144–145, 158, and 174–176.

MANAGEMENT WRAP-UP

Managers are ethical rule makers for their organizations. They are charged with creating the policies and procedures to establish ethical conduct, including the ethical use of information systems. Managers are also responsible for identifying, analyzing, and resolving the ethical dilemmas that invariably crop up as they balance conflicting needs and interests.

Rapid changes fueled by information technology are creating new situations where existing laws or rules of conduct may not be relevant. New "gray areas" are emerging in which ethical standards have not yet been codified into law. A new system of ethics for the information age is required to guide individual and organizational choices and actions.

Information technology is introducing changes that create new ethical issues for societies to debate and resolve. Increasing computing power, storage, and networking capabilities—including the Internet—can expand the reach of individual and organizational actions and magnify their impact. The ease and anonymity with which information can be communicated, copied, and manipulated in online environments are challenging traditional rules of right and wrong behavior.

For Discussion

1. Should producers of software-based services such as ATMs be held liable for economic injuries suffered when their systems fail?

2. Should companies be responsible for unemployment caused by their information systems? Why or why not?

SUMMARY

1. *What ethical, social, and political issues are raised by information systems?* Information technology has raised new possibilities for behavior for which laws and rules of acceptable conduct have not yet been developed. The main ethical, social, and political issues raised by information

systems center around information rights and obligations, property rights, accountability and control, system quality, and quality of life.

Ethical, social, and political issues are closely related. Ethical issues confront individuals who must choose a course of action, often in a situation in which two or more ethical principles are in conflict (a dilemma). Social issues spring from ethical issues as societies develop expectations in individuals about the correct course of action. Political issues spring from social conflict and have to do largely with laws that prescribe behavior and seek to use the law to create situations in which individuals behave correctly.

2. *Are there specific principles for conduct that can be used to guide decisions about ethical dilemmas?* Six ethical principles are available to judge conduct. These principles are derived independently from several cultural, religious, and intellectual traditions and include the Golden Rule, Immanuel Kant's Categorical Imperative, Descartes' rule of change, the Utilitarian Principle, the Risk Aversion Principle, and the ethical "no free lunch" rule. These principles should be used in conjunction with an ethical analysis is to guide decision making. The ethical analysis involves identifying the facts, values, stakeholders, options, and consequences of actions. Once completed, one can consider what ethical principle to apply to a situation to arrive at a judgment.

3. *Why does contemporary information systems technology pose challenges to the protection of individual privacy and intellectual property?* Contemporary information systems technology, including Internet technology, challenges traditional regimens for protecting individual privacy and intellectual property. Data storage and data analysis technology allows companies to easily gather personal data about individuals from many different sources and analyze these data to create detailed electronic profiles about individuals and their behavior. Data flowing over the Internet can be monitored at many points. The activities of Web site visitors can be closely tracked using "cookies" and other Web monitoring tools. Not all Web sites have strong privacy protection policies, and they do not always allow for informed consent regarding the use of personal information. The online industry prefers self-regulation to the U.S. government tightening privacy protection legislation.

Traditional copyright laws are insufficient to protect software piracy because digital material can be so easily copied. Internet technology also makes intellectual property even more difficult to protect because digital material can be so easily copied and transmitted to many different locations simultaneously over the Net. Web pages can be easily constructed by using pieces of content from other Web sites without permission.

4. *How have information systems affected everyday life?* Although computer systems have been sources of efficiency and wealth, they have some negative impacts. Errors in large computer systems are impossible to totally eradicate. Computer errors can cause serious harm to individuals and organizations, and existing laws and social practices are often unable to establish liability and accountability for these problems. Less serious errors are often attributable to poor data quality, which can cause disruptions and losses for businesses. Jobs can be lost when workers are replaced by computers or tasks become unnecessary in reengineered business processes. The ability to own and use a computer may be exacerbating socioeconomic disparities among different racial groups and social classes. Widespread use of computers increases opportunities for computer crime and computer abuse. Computers can also create health problems such as repetitive stress injury, computer vision syndrome, and technostress.

5. *How can organizations develop corporate polices for ethical conduct?* For each of the five moral dimensions of information systems, corporations should develop an ethics policy statement to assist individuals and to encourage the correct decisions. The policy areas are as follows. Individual information rights: Spell out corporate privacy and due process policies. Property rights: Clarify how the corporation will treat property rights of software owners. Accountability and control: Clarify who is responsible and accountable for corporate information. System quality: Identify methodologies and quality standards to be achieved. Quality of life: Identify corporate policies on family, computer crime, decision making, vulnerability, job loss, and health risks.

KEY TERMS

Accountability, 150
Carpal tunnel syndrome (CTS), 168
Computer abuse, 166
Computer crime, 166
Computer vision syndrome (CVS), 169
Cookie, 155
Copyright, 160
Descartes' rule of change, 151
Digital divide, 168

Digital Millennium Copyright Act (DMCA), 162
Due process, 150
Ethical "no free lunch" rule, 151
Ethics, 146
Fair Information Practices (FIP), 153
Framing, 161
Immanuel Kant's Categorical Imperative, 151
Information rights, 147

Informed consent, 154
Intellectual property, 159
Liability, 150
Non-obvious relationship awareness (NORA), 149
Opt-in, 156
Opt-out, 156
P3P, 157
Patent, 160
Privacy, 153

Profiling, 149
Repetitive stress injury (RSI), 168
Responsibility, 150
Risk Aversion Principle, 151
Spamming, 167
Technostress, 169
Trade secret, 159
Utilitarian Principle, 151
Web bugs, 155

REVIEW QUESTIONS

1. In what ways are ethical, social, and political issues connected? Give some examples.

2. What are the key technological trends that heighten ethical concerns?

3. What are the differences between responsibility, accountability, and liability?

4. What are the five steps in an ethical analysis?

5. Identify and describe six ethical principles.

6. What is a professional code of conduct?

7. What are meant by "privacy" and "fair information practices"?

8. How is the Internet challenging the protection of individual privacy?

9. What role can informed consent, legislation, industry self-regulation, and technology tools play in protecting individual privacy of Internet users?

10. What are the three different regimes that protect intellectual property rights? What challenges to intellectual property rights are posed by the Internet?

11. Why is it so difficult to hold software services liable for failure or injury?

12. What is the most common cause of system quality problems?

13. Name and describe four "quality of life" impacts of computers and information systems.

14. What is technostress, and how would you identify it?

15. Name three management actions that could reduce RSI injuries.

APPLICATION SOFTWARE EXERCISE

WORD PROCESSING AND WEB PAGE DEVELOPMENT TOOL EXERCISE: CREATING A SIMPLE WEB SITE

Build a simple Web site of your own design for a business using the Web page creation function of Microsoft Word, Microsoft FrontPage, or a Web page development tool of your choice. Your Web site should include a Home page with a description of your business and at least one picture or graphic. From the Home page you must be able to link to a second Web page and, from there, link to a third Web page. Make the Home page long enough so that when you arrive at the bottom of the page, you can no longer see the top. There you must include a link back to the top. Also include a link to one of the secondary Web pages. On that secondary page, include a link to the top of that page, and a link back to the top of the *Home* page. Also include a link to the third page, which should contain a link to its own top and a link back to the top of the *Home* page. Finally, on one of the secondary pages, include another picture or graphic, and on the other page include an object that you create using Microsoft Excel or other spreadsheet software. The Laudon Web site for Chapter 5 includes instructions for completing this project. If you have tested every function and all are now working to your satisfaction, save the pages you have created for submission to your instructor.

GROUP PROJECT

With three or four of your classmates, develop a corporate ethics code on privacy that addresses both employee privacy and the privacy of customers and users of the corporate Web site. Be sure to consider e-mail privacy and employer monitoring of work-sites, as well as corporate use of information about employees concerning their off-job behavior (e.g., lifestyle, marital arrangements, and so forth). If possible, use electronic presentation software to present your ethics code to the class.

TOOLS FOR INTERACTIVE LEARNING

■ INTERNET CONNECTION

The Internet Connection for this chapter will direct you to a series of Web sites where you can learn more about the privacy issues raised by the use of the Internet and the Web. You can complete an exercise to analyze the privacy implications of existing technologies for tracking Web site visitors.

■ INTERACTIVE STUDY GUIDE

You can use the Interactive Study Guide to test your knowledge of the topics in this chapter, and get instant feedback where you need more practice.

■ RUNNING CASE

The Running Case provides an opportunity for you to develop an online privacy policy for Dirt Bikes USA's Web site. You can find a complete description of this project on the Laudon Web site for Chapter 5 and on the Multimedia Edition CD-ROM.

■ ELECTRONIC COMMERCE PROJECT

At the Laudon Web site for Chapter 5, you will find an Electronic Commerce project that uses the interactive software at the Google Groups Web site to explore the use of Internet discussion groups for targeted marketing.

■ MANAGEMENT DECISION PROBLEM

At the Laudon Web site for Chapter 5, you will find a Management Decision Problem where you can analyze whether employees are spending too much personal time on the Web and address the ethical implications of monitoring their Web usage.

■ CD-ROM

If you use the Multimedia Edition CD-ROM with this chapter, you can find a video clip on software piracy and the activities of the Software Publishers Association (SPA), an audio overview of the major themes of this chapter, and bullet text summarizing the key points of the chapter.

CASE STUDY—*The FBI and Digital Surveillance: How Far Should It Go?*

In the 1960s the U.S. Federal Bureau of Investigation (FBI) began compiling files on citizens considered a threat to U.S. security. Its secret files included thousands of Vietnam War protestors, civil rights activists, and such well-known figures as Albert Einstein, Rock Hudson, and Henry Ford. The Privacy Act of 1974 later became law in order to forbid the collection of such information unless the Justice Department could show reason to suspect that the person had committed a crime.

Worries about the FBI secretly collecting data on ordinary citizens resurfaced in 1999 when the FBI admitted that it had developed and was using a computer product it named Carnivore (also known as DCS1000) to secretly collect e-mail information. However, the growing fear of the FBI may have been reversed when terrorists attacked the World Trade Center and the Pentagon on September 11, 2001. Many appear to be reevaluating how much privacy they are willing to surrender in order to gain more security.

Carnivore, which is used to eavesdrop on communication flowing through the Internet, is a computer-age version of wiretapping. Wiretaps gather analog information (voices) from telephones, whereas Carnivore gathers digital information from digital network traffic flowing to or from a specific user or Internet address. The FBI named it Carnivore because, they say, Carnivore finds the "meat" in "suspicious" or "interesting" communications. However, the two have two major differences. First, wiretaps require high-level court orders because they give the FBI the right to listen to all telephone call conversations on the tapped line of the person being investigated. Carnivore court orders are easier to obtain because they only grant permission to gather certain data from e-mail headers and not from the content of the message itself.

Second, the two differ in their methods of collection. Wiretaps are placed on the telephone line(s) of individuals under investigation. The FBI taps Internet communication by installing Carnivore on a special computer at the site of the target's Internet Service Provider (ISP). There it must review the headers of all messages that pass through the ISP's computer system (multiple millions of messages daily for larger ISPs) in order to identify those that fall within the court order. When identified, Carnivore will select those messages and their contents.

Why would the FBI seek only the header information? First, because the legal standard for court orders on collecting header information is much lower than that for the message itself. To meet the higher standard needed to read e-mail and other messages, the FBI would have to prove "probable cause" (strong evidence of possible criminal activity). Second, according to the FBI, header information has proven valuable in its pursuits.

Headers often contain more data than that allowed in the court order, illegally giving the FBI access to data it has no right to see. Also, because Carnivore must access every header for all e-mails to locate the ones authorized by the court order, the agents could illegally use it to select data from any of the headers they desire, and only the FBI would know. Donald Kerr, the director of the FBI lab division, agreed that Carnivore enables FBI agents to use the system illegally to check up on someone's ex-spouse or political enemy. Nonetheless, he claimed, it was very unlikely to happen because agents who acted illegally would face heavy fines and up to five years in prison.

Carnivore does not produce audit trails. Many have viewed the system as "the electronic equivalent of listening to everybody's phone calls to see if it's the phone call you should be monitoring," according to Mark Rasch, a former federal prosecutor. Opponents also feared that local law enforcement agencies could begin to use Carnivore, noting that the Fourth Amendment, used to protect privacy, only applies to the federal government and not to state or local governments. According to Paul Bresson, an FBI spokesperson, the FBI position was that it was seeking ways to modify Carnivore so that it would only collect information on targeted people. He said, "We never denied that it had the capability to capture more [data than an investigation requires]. What we maintained was that it had the filtering devices to capture only the data pertaining to the court order." The view of David Sobel, general counsel for the Electronic Privacy Information Center (EPIC), a Washington D.C.–based electronic privacy group, was, "If it's that easy for the FBI to accidentally collect too much data, imagine how simple it would be for agents to do so intentionally."

Technical problems with Carnivore may have actually impeded the FBI's anti-terrorism investigations several years ago. An internal FBI e-mail message dated April 5, 2000, described how Carnivore software failed to work correctly the previous month for the FBI's International Terrorism Operations Section investigating Osama Bin Laden. The Carnivore software captured not only the electronic communications of a court-authorized target but also the e-mail of individuals who were not under investigation. Sobel pointed out that "Carnivore is a powerful but clumsy tool that endangers the privacy of innocent American citizens…its imprecision can also jeopardize important investigations."

Before the September 11 terrorist attacks, congressional fears were strong, as expressed at a July 2000 House of Representatives hearing on Carnivore. "There's new legal ground that you all are trying to break here where you are saying you have the authority to harvest large quantities of information, then you filter out what you want," explained Bob Barr, a Republican Representative from Georgia. "Those are two very, very large steps we are taking here. I don't think this has been well thought out." However, on October 26, 2001, President George W. Bush signed a new bill to combat terrorism, a bill that had been overwhelmingly approved by both the U.S. Senate and House of Representatives. The bill, which was passed in reaction to the terrorist attacks, expands the government's ability not only to detain immigrants and penetrate money-laundering banks but also to conduct more electronic surveillance. For example, it authorizes the government to approve wiretaps even if intelligence gathering is only a minor purpose. (Previously, officials needed separate authorizations for each phone used by a person under surveillance.) Officials can subpoena the addresses and times of e-mail messages sent by suspected terrorists as they can with telephone messages. The new law does include a sunset provision, however. The increased power to keep more computers and telephones under surveillance will expire in 2005.

The FBI's position is simple: ISPs must allow the FBI to install and control Carnivore. Even at the 2000 Congressional hearings, the FBI refused to give any information on Carnivore technology or on its uses. It simply claimed Carnivore was necessary to catch drug dealers, pornographers, and terrorists. Most ISPs have been in opposition. EarthLink, the second-largest ISP in the United States with nearly five million subscribers, was served a court order for a Carnivore installation in December 1999. It was willing to supply the FBI the desired information, but its technicians realized the software was incompatible with EarthLink's new software system. EarthLink also feared Carnivore would illegally collect information beyond the scope of the court order. Les Seagraves, the chief privacy officer at EarthLink, offered a compromise. EarthLink's engineers would develop software to collect exactly what the court order requested and no more, thus protecting its systems and subscribers while giving the FBI the required information. The FBI agreed, but several weeks later it changed its mind and insisted EarthLink allow Carnivore to be installed. After the terrorist attacks, EarthLink spokesperson Dan Greenfield let it be known that the FBI agreed not to install Carnivore but instead would allow EarthLink to gather the information itself. EarthLink consented.

Even prior to the September 11 terrorist attacks, some organizations had agreed to use Carnivore because they believed they had no alternative even though they still did not like it. That view seems to have been strengthened for many people since September 11. But opposition does remain. Patrick Leahy, who headed the Senate Judiciary Committee, said, "We must not let the terrorists win." He explained, "If we abandon our democracy to battle them, they win." David Boaz, a vice president of the conservative Cato Institute still said after the attacks, "We need strong protections against government access to information about individuals."

Clearly, the FBI already does gather a lot of other information. For example, they use the immense LexisNexis database that contains legal briefs, newspaper articles, and other public records. They also gather such data as taxpayer assets, credit card charges (including activity locations), telephone numbers, and even driving histories. Because it is illegal for government organizations (including the FBI) to collect much of this type of information themselves, they outsource the collection, purchasing such data from commercial organizations that legally collect them for their own use or for sale to their customers, of which the government is one. However, many people have opposed this method.

One publicly held company that sells such data to the FBI is ChoicePoint Inc. of Alpharetta, Georgia. It supplies its commercial customers with information primarily to enable them to check out prospective clients and partners, and it claims its dealings with government organizations are "a natural extension" of its business. Derek Smith, ChoicePoint's CEO, maintains it helps the government to unearth fraud and to convict criminals. The FBI contends it has "located nearly 1,300 subjects of criminal cases using these kinds of searches." John Collingwood, another FBI spokesperson, adds that this method "saves countless hours of manual record checks, a process the FBI has relied on for decades." The federal Health Care Financing Administration also relies on information from ChoicePoint. It compares its data with ChoicePoint's 2 million "high-risk and fraudulent business addresses" to help locate fraud.

Many ways currently exist for criminals and terrorists to circumvent the use of Carnivore so that the FBI would not be able to collect header information. First, Carnivore cannot even read many Web-based e-mails, such as those sent from Hotmail and Yahoo! Second, effective software to encrypt messages is easily obtainable. Services such as Anonymizer.com enable users to send e-mail or surf the Web with their identification disguised. Plotters are also aware of keywords that might call attention to them and try to substitute code words or misspellings (spelling for America "Amreeka," for instance.)

One issue that has only emerged since the terrorist attacks is the great power of *steganography*, the embedding of secret messages within other more public messages. Computer technology now enables users to hide messages within digitized, written, graphics and even music documents, and they are virtually undetectable, making it even more difficult to find the message than to decode it. In 1998, referring not only to encryption but also to steganography, the then FBI director Louis Freeh told the U.S. Senate Judiciary committee, "Not just Bin Laden, but many other people who work against us in the area of terrorism, are becoming sophisticated enough to equip themselves with encryption devices."

Ultimately, the goal of new anti-terrorism laws and technologies is to allow the FBI and the CIA to collect more secret information. But a number of official studies have pointed out that U.S. intelligence agencies for years have collected far more information than they can analyze. E-mail communication in difficult foreign languages might easily wind up in a pile of untranslated, unread, unabsorbed information.

Sources: Michael Moss and Ford Fessenden, "New Tools for Domestic Spying and Qualms," *New York Times,* December 10, 2002; Debbie Gage, "FBI Bureaucracy Hobbles Tech Adoption," *Baseline*, September, 2002; James Risen and David Johnston, "FBI Report Found Agency Not Ready to Counter Terror," *New York Times*, June 1, 2002; Adam Liptak, Changing the Standard, *New York Times*, May 31, 2002 and "Self Criticism and Risk," *New York Times*, May 30, 2002; Eric Chabrow, "New Priorities, Information Week, June 3, 2002; John R. Wilke, "How Outdated Files Hamper FBI Effort to Fight Terrorism, " Wall Street Journal, July 9, 2002; Michael Duffy and Nancy Gibbs, "How Far Do We Want the FBI to Go?" *Time*, June 10, 2002; Dan Eggen, "'Carnivore' Glitches Blamed for FBI Woes," *Washington Post*, May 29, 2002; Susan Stellin, "Terror's Confounding Online Trail, *New York Times*, March 28, 2002; Electronic Privacy Information Center, "FBI's

Carnivore System Disrupted Anti-Terror Investigation," May 28, 2002; David Armstrong and Joseph Pereira, "FBI Gives Carriers Access to Watchlists; Database Plays New Role After Attacks," *Wall Street Journal*, October 23, 2001; Ariana Eunjung Cha and Jonathan Krim, "Privacy Trade-Offs Reassessed," *Washington Post*, September 13, 2001, and "Terrorists' Online Methods Elusive," *Washington Post*, September 19, 2001; Nick Wingfield, "Some Fear Fight Against Terror Will Imperil Privacy," *Wall Street Journal*, September 13, 2001; Adam Clymer, "Antiterrorism Bill Passes; U.S. Gets Expanded Powers," *New York Times*, October 26, 2001; Adam Clymer, "Bush Signs Bipartisan Bill to Combat Terrorism," *New York Times*, October 26, 2001; Larry Kahaner, "Hungry for Your E-Mail," *InformationWeek*, April 23, 2001, <www.informationweek.com>, and "Taking a Bite Out of Carnivore," *InformationWeek*, April 23, 2001, <www.informationweek.com>; Glenn R. Simpson, "FBI's Reliance on the Private Sector Has Raised Some Privacy Concerns," *Wall Street Journal*, April 13, 2001; Jennifer DiSabatino, "Carnivore Probe Mollifies Some," *The Industry Standard*," November 23, 2000; Bill Frezza, "Carnivore Takes a Bite Out of the Fourth Amendment, *TechWeb*, August 7, 2000; David Johnston, "Citing FBI Lapse, Ashcroft Delays McVeigh Execution," *New York Times*, May 13, 2001; Margaret Johnston, "Lawmakers Find Carnivore Unappetizing," *The Industry Standard*, July 25, 2000; Larry Kahaner, "Carnivore's Legal Teeth," *Informationweek.com*, April 23, 2001; Declan McCullagh, "Ashcroft to Chew on Carnivore" *Wired News*, January 27, 2001; Declan McCullagh, "Bin Laden: Steganography Master?" *Wired News*, February 7, 2001, and "Regulating Privacy: At What Cost?" *Wired News*, September 19, 2000; Mary Mosquera, "Lawmakers Want Privacy Protections with Carnivore," *TechWeb*, September 6, 2000; and Peter Rojas, "Is It Spam or Spammimic?" *Red Herring*, February 15, 2001.

CASE STUDY QUESTIONS

1. Does Carnivore present an ethical dilemma? Explain your answer.

2. Apply an ethical analysis to the issue of the FBI's use of information technology and U.S. citizens' privacy rights.

3. What are the ethical, social, and political issues raised by the FBI tapping the e-mails of individuals and collecting personal data on them?

4. How effective is Carnivore as a terrorism and crime-prevention tool?

5. State your views on ways to solve the problems of collecting the key data the FBI can gain through Carnivore without interfering with the privacy of people not related to the crime involved.

ANALYZING BUSINESS PROCESSES FOR AN ENTERPRISE SYSTEM

Your firm manufactures specialty chemicals and dyestuffs used in plastics, fibers, and coatings. It operates five different production facilities in the southeastern United States, with corporate headquarters in Memphis, Tennessee.

Rapid time-to-market of new products, strong customer service, and low costs are essential for remaining competitive in the chemical industry. Management is looking for ways to make the company operate more efficiently and would like to start by examining order processing.

This is how the firm's order processing currently operates: A customer can call, fax, or mail in an order. A customer service representative writes down order information on an order pad. This information includes the customer name, shipping address, billing address, product number, product description, quantity, and shipping instructions (such as to call the receiving manager to make an appointment for delivery). After gathering all the relevant information, the representative confirms the entire order with the customer.

While taking down the order information, the customer service representative accesses the company's order entry system and checks the inventory for each product ordered. The customer service representative first checks the warehouse closest to the customer's shipping address. If the product is not available there, the representative checks another warehouse. If the order is placed on the telephone, the customer service representative suggests a delivery date, which is four to five business days away. If the customer needs the order sooner, the customer service representative queries the existing order entry system to see which warehouse might have the inventory to fulfill the order. Generally the warehouse closest to the customer's shipping address will fill the order.

All current orders are collected manually and entered into the firm's order entry system. The order will not be accepted by the system unless it includes the customer's identification number, shipping address, and billing address. (If the order is from a new customer, the system can assign a new customer number.) If the order has a delivery date of 8 to 10 business days in the future, the order form will be held manually for several days and then inputted into the system. If an order is for more than 10 days in the future, it will be treated as a back order when it is input into the system. The system generates a back-order report daily to remind customer service representatives of orders that they have on back order.

When each order has been entered, the system performs a credit check on the customer. Some customers are assigned "credit hold" status and are not shipped their orders until payment has been received for the purchase. Other customer orders are processed immediately and the customer pays for the purchase after receiving the shipment and an invoice. A report on credit hold is forwarded to the credit department and the customer service representatives receive a daily report on orders placed on credit hold.

Different business units at your company use different identification systems for the same products. In other words, corporate headquarters might use a different product number for a product such as Purple Dye #211 than the product identification number used at the plant where it was manufactured.

1. Diagram the order process. What are the outputs of this process?

2. What other major business processes outside of the order process are likely to be impacted by the order process? Explain.

3. How could this process be made more efficient? Draw a diagram of your proposed process and information changes.

4. Prepare descriptions of two reports from this system, one that would be important to the order entry staff and one that would be important to corporate management.

5. Your company is thinking about installing enterprise software. You would like to learn more about enterprise software and how it could handle your order entry process. Explore the Solutions Map for the chemical industry on the SAP Web site (www.sap.com). Which SAP processes are likely to address the activities in order processing that we have described? What questions would you ask to see if SAP's software could handle your order process?

6. You have heard that enterprise software might not be able to handle the following situations:

   - When the system checks for available inventory, it treats material (batches of chemicals) that is still undergoing quality control inspection as available inventory as well as material in inventory that has already passed quality control inspection.

- There is no way to automatically check customer records to see which qualify for sales tax exemptions.
- The system assigns a different date for back-ordered items that are currently out of stock rather than the original requested date on the customer order.

What impact might this lack of functionality have on order processing and other parts of the company? How could you determine how serious a problem this creates? What questions would you ask?

MANAGING HARDWARE AND SOFTWARE ASSETS

objectives

As a manager, you'll face many decisions about using hardware and software to improve the performance of your firm. After completing this chapter, you will be able to answer the following questions:

1. *What computer processing and storage capability does our organization need to handle its information and business transactions?*

2. *What arrangement of computers and computer processing would best benefit our organization?*

3. *What kinds of software and software tools do we need to run our business? What criteria should we use to select our software technology?*

4. *Of what new software technologies should we be aware? How would they benefit our organization?*

5. *How should we acquire and manage the firm's hardware and software assets?*

Bank of America (Asia) Upgrades Its IT Infrastructure

Hong Kong-based Bank of America (Asia) is the largest and most profitable subsidiary of the Bank of America outside of the United States. It has 15 branches in Hong Kong and Macau and offers a wide range of consumer and commercial banking products and services, including deposit and loan products, trade finance, foreign exchange, leasing, insurance, investment, and online and wireless banking services. As the Bank introduced new products it found that it needed a more flexible and robust information technology (IT) infrastructure that could integrate the systems supporting all of its products and that could provide a consistent customer experience across channels. The bank also wanted to reduce the costs of supporting and owning its technology assets.

The Bank's Core Banking system has been using Fiserv's ICBS Banking application running on an IBM AS/400 midrange computer for many years. This application interfaces with Base24 software running on a Tandem computer which acts as a transaction processor and message switch for banking transactions coming in from ATMs, phone banking, and Internet banking channels that are open 24 hours a day. The system worked well for the Bank's core products but could not easily handle new products, such as securities, mutual funds, and bonds, and new service channels

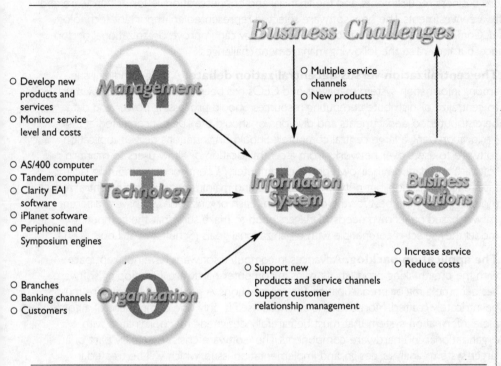

Business Challenges

○ Multiple service channels
○ New products

Management
○ Develop new products and services
○ Monitor service level and costs

Technology
○ AS/400 computer
○ Tandem computer
○ Clarity EAI software
○ iPlanet software
○ Periphonic and Symposium engines

Organization
○ Branches
○ Banking channels
○ Customers

Information System

○ Support new products and service channels
○ Support customer relationship management

Business Solutions

○ Increase service
○ Reduce costs

such as mobile phones and small handheld personal digital assistant computing devices.

Michael Leung, CIO for Bank of America (Asia) did not want to overhaul the entire system, but instead wanted to use middleware software products that could work with the bank's existing IT infrastructure while providing a platform that could handle new services and products. After a six-month search, Leung and his information systems staff selected Clarity Enterprise Application Integration (EAI) software and related middleware from Finesse Alliance. The Clarity EAI engine provides software that can integrate information from the new service channels with the systems supporting the bank's various financial products. The bank also installed other software tools, including iPlanet Web server software and Nortel Network's Periphonic IVR and Symposium CTI engines. The end result was an infrastructure with the flexibility to serve current and new demands from the bank's clients.

Sources: Winston Raj, "Are You Global-Proof?" *CIO Asia Magazine*, March 2002 and <www.bankofamerica.com.hk>, accessed July 5, 2002.

181

MANAGEMENT CHALLENGES

Bank of America (Asia) found that its efficiency and competitiveness were hampered by outdated technology. The company found it could offer more products and services to customers by using the right hardware and software. In order to select appropriate technology, the bank's management had to understand the capabilities of computer hardware and software technology, how to select hardware and software to meet current and future business requirements, and the financial and business rationale for its hardware and software investments. The new software selected represented an important technology asset. Computer hardware and software technology can improve organizational performance, but they raise the following management challenges:

1. **The centralization versus decentralization debate.** A long-standing issue among information system managers and CEOs has been the question of how much to centralize or distribute computing resources. Should processing power and data be distributed to departments and divisions, or should they be concentrated at a single location using a large central computer? Should organizations deliver application software to users over networks from a central location or allow users to maintain software and data on their own desktop computers? Client/server computing facilitates decentralization, but network computers and mainframes support a centralized model. Which is the best for the organization? Each organization will have a different answer based on its own needs. Managers need to make sure that the computing model they select is compatible with organizational goals (Schuff and St. Louis, 2001).

2. **The application backlog.** Advances in computer software have not kept pace with the breathtaking productivity gains in computer hardware. Developing software has become a major preoccupation for organizations. A great deal of software must be intricately crafted. Moreover, the software itself is only one component of a complete information system that must be carefully designed and coordinated with organizational and hardware components. The "software crisis" is actually part of a larger systems analysis, design, and implementation issue, which will be treated in detail later. Despite the gains from fourth-generation languages, personal desktop software tools, object-oriented programming, and software tools for the Web, many businesses continue to face a backlog of two to three years in developing the information systems they need, or they will not be able to develop them at all.

Although managers and business professionals do not need to be computer technology experts, they should have a basic understanding of the role of hardware and software in the organization's information technology (IT) infrastructure so that they can make technology decisions that promote organizational performance and productivity. This chapter surveys the capabilities of computer hardware and computer software and highlights the major issues in the management of the firm's hardware and software assets.

6.1 COMPUTER HARDWARE AND INFORMATION TECHNOLOGY INFRASTRUCTURE

Computer hardware, which we defined in Chapter 1, provides the underlying physical foundation for the firm's IT infrastructure. Other infrastructure components—software, data, and networks—require computer hardware for their storage or operation.

THE COMPUTER SYSTEM

Computer

Physical device that takes data as an input, transforms the data by executing stored instructions, and outputs information to a number of devices.

A **computer** is a physical device that takes data as input, transforms these data according to stored instructions, and outputs the processed information. A contemporary computer system consists of a central processing unit, primary storage, secondary storage, input devices, output devices, and communications devices (see Figure 6-1). The central processing unit manipulates raw data into a more useful form and controls the other parts of the computer system.

Figure 6-1 Hardware components of a computer system. A
contemporary computer system
can be categorized into six major
components. The central processing unit manipulates data and controls the other parts of the computer system; primary storage
temporarily stores data and program instructions during processing; secondary storage stores data
and instructions when they are not
used in processing; input devices
convert data and instructions for
processing in the computer; output devices present data in a form
that people can understand; and
communications devices control
the passing of information to and
from communications networks.

Primary storage temporarily stores data and program instructions during processing, whereas secondary storage devices (magnetic and optical disks, magnetic tape) store data and programs when they are not being used in processing. Input devices, such as a keyboard or mouse, convert data and instructions into electronic form for input into the computer. Output devices, such as printers and video display terminals, convert electronic data produced by the computer system and display them in a form that people can understand. Communications devices provide connections between the computer and communications networks. Buses are circuitry paths for transmitting data and signals among the parts of the computer system.

In order for information to flow through a computer system and be in a form suitable for processing, all symbols, pictures, or words must be reduced to a string of binary digits. A binary digit is called a **bit** and represents either a 0 or a 1. In the computer, the presence of an electronic or magnetic signal means 1, and its absence signifies 0. Digital computers operate directly with binary digits, either singly or strung together to form bytes. A string of 8 bits that the computer stores as a unit is called a **byte.** Each byte can be used to store a decimal number, a symbol, a character, or part of a picture (see Figure 6-2).

bit

A binary digit representing the smallest unit of data in a computer system. It can only have one of two states, representing 0 or 1.

byte

A string of bits, usually 8, used to store one number or character in a computer system.

central processing unit (CPU)

Area of the computer system that manipulates symbols, numbers, and letters, and controls the other parts of the computer system.

The CPU and Primary Storage

The **central processing unit (CPU)** is the part of the computer system where the manipulation of symbols, numbers, and letters occurs, and it controls the other parts of the computer system (see Figure 6-3). Located near the CPU is **primary storage** (sometimes called primary memory or main memory), where data and program instructions are stored temporarily during processing. Buses provide pathways for transmitting data and signals between the CPU, primary storage, and the other devices in the computer system. The characteristics of the CPU and primary storage are very important in determining a computer's speed and capabilities.

Figure 6-3 also shows that the CPU consists of an arithmetic-logic unit and a control unit. The **arithmetic-logic unit (ALU)** performs the computer's principal logical and arithmetic operations. It adds, subtracts, multiplies, and divides, determining whether a number is positive, negative, or zero. In addition to performing arithmetic functions, an ALU must be able to determine when one quantity is greater than or less than another and when two quantities are equal. The ALU can perform logic operations on letters as well as numbers.

primary storage

Part of the computer that temporarily stores program instructions and data being used by the instructions.

arithmetic-logic unit (ALU)

Component of the CPU that performs the computer's principal logic and arithmetic operations.

| 0 | or | 1 | One bit |

Characters are represented by one byte for each letter.

| 0 | 1 | 0 | 0 | 0 | 0 | 0 | 1 | One byte for character A

Figure 6-2 Bits and bytes. Bits are represented by either a 0 or 1. A string of 8 bits constitutes a byte, which represents a character or number. Illustrated here is a byte representing the letter "A" using the ASCII binary coding standard.

Figure 6-3 The CPU and primary storage. The CPU contains an arithmetic-logic unit and a control unit. Data and instructions are stored in unique addresses in primary storage that the CPU can access during processing. The data bus, address bus, and control bus transmit signals between the central processing unit, primary storage, and other devices in the computer system.

control unit
Component of the CPU that controls and coordinates the other parts of the computer system.

machine cycle
Series of operations required to process a single machine instruction.

RAM (random access memory)
Primary storage of data or program instructions that can directly access any randomly chosen location in the same amount of time.

ROM (read-only memory)
Semiconductor memory chips that contain program instructions. These chips can only be read from; they cannot be written to.

microprocessor
Very large scale integrated circuit technology that integrates the computer's memory, logic, and control on a single chip.

megahertz
A measure of cycle speed, or the pacing of events in a computer; one megahertz equals one million cycles per second.

The **control unit** coordinates and controls the other parts of the computer system. It reads a stored program, one instruction at a time, and directs other components of the computer system to perform the program's required tasks. The series of operations required to process a single machine instruction is called the **machine cycle.**

Primary storage has three functions. It stores all or part of the software program that is being executed. Primary storage also stores the operating system programs that manage the operation of the computer (see Section 6.3). Finally, the primary storage area holds data that the program is using. Internal primary storage is often called **RAM,** or **random access memory.** It is called RAM because it can directly access any randomly chosen location in the same amount of time.

Primary memory is divided into storage locations called *bytes*. Each location contains a set of eight binary switches or devices, each of which can store one bit of information. The set of eight bits found in each storage location is sufficient to store one letter, one digit, or one special symbol (such as $). Each byte has a unique address, similar to a mailbox, indicating where it is located in RAM. The computer can remember where the data in all of the bytes are located simply by keeping track of these addresses. Computer storage capacity is measured in bytes. Table 6-1 lists the primary measures of computer storage capacity and processing speed.

Primary storage is composed of *semiconductors*, which are integrated circuits made by printing thousands and even millions of tiny transistors on small silicon chips. There are several different kinds of semiconductor memory used in primary storage. RAM is used for short-term storage of data or program instructions. RAM is volatile: Its contents will be lost when the computer's electric supply is disrupted by a power outage or when the computer is turned off. **ROM,** or **read-only memory,** can only be read from; it cannot be written to. ROM chips come from the manufacturer with programs already burned in, or stored. ROM is used in general-purpose computers to store important or frequently used programs.

COMPUTER PROCESSING

The processing capability of the CPU plays a large role in determining the amount of work that a computer system can accomplish.

Microprocessors and Processing Power

Contemporary CPUs use semiconductor chips called **microprocessors,** which integrate all of the memory, logic, and control circuits for an entire CPU onto a single chip. The speed and performance of a computer's microprocessors help determine a computer's processing power and are based on the number of bits that can be processed at one time (*word length*), the amount of data that can be moved between the CPU, primary storage and other devices (data bus width), and cycle speed, measured in **megahertz.** (Megahertz is abbreviated MHz and stands for millions of cycles per second).

TABLE 6-1	KEY MEASURES OF COMPUTER STORAGE CAPACITY AND PROCESSING SPEED

Storage Capacity	
Byte	String of 8 bits
Kilobyte	1,000 bytes (actually 1,024 storage positions)
Megabyte	1,000,000 bytes
Gigabyte	1,000,000,000 bytes
Terabyte	1,000,000,000,000 bytes
Processing Speed	
Microsecond	1/1,000,000 second
Nanosecond	1/1,000,000,000 second
Picosecond	1/1,000,000,000,000 second
MIPS	Millions of instructions per second

Microprocessors can be made faster by using **reduced instruction set computing (RISC)** in their design. Conventional chips, based on complex instruction set computing, have several hundred or more instructions hard-wired into their circuitry, and they may take several cycles to execute a single instruction. If the little-used instructions are eliminated, the remaining instructions can execute much faster. RISC computers have only the most frequently used instructions embedded in them. A RISC CPU can execute most instructions in a single machine cycle and sometimes multiple instructions at the same time. RISC is often used in scientific and workstation computing.

Parallel Processing

Processing can also be sped up by linking several processors to work simultaneously on the same task. Figure 6-4 compares parallel processing to serial processing used in conventional computers. In **parallel processing,** multiple processing units (CPUs) break down a problem into smaller parts and work on it simultaneously. Getting a group of processors to attack the same problem at once requires both rethinking the problems and special software that can divide problems among different processors in the most efficient way possible, providing the needed data, and reassembling the many subtasks to reach an appropriate solution.

Massively parallel computers have huge networks of processor chips interwoven in complex and flexible ways to attack large computing problems. As opposed to parallel processing, where small numbers of powerful but expensive specialized chips are linked together, massively parallel machines link hundreds or even thousands of inexpensive, commonly used chips to break problems into many small pieces and solve them.

reduced instruction set computing (RISC)
Technology used to enhance the speed of microprocessors by embedding only the most frequently used instructions on a chip.

parallel processing
Type of processing in which more than one instruction can be processed at a time by breaking down a problem into smaller parts and processing them simultaneously with multiple processors.

massively parallel computers
Computers that use hundreds or thousands of processing chips to attack large computing problems simultaneously.

Figure 6-4 Sequential and parallel processing. During sequential processing, each task is assigned to one CPU that processes one instruction at a time. In parallel processing, multiple tasks are assigned to multiple processing units to expedite the result.

STORAGE, INPUT AND OUTPUT TECHNOLOGY

The capabilities of computer systems depend not only on the speed and capacity of the CPU but also on the speed, capacity, and design of storage, input and output technology. Storage, input and output devices are called *peripheral devices* because they are outside the main computer system unit.

Secondary Storage Technology

Electronic commerce and electronic business have made storage a strategic technology. Although electronic commerce and electronic business are reducing manual processes, data of all types must be stored electronically and available whenever needed. Most of the information used by a computer application is stored on secondary storage devices located outside of the primary storage area. **Secondary storage** is used for relatively long term storage of data outside the CPU. Secondary storage is nonvolatile and retains data even when the computer is turned off. The most important secondary storage technologies are magnetic disk, optical disk, and magnetic tape.

Magnetic Disk   The most widely used secondary storage medium today is **magnetic disk.** There are two kinds of magnetic disks: floppy disks (used in PCs) and **hard disks** (used on large commercial disk drives and PCs). Large mainframe or midrange computer systems have multiple hard disk drives because they require immense disk storage capacity in the gigabyte and terabyte range. PCs also use **floppy disks,** which are removable and portable, with lower storage capacities and access rates than hard disks. Removable disk drives are becoming popular backup storage alternatives for PC systems. Magnetic disks on both large and small computers permit direct access to individual records so that data stored on the disk can be directly accessed regardless of the order in which the data were originally recorded. Disk technology is useful for systems requiring rapid and direct access to data.

Disk drive performance can be further enhanced by using a disk technology called **RAID (Redundant Array of Inexpensive Disks).** RAID devices package more than a hundred disk drives, a controller chip, and specialized software into a single large unit. Traditional disk drives deliver data from the disk drive along a single path, but RAID delivers data over multiple paths simultaneously, improving disk access time and reliability. For most RAID systems, data on a failed disk can be restored automatically without the computer system having to be shut down.

Optical Disks   Optical disks, also called compact disks or laser optical disks, use laser technology to store massive quantities of data in a highly compact form. They are available for both PCs and large computers. The most common optical disk system used with PCs is called **CD-ROM (compact disk read-only memory).** A 4.75-inch compact disk for PCs can store up to 660 megabytes, nearly 300 times more than a high-density floppy disk. Optical disks are most appropriate for applications where enormous quantities of unchanging data must be stored compactly for easy retrieval or for applications combining text, sound, and images.

CD-ROM is read-only storage. No new data can be written to it; it can only be read. *WORM (write once/read many)* and *CD-R (compact disk-recordable)* optical disk systems allow users to record data only once on an optical disk. Once written, the data cannot be erased but can be read indefinitely. **CD-RW (CD-ReWritable)** technology has been developed to allow

---

secondary storage

Relatively long term, nonvolatile storage of data outside the CPU and primary storage.

magnetic disk

A secondary storage medium in which data are stored by means of magnetized spots on a hard or floppy disk.

hard disk

Magnetic disk resembling a metallic platter; used in large computer systems and in most PCs.

floppy disk

Removable magnetic disk storage primarily used with PCs.

RAID (Redundant Array of Inexpensive Disks)

Disk storage technology to boost disk performance by packaging more than 100 smaller disk drives with a controller chip and specialized software in a single large unit to deliver data over multiple paths simultaneously.

CD-ROM (compact disk read-only memory)

Read-only optical disk storage used for imaging, reference, and other applications with massive amounts of unchanging data and for multimedia.

CD-RW (CD-ReWritable)

Optical disk storage that can be rewritten many times by users

---

Secondary storage devices such as floppy disks, optical disks, and hard disks are used to store large quantities of data outside the CPU and primary storage. They provide direct access to data for easy retrieval.

users to create rewritable optical disks for applications requiring large volumes of storage where the information is occasionally updated.

Digital video disks (DVDs), also called digital versatile disks, are optical disks the same size as CD-ROMs but of even higher capacity. They can hold a minimum of 4.7 gigabytes of data, enough to store a full-length, high-quality motion picture. DVDs are initially being used to store movies and multimedia applications using large amounts of video and graphics, but they may replace CD-ROMs because they can store large amounts of digitized text, graphics, audio, and video data. Once read-only, writable and re-writable DVD drives and media are now available.

Magnetic Tape   **Magnetic tape** is an older storage technology that still is employed for secondary storage of large quantities of data that are needed rapidly but not instantly. Magnetic tape is very inexpensive and relatively stable. However, it stores data sequentially and is relatively slow compared to the speed of other secondary storage media. In order to find an individual record stored on magnetic tape, such as an employment record, the tape must be read from the beginning up to the location of the desired record.

Storage Networking   To meet the escalating demand for data-intensive graphics, Web transactions, and other digital firm applications, the amount of data that companies need to store is doubling every 12 to 18 months. Companies are turning to new kinds of storage infrastructures to deal with the complexity and cost of mushrooming storage requirements.

Large companies have many different storage resources—disk drives, tape backup drives, RAID, and other devices that may be scattered in many different locations. This arrangement is expensive to manage and makes it difficult to access data across the enterprise. Storage networking technology enables firms to manage all of their storage resources centrally by providing an overall storage plan for all the storage devices in the enterprise.

There are alternative storage networking arrangements. In *direct-attached storage*, storage devices are connected directly to individual server computers and must be accessed through each server, which can create bottlenecks. **Network-attached storage (NAS)** overcomes this problem by attaching high-speed RAID storage devices to a network so that the devices in the network can access this storage through a specialized server dedicated to file service and storage. **Storage-area networks (SANs)** go one step further by placing multiple storage devices on a separate high-speed network dedicated to storage purposes. The SAN creates a large central pool of storage that can be shared by multiple servers so that users can rapidly share data across the SAN. The storage area network (SAN) connects different kinds of storage devices, such as tape libraries and disk arrays. The SAN storage devices are located on their own network and connected using a high-transmission technology such as Fibre Channel. The network moves data among pools of servers and storage devices, creating an enterprise-wide infrastructure for data storage. Figure 6-5 illustrates how a SAN works.

SANs can be expensive and difficult to manage, but they are very useful for companies that need to share information across applications and computing platforms. SANs can help these companies consolidate their storage resources and provide rapid data access for widely distributed users.

Input and Output Devices

Human beings interact with computer systems largely through input and output devices. Input devices gather data and convert them into electronic form for use by the computer, whereas output devices display data after they have been processed. Table 6-2 describes the principal input and output devices.

The principal input devices consist of keyboards, pointing devices (such as the computer mouse and touch screens), and *source data automation* technologies (optical and magnetic ink character recognition, pen-based input, digital scanners, audio input, and sensors), which capture data in computer-readable form at the time and place they are created. They also include **radio-frequency identification (RFID)** devices that use tiny tags incorporating embedded microchips containing information about an item and its location to transmit signals over a short distance to special RFID readers. The information is then transferred to a processing device. RFID is especially useful for tracking the location of items as they move through the supply chain. The principal output devices are cathode ray tube terminals (CRTs), sometimes called video display terminals (VDTs), printers, and audio output.

Digital Video Disk (DVD)
High-capacity optical storage medium that can store full-length motion pictures and large amounts of data.

magnetic tape
Inexpensive, older secondary-storage medium in which large volumes of information are stored sequentially by means of magnetized and nonmagnetized spots on tape.

network-attached storage (NAS)
Attaching high-speed RAID storage devices to a network so that the devices in the network can access these storage devices through a specialized server dedicated to file service and storage.

storage area network (SAN)
A high-speed network dedicated to storage that connects different kinds of storage devices, such as tape libraries and disk arrays so that they can be shared by multiple servers across the enterprise.

radio-frequency identification (RFID)
Devices using tiny tags with embedded microchips containing information on an item and its location that is transmitted to special RFID readers.

Figure 6-5 A storage area network (SAN). A typical SAN consists of a server, storage devices, and networking devices and is used strictly for storage. The SAN stores data on many different types of storage devices, providing data to the enterprise. The SAN supports communication between any server and the storage unit as well as between different storage devices in the network.

Batch and Online Input and Processing

batch processing
A method of collecting and processing data in which transactions are accumulated and stored until a specified time when it is convenient or necessary to process them as a group.

online processing
A method of collecting and processing data in which transactions are entered directly into the computer system and processed immediately.

The manner in which data are input into the computer affects how the data can be processed. Information systems collect and process information in one of two ways: through batch or through online processing. In **batch processing,** transactions, such as orders or payroll time cards, are accumulated and stored in a group or batch until the time when, because of some reporting cycle, it is efficient or necessary to process them. Batch processing is found primarily in older systems where users need only occasional reports. In **online processing,** the user enters transactions into a device (such as a data entry keyboard or bar code reader) that is directly connected to the computer system. The transactions usually are processed immediately. Most processing today is online processing.

Figure 6-6 compares batch and online processing. Batch systems often use tape as a storage medium, whereas online processing systems use disk storage, which permits immediate access to specific records. In batch systems, transactions are accumulated in a *transaction file,* which contains all the transactions for a particular time period. Periodically, this file is used to update a *master file,* which contains permanent information on entities. (An example is a payroll master file with employee earnings and deduction data. It is updated with weekly time-card transactions.) Adding the transaction data to the existing master file creates a new master file. In online processing, transactions are entered into the system immediately using a keyboard, pointing device, or source data automation, and the system usually responds immediately. The master file is updated continually.

Multimedia combines text, graphics, sound, and video into a computer-based experience that permits two-way communication. Many organizations use this technology for interactive training.

Interactive Multimedia

The processing, input, output, and storage technologies we have just described can be used to cre-

TABLE 6-2   INPUT AND OUTPUT DEVICES

Input Device	Description
Keyboard	Principal method of data entry for text and numerical data.
Computer mouse	Handheld device with point-and-click capabilities that is usually connected to the computer by a cable. The computer user can move the mouse around on a desktop to control the cursor's position on a computer display screen, pushing a button to select a command. Trackballs and touch pads often are used in place of the mouse as pointing devices on laptop PCs.
Touch screen	Allows users to enter limited amounts of data by touching the surface of a sensitized video display monitor with a finger or a pointer. Often found in information kiosks in retail stores, restaurants, and shopping malls.
Optical character recognition	Devices that can translate specially designed marks, characters, and codes into digital form. The most widely used optical code is the *bar code*, which is used in point-of-sale systems in supermarkets and retail stores. The codes can include time, date, and location data in addition to identification data.
Magnetic ink character recognition (MICR)	Used primarily in check processing for the banking industry. Characters on the bottom of a check identify the bank, checking account, and check number and are preprinted using a special magnetic ink. A MICR reader translates these characters into digital form for the computer.
Pen-based input	Handwriting-recognition devices, such as pen-based tablets, notebooks, and notepads, convert the motion made by an electronic stylus pressing on a touch-sensitive tablet screen into digital form.
Digital scanner	Translates images such as pictures or documents into digital form and are an essential component of image-processing systems.
Audio input	Voice input devices that convert spoken words into digital form for processing by the computer. Microphones and tape cassette players can serve as input devices for music and other sounds.
Sensors	Devices that collect data directly from the environment for input into a computer system. For instance, today's farmers can use sensors to monitor the moisture of the soil in their fields to help them with irrigation.
Radio frequency identification (RFID)	Use of tags incorporating microchips to transmit information about items and their location to special RFID readers. Useful for tracking the location of items as they move through the supply chain.
Output Device	**Description**
Cathode ray tube (CRT)	Electronic gun that shoots a beam of electrons illuminating tiny points on a display screen. Laptop computers use flat panel displays, which are less bulky than CRT monitors.
Printers	Produce a printed hard copy of information output. They include impact printers (such as dot matrix printers) and nonimpact printers (laser, inkjet, and thermal transfer printers).
Audio output	Voice output devices convert digital output data back into intelligible speech. Other audio output, such as music, can be delivered by speakers connected to the computer.

ate **multimedia** applications that integrate sound and full-motion video, or animation with graphics and text into a computer-based application. Multimedia is becoming the foundation of new consumer products and services, such as electronic books and newspapers, electronic classroom-presentation technologies, full-motion videoconferencing, imaging, graphics design tools, and video and voice mail. PCs today come with built-in multimedia capabilities, including high-resolution color monitors, CD-ROM drives or DVD drives to store video, audio, and graphic data, and stereo speakers for amplifying audio output.

Interactive Web pages replete with graphics, sound, animations, and full-motion video have made multimedia popular on the Internet. For example, visitors to the CNN.com Web site can access news stories from CNN, photos, on-air transcripts, video clips, and audio clips. The video and audio clips are made available using **streaming technology,** which allows audio and video data to be processed as a steady and continuous stream as they are downloaded from the Web.

Multimedia Web sites are also being used to sell digital products, such as digitized music clips. A compression standard known as **MP3,** also called **MPEG3,** which stands for Motion Picture Experts Group, audio layer 3, can compress audio files down to one-tenth or one-twelfth of their original size with virtually no loss in quality. Visitors to Web sites such as MP3.com can download MP3 music clips over the Internet and play them on their own computers.

multimedia

The integration of two or more types of media such as text, graphics, sound, voice, full-motion video, or animation into a computer-based application.

streaming technology

Technology for transferring data so that they can be processed as a steady and continuous stream.

MP3 (MPEG3)

Compression standard that can compress audio files for transfer over the Internet with virtually no loss in quality.

Figure 6-6 A comparison of batch and online processing. In batch processing, transactions are accumulated and stored in a group. Because batches are processed at regular intervals, such as daily, weekly, or monthly, information in the system will not always be up to date. In online processing, transactions are input immediately and usually processed immediately. Information in the system is generally up to date. A typical online application is an airline reservation system.

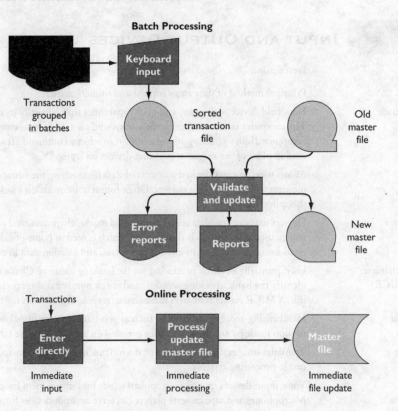

mainframe

Largest category of computer; used for major business processing.

midrange computer

Middle-size computer that is capable of supporting the computing needs of smaller organizations or of managing networks of other computers.

minicomputer

Middle-range computer used in systems for universities, factories, or research laboratories.

server

Computer specifically optimized to provide software and other resources to other computers over a network.

server farm

Large group of servers maintained by a commercial vendor and made available to subscribers for electronic commerce and other activities requiring heavy use of servers.

personal computer (PC)

Small desktop or portable computer.

workstation

Desktop computer with powerful graphics and mathematical capabilities and the ability to perform several complicated tasks at once.

6.2 CATEGORIES OF COMPUTERS AND COMPUTER SYSTEMS

Contemporary computers can be categorized as mainframes, midrange computers, PCs, workstations, and supercomputers. Managers need to understand the capabilities of each of these types of computers, and why some types are more appropriate for certain processing work than others.

CLASSIFYING COMPUTERS

A **mainframe** is the largest computer, a powerhouse with massive memory and extremely rapid processing power. It is used for very large business, scientific, or military applications where a computer must handle massive amounts of data or many complicated processes. A **midrange computer** is less powerful, less expensive, and smaller than a mainframe but capable of supporting the computing needs of smaller organizations or of managing networks of other computers. Midrange computers can be **minicomputers,** which are used in systems for universities, factories, or research laboratories, or they can be **servers,** which are used for managing internal company networks or Web sites. Server computers are specifically optimized to support a computer network, enabling users to share files, software, peripheral devices (such as printers), or other network resources. Servers have large memory and disk-storage capacity, high-speed communications capabilities, and powerful CPUs.

Servers have become important components of firms' IT infrastructures, because they provide the hardware platform for electronic commerce. By adding special software, they can be customized to deliver Web pages, process purchase and sale transactions, or exchange data with systems inside the company. Organizations with heavy electronic commerce requirements and massive Web sites are running their Web and electronic commerce applications on multiple servers in **server farms** in computing centers run by commercial vendors such as IBM.

A **personal computer (PC),** which is sometimes referred to as a *microcomputer,* is one that can be placed on a desktop or carried from room to room. Smaller laptop PCs are often used as portable desktops on the road. PCs are used as personal machines as well as in business. A **workstation** also fits on a desktop but has more powerful mathematical and graphics-processing capabilities than a PC and can perform more complicated tasks than a PC in the same amount of time. Workstations are used for scientific, engineering, and design work that requires powerful graphics or computational capabilities.

A **supercomputer** is a highly sophisticated and powerful computer that is used for tasks requiring extremely rapid and complex calculations with hundreds of thousands of variable factors. Supercomputers use parallel processors and traditionally have been used in scientific and military work, such as classified weapons research and weather forecasting, which use complex mathematical models. They are now starting to be used in business for the manipulation of vast quantities of data.

COMPUTER NETWORKS AND CLIENT/SERVER COMPUTING

Today, stand-alone computers have been replaced by computers in networks for most processing tasks. The use of multiple computers linked by a communications network for processing is called **distributed processing.** In contrast, with **centralized processing,** in which all processing is accomplished by one large central computer, distributed processing distributes the processing work among PCs, midrange computers, and mainframes linked together.

One widely used form of distributed processing is **client/server computing.** Client/server computing splits processing between "clients" and "servers." Both are on the network, but each machine is assigned functions it is best suited to perform. The **client** is the user point-of-entry for the required function and is normally a desktop computer, workstation, or laptop computer. The user generally interacts directly only with the client portion of the application, often to input data or retrieve data for further analysis. The *server* provides the client with services. The server could be a mainframe or another desktop computer, but specialized server computers are often used in this role. Servers store and process shared data and also perform back-end functions not visible to users, such as managing network activities. Figure 6-7 illustrates the client/server computing concept. Computing on the Internet uses the client/server model (see Chapter 9).

Figure 6-8 illustrates five different ways that the components of an application could be partitioned between the client and the server. The interface component is essentially the application interface—how the application appears visually to the user. The application logic component consists of the processing logic, which is shaped by the organization's business rules. (An example might be that a salaried employee is only to be paid monthly.) The data management component consists of the storage and management of the data used by the application. The exact division of tasks depends on the requirements of each application, including its processing needs, the number of users, and the available resources.

In some firms client/server networks with PCs have actually replaced mainframes and minicomputers. The process of transferring applications from large computers to smaller ones is called **downsizing.** Downsizing can potentially reduce computing costs, because memory and processing power on a PC cost a fraction of their equivalent on a mainframe. The decision to downsize involves many factors in addition to the cost of computer hardware, including the need for new software, training, and perhaps new organizational procedures (see the discussion of total cost of ownership in Section 6.4).

NETWORK COMPUTERS AND PEER-TO-PEER COMPUTING

In one form of client/server computing, client processing and storage capabilities are so minimal that the bulk of computer processing occurs on the server. The term *thin client* is sometimes

supercomputer
Highly sophisticated and powerful computer that can perform very complex computations extremely rapidly.

distributed processing
The distribution of computer processing work among multiple computers linked by a communications network.

centralized processing
Processing that is accomplished by one large central computer.

client/server computing
A model for computing that splits processing between "clients" and "servers" on a network, assigning functions to the machine most able to perform the function.

client
The user point-of-entry for the required function in client/server computing. Normally a desktop computer, workstation, or laptop computer.

downsizing
The process of transferring applications from large computers to smaller ones.

Figure 6-7 Client/server computing. In client/server computing, computer processing is split between client machines and server machines linked by a network. Users interface with the client machines.

Figure 6-8 Types of client/server computing. There are various ways in which an application's interface, logic, and data management components can be divided among the clients and servers in a network.

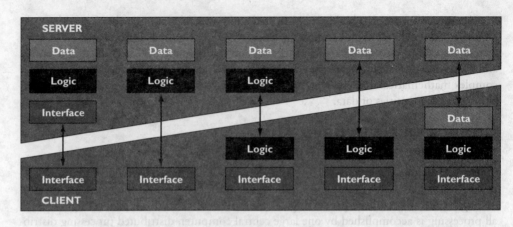

network computer (NC)
Simplified desktop computer that does not store software programs or data locally. Users download whatever software or data they need from a central computer over the Internet or an organization's own internal network.

used to refer to the client in this arrangement. Thin clients with minimal memory, storage and processor power and which are designed to work on networks are called **network computers (NCs).** NC users download whatever software or data they need from a central computer over the Internet or an organization's internal network. The central computer also saves information for the user and makes it available for later retrieval, effectively eliminating the need for secondary storage devices such as hard disks, floppy disks, CD-ROMs, and their drives.

NCs are less expensive to purchase than PCs with local processing and storage, and can be administered and updated from a central network server. Software programs and applications would not have to be purchased, installed, and upgraded for each user because software would be delivered and maintained from one central point. Network computers and centralized software distribution thus could increase management control over the organization's computing function.

However, PC prices have fallen so that units can be purchased for almost the same cost as NCs. If a network failure occurs, hundreds or thousands of employees would not be able to use their computers, whereas people could keep working if they had full-function PCs. Companies should closely examine how network computers might fit into their information technology infrastructure.

Peer-to-Peer Computing

peer-to-peer computing
Form of distributed processing that links computers via the Internet or private networks so that they can share processing tasks.

Another form of distributed processing, called **peer-to-peer computing,** puts processing power back on users' desktops, linking these computers so that they can share processing tasks. Individual PCs, workstations, or other computers can share data, disk space, and even processing power for a variety of tasks when they are linked in a network, including the Internet. The peer-to-peer computing model stands in contrast to the network computing model, because processing power resides only on individual desktops and these computers work together without a server or any central controlling authority.

It has been estimated that most companies—and individuals—use less than 25 percent of their processing and storage capacity. Peer-to-peer computing taps the unused disk space or processing power on PC or workstation networks for large computing tasks that previously could only be performed by large expensive server computers or even supercomputers.

grid computing
Applying the computational resources of many computers in the network to a single large and complex problem.

One form of peer-to-peer computing called **grid computing** uses special software to reclaim unused computing cycles on desktop computers and harness them into a "virtual supercomputer." This platform breaks down problems into small pieces that can run on many separate machines. For example, hundreds of engineers at Pratt & Whitney use grid computing to perform complex computations that simulate air flow through jet engines and test stress on materials, running their jobs on a computational "grid" consisting of 8,000 computer chips inside 5,000 workstations in three different cities (Ricadela, 2002).

Each form of computer processing can provide benefits, depending on the business needs of the organization. Peer-to-peer computing is especially useful for research and design collaboration work, while network computing may be appropriate for firms with a highly centralized information technology infrastructure.

6.3 TYPES OF SOFTWARE

To play a useful role in the firm's information technology infrastructure, computer hardware requires computer software. Chapter 1 defined computer *software* as the detailed instructions that control the operation of a computer system. Selecting appropriate software for the organization is a key management decision.

A software **program** is a series of statements or instructions to the computer. The process of writing or coding programs is termed *programming*, and individuals who specialize in this task are called *programmers*.

There are two major types of software: system software and application software. Each kind performs a different function. **System software** is a set of generalized programs that manage the computer's resources, such as the central processor, communications links, and peripheral devices. Programmers who write system software are called *system programmers*.

Application software describes the programs that are written for or by users to apply the computer to a specific task. Software for processing an order or generating a mailing list is application software. Programmers who write application software are called *application programmers*.

The types of software are interrelated and can be thought of as a set of nested boxes, each of which must interact closely with the other boxes surrounding it. Figure 6-9 illustrates this relationship. The system software surrounds and controls access to the hardware. Application software must work through the system software in order to operate. End users work primarily with application software. Each type of software must be specially designed for a specific machine to ensure its compatibility.

SYSTEM SOFTWARE AND PC OPERATING SYSTEMS

System software coordinates the various parts of the computer system and mediates between application software and computer hardware. The system software that manages and controls the computer's activities is called the **operating system.** Other system software consists of computer language translation programs that convert programming languages into machine language that can be understood by the computer and utility programs that perform common processing tasks.

The operating system is the computer system's chief manager. The operating system allocates and assigns system resources, schedules the use of computer resources and computer jobs, and monitors computer system activities. The operating system provides locations in primary memory for data and programs, and controls the input and output devices, such as printers, terminals, and telecommunication links. The operating system also coordinates the scheduling of work in various areas of the computer so that different parts of different jobs can

program
A series of statements or instructions to the computer.

system software
Generalized programs that manage the computer's resources, such as the central processor, communications links, and peripheral devices.

application software
Programs written for a specific application to perform functions specified by end users.

operating system
The system software that manages and controls the activities of the computer.

SYSTEM SOFTWARE

Operating System

Schedules computer events
Allocates computer resources
Monitors events

Language Translators

Interpreters
Compilers

Utility Programs

Routine operations (e.g., sort, list, print)
Manage data (e.g., create files, merge files)

APPLICATION SOFTWARE

Programming languages
Assembly language

FORTRAN   PASCAL
COBOL   C
BASIC   Fourth-generation languages and PC software tools

Figure 6-9 The major types of software. The relationship between system software, application software, and users can be illustrated by a series of nested boxes. System software—consisting of operating systems, language translators, and utility programs—controls access to the hardware. Application software, such as programming languages and "fourth-generation" languages, must work through the system software to operate. The user interacts primarily with the application software.

be worked on at the same time. Finally, the operating system keeps track of each computer job and may also keep track of who is using the system, of what programs have been run, and of any unauthorized attempts to access the system. Operating system capabilities, such as multi-programming, virtual storage, time sharing, and multiprocessing, enable the computer to handle many different tasks and users at the same time. Table 6-3 describes these capabilities.

Language Translation and Utility Software

System software includes special language translator programs that translate high-level language programs written in programming languages such as COBOL, FORTRAN, or C into machine language that the computer can execute. The program in the high-level language before translation into machine language is called **source code.** A **compiler** translates source code into machine code called *object code,* which is linked to other object code modules and then executed by the computer. Some programming languages, such as BASIC, do not use a compiler but an *interpreter,* which translates each source code statement one at a time into machine code and executes it.

System software includes *utility programs* for routine, repetitive tasks, such as copying, clearing primary storage, computing a square root, or sorting. Utility programs can be shared by all users of a computer system and can be used in many different information system applications when requested.

PC Operating Systems and Graphical User Interfaces

Like any other software, PC software is based on specific operating systems and computer hardware. Software written for one PC operating system generally cannot run on another. Table 6-4 compares the leading PC operating systems: Windows XP, Windows 98 and Windows Me, Windows 2000, Windows CE, UNIX, Linux, OS/2, the Macintosh operating system, and DOS.

When a user interacts with a computer, including a PC, the interaction is controlled by an operating system. A user communicates with an operating system through the user interface of that operating system. Contemporary PC operating systems use a **graphical user interface,** often called a GUI, which makes extensive use of icons, buttons, bars, and boxes to perform tasks. It has become the dominant model for the user interface of PC operating systems and for many types of application software.

Microsoft's Windows family of operating systems provides a streamlined graphical user interface that arranges icons to provide instant access to common tasks. They can perform multiple programming tasks simultaneously and have powerful networking capabilities, including the capability to integrate fax, e-mail, and scheduling programs. They include

---

source code

Program instructions written in a high-level programming language that must be translated into machine language to be executed by the computer.

compiler

Special system software that translates a high-level language into machine language for execution by the computer.

graphical user interface (GUI)

The part of an operating system users interact with that uses graphic icons and the computer mouse to issue commands and make selections.

TABLE 6-3   OPERATING SYSTEM CAPABILITIES

Operating System Capability	Description
Multiprogramming	Multiple programs can share a computer system's resources at any one time through concurrent use of the CPU. Only one program is actually using the CPU at any given moment, but the input/output needs of other programs can be serviced at the same time.
Virtual Storage	Handles programs more efficiently by breaking down the programs into tiny sections that are read into memory only when needed. The rest of each program is stored on disk until it is required. Virtual storage allows very large programs to be executed by small machines, or a large number of programs to be executed concurrently by a single machine.
Time Sharing	Allows many users to share computer processing resources simultaneously by allocating each a tiny slice of computer time to perform computing tasks and transferring processing from user to user. This arrangement permits many users to be connected to a CPU simultaneously, with each receiving only a tiny amount of CPU time.
Multiprocessing	Links together two or more CPUs to work in parallel in a single computer system. The operating system can assign multiple CPUs to execute different instructions from the same program or from different programs simultaneously, dividing the work between the CPUs.

TABLE 6-4   LEADING PC OPERATING SYSTEMS

Operating System	Features
Windows XP	Reliable, robust operating system for powerful PCs with versions for both home and corporate users. Features support of the Internet, multimedia, and group collaboration, along with powerful networking, security, and corporate management capabilities.
Windows 98/Me	Earlier versions of the Windows operating system for home users. Can be integrated with the information resources of the Web.
Windows 2000	Operating system for PCs, workstations, and network servers. Supports multitasking, multiprocessing, intensive networking, and Internet services for corporate computing.
Windows.NET server	Most recent Windows operating system for servers.
Windows CE	Pared-down version of the Windows operating system, including its graphical user interface, for small handheld computers and wireless communication devices.
UNIX	Used for powerful PCs, workstations, and network servers. Supports multitasking, multiuser processing, and networking. Is portable to different models of computer hardware.
Linux	Free, reliable alternative to UNIX and Windows 2000 that runs on many different types of computer hardware and can be modified by software developers.
OS/2	Robust 32-bit operating system for powerful IBM or IBM-compatible PCs with Intel microprocessors. Used for complex, memory-intensive applications or those that require networking, multitasking, or large programs.
Mac OS	Operating system for the Macintosh computer, featuring multitasking, powerful multimedia and networking capabilities, and a mouse-driven graphical user interface. Supports connecting to and publishing on the Internet.
DOS	16-bit operating system for older PCs based on the IBM PC standard. Does not support multitasking and limits the size of a program in memory to 640K.

tools for group collaboration, accessing information from the Internet, and creating and storing Web pages. **Windows XP** (for eXPerience), the most recent Windows operating system, is reliable, robust and relatively easy to use. The Windows XP Home Edition is for home users and the Windows XP Professional Edition targets mobile and business users. This operating system is meant for powerful new PCs with at least 400 megahertz of processing power and 128 megabytes of RAM. **Windows 98** and **Windows ME** are earlier versions of this operating system for home users.

Windows XP

Powerful Windows operating system that provides reliability, robustness, and ease of use for both corporate and home PC users.

Windows 98

Earlier version of the Windows operating system that is closely integrated with the Internet.

Windows Millennium Edition (Windows Me)

Earlier version of the Windows operating system enhanced for consumer users featuring tools for working with video, photos, music, and home networking.

Microsoft Windows XP is a robust and easy-to-use operating system for corporate and home applications.

Windows 2000

Windows operating system for high-performance PCs and network servers. Supports networking, multitasking, multiprocessing, and Internet services.

Windows .NET server

Most recent Windows operating system for servers.

UNIX

Operating system for all types of computers, which is machine independent and supports multiuser processing, multitasking, and networking. Used in high-end workstations and servers.

Linux

Reliable and compactly designed operating system that is an offshoot of UNIX and that can run on many different hardware platforms. Is available free or at very low cost as an alternative to UNIX and Windows operating system.

open-source software

Software that provides free access to its program code, allowing users to modify the program code to make improvements or fix errors.

machine language

A programming language consisting of the 1s and 0s of binary code.

COBOL (COmmon Business Oriented Language)

Major programming language for business applications because it can process large data files with alphanumeric characters.

Windows 2000 is used as an operating system for high-performance desktop and laptop computers and for network servers. Windows operating systems for network servers provide network management functions, including tools for creating and operating Web sites and other Internet services. In addition to Windows 2000, they include **Windows .NET server,** the most recent Windows server product, and *Windows NT,* which is an earlier version of this software. There are multiple editions of these server operating systems to meet the needs of small businesses, medium and large businesses, and businesses that have massive computer centers and processing requirements.

UNIX is an interactive, multiuser, multitasking operating system developed by Bell Laboratories in 1969 to help scientific researchers share data. UNIX was designed to connect various machines together and is highly supportive of communications and networking. UNIX is often used on workstations and servers and provides the reliability and scalability for running large systems on high-end servers. UNIX can run on many different kinds of computers and can be easily customized. Application programs that run under UNIX can be ported from one computer to run on a different computer with little modification.

UNIX is considered powerful but very complex, with a legion of commands. Graphical user interfaces have been developed for UNIX. UNIX also poses some security problems, because multiple jobs and users can access the same file simultaneously. Vendors have developed different versions of UNIX that are incompatible, thereby limiting software portability.

Linux is a UNIX-like operating system that can be downloaded from the Internet free of charge or purchased for a small fee from companies that provide additional tools for the software. It is free, reliable, compactly designed, and capable of running on many different hardware platforms, including servers, handheld computers, and consumer electronics. Linux has become popular during the past few years among sophisticated computer users and businesses as a robust low-cost alternative to UNIX and the Windows operating systems. Major hardware and software vendors are starting to provide versions of their products that can run on Linux. The software instructions for Linux are available along with the operating system software, so the software can be modified by software developers to fit their particular needs. The Window on Technology describes why business use of Linux is growing.

Linux is an example of **open-source software,** which provides all computer users with free access to its program code, so they can modify the code to fix errors or to make improvements. Open-source software such as Linux is not owned by any company or individual. A global network of programmers and users manages and modifies the software, usually without being paid to do so.

PROGRAMMING LANGUAGES AND CONTEMPORARY SOFTWARE TOOLS

Application software is primarily concerned with accomplishing the tasks of end users. Many different languages and software tools can be used to develop application software. Managers should understand which software tools and programming languages are appropriate for their organization's objectives.

Application Programming Languages for Business

The first generation of computer languages consisted of **machine language,** which required the programmer to write all program instructions in the 0s and 1s of binary code and to specify storage locations for every instruction and item of data used. Programming in machine language was a very slow, labor-intensive process. As computer hardware improved and processing speed and memory size increased, programming languages became progressively easier for humans to understand and use. From the mid-1950s to the mid-1970s, high-level programming languages emerged, allowing programs to be written with regular words using sentence-like statements.

Table 6-5 describes the major programming languages used for business and scientific work. For business applications, the most important languages have been COBOL, C, C++, and Visual Basic. **COBOL (Common Business Oriented Language)** was developed in the early 1960s for processing large data files with alphanumeric characters (mixed alphabetic and numeric data) and for performing repetitive tasks such as payroll. It is not well suited for complex, mathematical calculations but remains useful for many business processing and

CAN LINUX GO MAINSTREAM?

When the founders of Tradeworx, a hedge-fund firm and technology provider started their business in 1999, they had to decide whether to run mission-critical systems on proprietary platforms from established operating system vendors such as Microsoft or Sun Microsystems or to build their own applications using Linux. The difference in cost could amount to hundreds of thousands of dollars. Mike Beller, Tradeworx' chief technology officer, estimated that using a proprietary system could cost $6,000 or more per CPU, while a Linux-based system would only cost $1,000 to $2,000 per CPU. Cost savings could range from 20 to 70 percent. Beller decided to cluster a number of inexpensive Pentium CPUs together using the Linux operating system. Linux proved to be inexpensive and extremely stable.

Businesses using Linux used to be a tiny minority but their ranks are swelling. The Dreamworks motion picture studio clustered a series of Linux servers to program the complex graphics for the successful film *Shrek*. Similarly, Boeing's Phantom Works group has customized its server software to perform aircraft design tasks that previously required a supercomputer. Western Geco, the world's largest seismic services company based in Sussex, United Kingdom, is building clusters of Dell PC servers running Linux for the computer-intensive processing required by its research work. Since Linux is rooted in Unix, many of the tools the company used in its Unix environment port to Linux very easily.

The financial services industry has been willing to adopt Linux for mission-critical applications because they are less dependent on proprietary applications and operating systems than other industries. They tend to build more of their own applications in-house and that gives them greater flexibility to implement new technologies. CS First Boston converted a major worldwide financial trading system called Agora to Linux. Agora performs thousands of complex transactions and CS First Boston has been able to consolidate its processing operations from 20 RISC servers to a smaller number of servers with Intel processors. E*TRADE Group switched from Sun Microsystems to IBM servers running Linux to house its new Web site so that it did not have to be locked into a hardware vendor because of its operating system. E*TRADE can run its programs on Linux and can switch easily to another hardware vendor that supports Linux.

Hardware companies such as IBM, Hewlett-Packard, Dell, Sun, and Compaq are offering versions of their computers pre-loaded with Linux and are spending a significant amount of research dollars to make it easier and more effective to use. Oracle, SAP, Veritas, BEA and other leading software firms are marketing versions of their products that operate on Linux.

The area of greatest success for Linux has been as a server operating system. The International Data Corporation (IDC) calls Linux the fastest growing server operating system, expanding at a compounded annual rate near 30 percent. Linux is rapidly becoming the de facto operating system for server-appliances targeted at small business and home office users who want to easily network a few machines. Its low, $0 per copy price makes it extremely attractive to such users. China recently announced it was adopting Linux as the mainstream operating system for its server computers, and the governments of the United Kingdom and Germany have endorsed Linux.

Linux is also showing promise in software applications embedded in devices such as cell phones or set-top cable TV boxes. Linux is very economical in its use of computing resources, which are very limited in such devices.

One key area where Linux has yet to have an impact is desktop software. Some analysts believe that big corporations will still opt for Microsoft Windows and Microsoft Office because it presents a complete "soup to nuts" set of software tools for PC productivity. However, Microsoft recently changed its Office licensing policy, replacing fees for one-time upgrades with long-term "software maintenance" contracts that made its desktop productivity software even more expensive for businesses to own. Desktop productivity tools that run on Linux, such as Sun's StarOffice are much less expensive than Office and are becoming more competitive.

To Think About: Should a company select Linux as an operating system for its major business applications? What are the business as well as the technology issues that should be addressed when making that decision?

Sources: Don Clark, "Microsoft Faces New Challenge with Linux's Rising Popularity," *Wall Street Journal*, September 12, 2002; Alex Salkever, "Giant Steps for a Software Upstart," *BusinessWeek online*, May 16, 2002, <www.businessweed. com>; Jim Middlemiss, "IT Challenge: Can Linux Be Trusted?" *Wall Street & Technology*, March 2002; "Vendors Spur Linux On," *InformationWeek*, February 11, 2002; John Pallatto, "Linux Scoring Wins on Enterprise," *Internet World*, June 1, 2002; and John Pallato "Linux Finds Favor on Beijing Servers as Cheaper Option," *Wall Street Journal*, August 8, 2002.

TECHNOLOGY

reporting tasks. **C** is a powerful and efficient language developed in the early 1970s that combines machine portability with tight control and efficient use of computer resources. C is used primarily by professional programmers to create operating systems and application software, especially for PCs, and it can work on a variety of different computers. **C++** is a newer version of C that is object-oriented. (See the discussion of object-oriented programming later in this section). It has all the capabilities of C plus additional features for working with software

C

A powerful programming language with tight control and efficiency of execution; is portable across different microprocessors and is used primarily with PCs.

TABLE 6-5   Application Programming Languages

Programming Language	Description
COBOL	Designed for business administration to process large data files with alphanumeric characters (mixed alphabetic and numeric data).
C	Used primarily by professional programmers to create operating systems and application software, especially for PCs. Combines machine portability with tight control and efficient use of computer resources and can work on a variety of different computers.
C++	Object-oriented version of C that is used for developing application software.
Visual Basic	Visual programming tool for creating applications running on Windows.
FORTRAN (FORmula TRANslator)	Useful for processing numeric data. Some business applications can be written in FORTRAN, but it is primarily used for scientific and engineering applications.
BASIC (Beginners All-purpose Symbolic Instruction Code)	Developed in 1964 to teach students how to use computers. Easy to use but does few computer-processing tasks well, even though it does them all. Used primarily in education to teach programming.
Pascal	Developed in the late 1960s and used primarily in computer science courses to teach sound programming practices.
Assembly language	"Second-generation" language that is very close to machine language and is designed for a specific machine and specific microprocessors. Gives programmers great control, but it is difficult and costly to write and learn. Used primarily today in system software.

C++
Object-oriented version of the C programming language.

Visual Basic
Visual programming tool for creating applications running on Windows.

fourth-generation language
A programming language that can be employed directly by end users or less-skilled programmers to develop computer applications more rapidly than conventional programming languages.

natural language
Programming language that is very close to human language.

query language
Software tool that provides immediate online answers to requests for information that are not predefined.

objects. C++ is used for developing application software. **Visual Basic** is a widely used visual programming tool and environment for creating applications that run on Microsoft Windows. With Visual Basic, users develop programs by using a graphical user interface to choose and modify sections of code written in BASIC.

Fourth-Generation Languages

Fourth-generation languages consist of a variety of software tools that enable end users to develop software applications with minimal or no technical assistance or that enhance professional programmers' productivity. Fourth-generation languages tend to be nonprocedural, or less procedural, than conventional programming languages. Procedural languages require specification of the sequence of steps, or procedures, that tell the computer what to do and how to do it. Nonprocedural languages need only specify what has to be accomplished rather than provide details about how to carry out the task. Some of these nonprocedural languages are **natural languages** that enable users to communicate with the computer using conversational commands resembling human speech.

Table 6-6 shows that there are seven categories of fourth-generation languages: PC software tools, query languages, report generators, graphics languages, application generators, application software packages, and very high-level programming languages. The table shows the tools ordered in terms of ease of use by nonprogramming end users. End users are most likely to work with PC software tools and query languages. **Query languages** are software tools that provide immediate online answers to requests for information that are not predefined, such as "Who are the highest-performing sales representatives?" Query languages are often tied to data management software (discussed later in this section) and to database management systems (see Chapter 7.)

Contemporary Tools for Software Development

The need for businesses to fashion systems that are flexible or that can run over the Internet has stimulated approaches to software development based on object-oriented programming tools and new programming languages such as Java, hypertext markup language (HTML), and eXtensible Markup Language (XML).

Object-Oriented Programming   Traditional software development methods have treated data and procedures as independent components. A separate programming procedure must be written every time someone wants to take an action on a particular piece of data. The procedures act on data that the program passes to them.

TABLE 6-6   CATEGORIES OF FOURTH-GENERATION LANGUAGES

Fourth-Generation Tool	Description	Example	
PC software tools	General-purpose application software packages for PCs.	WordPerfect Internet Explorer Microsoft Access	**Oriented toward end users**
Query language	Languages for retrieving data stored in databases or files. Capable of supporting requests for information that are not predefined.	SQL	
Report generator	Extract data from files or databases to create customized reports in a wide range of formats not routinely produced by an information system. Generally provide more control over the way data are formatted, organized, and displayed than query languages.	RPG III	
Graphics language	Retrieve data from files or databases and display them in graphic format. Some graphics software can perform arithmetic or logical operations on data as well.	SAS Graph Systat	
Application generator	Contain preprogrammed modules that can generate entire applications, including Web sites, greatly speeding development. A user can specify what needs to be done, and the application generator will create the appropriate program code for input, validation, update, processing, and reporting.	FOCUS PowerBuilder Microsoft FrontPage	
Application software package	Software programs sold or leased by commercial vendors that eliminate the need for custom-written, in-house software.	PeopleSoft HRMS SAP R/3	
Very high-level programming language	Generate program code with fewer instructions than conventional languages, such as COBOL or FORTRAN. Designed primarily as productivity tools for professional programmers.	APL Nomad2	**Oriented toward IS professionals**

Object-oriented programming combines data and the specific procedures that operate on those data into one object. The object combines data and program code. Instead of passing data to procedures, programs send a message for an object to perform a procedure that is already embedded into it. (Procedures are termed *methods* in object-oriented languages.) The same message may be sent to many different objects, but each will implement that message differently. For example, an object-oriented financial application might have Customer objects sending debit and credit messages to Account objects. The Account objects in turn might maintain Cash-on-Hand, Accounts-Payable, and Accounts-Receivable objects.

An object's data are encapsulated from other parts of the system, so each object is an independent software building block that can be used in many different systems without changing the program code. Thus, object-oriented programming is expected to reduce the time and cost of writing software by producing reusable program code or software chips that can be reused in other related systems. Future software work can draw on a library of reusable objects, and productivity gains from object-oriented technology could be magnified if objects were stored in reusable software libraries and explicitly designed for reuse (Fayad and Cline, 1996). However, such benefits are unlikely to be realized unless organizations develop appropriate standards and procedures for reuse (Kim and Stohr, 1998).

Object-oriented programming is based on the concepts of *class* and *inheritance*. Program code is not written separately for every object but for classes, or general categories, of similar objects. Objects belonging to a certain class have the features of that class. Classes of objects in turn can inherit all the structure and behaviors of a more general class and then add variables and behaviors unique to each object. New classes of objects are created by choosing an existing class and specifying how the new class differs from the existing class, instead of starting from scratch each time.

We can see how class and inheritance work in Figure 6-10, which illustrates the relationships among classes concerning employees and how they are paid. Employee is the common ancestor, or superclass for the other three classes. Salaried, Hourly and Temporary are subclasses of Employee. The class name is in the top compartment, the attributes for each class are in the middle portion of each box, and the list of operations is in the bottom portion of each box. The features that are shared by all employees-id (identification number), name, address, date hired, position, and pay, are stored in the employee superclass, while each subclass stores features that

object-oriented programming

An approach to software development that combines data and procedures into a single object.

Figure 6-10 Class and inheritance. This figure illustrates how classes inherit the common features of their superclass.

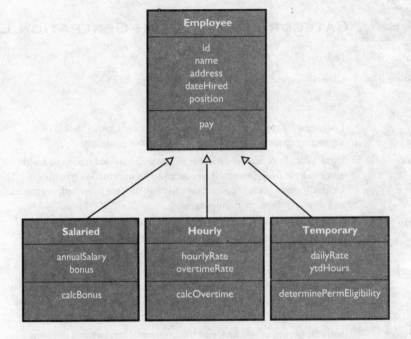

are specific to that particular type of employee. Specific to Hourly employees, for example, are their hourly rate and overtime rate. A solid line from the subclass to the superclass pointing to the superclass is a generalization path showing that the subclasses Salaried, Hourly, and Temporary have common features that can be generalized into the superclass Employee.

Object-oriented programming has spawned a new programming technology known as **visual programming.** With visual programming, programmers do not write code. Rather, they use a mouse to select and move around programming objects, copying an object from a library into a specific location in a program, or drawing a line to connect two or more objects.

Java   Java is a platform-independent, object-oriented programming language developed by Sun Microsystems. Java software is designed to run on any computer or computing device, regardless of the specific microprocessor or operating system it uses. A Macintosh PC, an IBM PC running Windows, a Sun server running UNIX, and even a smart cellular phone or personal digital assistant can share the same Java application.

Java can be used to create miniature programs called "applets" designed to reside on centralized network servers. The network delivers only the applets required for a specific function. With Java applets residing on a network, a user can download only the software functions and data that he or she needs to perform a particular task, such as analyzing the revenue from one sales territory. The user does not need to maintain large software programs or data files on his or her desktop machine. When the user is finished with processing, the data can be saved through the network.

Java is also a very robust language that can handle text, data, graphics, sound, and video, all within one program if needed. Java applets often are used to provide interactive capabilities for Web pages. For example, Java applets can be used to create animated cartoons or real-time news tickers for a Web site, or to add a capability to a Web page to calculate a loan payment schedule online in response to financial data input by the user.

Companies are starting to develop more extensive Java applications running over the Internet or over their private networks because such applications can potentially run in Windows, UNIX, IBM mainframe, Macintosh, and other environments without having to be rewritten for each computing platform. Java can let PC users manipulate data on networked systems using Web browsers, reducing the need to write specialized software.

Despite these benefits, Java has not yet fulfilled its early promise to revolutionize software development and use. Programs written in current versions of Java tend to run slower than "native" programs, although high-performance versions of Java are under development (Pancake and Lengauer, 2001). Vendors such as Microsoft are supporting alternative versions of Java that include subtle differences that affect Java's performance in different pieces of hardware and operating systems.

visual programming

The construction of software programs by selecting and arranging programming objects rather than by writing program code.

Java

Programming language that can deliver only the software functionality needed for a particular task, such as a small applet downloaded from a network; can run on any computer and operating system.

With visual programming tools, such as IBM's Visual Age Generator, working software programs can be created by drawing, pointing, and clicking instead of writing program code.

Hypertext Markup Language (HTML) and XML **Hypertext markup language (HTML)** is a page description language for creating hypertext or hypermedia documents such as Web pages. (See the discussions of hypermedia in Chapter 7 and of Web pages in Chapter 9.) HTML uses instructions called *tags* to specify how text, graphics, video, and sound are placed on a document and to create dynamic links to other documents and objects stored in the same or remote computers. Using these links, a user need only point at a highlighted key word or graphic, click on it, and immediately be transported to another document.

HTML programs can be custom written, but they also can be created using the HTML authoring capabilities of Web browsers or of popular word processing, spreadsheet, data management, and presentation graphics software packages. HTML editors, such as Microsoft FrontPage and Adobe GoLive, are more powerful HTML authoring tool programs for creating Web pages.

XML, which stands for **eXtensible Markup Language,** is a new specification originally designed to improve usefuless of Web documents. Whereas HTML only determines how text and images should be displayed on a Web document, XML describes what the data in these documents mean so the data can be used in computer programs. In XML, a number is not simply a number; the XML tag specifies whether the number represents a price, a date, or a ZIP code. Table 6-7 illustrates the differences between HTML and XML

By tagging selected elements of the content of documents for their meanings, XML makes it possible for computers to automatically manipulate and interpret their data and perform operations on the data without human intervention. Web browsers and computer programs, such as order processing or ERP software, can follow programmed rules for applying and displaying the data. XML provides a standard format for data exchange.

XML is already becoming a serious technology for Web-based applications. The key to XML is the setting of standards (or vocabulary) that enable both sending and receiving parties to describe data the same way. Each standard is contained in an XML Document Type Definition (DTD), usually simply called a dictionary. For example, RosettaNet is an XML

hypertext markup language (HTML)
Page description language for creating Web pages and other hypermedia documents.

XML (eXtensible Markup Language)
General-purpose language that describes the structure of a document and supports links to multiple documents, allowing data to be manipulated by the computer. Used for both Web and non-Web applications.

TABLE 6-7 COMPARISON OF HTML AND XML

Plain English	HTML	XML
Subcompact	<TITLE>Automobile</TITLE>	<AUTOMOBILETYPE="Subcompact">
4 passenger	<LI>4 passenger	<PASSENGER UNIT="PASS">4</PASSENGER>
$16,800	<LI>$16,800	<PRICE CURRENCY="USD">$16,800</PRICE>

dictionary developed by 34 leading companies within the PC industry. It defines all properties of a personal computer, such as modems, monitors, and cache memory. As a result the entire PC industry is now able to speak the same language. The entire supply chain of the industry can now easily be linked without requiring business partners or customers to use a particular programming language, application, or operating system to exchange data. Companies can also use XML to access and manipulate their own internal data without high software development costs.

XHTML (Extensible Hypertext Markup Language) is a hybrid combining features of HTML and XML that has been recommended as a replacement for HTML by the World Wide Web Consortium (which works with business and government to create Web standards.) XHTML reformulates HTML with XML document-type definitions, giving it additional flexibility and the ability to create Web pages that can be read by many different computing platforms and Net display devices.

XHTML (Extensible Hypertext Markup Language)

Hybrid of HTML and XML that provides more flexibility than HTML.

APPLICATION SOFTWARE PACKAGES AND PRODUCTIVITY SOFTWARE

Much of the software used in businesses today is not custom-programmed but consists of application software packages and desktop productivity tools. A **software package** is a prewritten, precoded, commercially available set of programs that eliminates the need for individuals or organizations to write their own software programs for certain functions. There are software packages for system software, but most package software is application software.

Software packages that run on mainframes and larger computers usually require professional programmers for their installation and support. However, there are also application software packages developed explicitly for end users. Productivity software packages for word processing, spreadsheet, data management, presentation graphics, integrated software packages, e-mail, Web browsers, and groupware are the most widely used software tools among business and consumer users.

software package

A prewritten, precoded, commercially available set of programs that eliminates the need to write software programs for certain functions.

Word Processing Software

Word processing software, which we introduced in Chapter 2, stores text data electronically as a computer file rather than on paper. The word processing software allows the user to make changes in the document electronically in memory. This eliminates the need to retype an entire page to incorporate corrections. The software has formatting options to make changes in line spacing, margins, character size, and column width. Microsoft Word and WordPerfect are popular word processing packages. Figure 6-11 illustrates a Microsoft Word screen displaying text, spelling and grammar checking, and major menu options.

Most word processing software has advanced features that automate other writing tasks: spelling checkers, style checkers (to analyze grammar and punctuation), thesaurus programs, and

Figure 6-11 Text and the spell-checking option in Microsoft Word. Word processing software provides many easy-to-use options to create and output a text document to meet a user's specifications.
Source: Courtesy of Microsoft.

mail merge programs, which link letters or other text documents with names and addresses in a mailing list. The newest versions of this software can create and access Web pages.

Businesses that need to create highly professional looking brochures, manuals, or books will likely use desktop publishing software for this purpose. *Desktop publishing* software provides more control over the placement of text, graphics, and photos in the layout of a page than does word processing software. Adobe PageMaker and QuarkXPress are two popular desktop publishing packages.

Spreadsheets

Electronic **spreadsheet** software provides computerized versions of traditional financial modeling tools, such as the accountant's columnar pad, pencil, and calculator. An electronic spreadsheet is organized into a grid of columns and rows. The power of the electronic spreadsheet is evident when one changes a value or values because all other related values on the spreadsheet will be automatically recomputed.

Spreadsheets are valuable for applications in which numerous calculations with pieces of data must be related to each other. Spreadsheets also are useful for applications that require modeling and what-if analysis. After the user has constructed a set of mathematical relationships, the spreadsheet can be recalculated instantaneously using a different set of assumptions. A number of alternatives can easily be evaluated by changing one or two pieces of data without having to rekey in the rest of the worksheet. Many spreadsheet packages include graphics functions that can present data in the form of line graphs, bar graphs, or pie charts. The most popular spreadsheet packages are Microsoft Excel and Lotus 1-2-3. The newest versions of this software can read and write Web files. Figure 6-12 illustrates the output from a spreadsheet for a break-even analysis and its accompanying graph.

Data Management Software

Although spreadsheet programs are powerful tools for manipulating quantitative data, **data management software** is more suitable for creating and manipulating lists and for combining

spreadsheet
Software displaying data in a grid of columns and rows, with the capability of easily recalculating numerical data.

data management software
Software used for creating and manipulating lists, creating files and databases to store data, and combining information for reports.

Figure 6-12 Spreadsheet software. Spreadsheet software organizes data into columns and rows for analysis and manipulation. Contemporary spreadsheet software provides graphing abilities for clear visual representation of the data in the spreadsheets. This sample break-even analysis is represented as numbers in a spreadsheet as well as a line graph for easy interpretation.

Total fixed cost	19,000.00				
Variable cost per unit	3.00				
Average sales price	17.00				
Contribution margin	14.00				
Breakeven point	1,357				

Custom Neckties Pro Forma Income Statement					
Units sold	0.00	679	1,357	2,036	2,714
Revenue	0	11,536	23,071	34,607	46,143
Fixed cost	19,000	19,000	19,000	19,000	19,000
Variable cost	0	2,036	4,071	6,107	8,143
Total cost	19,000	21,036	23,071	25,107	27,143
Profit/Loss	(19,000)	(9,500)	0	9,500	19,000

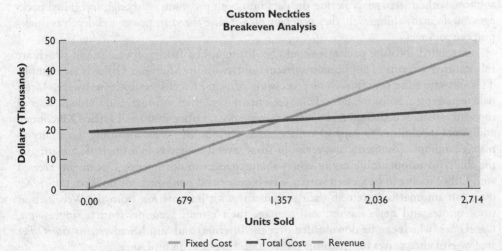

Figure 6-13 Data management software. This screen from Microsoft Access illustrates some of its powerful capabilities for managing and organizing information.

information from different files. PC data management packages have programming features and easy-to-learn menus that enable nonspecialists to build small information systems.

Data management software typically has facilities for creating files and databases and for storing, modifying, and manipulating data for reports and queries. A detailed treatment of data management software and database management systems can be found in Chapter 7. Popular database management software for the personal computer includes Microsoft Access, which has been enhanced to publish data on the Web. Figure 6-13 shows a screen from Microsoft Access illustrating some of its capabilities.

Presentation Graphics

presentation graphics
Software to create professional-quality graphics presentations that can incorporate charts, sound, animation, photos, and video clips.

Presentation graphics software allows users to create professional-quality graphics presentations. This software can convert numeric data into charts and other types of graphics and can include multimedia displays of sound, animation, photos, and video clips. The leading presentation graphics packages include capabilities for computer-generated slide shows and translating content for the Web. Microsoft PowerPoint and Lotus Freelance Graphics are popular presentation graphics packages.

Integrated Software Packages and Software Suites

integrated software package
A software package that provides two or more applications, such as word processing and spreadsheets, providing for easy transfer of data between them.

Integrated software packages combine the functions of the most important PC software packages, such as word processing, spreadsheets, presentation graphics, and data management. This integration provides a more general-purpose software tool and eliminates redundant data entry and data maintenance. For example, the break-even analysis spreadsheet illustrated in Figure 6-11 could be reformatted into a polished report with word processing software without separately keying the data into both programs. Although integrated packages can do many things well, they generally do not have the same power and depth as single-purpose packages.

Office 2000 and Office XP
Integrated software suites with capabilities for supporting collaborative work on the Web or incorporating information from the Web into documents.

Integrated software packages should be distinguished from software suites, which are full-featured versions of application software sold as a unit. Microsoft Office is an example. This software suite contains Word processing software, Excel spreadsheet software, Access data management software, PowerPoint presentation graphics software, and Outlook, a set of tools for e-mail, scheduling, and contact management. **Office 2000** and **Office XP** contain additional capabilities to support collaborative work on the Web, including the ability to manage multiple comments and revisions from several reviewers in a single document and the ability to automatically notify others about changes to documents. Documents created with Office tools can be viewed with a Web browser and published on the Web. Office XP users can automatically refresh their documents with information from the Web such as stock quotes and news flashes, and manage their e-mail accounts from a single view. *OpenOffice* (which can be downloaded over the Internet) and Sun Microsystems' *StarOffice* are low-cost alternatives to Microsoft Office tools that can run on Linux.

Users can create professional-looking electronic presentations incorporating text, diagrams, and other multimedia elements using presentation graphics software. This slide was created using Microsoft PowerPoint.

E-mail Software.

Electronic mail (e-mail) is used for the computer-to-computer exchange of messages and is an important tool for communication and collaborative work. A person can use a networked computer to send notes or lengthier documents to a recipient on the same network or a different network. Many organizations operate their own electronic-mail systems, but communications companies, such as MCI and AT&T, offer these services, along with commercial online information services, such as America Online and public networks on the Internet.

Web browsers and the PC software suites have e-mail capabilities, but specialized e-mail software packages are also available for use on the Internet. In addition to providing electronic messaging, e-mail software has capabilities for routing messages to multiple recipients, message forwarding, and attaching text documents or multimedia to messages.

electronic mail (e-mail)
The computer-to-computer exchange of messages.

Web Browsers

Web browsers are easy-to-use software tools for displaying Web pages and for accessing the Web and other Internet resources. Web browser software features a point-and-click graphical user interface that can be employed throughout the Internet to access and display information stored on computers at other Internet sites. Browsers can display or present graphics, audio, and video information as well as traditional text, and they allow you to click on-screen buttons or highlighted words to link to related Web sites. Web browsers have become the primary interface for accessing the Internet or for using networked systems based on Internet technology. You can see examples of Web browser software by looking at the illustrations of Web pages in each chapter of this text.

The two leading commercial Web browsers are Microsoft's Internet Explorer and Netscape. They include capabilities for using e-mail, file transfer, online discussion groups and bulletin boards, along with other Internet services. Newer versions of these browsers contain support for Web publishing and workgroup computing. (See the following discussion of groupware.)

Web browser
An easy-to-use software tool for accessing the World Wide Web and the Internet.

Groupware

Groupware provides functions and services to support the collaborative activities of work groups. Groupware includes software for group writing and commenting, information-sharing, electronic meetings, scheduling, and e-mail and a network to connect the members of the group as they work on their own desktop computers, often in widely scattered locations. Any group member can review the ideas of others at any time and add to them, or individuals can post a document for others to comment on or edit. Leading commercial groupware products include Lotus Notes and OpenText's Livelink. Groove is a new groupware tool based on peer-to-peer technology, which enables people to work directly with other people over the

groupware
Software that provides functions and services that support the collaborative activities of work groups.

Groupware facilitates collaboration by enabling members of a group to work collectively on documents, schedule meetings, and discuss activities, events, and issues. Illustrated here is OpenText LiveLink Meeting Zone, which enables users to set up online meetings to brainstorm new ideas, take notes, create tasks, and share documents.

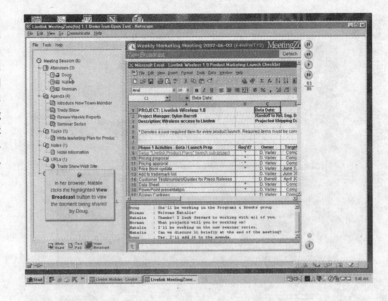

Internet without going through a central server. Microsoft Internet Explorer and Netscape Web browser software include groupware functions, such as e-mail, electronic scheduling and calendaring, audio and data conferencing, and electronic discussion groups and databases (see Chapter 10). Microsoft's Office 2000 and Office XP software suites include groupware features using Web technology.

SOFTWARE FOR ENTERPRISE INTEGRATION

Chapters 2 and 3 discussed the growing organizational need to integrate functions and business processes to improve organizational control, coordination, and responsiveness by allowing data and information to flow freely between different parts of the organization. Poorly integrated applications can create costly inefficiencies or slowed down customer service that become competitive liabilities. Alternative software solutions are available to promote enterprise integration.

One alternative, which we introduced in Chapter 2, is to replace isolated systems that cannot communicate with each other with an enterprise system. **Enterprise software** consists of a set of interdependent modules for applications such as sales and distribution, financial accounting, investment management, materials management, production planning, plant maintenance, and human resources that allow data to be used by multiple functions and business processes for more precise organizational coordination and control. The modules can communicate with each other directly or by sharing a common repository of data. Contemporary enterprise systems use a client/server computing architecture. Major enterprise software vendors include SAP, Oracle, PeopleSoft, and Baan. These vendors are now enhancing their products to provide more capabilities for supply chain management and exchange of data with other enterprises.

Individual companies can implement all of the enterprise software modules offered by a vendor or select only the modules of interest to them. They can also configure the software they select to support the way they do business. For example, they could configure the software to track revenue by product line, geographical unit, or distribution channel. However, the enterprise software may not be able to support some companies' unique business processes and often requires firms to change the way they work. Chapter 13 describes the challenges of implementing enterprise software in greater detail.

Most firms cannot jettison all of their existing systems and create enterprise-wide integration from scratch. Many existing legacy mainframe applications are essential to daily operations and very risky to change, but they can be made more useful if their information and business logic can be integrated with other applications (Noffsinger, Niedbalski, Blanks, and Emmart, 1998). One way to integrate various legacy applications is to use special software called **middleware** to create an interface or bridge between two different systems. Middleware is software that connects two otherwise separate applications, allowing them to

enterprise software

Set of integrated modules for applications such as sales and distribution, financial accounting, investment management, materials management, production planning, plant maintenance, and human resources that allow data to be used by multiple functions and business processes.

middleware

Software that connects two disparate applications, allowing them to communicate with each other and to exchange data.

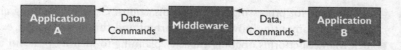

Figure 6-14 Middleware. Middleware is software that functions as a translation layer between two disparate applications so that they can work together.

communicate with each other and to pass data between them (see Figure 6-14). Middleware may consist of custom software written in-house or a software package.

There are many different types of middleware. One important use of middleware is to link client and server machines in client/server computing and increasingly to link a Web server to data stored on another computer. A **Web server** is the software for locating and managing stored Web pages. It locates the Web pages requested by a user on the computer where they are stored and delivers the Web pages to the user's computer. Middleware allows users to request data (such as an order) from the actual transaction system (such as an order processing system) housing the data using forms displayed on a Web browser, and it enables the Web server to return dynamic Web pages based on information users request.

Instead of custom-writing middleware software to connect one application to another, companies can now purchase **enterprise application integration software** to connect disparate applications or application clusters. There are a variety of commercial enterprise application integration software products, many featuring business process integration tools to link applications together through business process modeling. The software allows system builders to model their business processes graphically and define the rules that applications should follow to make these processes work. The software then generates the underlying program instructions to link existing applications to each other so they can exchange data via messages governed by the rules of the business processes. (An example of these rules might be "when an order has been placed, the order application should tell the accounting system to send an invoice and should tell shipping to send the order to the customer."). Because the enterprise application integration software is largely independent of the individual applications it connects, the organization can change its business processes and grow without requiring changes to the applications. A few enterprise application integration tools allow multiple businesses to integrate their systems into an extended supply chain.

6.4 MANAGING HARDWARE AND SOFTWARE ASSETS

Selection and use of computer hardware and software technology can have a profound impact on business performance. Computer hardware and software thus represent important organizational assets that must be properly managed. We now describe the most important issues in managing hardware and software technology assets: understanding the new technology requirements for electronic commerce and the digital firm, determining the total cost of ownership (TCO) of technology assets, and determining whether to own and maintain technology assets or use external technology service providers for the firm's IT infrastructure.

HARDWARE TECHNOLOGY REQUIREMENTS FOR ELECTRONIC COMMERCE AND THE DIGITAL FIRM

Electronic commerce and electronic business are placing heavy new demands on hardware technology because organizations are replacing so many manual and paper-based processes with electronic ones. Much larger processing and storage resources are required to process and store the escalating number of digital transactions flowing between different parts of the firm and between the firm and its customers and suppliers. Many people using a Web site simultaneously place great strains on a computer system, as does hosting large numbers of interactive Web pages with data-intensive graphics or video.

Capacity Planning and Scalability

Managers and information systems specialists now need to pay more attention to hardware capacity planning and scalability than they did in the past. **Capacity planning** is the process of predicting when a computer hardware system becomes saturated. It considers factors such as the maximum number of users that the system can accommodate at one time, the impact of existing and future software applications, and performance measures such as minimum

Web server

Software that manages requests for Web pages on the computer where they are stored and that delivers the page to the user's computer.

enterprise application integration software

Software that ties together multiple applications to support enterprise integration.

capacity planning

The process of predicting when a computer hardware system becomes saturated to ensure that adequate computing resources are available for work of different priorities and that the firm has enough computing power for its current and future needs.

response time for processing business transactions. Capacity planning ensures that the firm has enough computing power for its current and future needs. For example, the Nasdaq Stock Market performs ongoing capacity planning to identify peaks in the volume of stock trading transactions and to ensure it has enough computing capacity to handle large surges in volume when trading is very heavy.

Although capacity planning is performed by information system specialists, input from business managers is essential. Business managers need to determine acceptable levels of computer response time and availability for the firm's mission-critical systems to maintain the level of business performance they expect. New applications, mergers and acquisitions, and changes in business volume will all impact computer workload and must be taken into account when planning hardware capacity.

Scalability refers the ability of a computer, product, or system to expand to serve a large number of users without breaking down. Electronic commerce and electronic business both call for scalable IT infrastructures that have the capacity to grow with the business as the size of a Web site and number of visitors increase. Organizations must make sure they have sufficient computer processing, storage, and network resources to handle surging volumes of digital transactions and to make such data immediately available online.

TOTAL COST OF OWNERSHIP (TCO) OF TECHNOLOGY ASSETS

The purchase and maintenance of computer hardware and software is but one of a series of cost components that managers must consider when selecting and managing hardware and software technology assets. The actual cost of owning technology resources includes the original cost of acquiring and installing computers and software; ongoing administration costs for hardware and software upgrades, maintenance, technical support, and training; and even utility and real estate costs for running and housing the technology. The **total cost of ownership (TCO)** model can be used to analyze these direct and indirect costs to help firms determine the actual cost of specific technology implementations.

When all these cost components are considered, the TCO for a PC might run up to three times the original purchase price of the equipment. "Hidden costs" for support staff and additional network management can make distributed client/server architectures more expensive than centralized mainframe architectures.

Hardware and software acquisition costs account for only about 20 percent of TCO, so managers must pay close attention to administration costs to understand the full cost of the firm's hardware and software. It is possible to reduce some of these administration costs through better management. The investment bank Morgan Stanley estimated that businesses spent $130 billion in the last two years on unnecessary technology expenditures (Phillips, 2002). Many large firms are saddled with redundant, incompatible hardware and software because their departments and divisions have been allowed to make their own technology purchases. Their information technology infrastructures are excessively unwieldy and expensive to administer.

These firms could reduce their TCO by through greater centralization and standardization of their hardware and software resources (see the Window on Management). Companies could reduce the size of the information systems staff required to support their infrastructure if the firm minimizes the number of different computer models and pieces of software that employees are allowed to use. In a centralized infrastructure, systems can be administered from a central location and troubleshooting can be performed from that location (David, Schuff, and St. Louis, 2002).

The Manager's Toolkit describes the most important TCO components to help you to perform a TCO analysis.

RENT OR BUILD DECISIONS: USING TECHNOLOGY SERVICE PROVIDERS

Some of the most important questions facing managers are, "How should we acquire and maintain our technology assets? Should we build and run them ourselves or lease them from outside sources?" In the past, most companies built and ran their own computer facilities and

---

Scalability

The ability of a computer, product, or system to expand to serve a larger number of users without breaking down.

---

total cost of ownership (TCO)

Designates the total cost of owning technology resources, including initial purchase costs, the cost of hardware and software upgrades, maintenance, technical support, and training.

UNITED TECHNOLOGIES CORPORATION OVERHAULS ITS IT INFRASTRUCTURE

United Technologies Corporation (UTC) is a $28 billion company based in Hartford, Connecticut, providing high-technology products to the aerospace and building systems industries throughout the world. UTC operates in over 2000 locations in approximately 180 countries and has 152,000 employees, nearly 80,000 of which work outside the United States. UTC's major business units include Pratt & Whitney (aircraft engines), Sikorsky Aircraft Corporation (helicopters), Carrier Corporation (heating and air conditioning systems), Otis Elevator Corporation, Hamilton Sundstrand Corporation (aerospace and industrial systems), and UTC Fuel Cells.

After decades of growth, the company's information technology infrastructure was fragmented and redundant. Each business unit had its own standards and the quality of people varied from unit to unit. The business units used so many different pieces of hardware and software that they were difficult and costly to manage. UTC decided to make IT infrastructure standardization a major goal. In early June 2002, the company announced it would completely overhaul and consolidate its IT infrastructure.

UTC had computer centers and server farms with 8 mainframe computers, 11 IBM AS/400 servers and 2950 other servers dispersed throughout the United States. UTC consolidated 20 different computer centers into three—a mirrored computer center on the Pratt & Whitney campus in East Hartford and two other computer centers in Meriden and Norwich, Connecticut, owned by the consulting firm Computer Sciences Corporation (CSC), based in El Segundo California. CSC's computer center in Newington, Connecticut, is being used to host UTC's Web site. As a result of consolidation, the company only needs two mainframe computers and two AS/400 systems and could easily eliminate 350 servers by the end of 2002.

UTC had many different models of PCs running many different types of application and operating system software, which added to UTC's technology management costs. It standardized its PC platform on the Windows 2000 operating system and the Office 2000 desktop productivity software suite running on Dell PCs. UTC identified 160,000 pieces of software, of which only 5,000 were retained. It placed security restrictions on PCs so employees can't go to the Internet and download software on them, a practice that had contributed to UTC's technology inefficiencies.

UTC also selected Veritas Software Corporation's NetBackup storage software. UTC had been using a variety of products for backup and management of storage and processing that occasionally lost mission-critical data. Backups had been occurring haphazardly, depending on where a device was located. UTC is also creating two storage-area networks (SANs) on the East Hartford campus that will link to RAID (Redundant Array of Independent Disk) storage. Fifteen help desks running nine software applications were consolidated into one center running one system.

UTC thinks its infrastructure standardization has been worthwhile. Although its new technology could cost as much as $4.5 billion, it would create efficiencies that could save the firm $1 billion annually over the next 15 years.

To Think About: What were the management benefits of consolidating UTC's information technology infrastructure? What management, organization, and technology issues had to be addressed when making the decision to overhaul the infrastructure?

Sources: Lucas Mearian, "United Technologies in $4.5B IT Overhaul," *Computerworld*, June 10, 2002; Fred Sandsmark,"Building Efficiencies: United Technologies Corporation," *IQ Magazine*, July/August 2001; and United Technologies Corporation Web site, <www.utc.com>, accessed July 29, 2002.

MANAGEMENT

---

developed their own software. Today, more and more companies are obtaining their hardware and software technology from external service vendors. Online services for storage and for running application software have become especially attractive options for many firms.

On-Line Storage Service Providers

Some companies are using storage service providers (SSPs) to replace or supplement their own in-house storage infrastructure. A **storage service provider (SSP)** is a third-party provider that rents out storage space to subscribers over the Web (see Figure 6-15). Storage service providers sell storage as a pay-per-use utility, allowing customers to store their data on remote computers accessed via networks without having to purchase and maintain their own storage infrastructure and storage support staff. To be successful SSPs must offer very high availability and reliability and also must keep up with the latest technology. SSPs are responsible for monitoring the stored data and for managing their own capacity, response time, and reliability.

storage service provider (SSP)

Third-party provider that rents out storage space to subscribers over the Web, allowing customers to store and access their data without having to purchase and maintain their own storage technology.

MIS IN ACTION: MANAGER'S TOOLKIT

HOW TO CALCULATE THE TOTAL COST OF OWNERSHIP (TCO) OF TECHNOLOGY ASSETS

In order to determine the total cost of ownership (TCO) of an organization's technology assets, you will need to calculate the cost of the following components:

Hardware acquisition: Purchase price of computer hardware equipment, including computers, terminals, storage, printers

Software acquisition: Purchase or license of software for each user

Installation: Cost to install computers and software

Training: Cost to provide training to information system specialists and end users

Support: Cost to provide ongoing technical support, help desks, and so forth

Maintenance: Cost to upgrade the hardware and software

Infrastructure: Cost to acquire, maintain, and support related infrastructure such as networks and specialized equipment (including storage backup units)

Downtime: Lost productivity if hardware or software failures cause the system to be unavailable for processing and user tasks

Space and energy: Real estate and utility costs for housing and providing power for the technology

Application Service Providers (ASPs)

Section 6.2 described hardware capabilities for providing data and software programs to desktop computers and over networks. It is clear that software will be increasingly delivered and used over networks. Online application service providers (ASPs) are springing up to provide these software services over the Web and over private networks. An **application service provider (ASP)** is a business that delivers and manages applications and computer services from remote computer centers to multiple users via the Internet or a private network. Instead of buying and installing software programs, subscribing companies can rent the same functions from these services. Users pay for the use of this software either on a subscription or per transaction basis. The ASP's solution combines package software applications and all of the related hardware, system software, network, and other infrastructure services that the customer would have to purchase, integrate, and manage on his or her own. The ASP customer interacts with a single entity instead of an array of technologies and service vendors.

The "timesharing" services of the 1970s, which ran applications such as payroll on their computers for other companies, were an earlier version of this application hosting. But today's ASPs run a wider array of applications than these earlier services and deliver many of

application service provider (ASP)

Company providing software that can be rented by other companies over the Web or a private network.

Figure 6-15 How managed storage works. By enlisting the services of a storage service provider (SSP), companies do not have to maintain their own storage infrastructure on their premises. They can rent storage technology and management services from the vendor and access their data stored by the vendor over a network.
Source: *How Managed Storage Works* from COMPUTERWORLD, October 15, 2001. Copyright © 2001. Reprinted by permission of Reprint Management Service.

CUSTOMER PREMISES

Vendor-supplied portal software gives a customer the same view as the vendor operations center.

Firewall

Vendor's on-site hardware device

Storage infrastructure (may be direct-attached storage, SANs or NAS)

VENDOR OPS. CENTER

Using proprietary software, vendor employees monitor and manage a customer's storage.

SECURE NETWORK CONNECTION
The customer's actual data never passes through the firewall; rather, metadata needed to manage storage flows across a secure network connection.

these software services over the Web. At Web-based services, servers perform the bulk of the processing and the only essential program needed by users is their Web browser. Large and medium-size businesses are using ASPs for enterprise systems, sales force automation, or financial management, and small businesses are using them for functions such as invoicing, tax calculations, electronic calendars, and accounting.

Companies are turning to this "software service" model as an alternative to developing their own software. Some companies will find it much easier to "rent" software from another firm and avoid the expense and difficulty of installing, operating, and maintaining complex systems, such as enterprise resource planning (ERP). The ASP contracts guarantee a level of service and support to make sure that the software is available and working at all times. Today's Internet-driven business environment is changing so rapidly that getting a system up and running in three months instead of six could mean the difference between success and failure. Application service providers also enable small and medium-size companies to use applications that they otherwise could not afford.

Companies considering the software service model need to carefully assess application service provider costs and benefits, weighing all management, organizational, and technology issues. In some cases, the cost of renting software can add up to more than purchasing and maintaining the application in-house. Yet there may be benefits to paying more for software through an ASP if this decision allows the company to focus on core business issues instead of technology challenges. More detail on application service providers can be found in Chapter 12.

Other Types of Service Providers

Other types of specialized service providers provide additional resources for helping organizations manage their technology assets. *Management service providers* can be enlisted to manage combinations of applications, networks, storage, and security as well as to provide Web site and systems performance monitoring. *Business continuity service providers* offer disaster recovery and continuous Web availability services to help firms continue essential operations when their systems malfunction (see Chapter 14). Table 6-8 provides examples of the major types of technology service providers.

Utility Computing

Many of the service providers we have just described lease information technology services using fixed price contracts. IBM is championing a **utility computing** model in which companies pay only for the products and services they use, much as they would pay for electricity. In this "pay as you go" model of computing, which is sometimes called on-demand computing or usage-based pricing, customers would pay more or less for server capacity and storage depending on how much of these resources they actually use during a specified time period. IBM offers a full range of usage-based services, including server capacity, storage space, software applications, and Web hosting. Other vendors, including Compaq, Hewlett-Packard, and Electronic Data Systems (EDS) also offer some utility computing services.

Utility computing

Model of computing in which companies pay only for the information technology resources they actually use during a specified time period. Also called on-demand computing or usage-based pricing.

TABLE 6-8	EXAMPLES OF TECHNOLOGY SERVICE PROVIDERS

Type of Service Provider	Description	Example
Storage service provider	Provides online access over networks to storage devices and storage area network technology.	IBM Managed Storage Services (MSS)
Application service provider	Uses centrally managed facilities to host and manage access to package applications delivered over networks on a subscription basis.	Corio Inc. offers a suite of hosted enterprise application software.
Management service provider	Manages combinations of applications, networks, systems, storage, and security as well as providing Web site and systems performance monitoring to subscribers over the Internet.	Totality, Seven Space/Nuclio
Business continuity service provider	Defines and documents procedures for planning and recovering from system malfunctions that threaten vital business operations.	Comdisco disaster recovery, rapid recovery, and continuous Web availability services.

MAKE IT YOUR BUSINESS

FINANCE AND ACCOUNTING

One of the earliest tasks assigned to computers was to automate calculations for finance and accounting, and these functions have remained high-priority targets for computerization. Many application software packages for individuals as well as for large businesses support financial processes such as corporate accounting, tax calculations, payroll processing, or investment planning. Calculating the Total Cost of Ownership (TCO) of technology assets usually requires models and expertise supplied by finance and accounting. You can find examples of finance and accounting applications on pages 180–181, 197, and 209.

HUMAN RESOURCES

Because hardware and software technologies are changing very rapidly, providing many new productivity tools to employees and powerful software package and services for the human resources department, employees will need frequent retraining in order to use these tools effectively.

MANUFACTURING AND PRODUCTION

Many manufacturing applications are based on client/server networks, which use networked computers to control the flow of work on the

factory floor. Handheld computers and bar code scanners are widely used to track items in inventory and to track package shipments. XML provides a set of standards through which all systems of participants in an industry supply chain can exchange data with each other without high expenditures for specialized translation programs and middleware. You can find examples of manufacturing and production applications on pages 197, 209, 216–217.

SALES AND MARKETING

Sales and marketing has benefited from hardware and software technologies that provide customers and sales staff with rapid access to information, responses to customer questions, and order-taking. Web browser software provides an easy-to-use interface for accessing product information or placing orders over the Web, while e-mail software is a quick and inexpensive tool for answering customer queries. Web sites can be enhanced with Java applets that allow users to perform calculations or view interactive product demonstrations on Web sites using standard Web browser software. You can find examples of sales and marketing applications on pages 180–181 and 216–217.

MANAGEMENT WRAP-UP

Managers should know how to select and manage the organization's hardware and software assets in the firm's information technology (IT) infrastructure. General managers should understand the costs and capabilities of various hardware and software technologies and should understand the advantages and disadvantages of building and owning these assets or of renting them from outside services.

Computer hardware and software technology can either enhance or impede organizational performance. Computer hardware and software selection should be based on organizational and business needs, considering how well the technology meshes with the organization's culture and structure as well as information-processing requirements. Hardware and software services provided by outside vendors should fit into organizational computing plans.

A range of hardware and software technologies is available to organizations. Organizations have many computer processing options to choose from, including mainframes, workstations, PCs, servers, and network computers, and many different ways of configuring hardware components to create systems. Firms can also select among alternative operating systems and application software tools. Key technology decisions include the appropriateness of the hardware or software for the problem to be addressed and compatibility with other components of the firm's IT infrastructure.

For Discussion

1. Why is selecting computer hardware and software for the organization an important management decision? What management, organization, and technology issues should be considered when selecting computer hardware?

2. Should organizations use application service providers (ASPs) and storage service providers (SSPs) for all their software and storage needs? Why or why not? What management, organization, and technology factors should be considered when making this decision?

SUMMARY

1. *What computer processing and storage capability does our organization need to handle its information and business transactions?* Managers should understand the alternative computer hardware technologies available for processing and storing information so that they can select the right technologies for their business. Modern computer systems have six major components: a central processing unit (CPU), primary storage, input devices, output devices, secondary storage, and communications devices. All of these components need to work together to process information for the organization. The CPU is the part of the computer where the manipulation of symbols, numbers, and letters occurs. The CPU has two components: an arithmetic-logic unit and a control unit.

   The CPU is closely tied to primary memory, or primary storage, which stores data and program instructions temporarily before and after processing. Several different kinds of semiconductor memory chips are used with primary storage: RAM (random access memory) is used for short-term storage of data and program instructions and ROM (read-only memory) permanently stores important program instructions.

   Computer processing power depends in part on the speed of their microprocessors, which integrate the computer's logic and control on a single chip. Most conventional computers process one instruction at a time, but computers with parallel processing can process multiple instructions simultaneously. The principal secondary storage technologies are magnetic disk, optical disk, and magnetic tape. Optical disks can store vast amounts of data compactly. CD-ROM disk systems can only be read from, but CD-RW rewritable optical disk systems are now available.

   The principal input devices are keyboards, computer mice, touch screens, magnetic ink and optical character recognition, pen-based instruments, digital scanners, sensors, and audio input. The principal output devices are video display terminals, printers, and audio output devices. In batch processing, transactions are accumulated and stored in a group until the time when it is efficient or necessary to process them. In online processing, the user enters transactions into a device that is directly connected to the computer system. The transactions are usually processed immediately. Multimedia integrates two or more types of media, such as text, graphics, sound, voice, full-motion video, still video, and/or animation into a computer-based application.

2. *What arrangement of computers and computer processing would best benefit our organization?* Managers should understand the capabilities of various categories of computers and arrangements of computer processing. The type of computer and arrangement of processing power that should be used by the business depends on the nature of the organization and its problems.

   Computers are categorized as mainframes, midrange computers, PCs, workstations, or supercomputers. Mainframes are the largest computers; midrange computers can be mini-computers used in factory, university, or research lab systems or servers providing software and other resources to computers on a network. PCs are desktop or laptop machines; workstations are desktop machines with powerful mathematical and graphic capabilities; and supercomputers are sophisticated, powerful computers that can perform massive and complex computations rapidly. Because of continuing advances in microprocessor technology, the distinctions between these types of computers are constantly changing.

   Computers can be networked together to distribute processing among different machines. In the client/server model of computing, computer processing is split between "clients" and "servers" connected via a network. The exact division of tasks between client and server depends on the application. Network computers are pared-down desktop machines with minimal or no local storage and processing capacity. They obtain most or all of their software and data from a central network server. Whereas network computers help organizations maintain central control over computing, peer-to-peer computing puts processing power back on users' desktops, linking individual PCs, workstations, or other computers through the Internet or private networks to share data, disk space, and processing power for a variety of tasks.

3. *What kinds of software and software tools do we need to run our business? What criteria should we use to select our software technology?* Managers should understand the capabilities of various types of software so they can select software technologies that provide the greatest benefit for their firms. There are two major types of software: system software and application software. System software coordinates the various parts of the computer system and mediates between application software and computer hardware. Application software is used by application programmers and some end users to develop specific business applications.

   The system software that manages and controls the activities of the computer is called the operating system. The operating system acts as the chief manager of the information system, allocating, assigning, and scheduling system resources and monitoring the use of the computer. Multiprogramming, multiprocessing, virtual storage, and time sharing are operating system capabilities that enable computer system resources to be used more efficiently. Other system software includes computer-language translation programs that convert programming languages into machine language and utility programs that perform common processing tasks.

   PC operating systems have developed sophisticated capabilities such as multitasking and support for multiple users on networks. Leading PC operating systems include Windows XP, Windows 98 and Windows Me; Windows.NET Server and Windows 2000, Windows CE, UNIX, Linux, OS/2, Mac OS, and DOS. PC operating systems and many kinds of application software now use graphical user interfaces.

   The general trend in software is toward user-friendly, high-level languages that both increase professional programmer productivity and make it possible for end users to work directly with information systems. The principal programming languages used in business include COBOL, C, C++, and Visual Basic and each is designed to solve specific types of problems. Fourth-generation languages are less procedural than conventional programming languages and enable end users to perform many software tasks that previously required technical specialists. They include popular PC software tools such as word processing, spreadsheet, data management, presentation graphics, and e-mail software along with Web browsers and groupware. Enterprise software, middleware, and enterprise application integration software are all software tools for promoting enterprise-wide integration of business processes and information system applications.

Software selection should be based on criteria such as efficiency, compatibility with the organization's technology platform, vendor support, and whether the software tool is appropriate for the problems and tasks of the organization.

4. *Of what new software technologies should we be aware? How would they benefit our organization?* Object-oriented programming tools and new programming languages such as Java, hypertext markup language (HTML), and eXtensible Markup Language (XML) can help firms create software more rapidly and efficiently and produce applications based on the Internet or data in Web sites. Object-oriented programming combines data and procedures into one object, which can act as an independent software building block. Each object can be used in many different systems without changing program code.

Java is an object-oriented programming language designed to operate on the Internet. It can deliver precisely the software functionality needed for a particular task as a small applet that is downloaded from a network. Java can run on any computer and operating system. HTML is a page description language for creating Web pages. XML is a language for creating structured documents in which data are tagged for meanings. The tagged data in XML documents and Web pages can be manipulated and used by other computer systems. XML can thus be used to exchange data between Web sites and different legacy systems within a firm and between the systems of different partners in a supply chain.

5. *How should we acquire and manage the firm's hardware and software assets?* Both hardware and software are major organizational assets that must be carefully managed. Electronic commerce and electronic business have put new strategic emphasis on technologies that can store vast quantities of transaction data and make them immediately available online. Managers and information systems specialists need to pay special attention to hardware capacity planning and scalability to ensure that the firm has enough computing power for its current and future needs.

They also need to balance the costs and benefits of owning and maintaining their own hardware and software or renting these assets from external service providers. Online storage service providers (SSPs) rent out storage space to subscribers over the Web. Application service providers (ASPs) rent out software applications and computer services from remote computer centers to subscribers over the Internet or private networks. In the utility computing model, subscribers would only pay for the software and hardware services they actually use during a specified time period.

Calculating the total cost of ownership (TCO) of the organization's technology assets can help provide managers with the information they need to manage these assets and decide whether to rent or own these assets. The total cost of owning technology resources includes not only the original cost of computer hardware and software but also costs for hardware and software upgrades, maintenance, technical support, and training.

KEY TERMS

Application service provider (ASP), 210

Application software, 193

Arithmetic-logic unit (ALU), 183

Batch processing, 188

Bit, 183

Byte, 183

C, 197

C++, 198

Capacity planning, 207

CD-ROM (compact disk read-only memory), 186

CD-RW (CD-ReWritable), 186

Central processing unit (CPU), 183

Centralized processing, 191

Client, 191

Client/server computing, 191

COBOL (COmmon Business Oriented Language), 196

Compiler, 194

Computer, 182

Control unit, 184

Data management software, 203

Digital video disk (DVD), 187

Distributed processing, 191

Downsizing, 191

Electronic mail (e-mail), 207

Enterprise application integration software, 207

Enterprise software, 206

Floppy disk, 186

Fourth-generation language, 198

Graphical user interface (GUI), 194

Grid computing, 192

Groupware, 205

Hard disk, 186

Hypertext markup language (HTML), 201

Integrated software package, 204

Java, 200

Linux, 196

Machine cycle, 184

Machine language, 196

Magnetic disk, 186

Magnetic tape, 187

Mainframe, 190

Massively parallel computers, 185

Megahertz, 184

Microprocessor, 184

Middleware, 206

Midrange computer, 190

Minicomputer, 190

MP3 (MPEG3), 189

Multimedia, 189

Natural language, 198

Network-attached storage (NAS), 187

Network computer (NC), 192

Object-oriented programming, 200

Office 2000 and Office XP, 204

Online processing, 188

Open-source software, 196

Operating system, 193

Parallel processing, 185

Peer-to-peer computing, 192

Personal computer (PC), 190

Presentation graphics, 204

REVIEW QUESTIONS

1. What are the components of a contemporary computer system?

2. Name the major components of the CPU and the function of each.

3. Distinguish between serial, parallel, and massively parallel processing.

4. List the most important secondary storage media. What are the strengths and limitations of each?

5. List and describe the major computer input and output devices.

6. What is the difference between batch and online processing? Diagram the difference.

7. What is multimedia? What technologies are involved?

8. What is the difference between a mainframe, a minicomputer, a server, and a PC? Between a PC and a workstation?

9. Compare the client/server, network computer, and peer-to-peer models of computing.

10. What are the major types of software? How do they differ in terms of users and uses?

11. What is the operating system of a computer? What does it do? What roles do multiprogramming, virtual storage, time sharing, and multiprocessing play in the operation of an information system?

12. List and describe the major PC operating systems.

13. List and describe the major application programming languages for business. How do they differ from fourth-generation languages?

14. What is object-oriented programming? How does it differ from conventional software development?

15. What are Java, HTML, and XML? Compare their capabilities. Why are they becoming important?

16. Name and describe the most important PC productivity software tools.

17. Name and describe the kinds of software that can be used for enterprise integration.

18. List and describe the principal issues in managing hardware and software assets.

APPLICATION SOFTWARE EXERCISE

SPREADSHEET EXERCISE: EVALUATING COMPUTER HARDWARE AND SOFTWARE OPTIONS

You have been asked to obtain pricing information on hardware and software for an office of 30 people. Using the Internet, get pricing for 30 PC desktop systems (monitor, computer, and keyboard) manufactured by IBM, Dell, and Compaq as listed at their respective corporate Web sites. (For the purposes of this exercise, ignore the fact that desktop systems usually come with pre-loaded software packages.) Also get pricing on 15 monochrome desktop printers manufactured by Hewlett-Packard and by Xerox. Each desktop system must satisfy the minimum specifications shown in Table 1.

Each desktop printer must satisfy the minimum specifications shown in Table 2.

After getting pricing on the desktop systems and printers, obtain pricing on 30 copies of Microsoft's Office XP, Corel's WordPerfect Office 2002, and IBM's Lotus SmartSuite applica-

TABLE 1
MINIMUM DESKTOP SPECIFICATIONS

Processor speed (in gigahertz)	1.8GHz
Hard Drive (in gigabytes)	40GB
RAM (in megabytes)	256MB
CD-ROM speed	48 speed
Monitor (diagonal measurement)	17 inches

tion packages and on 30 copies of Microsoft Windows XP Professional edition. The application software suite packages come in various versions, so be sure that each package contains programs for word processing, spreadsheet analysis, database analysis, graphics preparation, and e-mail.

Prepare a spreadsheet showing your research results for the desktop systems, for the printers, and for the software. Use

TABLE 2	
MINIMUM MONOCHROME PRINTER SPECIFICATIONS	
Print speed (pages per minute)	12
Print quality	600 x 600
Network ready?	Yes
Maximum price/unit	$1000

your spreadsheet software to determine the desktop system, printer, and software combination that will offer both the best performance and pricing per worker. Since every two workers will share one printer (15 printers/30 systems), assume only half a printer cost per worker in the second spreadsheet. In both spreadsheets, assume that your company will take the standard warranty and servicing contract offered by each product's manufacturer.

GROUP PROJECT

Obtain a copy of OpenOffice <www.openoffice.org> which is downloadable for free or find a low-cost copy of Sun StarOffice and compare its capabilities to the Microsoft Office suite of desktop productivity tools. Evaluate their functions, ease of use, and compatibility with models of computer hardware and operating systems. Which would you purchase if you were an individual? A business? Justify your decision. If possible, use electronic presentation software to present your findings to the class.

TOOLS FOR INTERACTIVE LEARNING

▓ INTERNET CONNECTION

The Internet Connection for this chapter will direct you to a series of Web sites where you can complete an exercise to survey the products and services of major computer hardware vendors and the use of Web sites in the computer hardware industry.

▓ INTERACTIVE STUDY GUIDE

You can use the Interactive Study Guide to test your knowledge of the topics in this chapter and get instant feedback where you need more practice.

▓ RUNNING CASE

The Running Case provides an opportunity for you to evaluate new desktop hardware and software for Dirt Bikes USA and perform a Total Cost of Ownership analysis. You can find a complete description of this project on the Laudon Web site for Chapter 6 and on the Multimedia Edition CD-ROM.

▓ ELECTRONIC BUSINESS PROJECT

At the Laudon Web site for Chapter 6, you will find an Electronic Business Project for salesforce budgeting.

▓ MANAGEMENT DECISION PROBLEM

At the Laudon Web site for Chapter 6, you will find a Management Decision Problem on capacity planning for electronic commerce.

▓ CD-ROM

If you use the Multimedia Edition CD-ROM with this chapter, you can find a video clip by Intel showing the evolution of computer hardware, an audio overview of the key themes of this chapter, and bullet text summarizing the key points of the chapter.

CASE STUDY—*Consolidating Servers: A Wise Move for Mary Kay Inc.?*

Mary Kay Inc. is one of the largest sellers of skin care and cosmetic products in the United States. It manufactures such products as facial skin care, color cosmetics, nail care, body care, sun protection, fragrances, men's skin care, and even dietary supplements. In 2001, its global retail sales topped $2.5 billion. Over 80 percent came via the Internet. Its business model is to offer wide choices to its consumers through one-to-one personalized sales. To fulfill its model, its products are sold by members of its independent sales force of 850,000. They are called Independent Beauty Consultants (IBCs) and sell Mary Kay products in 33 countries. The company's focus is "on high-touch, personalized service," according to Kregg Jodie, Mary Kay's Senior Vice President and CIO.

In 1998 and 1999, Mary Kay was facing increasing competition, from traditional sources such as Avon and from upstart companies that offered direct cosmetic sales to consumers over the Internet. The business solution Jodie and others agreed upon was that Mary Kay needed a Web site where customers and their personal IBCs could shop directly whenever they chose. Mary Kay wanted a more modern ordering system that would be easier to use. The system had to automatically calculate discounts and detect the customer's eligibility for sales promotions.

Prior to its Internet system, Mary Kay had only taken orders via telephone or mail, or through their off-line desktop and laptop computers. Mary Kay worked with BEST Systems Inc. to build an Internet-based e-commerce system called InTouch to be used by the IBCs for ordering over the Web. The connection would be easy because using an Internet system meant the IBCs would only need Internet access and a Web browser. The system they built was Microsoft-based, and it was both very reliable and initially very scalable.

InTouch delivered many benefits. Being an Internet system, it had 24-hour availability. IBCs and customers working with them could view and browse Mary Kay's up-to-date product catalogue, and even access information on the current inventory. Current promotional information was always available, and each IBC could create a personalized sales Web site. Customers and IBCs could check the order status for all orders, whether they had been entered through the Internet or via one of the older methods. As products were ordered, the system checked and immediately reserved the products or informed the IBC that it was out of stock and placed a back order if the customer desired. The system immediately calculated and displayed the final cost including any cost reductions and enabled customers to pay using their credit cards.

Within two years, the system was supporting 125,000 personal Web sites. Mary Kay initially used four servers to handle the Web orders, but kept adding more servers to keep up with its mushrooming Internet business. At end of two years (December 2001), the company had 30 servers supporting its Web site. The company upgraded the system to run over Windows 2000 Advanced Server as its operating system, resulting in huge performance and stability improvements. Mary Kay also developed a script used to install new servers in just a few hours and used Windows 2000 to manage the servers remotely.

Despite its successes, the distributed Web order entry system was having problems. First, Mary Kay still had four separate order-entry systems—Web, telephone, mail, and desktop computers—and they needed to be unified. Moreover, the order entry clerk job for telephone and mail sales was too complex, and so it resulted in many errors. Mary Kay had different businesses rules for some locations, and they needed to be centralized. Finally, although the system had been very scalable, the company's business was still growing, and soon it needed to be able to handle many more orders daily. By late December 2001, the system was processing as many as 25,000 orders in one day, and by spring of 2002, it had climbed to 30,000 Internet orders in some days. The high number of daily orders came at the end of the month. Most orders during any day were entered at end of the day, spiking loads on the system within a short period of time. Each order consisted of up to 50 separate transactions. On heavy order days, the system was handling over 1.2 million transactions daily.

According to Jodie, adding more servers would no longer work because the storage and network management requirements of additional servers were becoming too unwieldy, and additional servers also required too much physical space. Mary Kay's home-grown supply chain software running on Compaq Alpha servers could not keep up with the growing load. More distributed hardware clearly would not solve these problems created by Mary Kay's growth. Instead Jodie, with management support, decided to move from the firm's current decentralized network system to a centralized system on a mainframe. The company then installed a Unisys Enterprise Server ES7000 mainframe with 32 Intel processors to run the whole system. Mary Kay was able to partition the Unisys mainframe with its 32

processors into multiple "virtual servers" which could be run separately. Yet they all share the ES7000's storage and networking resources. Galen Schreck, an enterprise infrastructure analyst at Forrester Research, explained, "The real question is where it fits in, versus racks full of smaller servers." Moreover, he explained, "A lot of data centers rely heavily on scripts and batch operations," and so the processes can't be broken up to run multiple tasks at the same time. The ES7000 was the first mainframe server hardware that was designed specifically for the MS Windows 2000 operating system, and Jodie wanted to stay with Microsoft because he believed it would be too difficult to move from Windows while also switching from servers to a mainframe.

Mary Kay subsequently added three more ES7000s so it could easily manage further expansion. It used two of them for its supply-chain system, OneWorld, which it purchased from J.D. Edwards. OneWorld had been developed working with Microsoft and Unisys, and Jodie said "We felt like there wasn't too much risk because of the level of work they [Unisys, Microsoft, and J.D. Edwards] were doing together."

The company started the conversion on June 10, 2002 and has already found that it takes the IBCs 50 percent less time to enter orders than previously. The system will also enable Mary Kay to more easily manage the online operations as its sales continued to multiply.

Sources: Sean Gallagher, "Mary Kay Trims Servers, Taps Windows Mainframe," *Baseline Magazine,* July 2, 2002; "Ross Systems Helps Mary Kay, Inc. Get Beautiful Global Results," <www.rossinc.com>, July 16, 2002; Unisys Corporation, "Mary Kay Gets I.T. Makeover from Unisys with Four ES7000 Servers and Windows 2000 Datacenter Server," June 10, 2002; Microsoft Case Study, "Mary Kay Centralizes Order Entry with Microsoft .NET," <www.microsoft.com>, April 2, 2002; Microsoft Case Study, "Mary Kay InTouch Community Scales Out and Up With Windows 2000 to Accommodate 1800 Percent Increase in Outline Orders over Two-year Period," <www.microsoft.com>, December 27, 2001.

CASE STUDY QUESTIONS:

1. Describe Mary Kay's business strategy before 1998. Did its strategy change? Explain your answer.

2. How did information technology fit in with and support Mary Kay's pre-1998 strategy? Why did Mary Kay change the role for information technology in 1998?

3. Why did Mary Kay choose a distributed network approach for handling its growing orders? What were its main strengths?

4. Why did the company abandon its distributed network approach for order entry when it had been successful?

5. Identify and describe the business as well as the technology issues that Mary Kay had to address when consolidating servers.

MANAGING DATA RESOURCES

As a manager, you'll want to know how to organize your company's data so that they can be easily accessed and utilized. After reading this chapter, you will be able to answer the following questions:

1. *Why do businesses have trouble finding the information they need in their information systems?*

2. *How does a database management system help businesses improve the organization of their information?*

3. *How do the principal types of database models affect the way businesses can access and use information?*

4. *What are the managerial and organizational requirements of a database environment?*

5. *What new tools and technologies can make databases more accessible and useful?*

Singapore's Tourism Board Learns to Manage Its Data

The Singapore Tourism Board (STB) collects, stores, and analyzes data on visitors to Singapore. Mainframe computers capture and process visitor arrival data to generate monthly and annual reports. As Singapore became increasingly popular as a global business and tourist destination, the Tourism Board's information systems department could not keep up with the Singapore government's demand for more accurate and timely statistical information. The Tourism board was using outdated data management and storage systems in which data were stored in disparate files and formats that were not integrated. It was difficult and time-consuming to consolidate the data from so many disparate sources. End users could not easily generate ad-hoc reports in their preferred formats.

Patrick, Lau Chen Chai, the CIO for the Singapore Tourism Board, initiated a project to create a powerful central repository for tourism data that could be used for all key statistical systems as well as the other needs of the Board and the industry. With the endorsement of senior management, Lau's group built a data warehouse called AIMS (Automated Information Management System), which is based on Oracle databases running on Sun and Siemens server computers. The system uses a three-tier client-server architecture so that processing power can be equally distributed

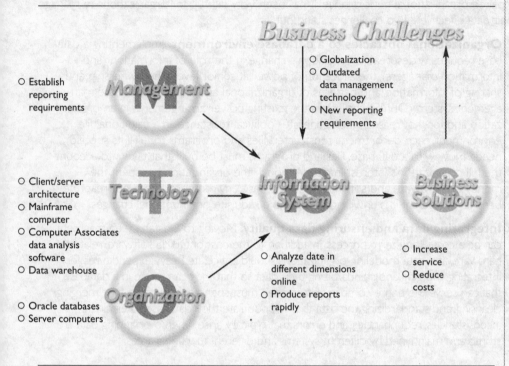

among user PCs, the application server, and the database server. To analyze the data in the warehouse, Lau selected tools from Computer Associates, including InfoPump, InfoBea-con, InfoReports, and WebBeacon analysis software. Info-Bea-con is an online analytical tool to analyze and present the data in a multi-dimensional format that allows the Tourism Board to generate the required information in different dimensions.

AIMS went live in April 1999. The warehouse has enabled STB to produce its reports much more efficiently and quickly, saving STB a total of 550 person-days that used to be spent producing reports and a total of 546 person-days that used to be spent servicing ad-hoc information requests from various departments of the Board. Now STB can get information on visitors within three days of their arrival in Singapore.

Sources: Winston Raj, "Constructing Potato Head," *CIO Asia*, January 2002 and <www.stb.com.sg>.

MANAGEMENT CHALLENGES

The Singapore Tourism Board's experience illustrates how much the effective use of information depends on how data are stored, organized, and accessed. Proper delivery of information not only depends on the capabilities of computer hardware and software but also on the organization's ability to manage data as an important resource. The Tourism Board's inability to assemble visitor data led to inefficient reporting processes that impaired organizational performance. It has been very difficult for organizations to manage their data effectively. Two challenges stand out.

1. **Organizational obstacles to a database environment.** Implementing a database requires widespread organizational change in the role of information (and information managers), the allocation of power at senior levels, the ownership and sharing of information, and patterns of organizational agreement. A database management system (DBMS) challenges the existing power arrangements in an organization and for that reason often generates political resistance. In a traditional file environment, each department constructed files and programs to fulfill its specific needs. Now, with a database, files and programs must be built that take into account the full organization's interest in data. Although the organization has spent the money on hardware and software for a database environment, it may not reap the benefits it should if it is unwilling to make the requisite organizational changes.

2. **Integrating data and ensuring data quality.** Moving to a database environment can be a costly long-term process. In addition to the cost of DBMS software, related hardware, and data modeling, organizations should anticipate heavy expenditures for integrating, merging and standardizing their data so that they can reside in a database that can serve the entire company. Firms often must spend considerable time merging, cleansing, and standardizing the data that will populate their database to eliminate inconsistencies, redundancies, and errors that typically arise when overlapping data are stored and maintained by different systems and different functional areas.

This chapter examines the managerial and organizational requirements as well as the technologies for managing data as a resource. Organizations need to manage their data assets very carefully to make sure that the data can be easily accessed and used by managers and employees across the organization. First we describe the typical challenges facing businesses trying to access information using traditional file management technologies. Then we describe the technology of database management systems, which can overcome many of the drawbacks of traditional file management and provide the firmwide integration of information required for digital firm applications. We include a discussion of the managerial and organizational requirements for successfully implementing a database environment.

7.1 ORGANIZING DATA IN A TRADITIONAL FILE ENVIRONMENT

An effective information system provides users with timely, accurate, and relevant information. This information is stored in computer files. When the files are properly arranged and maintained, users can easily access and retrieve the information they need. Well-managed, carefully arranged files make it easy to obtain data for business decisions, whereas poorly managed files lead to chaos in information processing, high costs, poor performance, and little, if any, flexibility. Despite the use of excellent hardware and software, many organizations have inefficient information systems because of poor file management. In this section we describe the traditional methods that organizations have used to arrange data in computer files. We also discuss the problems with these methods.

FILE ORGANIZATION TERMS AND CONCEPTS

A computer system organizes data in a hierarchy that starts with bits and bytes and progresses to fields, records, files, and databases (see Figure 7-1). A *bit* represents the smallest unit of data a computer can handle. A group of bits, called a *byte*, represents a single character, which

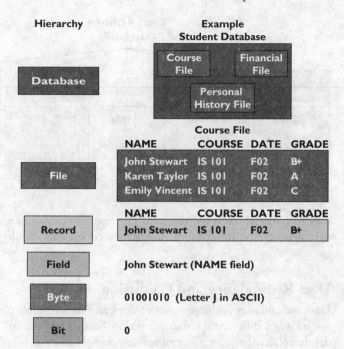

Figure 7-1 The data hierarchy. A computer system organizes data in a hierarchy that starts with the bit, which represents either a 0 or a 1. Bits can be grouped to form a byte to represent one character, number, or symbol. Bytes can be grouped to form a field, and related fields can be grouped to form a record. Related records can be collected to form a file, and related files can be organized into a database.

can be a letter, a number, or another symbol. A grouping of characters into a word, a group of words, or a complete number (such as a person's name or age) is called a **field.** A group of related fields, such as the student's name, the course taken, the date, and the grade, comprises a **record;** a group of records of the same type is called a **file.** For instance, the student records in Figure 7-1 could constitute a course file. A group of related files makes up a **database.** The student course file illustrated in Figure 7-1 could be grouped with files on students' personal histories and financial backgrounds to create a student database.

A record describes an entity. An **entity** is a person, place, thing, or event on which we maintain information. An order is a typical entity in a sales order file, which maintains information on a firm's sales orders. Each characteristic or quality describing a particular entity is called an **attribute.** For example, order number, order date, order amount, item number, and item quantity would each be an attribute of the entity order. The specific values that these attributes can have can be found in the fields of the record describing the entity order (see Figure 7-2).

Every record in a file should contain at least one field that uniquely identifies instances of that record so that the record can be retrieved, updated, or sorted. This identifier field is called a **key field.** An example of a key field is the order number for the order record illustrated in Figure 7-2 or an employee number or social security number for a personnel record (containing employee data such as the employee's name, age, address, job title, and so forth).

PROBLEMS WITH THE TRADITIONAL FILE ENVIRONMENT

In most organizations, systems tended to grow independently and not according to some grand plan. Each functional area tended to develop systems in isolation from other functional areas. Accounting, finance, manufacturing, human resources, and sales and marketing all developed their own systems and data files. Figure 7-3 illustrates the traditional approach to information processing.

Each application, of course, required its own files and its own computer program to operate. For example, the human resources functional area might have a personnel master file, a payroll file, a medical insurance file, a pension file, a mailing list file, and so forth until tens, perhaps hundreds, of files and programs existed. In the company as a whole, this process led to multiple master files created, maintained, and operated by separate divisions or departments. As this process goes on for 5 or 10 years, the organization is saddled with hundreds of programs and applications, with no one who knows what they do, what data

field
A grouping of characters into a word, a group of words, or a complete number, such as a person's name or age.

record
A group of related fields.

file
A group of records of the same type.

database
A group of related files.

entity
A person, place, thing, or event about which information must be kept.

attribute
A piece of information describing a particular entity.

key field
A field in a record that uniquely identifies instances of that record so that it can be retrieved, updated, or sorted.

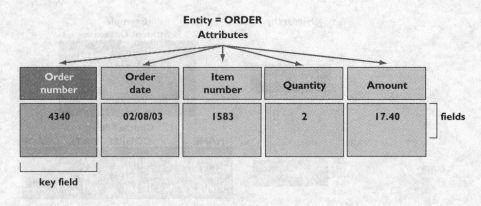

Figure 7-2 Entities and attributes. This record describes the entity called ORDER and its attributes. The specific values for order number, order date, item number, quantity, and amount for this particular order are the fields for this record. Order number is the key field because each order is assigned a unique identification number.

they use, and who is using the data. The resulting problems are data redundancy, program-data dependence, inflexibility, poor data security, and inability to share data among applications.

Data Redundancy and Confusion

data redundancy

The presence of duplicate data in multiple data files.

Data redundancy is the presence of duplicate data in multiple data files. Data redundancy occurs when different divisions, functional areas, and groups in an organization independently collect the same piece of information. Because it is collected and maintained in so many different places, the same data item, such as employee, fiscal year, or product identification code may have different meanings in different parts of the organization. Different systems might use different names for the same item. For instance, the sales, inventory, and manufacturing systems of a clothing retailer might use different codes to represent clothing size. One system might represent clothing size as "extra large" while another might use the code XL for the same purpose. The resulting confusion would make it difficult for companies to create customer relationship management, supply chain management, or enterprise systems that integrate data from different sources.

Program-Data Dependence

program-data dependence

The close relationship between data stored in files and the software programs that update and maintain those files. Any change in data organization or format requires a change in all the programs associated with those files.

Program-Data dependence is the tight relationship between data stored in files and the specific programs required to update and maintain those files. Every traditional computer program has to describe the location and nature of the data with which it works. In a traditional file environment, any change in data requires a change in all programs that access the data. Changes,

Figure 7-3 Traditional file processing. The use of a traditional approach to file processing encourages each functional area in a corporation to develop specialized applications. Each application requires a unique data file that is likely to be a subset of the master file. These subsets of the master file lead to data redundancy, processing inflexibility, and wasted storage resources.

for instance, in tax rates or ZIP code length require changes in programs. Such programming changes may cost millions of dollars to implement in programs that require the revised data.

Lack of Flexibility

A traditional file system can deliver routine scheduled reports after extensive programming efforts, but it cannot deliver ad hoc reports or respond to unanticipated information requirements in a timely fashion. The information required by ad hoc requests is somewhere in the system but too expensive to retrieve. Several programmers would have to work for weeks to put together the required data items in a new file.

Poor Security

Because there is little control or management of data, access to and dissemination of information may be out of control. Management may have no way of knowing who is accessing or even making changes to the organization's data.

Lack of Data-Sharing and Availability

The lack of control over access to data in this confused environment does not make it easy for people to obtain information. Because pieces of information in different files and different parts of the organization cannot be related to one another, it is virtually impossible for information to be shared or accessed in a timely manner. Information cannot flow freely across different functional areas or different parts of the organization.

7.2 THE DATABASE APPROACH TO DATA MANAGEMENT

Database technology can cut through many of the problems a traditional file organization creates. A more rigorous definition of a **database** is a collection of data organized to serve many applications efficiently by centralizing the data and minimizing redundant data. Rather than storing data in separate files for each application, data are stored physically to appear to users as being stored in only one location. A single database services multiple applications. For example, instead of a corporation storing employee data in separate information systems and separate files for personnel, payroll, and benefits, the corporation could create a single common human resources database. Figure 7-4 illustrates the database concept.

database (rigorous definition)
A collection of data organized to service many applications at the same time by storing and managing data so that they appear to be in one location.

Figure 7-4 The contemporary database environment. A single human resources database serves multiple applications and also allows a corporation to easily draw together all the information for various applications. The database management system acts as the interface between the application programs and the data.

Database Management Systems

database management system (DBMS)

Special software to create and maintain a database and enable individual business applications to extract the data they need without having to create separate files or data definitions in their computer programs.

logical view

A representation of data as they would appear to an application programmer or end user.

physical view

The representation of data as they would actually be organized on physical storage media.

data definition language

The component of a database management system that defines each data element as it appears in the database.

data manipulation language

A language associated with a database management system that end users and programmers use to manipulate data in the database.

Structured Query Language (SQL)

The standard data manipulation language for relational database management systems.

data dictionary

An automated or manual tool for storing and organizing information about the data maintained in a database.

data element

A field.

A **database management system (DBMS)** is simply the software that permits an organization to centralize data, manage them efficiently, and provide access to the stored data by application programs. The DBMS acts as an interface between application programs and the physical data files. When the application program calls for a data item such as gross pay, the DBMS finds this item in the database and presents it to the application program. Using traditional data files the programmer would have to specify the size and format of each data element used in the program and then tell the computer where they were located. A DBMS eliminates most of the data definition statements found in traditional programs.

The DBMS relieves the programmer or end user from the task of understanding where and how the data are actually stored by separating the logical and physical views of the data. The **logical view** presents data as they would be perceived by end users or business specialists, whereas the **physical view** shows how data are actually organized and structured on physical storage media. There is only one physical view of the data, but there can be many different logical views. The database management software makes the physical database available for different logical views presented for various application programs. For example, an employee retirement benefits program might use a logical view of the human resources database illustrated in Figure 7-4 that requires only the employee's name, address, social security number, pension plan, and retirement benefits data.

A database management system has three components:

1. A data definition language
2. A data manipulation language
3. A data dictionary

The **data definition language** is the formal language programmers use to specify the content and structure of the database. The data definition language defines each data element as it appears in the database before that data element is translated into the forms required by application programs.

Most DBMS have a specialized language called a **data manipulation language** that is used in conjunction with some conventional application programming languages to manipulate the data in the database. This language contains commands that permit end users and programming specialists to extract data from the database to satisfy information requests and develop applications. The most prominent data manipulation language today is **Structured Query Language,** or **SQL.** End users and information systems specialists can use SQL as an interactive query language to access data from databases, and SQL commands can be embedded in application programs written in conventional programming languages.

The third element of a DBMS is a **data dictionary.** This is an automated or manual file that stores definitions of data elements and data characteristics such as usage, physical representation, ownership (who in the organization is responsible for maintaining the data), authorization, and security. Many data dictionaries can produce lists and reports of data use, groupings, program locations, and so on. Figure 7-5 illustrates a sample data dictionary report that shows the size, format, meaning, and uses of a data element in a human resources database. A **data element** represents a field. In addition to listing the standard name (AMT-PAY-BASE), the dictionary lists the names that reference this element in specific systems and identifies the individuals, business functions, programs, and reports that use this data element.

By creating an inventory of data contained in the database, the data dictionary serves as an important data management tool. For instance, business users could consult the dictionary to find out exactly what pieces of data are maintained for the sales or marketing function or even to determine all the information maintained by the entire enterprise. The dictionary could supply business users with the name, format, and specifications required to access data for reports. Technical staff could use the dictionary to determine what data elements and files must be changed if a program is changed.

Most data dictionaries are entirely passive; they simply report. More advanced types are active; changes in the dictionary can be automatically used by related programs. For

NAME: AMT-PAY-BASE
FOCUS NAME: BASEPAY
PC NAME: SALARY

DESCRIPTION: EMPLOYEE'S ANNUAL SALARY

SIZE: 9 BYTES
TYPE: N (NUMERIC)
DATE CHANGED: 01/01/95
OWNERSHIP: COMPENSATION
UPDATE SECURITY: SITE PERSONNEL
ACCESS SECURITY: MANAGER, COMPENSATION PLANNING AND RESEARCH
MANAGER, JOB EVALUATION SYSTEMS
MANAGER, HUMAN RESOURCES PLANNING
MANAGER, SITE EQUAL OPPORTUNITY AFFAIRS
MANAGER, SITE BENEFITS
MANAGER, CLAIMS PAYING SYSTEMS
MANAGER, QUALIFIED PLANS
MANAGER, SITE EMPLOYMENT/EEO
BUSINESS FUNCTIONS USED BY: COMPENSATION
HR PLANNING
EMPLOYMENT
INSURANCE
PENSION
401K

PROGRAMS USING: PI01000
PI02000
PI03000
PI04000
PI05000

REPORTS USING: REPORT 124 (SALARY INCREASE TRACKING REPORT)
REPORT 448 (GROUP INSURANCE AUDIT REPORT)
REPORT 452 (SALARY REVIEW LISTING)
PENSION REFERENCE LISTING

Figure 7-5 Sample data dictionary report. The sample data dictionary report for a human resources database provides helpful information such as the size of the data element, which programs and reports use it, and which group in the organization is the owner responsible for maintaining it. The report also shows some of the other names that the organization uses for this piece of data.

instance, to change ZIP codes from five to nine digits, one could simply enter the change in the dictionary without having to modify all application programs using ZIP codes.

In an ideal database environment, the data in the database are defined only once and used for all applications whose data reside in the database, thereby eliminating data redundancy and inconsistency. Application programs, which are written using a combination of the data manipulation language of the DBMS and a conventional programming language, request data elements from the database. Data elements called for by the application programs are found and delivered by the DBMS. The programmer does not have to specify in detail how or where the data are to be found.

A DBMS can reduce program-data dependence along with program development and maintenance costs. Access and availability of information can be increased because users and programmers can perform ad hoc queries of data in the database. The DBMS allows the organization to centrally manage data, their use, and security. The Window on Management illustrates some of these benefits.

TYPES OF DATABASES

Contemporary DBMS use different database models to keep track of entities, attributes, and relationships. Each model has certain processing advantages and certain business advantages.

Relational DBMS

The most popular type of DBMS today for PCs as well as for larger computers and mainframes is the **relational DBMS.** The relational data model represents all data in the database as simple two-dimensional tables called relations. The tables appear similar to flat files, but the information in more than one file can be easily extracted and combined. Sometimes the tables are referred to as files.

relational DBMS

A type of logical database model that treats data as if they were stored in two-dimensional tables. It can relate data stored in one table to data in another as long as the two tables share a common data element.

A DATABASE SHOWS THE WORLD AWASH IN STOLEN NUCLEAR MATERIAL

The September 11, 2001, terrorist attacks in New York City and Washington, D.C. heightened fears about weapons-grade nuclear material that may have fallen into the wrong hands. In March 2002, Lyudmila Zaitseva, a visiting fellow at Stanford University's Institute for International Studies, observed "We can only guess by the routes where the [missing nuclear] material is going. We can't be sure if it is Iraq, Iran, North Korea, al Qaeda, or Hezbollah."

The problem began at least 10 years ago with the collapse of the Soviet Union. Since that time, those with knowledge about this issue have expressed fear that the nuclear material has not been well protected or even accounted for. No one even knew just what material was missing, much less where that material is. In recent months the Strategic Security Project at Stanford University (nicknamed the Database on Nuclear Smuggling, Theft, and Orphan Radiation Sources) began to collect data on what nuclear material was missing and what has happened to it. "It blows the mind, the lack of information," stated George Bunn, an experienced arms control negotiator. "What we're trying to say is: 'What are the facts?'"

The data about stolen radioactive material come from two existing unclassified databases and additional data from sources ranging from government agencies to local media reports. The Strategic Security Project evaluates each entry for accuracy and probability. The data are being stored in a database where DBMS security features can be used to limit access only to approved researchers. The database contains data on illicitly obtained weapons-grade nuclear material as well as scientific and medical material that may have been lost, misplaced, or simply thrown away but nevertheless could pose health and security threats. Members of the

Stanford group have begun informing appropriate government agencies in the United States and Europe of the existence of the database and offering access to the data to approved organizations.

By assembling all the data about lost, misplaced, or stolen nuclear material into a single database, analysts have a more comprehensive and precise picture of how serious a problem wayward nuclear material poses. According to Zaitseva, at least 88 pounds (40 kg) of weapons-usable uranium and plutonium have been stolen from poorly protected nuclear facilities in the former Soviet Union. Most of this material was subsequently retrieved, but 4.4 pounds (2 kg) of highly enriched uranium stolen from a reactor remains missing. One of several fuel rods that disappeared from a research reactor in the Congo was found to have later resurfaced in Italy, reportedly in the hands of Mafia, but the others still cannot be accounted for.

"This is a smart step," exclaimed Michael Levi, the director of the Strategic Security Project. "Knowing what's out there is the first step to bringing it back in." Research to this point has discovered where some of the critical material was initially transported, but we do not know where any of it ended up. Research is continuing, and the information is being securely guarded in the tightly protected DBMS.

Think About: What are the advantages of using a database to track stolen or lost nuclear material? How can such data be better managed using a DBMS?

Source: Andrew Quinn, "Data Show World Awash in Stolen Nuclear Material," *Reuters*, March 6, 2002 and "Fears Over Missing Nuclear Material," *BBC News*, March 7, 2002.

MANAGEMENT

---

tuple

A row or record in a relational database.

Figure 7-6 shows a supplier table, a part table, and an order table. In each table the rows are unique records and the columns are fields. Another term for a row or record in a relation is a **tuple.** Often a user needs information from a number of relations to produce a report. Here is the strength of the relational model: It can relate data in any one file or table to data in another file or table as long as both tables share a common data element.

To demonstrate, suppose we wanted to find in the relational database in Figure 7-6 the names and addresses of suppliers who could provide us with part number 137 or part number 152. We would need information from two tables: the supplier table and the part table. Note that these two files have a shared data element: Supplier_Number.

In a relational database, three basic operations as shown in Figure 7-7 are used to develop useful sets of data: select, project, and join. The *select* operation creates a subset consisting of all records in the file that meet stated criteria. Select creates, in other words, a subset of rows that meet certain criteria. In our example, we want to select records (rows) from the part table where the part number equals 137 or 152. The *join* operation combines relational tables to provide the user with more information than is available in individual tables. In our example we want to join the now-shortened part table (only parts numbered 137 or 152 will be presented) and the supplier table into a single new result table.

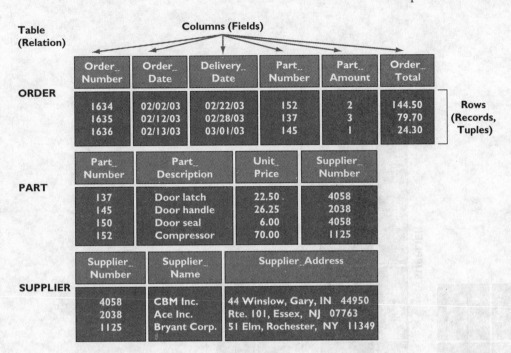

Table (Relation)

Columns (Fields)

ORDER

Order_ Number	Order_ Date	Delivery_ Date	Part_ Number	Part_ Amount	Order_ Total
1634	02/02/03	02/22/03	152	2	144.50
1635	02/12/03	02/28/03	137	3	79.70
1636	02/13/03	03/01/03	145	1	24.30

Rows (Records, Tuples)

PART

Part_ Number	Part_ Description	Unit_ Price	Supplier_ Number
137	Door latch	22.50	4058
145	Door handle	26.25	2038
150	Door seal	6.00	4058
152	Compressor	70.00	1125

SUPPLIER

Supplier_ Number	Supplier_ Name	Supplier_Address
4058	CBM Inc.	44 Winslow, Gary, IN 44950
2038	Ace Inc.	Rte. 101, Essex, NJ 07763
1125	Bryant Corp.	51 Elm, Rochester, NY 11349

Figure 7-6 The relational data model. Each table is a relation and each row or record is a tuple. Each column corresponds to a field. These relations can easily be combined and extracted to access data and produce reports, provided that any two share a common data element. In this example, the ORDER file shares the data element "Part_Number" with the PART file. The PART and SUPPLIER files share the data element "Supplier_Number."

The *project* operation creates a subset consisting of columns in a table, permitting the user to create new tables (also called views) that contain only the information required. In our example, we want to extract from the new result table only the following columns: Part_Number, Supplier_Number, Supplier_Name, and Supplier_Address (see Figure 7-7).

Leading mainframe relational database management systems include IBM's DB2 and Oracle from the Oracle Corporation. DB2, Oracle, and Microsoft SQL Server are used as DBMS for midrange computers. Microsoft Access is a PC relational database management system, and Oracle Lite is a DBMS for small handheld computing devices.

Hierarchical and Network DBMS

One can still find older systems that are based on a hierarchical or network data model. The **hierarchical DBMS** presents data to users in a treelike structure. Within each record, data elements are organized into pieces of records called *segments*. To the user, each record looks like an organization chart with one top-level segment called the *root*. An upper segment is connected logically to a lower segment in a parent–child relationship. A parent segment can have more than one child, but a child can have only one parent.

Figure 7-8 shows a hierarchical structure that might be used for a human resources database. The root segment is Employee, which contains basic employee information such as name, address, and identification number. Immediately below it are three child segments: Compensation (containing salary and promotion data), Job Assignments (containing data about job positions and departments), and Benefits (containing data about beneficiaries and benefit options). The Compensation segment has two children below it: Performance Ratings (containing data about employees' job performance evaluations) and Salary History (containing historical data about employees' past salaries). Below the Benefits segment are child segments for Pension, Life Insurance, and Health Care, containing data about these benefit plans.

Whereas hierarchical structures depict one-to-many relationships, **network DBMS** depict data logically as many-to-many relationships. In other words, parents can have multiple children, and a child can have more than one parent. A typical many-to-many relationship for a network DBMS is the student–course relationship (see Figure 7-9). There are many courses in a university and many students. A student takes many courses and a course has many students.

Hierarchical and network DBMS are considered outdated and are no longer used for building new database applications. They are much less flexible than relational DBMS and do not support ad hoc, English language-like inquiries for information. All paths for accessing data must be specified in advance and cannot be changed without a major programming

hierarchical DBMS

Older logical database model that organizes data in a treelike structure. A record is subdivided into segments that are connected to each other in one-to-many parent–child relationships.

network DBMS

Older logical database model that is useful for depicting many-to-many relationships.

ORDER

Order_Number	Order_Date	Delivery_Date	Part_Number	Part_Amount	Order_Total
1634	02/02/03	02/22/03	152	2	144.50
1635	02/12/03	02/28/03	137	3	79.70
1636	02/13/03	03/01/03	145	1	24.30

SUPPLIER

Supplier_Number	Supplier_Name	Supplier_Address
4058	CBM Inc.	44 Winslow, Gary, IN 44950
2038	Ace Inc.	Rte. 101, Essex, NJ 07763
1125	Bryant Corp.	51 Elm, Rochester, NY 11349

Join by Supplier_Number

PART

Part_Number	Part_Description	Unit_Price	Supplier_Number
137	Door latch	22.50	4058
145	Door handle	26.25	2038
150	Door seal	6.00	4058
152	Compressor	70.00	1125

Select Part_Number = 137 or 152

Part_Number	Supplier_Number	Supplier_Name	Supplier_Address
137	4058	CBM Inc.	44 Winslow, Gary, IN 44950
152	1125	Bryant Corp.	51 Elm, Rochester, NY 11349

Project selected columns

Figure 7-7   The three basic operations of a relational DBMS. The select, project, and join operations allow data from two different tables to be combined and only selected attributes to be displayed.

Figure 7-8 A hierarchical database for a human resources system. The hierarchical database model looks like an organizational chart or a family tree. It has a single root segment (Employee) connected to lower level segments (Compensation, Job Assignments, and Benefits). Each subordinate segment, in turn, may connect to other subordinate segments. Here, Compensation connects to Performance Ratings and Salary History. Benefits connects to Pension, Life Insurance, and Health Care. Each subordinate segment is the child of the segment directly above it.

effort. For instance, if you queried the human resources database illustrated in Figure 7-8 to find out the names of the employees with the job title of administrative assistant, you would discover that there is no way that the system can find the answer in a reasonable amount of time. This path through the data was not specified in advance.

Relational DBMS, in contrast have much more flexibility in providing data for ad hoc queries, combining information from different sources, and providing capability to add new data and records without disturbing existing programs and applications. However, these systems can be slowed down if they require many accesses to the data stored on disk to carry out the select, join, and project commands. Selecting one part number from among millions, one record at a time, can take a long time. Of course the database can be tuned to speed up prespecified queries.

Hierarchical DBMS can still be found in large legacy systems that require intensive high-volume transaction processing. A **legacy system** is a system that has been in existence for a long time and that continues to be used to avoid the high cost of replacing or redesigning it. Banks, insurance companies, and other high-volume users continue to use reliable hierarchical DBMS such as IBM's IMS (Information Management System), developed in 1969. As relational products acquire more muscle, firms will shift away completely from hierarchical DBMS, but this will happen over a long period of time.

legacy system
A system that has been in existence for a long time and that continues to be used to avoid the high cost of replacing or redesigning it.

Object-Oriented Databases

Conventional database management systems were designed for homogeneous data that can be easily structured into predefined data fields and records organized in rows or tables. But many applications today and in the future will require databases that can store and retrieve not only structured numbers and characters but also drawings, images, photographs, voice, and full-motion video. Conventional DBMS are not well suited to handling graphics-based or multimedia applications. For instance, design data in a computer-aided design (CAD) database consist of complex relationships among many types of data. Manipulating these kinds of data in a relational system requires extensive programming to translate these complex data structures into tables and rows. An **object-oriented DBMS,** however, stores the data and procedures as objects that can be automatically retrieved and shared.

Object-oriented database management systems (OODBMS) are becoming popular because they can be used to manage the various multimedia components or Java applets used in Web applications, which typically integrate pieces of information from a variety of sources. OODBMS also are useful for storing data types such as recursive data. (An example would be parts within parts as found in manufacturing applications.) Finance and trading applications often use OODBMS because they require data models that must be easy to change to respond to new economic conditions.

Although object-oriented databases can store more complex types of information than relational DBMS, they are relatively slow compared with relational DBMS for processing

object-oriented DBMS
An approach to data management that stores both data and the procedures acting on the data as objects that can be automatically retrieved and shared; the objects can contain multimedia.

Figure 7-9 The network data model. This illustration of a network data model showing the relationship the students in a university have to the courses they take represents an example of logical many-to-many relationships.

Figure 7-10 The results of using the SELECT statement to select only the columns Part_Number, Part_Description and Unit_Price from all rows in the PART table.

Part_ Number	Part_ Description	Unit_ Price
137	Door latch	22.50
145	Door handle	26.25
150	Door seal	6.00
152	Compressor	70.00

object-relational DBMS

A database management system that combines the capabilities of a relational DBMS and the capabilities of an object-oriented DBMS.

large numbers of transactions. Hybrid **object-relational DBMS** systems are now available to provide capabilities of both object-oriented and relational DBMS. A hybrid approach can be accomplished in three different ways: by using tools that offer object-oriented access to relational DBMS, by using object-oriented extensions to existing relational DBMS, or by using a hybrid object-relational database management system.

QUERYING DATABASES: ELEMENTS OF SQL

Structured query language (SQL) is the principal data manipulation language for relational DBMS and a major tool for querying, reading, and updating a relational database. There are versions of SQL that can run on almost any operating system and computer, so that computers are able to exchange data by passing SQL commands to each other. End users and information systems specialists can use SQL as an interactive query language to access data from databases, and SQL commands can also be embedded in application programs written in COBOL, C, and other programming languages.

We now describe the most important basic SQL commands. Convention calls for certain SQL reserved words with special meanings, such as SELECT and FROM, to be capitalized and for SQL statements to be written in multiple lines. Most SQL statements to retrieve data contain the following three clauses

SELECT	Lists the columns from tables that the user would like to see in a result table
FROM	Identifies the tables or views from which the columns will be selected
WHERE	Includes conditions for selecting specific rows (records) within a single table and conditions for joining multiple tables

The SELECT Statement

The SELECT statement is used to query data from a relational table for specific information. The general form for a SELECT statement that retrieves specified columns for all of the rows in the table is:

    SELECT Column_Name, Column_Name, . . .
    FROM Table_Name;

The columns to be obtained are listed after the keyword SELECT and the table to be used is listed after the keyword FROM. Note that column and table names do not have spaces and must be typed as one word or with an underscore and that the statement ends with a semicolon. Review Figure 7-6. Suppose you wanted to see the Part_Number, Part_Description, and Unit_Price for each part in the PART table. You would specify:

    SELECT Part_Number, Part_Description, Unit_Price
    FROM PART;

Figure 7-10 illustrates the results of your projection.

Conditional Selection

The WHERE clause is used to specify that only certain rows of the table are displayed, based on the criteria described in that WHERE clause. Suppose, for example, you wanted to see the same data only for parts in the PART table with unit prices less than $25.00. You would specify:

    SELECT Part_Number, Part_Description, Unit_Price
    FROM PART
    WHERE Unit_Price < 25.00;

Your query would return the results illustrated in Figure 7-11.

Joining Two Tables

Suppose we wanted to obtain information on the names, identification numbers, and addresses of suppliers for each part in the database. We can do this by joining the PART table with the SUPPLIER table and then extracting the required information. The query would look like this:

Part_ Number	Part_ Description	Unit_ Price
137 150	Door latch Door seal	22.50 6.00

Figure 7-11 The results of using a conditional selection to select only parts that meet the condition of having unit prices less than $25.

```
SELECT PART.Part_Number, SUPPLIER.Supplier_Number, SUPPLIER.Supplier_Name,
    SUPPLIER.Supplier_Address
FROM PART, SUPPLIER
WHERE PART.Supplier_Number = SUPPLIER.Supplier_Number;
```

The results would look like Figure 7-12. And if we only wanted to see the name, address, and supplier numbers for the suppliers of part numbers 137 or 152, the query would be:

```
SELECT PART.Part_Number, SUPPLIER.Supplier_Number, SUPPLIER.Supplier_Name,
    SUPPLIER.Supplier_Address
FROM PART, SUPPLIER
WHERE PART.Supplier_Number = SUPPLIER.Supplier_Number AND Part_Number = 137 OR
    Part_Number = 152;
```

The results would look like the result of the join operation depicted in Figure 7-7. Note that several conditions can be expressed in the WHERE clause.

7.3 CREATING A DATABASE ENVIRONMENT

In order to create a database environment, one must understand the relationships among the data, the type of data that will be maintained in the database, how the data will be used, and how the organization will need to change to manage data from a company-wide perspective. Increasingly, database design will also have to consider the how the organization can share some of its data with its business partners (Jukic, Jukic, and Parameswaran, 2002). We now describe important database design principles and the management and organizational requirements of a database environment.

DESIGNING DATABASES

To create a database, one must go through two design exercises: a conceptual design and a physical design. The conceptual, or logical, design of a database is an abstract model of the database from a business perspective, whereas the physical design shows how the database is actually arranged on direct access storage devices. Logical design requires a detailed description of the business information needs of the actual end users of the database. Ideally, database design will be part of an overall organizational data planning effort (see Chapter 12).

The conceptual database design describes how the data elements in the database are to be grouped. The design process identifies relationships among data elements and the most efficient way of grouping data elements together to meet information requirements. The process also identifies redundant data elements and the groupings of data elements required for specific application programs. Groups of data are organized, refined, and streamlined until an overall logical view of the relationships among all the data elements in the database emerges.

Part_ Number	Supplier_ Number	Supplier_ Name	Supplier_Address
137	4058	CBM Inc.	44 Winslow, Gary, IN 44950
145	2038	Ace Inc.	Rte. 101, Essex, NJ 07763
150	4058	CBM Inc.	44 Winslow, Gary, IN 44950
152	1125	Bryant Corp.	51 Elm, Rochester, NY 11349

Figure 7-12 A projection from joining the PART and SUPPLIER tables.

Figure 7-13 An entity-relationship diagram. This diagram shows the relationships between the entities ORDER, PART, and SUPPLIER that were used to develop the relational database illustrated in Figure 7-6.

entity-relationship diagram
A methodology for documenting databases illustrating the relationship between various entities in the database.

normalization
The process of creating small stable data structures from complex groups of data when designing a relational database.

Entity Attributes

Order_Number

Order_Date
Delivery_Date
Part_Number
Part_Amount
Order_Total

Part_Number

Part_Description
Unit_Price
Supplier_Number

Supplier_Number

Supplier_Name
Supplier_Address

Database designers document the conceptual data model with an **entity-relationship diagram,** illustrated in Figure 7-13. The boxes represent entities and the diamonds represent relationships. The 1 or M on either side of the diamond represents the relationship among entities as either one-to-one, one-to-many, or many-to-many. Figure 7-13 shows that the entity ORDER can have more than one PART and a PART can only have one SUPPLIER. Many parts can be provided by the same supplier. The attributes for each entity are listed next to the entity and the key field is underlined.

To use a relational database model effectively, complex groupings of data must be streamlined to eliminate redundant data elements and awkward many-to-many relationships. The process of creating small, stable data structures from complex groups of data is called **normalization.** Figures 7-14 and 7-15 illustrate this process. In the particular business modeled here, an order can have more than one part but each part is provided by only one supplier. If we built a relation called ORDER with all the fields included here, we would have to repeat the name, description, and price of each part on the order and the name and address of each part vendor. This relation contains what are called repeating groups because there can be many parts and suppliers for each order, and it actually describes multiple entities—parts and suppliers as well as orders. A more efficient way to arrange the data is to break down ORDER into smaller relations, each of which describes a single entity. If we go step by step and normalize the relation ORDER, we emerge with the relations illustrated in Figure 7-15.

If a database has been carefully considered, with a clear understanding of business information needs and usage, the database model will most likely be in some normalized form. Many real-world databases are not fully normalized because this may not be the most sensible way to meet business information requirements. Note that the relational database illustrated in Figure 7-6 is not fully normalized because there could be more than one part for each order. The designers chose to not use the four relations described in Figure 7-15 because most of the orders handled by this particular business are only for one part. The designers might have felt that for this particular business it was inefficient to maintain four different tables.

DISTRIBUTING DATABASES

distributed database
A database that is stored in more than one physical location. Parts or copies of the database are physically stored in one location, and other parts or copies are stored and maintained in other locations.

Database design also considers how the data are to be distributed. Information systems can be designed with a centralized database that is used by a single central processor or by multiple processors in a client/server network. Alternatively, the database can be distributed. A **distributed database** is one that is stored in more than one physical location. Parts of the database are stored physically in one location, and other parts are stored and maintained in other locations. There are two main ways of distributing a database (see Figure 7-16.) The central database can be partitioned (see Figure 7-16a) so that each remote processor has the necessary data to serve its local area. Changes in local files can be justified with the central

ORDER										
Order_ Number	Part_ Amount	Part_ Number	Part_ Description	Unit_ Price	Supplier_ Number	Supplier_ Name	Supplier_ Address	Order_ Date	Delivery_ Date	Order_ Total

Figure 7-14 An unnormalized relation for ORDER. In an unnormalized relation there are repeating groups. For example, there can be many parts and suppliers for each order. There is only a one-to-one correspondence between Order_Number and Order_Date, Order_Total, and Delivery_Date.

Figure 7-15 A normalized relation for ORDER. After normalization, the original relation ORDER has been broken down into four smaller relations. The relation ORDER is left with only three attributes and the relation ORDERED_PARTS has a combined, or concatenated, key consisting of Order_Number and Part_Number.

database on a batch basis, often at night. Another strategy is to replicate the central database (Figure 7-16b) at all remote locations. For example, Lufthansa Airlines replaced its centralized mainframe database with a replicated database to make information more immediately available to flight dispatchers. Any change made to Lufthansa's Frankfort DBMS is automatically replicated in New York and Hong Kong. This strategy also requires updating of the central database on off hours.

Distributed systems reduce the vulnerability of a single, massive central site. They increase service and responsiveness to local users and often can run on smaller, less expensive computers. Distributed systems, however, are dependent on high-quality telecommunications lines, which themselves are vulnerable. Moreover, local databases can sometimes depart from central data standards and definitions, and they pose security problems by widely distributing access to sensitive data. Database designers need to weigh these factors in their decisions.

MANAGEMENT REQUIREMENTS FOR DATABASE SYSTEMS

Much more is required for the development of database systems than simply selecting a logical database model. The database is an organizational discipline, a method, rather than a tool or technology. It requires organizational and conceptual change. Without management support and understanding, database efforts fail. The critical elements in a database environment are (1) data administration, (2) data planning and modeling methodology, (3) database technology and management, and (4) users. This environment is depicted in Figure 7-17.

Figure 7-16 Distributed databases. There are alternative ways of distributing a database. The central database can be partitioned (a) so that each remote processor has the necessary data to serve its local needs. The central database also can be duplicated (b) at all remote locations.

Figure 7-17 Key organizational elements in the database environment. For a database management system to flourish in any organization, data administration functions and data planning and modeling methodologies must be coordinated with database technology and management. Resources must be devoted to train end users to use databases properly.

data administration
A special organizational function for managing the organization's data resources, concerned with information policy, data planning, maintenance of data dictionaries, and data quality standards.

information policy
Formal rules governing the maintenance, distribution, and use of information in an organization.

Data Administration

Database systems require that the organization recognize the strategic role of information and begin actively to manage and plan for information as a corporate resource. This means that the organization must develop a **data administration** function with the power to define information requirements for the entire company and with direct access to senior management. The chief information officer (CIO) or vice president of information becomes the primary advocate in the organization for database systems.

Data administration is responsible for the specific policies and procedures through which data can be managed as an organizational resource. These responsibilities include developing information policy, planning for data, overseeing logical database design and data dictionary development, and monitoring how information system specialists and end-user groups use data.

The fundamental principle of data administration is that all data are the property of the organization as a whole. Data cannot belong exclusively to any one business area or organizational unit. All data are to be made available to any group that requires them to fulfill its mission. An organization needs to formulate an **information policy** that specifies its rules for sharing, disseminating, acquiring, standardizing, classifying, and inventorying information throughout the organization. Information policy lays out specific procedures and accountabilities, specifying which organizational units share information, where information can be distributed, and who has responsibility for updating and maintaining the information. Although data administration is a very important organizational function, it has proved very challenging to implement.

Data Planning and Modeling Methodology

The organizational interests served by the DBMS are much broader than those in the traditional file environment; therefore, the organization requires enterprise-wide planning for data. Enterprise analysis, which addresses the information requirements of the entire organization (as opposed to the requirements of individual applications), is needed to develop databases. The purpose of enterprise analysis is to identify the key entities, attributes, and relationships that constitute the organization's data. These techniques are described in greater detail in Chapter 12.

Database Technology, Management, and Users

Databases require new software and a new staff specially trained in DBMS techniques, as well as new data management structures. Most corporations develop a database design and management group within the corporate information system division that is responsible for defining and organizing the structure and content of the database and maintaining the database. In close cooperation with users, the design group establishes the physical database, the logical relations among elements, and the access rules and procedures. The functions it performs are called **database administration.**

A database serves a wider community of users than traditional systems. Relational systems with fourth-generation query languages permit employees who are not computer specialists to access large databases. In addition, users include trained computer specialists. To optimize access for nonspecialists, more resources must be devoted to training end users.

database administration
Refers to the more technical and operational aspects of managing data, including physical database design and maintenance.

7.4 Database Trends

Organizations are installing powerful data analysis tools and data warehouses to make better use of the information stored in their databases and are taking advantage of database technology linked to the World Wide Web. We now explore these developments.

Online analytical processing (OLAP) gives users quick, unlimited views of multiple relationships in large quantities of data. This report from Cognos PowerPlay shows revenue for multiple product lines by quarter for 2000 and 2001.

MULTIDIMENSIONAL DATA ANALYSIS

Sometimes managers need to analyze data in ways that traditional database models cannot represent. For example, a company selling four different products—nuts, bolts, washers, and screws—in the East, West, and Central regions, might want to know actual sales by product for each region and might also want to compare them with projected sales. This analysis requires a multidimensional view of data.

To provide this type of information, organizations can use either a specialized multidimensional database or a tool that creates multidimensional views of data in relational databases. Multidimensional analysis enables users to view the same data in different ways using multiple dimensions. Each aspect of information—product, pricing, cost, region, or time period—represents a different dimension. So a product manager could use a multidimensional data analysis tool to learn how many washers were sold in the East in June, how that compares with the previous month and the previous June, and how it compares with the sales forecast. Another term for multidimensional data analysis is **online analytical processing (OLAP).**

Figure 7-18 shows a multidimensional model that could be created to represent products, regions, actual sales, and projected sales. A matrix of actual sales can be stacked on top of a matrix of projected sales to form a cube with six faces. If you rotate the cube 90 degrees one way, the face showing will be product versus actual and projected sales. If you rotate the cube 90 degrees again, you can see region versus actual and projected sales. If you rotate 180 degrees from the original view, you can see projected sales and product versus region. Cubes can be nested within cubes to build complex views of data.

online analytical processing (OLAP)
Capability for manipulating and analyzing large volumes of data from multiple perspectives.

Figure 7-18 Multidimensional data model. The view that is showing is product versus region. If you rotate the cube 90 degrees, the face that will be showing is product versus actual and projected sales. If you rotate the cube 90 degrees again, you can see region versus actual and projected sales. Other views are possible. The ability to rotate the data cube is the main technique for multidimensional reporting. It is sometimes called "slice and dice."

DATA WAREHOUSES AND DATAMINING

Decision makers need concise, reliable information about current operations, trends, and changes. What has been immediately available at most firms is current data only (historical data were available through special IS reports that took a long time to produce). Data often are fragmented in separate operational systems, such as sales or payroll, so that different managers make decisions from incomplete knowledge bases. Users and information system specialists may have to spend inordinate amounts of time locating and gathering data (Watson and Haley, 1998). Data warehousing addresses this problem by integrating key operational data from around the company in a form that is consistent, reliable, and easily available for reporting.

What Is a Data Warehouse?

data warehouse

A database, with reporting and query tools, that stores current and historical data extracted from various operational systems and consolidated for management reporting and analysis.

A **data warehouse** is a database that stores current and historical data of potential interest to managers throughout the company. The data originate in many core operational systems and external sources, including Web site transactions, each with different data models. They may include legacy systems, relational or object-oriented DBMS applications, and systems based on HTML or XML documents. The data from these diverse applications are copied into the data warehouse database as often as needed—hourly, daily, weekly, monthly. The data are standardized into a common data model and consolidated so that they can be used across the enterprise for management analysis and decision making. The data are available for anyone to access as needed but cannot be altered.

Figure 7-19 illustrates the data warehouse concept. The data warehouse must be carefully designed by both business and technical specialists to make sure it can provide the right information for critical business decisions. The firm may need to change its business processes to benefit from the information in the warehouse (Cooper, Watson, Wixom, and Goodhue, 2000). The Manager's Toolkit describes how to conduct a business analysis that addresses these issues.

Companies can build enterprise-wide data warehouses where a central data warehouse serves the entire organization, or they can create smaller, decentralized warehouses called data marts. A **data mart** is a subset of a data warehouse in which a summarized or highly focused portion of the organization's data is placed in a separate database for a specific population of users. For example, a company might develop marketing and sales data marts to deal with customer information. A data mart typically focuses on a single subject area or line of business, so it usually can be constructed more rapidly and at lower cost than an enterprise-wide data warehouse. However, complexity, costs, and management problems will rise if an organization creates too many data marts.

data mart

A small data warehouse containing only a portion of the organization's data for a specified function or population of users.

Datamining

A data warehouse system provides a range of ad hoc and standardized query tools, analytical tools, and graphical reporting facilities, including tools for OLAP and datamining.

Figure 7-19 Components of a data warehouse. A data warehouse extracts current and historical data from operational systems inside the organization. These data are combined with data from external sources and reorganized into a central database designed for management reporting and analysis. The information directory provides users with information about the data available in the warehouse.

MIS IN ACTION: MANAGER'S TOOLKIT

HOW TO MAKE A DATA WAREHOUSE SERVE THE BUSINESS

The first steps in building a data warehouse involve conducting a thorough business analysis of the information requirements that could be satisfied by a data warehouse. Here are some of the questions managers should ask:

1. *Users:* Who are the primary users of the data warehouse? What levels of the organization and business functions do they represent?
2. *Ownership:* What organizational group or groups own the data? Who is responsible for maintaining the data? Who is authorized to access the data?
3. *Information requirements:* What types of reports should the data warehouse provide? What pieces of data are used in these reports? Do these reports require the data to be detailed or summarized?
4. *Data sources:* What are the sources of data required by the reports? Which pieces come from internal TPS and other systems? Which come from sources outside the company? How can the company obtain the data for these reports?

5. *Currency:* How often do the data in the warehouse need to be updated? How long should historical data in the warehouse be maintained?
6. *Data standards:* Applications that were designed to support different functions or organizational units may use the same term in different ways. These discrepancies must be identified so that each data element is defined and used the same way in the data warehouse system. Does everyone agree on how each piece of data is defined and used?
7. *Quality expectations:* What level of accuracy and completeness of the data in the warehouse is sufficient to meet business needs?
8. *Benefits:* Precisely what are the business benefits of building this data warehouse? To what extent can these benefits be quantified? Are the benefits greater than the costs? (See Chapter 13.)
9. *Business process change:* Does the company need to change its business processes in order to use the information from the data warehouse effectively? How much change is required?

Datamining uses a variety of techniques to find hidden patterns and relationships in large pools of data and infer rules from them that can be used to predict future behavior and guide decision making (Fayyad et al., 2002; Hirji, 2001). Datamining is often used to provide information for targeted marketing where personalized or individualized messages can be created based on individual preferences and there are many other datamining applications in both business and scientific work. These systems can perform high-level analyses of patterns or trends, but they can also drill into more detail where needed. Table 7-1 describes how some organizations are benefiting from datamining and Chapter 11 provides more detail on how datamining is being used to guide business decisionmaking.

Datamining is both a powerful and profitable tool, but it poses challenges to the protection of individual privacy. Datamining technology can combine information from many diverse sources to create a detailed "data image" about each of us—our income, our driving habits, our hobbies, our families, and our political interests. The question of whether companies should be allowed to collect such detailed information about individuals is explored in Chapter 5.

datamining

Analysis of large pools of data to find patterns and rules that can be used to guide decision making and predict future behavior.

TABLE 7-1	HOW BUSINESSES ARE USING DATAMINING
Organization	**Datamining Application**
Disco S.A.	Argentine supermarket chain uses datamining to analyze purchasing patterns of more than 1.5 million customers who participate in a frequent buyer program in over 200 stores.
Red Robin Restaurants	Greenwood Village, Colorado-based chain uses OLAP and datamining to analyze the menus for its 87 corporate restaurants and over 100 franchise locations. By analyzing the price, cost, and quality of each item in all the meals the restaurant serves, Red Robin can identify the menu items that offer both high volume and high profit margin.
Carrier Corporation	Analyzes data generated by online purchasers and visitors to its Web site, combined with third-party demographic data to create profiles of online customers. Uses these profiles to target customers with appropriate products, such as multiroom air conditioners for suburban homeowners or compact models for apartment dwellers.
Verizon Wireless	Analyzes Verizon's customer database to identify new customers so that customer-service representatives can determine whether they need special help or services. Also uses datamining to identify mobile phone customers who might benefit from switching calling plans and mails them special promotions. Verizon uses such initiatives to increase customer satisfaction and thus reduce customer churn.

Benefits of Data Warehouses

Data warehouses not only offer improved information but they also make it easy for decision makers to obtain it. They even include the ability to model and remodel the data. It has been estimated that 70 percent of the world's business information resides on mainframe databases, many of which are for older legacy systems. Many of these legacy systems are critical production applications that support the company's core business processes. As long as these systems can efficiently process the necessary volume of transactions to keep the company running, firms are reluctant to replace them to avoid disrupting critical business functions and high system replacement costs. Many of these legacy systems use hierarchical DBMS or even older nondatabase files where information is difficult for users to access. Data warehouses enable decision makers to access data as often as they need without affecting the performance of the underlying operational systems. Many organizations are making access to their data warehouses even easier by using Web technology. Organizations such as Harrah's described in the chapter-ending case study, have used the information gleaned from data warehouses and datamining to help them refocus their businesses.

DATABASES AND THE WEB

Database technology plays an important role in making organizations' information resources available on the World Wide Web. We now explore the role of hypermedia databases in the Web and the growing use of Web sites to access information stored in conventional databases inside the firm.

The Web and Hypermedia Databases

Web sites store information as interconnected pages containing text, sound, video, and graphics using a hypermedia database. The **hypermedia database** approach to information management stores chunks of information in the form of nodes connected by links the user specifies (see Figure 7-20). The nodes can contain text, graphics, sound, full-motion video, or executable computer programs. Searching for information does not have to follow a predetermined organization scheme. Instead, one can branch instantly to related information in any kind of relationship the author establishes. The relationship between records is less structured than in a traditional DBMS.

The hypermedia database approach enables users to access topics on a Web site in whatever order they wish. For instance, from the Web page from the U.S. National Oceanic and Atmospheric Administration (NOAA) illustrated on page 239, one could branch to other Web pages by clicking on the topics highlighted in blue below the illustration and or by clicking on HOME, Site Map, Contacts, and Search at the top of the page. We provide more detail on these and other features of Web sites in Chapter 9.

hypermedia database

An approach to data management that organizes data as a network of nodes linked in any pattern the user specifies; the nodes can contain text, graphics, sound, full-motion video, or executable programs.

Figure 7-20 A hypermedia database. In a hypermedia database, the user can choose his or her own path to move from node to node. Each node can contain text, graphics, sound, full-motion video, or executable programs.

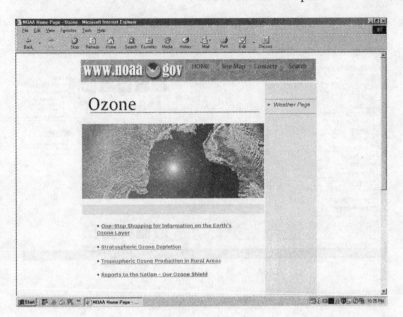

From the U.S. National Oceanic and Atmospheric Administration Web page, you can branch to other Web pages by clicking on the topics highlighted in blue or by clicking on the options to the right of the NOAA logo. Web sites store information as interconnected pages containing text, sound, graphics, and video using a hypermedia approach to data management.

Linking Internal Databases to the Web

A series of middleware and other software products has been developed to help users gain access to organizations' legacy data through the Web. For example, a customer with a Web browser might want to search an online retailer's database for pricing information. Figure 7-21 illustrates how that customer might access the retailer's internal database over the Web. The user would access the retailer's Web site over the Internet using Web browser software on his or her client PC. The user's Web browser software would request data from the organization's database, using HTML commands to communicate with the Web server. Because many back-end databases cannot interpret commands written in HTML, the Web server would pass these requests for data to special software that would translate HTML commands into SQL so that they could be processed by the DBMS working with the database. In a client/server environment, the DBMS often resides on a special dedicated computer called a **database server.** The DBMS receives the SQL requests and provides the required data. The middleware would transfer information from the organization's internal database back to the Web server for delivery in the form of a Web page to the user.

Figure 7-21 shows that the software working between the Web server and the DBMS could be an application server, a custom program, or a series of software scripts. An **application server** is a software program that handles all application operations, including transaction processing and data access, between browser-based computers and a company's back-end business applications or databases. The application server takes requests from the Web server, runs the business logic to process transactions based on those requests, and provides connectivity to the organization's back-end systems or databases. *Common Gateway Interface (CGI)* is a specification for transferring information between a Web server and a

database server
A computer in a client/server environment that is responsible for running a DBMS to process SQL statements and perform database management tasks.

application server
Software that handles all application operations between browser-based computers and a company's back-end business applications or databases.

Figure 7-21 Linking internal databases to the Web. Users can access an organization's internal database through the Web using their desktop PCs and Web browser software.

The ThomasRegister.com Web site links to a database of more than 170,000 companies, 400,000 products, thousands of on-line catalogs, and millions of CAD drawings searchable by product, company, or brand name. More and more organizations are using the Web to provide an interface to internal databases.

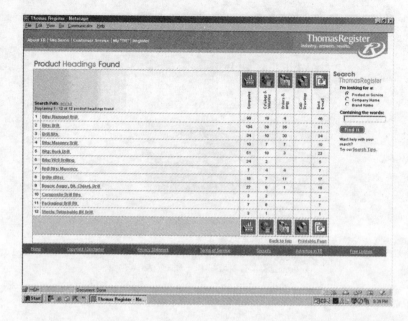

program designed to accept and return data. The program could be written in any programming language, including C, Perl, Java, or Visual Basic.

There are a number of advantages to using the Web to access an organization's internal databases. Web browser software is extremely easy to use, requiring much less training than even user-friendly database query tools. The Web interface requires no changes to the internal database. Companies leverage their investments in older systems because it costs much less to add a Web interface in front of a legacy system than to redesign and rebuild the system to improve user access.

Accessing corporate databases through the Web is creating new efficiencies and opportunities; in some cases even changing the way business is being done. Some companies have created new businesses based on access to large databases via the Web. Others are using Web technology to provide employees with integrated firmwide views of information. The major enterprise system vendors have enhanced their software so that users can access enterprise data through a Web interface. Table 7-2 describes some of these applications of Web-enabled databases.

Database technology has provided many organizational benefits, but it allows businesses and government agencies to maintain large databases with detailed personal information that pose a threat to individual privacy. The Window on Organizations describes some privacy issues raised by public motor vehicle databases that are used by business for marketing and other purposes.

TABLE 7-2   EXAMPLES OF WEB-ENABLED DATABASES

Organization	Use of Web-Enabled Database
Thomas Register Advanced Order Online	Web site links to Thomas's database of more than 170,000 companies, 400,000 products, thousands of product catalogs, and millions of CAD drawings searchable by product, part number, or brand name. Visitors can search for products, view a company's catalog, request price quotes, make purchases online using a credit card or company purchasing card, and track orders.
IGo.com	Web site is linked to a giant relational database housing information about batteries and peripherals for computers and other portable electronic devices. Visitors can immediately find online information about each electronic device and the batteries and parts it uses and place orders for these parts over the Web.
Australian National University Bioinformatics Group	Web site links to a Universal Viral Database, which describes all viruses of animals and plants. Visitors can search the database for descriptions of viruses, images of viruses, and links to genomic and protein databanks.
St. Luke's Hospital in Chesterfield, Mo.	Web-enabled Patient Information Network System (WebPINS) uses a Web front end to enable physicians to obtain a unified view of patient information that has been consolidated in a Sybase database.

PUBLIC DATABASES FOR SALE: BOON TO BUSINESS OR THREAT TO PRIVACY?

Window on Organizations

MIS In Action

If you look young, you may have used your driver's license to prove your age before buying cigarettes or liquor or to see some movies. However, you probably don't realize all the information it carries that can be used by others without your approval. At least 40 states issue driver's licenses with bar codes or magnetic strips (check your driver's license to see if it has one). Your license may carry your birthday, age, name, address, an identification number, driving restrictions, and possibly your sex, eye color, height, and social security number. Some states even include your photograph in its coding. Scanners are now being used to check that data. Some bars and liquor stores scan your license to verify your age. Some hospitals scan that information for their records, while airports and government buildings are starting to scan it to locate suspected terrorists or criminals. Many of those scanners not only check the needed data, but also store that data on a database where it becomes useful for other purposes. As Paul Barclay, the owner of The Rack, a popular Boston bar that scans licenses, says, "It's not just an ID check. It's a tool." For example, police departments are calling bars to see if someone on their lists is at their establishments. Bars are using the data to give special treatment to repeated customers. Some users of these scanners sell their information to companies for use in marketing.

Experian, a unit of London-based GUS PLC, is one of the largest credit reporting agencies in the United States. Experian realized that it could expand its business beyond credit checks for automobile loans if it collected vehicle data from all 51 state departments of motor vehicles (DMVs) and blended these data with other data such as change-of-address and credit records. Experian was thus able to create a database that combines the motor vehicle data with its own records on individuals' credit histories, address-change information from the U.S. Postal Service, and accident and emission reports. The database could be used to help auto makers and auto parts companies contact vehicle owners affected by recalls, perhaps averting injuries or loss of lives due to defective cars or car parts. Retailers could use the data to expedite processing of loans to auto purchasers. Each 17-digit vehicle identification number contains references to the vehicle model, make, and color, allowing car dealers to determine what kind of vehicles would sell best in their regions.

Experian built a database of 65 terabytes of data covering 335 million vehicles around the United States. It is the tenth largest database in the world. Because these data come from so many sources, Experian receives them in 175 different formats. Experian transforms all of the data into a DB2 format, using UTI Extract software from Evolutionary Technologies. The database processes 175 million transactions per month. For $10.99 per query, Experian can make the ownership history for any vehicle bought or sold in the United States available on the Web.

Privacy advocates worry that the unregulated use of public databases allows personal information to be used in ways that the owners have not authorized. In 1994, Congress passed the Driver's Privacy Protection Act to prevent departments of motor vehicles from selling driver's license information to direct marketing companies. But this law does not control how businesses can use driver license and other motor vehicle data to create databases on their own.

MAKE IT YOUR BUSINESS

To Think About: Considering these examples along with your own views on regulating the use of public databases, argue in support of the unregulated use of these databases, and then argue in support of those who believe their unregulated use is a violation of one's privacy.

Sources: Pimm Fox, "Extracting Dollars from Data," *ComputerWorld*, April 15, 2002 and Jennifer B. Lee, "Welcome to the Database Lounge," *New York Times*, March 21, 2002.

ORGANIZATIONS

MAKE IT YOUR BUSINESS

FINANCE AND ACCOUNTING

Banks and financial services have benefited from a database approach to information management. Much of their data were traditionally organized along product lines in a number of different systems where it was difficult to provide a complete picture of a customer's transactions with the organization. Database management software and data warehouses have enabled these firms to organize their data more flexibly so that they can view information by customer, financial product, or other criteria. Financial firms are also intensive users of datamining for analyzing credit risk or for identifying profitable customers.

HUMAN RESOURCES

Companies typically maintain human resources databases enabling them to maintain data on employees, benefits plans and training programs and to provide reports to the government concerning compliance with health, safety, and equal employment opportunity regulations. Since these human resources databases contain sensitive information, such as salaries, job performance evaluations, and medical history, companies must be very careful about distributing this information. The security and data access rules for DBMS can help protect confidentiality and privacy.

MANUFACTURING AND PRODUCTION

Many manufacturing and production processes rely on database technology. Companies maintain large databases of finished goods, raw materials in inventory, and goods in transit that can be used for supply chain management. The manufacturing process makes use of numerous databases on suppliers, jobs in progress, product components, product quality, and costs. You can find examples of manufacturing and production applications on page 226.

SALES AND MARKETING

Database, data warehouse, and datamining technologies have been powerful tools for marketers because they enable firms to assemble and analyze vast quantities of data about customers from many different sources. By querying these customer databases, analysts can identify customers most interested in specific products or highly profitable customers. They can target specialized products and promotions based on these detailed customer profiles. The sales function can benefit from allowing customers to access corporate databases linked to the Web to place orders or to find out product information. You can find examples of sales and marketing applications on pages 218–219, 241, and 245–247.

MANAGEMENT WRAP-UP

Selecting an appropriate data model and data management technology for the organization is a key management decision. Managers will need to evaluate the costs and benefits of implementing a database environment and the capabilities of various DBMS or file management technologies. Management should ascertain that organizational databases are designed to meet management information objectives and the organization's business needs.

The organization's data model should reflect its key business processes and decision-making requirements. Data planning may need to be performed to make sure that the organization's data model delivers information efficiently for its business processes and enhances organizational performance. Designing a database is an organizational endeavor.

Multiple database and file management options are available for organizing and storing information. Key technology decisions should consider the efficiency of accessing information, flexibility in organizing information, the type of information to be stored and arranged, compatibility with the organization's data model, and compatibility with the organization's hardware and operating systems.

For Discussion

1. It has been said that you do not need database management software to create a database environment. Discuss.

2. To what extent should end users be involved in the selection of a database management system and database design?

SUMMARY

1. *Why do businesses have trouble finding the information they need in their information systems?* A computer system organizes data in a hierarchy that starts with bits and bytes and progresses to fields, records, files, and databases. Traditional file management techniques make it difficult for organizations to keep track of all of the pieces of data they use in a systematic way or to organize these data so that they can be easily accessed. Different functional areas and groups were allowed to develop their own files independently. Over time, this traditional file environment creates problems such as data redundancy and inconsistency, program-data dependence, inflexibility, poor security, and lack of data-sharing and availability.

2. *How does a database management system help businesses improve the organization of their information?* A database management system (DBMS) consists of software that permits centralization of data and data management so that businesses have a single consistent source for all their data needs. A single database services multiple applications. A DBMS includes a data definition language, a data manipulation language, and a data dictionary capability. The most important feature of the DBMS is its ability to separate the logical and physical views of data. The user works with a logical view of data. The DBMS retrieves information so that the user does not have to be concerned with its physical location.

3. *How do the principal types of database models affect the way businesses can access and use their information?* The principal types of databases today are relational DBMS and object-oriented DBMS. Relational systems are very flexible for supporting ad hoc requests for information and for combining information from different sources. They support many-to-many relationships among entities and are efficient for storing alphanumeric data that can be organized into structured fields and records. This flexibility was not possible with the older hierarchical and network database models. Object-oriented DBMS can store graphics and other types of data in addition to conventional text data to support multimedia applications. Organizations should use the DBMS that is best suited for their data model.

Designing a database requires both a logical design and a physical design. The logical design models the database from a business perspective. The process of creating small, stable data structures from complex groups of data when designing a relational database is termed *normalization*. Database design also considers whether a complete database or portions of the database can be distributed to more than one location to increase responsiveness and reduce vulnerability and costs. There are two major types of distributed databases: replicated databases and partitioned databases.

4. *What are the management and organizational requirements of a database environment?* Developing a database environment requires much more than selecting database technology. It requires a formal information policy governing the maintenance, distribution, and use of information in the organization. The organization must also develop a data administration function and a data planning methodology. There is political resistance in organizations to many key database concepts, especially to sharing of information that has been controlled exclusively by one organizational group.

5. *What new tools and technologies can make databases more accessible and useful?* There are powerful tools available to analyze the information in databases and to take advantage of the information resources on the World Wide Web. Multidimensional data analysis, also known as online analytical processing (OLAP), can represent relationships among data as a multidimensional structure, which can be visualized as cubes of data and cubes within cubes of data, allowing for more sophisticated data analysis. Data can be more conveniently analyzed across the enterprise by using a data warehouse, in which current and historical data are extracted from many different operational systems and consolidated for management decision making. Datamining analyzes large pools of data, including the contents of data warehouses, to find patterns and rules that can be used to predict future behavior and guide decision making. Hypermedia databases allow data to be stored in nodes linked together in any pattern the user establishes and are used for storing information at Web sites. Conventional databases can be linked to the Web to facilitate user access to an organization's internal data.

KEY TERMS

Application server, 239

Attribute, 221

Data administration, 234

Data definition language, 224

Data dictionary, 224

Data element, 224

Data manipulation language, 224

Data mart, 237

Data redundancy, 222

Data warehouse, 236

Database, 221

Database (rigorous definition), 223

Database administration, 234

Database management system (DBMS), 224

Database server, 239

Datamining, 236

Distributed database, 232

Entity, 221

Entity-relationship diagram, 232

Field, 221

File, 221

Hierarchical DBMS, 227

Hypermedia database, 238

Information policy, 234

Key field, 221

Legacy system, 229

Logical view, 224

Network DBMS, 227

Normalization, 232

Object-oriented DBMS, 229

Object-relational DBMS, 230

Online analytical processing (OLAP), 235

Physical view, 224

Program-data dependence, 222

Record, 221

Relational DBMS, 225

Structured Query Language (SQL), 224

Tuple, 226

Review Questions

1. Why is file management important for overall system performance?

2. List and describe each of the components in the data hierarchy.

3. Define and explain the significance of entities, attributes, and key fields.

4. List and describe some of the problems of the traditional file environment.

5. Define a database and a database management system.

6. Name and briefly describe the three components of a DBMS.

7. What is the difference between a logical and a physical view of data?

8. List some benefits of a DBMS.

9. Describe the principal types of databases and the advantages and disadvantages of each.

10. Name and describe the three most important SQL commands.

11. What is normalization? How is it related to the features of a well-designed relational database?

12. What is a distributed database, and what are the two main ways of distributing data?

13. What are the four key organizational elements of a database environment? Describe each briefly.

14. Describe the capabilities of online analytical processing (OLAP) and datamining.

15. What is a data warehouse? How can it benefit organizations?

16. What is a hypermedia database? How does it differ from a traditional database? How is it used for the Web?

17. How can users access information from a company's internal databases via the Web?

Application Software Exercise

DATABASE EXERCISE: BUILDING A RELATIONAL DATABASE FOR A SMALL BUSINESS

Sylvester's Bike Shop, located in San Francisco, California, sells road, mountain, hybrid, leisure, and children's bicycles. Currently, Sylvester's purchases bikes from three suppliers, but plans to add new suppliers in the near future. This rapidly growing business needs a database system to manage this information.

Initially, the database should house information about suppliers and products. The database will contain two tables: a supplier table and a product table. The reorder level refers to the number of items in inventory that triggers a decision to order more items to prevent a stockout. (In other words, if the number of units of a particular product in inventory falls below the reorder level, the item should be reordered.) The user should be able to perform several queries and produce several managerial reports based on the data contained in the two tables.

Using the information found in the tables on the Laudon Web site for Chapter 7, build a simple relational database for Sylvester's. Once you have built the database, perform the following activities.

a. Prepare a report that identifies the five most expensive bicycles. The report should list the bicycles in descending order from most expensive to least expensive, the quantity on hand for each and the markup percentage for each.

b. Prepare a report that lists each supplier, its products, quantity on hand, and associated reorder levels. The report should be sorted alphabetically by supplier. Within each supplier category, the products should be sorted alphabetically.

c. Prepare a report listing only the bicycles that are low in stock and need to be reordered. The report should provide supplier information for the items identified.

d. Write a brief description of how the database could be enhanced to further improve management of the business. What tables or fields should be added? What additional reports would be useful?

Group Project

Review Figure 7-4, which provides an overview of a human resources database. Some additional information that might be maintained in such a database are an employee's date of hire, date of termination, number of children, date of birth, educational level, sex code, Social Security tax, Medicare tax, year-to-date gross pay and net pay, amount of life insurance coverage, healthcare plan payroll-deduction amount, life insurance plan payroll-deduction amount, and pension plan payroll-deduction amount.

Form a group with three or four of your classmates. Prepare two sample reports using the data in the database that might be of interest to either the employer or the employee. What pieces of information should be included on each report? In addition, prepare a data dictionary entry for one of the data elements in the database similar to the entry illustrated in Figure 7-5.

Your group's analysis should determine what business functions use this data element, which function has the primary responsibility for maintaining the data element, and which positions in the organization can access that data element. If possible, use electronic presentation software to present your findings to the class.

TOOLS FOR INTERACTIVE LEARNING

■ INTERNET CONNECTION

The Internet Connection for this chapter will direct you to a series of Web sites where you can complete an exercise to evaluate various commercial database management system products.

■ INTERACTIVE STUDY GUIDE

You can use the Interactive Study Guide to test your knowledge of the topics in this chapter and get instant feedback where you need more practice.

■ RUNNING CASE

The Running Case provides an opportunity for you to use database software to redesign Dirt Bikes USA's customer database so that can be more easily used for marketing. You can find a complete description of this project on the Laudon Web site for Chapter 7 and on the Multimedia Edition CD-ROM.

■ ELECTRONIC COMMERCE PROJECT

At the Laudon Web site for Chapter 7, you will find an Electronic Commerce project for setting up a business in Australia that requires searches of online databases.

■ MANAGEMENT DECISION PROBLEM

At the Laudon Web site for Chapter 7, you will find a Management Decision Problem on developing companywide data standards.

■ CD-ROM

If you use the Multimedia Edition CD-ROM with this chapter, you can find a video clip illustrating Acxiom's database marketing application, an audio overview of the major themes of this chapter, and bullet text summarizing the key points of the chapter.

CASE STUDY—*Harrah's Big Database Gamble*

Harrah's, with around 25 million customers in 2001, is headquartered in Memphis, Tennessee, and operates 25 casinos with 40,000 gambling machines in 12 states. For years it had been a fairly small gambling company but, by 2001, had emerged as the second largest in the industry. It is flourishing at a time when competition is more intense than ever.

By the mid-1990s, the gambling expansion appeared to reach the point of diminishing returns. The number of casinos in the United States swelled, thanks to changes in federal and state laws permitting gambling on riverboats and Indian reservations. There are only so many gamblers in the population, and so for the casinos to continue to grow they had to move some gamblers from competitors' casinos to their own. How could Harrah's succeed in this environment?

While other gambling companies have spent their investment dollars trying to lure customers by building flashy casinos with extravagant rooms and entertainment, Harrah's has focused on technology that allows it to identify, track, and cultivate its most profitable customers. Harrah's COO Gary Loveman explained the strategy this way: "The prevailing wisdom in this business is that the attractiveness of a property drives customers. Our approach is different. We stimulate demand by knowing our customers."

By the early 1990s, casino operators had found that the slots and other machines surpassed the table games (such as dice and blackjack) as their biggest source of income. About the same time, the casinos began to use computers to keep records on individual gamblers, and they began recognizing the most profitable customers and giving them very special treatment while others would only get an occasional drink or sandwich. But Harrah's has focused on customer relationship management much more intensively than its rivals. According to William Schmitt, executive director of CIBC World Markets in New York City, "Everyone tracks their customers' play on a real time

basis (using computers)." However, "Harrah's matches what its customers are worth (as gamblers) with what they might be worth and has a 90 percent hit ratio in turning customers who are presently worth $500 into customers who are worth $5000."

COO Loveman, a former Harvard business school professor, is the person primarily responsible for Harrah's change to a customer-centered strategy. He recognized an opportunity in the gambling industry to apply what he taught about customer loyalty in the classroom. Loveman believes in treating each person as a long-range customer, whether or not that person is staying at a Harrah's hotel, and whether or not that person is a big spender. He pointed out that Harrah's got 36 cents out of every dollar their customers spent in casinos, and a rise to 40 cents "would be monstrous."

After presenting his ideas to Harrah's management, Loveman was immediately hired as COO. In fact, by applying Loveman's strategy, Harrah's "wallet share" had risen to 42 cents in 2001, and for each percentage point gained, Harrah's had shown a profit increase of $125 million. Since then, by carefully analyzing its customer data, Harrah's has learned that 80 percent of its casino revenues comes from customers who only spend between $100 and $500 per visit. The data showed that many Harrah's customers are relatively local and can come more often without expensive plane fares.

The centerpiece of the Harrah's strategy is its Total Rewards program. When gamblers arrive at a Harrah's hotel or casino, they are asked to apply for a Total Rewards card, although its use is voluntary. Total Rewards applicants must provide information on their gender, age, home location, and the games they like to play. If gamblers choose to insert their card into the slot machine they are playing (or other machines such as poker), the machine will record on the card the amount of money put into the machine, the total number of bets the customer placed, the average size of the bet, and the total amount of money deposited ("coin-in"). Gamblers are rewarded points based on the amount of time a customer spends gambling. Points are not given based on winning or losing or the amount of money deposited in the machine. The points are saved on each customer's record, and the gamblers can exchange their points for rewards or cash. Each time a Total Rewards customer returns to a Harrah's hotel or casino, his or her record will be updated.

These data are stored in a data warehouse. Harrah's combines its gambling transaction data with data from other sources such as its hotel reservation system. The company then analyzes these data using customer relationship management (CRM) software, which views customers as long-term assets. A CRM system coordinates all business processes for dealing with customers, which in Harrah's case includes both gambling and hotel customers. The company uses Cognos Impromptu, a CRM query tool from the Cognos Corp. of Burlington, Massachusetts, running over its data warehouse. For marketing managers to analyze the data, the company uses modeling tools from SAS Institute Inc., located in Cary, N.C. The overall system Harrah's developed has been named WINet (Winner's Information Network).

Using these tools, Harrah's marketing department builds a detailed gambling profile on each customer. It then will create a personalized marketing program, including a plan to entice the gambler back. "We wanted to track what our customers are spending with us in a retail environment so that we can reward loyal ones with complimentary perks such as hotel discounts," explains Tracy Austin, Harrah's vice president of IT development. Loveman points out that "Age and distance from the casino are critical predictors of frequency (of visits to the nearest Harrah's casino), coupled with the kind of game you play and how many coins you play per game." Thus, using this information, the computer estimates how much money the company can earn from the individual person over time, viewing the cost of this information and the rewards from Total Rewards as an investment.

Harrah's has established 90 targeted demographic segments to identify the customer's value to the company. According to its profile studies, the "perfect" player is a 62-year-old woman who lives within 30 minutes of a casino and plays the dollar video poker. Harrah's analysts say such customers have time on their hands, ample disposable cash, and easy access to a casino. The more likely a customer will return often and the more that customer is predicted to spend, the higher the demographic segment assigned to that customer. The Harrah's rewards depend upon which segment the customer is in, although just by returning everyone will get some extra treatment. Those who return regularly will receive an enticing promotional mailing a month or two before the customer is expected to return, giving that person something that can be used when the customer arrives. When a repeat customer calls Harrah's to make a reservation, information from the customer's record comes up on the reservation computer screen. If the customer has received an offer in the mail, that information will be displayed on the screen. Possible rewards can include cash, complimentary trips, meals, hotel room upgrades, free hotel weekends, welcome gifts such as flowers or candy in the hotel room, tickets to sporting and entertainment events, and possibly even being met at the airport and transported to the hotel.

As Harrah's expanded, each casino was being operated independently. John Boushy, Harrah's CIO, said "While management at each of our properties had been thinking, 'This is my customer,' customers had been wondering why they didn't get the same treatment at different Harrah's properties." Management decided that all Harrah's sites had to be on WINet so that when a customer at one casino (or hotel) goes to another Harrah's, he or she will receive the same treatment. Moreover, that person's record will show the same segment and the same number of points the individual has collected at the other site or sites. Another problem management faced was that the company also had to change Harrah's corporate culture, and do so at all 25 locations. Their staff had to switch from a focus only on their own casino and that casino's profit to a customer-focused corporation regardless of which Harrah's casino they are working in. One result of this change was that more than half of Harrah's three Las Vegas casinos' revenue comes from gamblers already known to the company because they had previously gambled in one or more of its non-Las Vegas casinos.

Harrah's CRM-based strategy appears to be a great success. The company showed a 13 percent profit gain in the first year it was used, even though it gave out $251 million in Total Rewards that year. Harrah's same location 1999 sales increased by 14 percent over 1998. Harrah's has seen a 23 percent gain in customers who gambled in more than one location. Moreover, customers spend more on each visit than in previous years. In 2001, it achieved $3.7 billion in revenue, an 11 percent gain from 2000. Slots and other gaming machines, which are linked to the Total Rewards program, account for 80 percent of Harrah's operating profit.

Harrah's insists that it keeps the customer information it collects confidential, that it will never sell its customer list to other organizations, and that it is not out to exploit gamblers. However, opponents of the gambling industry have criticized Harrah's use of customer data. Richard Thomas Grey, director of the National Coalition Against Legalized Gambling, said that Harrah's goal is to separate people from their money. The Council on Compulsive Gambling of New Jersey, an advocacy organization, also opposes Harrah's approach.

Harrah's CEO Philip G. Satre defends his company by pointing out that the company does not pursue those who are poor. Instead, it reaches out to people who will spend $1,000 to $2,000 per trip gambling. He also claims the Total Rewards program actually gives these people rewards instead of encouraging them to gamble more. Harrah's just encourages them to do whatever gambling they choose to do at Harrah's rather than at another casino. Harrah's claims it would never push a customer to do more gambling. "It's all about customers bringing their existing gaming business to us," says Loveman. He further points out that the purpose is to get to know those who already want to gamble and give them reasons to spend their money at Harrah's. His explanation is "All we used to know was how much money we made on each machine, but we couldn't connect what kind of customer used them. Now, I can get on the system and say, 'Where are all the 60-or-older females from North Carolina playing?' This is the replacement of intuition and hunch with science." If customers don't want their play tracked, they don't have to use the card.

Sources: Joe Ashbrook Nickell, "Welcome to Harrah's," *Business 2.0*, April 2002; Meridith Levinson, "How It Works," *Darwin Magazine*, May 2001; Meridith Levinson, "Harrah's Knows What You Did Last Night," *Darwin Magazine*, May 2001; Meridith Levinson, "Technology's Potential Dark Side," *Darwin Magazine*, May 2001; Anne Chen, "Harrah's Places Its CRM Bet," *eWEEK.com*, April 2, 2001.

CASE STUDY QUESTIONS

1. Analyze Harrah's using the competitive forces and value chain models.

2. Describe Harrah's business model and business strategy. How do they differ from those of other gambling companies?

3. What role has database technology played in Harrah's strategy? How critical is it to the success of the company?

4. How did Harrah's use CRM software and modeling tools to address the company's problem?

5. Are there any ethical problems raised by Harrah's use of customer data? Explain your answer.

6. What problems can database technology and customer relationship management software solve for Harrah's? What problems can't they address?

8

CHAPTER

TELECOMMUNICATIONS AND NETWORKS

objectives

At many points in your career, you will need to make decisions about how to use telecommunications technology and services in your business. After reading this chapter, you will be able to answer these questions:

1. *What technologies are used in telecommunications systems?*

2. *What telecommunications transmission media should our organization use?*

3. *How should our organization design its networks?*

4. *What alternative network services are available to our organization?*

5. *What telecommunications applications can be used for electronic business and electronic commerce?*

Wireless Communication Speeds Up Ford's Supply Chain

Automobile manufacturers are continually trying to find ways of cutting their supply chain costs. Figuring out how to track inventory, assets, materials, and workflow are among the most challenging aspects of supply chain management. Addressing these issues has become a top priority for Ford Motor Company in its effort to remain competitive. Looking for ways to cut costs and make its factories more flexible, Ford examined the firm's business processes for delivering parts to the factory floor. Management found that the communication between the workers who build its cars and trucks and the constantly moving handlers who deliver parts from plant warehouses created production inefficiencies. When parts ran low the line workers had to physically flag down a parts handler as he was riding on his forklift. Sometimes the production line had to grind to a halt until the required parts were delivered.

Ford could, of course, stockpile parts on the shop floor, but piling enough car doors at each workstation for an entire work shift was impractical and expensive, preventing Ford from realizing just-in-time inventory economies. Ford's goal was to keep only two hours worth of supplies on the shop floor and replenish them when only enough for 20 or 30 minutes of work was left.

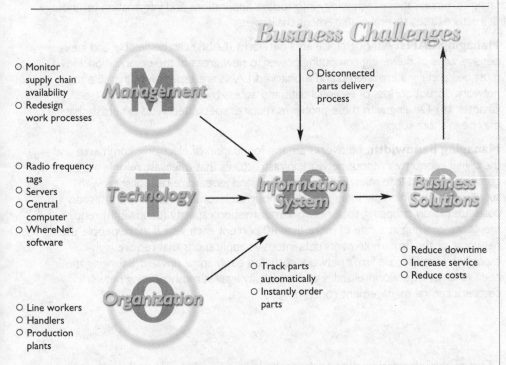

Ford found a solution in a wireless communication system from WhereNet, a supply chain solutions provider. When any of 20,000 line workers are low on parts, they press a button to activate a radio frequency tag. Each tag sends its own unique tracking signal to ceiling antennae which then transmit it to specialized servers feeding a central warehouse computer. The signal tells where the worker is located, what part he or she needs and the time the request was made to the order queue. Ford has installed this wireless system in 41 plants in the United States, Europe, and Latin America and most have met Ford's two-hour supply goal. The system has also made Ford's manufacturing operations more flexible. Because it allows line workers to get new parts easily throughout the day, Ford can assemble smaller batches of more different kinds of vehicles. Plants can also make vehicles that need additional parts without having to expand their warehouses.

Sources: Eileen Gunn, "Blue-Collar Wireless," *Smart Business Magazine*, June 2002; "Beyond Explorer Woes, Ford Misses Key Terms in Buyers, Technology," *Wall Street Journal*, January 14, 2002; and <www.wherenet.com>, accessed October 16, 2002.

MANAGEMENT CHALLENGES

Ford Motor Company, like many organizations all over the world, has found ways to benefit from communications technology to coordinate its business processes and to communicate more efficiently. It would be virtually impossible to conduct business today without using communications technology, and applications of networks and communications technology for electronic business and electronic commerce are multiplying. However, incorporating communications technology into today's applications and information technology infrastructure raises several management challenges:

1. **Managing LANs.** Although local area networks (LANs) can be flexible and inexpensive ways of delivering computing power to new areas of the organization, they must be carefully administered and monitored. LANs are especially vulnerable to network disruption; loss of essential data, and access by unauthorized users (see Chapter 14). Dealing with these problems requires special technical expertise that may be in short supply.

2. **Managing bandwidth.** Networks are the foundation of electronic commerce and the digital economy. Without network infrastructures that offer fast, reliable access, companies would lose many online customers and jeopardize relationships with suppliers and business partners as well. Although telecommunication transmission costs are rapidly dropping, total network transmission capacity (bandwidth) requirements are growing at a rate of more than 40 percent each year. If more people use networks or the firm implements data-intensive applications that require high-capacity transmission, a firm's network costs can easily spiral upward. Balancing the need to ensure network reliability and availability against mushrooming network costs is a central management concern.

Most of the information systems we use today require networks and communications technology. Companies, large and small from all over the world, are using networked systems and the Internet to locate suppliers and buyers, to negotiate contracts with them, and to service their trades. Applications of networks are multiplying in research, organizational coordination, and control. Networked systems are fundamental to electronic commerce and electronic business.

Today's computing tasks are so closely tied to networks that some believe "the network is the computer." This chapter describes the components of telecommunications systems, showing how they can be arranged to create various types of networks and network-based applications that can increase an organization's efficiency and competitiveness.

8.1   COMPONENTS AND FUNCTIONS OF A TELECOMMUNICATIONS SYSTEM

telecommunications

The communication of information by electronic means, usually over some distance.

Telecommunications is the communication of information by electronic means, usually over some distance. Previously, telecommunications meant voice transmission over telephone lines. Today, a great deal of telecommunications transmission is digital data transmission, using computers to transmit data from one location to another. Deregulation of the telecommunications industry and technology advances have led to an explosion of telecommunications products and services that can create the foundation for a digital business environment. Managers continually will be faced with decisions about selecting telecommunications technologies and services to enhance the performance of their firm and how best to incorporate them into their information systems and business processes.

TELECOMMUNICATIONS SYSTEM COMPONENTS

telecommunications system

A collection of compatible hardware and software arranged to communicate information from one location to another.

A **telecommunications system** is a collection of compatible hardware and software arranged to communicate information from one location to another. Figure 8-1 illustrates the components of a large traditional telecommunications system where processing power is concen-

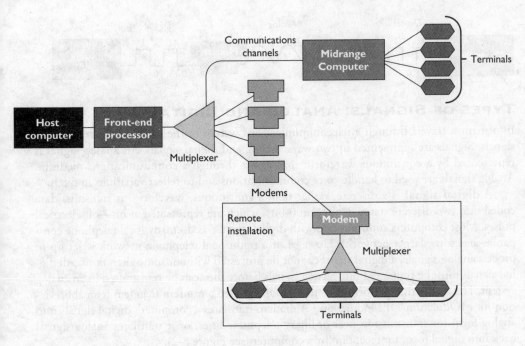

Figure 8-1 Components of a telecommunications system. This figure illustrates some of the hardware components that would be found in a traditional large telecommunications system. They include computers, terminals, communications channels, and communications processors, such as modems, multiplexers, and the front-end processor. Special communications software controls input and output activities and manages other functions of the communications system.

trated at a central computer . Telecommunications systems can transmit text, graphic images, voice, or video information. This section describes the major components of telecommunications systems. Subsequent sections describe how the components can be arranged into various types of networks.

The following are essential components of a telecommunications system:

1. Computers to process information

2. Terminals or any input/output devices that send or receive data

3. Communications channels, the links by which data or voice are transmitted between sending and receiving devices in a network. Communications channels use various communications media, such as telephone lines, coaxial cable, fiber-optic cable, and wireless transmission.

4. Communications processors, such as modems, multiplexers, controllers, and front-end processors, which provide support functions for data transmission and reception

5. Communications software, which controls input and output activities and manages other functions of the communications network

FUNCTIONS OF TELECOMMUNICATIONS SYSTEMS

In order to send and receive information from one place to another, a telecommunications system must perform a number of separate functions. The system transmits information, establishes the interface between the sender and the receiver, routes messages along the most efficient paths, performs elementary processing of the information to ensure that the right message gets to the right receiver, performs editorial tasks on the data (such as checking for transmission errors and rearranging the format), and converts messages from one speed (say, the speed of a computer) into the speed of a communications line or from one format to another. Finally, the telecommunications system controls the flow of information.

A telecommunications network typically contains diverse hardware and software components that need to work together to transmit information. Different components in a network can communicate by adhering to a common set of rules that enable them to "talk" to each other. This set of rules and procedures governing transmission between two points in a network is called a **protocol.** Each device in a network must be able to interpret the other device's protocol. The principal functions of protocols in a telecommunications network are to identify each device in the communication path, to secure the attention of the other device, to verify correct receipt of the transmitted message, to verify that a message requires retransmission because it cannot be correctly interpreted, and to perform recovery when errors occur.

protocol
A set of rules and procedures that govern transmission between the components in a network.

Figure 8-2 Functions of the modem. A modem is a device that translates digital signals from a computer into analog form so that they can be transmitted over analog telephone lines. The modem also is used to translate analog signals back into digital form for the receiving computer.

analog signal

A continuous waveform that passes through a communications medium; used for voice communications.

digital signal

A discrete waveform that transmits data coded into two discrete states as 1-bits and 0-bits, which are represented as on–off electrical pulses; used for data communications.

modem

A device for translating digital signals into analog signals and vice versa.

channels

The links by which data or voice are transmitted between sending and receiving devices in a network.

twisted wire

A transmission medium consisting of pairs of twisted copper wires; used to transmit analog phone conversations but can be used for data transmission.

coaxial cable

A transmission medium consisting of thickly insulated copper wire; can transmit large volumes of data quickly.

fiber-optic cable

A fast, light, and durable transmission medium consisting of thin strands of clear glass fiber bound into cables. Data are transmitted as light pulses.

TYPES OF SIGNALS: ANALOG AND DIGITAL

Information travels through a telecommunications system in the form of electromagnetic signals. Signals are represented in two ways: analog and digital signals. An **analog signal** is represented by a continuous waveform that passes through a communications medium. Analog signals are used to handle voice communications and to reflect variations in pitch.

A **digital signal** is a discrete, rather than a continuous, waveform. It transmits data coded into two discrete states: 1-bits and 0-bits, which are represented as on—off electrical pulses. Most computers communicate with digital signals, as do many local telephone companies and some larger networks. However, if a traditional telephone network is set up to process analog signals, a digital signal cannot be processed without some alterations. All digital signals must be translated into analog signals before they can be transmitted in an analog system. The device that performs this translation is called a **modem** (Modem is an abbreviation for MOdulation/DEModulation.) A modem translates a computer's digital signals into analog form for transmission over ordinary telephone lines, or it translates analog signals back into digital form for reception by a computer (see Figure 8-2).

COMMUNICATIONS CHANNELS

Communications **channels** are the means by which data are transmitted from one device in a network to another. A channel can use different kinds of telecommunications transmission media: twisted wire, coaxial cable, fiber optics, terrestrial microwave, satellite, and other wireless transmission. Each has advantages and limitations. High-speed transmission media are more expensive in general, but they can handle higher volumes, which reduces the cost per bit. For instance, the cost per bit of data can be lower via satellite link than via leased telephone line if a firm uses the satellite link 100 percent of the time. There is also a wide range of speeds possible for any given medium depending on the software and hardware configuration.

Twisted Wire

Twisted wire consists of strands of copper wire twisted in pairs and is an older transmission medium. Many of the telephone systems in buildings had twisted wires installed for analog communication, but they can be used for digital communication as well. Although it is low in cost and already is in place, twisted wire can be relatively slow for transmitting data, and high-speed transmission causes interference called *crosstalk*. There are limits to the amount of data that a twisted wire channel can carry, but new software and hardware have raised the twisted-wire transmission capacity to make it useful for local- and wide-area computer networks as well as telephone systems.

Coaxial Cable

Coaxial cable, like that used for cable television, consists of thickly insulated copper wire, which can transmit a larger volume of data than twisted wire. It often is used in place of twisted wire for important links in a telecommunications network because it is a faster, more interference-free transmission medium, with speeds of up to 200 megabits per second. However, coaxial cable is thick, is hard to wire in many buildings, and cannot support analog phone conversations. It must be moved when computers and other devices are moved.

Fiber Optics and Optical Networks

Fiber-optic cable consists of strands of clear glass fiber, each the thickness of a human hair, which are bound into cables. Data are transformed into pulses of light, which are sent through the fiber-optic cable by a laser device at a rate from 500 kilobits to several trillion bits per second. Fiber-optic cable is considerably faster, lighter, and more durable than wire media and is well suited to systems requiring transfers of large volumes of data. However, fiber-optic cable is more difficult to work with, more expensive, and harder to install.

Until recently, fiber-optic cable has been used primarily as the high-speed network **backbone,** whereas twisted wire and coaxial cable have been used to connect the backbone to individual businesses and households. A backbone is the part of a network that handles the major traffic. It acts as the primary path for traffic flowing to or from other networks. Now telecommunications carriers are working on bringing fiber all the way into the basement of buildings so they can provide a variety of new services to business and eventually residential customers. These **optical networks** can transmit all types of traffic—voice, data, and video—over fiber cables and provide the

Fiber-optic cable can transmit data that have been transformed into pulses of light at speeds up to 6 terabits per second. Fiber-optic technology is used in high-capacity optical networks.

backbone
Part of a network handling the major traffic and providing the primary path for traffic flowing to or from other networks.

optical network
High-speed networking technologies for transmitting data in the form of light pulses.

massive transmission capacity for new types of services and software. Using optical networks, on-demand video, software downloads, and high-quality digital audio can be accessed using set-top boxes and other information appliances without any degradation in quality or delays.

Currently, fiber-optic networks are slowed down by the need to convert electrical data to optics to send it over a fiber line and then reconvert it back. The long-term goal is to create pure optical networks in which light packets shuttle digital data at tremendous speed without ever converting them to electrical signals. Many new optical technologies are in development for this purpose. Next-generation optical networks will also boost capacity by using **dense wavelength division multiplexing (DWDM).** DWDM boosts transmission capacity by using many different colors of light, or different wavelengths, to carry separate streams of data over the same fiber strand at the same time. DWDM combines up to 160 wavelengths per strand and can transmit up to 6.4 terabits per second over a single fiber. This technology will enable communications service providers to add bandwidth to an existing fiber-optic network without having to lay more fiber-optic cable. Before wavelength division multiplexing, optical networks could only use a single wavelength per strand.

dense wavelength division multiplexing (DWDM)
Technology for boosting transmission capacity of optical fiber by using many different wavelengths to carry separate streams of data over the same fiber strand at the same time.

Wireless Transmission

Wireless transmission that sends signals through air or space without being tied to a physical line, has become an increasingly popular alternative to tethered transmission channels, such as twisted wire, coaxial cable, and fiber optics. Today, common technologies for wireless data transmission include microwave transmission, communication satellites, pagers, cellular telephones, personal communication services (PCS), smart phones, personal digital assistants (PDAs), and mobile data networks.

The wireless transmission medium is the electromagnetic spectrum, illustrated in Figure 8-3. Some types of wireless transmission, such as microwave or infrared, by nature occupy specific spectrum frequency ranges (measured in megahertz). Other types of wireless transmissions are actually functional uses, such as cellular telephones and paging devices, that have been assigned a specific range of frequencies by national regulatory agencies and international agreements. Each frequency range has its own strengths and limitations, and these have helped determine the specific function or data communications niche assigned to it.

Microwave systems, both terrestrial and celestial, transmit high-frequency radio signals through the atmosphere and are widely used for high-volume, long-distance, point-to-point communication. Microwave signals follow a straight line and do not bend with the curvature of the earth; therefore, long-distance terrestrial transmission systems require that transmission stations be positioned about 37 miles apart, adding to the expense of microwave.

microwave
A high-volume, long-distance, point-to-point transmission in which high-frequency radio signals are transmitted through the atmosphere from one terrestrial transmission station to another.

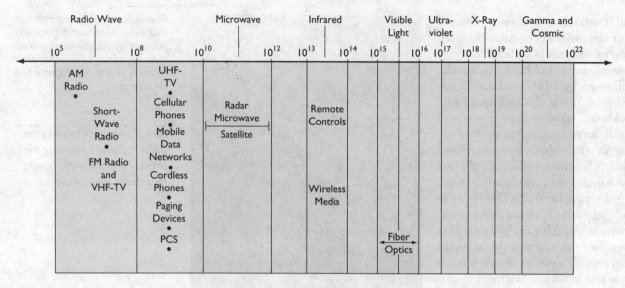

Figure 8-3 Frequency ranges for communications media and devices. Each telecommunications transmission medium or device occupies a different frequency range, measured in megahertz, on the electromagnetic spectrum.

satellite

The transmission of data using orbiting satellites that serve as relay stations for transmitting microwave signals over very long distances.

This problem can be solved by bouncing microwave signals off communication **satellites,** enabling them to serve as relay stations for microwave signals transmitted from terrestrial stations. Communication satellites are cost effective for transmitting large quantities of data over very long distances. Satellites are typically used for communications in large, geographically dispersed organizations that would be difficult to tie together through cabling media or terrestrial microwave. For instance, Amoco uses satellites for real-time data transfer of oil field exploration data gathered from searches of the ocean floor. Exploration ships transfer these data using geosynchronous satellites to central computing centers in the United States for use by researchers in Houston, Tulsa, and suburban Chicago. Figure 8-4 illustrates how this system works.

Conventional communication satellites move in stationary orbits approximately 22,000 miles above the earth. A newer satellite medium, the low-orbit satellite, is beginning to be deployed. These satellites travel much closer to the earth and are able to pick up signals from weak transmitters. They also consume less power and cost less to launch than conventional satellites. With such wireless networks, businesspeople will be able to travel virtually anywhere in the world and have access to full communication capabilities including videoconferencing and multimedia-rich Internet access.

Other wireless transmission technologies are being used in situations requiring remote access to corporate systems and mobile computing power. **Paging systems** have

paging system

A wireless transmission technology in which the pager beeps when the user receives a message; used to transmit short alphanumeric messages.

Figure 8-4 Amoco's satellite transmission system. Satellites help Amoco transfer seismic data between oil exploration ships and research centers in the United States.

been used for several decades, originally simply beeping when the user received a message and requiring the user to telephone an office to learn about the message. Today, paging devices can send and receive short alphanumeric messages that the user reads on the pager's screen. Paging is useful for communicating with mobile workers, such as repair crews; one-way paging also can provide an inexpensive way of communicating with workers in offices. For example, Computer Associates distributes two-way pagers with its CA Unicenter software, which allows computer network operators to monitor and respond to problems.

Cellular telephones (cellphones) work by using radio waves to communicate with radio antennas (towers) placed within adjacent geographic areas called *cells*. A telephone message is transmitted to the local cell by the cellular telephone and then is handed off from antenna to antenna—cell to cell—until it reaches the cell of its destination, where it is transmitted to the receiving telephone. As a cellular signal travels from one cell into another, a computer that monitors signals from the cells switches the conversation to a radio channel assigned to the next cell. The radio antenna cells normally cover eight-mile hexagonal areas, although their radius is smaller in densely populated localities.

Older cellular systems are analog and newer cellular systems are digital. **Personal communication services (PCS)** are one popular type of digital cellular service. PCS are entirely digital. They can transmit both voice and data and operate in a higher frequency range than analog cellular telephones. PCS cells are much smaller and more closely spaced than analog cells, and can accommodate higher traffic demands.

Newer models of digital cellular phones can handle voice mail, e-mail, and faxes, save addresses, access a private corporate network, and access information from the Internet as well as provide wireless voice transmission. These **smart phones** are being equipped with Web browser software that lets digital cellular phones or other wireless devices access Web pages formatted to send text or other information that is suitable for tiny screens. Some smart phone models offer larger screens and keypads to make Internet access easier.

Personal digital assistants (PDA) are small handheld computers capable of entirely digital communications transmission. They have built-in wireless telecommunications capabilities as well as work-organization software. A well-known example is the Palm i705 handheld organizer. It can display, compose, send, and receive e-mail messages and can provide access to the Internet. The handheld device includes applications such as an electronic scheduler, address book, and expense tracker, and can accept data entered with a special stylus through an on-screen writing pad.

Wireless networks explicitly designed for two-way transmission of data files are called **mobile data networks.** These radio-based networks transmit data to and from handheld computers. One type of mobile data network is based on a series of radio towers constructed specifically to transmit text and data. Motient is a publicly available network that uses such media for wide area two-way data transmission. Otis Elevators has used this network to dispatch repair technicians around the country from a single office in Connecticut and to receive the technicians' reports.

Wireless networks and transmission devices can be more expensive, slower, and more error prone than transmission over wired networks, although the major digital cellular networks are upgrading their speed of their services. Transmission capacity and energy supply in wireless devices require careful management from both hardware and software standpoints. Security and privacy will be more difficult to maintain because wireless transmission can be easily intercepted (see Chapter 14).

Data cannot be transmitted seamlessly between different wireless networks if they use incompatible standards. For example, digital cellular service in the United States is provided by different operators using one of several competing digital cellular technologies— CDMA (Code Division Multiple Access), GSM (Global System for Mobile Communications), and TDMA (Time Division Multiple Access)—that do not interoperate with each other. Many digital cellular handsets that use one of these technologies cannot operate in other countries outside North America, which operate at different frequencies with still another set of standards. We provide a detailed discussion of these standards and other standards for networking in Chapter 9.

cellular telephone (cellphone)
A device that transmits voice or data, using radio waves to communicate with radio antennas placed within adjacent geographic areas called cells.

personal communication services (PCS)
A wireless cellular technology that uses lower power, higher frequency radio waves than does cellular technology and so can be used with smaller size telephones.

smart phone
Wireless phone with voice, text, and Internet capabilities.

personal digital assistants (PDA)
Small, pen-based, handheld computers with built-in wireless telecommunications capable of entirely digital communications transmission.

mobile data networks
Wireless networks that enable two-way transmission of data files cheaply and efficiently.

The Palm i705 handheld, Nokia mobile phone and the BlackBerry wireless e-mail solution are examples of handheld devices for wireless communication. Some of these devices can provide wireless access to the Internet.

baud

A change in signal from positive to negative or vice versa that is used as a measure of transmission speed.

bandwidth

The capacity of a communications channel as measured by the difference between the highest and lowest frequencies that can be transmitted by that channel.

Transmission Speed

The total amount of information that can be transmitted through any telecommunications channel is measured in bits per second (bps). Digital transmission speed has also been measured by the baud rate. A **baud** is a binary event representing a signal change from positive to negative or vice versa. The baud rate is not always the same as the bit rate. At higher speeds a single signal change can transmit more than one bit at a time, so the bit rate generally will surpass the baud rate.

One signal change, or cycle, is required to transmit one or several bits per second; therefore, the transmission capacity of each type of telecommunications medium is a function of its frequency. The number of cycles per second that can be sent through that medium is measured in hertz (see Chapter 6). The range of frequencies that can be accommodated on a particular telecommunications channel is called its **bandwidth.** The bandwidth is the difference between the highest and lowest frequencies that can be accommodated on a single channel. The greater the range of frequencies, the greater the bandwidth and the greater the channel's transmission capacity. Table 8-1 compares the transmission speed and relative costs of the major types of transmissions media.

COMMUNICATIONS PROCESSORS AND SOFTWARE

Communications processors, such as front-end processors, concentrators, controllers, multiplexers, and modems, support data transmission and reception in a telecommunications net-

TABLE 8-1	TYPICAL SPEEDS AND COSTS OF TELECOMMUNICATIONS TRANSMISSION MEDIA	
Medium	Speed	Cost
Twisted wire	up to 100 Mbps	Low
Microwave	up to 200+ Mbps	
Satellite	up to 200+ Mbps	
Coaxial cable	up to 200 Mbps	
Fiber-optic cable	up to 6+ Tbps	High
Mbps = megabits per second		
Gbps = gigabits per second		
Tbps = terabits per second		

work. In large computer systems, such as those from IBM, the **front-end processor** is a special purpose computer dedicated to communications management and is attached to the main, or host, computer. The front-end processor performs communications processing such as error control, formatting, editing, controlling, routing, and speed and signal conversion.

A **concentrator** is a programmable telecommunications computer that collects and temporarily stores messages from terminals until enough messages are ready to be sent economically. The concentrator bursts signals to the host computer.

A **controller** is a specialized computer that supervises communications traffic between the CPU and peripheral devices, such as terminals and printers. The controller manages messages from these devices and communicates them to the CPU. It also routes output from the CPU to the appropriate peripheral device.

A **multiplexer** is a device that enables a single communications channel to carry data transmissions from multiple sources simultaneously. The multiplexer divides the communications channel so that it can be shared by multiple transmission devices. The multiplexer may divide a high-speed channel into multiple channels of slower speed or may assign each transmission source a very small slice of time for using the high-speed channel.

Special telecommunications software residing in the host computer, front-end processor, and other processors in the network is required to control and support network activities. This software is responsible for functions such as network control, access control, transmission control, error detection/correction, and security. More detail on security software can be found in Chapter 14.

8.2 COMMUNICATIONS NETWORKS

A number of different ways exist to organize telecommunications components to form a network and hence provide multiple ways of classifying networks. Networks can be classified by the way their components are connected, or **topology.** Networks also can be classified by their geographic scope and the type of services provided. This section describes different networks and the management and technical requirements of creating networks that link entire enterprises.

NETWORK TOPOLOGIES

One way of describing networks is by the way their components are connected, or topology. As illustrated in Figures 8-5 to 8-7, the three most common topologies are the star, bus, and ring.

The Star Network

The **star network** (see Figure 8-5) consists of a central host computer connected to a number of smaller computers or terminals. This topology is useful for applications where some processing must be centralized and some can be performed locally. One problem with the star network is its vulnerability. All communication between points in the network must pass

front-end processor
A special purpose computer dedicated to managing communications for the host computer in a network.

concentrator
Telecommunications computer that collects and temporarily stores messages from terminals for batch transmission to the host computer.

controller
A specialized computer that supervises communications traffic between the CPU and the peripheral devices in a telecommunications system.

multiplexer
A device that enables a single communications channel to carry data transmissions from multiple sources simultaneously.

topology
The way in which the components of a network are connected.

star network
A network topology in which all computers and other devices are connected to a central host computer. All communications between network devices must pass through the host computer.

Figure 8-5 A star network topology. In a star network configuration, a central host computer acts as a traffic controller for all other components of the network. All communication between the smaller computers, terminals, and printers must first pass through the central computer.

Figure 8-6 A bus network topology. This topology allows for all messages to be broadcast to the entire network through a single circuit. There is no central host, and messages can travel in both directions along the cable.

bus network

Network topology linking a number of computers by a single circuit with all messages broadcast to the entire network.

ring network

A network topology in which all computers are linked by a closed loop in a manner that passes data in one direction from one computer to another.

through the central computer. Because the central computer is the traffic controller for the other computers and terminals in the network, communication in the network will come to a standstill if the host computer stops functioning.

The Bus Network

The **bus network** (see Figure 8-6) links a number of computers by a single circuit made of twisted wire, coaxial cable, or fiber-optic cable. All of the signals are broadcast in both directions to the entire network, with special software to identify which components receive each message (there is no central host computer to control the network). If one of the computers in the network fails, none of the other components in the network are affected. However, the channel in a bus network can handle only one message at a time, so performance can degrade if there is a high volume of network traffic. When two computers transmit messages simultaneously, a "collision" occurs, and the messages must be re-sent.

The Ring Network

Like the bus network, the **ring network** (see Figure 8-7) does not rely on a central host computer and will not necessarily break down if one of the component computers malfunctions. Each computer in the network can communicate directly with any other computer, and each processes its own applications independently. However, in a ring topology, the connecting wire, cable, or optical fiber forms a closed loop. Data are passed along the ring from one computer to another and always flow in one direction. Both ring and bus topologies are used in local area networks (LANs), which are discussed in the next section.

PRIVATE BRANCH EXCHANGES, LOCAL AREA NETWORKS (LANS), AND WIDE AREA NETWORKS (WANS)

Networks may be classified by geographic scope into local networks and wide area networks. Wide area networks encompass a relatively wide geographic area, from several miles to thousands of miles, whereas local networks link local resources, such as computers and terminals, in the same department or building of a firm. Local networks consist of private branch exchanges and local area networks.

Figure 8-7 A ring network topology. In a ring network configuration, messages are transmitted from computer to computer, flowing in a single direction through a closed loop. Each computer operates independently so that if one fails, communication through the network is not interrupted.

Private Branch Exchanges

A **private branch exchange (PBX)** is a special-purpose computer designed for handling and switching office telephone calls at a company site. It can belong to the company or to a telecommunications provider. Today's PBXs can carry voice and data to create local networks. PBXs can store, transfer, hold, and redial telephone calls, and they also can be used to switch digital information among computers and office devices. Using a PBX, you can write a letter on a PC in your office, send it to the printer, then dial up the local copying machine and have multiple copies of your letter created.

The advantage of digital PBXs over other local networking options is that they do not require special wiring. A PC connected to a network by telephone can be plugged or unplugged anywhere in a building, using the existing telephone lines. Commercial vendors support PBXs, so the organization does not need special expertise to manage them.

The geographic scope of PBXs is limited, usually to several hundred feet, although the PBX can be connected to other PBX networks or to packet-switched networks (see the discussion of packet switching in this section) to encompass a larger geographic area. The primary disadvantages of PBXs are that they are limited to telephone lines and they cannot easily handle very large volumes of data.

Local Area Networks

A **local area network (LAN)** encompasses a limited distance, usually one building or several buildings in close proximity. Most LANs connect devices located within a 2,000-foot radius, and they have been widely used to link PCs. LANs require their own communications channels and are often controlled and operated by end user groups or departments in a firm.

LANs generally have higher transmission capacities than PBXs, using bus or ring topologies and a high bandwidth. They are recommended for applications transmitting high volumes of data and other functions requiring high transmission speeds, including video transmissions and graphics. LANs often are used to connect PCs in an office to shared printers and other resources or to link computers and computer-controlled machines in factories.

Figure 8-8 illustrates one model of a LAN. The server acts as a librarian, storing programs and data files for network users. The server determines who gets access to what and in what sequence. Servers may be powerful PCs with large hard-disk capacity, workstations, minicomputers, or mainframes, although specialized computers are available for this purpose.

The network gateway connects the LAN to public networks, such as the telephone network, or to other corporate networks so that the LAN can exchange information with networks external to it. A **gateway** is generally a communications processor that can connect dissimilar networks by translating from one set of protocols to another. A **router** is used to route packets of data through several connected LANs or to a wide area network.

private branch exchange (PBX)
A central switching system that handles a firm's voice and digital communications.

local area network (LAN)
A telecommunications network that requires its own dedicated channels and that encompasses a limited distance, usually one building or several buildings in close proximity.

gateway
A communications processor that connects dissimilar networks by providing the translation from one set of protocols to another.

router
Device that forwards packets of data from one LAN or WAN to another.

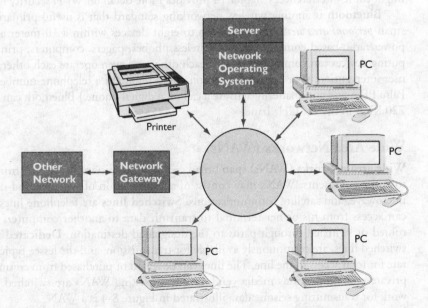

Figure 8-8 A local area network (LAN). A typical local area network connects computers and peripheral devices that are located close to each other, often in the same building.

LAN technology consists of cabling (twisted wire, coaxial, or fiber-optic cable) or wireless technology that links individual computer devices, network interface cards (which are special adapters serving as interfaces to the cable), and software to control LAN activities. The LAN network interface card specifies the data transmission rate, the size of message units, the addressing information attached to each message, and network topology (Ethernet uses a bus topology, for example).

LAN capabilities also are defined by the **network operating system (NOS).** The network operating system can reside on every computer in the network, or it can reside on a single designated server for all the applications on the network. The NOS routes and manages communications on the network and coordinates network resources. Novell NetWare, Microsoft Windows .NET Server 2003, the server versions of Windows 2000, and IBM's OS/2 Warp Server are popular network operating systems.

LANs may take the form of client/server networks, in which the server provides data and application programs to "client" computers on the network (see the Chapter 6 discussion of client/server computing) or they may use a peer-to-peer architecture. A **peer-to-peer** network treats all processors equally. The various computers on the network can exchange data by direct access and can share peripheral devices without going through a separate server.

LANs require new wiring each time a LAN is moved. One way to solve this problem is to create a wireless LAN. Wireless LANs have become easier to create and maintain and are starting to provide flexible, low-cost networking for firms and work groups. The **802.11b** network standard (also known as 802.11 High Rate or **Wi-Fi**) can be used to create wireless LANs in homes and offices. Wi-Fi stands for Wireless Fidelity and can transmit up to 11 megabits per second in the 2.4 GHz frequency range. Wi-Fi can also provide high-speed Internet access to specially outfitted PCs within a few hundred feet of a Wi-Fi access point, or transmitter. Wi-Fi "hot spots" are springing up in hotels, airport lounges, libraries, and college dorms to provide mobile access to the Internet. Businesses are using Wi-Fi networks to create low-cost wireless LANs and to provide Internet access from conference rooms and temporary workstations.

The cost of a Wi-Fi network runs less than $300 per installation, much less than a stationary LAN. Most high-end laptop computers are now Wi-Fi enabled and special adapters can be purchased to equip other PCs with Wi-Fi capabilities. A simple wireless network can be created by linking several computers that are equipped with Wi-Fi adapters and a wireless access point—a radio receiver/transmitter and antennae that link to a wired network, router or hub. Access points can be mounted indoors on ceilings or outdoors on poles or towers. These wireless LANs have a range of several hundred feet, although the range can be extended by mounting antennae on towers or by adding access points, with users roaming among them as they would in a cellular phone system. There are a few drawbacks to this technology, however. Wi-Fi networks are susceptible to interference from nearby systems operating in the same spectrum and there is no way to control additional new devices in the same area that might cause interference. Chapter 14 provides more detail on Wi-Fi security issues.

Bluetooth is another wireless networking standard that is useful primarily for creating small *personal area networks* linking up to eight devices within a 10-meter area using low-power radio-based communication. Wireless phones, pagers, computers, printers, and computing devices can communicate with each other and even operate each other without direct user intervention. (For example, a person could highlight a telephone number on a wireless Palm PDA and automatically activate a call on a digital phone.) Bluetooth can transmit up to 720 Kbps in the 2.4 GHz band.

Wide Area Networks (WANs)

Wide area networks (WANs) span broad geographical distances, ranging from several miles to entire continents. WANs may consist of a combination of switched and dedicated lines, microwave, and satellite communications. **Switched lines** are telephone lines that a person can access from his or her terminal to transmit data to another computer, the call being routed or switched through paths to the designated destination. **Dedicated lines,** or nonswitched lines, are continuously available for transmission, and the lessee typically pays a flat rate for total access to the line. The lines can be leased or purchased from common carriers or private communications media vendors. Most existing WANs are switched. Amoco's network for transmitting seismic data illustrated in Figure 8-4 is a WAN.

---

network operating system (NOS)
Special software that routes and manages communications on the network and coordinates network resources.

peer-to-peer
Network architecture that gives equal power to all computers on the network.

802.11b (Wi-Fi)
Standard for high-speed wireless LANs that can transmit up to 11 Mbps within a 100-meter area, providing a low-cost flexible technology for connecting work groups and providing mobile Internet access.

Bluetooth
Standard for wireless personal area networks that can transmit up to 720 Kbps within a 10-meter area.

wide area network (WAN)
Telecommunications network that spans a large geographical distance. May consist of a variety of cable, satellite, and microwave technologies.

switched lines
Telephone lines that a person can access from a terminal to transmit data to another computer, the call being routed or switched through paths to the designated destination.

dedicated lines
Telephone lines that are continuously available for transmission by a lessee. Typically conditioned to transmit data at high speeds for high-volume applications.

Individual business firms may maintain their own wide area networks. The firm is responsible for telecommunications content and management. However, private wide area networks are expensive to maintain, or firms may not have the resources to manage their own wide area networks. In such instances, companies may choose to use commercial network services to communicate over vast distances.

NETWORK SERVICES AND BROADBAND TECHNOLOGIES

In addition to topology and geographic scope, networks can be classified by the types of service they provide.

Value-Added Networks (VANs)

Value-added networks are an alternative to firms designing and managing their own networks. **Value-added networks (VANs)** are private, third-party-managed networks that offer data transmission and network services to subscribing firms. Subscribers pay only for the amount of data they transmit plus a subscription fee. Customers do not have to invest in network equipment and software and may achieve savings in line charges and transmission costs because the costs of using the network are shared among many users.

Many companies are now using the Internet to transmit their data because it is less expensive than using VANs. In response, today's value-added networks are providing extra services for secure e-mail management and data transmission, management reporting, and electronic document interchange translation (see the discussion of electronic document interchange in Section 8.3).

Other Network Services

Traditional analog telephone service is based on circuit switching, where a direct connection must be maintained between two nodes in a network for the duration of the transmission session. **Packet switching** is a basic switching technique that can be used to achieve economies and higher speeds in long-distance transmission. VANs and the Internet use packet switching. Packet switching breaks up a lengthy block of data into small, fixed bundles called packets. There are many different packet sizes, some of them variable, depending on the communications standard being used. (The X.25 packet switching standard uses packets of 128 bytes each.) The packets include information for directing the packet to the right address and for checking transmission errors along with the data. Data are gathered from many users, divided into small packets, and transmitted via various communications channels. Each packet travels independently through the network. Packets of data originating at one source can be routed through different paths in the network before being reassembled into the original message when they reach their destination. Figure 8-9 illustrates how packet switching works.

value-added network (VAN)
Private, multipath, data-only, third-party-managed network that multiple organizations use on a subscription basis.

packet switching
Technology that breaks blocks of data into fixed bundles and routes them in the most economical way through any available communications channel.

Figure 8-9 Packet-switched networks and packet communications. Data are grouped into small packets, which are transmitted independently via various communications channels and reassembled at their final destination.

frame relay

A shared network service technology that packages data into bundles for transmission but does not use error-correction routines. Cheaper and faster than packet switching.

asynchronous transfer mode (ATM)

A networking technology that parcels information into 8-byte cells, allowing data to be transmitted between computers from different vendors.

Integrated Services Digital Network (ISDN)

International standard for transmitting voice, video, image, and data to support a wide range of service over the public telephone lines.

digital subscriber line (DSL)

A group of technologies providing high-capacity transmission over existing copper telephone lines.

cable modem

Modem designed to operate over cable TV lines to provide high-speed access to the Web or corporate intranets.

T1 line

A dedicated telephone connection comprising 24 channels that can support a data transmission rate of 1.544 Mbps. Each channel can be configured to carry voice or data traffic.

broadband

High-speed transmission technology. Also designates a single communications medium that can carry multiple channels of data simultaneously.

converged network

Network with technology to enable voice, video, and data to run over a single network.

unified messaging

System combining voice messages, e-mail, and fax so that they can all be obtained from a single system.

Frame relay is a shared network service that is faster and less expensive than packet switching and can achieve transmission speeds up to 1.544 megabits per second. Frame relay packages data into frames that are similar to packets, but it does not perform error correction. It works well on reliable lines that do not require frequent retransmissions because of error.

Most corporations today use separate networks for voice, private-line services, and data, each of which is supported by a different technology. A service called **asynchronous transfer mode (ATM)** may overcome some of these problems because it can seamlessly and dynamically switch voice, data, images, and video between users. ATM also promises to tie LANs and WANs together more easily. ATM technology parcels information into uniform cells, each with 53 groups of 8 bytes, eliminating the need for protocol conversion. It can pass data between computers from different vendors and permits data to be transmitted at any speed the network handles. ATM can transmit up to 10 gigabits per second.

Integrated Services Digital Network (ISDN) is an international standard for dial-up network access that integrates voice, data, image, and video services in a single link. There are two levels of ISDN service: Basic Rate ISDN and Primary Rate ISDN. Each uses a group of B (bearer) channels to carry voice or data along with a D (delta) channel for signaling and control information. Basic Rate ISDN can transmit data at a rate of 128 kilobits per second on an existing local telephone line. Organizations and individuals requiring the ability to provide simultaneous voice or data transmission over one physical line might choose this service. Primary Rate ISDN offers transmission capacities in the megabit range and is designed for large users of telecommunications services.

Other high-capacity services include digital subscriber line (DSL) technologies, cable modems, and T1 lines. Like ISDN, **digital subscriber line (DSL)** technologies also operate over existing copper telephone lines to carry voice, data, and video, but they have higher transmission capacities than ISDN. There are several categories of DSL. Asymmetric digital subscriber line (ADSL) supports a transmission rate of 1.5 to 9 megabits per second when receiving data and up to 640 kilobits per second when sending data. Symmetric digital subscriber line (SDSL) supports the same transmission rate for sending and receiving data of up to 3 megabits per second. **Cable modems** are modems designed to operate over cable TV lines. They can provide high-speed access to the Web or corporate intranets of up to 4 megabits per second. However, cable modems use a shared line so that transmission will slow down if there are a large number of local users sharing the cable line. A cable modem at present has stronger capabilities for receiving data than for sending data. A **T1 line** is a dedicated telephone connection comprising 24 channels that can support a data transmission rate of 1.544 megabits per second. Each of these 64-kilobit-per-second channels can be configured to carry voice or data traffic. These services often are used for high-capacity Internet connections. Table 8-2 summarizes these network services.

High-speed transmission technologies are sometimes referred to as **broadband.** The term broadband is also used to designate transmission media that can carry multiple channels simultaneously over a single communications medium.

NETWORK CONVERGENCE

Most companies maintain separate networks for voice, data, and video, but products are now available to create **converged networks,** which can deliver voice, data, and video in a single network infrastructure. These multiservice networks can potentially reduce networking costs by eliminating the need to provide support services and personnel for each different type of network. Multiservice networks can be attractive solutions for companies running multimedia applications, such as video collaboration, voice-data call centers, distance learning (see the following section), or **unified messaging,** or for firms with high costs for voice services. Unified messaging systems combine voice mail, e-mail, and faxes so they can all be obtained from one system.

TABLE 8-2 NETWORK SERVICES

Service	Description	Bandwidth
X.25	Packet-switching standard that parcels data into packets of 128 bytes	Up to 1.544 Mbps
Frame relay	Packages data into frames for high-speed transmission over reliable lines but does not use error-correction routines	Up to 1.544 Mbps
ATM (asynchronous transfer mode)	Parcels data into uniform cells to allow high-capacity transmission of voice, data, images, and video between different types of computers	25 Mbps–10 Gbps
ISDN	Digital dial-up network access standard that can integrate voice, data, and video services	Basic Rate ISDN: 128 Kbps; Primary Rate ISDN: 1.5 Mbps
DSL (digital subscriber line)	Series of technologies for high-capacity transmission over copper wires	ADSL—up to 9 Mbps for receiving and up to 640 Kbps for sending data; SDSL—up to 3 Mbps for both sending and receiving
T1	Dedicated telephone connection with 24 channels for high-capacity transmission	1.544 Mbps
Cable modem	Service for high-speed transmission of data over cable TV lines that are shared by many users	Up to 4 Mbps

8.3 ELECTRONIC BUSINESS AND ELECTRONIC COMMERCE TECHNOLOGIES

Baxter Healthcare International, described in Chapter 3, realized the strategic significance of telecommunications. The company placed its own computer terminals in hospital supply rooms. Customers could dial up a local VAN and send their orders directly to the company. Other companies also are achieving strategic benefits by developing electronic commerce and electronic business applications based on networking technologies.

Electronic mail (e-mail), groupware, voice mail, facsimile machines (fax), digital information services, teleconferencing, dataconferencing, videoconferencing, and electronic data interchange are key applications for electronic commerce and electronic business because they provide network-based capabilities for communication, coordination, and speeding the flow of purchase and sale transactions.

Netscape Communicator includes e-mail functions such as attaching files, displaying messages, and providing logs of all incoming and outgoing messages. E-mail has become an important tool for organizational communication.

MONITORING EMPLOYEES ON NETWORKS: UNETHICAL OR GOOD BUSINESS?

E-mail usage has exploded as hundreds of millions of people the world over turn to it for speedy, convenient, and inexpensive business and personal communications. Not surprisingly the use of e-mail for personal reasons at the workplace has also grown, as has use of the Web for personal purposes. A number of studies have concluded that at least 25 percent of employee online time is spent on non–work related Web surfing.

Many companies are starting to monitor their employees' use of e-mail and the Internet. A study by the American Management Association concluded that more than 75 percent of large U.S. companies are recording and reviewing employee communications and activities on the job, including e-mail, Internet connections, and computer files. Although U.S. companies have the legal right to monitor employee Internet and e-mail activity, is such monitoring unethical, or is it simply good business?

Managers worry about the loss of time and employee productivity when employees are focusing on personal rather than company business. If personal traffic on company networks is too high, it can also clog the company's network so that business work cannot be performed. Some employees at Xerox had sent so much junk and pornographic e-mail while on the job that the company's e-mail system shut down. Too much time on personal business, Internet or not, can mean lost revenue or overcharges to clients. Some employees may be charging time they spend trading stocks over the Web or pursuing other personal business to clients, thus overcharging the clients.

When employees use e-mail or the Web with employer facilities, anything they do, including anything illegal, carries the company's name. Therefore, the employer can be traced and held liable. Managements fear that racist, sexually explicit, or other potentially offensive material could result in adverse publicity and even lawsuits. Even if the company is found not to be liable, responding to lawsuits will cost the company tens of thousands of dollars at a minimum. Companies also fear e-mail leakage of trade secrets.

Some companies try to ban all personal activities on corporate networks—zero tolerance. Others block employee access to specific Web sites or limit personal time on the Web using software that allows them to track the Web sites their employees visit, the amount of time they spend at these sites, and the files they download. New Web monitoring software tools even allow employees to see how their activity is being monitored. Fatline Inc.'s FastTracker includes an "employee view" for workers to see what is being recorded about them. Some firms have fired employees that have stepped out of bounds. No solution is problem-free, but many consultants believe companies should have a written corporate policy on employee e-mail and Internet use. The policy should include explicit ground rules that state, by position or level, under what circumstances employees can use company facilities for e-mail or Internet use. The policy should also inform employees if these activities are monitored and explain why. The rules may need to be tailored to the specific organization because different companies may need to access different Web materials as part of their businesses. For example, although some companies may exclude anyone from visiting sites that have explicit sexual material, law firm or hospital employees may require access, whereas investment firms will need to allow many of their employees access to other investment sites.

To Think About: Should managers monitor employee e-mail and Internet usage? Why or why not? Describe an effective e-mail and Web use policy for a company.

Sources: Sandra Swanson, "Employers Take a Closer Look," *Information-Week,* July 15, 2002; Laura Hunt, "E-mail Monitoring: Why You Should Pry," *SearchEbusiness.com,* April 16, 2002; Brett Glass, "Are You Being Watched?" *PC Magazine,* April 2002; Lou Hirsch, "The Boss Is Watching: Workplace Monitoring on the Rise," *NewsFactor Network,* June 29, 2001; Stephen Shankland, "Study: Web, E-Mail Monitoring Spreads," *CNET News,* July 8, 2001; and "U.S. Web Use Mostly at Work," *Reuters,* April 6, 2000.

MANAGEMENT

ELECTRONIC MAIL AND GROUPWARE

We described the capabilities of electronic mail, or e-mail, in Chapter 6. E-mail eliminates costly long-distance telephone charges, expediting communication between different parts of an organization. Nestlé SA, the Swiss-based multinational food corporation, installed an electronic-mail system to connect its 60,000 employees in 80 countries. Nestlé's European units can use the electronic-mail system to share information about production schedules and inventory levels to ship excess products from one country to another.

Many organizations operate their own internal electronic-mail systems, but communications companies, such as AT&T, offer these services as do commercial online information services, such as America Online and public networks on the Internet (see Chapter 9). Employee use of e-mail and the Internet has become an important management issue, as described in the Window on Management, which examines whether monitoring employees using e-mail, the Internet, and other network facilities is ethical.

Although e-mail has become a valuable tool for communication, groupware provides additional capabilities for supporting enterprise-wide communication and collaborative work. Individuals, teams, and work groups at different locations in the organization can use groupware to participate in discussion forums and work on shared documents and projects. More details on the use of groupware for collaborative work can be found in Chapters 6 and 12.

VOICE MAIL AND FAX

A **voice mail** system digitizes the sender's spoken message, transmits it over a network, and stores the message on disk for later retrieval. When the recipient is ready to listen, the messages are reconverted to audio form. Various store-and-forward capabilities notify recipients that messages are waiting. Recipients have the option of saving these messages for future use, deleting them, or routing them to other parties.

Facsimile (fax) machines can transmit documents containing both text and graphics over ordinary telephone lines. A sending fax machine scans and digitizes the document image. The digitized document is transmitted over a network and reproduced in hard copy form by a receiving fax machine. The process results in a duplicate, or facsimile, of the original.

TELECONFERENCING, DATACONFERENCING, AND VIDEOCONFERENCING

People can meet electronically, even though they are hundreds or thousands of miles apart, by using teleconferencing, dataconferencing, or videoconferencing. **Teleconferencing** allows a group of people to confer simultaneously via telephone or via e-mail group communication software. Teleconferencing that includes the ability of two or more people at distant locations to work on the same document or data simultaneously is called **dataconferencing.** With dataconferencing, users at distant locations are able to edit and modify data (text, such as word processing documents; numeric, such as spreadsheets; and graphic) files. Teleconferencing in which participants see each other over video screens is termed *video teleconferencing*, or **videoconferencing.**

These forms of electronic conferencing are growing in popularity because they save travel time and cost. Legal firms might use videoconferencing to take depositions and to convene meetings between lawyers in different branch offices. Videoconferencing can help companies promote remote collaboration from different locations or fill in personnel expertise gaps. Electronic conferencing is useful for supporting telecommuting, enabling home workers to meet with or collaborate with their counterparts working in the office or elsewhere. The Window on Organizations describes how such technologies can improve medical care throughout the world.

Videoconferencing usually has required special videoconference rooms and equipment that used to be very expensive. Falling prices for room-based videoconferencing and the

voice mail
A system for digitizing a spoken message and transmitting it over a network.

facsimile (fax)
A machine that digitizes and transmits documents with both text and graphics over telephone lines.

teleconferencing
The ability to confer with a group of people simultaneously using the telephone or electronic-mail group communication software.

dataconferencing
Teleconferencing in which two or more users are able to edit and modify data files simultaneously.

videoconferencing
Teleconferencing in which participants see each other over video screens.

With PC desktop videoconferencing systems, users can see each other and simultanousely work on the same document. Organizations are using videoconferencing to improve coordination and save travel time and costs.

CLOSING THE HEALTHCARE GAP WITH VIDEOCONFERENCING

About 11 million children younger than five years old die each year, and 8 out of 10 of them live in medically underserved nations. According to the World Health Organization, the death rate for children in underdeveloped nations is 20 percent to 50 percent, compared to less than 4 percent in the United States.

In Panama, for example, a mother living deep in the country might have to walk for days to take her child to a hospital. By the time she gets there, the infection is much worse and harder to treat. Hospital del Nino, Panama's largest children's hospital, is trying to address this challenge by staging live videoconferences with physicians in the United States. Every other month, Panamanian doctors hold live videoconferences with medical specialists from St. Joseph's Children's Hospital in Paterson, New Jersey, Mount Sinai New York University Medical Center in New York, and Johns Hopkins Hospital in Baltimore to examine patients and CT scans electronically. The videoconferencing sessions enable local doctors to work in consultation with U.S. specialists so that Panamanian children can often be treated without costly flights abroad. Through videoconferencing, they have dealt directly with more than 200 severely ill children and disseminated information to help about 2,500 more children in other parts of the country with similar illnesses.

If the children do need medical treatment in the United States, videoconferencing helps local doctors do as much of the preparatory work as possible in their native country. Yordano, for example, was born in rural Panama with a deformed skull that left him with only one eye and trouble swallowing. In November 2000, doctors from St. Joseph's Children's Hospital in Paterson examined him via videoconferencing. During the videoconferencing session, the Panamanian doctors used visual CT scans to collect head measurements, which were then used to create a computer model of

Yordano's head to plan the surgery in the United States that reshaped the boy's skull.

The telemedicine project is sponsored by Medical Missions for Children, a nonprofit organization based in Paterson, New Jersey. Medical Missions is expanding the telemedicine program to eight more U.S. hospitals and 20 countries, including Nicaragua, Bolivia, Uzbekistan, and Georgia. Medical Missions uses videoconferencing equipment from Polycom Inc. because it works with a wide spectrum of applications and interfaces. (Communication infrastructures vary from country to country.) A point-to-point telemedicine session between a U.S. hospital and one in Panama or another country requires a Polycom ViewStation videoconferencing system at both sites. The World Bank has donated its satellite network for countries without satellite services. In addition to videoconferences, the satellite network allows physicians to transfer electronic medical records and digital images such as X-rays and MRIs.

Such telemedicine projects have accelerated the process of spreading medical knowledge. Physicians in third world countries such as Panama get advice on conditions with which they are not familiar, while their colleagues in the United States see and learn about illnesses that no longer show up in the U.S., such as advanced stages of tuberculosis. Telemedicine applications are also helping medical practitioners to diagnose and treat U.S. soldiers in faraway locations and civilians living in remote rural areas.

To Think About: What are the benefits of videoconferencing in medicine? How has videoconferencing changed the way medicine is practiced?

Sources: Marianne Kolbasuk McGee, "The Doctor Is In," *InformationWeek,* June 10, 2002; and Alex Salkever, "The MD Meets IT," *BusinessWeek Online,* April 15, 2002, <www.businessweek.com>.

ORGANIZATIONS

availability of inexpensive PC-based, desktop videoconferencing systems have reduced videoconferencing costs so that more organizations can benefit from this technology.

Desktop videoconferencing systems typically provide windows for users to see each other and capabilities for participants to work on the same document from different locations. Most desktop systems provide audio capabilities for two-way, real-time conversations and a whiteboard. The whiteboard is a shared drawing program that lets multiple users collaborate on projects by modifying images and text online. Software products such as Microsoft NetMeeting (a feature of the Windows operating system) and CU-SeeMe (available in both shareware and commercial versions) provide low-cost tools for desktop videoconferencing over the Internet.

DIGITAL INFORMATION SERVICES, DISTANCE LEARNING, AND E-LEARNING

Powerful and far-reaching digital electronic services enable networked PC and workstation users to obtain information from outside the firm instantly without leaving their desks. Stock

America Online gives subscribers access to extensive information resources, including news reports, weather, education, financial services, and information on the Web. Companies and individuals can use such digital information services to obtain information instantly from the desktop.

prices, periodicals, competitor data, industrial supplies catalogs, legal research, news articles, reference works, and weather forecasts are some of the information that can be accessed online. Many of these services provide capabilities for e-mail, electronic bulletin boards, online discussion groups, shopping, and travel reservations as well as Internet access. Table 8-3 describes the leading commercial digital information services. The following chapter describes how organizations can access even more information resources using the Internet.

Organizations can also use communications technology to run distance learning programs where they can train employees in remote locations without requiring the employees to be physically present in a classroom. **Distance learning** is education or training delivered over a distance to individuals in one or more locations. Although distance learning can be accomplished with print-based materials, the distance learning experience is increasingly based on information technology, including videoconferencing, satellite or cable television, or interactive multimedia, including the Web. The term **e-learning** is increasingly being used to describe instruction using purely digital technology such as CD-ROMs, the Internet, or private networks. Some distance learning programs use *synchronous communication,* where teacher and student are present at the same time during the instruction, even if they are in different places. Other programs use *asynchronous communication*, where teacher and student don't have person-to-person interaction at the same time or place. For example, students might access a Web site to obtain their course materials and communicate with their instructors via e-mail.

distance learning

Education or training delivered over a distance to individuals in one or more locations.

e-learning

Instruction delivered through purely digital technology such as CD-ROMs, the Internet or private networks.

ELECTRONIC DATA INTERCHANGE

Electronic data interchange (EDI) is a key technology for electronic commerce because it allows the computer-to-computer exchange between two organizations of standard transaction documents such as invoices, bills of lading, or purchase orders. EDI lowers transaction

electronic data interchange (EDI)

The direct computer-to-computer exchange between two organizations of standard business transaction documents.

TABLE 8-3	COMMERCIAL DIGITAL INFORMATION SERVICES
Provider	Type of Service
America Online	General interest/business information
Microsoft Network	General interest/business information
Dow Jones News Retrieval	Business/financial information
Dialog	Business/scientific/technical information
LexisNexis	News/business/legal information

Instructors can use Prometheus Web-based software to provide their students with course materials and a dedicated academic resource center on the Web. Such tools can be used to support distance learning.

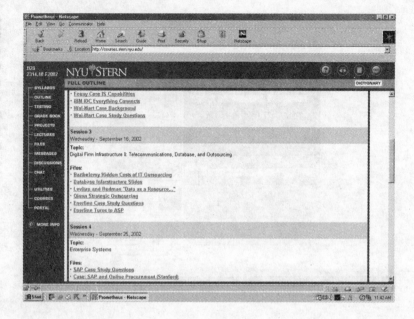

costs because transactions can be automatically transmitted from one information system to another through a telecommunications network, eliminating the printing and handling of paper at one end and the inputting of data at the other. EDI also may provide strategic benefits by helping a firm lock in customers, making it easier for customers or distributors to order from them rather than from competitors. EDI can curb inventory costs by minimizing the amount of time components are in inventory.

EDI differs from e-mail in that it transmits an actual structured transaction (with distinct fields such as the transaction date, transaction amount, sender's name, and recipient's name) as opposed to an unstructured text message such as a letter. Figure 8-10 illustrates how EDI works.

Organizations can most fully benefit from EDI when they integrate the data supplied by EDI with applications such as accounts payable, inventory control, shipping, and production planning, and when they have carefully planned for the organizational changes surrounding new business processes (Premkumar, Ramamurthy, and Nilakanta, 1994). Management support and training in the new technology are essential (Raymond and Bergeron, 1996). Companies also must standardize the form of the transactions they use with other firms and comply with legal requirements for verifying that the transactions are authentic. Many organizations prefer to use private networks for EDI transactions but are increasingly turning to the Internet for this purpose (see Chapters 4 and 9).

Figure 8-10 Electronic data interchange (EDI). Companies can use EDI to automate electronic commerce transactions. Purchase orders and payments can be transmitted directly from the customer's computer to the seller's computer. The seller can transmit shipping notices, price changes, and invoices electronically back to the customer.

MIS IN ACTION: Manager's Toolkit

DEVELOPING A BUSINESS-DRIVEN TELECOMMUNICATIONS PLAN

Throughout your career you may be asked to find ways to use telecommunications technology to enhance your firm's competitive position. Here are the steps you need to take to develop a strategic telecommunications plan.

1. Determine the role of telecommunications in your firm's strategy. If your firm's long-range business plan requires increasing the scale and scope of operations, creating new products or services, or lowering operational costs, consider whether new telecommunications applications and services could promote these objectives.

2. Assess your firm's existing voice, data, and video communications capabilities. Are they sufficient to meet future business goals? What areas need improvement?

3. If additional telecommunications capabilities are required, establish the scope of these capabilities. You will need to consider:

   ▪ Distance: Are future communications needs primarily local or long distance?

   ▪ Services: What range of telecommunications services are needed: Do they include e-mail, EDI, Web access, voice mail, videoconferencing, graphics transmission, and internally generated transactions? Do these services need to be integrated?

   ▪ Points of access: How many different locations and users in the organization require access to new communications services and capabilities?

   ▪ Utilization: What frequency and volume of communications does your firm anticipate?

   ▪ Cost: How much do proposed telecommunications technology options cost? Which cost components are fixed? Which are variable?

   ▪ Security: What level of security and reliability do proposed networks have to maintain?

   ▪ Connectivity: How much time, money, and effort would be required to make sure all of the disparate components of a network or multiple networks can communicate with each other (see Chapter 9)?

MAKE IT YOUR BUSINESS

FINANCE AND ACCOUNTING

Telecommunications is widely used in specialized financial services firms and in other businesses to expedite funds transfer. Many nonfinancial companies use electronic data interchange (EDI) to transfer payments to suppliers and invoices to large corporate customers. Banks maintain networks to link their automated teller machines (ATMs) and branch offices to central computers that keep track of deposit, withdrawal, and fund transfer transactions occurring at remote locations. Financial services firms today depend on networked systems to provide their managers and clients with instant access to account information. These firms are heavy users of online digital information services, such as Dow Jones, to obtain data on firms' financial positions and on financial markets.

HUMAN RESOURCES

Contemporary human resources systems have realized great efficiencies by using communications technology to provide authorized human resources professionals and employees with direct online access to employee information. Employees can use telephone-based systems, the Web, or private corporate networks to review their employment records or to make changes to their benefits plans. Managers can use e-mail and videoconferencing to communicate with employees and work teams. Input from human resource specialists is essential when developing a corporate policy for employee use of networks and computing resources. You can find examples of human resources applications on pages 264 and 266.

MANUFACTURING AND PRODUCTION

The manufacturing and production function has become highly networked and communications-driven. Computers and computer-controlled machines on the factory floor are often linked in LANs. In companies with advanced manufacturing systems, each step in the manufacturing process uses networks to transmit data to the next step. Data from orders triggers transactions that can be transmitted via networks directly to manufacturing scheduling systems, to supply chain management systems, to the assembly line, and to systems for warehousing and delivery. You can find examples of manufacturing and production applications on pages 248–249.

SALES AND MARKETING

Many sales transactions today take place using point-of-sale systems that capture sales transaction data at the checkout counter using bar code scanners or other devices. These data are often transmitted via networks to the firm's central computer where they update the firm's order processing and inventory systems. Once consolidated in corporate systems, these data can be analyzed to identify high-performing and low-performing items, buying trends, and items needing rapid replenishment from suppliers. E-mail and call centers where customers' telephone calls are directed to service representatives have become popular technologies for customer service and support. You can find examples of sales and marketing applications on pages 273–275.

MANAGEMENT WRAP-UP

Managers need to be continuously involved in telecommunications decisions because so many important business processes are based on telecommunications and networks. Management should identify the business opportunities linked to telecommunications technology and establish the business criteria for selecting the firm's telecommunications platform.

Telecommunications technology enables organizations to reduce transaction and coordination costs, promoting electronic commerce and electronic business. The organization's telecommunications infrastructure should support its business processes and business strategy.

Communications technology is intertwined with all the other information technologies and deeply embedded in contemporary information systems. Networks are becoming more pervasive and powerful, with capabilities to transmit voice, data, and video over long distances. Many alternative network designs, transmission technologies, and network services are available to organizations.

For Discussion

1. Network design is a key business decision as well as a technology decision. Why?

2. If you were an international company with global operations, what criteria would you use to determine whether to use a VAN service or a private WAN?

SUMMARY

1. *What technologies are used in telecommunications systems?* A telecommunications system consists of devices that create a network for communication from one location to another by electronic means. The essential components of a telecommunications system are computers, terminals, other input/output devices, communications channels, communications processors (such as modems, multiplexers, controllers, concentrators, and front-end processors), and telecommunications software. Different components of a telecommunications network can communicate with each other with a common set of rules termed protocols. Data are transmitted throughout a telecommunications network using either analog signals or digital signals. A modem is a device that translates analog signals to digital signals and vice versa.

2. *What telecommunications transmission media should our organization use?* The capacity of a telecommunications channel is determined by the range of frequencies it can accommodate. The higher the range of frequencies, called bandwidth, the higher the capacity (measured in bits per second). The principal transmission media are twisted copper telephone wire, coaxial copper cable, fiber-optic cable, and wireless transmission using microwave, satellite, low-frequency radio waves, or infrared waves. The choice of transmission medium depends on the distance and volume of communication

required by the organization and its financial resources. Fiber-optic and coaxial cable are used for high-volume transmission but are expensive to install. Twisted wire can usually transmit low volumes of data, but it is less expensive than other media, allowing companies to use the existing wiring for telephone systems for digital communication. Terrestrial microwave and satellite are used for wireless communication over long distances and can be cost-effective for transmitting large volumes of data to and from faraway locations.

3. *How should our organization design its networks?* Network design should be based on the organization's information requirements and the distance required for transmission. The three common network topologies are the star network, the bus network, and the ring network. In a star network, all communications must pass through a central computer, and star networks are primarily used when some centralized processing is required. The bus network links a number of devices to a single channel and broadcasts all of the signals to the entire network with special software to identify which components receive each message. In a ring network, each computer in the network can communicate directly with any other computer but the channel is a closed loop. Data are passed along the ring from one computer to another. Network design should also consider geographic scope. Local area networks (LANs) and private branch exchanges

(PBXs) are used to link offices and buildings in close proximity. PBXs are limited to existing telephone lines and low transmission speeds. Conventional LANs require special wiring, but technology such as 802.11b (Wi-Fi) can be used to construct low-cost, high-speed wireless LANs. Wide area networks (WANs) span a broad geographical distance, ranging from several miles to continents, and are private networks that are independently managed.

4. *What alternative network services are available to our organization?* A number of services are available to organizations for network management and Internet access. Value-added networks (VANs) sell wide area networking services to companies that do not want to build or maintain their own private networks. VANs (and the Internet) achieve economies and higher speeds in long-distance transmission by using packet switching, which breaks messages into small packets that are sent independently along different paths in a network and then reassembled at their destination.

Integrated Services Digital Network (ISDN) is an international standard for dial-up network access that integrates voice, data, image, and video services in a single link. Basic Rate ISDN can transmit data at a rate of 128 kilobits per second (Kbps) on an existing local telephone line.

Firms have the option of using frame relay, asynchronous transfer mode (ATM), digital subscriber line, cable modem, and T1 lines for high transmission capacity. Frame relay is a shared network service that is faster and less expensive than packet switching because it does not perform error correction routines. ATM can seamlessly and dynamically switch voice, data, images, and video between computers from different vendors and can tie LANs and WANs together. ATM can transmit up to 10 gigabits per second.

Digital subscriber line (DSL) technologies, cable modems, and T1 lines are often used for high-capacity Internet connections. Like ISDN, DSL technologies also operate over existing copper telephone lines to carry voice, data, and video, but they have higher transmission capacities than ISDN. Asymmetric digital subscriber line (ADSL) supports a transmission rate of 1.5 to 9 megabits per second (Mbps) when receiving data and up to 640 Kbps when sending data. Symmetric digital subscriber line (SDSL) supports the same transmission rate for sending and receiving data of up to 3 Mbps. Cable modems are modems designed to operate over cable TV lines. They can provide high-speed access to the Web or corporate intranets of up to 4 Mbps. A T1 line is a dedicated telephone connection comprising 24 channels that can support a data transmission rate of 1.544 Mbps. Each of these 64-Kbps channels can be configured to carry voice or data traffic.

5. *What telecommunications applications can be used for electronic business and electronic commerce?* The principal telecommunications applications for electronic commerce and electronic business are electronic mail, voice mail, fax, digital information services, distance learning, teleconferencing, dataconferencing, videoconferencing, electronic data interchange (EDI), and groupware. EDI is the computer-to-computer exchange between two organizations of standard transaction documents such as invoices, bills of lading, and purchase orders.

KEY TERMS

REVIEW QUESTIONS

1. Why has telecommunications technology become such an important issue for managers and organizations?

2. What is a telecommunications system? What are the principal functions of all telecommunications systems?

3. Name and briefly describe each of the components of a telecommunications system.

4. Distinguish between an analog and a digital signal.

5. Name the different types of telecommunications transmission media and compare them in terms of speed and cost.

6. Name and describe the technologies used for wireless transmission.

7. What are optical networks? Why are they becoming important?

8. What is the relationship between bandwidth and a channel's transmission capacity?

9. Name and briefly describe the different kinds of communications processors.

10. Name and briefly describe the three principal network topologies.

11. Distinguish between a PBX and a LAN.

12. What are the components of a typical LAN? What are the functions of each component? Describe the technologies for wireless LANs.

13. List and describe the various network services.

14. Distinguish between a WAN and a VAN.

15. Define the following: modem, baud, protocol, converged network, and broadband.

16. Name and describe the telecommunications applications that can support electronic commerce and electronic business.

APPLICATION SOFTWARE EXERCISE

You can find a spreadsheet exercise on Analyzing Telecommunications Costs at the Laudon Web site for Chapter 8.

GROUP PROJECT

With a group of two or three of your fellow students, describe in detail the ways that telecommunications technology can provide a firm with competitive advantage. Use the companies described in Chapter 3 or other chapters you have read so far to illustrate the points you make, or select examples of other companies using telecommunications from business or computer magazines. If possible, use electronic presentation software to present your findings to the class.

TOOLS FOR INTERACTIVE LEARNING

▓ INTERNET CONNECTION

The Internet Connection for this chapter will take you to the Rosenbluth Travel Web site where you can complete an exercise to analyze how Rosenbluth International uses the Web and communications technology in its daily operations.

▓ INTERACTIVE STUDY GUIDE

You can use the Interactive Study Guide to test your knowledge of the topics in the chapter and get instant feedback where you need more practice.

▓ RUNNING CASE

The Running Case provides an opportunity for you to develop a plan to use information technology to cut down and better manage Dirt Bikes USA's corporate travel expenses. You can find a complete description of this project on the Laudon Web site for Chapter 8 and on the Multimedia Edition CD-ROM.

▓ ELECTRONIC BUSINESS PROJECT

At the Laudon Web site for Chapter 8, you can find an Electronic Business project to compare and evaluate the supply chain management services of Schneider National and J.B. Hunt.

▓ MANAGEMENT DECISION PROBLEM

At the Laudon Web site for Chapter 8, you can find a Management Decision Problem on selecting an Internet connection service.

▓ CD-ROM

If you purchase and use the Multimedia Edition CD-ROM with this chapter, you can find a video demonstrating the capabilities of personal communication services, an audio overview of the major themes of this chapter, and bullet text summarizing the key points of the chapter.

CASE STUDY—*Rosenbluth International Travels a Telecommunications Route to Success*

The travel-service industry is in trouble. Airlines have capped the commissions they will pay to travel agents, and these commissions have been the main source of their income. Travel agents can no longer assume that clients will pay them for the right to handle their travel business. In addition, global competition has forced many corporations to cut back on all expenses, including travel. Finally, the World Wide Web now makes it easy for individuals, whether as private persons or employees, to investigate and book their own travel. Management at Rosenbluth International had to face this formidable reality and find a way to thrive.

Rosenbluth, a privately held, family-owned company, is the second largest travel-services firm in the world, with American Express being number one. It has more than $6 billion in annual sales and 5,200 employees in 24 countries. Headquartered in Philadelphia, Pennsylvania, the company was founded in 1892, and it was a relatively small company when Hal Rosenbluth joined the firm in 1974. In 1984, he obtained a contract to provide all of DuPont Corporation's travel services, and the company's explosive growth began. Rosenbluth was a success with DuPont because he managed to save the company $150 million in travel and entertainment (T&E) expenses.

Hal Rosenbluth believes that by creating a humane working environment, and by genuinely putting employees (called "associates" at Rosenbluth) first, they will give more to the company and offer better service to its customers. "Our only sustainable competitive advantages," Rosenbluth maintains, "are the associates and the environment in which we work." Although his approach remains central to the company, by itself it would not continue to make the company successful in the radically new environment. The strategy that has worked begins with understanding the value that Rosenbluth International can give to its clients by helping them manage costs.

Rosenbluth relies heavily on an array of information technology-based services for implementing cost-effective business travel programs. First, at the level of the individual trip, it has lowered airline costs by developing a way to search for the lowest fares that will meet the requirements of the traveler. DACODA (Discount Analysis Containing Optimal Decision Algorithms) is Rosenbluth's yield-management system. Yield management enables airlines to fill their airplanes while obtaining the highest possible price per seat for a specified destination and departure time. DACODA reverses the process, focusing on the client company's optimal air program worldwide. One of its functions is to sort through all the complex airline databases, analyzing

their pricing and discounting schemes. Travelers are given a list of choices to select from within the time, date, and location parameters they have selected. Through its software, Rosenbluth also tracks and manages a series of qualitative preferences that can offer clients a better trip for the same cost. For example, the system combines personal preference information with flight data to enable many travelers to spend less time on the ground between connections. The software also maintains such data as seating preferences for each client, including traveler concerns about placement related to plane wings.

As client employees travel, much of their travel data, both booked and billed, is automatically stored in Rosenbluth's databases, making it very easy for travelers and their employers to record and monitor expenses. VISION is the proprietary Rosenbluth real-time software package that instantly collects client travel data. The traveler is presented with a simple, easy-to-use interface to enter, submit, and track expenses during the trip. This software package even enforces the client company's travel policies for each trip. It integrates the data regardless of where the reservation is made or which airline reservation system is used. This software is the source of management reports that are customized to meet client-specific needs. Thus, management can easily monitor and control all of its corporate travel and entertainment expenses. Rosenbluth will work with clients to develop a strategy that saves money at each stage of the procurement process for travel services.

Rosenbluth's Global Distribution Network (GDN) is a worldwide telecommunications network through which the airline reservation systems are accessible. All Rosenbluth agents are connected to GDN, as are most of the company's travel software applications. Clients planning trips can either use the network to research and book their travel arrangements, or they can work through a Rosenbluth agent. Moreover, clients can choose to use a local Rosenbluth agent, or they can turn to specific agents of their choice anywhere in the world.

Wal-Mart is a good example of a satisfied customer. Every traveler within the giant retailing company has access to a Rosenbluth reservation through a desktop or laptop computer connected to Wal-Mart's local area network. The company's 7,000 frequent travelers book their own hotel, air, and auto-rental reservations by calling up Rosenbluth's reservation system. They enter their name, travel dates, times, and cities of origin, destination, and stopover. Rosenbluth's software creates a grid of flight options that adhere to Wal-Mart travel policies. The employee clicks a few buttons and the reservations are completed. Some other companies accomplish the same thing by having their employees access Rosenbluth software through Rosenbluth's Web site. This approach is particularly cost effective for Rosenbluth clients because all the clients need to do is give their employees Web browser software and a connection to the Internet. Business travelers on the go can obtain information from the Web site, such as airline numbers or the location of restaurants and copy centers at their destinations, using a handheld Palm personal digital assistant.

In addition to helping clients, Rosenbluth has relied on technology to cut its own costs to the bone in order to survive. For example, Rosenbluth agents use the same software as clients so that they, too, can easily and quickly locate the lowest fares, book flights, and serve clients quickly. The company also has examined the working methods of their agents in order to find ways for them to work more efficiently. Rosenbluth noticed that his agents typed the same words over and over, so he ordered their computer interface be modified where possible to present prompts that required only "yes" and "no" responses. The developers also changed the programs to display the client company's travel guidelines on the screen so that the agent would not waste time creating options for a client that were outside the company guidelines. As a result of these changes, agents experienced a 75 percent reduction in keystrokes, a significant increase in productivity.

The global network also makes an enormous contribution to reducing Rosenbluth costs. Because of the network, it does not matter where the travel agent is physically located. As a result, Rosenbluth has been able to establish a series of centralized reservation centers known as "intellicenters." These centers are located in North Dakota, Delaware, and Pennsylvania, all locations where labor costs are low but the work ethic is high. Costs are low enough in these centers that Rosenbluth is able to offer clients a significant reduction in costs for booking through one of the intellicenters. The network also is managed so that if one reservation center becomes overloaded, excess calls are immediately and automatically routed to another center where current volume is lower. For example, during the great East Coast blizzard of January 1996, about 21,000 calls were rerouted without any problem. Customers did not even know they were being rerouted.

Rosenbluth has continued to expand its services for clients to take better advantage of the Web. A Web Fares Solution system for Rosenbluth's corporate clients automatically searches for cheap Web airfares and compares them with published or corporate negotiated fares so that firms can always obtain the best price. Travel managers can use Rosenbluth's data warehousing and reporting capabilities to evaluate the impact of Web fares on their overall travel program.

In August 1999, Rosenbluth announced the acquisition of Biztravel.com, an award-winning Web site for the planning and booking of business travel, and started targeting small and medium-size businesses that do not have their own travel departments. Medium and small businesses spending $5 million or less on travel each year comprise 60 percent of total annual corporate travel expenditures in the United States and thus represent a profitable new market for Rosenbluth to move into. Biztravel.com was unable to survive the sharp drop in travel after September 11, 2001 and ceased operations a few weeks after the terrorist attacks.

Rosenbluth is now trying to penetrate the medium and small business market through other means. It bundled some of its services for booking cost-effective reservations and for Web-based reporting into a packaged solution called e-PAC that can be quickly and easily implemented by small businesses. In June 2002, Rosenbluth announced a Net marketplace called Rosenbluth Exchange for procuring travel services. The Rosenbluth Exchange uses an electronic Request for Proposal (RFP) system that can capture companies' travel policy information and historical data to identify targeted discount areas. Travel suppliers can then bid for the company's business. Negotiations can take place online until a deal has been reached. By obtaining travel upgrades and discounted airfares that were previously available only to very large companies, smaller firms using Rosenbluth Exchange could achieve double-digit percentage savings.

Rosenbluth's new services even include one for helping clients figure out whether they need to travel in the first place. The company now provides "business interaction management" services designed to help clients achieve their business goals by identifying the best methods for connecting people and ideas. Using the results of research conducted by the Wharton School of the University of Pennsylvania, Rosenbluth will be able to help each client determine when and if a business trip is necessary. Rosenbluth agents can then provide alternatives such as videoconferencing or teleconferencing when travel is not necessary. Rosenbluth can earn revenue from these alternative services and offers an advanced teleconferencing suite called TeleSuite, which displays life-size images on screens. The technology is so lifelike that users can react to meeting participants in other locations as if they were all sitting in the same conference room. A TeleSuite session for an afternoon meeting costs around $600 per person compared with a business trip costing $2,000 or more. Sometimes employees such as sales staff should travel more and Rosenbluth's service will point that out to clients as well.

Hal Rosenbluth has said, "We've evolved from a travel management company to a business interaction management company. We view our job as 'connecting people.' Now we will not only connect people by planes or trains but we will connect them through technology."

Sources: Joe Sharkey, "When Having a Meeting Is Like Going to a Movie," *New York Times*, September 24, 2002; Christina Binkley, "Rosenbluth to Offer Tool to Help Companies Reduce Travel Costs," *Wall Street Journal*, April 22, 2002; Rosenbluth International, "Millions of Small and Mid-Sized Companies Can Now Save on the $66 Billion Spent Annually on Travel in the United Sates through Rosenbluth International Exchange," June 25, 2002; Rosenbluth International, "Rosenbluth International Brings 'Simplicity' to Travel Management," June 12, 2002; Aisha M. Williams, "Travel Service Helps Small Businesses Trim Expenses," *InformationWeek*, March 20, 2000; Jim Graham, "You Don't Have to Travel to Do Business," *USA Today*, February 9, 1999; and <www.rosenbluth.com>, accessed July 11, 2002.

CASE STUDY QUESTIONS

1. What problems did Rosenbluth Travel face? Analyze the company using the competitive forces and value chain models.

2. What competitive strategy did the company follow to address its problems? How effective is that strategy?

3. How do Rosenbluth's information systems and telecommunications technology fit in with and contribute to its strategy? How did these systems change the company's business processes? How do these systems provide value?

4. What management, organization, and technology issues were addressed when Rosenbluth implemented the DACODA, VISION, and its other systems?

THE INTERNET AND THE NEW INFORMATION TECHNOLOGY INFRASTRUCTURE

objectives

As a manager, you'll need to know how to maximize the benefits of Internet technology in your firm's information technology infrastructure. After reading this chapter, you will be able to answer the following questions:

1. *What is the new information technology (IT) infrastructure for business? Why is connectivity so important in this infrastructure?*

2. *How does the Internet work? What are its major capabilities?*

3. *How can organizations benefit from using the World Wide Web and Web technology? How can businesses benefit from the Wireless Web?*

4. *What are the principal technologies for supporting electronic commerce and electronic business?*

5. *What management problems are raised by the new information technology (IT) infrastructure? How can businesses solve these problems?*

Wireless Technology Comes to the Rescue for San Mateo Firefighters

Firefighters face a very hazardous job. When a fire call comes in to the firehouse, they must move quickly, have all equipment at hand, and know immediately what their assignments will be. Others need that information as well, including not only the other firefighters and emergency workers at the scene, but also fire department staff at dispatch centers. To expedite emergency dispatching, San Mateo County's Public Safety Commission has equipped all of its fire trucks with a Palm handheld computer with wireless access to the Web.

The software for this application was developed by Telecommunications Engineering Associates (TEA), which had created Web-based systems for public safety departments to let fire crews and citizens keep track of incidents in the community. TEA's CEO, Daryl Jones came up with the idea to add a wireless gateway to a Web site to help people in the field access real-time information about incidents. The Web site consolidates this real-time information and transmits it to authorized mobile wireless devices used by fire crews

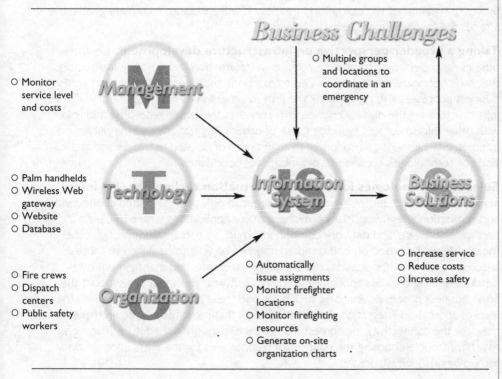

Business Challenges

○ Multiple groups and locations to coordinate in an emergency

Management
○ Monitor service level and costs

Technology
○ Palm handhelds
○ Wireless Web gateway
○ Website
○ Database

Organization
○ Fire crews
○ Dispatch centers
○ Public safety workers

Information System
○ Automatically issue assignments
○ Monitor firefighter locations
○ Monitor firefighting resources
○ Generate on-site organization charts

Business Solutions
○ Increase service
○ Reduce costs
○ Increase safety

When a call is made to one of two county dispatch centers, the relevant information is entered into a central database. The data are reformatted and supplied to authorized fire and public safety personnel along with information about any hazardous material on the premises. Battalion chief Richard Price uses information from FireDispatch.com to build an on-site organization chart showing each unit's assignment and each firefighter's position while fighting the fire. FireDispatch.com is a TEA application that uses streaming audio, video, digital images, and dynamic mapping to broadcast live fire department emergencies. That capability proved to be particularly valuable in late 2001 when Price used the system to determine the location of every firefighter when a building collapsed during a fire. If additional firefighters are required, Price can use the system to see what resources are still available throughout the county.

The original system was built for laptops, all of which had to be mounted on each fire truck. The installation on these trucks took eight weeks and cost about $10,000 each. When the system was redesigned for handheld devices, the total cost was less, and the handhelds proved much more portable and easy to use. None of the applications are complex and even the most technophobic fire chief can feel comfortable using the system.

Sources: Howard Baldwin, "2001 Mobile Master Awards for Enterprise Deployment," *M-BusinessDaily*, January 10, 2002; <www.firedispatch.com> and <www.tcomeng.com>.

277

MANAGEMENT CHALLENGES

Like the San Mateo County Public Safety Commission, many organizations are extending their information technology infrastructures to include mobile computing devices, access to the Internet, and electronic links to other organizations. Electronic commerce, electronic business, and the emerging digital firm require a new information technology infrastructure that can integrate information from a variety of sources and applications. However, using Internet technology and this new IT infrastructure to digitally enable the firm raises the following management challenges:

1. **Taking a broader perspective on infrastructure development.** Electronic business and electronic commerce require an information technology infrastructure that can coordinate commerce-related transactions and operational activities across business processes and perhaps link the firm to others in its industry. The new IT infrastructure for the digitally enabled firm connects the whole enterprise and links with other infrastructures, including those of other organizations and the public Internet. Management can no longer think in terms of isolated networks and applications, or technologies confined to organizational boundaries.

2. **Selecting technologies for the new information technology (IT) infrastructure.** Internet technology, XML, and Java can only provide limited connectivity and application integration. Many firms have major applications where disparate hardware, software, and network components must be coordinated through other means. Networks based on one standard may not be able to be linked to those based on another without additional equipment, expense, and management overhead. Integrating business applications requires software tools that can support the firm's business processes and data structures, and these may not always provide the level of application integration desired. Networks that meet today's requirements may lack the connectivity for domestic or global expansion in the future. Managers may have trouble choosing the right set of technologies for the firm's information technology (IT) infrastructure.

9.1 THE NEW INFORMATION TECHNOLOGY (IT) INFRASTRUCTURE FOR THE DIGITAL FIRM

Today's firms can use the information technologies we have described in previous chapters to create an information technology (IT) infrastructure capable of coordinating the activities of entire firms and even entire industries. By enabling companies to radically reduce their agency and transaction costs, this new IT infrastructure provides a broad platform for electronic commerce, electronic business, and the emerging digital firm. This new IT infrastructure is based on powerful networks and Internet technology.

ENTERPRISE NETWORKING AND INTERNETWORKING

Figure 9-1 illustrates the new information technology (IT) infrastructure. The new IT infrastructure uses a mixture of computer hardware supplied by different vendors. Large, complex databases that need central storage are found on mainframes or specialized servers, whereas smaller databases and parts of large databases are loaded on PCs and workstations. Client/server computing often is used to distribute more processing power to the desktop. The desktop itself has been extended to a larger workspace that includes programmable cell phones, PDAs, pagers, and other mobile computing devices. This new IT infrastructure also incorporates public infrastructures such as the telephone system, the Internet, and public network services. Internet technology plays a pivotal role in this new infrastructure as the principal communication channel with customers, employees, vendors, and distributors.

In the past, firms generally built their own software and developed their own computing facilities. As today's firms move toward this new infrastructure, their information systems departments are changing their roles to managers of software packages and software and networking services provided by outside vendors.

Figure 9-1 The new information technology (IT) infrastructure: The new IT infrastructure links desktop workstations, network computers, LANs, and server computers in an enterprise network so that information can flow freely throughout different parts of the organization. The enterprise network may also be linked to kiosks, point-of-sale (POS) terminals, PDAs, digital cellphones and PCS, and other mobile computing devices as well as to the Internet using public infrastructures. Customers, suppliers, and business partners may also be linked to the organization through this new IT infrastructure.

Through enterprise networking and internetworking, information flows smoothly between all of these devices within the organization and between the organization and its external environment. In **enterprise networking,** the organization's hardware, software, network, and data resources are arranged to put more computing power on the desktop and to create a company-wide network linking many smaller networks. The system is a network. In fact, for all but the smallest organizations, the system is composed of multiple networks. A high-capacity backbone network connects many local area networks and devices.

The backbone may be connected to the networks of other organizations outside the firm, to the Internet, to the networks of public telecommunication service providers, or to other public networks. The linking of separate networks, each of which retains its own identity, into an interconnected network is called **internetworking.**

STANDARDS AND CONNECTIVITY FOR DIGITAL INTEGRATION

The new IT infrastructure is most likely to increase productivity and competitive advantage when digitized information can move seamlessly through the organization's web of electronic networks, connecting different kinds of machines, people, sensors, databases, functional divisions, departments, and work groups. This ability of computers and computer-based devices to communicate with one another and "share" information in a meaningful way without human intervention is called **connectivity.** Internet technology, XML, and Java software provide some of this connectivity, but these technologies cannot be used as a foundation for all of the organization's information systems. Most organizations still use proprietary networks. They need to develop their own connectivity solutions to make different kinds of hardware, software, and communications systems work together.

Achieving connectivity requires standards for networking, operating systems, and user interfaces. Open systems promote connectivity because they enable disparate equipment and

enterprise networking
An arrangement of the organization's hardware, software, network, and data resources to put more computing power on the desktop and create a company-wide network linking many smaller networks.

internetworking
The linking of separate networks, each of which retains its own identity, into an interconnected network.

connectivity
A measure of how well computers and computer-based devices communicate and share information with one another without human intervention.

open systems

Software systems that can operate on different hardware platforms because they are built on public nonproprietary operating systems, user interfaces, application standards, and networking protocols.

Transmission Control Protocol/Internet Protocol (TCP/IP)

U.S. Department of Defense reference model for linking different types of computers and networks; used in the Internet.

services to work together. **Open systems** are built on public, nonproprietary operating systems, user interfaces, application standards, and networking protocols. In open systems, software can operate on different hardware platforms and in that sense can be "portable." Java software, described in Chapter 6, can create an open system environment. The UNIX operating system supports open systems because it can operate on many different kinds of computer hardware. However, there are different versions of UNIX and no one version has been accepted as an open systems standard. Linux also supports open systems.

Models of Connectivity for Networks

There are different models for achieving connectivity in telecommunications networks. The **Transmission Control Protocol/Internet Protocol (TCP/IP)** model was developed by the U.S. Department of Defense in 1972 and is used in the Internet. Its purpose was to help scientists link disparate computers. Figure 9-2 shows that TCP/IP has a five-layer reference model.

1. *Application:* Provides end-user functionality by translating the messages into the user/host software for screen presentation.

2. *Transmission Control Protocol (TCP):* Performs transport, breaking application data from the end user down into TCP packets called datagrams. Each packet consists of a header with the address of the sending host computer, information for putting the data back together, and information for making sure the packets do not become corrupted.

3. *Internet Protocol (IP):* The Internet Protocol receives datagrams from TCP and breaks the packets down further. An IP packet contains a header with address information and carries TCP information and data. IP routes the individual datagrams from the sender to the recipient. IP packets are not very reliable, but the TCP level can keep resending them until the correct IP packets get through.

4. *Network interface:* Handles addressing issues, usually in the operating system, as well as the interface between the initiating computer and the network.

5. *Physical net:* Defines basic electrical-transmission characteristic for sending the actual signal along communications networks.

Two computers using TCP/IP would be able to communicate even if they were based on different hardware and software platforms. Data sent from one computer to the other would pass downward through all five layers, starting with the sending computer's application layer and passing through the physical net. After the data reached the recipient host computer, they would travel up the layers. The TCP level would assemble the data into a format the receiving host computer could use. If the receiving computer found a damaged packet, it would ask the sending computer to retransmit it. This process would be reversed when the receiving computer responded.

Figure 9-2 The Transmission Control Protocol/Internet Protocol (TCP/IP) reference model. This figure illustrates the five layers of the TCP/IP reference model for communications.

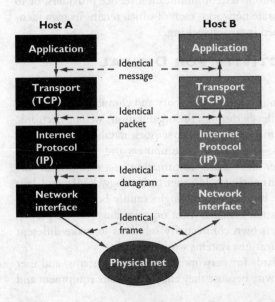

The **Open Systems Interconnect (OSI)** model is an alternative model developed by the International Standards Organization for linking different types of computers and networks. It was designed to support global networks with large volumes of transaction processing. Like TCP/IP, OSI enables a computer connected to a network to communicate with any other computer on the same network or a different network, regardless of the manufacturer, by establishing communication rules that permit the exchange of information between dissimilar systems. OSI divides the telecommunications process into seven layers.

Other connectivity-promoting standards have been developed for graphical user interfaces, electronic mail, packet switching, wireless networks, and electronic data interchange (EDI) (see Chapter 8). Any manager wishing to achieve some measure of connectivity in his or her organization should try to use these standards when designing networks, purchasing hardware and software, or developing information system applications.

Open Systems Interconnect (OSI)

International reference model for linking different types of computers and networks.

TECHNOLOGY AND BUSINESS STANDARDS WORK HAND-IN-HAND

Supply chain management systems, private exchanges and Net marketplaces enable companies to automate procurement of goods and services, but a surprising number of many firms can't fully benefit from their connectivity. About 30 percent of the data exchanged between suppliers and retailers doesn't match up, costing the consumer goods industry $40 billion each year. Orders placed electronically or manually based on erroneous or inconsistent information cannot be fulfilled, and must be placed over and over again until the information has been corrected and synchronized.

In the consumer goods business, identification numbers and product configurations change so frequently that manufacturers and retailers have an extremely hard time keeping product information up to date, especially if they order using paper, phone, and fax. "If a customer makes a one-digit error in the code for a product, they may repeatedly place orders for the product to be replenished and not receive it until they [or we] get on the phone and straighten that out," explains Milan Turk, P&G's director of customer e-business.

Proctor & Gamble (P&G) produces 60,000 items, and its record on each item contains many fields, including product identification number, description, and package size. Most retail customers use their own codes to maintain this information. When P&G changes existing products, it changes many fields, including identification numbers and product configurations, and it then notifies retailers of these new codes. Turk says it can currently take up to 5 weeks to distribute product data to retailers using conventional electronic document interchange (EDI), telephone, fax, or paper documents.

What is needed is a common product-description language, and one has just been developed for the retail industry. The Uniform Code Council Inc. of Lawrence, Kansas, a standards organization, has developed UCCnet Global Registry, a central product information registry and data synchronization hub, to standardize product names and description codes so

wholesalers and retailers can use the same data. The registry contains 62 data fields per product, such as manufacturer, part number, price, and package size, providing a common language for companies to talk about an item. UCCnet matches product data from across the industry in a single searchable database.

The WorldWide Retail Exchange and Transora have both decided to use the UCCnet registry, as have major retailers such as Wal-Mart Stores. The WorldWide Retail Exchange serves 62 of the largest retailers, while Transora is a manufacturer-founded exchange serving over 60 of the largest consumer products manufacturers. Transora hosts product catalogs for participating manufacturers, such as P&G and Hershey Foods, and offers services to synchronize these catalogs with the UCCnet registry, which catalogs the data for retailers. The data from the Transora catalog are converted into XML documents that are fed into UCCnet's systems.

The benefits for large consumer goods suppliers and retailers are very clear. Once both manufacturers such as P&G and its retail customers use the UCC data registry, the process of providing updated product information could take hours or minutes instead of days or weeks. One potential sticking point: companies may have to redesign and rebuild their databases to confirm with the UCCnet data standards, an expensive proposition for small companies.

To Think About: What are the organizational benefits of using UCCnet? What management, organization, and technology issues must be addressed in order to participate in UCCNet?

Sources: Steve Konicki, "Shopping for Savings," *InformationWeek*," July 1, 2002; Michael Meehan, "Big Retailers Push Data Ties," *Computerworld*, June 10, 2002; Brian Sullivan and Michael Meehan, "UCCnet Standard Could Squeeze Small Retail Suppliers," *Computerworld*, June 6, 2002; and Brian Sullivan and Michael Meehan "UCCnet's Promise: Synchronized Product Data, *Computerworld*, June 10 2002.

The Importance of Business Standards

Even if firms adopt the technologies we have just described they may not be able to solve their connectivity problems. Information cannot flow seamlessly from one system to another or one organization to another unless all interconnected applications use the same standards for representing data. Even if a firm has company-wide data standards, companies within the same industry may not be able to exchange data if their product descriptions do not correspond to those of other firms. This is one reason why manufacturers have not been able to achieve the level of interorganizational coordination of supply chain processes that they wish even though they have spent $1 billion on information technology since 1999 to make their supply chains more collaborative. Industry-wide standards for describing product data are starting to address this problem, as described in The Window on Organizations.

9.2   THE INTERNET: INFORMATION TECHNOLOGY INFRASTRUCTURE FOR THE DIGITAL FIRM

The Internet is perhaps the most well-known, and the largest, implementation of internetworking, linking hundreds of thousands of individual networks all over the world. The Internet has a range of capabilities that organizations are using to exchange information internally or to communicate externally with other organizations. Internet technology provides the primary infrastructure for electronic commerce, electronic business, and the emerging digital firm.

WHAT IS THE INTERNET?

The Internet began as a U.S. Department of Defense network to link scientists and university professors around the world. Even today individuals cannot connect directly to the Net, although anyone with a computer, a modem, and the willingness to pay a small monthly usage fee can access it through an Internet Service Provider. An **Internet Service Provider (ISP)** is a commercial organization with a permanent connection to the Internet that sells temporary connections to subscribers. Individuals also can access the Internet through such popular online services as America Online and Microsoft Network (MSN).

No one owns the Internet and it has no formal management organization. As a creation of the Defense Department for sharing research data, this lack of centralization was purposeful to make it less vulnerable to wartime or terrorist attacks. To join the Internet, an existing network needs only to pay a small registration fee and agree to certain standards based on the TCP/IP reference model. Costs are low. Each organization, of course, pays for its own networks and its own telephone bills, but those costs usually exist independent of the Internet. Regional Internet companies have been established to which member networks forward all transmissions. These Internet companies route and forward all traffic, and the cost is still only that of a local telephone call. The result is that the costs of e-mail and other Internet connections tend to be far lower than equivalent voice, postal, or overnight delivery, making the Internet a very inexpensive communications medium. It is also a very fast method of communication, with messages arriving anywhere in the world in a matter of seconds, or a minute or two at most. We now briefly describe the most important Internet capabilities.

INTERNET TECHNOLOGY AND SERVICES

The Internet is based on client/server technology. Individuals using the Internet control what they do through client applications, such as Web browser software. All the data, including e-mail messages and Web pages, are stored on servers. A client uses the Internet to request information from a particular Web server on a distant computer and the server sends the requested information back to the client via the Internet.

Client platforms today include not only PCs and other computers but also a wide array of handheld devices and information appliances, some of which can even provide wireless Internet access. An **information appliance** is a device such as an Internet-enabled cell phone or a TV Internet receiver for Web access and e-mail that has been customized to perform a few specialized computing tasks well with minimal user effort. Table 9-1 lists examples of some of these client platforms, most of which were described in Chapters 6 and 8. Experts believe that the role

Internet Service Provider (ISP)
A commercial organization, with a permanent connection to the Internet, that sells temporary connections to subscribers.

information appliance
Device that has been customized to perform a few specialized computing tasks well with minimal user effort.

TABLE 9-1   EXAMPLES OF INTERNET CLIENT PLATFORMS

Device	Description	Example
PC	General purpose computing platform that can perform many different tasks, but can be complex to use	Dell, Compaq, IBM PCs
Net PC	Network computer with minimal local storage and processing capability; designed to use software and services delivered over networks and the Internet	Sun Ray
Smart Phone	Has a small screen and keyboard for browsing the Web and exchanging e-mail in addition to providing voice communication	Nokia 8390
Video Game Console	Video game console with a modem, keyboard, and capabilities to function as a Web access terminal	Sega Dreamcast Microsoft Xbox
PDA	Wireless handheld personal digital assistant with e-mail and Internet service	Palm i705
Wireless E-Mail Handheld	Tablet with keyboard that provides textual e-mail capabilities. Requires linking to an e-mail service	BlackBerry
TV Internet Receiver	Provides Web surfing and e-mail capabilities using a television set, receiver, and a wireless keyboard	MSNTV

of the PC or desktop computer as the Internet client is diminishing as people turn to these easy-to-use specialized information appliances to connect to the Internet.

Servers dedicated to the Internet or even to specific Internet services are the heart of the information on the Net. Each Internet service is implemented by one or more software programs. All of the services may run on a single server computer, or different services may be allocated to different machines. There may be only one disk storing the data for these services, or there may be multiple disks for each type, depending on the amount of information being stored. Figure 9-3 illustrates one way that these services might be arranged in a multitiered client/server architecture.

Web server software receives requests for Web pages from the client and accesses the Web pages from the disk where they are stored. Web servers can also access other information from an organization's internal information system applications and their associated databases and return that information to the client in the form of Web pages if desired. Specialized middleware, including application servers, is used to manage the interactions between the Web server and the organization's internal information systems for processing orders, tracking inventory, maintaining product catalogs, and other electronic commerce functions. For example, if a customer filled out an online form on a Web page to order a product such as a light fixture, the middleware would translate the request on the Web page into commands that could be used by the company's internal order processing system and customer database.

The most important Internet services for business include e-mail, Usenet newsgroups, LISTSERVs, chatting, Telnet, FTP, and the World Wide Web. They can be used to retrieve and offer information. Table 9-2 lists these capabilities and describes the functions they support.

Communication on the Internet

The Internet provides an array of capabilities for electronic communication that can help companies reduce their communication costs.

Electronic Mail (E-Mail).   The Internet has become the most important e-mail system in the world because it connects so many people worldwide, creating a productivity gain that observers have compared to Gutenberg's development of movable type in the fifteenth century. Organizations use it to facilitate communication between employees and offices, and to communicate with customers and suppliers. Researchers use this facility to share ideas, information, even documents and graphic images. Businesses now treat e-mail as an essential communication and collaboration tool.

Figure 9-4 illustrates the components of an Internet e-mail address. The portion of the address to the left of the @ symbol in an e-mail address is the name or identifier of the specific individual or organization. To the right of the @ symbol is the domain name. The **domain name** is the name that identifies a unique node on the Internet. The domain name corresponds to a unique four-part numeric **Internet Protocol (IP) address** for each computer connected to the Internet.

domain name

The name identifying a unique node on the Internet.

Internet Protocol (IP) address

Four-part numeric address indicating a unique computer location on the Internet.

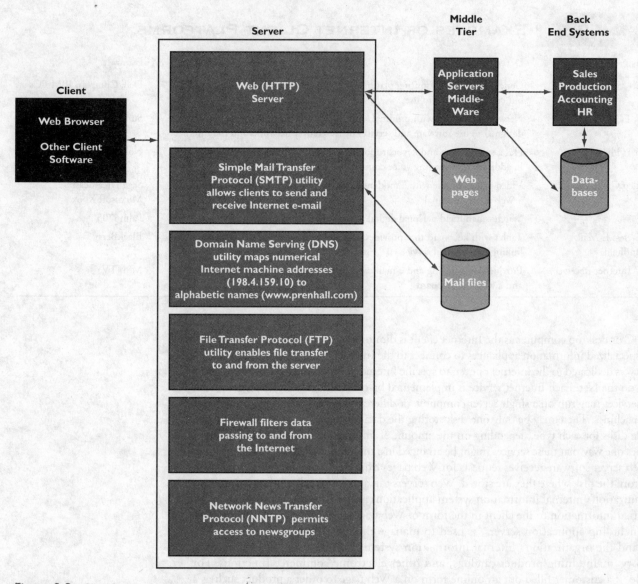

Figure 9-3 Client/server computing on the Internet. Client computers running Web browser and other software can access an array of services on servers via the Internet. These services may all run on a single server or on multiple specialized servers.

Domain Name System (DNS)

A hierarchical system of servers maintaining databases enabling the conversion of domain names to their IP addresses.

Usenet

Forums in which people share information and ideas on a defined topic through large electronic bulletin boards where anyone can post messages on the topic for others to see and to which others can respond.

(For example, the domain name *www.prenhall.com* has the IP address 198.4.159.10) A **Domain Name System (DNS)** maps domain names to their IP addresses.

The domain name contains subdomains separated by a period. The domain that is farthest to the right is the top-level domain, and each domain to the left helps further define the domain by network, department, and even specific computer. The top-level domain name may be either a country indicator or a function indicator, such as *com* for a commercial organization or *gov* for a government institution. All e-mail addresses end with a country indicator except those in the United States, which ordinarily do not use one. In Figure 9-4, *it*, the top-level domain, is a country indicator, indicating that the address is in Italy. *Edu* indicates that the address is an educational institution; *univpisa* (in this case, University of Pisa) indicates the specific location of the host computer.

Usenet Newsgroups (Forums)   **Usenet** newsgroups are worldwide discussion groups in which people share information and ideas on a defined topic such as radiology or rock bands. Discussion takes place in large electronic bulletin boards where anyone can post messages for others to read. Many thousands of groups exist discussing almost all conceivable topics. Each Usenet site is financed and administered independently.

TABLE 9-2   MAJOR INTERNET SERVICES

Capability	Functions Supported
E-mail	Person-to-person messaging; document sharing
Usenet newsgroups	Discussion groups on electronic bulletin boards
LISTSERVs	Discussion groups using e-mail mailing list servers
Chatting	Interactive conversations
Telnet	Log on to one computer system and do work on another
FTP	Transfer files from computer to computer
World Wide Web	Retrieve, format, and display information (including text, audio, graphics, and video) using hypertext links

LISTSERV   A second type of public forum, **LISTSERV,** allows discussions or messaging to be conducted through predefined groups but uses e-mail mailing list servers instead of bulletin boards for communications. If you find a LISTSERV topic you are interested in, you may subscribe. From then on, through your e-mail, you will receive all messages sent by others concerning that topic. You can, in turn, send a message to your LISTSERV and it will automatically be broadcast to the other subscribers. Tens of thousands of LISTSERV groups exist.

Chatting   **Chatting** allows two or more people who are simultaneously connected to the Internet to hold live, interactive conversations. Chat groups are divided into channels, and each is assigned its own topic of conversation. The first generation of chat tools was for written conversations in which participants type their remarks using their keyboard and read responses on their computer screen. Systems featuring voice chat capabilities, such as those offered by Yahoo! Chat, are now becoming popular.

A new enhancement to chat service called **instant messaging** even allows participants to create their own private chat channels. The instant messaging system alerts a person whenever someone on his or her private list is online so that the person can initiate a chat session with that particular individual. There are a number of competing instant messaging systems for consumers, including Yahoo! Messenger, MSN Messenger, and AOL Instant Messenger. Some of these systems can provide voice-based instant messages so that a user can click on a "talk" button and have an online conversation with another person. Companies concerned with security are building proprietary instant messaging systems using tools such as Lotus Sametime.

Chatting and instant messaging can be effective business tools if people who can benefit from interactive conversations set an appointed time to "meet" and "talk" on a particular topic. For instance, Totality, a San Francisco Web-service company, uses instant messaging to help team members collaborate more efficiently while working to keep clients' Web sites running smoothly (Bhattacharjee, 2002). Many online retailers are enhancing their Web sites with chat services to attract visitors, to encourage repeat purchases, and to improve customer service.

Telnet   **Telnet** allows someone to be on one computer system while doing work on another. Telnet is the protocol that establishes an error-free, rapid link between the two computers, allowing you, for example, to log on to your business computer from a remote computer when you are on the road or working from your home. You can also log in and use third-party computers that have been made accessible to the public, such as using the catalog of the

LISTSERV

Online groups using e-mail broadcast from mailing list servers for discussions or messaging.

chatting

Live, interactive conversations over a public network.

instant messaging

Chat service that allows participants to create their own private chat channels so that a person can be alerted whenever someone on his or her private list is online to initiate a chat session with that particular individual.

Telnet

Network tool that allows someone to log on to one computer system while doing work on another.

Figure 9-4 Analysis of an Internet address. In English, the e-mail address of physicist and astronomer Galileo Galilei would be translated as "G. Galileo, University of Pisa, educational institution, Italy." The domain name to the right of the @ symbol contains a country indicator, a function indicator, and the location of the host computer.

Nordstrom.com provides on-line chat capabilities to answer visitors' questions and to help them find items for which they are looking. This Web site can even display Web pages for products recommended by Nordstrom's customer service representative while the chat session is taking place.

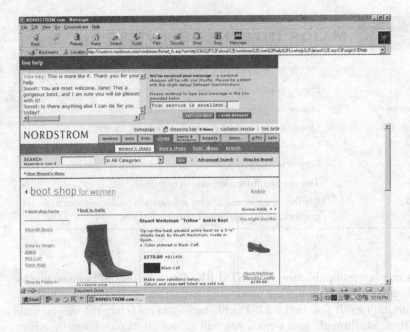

Internet telephony

Two-way voice transmission over the Internet using the Internet Protocols' packet-switched connections.

voice over IP (VoIP)

Voice transmission using the Internet Protocol (IP) in a private intranet or WAN.

virtual private network (VPN)

A secure connection between two points across the Internet to transmit data. Provides a low-cost alternative to a private network.

Figure 9-5 How IP telephony works. An IP phone call digitizes and breaks up a voice message into data packets that may travel along different routes before being reassembled at their final destination. A server nearest the call's destination, called a gateway, arranges the packets in the proper order and directs them to the telephone number of the receiver or the IP address of the receiving computer.
Source: "Using the Internet to Cut Phone Calls Down to Size" by David G. Wallace, *New York Times*, July 19, 2001.

U.S. Library of Congress. Telnet will use the computer address you supply to locate the computer you want to reach and connect you to it.

Internet Telephony   Hardware and software have been developed for **Internet telephony,** allowing companies to use the Internet for telephone voice transmission. (Internet telephony products sometimes are called IP telephony products.) IP telephony uses the Internet Protocol (IP) to deliver voice information in digital form using packet switching, avoiding the tolls charged by the circuit-switched telephone network (see Figure 9-5). IP telephony calls can be made and received with a desktop computer equipped with microphone and speakers or with a standard telephone or cell phone. When used in a private intranet or WAN, this technology is known as **voice over IP** (abbreviated **voIP**). New high-bandwidth networks will eliminate many of the early sound quality problems of this technology and enable the integration of voice with other Internet services.

Companies with multiple sites worldwide that are connected through a private or public IP network, or that have seasonally variable demand for voice services are the most likely to benefit initially from this technology (Varshney, Snow, McGivern, and Howard, 2002). Firms can also lower their network management costs by consolidating voice and data into a single communications infrastructure (see the Window on Technology). Businesses can use this technology for applications such as Internet conference calls using video or Web sites that allow users to reach a live customer service representative by clicking a link on a Web page.

Virtual Private Networks   Internet technology can also reduce communication costs by allowing companies to create virtual private networks as low-cost alternatives to private WANs. A **virtual private network (VPN)** is a secure connection between two points across the Internet, enabling private communications to travel securely over the public infrastructure. VPN services are available through Internet Service Providers (ISPs). The

SPORTS SOCCER SCORES WITH VOIP

The perturbed management at Sports Soccer found its staff spending too much time dealing with technology rather then on selling sports equipment. This 126-store sports retail chain in the United Kingdom and Belgium had immense communications problems, starting with telephone bills that surpassed £250,000 (approximately U.S. $375,000) each year because of the multiple telephone lines at most stores. In addition, customers were often frustrated when they had to wait an average of 24 seconds for a simple credit card approval, even for purchases as small as a T-shirt. Inventory replenishment was usually delayed because clogged transmission lines required each store to wait until late afternoon to transmit its daily store sales information via modems, leaving warehouse staff with insufficient time to finish their work. Headquarters also depended on closed circuit TV to transmit and receive important information to and from each store, further clogging corporate and store communication. To make matters worse, Sports Soccer is a growing corporation. What would adding more sites do to all of these vital communications?

After exploring various alternatives, the company settled on a wide area network (WAN) based on Cisco Systems' Architecture for Voice, Video, and Integrated Data (AVVID). This solution centralizes management of voice, data, and closed-circuit TV (CCTV) so that store employees are freed up to concentrate on customers. The new system also has adequate bandwidth to carry the traffic required.

The company installed Cisco's CallManager software to set up two redundant configurations in two separate headquarter buildings connected to two separate phone lines through different phone exchanges. Should one fail, the system can switch to the other. Once the basic network infrastructure had been built, 500 IP telephones were easily installed in Sports Soccer's head office and all its stores and automatically assigned appropriate local telephone numbers. The company decided to compress all voice calls to save bandwidth, an act that did not degrade the voices because of the high quality of the system.

The new system has reduced credit card transmission approval time to an acceptable average of eight seconds and has solved the stock replenishment problem. With adequate bandwidth, the central system is able to collect sales information in real time so that the central warehouse system can pick items that need replenishment throughout the day and ship them to individual stores in time for store openings the next day. The new system can also monitor information such as price changes occurring at checkout counters. If bandwidth-hungry video has to be transmitted over the WAN, Cisco's AVVID software enables the company to set priorities for the transmission of different types of IP traffic and applications. That way, the company can assign top priority to credit card transactions so that customer service is not degraded when the network is transmitting video. Sports Soccer's IT director John Ashley reported that using the VoIP network cost less than half of the other alternative solutions the company considered, such as installing PBX systems in every store.

Sports Soccer appears to be no exception. According to researchers, companies can lower their network management costs by consolidating voice and data into a single communications infrastructure while saving 50 percent or more on international voice and fax calls over an IP telephony network. The savings are especially clear for companies that make a large number of high-cost calls to developing nations. For example, VoIP technology helped Relativity Technologies, a North Carolina software company, cut $2,000 per month in telephone expenses. Relativity maintained skilled teams of software developers in Novosibirsk, Siberia and in St. Petersburg, Russia, and often needed to use the telephone to make two-hour conference calls with these groups. Relativity was able to reduce its international long distance charges to next to nothing by using VoIP software from Vedic Technologies for conference calling and by routing the calls over Relativity's IP network.

Think About: What are the business benefits of using VoIP? What management, technology, and organization issues did Sports Soccer have to address when implementing this technology?

Source: Rhonda Raider, "VoIP Bargain for Retailer," *Packet Magazine*, First Quarter 2002; and Rhonda Raider "Redialing Internet Telephony," *BusinessWeek Online*, May 1, 2002.

TECHNOLOGY

VPN provides many features of a private network at much lower cost than using private leased telephone lines or frame-relay connections. Companies can save on long-distance communication costs because workers can access remote locations for the cost of making a local call to an ISP.

There are several competing protocols used to protect data transmitted over the public Internet, including point-to-point tunneling protocol (PPTP). In a process called tunneling, packets of data are encrypted and wrapped inside IP packets so that non-IP data can travel through the Internet. By adding this "wrapper" around a network message to hide its content, organizations can create a private connection that travels through the public Internet.

Information Retrieval on the Internet

Information retrieval is a second basic Internet function. Many hundreds of library catalogs are online through the Internet, including those of such giants as the Library of Congress, the University of California, and Harvard University. In addition, users are able to search many thousands of databases that have been opened to the public by corporations, governments, and nonprofit organizations. Individuals can gather information on almost any conceivable topic stored in these databases and libraries. Many use the Internet to locate and download some of the free, quality computer software that has been made available by developers on computers all over the world.

file transfer protocol (FTP)
Tool for retrieving and transferring files from a remote computer.

FTP   **File transfer protocol (FTP)** is used to access a remote computer and retrieve files from it. FTP is a quick and easy method if you know the remote computer site where the file is stored. After you have logged on to the remote computer, you can move around directories that have been made accessible for FTP to search for the file(s) you want to retrieve. Once located, FTP makes transfer of the file to your own computer very easy.

NEXT GENERATION NETWORKS AND INTERNET2

The public Internet was not originally designed to handle massive quantities of data flowing through hundreds of thousands of networks. Experimental national research networks (NRNs) are developing high-speed next generation networks to address this problem. These private networks do not replace the public Internet, but provide test beds for leading-edge technology for research institutions, universities, and corporations that may eventually migrate to the public Internet. These technologies will make it possible for companies to distribute video, audio, three-dimensional simulations, or life-size video teleconferencing that are too data-intensive for today's public Internet without any degradation in performance. Table 9-3 describes the activities of some of these national research networks.

Internet2
Research network with new protocols and transmission speeds that provides an infrastructure for supporting high-bandwidth Internet applications.

In the United States Internet2 and Next Generation Internet (NGI) are NRN consortia representing 180 universities, private businesses, and government agencies working on a new robust high-bandwidth version of the Internet. The **Internet2** infrastructure is based on a series of interconnected *gigapops*, which are regional high-speed points-of-presence that serve as aggregation points for traffic from participating institutions. These gigapops in turn are connected to backbone networks with bandwidths exceeding 2.5 gigabits per second (Gbps). Internet2 connection speeds are in the hundreds of megabits per second range (Mbps), with at least 100 Mbps connections to servers and at least 10 Mbps to the desktop.

These research groups are developing protocols for permitting different quality-of-service levels. Today's Internet transmissions are "best effort"—packets of data arrive when they arrive without any regard to the priority of their contents. Different types of packets could be assigned different levels of priority as they travel over the network. For example, packets for applications such as videoconferencing, which need to arrive simultaneously without any break in service, would receive higher priority than e-mail messages, which do not have to be delivered instantaneously.

TABLE 9-3   EXAMPLES OF NATIONAL RESEARCH NETWORKS

National Research Network	Activities
6NET	European research network that is the world's largest test bed for Internet protocol version 6 (Ipv6), which greatly increases the number of available IP addresses.
Welsh Video Network	Runs across the SuperJANET network run by the United Kingdom Education and Research Networking Association and supports high-speed videoconferencing and other digital video for 80 universities and research facilities.
Asia Pacific Advanced Network	Pan-Asian network based in Japan that connects the national research networks of Australia, Hong Kong, Korea, the Philippines, Thailand, China, and Malaysia along with NRNs in Europe, Latin America, and North America.
CANARIE	Canadian project managing the CA*Net2 and CA*Net3 national research networks for developing leading-edge Internet capabilities.

The existing Internet is being enhanced to provide higher transmission speed, different levels of service, and increased security; the transition to next generation Internet technology will occur slowly (Weiser, 2001).

9.3 THE WORLD WIDE WEB

The World Wide Web (the Web) is at the heart of the explosion in the business use of the Internet. The Web is a system with universally accepted standards for storing, retrieving, formatting, and displaying information using a client/server architecture. The Web combines text, hypermedia, graphics, and sound. It can handle all types of digital communication while making it easy to link resources that are half-a-world apart. The Web uses graphical user interfaces for easy viewing. It is based on a standard hypertext language called hypertext markup language (HTML), which formats documents and incorporates dynamic links to other documents and pictures stored in the same or remote computers. (We described HTML in Chapter 6.) Using these links, the user need only point at a highlighted key word or graphic, click on it, and immediately be transported to another document, probably on another computer somewhere else in the world. Users are free to jump from place to place following their own logic and interest.

Web browser software is programmed according to HTML standards (see Chapter 6). The standard is universally accepted, so anyone using a browser can access any of millions of Web sites. Browsers use hypertext's point-and-click ability to navigate or *surf*—move from site to site on the Web—to another desired site. The browser also includes an arrow or back button to enable the user to retrace his or her steps, navigating back, site by site.

Those who offer information through the Web must establish a **home page**—a text and graphical screen display that usually welcomes the user and explains the organization that has established the page. For most organizations, the home page will lead the user to other pages, with all the pages of a company being known as a Web site. For a corporation to establish a presence on the Web, therefore, it must set up a Web site of one or more pages. Most Web pages offer a way to contact the organization or individual. The person in charge of an organization's Web site is called a **Webmaster.**

To access a Web site, the user must specify a **uniform resource locator (URL),** which points to the address of a specific resource on the Web. For instance, the URL for Prentice Hall, the publisher of this text, is http://www.prenhall.com. *Http* stands for **hypertext transport protocol,** which is the communications standard used to transfer pages on the Web. Http defines how messages are formatted and transmitted and what actions Web servers and browsers should take in response to various commands. *Prenhall.com* is the domain name identifying the Web server storing the Web pages.

SEARCHING FOR INFORMATION ON THE WEB

Locating information on the Web is a critical function; billions of Web pages are in existence, and this number will quickly double. No comprehensive catalog of Web sites exists. The principal methods of locating information on the Web are Web site directories, search engines, and broadcast or "push" technology.

Several companies have created directories of Web sites and their addresses, providing search tools for finding information. Yahoo! is an example. People or organizations submit sites of interest, which then are classified. To search the directory, you enter one or more key words and then see displayed a list of categories and sites with those key words in the title.

Other search tools do not require Web sites to be preclassified and will search Web pages on their own automatically. Such tools, called **search engines,** can find Web sites that may be little known. They contain software that looks for Web pages containing one or more of the search terms; then they display matches ranked by a method that usually involves the location and frequency of the search terms. (Some search engine sites use human experts to help with the ranking.) These search engines create indexes of the Web pages they visit. The search engine software then locates Web pages of interest by searching through these indexes. Some search engines are more comprehensive or current than others, depending on how their components are tuned, and some also classify Web sites by subject categories. Google uses special

home page
A World Wide Web text and graphical screen display that welcomes the user and explains the organization that has established the page.

Webmaster
The person in charge of an organization's Web site.

uniform resource locator (URL)
The address of a specific resource on the Internet.

hypertext transport protocol
The communications standard used to transfer pages on the Web. Defines how messages are formatted and transmitted.

search engine
A tool for locating specific sites or information on the Internet.

AltaVista provides a powerful search engine for accessing Web information resources, including images, video, and audio files as well as text. Users can search for sites of interest by entering key words or by exploring the categories.

software that indexes and ranks sites based on relevance measured by the number of users who access them and the number of outside links to a particular page. Specialized search engines are also available to help users locate specific types of information easily. For example, PubMed specializes in searches for articles in medical journals. Some Web sites for locating information such as Yahoo! and AltaVista have become so popular and easy to use that they also serve as portals for the Internet (see Chapter 4).

There are two ways of identifying Web pages to be tracked by search engines. One is to have Web page owners register their URLs with search engine sites. The other is to use software agents known as spiders, bots, and Web crawlers to traverse the Web and identify the Web pages for indexing. Chapter 10 details the capabilities of software agents with built-in intelligence, which can also help users search the Internet for shopping information. **Shopping bots** can help people interested in making a purchase filter and retrieve information about products of interest, evaluate competing products according to criteria they have established, and negotiate with vendors for price and delivery terms (Maes, Guttman, and Moukas, 1999). Many of these shopping agents search the Web for pricing and availability of products specified by the user and return a list of sites that sell the item along with pricing information and a purchase link. Table 9-4 compares various types of electronic commerce agents.

Broadcast and "Push" Technology

Instead of spending hours surfing the Web, users can have the information they are interested in delivered automatically to their desktops through **"push" technology.** A computer

shopping bot

Software with varying levels of built-in intelligence to help electronic commerce shoppers locate and evaluate products or services they might wish to purchase.

"push" technology

Method of obtaining relevant information on networks by having a computer broadcast information directly to the user based on prespecified interests.

TABLE 9-4	EXAMPLES OF ELECTRONIC COMMERCE AGENTS
Agent	Description
MySimon	Real-time shopping bot that searches more than 1,000 affiliated and unaffiliated merchants in 90 categories.
BestBookBuys.com	Shopping bot searches 26 online bookstores to help users find the lowest prices for titles they specify.
Bottom Dollar	Bot simultaneously queries many online retailers to obtain the best prices for products specified by the user.
Valuefind	Searches for the best deal from retail vendors, auctions, and classified ads. Users can limit the search to a specific price range and to certain Web sites.

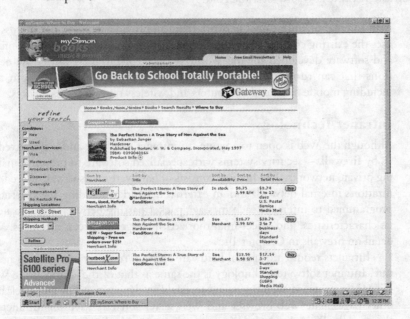

MySimon features a shopping bot that can search Internet retailers for price and availability of products specified by the user. Displayed here are the results of a search of prices and sources for a popular book.

broadcasts information of interest directly to the user, rather than having the user "pull" content from Web sites.

Special client software allows the user to specify the categories of information he or she wants to receive, such as news, sports, financial data, and so forth, and how often this information should be updated. After finding the kind of information requested, push server programs serve it to the push client. The streams of information distributed through push technology are known as channels. Microsoft's Internet Explorer and Netscape Communicator include push tools that automatically download Web pages, inform the user of updated content, and create channels of user-specified sites. Using push technology to transmit information to a select group of individuals is one example of **multicasting.** (LISTSERVs sending e-mail to members of specific mailing lists is another.)

Online marketplaces and exchanges can use push services to alert buyers to price change and special deals. Companies are using internal push channels to broadcast important information, such as price updates or new competitor products, on their own private networks.

multicasting
Broadcasting data to a selected group of recipients.

INTRANETS AND EXTRANETS

Organizations can use Internet networking standards and Web technology to create private networks called *intranets*. We introduced intranets in Chapter 1, explaining that an intranet

MicroStrategy's Narrowcast Server uses "push" technology to automatically deliver information on topics of interest to users via the Web, e-mail, pagers, or mobile phones.

is an internal organizational network that can provide access to data across the enterprise. It uses the existing company network infrastructure along with Internet connectivity standards and software developed for the World Wide Web. Intranets can create networked applications that can run on many different kinds of computers throughout the organization, including mobile handheld computers and wireless remote access devices.

Intranet Technology

Although the Web is open to anyone, an intranet is private and is protected from public visits by **firewalls**—security systems with specialized software to prevent outsiders from invading private networks. The firewall consists of hardware and software placed between an organization's internal network and an external network, including the Internet. The firewall is programmed to intercept each message packet passing between the two networks, examine its characteristics, and reject unauthorized messages or access attempts. We provide more detail on firewalls in Chapter 14.

Intranets require no special hardware and can run over any existing network infrastructure. Intranet software technology is the same as that of the World Wide Web. Intranets use HTML to program Web pages and to establish dynamic, point-and-click hypertext links to other pages. The Web browser and Web server software used for intranets are the same as those on the Web. A simple intranet can be created by linking a client computer with a Web browser to a computer with Web server software via a TCP/IP network. A firewall keeps unwanted visitors out.

Extranets

Some firms are allowing people and organizations outside the firm to have limited access to their internal intranets. Private intranets that are extended to authorized users outside the company are called *extranets*, which we also introduced in Chapter 1. For example, authorized buyers could link to a portion of a company's intranet from the public Internet to obtain information about the cost and features of its products. The company can use firewalls to ensure that access to its internal data is limited and remains secure; firewalls can also authenticate users, making sure that only authorized people can access the site.

Extranets are especially useful for linking organizations with suppliers, customers, or business partners. They often are used for collaborating with other companies for supply chain management, product design and development, or training efforts. Private industrial networks are based on extranets. Figure 9-6 illustrates one way that an extranet might be set up.

THE WIRELESS WEB

Chapter 8 described how wireless LAN technology can be used to access the Internet from an untethered PC or handheld computing device. This is one aspect of the wireless Web, but users can only access the Web if they are in range of their wireless networks. The term **Wireless Web** is more often applied to technologies that allow Internet-enabled cell phones, PDAs, and other wireless computing devices to access digital information from the Internet

Sidebar definitions

firewall
Hardware and software placed between an organization's internal network and an external network to prevent outsiders from invading private networks.

Wireless Web
Technologies enabling users to access digital information from the Internet using wireless mobile computing devices.

Figure 9-6 Model of an extranet. In this model of an extranet, selected customers, suppliers, and business partners can access a company's private intranet from the public Internet. A firewall allows access only to authorized outsiders.

Kyocera's smart phone can be used for wireless e-mail and Web surfing as well as for voice communication. Shown here is a Web page that has been specially formatted for small display screens on handheld mobile devices.

from any location. Mobile Internet access from wireless devices will not replace Internet access through PCs, but it will enable millions of people to obtain Web information services wherever they go. Businesses will increasingly incorporate wireless Internet access into their information technology infrastructures so that employees can access information wherever they are and make decisions instantly without being tethered to a desk or computer.

Figure 9-7 illustrates how business processes using this wireless technology can become more efficient. First Service Networks (FSN), a national maintenance contractor based in Stamford, Connecticut, was hampered by its manual call center network, manual dispatch of independent service technicians, and manual invoicing process. Coordinating thousands of local subcontractors often strained the company's 15-person customer service call center. To solve this problem FSN revamped its IT infrastructure to link Web-enabled mobile phones to its customer relationship management (CRM) and financial applications.

Clients have three alternative ways of notifying FSN—via telephone by entering a service call, over the Internet, or by using a remote sensing device that automatically signals the system when there is a problem. Siebel Systems Field Service software automatically routes

Figure 9-7   Before-after diagram of change in First Service Networks' business processes. By wirelessly automating most service requests, FSN can handle five times as many service requests without increasing its call center staff and respond more quickly to customers and contract repair staff.
Source: "Cutting Cost with Direct Customers," *mBusiness* 10/01 p. 36. Used with permission.

service requests accompanied by the history of the equipment being serviced to the mobile phone of the appropriate local contractor. Upon receiving the service request as an electronic message on their mobile phones, the repair technicians enter their estimated arrival time using their mobile phone keypads. This information is immediately transmitted to FSN's main server for both FSN and its customers to view on the Web. Once the service technicians arrive on the job and determine the needed repairs, they use their phones to key in service status and service codes for transmittal to FSN's server and online review and approval by the client and FSN. After the work is completed, the service technician electronically initiates an invoice, which is transmitted back to FSN's home office for approval.

With the old telephone-based system, FSN might not receive bills from subcontractors until 12 weeks after the work was finished. The new system passes information on the completed repair directly from the customer site to FSN's financial software, so that the contractor can be paid within 30 days. About 80 percent of service requests can now be handled without the old call center, so that each customer service employee can handle five times more requests than in the past.

Web content is being reformatted for wireless devices, and new content and services are being developed specifically for those devices. Specialized portals can steer users of Web-enabled wireless devices to the information they are most likely to need.

Chapter 4 introduced *m-commerce*—the use of the Internet for purchasing goods and services as well as for transmitting messages using handheld wireless devices. Table 9-5 describes what are likely to be the most popular categories of m-commerce services and applications. Location-based applications are of special interest because they take advantage of the unique capabilities of mobile technology. Whenever a user is connected to the Internet via a wireless device (cell phone, PDA, laptop), the transmission technology can be leveraged to determine that person's location and beam location-specific services or product information. For example, drivers could use this capability to obtain local weather data and traffic information along with alternate route suggestions and descriptions of nearby restaurants.

Although m-commerce is just starting up in the United States, millions of users in Japan and Scandinavia already use cell phones to purchase goods, trade files, exchange short text messages, and obtain updated weather and sports reports.

Wireless Web Standards

There are a plethora of standards governing every area of wireless communications. The two main standards for the Wireless Web are Wireless Application Protocol (WAP) and I-mode (see Figure 9-8).

Wireless Application Protocol (WAP) is a system of protocols and technologies that lets cell phones and other wireless devices with tiny display screens, low-bandwidth connections, and minimal memory access Web-based information and services. WAP uses **WML (Wireless Markup Language),** which is based on XML (see Chapter 6) and optimized for tiny displays. A person with a WAP-compliant phone uses the built-in microbrowser to make

Wireless Application Protocol (WAP)

System of protocols and technologies that lets cell phones and other wireless devices with tiny displays, low-bandwidth connections, and minimal memory access Web-based information and services.

WML (Wireless Markup Language)

Markup language for wireless Web sites; based on XML and optimized for tiny displays.

TABLE 9-5	M-COMMERCE SERVICES AND APPLICATIONS

Type of M-Commerce Service	Applications
Information-based services	Instant messaging, e-mail, searching for a movie or restaurant using a cell phone or handheld PDA
Transaction-based services	Purchasing stocks, concert tickets, music, or games; searching for the best price of an item using a cell phone and buying it in a physical store or on the Web
Personalized services	Services that anticipate what you want based on your location or data profile, such as updated airline flight information or beaming coupons for nearby restaurants

Figure 9-8 WAP versus I-Mode. WAP and I-mode are two competing standards for accessing information from the Wireless Web.

a request in WML. A **microbrowser** is an Internet browser with a small file size that can work with the low-memory constraints of handheld wireless devices and the low bandwidth of wireless networks. The request is passed to a WAP gateway, which retrieves the information from an Internet server in either standard HTML format or WML. The gateway translates HTML content back into WML so that it can be received by the WAP client. The complexity of the translation process can affect the speed of information delivery. WAP supports most wireless network standards and operating systems for handheld computing devices such as PalmOS and Windows CE.

I-mode is a rival standard developed by Japan's NTT DoCoMo mobile phone network; it is widely used in Japan and is being introduced to Europe. I-mode uses compact HTML to deliver content, making it easier for businesses to convert their HTML Web sites to mobile service. I-mode uses packet switching, which allows users to be constantly connected to the network and content providers to broadcast relevant information to users. (WAP users have to dial in to see if a site has changed.) I-mode can handle color graphics not available on WAP handsets, although WAP is being modified to handle color graphics.

M-Commerce Challenges

Rollout of m-commerce services has not been as rapid in the United States as in Japan and Europe. Keyboards and screens on cell phones are tiny and awkward to use. The data transfer speeds on existing wireless networks are very slow, ranging from 9.6 to 14.4 kilobits per second (Kbps), compared to 56 Kbps for a dial-up connection to the Internet via a PC. Each second waiting for data to download costs the customer money. Most Internet-enabled phones have minimal memory and limited power supplies. Web content for wireless devices is primarily in the form of text with very little graphics. Not enough Web sites have reconfigured their services to display only the few lines of text that can be accommodated by cell phone screens.

Unlike Europe, U.S. wireless networks are based on several incompatible technologies. (Europe uses the GSM standard, whereas wireless carriers in the United States primarily use CDMA or TDMA standards.) For the Wireless Web to take off, more Web sites need to be designed specifically for wireless devices that are more Web friendly.

Some of the limitations of m-commerce may be overcome by using voice recognition and personalization technology. **Voice portals** accept voice commands for accessing information from the Web. Voice portals offer customers a combination of content and services, with users accessing the content by speaking into a telephone. The user can orally request

microbrowser

Web browser software with a small file size that can work with low-memory constraints, tiny screens of handheld wireless devices, and low bandwidth of wireless networks.

I-mode

Standard developed by Japan's NTT DoCoMo mobile phone network for enabling cell phones to receive Web-based content and services.

voice portal

Portal that can accept voice commands for accessing information from the Web.

information, such as stock quotes, weather reports, airlines schedules, or news stories. For example, TellMe provides direct access to the Web using voice commands so that users can contact taxis, hotels, and friends as well as obtain weather reports, ski reports, and traffic information. Sophisticated voice recognition software processes the requests, which are translated back into speech for the customer. Personalization technology can organize and filter Web content so that only the information of greatest relevance to users appears on wireless display screens (Billsus et al., 2002).

M-commerce will also benefit from faster wireless networks. Cellular network providers are speeding up their services, preparing new versions of the three main digital standards to double their speed. Third-generation (3G) mobile communication networks will offer transmission speeds ranging from several hundred Kbps to 2 Mbps, depending on the nature of the application. Faster wireless networks will make it possible to stream high-quality video and audio to mobile devices along with new services.

Businesses will need to review all of these issues when determining the role of Wireless Web technology in their business strategy. The Manager's Toolkit provides questions to guide management analysis.

9.4   SUPPORT TECHNOLOGY FOR ELECTRONIC COMMERCE AND ELECTRONIC BUSINESS

Businesses seriously pursuing electronic commerce and electronic business need special tools for maintaining their Web sites. These tools include Web server and electronic commerce server software, customer tracking and personalization tools, Web content management tools, and Web site performance monitoring tools.

WEB SERVERS AND ELECTRONIC COMMERCE SERVERS

In Chapter 6 we introduced Web servers as the software necessary to run Web sites, intranets, and extranets. The core capabilities of Web server software revolve around locating and managing stored Web pages. Web server software locates the Web pages requested by client computers by translating the URL Web address into the physical file address for the requested Web page. The Web server then sends the requested pages to the client. Many Web servers also include tools for authenticating users, support for file transfer protocol (FTP), search engines and indexing programs, and capabilities for capturing Web site visitor information in log files. (Each request to the server for a file is recorded as an entry in the Web server log and is called a **hit**.) Apache HTTP Server and Microsoft's Internet Information Services (IIS) are currently the most popular Web servers. Management will have to examine carefully the servers available in order to determine which server offers the functionality that best fits the needs of its site.

hit

An entry into a Web server's log file generated by each request to the server for a file.

MIS IN ACTION: MANAGER'S TOOLKIT

HOW TO INTEGRATE THE WIRELESS WEB INTO BUSINESS STRATEGY

Some businesses will benefit from incorporating the Wireless Web into their business strategy; other may not. Before investing heavily in Wireless Web technology and m-commerce, here are some key questions to ask:

1. *Wireless value proposition:* Does adopting wireless technology enhance the company's existing business model? Can using wireless technology produce substantial gains in sales, customer loyalty, or customer service?

2. *User benefits:* Does using the wireless technology provide a valuable service to the user? How valuable is this service? Does it save customers or employees substantial amounts of time?

3. *Rationale for switching:* Does the wireless technology create a product, service, or business process improvement that is so compelling that it will be enthusiastically adopted? How willing would users be to give up working at their desktops to use the new mobile technology?

4. *Business process change:* What business processes will change as a result of using wireless technology? What jobs and work practices will be affected? Will these changes be easy to make? Will employees require additional training in order to use the new technology? Will business processes of customers and suppliers have to change as well as those of the firm?

Web server computers range in size from small desktop PCs to mainframes, depending on the size of the Web sites. The Web server computer must be large enough to handle the Web server software and the projected traffic of the particular site.

Servers differ in the number of simultaneous users they can handle, how quickly they can service their requests, and the technologies they support in Web applications. Server scalability is a major issue if a company is looking forward to rapid growth.

Specialized **electronic commerce server software** provides functions essential for e-commerce Web sites, often running on computers dedicated to this purpose. Functions the software must perform for both business-to-consumer and business-to-business e-commerce include:

electronic commerce server software
Software that provides functions essential for running e-commerce Web sites, such as setting up electronic catalogs and storefronts, and mechanisms for processing customer purchases.

- Setting up electronic storefronts and electronic catalogs to display product and pricing information.
- Designing electronic shopping carts so customers can collect and pay for the items they wish to purchase.
- Making shipping arrangements.
- Linking to electronic payment processing systems.
- Displaying product availability and tracking shipments.
- Connecting to back-office systems where necessary.

Systems designed for small business-to-consumer (B2C) e-commerce usually include wizards and templates to aid in the setting up of the storefronts and catalogs. However, high-end B2C and B2B systems, such as Microsoft's Commerce Server and IBM's WebSphere Commerce Suite, require the help of IT professionals for installation and support.

CUSTOMER TRACKING AND PERSONALIZATION TOOLS

Customer tracking and personalization tools have several main goals:

- Collecting and storing data on the behavior of online customers and combining that data with data already stored in the company's back-office systems.
- Analyzing the data in order better to understand the behavior of online customers.
- Identifying customer preferences and trends.

Chapter 4 described some of the benefits of personalizing Web sites to deliver content specific to each user. Online personalization systems often use **clickstream tracking** tools to collect data on customer activities at Web sites and store them in a log. The tools record the site that users last visited before coming to your Web site and where these users go when they leave your site. They also record the specific pages visited on your site, the time spent on each page of the site, the types of pages visited, and what the visitors purchased. Web sites can also populate databases with explicit data gained when visitors fill out registration forms on the site or purchase products.

clickstream tracking
Tracking data about customer activities at Web sites and storing them in a log.

Collaborative filtering software tracks users' movements on a Web site, comparing the information it gains about a user's behavior against data about other customers with similar interests to predict what the user would like to see next. The software then makes recommendations to users based on their assumed interests. For example, Amazon.com uses collaborative filtering software to prepare personalized book recommendations: "Customers who bought this book also bought . . . ."

collaborative filtering
Tracking users' movements on a Web site, comparing the information gleaned about a user's behavior against data about other customers with similar interests to predict what the user would like to see next.

Segmentation and rules-based systems use business rules to deliver certain types of information based on a user's profile, classifying users into smaller groups or segments based on these rules. The software uses demographic, geographic, income, or other information to divide, or segment, large populations into smaller groups for targeted content. Broadvision's electronic commerce system for offering personalized content to Web site visitors is a rules-based product.

Data collected from Web site visitors can be stored in databases or data warehouses where the data can be more easily analyzed to unearth customer preferences and trends. Some of these databases combine clickstream data with data from back-office systems and relevant external data to gain a fuller understanding of each customer. Chapter 11 provides additional detail on Web customer data analysis.

WEB CONTENT MANAGEMENT TOOLS

Web content management tools

Software to facilitate the collection, assembly, and management of content on a Web site, intranet, or extranet.

Web content management tools exist because many companies have sites with thousands or hundreds of thousands of pages to manage, a task too great for a Webmaster. Web content management software has emerged to assist the Webmaster and other authorized staff in the collection, assembly, and management of content on a Web site, intranet, or extranet.

Dynamic page generation

Technology for storing the contents of Web pages as objects in a database rather where they can be accessed and assembled to create constantly changing Web pages.

The materials on Web sites are often very complex and include many forms of data such as documents, graphics, and sound. Often the content must be dynamic, and parts of it must be capable of changing, depending on circumstances such as the identification of the visitor, the day of the month, the price of a product, or the requests of the visitor. **Dynamic page generation** tools store the contents of Web pages as objects in a database rather than as static HTML documents. When a user requests a Web page, the contents of the page are fetched from the database. Web content management tools help users organize and modify this material when needed, and ensure that only those responsible for the specific content are able to update or change it.

WEB SITE PERFORMANCE MONITORING TOOLS

Most Web sites are plagued by problems such as slow performance, major outages, content errors, broken links between Web pages, transaction failures, and slow-loading pages. To address these problems, companies can use their own **Web site performance monitoring tools** or rely on Web site performance monitoring services.

Web site performance monitoring tools

Software tools for monitoring the time to download Web pages and perform Web transactions, identifying broken links between Web pages, and pinpointing other Web site problems and bottlenecks.

Web site performance monitoring tools measure the response times of specific transactions such as inquiries, checking out purchases, or authorizing credit through a credit card. They can pinpoint the location of bottlenecks that slow down a Web site, such as at the Web or application server, a specific database, or a network router. Some tools test the site scalability through stressing the site by creating many test site visitors. Some tools also identify the causes for slow page loading speeds, such as loading too many banners, too many dense graphics files, or disk-space problems.

WEB HOSTING SERVICES

Web hosting service

Company with large Web server computers to maintain the Web sites of fee-paying subscribers.

Companies that lack the financial or technical resources to operate their own Web sites or electronic commerce services can use Web hosting services. A **Web hosting service** maintains a large Web server computer or series of servers and provides fee-paying subscribers with space to maintain their Web sites. The subscribing companies may create their own Web pages or have the hosting service or a Web design firm create them. Some services offer *co-location*, in which the firm actually purchases and owns the server computer housing its Web site, but locates the server in the physical facility of the hosting service.

The AlertSite Web Site Monitoring System monitors Web sites and other Internet-connected devices to ensure that they are performing optimally. Displayed here is one of its reports showing hourly changes in Web site response time (in seconds).

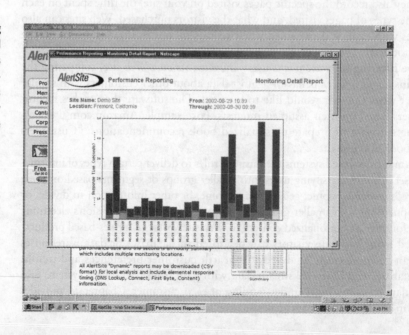

Companies can also use specialized e-commerce application service providers to set up and operate their e-commerce sites or intranets. Companies such as FreeMerchant.com, Yahoo! Store, and Bigstep.com provide low-cost e-commerce sites to small businesses with very simple e-commerce requirements that can use a predefined template for displaying and selling their wares.

Web hosting services offer solutions to small companies that do not have the resources to operate their own Web sites or to companies that still are experimenting with electronic commerce. Such services cost much less than running one's own Web site, and the hosting services have technical staff who can design, develop, manage, and support the site.

Many large companies use Web hosting services because they offer highly experienced technical staff and servers in multiple global locations, and backup server capacity to ensure 100 percent Web site availability. Companies such as IBM Global Services and Electronic Data Systems Corporation (EDS) provide fully managed Web hosting services. High-end managed hosting can range from $50,000 to $1 million per month.

9.5 MANAGEMENT ISSUES AND DECISIONS

An information technology infrastructure for digitally enabling the enterprise requires coordinating many different types of computing and networking technologies, public and private infrastructures, and organizational processes. Careful management and planning are essential.

THE CHALLENGE OF MANAGING THE NEW INFORMATION TECHNOLOGY INFRASTRUCTURE

Implementing enterprise networking and the new information technology (IT) infrastructure has created problems as well as opportunities for organizations. Managers need to address these problems to create an IT infrastructure for digitally enabling their firms.

E-commerce and e-business are forcing companies to reassess their information technology infrastructures in order to remain competitive. Many organizations are saddled with a maze of old legacy applications, hardware, and networks that don't talk to each other. In order to support enterprise-wide business processes that can smoothly link to customers or suppliers via the Internet, they must rebuild their information architectures and information technology infrastructures. Five problems stand out: loss of management control over information systems, connectivity and application integration challenges, the need for organizational change, the hidden costs of enterprise computing, and the difficulty of ensuring infrastructure scalability, reliability, and security (see Table 9-6).

Loss of Management Control

Managing information systems technology and corporate data are proving much more difficult in a distributed environment because of the lack of a single, central point where needed management can occur. Distributed client/server networks, new mobile wireless networks, and Internet computing have empowered end users to become independent sources of computing power capable of collecting, storing, and disseminating data and software. Data and software no longer are confined to the mainframe and under the management of the traditional information systems department, but reside on many different computing platforms throughout the organization.

TABLE 9-6   **PROBLEMS POSED BY THE NEW INFORMATION TECHNOLOGY (IT) INFRASTRUCTURE**

Loss of management control over systems

Connectivity and application integration challenges

Organizational change requirements

Hidden costs of enterprise computing

Scalability, reliability, and security

An enterprise-wide information technology infrastructure requires that the business know where all of its data are located and ensure that the same piece of information, such as a product number, is used consistently throughout the organization (see Chapter 7). These data may not always be in a standard format or may reside on incompatible computing platforms. However, observers worry that excess centralization and management of information resources will reduce users' ability to define their own information needs. The dilemma posed by the enterprise networking and the new information technology infrastructure is one of central-management control versus end-user creativity and productivity.

Connectivity and Application Integration Challenges

We have already described the connectivity problems created by incompatible networks and standards, including connectivity problems for wireless networks. Digital firm organizations depend on enterprise-wide integration of their business processes and applications so that they can obtain their information from any point in the value chain. An order from a Web site should be able to trigger events automatically in the organization's accounting, inventory, and distribution applications to speed the product swiftly to the customer. This end-to-end process and application integration is extremely difficult to achieve and beyond the reach of many firms.

Organizational Change Requirements

Enterprise-wide computing is an opportunity to reengineer the organization into a more effective unit, but it will only create problems or chaos if the underlying organizational issues are not fully addressed. Behind antiquated legacy infrastructures are old ways of doing business, which must also be changed to work effectively in a new enterprise-wide IT infrastructure. Infrastructure and architecture for a business that can respond to rapidly changing marketplace demands and industry changes require changes in corporate culture and organizational structure that are not easy to make. It took several years of hard work and large financial investments for IBM to Web enable its business processes and convince disparate business units to adopt a "One IBM" mindset where everyone uses common tools. Sun Microsystems, the networking technology giant, experienced a painful two-year conversion of its own information systems to make them run on its own networks (Kanter, 2001).

Hidden Costs of Enterprise Computing

Many companies have found that the savings they expected from distributed client/server computing did not materialize because of unexpected costs. Hardware-acquisition savings resulting from downsizing often are offset by high annual operating costs for additional labor and time required for network and system management. Considerable time must be spent on tasks such as network maintenance; data backup; technical problem solving; and hardware, software, and software-update installations. Gains in productivity and efficiency from equipping employees with wireless mobile computing devices must be balanced against increased costs associated with integrating these devices into the firm's IT infrastructure and providing technical support.

Scalability, Reliability, and Security

Companies seeking to digitally enable their businesses require robust information technology infrastructures providing plentiful bandwidth and storage capacity for transmitting and maintaining all of the data generated by electronic commerce and electronic business transactions. Network infrastructures need not only to be able to handle current e-business and e-commerce demands but also to be able to scale rapidly to meet future demands while providing high levels of performance and availability for mission-critical applications.

Enterprise networking is highly sensitive to different versions of operating systems and network management software, with some applications requiring specific versions of each. It is difficult to make all of the components of large, heterogeneous networks work together as smoothly as management envisions. **Downtime**—periods of time in which the system is not operational—remains much more frequent in distributed systems than in established mainframe systems and should be considered carefully before taking essential applications off a mainframe.

downtime

Period of time in which an information system is not operational.

Security is of paramount importance in firms with extensive networking and electronic transactions with individuals or other businesses outside organizational boundaries. Networks present end users, hackers, and thieves with many points of access and opportunities to steal or modify data in networks. Systems linked to the Internet are even more vulnerable because the Internet was designed to be open to everyone. Wireless computing devices linked to corporate applications create new areas of vulnerability. We discuss these issues in greater detail in Chapter 14.

SOME SOLUTIONS

Organizations can meet the challenges posed by the new IT infrastructure by planning for and managing business and organizational changes; increasing end-user training; asserting data administration disciplines; and considering connectivity, application integration, bandwidth, and cost controls in their technology planning.

Managing the Change

To gain the full benefit of any new technology, organizations must carefully plan for and manage the change. Business processes may need to be reengineered to accompany infrastructure changes (see Chapter 12). For example, equipping the sales force with wireless handheld devices for entering orders in the field provides an opportunity for management to review the sales process to see if redundant order entry activities or a separate order entry staff can be eliminated. Management must address the organizational issues that arise from shifts in staffing, function, power, and organizational culture attending a new information technology infrastructure.

Education and Training

A well-developed training program can help end users overcome problems resulting from the lack of management support and understanding of networked computing (Westin et al., 1985; Bikson et al., 1985). Technical specialists will need training in Web site, wireless, and client/server development and network support methods.

Data Administration Disciplines

The role of data administration (see Chapter 7) becomes even more important when networks link many different applications, business areas, and computing devices. Organizations must systematically identify where their data are located, which group is responsible for maintaining each piece of data, and which individuals and groups are allowed to access and use that data. They need to develop specific policies and procedures to ensure that their data are accurate, available only to authorized users, and properly backed up.

Planning for Connectivity and Application Integration

Senior management must take a long-term view of the firm's IT infrastructure and information architecture, making sure they can support the required level of process and information integration for current and future needs. Infrastructure planning should consider how much connectivity would be required to digitally enable core strategic business processes. To what extent should network services be standardized throughout the organization? Will the firm be communicating with customers and suppliers using different technology platforms? How should wireless mobile computing networks be integrated with the rest of the firm?

Although some connectivity problems can be solved by using intranets or the Internet, the firm will need to establish enterprise-wide standards for other systems and applications. Management can establish policies to keep networks and telecommunications services as

MAKE IT YOUR BUSINESS

FINANCE AND ACCOUNTING

Wireless Web technology has been the source of new financial services. Individual investors and investment professionals can use their mobile phones to obtain stock quotes and financial market news, to make stock trades, and to review their portfolios. Wireless Web and Internet technology are also making it possible to speed up fund flows by providing capabilities for immediate billing and invoicing. You can find examples of financial and accounting applications on pages 293–294.

HUMAN RESOURCES

Internet technology has created new efficient and cost-effective tools for employee communication and coordination. Managers can use e-mail, chat, and instant messaging to communicate with employees that are in many different locations. Companies can use intranets to publish employee bulletins, policy manuals, directories, and other human resources documents. You can find examples of human resources applications on pages 276–277.

MANUFACTURING AND PRODUCTION

Extranets are especially useful for collaborative commerce and supply chain management, and are the primary platform for private industrial networks. They are often used for providing product availability, pricing, and shipment data; for exchanging purchase orders and invoices; and for joint product development activities with other companies. You can find examples of manufacturing and production applications on pages 281, 287, and 305–308.

SALES AND MARKETING

The Web is an especially powerful medium for sales and marketing because it provides capabilities for personalization and interacting with customers that cannot be found in other channels. Companies can engage in ongoing dialogues with customers using e-mail, chat, and electronic discussion groups to solidify their customer relationships. Wireless Web technology provides new information and location-based services for companies to sell, which could provide major new sources of revenue. You can find examples of sales and marketing applications on pages 281 and 305–308.

homogeneous as possible, setting standards for data, voice, e-mail, and videoconferencing services along with hardware, software, and network operating systems.

An enterprise-wide architecture for integrated business applications and processes cannot be created through piecemeal changes. It represents a long-term endeavor that should be supported by top management and coordinated with the firm's strategic plans.

MANAGEMENT WRAP-UP

Planning the firm's IT infrastructure is a key management responsibility. Managers need to consider how the IT infrastructure supports the firm's business goals and whether the infrastructure should incorporate public infrastructures and links to other organizations. Planning should also consider the need to maintain some measure of management control as computing power becomes more widely distributed throughout the organization.

The new information technology infrastructure can enhance organizational performance by making information flow more smoothly between different parts of the organization and between the organization and its customers, suppliers, and other value partners. Organizations can use Internet technology and tools to reduce communication and coordination costs, create interactive products and services, and accelerate the distribution of knowledge.

Internet technology is providing the connectivity for the new information technology infrastructure and the emerging digital firm using the TCP/IP reference model and other standards for retrieving, formatting, and displaying information. Key technology decisions should consider the capabilities of Internet, electronic commerce, and new wireless technologies along with connectivity, scalability, reliability, and requirements for application integration.

For Discussion

1. It has been said that developing an IT infrastructure for electronic commerce and electronic business is, above all, a business decision, as opposed to a technical decision. Discuss.

2. A fully integrated IT infrastructure is essential for business success. Do you agree? Why or why not?

SUMMARY

1. *What is the new information technology (IT) infrastructure for business? Why is connectivity so important in this infrastructure?* The new information technology (IT) infrastructure uses a mixture of computer hardware supplied by different vendors, including mainframes, PCs, and servers, which are networked to each other. More processing power is available on the desktop through client/server computing and mobile personal information devices that provide remote access to the desktop from outside the organization. The new IT infrastructure also incorporates public infrastructures, such as the telephone system, the Internet, and public network services.

Connectivity is a measure of how well computers and computer-based devices can communicate with one another and "share" information in a meaningful way without human intervention. It is essential in enterprise networking in the new IT infrastructure, where different hardware, software, and network components must work together to transfer information seamlessly from one part of the organization to another. TCP/IP and OSI are important reference models for achieving connectivity in networks. Each divides the communications process into layers. UNIX is an operating system standard that can be used to create open systems, as can the Linux operating system. Connectivity also can be achieved by using Internet technology, XML, and Java.

2. *How does the Internet work? What are its major capabilities?* The Internet is a worldwide network of networks that uses the client/server model of computing and the TCP/IP network reference model. Using the Internet, any computer (or computing appliance) can communicate with any other computer connected to the Internet throughout the world. The Internet has no central management. The Internet is used for communications, including e-mail, public forums on thousands of topics, and live, interactive conversations. It also is used for information retrieval from hundreds of libraries and thousands of corporate, government, and nonprofit databases. It has developed into an effective way for individuals and organizations to offer information and products through a Web of graphical user interfaces and easy-to-use links worldwide. Major Internet capabilities include e-mail, Usenet, LIST-SERV, chatting, Telnet, FTP, and the World Wide Web.

Many organizations use Internet e-mail, chat, and Usenet services to reduce communications costs when they must manage organizational activities and communicate with many employees. Firms are also starting to realize economies by using Internet telephony, which enables Internet technology to be used for telephone voice transmission. Internet technology can also reduce communication costs by allowing companies to create virtual private networks as low-cost alternatives to private WANs.

3. *How can organizations benefit from using the World Wide Web and Web technology? How can businesses benefit from the Wireless Web?* The World Wide Web provides a universal set of standards for storing, retrieving, and displaying information in a client/server environment, enabling users to link to information resources housed in many different computer systems around the world. Web pages featuring text, graphics, video, and sound can be used to create new products and services and closer relationships with customers. Web site directories, search engines, and "push" technology can help users locate the information they need on the Web. Web technology and Internet networking standards provide the connectivity and interfaces for internal private intranets and private extranets that be accessed by many different kinds of computers both inside and outside the organization.

Wireless Web technologies enable Internet-enabled cell phones, PDAs, and other wireless computing devices to access digital information from the Internet from any location. Employees of businesses equipped with wireless Internet connections can access Web information from any location and make decisions instantly without being tethered to a desk or computer. Wireless Web applications, especially those that are location-based, also represent a source of new products, services, and revenue. However, Wireless Web applications have not yet been widely adopted because keyboards and display screens on cell phones are tiny and awkward to use and data transfer speeds on existing wireless networks are still quite slow.

4. *What are the principal technologies for supporting electronic commerce and electronic business?* Businesses need a series of software tools for maintaining a Web site. Web server software locates and manages Web pages stored on Web server computers. Electronic commerce server software provides capabilities for setting up electronic storefronts and arranging for payments and shipping. Customer tracking and personalization tools collect, store, and analyze data on Web site visitors. Content management tools facilitate the collection, assembly, and management of Web site content. Web site performance monitoring tools monitor the speed of Web site transactions and identify Web site performance problems. Businesses can use an external vendor's Web hosting service as an alternative to maintaining their own Web sites.

5. *What management problems are raised by the new information technology (IT) infrastructure? How can businesses solve these problems?* Problems posed by the new IT infrastructure include: loss of management control over systems; the need to carefully manage organizational change; connectivity and application integration challenges; the difficulty of ensuring network scalability, reliability, and security; and controlling the hidden costs of enterprise computing.

Solutions include planning for and managing the business and organizational changes associated with enterprise-wide computing; increasing end-user training; asserting data administration disciplines; and considering connectivity, application integration, bandwidth, and cost controls when planning the IT infrastructure.

Key Terms

Review Questions

1. What are the features of the new information technology infrastructure?

2. Why is connectivity so important for the digital firm? List and describe the major connectivity standards for networking and the Internet.

3. What is the Internet? List and describe alternative ways of accessing the Internet

4. List and describe the principal Internet capabilities.

5. Describe the capabilities of next generation networks, including Internet2? How do they differ from those of the existing public Internet? What benefits can they provide?

6. Why is the World Wide Web so useful for individuals and businesses?

7. Define and describe the following: home page, uniform resource locator (URL), Internet telephony, virtual private network (VPN), and voice portal.

8. List and describe alternative ways of locating information on the Web.

9. What are intranets and extranets? How do they differ from the Web?

10. What is the Wireless Web? How does it differ from the conventional Web?

11. List and describe the types of m-commerce services and applications supported by the Wireless Web.

12. Compare the WAP and I-mode Wireless Web standards.

13. List and describe the principal technologies for supporting electronic commerce and electronic business.

14. Under what conditions should firms consider Web hosting services?

15. Describe five problems posed by the new IT infrastructure.

16. Describe some solutions to the problems posed by the new IT infrastructure.

Application Software Exercise

SPREADSHEET EXERCISE: ANALYZING WEB SITE VISITORS

Your firm, Marina Clothiers, makes casual pants, shirts, and other clothes for both men and women. Your firm has been attempting to increase the number of online customers by placing advertising banners for your Web site at other Web sites. When users click on these banner ads, they automatically are transported to your Web site. Data from your advertising campaign are summarized in the weekly Marketing Trends Report (MTR) produced by your Web site analysis software, which appears on the Laudon Web site for Chapter 9.

■ *Visitors* are the number of people who visited your Web site by clicking on a banner ad for your site that was placed on an affiliated Web site.

■ *Shoppers* are the number of visitors referred by banner ads who reached a page in your Web site designated as a shopping page.

■ *Attempted buyers* are the number of potential buyers referred by banner ads who reached a Web page designated as a page for summarizing and paying for purchases.

■ *Buyers* are the number of buyers referred by banner ads who actually placed an order from your Web site.

■ *Source* indicates the specific Web site from which visitors came to your Web site.

In trying to increase the number of online customers, you must determine your Web site's success in converting visitors to actual buyers. You must also look at the abandonment rate—the percentage of attempted buyers who abandon your Web site just as they were about to make a purchase. Low conversion rates and high abandonment rates are indicators that a Web site is not very effective. You also must identify likely Web site partners for a new advertising campaign. Use the MTR with your spreadsheet software to help you answer the questions below. Include a graphics presentation to support your findings:

1. What are the total number of visitors, shoppers, attempted buyers, and buyers at your Web site?
2. Which sources provided the highest conversion rate to buyers at your Web site—that is, the percentage of visi-

tors from a previous site that become buyers on your site? What is the average conversion rate for your Web site?
3. Which sources provided the highest abandonment rate at your Web site—that is the percentage of attempted buyers that abandoned their shopping cart at your Web site before completing a purchase. What is the average abandonment rate for your Web site?
4. On which Web sites (or types of Web sites) should your firm purchase more banner ads?

GROUP PROJECT

Form a group with three or four of your classmates. Prepare evaluations of the wireless Internet capabilities of a Palm and a PocketPC handheld computing device. Your analysis should consider the purchase cost of each device, any additional software required to make it Internet enabled, the cost of wireless Internet services, and what Internet services are available for each device. You should also consider other capabilities of each device, including the ability to integrate with existing corporate or PC applications. Which device would you select? What criteria would you use to guide your selection? If possible, use electronic presentation software to present your findings to the class.

TOOLS FOR INTERACTIVE LEARNING

■ INTERNET CONNECTION

The Internet Connection for this chapter will take you to a series of Web sites where you can evaluate tools for providing Wireless Web access.

■ INTERACTIVE STUDY GUIDE

You can use the Interactive Study Guide to test your knowledge of the topics in the chapter and get instant feedback where you need more practice

■ RUNNING CASE

The Running Case provides an opportunity for you to develop a plan that will enable Dirt Bikes USA to realize new efficiencies by making better use of Internet tools and services. You can find a complete description of this project on the Laudon Web site for Chapter 9 and on the Multimedia Edition CD-ROM.

■ ELECTRONIC COMMERCE PROJECT

At the Laudon Web site for Chapter 9, you will find an Electronic Commerce Project where you can evaluate various Web search engines for business research.

■ MANAGEMENT DECISION PROBLEM

At the Laudon Web site for Chapter 9, you will find a Management Decision Problem on reducing agency costs.

■ CD-ROM

If you use the Multimedia Edition CD-ROM with this chapter, you can find a video demonstrating PeopleSoft's Web-based global human resources system, an audio overview of the major themes of this chapter, and bullet text summarizing the key points of the chapter.

CASE STUDY—*Does Wine Retailing Have a Future on the Internet?*

In the early days of the Web, wine retailing looked like it could be a very successful Internet business. Annual wine sales today in the United States run about $17 billion and worldwide about $100 billion. Some analysts have predicted that Internet sales could reach five-to-ten percent of that market by 2005.

In January 1995, a master sommelier named Peter Granoff partnered with computer expert Robert Olson to launch Virtual Vineyards, the first company to sell wine over a Web site. Their goal was to give wine shoppers direct access to limited-production wines that are often not available through most wine retail superstores. They focused on boutique wines for those who really cared about wines rather than marketing to occasional or new wine drinkers. They offered wines from the finest wineries, and screened them for

quality. Their strategy was to expand slowly, working with wholesalers and retailers to enable them to sell wines eventually in many states. Virtual Vineyards provided additional value by offering information to educate buyers about each label for sale as well as Granoff's tasting chart and personal guarantee of each wine's quality. The company obtained $20 million in funding. However, Virtual Vineyards had no licenses to make sales legally, so it paid high handling fees to wholesalers and retailers who acted as its fulfillment agents. The company had trouble aggregating orders in a meaningful way and had big empty trucks shipping orders all over the country. It also became embroiled in legal court battles because of its lack of licenses in some states. These high operating costs were passed on to consumers, and the company never attracted enough customers to become profitable.

Virtual Vineyards initially looked like such a promising business that it inspired other competitors, including WineShopper, Wine.com, and eVineyard. Every new site serving the United States had to address the 70-year-old and very convoluted three-tiered liquor and wine distribution system. When the 21st amendment ended Prohibition in the United States in 1933, control over production, distribution, and sale of alcoholic beverages was left to the individual states. They independently developed or followed a three-tiered system for wine. The first tier is the suppliers to each state (the producers and importers). Suppliers can only sell to the second tier, wholesalers, which in turn can only distribute to retailers, the third tier. Retailers, including bars, restaurants, hotels, and liquor stores, are the only ones who legally can sell to the public. The system differs between each state, sometimes dramatically.

Today 13 states prohibit direct interstate shipping of wine even to its own citizens who are outside their home state. The remaining states regulate importing and require permits. Some states allow wine sales in grocery stores, while others allow sales only in state-operated stores or in private liquor stores. Some prevent sales on certain holidays. Some states limit the amount an individual can purchase within any one month or year. Several now prohibit sales via the Internet. Thus each of the fifty states has its own laws and regulations governing the production, sale, distribution, and delivery of wine as well as for tax collection from all three tiers. To control this, every state requires every company to have a state license for each of the three levels that company operates in. These intricate and arcane sets of laws were developed for bricks-and-mortar sales, not for the Internet.

Those selling wines on the Internet have two choices—either work through bricks-and-mortar companies, paying all three levels a fee for each sale, a costly alternative, or develop their own computer systems to obtain their own licenses and maintain full compliance with all state laws and regulations. Such a system must support laws governing alcohol supplying, sales, distribution, and delivery in each state, linking and fully integrating the producers, wholesalers, and retailers—a very complicated requirement. Moreover, to develop one's own system today, a company must use computers to maintain adequate legal and tax records for every tier in every state in which it operates.

Other noncomputer problems faced by Web-based wine sales include age verification. The purchaser or delivery recipient has to be age 21 or older, which means that someone of age has to be home to receive any delivery. Large numbers of consumers might use Wine sites to learn about and experiment with new wines, and if they like any, locate less expensive ways to purchase them. Given the legal complexities of wine retailing, orders could easily take weeks to be processed and delivered.

One company that opted to build its own system to obtain its own licenses and control its own sales was WineShopper.com, founded in 1997 by Peter Sisson. He raised $46 million in venture capital from several investors including Amazon.com. He also had the support of Wine & Spirits Wholesalers of America, a trade organization, and so he decided to sell exclusively from the listings in these wholesalers' databases. The wholesalers set the price. These wholesalers are not necessarily cheaper than specialty shops, but they claim they can deliver any bottle from anywhere in the world. The

company's goals were to sell any wine available anywhere to anyone, offering customers satisfaction and convenience. Sisson said he would be making products accessible in areas where they are not currently available, listing all wines available from all U.S. wholesalers' catalogues. (Over 250 wholesalers from 47 states, plus 550 wine producers, had already agreed to work with WineShopper). He decided to provide information and independent expertise on wine from such sources as *Wine Spectator*, *Food & Wine*, and *The Connoisseurs' Guide to California Wine*. He wanted his site to become the first destination for consumers seeking wine information or product. His plan included a distribution network that followed the three-tier system, and it would have its computer environment support the complex needs of the state laws and regulations.

The WineShopper.com Web site was designed to look the same to customers from any location in the United States while maintaining a separate computer backend system for each state where it executed a transaction. To support the unique legal requirements of each state, WineShopper used a massive database mapping mechanism that was capable of handling and codifying all of the laws in such a way that it could be mapped to a nine digit zip code based on a shipping address. The laws are very complex and go way beyond just the state level. Even county and city laws within states can come into play, notes Dennis Riley, WineShopper's director of information systems. The whole WineShopper system ran on Sun hardware and partially on Sun software, and it even included wide use of Sun's Java programming language.

WineShopper.com used a three-tired IT infrastructure consisting of a front end of Web servers, a middle layer of application servers, and backend database servers. The Web servers directed order transactions placed by users over the Internet to the application servers running various applications, including an e-commerce storefront application cluster and an enterprise resource planning (ERP) application cluster. These application servers communicated with database servers. The ERP application cluster sent the order to the warehouse for fulfillment. To store all the data for so many different business rules and state regulations, WineShopper used Oracle databases and almost 1 terabyte of storage. The company maintained a separate database for the current inventory within each state as well as files for the prices in each state. The system was load-balanced to maximize response time for WineShopper customers. The company had redundant backup systems to prevent any service interruption. The system was also designed for easy expansion when needed. "One of our biggest expenditures has been on multimillion-dollar technical development of compliance engines," explained Suzanne Gannon, the director of public relations and corporate communications for WineShopper. The company was geographically distributed, with the production environment and main data center in Sunnyvale, California, the development and integration environment in San Francisco, and the warehouse in Napa, California, in the heart of California's wine country.

In addition to the challenge of handling unique state laws, the Wineshopper.com system had trouble dealing with the legacy systems for inventory and products in distribution used by its wholesalers. The various wine wholesalers use different systems with different SKUs (stock-keeping unit identification numbers for items) so that there was no uniform coding structure that could be used by WineShopper and its distributors. WineShopper tried to develop a coding system to eliminate data inconsistencies and provide a single standard view of data concerning products in distribution.

Sun claimed that this convoluted three-tiered system was the most complicated Web site it had ever seen. WineShopper.com experienced many delays in going live and in expanding because of software problems, although it finally went live in California in April 2000 and in New York in July. By mid-August the site was also operating for Colorado, Florida, Illinois, Missouri, and Wisconsin, and it had achieved regulatory approval in over 30 states. Its goal was to have a system running in the states that reached 70 percent of the U.S. market by the December holiday season. However the company took too long to go live, blaming its problems on software. It was spending so much money that in August 2000 it merged with Wine.com.

Wine.com had been founded in 1995. It targeted knowledgeable wine drinkers who had both money and good credit records. It kept itself small, selling high-end wines, and focusing on the convenience of delivering wines rather than on offering the lowest price. However, it changed its target over time because of the growing competition from WineShopper with its high spending. Wine.com felt pushed to spend a lot of money and hire a large staff. In September 1999, with no money left, Virtual Vineyards purchased Wine.com's name and domain name and changed its name to Wine.com. The new Wine.com emphasized customer satisfaction and reliable delivery. By early 2000, this company had received another $92 million in investments.

In early 2000, WineShopper and Wine.com were in stiff competition, spending a lot of money. In August 2000, they decided to end the competition and reduce the expenditures by merging. "We have very complementary strengths and assets and realized we could focus our resources on growing the wine market instead of fighting each other," explained Sisson. "The new company used the Wine.com name and Web address. The two companies continued separate operations until the end of 2000, giving them time to merge their computer systems and concentrate on developing their Wine.com name. They estimated they were offering about 2,000 wines, domestic and foreign, including both well-known and boutique wines as well as about 1,000 old and rare wines. The company closed a key office in Fremont, California, and consolidated operations in Napa. The new Web site contained a great deal of wine information, including editorials, ratings, and tasting notes from *Wine Spectator*. The new Wine.com was now considered the dominant force in the Internet wine business.

In January 2001, Wine.com laid off 75 of its 310 employees, claiming the cuts reduced staff redundancy because of the merger. At that time, according to Granoff, sales were up 300 percent in 2000, and they were selling in 40 states.

In 1998, eVineyard was established with only $20 million of private equity. Its strategy was different: buy wine only when a customer ordered it, giving eVineyard only a virtual inventory. It ordered its goods from wholesalers, shipping them to customers either from its Portland, Oregon, office or from small logistics centers it established in states that required a physical location. Its strategy also included expanding one state at a time, obtaining retail licenses in each state. This process was often very slow; for example it took 10 months in New York. In some states, such as New Jersey, the company could only obtain a license by purchasing an existing one. It was only able to sell the wines that its

regional distributors handled. According to Brett Lauter, eVineyard's chief marketing officer, the company served 77 percent of the premium wine-drinking market when it was only operating in 27 states. In 2000, he estimated the company grew 1,000 percent from its previous year and was now selling at between $5 million and $10 million annually.

Lauter estimated that his competitor Wine.com was probably spending over $2 million each month to stay in business. "It takes a lot of wine sales to make up for that burn rate," he observed. In April 2001, Wine.com officials announced the company might file for bankruptcy protection, and it announced a layoff of 160 of the remaining 235 employees, including Granoff and Sisson. EVineyard purchased Wine.com for $9 million, taking only its domain name and customer list. It did not assume any of Wine.com's $17 million debt, and it did not retain any of Wine.com's 85 remaining employees. This left eVineyard (now called Wine.com) as the only major company in the Web-based wine retail business.

Several industry analysts noted that the while others believed they could change the whole wine distribution system, eVineyard (now Wine.com) kept its costs low. "We didn't spend money like drunken sailors," said Michael Osborn, the founder and vice president of eVineyard. "We're a retailer. Fundamental business principles apply." Wine.com had over 400 employees, while we have 60 employees. They raised $200 million in venture capital, while we raised $35 million." EVineyard also retained its own distribution system.

Today, the whole wine market has changed, and Web-based wine merchants or entrepreneurs are facing other problems. Most of the money invested in wine Web sites was lost in the 2000–2002 stock market crash, and new dot-com investments will be difficult to find. Moreover, a number of Sonoma and Napa wineries are selling their own wines through their own Internet sites. New e-commerce technology makes selling wine on the Web more profitable than selling through traditional wholesaler-distribution channels. An online shopping cart appropriate for wine retailing, which used to cost $50,000 to set up, now costs only about $1,000. What will the future hold for Internet wine retailers?

Sources: Eric Schoeniger, "Redefining Leadership," *The Chief Executive*, March 2002; Michael Totty and Ann Grimes, "If At First You Don't Succeed," *Wall Street Journal*, February 11, 2002; Janice Fuhrmen, "Web Still Catching Some Wine Business," *San Francisco Chronicle*, February 1, 2002; Paul Tincknett, "10.11.01: A Binary Moment in Time; Is Dot-com Wine Dead?" *Ferment*, November 2001; "eVineyard Inc. Leverages Wine.com Purchase," *PR Newswire*, July 17, 2001; "eVineyard Acquires Wine.com," *PR Newswire*, April 27, 2001; Tim Fish, "Internet Wine Retailer Wine.com Sold to eVineyard.com," *Wine Spectator*, April 27, 2001; Keith Regan, "Internet Wine Sellers Still Woozy on Web Fumes," *E-Commerce Times*, April 13, 2001; Tim Fish, "Internet Wine Retailer Wine.com Lays Off Two-Thirds of Staff," *Daily Wine News*, April 3, 2001; Peter Simon, "Wine.com Fires 75 after Merger with WineShopper.com," *SF Gate*, January 11, 2001; "Wine.com and WineShopper.com Join Forces to Succeed Online," *Food & Drink Weekly*, August 21, 2000; Dana Nigro, "Online Retailers Wine.com and WineShopper.com to Merge," *Wine Spectator*, August 15, 2000; "The Cat Chasing Its Tail; WineAccess.com Announces an Analysis of the Wine.com/Wineshopper.com Merger," *Business Wire*, August 16, 2000; "No Sour Grapes for Online Wine Lovers; Sun Microsystems Powers WineShopper.com's Internet Wine Resource," *PR Newswire*, October 18,

2000; "Free the Grapes!" *Business Wire*, August 15, 2000; "Start Spreading the News, WineShopper.com Goes Live in New York; Brings New Yorkers Access to Wines Not Previously Available in State," *Business Wire*, July 31, 2000; Lisa Terry, "Bottled Courage," *Upside Today*, March 20, 2000; Dennis Riley, "Premier Destination in Burgeoning Online Wine Market Based on Sun Enterprise Server and Sun StorEdge Solutions,"Sun Microsystems Web site, accessed July 1, 2002, <www.sun.com>.

CASE STUDY QUESTIONS:

1. Use the competitive forces and value chain models to analyze wine retailing as an Internet business model.

2. Compare the business models and strategies for Internet wine retailing used by WineShopper, eVineyard, and Virtual Vineyards. Discuss the flaws and strengths of each company.

3. Do you think WineShopper.com's business model was a difficult model to work with, and why? What management, organization, and technology issues contributed to this company's failure?

4. How important to eVineyard's success to-date were the timing, management, and the strategy? How important was the role of technology? In your opinion, why was eVineyard the eventual winner in the race for online wine sales?

5. Do you think wine retailing can succeed on the Internet? Explain your answer.

CREATING A NEW INTERNET BUSINESS

We have prepared a list of new businesses that could benefit from going on the Web. Select one of the businesses from the list and develop an Internet strategy for that business. You will need to identify the Internet business model to be pursued, use the Internet to research and analyze markets and competitors, and design part of the Web site for that business.

VIRTUAL TOUR OF ELECTRONIC COMMERCE SITES

To prepare for this project, review Internet business models by taking the virtual tour of the electronic commerce sites described in the following table. To take the tour, visit the Web site representing each business model. Explore the Web site so that you have a clear idea of how that business uses the Web for electronic commerce.

VIRTUAL TOUR OF ELECTRONIC COMMERCE SITES

Business Model	Description	Organization	URL
Virtual Storefront	Sells physical goods online instead of through a physical storefront or retail outlet. The goods are then shipped to the customer.	Amazon.com	www.amazon.com
Information Broker	Provides primarily product, pricing, and availability information. The final purchase transaction is usually conducted elsewhere.	Edmunds.com	www.edmunds.com
Transaction Broker	Provides services that allow people to complete transactions, such as buying and selling securities.	E*TRADE	www.etrade.com
Online Marketplace	Provides digital environment where buyers and sellers can meet, search for products, display products, and establish prices for those products. Can provide online auctions or reverse auctions as well as negotiated or fixed pricing.	eBay	www.ebay.com
Content Provider	Creates revenue by providing digital content, such as digital news, music, photos, or video, over the Web.	*Wall Street Journal* Interactive	www.wsj.com
Online Service Provider	Provides online hardware and software services for individuals and businesses.	Xdrive	www.xdrive.com
Portal	Provides an initial point of entry to the Web along with specialized content and other services.	Yahoo!	www.yahoo.com
Virtual Community	Provides an online meeting place where people with similar interests can communicate and find useful information.	iVillage	www.ivillage.com

SELECTING AN INTERNET BUSINESS MODEL AND DESIGNING A WEB STRATEGY

The five businesses we describe are fictitious but are based on real-world scenarios. Review each of them. Then select one business and answer the following questions:

1. What Internet business model would be appropriate for the company to follow in creating a Web site?

2. In what ways can the company benefit from a Web site? How would it provide value to the firm? What functions should it perform for the company (marketing, sales, customer support, internal communications, etc.)?

3. In what other ways might the company use the Internet for its own benefit?

4. Prepare functional specifications for the company's use of the Web and the Internet. Include links to and from other sites in your design.

5. Prepare a cost–benefit analysis of a proposal to implement the company's use of the Internet.

For each of the five businesses, we list a Web site of a real-world company in the same or a related business to help you understand that type of business. Visit the Web site related to the business you have selected and review it carefully.

Business 1: InfoInc

InfoInc is a start-up company that would like to provide a service by offering easy access to needed information in specialized fields such as accounting, finance, or medicine. Although its business plan calls for moving into a number of fields, InfoInc would like to begin by addressing the needs of people in the accounting and tax fields. Its first two target groups are accounting professionals and the general public. For the general public, the plan is to provide a Web site with advice on various issues such as tax laws and IRA savings rules. The site would also contain links to other sites where visitors will be able to obtain advice on such issues as how to establish a new business. For accounting professionals, such as certified public accountants (CPAs) and corporate financial officers, InfoInc would like to offer more detailed information services. In addition, the company wants to provide capabilities that might help the CPAs and financial officers manage their e-mail, voice mail, and fax.

Web reference: WebMD Inc. <http://webmd.com/>

Business 2: Aerospace Metal Alloys

Aerospace Metal is a distributor of exotic steel, aluminum, and titanium alloys to the aerospace industry and to other specialty industries. These metals, such as kovar and inconel, must meet exceptionally exacting standards because they become parts in airplanes, rockets, industrial furnaces, and other high-performance products. Aerospace sells raw materials produced in the form of bars, sheets, rings, and forgings. In turn, Aerospace customers use these materials to fabricate their final products. Many Aerospace customers are actually parts suppliers to end-product assemblers such as Boeing Aircraft. Aerospace Metal maintains a sales staff to sell these metals, and the company stores its products in seven warehouses throughout the country. They obtain their products from steel and metal manufacturers throughout North America. If a customer requests a product not carried by Aerospace, the company will special-order it from an appropriate supplier.

Web reference: Specialty Steel and Storage <www.steelforge.com>

Business 3: Columbiana

Columbiana is a small, independent island in the Caribbean. It is underdeveloped and is also off the tourist path for most visitors to that area despite its many attractions. The island has a unique his-tory, with Indian ruins dating back 800 years and with many historical buildings, forts, and other sites built during its centuries as a British colony. A few first-class hotels have been built along some of its beautiful white beaches, and less expensive accommodations are also available along beaches, in several towns, and near several fishing villages. Its rain forests, rivers, striking mountains, and volcano cone all could be of interest to tourists. In addition, it has many restaurants that specialize in native dishes and fresh fish. The government not only wants to increase tourism but it also wants to increase trade by developing new markets for its tropical agricultural products. In addition, leaders hope to attract investment capital so that many of the unemployed residents can find jobs. Two major airlines have regular flights to Columbiana, as do several small Caribbean airlines. The island is on the tourist itinerary of only one cruise ship company. The Web site will not transact any business, but it will offer information and links to other appropriate sites.

Web reference: Dominica <http://dominica.dm>

Business 4: Home Do-It-Yourself Tools Inc.

As more and more people are turning to do-it-yourself home repairs, the market for tools of all kinds for home use has grown rapidly. The buyer has thousands of tools to choose from, and so the search can be time consuming and the prices paid can be very high. Home Do-It-Yourself Tools Inc. (Home Tools) was founded to capitalize on this trend. The founder initially opened a small store in Atlanta, Georgia, and soon thereafter established a catalog to try to expand the business. Home Tools uses a toll-free 800 telephone number to take orders and to answer potential customers' technical and product questions. It solicits new customers through advertisements in magazines read by home repair enthusiasts. The owners now wants to make better use of the Internet to reach out to new customers, reduce Home Tools' cost per sale, and improve service quality. The heart of the business is a database listing several thousand tools and the tasks for which they are commonly used.

Web reference: iGo.com <www.igo.com>

Business 5: Low Cost Tires Inc.

Low Cost Tires Inc. (Tires Inc.) began as a small auto repair and tire shop in a small city outside of Chicago. While the original goal of the shop was to gain a reputation for quality repair, the owner also stressed meeting customer needs on the sale of tires. Tires Inc. carries a very wide selection of tires so that customers can always be served on the spot. Its staff is highly trained and very knowledgeable about tires. Selling tires has turned out to be more profitable than auto repairs. Although the owner plans to maintain the auto repair business, he wants to use the Internet to expand tire sales and to capitalize on his staff's understanding of customer needs. Management believes the correct Web strategy could help Tires Inc. improve customer service locally, increase its customer base, and help it create retail outlets in new locations.

Web reference: The Luggage Factory <www.luggagefactory outlet.com>

MANAGEMENT AND ORGANIZATIONAL SUPPORT SYSTEMS FOR THE DIGITAL FIRM

MANAGING KNOWLEDGE FOR THE DIGITAL FIRM

CHAPTER 10

objectives

As a manager, you'll want to know how your firm can benefit from information systems for knowledge management. After completing this chapter, you will be able to answer the following questions:

1. *Why do businesses today need knowledge management programs and systems for knowledge management?*

2. *Which information system applications are most useful for distributing, creating, and sharing knowledge in the firm?*

3. *What are the business benefits of using artificial intelligence technology for knowledge management?*

4. *How can businesses use expert systems and case-based reasoning to capture knowledge?*

5. *How can organizations benefit from using neural networks and other intelligent techniques?*

Quaker Chemical Concocts a New Formula for Collaboration

Quaker Chemical, based in Conshohocken, Pennsylvania, is a worldwide producer of custom-formulated chemical specialty products and fluid management services. Its clients include makers of automotive and aerospace products, and firms in the environment, can, and pulp and paper industries. It recently underwent a global reorganization so that its sales staff now sells by business line rather than by geographic region. In order to maximize the benefits from this reorganization, Quaker needed a system that could transcend regional barriers and help its sales force track, manage, and collaborate on client services and accounts. Developing new chemical formulas for automakers, determining why sales at certain North American mills are down, or tracking 55-gallon drums of chemicals—all of these problems could be more easily solved if the company could gather information stored on workers' computers and in their heads and make it more widely available. Quaker doesn't have off-the-shelf products, and Quaker formulates unique products for every customer, so capturing what Quaker's laboratory workers know about Quaker formulas is especially critical.

In mid-2000, Quaker launched a knowledge management system called Quaker Business Intelligence, or QBI. The system is a global intranet with collaborative software from Intraspect Software of Brisbane, California, working in

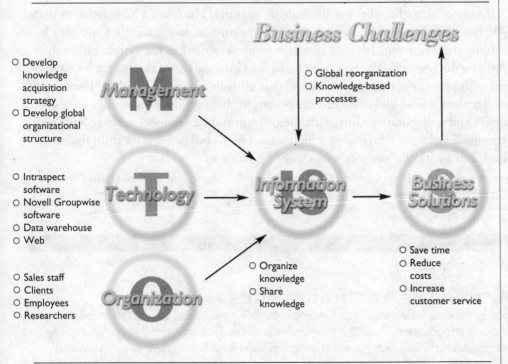

conjunction with Quaker's Novell GroupWise collaboration system. Employees can drop word processing documents, e-mail, Web pages, presentations, and spreadsheets in central files into the system. They can subscribe to certain folders relating to their jobs in the same way they would subscribe to an e-mail mailing list. The system alerts them automatically when changes are made to the individual files relating to their job tasks. About 60 percent of these files are used by research and development staff, the rest being shared by employees in sales, finance, and other areas. Employees can also search through thousands of e-mail messages captured by the system. When an employee logs on to his or her computer, the Intraspect software pops up with the look and feel of a simple Web page. Employees can control what is added to their "home page" or to the files belonging to their group and they can customize their home page to fit their job needs. The Intraspect system can be integrated with a data warehouse that Quaker uses to track its financial information. Eventually both of these systems will work with an enterprise system from J.D. Edwards that the company is in the process of implementing.

About 800 of Quaker's 1,100 workers use the Intraspect system. According to Thomas Baker, Quaker's manager of business intelligence development, the system stores nearly 27,000 documents in over 7,000 folders. "We don't want people to just send statistics," he noted ". . . we are trying to find out what people said and what they learned from their mistakes." In one instance, Quaker developed a formula for automaker Mercedes-Benz in the Netherlands and the system helped the company re-use data gathered during that product-development cycle in another plant in South America. Quaker's "steel product managers' forum" is another effective use of the system Previously, if a manager had trouble finding out why a customer experienced surface imperfections while rolling steel in a specific type of mill, he or she would e-mail other Quaker colleagues. Now that manager can initiate a discussion within QBI, sending an alert to all managers in the company's steel division. The system archives the message threads from that discussion and these threads can be accessed later by workers trying to answer a similar question.

Many of these benefits are difficult to quantify. However, Quaker claims that QBI has already saved the company four months of labor worth $300,000 by enabling three different lab sites to access formulas stored in the system rather than duplicate the research. The company's goal is to increase use of the system by 30 percent each year for the next two years so that all employees work with it. Eventually management would like to extend the system to share product knowledge with customers and collaborate online with them. Important customers such as Ford and DaimlerChrysler are demanding a higher-level of Web-based service from their suppliers, and such collaboration is one way to provide it.

Sources: Kim Girard, "Quaker Chemical's Collaboration Formula," *Baseline*, May 15, 2002; Quaker Chemical Corporation Web site, accessed August 22, 2002, <www.quakerchem.com>; and Intraspect Corporate Web site, accessed August 21, 2002, <www.intraspect.com>.

MANAGEMENT CHALLENGES

Quaker Business Intelligence is one example of how systems can be used to leverage organizational knowledge by making it more easily available. Collaborating and communicating with practitioners and experts and sharing ideas and information have become essential requirements in business, science, and government. In an information economy, capturing and distributing intelligence and knowledge and enhancing group collaboration have become vital to organizational innovation and survival. Special systems can be used for managing organizational knowledge, but they raise the following management challenges:

1. **Designing knowledge systems that genuinely enhance organizational performance.** Managers have encountered problems when attempting to transform their firms through knowledge management programs (Gold, Malhotra, and Segars, 2001). Information systems that truly enhance the productivity of knowledge workers may be difficult to build because the manner in which information technology can enhance higher-level tasks, such as those performed by managers and professionals, is not always clearly understood. Some aspects of organizational knowledge cannot be captured easily or codified, or the information that organizations finally manage to capture may become outdated as environments change. It is very difficult to integrate knowledge management programs with business strategy. Processes and interactions between information technology and social elements in organizations must be carefully managed (Davenport, Thomas, and Cantrell, 2002; Grover and Davenport, 2001).

2. **Identifying and implementing appropriate organizational applications for artificial intelligence.** Only certain kinds of information problems are appropriate for artificial intelligence (AI) applications. AI tools work best with complex, repetitive information-based activities. Many AI applications improve performance through trial and error and may not be reliable enough for mission-critical problems (Booth and Boluswar, 2002). Expert systems are expensive and time-consuming to maintain because their rules must be reprogrammed every time there is a change in the organizational environment. Many thousands of businesses have undertaken experimental projects in expert systems, but only a small percentage have created expert systems that actually can be used on a production basis. Organizations need to determine exactly how they can benefit from AI and whether the benefits are realistic.

This chapter examines information system applications specifically designed to help organizations create, capture, distribute, and apply knowledge and information. First, we examine information systems for supporting information and knowledge work. Then we look at the ways that organizations can use artificial intelligence technologies for capturing and storing knowledge and expertise.

10.1 KNOWLEDGE MANAGEMENT IN THE ORGANIZATION

Chapter 1 described the emergence of the information economy and the digital firm in which the major source of wealth and prosperity is the production and distribution of information and knowledge, and firms increasingly rely on digital technology to enable business processes. For example, 55 percent of the U.S. labor force consists of knowledge and information workers, and 60 percent of the gross domestic product of the United States comes from the knowledge and information sectors, such as finance and publishing.

In an information economy, knowledge-based core competencies—the two or three things that an organization does best—are key organizational assets. Producing unique products or services or producing them at a lower cost than competitors is based on superior knowledge of the production process and superior design. Knowing how to do things effectively and efficiently in ways that other organizations cannot duplicate is a primary source of value and a factor in production that cannot be purchased in external markets. Some management theorists believe that these **knowledge assets** are as important for competitive advantage and survival, if not more important, than physical and financial assets.

As knowledge becomes a central productive and strategic asset, organizational success increasingly depends on the firm's ability to produce, gather, store, and disseminate knowledge. With knowledge, firms become more efficient and effective in their use of scarce resources. Without knowledge, firms become less efficient and effective in their use of resources and ultimately fail.

knowledge assets
Organizational knowledge regarding how to efficiently and effectively perform business processes and create new products and services that enables the business to create value.

ORGANIZATIONAL LEARNING AND KNOWLEDGE MANAGEMENT

How do firms obtain knowledge? Like humans, organizations create and gather knowledge through a variety of **organizational learning** mechanisms. Through trial and error, careful measurement of planned activities, and feedback from customers and the environment in general, organizations create new standard operating procedures and business processes that reflect their experience. This is called "organizational learning." Arguably organizations that can sense and respond to their environments rapidly will survive longer than organizations that have poor learning mechanisms.

Knowledge management increases the ability of the organization to learn from its environment and to incorporate knowledge into its business processes. **Knowledge management** refers to the set of processes developed in an organization to create, gather, store, transfer, and apply knowledge. Information technology plays an important role in knowledge management by supporting these business processes for creating, identifying, and leveraging knowledge throughout the organization. Developing procedures and routines—business processes—to optimize the creation, flow, learning, protection, and sharing of knowledge in the firm is now a core management responsibility.

Companies cannot take advantage of their knowledge resources if they have inefficient processes for capturing and distributing knowledge, or if they fail to appreciate the value of the knowledge they already possess (Davenport and Prusak, 1998). Some corporations have created explicit knowledge management programs for protecting and distributing knowledge resources that they have identified and for discovering new sources of knowledge. These programs are often headed by a **chief knowledge officer (CKO).** The chief knowledge officer is a senior executive who is responsible for the firm's knowledge management program. The CKO helps design programs and systems to find new sources of knowledge or to make better use of existing knowledge in organizational and management processes (Flash, 2001; Earl and Scott, 1999).

organizational learning
Creation of new standard operating procedures and business processes that reflect organizations' experience.

knowledge management
The set of processes developed in an organization to create, gather, store, maintain, and apply the firm's knowledge.

chief knowledge officer (CKO)
Senior executive in charge of the organization's knowledge management program.

SYSTEMS AND INFRASTRUCTURE FOR KNOWLEDGE MANAGEMENT

All the major types of information systems described in this text facilitate the flow of information and the management of a firm's knowledge. Earlier chapters described systems that help firms understand and respond to their environments more effectively, notably enterprise systems, external and internal networks, databases, datamining, and communication-based applications. The concept of a "digital firm" refers to a firm with substantial use of information technology to enhance its ability to sense and respond to its environment.

Although all the information systems we have described help an organization sense and respond to its environment, some technologies uniquely and directly address the organizational learning and knowledge management task. Office systems, knowledge work systems (KWS), group collaboration systems, and artificial intelligence applications are especially useful for knowledge management because they focus on supporting information and knowledge work and on defining and capturing the organization's knowledge base. This knowledge base may include (1) structured internal knowledge (explicit knowledge), such as product manuals or research reports; (2) external knowledge of competitors, products, and markets, including competitive intelligence; and (3) informal internal knowledge, often called **tacit knowledge,** which resides in the minds of individual employees but has not been documented in structured form (Davenport, DeLong, and Beers, 1998).

Information systems can promote organizational learning by identifying, capturing, codifying, and distributing both explicit and tacit knowledge. Once information has been collected and organized in a system, it can be leveraged and reused many times. Companies can use information systems to codify their best practices and make knowledge of these practices more widely available to employees. **Best practices** are the most successful solutions or problem-solving methods that have been developed by a specific organization or industry. In addition to improving existing work practices, the knowledge can be preserved as organizational memory to train future employees or to help them with decision making. **Organizational memory** is the stored learning from an organization's history that can be used for decision-making and other purposes. Information systems can also provide *knowledge networks* for linking people so that individuals with special areas of expertise can be easily identified and tacit knowledge can be shared.

Figure 10-1 illustrates the information systems and information technology (IT) infrastructure for supporting knowledge management. Knowledge work systems support the activities of highly skilled knowledge workers and professionals as they create new knowledge

tacit knowledge
Expertise and experience of organizational members that has not been formally documented.

best practices
The most successful solutions or problem-solving methods that have been developed by a specific organization or industry.

organizational memory
The stored learning from an organization's history that can be used for decision making and other purposes.

Figure 10-1 Knowledge management requires an information technology (IT) infrastructure that facilitates the collection and sharing of knowledge as well as software for distributing information and making it more meaningful. The information systems illustrated here give close-in support to information workers at many levels in the organization.

and try to integrate it into the firm. Group collaboration and support systems support the creation, identification, and sharing of knowledge among people working in groups. Office systems help disseminate and coordinate the flow of information in the organization. Artificial intelligence systems capture new knowledge and provide organizations and managers with codified knowledge that can be reused by others in the organization. These systems require an IT infrastructure that makes heavy use of powerful processors, networks, databases, and Internet tools.

10.2 INFORMATION AND KNOWLEDGE WORK SYSTEMS

Information work is work that consists primarily of creating or processing information. It is carried out by information workers who usually are divided into two subcategories: **data workers,** who primarily process and disseminate information; and **knowledge workers,** who primarily create knowledge and information.

Examples of data workers include secretaries, sales personnel, bookkeepers, and draftspeople. Researchers, designers, architects, writers, and judges are examples of knowledge workers. Data workers usually can be distinguished from knowledge workers because knowledge workers usually have higher levels of education and memberships in professional organizations. In addition, knowledge workers exercise independent judgment as a routine aspect of their work. Data and knowledge workers have different information requirements and different systems to support them.

DISTRIBUTING KNOWLEDGE: OFFICE AND DOCUMENT MANAGEMENT SYSTEMS

Most data work and a great deal of knowledge work takes place in offices, including most of the work done by managers. The office plays a major role in coordinating the flow of information throughout the entire organization. The office has three basic functions (see Figure 10-2):

▪ Managing and coordinating the work of data and knowledge workers

▪ Connecting the work of local information workers with all levels and functions of the organization

▪ Connecting the organization to the external world, including customers, suppliers, government regulators, and external auditors.

Office workers span a very broad range: professionals, managers, sales, and clerical workers working alone or in groups. Their major activities include the following:

▪ Managing documents, including document creation, storage, retrieval, and dissemination

▪ Scheduling for individuals and groups

▪ Communicating, including initiating, receiving, and managing voice, digital, and document-based communications for individuals and groups

▪ Managing data, such as on employees, customers, and vendors

information work

Work that primarily consists of creating or processing information.

data workers

People, such as secretaries or bookkeepers, who process and disseminate the organization's information and paperwork.

knowledge workers

People, such as engineers, scientists, or architects, who design products or services or create knowledge for the organization.

Figure 10-2 The three major roles of offices. Offices perform three major roles. (1) They coordinate the work of local professionals and information workers. (2) They coordinate work in the organization across levels and functions. (3) They couple the organization to the external environment.

TABLE 10-1   TYPICAL OFFICE SYSTEMS

Office Activity	Technology
Managing documents	Word processing, desktop publishing, document imaging, Web publishing, work flow managers
Scheduling	Electronic calendars, groupware, intranets
Communicating	E-mail, voice mail, digital answering systems, groupware, intranets
Managing data	Desktop databases, spreadsheets, user-friendly interfaces to mainframe databases

office systems

Computer systems, such as word processing, voice mail, and imaging, that are designed to increase the productivity of information workers in the office.

These activities can be supported by office systems (see Table 10-1). **Office systems** are any application of information technology that intends to increase productivity of information workers in the office. Fifteen years ago, office systems handled only the creation, processing, and management of documents. Today professional knowledge and information work remains highly document centered. However, digital image processing—words and documents—is also at the core of systems, as are high-speed digital communications services. Because office work involves many people jointly engaged in projects, contemporary office systems have powerful group assistance tools such as networked digital calendars. An ideal office environment would be based on a seamless network of digital machines linking professional, clerical, and managerial work groups and running a variety of types of software.

Although word processing and desktop publishing address the creation and presentation of documents, they only exacerbate the existing paper avalanche problem. Work flow problems arising from paper handling are enormous. It has been estimated that up to 85 percent of corporate information is stored on paper. Locating and updating information in that format is a great source of organizational inefficiency.

One way to reduce problems stemming from paper work flow is to employ document imaging systems. *Document imaging systems* (which we defined in Chapter 2) are systems that convert paper documents and images into digital form so they can be stored and accessed by a computer. Such systems store, retrieve, and manipulate a digitized image of a document, allowing the document itself to be discarded. Once the document has been stored electronically, it can be immediately retrieved or shared with others. The system must contain a scanner that converts the document image into a digitized image, storing that image as a graphic. If the document is not in active use, it usually is stored on an optical disk system that may use a *jukebox* device for storing and retrieving many optical disks.

An imaging system also requires indexes that allow users to identify and retrieve a document when needed. Index data are entered so that a document can be retrieved in a variety of ways, depending upon the application. For example, the index may contain the document scan date, the customer name and number, the document type, and some subject information. Finally, the system must include retrieval equipment, primarily workstations capable of handling graphics, although printers usually are included. Figure 10-3 illustrates the components of a typical imaging system.

Traditional document-management systems can be expensive, requiring proprietary client/server networks, special client software, and storage capabilities. Intranets provide a low-cost and universally available platform for basic document publishing, and many companies are using them for this purpose. Employees can publish information using Web-page authoring tools and post it to an intranet Web server where it can be shared and accessed throughout the company with standard Web browsers. These Web-like "documents" can be multimedia objects combining text, graphics, audio, and video along with hyperlinks. After a document has been posted to the server, it can be indexed for quicker access and linked to other documents (see Figure 10-4). For more sophisticated document-management functions, such as controlling changes to documents, maintaining histories of activity and changes in the managed documents, and the ability to search documents on either content or

Figure 10-3 Components of an imaging system. A typical imaging system stores and processes digitized images of documents, using scanners, an optical disk system, an index server, workstations, and printers. A midrange or small mainframe computer may be required to control the activities of a large imaging system.

index terms, commercial Web-based systems such as those from IntraNet Solutions or Open Text are available.

In addition to streamlining work flow, Web-based and traditional document management systems provide tools for creating knowledge repositories to help organizations consolidate and leverage their knowledge. A **knowledge repository** is a collection of internal and external knowledge in a single location for more efficient management and utilization by the organization. Using these tools, knowledge from many different sources that can be documented in the form of memos, reports, presentations, and articles can be digitized and placed in a central location for easy storage and retrieval. Organizational knowledge repositories may also include tools for accessing information from corporate databases.

knowledge repository

Collection of documented internal and external knowledge in a single location for more efficient management and utilization by the organization.

The Window on Management describes the benefits of Web-based systems for work flow management, document control, and project management in the architectural, engineering, and construction industries.

CREATING KNOWLEDGE: KNOWLEDGE WORK SYSTEMS

Knowledge work is that portion of information work that creates new knowledge and information. For example, knowledge workers create new products or find ways to improve existing ones. Knowledge work is segmented into many highly specialized fields, and each field has a different collection of **knowledge work systems (KWS)** to support workers in that field. Knowledge workers perform three key roles that are critical to the organization and to the managers who work within the organization:

knowledge work systems (KWS)

Information systems that aid knowledge workers in the creation and integration of new knowledge in the organization.

- Keeping the organization up-to-date in knowledge as it develops in the external world—in technology, science, social thought, and the arts.

- Serving as internal consultants regarding the areas of their knowledge, the changes taking place, and the opportunities.

- Acting as change agents evaluating, initiating, and promoting change projects.

Knowledge workers and data workers have somewhat different information systems support needs. Most knowledge workers rely on office systems such as word processors, voice mail, and calendars, but they also require more specialized knowledge work systems. Knowledge work systems are specifically designed to promote the creation of knowledge and to ensure that new knowledge and technical expertise are properly integrated into the business.

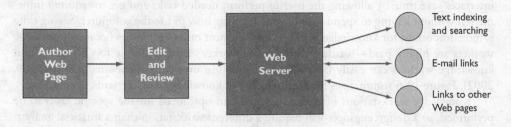

Figure 10-4 Web publishing and document management. An author can post information on an intranet Web server, where it can be accessed through a variety of mechanisms.

MANAGING CONSTRUCTION PROJECTS WITH THE INTERNET

Many people think that the most widely used tool in a construction project is a hammer, but it's probably a filing cabinet or fax machine. The $3.4 trillion U.S. construction industry is highly paper intensive. A complex project such as a large building requires the coordination of many different groups and hundreds of architectural drawings and design documents, which can change daily. Costly delays because of misplaced documents could make or break a company in an industry with razor-thin profit margins of 1 to 2 percent.

Web technology is starting to address this problem. New Web-based construction project management systems enable project managers to exchange documents and work online wherever they are using Web browser software. Autodesk Building Collaboration Services (formerly Buzzsaw.com), for example, offers customers a shared central space where project managers can exchange documents with engineers and architects, bid for subcontractor services, track scheduling and performance, and hold online meetings.

Toys R Us used Autodesk's services to better manage and speed up construction while reducing costs. In one project, it remodeled two dilapidated theaters in New York's Times Square into the largest toy store in the world. This Times Square project, headed by Tracy LeBlanc, held weekly meetings with 15 project consultants, partly to decide on design changes. Once finished, agreements on changes were sent to the architects to integrate them into the plans, which were returned to the consultants who then made more detailed documents and passed them to the general construction contractor.

In the past all plans were hand drawn and then sent by mail or overnight express to the next person involved, who would have to have new plans drawn. The same process would be repeated until the final detailed documents were in the hands of the general contractor. This took a great deal of time and labor. Now, changes can be uploaded to the Autodesk Building Collaboration Services Web site for instant communication and immediate revision. Depending on the size of the project and the distance between the various individuals, using the Internet can save days or weeks and reduce the number of errors made in manual redrawing. Toys R Us claimed the service would save $100,000 a year in messaging, printing, and photo processing costs alone. Figure 10-5 illustrates how the business processes for construction projects changed as a result of this system.

Even more significant savings resulted from using the service to keep a complicated project, such as the Toys R Us building, on time and within budget. For example, LeBlanc used the system to monitor progress at the Times Square site from two Webcams installed at the construction site, controlling the rotation of the cameras from his computer keyboard. He and other members of the architectural, design, and construction team also used the Building Collaboration Services Web site to view digital photos of the building.

To Think About: What are the management benefits of using Web-based construction management software? How do such tools provide value? What are the possible drawbacks?

Sources: Donna Fuscaldo, "Building a Market," *Wall Street Journal*, April 15, 2002; Tony Kontzer, "Buzzsaw Gets the Job Done," *InternetWorld*, December 16, 2002; and Mark Roberti, "Cutting Construction Chaos," *The Industry Standard*, June 11, 2001.

MANAGEMENT

Requirements of Knowledge Work Systems

Knowledge work systems have characteristics that reflect the special needs of knowledge workers. First, knowledge work systems must give knowledge workers the specialized tools they need, such as powerful graphics, analytical tools, and communications and document-management tools. These systems require great computing power in order to rapidly handle the sophisticated graphics or complex calculations necessary to such knowledge workers as scientific researchers, product designers, and financial analysts. Because knowledge workers are so focused on knowledge in the external world, these systems also must give the worker quick and easy access to external databases.

A user-friendly interface is very important to a knowledge worker's system. User-friendly interfaces save time by allowing the user to perform needed tasks and get to required information without having to spend a lot of time learning how to use the computer. Saving time is more important for knowledge workers than for most other employees because knowledge workers are highly paid—wasting a knowledge worker's time is simply too expensive and knowledge workers can easily fall prey to information overload (Farhoomand and Drury, 2002). Figure 10-6 summarizes the requirements of knowledge work systems.

Knowledge workstations often are designed and optimized for the specific tasks to be performed, so a design engineer will require a different workstation than a financial analyst. Design engineers need graphics with enough power to handle three-dimensional computer-

BEFORE

AFTER

Figure 10-5 Changes in the construction project management process. Toys R Us replaced its multi-step paper-based process for generating and revising construction design plans with a much simpler process using Web-based project management tools for the construction industry.

aided design (CAD) systems. However, financial analysts are more interested in having access to a myriad of external databases and in optical disk technology for efficiently storing and accessing massive amounts of financial data.

Examples of Knowledge Work Systems

Major knowledge work applications include computer-aided design (CAD) systems, virtual reality systems for simulation and modeling, and financial workstations. **Computer-aided design (CAD)** automates the creation and revision of designs, using computers and sophisticated graphics software. Using a more traditional physical design methodology, each design modification requires a mold to be made and a prototype to be physically tested. That process must be repeated many times, which is very expensive and time-consuming. Using a CAD workstation, the designer only needs to make a physical prototype toward the end of the design process because the design can be easily tested and changed on the computer. The ability of CAD software to provide design specifications for the tooling and the manufacturing process also saves a great deal of time and money while producing a manufacturing process with far fewer problems. The architect Frank Gehry used CATIA computer-aided design software to create the flowing curves on the innovative Guggenheim Museum in Bilbao, Spain. Drafting this design alone with traditional paper and pencil tools could have taken decades. Hawkes Ocean Technology used Autodesk's Inventor three-dimensional design and engineering program to create and manipulate flowing shapes when designing the revolutionary Deep Flight Aviator submarine for the U.S. Navy. The software allowed Hawkes to create and manipulate flowing shapes, test their stress points, and refine them without ever having to touch a lathe or mold. The system also enabled Hawkes to cut design costs by one-third, reduce engineering staff from 10 to 3, and bypass the prototyping stage when developing new products (Salkever, 2002). The chapter-ending case study describes how CAD is transforming the design and production of aircraft.

Virtual reality systems have visualization, rendering, and simulation capabilities that go far beyond those of conventional CAD systems. They use interactive graphics software to create computer-generated simulations that are so close to reality that users almost believe they are participating in a real-world situation. In many virtual reality systems, the user dons special clothing, headgear, and equipment, depending on the application. The

computer-aided design (CAD)
Information system that automates the creation and revision of designs using sophisticated graphics software.

virtual reality systems
Interactive graphics software and hardware that create computer-generated simulations that provide sensations that emulate real-world activities.

Figure 10-6 Requirements of knowledge work systems. Knowledge work systems require strong links to external knowledge bases in addition to specialized hardware and software.

Computer-aided design (CAD) systems improve the quality and precision of product design by performing much of the design and testing work on the computer.

clothing contains sensors that record the user's movements and immediately transmit that information back to the computer. For instance, to walk through a virtual reality simulation of a house, you would need garb that monitors the movement of your feet, hands, and head. You also would need goggles containing video screens and sometimes audio attachments and feeling gloves so that you could be immersed in the computer feedback.

Virtual reality is just starting to provide benefits in educational, scientific, and business work. For example, neuroradiologists at New York's Beth Israel Medical Center can use the Siemens Medical Systems 3D Virtuoso System to peek at the interplay of tiny blood vessels or take a fly-through of the aorta. Surgeons at New York University School of Medicine can use three-dimensional modeling to target brain tumors more precisely, thereby reducing bleeding and trauma.

Virtual Reality Modeling Language (VRML)

A set of specifications for interactive three-dimensional modeling on the World Wide Web.

Virtual reality applications are being developed for the Web using a standard called **Virtual Reality Modeling Language (VRML).** VRML is a set of specifications for interactive, three-dimensional modeling on the World Wide Web that can organize multiple media types, including animation, images, and audio to put users in a simulated real-world environment. VRML is platform independent, operates over a desktop computer, and requires little bandwidth. Users can download a three-dimensional virtual world designed using VRML from a server over the Internet using their Web browser.

DuPont, the Wilmington, Delaware, chemical company, created a VRML application called HyperPlant, which allows users to access three-dimensional data over the Internet with Netscape Web browsers. Engineers can go through three-dimensional models as if they were physically walking through a plant, viewing objects at eye level. This level of detail reduces the number of mistakes they make during construction of oil rigs, oil plants, and other structures.

investment workstation

Powerful desktop computer for financial specialists, which is optimized to access and manipulate massive amounts of financial data.

The financial industry is using specialized **investment workstations** to leverage the knowledge and time of its brokers, traders, and portfolio managers. Firms such as Merrill Lynch and Paine Webber have installed investment workstations that integrate a wide range of data from both internal and external sources, including contact management data, real-time and historical market data, and research reports. Previously, financial professionals had to spend considerable time accessing data from separate systems and piecing together the information they needed. By providing one-stop information faster and with fewer errors,

Women can create a VRML "virtual model" that approximates their physical proportions to help them visualize how they will look in clothing sold in the Lands' End Web site. The digitized image can be rotated to show how the outfits will look from all angles and users can click to change the clothes' color.

TABLE 10-2	EXAMPLES OF KNOWLEDGE WORK SYSTEMS

Knowledge Work System	Function in Organization
CAD/CAM (Computer-aided design/ computer-aided manufacturing)	Provides engineers, designers, and factory managers with precise control over industrial design and manufacturing
Virtual reality systems	Provide drug designers, architects, engineers, and medical workers with precise, photorealistic simulations of objects
Investment workstations	High-end PCs used in financial sector to analyze trading situations instantaneously and facilitate portfolio management

the workstations streamline the entire investment process from stock selection to updating client records. Table 10-2 summarizes the major types of knowledge work systems.

SHARING KNOWLEDGE: GROUP COLLABORATION SYSTEMS AND ENTERPRISE KNOWLEDGE ENVIRONMENTS

Although many knowledge and information work applications have been designed for individuals working alone, organizations have an increasing need to support people working in groups. These groups include not only formal work groups but, increasingly, informal communities of practice that are important sources of organizational expertise. A **community of practice** is an informal group of people in an organization with a common professional interest, such as a group in an international bank with a special interest in lending activities in Southeast Asia or a Linux user's group in a corporation that primarily uses the Windows operating system. Its members may live or work in many different locations. In contrast to project teams, communities of practice often do not have responsibility for the production of a specific deliverable within a given time span and set their own agendas, such as education sessions, conferences, or assisting other members with problems they encounter in their work.

community of practice
Informal group of people that may live or work in many different locations but who share a common professional interest. An important source of expertise for organizations.

Groupware and Web Collaboration Tools

Chapters 6, 8 and 9 introduced the key technologies for group coordination and collaboration: e-mail, teleconferencing, dataconferencing, videoconferencing, and groupware. *Groupware* (which we introduced in Chapter 6) has been a primary tool for creating collaborative work environments. Groupware is built around three key principles: communication, collaboration, and coordination. It allows groups to work together on documents, schedule meetings, route electronic forms, access shared folders, participate in electronic discussions, develop shared databases, and send e-mail. Information-intensive companies, such as consulting firms, law firms, and financial management companies, have found groupware an especially powerful tool for leveraging their knowledge assets.

Internet tools for e-mail, newsgroup discussions, group scheduling, Web publishing, and point-to-point conferencing offer low-cost alternatives to proprietary groupware for collaborative work. These tools are best suited for simple tasks in small and medium businesses. Commercial software tools called teamware make intranets more useful for working in teams. **Teamware** consists of intranet-based applications for building a work team, sharing ideas and documents, brainstorming, scheduling, tracking the status of tasks and projects, and archiving decisions made or rejected by project team members for future use. Teamware is similar to groupware, although its application development capabilities are not as powerful as those provided by sophisticated groupware products. However, it lets companies easily implement collaboration applications that can be accessed using a Web browser. eRoom Technology's eRoom and Lotus Quickplace are examples of commercial teamware products.

teamware
Group collaboration software that is customized for teamwork.

Proprietary groupware remains a key tool for applications requiring extensive coordination, frequent updating and document tracking, and a high-level of security. Lotus Notes, OpenText Livelink, and other conventional groupware products have been enhanced so they can be integrated with the Internet or private intranets and used for collaborative commerce and supply chain management. Groove Networks provides a peer-to-peer collaboration platform that enables workers on the fly to collaborate and share data without going through a central Web server. The basic Groove interface lets users create or join shared workspaces that can be customized with tools for instant messaging, chat, streaming voice and video communication, a notepad, a calendar, shared file repositories, and a shared browser that allows multiple users to jointly surf the Web. Members of groups defined by Groove can be limited to specific applications, files, and discussions.

A growing number of companies are using Web conferencing tools to stage meetings, conferences, and presentations online. Web conferencing and collaboration software provides a "virtual" conference table where participants can view and modify documents and slides and share their thoughts and comments using chat, telephone, or video. The current generation of such tools from Lotus, Microsoft, PlaceWare, and WebEx, work through a standard Web browser. Participants from many different locations can use these Web conferencing tools, which include a virtual whiteboard, to annotate, edit, or view documents, slides, video, and Web pages as part of a presentation. Salespeople might use such tools for offering online product demonstrations, while senior executives might use them to analyze a contract proposal or to stage a presentation for hundreds of investors.

Intranets and Enterprise Knowledge Environments

Chapters 4 and 9 described how some organizations are using intranets and Internet technologies for group collaboration and coordination. Some of these intranets are providing the foundation for enterprise knowledge environments in which information from a variety of sources and media, including text, sound, video, and even digital slides, can be shared, displayed, and accessed across an enterprise through a simple common interface. If properly designed, these knowledge environments can serve as organizational **knowledge maps.** Knowledge maps are tools for identifying and locating the organization's knowledge resources, and they can point to people as sources of knowledge as well as to documents and databases. Examples of enterprise knowledge environments can be found in Table 10-3. These comprehensive intranets can transform decades-old processes, allowing people to inventory and disseminate information, share best practices, communicate, conduct research, and collaborate in ways that were never before possible.

Enterprise knowledge environments are so rich and vast that many organizations have built specialized corporate portals to help individuals navigate through various knowledge resources. These **enterprise information portals,** also known as *enterprise knowledge portals* direct individuals to digital knowledge objects and information system applications, helping them make sense of the volume of information that is available and also showing how organizational knowledge resources are interconnected. Figure 10-7 illustrates what an enterprise

---

knowledge map

Tool for identifying and locating the organization's knowledge resources.

enterprise information portal

Application that enables companies to provide users with a single gateway to internal and external sources of information.

Groove Networks provides peer-to-peer desktop collaboration software enabling users to work online or offline in virtual workspaces they create and control. Illustrated here is a sample Groove shared space, which can show who's active or inactive in a space, which tool they are using, and the assigned role of each group member. Each shared space can be customized with the tools selected by users.

TABLE 10-3   EXAMPLES OF ENTERPRISE KNOWLEDGE ENVIRONMENTS

Organization	Knowledge Management Capabilities
Ford Motor Company	Intranet delivers information about news, people, processes, products, and competition to 95,000 professional employees. Employees can access online libraries and a Web Center of Excellence with information on best practices, standards, and recommendations.
Roche Laboratories	Global Healthcare Intelligence Platform integrates documents from multiple sources to provide its professional services group with up-to-date information and expertise relating to new Hoffman-La Roche pharmaceutical products. The system gathers relevant information from global news sources, specialty publishers, healthcare Web sites, government sources, and the firm's proprietary internal information systems, indexing, organizing, linking, and updating the information as it moves through the system. Users can search multiple sources and drill down through layers of detail to see relationships among pieces of data.
Shell Oil Company	Knowledge Management System (KMS) provides a communications and collaboration environment where employees can learn about and share information about best practices. Includes information from internal sources and from external sources, such as universities, consultants, other companies, and research literature. A Lotus Domino groupware application allows employees to carry on dialogues through the company intranet. The author of a best practice in the repository might use this tool to talk with colleagues about his or her experiences.
Booz Allen Hamilton	Knowledge Online intranet provides an online repository of consultants' knowledge and experience, including a searchable database organized around the firm's best specialties and best practices; other intellectual capital such as research reports, presentations, graphs, images, and interactive training material; and links to resumes and job histories.

information portal might look like. It might include access to external sources of information, such as news feeds and research, as well as internal knowledge resources and capabilities for e-mail, chat (including instant messaging), discussion groups, and videoconferencing. Commercial software tools are available to build and personalize these portals, providing users with a single point of access to multiple types of information from wireless as well as wired devices. Many of these tools include capabilities for categorizing, indexing, and searching content and for linking to business applications such as enterprise and customer relationship management systems.

A corporate portal can enhance employee productivity by presenting a seamless single point of access to all of the information resources employees need to do their jobs. Portals or portions of portals extended to customers, suppliers, and business partners can help these groups understand the company's business or unique value proposition.

Figure 10-7 An enterprise information portal. The portal provides a single point of access to the firm's knowledge resources, and helps the firm coordinate information and people to make decisions and take action.

A KNOWLEDGE PORTAL BECOMES DEACONS' COMPETITIVE WEAPON

Deacons is a 150-year law firm with offices in Hong Kong, the People's Republic of China, Thailand, Vietnam, Indonesia, Singapore, Taiwan, and Australia. It provides lawyers fluent in the host country's language who also have local contacts and expertise. Deacons is one of Hong Kong's largest legal practices. Its Hong Kong office has 180 attorneys and has recently encountered mounting competition from London law firms as well as other firms in Hong Kong. CIO Philip Scorgie concluded that one way to be more competitive would be to install an information system that would help the company preserve and share its knowledge.

Deacons modeled its system after portals such as Yahoo! where millions of documents are indexed and powerful search engines help users locate what they want. Deacons began its knowledge portal project in 1999 when search engines had been vastly improved and could now rapidly search through millions of documents. However, because quality indexing, Chinese text searching, and other requisite portal technology were not yet easily available, the firm decided to develop these capabilities in-house. The company turned to Microsoft and Oracle to develop the software and purchased Sun and Compaq hardware.

Eliciting the cooperation of Deacons' lawyers was the tougher challenge. Deacons wanted to load and search over two million documents just to start with, with many more to be added later. The firm hired a special knowledge management team of six non-practicing attorneys to index each existing document in its computer systems and organize the documents into folders where they could be much more easily located and accessed. This allowed the system to demonstrate its usefulness without requiring the cooperation of practicing lawyers. Staff usage of the system was logged to determine what information was most frequently requested and the search engines were tuned so they would more easily locate the information people most wanted.

Deacons credited contributors of materials. Many younger lawyers were willing to share their work as a way to achieve some recognition in the firm. However many experienced lawyers opposed sharing their work, such as contracts for the purchase or financing of ships, because they viewed it as proprietary. The firm considered these documents valuable corporate assets because they could serve as templates that could be modified for others to use. These lawyers had to be convinced to allow their work to be seen by others. When other features were added, many of the less eager lawyers were intrigued, and that helped also. By 2002, contributions from lawyers were increasing at a rate of 25 percent per year.

Deacons' knowledge portal was linked to other Deacons systems so that, for example, one could obtain human resources information about other internal staff members, organization charts, and floor plans. The portal was also connected to other information on the corporate computers, such as company financials and information on case management. It also enabled newly hired lawyers to be trained more quickly, partly because the information needed to do their jobs was immediately available. Almost no training is required to use the system's standardized Web interface. The system is personalized for each user's position in the organization, and when individuals change jobs, the kind of information they can access changes automatically.

The company also made the system into a free-of-charge extranet for clients to access documents, issue new instructions, and check the status of cases online. Deacons initially made its extranet available only to a few of its largest clients, but has been gradually giving access to others. Soon the clients will be given customized portals that enable each to access the work being done for them. By adding even more value to company knowledge for its employees and clients, Deacons' portal has enhanced the firm's image in the marketplace.

Think About: How did Deacons obtain value from using a knowledge portal? How did this system change the way the company conducted business? What management, organization, and technology issues had to be addressed to use this portal successfully?

Sources: Ann Toh, "They've Got Knowledge," *CIO-ASIA*, January 2002; and Deacons' Web site at <www.deaconslaw.com>.

ORGANIZATIONS

The Window on Organizations describes some of the benefits of a knowledge portal for a law firm. The Manager's Toolkit describes the business issues that must be addressed when developing a portal.

Another application for knowledge intranets is to provide a platform for *e-learning*, which we introduced in Chapter 8. For example, Johnson & Johnson created an Internet-based program called J&J Law School Online to help employees recognize and deal with legal issues they encounter in their daily work. A series of Web-based courses covers a variety of legal and ethical topics selected to match an employee's role within the company. APL Inc., the international subsidiary of the giant transportation firm NOL Group of Singapore, implemented a Web-based platform to train over 1,500 sales representatives in more than

MIS IN ACTION: MANAGER'S TOOLKIT

ESTABLISHING THE BUSINESS REQUIREMENTS OF AN ENTERPRISE INFORMATION PORTAL

Portals can be viewed as electronic doorways into a company. They help users access essential information and collaborate with each other, and they can enhance business performance if they are carefully thought out. When designing a portal, here are some key questions business managers should ask:

1. *Content:* To what information should the portal point? How is this information used in the organization's business processes? Which sources of this information are internal? Which are external? Should the external sources be provided by a content aggregation service or gathered by the organization itself? Does any of this content have to be edited or repackaged to be used effectively?
2. *Users:* Who are the users of the portal? All employees or specific groups of employees? Should the portal or parts of the portal be accessible to people outside the organization?
3. *Personalization:* Does the portal page need to be personalized for specific users or groups in the organization? How much customization is required?
4. *Collaboration support:* Should the portal provide capabilities for communication and collaboration, such as e-mail, newsgroups, chat, or groupware?
5. *Ease of use:* How can the portal be designed so that it is easy to use and to navigate from one source of information to another? Do users need special search engines or knowledge maps to help them find information?
6. *Updating and editing:* How often does the information feeding the portal need to be updated? Which individuals in the organization will be responsible for updating this information or editing content?
7. *Management and administration:* Who is responsible for administering the portal and for approving and reviewing content? Who is responsible for editing the content if this is required?
8. *Benefits and costs:* What are the business benefits to be provided by the portal? Can they be quantified? Can these benefits justify the cost of building and maintaining the portal? (See the discussion of information system costs and benefits in Chapter 13.)

---

126 countries in Siebel System's customer relationship management software along with other key sales and financial software.

Group collaboration and knowledge-sharing technologies alone cannot promote information sharing if team members do not believe it is in their interest to share, especially in organizations that encourage competition among employees. This technology can best enhance the work of a group if the applications are properly designed to fit the organization's needs and work practices and if management encourages a collaborative atmosphere. Successful knowledge sharing requires an appropriate knowledge sharing environment (Pan, Hsieh, and Chen, 2001).

10.3 ARTIFICIAL INTELLIGENCE

Organizations are using artificial intelligence technology to capture individual and collective knowledge and to codify and extend their knowledge base.

WHAT IS ARTIFICIAL INTELLIGENCE?

Artificial intelligence (AI) is the effort to develop computer-based systems (both hardware and software) that behave as humans. Such systems would be able to learn natural languages, accomplish coordinated physical tasks (robotics), use a perceptual apparatus that informs their physical behavior and language (visual and oral perception systems), and emulate human expertise and decision making (expert systems). Such systems also would exhibit logic, reasoning, intuition, and the just-plain-common-sense qualities that we associate with human beings. Figure 10-8 illustrates the elements of the artificial intelligence family. Another important element is intelligent machines, the physical hardware that performs these tasks.

Successful artificial intelligence systems are based on human expertise, knowledge, and selected reasoning patterns, but they do not exhibit the intelligence of human beings.

artificial intelligence (AI)
The effort to develop computer-based systems that can behave like humans, with the ability to learn languages, accomplish physical tasks, use a perceptual apparatus, and emulate human expertise and decision making.

Figure 10-8 The artificial intelligence family. The field of AI currently includes many initiatives: natural language, robotics, perceptive systems, expert systems, and intelligent machines.

Existing artificial intelligence systems do not come up with new and novel solutions to problems. Existing systems extend the powers of experts but in no way substitute for them or capture much of their intelligence. Briefly, existing systems lack the common sense and generality of naturally intelligent human beings.

Human intelligence is vastly complex and much broader than computer intelligence. A key factor that distinguishes human beings from other animals is their ability to develop associations and to use metaphors and analogies such as *like* and *as*. Using metaphor and analogy, humans create new rules, apply old rules to new situations, and, at times, act intuitively and/or instinctively without rules. Much of what we call common sense or generality in humans resides in the ability to create metaphor and analogy.

Human intelligence also includes a unique ability to impose a conceptual apparatus on the surrounding world. Metaconcepts such as cause-and-effect and time, and concepts of a lower order such as breakfast, dinner, and lunch, are all imposed by human beings on the world around them. Thinking in terms of these concepts and acting on them are central characteristics of intelligent human behavior.

WHY BUSINESS IS INTERESTED IN ARTIFICIAL INTELLIGENCE

Although artificial intelligence applications are much more limited than human intelligence, they are of great interest to business for the following reasons:

- To store information in an active form as organizational memory, creating an organizational knowledge base that many employees can examine and preserving expertise that might be lost when an acknowledged expert leaves the firm.

- To create a mechanism that is not subject to human feelings, such as fatigue and worry. This may be especially useful when jobs may be environmentally, physically, or mentally dangerous to humans. These systems also may be useful advisers in times of crisis.

- To eliminate routine and unsatisfying jobs held by people.

- To enhance the organization's knowledge base by generating solutions to specific problems that are too massive and complex to be analyzed by human beings in a short period of time.

CAPTURING KNOWLEDGE: EXPERT SYSTEMS

In limited areas of expertise, such as diagnosing a car's ignition system or classifying biological specimens, the rules of thumb used by real-world experts can be understood, codified, and placed in a machine. Information systems that solve problems by capturing knowledge for a very specific and limited domain of human expertise are called **expert systems.** Expert systems capture the knowledge of skilled employees in the form of a set of rules. The set of rules in the expert system adds to the memory, or stored learning of the firm. An expert system can assist decision making by asking relevant questions and explaining the reasons for adopting certain actions.

Expert systems lack the breadth of knowledge and the understanding of fundamental principles of a human expert. They are quite narrow, shallow, and brittle. They typically perform very limited tasks that can be performed by professionals in a few minutes or hours. Problems that cannot be solved by human experts in the same short period of time are far too difficult for an expert system. However, by capturing human expertise in limited areas, expert systems can provide benefits, helping organizations make high-quality decisions with fewer people.

How Expert Systems Work

Human knowledge must be modeled or represented in a way that a computer can process. The model of human knowledge used by expert systems is called the **knowledge base.** A standard structured programming construct (see Chapter 14) is the IF–THEN construct, in which a condition is evaluated. If the condition is true, an action is taken. For instance,

IF INCOME > $45,000 (condition)
THEN PRINT NAME AND ADDRESS (action)

expert system
Knowledge-intensive computer program that captures the expertise of a human in limited domains of knowledge.

knowledge base
Model of human knowledge that is used by expert systems.

Figure 10-9 Rules in an AI program. An expert system contains a number of rules to be followed when used. The rules themselves are interconnected; the number of outcomes is known in advance and is limited; there are multiple paths to the same outcome; and the system can consider multiple rules at a single time. The rules illustrated are for simple credit-granting expert systems.

A series of these rules can be a knowledge base. Any reader who has written computer programs knows that virtually all traditional computer programs contain IF–THEN statements. The difference between a traditional program and a **rule-based expert system** program is one of degree and magnitude. AI programs can easily have 200 to 10,000 rules, far more than traditional programs, which may have 50 to 100 IF–THEN statements. Moreover, in an AI program the rules tend to be interconnected and nested to a far greater degree than in traditional programs, as shown in Figure 10-9. Hence the complexity of the rules in a rule-based expert system is considerable.

Could you represent the knowledge in the Encyclopedia Britannica this way? Probably not, because the **rule base** would be too large, and not all the knowledge in the encyclopedia can be represented in the form of IF–THEN rules. In general, expert systems can be efficiently used only in those situations in which the domain of knowledge is highly restricted (such as in granting credit) and involves no more than a few thousand rules.

The **AI shell** is the programming environment of an expert system. In the early years of expert systems, computer scientists used specialized artificial intelligence programming languages, such as LISP or Prolog, that could process lists of rules efficiently. Today a growing number of expert systems use AI shells that are user-friendly development environments. AI shells can quickly generate user-interface screens, capture the knowledge base, and manage the strategies for searching the rule base.

The strategy used to search through the rule base is called the **inference engine.** Two strategies are commonly used: forward chaining and backward chaining (see Figure 10-10).

In **forward chaining** the inference engine begins with the information entered by the user and searches the rule base to arrive at a conclusion. The strategy is to fire, or carry out, the action of the rule when a condition is true. In Figure 10-10, beginning on the left, if the user enters a client with income greater than $100,000, the engine will fire all rules in sequence from left to right. If the user then enters information indicating that the same client owns real estate, another pass of the rule base will occur and more rules will fire. Processing continues until no more rules can be fired.

In **backward chaining** the strategy for searching the rule base starts with a hypothesis and proceeds by asking the user questions about selected facts until the hypothesis is either confirmed or disproved. In our example, in Figure 10-10, ask the question, "Should we add

rule-based expert system
An AI program that has a large number of interconnected and nested IF–THEN statements, or rules, that are the basis for the knowledge in the system.

rule base
The collection of knowledge in an AI system that is represented in the form of IF–THEN rules.

AI shell
The programming environment of an expert system.

inference engine
The strategy used to search through the rule base in an expert system; can be forward or backward chaining.

forward chaining
A strategy for searching the rule base in an expert system that begins with the information entered by the user and searches the rule base to arrive at a conclusion.

backward chaining
A strategy for searching the rule base in an expert system that acts like a problem solver by beginning with a hypothesis and seeking out more information until the hypothesis is either proved or disproved.

Figure 10-10 Inference engines in expert systems. An inference engine works by searching through the rules and "firing" those rules that are triggered by facts gathered and entered by the user.

this person to the prospect database?" Begin on the right of the diagram and work toward the left. You can see that the person should be added to the database if a sales representative is sent, term insurance is granted, or a financial advisor visits the client.

An AI development team is composed of one or more experts, who have a thorough command of the knowledge base, and one or more knowledge engineers, who can translate the knowledge (as described by the expert) into a set of rules. A **knowledge engineer** is similar to a traditional systems analyst but has special expertise in eliciting information and expertise from other professionals.

The team members must select a problem appropriate for an expert system. The project will balance potential savings from the proposed system against the cost. The team members will develop a prototype system to test assumptions about how to encode the knowledge of experts. Next, they will develop a full-scale system, focusing mainly on the addition of a very large number of rules. The complexity of the entire system grows with the number of rules, so the comprehensibility of the system may be threatened. Generally, the system will be pruned to achieve simplicity and power. The system is tested by a range of experts within the organization against the performance criteria established earlier. Once tested, the system will be integrated into the data flow and work patterns of the organization.

knowledge engineer

A specialist who elicits information and expertise from other professionals and translates it into a set of rules for an expert system.

Examples of Successful Expert Systems

The following are examples of expert systems that provide organizations with an array of benefits, including reduced errors, reduced costs, reduced training time, improved decisions, and improved quality and service.

Countrywide Funding Corp. in Pasadena, California, is a loan-underwriting firm with about 400 underwriters in 150 offices around the country. The company developed a PC-based expert system in 1992 to make preliminary creditworthiness decisions on loan requests. The company had experienced rapid, continuing growth and wanted the system to help ensure consistent, high-quality loan decisions. CLUES (Countrywide's Loan Underwriting Expert System) has about 400 rules. Countrywide tested the system by sending every loan application handled by a human underwriter to CLUES as well. The system was refined until it agreed with the underwriters in 95 percent of the cases.

Countrywide will not rely on CLUES to reject loans, because the expert system cannot be programmed to handle exceptional situations such as those involving a self-employed person or complex financial schemes. An underwriter will review all rejected loans and will make the final decision. CLUES has other benefits. Traditionally, an underwriter could handle six or seven applications a day. Using CLUES, the same underwriter can evaluate at least 16 per day. Countrywide now is using the rules in its expert system to answer e-mail inquiries from visitors to its Web site who want to know if they qualify for a loan.

Galeria Kaufhof, a German superstore chain, uses a rule-based system to help it manage over 110,000 deliveries of goods that it receives each day, ranging from clothing to complex

Countrywide Funding Corporation developed an expert system called CLUES to evaluate the creditworthiness of loan applicants. Countrywide is using the rules in this system to answer inquiries from visitors to its Web site who want to know if they qualify for a loan.

electronics and fine china. Inspecting each delivery is time-consuming and expensive, but the company wants to make sure that it is receiving goods that are not damaged or defective. Kaufhof implemented a rule-based system that identifies high-risk deliveries and passes along lower-risk ones automatically. The system scans delivery labels and identifies each delivery in terms of its size, type of product, whether the product is a new product, and the supplier's past history of deliveries to Kaufhof. Deliveries of large numbers of complex products that are new or that have suppliers with unfavorable delivery histories are carefully inspected while other deliveries are passed on without inspection (Booth and Buluswar, 2002).

The investment banking firm Goldman Sachs uses a rule-based expert system to keep unwanted stocks out of individual portfolios. Almost all of its client portfolios have restrictions specified by owners on which stocks or even entire sectors to exclude. Goldman wanted to make sure its global network of financial advisers respected these restrictions so that they did not make any purchases that clients didn't want. Goldman's business managers, compliance officers, and private wealth managers all play roles in deciding which stocks to purchase for a portfolio. The company developed a rule-based system that maintains rules for keeping a particular stock from entering a client's portfolio. By creating a centralized portfolio filtering system, Goldman is better able to catch mistakes before erroneous trades go through (Guerra, 2001).

Although expert systems lack the robust and general intelligence of human beings, they can provide benefits to organizations if their limitations are well understood. Only certain classes of problems can be solved using expert systems. Virtually all successful expert systems deal with problems of classification in which there are relatively few alternative outcomes and in which these possible outcomes are all known in advance. Many expert systems require large, lengthy, and expensive development efforts. Hiring or training more experts may be less expensive than building an expert system. Typically, the environment in which an expert system operates is continually changing so that the expert system must also continually change. Some expert systems, especially large ones, are so complex that in a few years the maintenance costs equal or surpass the development costs.

The knowledge base of expert systems is fragile and brittle; they cannot learn or change over time. In fast-moving fields, such as medicine or the computer sciences, keeping the knowledge base up to date is a critical problem. For example, Digital Equipment Corporation stopped using its XCON expert system for configuring VAX computers because its product line was constantly changing and it was too difficult to keep updating the system to capture these changes. Expert systems can only represent limited forms of knowledge. IF–THEN knowledge exists primarily in textbooks. There are no adequate representations for deep causal models or temporal trends. No expert system, for instance, can write a textbook on information systems or engage in other creative activities not explicitly foreseen by system designers. Many experts cannot express their knowledge using an IF–THEN format.

Expert systems cannot yet replicate knowledge that is intuitive, based on analogy and on a sense of things.

Contrary to early promises, expert systems are most effective in automating lower-level clerical functions. They can provide electronic checklists for lower-level employees in service bureaucracies such as banking, insurance, sales, and welfare agencies. The applicability of expert systems to managerial problems is very limited. Managerial problems generally involve drawing facts and interpretations from divergent sources, evaluating the facts, and comparing one interpretation of the facts with another; they are not limited to simple classification. Expert systems based on the prior knowledge of a few known alternatives are unsuitable to the problems managers face on a daily basis.

ORGANIZATIONAL INTELLIGENCE: CASE-BASED REASONING

Expert systems primarily capture the knowledge of individual experts, but organizations also have collective knowledge and expertise that they have built up over the years. This organizational knowledge can be captured and stored using case-based reasoning. In **case-based reasoning (CBR),** descriptions of past experiences of human specialists, represented as cases, are stored in a database for later retrieval when the user encounters a new case with similar parameters. The system searches for stored cases with problem characteristics similar to the new one, finds the closest fit, and applies the solutions of the old case to the new case. Successful solutions are tagged to the new case and both are stored together with the other cases in the knowledge base. Unsuccessful solutions also are appended to the case database along with explanations as to why the solutions did not work (see Figure 10-11).

Expert systems work by applying a set of IF–THEN–ELSE rules against a knowledge base, both of which are extracted from human experts. Case-based reasoning, in contrast, represents knowledge as a series of cases, and this knowledge base is continuously expanded and refined by users.

Compaq Computer of Houston, Texas, gave purchasers of its Pagemarq printer case-based reasoning software to help reduce customer service costs. The software knowledge base is a series of several hundred actual cases of Pagemarq printer problems—actual stories about

case-based reasoning (CBR)
Artificial intelligence technology that represents knowledge as a database of cases and solutions.

Figure 10-11 How case-based reasoning works. Case-based reasoning represents knowledge as a database of past cases and their solutions. The system uses a six-step process to generate solutions to new problems encountered by the user.

smudged copies, printer memory problems, and jammed printers—all the typical problems people face with laser printers. Trained CBR staff entered case descriptions in textual format into the CBR system. They entered key words necessary to categorize the problem, such as smudge, smear, lines, streaks, and paper jam. They also entered a series of questions that might be needed to allow the software to further narrow the problem. Finally, solutions were attached to each case.

With the Compaq-supplied CBR system running on their computer, owners seldom need to call Compaq's service department. Instead, they run the software and describe the problem to the software. The system swiftly searches actual cases, discarding unrelated ones, selecting related ones. If necessary to further narrow the search results, the software will ask the user for more information. In the end, one or more cases relevant to the specific problem are displayed, along with their solutions. Now, customers can solve most of their own problems quickly without a telephone call, and Compaq has saved $10 million to $20 million annually in customer-support costs.

10.4 OTHER INTELLIGENT TECHNIQUES

Organizations are using other intelligent computing techniques to extend their knowledge base by providing solutions to problems that are too massive or complex to be handled by people with limited resources. Neural networks, fuzzy logic, genetic algorithms, and intelligent agents are developing into promising business applications.

NEURAL NETWORKS

Neural networks are designed to imitate the physical thought process of the biological brain. Figure 10-12 shows two neurons from a leech's brain. The soma, or nerve cell, at the center acts like a switch, stimulating other neurons and being stimulated in turn. Emanating from the neuron is an axon, which is an electrically active link to the dendrites of other neurons. Axons and dendrites are the "wires" that electrically connect neurons to one another. The junction of the two is called a synapse. This simple biological model is the metaphor for the development of neural networks. A **neural network** consists of hardware or software that attempts to emulate the processing patterns of the biological brain.

Figure 10-13 shows an artificial neural network with two neurons. The resistors in the circuits are variable and can be used to teach the network. When the network makes a mistake (i.e., chooses the wrong pathway through the network and arrives at a false conclusion), resistance can be raised on some circuits, forcing other neurons to fire. If this learning process continues for thousands of cycles, the machine learns the correct response. The neurons are highly interconnected and operate in parallel, as does the human brain, allowing the neural network to process very large amounts of data efficiently.

A neural net has a large number of sensing and processing nodes that continuously interact with each other. Figure 10-14 represents one type of neural network comprising an input layer, an output layer, and a hidden processing layer. Humans "train" the network by feeding it a set of training data for which the inputs produce a known set of outputs or conclusions.

neural network

Hardware or software that attempts to emulate the processing patterns of the biological brain.

Figure 10-12 Biological neurons of a leech. Simple biological models, like the neurons of a leech, have influenced the development of artificial or computational neural networks in which the biological cells are replaced by transistors or entire processors.
Source: Defense Advance Research Projects Agency (DARPA), 1988. Unclassified.

Figure 10-13 Artificial neural network with two neurons. In artificial neurons, the biological neurons become processing elements (switches), the axons and dendrites become wires, and the synapses become variable resistors that carry weighted inputs (currents) that represent data. *Source:* DARPA, 1988. Unclassified.

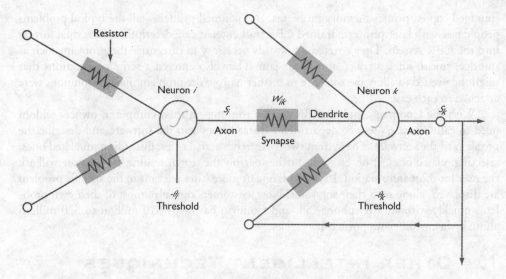

This helps the computer learn the correct solution by example. As the computer is fed more data, each case is compared with the known outcome. If it differs, a correction is calculated and applied to the nodes in the hidden processing layer. These steps are repeated until a condition, such as corrections being less than a certain amount, is reached. The neural network in Figure 10-14 has "learned" how to identify a good credit risk. There are also self-organizing neural networks that can be "trained" by exposing them to large amounts of data and allowing them to discover the patterns and relationships in the data.

The Difference Between Neural Networks and Expert Systems

What is different about neural networks? Expert systems seek to emulate or model a human expert's way of solving problems, but neural network builders claim that they do not model human intelligence, do not program solutions, and do not aim to solve specific problems per se. Instead, neural network designers seek to put intelligence into the hardware in the form of a generalized capability to learn. In contrast, the expert system is highly specific to a given problem and cannot be easily retrained.

Neural network applications are emerging in medicine, science, and business to address problems in pattern classification, prediction and financial analysis, and control and optimization. Papnet is a neural net-based system that distinguishes between normal and abnormal cells when examining Pap smears for cervical cancer and has far greater accuracy than visual examinations by technicians. The computer is not able to make a final decision, so a technician will review any selected abnormal cells. Using Papnet, a technician requires one-fifth the time to review a smear while attaining perhaps 10 times the accuracy of the existing manual method.

Neural networks are being used by the financial industry to discern patterns in vast pools of data that might help investment firms predict the performance of equities, corporate bond ratings, or corporate bankruptcies. Visa International Inc. is using a neural network to help

Figure 10-14 A neural network uses rules it "learns" from patterns in data to construct a hidden layer of logic. The hidden layer then processes inputs, classifying them based on the experience of the model. *Source:* Herb Edelstein, "Technology How-To: Mining Data Warehouses," *InformationWeek*, January 8, 1996. Copyright © 1996 CMP Media, Inc., 600 Community Drive, Manhasset, NY 11030. Reprinted with permission.

Ward Systems' NeuroShell Predictor uses neural network technology to make predictions by "learning" patterns in the user's data file. The Predictor allows users to select columns from their data file which will be used as inputs to the model and to select the output column which contains the values they are trying to predict.

detect credit card fraud by monitoring all Visa transactions for sudden changes in the buying patterns of cardholders.

Unlike expert systems, which typically provide explanations for their solutions, neural networks cannot always explain why they arrived at a particular solution. Moreover, they cannot always guarantee a completely certain solution, arrive at the same solution again with the same input data, or always guarantee the best solution (Trippi and Turban, 1989–1990). They are very sensitive and may not perform well if their training covers too little or too much data. In most current applications, neural networks are best used as aids to human decision makers instead of substitutes for them.

FUZZY LOGIC

Traditional computer programs require precision: on–off, yes–no, right–wrong. However, we human beings do not experience the world this way. We might all agree that +120 degrees is hot and −40 degrees is cold; but is 75 degrees hot, warm, comfortable, or cool? The answer depends on many factors: the wind, the humidity, the individual experiencing the temperature, one's clothing, and one's expectations. Many of our activities also are inexact. Tractor-trailer drivers would find it nearly impossible to back their rigs into spaces precisely specified to less than an inch on all sides.

Fuzzy logic is a rule-based technology that tolerates imprecision and even uses it to solve problems we could not have solved before. Fuzzy logic consists of a variety of concepts and techniques for representing and inferring knowledge that is imprecise, uncertain, or unreliable. Fuzzy logic can create rules that use approximate or subjective values and incomplete or ambiguous data. By expressing logic with some carefully defined imprecision, fuzzy logic is closer to the way people actually think than traditional IF–THEN rules.

Ford Motor Co. developed a fuzzy logic application that backs a simulated tractor-trailer into a parking space. The application uses the following three rules:

IF the truck is *near* jackknifing, THEN *reduce* the steering angle.

IF the truck is *far away* from the dock, THEN steer *toward* the dock.

IF the truck is *near* the dock, THEN point the trailer *directly* at the dock.

This logic makes sense to us as human beings, for it represents how we think as we back that truck into its berth.

How does the computer make sense of this programming? The answer is relatively simple. The terms (known as membership functions) are imprecisely defined so that, for example, in Figure 10-15, cool is between 50 degrees and 70 degrees, although the temperature is most clearly cool between about 60 degrees and 67 degrees. Note that cool is overlapped by cold or norm. To control the room environment using this logic, the programmer would develop

fuzzy logic

Rule-based AI that tolerates imprecision by using nonspecific terms called membership functions to solve problems.

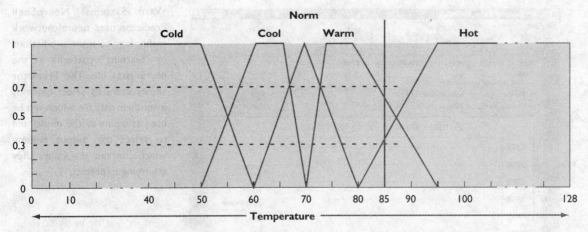

Figure 10-15 Implementing fuzzy logic rules in hardware. The membership functions for the input called temperature are in the logic of the thermostat to control the room temperature. Membership functions help translate linguistic expressions such as "warm" into numbers that the computer can manipulate.

Source: James M. Sibigtroth, "Implementing Fuzzy Expert Rules in Hardware," *AI Expert,* April 1992. © 1992 Miller Freeman, Inc. Reprinted with permission.

similarly imprecise definitions for humidity and other factors such as outdoor wind and temperature. The rules might include one that says: "If the temperature is cool or cold and the humidity is low while the outdoor wind is high and the outdoor temperature is low, raise the heat and humidity in the room." The computer would combine the membership function readings in a weighted manner and, using all the rules, raise and lower the temperature and humidity.

Fuzzy logic is widely used in Japan and is gaining popularity in the United States. Its popularity has occurred partially because managers find they can use it to reduce costs and shorten development time. Fuzzy logic code requires fewer IF–THEN rules, making it simpler than traditional code. The rules required in the previous trucking example, plus its term definitions, might require hundreds of IF–THEN statements to implement in traditional logic. Compact code requires less computer capacity, allowing, for example, Sanyo Fisher USA to implement camcorder controls without adding expensive memory to their product.

Fuzzy logic also allows us to solve problems not previously solvable, thus improving product quality. In Japan, Sendai's subway system uses fuzzy logic controls to accelerate so smoothly that standing passengers need not hold on. Mitsubishi Heavy Industries in Tokyo has been able to reduce the power consumption of its air conditioners by 20 percent by implementing control programs in fuzzy logic. The autofocus device in cameras is only possible because of fuzzy logic. Williams-Sonoma sells an "intelligent" steamer made in Japan that uses fuzzy logic. A variable heat setting detects the amount of grain, cooks it at the preferred temperature, and keeps the food warm up to 12 hours.

Management also has found fuzzy logic useful for decision making and organizational control. A Wall Street firm had a system developed that selects companies for potential acquisition, using the language stock traders understand. Recently, a system has been developed to detect possible fraud in medical claims submitted by healthcare providers anywhere in the United States.

GENETIC ALGORITHMS

genetic algorithms

Problem-solving methods that promote the evolution of solutions to specified problems using the model of living organisms adapting to their environment.

Genetic algorithms (also referred to as adaptive computation) refer to a variety of problem-solving techniques that are conceptually based on the method that living organisms use to adapt to their environments—the process of evolution. They are programmed to work the way populations solve problems—by changing and reorganizing their component parts using processes such as reproduction, mutation, and natural selection. Thus, genetic algorithms promote the evolution of solutions to particular problems, controlling the generation, variation, adaptation, and selection of possible solutions using genetically based processes. As solutions alter and combine, the worst ones are discarded and the better ones survive to go on to produce even better solutions. Genetic algorithms breed programs that solve problems even when no person can fully understand their structure (Holland, 1992).

		Color	Speed	Intelligence	Fitness
1 0 1 1 0 1	1	White	Medium	Dumb	40
0 1 0 1 0 1	2	Black	Slow	Dumb	43
1 1 0 1 1 0	3	White	Slow	Very Dumb	22
0 0 0 1 0 1	4	Black	Fast	Dumb	71
1 0 1 0 0 0	5	White	Medium	Very Smart	53
A population of chromosomes			**Decoding of chromosomes**	**Evaluation of chromosomes**	

Figure 10-16 The components of a genetic algorithm. This example illustrates an initial population of "chromosomes," each representing a different solution. The genetic algorithm uses an iterative process to refine the initial solutions so that the better ones, those with the higher fitness, are more likely to emerge as the best solution.
Source: From *Intelligent Decision Support Methods* by Vasant Dhar and Roger Stein, p. 65 © 1997. Reprinted by permission of Prentice Hall, Upper Saddle River, N.J.

A genetic algorithm works by representing information as a string of 0s and 1s. A possible solution can be represented by a long string of these digits. The genetic algorithm provides methods of searching all possible combinations of digits to identify the right string representing the best possible structure for the problem.

In one method, the programmer first randomly generates a population of strings consisting of combinations of binary digits (see Figure 10-16). Each string corresponds to one of the variables in the problem. One applies a test for fitness, ranking the strings in the population according to their level of desirability as possible solutions. After the initial population is evaluated for fitness, the algorithm then produces the next generation of strings, consisting of strings that survived the fitness test plus offspring strings produced from mating pairs of strings, and tests their fitness. The process continues until a solution is reached.

Solutions to certain types of problems in areas of optimization, product design, and the monitoring of industrial systems are especially appropriate for genetic algorithms. Many business problems require optimization because they deal with issues such as minimization of costs, maximization of profits, efficient scheduling, and use of resources. If these situations are very dynamic and complex, involving hundreds or thousands of variables or formulas, genetic algorithms can expedite the solution because they can evaluate many different solution alternatives quickly to find the best one. For example, General Electric engineers used genetic algorithms to help optimize the design for jet turbine aircraft engines, where each design change required changes in up to 100 variables. The supply chain management software from i2 Technologies uses genetic algorithms to optimize production scheduling models incorporating hundreds of thousands of details about customer orders, material and resource availability, manufacturing and distribution capability, and delivery dates. International Truck and Engine used this software to iron out snags in production, reducing costly schedule disruptions by 90 percent in five of its plants (Wakefield, 2001; Burtka, 1993).

Hybrid AI Systems

Genetic algorithms, fuzzy logic, neural networks, and expert systems can be integrated into a single application to take advantage of the best features of these technologies. Such systems are called **hybrid AI systems.** Hybrid applications in business are growing. In Japan, Hitachi, Mitsubishi, Ricoh, Sanyo, and others are starting to incorporate hybrid AI in products such as home appliances, factory machinery, and office equipment. Matsushita has developed a "neurofuzzy" washing machine that combines fuzzy logic with neural networks. Nikko Securities has been working on a neurofuzzy system to forecast convertible-bond ratings.

hybrid AI systems

Integration of multiple AI technologies into a single application to take advantage of the best features of these technologies.

INTELLIGENT AGENTS

Intelligent agents are software programs that work in the background without direct human intervention to carry out specific, repetitive, and predictable tasks for an individual user, business process, or software application. The agent uses a built-in or learned knowledge base to accomplish tasks or make decisions on the user's behalf. Intelligent agents can be programmed to make decisions based on the user's personal preferences—for example, to delete junk e-mail, schedule appointments, or travel over interconnected networks to find the cheapest airfare to California. The agent can be likened to a personal digital assistant collaborating with

intelligent agent

Software program that uses a built-in or learned knowledge base to carry out specific, repetitive, and predictable tasks for an individual user, business process, or software application.

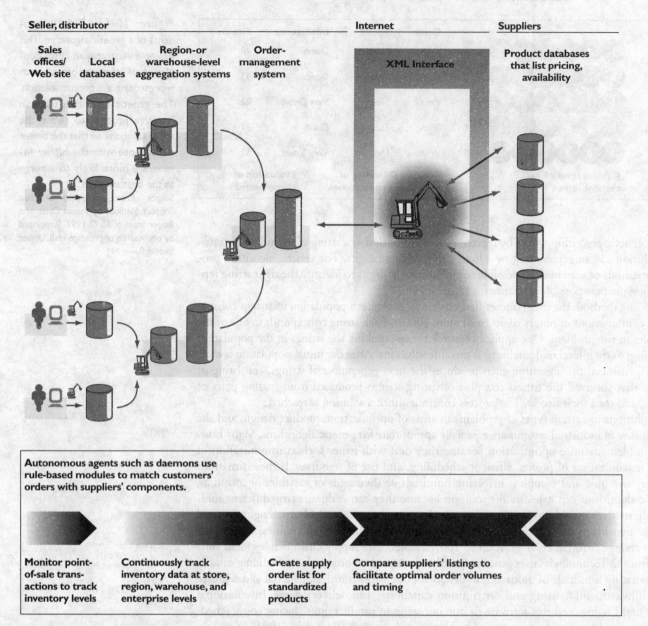

Figure 10-17 Intelligent agent technology at work. This autonomous execution system uses intelligent agent and XML technology to automate the process of matching orders with data on the availability of components. Daemons are computer programs that lie dormant until activated to perform specified operations at predefined times or in response to certain events.
Source: Corey Booth and Sashi Buluswar, *The Return of Artificial Intelligence*, The McKinsey Quarterly, 2002 No. 2.

the user in the same work environment. It can help the user by performing tasks on the user's behalf, training or teaching the user, hiding the complexity of difficult tasks, helping the user collaborate with other users, or monitoring events and procedures.

There are many intelligent agent applications today in operating systems, application software, e-mail systems, mobile computing software, and network tools. For example, the Wizards found in Microsoft Office software tools have built-in capabilities to show users how to accomplish various tasks, such as formatting documents or creating graphs, and to anticipate when users need assistance. Of special interest to business are intelligent agents for cruising networks, including the Internet, in search of information. Chapter 9 described how these *shopping bots* can help consumers find products they want and assist them in comparing prices and other features. Because these mobile agents are personalized, semiautonomous, and continuously running, they can help automate several of the most time-consuming stages of the buying process and thus reduce transaction costs.

Figure 10-17 illustrates the use of intelligent agents in an *autonomous execution system,* which runs continuously, monitors information as it arrives from multiple distributed locations, and

MAKE IT YOUR BUSINESS

FINANCE AND ACCOUNTING

Many expert system, neural network, and hybrid AI applications as well as knowledge work systems have been developed for the finance and accounting function. Rule-based expert systems have been widely used tools for evaluating the credit risk of loan applicants and for investment portfolio selection. A number of financial services firms use neural networks for stock and bond trading strategies, commodity trading, and detecting credit card fraud. Financial professionals use investment workstations that integrate a wide range of financial data from internal and external sources to support their research and analysis.

HUMAN RESOURCES

The human resources function uses Web publishing tools and intranets to communicate company policies to employees and to provide online directories to human resource policies and training programs. You can find examples of human resources applications on page 326.

MANUFACTURING AND PRODUCTION

The manufacturing and production function is replete with knowledge system applications. Many companies are using intranets and group collaboration tools for sharing product design and manufacturing specifications among team members in many different locations and for project management. Robotic equipment now performs man-

ufacturing tasks, such as welding or lifting heavy parts, that are too difficult or tedious for humans. Expert systems have been used to guide the configuration of orders when products with many different parts or features are being assembled. Both expert systems and case-based reasoning systems are used for assisting diagnostic and repair work on malfunctioning products and equipment. Fuzzy logic helps improve the performance of products such as camcorders, air conditioners, washing machines, and subway cars. Genetic algorithms have generated solutions for problems in optimizing scheduling or design. You can find examples of manufacturing and production applications on pages 312–314, 320, and 342–345.

SALES AND MARKETING

Specialized corporate portals and knowledge repositories have been created for sales and marketing staff to help them access and share information about customers, sales leads, competitors, and changes in product pricing and specifications. Virtual reality and VRML simulations can help customers experience the "look and feel" of products and even tailor some of these products more precisely to their needs. Case-based reasoning systems have been widely used for customer service and support. Many online intelligent agent tools and services have been developed to search the Web for products and services specified by users and to assist them in comparing prices and features. You can find examples of sales and marketing applications on pages 312–314.

executes specific tasks in response to what they find. Arrow Electronics, a $10 billion components distributor uses such a system to match orders from 200,000 customers with data on the availability of components from 600 suppliers. The system uses XML to exchange data using the RosettaNet standard for the electronics industry and handles 10 million transactions around the world each day. By automatically notifying suppliers about orders and customers about the availability and shipment of parts, the system has reduced Arrow's order times by 50 to 75 percent.

MANAGEMENT WRAP-UP

Leveraging and managing organizational knowledge have become core management responsibilities. Managers need to identify the knowledge assets of their organizations and make sure that appropriate systems and processes are in place to maximize their use.

Systems for knowledge and information work and artificial intelligence can enhance organizational processes in a number of ways. They can facilitate communication, collaboration, and coordination; bring more analytical power to bear in the development of solutions; or reduce the amount of human intervention in organizational processes.

An array of technologies is available to support knowledge management, including artificial intelligence technologies and tools for knowledge and information work and group collaboration. Managers should understand the costs, benefits, and capabilities of each technology and the knowledge management problem for which each is best suited.

For Discussion

1. Knowledge management is a business process, not a technology. Discuss.
2. How much can the use of artificial intelligence change the management process?

Summary

1. *Why do businesses today need knowledge management programs and systems for knowledge management?* Businesses need knowledge management programs because knowledge has become a central productive and strategic asset in today's information economy and a potential source of strategic advantage. Knowledge management is a set of processes for systematically and actively managing and leveraging the stores of knowledge in an organization. Information systems can play a valuable role in knowledge management, helping the organization create, store, disseminate, and apply knowledge and capture its knowledge base. Knowledge management systems include support for knowledge repositories, knowledge networks, and communities of practice. Office systems, knowledge work systems (KWS), group collaboration systems, and artificial intelligence applications are especially useful for knowledge management because they focus on supporting information and knowledge work and on defining and codifying the organization's knowledge base.

2. *Which information system applications are most useful for distributing, creating, and sharing knowledge in the firm?* Offices coordinate information work in the organization, link the work of diverse groups in the organization, and couple the organization to its external environment. Office systems support these functions by automating document management, communications, scheduling, and data management. Word processing, desktop publishing, Web publishing, and digital imaging systems support document management activities. Electronic-mail systems and groupware support communications activities. Electronic calendar applications and groupware support scheduling activities. Desktop data-management systems support data-management activities.

   Knowledge work systems (KWS) support the creation of knowledge and its integration into the organization. KWS require easy access to an external knowledge base; powerful computer hardware that can support software with intensive graphics, analysis, document management, and communications capabilities; and a user-friendly interface. KWS often run on workstations that are customized for the work they must perform. Computer-aided design (CAD) systems and virtual reality systems which create interactive simulations that behave like the real world, and require graphics and powerful modeling capabilities. KWS for financial professionals provide access to external databases and the ability to analyze massive amounts of financial data very quickly.

   Groupware is special software to support information-intensive activities in which people work collaboratively in groups. Intranets can perform many group collaboration and support functions and allow organizations to use Web publishing capabilities for document management.

3. *What are the business benefits of using artificial intelligence technology for knowledge management?* Artificial intelligence is the development of computer-based systems that behave like humans. There are five members of the artificial intelligence family tree: natural language, robotics, perceptive systems, expert systems, and intelligent machines. Artificial intelligence lacks the flexibility, breadth, and generality of human intelligence, but it can be used to capture and codify organizational knowledge. Businesses can use artificial intelligence to help them create an organizational knowledge base to preserve expertise; to perform routine, unsatisfying, or dangerous jobs; and to generate solutions to specific problems that are too massive and complex to be analyzed by human beings in a short period of time.

4. *How can businesses use expert systems and case-based reasoning to capture knowledge?* Expert systems are knowledge-intensive computer programs that solve problems that heretofore required human expertise. The systems capture a limited domain of human knowledge using rules. The strategy to search through the knowledge base, called the *inference engine*, can use either forward or backward chaining. Expert systems are most useful for problems of classification or diagnosis. Case-based reasoning represents organizational knowledge as a database of cases that can be continually expanded and refined. When the user encounters a new case, the system searches for similar cases, finds the closest fit, and applies the solutions of the old case to the new case. The new case is stored with successful solutions in the case database.

5. *How can organizations benefit from using neural networks and other intelligent techniques?* Neural networks consist of hardware and software that attempt to mimic the thought processes of the human brain. Neural networks are notable for their ability to learn without programming and to recognize patterns that cannot be easily described by humans. They are being used in science, medicine, and business primarily to discriminate patterns in massive amounts of data.

   Fuzzy logic is a software technology that expresses logic with some carefully defined imprecision so that it is closer to the way people actually think than traditional IF–THEN rules. Fuzzy logic has been used for controlling physical devices and is starting to be used for limited decision-making applications.

   Genetic algorithms develop solutions to particular problems using genetically based processes such as fitness, crossover, and mutation. Genetic algorithms are beginning to be applied to problems involving optimization, product design, and monitoring industrial systems where many alternatives or variables must be evaluated to generate an optimal solution.

   Intelligent agents are software programs with built-in or learned knowledge bases that carry out specific, repetitive, and predictable tasks for an individual user, business process, or software application. Intelligent agents can be programmed to search for information or conduct transactions on networks, including the Internet.

KEY TERMS

AI shell, 329

Artificial intelligence, 327

Backward chaining, 329

Best practices, 316

Case-based reasoning (CBR), 332

Chief knowledge officer (CKO), 315

Community of practice, 323

Computer-aided design (CAD), 321

Data workers, 317

Enterprise information portal, 324

Expert system, 328

Forward chaining, 329

Fuzzy logic, 335

Genetic algorithms, 336

Hybrid AI systems, 337

Inference engine, 329

Information work, 317

Intelligent agent, 337

Investment workstation, 322

Knowledge assets, 315

Knowledge base, 328

Knowledge engineer, 330

Knowledge management, 315

Knowledge map, 324

Knowledge repository, 319

Knowledge workers, 317

Knowledge work systems (KWS), 319

Neural network, 333

Office systems, 318

Organizational learning, 315

Organizational memory, 316

Rule base, 329

Rule-based expert system, 329

Tacit knowledge, 316

Teamware, 323

Virtual Reality Modeling Language (VRML), 322

Virtual reality systems, 321

REVIEW QUESTIONS

1. What is knowledge management? List and briefly describe the information systems that support it and the kind of information technology (IT) infrastructure it requires.

2. How does knowledge management promote organizational learning? How do knowledge management systems support knowledge networks, knowledge repositories, and communities of practice?

3. Describe the roles of the office in organizations. What are the major activities that take place in offices?

4. What are the principal types of information systems that support information worker activities in the office?

5. What are the generic requirements of knowledge work systems? Why?

6. Describe how the following systems support knowledge work: computer-aided design (CAD), virtual reality, and investment workstations.

7. How does groupware support information work? Describe its capabilities and Internet and intranet capabilities for collaborative work.

8. What is artificial intelligence? Why is it of interest to businesses?

9. What is the difference between artificial intelligence and natural or human intelligence?

10. Define an expert system and describe how it can help organizations use their knowledge assets.

11. Define and describe the role of the following in expert systems: rule base, AI shell, and inference engine.

12. What is case-based reasoning? How does it differ from an expert system?

13. Describe three problems of expert systems.

14. Describe a neural network. With what kinds of tasks would a neural network excel?

15. Define and describe fuzzy logic. For what kinds of applications is it suited?

16. What are genetic algorithms? How can they help organizations solve problems? For what kinds of problems are they suited?

17. What are intelligent agents? How can they be used to benefit businesses?

APPLICATION SOFTWARE EXERCISE

EXPERT SYSTEM EXERCISE: BUILDING A SIMPLE EXPERT SYSTEM FOR RETIREMENT PLANNING

When employees at your company retire, they are given cash bonuses. These cash bonuses are based on the length of employment and the retiree's age. In order to receive a bonus, an employee must be at least 50 years of age and have worked for the company for five years. The following table summarizes the criteria for determining bonuses.

Using the information provided, build a simple expert system. Find a demonstration copy of an expert system software

LENGTH OF EMPLOYMENT	BONUS
< 5 years	No bonus
6–10 years	20 percent of current annual salary
11–15 years	30 percent of current annual salary
16–20 years	40 percent of current annual salary
20–25 years	50 percent of current annual salary
26 or more years	100 percent of current annual salary

tool on the Web that you can download (see the recommendations at the Laudon Web site for Chapter 10). Alternatively, use your spreadsheet software to build the expert system.

GROUP PROJECT

With a group of classmates, select two groupware products such as Lotus Notes, OpenText LiveLink, or Groove and compare their features and capabilities. To prepare your analysis, use arti-

cles from computer magazines and the Web sites for the groupware manufacturers. If possible, use electronic presentation software to present your findings to the class.

TOOLS FOR INTERACTIVE LEARNING

▇ INTERNET CONNECTION

The Internet Connection for this chapter will take you to the National Aeronautics and Space Administration (NASA) Web site, where you can complete an exercise showing how this Web site can be used by knowledge workers.

▇ INTERACTIVE STUDY GUIDE

You can use the Interactive Study Guide to test your knowledge of the topics in this chapter and get instant feedback where you need more practice.

▇ RUNNING CASE

The Running Case provides an opportunity for you to investigate opportunities for identifying information system applications to help Dirt Bikes USA better manage its knowledge assets. You can find a complete description of this project on the Laudon Web site for Chapter 10 and on the Multimedia Edition CD-ROM.

▇ ELECTRONIC COMMERCE PROJECT

The Electronic Commerce project for this chapter will direct you to Web sites where you can compare the capabilities of two shopping bots for the Web.

▇ MANAGEMENT DECISION PROBLEM

At the Laudon Web site for Chapter 10, you can find a Management Decision Problem on measuring productivity from a knowledge intranet.

▇ CD-ROM

If you use the Multimedia Edition CD-ROM with this chapter, you will find a video clip illustrating how the Papnet neural network is used for medical testing, an audio overview of the major themes of this chapter, and bullet text summarizing the key points of the chapter.

CASE STUDY—*Can Boeing Keep Flying High?*

The Boeing Company has been critical to the United States for over 60 years in both war and peace. During World War II, it produced the B17 and B29 bombers that were the heart of the military bombing campaign against the Axis powers. In 1958, the 707, Boeing's first successful civilian passenger plane, began commercial operation and was so successful that 348 of that model are still flying today. When in 1969 Boeing came out with its long-range 747 jumbo jet, the company became the largest exporter of any corporation in the United States. During the 1990s, the company underwent rapid expansion, acquiring Rockwell International, a major aerospace and defense company in 1996, competing aircraft manufacturer McDonnell Douglas in 1997, and Hughes Aircraft, a leading space and communications company in 2000. Today, with over 180,000 employees, Boeing is a giant producer of passenger planes, business jets, fighter planes, helicopters, flight instruments, and even satellites and missiles.

Although Boeing is a major force in the aerospace, defense, and communications industries as well as the commercial airline industry, its path to growth and prosperity has become clouded. In its commercial airline business it faces a formidable competitor. Airbus Industrie had been established in 1971 by the British and French governments and was immediately subsidized by these governments. In 1996, Airbus decided to challenge Boeing for the jumbo jet market, then ruled exclusively by Boeing with its 416-seat long-distance 747-400. Airbus predicts air travel will expand rapidly during the next decade, requiring many giant jumbo jets. Its Airbus A380 seats 555 passengers, and is the world's largest jetliner. It features a full double-deck rather than the 747's shorter second story "hump," and later versions could eventually be stretched to accommodate over 650 seats. The A380's major benefit would be that by carrying more passengers, it will not require additional landing slots at the overcrowded hub airports. Moreover, Airbus claims the operating costs for its A380 will be 17 percent lower compared to the Boeing 747. Airbus, as a newer company, could also build more modern technology into

its planes. Its cockpit designs are similar in all of its jets, so pilots need only a few days of extra training to fly another model. Airbus has steadily taken market share away from Boeing, and by 1999 had surpassed Boeing in the number of planes sold.

At first, Boeing decided to compete with Airbus in the giant jumbo jetliner market by "stretching" its existing 747 at a development cost of only $3 to $4 billion, far lower than the $12 billion price tag for developing the Airbus plane. In March 2001, however, Boeing withdrew from the competition. Its management developed a very different vision of the market for jumbo jets. Boeing's management foresees a turn to smaller airliners that will fly close to the speed of sound, enabling passengers to fly nonstop from departure to destination, bypassing the overcrowded hubs. This would stimulate the growth of smaller regional airlines and reduce the need for huge jumbo jets. Boeing announced it was designing a new 230 to 250 passenger aircraft, dubbed the Sonic Cruiser. It will fly fast enough to cut one hour out of each 3,000 miles of flight, enabling many more direct flights, greatly reducing the need for flight transfers at the large hubs. Moreover, while the current coast-to-coast and overseas jumbo jet flights enable a plane to make one round-trip daily, Boeing claims its faster new plane will fly two round trips daily, making it a valuable investment. Further, management claims, these planes will especially attract the profitable first- and business-class passengers. For airlines struggling with lower-cost competitors, Boeing is also considering an ultra-efficient 250-seat airplane built from lightweight materials that travels at the same speed as existing jetliners but would be 20 percent cheaper to operate. All in all, Boeing foresees a strong expansion of smaller jet sales rather than of jumbo jet sales.

In addition to Airbus competition, Boeing has been facing difficult conditions because the market for commercial airplanes has been shrinking due to airline mergers and the downturn in air travel after the September 11, 2001, terrorist attacks. Boeing's CEO Phil Condit is pushing Boeing into the lucrative services area: maintenance, modifications, financing, and pilot training. He is also looking beyond aircraft and related services to steer Boeing into a variety of high technology businesses, including airborne Internet services and digital movie distribution. This diversification is one reason why Boeing moved its global headquarters from Seattle, Washington, to Chicago, Illinois.

Boeing now sees its military and space business as its biggest growth area as it switches from commercial airplane production to newer businesses based on information and communications technologies. In July 2002, it announced it was merging its satellite and communications businesses with its military manufacturing unit, creating an operation equal in size to its commercial airplane division. Boeing is a contractor for the U.S. government's National Missile Defense project. The company is also working on projects related to "network centric warfare," in which the United States would use a global information grid to orchestrate all of its missiles, planes, tanks, and ships in battle from a central command post. Boeing makes satellites, AWACS (Airborne Warning and Control System) airplanes, unmanned surveillance aircraft, guided missiles, and Global Positioning System (GPS)-equipped handheld radios. The company is developing broadband technology and standards that could network all of these "smart" devices and every element of warfare so that they could be visually displayed on the "data wall" at a command-and-control center. If Boeing's infrastructure becomes adopted, the company could see $20 to $30 billion in defense business opportunities over the next ten years. Analysts warn, however, that the U.S. government may not like depending on Boeing alone to construct such systems.

Another Boeing initiative is in air traffic management. Boeing set up a separate business unit to overhaul the way air traffic is controlled. It would like to see the United States air traffic controller system transformed from ground-based traffic control to air-based traffic control relying on the Global Positioning System (GPS). Navigation computers would be required on all jetliners, enabling every airplane continually to transmit its exact position, direction, and speed to nearby aircraft. This method would permit planes to fly shorter distances on each flight while also reducing the long waits for takeoffs. Some air traffic controllers would still be needed, particularly at larger airports. Inexpensive computer and GPS technology already exists, and both Boeing and Airbus airplanes are already equipped for flying without using ground-based systems.

In these new initiatives and its commercial airplane business, Boeing's management is trying to lower costs by using technology to reform inefficient business processes. Boeing's airplane production process was paper-intensive, with a final design of the Boeing 747 consisting of approximately 75,000 paper engineering drawings. Boeing designers long ago realized they would save much production time if they reused existing designs rather than designing each aircraft from scratch. The process of design customization was manual and took more than 1,000 engineers a year of full-time work to complete. For every customization choice on every airplane built, hundreds of pages of detailed drawings needed to be drawn manually. To reuse old paper aircraft configurations and parts designs, the engineers first needed to search through an immense number of paper drawings to find appropriate designs to reuse for the specific configuration. They then laboriously copied the old designs to use for the new plane. Inevitably, errors crept into the new designs—large numbers of errors, given the large numbers of design sheets—because of unavoidable copying mistakes.

It used to take 800 computers to manage the coordination of engineering and manufacturing and many of these did not communicate directly with each other. The list of parts produced by engineering for a given airplane was configured differently from the lists used by manufacturing and customer service. Ultimately the parts list had to be broken down, converted, and recomputed up to 13 times during the production of a single plane.

Another problem with manual design was that the staff needed to create life-size mock-ups in plywood and plastic to ensure that everything fit and that the pipes and wires that run through the plane are placed properly and do not interfere with other necessary equipment. They were also needed to verify the accuracy of part specifications. Building mock-ups was a slow, expensive, laborious process. At production time, errors would again occur when part numbers of specifications were manually copied and at times miscopied onto order sheets, resulting in many wrong or mis-sized parts arriving.

Engineers worked in separate fiefdoms based on their field of specialization. Some engineers designed the plane's parts, others assembled them, and others designed the parts' packing crates. They rarely compared notes. If production engineers discovered a part that didn't fit, they sent a complaint back to the designers located in another plant. The designers then pulled out their drawings, reconfigured the part to make it match drawings of the surrounding parts, and sent the new design back to the plant. Warehouses were filled with paper.

In the early 1990s, Boeing began switching to a "paperless design" model, which it used to computerize the design and production of its 777 aircraft. The 777 aircraft carries 300 to 440 passengers and has lower operating, maintenance, and fuel costs because it uses lighter materials and can fly with only two pilots and two engines. The "paperless design" system employs nine IBM mainframes, a Cray supercomputer, and 2,200 workstations, storing 3,500 billion bits of information. It enables engineers to call up any of the 777's millions of parts, modify them, fit them into the surrounding structure, and put them back into the plane's "electronic box" so that other engineers can make their own adjustments. Boeing assembled a single parts list that can be used by every division without modification and without tabbing. In addition management established design–production teams that brought together designers and fabricators from a range of specialties throughout the whole process. Ultimately the airplane was designed entirely on the computer screen and was initially assembled without expensive mock-ups. The company cut overall engineering design errors by 50 percent while designing and building a 777 in 10 months.

Boeing has been using systems to address its massive supply chain problem. Five to six million parts are required for its large twin-aisle airplanes alone. Inventory of these parts has been handled manually, and the production sites became infamous for the large piles of parts not being used. Not surprisingly, Boeing inventory turned over only two to three times per year compared to 12 times a year in an efficient manufacturing operation. Needed parts often arrived late. Boeing had to assign about 300 materials planners in different plants just to find needed parts on the shop floor.

In 1994, Boeing launched a process improvement program known as Define and Control Airplane Configuration/Manufacturing Resource Management (DCAC/MRM) to streamline and simplify the processes of configuring and assembling airplanes. Boeing had been using 400 software programs, each with its own independent database, to support production. The management team decided to replace these 400 programs with four interconnected, off-the-shelf software packages, one each for configuration, manufacturing, purchasing, and inventory control. This would enable everyone to work from the same database, offering data integrity and coordination. Each airplane was assigned its own unique identification number that could be used to identify all the parts required by that plane. Each airplane would have only one parts list, and it would be updated electronically during the production cycle. Management estimated that the project would cost $1 billion and would require more than 1,000 employees but would pay for itself within two years.

Boeing decided to purchase enterprise resource planning (ERP) software from Baan Co., of Putten, Netherlands, because this software could be used to control the flow of parts and was considered particularly well suited for companies with multi-site hybrid manufacturing processes such as Boeing. The software also includes EDI links with external suppliers and database links for internal suppliers. "As soon as our ERP system determines we don't have enough of a certain part in the assembly line to satisfy an airplane," explained one production manager, "we can identify which supplier we need and where that supplier's part needs to be delivered." Boeing's goal was that 45,000 persons would use the system at 70 plants to coordinate commercial airplane manufacturing. Rollout completion was targeted for the end of 1997. In addition to Baan's software, Boeing selected forecasting software from i2 Technologies, factory floor process planning software from CimLinc, product data management software from Structural Dynamics Research, and a product configuration system from Trilogy.

This project encountered serious problems, nearly causing a "manufacturing nervous breakdown." Parts shortages, defective parts, rework, and overtime approached all-time highs. Managers calculated that Boeing's production system was more than $1 billion over initial cost projections. The company was forced to make late deliveries, jeopardizing Boeing's standing with clients and its financial performance.

Eventually these problems were solved and Boeing went on to make other process improvements. At "moonshine shops," mechanics and assemblers are experimenting on innovations to improve efficiency, such as redesigning parts so that they are easier to assemble and load. Management is also working to standardize designs, to design units that require fewer parts, and to emphasize just-in-time parts delivery. Overall Boeing has already been able to decrease its 777 assembly time from 71 days to 31 days.

Boeing is trying to use Internet technology to reduce procurement costs by moving all purchasing online, reducing the number of suppliers to 18,000, and eliminating EDI. Boeing's old procurement processes were excessively paper-driven, with about 90 percent of all transactions such as purchase orders, contracts, invoices, requests for proposal (RFP), and shipping notices involving paper. Just removing reliance on paper could potentially save Boeing 20 to 27 percent of its internal costs. As a result of Boeing's recent corporate acquisitions, Boeing absorbed a number of different divisional order processing systems, many of which were left unchanged. This meant that Boeing now had 18 separate EDI connections for each of its many suppliers.

Boeing's launched its Commercial Aviation Web portal called myboeingfleet.com in May 2000. Boeing has 850 customers, including airlines, governments, and leasing companies. The new portal is a customer source of tools, parts and information about specific planes. Customers can access 1.5 million engineering drawings, 70,000 maintenance manuals, official service bulletins, and even a Web page where customers can discuss their problems with Boeing engineers. Prior to the portal, customers had to go to different sites for different functions such as part purchases. Using the unified Web site reduced the cost and the amount of paper needed in each transaction. Boeing now involves only nine people in each transaction rather than the 38 previously needed. The portal has reduced the amount of paper exchanged between Boeing and its airplane customers, and improved customer relations, but it has not inspired new customer service programs that might create additional revenue.

Boeing's next B2B step was joining BAE Systems, Lockheed Martin, Raytheon Company, and Rolls-Royce to launch Exostar, a global Net marketplace for the aerospace and defense industry in September 2000. The founders had all been building their own e-commerce supply-chain Web sites, investing millions of dollars, and they realized it would be cheaper and easier to join together to create a global electronic marketplace for their industry. While these companies are intense rivals for supplies and for commercial military aircraft and space contracts, they are also suppliers to and customers of each other. Their goal is to reduce costs while making their supply chains more efficient. In the past processing a purchase order cost Boeing about $150 manually. Today the standardized and automated contracts now cost around $1.50 each.

Quickly more than 8,000 suppliers joined Exostar out of the approximately 37,000 industry suppliers worldwide. Exostar gave suppliers a single connection point, improving their relationship with their buyers. Exostar uses the XML language, making it much easier for all suppliers and purchasers to join and use. It also enables Boeing and its suppliers to keep their internal systems, including Boeing's 18 legacy purchasing systems. Its suppliers now never have to deal with multiple systems. Moreover, it is now much easier for Boeing to know how much business the whole company is doing with its major suppliers. It also means future merger and acquisition integrations will be much easier. Exostar also includes a facility for suppliers and producers to work together in real time to plan schedules and to design or redesign products. Finally, Exostar is a much cheaper and easier system than is EDI.

Boeing hopes Exostar will eventually wean all suppliers off EDI. However, small suppliers have been reluctant to switch to Exostar because they do not have the technical sophistication or financial incentive to change their business processes and systems to work with an online marketplace. Industry analysts also point out that using an industry consortium Net marketplace may not work to Boeing's competitive advantage. Boeing has unique products and has used its status as a major industry player to set procurement standards that were in its best interests. While working on common solutions, each Exostar partner will try to protect its supply chain practices. The four companies compete for business, and the question is whether they will be able to separate their individual interests from their common goals for Exostar. To date, the bulk of Exostar purchases have been for indirect maintenance, repair, and operation goods.

Boeing also hopes to gain efficiencies from stepped-up use of knowledge management systems. Its Commercial Airplanes division, for example, must provide maintenance and support for a wide range of equipment with long lifespans. The company's global field workforce needs to refer 50 percent of its questions to Boeing's service engineers. It would cost Boeing up to thousands of dollars each time an engineer had to answer a query, because they were spending hours retrieving data and records. About half of the queries engineers receive each day have been previously answered, sometimes several times before. But unless the engineer remembered that a query had been previously answered, he or she would treat the inquiry as an entirely new investigation. Boeing implemented software from Primus Knowledge Solutions that includes an electronic repository of answers to a specified set of questions. This system can capture engineers' knowledge more easily, putting documents, messages, and drawings into folders that can be accessed with a sophisticated search engine. This saves engineers as much as several hours per day, since they no longer have to manually organize and coordinate information gathering. Every time a field service person answers a question, it can be funneled to the knowledge management system and indexed for future users.

In the summer of 2001, Boeing started rolling out an employee portal, starting first with 2,000 finance and engineering employees. All employees can access the portal, including nearly 50,000 factory employees given access through factory floor kiosks. For software, the company turned to Plumtree Software's Corporate Portal system. One problem that hopefully this portal would solve was that 172,000 employees were already connected, but to literally hundreds of intranets. The new portal is linking common data from Boeing's four big divisions, enabling the divisions to share significant data and applications over the Web. The company's plan is to identify the best-of-breed products in use in various units, and standardize the company's software on them. The portal gives employees access to large amounts of information, including: technical information, such as design data; personalized tools like calendars; human resources information such as retirement systems; and library items such as a glossary of aerospace industry acronyms. In addition, it gives employees such as aircraft designers an easy way to collaborate with other Boeing designers at home or abroad. The Boeing designers will also be able to collaborate with supplier designers when Boeing links its employee portal up with Exostar.

Overall, Boeing's aircraft production costs are still higher than the competition and the company is trying to reduce its U.S. workforce so that it can outsource more of its parts production work with components suppliers in China, Malaysia, and other countries. Jerry Calhoun, Boeing's lead labor negotiator stated that ". . . even with our efficiencies, even with our abilities to squeeze cost out of our product, we're still not cost-effective." According to Calhoun, Boeing would never win a sales campaign strictly on price.

CIO Scott Griffin has said, "The interesting issue for a big company is that when you're big, it is very hard to be fast. . . . We want to be big and fast." While Boeing has made many changes, the question remains whether these changes will make Boeing a strong yet nimble competitor in both its traditional and new lines of business. Can Boeing go fast enough to keep on flying?

Sources: Edward Wong, "For Jet Rivals, Caution Here, Swagger There," *New York Times*, July 28, 2002; "Airbus Claims Lead Over Boeing Despite Lost Orders," Ananova Web site January 17, 2002, <www.ananova.com>; Demir Barias, "Exostar Appoints CEO," *Line56*, January 8, 2002; Stanley Holmes and Mike France, "Boeing's Secret," *BusinessWeek*, May 20, 2002; Steven Greenhouse, "Mediator Joins Stalled Talks by Boeing Co. and Its Unions," *New York Times*, August 17, 2002; Pimm Fox, "Making Support Pay," *Computerworld*, March 11, 2002; "Boeing Shows How XML Can Help Business," *ITworld.com*, March 12, 2001; J. Lynn Lunsford, "Boeing's Planned Sonic Cruiser Is Buzz of Aerospace Industry, *Wall Street Journal*, February 27, 2002; "Boeing Explores Plan 'B,'" *Wall Street Journal*, June 11, 2002; "Lean Times: With Airbus on Its Tail, Boeing Is Rethinking How It Builds Planes," *Wall Street Journal*, September 5, 2001; "Boeing Plan to Unsnarl Air Traffic: Cede Ground Control to Satellites," *Wall Street Journal*, May 17, 2001; Dominic Gates, "Boeing's Big Move," *The Industry Standard*, April 2, 2001; Tom Kaneshige, "Exostar Unwraps 4.0," *Line56*, November 29, 2001; Richard Karpinski, "Web Supply Chains Revised," *InternetWeek.com*, September 28, 2001; Stephanie Sanborn and Heather Harreld, "U.S. Recovery: Airline Industry Exchanges Adopt 'Wait and See' Approach," *InfoWorld*, September 21, 2001; David Lewis, "Boeing Portal to Serve Employees, Partners," *InternetWeek*, July 30, 2001; Sandra Swanson, "Boeing: Design Anywhere, Build Anywhere, Share Freely," *InformationWeek*, December 10, 2001; J. Lynn Lunsford, Daniel Michaels, and Andy Pasztor, "Industry Focus: At Paris Air Show, Boeing-Airbus Duel Has New Twist," *Wall Street Journal*, June 15, 2001; Stanley Holmes, "Boeing Goes Lean," *BusinessWeek online*, June 4, 2001, <www.businessweek.com>; Daniel Michaels, "New Approach: Airbus Revamp Brings Sense to Consortium, Fuels Boeing Rivalry," *Wall Street Journal*, April 30, 2001; David Gauthier-Villars, Andy Pasztor, Anne Marie Squeo, and Scott McCartney, "Flight Plan: Boeing Revamp Cuts Ties to Seattle, Puts Focus on News Services," *Wall Street Journal*, March 22, 2001; Stuart F. Brown, "How to Build a Really, Really, Really Big Plane," *Fortune*, March 5, 2001; Amy Helen Johnson, "Boeing's Flight Plan," *Line56*, January 15, 2001; Jeff Cole, "Wing Commander: At Boeing, an Old Hand Provides New Tricks to Battle with Airbus," *Wall Street Journal*, January 10, 2001; Phillip L. Zweig, "Can Exostar Transform the Aerospace Industry?" *Outlook 2001*, 2, January 2001.

CASE STUDY QUESTIONS:

1. Analyze Boeing and its business strategy using the value chain and competitive forces models.

2. Summarize the business and technology conditions that caused Boeing to change its business strategy. What management, organization, and technology problems prompted this change?

3. How did Boeing change its business processes and information systems to support its new strategy? How do Boeing's information systems provide value?

4. What is the relationship of knowledge management to Boeing's business strategy? How is Boeing using knowledge management to execute its business model and business strategy?

5. Evaluate Boeing's new business strategy. What management, organization, and technology issues will Boeing face as it attempts to implement the strategy? How successful will Boeing be in pursuing that strategy?

CHAPTER 11

ENHANCING MANAGEMENT DECISION MAKING FOR THE DIGITAL FIRM

As a manager, you will be asked to make many different kinds of decisions. You will want to know how you can use information systems to improve your decision making, whether you are working alone or in a group. After completing this chapter, you will be able to answer the following questions:

1. *How can information systems help individual managers make better decisions when the problems are nonroutine and constantly changing?*

2. *How can information systems help people working in a group make decisions more efficiently?*

3. *Are there any special systems that can facilitate decision making among senior managers? Exactly what can these systems do to help high-level management?*

4. *What benefits can systems to support management decision making provide for the organization as a whole?*

objectives

The Gap Uses DSS for More Efficient Decision Making

During the 1990s, corporate America was smitten with the California dress style. The Gap led the charge to outfit everyone in khaki pants and corporate casual attire. Sales rose, and the company launched Gap and Banana Republic stores overseas, opened Old Navy stores, and started selling on the Web. While Gap sales grew in 2001, net income started to fall because the inventories and merchandising at its 4,100 stores became difficult to manage. Corporate buyers could not predict how many boot-cut jeans to buy or when they should arrive at stores. They were forced to gather current and past sales information from separate planning and inventory allocation systems and analyze this information on their own. Deciding what to buy, how much and when to stock clothes was a slow and tedious process. Often the data were duplicated among those different systems, making accurate forecasts even more difficult.

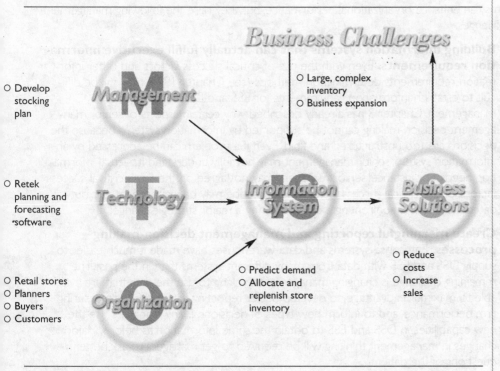

According to Michael Barrie, Gap's vice president of planning and forecasting systems, "Every item in a store is an investment." Given the number of Gap stores, these items amounted to huge investments, so if they remain on store shelves too long, the company's return on its inventory investment is much lower. In March 2001, the Gap decided to address this problem by implementing Retek's planning and forecasting software. The Retek software provides a common set of tools for all activities across all divisions. It integrates preseason-planning activities such as determining how many denim trench coats to stock in Chicago stores with end-of-season activities such as clearance pricing. Planners can use the software to measure customer reactions to repricing items and to speed up or slow down the shipment of clothes. Forecasts can be made for specific styles and colors based on factors such as how fast an item sells, the date it is placed on a store shelf, and seasonal sales patterns. Using software on their desktops, merchants and planners will be able to see the current status of each others' plans and forecasts so that they can collaborate and make better decisions about what to allocate, when to mark down, and how much to mark down. The system, however, "won't help us pick a better product," Barrie observes. That's up to the Gap's buyers who select items to sell based on their sense of fashion and style. But the software has clearly promoted more efficient decision making.

Sources: Meridith Levinson, "They Know What You'll Buy Next Summer (They Hope)," *CIO Magazine*, May 1, 2002; and Bob Tedeschi, "The Price is Right," *Smart Business Magazine*, May 2002.

MANAGEMENT CHALLENGES

The Gap's planning and forecasting system is an example of a decision-support system (DSS). Such systems have powerful analytic capabilities to support managers during the process of arriving at a decision. Other systems in this category are group decision-support systems (GDSS), which support decision making in groups, and executive support systems (ESS), which provide information for making strategic-level decisions. These systems can enhance organizational performance, but they raise the following management challenges:

1. **Building information systems that can actually fulfill executive information requirements.** Even with the use of critical success factors and other information requirements determination methods (see Chapter 13), it may still be difficult to establish information requirements for ESS and DSS serving senior management. Chapter 3 has already described why certain aspects of senior management decision making cannot be supported by information systems because the decisions are too unstructured and fluid. Even if a problem can be addressed by an information system, senior management may not fully understand its actual information needs. For instance, senior managers may not agree on the firm's critical success factors, or the critical success factors they describe may be inappropriate or outdated if the firm is confronting a crisis requiring a major strategic change.

2. **Create meaningful reporting and management decision-making processes.** Enterprise systems and data warehouses have made it much easier to supply DSS and ESS with data from many different systems than in the past. The remaining challenge is changing management thinking to use the data that are available to maximum advantage, to develop better reporting categories for measuring firm performance, and to inform new types of decisions. Many managers use the new capabilities in DSS and ESS to obtain the same information as before. Major changes in management thinking will be required to get managers to ask better questions of the data.

business intelligence

Applications and technologies that focus on gathering, storing, analyzing, and providing access to data from many different sources to help users make better business decisions.

Most information systems described throughout this text help people make decisions in one way or another, but DSS, GDSS, and ESS are part of a special category of information systems that are explicitly designed to enhance managerial decision making. Some of these systems represent **business intelligence** applications that focus on gathering, storing, analyzing, and providing access to data from many different sources to help users make better business decisions. By taking advantage of more accurate firm-wide data provided by enterprise systems and the new information technology infrastructure, these systems can support very fine-grained decisions for guiding the firm, coordinating work activities across the enterprise, and responding rapidly to changing markets and customers. Many of these managerial decision-making applications are now Web-enabled. This chapter describes the characteristics of each of these types of information systems, showing how each enhances the managerial decision-making process and ultimately the performance of the organization.

DSS, GDSS, and ESS can support decision making in a number of ways. They can automate certain decision procedures (for example, determining the highest price that can be charged for a product to maintain market share or the right amount of materials to maintain in inventory to maximize efficient customer response and product profitability). They can provide information about different aspects of the decision situation and the decision process, such as what opportunities or problems triggered the decision process, what solution alternatives were generated or explored, and how the decision was reached. Finally, they can stimulate innovation in decision making by helping managers question existing decision procedures or explore different solution designs (Dutta, Wierenga, and Dalebout, 1997). The ability to explore the outcomes of alternative organizational scenarios, use precise firm-wide information, and provide tools to facilitate group decision processes can help managers make decisions that help the firm achieve its strategic objectives (Forgionne and Kohli, 2000).

11.1 DECISION-SUPPORT SYSTEMS (DSS)

As noted in Chapter 2, *decision-support systems (DSS)* assist management decision making by combining data, sophisticated analytical models and tools, and user-friendly software into single powerful systems that can support semistructured or unstructured decision making. DSS provide users with flexible sets of tools and capabilities for analyzing important blocks of data.

MIS AND DSS

Some of the earliest applications for supporting management decision making were *management information systems (MIS)*, which we introduced in Chapter 2. MIS primarily provide information on the firm's performance to help managers in monitoring and controlling the business. They typically produce fixed, regularly scheduled reports based on data extracted and summarized from the organization's underlying transaction processing systems (TPS). The format from these reports is often specified in advance. A typical MIS report might show a summary of monthly sales for each of the major sales territories of a company. Sometimes MIS reports are exception reports, highlighting only exceptional conditions, such as when the sales quotas for a specific territory fall below an anticipated level or employees who have exceeded their spending limit in a dental care plan. Traditional MIS produced primarily hard copy reports. Today, these reports might be available online through an intranet, and more MIS reports can be generated on demand. Table 11-1 provides some examples of MIS applications.

DSS provide new sets of capabilities for nonroutine decisions and user control. MIS provide managers with reports based on routine flows of data and assist in the general control of organizations, whereas DSS emphasize change, flexibility, and rapid response. With a DSS there is less of an effort to link users to structured information flows and a correspondingly greater emphasis on models, assumptions, ad hoc queries, and display graphics.

Chapter 3 introduced the distinction between structured, semistructured, and unstructured decisions. Structured problems are repetitive and routine, for which known algorithms provide solutions. Unstructured problems are novel and nonroutine, for which there are no algorithms for solutions. One can discuss, decide, and ruminate about unstructured problems, but they are not solved in the sense that one finds an answer to an equation. Semistructured problems fall between structured and unstructured problems. While MIS primarily address structured problems, DSS support semistructured and unstructured problem analysis. Chapter 3 also introduced Simon's description of decision making, which consists of four stages: intelligence, design, choice, and implementation. DSS are intended to help design and evaluate alternatives and monitor the adoption or implementation process.

TABLE 11-1	EXAMPLES OF MIS APPLICATIONS
Organization	**MIS Application**
California Pizza Kitchen	Inventory Express application "remembers" each restaurant's ordering patterns, and compares the amount of ingredients used per menu item to predefined portion measurements established by management. The system identifies restaurants with out-of-line portions and notifies their management so that corrective action can be taken.
PharMark	Extranet MIS identifies patients with drug-use patterns that place them at risk for adverse outcomes.
Black & Veatch	Intranet MIS tracks construction costs for its various projects across the United States.
Taco Bell	TACO (Total Automation of Company Operations) system provides information on food, labor, and period-to-date costs for each restaurant.

Types of Decision-Support Systems

The earliest DSS tended to draw on small subsets of corporate data and were heavily model driven. Recent advances in computer processing and database technology have expanded the definition of a DSS to include systems that can support decision making by analyzing vast quantities of data, including firm-wide data from enterprise systems and transaction data from the Web.

Today, there are two basic types of decision-support systems, model-driven and data-driven (Dhar and Stein, 1997). **Model-driven DSS** were primarily stand-alone systems isolated from major organizational information systems that used some type of model to perform "what-if" and other kinds of analyses. Such systems were often developed by end-user divisions or groups not under central information system control. Their analysis capabilities were based on a strong theory or model combined with a good user interface that made the model easy to use.

The voyage-estimating DSS described in Chapter 2 and the Gap's planning and forecasting system described in the chapter-opening vignette are examples of model-driven DSS. Another is Continental Airlines Inc.'s system for cargo revenue optimization. Continental's cargo division developed a software application called CargoProf to maximize revenue from its aircraft freight compartments. The software is a customized package from Manugistics Inc. of Rockville, Maryland, and ensures that Continental sells all available freight space on its carriers at the most profitable price. The system forecasts cargo capacity and sets an optimal value each night on what they need.

Figure 11-1 shows how this system works. Continental booking agents transmit freight order requests for reservations on a given flight. Continental's legacy reservation system captures order data such as a shipment's weight, dimensions, and contract price and forwards the data to CargoProf. The CargoProf software checks available capacity in the airplane's bays, taking into account both the size and weight of the cargo, and compares it against a present pricing model. The software then considers several other variables such as anticipated passenger baggage and extra fuel requirements based on seasonal factors. CargoProf then analyzes these numbers and either accepts the reservation at the customer's contract price or rejects it if taking on the shipment is not cost effective. If the customer's order is rejected for one flight, CargoProf can check other flights to see if they could profitably carry the cargo. CargoProf can also handle incremental price changes for rush shipments. Users can override CargoProf capacity forecasts on certain flights if, for example, unanticipated head winds require a greater fuel load. By making freight bookings more efficient, CargoProf saved Continental $9 million over a two-year period (Songini, 2002).

The second type of DSS is a **data-driven DSS.** These systems analyze large pools of data found in major organizational systems. They support decision making by allowing users to extract useful information that was previously buried in large quantities of data. Often data from transaction processing systems (TPS) are collected in data warehouses for this purpose. Online analytical processing (OLAP) and datamining can then be used to analyze the data. Companies are starting to build data-driven DSS to mine customer data gathered from their Web sites as well as data from enterprise systems. WH Smith PLC's system for online sales and profitability analysis described in the Window on Organizations is an example of a data-driven DSS.

Traditional database queries answer such questions as, "How many units of product number 403 were shipped in November 2002?" OLAP, or multidimensional analysis, supports much more complex requests for information, such as, "Compare sales of product 403 relative to plan by quarter and sales region for the past two years." We described OLAP (online analytical processing) and multidimensional data analysis in Chapter 7. With OLAP and query-oriented data analysis, users need to have a good idea about the information for which they are looking.

Datamining, which we introduced in Chapter 7, is more discovery driven. Datamining provides insights into corporate data that cannot be obtained with OLAP by finding hidden patterns and relationships in large databases and inferring rules from them to predict future behavior. The patterns and rules then can be used to guide decision making and forecast the effect of those decisions. The types of information that can be yielded from datamining include associations, sequences, classifications, clusters, and forecasts.

Associations are occurrences linked to a single event. For instance, a study of supermarket purchasing patterns might reveal that when corn chips are purchased, a cola

---

model-driven DSS

Primarily stand-alone system that uses some type of model to perform "what-if" and other kinds of analyses.

data-driven DSS

A system that supports decision making by allowing users to extract and analyze useful information that was previously buried in large databases.

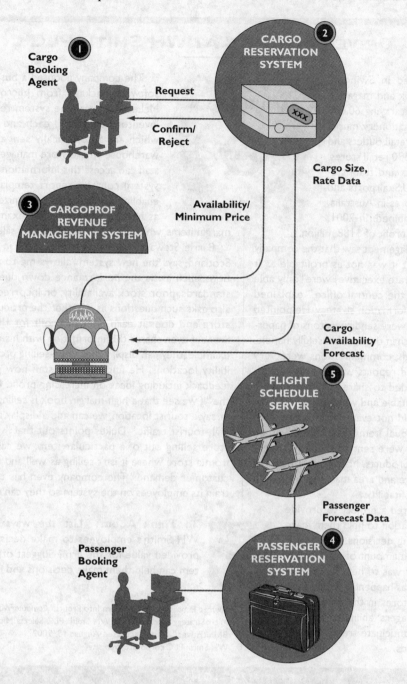

Figure 11-1 Cargo Revenue Optimization at Continental Airlines. When a booking agent (1) requests a cargo reservation, the cargo reservation system (2) passes the shipment details and customer contract rate to CargoProf (3). Meanwhile, the passenger reservation system (4) feeds a passenger forecast to the flight schedule server's cargo capacity forecaster (5), which calculates expected cargo capacity each night for every flight. It passes this capacity data to CargoProf, which calculates for each flight with available cargo space the minimum prices that a booking must meet or exceed in order to be profitable. The cargo reservation system then accepts or rejects the request. Agents with rejected requests can then either try a different day or route to sell the customer into a higher rate class.

drink is purchased 65 percent of the time, but when there is a promotion, cola is purchased 85 percent of the time. With this information, managers can make better decisions because they have learned the profitability of a promotion.

In *sequences,* events are linked over time. One might find, for example, that if a house is purchased, then a new refrigerator will be purchased within two weeks 65 percent of the time, and an oven will be bought within one month of the home purchase 45 percent of the time.

Classification recognizes patterns that describe the group to which an item belongs by examining existing items that have been classified and by inferring a set of rules. For example, businesses such as credit card or telephone companies worry about the loss of steady customers. Classification can help discover the characteristics of customers who are likely to leave and can provide a model to help managers predict who they are so that they can devise special campaigns to retain such customers.

Clustering works in a manner similar to classification when no groups have yet been defined. A datamining tool will discover different groupings within data, such as

DATA DRIVES INSIGHTS AT WH SMITH PLC

WH Smith PLC, headquartered in Swindon, England, is the number one book and magazine retailer in the United Kingdom, carrying 60,000 items such as reading material, stationery, music, computer games, and gifts at its retail outlets and Web site. It runs approximately 530 retail stores, 190 stores in European airports and train stations, more than 500 stores in U.S. airports and hotels, and approximately 20 stores in Australia, Singapore, and Hong Kong combined. In 2001, sales reached $3.9 billion with a profit of $188 million.

Several years ago, Smith's management saw that the company was running into trouble in that it was not as profitable as it could be. At that time its corporate executives were "only able to monitor sales and stock at the central office," explained Trevor Dukes, Smith's head of information strategy. He pointed out that "senior store managers were sending us tons of paperwork about their stores," more than they could usefully handle. Using such paper-based methods, communications were very slow and information in printed reports was already out-of-date. Moreover, the stores needed to share information with other stores about what is profitable and what is not, and how trends are changing. Stores could not even obtain information about the profitability of individual items. Even directives on promotions and incentives that were sent to the stores were not integrated with the stores' products. Management believed that employees, particularly store and area managers, needed a stronger focus on improving profitability.

Company management initiated a project to provide managers with tools and information to help them make better merchandise and stocking decisions. One major goal was to reduce the immense amount of paper being passed back and forth. Another was to help store managers better understand what was happening within their own stores and within other stores in the company. A third goal was to improve managers' ability to recognize customer buying patterns and to anticipate trends so they could align their inventory to the trends.

The company adopted a business intelligence software package from MicroStrategy Inc. of McLean, Virginia. The system relies on sales and inventory data from each and every purchase, which are automatically sent to a central data warehouse where store managers and corporate staff can access this information via the Web. The system contains report templates and wizards, enabling managers to customize the information as needed, identifying, for example, the highest-margin items, which can then be ranked by sales.

Barrie Stewart, the manager of a store in Dunbartonshire, Scotland, says the new system "allows me to ask several questions, such as, 'Is the performance down due to poor display standards, poor stock availability, or incorrect location?'" He also asks such questions as whether the product is right for his store and does it earn enough profit for the space it uses? Stewart even shares this information with his employees so, for example, they can display their best-selling products in high visibility locations. He finds that his staff now gives him helpful feedback including ideas on increasing profit. Rowley even says the "if we see that a high-margin book is selling particularly well in, say, a tourist location, we can add a display at a shop that has high tourist traffic." Dukes points out that "when we see one store selling out of a particular item, we can shift inventory from a store where it isn't selling as well and take advantage of customer demand." The company even has taken the time to train its employees on the system so they can use it themselves.

To Think About: List the ways this DSS helps WH Smith's employees to make decisions. How has it provided value for the firm? Suggest other ways the system can help them make decisions and increase profits.

Sources: Pimm Fox, "Insights Turn Into Profits," *ComputerWorld*, February 10, 2002; MicroStrategy Incorporated, "WH Smith PLC Selects Microstrategy to Anchor BI Initiatives," *DSstar*, accessed August 15, 2002, <www.tgc.com/dsstar>; and WH Smith PLC corporate Web site, <www.whsmithplc.com>.

ORGANIZATIONS

finding affinity groups for bank cards or partitioning a database into groups of customers based on demographics and types of personal investments.

Although these applications involve predictions, *forecasting* uses predictions in a different way. It uses a series of existing values to forecast what other values will be. For example, forecasting might find patterns in data to help managers estimate the future value of continuous variables such as sales figures.

Datamining uses statistical analysis tools as well as neural networks, fuzzy logic, genetic algorithms, or rule-based and other intelligent techniques (described in Chapter 12). It is an important aspect of **knowledge discovery,** which includes selection, preparation, and interpretation of the contents of large databases to identify novel and valuable patterns in the data.

knowledge discovery

The process of identifying novel and valuable patterns in large volumes of data through the selection, preparation, and evaluation of the contents of large databases.

Lucent Technologies Visual Insights software can help businesses detect patterns in their data. Each dot in this example represents items purchased at one supermarket, with lines drawn between purchases of individual shoppers. The software shows links between different purchase items, such as cookies and milk.

As noted in Chapter 3, it is a mistake to think that only individuals in large organizations make decisions. In fact, most decisions are made collectively. Frequently, decisions must be coordinated with several groups before being finalized. In large organizations, decision making is inherently a group process, and a DSS can be designed to facilitate group decision making. (Section 11.2 deals with this issue.)

COMPONENTS OF DSS

Figure 11-2 illustrates the components of a DSS. They include a database of data used for query and analysis, a software system with models, datamining, and other analytical tools and a user interface.

The **DSS database** is a collection of current or historical data from a number of applications or groups. It may be a small database residing on a PC that contains a subset of corporate data that has been downloaded and possibly combined with external data. Alternatively, the DSS database may be a massive data warehouse that is continuously updated by major organizational TPS (including enterprise systems and data generated by Web site transactions.) The data in DSS databases are generally extracts or copies of production databases so that using the DSS does not interfere with critical operational systems.

The **DSS software system** contains the software tools that are used for data analysis. It may contain various OLAP tools, datamining tools, or a collection of mathematical and analytical models that easily can be made accessible to the DSS user. A **model** is an abstract representation that illustrates the components or relationships of a phenomenon. A model can be a physical model (such as a model airplane), a mathematical model (such as an equation), or a verbal model (such as a description of a procedure for writing an order). Each decision-support system is built for a specific set of purposes and will make different collections of models available depending on those purposes.

Perhaps the most common models are libraries of statistical models. Such libraries usually contain the full range of expected statistical functions including means, medians, deviations, and scatter plots. The software has the ability to project future outcomes by analyzing a series of data. Statistical modeling software can be used to help establish relationships, such as relating product sales to differences in age, income, or other factors between communities. Optimization models, often using

DSS database

A collection of current or historical data from a number of applications or groups. Can be a small PC database or a massive data warehouse.

DSS software system

Collection of software tools that are used for data analysis, such as OLAP tools, datamining tools, or a collection of mathematical and analytical models.

model

An abstract representation that illustrates the components or relationships of a phenomenon.

Figure 11-2 Overview of a decision-support system (DSS). The main components of the DSS are the DSS database, the DSS software system, and the user interface. The DSS database may be a small database residing on a PC or a massive data warehouse.

Figure 11-3 Sensitivity analysis. This table displays the results of a sensitivity analysis of the effect of changing the sales price of a necktie and the cost per unit on the product's breakeven point. It answers the question "What happens to the breakeven point if the sales price and the cost to make each unit increase or decrease?"

Total fixed costs	19000
Variable cost per unit	3
Average sales price	17
Contribution margin	14
Breakeven point	1357

		Variable Cost per Unit				
Sales	1357	2	3	4	5	6
Price	14	1583	1727	1900	2111	2375
	15	1462	1583	1727	1900	2111
	16	1357	1462	1583	1727	1900
	17	1267	1357	1462	1583	1727
	18	1188	1267	1357	1462	1583

sensitivity analysis

Models that ask "what-if" questions repeatedly to determine the impact of changes in one or more factors on the outcomes.

linear programming, determine optimal resource allocation to maximize or minimize specified variables such as cost or time. A classic use of optimization models is to determine the proper mix of products within a given market to maximize profits.

Forecasting models often are used to forecast sales. The user of this type of model might supply a range of historical data to project future conditions and the sales that might result from those conditions. The decision-maker could vary those future conditions (entering, for example, a rise in raw materials costs or the entry of a new, low-priced competitor in the market) to determine how these new conditions might affect sales. Companies often use this software to predict the actions of competitors. Model libraries exist for specific functions, such as financial and risk analysis models.

Among the most widely used models are **sensitivity analysis** models that ask "what-if" questions repeatedly to determine the impact of changes in one or more factors on outcomes. "What-if" analysis—working forward from known or assumed conditions—allows the user to vary certain values to test results in order to better predict outcomes if changes occur in those values. "What happens if" we raise the price by 5 percent or increase the advertising budget by $100,000? What happens if we keep the price and advertising budget the same? Desktop spreadsheet software, such as Microsoft Excel or Lotus 1-2-3, is often used for this purpose (see Figure 11-3). Backward sensitivity analysis software is used for goal seeking: If I want to sell one million product units next year, how much must I reduce the price of the product?

The DSS user interface permits easy interaction between users of the system and the DSS software tools. A graphic, easy-to-use, flexible user interface supports the dialogue between the user and the DSS. The DSS users can be managers or employees with no patience for learning a complex tool, so the interface must be relatively intuitive. Many DSS today are being built with Web-based interfaces to take advantage of the Web's ease of use, interactivity, and capabilities for personalization and customization. Building successful DSS requires a high level of user participation to make sure the system provides the information managers need. The Manager's Toolkit provides some guidelines for developing DSS solutions.

MIS IN ACTION: MANAGER'S TOOLKIT

HOW TO EVALUATE A DSS PROJECT

If your company is interested in using a DSS to support management decision making, here are some key questions to ask:

1. What kind of problem do you expect this system to solve?
2. Does the solution require the use of models? If so, which ones? What are the variables in the problem?
3. Does the solution require the use of query and data analysis tools? If so, which ones?
4. What data do you need to arrive at a solution? Can all of the data be found from within the company or does some data come

from external sources? Can you obtain the data automatically from corporate and external databases or must the data be entered separately? How much effort would be required to assemble the required data for the system?

5. What type of user interface is required? Must users use it to input data as well as ask questions of the data? Is the interface easy to use?
6. What computer hardware and operating system are required to run this system?
7. How long does it take to get answers from the data? How clear are the results?

TABLE 11-2	EXAMPLES OF DECISION-SUPPORT SYSTEMS
Organization	DSS Application
General Accident Insurance	Customer buying patterns and fraud detection
Bank of America	Customer profiles
Frito-Lay, Inc.	Price, advertising, and promotion selection
Burlington Coat Factory	Store location and inventory mix
KeyCorp	Targeting direct mail marketing customers
National Gypsum	Corporate planning and forecasting
Southern Railway	Train dispatching and routing
ShopKo Stores	Optimizing price markdowns
Texas Oil and Gas Corporation	Evaluation of potential drilling sites
United Airlines	Flight scheduling and passenger demand forecasting
U.S. Department of Defense	Defense contract analysis

DSS APPLICATIONS AND THE DIGITAL FIRM

There are many ways in which DSS can be used to support decision making. Table 11-2 lists examples of DSS in well-known organizations. Both data-driven and model-driven DSS have become very powerful and sophisticated, providing fine-grained information for decisions that enable the firm to coordinate both internal and external business processes much more precisely. Some of these DSS are helping companies improve supply chain management or customer relationship management. Some take advantage of the company-wide data provided by enterprise systems. DSS today can also harness the interactive capabilities of the Web to provide decision-support tools to both employees and customers.

To illustrate the range of capabilities of a DSS, we now describe some successful DSS applications. IBM and San Miguel Corporation's supply chain management systems, Continental Airlines' cargo revenue optimization system, and Federated Department Stores' inventory replenishment system are examples of model-driven DSS. Royal Bank of Canada's customer segmentation system and the customer analysis systems used by WH Smith PLC, Kinki Nippon Tourist, and The Body Shop are examples of data-driven DSS. We will also examine some applications of geographic information systems (GIS), a special category of DSS for visualizing data geographically.

DSS for Supply Chain Management

Supply chain decisions involve determining "who, what, when, and where" from purchasing and transporting materials and parts through manufacturing products and distributing and delivering those products to customers. Supply chain management systems contain data about inventory, supplier performance, and logistics of materials and finished goods. DSS can draw on such data to help managers examine this complex chain comprehensively and search among a huge number of alternatives for the combinations that are most efficient and cost-effective. The prime management goal might be to reduce overall costs while increasing the speed and accuracy of filling customer orders.

In 1994, IBM Research developed an advanced supply chain optimization and simulation tool called the Asset Management Tool (AMT) to reduce inventory levels, yet maintain enough inventory in the supply chain to respond quickly to customer demands. AMT deals with a range of entities in the supply chain, including targets for inventory and customer service levels, product structure, channel assembly, supplier terms and conditions, and lead-time reduction. Users of AMT can evaluate supply chains in terms of financial tradeoffs associated with various configurations and operational policies.

The IBM Personal Systems Group (PSG) used AMT to reduce supply chain costs to cope with the large volumes, dropping prices, and slim profit margins in the personal computer market. PSG was able to reduce overall pipeline inventory by over 50 percent in 1997 and 1998. The system helped PSG reduce payments made to distributors and resellers to compensate for product price reductions by more than $750 million in 1998. PSG's cycle time from component procurement to product sale was reduced by four to six weeks, bringing reductions of 5 to 7 percent in overall product cost.

IBM's AS/400 midrange computer division used AMT to analyze and quantify the impact of product complexity. Information from the system helped IBM reduce the number of product features, substitute alternate parts, and delay customization. AMT also provided an analysis of the tradeoff between serviceability and inventory in IBM's QuickShip Program, helping the company reduce operational cost by up to 50 percent. IBM has also been able to use AMT to help its business partners improve management of their supply chains. For instance, supply chain analysis helped Piancor, one of IBM's major distributors, identify opportunities for optimizing the product flow between the two companies (Dietrich et al., 2000).

Federated Department Stores owns over 450 department stores belonging to such well-known chains as Macy's, Bloomingdale's, Burdines, Goldsmith's, Rich's and The Bon Marché. Federated used to stock these stores with the same number, say eight of a certain style of men's shirts, and keep those levels consistent throughout the year. Its systems would regularly reorder 10 percent of staple items such as socks, underwear, cosmetics, hosiery, men's dress shirts, and cookware. Inventories did not match customer demand and buying patterns. Sometimes, consumers could not find the items they wanted and Federated lost sales. Other times, goods sat on store shelves because customers didn't want them and Federated lost money on inventory and unproductive displays.

In 1995, Federated started using Inforem software for automatic inventory replenishment. Today, about 30 percent of Federated's total sales are generated from items that are automatically restocked using Inforem. Inforem has halved the amount of items that are out of stock each month from 10 percent to 5 percent while also decreasing the number of unsold items in inventory. Since inventory carrying costs account for approximately 15 percent of the cost of goods sold, Inforem has saved Federated millions of dollars each year. Inforem can react to sudden changes in the demand chain: When women began regularly wearing pants to work, the system noticed a corresponding decrease in hosiery sales and a corresponding increase in sales of trouser socks, enabling the company to adjust its sock and panty hose orders to reflect these changes in demand. The system also takes individual store profiles into account so that if a manufacturer is in short supply of socks, it can select the stores where these items will sell the best (Levinson, 2002).

San Miguel Corporation uses DSS for supply chain management to help it distribute more than 300 products, such as beer, liquor, dairy products, and feedgrains to every corner of the Philippine archipelago. A production load allocation system determines the quantity of products to produce for each bottling line and how production output should be assigned to warehouses. It balances ordering, carrying, and stock-out costs while considering frequency of deliveries and minimum order quantities, saving the company $180,000 in inventory costs in one year. The DSS can generate optimal production allocation plans based on either minimizing cost or maximizing profit. San Miguel's system also helps it reassign deliveries and warehouse facilities to counter imbalances in capacity and demand. Managers used information from the system to move more of San Miguel's delivery business to third-party logistics providers so that its own delivery trucks could be used more efficiently. The company found that it could reduce the number of routes serving sales districts in metropolitan Manila alone by 43 percent (del Rosario, 1999).

DSS for Customer Relationship Management

DSS for customer relationship management use datamining to guide decisions about pricing, customer retention, market share, and new revenue streams. These systems typically consolidate customer information from a variety of systems into massive data warehouses and use various analytical tools to slice it into tiny segments for one-to-one marketing (see Figure 11-4).

Instead of sending customers the same marketing information, Royal Bank of Canada has developed a DSS for customer segmentation that can tailor messages to very small groups of people and offer them products, services, and prices that are more likely to appeal to them. This DSS consolidates data from various systems in the organization into a data warehouse. The Royal Bank's main customer database is its marketing information file (MIF) which also

Questions

1. Who are our most frequent customers?

2. Do they live close to our retail outlets?

3. How can we re-segment those customers?

4. How can we better reach those segments?

Customer data warehouse

- Legacy data
- Web site transaction data
- Call center data
- Third party data
- ERP data

Analysis

1. Use statistical analysis to identify the top 25% of frequent shoppers

2. Establish correlation between location and sales frequency

3. Verify new customer segments
   - frequent customers not living near a store
   - frequent customers living near a store
   - infrequent customers living near a store

4. Query the database for detailed information on each customer segment

Figure 11-4 DSS for customer analysis and segmentation. This DSS allows companies to segment their customer base with a high level of precision where it can be used to drive a marketing campaign. Based on the results of datamining, a firm can develop specific marketing campaigns for each customer segment. For example, it could target frequent customers living near a store with coupons for products of interest and with rewards for frequent shoppers.

contains data from every document a customer fills out as well as data from checking accounts, credit cards, and the Royal Bank's enterprise and billing systems.

By querying the database, analysts can identify customers based on the products they might buy and the likelihood they will leave the bank and combine these data with demographic data from external sources. Royal Bank can then identify one or a group of profitable customers who appear to be getting ready to leave the bank. To identify such customers, the bank will look at the customer's bank balance (if it was recently kept low), credit card payments (if they were reduced in amount and perhaps paid later than in the past), and deposits (if they have become sporadic). These signs could indicate a customer who is recently unemployed, but they could also highlight a profitable customer preparing to switch to another bank. The Royal Bank, using its vast stored data, can quickly learn whether it has profited from this customer's business. They measure profitability looking at the customer's past ongoing balances, personal use of his or her Royal Bank line of credit, and the car loan and/or mortgage that person holds from the bank. The bank can also deduce from personal data whether the customer is at a stage in life when he or she will need more bank loans and other bank services.

Having identified such customer(s), the bank's marketing department might put together a tempting package of banking services at a low price, such as Internet banking, bill payment, unlimited ATM access, and a limited number of branch transactions, all for a fee of $9.95 per month. The bank knows that customers who use such service packages stay with the bank for about three years longer than do those who have no such package. If the customer is not satisfied with the specific package, marketing can even tailor a package specifically for that individual. Royal Bank is linking its customer database and legacy systems to the Web so that it can offer customers service packages instantly online as they access their accounts over the Internet. Royal Bank's customer segmentation is so effective that it can achieve a response rate as high as 30 percent to its marketing campaigns, compared to an average of 3 percent for the banking industry (Wilson, 2000 and Radding, 2000).

Kinki Nippon Tourist (KNT), Japan's second largest travel agency, revolutionized Japanese tourism in the early 1980s by providing newspaper advertising and magazines explicitly customized for repeat customers that would allow them to purchase trips over the telephone. (Until KNT opened these new channels, tourists had to arrange their trips through a travel agency). When competitors followed, KNT tried to develop a one-to-one marketing strategy to retain core customers and increase customer loyalty. To store and analyze detailed information on customer preferences, behavior, and opinions of tours, KNT implemented a massive data warehouse based on a Teradata relational database. The system runs on a WorldMark Massively Parallel Processor and includes data on 1.5 million customers. The data come from telephone calls, conversations with tour operators, and customer questionnaires as well as transactions. Nearly 500 users can access the system directly through individual workstations.

By analyzing the detailed customer data, KNT uncovered new patterns that were previously undetectable in its old legacy systems. For example, it found that customers whose first tour was made by bus were likely to be repeat bus customers. The company can use this finding to target appropriate tours, events, and hospitality to these customers. KNT can also use the data warehouse to determine which newspaper ads work the best for certain tours and which tours are better promoted through direct mail. KNT's call center operators can use the information from the data warehouse to improve customer service. And KNT uses data from the system to customize its magazines to specific customer segments (NCR, 2001).

The U.S. division of The Body Shop International plc, the U.K. skin and hair product vendor, wanted to boost the efficiency of its mail order business. When the economy took a downturn in 2001, the company cut back on catalog circulation by 50 percent to reduce costs. But it wanted to find a way to improve the response rates for the catalogs it did mail out. The Body Shop had been building mailing lists using customer sales data from previous mailings. The company acquired predictive analysis software tools from Sightward to improve the analysis of its database of catalog, Web, and store customers. The Sightward tools helped The Body Shop identify consumers who were more likely to make catalog purchases so that it could build a more precise and targeted mailing list for the 120,000 copies of its fall 2001 catalog. Revenue per catalog increased 10 to 20 percent (Whiting, 2002).

Some of these DSS for customer relationship management use data gathered from the Web. Chapter 9 has described how each action a visitor has taken when visiting a particular Web site can be captured on that Web site's log. Companies can mine these data to answer questions such as what customers are purchasing and what promotions are generating the most traffic. The results can help companies tailor marketing programs more effectively, redesign Web sites to optimize traffic, and create personalized buying experiences for Web site visitors. Other DSS combine Web site transaction data with data from enterprise systems.

Data Visualization and Geographic Information Systems (GIS)

Data from information systems can be made easier for users to digest and act upon by using charts, tables, graphs, maps, digital images, three-dimensional presentations, animations, and other data visualization technologies. By presenting data in graphical form, **data visualization** tools help users see patterns and relationships in large amounts of data that would be difficult to discern if the data were presented as traditional lists of text. Some data visualization tools are interactive, allowing users to manipulate data and see the graphical displays change in response to the changes they make.

Geographic information systems (GIS) are a special category of DSS that use data visualization technology to analyze and display data for planning and decision making in the form of digitized maps. The software can assemble, store, manipulate, and display geographically referenced information, tying data to points, lines, and areas on a map. GIS can thus be used to support decisions that require knowledge about the geographic distribution of people or other resources in scientific research, resource management, and development planning. For example, GIS might be used to help state and local governments calculate emergency response times to natural disasters or to help banks identify the best locations for installing new branches or ATM terminals. GIS tools have become affordable even for small businesses and some can be used on the Web.

GIS have modeling capabilities, allowing managers to change data and automatically revise business scenar-

---

data visualization

Technology for helping users see patterns and relationships in large amounts of data by presenting the data in graphical form.

geographic information system (GIS)

System with software that can analyze and display data using digitized maps to enhance planning and decision making.

The U.S. National Forest service was offered a land swap by a mining company seeking development rights to a mineral deposit in the Prescott National Forest of Arizona. Using a geographic information system (GIS) and a variety of digital maps, the U.S. Geological Survey and the Forest Service created perspective views of the terrain before and after mining. The GIS showed that mining would cause dramatic changes to the topography.

ios to find better solutions. Johanna Dairies of Union, New Jersey, used GIS software to display its customers on a map and then design the most efficient delivery routes, saving the company $100,000 annually for each route that was eliminated. Sonny's Bar-B-Q, the Gainesville, Florida-based restaurant chain, used GIS with federal and local census data on median age, household income, total population, and population distribution to help management decide where to open new restaurants. The company's growth plan specifies that it will only expand into regions where barbecue food is very popular but where the number of barbecue restaurants is very small. Sonny's restaurants must also be at least seven miles away from each other. Champion Printing & Advertising, Inc., used MapInfo Corporation's GIS tools to improve the results of the direct-mail campaigns it runs for its financial institution customers. The company used customer demographic data and MapInfo mapping capabilities to locate people who are more likely to become customers for the banks' services. By using this GIS, the bank was able to reshape its direct mailing campaigns to achieve a response rate of 15 percent. In the past the response rate to direct mailings had been less than 2 percent (Lais, 2002).

WEB-BASED CUSTOMER DECISION-SUPPORT SYSTEMS

The growth of electronic commerce has encouraged many companies to develop DSS where customers and employees can take advantage of Internet information resources and Web capabilities for interactivity and personalization. DSS based on the Web and the Internet can support decision making, by providing online access to various databases and information pools along with software for data analysis. Some of these DSS are targeted toward management, but many have been developed to attract customers by providing information and tools to assist their decision making as they select products and services. Companies are finding that deciding which products and services to purchase has become increasingly information-intensive. People are now using more information from multiple sources to make purchasing decisions (such as purchasing a car or computer) before they interact with the product or sales staff. **Customer decision-support systems (CDSS)** support the decision-making process of an existing or potential customer.

People interested in purchasing a product or service can use Internet search engines, intelligent agents, online catalogs, Web directories, newsgroup discussions, e-mail, and other

customer decision-support system (CDSS)
System to support the decision-making process of an existing or potential customer.

SmartMoney.com features online tools to help families with children make decisions about allocating their financial assets. DSS based on the Web can provide information from multiple sources and analytical tools to help potential customers select products and services.

TABLE 11-3   EXAMPLES OF WEB-BASED DSS

DSS	Description
General Electric Plastics	Web site provides a Design Solutions Center with a Web-based suite of online engineering tools for materials developers in the plastics industry. Visitors can select plastics materials, perform production costs estimates, search for product-specification information, and take online training.
Fidelity Investments	Web site features an online, interactive decision-support application to help clients make decisions about investment savings plans and investment portfolio allocations. The application allows visitors to experiment with numerous "what-if" scenarios to design investment savings plans for retirement or a child's college education. If the user enters information about his or her finances, time horizon, and tolerance for risk, the system will suggest appropriate portfolios of mutual funds. The application performs the required number crunching and displays the changing return on investment as the user alters these assumptions.
Homes.com	Provides a nationwide listing of homes for sale, apartments for rent, and mortgages available. Visitors can find out what mortgages they qualify for and calculate the maximum mortgage they can afford and alternative monthly mortgage payments. They can also use tools to help them determine whether they should rent or buy.

tools to help them locate the information they need to help with their decision. Information brokers, such as Edmunds.com, described in Chapter 4, are also sources of summarized, structured information for specific products or industries and may provide models for evaluating the information. Companies also have developed specific customer Web sites where all the information, models, or other analytical tools for evaluating alternatives are concentrated in one location. Web-based DSS have become especially popular in the financial services area because so many people are trying to manage their own assets and retirement savings. Table 11-3 lists some examples.

11.2 GROUP DECISION-SUPPORT SYSTEMS (GDSS)

The DSS we have just described focus primarily on individual decision making. However, so much work is accomplished in groups within organizations that a special category of systems called group decision-support systems (GDSS) has been developed to support group and organizational decision making.

WHAT IS A GDSS?

group decision-support
system (GDSS)
An interactive computer-based
system to facilitate the solution
to unstructured problems by a
set of decision-makers working
together as a group.

A **group decision-support system (GDSS)** is an interactive computer-based system to facilitate the solution of unstructured problems by a set of decision-makers working together as a group (DeSanctis and Gallupe, 1987). Groupware and Web-based tools for videoconferencing and electronic meetings described earlier in this text can support some group decision processes, but their focus is primarily on communication. GDSS, however, provide tools and technologies geared explicitly toward group decision making and were developed in response to a growing concern over the quality and effectiveness of meetings. The underlying problems in group decision making have been the explosion of decision-maker meetings, the growing length of those meetings, and the increased number of attendees. Estimates on the amount of a manager's time spent in meetings range from 35 percent to 70 percent.

Components of GDSS

GDSS make meetings more productive by providing tools to facilitate planning, generating, organizing, and evaluating ideas, establishing priorities, and documenting meeting proceedings for others in the organization. GDSS consist of three basic elements: *hardware, software tools,* and *people. Hardware* refers to the conference facility itself, including the room, the tables, and the chairs. Such a facility must be physically laid out in a manner that supports group collaboration. It also must include some electronic hardware, such as electronic display boards, as well as audiovisual, computer, and networking equipment.

Although groupware tools for collaborative work described in Chapters 6 and 10 can be used to support group decision making, there are specific GDSS *software tools* for supporting group meetings. These tools were originally developed for meetings in which all participants are in the same room, but they also can be used for networked meetings in which participants are in different locations. Specific GDSS software tools include the following:

■ *Electronic questionnaires* aid the organizers in premeeting planning by identifying issues of concern and by helping to ensure that key planning information is not overlooked.

■ *Electronic brainstorming tools* allow individuals, simultaneously and anonymously, to contribute ideas on the topics of the meeting.

■ *Idea organizers* facilitate the organized integration and synthesis of ideas generated during brainstorming.

■ *Questionnaire tools* support the facilitators and group leaders as they gather information before and during the process of setting priorities.

■ *Tools for voting or setting priorities* make available a range of methods from simple voting, to ranking in order, to a range of weighted techniques for setting priorities or voting.

■ *Stakeholder identification and analysis tools* use structured approaches to evaluate the impact of an emerging proposal on the organization and to identify stakeholders and evaluate the potential impact of those stakeholders on the proposed project.

■ *Policy formation tools* provide structured support for developing agreement on the wording of policy statements.

■ *Group dictionaries* document group agreement on definitions of words and terms central to the project.

■ *People* refers not only to the participants but also to a trained facilitator and often to a staff that supports the hardware and software.

Together these elements have led to the creation of a range of different kinds of GDSS, from simple electronic boardrooms to elaborate collaboration laboratories. In a collaboration laboratory, individuals work on their own desktop PCs or workstations. Their input is integrated on a file server and is viewable on a common screen at the front of the room; in most systems the integrated input is also viewable on the individual participant's screen.

OVERVIEW OF A GDSS MEETING

In a GDSS electronic meeting, each attendee has a workstation. The workstations are networked and are connected to the facilitator's console, which serves as both the facilitator's workstation and control panel and the meeting's file server. All data that the attendees forward from their workstations to the group are collected and saved on the file server. The facilitator is able to project computer images onto the projection screen at the front center of the room. The facilitator also has an overhead projector available. Whiteboards are visible on

An electronic meeting system provides capabilities for group decision support, such as networked workstations, projection screens, whiteboards, and software tools.

Figure 11-5 Group system tools. The sequence of activities and collaborative support tools used in an electronic meeting system facilitates communication among attendees and generates a full record of the meeting. [Source: From Nunamaker et al., "Electronic Meeting Systems to Support Group Work" in Communications of the ACM, July 1991. Reprinted by permission.]

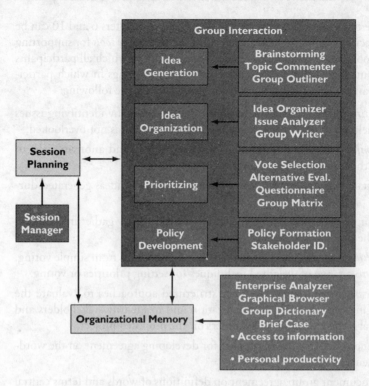

either side of the projection screen. Many electronic meeting rooms are arranged in a semi-circle and are tiered in legislative style to accommodate a large number of attendees. The facilitator controls the use of tools during the meeting.

Attendees have full control over their own desktop computers. An attendee is able to view the agenda (and other planning documents), look at the integrated screen (or screens as the session progresses), use ordinary desktop PC tools (such as a word processor or a spreadsheet), tap into production data that have been made available, or work on the screen associated with the current meeting step and tool (such as a brainstorming screen). During the meeting all input to the integrated screens is saved on the file server and participants' work is kept confidential. When the meeting is completed, a full record of the meeting (both raw material and resultant output) is available to the attendees and can be made available to anyone else with a need for access. Figure 11-5 illustrates the sequence of activities at a typical electronic meeting along with the types of tools used and the output of those tools.

How GDSS Can Enhance Group Decision Making

Studies show that in traditional decision-making meetings without GDSS support the optimal meeting size is three to five attendees. Beyond that size, the meeting process begins to break down. Using GDSS software, studies show the meeting size can increase while productivity also increases. One reason for this is that attendees contribute simultaneously rather than one at a time, which makes more efficient use of meeting time.

A GDSS contributes to a more collaborative atmosphere by guaranteeing contributors' anonymity so that attendees can focus on evaluating the ideas themselves. Attendees can contribute without fear of personally being criticized or of having their ideas rejected because of the identity of the contributor. GDSS software tools follow structured methods for organizing and evaluating ideas and for preserving the results of meetings, allowing nonattendees to locate needed information after the meeting. The documentation of a meeting by one group at one site can also be used as input to another meeting on the same project at another site.

If properly designed and supported, GDSS meetings can increase the number of ideas generated and the quality of decisions while producing the desired results in fewer meetings. However, their outcomes are not necessarily better than face-to-face meetings. GDSS seem most useful for tasks involving idea generation, complex problems, and large groups (Fjermestad and Hiltz, 2000–2001, 1998–1999). One problem with understanding the value of GDSS is their complexity. A GDSS can be configured in an almost infinite variety of ways and the nature of electronic meeting technology is only one of a number of factors that affect meeting processes and output. The outcome of group meetings depends upon the composition of the group, the manner in which the problem is presented to the group, the facilitator's effectiveness, the organization's culture and environment, the quality of the planning, the cooperation of the attendees, and the appropriateness of tools selected for different types of meetings and decision problems (Hender, Dean, Rodgers, and Nunamaker, 2002; Dennis and Wixom, 2001–2002; Dennis, Wixom, and Vandenberg, 2001).

11.3 EXECUTIVE SUPPORT IN THE ENTERPRISE

We have described how DSS and GDSS help managers make unstructured and semi-structured decisions. *Executive support systems (ESS)*, which we introduced in Chapter 2, also help managers with unstructured problems, focusing on the information needs of senior management. Combining data from internal and external sources, ESS create a generalized computing and communications environment that can be focused and applied to a changing array of problems. ESS help senior executives monitor organizational performance, track activities of competitors, spot problems, identify opportunities, and forecast trends.

THE ROLE OF EXECUTIVE SUPPORT SYSTEMS IN THE ORGANIZATION

Contemporary ESS can bring together data from all parts of the organization and allow managers to select, access, and tailor them as needed using easy-to-use desktop analytical tools and online data displays. Use of the systems has migrated down several organizational levels so that the executive and any subordinates are able to look at the same data in the same way.

Today's systems try to avoid the problem of data overload so common in paper reports because the data can be filtered or viewed in graphic format (if the user so chooses). ESS have the ability to **drill down,** moving from a piece of summary data to lower and lower levels of detail. The ability to drill down is useful not only to senior executives but to employees at lower levels of the organization who need to analyze data. OLAP tools for analyzing large databases provide this capability.

> **drill down**
> The ability to move from summary data to lower and lower levels of detail.

A major challenge of building executive support systems has been to integrate data from systems designed for very different purposes so that senior executives can review organizational performance from a firm-wide perspective. In the traditional firm, which typically had hundreds or even thousands of incompatible systems, pulling such information together and making sense out of it was a major task. Today, properly configured and implemented enterprise systems can provide managers with timely, comprehensive, and accurate firm-wide information. ESS based on such data can be considered logical extensions of enterprise system functionality.

External data, including data from the Web, are now more easily available in many ESS as well. Executives need a wide range of external data from current stock market news to competitor information, industry trends, and even projected legislative action. Through their ESS, many managers have access to news services, financial market databases, economic information, and whatever other public data they may require.

Contemporary ESS include tools for modeling and analysis. With only a minimum of experience, most managers find they can use these tools to create graphic comparisons of data by time, region, product, price range, and so on. (Whereas DSS use such tools primarily for modeling and analysis in a fairly narrow range of decision situations, ESS use them primarily to provide status information about organizational performance.)

ESS must be designed so that high-level managers and others can use them without much training. One area that merits special attention is the determination of executive information requirements. ESS need to have some facility for environmental scanning. A key information requirement of managers at the strategic level is the capability to detect signals of problems in the organizational environment that indicate strategic threats and opportunities (Walls et al., 1992). The ESS need to be designed so that both external and internal sources of information can be used for environmental scanning purposes.

ESS potentially could give top executives the capability of examining other managers' work without their knowledge, so there may be some resistance to ESS at lower levels of the organization. Implementation of ESS should be carefully managed to neutralize such opposition (see Chapter 13).

BENEFITS OF EXECUTIVE SUPPORT SYSTEMS

Much of the value of ESS is found in their flexibility. These systems put data and tools in the hands of executives without addressing specific problems or imposing solutions. Executives are free to shape the problems as necessary, using the system as an extension of their own thinking processes. These are not decision-making systems; they are tools to aid executives in making decisions.

The most visible benefit of ESS is their ability to analyze, compare, and highlight trends. The easy use of graphics allows the user to look at more data in less time with greater clarity and insight than paper-based systems can provide. In the past, executives obtained the same information by taking up days and weeks of their staffs' valuable time. By using ESS, those staffs and the executives themselves are freed up for the more creative analysis and decision making in their jobs. ESS capabilities for drilling down and highlighting trends also may enhance the quality of such analysis and can speed up decision making (Leidner and Elam, 1993–1994).

Executives are using ESS to monitor performance more successfully in their own areas of responsibility. Some companies are using these systems to monitor key performance indicators for the entire firm and to measure firm performance against changes in the external environment (see the Window on Management). The timeliness and availability of the data result in needed actions being identified and taken earlier. Problems can be handled before they become too damaging; opportunities can also be identified earlier. These systems can thus help organizations move toward a "sense and respond" strategy.

A well-designed ESS could dramatically improve management performance and increase upper management's span of control. Immediate access to so much data allows executives to better monitor activities of lower units reporting to them. That very monitoring ability could allow decision making to be decentralized and to take place at lower operating levels. Executives are often willing to push decision making further down into the organization as long as they can be assured that all is going well. Alternatively, executive support systems based on enterprise-wide data could potentially increase management centralization, enabling senior executives to monitor the performance of subordinates across the company and direct them to take appropriate action when conditions change.

EXECUTIVE SUPPORT SYSTEMS AND THE DIGITAL FIRM

To illustrate the different ways in which an ESS can enhance management decision making, we now describe important types of ESS applications for gathering business intelligence and monitoring corporate performance, including ESS based on enterprise systems.

ESS for Business Intelligence

Today, customer expectations, Internet technology, and new business models can alter the competitive landscape so rapidly that managers need special capabilities for competitive intelligence gathering. ESS can help managers identify changing market conditions, formulate responses, track implementation efforts, and learn from feedback.

BP Sony NV, the Netherlands branch of the multinational electronics giant, wanted more insight from the marketplace to drive its competitive strategy. Until recently, its management reports were based primarily on financial and administrative data that took at least 24 hours to generate. Management wanted to be able to make meaningful decisions based on marketing and sales data as well so it could respond quickly to marketplace changes. Sony Netherlands constructed a data warehouse and Executive Information System for this purpose.

The system is now available to 78 users in management, marketing, and sales. They can use the system to help them define strategies, search for opportunities, identify problems, and substantiate actions. Using a drill-down function, they can examine the underlying numbers behind the total result. For instance, while senior management can obtain sales

DIGITAL COCKPITS HELP STEER
THE ENTERPRISE

Jeffrey Immelt, General Electric's (GE) chairman and chief executive officer (CEO), is faced with the difficult task of keeping up with all 11 of GE's primary divisions. Even though GE is one of the world's largest corporations, he and his senior managers now can obtain a solid overview of each division and of the whole corporation in a matter of minutes, using GE's intranet. His secret? The corporate cockpit, which is GE's name for its version of a digital dashboard. A digital dashboard presents key performance indicators that give top executives quick but clear pictures of their company's financial health.

This corporate information is extremely vital and yet so confidential that only 45 top GE executives are allowed access to it, although more have access to the digital dashboard of their own divisions. GE began development of its corporate cockpit in 2000, completing it in June 2002. The software is a combination of digital and graphics data, and its users can see them either way through tabs at the top of the screen. The top-level corporate data are mostly distillations of data from the digital dashboards of each of the 11 divisions. It presents information in nine categories, including headcounts, sales, orders, and pricing.

Naturally the divisional dashboards display differing critical information that is specific to their own units. For example, NBC includes its TV ratings while GE's card services division displays the number of delinquent credit card accounts. GE's plastics division shows three basic categories: manufacturing, selling, and procurement, with more specific measurements being displayed under these categories. So, for example, manufacturing data includes the number of days without a major production incident, while procurement displays the current price of benzene, which is a critical commodity for its plastics. If a specific measurement goes above or below a predetermined number, it is displayed in red, and if it is too far out of the range, executives are automatically alerted to the problem either through e-mail or paging.

Executives can click on any specific number and another screen pops up that displays its underlying data.

Electronic Data Systems' (EDS) dashboard application version is called Pole Position and uses automobile graphics on a four-quadrant chart to represent the data flowing in from an automated sales force program that tracks where revenues come from. In the top right quadrant is a Formula One racer representing EDS service offerings such as Web design or database consulting that frequently prevail over fierce competitors. A dump truck in the top left quadrant represents wins against easy competition, and the bottom right quadrant shows a sporty roadster, representing wins against good competition that do not generate significant revenue. The bottom left quadrant displays a clunker with the hood up, for which the message is obvious. Each vehicle is color-coded for profitability.

According to Larry Biagini, GE's chief technology officer, "These things are all about making sure we react before things get out of hand," because these numbers are how the executives "feel the pulse" of their businesses. . . . "With this, Jeff [Immelt] and the [divisional] CEOs can get together and, without setting up a formal agenda, sit down and look around and take different paths in their discussions." His point is that "It allows flexibility we haven't had in the past, and it absolutely allows faster decision times."

To Think About: What are the management benefits of digital dashboards? How do these dashboard systems provide value for the firm? What technical, organization and management issues did the companies described here have to address in developing and installing their digital dashboards?

Source: Bob Tedeschi, "E-Commerce Report: Digital Cockpits Are a Faster, Much Closer Way of Tracking Performance in a Corporation's Every Corner," *New York Times,* July 29, 2002; and Alex Salkever and Olga Kharif, "Business' Killer App: The Web," *BusinessWeek,* April 15, 2002.

MANAGEMENT

results by business unit or product group, a marketing manager can use the system to look only at the group of products he or she was responsible for. The manager can produce a report to indicate exactly which products are strong or weak performers or to rank dealers by performance. The system is flexible, easy to use, and can provide much of this information to the user online (Information Builders, 2000).

Cookson Electronics of Foxborough, Massachusetts, a supplier of materials used in printed circuit boards and semiconductor packaging, has 14 divisions around the world. Each is responsible for a different point in the electronics lifecycle, providing parts for computers, cellphones, and other consumer electronics. The semiconductor field has highly cyclical fluctuations in business, and Cookson divisions responsible for this part of the business can help the entire firm predict demand by anticipating industry cycles. Working with senior managers, Cookson's senior intelligence officer Yann Morvan developed a list of key

Cognos Visualizer dashboards use a diverse selection of maps and charts to display multiple metrics simultaneously, enabling decision-makers to view some or all key business measures in one place. Digital dashboards use easy-to-understand displays to provide management with a comprehensive view of firm performance.

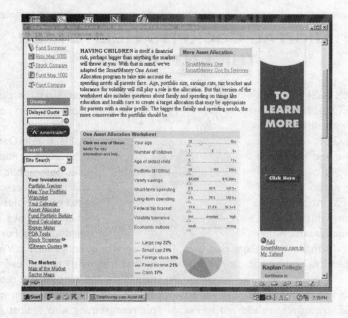

intelligence topics (KITs) linked to strategic decisions. For example, a KIT might cover the firm's top five competitors, suppliers, customers, or technologies.

The Cookson Electronic Business Intelligence System (CEBIS), based on Lotus Notes, enables Cookson's 6,000 worldwide employees to access and contribute competitive intelligence information, such as competitor strategic alliances or geographic extensions or significant investments in research and development. Senior managers can use CEBIS to subscribe to the latest information on a specific KIT and receive news and analysis via e-mail or fax. Cookson expects the information from CEBIS will help managers counter threats and anticipate changes (Shand, 2000).

Monitoring Corporate Performance: Balanced Scorecard Systems

Companies have traditionally measured value using financial metrics such as return on investment (ROI), which we describe in Chapter 13. Many firms are now implementing a **balanced scorecard** model that supplements traditional financial measures with measurements from additional perspectives such as customers, internal business processes, and learning and growth. Managers can use balanced scorecard systems to see how well the firm is meeting its strategic goals. The goals and measures for the balanced scorecard vary from company to company. Companies are setting up information systems to populate the scorecard for management.

Aurora Consolidated Laboratories, a division of Aurora Health Care, is Wisconsin's largest private employer, with 13 hospitals, dozens of clinics and health centers, and 3,500 physicians reporting through over 100 cost centers. In addition to monitoring costs closely, management wanted to measure customer satisfaction, the efficiency of Aurora's lab processes, satisfaction of key partners and suppliers, and employee motivation and productivity. The company implemented a Web-based reporting and communications system based on WebFOCUS from Information Builders Inc., which uses data from more than 35 databases consolidated in a data warehouse to give managers a scorecard on how well they are progressing. The system provides up-to-date data on corporate performance, graphs and charts to spot trends and anomalies, and the capability to drill down to see detailed data behind the trends. Users can save reports from the system as HTML files for later viewing with their Web browsers. The system was initially available to 25 users, including senior managers, vice presidents, and selected supervisors but is being gradually opened to other managers (Information Builders, 2000).

Amsterdam-based ING Bank, which is part of the ING Group global financial services firm, adopted a balanced scorecard approach when it reorganized. Management wanted to shift from a product to a client orientation and develop appropriate performance indicators to measure progress in this new direction. In 1997, the bank built a Web-based balanced scorecard application using SAS tools for data warehousing and statistical analysis to mea-

---

balanced scorecard

Model for analyzing firm performance that supplements traditional financial measures with measurements from additional business perspectives, such as customers, internal business processes, and learning and growth.

| TABLE 11-4 | STRATEGIC PERFORMANCE MANAGEMENT TOOLS FOR ENTERPRISE SYSTEMS |

Enterprise System Vendor	Description
SAP	Web-enabled mySAP Strategic Enterprise Management™ module provides reports giving managers a comprehensive view of firm performance. Features corporate performance metrics, simulation, and planning tools. Managers can model and communicate key performance indicators for a Balanced Scorecard. Another measurement tool called the Management Cockpit can be used to monitor strategic performance indicators using internal and external benchmarks.
PeopleSoft	Web-enabled Enterprise Performance Management (EPM) features modules for workforce analytics, customer relationship analytics, financial analytics, supply chain analytics, and profitability management for financial services. The Financial Analytics module supports Activity-Based Management and the Balanced Scorecard.
Oracle	Strategic Enterprise Management includes support for the Balanced Scorecard, activity-based management, and budgeting. A value-based management module under development will help companies develop and apply new accounting methods for quantifying intellectual capital.

sure progress with 21 indicators. Data to fill out the scorecard, from sources such as financial ledger applications and client retention and market penetration ratios, feed a central data warehouse. The data come from systems running on Lotus Notes, Microsoft Excel spreadsheets, and Oracle and DB2 databases. The data warehouse and balanced scorecard software run on IBM RS/6000 servers. ING initially made the balanced scorecard system available only to midrange executives in sales, but later extended it to 3,000 users, including people at nearly every level of its relationship management group. Users regularly check progress with the scorecard. For example, by comparing how many visits they have made to different clients, sales people can make better decisions about how to allocate their time (McCune, 2000).

Enterprise-wide Reporting and Analysis

Enterprise system vendors are now providing capabilities to extend the usefulness of data captured in operational systems to give management a picture of the overall performance of the firm. Some provide reporting of metrics for balanced scorecard analysis as well as more traditional financial and operating metrics. Table 11-4 describes strategic performance management tools for each of the major enterprise system vendors.

Companies can use these new enterprise-reporting capabilities to create measures of firm performance that were not previously available. The head of Strategic Planning at Dow Chemical led a cross-functional steering team to develop a set of measures and reports based on data from the company's SAP enterprise system. Process experts in different areas of the company defined reporting categories such as expense management, inventory management, and sales. Dow then developed a data mart for each type of data, amounting to over 20 data marts. The data marts are integrated so that the numbers for the "business results" mart balance with numbers in the expenses and sales marts. Dow also implemented a new set of performance measures based on shareholder value and activity-based costing. **Activity-based costing** is a budgeting and analysis model that identifies all the resources, processes, and costs, including overhead and operating expenses, required to produce a specific product or service. It focuses on determining firm activities that cause costs to occur rather than on merely tracking what has been spent. It allows managers to see which products or services are profitable or losing money so they can determine the changes required to maximize firm profitability. Instead of reporting in terms of product and income, the system can focus on contribution margins and customer accounts, with the ability to calculate the current and lifetime value of each account. The system is used by over 5,000 people, ranging from Dow's CEO to plant floor workers (Davenport, 2000).

Detroit Edison, the seventh-largest electric utility company in the United States, decided it needed a more in-depth understanding of the true nature of its costs to cope with deregulation and new sources of competition. It implemented PeopleSoft's Activity-Based Management (ABM) analytics software, which provides management with operational

activity-based costing
Model for identifying all the company activities that cause costs to occur while producing a specific product or service so that managers can see which products or services are profitable or losing money and make changes to maximize firm profitability.

MAKE IT YOUR BUSINESS

FINANCE AND ACCOUNTING

The finance and accounting function is replete with DSS and ESS applications. Many DSS are based on financial models for breakeven analysis, profitability analysis, capital budgeting, and financial forecasting. Retail financial service firms depend on model-based DSS for client portfolio analysis and investment recommendations. ESS often provide overviews of firm-wide financial performance, including activity-based costing and financial measures for balanced scorecard reporting. Reporting monthly or yearly cash flows and balances is a typical MIS for the finance and accounting function. You can find examples of finance and accounting applications on pages 364–368 and 371–373.

HUMAN RESOURCES

The human resources function uses model-based decision-support systems for analysis of labor contract costs or alternative compensation plans for nonunion employees. Executive information systems are used for human resources planning to project the firm's long-term labor force requirements. Comparing employee salaries to budgeted compensation amounts is a typical MIS for human resources.

MANUFACTURING AND PRODUCTION

The manufacturing and production function requires many decisions about the optimization of production, logistics, and maintenance that must evaluate many interrelated variables. Model-based DSS have been guiding decisions about supply chain management, including the development of optimal production plans, delivery schedules, and

inventory allocations. Recommending optimal plans for dispatching and routing vehicles and for facilities management are popular GIS applications. ESS can provide overviews of the firm's production resources. Comparing actual production amounts to targeted amounts for a monthly or yearly period is a typical MIS for manufacturing and production. You can find examples of manufacturing and production applications on pages 355–356, 358–359, and 365.

SALES AND MARKETING

DSS applications abound in sales and marketing. Model driven DSS support decisions about product pricing, sales forecasting, and advertising and promotional campaigns. Companies increasingly use data-driven DSS for customer relationship management (CRM) to analyze customer purchasing patterns, detect customer retention problems, identify profitable customers, and develop targeted marketing campaigns. Some of these DSS for CRM combine customer data from Web transactions with customer transaction data from offline sources. Many Web-based DSS provide access to information and products to influence customer purchasing decisions. ESS can be used for competitor analysis and identification of opportunities for new products or sales channels. GIS can analyze sales patterns and market data by location, supporting decisions on where to locate retail outlets or target marketing campaigns. Listing the best- and worst-performing sales territories for a monthly or yearly period is a typical MIS for sales and marketing. You can find examples of sales and marketing applications on pages 346–347, 352, 356–359, 371–373.

views of the process and activity costs for which they are personally responsible. ABM is part of PeopleSoft's Enterprise Performance Management application package, which extracts information from existing enterprise resource planning systems to provide high-level, industry-specific, and role-based performance and profitability measurement, analysis, and reporting. Detroit Edison used PeopleSoft ABM to create five cost models for three different lines of business-power generation, transmission and distribution, and corporate support. The software helped the company analyze the processes involved in the production of a product as well as product costs so that it could identify process improvements as well as cost reduction opportunities to save millions of dollars (PeopleSoft, 2002).

Management of Nissan Motor Company of Australia must oversee the activities of 550 people in 23 sites across the Australian continent. The company is primarily involved in Nissan's import and distribution activities for 35,000 automobiles each year. Like other automotive companies, Nissan Australia has extensive reporting requirements, including detailed controlling reports for financial accounts and monthly accounts. Managers need detailed reports down to the model level, with controlling reports for each department. When Nissan used an old legacy mainframe system, it would take up to two weeks to create and distribute reports to the company's board of directors.

In 1997, Nissan Australia installed SAP's R/3 enterprise software, serving as a pilot for the rest of the Nissan organization. The company also installed Information Builders' SNAPpack Power Reporter to create custom reports with a Web interface and powerful drill-down capabilities that did not require extensive programming to produce. These reports can be generated immediately and include profit-and-loss reports, gross margin analysis, balance sheets, and wholesale and retail vehicles. Management requests for more profit analysis reports by model, state, and other variables can be easily satisfied (Information Builders, 2000).

Management is responsible for determining where management support systems can make their greatest contribution to organizational performance and for allocating the resources to build them. Management needs to work closely with system builders to make sure that these systems effectively capture the right set of information requirements and decision processes for guiding the firm.

Management support systems can improve organizational performance by speeding up decision making or improving the quality of management decisions. However, some of these decision processes may not be clearly understood. A management support system will be most effective when system builders have a clear idea of its objectives, the nature of the decisions to be supported, and how the system will actually support decision making.

Systems to support management decision making can be developed with a range of technologies, including the use of large databases, modeling tools, graphics tools, datamining and analysis tools, and electronic meeting technology. Identifying the right technology for the decision or decision process to be supported is a key technology decision.

For Discussion

1. As a manager or user of information systems, what would you need to know to participate in the design and use of a DSS or an ESS? Why?

2. If businesses used DSS, GDSS, and ESS more widely, would they make better decisions? Explain.

SUMMARY

1. *How can information systems help individual managers make better decisions when the problems are nonroutine and constantly changing?* A special category of systems called decision-support systems (DSS) combines data, sophisticated analytical models and tools, and user-friendly software into a single powerful system that can support semistructured or unstructured decision making. There are two kinds of DSS: model-driven DSS and data-driven DSS. A DSS provides results of model-based or data-driven analysis that help managers design and evaluate alternatives and monitor the progress of the solution that was adopted.

DSS can help support decisions for supply chain management and customer analysis as well as model alternative business scenarios. DSS targeted toward customers as well as managers are becoming available on the Web. A special category of DSS called geographic information systems (GIS) uses data visualization technology to analyze and display data for planning and decision making with digitized maps. The components of a DSS are the DSS database, the DSS software system, and the user interface. The DSS database is a collection of current or historical data from a number of applications or groups that can be used for analysis. The data can come from both internal and external sources including enterprise systems and the Web. The DSS software system consists of OLAP and datamining tools or mathematical and analytical models

that are used for analyzing the data in the database. The user interface allows users to interact with the DSS software tools directly.

2. *How can information systems help people working in a group make decisions more efficiently?* People working together in a group can use group decision-support systems to help them in the process of arriving at a decision. A group decision-support system (GDSS) is an interactive computer-based system to facilitate the solution of unstructured problems by a set of decision-makers working together as a group rather than individually. Group decision-support systems (GDSS) have hardware, software, and people components. Hardware components consist of the conference room facilities, including seating arrangements and computer and other electronic hardware. Software components include tools for organizing ideas, gathering information, ranking and setting priorities, and documenting meeting sessions. People components include participants, a trained facilitator, and staff to support the hardware and software.

A GDSS helps decision-makers meeting together to arrive at a decision more efficiently and is especially useful for increasing the productivity of meetings larger than four or five people. However, the effectiveness of GDSS is contingent on the composition of the group, the task, appropriate tool selection and meeting support, and the organizational context of the meeting.

3. *Are there any special systems that can facilitate decision making among senior managers? Exactly what can these systems do to help high-level management?* Executive support systems help senior managers with unstructured problems that occur at the strategic level of the organization. ESS provide data from both internal and external sources and provide a generalized computing and communications environment that can be focused and applied to a changing array of problems. ESS help senior executives monitor firm performance, spot problems, identify opportunities, and forecast trends. These systems can filter out extraneous details for high-level overviews, or they can drill down to provide senior managers with detailed transaction data if required. ESS are starting to take advantage of firm-wide data provided by enterprise systems.

ESS help senior managers analyze, compare, and highlight trends so that they may more easily monitor organizational performance or identify strategic problems and opportunities. They are very useful for environmental scanning, providing business intelligence to help management detect signals of strategic threats or opportunities from the organization's environment. ESS can increase the span of control of senior management, allowing them to oversee more people with fewer resources.

4. *What benefits can systems to support management decision making provide for the organization as a whole?* DSS, GDSS, and ESS are starting to take advantage of more accurate firm-wide data provided by enterprise systems and the new information technology infrastructure to support very fine-grained decisions for guiding the firm, coordinating work activities across the enterprise, and responding rapidly to changing markets and customers. DSS can be used to guide company-wide decisions in supply chain management, customer relationship management, and planning business scenarios. ESS can be used to monitor company-wide performance using both traditional financial metrics and the balanced scorecard model. The ability to explore the outcomes of alternative organizational scenarios, use precise firm-wide information, and provide tools to facilitate group decision processes can help managers make decisions that help the firm achieve its strategic objectives.

KEY TERMS

Activity-based costing, 367	Data-driven DSS, 350	DSS software system, 353	Knowledge discovery, 352
Balanced scorecard, 366	Data visualization, 358	Geographic information system (GIS), 358	Model, 353
Business intelligence, 348	Drill down, 363		Model-driven DSS, 350
Customer decision-support system (CDSS), 359	DSS database, 353	Group decision-support system (GDSS), 360	Sensitivity analysis, 354

REVIEW QUESTIONS

1. What is a decision-support system (DSS)? How does it differ from a management information system (MIS)?

2. How can a DSS support unstructured or semistructured decision making?

3. What is the difference between a data-driven DSS and a model-driven DSS? Give examples.

4. What are the three basic components of a DSS? Briefly describe each.

5. How can DSS help firms with supply chain management and customer relationship management?

6. What is a geographic information system (GIS)? How does it use data visualization technology? How can it support decision making?

7. What is a customer decision-support system? How can the Internet be used for this purpose?

8. What is a group decision-support system (GDSS)? How does it differ from a DSS?

9. What underlying problems in group decision making have led to the development of GDSS?

10. Describe the three elements of a GDSS.

11. Name five GDSS software tools.

12. How can GDSS facilitate group decision making?

13. Define and describe the capabilities of an executive support system (ESS).

14. How can the Internet and enterprise systems provide capabilities for executive support systems?

15. What are the benefits of ESS? How do these systems enhance managerial decision making?

APPLICATION SOFTWARE EXERCISE

SPREADSHEET EXERCISE: PERFORMING BREAKEVEN ANALYSIS AND SENSITIVITY ANALYSIS

Selmore Collectible Toy Company (SCTC) makes toy sets consisting of collectible trucks, vans, and cars for the retail market. The firm is developing a new toy set that includes a battery-powered tractor-trailer, complete with cab and trailer, sports car, and motorcycle. Each set sells for $100. Table 1 shows the major components of SCTC's annual fixed costs for the toy set. Each component

TABLE 1
SCTC FIXED COSTS

Category	Amount
Land	$ 42,500
Buildings	332,500
Manufacturing machinery	532,000
Office equipment	212,800
Utilities	30,500
Insurance	99,700
Total	**$1,250,000**

TABLE 2
SCTC VARIABLE COSTS

Category	Amount
Labor	$15.00
Advertising	1.00
Shipping & receiving	5.00
Total	**$21.00**

includes the cost of purchases, depreciation and operating expenses. Table 2 shows the major components of SCTC's variable costs.

Prepare a spreadsheet to support the decision-making needs of SCTC's managers. The spreadsheet should show the fixed costs, variable costs per unit, the contribution margin, and the breakeven point for this product. How many sets does SCTC have to sell before it can start turning a profit? Include a data table to show alternative breakeven points, assuming variations in insurance costs and labor costs. How would increasing the sale price to $125 affect the breakeven point? The Laudon Web site for Chapter 11 provides more detail on the range of costs to include in your sensitivity analysis and on the calculations required for a simple breakeven analysis.

GROUP PROJECT

With three or four of your classmates, identify several groups in your university that could benefit from a GDSS. Design a GDSS for one of those groups, describing its hardware, software, and people elements. Present your findings to the class.

TOOLS FOR INTERACTIVE LEARNING

■ INTERNET CONNECTION

The Internet Connection for this chapter will take you to a series of Web sites where you can complete an exercise using Web-based DSS.

■ INTERACTIVE STUDY GUIDE

You can use the Interactive Study Guide to test your knowledge of the topics in this chapter and get instant feedback where you need more practice.

■ RUNNING CASE

The Running Case provides an opportunity for you to build a DSS to explore the impact of changes in component prices on Dirt Bikes USA's production costs. You can find a complete description of this project on the Laudon Web site for Chapter 11 and on the Multimedia Edition CD-ROM.

■ ELECTRONIC COMMERCE

At the Laudon Web site for Chapter 11, you will find an Electronic Commerce project that will use the interactive software at the Fidelity Investments Web site for investment portfolio analysis.

■ MANAGEMENT DECISION PROBLEM

At the Laudon Web site for Chapter 11, you can find a Management Decision Problem on analyzing a capital budgeting decision.

■ CD-ROM

If you use the Multimedia Edition CD-ROM with this chapter, you can find a video clip illustrating PeopleSoft's integrated system for measuring corporate performance, an audio overview of the major themes of this chapter, and bulleted text summarizing the key points of the chapter.

CASE STUDY—*Can DSS Help MasterCard Master the Credit Card Business?*

Credit (charge) cards have been very big business for several decades. In 2001, over $30 trillion in payments for goods and services were charged using credit cards. The cards have made life easier for many people because they do not need to carry large amounts of cash for most purchases. Many people also use the cards as a way to borrow money because they need only pay a small percentage of the amount they owe each month, although they are usually charged very high interest rates for the unpaid balance. The interest goes to the issuing bank, making credit cards a

very profitable service for them. However, the credit card industry is intensely competitive, highly fragmented, and growing at a rate of 3 to 4 percent per year, making those profits difficult to achieve.

Visa and MasterCard are associations of banks that issue the credit cards. They market their cards, often several different cards, and provide support for the transactions, making networks available to collect and use the data. The most popular credit card has been Visa, with 44.5 percent of the business in 2001, while MasterCard is number two with 31.6 percent. Being very much second to Visa, MasterCard is trying to overtake it. While it had been number two since the beginning, MasterCard began to emerge from "its doldrums" in 1997, according to Robert Selander, MasterCard's CEO. It began to realize it might really be able to overtake Visa and become number one. To reach that goal, MasterCard needed to present itself so that potential users will choose a MasterCard rather than a Visa. It also had to spur the bank issuers to promote MasterCard cards rather than those of their competition.

In 1998, when MasterCard had only 28.8 percent of the credit card charge volume while Visa's was over 50 percent, MasterCard decided it needed a new computer center, partially to handle all the data as the company's business expanded as a result of its drive to overtake Visa. It also foresaw growth as a result of its change in strategy. The company's new strategy required a system that would be able to keep a record of every transaction of every customer for three years. The strategy included ways MasterCard and its member banks could use that data to increase their credit card business. MasterCard wanted to increase its daily volume of 30 million transactions in 1997. At the time it had three separate computer centers on four floors in the suburbs of St. Louis, Missouri, and it wanted to consolidate the computer centers while enlarging the new center so that it would be able to handle both the current volume and the planned volume as it expanded. At that time it was storing nearly 50 terabytes (50 trillion numbers and letters) of data, including the dollar amount, merchant, location, and card number. MasterCard also planned to add other data fields, such as ZIP codes, to make the data more useful. However, to protect MasterCard users, it did decide not to include demographic data such as incomes and ages. Nonetheless, "The credit card business lives and dies by data," said Ted Iacobuzio, director of consumer credit research for the consulting and research firm, TowerGroup.

While both Visa and MasterCard had already been warehousing so much data, they were both moving toward providing reports to their member banks. MasterCard's goal was to give its members (the banks) direct access to their customers' data as well as tools to analyze all of this data, all in order to persuade the banks to choose MasterCard over Visa. For example, if banks could use MasterCard tools to improve their analysis of the profitability of the cards in their portfolios or gain more customers and transactions to process, they would be inclined to push MasterCard more often. Such analysis could help banks determine the types of customers that were most profitable or find ways to appeal to more potential MasterCard customers. Many banks issue both Visa cards and MasterCard cards (sometimes several of each), and if the banks can use this information from MasterCard while Visa does not have or make available such information, the MasterCard company can gain a strategic advantage. For example, in 2001, MasterCard persuaded Citigroup, the largest issuer of credit cards, to push MasterCard over Visa so that 85 percent of its credit cards came from MasterCard versus only 15 percent from Visa. J.P. Morgan Chase likewise was convinced to use MasterCard for 80 percent of the cards it issued.

MasterCard hoped it could persuade banks to use these data if they could see value (increased profit) in the process. Joseph Caro, MasterCard's vice president of Internet technology ser-

vices, said that "little percentages" can be very profitable to banks. In one case, a bank was requiring its merchants to verify the whole process by using the telephone to call in one transaction out of 50 for approval (rather than using a telecommunications method), while most banks were requiring only one transaction in 500. Because call-ins cost about $3 each, that bank could save $300,000 a year by switching over to the one in 500 method. Another bank was turning down one transaction out of five because so many call-ins were timing out. The bank was able to discover that most of the customers turned down were actually creditworthy. By changing its set up, the bank would be able to eliminate thousands of unnecessary lost transactions.

About 28,000 banks and financial service companies issue MasterCard credit cards. To draw these customers into using its credit card transaction data, MasterCard needed not only to make each bank's data available to them, but it also needed to make available appropriate analytic software. MasterCard assigned 35 full-time developers to the task of identifying and creating software tools to accomplish this task. Drawing on Business Objects' WebIntelligence software in 2001, these developers created and programmed 27 tools for the banks to use. (These tools are not free and they are not available to merchants.) One of MasterCard's new tools, called the Business Performance Intelligence, is for operational reporting and includes a suite of 70 standard reports that banks can use to analyze their daily, weekly, or monthly transactions. The banks can then compare the results from one market (such as a United States state or region, or a single country) with that of another market. MasterCard also works with individual banks to create their own custom reports, enabling them to concentrate on their own issues and concerns. Subscribing banks access the MasterCard business intelligence system via a secure extranet.

The developers also created MarketScope, which are applications that have the goal of helping banks and merchants work together to generate more purchases from the merchants if they are paid for by MasterCard. One example they give is to enable Wal-Mart stores to determine how many MasterCard holders spend $25 or more on sporting goods in January and February. Then, MasterCard's vice president of systems development, Andrew Clyne, suggested that Wal-Mart could send these cardholders the right to obtain tickets to their closest major league baseball team based upon future sporting goods purchases above a certain dollar minimum. Iacobuzio said that such a strategy should appeal to state and regional banks. However, he believes it is likely that national and international banks would have already developed and are using their own analytical software. But even they would have a use for MasterCard's software as a kind of benchmark against which to measure the effectiveness of their own systems.

MasterCard's new data storage site, which was opened in May 2002, is also in St. Louis, in a single 525,000-square-foot building. The complex, which was built on open land, cost MasterCard $135 million. The changeover to the new site happened over a weekend with almost no problems, despite the purchases of about $4 billion each day. Moreover, despite the increasing volume, the processing was much faster. As Caro said, "If we can do things faster, little percentages start moving in our direction."

Visa, however, is not sitting still, and is managing about 100 trillion terabytes of data for its clients. Until recently, it mainly supplied the data online or on disks to its bank customers, who used their own software and computers to analyze the data. Recently, Visa started to run analyses for the banks on its own computers. In May 2002, Visa also introduced a Web service called Resolve Online to help banks deal with disputed payments and is working on providing banks with online analytic tools. "If MasterCard is ahead of the game in any of this," says Iacobuzio, Visa "will have it in six months."

Sources: Tom Steinert-Threlkeld, "MasterCard Tools Up Data Handling," *Baseline*, June 17, 2002; Rick Whiting, "Extranets Go the Extra Mile," *InformationWeek*, May 20, 2002; and Kenneth N. Gilpin, "Market Insight: One Rule of Plastic: Recovery Has a Dark Side," *New York Times*, February 24, 2002.

CASE STUDY QUESTIONS:

1. Analyze MasterCard using the competitive forces and value chain models. Briefly summarize the problems that MasterCard was facing before 1998 that caused it to change its business strategy.

2. Describe the new business strategy MasterCard developed. What is the role of information systems in its new strategy?

3. What kind of decision-support systems did MasterCard develop? How are they related to its business strategy? How do they provide value for MasterCard and its clients?

4. Has MasterCard's strategy been successful? Can MasterCard hold on to its strategic advantage? Explain your answer.

DESIGNING AN ENTERPRISE INFORMATION PORTAL

You are the CIO of a major corporation that researches, develops, manufactures, and distributes pharmaceuticals. Your company, which is named United States Pharma Corp., is headquartered in the state of New Jersey in the United States, but it has sites in many countries around the world. Many of the research sites are in the United States, Germany, France, Great Britain, Australia, and Switzerland. Distribution sites are not only in the United States and Europe but also in a number of countries in East and South Asia, Africa, and the Middle East.

Your company is involved with much more than research and development of new drugs. For example, it owns two companies that produce and sell generic drugs (drugs that are no longer protected by a patent and so are copied and sold under other names). It also produces many over-the-counter drugs to combat such problems as headaches, pain, athlete's foot, and allergic reactions. The company also produces and sells some drugs that help to cure or improve some animal diseases such as heartworms and fleas.

The key to the ongoing profits of the company is the research and development of new pharmaceuticals. The company researches thousands of possible drugs in order to finally develop and patent just one that is successful and so becomes a widely sold pharmaceutical product. Such products take 8 to 15 years to research, develop, and test, followed by clinical trials and finally approval by the Food and Drug Administration (FDA). The staff must research both diseases and their treatments and the potential pharmaceuticals that could become innovative new drugs. Experts who are working on the cutting edge of medical, chemical, and other fields are carrying out research in order to develop possible new drugs and medical treatments.

To undertake the research, test the new products, and eventually obtain FDA approval, the researchers and other scientists must test all the possible pharmaceuticals. They must also turn to many places to obtain and share information with others both within and outside of the company. For example they will want to communicate with the World Health Organization, the FDA, and the Centers for Disease Control and Prevention. In addition they will need to connect to the pharmaceutical industry's organizations such as the International Federation of Pharmaceutical Manufacturers Associations (IFPMA). Health education and information sites are also critical, such as the U.S. National Library of Medicine and such private organizations as the Mayo Clinic Health Oasis.

As the CIO, you have concluded that your company needs a corporate knowledge environment portal that can provide many of the corporate employees with easy access to the information they need. The users of the portal would primarily be chemical, biological, and pharmaceutical researchers as well as medical personnel involved in research, tests, and eventually clinical trials.

1. Write a brief description of the company, its key functions and systems.

2. Design the corporate portal, providing a description that can be reviewed and approved by your senior executive committee. Your design specifications should include:

   ▌ Internal systems and databases that users of the portal would need to access

   ▌ External sources researchers would need to access to further their research

   ▌ Internal and external communication and collaboration facilities the researchers would need to develop their ideas, pursue their research, and share their research and ideas with others

   ▌ Intranet and Internet search tools to support research

   ▌ Sources for relevant news relating to the company and research

   ▌ FDA rules and regulations regarding clinical programs, clinical trials, and patent applications

   ▌ Connections to pharmaceutical conferences and forums as well as professional organizations and appropriate professional journals

   ▌ Any additional sources of information that would prove helpful to users

   Use the Web to research these features. Your analysis should include the qualities of a good corporate portal and describe commercially available tools for building your portal.

3. Design a home page for your portal that you can present to management.

BUILDING INFORMATION SYSTEMS IN THE DIGITAL FIRM

12

CHAPTER

REDESIGNING THE ORGANIZATION WITH INFORMATION SYSTEMS

objectives

During your career, you will undoubtedly be looking for ways to use new information systems to improve the performance of your firm. You may be asked to help your organization build a new information system. After reading this chapter, you will be able to answer the following questions:

1. *How could building a new system change the way an organization works?*

2. *How can a company make sure that the new information systems it builds fit its business plan?*

3. *What are the steps required to build a new information system?*

4. *What alternative methods for building information systems are available?*

5. *Are there any techniques or system-building approaches to help us build e-commerce and e-business applications more rapidly?*

FleetBoston Builds a New Lead Management System

In the cutthroat financial services industry, customer retention is essential. FleetBoston Financial Corporation wanted to expand its customer base and also increase the number of financial products and services it sells to new and existing customers by about 35 percent. This $200 billion financial services and retail banking company became the seventh largest financial holding company in the United States by acquiring at least 10 banks, merging in 1999 with BankBoston. It also acquired investment firm Quick & Reilly in 1998. FleetBoston was faced with numerous disparate systems within each of its business units that prevented it from consolidating information about customers. The lead management process was largely manual. Employees faxed or e-mailed sales leads to other departments, but they had little knowledge of appropriate contacts and could not track what happened to the lead. In some instances, customers were lost in the process.

376

FleetBoston decided to implement a new lead management system based on an application software package from MarketSoft Corp. called DemandMore Leads that can pull together information from all of the salesforce automation systems in all of the company's business units for the routing and management of referrals.

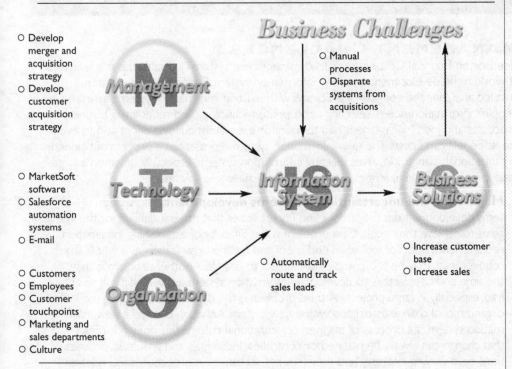

Business Challenges

Management
- Develop merger and acquisition strategy
- Develop customer acquisition strategy

Technology
- MarketSoft software
- Salesforce automation systems
- E-mail

Organization
- Customers
- Employees
- Customer touchpoints
- Marketing and sales departments
- Culture

Information System
- Automatically route and track sales leads

- Manual processes
- Disparate systems from acquisitions

Business Solutions
- Increase customer base
- Increase sales

The new system connects five customer touchpoints—the call center, service desk, branch locations, campaign-management application, and online self-service within the company's mortgage, small-business banking, personal finance, and Quick & Reilly investment divisions to channel customer data throughout the organization. Mortgage representatives can use this system to send Quick & Reilly contact information via a Web interface about a mortgage customer interested in investment advice. The system accepts sales lead information from all of these touchpoints, assigns priority to the leads, and delivers the lead data to the salesforce automation system in the division where the most appropriate sales representative works. Employees in all of Fleet's divisions can share the customer data. The system places an identifying watermark on each lead and can track the lead as it moves throughout the salesforce automation applications. The corporate marketing and sales departments can thereby monitor whether a representative followed up with the lead and addressed the prospect's needs and whether the lead produced a sale. Sales representatives can access more data about a specific customer from other divisions to help close a sale. When representatives don't follow up on a lead within a preset amount of time, the system automatically reroutes the lead to another sales representative.

One requirement that had to be met was that employees had to be able to enter customer leads using their existing systems. Fleet also had to address some cultural issues. Employees working in one division might be reluctant to share their customer information with other lines of business. Fleet developed a training program to help employees spot potential leads for different parts of the company as well as an incentive program to reward employees when cross-divisional referrals are converted into sales. When the company starts converting to the DemandMore system, Fleet will start to measure its success.

Sources: Eileen Colkin, "Fleet Moving to Consolidate Leads Across Systems," *InformationWeek,* January 28, 2002; Jim Middlemiss, "The Challenge," *Wall Street & Technology*, August 13, 2002; and <www.fleet.com>, accessed September 2, 2002.

MANAGEMENT CHALLENGES

FleetBoston Financial Corporation's lead management system illustrates the many factors at work in the development of a new information system. Building the new system entailed analyzing the company's problems with existing information systems, assessing people's information needs, selecting appropriate technology, and redesigning business processes and jobs. Management had to monitor the system-building effort and to evaluate its benefits and costs. The new information system represented a process of planned organizational change. However, building information systems, especially those on a large scale, presents many challenges. Here are several challenges to consider:

1. **Major risks and uncertainties in systems development.** Information systems development has major risks and uncertainties that make it difficult for the systems to achieve their goals. One problem is the difficulty of establishing information requirements, both for individual end users and for the organization as a whole. The requirements may be too complex or subject to change. Another problem is that the time and cost factors to develop an information system are very difficult to analyze, especially in large projects. A third problem is the difficulty of managing the organizational change associated with a new system. Although building a new information system is a process of planned organizational change, this does not mean that change can always be planned or controlled. Individuals and groups in organizations have varying interests, and they may resist changes in procedures, job relationships, and technologies. Although this chapter describes some ways of dealing with these risks and uncertainties, the issues remain major management challenges.

2. **Determining where new systems and business processes can have the greatest strategic impact.** One of the most important strategic decisions that a firm can make is not deciding how to use computers to improve business processes, but instead understanding what business processes need improvement. When systems are used to strengthen the wrong business model or business processes, the business can become more efficient at doing what it should not do (Hammer, 2002). As a result, the firm becomes vulnerable to competitors who may have discovered the right business model. Considerable time and cost can also be spent improving business processes that have little impact on overall firm performance and revenue. Managers need to determine what business processes are the most important to focus on when applying new information technology and how improving these processes will help the firm execute its strategy.

This chapter describes how new information systems are conceived, built, and installed, with special attention to the issues of organizational design, business process reengineering, and total quality management. It describes the core systems development activities and how to ensure that new systems are linked to the organization's business plan and information requirements. This chapter also examines alternative approaches for building systems.

12.1 SYSTEMS AS PLANNED ORGANIZATIONAL CHANGE

This text has emphasized that an information system is a sociotechnical entity, an arrangement of both technical and social elements. The introduction of a new information system involves much more than new hardware and software. It also includes changes in jobs, skills, management, and organization. In the sociotechnical philosophy, one cannot install new technology without considering the people who must work with it (Bostrom and Heinen, 1977). When we design a new information system, we are redesigning the organization.

One important thing to know about building a new information system is that this process is one kind of planned organizational change. System builders must understand how a system will affect the organization as a whole, focusing particularly on organizational conflict and changes in the locus of decision making. Builders must also consider how the nature of work groups will change under the new system. Systems can be technical successes but organizational failures because of a failure in the social and political process of building the system. Analysts and designers are responsible for ensuring that key members of the organization participate in the design process and are permitted to influence the system's ultimate shape.

Linking Information Systems to the Business Plan

Deciding which new systems to build should be an essential component of the organizational planning process. Organizations need to develop an information systems plan that supports their overall business plan and in which strategic systems are incorporated into top-level planning. Once specific projects have been selected within the overall context of a strategic plan for the business and the systems area, an **information systems plan** can be developed. The plan serves as a road map indicating the direction of systems development, the rationale, the current situation, the management strategy, the implementation plan, and the budget (see the Manager's Toolkit).

information systems plan
A road map indicating the direction of systems development: the rationale, the current situation, the management strategy, the implementation plan, and the budget.

MIS in Action: Manager's Toolkit

HOW TO DEVELOP AN INFORMATION SYSTEMS PLAN
A good information systems plan should address the following topics:

1. Purpose of the Plan
   - Overview of plan contents
   - Changes in firm's current situation
   - Firm's strategic plan
   - Current business organization and future organization
   - Key business processes
   - Management strategy
2. Strategic Business Plan
   - Current situation
   - Current business organization
   - Changing environments
   - Major goals of the business plan
3. Current Systems
   - Major systems supporting business functions and processes
   - Current infrastructure capabilities
     - Hardware
     - Software
     - Database
     - Telecommunications and Internet
   - Difficulties meeting business requirements
   - Anticipated future demands
4. New Developments
   - New system projects
     - Project descriptions
     - Business rationale
   - New infrastructure capabilities required
     - Hardware
     - Software

Database
Telecommunications and Internet
5. Management Strategy
   - Acquisition plans
   - Milestones and timing
   - Organizational realignment
   - Internal reorganization
   - Management controls
   - Major training initiatives
   - Personnel strategy
6. Implementation Plan
   - Anticipated difficulties in implementation
   - Progress reports
7. Budget Requirements
   - Requirements
   - Potential savings
   - Financing
   - Acquisition cycle

The plan contains a statement of corporate goals and specifies how information technology supports the attainment of those goals. The report shows how general goals will be achieved by specific systems projects. It lays out specific target dates and milestones that can be used later to evaluate the plan's progress in terms of how many objectives were actually attained in the time frame specified in the plan. The plan indicates the key management decisions concerning hardware acquisition; telecommunications; centralization/decentralization of authority, data, and hardware; and required organizational change. Organizational changes are usually described, including management and employee training requirements; recruiting efforts; changes in business processes; and changes in authority, structure, or management practice.

ESTABLISHING ORGANIZATIONAL INFORMATION REQUIREMENTS

In order to develop an effective information systems plan, the organization must have a clear understanding of both its long- and short-term information requirements. Two principal methodologies for establishing the essential information requirements of the organization as a whole are enterprise analysis and critical success factors.

Enterprise Analysis (Business Systems Planning)

enterprise analysis

An analysis of organization-wide information requirements that examines the entire organization in terms of organizational units, functions, processes, and data elements; helps identify the key entities and attributes in the organization's data.

Enterprise analysis (also called *business systems planning*) argues that the firm's information requirements can only be understood by looking at the entire organization in terms of organizational units, functions, processes, and data elements. Enterprise analysis can help identify the key entities and attributes of the organization's data.

The central method used in the enterprise analysis approach is to take a large sample of managers and ask them how they use information, where they get the information, what their environments are like, what their objectives are, how they make decisions, and what their data needs are. The results of this large survey of managers are aggregated into subunits, functions, processes, and data matrices. Data elements are organized into logical application groups— groups of data elements that support related sets of organizational processes. Figure 12-1 is an output of enterprise analysis conducted by the Social Security Administration as part of a massive systems redevelopment effort. It shows what information is required to support a particular process, which processes create the data, and which use them. The shaded boxes in the figure indicate a logical application group. In this case, actuarial estimates, agency plans, and budget data are created in the planning process, suggesting that an information system should be built to support planning.

The weakness of enterprise analysis is that it produces an enormous amount of data that is expensive to collect and difficult to analyze. Most of the interviews are conducted with senior or middle managers, but there is little effort to collect information from clerical workers and supervisory managers. Moreover, the questions frequently focus not on management's critical objectives and where information is needed but rather on what existing information is used. The result is a tendency to automate whatever exists. But in many instances, entirely new approaches to how business is conducted are needed, and these needs are not addressed.

Strategic Analysis or Critical Success Factors

critical success factors (CSFs)

A small number of easily identifiable operational goals shaped by the industry, the firm, the manager, and the broader environment that are believed to assure the success of an organization. Used to determine the information requirements of an organization.

The strategic analysis, or critical success factors approach argues that an organization's information requirements are determined by a small number of **critical success factors (CSFs)** of managers. If these goals can be attained, the firm's or organization's success is assured (Rockart, 1979; Rockart and Treacy, 1982). CSFs are shaped by the industry, the firm, the manager, and the broader environment. An important premise of the strategic analysis approach is that there are a small number of objectives that managers can easily identify and on which information systems can focus.

The principal method used in CSF analysis is personal interviews—three or four—with a number of top managers to identify their goals and the resulting CSFs. These personal CSFs are aggregated to develop a picture of the firm's CSFs. Then systems are built to deliver information on these CSFs. (See Table 12-1 for an example of CSFs. For the method of developing CSFs in an organization, see Figure 12-2.)

The strength of the CSF method is that it produces a smaller data set to analyze than does enterprise analysis. Only top managers are interviewed, and the questions focus on a small number of CSFs rather than a broad inquiry into what information is used or needed. The CSF method takes into account the changing environment with which organizations and managers must deal. This method explicitly asks managers to look at the environment and consider how their analysis of it shapes their information needs. It is especially suitable for top management and for the development of DSS and ESS. Unlike enterprise analysis, the CSF method focuses organizational attention on how information should be handled.

The method's primary weakness is that the aggregation process and the analysis of the data are art forms. There is no particularly rigorous way in which individual CSFs can be aggregated into a clear company pattern. Second, there is often confusion among interviewees

Process/data class matrix (Data Classes across the top; Processes down the side). Key: C = creators of data, U = users of data.

Logical Application Group	Process	Actuarial estimates	Agency plans	Budget	Program regs./policy	Admin. regs./policy	Labor agreements	Data standards	Procedures	Automated systems documentation	Educational media	Public agreements	Intergovernmental agreements	Grants	External	Exchange control	Administrative accounts	Program expenditures	Audit reports	Organization/position	Employee identification	Recruitment/placement	Complaints/grievances	Training resources	Security	Equipment utilization	Space utilization	Supplies utilization	Workload schedules	Work measurement	Enumeration I.D.	Enumeration control	Earnings	Employer I.D.	Earnings control	Claims characteristics	Claims control	Decisions	Payment	Collection/waiver	Notice	Inquiries control	Quality appraisal
PLANNING	Develop agency plans	C	C	C	U	U	U								C																												
	Administer agency budget	C	C	C	U	U							U	U	U		U	U	U	U	U				U	U	U			U		U			U	U					U	U	U
	Formulate program policies	U	U		C				U						U					U				U														U					U
	Formulate admin. policies		U		U	C	C		U						U					U		U		U																			
	Formulate data policies		U	U	U			C	U	U																U	U	U	U														
	Design work processes		U		U	U			C	C		U	U							U																		U					U
GENERAL MANAGEMENT	Manage public affairs		U		U	U			U		C	C	C																														
	Manage intrgovt. affairs	U	U		U	U			U		U		C	C	C																U	U	U	U	U	U		U		U			
	Exchange data			U					U			U	U	U	U	C	U	U													U												
	Maintain admin. accounts			U	U				U			U	U			C		U								U	U	U							U		U						
	Maintain prog. accounts		U	U					U			U	U				C												U							U	U	U	U	U		U	
	Conduct audits			U	U			U	U							U	U	C		U									U														
	Establish organizations		U		U				U											C	U								U	U													U
	Manage human resources		U		U	U	U		U											C	C	C	C	C																			
	Provide security			U	U			U	U	U	U														C	C	C	C			U												
	Manage equipment		U		U			U	U	U	U														C	C	C	C															
	Manage facilities		U		U				U																U	U	C																
	Manage supplies		U		U				U																C	U	U	C															
	Manage workloads	U		U	U	U			U						U										U	U	U		C	C		U			U		U					U	U
PROGRAM ADMIN.	Issue Social Security nos.								U				U	U																	C	C											
	Maintain earnings								U				U	U	U																U		C	C	C	U							
	Collect claims information				U	U			U						U																U	U				C	C	U	U	U			
	Determine elig./entlmt.								U																						U	U	U			U		C	U	U			
	Compute payments			U					U										U												U	U	U			U		U	C	C			
	Administer debt mgmt.			U					U										U														U							C			
SUPPORT	Generate notices								U						U																U	U			U		U	U	U	C			
	Respond to prog. inquiries			U					U	U	U																				U	U			U		U	U	U	U	U	C	
	Provide quality assessment			U	U				U	U																					U	U			U		U	U			U		C

Figure 12-1 Process/data class matrix. This chart depicts which data classes are required to support particular organizational processes and which processes are the creators and users of data.

KEY
C = creators of data   U = users of data

TABLE 12-1 CRITICAL SUCCESS FACTORS AND ORGANIZATIONAL GOALS

Example	Goals	CSF
Profit concern	Earnings/share	Automotive industry
	Return on investment	Styling
	Market share	Quality dealer system
	New product	Cost control
		Energy standards
Nonprofit	Excellent healthcare	Regional integration with other hospitals
	Meeting government regulations	Improved monitoring of regulations
	Future health needs	Efficient use of resources

Source: Rockart (1979).

Figure 12-2 Using CSFs to develop systems. The CSF approach relies on interviews with key managers to identify their CSFs. Individual CSFs are aggregated to develop CSFs for the entire firm. Systems can then be built to deliver information on these CSFs.

(and interviewers) between *individual* and *organizational* CSFs. They are not necessarily the same. What can be critical to a manager may not be important for the organization. Moreover, this method is clearly biased toward top managers because they are the ones (generally the only ones) interviewed.

SYSTEMS DEVELOPMENT AND ORGANIZATIONAL CHANGE

New information systems can be powerful instruments for organizational change, enabling organizations to redesign their structure, scope, power relationships, work flows, products, and services. Table 12-2 describes some of the ways that information technology is being used to transform organizations and business processes.

The Spectrum of Organizational Change

Information technology can promote various degrees of organizational change, ranging from incremental to far-reaching. Figure 12-3 shows four kinds of structural organizational change

TABLE 12-2	HOW INFORMATION TECHNOLOGY CAN TRANSFORM ORGANIZATIONS
Information Technology	**Organizational Change**
Global networks	International division of labor: The operations of a firm and its business processes are no longer determined by location; the global reach of firms is extended; costs of global coordination decline. Transaction costs decline.
Enterprise networks	Collaborative work and teamwork: The organization of work can now be coordinated across divisional boundaries; the costs of management (agency costs) decline. Multiple tasks can be worked on simultaneously from different locations.
Distributed computing	Empowerment: Individuals and work groups now have the information and knowledge to act. Business processes can be streamlined. Management costs decline. Hierarchy and centralization decline.
Portable computing	Virtual organizations: Work is no longer tied to physical location. Knowledge and information can be delivered anywhere they are needed, anytime. Work becomes portable.
Multimedia, Graphical interfaces	Accessibility: Everyone in the organization—even senior executives—can access information and knowledge. Organizational costs decline as work flows move from paper to digital image, documents, and voice. Complex knowledge objects can be stored and represented as objects containing graphics, audio, video, or text.

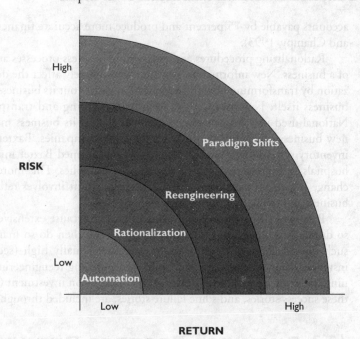

High

RISK

Paradigm Shifts

Reengineering

Rationalization

Low

Automation

Low   High

RETURN

Figure 12-3 Organizational change carries risks and rewards. The most common forms of organizational change are automation and rationalization. These relatively slow moving and slow changing strategies present modest returns but little risk. Faster and more comprehensive change—like reengineering and paradigm shifts—carries high rewards but offers substantial chances of failure.

that are enabled by information technology: (1) automation, (2) rationalization, (3) reengineering, and (4) paradigm shifts. Each carries different rewards and risks.

The most common form of IT-enabled organizational change is **automation.** The first applications of information technology involved assisting employees with performing their tasks more efficiently and effectively. Calculating paychecks and payroll registers, giving bank tellers instant access to customer deposit records, and developing a nationwide network of airline reservation terminals for airline reservation agents are all examples of early automation.

A deeper form of organizational change—one that follows quickly from early automation—is **rationalization of procedures.** Automation frequently reveals new bottlenecks in production and makes the existing arrangement of procedures and structures painfully cumbersome. Rationalization of procedures is the streamlining of standard operating procedures, eliminating obvious bottlenecks, so that automation can make operating procedures more efficient. For example, FleetBoston Financial Corporation's new lead management system described in the chapter-opening vignette is effective not only because it uses computer technology but also because its design allows the organization to operate more efficiently. The procedures of FleetBoston, or any organization, must be rationally structured to achieve this result. FleetBoston had to have standard identification codes for customers, sales representatives, and sales departments, and standard rules for routing leads to the appropriate sales or marketing resource. Without a certain amount of rationalization in FleetBoston's organization, its computer technology would have been useless.

A more powerful type of organizational change is **business process reengineering,** in which business processes are analyzed, simplified, and redesigned. Using information technology, organizations can rethink and streamline their business processes to improve speed, service, and quality. Business process reengineering reorganizes work flows, combining steps to cut waste and eliminating repetitive, paper-intensive tasks (sometimes the new design eliminates jobs as well). It is much more ambitious than rationalization of procedures, requiring a new vision of how the process is to be organized.

A widely cited example of business process reengineering is Ford Motor Company's *invoiceless processing.* Ford employed more than 500 people in its North American Accounts Payable organization. The accounts payable clerks spent most of their time resolving discrepancies between purchase orders, receiving documents, and invoices. Ford reengineered its accounts payable process, instituting a system wherein the purchasing department enters a purchase order into an online database that can be checked by the receiving department when the ordered items arrive. If the received goods match the purchase order, the system automatically generates a check for accounts payable to send to the vendor. There is no need for vendors to send invoices. After reengineering, Ford was able to reduce head count in

automation

Using the computer to speed up the performance of existing tasks.

rationalization of procedures

The streamlining of standard operating procedures, eliminating obvious bottlenecks, so that automation makes operating procedures more efficient.

business process reengineering

The radical redesign of business processes, combining steps to cut waste and eliminating repetitive, paper-intensive tasks in order to improve cost, quality, and service, and to maximize the benefits of information technology.

accounts payable by 75 percent and produce more accurate financial information (Hammer and Champy, 1993).

Rationalizing procedures and redesigning business processes are limited to specific parts of a business. New information systems can ultimately affect the design of the entire organization by transforming how the organization carries out its business or even the nature of the business itself. For instance, the long-haul trucking and transportation firm Schneider National used new information systems to change its business model. Schneider created a new business managing the logistics for other companies. Baxter International's stockless inventory system (described in Chapter 3) transformed Baxter into a working partner with hospitals and into a manager of its customers' supplies. This more radical form of business change is called a **paradigm shift.** A paradigm shift involves rethinking the nature of the business and the nature of the organization itself.

Paradigm shifts and reengineering often fail because extensive organizational change is so difficult to orchestrate (see Chapter 13). Why then do so many corporations entertain such radical change? Because the rewards are equally high (see Figure 12-3). In many instances firms seeking paradigm shifts and pursuing reengineering strategies achieve stunning, order-of-magnitude increases in their returns on investment (or productivity). Some of these success stories, and some failure stories, are included throughout this book.

paradigm shift

Radical reconceptualization of the nature of the business and the nature of the organization.

12.2 BUSINESS PROCESS REENGINEERING AND PROCESS IMPROVEMENT

Many companies today are focusing on building new information systems that will improve their business processes. Some of these system projects represent radical restructuring of business processes, whereas others entail more incremental change.

BUSINESS PROCESS REENGINEERING

If organizations rethink and radically redesign their business processes before applying computing power, they can potentially obtain very large payoffs from their investments in information technology. The home mortgage industry is a leading example in the United States of how major corporations have implemented business process reengineering. The application process for a home mortgage took about six to eight weeks and cost about $3,000. The goal of many mortgage banks has been to lower that cost to $1,000 and the time to obtain a mortgage to about one week. Leading mortgage banks, such as Fleet Bank, Countrywide Funding Corporation, and Banc One Corporation, have redesigned the mortgage application process.

The mortgage application process is divided into three stages: origination, servicing, and secondary marketing. Figure 12-4 illustrates how business process redesign has been used in each of these stages.

In the past, a mortgage applicant filled out a paper loan application. The bank entered the application into its computer system. Specialists, such as credit analysts and underwriters from perhaps eight different departments, accessed and evaluated the application individually. If the loan application was approved, the closing was scheduled. After the closing, bank specialists dealing with insurance or funds in escrow serviced the loan. This "desk-to-desk" assembly-line approach might take up to 17 days.

Leading banks have replaced the sequential desk-to-desk approach with a speedier "work cell" or team approach. Now, loan originators in the field enter the mortgage application directly into laptop computers. Software checks the application transaction to make sure that all of the information is correct and complete. The loan originators transmit the loan applications using a dial-up network to regional production centers. Instead of working on the application individually, the credit analysts, loan underwriters, and other specialists convene electronically, working as a team to approve the mortgage. Some banks provide customers with a nearly instant credit lock-in of a guaranteed mortgage so they can find a house that meets their budget immediately. Such preapproval of a credit line is truly a radical reengineering of the traditional business process.

After closing, another team of specialists sets up the loan for servicing. The entire loan application process can take as little as two days. Loan information is easier to access than before, when the loan application could be in eight or nine different departments. Loan

Figure 12-4 Redesigning mortgage processing in the United States. By redesigning their mortgage processing systems and the mortgage application process, mortgage banks can reduce the costs of processing the average mortgage from $3,000 to $1,000, and reduce the time of approval from six weeks to one week or less. Some banks are even preapproving mortgages and locking interest rates on the same day the customer applies.

originators also can dial into the bank's network to obtain information on mortgage loan costs or to check the status of a loan for the customer.

By redesigning their approach to mortgage processing, mortgage banks have achieved remarkable efficiencies. They have not focused on redesigning a single business process but instead they have reexamined the entire set of logically connected processes required to obtain a mortgage. Instead of automating the previous method of mortgage processing, the banks have completely rethought the entire mortgage application process.

Work Flow Management

work flow management
The process of streamlining business procedures so that documents can be moved easily and efficiently from one location to another.

To streamline the paperwork in the mortgage application process, banks have turned to work flow and document management software. By using this software to store and process documents electronically, organizations can redesign their work flows so that documents can be worked on simultaneously or moved more easily and efficiently from one location to another. The process of streamlining business procedures so that documents can be moved easily and efficiently is called **work flow management.** Work flow and document management software automates processes such as routing documents to different locations, securing approvals, scheduling, and generating reports. Two or more people can work simultaneously on the same document, allowing much quicker completion time. Work need not be delayed because a file is out or a document is in transit. And with a properly designed indexing system, users will be able to retrieve files in many different ways, based on the content of the document.

STEPS IN EFFECTIVE REENGINEERING

To reengineer effectively, senior management needs to develop a broad strategic vision that calls for redesigned business processes. For example, Mitsubishi Heavy Industries management looked for breakthroughs to lower costs and accelerate product development that would enable the firm to regain world market leadership in shipbuilding. The company redesigned its entire production process to replace expensive labor-intensive tasks with robotic machines and computer-aided design tools. Companies should identify a few core business processes to be redesigned, focusing on those with the greatest potential payback and strategic value (Davenport and Short, 1990).

Management must understand and measure the performance of existing processes as a baseline. If, for example, the objective of process redesign is to reduce time and cost in developing a new product or filling an order, the organization needs to measure the time and cost consumed by the unchanged process. For example, before reengineering, it cost C. R. England & Sons Inc. $5.10 to send an invoice; after processes were reengineered the cost per invoice dropped to 15 cents (Davidson, 1993).

The conventional method of designing systems establishes the information requirements of a business function or process and then determines how they can be supported by information technology. However information technology can create new design options for various processes because it can be used to challenge long-standing assumptions about work arrangements that used to inhibit organizations. For example, the mortgage processing application we have just described shows that it is no longer necessary for people to be in the same physical location in order to work together on a document. Using networks and document management technology, they can access and work on the same document from many different locations. Information technology should be allowed to influence process design from the start.

Following these steps does not automatically guarantee that reengineering will always be successful. The organization's IT infrastructure should have capabilities to support business process changes that span boundaries between functions, business units, or firms (Broadbent, Weill, and St. Clair, 1999). The majority of reengineering projects do not achieve breakthrough gains in business performance. A reengineered business process or a new information system inevitably affects jobs, skill requirements, work flows, and reporting relationships. Fear of these changes breeds resistance, confusion, and even conscious efforts to undermine the change effort. Managing change is neither simple nor intuitive.

The scope of reengineering projects has widened, adding to their complexity. Today's digital firm environment involves much closer coordination of a firm's business processes with those of customers, suppliers, and other business partners than in the past. Organizations are required to make business process changes that span organizational boundaries and stand to derive substantial benefits from reengineering inefficient interorganizational processes. These interorganizational processes, such as those for supply chain management, not only need to be streamlined but also coordinated and integrated with those of other business partners. In such cases, reengineering will involve many companies working together to jointly redesign their shared processes. Reengineering expert James Champy calls the joint redesign of interorganizational business processes *X-engineering* and it will be even more challenging to implement successfully than reengineering processes for a single company. We examine the organizational change issues surrounding reengineering more carefully in Chapter 13.

PROCESS IMPROVEMENT: TOTAL QUALITY MANAGEMENT (TQM) AND SIX SIGMA

In addition to increasing organizational efficiency, companies are also changing their business processes to improve the quality in their products, services, and operations. Many are using the concept of **total quality management (TQM)** to make quality the responsibility of all people and functions within an organization. TQM holds that the achievement of quality control is an end in itself. Everyone is expected to contribute to the overall improvement of quality—the engineer who avoids design errors, the production worker who spots defects, the sales representative who presents the product properly to potential customers, and even the secretary who avoids typing mistakes. TQM derives from quality management concepts developed by American quality experts such as W. Edwards Deming and Joseph Juran, but it was popularized by the Japanese. Another quality concept that is being widely implemented today is six sigma. **Six sigma** is a specific measure of quality, representing 3.4 defects per million opportunities. Most companies cannot achieve this level of quality but use six sigma as a goal in order to implement a set of methodologies and techniques for improving quality and reducing costs. Studies have repeatedly shown that the earlier in the business cycle a problem is eliminated, the less it costs the company. Thus quality improvements cannot only raise the level of product and service quality but they can also lower costs.

total quality management (TQM)
A concept that makes quality control a responsibility to be shared by all people in an organization.

six sigma
A specific measure of quality, representing 3.4 defects per million opportunities; used to designate a set of methodologies and techniques for improving quality and reducing costs.

How Information Systems Support Quality Improvements

TQM and six sigma are considered to be more incremental than business process reengineering (BPR). TQM typically focuses on making a series of continuous improvements rather than dramatic bursts of change. Six sigma uses statistical analysis tools to detect flaws in the execution of an existing process and make minor adjustments. Sometimes, however, processes may have to be fully reengineered to achieve a specified level of quality. Information systems can help firms achieve their quality goals by helping them simplify products or processes, meet benchmarking standards, make improvements based on customer demands, reduce cycle time, and increase the quality and precision of design and production.

Simplifying the product or the production process. The fewer steps in a process, the less time and opportunity for an error to occur. Ten years ago, 1-800-FLOWERS, a multimillion-dollar telephone and Web-based floral service with a global reach, was a much smaller company that spent too much on advertising because it could not retain its customers. It had poor service, inconsistent quality, and a cumbersome manual order-taking process. Telephone representatives had to write the order, obtain credit card approval, determine which participating florist was closest to the delivery location, select a floral arrangement, and forward the order to the florist. Each step in the manual process increased the chance of human error, and the whole process took at least a half hour. Owners Jim and Chris McCann installed a new computer system that downloads orders taken at telecenters into a central computer and electronically transmits them to local florists. Orders are more accurate and arrive at the florist within one to two minutes (Gill, 1998).

Benchmarking. Many companies have been effective in achieving quality by setting strict standards for products, services, and other activities, and then measuring performance against those standards. This procedure is called **benchmarking.** Companies may use external industry standards, standards set by other companies, internally developed high standards, or some combination of the three. L. L. Bean, Inc., the Freeport, Maine, outdoor catalog

benchmarking
Setting strict standards for products, services, or activities and measuring organizational performance against those standards.

Delta Airlines developed information systems to improve service to customers when they are checking in or connecting flights. Improving customer service is one way that information systems can support Total Quality Management (TQM).

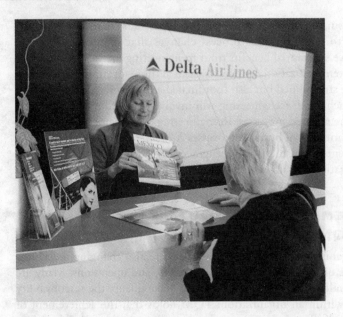

company, used benchmarking to achieve an order shipping accuracy of 99.9 percent. Its old batch order fulfillment system could not handle the surging volume and variety of items to be shipped. After studying German and Scandinavian companies with leading-edge order fulfillment operations, L. L. Bean carefully redesigned its order fulfillment process and information systems so that orders could be processed as soon as they were received and shipped out within 24 hours.

Use customer demands as a guide to improving products and services. Improving customer service, making customer service the number one priority, will improve the quality of the product itself. Delta Airlines decided to focus more on its customers, installing a customer care system at its airport gates. For each flight, the airplane seating chart, reservations, check-in information, and boarding data are linked in a central database. Airline personnel can track which passengers are on board regardless of where they checked in and use this information to make sure that passengers reach their destinations quickly even if delays cause them to miss connecting flights.

Reduce cycle time. Reducing the amount of time from the beginning of a process to its end (cycle time) usually results in fewer steps. Shorter cycles mean that errors are often caught earlier in production (or logistics or design or whatever the function), often before the process is complete, eliminating many hidden costs. Iomega Corporation in Roy, Utah, a manufacturer of disk drives, was spending $20 million a year to fix defective drives at the end of its 28-day production cycle. Reengineering the production process allowed the firm to reduce cycle time to a day and a half, eliminating this problem and winning the prestigious Shingo Prize for Excellence in American Manufacturing.

Improve the quality and precision of the design. Computer-aided design (CAD) software has made dramatic quality improvements possible in a wide range of businesses from aircraft manufacturing to production of razor blades. Alan R. Burns, head of the Airboss Company in Perth, Australia, used CAD to invent and design a new modular tire made up of a series of replaceable modules or segments so that if one segment were damaged, only that segment, not the whole tire, would need replacing. Burns established quality performance measurements for such key tire characteristics as load, temperature, speed, wear life, and traction. He entered these data into a CAD software package, which he used to design the modules. Using the software, he was able iteratively to design and test until he was satisfied with the results. He did not need to develop an actual working model until the iterative design process was almost complete. Because of the speed and accuracy of the CAD software, the product he produced was of much higher quality than would have been possible through manual design and testing.

Increase the precision of production. For many products, one key way to achieve quality is to make the production process more precise, thereby decreasing the amount of variation from one part to another. GE Medical Systems performed a rigorous quality analysis to improve the reliability and durability of its Lightspeed diagnostic scanner. It broke the processes of designing and producing the scanner into many distinct steps and established optimum specifications for each component part. By understanding these processes precisely, engineers learned that a few simple changes would significantly improve the product's reliability and durability (Deutsch, 1998).

12.3 OVERVIEW OF SYSTEMS DEVELOPMENT

Whatever their scope and objectives, new information systems are an outgrowth of a process of organizational problem solving. A new information system is built as a solution to some type of problem or set of problems the organization perceives it is facing. The problem may be one where managers and employees realize that the organization is not performing as well as expected, or it may come from the realization that the organization should take advantage of new opportunities to perform more successfully.

The activities that go into producing an information system solution to an organizational problem or opportunity are called **systems development.** Systems development is a structured kind of problem solving with distinct activities. These activities consist of systems analysis, systems design, programming, testing, conversion, and production and maintenance.

Figure 12-5 illustrates the systems development process. The systems development activities depicted here usually take place in sequential order. But some of the activities may need to be repeated or some may be taking place simultaneously, depending on the approach to system building that is being employed (see Section 12.4). Note also that each activity involves interaction with the organization. Members of the organization participate in these activities and the systems development process creates organizational changes.

systems development
The activities that go into producing an information systems solution to an organizational problem or opportunity.

SYSTEMS ANALYSIS

Systems analysis is the analysis of the problem that the organization will try to solve with an information system. It consists of defining the problem, identifying its causes, specifying the solution, and identifying the information requirements that must be met by a system solution.

The systems analyst creates a road map of the existing organization and systems, identifying the primary owners and users of data in the organization. These stakeholders have a direct interest in the information affected by the new system. In addition to these organizational aspects, the analyst also briefly describes the existing hardware and software that serve the organization.

From this organizational analysis, the systems analyst details the problems of existing systems. By examining documents, work papers, and procedures; observing system operations; and interviewing key users of the systems, the analyst can identify the problem areas

systems analysis
The analysis of a problem that the organization will try to solve with an information system.

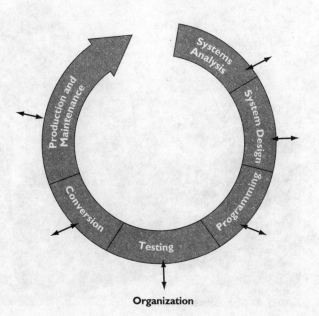

Figure 12-5 The systems development process. Each of the core systems development activities entails interaction with the organization.

and objectives a solution would achieve. Often the solution requires building a new information system or improving an existing one.

The systems analysis would include a **feasibility study** to determine whether that solution was feasible, or achievable, from a financial, technical, and organizational standpoint. The feasibility study would determine whether the proposed system was a good investment, whether the technology needed for the system was available and could be handled by the firm's information systems specialists, and whether the organization could handle the changes introduced by the system.

Normally, the systems analysis process will identify several alternative solutions that the organization can pursue. The process then will assess the feasibility of each. A written systems proposal report will describe the costs and benefits, advantages and disadvantages of each alternative. It is up to management to determine which mix of costs, benefits, technical features, and organizational impacts represents the most desirable alternative.

Establishing Information Requirements

Perhaps the most challenging task of the systems analyst is to define the specific information requirements that must be met by the system solution selected. At the most basic level, the **information requirements** of a new system involve identifying who needs what information, where, when, and how. Requirements analysis carefully defines the objectives of the new or modified system and develops a detailed description of the functions that the new system must perform. Faulty requirements analysis is a leading cause of systems failure and high systems development costs (see Chapter 13). A system designed around the wrong set of requirements will either have to be discarded because of poor performance or will need to undergo major modifications. Section 12.4 describes alternative approaches to eliciting requirements that help minimize this problem.

In many instances, building a new system creates an opportunity to redefine how the organization conducts its daily business. Some problems do not require an information system solution but instead need an adjustment in management, additional training, or refinement of existing organizational procedures. If the problem is information related, systems analysis still may be required to diagnose the problem and arrive at the proper solution.

SYSTEMS DESIGN

Systems analysis describes what a system should do to meet information requirements, and **systems design** shows how the system will fulfill this objective. The design of an information system is the overall plan or model for that system. Like the blueprint of a building or house, it consists of all the specifications that give the system its form and structure.

feasibility study
As part of the systems analysis process, the way to determine whether the solution is achievable, given the organization's resources and constraints.

information requirements
A detailed statement of the information needs that a new system must satisfy; identifies who needs what information, and when, where, and how the information is needed.

systems design
Details how a system will meet the information requirements as determined by the systems analysis.

Building successful information systems requires close cooperation among end users and information systems specialists throughout the systems development process.

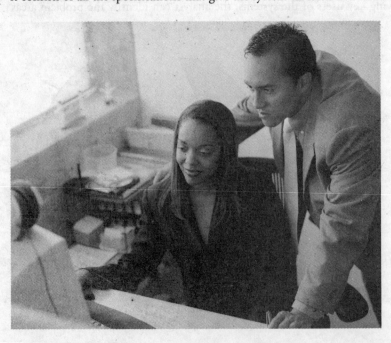

TABLE 12-3   DESIGN SPECIFICATIONS

Output

Medium
Content
Timing

Input

Origins
Flow
Data entry

User interface

Simplicity
Efficiency
Logic
Feedback
Errors

Database design

Logical data model
Volume and speed requirements
File organization and design
Record specifications

Processing

Computations
Program modules
Required reports
Timing of outputs

Manual procedures

What activities
Who performs them
When
How
Where

Controls

Input controls (characters, limit, reasonableness)
Processing controls (consistency, record counts)
Output controls (totals, samples of output)
Procedural controls (passwords, special forms)

Security

Access controls
Catastrophe plans
Audit trails

Documentation

Operations documentation
Systems documents
User documentation

Conversion

Transfer files
Initiate new procedures
Select testing method
Cut over to new system

Training

Select training techniques
Develop training modules
Identify training facilities

Organizational changes

Task redesign
Job design
Process design
Organization structure design
Reporting relationships

The systems designer details the system specifications that will deliver the functions identified during systems analysis. These specifications should address all of the managerial, organizational, and technological components of the system solution. Table 12-3 lists the types of specifications that would be produced during systems design.

Like houses or buildings, information systems may have many possible designs. Each design represents a unique blend of technical and organizational components. What makes one design superior to others is the ease and efficiency with which it fulfills user requirements within a specific set of technical, organizational, financial, and time constraints.

The Role of End Users

User information requirements drive the entire system-building effort. Users must have sufficient control over the design process to ensure that the system reflects their business priorities and information needs, not the biases of the technical staff (Hunton and Beeler, 1997). Working on design increases users' understanding and acceptance of the system, reducing problems caused by power transfers, intergroup conflict, and unfamiliarity with new system functions and procedures. As we describe in Chapter 13, insufficient user involvement in the design effort is a major cause of system failure. However, some systems require more user participation in design than others and Section 12.4 shows how alternative systems development methods address the user participation issue.

COMPLETING THE SYSTEMS DEVELOPMENT PROCESS

The remaining steps in the systems development process translate the solution specifications established during systems analysis and design into a fully operational information system. These concluding steps consist of programming, testing, conversion, production, and maintenance.

Programming

During the **programming** stage, system specifications that were prepared during the design stage are translated into software program code. On the basis of detailed design documents for files, transaction and report layouts, and other design details, specifications for each program in the system are prepared. Organizations write the software programs themselves or purchase application software packages for this purpose.

Testing

Exhaustive and thorough **testing** must be conducted to ascertain whether the system produces the right results. Testing answers the question, "Will the system produce the desired results under known conditions?"

The amount of time needed to answer this question has been traditionally underrated in systems project planning (see Chapter 14). Testing is time consuming: Test data must be carefully prepared, results reviewed, and corrections made in the system. In some instances parts of the system may have to be redesigned. The risks of glossing over this step are enormous.

Testing an information system can be broken down into three types of activities: unit testing, system testing, and acceptance testing. **Unit testing,** or program testing, consists of testing each program separately in the system. It is widely believed that the purpose of such testing is to guarantee that programs are error free, but this goal is realistically impossible. Testing should be viewed instead as a means of locating errors in programs, focusing on finding all the ways to make a program fail. Once pinpointed, problems can be corrected.

System testing tests the functioning of the information system as a whole. It tries to determine if discrete modules will function together as planned and whether discrepancies exist between the way the system actually works and the way it was conceived. Among the areas examined are performance time, capacity for file storage and handling peak loads, recovery and restart capabilities, and manual procedures.

Acceptance testing provides the final certification that the system is ready to be used in a production setting. Systems tests are evaluated by users and reviewed by management. When all parties are satisfied that the new system meets their standards, the system is formally accepted for installation.

The systems development team works with users to devise a systematic test plan. The **test plan** includes all of the preparations for the series of tests we have just described.

---

programming

The process of translating the system specifications prepared during the design stage into program code.

testing

The exhaustive and thorough process that determines whether the system produces the desired results under known conditions.

unit testing

The process of testing each program separately in the system. Sometimes called program testing.

system testing

Tests the functioning of the information system as a whole in order to determine if discrete modules will function together as planned.

acceptance testing

Provides the final certification that the system is ready to be used in a production setting.

test plan

Prepared by the development team in conjunction with the users; it includes all of the preparations for the series of tests to be performed on the system.

Figure 12-6 A sample test plan to test a record change. When developing a test plan, it is imperative to include the various conditions to be tested, the requirements for each condition tested, and the expected results. Test plans require input from both end users and information system specialists.

Procedure	Address and Maintenance "Record Change Series"		Test Series 2		
Prepared By:			Date:	Version:	
Test Ref.	Condition Tested	Special Requirements	Expected Results	Output On	Next Screen
2.0	Change records				
2.1	Change existing record	Key field	Not allowed		
2.2	Change nonexistent record	Other fields	"Invalid key" message		
2.3	Change deleted record	Deleted record must be available	"Deleted" message		
2.4	Make second record	Change 2.1 above	OK if valid	Transaction file	V45
2.5	Insert record		OK if valid	Transaction file	V45
2.6	Abort during change	Abort 2.5	No change	Transaction file	V45

OVERSEAS-CHINA BANKING CORPORATION SPEARHEADS A MASTERFUL SYSTEMS CONVERSION

Singapore-based Overseas-Chinese Banking Corporation (OCBC) is one of Singapore's leading financial institutions, with branches and offices in 14 countries, including Malaysia, China, Hong Kong, Japan, Australia, the United Kingdom, and the United States. To further expand in its core markets in Asia, OCBC acquired Keppel Capital Holdings, Ltd., on August 16, 2001. As part of this deal, OCBC acquired the systems and 1.5 million customers of Keppel's Tatlee Bank (KTB). KTB gave OCBC, which specialized in large corporate clients, a share in the consumer and small and medium-sized banking market, and had very good information systems for supporting these lines of business. OCBC developed a very aggressive six-month timetable for integrating these systems with its own so that it could leverage the best capabilities of both banks.

It was one of the most ambitious bank merger integration projects ever attempted. OCBC had to completely align staff, operations, products, services, and technology encompassing 30 key systems, 2,000 enhancement and conversion programs, 86 banking outlets, 22 finance company branches, 22 overseas branches, and 473 ATMs—with no degradation in customer service. OCBC modified some of its own systems to support KTB products, while wholly adopting KTB's retail systems for consumer and small and medium-size enterprise (SME) banking. How was this accomplished?

Obviously, careful planning was essential. During the first month a team comprised of KTB and OCBC staff and consultants from Accenture developed a blueprint Target Operating Model for the integration exercise. Information technology and business members worked together to define the systems and products to be retained or terminated, the organizational structure of the combined bank, the problems that were likely to be encountered, and the integration strategy. All the divisional heads and the CEO signed off on the plan. About 500 staff members from all divisions were asked to work together on weekends.

The enhanced and combined systems had to be thoroughly tested to make sure that their modifications worked and that they could scale up to handle both OCBC and KTB's combined customers. OCBC named Lim Lay Hock as the User Acceptance Testing Commander in charge of coordinating testing and verifying converted data in the various units. His teams designed the required changes in software programs and the programs required to convert the data from the old systems to the new systems that would be used by the bank. These activities were completed in four weeks and went into user acceptance testing. Andrew Lee was appointed the Cutover Commander serving as the single point of contact to manage the actual cutover. He monitored all the various work streams, key activities, and dependencies, and was responsible for making the call as to whether the final cutover to the new systems could proceed.

The bank conducted two mock runs in January 2002 to simulate the data conversion and the pre-live systems test, which was designed to ensure that the combined bank could operate on a single set of systems once the conversion had been completed. These mock runs rehearsed all processes, steps, and timings to make sure they would function like clockwork and that everyone understood their responsibilities and roles. The information systems staff conducted a few mock runs of its own to ensure that reconciliation and validation reports were flawless. The bank conducted training for 2,000 KTB and OCBC employees on the new systems. Business simulations identified various scenarios so that the bank staff would know how to respond when asked by customers about product changes.

The final conversion of major systems took place over the weekend of February 23 and 24, 2002, monitored by a 24-hour Command Center. OCBC's chief financial officer Chris Matten was present to oversee the reconciliation of financial records. For each system that needed to be cut over, teams checked the data to make sure they reflected the combined positions of OCBC and KTB precutover. An IT War Room kept watch on all the vast processes, data uploads and downloads, and conversion programs. Four teams of mobile ATMs were on standby to deliver money to customers if there was any downtime while the systems were being converted over. Given the enormity and complexity of the project, the conversion proceeded smoothly and swiftly. "Plan carefully, execute swiftly," the motto of the integration project, had been well chosen.

To Think About: What factors explain why this conversion was so successful? What role did management play?

Sources: Ann Toh, "1+1 = ONE," *CIO Asia*, May 2002 and <www.ocbc.com.sg>, accessed September 3, 2002.

MANAGEMENT

Figure 12-6 shows an example of a test plan. The general condition being tested is a record change. The documentation consists of a series of test-plan screens maintained on a database (perhaps a PC database) that is ideally suited to this kind of application.

Conversion

Conversion is the process of changing from the old system to the new system. Four main conversion strategies can be employed: the parallel strategy, the direct cutover strategy, the pilot study strategy, and the phased approach strategy.

conversion
The process of changing from the old system to the new system.

TABLE 12-4	Systems Development

Core Activity	Description
Systems analysis	Identify problem(s)
	Specify solution
	Establish information requirements
Systems design	Create design specifications
Programming	Translate design specifications into program code
Testing	Unit test
	Systems test
	Acceptance test
Conversion	Plan conversion
	Prepare documentation
	Train users and technical staff
Production and maintenance	Operate the system
	Evaluate the system
	Modify the system

parallel strategy

A safe and conservative conversion approach where both the old system and its potential replacement are run together for a time until everyone is assured that the new one functions correctly.

direct cutover

A risky conversion approach whereby the new system completely replaces the old one on an appointed day.

pilot study

A strategy to introduce the new system to a limited area of the organization until it is proven to be fully functional; only then can the conversion to the new system across the entire organization take place.

phased approach

Introduces the new system in stages either by functions or by organizational units.

documentation

Descriptions of how an information system works from both a technical or an end-user standpoint.

production

The stage after the new system is installed and the conversion is complete; during this time the system is reviewed by users and technical specialists to determine how well it has met its original goals.

postimplementation audit

Formal review process conducted after a system has been placed in production to determine how well the system has met its original objectives.

In a **parallel strategy** both the old system and its potential replacement are run together for a time until everyone is assured that the new one functions correctly. This is the safest conversion approach because, in the event of errors or processing disruptions, the old system can still be used as a backup. However, this approach is very expensive, and additional staff or resources may be required to run the extra system.

The **direct cutover** strategy replaces the old system entirely with the new system on an appointed day. At first glance, this strategy seems less costly than the parallel conversion strategy. However, it is a very risky approach that can potentially be more costly than parallel activities if serious problems with the new system are found. There is no other system to fall back on. Dislocations, disruptions, and the cost of corrections may be enormous.

The **pilot study** strategy introduces the new system to only a limited area of the organization, such as a single department or operating unit. When this pilot version is complete and working smoothly, it is installed throughout the rest of the organization, either simultaneously or in stages.

The **phased approach** strategy introduces the new system in stages, either by functions or by organizational units. If, for example, the system is introduced by functions, a new payroll system might begin with hourly workers who are paid weekly, followed six months later by adding salaried employees (who are paid monthly) to the system. If the system is introduced by organizational units, corporate headquarters might be converted first, followed by outlying operating units four months later.

Moving from an old system to a new one requires that end users be trained to use the new system. Detailed **documentation** showing how the system works from both a technical and end-user standpoint is finalized during conversion time for use in training and everyday operations. Lack of proper training and documentation contributes to system failure, so this portion of the systems development process is very important. The Window on Management shows how the Overseas-Chinese Banking Corporation's handling of conversion, testing, and training contributed to the success of its system projects when it acquired Keppel Tatlee Bank.

Production and Maintenance

After the new system is installed and conversion is complete, the system is said to be in **production.** During this stage the system will be reviewed by both users and technical specialists to determine how well it has met its original objectives and to decide whether any revisions or modifications are in order. In some instances, a formal **postimplementation audit** document will be prepared. After the system has been fine-tuned, it will need to be maintained while it is in production to correct errors, meet requirements, or improve processing efficiency. Changes in hardware, software, documentation, or procedures to a production system to correct errors, meet new requirements, or improve processing efficiency are termed **maintenance.**

Studies of maintenance have examined the amount of time required for various maintenance tasks. Approximately 20 percent of the time is devoted to debugging or correcting emergency production problems; another 20 percent is concerned with changes in data, files, reports, hardware, or system software. But 60 percent of all maintenance work consists of making user enhancements, improving documentation, and recoding system components for greater processing efficiency. The amount of work in the third category of maintenance problems could be reduced significantly through better systems analysis and design practices. Table 12-4 summarizes the systems development activities.

12.4 ALTERNATIVE SYSTEM-BUILDING APPROACHES

Systems differ in terms of their size and technological complexity, and in terms of the organizational problems they are meant to solve. Because there are different kinds of systems, a number of methods have been developed to build systems. This section describes these alternative methods: the traditional systems lifecycle, prototyping, application software packages, end-user development, and outsourcing.

TRADITIONAL SYSTEMS LIFECYCLE

The **systems lifecycle** is the oldest method for building information systems and is still used today for medium or large complex systems projects. The lifecycle methodology is a phased approach to building a system, dividing systems development into formal stages. There are different opinions among systems development specialists on how to partition the systems-building stages, but they roughly correspond to the stages of systems development that we have just described. The systems lifecycle methodology maintains a very formal division of labor between end users and information systems specialists. Technical specialists, such as systems analysts and programmers, are responsible for much of the systems analysis, design, and implementation work; end users are limited to providing information requirements and reviewing the technical staff's work. The lifecycle also emphasizes formal specifications and paperwork, so many documents are generated during the course of a systems project.

The systems lifecycle is still used for building large complex systems that require a rigorous and formal requirements analysis, predefined specifications, and tight controls over the systems-building process. However, the systems lifecycle approach can be costly, time consuming, and inflexible. Although system-builders can go back and forth among stages in the lifecycle, the systems lifecycle is predominantly a "waterfall" approach in which tasks in one stage are completed before work for the next stage begins. Activities can be repeated, but volumes of new documents must be generated and steps retraced if requirements and specifications need to be revised. This encourages freezing of specifications relatively early in the development process. The lifecycle approach is also not suitable for many small desktop systems, which tend to be less structured and more individualized.

PROTOTYPING

Prototyping consists of building an experimental system rapidly and inexpensively for end users to evaluate. By interacting with the prototype, users can get a better idea of their information requirements. The prototype endorsed by the users can be used as a template to create the final system.

The **prototype** is a working version of an information system or part of the system, but it is meant to be only a preliminary model. Once operational, the prototype will be further refined until it conforms precisely to users' requirements. Once the design has been finalized, the prototype can be converted to a polished production system.

The process of building a preliminary design, trying it out, refining it, and trying again has been called an **iterative** process of systems development because the steps required to build a system can be repeated over and over again. Prototyping is more explicitly iterative

maintenance
Changes in hardware, software, documentation, or procedures to a production system to correct errors, meet new requirements, or improve processing efficiency.

systems lifecycle
A traditional methodology for developing an information system that partitions the systems development process into formal stages that must be completed sequentially with a very formal division of labor between end users and information systems specialists.

prototyping
The process of building an experimental system quickly and inexpensively for demonstration and evaluation so that users can better determine information requirements.

prototype
The preliminary working version of an information system for demonstration and evaluation purposes.

iterative
A process of repeating over and over again the steps to build a system.

Figure 12-7 The prototyping process. The process of developing a prototype can be broken down into four steps. Because a prototype can be developed quickly and inexpensively, system builders can go through several iterations, repeating steps 3 and 4, to refine and enhance the prototype before arriving at the final operational one.

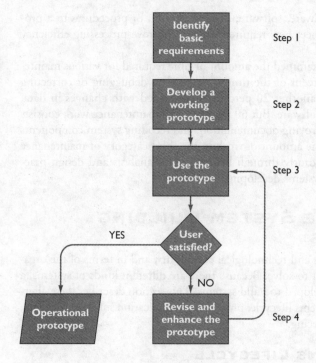

than the conventional lifecycle, and it actively promotes system design changes. It has been said that prototyping replaces unplanned rework with planned iteration, with each version more accurately reflecting users' requirements.

Steps in Prototyping

Figure 12-7 shows a four-step model of the prototyping process, which consists of the following:

Step 1: *Identify the user's basic requirements.* The system designer (usually an information systems specialist) works with the user only long enough to capture his or her basic information needs.

Step 2: *Develop an initial prototype.* The system designer creates a working prototype quickly, using fourth-generation software, interactive multimedia, or computer-aided software engineering (CASE) tools described in Chapter 14.

Step 3: *Use the prototype.* The user is encouraged to work with the system in order to determine how well the prototype meets his or her needs and to make suggestions for improving the prototype.

Step 4: *Revise and enhance the prototype.* The system builder notes all changes the user requests and refines the prototype accordingly. After the prototype has been revised, the cycle returns to step 3. Steps 3 and 4 are repeated until the user is satisfied.

When no more iterations are required, the approved prototype then becomes an operational prototype that furnishes the final specifications for the application. Sometimes the prototype itself is adopted as the production version of the system.

Advantages and Disadvantages of Prototyping

Prototyping is most useful when there is some uncertainty about requirements or design solutions. Prototyping is especially useful in designing an information system's **end-user interface** (the part of the system that end users interact with, such as online display and data-entry screens, reports, or Web pages). Because prototyping encourages intense end-user involvement throughout the systems development process (Cerveny et al., 1986), it is more likely to produce systems that fulfill user requirements.

However, rapid prototyping can gloss over essential steps in systems development. If the completed prototype works reasonably well, management may not see the need for reprogramming, redesign, or full documentation and testing to build a polished production sys-

---

end-user interface

The part of an information system through which the end user interacts with the system, such as on-line screens and commands.

Figure 12-8 The effects of customizing a software package on total implementation costs. As the modifications to a software package rise, so does the cost of implementing the package. Savings promised by the package can be whittled away by excessive changes.

tem. Some of these hastily constructed systems may not easily accommodate large quantities of data or a large number of users in a production environment.

APPLICATION SOFTWARE PACKAGES

Information systems can be built using software from **application software packages,** which we introduced in Chapter 6. There are many applications that are common to all business organizations—for example, payroll, accounts receivable, general ledger, or inventory control. For such universal functions with standard processes that do not change a great deal over time, a generalized system will fulfill the requirements of many organizations.

If a software package can fulfill most of an organization's requirements, the company does not have to write its own software. The company can save time and money by using the prewritten, predesigned, pretested software programs from the package. Package vendors supply much of the ongoing maintenance and support for the system, including enhancements to keep the system in line with ongoing technical and business developments.

If an organization has unique requirements that the package does not address, many packages include capabilities for customization. **Customization** features allow a software package to be modified to meet an organization's unique requirements without destroying the integrity of the package software. If a great deal of customization is required, additional programming and customization work may become so expensive and time consuming that they eliminate many of the advantages of software packages. Figure 12-8 shows how package costs in relation to total implementation costs rise with the degree of customization. The initial purchase price of the package can be deceptive because of these hidden implementation costs. If the vendor releases new versions of the package, the overall costs of customization will be magnified because these changes will need to be synchronized with future versions of the software.

Selecting Software Packages

When a system is developed using an application software package, systems analysis will include a package evaluation effort. The most important evaluation criteria are the functions provided by the package, flexibility, user-friendliness, hardware and software resources, database requirements, installation and maintenance effort, documentation, vendor quality, and cost. The package evaluation process often is based on a **Request for Proposal (RFP),** which is a detailed list of questions submitted to packaged software vendors.

When a software package solution is selected, the organization no longer has total control over the system design process. Instead of tailoring the system design specifications directly to user requirements, the design effort will consist of trying to mold user requirements to conform to the features of the package. If the organization's requirements conflict with the way the package works and the package cannot be customized, the organization will have to adapt to the package and change its procedures. Even if the organization's business

application software package

A set of prewritten, precoded application software programs that are commercially available for sale or lease.

customization

The modification of a software package to meet an organization's unique requirements without destroying the package software's integrity.

Request for Proposal (RFP)

A detailed list of questions submitted to vendors of software or other services to determine how well the vendor's product can meet the organization's specific requirements.

processes seem compatible with those supported by a software package, the package may be too constraining if these business processes are continually changing (Prahalad and Krishnan, 2002).

A new company that was just being set up could adopt the business processes and information flows provided by the package as its own business processes. But organizations that have been in existence for some time may not be able to easily change the way they work to conform to the package.

END-USER DEVELOPMENT

end-user development

The development of information systems by end users with little or no formal assistance from technical specialists.

Some types of information systems can be developed by end users with little or no formal assistance from technical specialists. This phenomenon is called **end-user development.** Using fourth-generation languages, graphics languages, and PC software tools, end users can access data, create reports, and develop entire information systems on their own, with little or no help from professional systems analysts or programmers. Many of these end-user developed systems can be created much more rapidly than with the traditional systems lifecycle. Figure 12-9 illustrates the concept of end-user development.

Benefits and Limitations of End-User Development

Many organizations have reported gains in application development productivity by using fourth-generation tools that in a few cases have reached 300 to 500 percent. Allowing users to specify their own business needs improves requirements gathering and often leads to a higher level of user involvement and satisfaction with the system. However, fourth-generation tools still cannot replace conventional tools for some business applications because they cannot easily handle the processing of large numbers of transactions or applications with extensive procedural logic and updating requirements.

End-user computing also poses organizational risks because it occurs outside of traditional mechanisms for information system management and control. When systems are created rapidly, without a formal development methodology, testing and documentation may be inadequate. Control over data can be lost in systems outside the traditional information systems department (see Chapter 7).

Managing End-User Development

To help organizations maximize the benefits of end-user applications development, management should control the development of end-user applications by requiring cost justification

Figure 12-9 End-user versus system lifecycle development. End users can access computerized information directly or develop information systems with little or no formal technical assistance. On the whole, end-user-developed systems can be completed more rapidly than those developed through the conventional systems lifecycle.
Source: From *Application Development Without Programmers*, by James Martin, © 1982. Reprinted by permission of Prentice Hall Inc., Upper Saddle River, NJ.

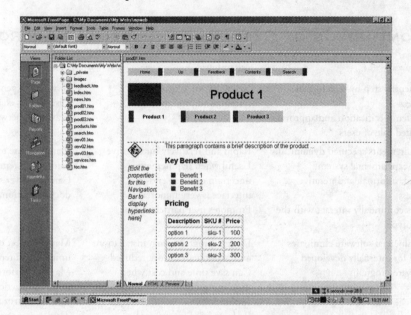

Microsoft FrontPage is a development tool with many features that can be employed by end users to create Web pages and Web sites without writing program code.

of end-user information system projects and by establishing hardware, software, and quality standards for user-developed applications.

When end-user computing first became popular, organizations used information centers to promote standards for hardware and software so that end users could not introduce many disparate and incompatible technologies into the firm (Fuller and Swanson, 1992). **Information centers** are special facilities housing hardware, software, and technical specialists to supply end users with tools, training, and expert advice so they can create information system applications on their own or increase their productivity. The role of information centers is diminishing as end-users become more computer literate, but organizations still need to closely monitor and manage end-user development.

information center
A special facility within an organization that provides training and support for end-user computing.

Outsourcing

If a firm does not want to use its internal resources to build or operate information systems, it can hire an external organization that specializes in providing these services to do the work. The process of turning over an organization's computer center operations, telecommunications networks, or applications development to external vendors is called **outsourcing.** The application service providers (ASPs) described in Chapter 6 are one form of outsourcing. Subscribing companies would use the software and computer hardware provided by the ASP as the technical platform for their system. In another form of outsourcing, a company would hire an external vendor to design and create the software for its system, but that company would operate the system on its own computer.

outsourcing
The practice of contracting computer center operations, telecommunications networks, or applications development to external vendors.

Outsourcing has become popular because some organizations perceive it as more cost effective than maintaining their own computer center or information systems staff. The provider of outsourcing services benefits from economies of scale (the same knowledge, skills, and capacity can be shared with many different customers) and is likely to charge competitive prices for information systems services. Outsourcing allows a company with fluctuating needs for computer processing to pay for only what it uses rather than to build its own computer center, which would be underutilized when there is no peak load. Some firms outsource because their internal information systems staff cannot keep pace with technological change or innovative business practices or because they want to free up scarce and costly talent for activities with higher payback.

Not all organizations benefit from outsourcing, and the disadvantages of outsourcing can create serious problems for organizations if they are not well understood and managed (Earl, 1996). Many firms underestimate costs for identifying and evaluating vendors of information technology services, for transitioning to a new vendor, and for monitoring vendors to make sure they are fulfilling their contractual obligations. These "hidden costs" can easily undercut anticipated benefits from outsourcing (Barthelemy, 2001). When a

| TABLE 12-5 | COMPARISON OF SYSTEMS-DEVELOPMENT APPROACHES | | |

Approach	Features	Advantages	Disadvantages
Systems lifecycle	Sequential step-by-step formal process Written specification and approvals Limited role of users	Necessary for large complex systems and projects	Slow and expensive Discourages changes Massive paperwork to manage
Prototyping	Requirements specified dynamically with experimental system Rapid, informal, and iterative process Users continually interact with the prototype	Rapid and relatively inexpensive Useful when requirements uncertain or when end-user interface is very important Promotes user participation	Inappropriate for large, complex systems Can gloss over steps in analysis, documentation, and testing
Applications software package	Commercial software eliminates need for internally developed software programs	Design, programming, installation, and maintenance work reduced Can save time and cost when developing common business applications Reduces need for internal information systems resources	May not meet organization's unique requirements May not perform many business functions well Extensive customization raises development costs
End-user development	Systems created by end users using fourth-generation software tools Rapid and informal Minimal role of information systems specialists	Users control systems-building Saves development time and cost Reduces application backlog	Can lead to proliferation of uncontrolled information systems and data Systems do not always meet quality assurance standards
Outsourcing	Systems built and sometimes operated by external vendor	Can reduce or control costs Can produce systems when internal resources are not available or technically deficient	Loss of control over the information systems function Dependence on the technical direction and prosperity of external vendors

firm allocates the responsibility for developing and operating its information systems to another organization, it can lose control over its information systems function. If the organization lacks the expertise to negotiate a sound contract, the firm's dependency on the vendor could result in high costs or loss of control over technological direction (Lacity, Willcocks, and Feeny, 1996). Firms should be especially cautious when using an outsourcer to develop or to operate applications that give it some type of competitive advantage.

Table 12-5 compares the advantages and disadvantages of each of the system-building alternatives.

12.5 APPLICATION DEVELOPMENT FOR THE DIGITAL FIRM

Electronic commerce, electronic business, and the emerging digital firm pose new challenges for system building. Technologies and business conditions are changing so rapidly that agility and scalability have become a critical success factor and primary goal of system design. Businesses need software components that can be added, modified, replaced, or reconfigured to enable them to respond rapidly to new opportunities. Systems must be scalable to accommodate growing numbers of users and to deliver data over multiple platforms—client/server networks, desktop computers with Web browsers, cellphones, and other mobile devices. E-commerce and e-business systems may also need to be designed so that they can run in hosted environments as well as on the company's own hardware and software platforms. To remain competitive, some firms feel pressured to design, develop, test, and deploy Internet or intranet applications in a matter of weeks or months (Earl and Khan, 2001).

Older development methods were based on a much more static view of systems. In the past, systems development would be based on a formal design document with functional specifications that was handed off to a development team. Alternatively, applications might be loosely designed and iteratively developed with multiple passes going to users for review and revision. Such development processes often took months or years and were ill suited to the pace and profile of Internet or intranet projects. Traditional methods did not adequately address the new features of Internet-based applications, which might have multiple tiers of clients and servers with different operating systems linked to transaction processing systems, as well as business processes that had to be coordinated with those of customers or suppliers.

In the digital firm environment, organizations need to be able to add, change, and retire their technology capabilities very rapidly. Companies are adopting shorter, more informal development processes for many of their e-commerce and e-business applications, processes that provide fast solutions that do not disrupt their core transaction processing systems and organizational databases. They are relying more heavily on fast-cycle techniques such as JAD, prototypes, and reusable standardized software components that can be assembled into a complete set of services for e-commerce and e-business.

OBJECT-ORIENTED DEVELOPMENT

Object-oriented development provides an approach that is believed to be well-suited for building systems that can respond to rapidly changing business environments, including Web applications. Chapter 6 introduced *object-oriented programming*, which combines data and the actions that can be performed on the data into a single object. **Object-oriented development** uses the object as the basic unit of systems analysis and design. The system is modeled as a collection of objects and the relationships between them. (Review Figure 6-10 in Chapter 6.) Data encapsulated in an object can only be accessed and modified by the operations, or *methods* associated with that object. Since processing logic resides within objects rather that in software programs, objects must collaborate with each other to make the system work. This system-building approach contrasts with the traditional structured development approach we described earlier, which models a system by separating data and the processes that act on the data.

The phases of object-oriented development (see Figure 12-10) are similar to those of conventional systems development, consisting of analysis, design and implementation. However, object-oriented development is more iterative and incremental than traditional structured development. During analysis, system-builders document the functional requirements of the system, specifying its most important properties and what the proposed system must do. Interactions between the system and its users are analyzed to identify objects, which include both data and processes. The object-oriented design phases describe how the objects will behave and how they will interact with one other. Similar objects are grouped together to form a class and classes are grouped into hierarchies where a subclass inherits the attributes and methods from its superclass. Chapter 14 provides additional detail on the tools used for object-oriented analysis and design.

object-oriented development
Approach to systems development that uses the object as the basic unit of systems analysis and design. The system is modeled as a collection of objects and the relationships between them.

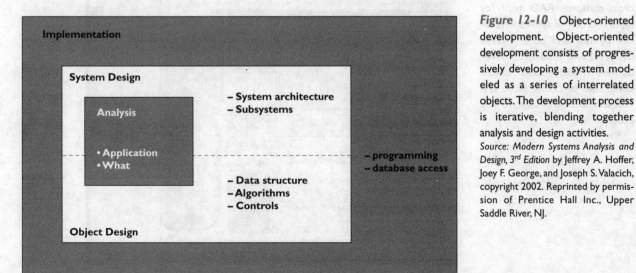

Figure 12-10 Object-oriented development. Object-oriented development consists of progressively developing a system modeled as a series of interrelated objects. The development process is iterative, blending together analysis and design activities.
Source: Modern Systems Analysis and Design, 3rd Edition by Jeffrey A. Hoffer, Joey F. George, and Joseph S. Valacich, copyright 2002. Reprinted by permission of Prentice Hall Inc., Upper Saddle River, NJ.

The information system is implemented by translating the design into program code, reusing classes that are already available in a library of reusable software objects and adding new ones created during the object-oriented design phase. Implementation may also involve the creation of an object-oriented database. The resulting system must be thoroughly tested and evaluated.

Since objects are reusable, object-oriented development could potentially reduce the time and cost of writing software because organizations could reuse software objects that have already been created as building blocks for other applications. New systems could be created by using some existing objects, changing others, and adding a few new objects.

Object-oriented frameworks have been developed to provide reusable, semicomplete applications that the organization can further customize into finished applications (Fayad and Schmidt, 1997). However, information systems specialists must learn a completely new way of modeling a system (Sircar, Nerur, and Mahapatra, 2001), and object-oriented models of systems aren't always more usable than process-oriented models (Agarwal, De, Sinha, and Tanniru, 2000). The benefits from object re-use deteriorate when the object must be modified for the new application (Irwin, 2002). Conversion to an object-oriented approach may require large-scale organizational investments, which management must balance against the anticipated payoffs.

RAPID APPLICATION DEVELOPMENT (RAD)

Object-oriented software tools, reusable software, prototyping, and fourth-generation tools are helping system builders create working systems much more rapidly than they could using traditional system-building methods and software tools. The term **rapid application development (RAD)** is used to describe this process of creating workable systems in a very short period of time. RAD can include the use of visual programming and other tools for building graphical user interfaces, iterative prototyping of key system elements, the automation of program code generation, and close teamwork among end users and information systems specialists. Simple systems often can be assembled from prebuilt components. The process does not have to be sequential, and key parts of development can occur simultaneously.

Sometimes a technique called **JAD (joint application design)** is used to accelerate the generation of information requirements and to develop the initial systems design. JAD brings end users and information systems specialists together in an interactive session to discuss the system's design. Properly prepared and facilitated, JAD sessions can significantly speed the design phase while involving users at an intense level.

WEB SERVICES

We have already described how firms are basing portions of their information technology infrastructure on services supplied by external vendors. Increasingly, new information system

---

rapid application development (RAD)
Process for developing systems in a very short time period by using prototyping, fourth-generation tools, and close teamwork among users and systems specialists.

joint application design (JAD)
Process to accelerate the generation of information requirements by having end users and information systems specialists work together in intensive interactive design sessions.

Simplicity for Mobile Devices is a cross-platform RAD tool for rapid creation of applications for cell phones and other mobile devices. Rapid application development (RAD) tools enable companies to create rapid system solutions without extensive programming.

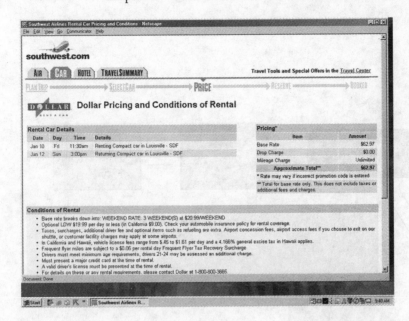

Visitors to the Southwestair.com Web site can make on-line reservations for Dollar Rent A Car directly from Southwest's Web site. Both companies use Web services to link their information systems.

applications will be built using Web services. **Web services** are software components deliverable over the Internet that enable one application to communicate with another with no translation required. By allowing applications to communicate and share data regardless of operating system, programming language, or client device, Web services can provide significant cost savings over traditional in-house systems while opening up new opportunities for collaboration with other companies (Patel and Saigal, 2002; Hagel and Brown, 2001). IBM has included Web services tools in its WebSphere e-business software, and Microsoft has incorporated Web services tools in its .NET platform.

For example, Dollar Rent A Car Systems uses Web services to integrate its online booking system with Southwest Airlines Co.'s Web site. Although both companies' systems are based on different technology platforms, a person booking a flight on Southwestair.com can reserve a car from Dollar without leaving the airline's Web site. Instead of struggling to get Dollar's reservation system to share data with Southwest's information systems, Dollar used Microsoft's .NET Web services technology as an intermediary. Reservations from Southwest are translated into Web services protocols, which are then translated into formats that can be understood by Dollar's computers. Other car rental companies have linked their information systems to airline companies' Web sites before. But without Web services, these connections had to be built one at a time. Web services provide a standard way for Dollar's computers to talk to other companies' information systems without having to build special links to each one. Dollar is now expanding its use of Web services to link directly to the systems of a small tour operator and a large travel reservation system as well as a wireless Web site for mobile phones and PDAs. It does not have to write new software code for each new partner's information systems or each new wireless device (see Figure 12-11).

Web services use an open "plug and play" architecture rather than a proprietary architecture. This architecture has three layers (see Figure 12-12). The first consists of software standards and communication protocols such as XML, SOAP, WSDL, and UDDI, that allow information to be exchanged easily among different applications. *XML (eXtensible Markup Language)*, introduced in Chapter 6, provides a standard description of data in Web pages and databases that makes it easier to exchange data among disparate applications and systems. Web services communicate through XML messages over standard Web protocols. **SOAP,** which stands for **Simple Object Access Protocol,** is a set of rules that allows applications to pass data and instructions to one another. **WSDL** stands for **Web Services Description Language,** which is a common framework for describing the tasks performed by a Web service so that it can be used by other applications. **UDDI,** standing for **Universal Description, Discovery, and Integration,** allows a Web service to be listed in a directory of Web services so that it can be easily located. Companies discover and locate Web services through this directory much as they would locate services in the Yellow Pages of a telephone book. Using these standards and protocols, a software application can connect freely to other

Web services

Software components deliverable over the Internet that enable one application to communicate with another with no translation required using a standard "plug and play" architecture.

SOAP (Simple Object Access Protocol)

Set of rules that allows Web services applications to pass data and instructions to one another.

WSDL (Web Services Description Language)

Common framework for describing the tasks performed by a Web service so that it can be used by other applications.

UDDI (Universal Description, Discovery, and Integration)

Allows a Web service to be listed in a directory of Web services so that it can be easily located by other organizations and systems.

Figure 12-11 How Dollar Rent A Car uses Web services. Dollar Rent A Car uses Web services to provide a standard intermediate layer of software to "talk" to other companies information systems. Dollar Rent A Car can use this set of Web services to link to other companies' information systems without having to build a separate link to each firm's systems.

Figure 12-12 The Web Services Architecture. The architecture for Web services has three layers. The most fundamental layer consists of software standards and communication protocols that make it possible for diverse systems to communicate electronically. The middle layer is a service grid where special utilities provide important services and tools. The third layer consists of application services that support common business processes, such as supply chain management or marketing. *Source:* from "Your Next IT Strategy" by John Hagel, III, and John Seeley Brown, *Harvard Business Review*, October 2001. Reprinted by permission.

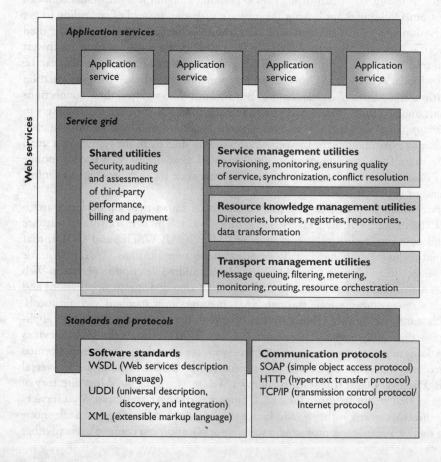

THE LURE OF WEB SERVICES

Singapore Exchange Ltd (SGX) is Asia Pacific's first demutualized, integrated, securities and derivatives exchange. SGX provides a diverse array of securities and derivative products and financial market information to its global network of broker members. "We are not directly connected to the investors themselves," says Daniel Tan, SGX's executive vice president and head of its information technology (IT) division. Instead, his company supplies time-sensitive investment information to brokers who then pass it on to appropriate customers equipped with MSN Messenger, a communication tool bundled with the latest version of Windows that is often used for chatting. To be successful in its business, SGX had to spend millions of dollars to develop the security such a system requires. In addition the company originally might have had to spend millions more to develop the Internet connections necessary to communicate with all of its customers' systems. Instead, Tan turned to Web Services, enabling SGX to make those connections at a much lower cost.

Web Services provides a set of standards that enable companies to communicate with each other without having to significantly modify their current software programs. In earlier times, one or both of the parties would have to write or rewrite their systems so they could communicate. Web Services use XML for the common language in their communication. Bill Burnham, a Softbank Venture Capital partner, explains the system this way: "Rather than think about individual Web sites, think about the Web holistically, where people create software by linking different applications across the Web." Thus, the Web has expanded way beyond just being a compilation of HTML pages from which people can collect information.

SGX's move to Microsoft.NET Web services technology and establishing connections with its clients took only three months, leaving all of its own systems all but unchanged. Tan says, "I do not have to invest in building the different delivery channels [required to communicate with each one of my customers]." SGX can reach customers without

knowing whether they are using pagers or mobile phones. Information from the SGX Web site goes through several layers to reach the investors, allowing customers to continue operating the way they did before SGX turned to .NET.

SembCorp Logistics also turned to .NET to provide customized services for its customers. This company is Asia's leading integrated logistics services provider, focusing on offshore logistics and supply chain management. It is developing a global logistics network and system to support customers around the globe. Customers can use its Web site to check inventory and to track their shipments. The logistics industry deals with a wide spectrum of customers. Using Web services allowed SembCorp to reduce the complexity involved in linking to customers using different technology platforms without worrying about the delivery mechanism. According to SemCorp's Chief Technology Officer Ng Han Kim, "With .NET, we can lower the integration costs for the customer, and we can put more functionalities and features into our services on the Web," thereby attracting more customers to subscribe to the company's logistics services. SembCorp chose Microsoft .NET over Sun's Java because it had committed so much money and resources to developing its Web services plaform. SembCorp will take longer to implement Web services than SGX because its .NET applications will penetrate more deeply into the firm's IT infrastructure. SembCorp must streamline and modularize processes involving networks, applications, and backend servers.

To Think About: What are the benefits of using Web services technology? How can they provide value to firms? What management, organization, and technology issues must be addressed when implementing Web services?

Sources: Winston Raj, "The Joys & Pains of .NET," CIO-Asia, May 2002; Singapore Exchange Ltd, accessed August 31, 2002, <www.ses.com.sg>; www. SembCorp Logistics Online, accessed August 31, 2002, semblog.com.; and Sari Kalin, "The Essential Guide to Web Services," *Darwin Magazine,* January 2002.

TECHNOLOGY

applications without custom programming for each different application with which it wants to communicate. Everyone shares the same standards.

The middle layer of Web services consists of a service grid to create environments essential for carrying out critical business activities. This middle layer provides a set of shared utilities, such as security, third party billing and payment that are used for critical business functions and transactions over the Internet. The service grid also includes utilities for transporting messages and identifying available services.

The third layer consists of application services, such as credit card processing or production scheduling, that automate specific business functions. Some application services will be proprietary to a particular company and others will be shared among all companies. A company may also develop its own application services and then sell them to other

MAKE IT YOUR BUSINESS

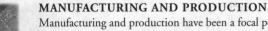

FINANCE AND ACCOUNTING

The finance and accounting function helps system builders identify the costs and benefits of new information system projects and assess their economic feasibility. It also assists with the financial analysis of system-building alternatives, comparing the costs of custom in-house development to the costs of developing with application software packages or outsourcing to external vendors. You can find examples of finance and accounting applications on pages 376–378 and 393.

HUMAN RESOURCES

The human resources function assists with the analysis of changes in work flows and job responsibilities resulting from new information systems. Human resource specialists may also be involved with corporate programs to educate employees in Total Quality Management (TQM) principles as well as efforts to train employees to use new information systems. You can find examples of human resources applications on page 393.

MANUFACTURING AND PRODUCTION

Manufacturing and production have been a focal point for process improvements to improve quality. Information systems have been used to identify defects and variances from quality standards, to reduce cycle time, and to increase precision in design and production. When firms are installing new enterprise systems, one of their major objectives is to improve coordination of business processes for manufacturing and production and between manufacturing and production and the other functional areas. You can find examples of manufacturing and production applications on pages 405 and 410–413.

SALES AND MARKETING

Information systems have supported quality improvements in sales and marketing that provide better customer service as well as products and sales experiences that increase customer satisfaction. Web-based information systems for online sales and marketing have become a high priority for corporate system building during the last few years. You can find examples of sales and marketing applications on pages 376–378, 405, and 410–413.

companies on a subscription basis. For instance, Citibank developed and markets CitiConnect, an XML-based payment processing service that plugs into existing B2B Net marketplaces.

Organizations can use Web services to automate interactions with each other and they can also use Web services to obtain software components from other organizations to accomplish specific tasks, such as billing services or payment processing (see the Window on Technology). They can use Web services to connect their traditional applications to outside services one by one as the need arises, paying only for the software functionality they need at the moment. Web services promise substantial savings in systems integration costs by reducing the cost of developing separate interfaces among systems. However, Web services and development tools are still in their infancy, and some key standards remain unresolved.

Looking Beyond the Organization

Building new systems for a digital firm environment requires more than innovative development approaches. E-commerce and e-business require systems planning and systems analysis based on a broader view of the organization, one that encompasses business processes extended beyond firm boundaries (Fingar, 2000). Firms can no longer execute their business and system plans alone because they need to forge new electronic relationships with suppliers, distributors, and customers. Their business processes often need to be integrated with customer and supplier business processes.

MANAGEMENT WRAP-UP

Selection of a systems-building approach can have a big impact on the time, cost, and end product of systems development. Managers should be aware of the strengths and weaknesses of each systems-building approach and the types of problems for which each is best suited.

Organizational needs should drive the selection of a systems-building approach. The impact of application software packages and of outsourcing should be carefully evaluated before they are selected because these approaches give organizations less control over the systems-building process.

Various software tools are available to support the systems-building process. Key technology decisions should be based on the organization's familiarity with the technology and its compatibility with the organization's information requirements, IT infrastructure, and information architecture.

For Discussion

1. Why is selecting a systems development approach an important business decision? Who should participate in the selection process?

2. Some have said that the best way to reduce system development costs is to use application software packages or fourth-generation tools. Do you agree? Why or why not?

SUMMARY

1. *How could building a new system change the way an organization works?* Building a new information system is a form of planned organizational change that involves many different people in the organization. Because information systems are sociotechnical entities, a change in information systems involves changes in work, management, and the organization. Four kinds of technology-enabled change are (1) automation, (2) rationalization of procedures, (3) business reengineering, and (4) paradigm shift, with far-reaching changes carrying the greatest risks and rewards. Many organizations are attempting business process reengineering to redesign work flows and business processes in the hope of achieving dramatic productivity breakthroughs. Information systems can also be used to support Total Quality Management (TQM), six sigma, and other initiatives for incremental process improvement.

2. *How can a company make sure that the new information systems it builds fit its business plan?* Organizations should develop information systems plans that describe how information technology supports the attainment of their business goals. The plans indicate the direction of systems development, the rationale, implementation strategy, and budget. Enterprise analysis and critical success factors (CSFs) can be used to elicit organization-wide information requirements that must be addressed by the plans.

3. *What are the steps required to build a new information system?* The core activities in systems development are systems analysis, systems design, programming, testing, conversion, production, and maintenance. Systems analysis is the study and analysis of problems of existing systems and the identification of requirements for their solutions. Systems design provides the specifications for an information system solution, showing how its technical and organizational components fit together.

4. *What alternative methods for building information systems are available?* There are a number of alternative methods for building information systems, each suited to different types of problems. The oldest method for building systems is the systems lifecycle, which requires that information

systems be developed in formal stages. The stages must proceed sequentially and have defined outputs; each requires formal approval before the next stage can commence. The system lifecycle is useful for large projects that need formal specifications and tight management control over each stage of system building. However, this approach is very rigid and costly and is not well suited for unstructured, decision-oriented applications where requirements cannot be immediately visualized.

Prototyping consists of building an experimental system rapidly and inexpensively for end users to interact with and evaluate. The prototype is refined and enhanced until users are satisfied that it includes all of their requirements and can be used as a template to create the final system. Prototyping encourages end-user involvement in systems development and iteration of design until specifications are captured accurately. The rapid creation of prototypes can result in systems that have not been completely tested or documented or that are technically inadequate for a production environment.

Developing an information system using an application software package eliminates the need for writing software programs when developing an information system. Using a software package reduces the amount of design, testing, installation, and maintenance work required to build a system. Application software packages are helpful if a firm does not have the internal information systems staff or financial resources to custom-develop a system. To meet an organization's unique requirements, packages may require extensive modifications that can substantially raise development costs.

End-user development is the development of information systems by end users, either alone or with minimal assistance from information systems specialists. End-user-developed systems can be created rapidly and informally using fourth-generation software tools. The primary benefits of end-user development are improved requirements determination; reduced application backlog; and increased end-user participation in, and control of, the systems development process. However, end-user development, in conjunction with distributed computing, has introduced new organizational risks by propagating information systems and data resources that do not necessarily meet quality assurance standards and that are not easily controlled by traditional means.

Outsourcing consists of using an external vendor to build (or operate) a firm's information systems. The work is done by the vendor rather than by the organization's internal information systems staff. Outsourcing can save application development costs or allow firms to develop applications without an internal information systems staff. However, firms risk losing control over their information systems and becoming too dependent on external vendors.

5. *Are there any techniques or system-building approaches to help us build e-commerce and e-business applications more rapidly?* Businesses today are often required to build e-commerce and e-business applications very rapidly in order to remain competitive. They are relying more heavily on rapid application

design, joint application design (JAD), and reusable software components to speed up the systems development process. Object-oriented software development is expected to reduce the time and cost of writing software and of making maintenance changes because it models a system as a series of reusable objects that combine both data and procedures. Rapid application development (RAD) uses object-oriented software, visual programming, prototyping, and fourth-generation tools for very rapid creation of systems. Web services will enable organizations to build and enhance systems by obtaining the functionality they need as software application components delivered over the Internet. Web services provide a common set of standards that allows organizations to link their systems regardless of their technology platform through a standard "plug and play" architecture.

KEY TERMS

Acceptance testing, 392

Application software package, 397

Automation, 383

Benchmarking, 387

Business process
  reengineering, 383

Conversion, 393

Critical success factors
  (CSFs), 380

Customization, 397

Direct cutover, 394

Documentation, 398

End-user development, 396

End-user interface, 396

Enterprise analysis, 380

Feasibility study, 390

Information center, 399

Information requirements, 390

Information systems plan, 379

Iterative, 395

Joint application design
  (JAD), 402

Maintenance, 395

Object-oriented development, 401

Outsourcing, 399

Paradigm shift, 384

Parallel strategy, 394

Phased approach, 394

Pilot study, 394

Postimplementation audit, 394

Production, 394

Programming, 392

Prototype, 395

Prototyping, 395

Rapid application development
  (RAD), 402

Rationalization of procedures, 383

Request for Proposal (RFP), 397

Six sigma, 387

SOAP (Simple Object Access
  Protocol), 403

Systems analysis, 389

Systems design, 390

Systems development, 389

Systems lifecycle, 395

System testing, 392

Test plan, 392

Testing, 392

Total quality management
  (TQM), 387

UDDI (Universal Description,
  Discovery and Integration), 403

Unit testing, 392

WSDL (Web Services
  Description Language), 403

Web services, 403

Work flow management, 386

REVIEW QUESTIONS

1. Why can an information system be considered planned organizational change?

2. What are the major categories of an information systems plan?

3. How can enterprise analysis and critical success factors be used to establish organization-wide information system requirements?

4. Describe each of the four kinds of organizational change that can be promoted with information technology.

5. What is business process reengineering? What steps are required to make it effective?

6. What is the difference between systems analysis and systems design? What activities do they comprise?

7. What are information requirements? Why are they difficult to determine correctly?

8. Why is the testing stage of systems development so important? Name and describe the three stages of testing for an information system.

9. What role do programming, conversion, production, and maintenance play in systems development?

10. What is the traditional systems lifecycle? Describe each of its steps and its advantages and disadvantages for system building.

11. What do we mean by information system prototyping? What are its benefits and limitations? List and describe the steps in the prototyping process.

12. What is an application software package? What are the advantages and disadvantages of developing information systems based on software packages?

13. What do we mean by end-user development? What are its advantages and disadvantages? Name some policies and procedures for managing end-user development.

14. What is outsourcing? Under what circumstances should it be used for building information systems?

15. What is the difference between object-oriented development and traditional systems development? What are the advantages of using object-oriented software development in building systems?

16. What is rapid application development (RAD)? How can it help system builders?

17. What are Web services? How can they help firms build and enhance their information systems?

APPLICATION SOFTWARE EXERCISE

DATABASE EXERCISE: DESIGNING A CUSTOMER SYSTEM FOR AUTO SALES

Ace Auto Dealers specializes in selling new vehicles from Subaru. The company advertises in local newspapers and also is listed as an authorized dealer on the Subaru Web site and the major Web sites for auto buyers. The company benefits from good local word of mouth reputation and name recognition and is a leading source for Subaru vehicles in the Portland, Oregon area.

When a prospective customer enters the showroom, he or she is greeted by an Ace sales representative. The sales representative manually fills out a form with information such as the prospective customer's name, address, telephone number, date of visit, and model and make of vehicle in which he or she is interested. The representative also asks where the prospect heard about Ace—whether it was from a newspaper ad, the Web, or word of mouth and this information is noted on the form also.

If the customer decides to purchase an auto, the dealer fills out a bill of sale form, listing the vehicle identification number, vehicle make and model, color, options selected, the base price, the total price, and the date of the sale along with the purchaser's name, address, and telephone number. This form also shows the amount of the total purchase price that was financed. Both forms are filed in manual folders—one for sales prospects and another for actual purchases.

Ace does not feel it knows enough about its customers. It cannot easily identify repeat customers at its dealership or customers who have purchased a Subaru in the past from another dealer. It cannot easily determine which prospects have made auto purchases or the percentage of prospects that has been con-

verted into buyers. Nor can it identify which customer touch-points have produced the greatest number of sales leads or actual sales so it can focus advertising and marketing more on the channels that generate the most revenue. Are purchasers coming from newspaper ads, from word of mouth, or from the Web? Additionally, the firm cannot tell whether its customers are more interested in no-frills cars or ones with luxury options.

Prepare a systems analysis report detailing Ace's problem, and a system solution that can be implemented using PC database management software. Then use database software to develop a simple system solution. Your systems analysis report should include the following:

1. Description of the problem and its organizational and business impact.

2. Proposed solution, solution objectives, and solution feasibility.

3. Costs and benefits of the solution you have selected. The company has a PC with Internet access and the full suite of Microsoft Office desktop productivity tools.

4. Information requirements to be addressed by the solution.

5. Management, organization and technology issues to be addressed by the solution, including changes in business processes.

On the basis of the requirements you have identified, design the database and populate it with at least 20 records per table. Print out the database design. Then use the system you have created to generate queries and reports that would be of most interest to management. Create several prototype data input forms for the system and review them with your instructor. Then revise the prototypes.

GROUP PROJECT

With three or four of your classmates, select a system described in this text that uses the Web. Examples might include the Kmart Web site in Chapter 3, the GM Web site in Chapter 4, or the Rosenbluth Web site in Chapter 8. Review the Web site for

the system you select. Use what you have learned from the Web site and the description in this book to prepare a report describing some of the design specifications for the system you select. Present your findings to the class.

TOOLS FOR INTERACTIVE LEARNING

▮ INTERNET CONNECTION

The Internet Connection for this chapter will direct you to the SAP Web site where you can complete an exercise to evaluate the capabilities of this major multinational software package and learn more about enterprise systems.

▮ INTERACTIVE STUDY GUIDE

You can use the Interactive Study Guide to test your knowledge of the topics in this chapter and get instant feedback where you need more practice.

▮ RUNNING CASE

The Running Case provides an opportunity for you to develop and build a system for tracking employee training and skills that would help Dirt Bikes USA better manage its human resources. You can find a complete description of this project on the Laudon Web site for Chapter 12 and on the Multimedia Edition CD-ROM.

▮ ELECTRONIC BUSINESS PROJECT

At the Laudon Web site for Chapter 12, you can complete an Electronic Business Project to redesign business processes to participate in a Net marketplace.

▮ MANAGEMENT DECISION PROBLEM

At the Laudon Web site for Chapter 12, you can find a Management Decision Problem on using a scoring model to evaluate alternative ERP systems.

▮ CD-ROM

If you use the Multimedia Edition CD-ROM with this chapter, you can find a video clip illustrating how General Motors used Palm handheld computing devices to redesign its healthcare delivery system, an audio overview of the introduction to this chapter, and bullet text summarizing the key points of the chapter.

CASE STUDY—*Can Brady Corporation Redesign Its Systems for Success?*

The Brady Corporation, one of the oldest and most successful companies in Milwaukee, Wisconsin, was founded in 1915 and is a leader in high-performance labels, signs, and related industrial safety products. It produces ultra-thin identification labels for handheld electronic devices and an adhesive that when removed leaves a pattern police use to identify such stolen objects as laptop computers. Another label it manufactures protects electronic devices by dissipating their heat or static. Some labels work in temperatures colder than 50 below zero, others glow or emit sounds in the dark, laminate themselves, or even stick to oily or greasy products.

In recent years, Brady has purchased many of its smaller competitors so that it now has 44 business units and produces and distributes its labels from 47 locations in 20 countries on five continents around the world, including the United States, the United Kingdom, Europe, Asia, and Australia. Brady has doubled its workforce from 1,500 in 1994 to 3,000 today. Its net sales increased from $260 million in 1994 to $479 million in 1999, while its 1994 net income grew from $18.5 million to $39.6 million in 1999. One unit, Seton Identification Products, does 30 percent of Brady's business with sales in 2000 of $150 million. Seton sells custom, made-to-order signs mostly directly to customers while other divisions mostly sell through distributors. Seton's average order size is $650.

Despite its growing success, the company found it was running into trouble in the mid-1990s. Katherine Hudson, Brady's CEO since 1994, came to fear that her company was falling behind small nimble new competitors who could use the Internet to shave costs on already-low profit margins. Brady's clients, such as maintenance supplies distributor W.W. Grainger and abrasive and adhesive distributor R.S. Hughes, needed immediate and reliable sources of supply as they moved into Asian and Latin American markets.

In 1997, Brady launched a major Web project in its Seton Identification Products division. The new digital system, called

Web-to-Workbench, enabled customers to be able to design and order their own signs online and the Web site would automatically forward the new order to the appropriate production facility. Management claims the project reduced online order processing costs by 88 percent. In 2000, about two-thirds of its online orders came from new customers. By December 2000, 20 percent of all orders were coming through the Internet.

The success of Web-to-Workbench was, however, insufficient to solve all of Brady's problems. Brady relied heavily on information systems to support most of its business processes but its systems were antiquated and could not communicate with each other. Customers were not paying invoices on time, leaving too much money sitting in accounts receivable. Employees were making frequent errors, resulting in duplicated work, partly because Brady business processes had too many steps. In addition, the company had become "sprawling and fragmented." For example it had 19 separate databases, each with its own file servers and transaction software. And these platforms could not communicate with each other. Each unit had its own sales tracking system, causing confusion among Brady employees and customers. Customers found differing prices and discounts depending upon where they placed their order. Each plant used different product identification numbers for the same items. Moreover, Brady had no way to determine its total business with a specific customer. For example a plant in Brazil might produce and ship the same products to the same customers as did a plant in New Hampshire, but no one would know. "We [have] to be much more customer-focused than we are," exclaimed Hudson. "We needed much more information about our customers." She also saw that too much of Brady's work was being handled manually.

Hudson's assessment at a management meeting in February 1999 was that the company could not continue growing because it was "stymied by an infrastructure that had reached well beyond its practical limits." She pointed out that the Internet enabled competition to come from anywhere, and so Brady's competitors were undercutting them. She said Brady's information technology controlled everything from production to payroll, but filling orders was expensive and very slow. Engineering was hampered in its efforts to develop new and profitable products because these systems could not communicate with each other. She concluded that the company must overhaul its business processes totally to move fully into the digital age. Brady needed to revamp all of its systems.

Brady's goals became clear. It needed a "business-led project for the whole company," and not just a software or information technology project, according to David Schroeder, Brady's CFO. Management allocated $30 million for a new project called Eclipse (Earning Customer Loyalty through Integrated Processes and Systems Everywhere) and expected the project to pay for itself by 2003. Hudson called for an annual revenue growth of 15 percent, reaching $1 billion in sales by 2004. She wanted half of all orders to come through the Internet by 2003, thereby reducing operating expenses by 2 percent or $10 million annually. She called for all 44 Brady business units worldwide to be connected with each other and its 1,400 business processes to be integrated in a single system. Such integration would give the company an easier and faster production process. She called for globally unified price lists and distributor discounts, and corporate-wide processes for purchasing raw materials. With such integration management could track orders, analyze sales trends, and run financial reports while customers could obtain answers for at least 60 percent of their questions on their first calls. For example customers should no longer need to wait a week just to get a price quote.

Eclipse's first and most fundamental task was to educate the key managers and employees on the importance of the project and the way it would be accomplished. As Hudson put it, "We can't expect everybody else to follow us if we don't understand it." Leadership spent a great deal of time attending meetings, courses, and seminars. According to Dr. Michael Hammer, the famous reengineering expert who led the first Eclipse seminar, "At Brady, a larger fraction of the managers really got into it. It wasn't a handful trying to push it down the throats of the rest." In May 1999, they began, finding "our best and brightest" to be the fulltime leaders in Eclipse, according to Hudson. Keith Kaczanowski was chosen to be the project leader. He was Brady's vice president of business process development and had very broad experience with Brady, including accounting information technology. Choosing other leaders was a problem because division managers had to be persuaded to give up some of their best employees to the project. However, Hudson believed that "If it didn't hurt to give up these people then we probably were not getting the right people for the project." Altogether 35 were selected and divided into six Eclipse groups.

The six Eclipse teams moved to a new office several miles from Brady headquarters, and they immediately began setting very clear measurable goals. For example, converting orders to cash (collecting payment from the sales) was 54 days, and their goal was to reduce it to 42 days. Inventory turnover was 4.39 times annual sales, but with Hudson's pushing, the new goal was set at 15 times per year to turn a product into a sale. Fifty percent of sales were to be conducted electronically by 2003. The

goals also reflected Brady's demand that Eclipse standardize processes throughout the company, making pricing and delivery more consistent. Whenever possible, Brady would use the Internet to facilitate dealing with suppliers, to make pricing and delivery time more consistent, and to increase sales of different products form different divisions to the same customer.

Brady chose SAP software for planning and operations and then selected IBM Global Services for consultant support in integrating the new software. SAP was already installed in 17,000 companies in 160 countries, while IBM had consulted on SAP installations in 1,900 companies. The Eclipse team decided it must do very little customization of SAP software so as to prevent problems. However, the team did decide not to use SAP software in two key areas—product design and customer relationship management (CRM). It concluded SAP functionality was not adequate in both of these areas. So Eclipse rewrote some of its own systems in the SAP software development language so the Brady systems could communicate well with SAP.

The project team then held 15 workshops with various experts in specific business functions to dissect key processes and diagram them. Brady discovered how inefficient and inconsistent the company really was in processing orders, with far too many steps and information handoffs. They also found that the average order was very small at about $250, indicating that Brady was selling to a large number of customers in small volume. Brady needed to centralize the price lists and computerize them. Kaczanowski had his teams focus on the actual processes in making a label, not on information systems, enabling them to eliminate many steps. In working on the cash conversion cycle, Maureen Casey's global training team worked on converting orders into cash by focusing on moving raw material through production to delivery and payment. This process had been extremely disorganized prior to Eclipse because Brady's manufacturing, delivery, and billing systems did not communicate with each other, resulting in orders being missed, late, or duplicated. The team simplified it and speeded it up. They developed a uniform system for price breaks while also eliminating minimum orders—a customer can even order just one of something, although with higher prices. They installed SAP's Variant Configurator system with product and pricing data, enabling sales reps to develop prices while making sales calls. By inputting the type of tag, its material, size, color and layout, the Configurator returned a price quote.

Brady's leadership examined and reshaped how everyone, from executives to factory workers, did their job. For example, manufacturing engineer Mike Sweeney complained that the queries about existing orders generated standardized responses, and he wanted something more precise. On the other hand, the order processing team ended up with more SAP data on purchase order histories, raw materials schedules, and accounting figures than the customer reps could handle. Planning for demand was new and difficult to get used to because it required more rigor than in the past. The team learned it had to do very careful training so employees would know how to obtain just the information they needed.

Eclipse was first implemented in October 1999 at Worldwide-Varitronics, a plant of 250 employees in Brooklyn, Minnesota. Its primary purpose was to shake-out problems and fix them before installing the systems in the other, larger units. While the pilot was considered a success, there were many problems. For instance there were large problems in SAP data, such as delivery time errors. Customer order problems also surfaced. For example, one customer ordered 25 cards and received 25 boxes of cards. The site's backlogs grew by 25 percent while on-time deliveries fell from 95 percent to 80 percent. Also the Variant Configurator software produced wrong prices. Many more customers called with problems or complaints. According to CFO Schroeder, call wait times increased.

The sales reps found that learning the two new pieces of software was extremely difficult. "There was a 'this isn't my problem' mentality,'" said Elizabeth Belmonte, global leader for customer value creation. "It has taken a year to 18 months to get to the point where they are now comfortable." The system required information the reps were not used to supplying, such as e-mail addresses and verification of telephone numbers. Moreover, the screens were packed with quoting, ordering, and tracking information requiring that the reps take a quick course in accounting basics. The result was that where data had errors or were missing, people down the line had to deal with them. Also, during the first conversion they found that "SAP requires quite a bit more discipline than they're used to," said Chris McElfresh, the Eclipse global order-to-cash process leader. A major challenge they faced was that the team and the specific unit being converted needed to accomplish the project without losing even one day of operations. For example, in the first conversion at Worldwide-Varitronics, they closed the plant on a Friday afternoon, worked very hard over the weekend, and opened Monday morning with the new system. "We [the Eclipse team] basically took over the businesses for a week," commented John Cullen, Eclipse project leader for customer and order acquisition. However, 10 days later, all of the systems had been converted. Brady employees still had to work overtime in evenings and weekends during the first 60 days just to do their normal job while also helping to fix problems.

The Eclipse team did take many steps during the conversion period to fix the problems. They held dozens of workshops so the employees would better understand how the processes worked. They recorded every step of every function, including even returned merchandise, and showed how the processes worked. They recorded suggestions from the employees and adopted them when they seemed useful. They had team members wear red shirts so they were easily identified when anyone needed help.

Eventually the new systems worked fine at Worldwide-Varitronics, no customers were lost, and Brady learned a great deal for future installations. The cost of processing an order fell from $16 to $2. Worldwide-Varitronics experienced a 66 percent increase in new business while accounts receivables were greatly reduced by requiring on-line credit card payments. Previously an order took three people to fulfill, but now only a machine operator was required. Inventory size was greatly reduced, partly because many products are now digitally produced and so can be built to order. The CFO said he expects most inventory will almost be eliminated during 2003. The unit also experienced a great reduction of errors, which had cost millions of dollars in returns. Previously many orders were faxed, requiring several employees to type in the information, and then

set the type prior to printing the sign. With the new system customers can design and input their own text online, viewing and approving it before it is printed.

After completing the first installation, Brady took steps to prevent future problems, including loading the master data seven months early and verifying it several weeks before going live. The company updated cost data three weeks before conversion and then double-checked it in the Variant Configurator. Brady expanded training on the new system from 60 days to 90 days.

Brady units, which have installed the new systems, are usually able to ship a new order within 24 hours. By mid-2002, more than 20 percent of monthly sales came from Web-to-Workbench. Sales reps usually are able to answer customers' questions from a computer screen using SAP's Available to Promise (ATP) platform, eliminating many telephone calls to factories. Reps can now provide 60 percent of quotes on the first call and are aiming for 90 percent. Reps can now see and follow an individual's order from the beginning through delivery including the invoice. The new system freed many employees from manual tasks such as most order-taking work, enabling them to be used in more productive, creative activities.

The new production system includes scheduling, availability, and purchase of raw materials, the manufacturing process, product reporting, and delivery. It has standardized production across factories, including the same product numbers in different plants. The system now is able to track raw materials through the plants, automatically ordering replenishments through the Web when needed. It can initiate production when a new order is entered by Brady or by a customer. The system includes forecasting of future orders. The company is already seeing a saving of about 2 percent annually with a goal of 10 percent ($8.8 million) over seven years. Purchase order costs as a percentage of total purchases have been cut to 3 percent, with the eventual target of 1.5 percent of purchases.

According to documents filed with the Securities and Exchange Commission, $30 million was budgeted for the Eclipse project—$15 million for consulting, $3 million for hardware, $4 million for SAP software licenses, and $8 million on project administration and training. As of the writing of this case, Brady has spent $25.6 million on Eclipse and expects to recoup its investment by 2003, primarily through savings generated by more frequent inventory turnover, reducing the time to convert sales to cash, cutting the cost to fill orders, and more efficient finance, sales, and marketing processes.

But Brady's inventory turnover is still only five times annual sales, profits are at 1998 levels, and sales have recently declined, partly because of the slowdown in global economic activity. Will Brady make its gigantic system-building effort pay off?

Sources: Randy Barrett and Dan Luzadder, "The Brady Bunch Rewrites All Its Scripts," *Baseline Magazine*, May 1, 2002; Randy Barrett, "Behind the Label: Making a Mark—That Sticks," "Gotcha! Where the Process of Changing Processes Fails," and "SAP: Not Always the Answer," *Baseline Magazine*, May 1, 2002; Dan Luzadder, "Go Live: Educate, Educate, and Educate, Again," *Baseline Magazine*, May 1,

2002; Kim Nash, "IBM's SAP Practice: Win Some, Lose Some," *Baseline Magazine*, May 1, 2002; and Maria Atanasov, "Killer App: A Good Sign," *Smart Business Magazine*, February 1, 2002.

CASE STUDY QUESTIONS

1. Analyze the Brady Corporation using the competitive forces and value chain models.

2. How well did Brady's systems support its business model? What management, organization, and technology factors were responsible for its problems?

3. Analyze the Internet as a source of problems and opportunity for Brady.

4. Was SAP's enterprise software package a good foundation for Brady's new systems? Explain your answer.

5. Describe the management, organizational, and technology changes Brady was making by its Web-to-Workbench and Eclipse projects. How extensive were they? Why do you think Brady took so long to implement its changes?

6. How successful were Brady Corporation's systems projects? How much value did they provide? Explain your answer.

13

UNDERSTANDING THE BUSINESS VALUE OF SYSTEMS AND MANAGING CHANGE

objectives

At many points during your career, you will be involved in projects to build new information systems. You will need to know how to measure the business benefits of these investments and how to make sure that these systems work successfully in your organization. After reading this chapter, you will be able to answer the following questions:

1. *How can our company measure the business benefits of our information systems? What models should be used to measure that business value?*

2. *Why do so many system projects fail? What are the principal reasons for system failures?*

3. *How should the organizational change surrounding a new system be managed to ensure success?*

4. *What strategies can our organization use to manage the system implementation process more effectively?*

The Navy/Marine Corps Intranet Becomes a Battleground

The project was unprecedented. The U.S. Navy/Marine Corps Intranet (N/MCI) project was designed to consolidate hundreds of disparate Navy and Marine Corps networks and 80,000 legacy applications into a single, integrated, secure architecture managed by outsourcer Electronic Data Systems (EDS). Its initial price tag was $6.9 billion. The project has been fraught with delays and implementation problems since its inception.

The project had to surmount serious cultural hurdles. Insiders describe the Navy as a conglomerate of hundreds of information technology fiefdoms that would fiercely resist losing control over their systems and networks. Massive cultural change would be required to get them to accept the intranet in the interests of the enterprise as a whole.

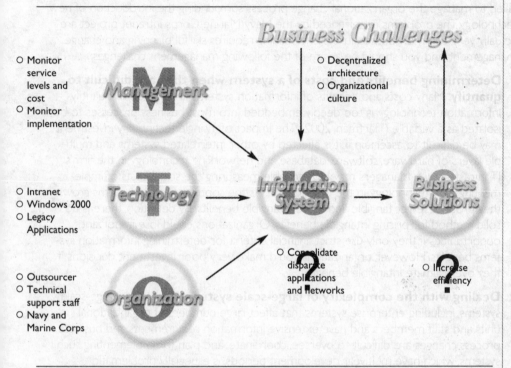

Business Challenges

O Monitor service levels and cost
O Monitor implementation

Management

O Intranet
O Windows 2000
O Legacy Applications

Technology

O Outsourcer
O Technical support staff
O Navy and Marine Corps

Organization

O Decentralized architecture
O Organizational culture

Information System

O Consolidate disparate applications and networks

Business Solutions

O Increase efficiency

Critics charged the initial implementation plans for the intranet were overly ambitious and mismanaged. The scope of the project was increased to add another 100,000 seats to the 60,000 seats originally served by the network. Although EDS had met project targets during the initial testing and evaluation phase, the remainder of the project started to fall behind schedule. It took two years to deploy 1,000 seats, when this task should only have taken 90 days. The Naval Air Systems Command (NAVAIR), one of the first Navy groups to use N/MCI halted deployment until significant technical problems could be fixed. Problems with the intranet's Remote Access Service forced two-thirds of NAVAIR users to use two separate computers, one to access N/MCI and another to access their legacy applications that hadn't passed security testing or didn't run on Windows 2000. The large number of legacy applications that had to be integrated into the intranet, combined with testing delays, caused the intranet implementation to fall further and further behind. Technical support personnel were not available to help users with repairs and upgrades to their other systems because they had been told to focus on N/MCI.

EDS program executive Rick Rosenberg stated that all the NAVAIR problems had been fixed and that secure Web site access was a Navy policy issue. To forestall further criticism and political attacks on the project, Rear Admiral Charles Munns, director of the Navy/Marine Corps intranet project and EDS called for an aggressive "scorched earth" rollout for the rest of the network.

Sources: Dan Verton, "DOD IT Projects Come Under Fire, " *Computerworld*, May 20, 2002; and "Insiders Slam Navy Intranet," *Computerworld*, May 27, 2002.

415

MANAGEMENT CHALLENGES

One of the principal challenges posed by information systems is ensuring they can deliver genuine business benefits. Organizations need to find ways of measuring the business value of their information systems and ensuring that these systems actually deliver the benefits they promise. There is a very high failure rate among information systems projects because organizations have incorrectly assessed their business value or because firms have failed to manage the organizational change process surrounding the introduction of new technology. The problems experienced by the Navy/Marine Corps intranet project are actually very common. Successful system-building requires skillful planning and change management, and you should be aware of the following management challenges:

1. **Determining benefits and costs of a system when they are difficult to quantify.** Many costs and benefits of information systems are difficult to quantify. Information technology is too deeply embedded into most business processes to be isolated as a variable (Hartman, 2002). The impact of a single technology investment may be difficult to ascertain if it is affected by other interrelated systems and multiple layers of hardware, software, database and networking technology in the firm's IT infrastructure. Managers may have trouble measuring the social costs of implementing new technology in the organization. As the sophistication of systems grows, they produce fewer tangible and more intangible benefits. By definition, there is no solid method for pricing intangible benefits. Organizations could lose important opportunities if they only use strict financial criteria for determining information systems benefits. However, organizations could make very poor investment decisions if they overestimate intangible benefits.

2. **Dealing with the complexity of large-scale systems projects.** Large-scale systems, including enterprise systems that affect large numbers of organizational units and staff members and have extensive information requirements and business process changes are difficult to oversee, coordinate, and plan for. Implementing such systems, which have multiyear development periods, is especially problematic because the systems are so complex. In addition, there are few reliable techniques for estimating the time and cost to develop large-scale information systems. Guidelines presented in this chapter are helpful but cannot guarantee that a large information system project can be precisely planned with accurate cost figures.

In this chapter we examine various ways of measuring the business value provided by information systems, describing both financial and nonfinancial models. We then examine the role of change management in successful system implementation. Finally we present strategies for reducing the risks in systems projects and improving project management.

13.1 UNDERSTANDING THE BUSINESS VALUE OF INFORMATION SYSTEMS

Information systems can have several different values for business firms. A consistently strong information technology infrastructure can, over the long term, play an important strategic role in the life of the firm. Considered less grandly, information systems can simply facilitate a firm's survival.

It is important also to realize that systems can have value but that the firm may not capture all or even some of the value. Although system projects can result in firm benefits, such as profitability and productivity, some or all of the benefits can go directly to the consumer in the form of lower prices or more reliable services and products (Hitt and Brynjolfsson, 1996). Society can reward firms that enhance consumer surplus by allowing them to survive or by rewarding them with increases in business revenues. But from a management point of view, the challenge is to retain as much of the benefit of systems investments as is feasible in current market conditions.

The worth of systems from a financial perspective essentially revolves around the question of return on invested capital. The value of systems comes down to one question: Does a particular IS investment produce sufficient returns to justify its costs? There are many problems with this approach, not the least of which is how to estimate benefits and count the costs.

TRADITIONAL CAPITAL BUDGETING MODELS

Capital budgeting models are one of several techniques used to measure the value of investing in long-term capital investment projects. The process of analyzing and selecting various proposals for capital expenditures is called **capital budgeting.** Firms invest in capital projects to expand production to meet anticipated demand or to modernize production equipment to reduce costs. Firms also invest in capital projects for many noneconomic reasons, such as installing pollution control equipment, converting to a human resources database to meet some government regulations, or satisfying nonmarket public demands. Information systems are considered long-term capital investment projects.

capital budgeting
The process of analyzing and selecting various proposals for capital expenditures.

Six capital budgeting models are used to evaluate capital projects:

The payback method

The accounting rate of return on investment (ROI)

The cost–benefit ratio

The net present value

The profitability index

The internal rate of return (IRR)

All capital budgeting methods rely on measures of cash flows into and out of the firm. Capital projects generate cash flows into and out of the firm. The investment cost is an immediate cash outflow caused by the purchase of the capital equipment. In subsequent years, the investment may cause additional cash outflows that will be balanced by cash inflows resulting from the investment. Cash inflows take the form of increased sales of more products (for reasons such as new products, higher quality, or increasing market share) or reduced costs in production and operations. The difference between cash outflows and cash inflows is used for calculating the financial worth of an investment. Once the cash flows have been established, several alternative methods are available for comparing different projects and deciding about the investment.

Financial models assume that all relevant alternatives have been examined, that all costs and benefits are known, and that these costs and benefits can be expressed in a common metric, specifically, money. When one has to choose among many complex alternatives, these assumptions are rarely met in the real world, although they may be approximated. Table 13-1 lists some of the more common costs and benefits of systems. **Tangible benefits** can be

tangible benefits
Benefits that can be quantified and assigned a monetary value; they include lower operational costs and increased cash flows.

TABLE 13-1	COSTS AND BENEFITS OF INFORMATION SYSTEMS

Costs	Intangible Benefits
Hardware	Improved asset utilization
Telecommunications	Improved resource control
Software	Improved organizational planning
Services	Increased organizational flexibility
Personnel	More timely information
	More information
Tangible Benefits (cost savings)	Increased organizational learning
Increased productivity	Legal requirements attained
Lower operational costs	Enhanced employee goodwill
Reduced workforce	Increased job satisfaction
Lower computer expenses	Improved decision making
Lower outside vendor costs	Improved operations
Lower clerical and professional costs	Higher client satisfaction
Reduced rate of growth in expenses	Better corporate image
Reduced facility costs	

intangible benefits

Benefits that are not easily quantified; they include more efficient customer service or enhanced decision making.

quantified and assigned a monetary value. **Intangible benefits,** such as more efficient customer service or enhanced decision making, cannot be immediately quantified but may lead to quantifiable gains in the long run.

Chapter 6 introduced the concept of total cost of ownership (TCO), which is designed to identify and measure the components of information technology expenditures beyond the initial cost of purchasing and installing hardware and software. However, TCO analysis provides only part of the information needed to evaluate an information technology investment because it does not typically deal with benefits, cost categories such as complexity costs, and "soft" and strategic factors discussed later in this section.

Limitations of Financial Models

Many well-known problems emerge when financial analysis is applied to information systems (Dos Santos, 1991). Financial models do not express the risks and uncertainty of their own cost and benefits estimates. Costs and benefits do not occur in the same time frame—costs tend to be upfront and tangible, whereas benefits tend to be back loaded and intangible. Inflation may affect costs and benefits differently. Technology—especially information technology—can change during the course of the project, causing estimates to vary greatly. Intangible benefits are difficult to quantify. These factors play havoc with financial models.

The difficulties of measuring intangible benefits give financial models an application bias: Transaction and clerical systems that displace labor and save space always produce more measurable, tangible benefits than management information systems, decision-support systems, or computer-supported collaborative work systems (see Chapters 10 and 11.) Traditional approaches to valuing information systems investments tend to assess the profitability of individual system projects for specific business functions. These approaches do not adequately address investments in IT infrastructure, testing new business models or other enterprise-wide capabilities that could benefit the organization as a whole (Ross and Beath, 2002).

The traditional focus on the financial and technical aspects of an information system tends to overlook the social and organizational dimensions of information systems that may affect the true costs and benefits of the investment. Many companies' information system investment decisions do not adequately consider costs from organizational disruptions created by a new system, such as the cost to train end users, the impact that users' learning curve for a new system will have on productivity, or the time managers will need to spend overseeing new system-related changes. Benefits such as more timely decisions from a new system or enhanced employee learning and expertise may also be overlooked in a traditional financial analysis (Ryan, Harrison, and Schkade, 2002).

There is some reason to believe that investment in information technology requires special consideration in financial modeling. Capital budgeting historically concerned itself with manufacturing equipment and other long-term investments, such as electrical generating facilities and telephone networks. These investments had expected lives of more than one year and up to 25 years. However, information systems differ from manufacturing systems in that their life expectancy is shorter. The very high rate of technological change in computer-based information systems means that most systems are seriously out of date in five to eight years. The high rate of technological obsolescence in budgeting for systems means simply that the payback period must be shorter and the rates of return higher than typical capital projects with much longer useful lives.

The bottom line with financial models is to use them cautiously and to put the results into a broader context of business analysis. Let us look at an example to see how these problems arise and can be handled. The following case study is based on a real-world scenario, but the names have been changed.

CASE EXAMPLE: PRIMROSE, MENDELSON, AND HANSEN

Primrose, Mendelson, and Hansen is a 250-person law partnership on Manhattan's West Side with branch offices in London, Los Angeles, and Paris. Founded in 1923, Primrose has excelled in corporate, taxation, environmental, and health law. Its litigation department is also well known.

The Problem

The firm occupies three floors of a new building. Many partners still have five-year-old PCs on their desktops but rarely use them except to read e-mail. Virtually all business is conducted face-to-face in the office, or when partners meet directly with clients on the clients' premises. Most of the law business involves marking up (editing), creating, filing, storing, and sending documents. In addition, the tax, pension, and real estate groups do a considerable amount of spreadsheet work.

With overall business off 15 percent since 2001, the chair, Edward W. Hansen, III, is hoping to use information systems to cope with the flood of paperwork, enhance service to clients, and slow the growth in administrative costs.

First, the firm's income depends on billable hours, and every lawyer is supposed to keep a diary of his or her work for specific clients in 30-minute intervals. Generally, senior lawyers at this firm charge about $500 an hour for their time. Unfortunately, lawyers often forget what they have been working on and must reconstruct their time diaries. The firm hopes that there will be some automated way of tracking billable hours.

Second, much time is spent communicating with clients around the world, with other law firms both in the United States and overseas, and with the Primrose branch offices. The fax machine has become the communication medium of choice, generating huge bills and developing lengthy queues. The firm looks forward to using some sort of secure e-mail, or even the Internet, for communication. Law firms are wary of breaches in the security of confidential client information.

Third, Primrose has no client database! A law firm is a collection of fiefdoms—each lawyer has his or her own clients and keeps the information about them private. This, however, makes it impossible for management to find out who is a client of the firm, who is working on a deal with whom, and so forth. The firm maintains a billing system, but the information in the system is too difficult to search. What Primrose needs is an integrated client management system that will take care of billing, monitor hourly charges, and make client information available to others in the firm. Even overseas offices want to have information on who is taking care of a particular client in the United States.

Fourth, there is no system to track costs. The head of the firm and the department heads who compose the executive committee cannot identify what the costs are, where the money is being spent, who is spending it, and how the firm's resources are being allocated. A decent accounting system that could identify the cash flows and the costs a bit more clearly than the firm's existing journal would be a big help.

The Solution

Information systems could obviously have some survival value and perhaps could grant a strategic advantage to Primrose if a system were correctly built and implemented. We can detail the costs of a new system solution by department and estimated benefits.

The technical solution adopted was to create a local area network composed of 300 fully configured Pentium 4 desktop PCs, three Windows .NET servers, and a 10 megabit per second (Mbps) Ethernet local area network on a coaxial cable. The network connects all the lawyers and their secretaries to a single, integrated system yet permits each lawyer to configure his or her desktop with specialized software and hardware. The older machines were given away to charity.

All desktop machines were configured with Windows XP Professional and Office XP software. Lotus Notes was chosen to handle client accounting, document management, group collaboration, and e-mail because it provided an easy-to-use interface and secure links to external networks (including the Internet). The Internet was rejected as an e-mail technology because of its uncertain security. The Primrose local area network is linked to external networks so that the firm can obtain information online from Lexis (a legal database) and several financial database services.

The new system required Primrose to hire a director of systems—a new position for most law firms. Two systems personnel were required to operate the system and train lawyers. An outside trainer was also hired for a short period.

Figure 13-1 shows the estimated costs and benefits of the system. The system had an actual investment cost of $1,733,100 in the first year (Year 0) and a total cost over six years

	A	B	C	D	E	F	G	H	I	J	K	L
				Estimated Costs and Benefits 2002–2007								
1	Year :				0	1	2	3	4	5		
2					2002	2003	2004	2005	2006	2007		
3	**Costs Hardware**											
4		Servers		3@ 20,000	60,000	10,000	10,000	10,000	10,000	10,000		
5		PCs		300@3,000	900,000	10,000	10,000	10,000	10,000	10,000		
6		Network cards		300@100	30,000	0	0	0	0	0		
7		Scanners		6@100	600	500	500	500	500	500		
8												
9	Telecommunications											
10		Routers		10@500	5,000	1,000	1,000	1,000	1,000	1,000		
11		Cabling		150,000	150,000	0	0	0	0	0		
12		Telephone connect costs		50,000	50,000	50,000	50,000	50,000	50,000	50,000		
13												
14	Software											
15		Database		15,000	15,000	15,000	15,000	15,000	15,000	15,000		
16		Network		10,000	10,000	2,000	2,000	2,000	2,000	2,000		
17		Groupware		300@500	150,000	3,000	3,000	3,000	3,000	3,000		
18												
19	Services											
20		Lexis		50,000	50,000	50,000	50,000	50,000	50,000	50,000		
21		Training		300hrs@75/hr	22,500	10,000	10,000	10,000	10,000	10,000		
22		Director of Systems		100,000	100,000	100,000	100,000	100,000	100,000	100,000		
23		Systems Personnel		2@70,000	140,000	140,000	140,000	140,000	140,000	140,000		
24		Trainer		1@50,000	50,000	0	0	0	0	0		
25												
26	**Total Costs**				1,733,100	391,500	391,500	391,500	391,500	391,500	3,690,600	
27	Benefits											
28		1. Billing enhancements			300,000	500,000	600,000	600,000	600,000	500,000		
29		2. Reduced paralegals			50,000	100,000	150,000	150,000	150,000	150,000		
30		3. Reduced clerical			50,000	100,000	100,000	100,000	100,000	100,000		
31		4. Reduced messenger			15,000	30,000	30,000	30,000	30,000	30,000		
32		5. Reduced telecommunications			5,000	10,000	10,000	10,000	10,000	10,000		
33		6. Lawyer efficiencies			120,000	240,000	360,000	360,000	360,000	360,000		
34												
35	**Total Benefits**				540,000	980,000	1,250,000	1,250,000	1,250,000	1,150,000	6,420,000	

Sheet1 / Sheet2 / Sheet3

Figure 13-1   Costs and benefits of the Legal Information System. This spreadsheet analyzes the basic costs and benefits of implementing an information system for the law firm. The costs for hardware, telecommunications, software, services, and personnel are analyzed over a six-year period.

of $3,690,600. The estimated benefits total $6,420,000 after six years. Was the investment worthwhile? If so, in what sense? There are financial and nonfinancial answers to these questions. Let us look at the financial models first. They are depicted in Figure 13-2.

The Payback Method

payback method

A measure of the time required to pay back the initial investment on a project.

The **payback method** is quite simple: It is a measure of the time required to pay back the initial investment of a project. The payback period is computed as

$$\frac{\text{Original investment}}{\text{Annual net cash inflow}} = \text{Number of years to pay back}$$

In the case of Primrose, it will take more than two years to pay back the initial investment. (Because cash flows are uneven, annual cash inflows are summed until they equal the original investment in order to arrive at this number.) The payback method is a popular method because of its simplicity and power as an initial screening method. It is especially good for high-risk projects in which the useful life of a project is difficult to determine. If a project pays for itself in two years, then it matters less how long after two years the system lasts.

The weakness of this measure is its virtues: The method ignores the time value of money, the amount of cash flow after the payback period, the disposal value (usually zero with computer systems), and the profitability of the investment.

Accounting Rate of Return on Investment (ROI)

Firms make capital investments to earn a satisfactory rate of return. Determining a satisfactory rate of return depends on the cost of borrowing money, but other factors can enter into the equation. Such factors include the historic rates of return expected by the firm. In the long run, the desired rate of return must equal or exceed the cost of capital in the marketplace. Otherwise, no one will lend the firm money.

	Estimated Costs and Benefits 2002–2007											
	A	B	C	D	E	F	G	H	I	J	K	L
1	Year :			0	1	2	3	4	5			
2	Net Cash Flow (not including orig. investment)			540,000	588,500	858,500	858,500	858,500	758,500			
3	Net Cash Flow (including orig. investment)			–1,193,100	588,500	858,500	858,500	858,500	758,500			
4												
5	(1) Payback Period = 2.5 years					Cumulative Cash Flow						
6	Initial investment = 1,733,100			Year 0	540,000	540,000						
7				Year 1	588,500	1,128,500						
8				Year 2	858,500	1,987,000						
9				Year 3	858,500	2,845,500						
10				Year 4	858,500	3,704,000						
11				Year 5	758,500	4,462,500						
12												
13	(2) Accounting rate of return											
14												
15	(Total benefits-Total Costs-Depreciation)/Useful life				Total Benefits	6,420,000						
16	--				Total Costs	3,690,600						
17	Total initial investment				Depreciation	1,733,100						
18				Tot. benefits-tot. costs-depreciation		996,300						
19					Life	6 years						
20												
21					Initial investment		1,733,100					
22	ROI =	(996,300/6)	9.58%									
23		1,733,100										
24												
25	(3) Cost–Benefit Ratio		Total Benefits	6,420,000	1.74							
26			Total Costs	3,690,600								
27												
28	(4) Net Present Value											
29			= NPV (0.05,D2:I2)–1,733,100			2,001,529						
30												
31	(5) Profitability Index											
32			PV/Investment	NPV(0.05,D2:I2)/1733100		2.15						
33												
34	(6) Internal Rate of Return											
35												
36			= IRR(D3:I3)			55%						

Sheet1   **Sheet2**   Sheet3

Figure 13-2   Financial models. To determine the financial basis for a project a series of financial models helps determine the return on invested capital. These calculations include the payback period, the accounting rate of return (ROI), the cost–benefit ratio, the net present value, the profitability index, and the internal rate of return (IRR).

The **accounting rate of return on investment (ROI)** calculates the rate of return from an investment by adjusting the cash inflows produced by the investment for depreciation. It gives an approximation of the accounting income earned by the project.

To find the ROI, first calculate the average net benefit. The formula for the average net benefit is as follows:

$$\frac{\left(\text{Total benefits} - \text{Total cost} - \text{Depreciation}\right)}{\text{Useful life}} = \text{Net benefit}$$

This net benefit is divided by the total initial investment to arrive at ROI. The formula is

$$\frac{\text{Net benefit}}{\text{Total initial investment}} = \text{ROI}$$

In the case of Primrose, the average rate of return on the investment is 9.58 percent, which could be a good return on investment if the cost of capital (the prime rate) has been hovering around 6 to 8 percent.

The weakness of ROI is that it can ignore the time value of money. Future savings are simply not worth as much in today's dollars as are current savings. However, ROI can be modified (and usually is) so that future benefits and costs are calculated in today's dollars. (The present value function on most spreadsheets will perform this conversion.)

Net Present Value

Evaluating a capital project requires that the cost of an investment (a cash outflow usually in year 0) be compared with the net cash inflows that occur many years later. But these

accounting rate of return on investment (ROI)
Calculation of the rate of return on an investment by adjusting cash inflows produced by the investment for depreciation. Approximates the accounting income earned by the investment.

two kinds of inflows are not directly comparable because of the time value of money. Money you have been promised to receive three, four, and five years from now is not worth as much as money received today. Money received in the future has to be discounted by some appropriate percentage rate—usually the prevailing interest rate, or sometimes the cost of capital. **Present value** is the value in current dollars of a payment or stream of payments to be received in the future. It can be calculated by using the following formula:

$$\text{Payment} \times \frac{1 - (1 + \text{interest})^{-n}}{\text{Interest}} = \text{Present value}$$

Thus, to compare the investment (made in today's dollars) with future savings or earnings, you need to discount the earnings to their present value and then calculate the net present value of the investment. The **net present value** is the amount of money an investment is worth, taking into account its cost, earnings, and the time value of money. The formula for net present value is

Present value of expected cash flows − Initial investment cost = Net present value

In the case of Primrose, the present value of the stream of benefits is $3,734,629, and the cost (in today's dollars) is $1,733,100, giving a net present value of $2,001,529. In other words, for a $1.7 million investment today, the firm will receive more than $2 million. This is a fairly good rate of return on an investment.

Cost–Benefit Ratio

A simple method for calculating the returns from a capital expenditure is to calculate the **cost–benefit ratio,** which is the ratio of benefits to costs. The formula is

$$\frac{\text{Total benefits}}{\text{Total costs}} = \text{Cost–benefit ratio}$$

In the case of Primrose, the cost–benefit ratio is 1.74, meaning that the benefits are 1.74 times greater than the costs. The cost–benefit ratio can be used to rank several projects for comparison. Some firms establish a minimum cost–benefit ratio that must be attained by capital projects. The cost–benefit ratio can, of course, be calculated using present values to account for the time value of money.

Profitability Index

One limitation of net present value is that it provides no measure of profitability. Neither does it provide a way to rank order different possible investments. One simple solution is provided by the profitability index. The **profitability index** is calculated by dividing the present value of the total cash inflow from an investment by the initial cost of the investment. The result can be used to compare the profitability of alternative investments.

$$\frac{\text{Present value of cash inflows}}{\text{Investment}} = \text{Profitability index}$$

In the case of Primrose, the profitability index is 2.15. The project returns more than its cost. Projects can be rank ordered on this index, permitting firms to focus on only the most profitable projects.

Internal Rate of Return (IRR)

Internal rate of return is a variation of the net present value method. It takes into account the time value of money. **Internal rate of return (IRR)** is defined as the rate of return or profit that an investment is expected to earn. IRR is the discount (interest) rate that will equate the present value of the project's future cash flows to the initial cost of the project (defined here as a negative cash flow in year 0 of $1,193,100). In other words, the value of R (discount rate) is such that Present value − Initial cost = 0. In the case of Primrose, the IRR is 55 percent.

present value

The value, in current dollars, of a payment or stream of payments to be received in the future.

net present value

The amount of money an investment is worth, taking into account its cost, earnings, and the time value of money.

cost–benefit ratio

A method for calculating the returns from a capital expenditure by dividing total benefits by total costs.

profitability index

Used to compare the profitability of alternative investments; it is calculated by dividing the present value of the total cash inflow from an investment by the initial cost of the investment.

internal rate of return (IRR)

The rate of return or profit that an investment is expected to earn.

Results of the Capital Budgeting Analysis

Using methods that take into account the time value of money, the Primrose project is cash-flow positive over the time period and returns more benefits than it costs. Against this analysis, one might ask what other investments would be better from an efficiency and effectiveness standpoint? Also, one must ask if all the benefits have

been calculated. It may be that this investment is necessary for the survival of the firm, or necessary to provide a level of service demanded by its clients. What are other competitors doing? In other words, there may be other intangible and strategic business factors to take into account.

Figure 13-3 A system portfolio. Companies should examine their portfolio of projects in terms of potential benefits and likely risks. Certain kinds of projects should be avoided altogether and others developed rapidly. There is no ideal mix. Companies in different industries have different profiles.

STRATEGIC CONSIDERATIONS

Other methods of selecting and evaluating information system investments involve strategic considerations that are not addressed by traditional capital budgeting methods. When the firm has several alternative investments from which to select, it can employ portfolio analysis and scoring models. It can apply real options pricing models to IT investments that are highly uncertain or use a knowledge value-added approach to measure the benefits of changes to business processes. Several of these methods can be used in combination.

Portfolio Analysis

Rather than using capital budgeting, a second way of selecting among alternative projects is to consider the firm as having a portfolio of potential applications. Each application carries risks and benefits. The portfolio can be described as having a certain profile of risk and benefit to the firm (see Figure 13-3). Although there is no ideal profile for all firms, information-intensive industries (e.g., finance) should have a few high-risk, high-benefit projects to ensure that they stay current with technology. Firms in non-information-intensive industries should focus on high-benefit, low-risk projects.

Risks are not necessarily bad. They are tolerable as long as the benefits are commensurate. Section 13.2 describes the factors that increase the risks of systems projects.

Once strategic analyses have determined the overall direction of systems development, a **portfolio analysis** can be used to select alternatives. Obviously, one can begin by focusing on systems of high benefit and low risk. These promise early returns and low risks. Second, high-benefit, high-risk systems should be examined; low-benefit, high-risk systems should be totally avoided; and low-benefit, low-risk systems should be reexamined for the possibility of rebuilding and replacing them with more desirable systems having higher benefits.

portfolio analysis
An analysis of the portfolio of potential applications within a firm to determine the risks and benefits, and to select among alternatives for information systems.

Scoring Models

A quick and sometimes compelling method for arriving at a decision on alternative systems is a **scoring model.** Scoring models give alternative systems a single score based on the extent to which they meet selected objectives (Matlin, 1989; Buss, 1983).

In Table 13-2 the firm must decide among three alternative office systems: (1) an IBM AS/400 client/server system with proprietary software, (2) a UNIX-based client/server system using an Oracle database, and (3) a Windows client/server system using Windows XP, Windows .NET Server, and Lotus Notes. Column 1 lists the criteria that decision makers may apply to the systems. These criteria are usually the result of lengthy discussions among the decision-making group. Often the most important outcome of a scoring model is not the score but simply agreement on the criteria used to judge a system (Ginzberg, 1979; Nolan, 1982). Column 2 lists the weights that decision makers attach to the decision criterion. The scoring model helps to bring about agreement among participants concerning the rank of the criteria. Columns 3 to 5 use a 1-to-5 scale (lowest to highest) to express the judgments of participants on the relative merits of each system. For example, concerning the percentage of user needs that each system meets, a score of 1 for a system argues that this system when compared with others being considered will be low in meeting user needs.

scoring model
A quick method for deciding among alternative systems based on a system of ratings for selected objectives.

TABLE 13-2 SCORING MODEL USED TO CHOOSE AMONG ALTERNATIVE OFFICE SYSTEMS[A]

Criterion	Weight	AS/400		UNIX		Windows XP	
Percentage of user needs met	0.40	2	0.8	3	1.2	4	1.6
Cost of the initial purchase	0.20	1	0.2	3	0.6	4	0.8
Financing	0.10	1	0.1	3	0.3	4	0.4
Ease of maintenance	0.10	2	0.2	3	0.3	4	0.4
Chances of success	0.20	3	0.6	4	0.8	4	0.8
Final score			1.9		3.2		4.0

Scale: 1 = low, 5 = high

[a]One of the major uses of scoring models is in identifying the criteria of selection and their relative weights. In this instance, an office system based on Windows XP appears preferable.

As with all objective techniques, there are many qualitative judgments involved in using the scoring model. This model requires experts who understand the issues and the technology. It is appropriate to cycle through the scoring model several times, changing the criteria and weights, to see how sensitive the outcome is to reasonable changes in criteria. Scoring models are used most commonly to confirm, to rationalize, and to support decisions, rather than as the final arbiters of system selection.

If Primrose had other alternative systems projects to select from, it could have used the portfolio and scoring models as well as financial models to establish the business value of its systems solution.

Primrose did not have a portfolio of applications that could be used to compare the proposed system. Senior lawyers believed the project was low in risk using well-understood technology. They believed the rewards were even higher than the financial models stated because the system might enable the firm to expand its business. For instance, the ability to communicate with other law firms, with clients, and with the international staff of lawyers in remote locations was not even considered in the financial analysis.

Real Options Pricing Models

Some information system projects are highly uncertain. Their future revenue streams are unclear and their up-front costs are high. Suppose, for instance, that a firm is considering a $20 million investment to upgrade its information technology infrastructure. If this infrastructure were available, the organization would have the technology capabilities to respond to future problems and opportunities. Although the costs of this investment can be calculated, not all of the benefits of making this investment can be established in advance. But if the firm waits a few years until the revenue potential becomes more obvious, it might be too late to make the infrastructure investment. In such cases, managers might benefit from using real options pricing models to evaluate information technology investments.

Real options pricing models use the concept of options valuation borrowed from the financial industry. An option is essentially the right, but not the obligation, to act at some future date. A typical call option, for instance, is a financial option in which a person buys the right (but not the obligation) to purchase an underlying asset (usually a stock) at a definite price (strike price) for a limited period of time. For instance, on January 22, 2002, for $1.50 one could purchase the right (a call option) to buy 100 shares of Wal-Mart common stock at $60 per share in March 2002. If, by March 2002, the price of Wal-Mart stock did not rise above $60, you would not exercise the option, and the value of the option would fall to zero on the strike date. If, however, the price of Wal-Mart common stock rose to, say, $100 per share, you could purchase the stock for the strike price of $60, and retain the profit of $40 per share. The stock option enables the owner to benefit from the upside potential of an opportunity while limiting the downside risk.

Real options pricing models value information systems projects similar to stock options, giving managers the flexibility to make a small capital investment today to create an opportunity in the future. Using ROPM, every information systems project can be treated as an option as long as management has the freedom to cancel, defer, restart, expand, or contract

real options pricing models

Models for evaluating information technology investments with uncertain returns by using techniques for valuing financial options.

the project. Real options involving investments in capital projects are different from financial options in that they cannot be traded on a market and they differ in value based on the firm in which they are made. Thus, an investment in an enterprise system will have very different real option values in different firms because the ability to derive value from even identical enterprise systems depends on firm factors, for example, prior expertise, skilled labor force, market conditions, and other factors. Nevertheless, several scholars have argued that the real options theory can be useful when considering highly uncertain IT investments, and potentially the same techniques for valuing financial options can be used (Benaroch and Kauffman, 2000; Taudes, Feurstein, and Mild, 2000).

Real options pricing models (ROPM) offer an approach to thinking about information technology projects that takes into account the value of management learning over time and the value of delaying investment. In real options theory, the value of the IT project (real option) is a function of the value of the underlying IT asset (present value of expected revenues from the IT project), the volatility of the value in the underlying asset, the cost of converting the option investment into the underlying asset (the exercise price), the risk free interest rate, and the option time to maturity (length of time the project can be deferred).

The real options model addresses some of the limitations of the discounted cash flow models described earlier, which essentially call for investing in an information technology project only when the value of the discounted cash value of the entire investment is greater than zero. ROPM allows managers to systematically take into account the volatility in the value of IT projects over time, the optimal timing of the investment, and the changing cost of implementation as technology prices or interest rates rise or fall over time. This model gives managers the flexibility to stage their IT investment or test the waters with small pilot projects to gain more knowledge about the risks of a project before investing in the entire implementation. Briefly, the ROPM places a value on management learning, and the use of an unfolding investment technique (investing in chunks) based on learning over time.

The disadvantages of this model are primarily in estimating all the key variables, especially the expected cash flows from the underlying asset, and changes in the cost of implementation. Several rule-of-thumb approaches are being developed (McGrath and MacMillan, 2000). ROPM can be useful when there is no experience with a technology and its future is highly uncertain.

Knowledge Value Added Approach

A different approach to traditional capital budgeting is to focus on the knowledge input into a business process as a way of determining the costs and benefits of changes in business processes from new information systems. Any program that uses information technology to change business processes requires knowledge input. The value of the knowledge used to produce improved outputs of the new process can be used as a measure of the value added. Knowledge inputs can be measured in terms of learning time to master a new process and a return on knowledge can be estimated. This method makes certain assumptions that may not be valid in all situations, especially product design and research and development, where processes do not have predetermined outputs (Housel, El Sawy, Zhong, and Rodgers, 2001).

INFORMATION TECHNOLOGY INVESTMENTS AND PRODUCTIVITY

Information technology now accounts for about 50 percent of total business expenditures on capital equipment in the United States. Whether this investment has translated into genuine productivity gains remains open to debate. Productivity is a measure of the firm's efficiency in converting inputs to outputs. It refers to the amount of capital and labor required to produce a *unit of output*. For over a decade, researchers have been trying to quantify the benefits from information technology investments by analyzing data collected at the economy level, industry level, firm level, and information system application level. The results of these studies have been mixed and the term "productivity paradox" was coined to describe such findings.

Information technology has increased productivity in manufacturing, especially the manufacture of information technology products, as well as in retail. Wal-Mart, which dominates U.S. retailing, has experienced increases in both productivity and profitability over the last decade through managerial innovations and powerful supply chain management systems. Competitors such as Sears, Kmart, and Costco are trying to emulate these practices. A 2002 study estimated that Wal-Mart's productivity alone accounted for over half of the productivity acceleration in U.S. general merchandise retailing (Johnson, 2002).

However, the extent to which computers have enhanced the productivity of the service sector remains unclear. Some studies show that investment in information technology has not led to any appreciable growth in productivity among office workers. The banking industry, which has been one of the most intensive users of information technology, did not experience any gains in productivity throughout the 1990s (Olazabal, 2002). Corporate downsizings and cost-reduction measures have increased worker efficiency but have not yet led to sustained enhancements signifying genuine productivity gains (Roach, 2000, 1996, and 1988). Cellphones, home fax machines, laptop computers, and information appliances allow highly paid knowledge workers to get more work done by working longer hours and bringing their work home, but they are not necessarily getting more work done in a specified unit of time.

The contribution of information technology to productivity in information and knowledge industries may be difficult to measure because of the problems of identifying suitable units of output for information work (Panko, 1991). How does one measure the output of a law office? Should one measure productivity by examining the number of forms completed per employee (a measure of physical unit productivity) or by examining the amount of revenue produced per employee (a measure of financial unit productivity) in an information- and knowledge-intense industry?

Other studies have focused on the value of outputs (essentially revenues), profits, ROI, and stock market capitalization as the ultimate measures of firm efficiency. A number of researchers have found that information technology investments have resulted in increased productivity and better financial performance, including higher stock valuations. (Brynjolfsson and Hitt, 1998 and 1993; Davamanirajan, Mukhopadhyay and Kriebel, 2002; Hitt, Wu and Zhou, 2002; Banker, 2001; Chatterjee, Pacini, and Sambamurthy, 2002; Brynjolfsson and Yang, 2000). Information technology investments were more likely to improve firm performance if they were accompanied by complementary investments in new business processes, organizational structures, and organizational learning that could unleash the potential of the new technology. In addition to this "organizational capital," complementary resources such as up-to-date IT infrastructures have been found to make e-commerce investments more effective in improving firm performance (Kraemer and Zhu, 2002). Firms that have built appropriate infrastructures—and view their infrastructures as sets of services providing strategic agility— have faster times to market, higher growth rates, and more sales from new products (Weill, Subramani and Broadbent, 2002; Weill and Broadbent, 1998).

In addition to reducing costs, computers may increase the quality of products and services for consumers or may create entirely new products and revenue streams. These intangible benefits are difficult to measure and consequently are not addressed by conventional productivity measures. Moreover, because of competition, the value created by computers may primarily flow to customers rather than to the company making the investments (Brynjolfsson, 1996). For instance, the investment in ATM machines by banks has not resulted in higher profitability for any single bank, although the industry as a whole has prospered and consumers enjoy the benefits without paying higher fees. Productivity may not necessarily increase firm profitability. Hence, the returns of information technology investments should be analyzed within the competitive context of the firm, the industry, and the specific way in which information technology is being applied.

13.2 THE IMPORTANCE OF CHANGE MANAGEMENT IN INFORMATION SYSTEM SUCCESS AND FAILURE

Benefits from information technology investments will be reduced if firms do not consider the costs of organizational change associated with a new system or make these changes effectively (Ryan and Harrison, 2000; Irani and Love, 2000–2001). The introduction or alteration of an information system has a powerful behavioral and organizational impact. It transforms how various individuals and groups perform and interact. Changes in the way that information is defined, accessed, and used to manage the organization's resources often lead to new distributions of authority and power. This internal organizational change breeds resistance and opposition and can lead to the demise of an otherwise good system.

A very large percentage of information systems fail to deliver benefits or to solve the problems for which they were intended because the process of organizational change surrounding system-building was not properly addressed. Successful system-building requires careful change management.

INFORMATION SYSTEM PROBLEM AREAS

The problems causing information **system failure** fall into multiple categories, as illustrated by Figure 13-4. The major problem areas are design, data, cost, and operations.

Figure 13-4 Information system problem areas. Problems with an information system's design, data, cost, or operations can be evidence of a system failure.

Design

The actual design of the system may fail to capture essential business requirements or improve organizational performance. Information may not be provided quickly enough to be helpful; it may be in a format that is impossible to digest and use; or it may represent the wrong pieces of data.

The way in which nontechnical business users must interact with the system may be excessively complicated and discouraging. A system may be designed with a poor **user interface.** The user interface is the part of the system with which end users interact. For example, an input form or an online data entry screen may be so poorly arranged that no one wants to submit data. The procedures to request online information retrieval may be so unintelligible that users are too frustrated to make requests. Web sites may discourage visitors from exploring further if Web pages are cluttered and poorly arranged, if users can't easily find the information they are seeking (see the Window on Organizations), or if it takes too long to access and display the Web page on the user's computer (Palmer, 2002). The Manager's Toolkit provides some guidelines for effective Web page design.

An information system will be judged a failure if its design is not compatible with the structure, culture, and goals of the organization as a whole. Historically, information system

---

system failure

An information system that either does not perform as expected, is not operational at a specified time, or cannot be used in the way it was intended.

user interface

The part of the information system through which the end user interacts with the system; type of hardware and the series of on-screen commands and responses required for a user to work with the system.

Before RedEnvelope.com redesigned its Web site, 81 percent of visitors abandoned full shopping carts without completing their purchase, frustrated by inconsistent navigation bars, slow loading Web pages and a complicated checkout process. The redesigned Web site illustrated here displays navigation bars clearly at the top of each page, loads quickly, and features a streamlined checkout process. After RedEvelope improved its Web site, sales increased by 95 percent.

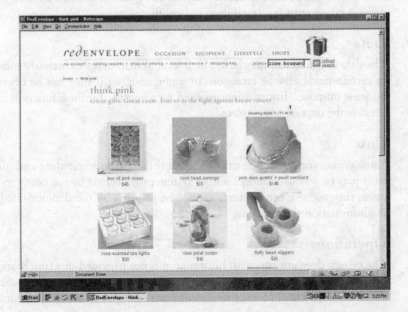

Is the Premium at InsWeb Too High for Users?

InsWeb operates an online insurance Web marketplace that enables consumers to shop for a variety of insurance products, including automobile, term life, homeowners, renters, and health insurance. Visitors to the InsWeb site can obtain competing quotes from over 40 well-known and respected insurance companies, including AIG, Allstate, CAN, GE Auto Insurance Program, and Travelers Property Casualty.

InsWeb provides a low-cost channel for insurance companies to acquire new customers who are pre-screened and come from the growing population of technology-oriented consumers who shop online. InsWeb acts as an agent for 11 auto insurers and a conduit for 25 more. The firms that use InsWeb as an agent pay it a commission while the other pay InsWeb a fee for providing leads that usually help them to close a deal with customers offline.

The site provides a great deal of useful information and users can, in theory, use it for one-stop comparison shopping for most of their insurance needs. InsWeb can, for example, show comparative rates on auto insurance and make recommendations on the level of coverage that would be most appropriate, given the policy-holder's home and other assets. But making the online application can be tedious and confusing if the multiple-choice options offered as answers to some questions do not correspond to the user's information.

Some business models translate to the Web more easily than others. Products such as books or CDs are relatively straightforward to sell to consumers online. But insurance by

Window on Organizations

MIS In Action

nature is a very complex product, requiring users to be armed with a great deal of information in order to understand exactly what they are buying. That is one reason why the insurance business traditionally relied on live agents to work with customers. How well could InsWeb perform this task?

For health insurance, InsWeb provides some general information but can't effectively help users compare policies side by side. InsWeb has a tool for this purpose, but it doesn't provide space for enough information on the policies for which it quotes prices. Users would need to click on each policy individually and read the details to find out important information. InsWeb could make this process more user-friendly by adopting some of the features of other e-commerce sites offering a large number of similar products: It could have provided a rating system for each policy's coverage or benefits, or it could perhaps include brief comments on the strengths and weaknesses of each policy option. While InsWeb could point users to lower-cost policies, working with this Web site was a great deal of work—perhaps too much work.

MAKE IT YOUR BUSINESS

To Think About: What organization and technology issues affected the usability of InsWeb's Web site? Why is Web site usability so important in electronic commerce?

Sources: Susan J. Marks, "InsWeb: Too High a Premium? *Business Week Online* April 15, 2002; and InsWeb Insurance Online, accessed July 28, 2002, <www.insweb.com>.

ORGANIZATIONS

design has been preoccupied with technical issues at the expense of organizational concerns. The result has often been information systems that are technically excellent but incompatible with their organization's structure, culture, and goals. Without a close organizational fit, such systems create tensions, instability, and conflict.

Data

The data in the system may have a high level of inaccuracy or inconsistency. The information in certain fields may be erroneous or ambiguous, or it may not be organized properly for business purposes. Information required for a specific business function may be inaccessible because the data are incomplete.

Cost

Some systems operate quite smoothly, but their cost to implement and run on a production basis may be way over budget. Other system projects may be too costly to complete. In both cases, the excessive expenditures cannot be justified by the demonstrated business value of the information they provide.

Operations

The system does not run well. Information is not provided in a timely and efficient manner because the computer operations that handle information processing break down. Jobs that abort too often lead to excessive reruns and delayed or missed schedules for delivery of

MIS IN ACTION: MANAGER'S TOOLKIT

DESIGNING A USER-FRIENDLY WEB SITE

The design and user friendliness of a Web site can mean the difference between e-commerce and e-business success and failure. Studies have found that poor design is more common than good design and that close to 50 percent of Web shoppers gave up purchasing items online because they could not easily locate the products they wanted on a Web site. Here are the most important factors to consider when designing an effective Web site:

Content: Content should be appropriate to the purpose of the site and its intended audience. Short sentences and paragraphs and bulleted lists should be used so that content can be scanned easily. A search function should be available if the site has large amounts of information.

Page design and layout: Graphics and design convey function and meaning and are an integral part of the user's Web site experience. Page design and layout, including color, fonts, and images, should be balanced, clean, and uncluttered. Both graphic and text elements should be clearly legible and pages should be short enough so that users don't have to do a great deal of vertical scrolling. The colors used in the Web site design should be carefully chosen, because certain colors convey specific messages.

Navigation: Most user interactions with Web sites require navigating hypertext links between Web pages. Web sites should be designed so that users have a clear sense of where they are within the local organization of information. Navigating from page to page should be simple. Users should be able to easily backtrack or return to the home page. Basic navigation links should be present on every page of the Web site.

Accessibility: Users should be able to obtain the information they want with the fewest possible steps in the shortest time. Information on Web sites should be organized to minimize the number of steps through menu pages.

Load factors: Users are frustrated by long delays, so Web pages should load quickly. The loading time for a Web page will be slowed down by large numbers of simultaneous visitors to a Web site and extensive multimedia graphics and dynamic content. Therefore, Web page designs need to be "tuned" to the network access speeds of most users as well as the capabilities of systems where they are hosted.

Standards: The Web site should work with the most popular Web browser software, including Microsoft Internet Explorer and Netscape Navigator, and with Macintosh operating systems as well as computers using the Intel hardware standard and Windows operating systems.

---

information. An online system may be operationally inadequate because the response time is too long.

Some of these problems can be attributed to technical features of information systems but most stem from organizational factors (Keil, Cule, Lyytinen, and Schmidt, 1998). System builders need to understand these organizational issues and learn how to manage the change associated with a new information system.

CHANGE MANAGEMENT AND THE CONCEPT OF IMPLEMENTATION

To effectively manage the organizational change surrounding the introduction of a new information system, one must examine the process of implementation. **Implementation** refers to all organizational activities working toward the adoption, management, and routinization of an innovation such as a new information system. In the implementation process, the systems analyst is a **change agent.** The analyst not only develops technical solutions but also redefines the configurations, interactions, job activities, and power relationships of various organizational groups. The analyst is the catalyst for the entire change process and is responsible for ensuring that the changes created by a new system are accepted by all parties involved. The change agent communicates with users, mediates between competing interest groups, and ensures that the organizational adjustment to such changes is complete.

One model of the implementation process is the Kolb/Frohman model of organizational change. This model divides the process of organizational change into a seven-stage relationship between an organizational *consultant* and his or her *client.* (The consultant corresponds to the information system designer and the client to the user.) The success of the change effort is determined by how well the consultant and client deal with the key issues at each stage (Kolb and Frohman, 1970). Other models of implementation describe the relationship as one between designers, clients, and decision makers, who are responsible for managing the implementation effort to bridge the gap between design and utilization (Swanson, 1988). Recent work on

implementation
All organizational activities working toward the adoption, management, and routinization of an innovation.

change agent
In the context of implementation, the individual acting as the catalyst during the change process to ensure successful organizational adaptation to a new system or innovation.

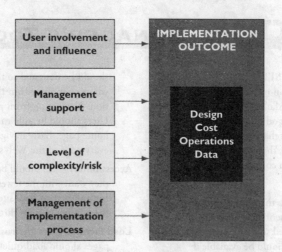

Figure 13-5 Factors in information system success or failure. The implementation outcome can be largely determined by the role of users; the degree of management support; the level of risk and complexity in the implementation project; and the quality of management of the implementation process. Evidence of success or failure can be found in the areas of design, cost, operations, or data of the information system.

implementation stresses the need for flexibility and improvisation with organizational actors not limited to rigid prescribed roles (Markus and Benjamin, 1997; Orlikowski and Hofman, 1997).

CAUSES OF IMPLEMENTATION SUCCESS AND FAILURE

Implementation outcome can be largely determined by the following factors:

- The role of users in the implementation process
- The degree of management support for the implementation effort
- The level of complexity and risk of the implementation project
- The quality of management of the implementation process

These are largely behavioral and organizational issues and are illustrated in Figure 13-5.

User Involvement and Influence

User involvement in the design and operation of information systems has several positive results. First, if users are heavily involved in systems design, they have more opportunities to mold the system according to their priorities and business requirements, and more opportunities to control the outcome. Second, they are more likely to react positively to the completed system because they have been active participants in the change process itself. Incorporating the user's knowledge and expertise leads to better solutions.

Thanks to widespread use of the Internet and fourth-generation tools, today's users are assuming more of a leadership role in articulating the adoption, development and implementation of information technology innovations (Kettinger and Lee, 2002). However, users often take a very narrow and limited view of the problem to be solved and may overlook important technology issues or alternative information system solutions. The skills and vision of professional system designers are still required much the same way that the services of an architect are required when building a new house (Markus and Keil, 1994).

The relationship between consultant and client has traditionally been a problem area for information system implementation efforts. Users and information systems specialists tend to have different backgrounds, interests, and priorities. This is referred to as the **user–designer communications gap.** These differences lead to divergent organizational loyalties, approaches to problem solving, and vocabularies. Information systems specialists, for example, often have a highly technical, or machine, orientation to problem solving. They look for elegant and sophisticated technical solutions in which hardware and software efficiency is optimized at the expense of ease of use or organizational effectiveness. Users prefer systems that are oriented to solving business problems or facilitating organizational tasks. Often the orientations of both groups are so at odds that they appear to speak in different tongues. These differences are illustrated in Table 13-3, which depicts the typical concerns of end users and technical specialists (information system designers) regarding the development of a new information system. Communication problems between end users and designers are a major reason why user requirements are not properly incorporated into information systems and why users are driven out of the implementation process.

user–designer communications gap

The difference in backgrounds, interests, and priorities that impede communication and problem solving among end users and information systems specialists.

TABLE 13-3	THE USER–DESIGNER COMMUNICATIONS GAP

User Concerns	Designer Concerns
Will the system deliver the information I need for my work?	How much disk storage space will the master file consume?
How quickly can I access the data?	How many lines of program code will it take to perform this function?
How easily can I retrieve the data?	How can we cut down on CPU time when we run the system?
How much clerical support will I need to enter data into the system?	What is the most efficient way of storing these data?
How will the operation of the system fit into my daily business schedule?	What database management system should we use?

Systems development projects run a very high risk of failure when there is a pronounced gap between users and technicians and when these groups continue to pursue different goals. Under such conditions, users are often driven out of the implementation process. Because they cannot comprehend what the technicians are saying, users conclude that the entire project is best left in the hands of the information specialists alone. With so many implementation efforts guided by purely technical considerations, it is no wonder that many systems fail to serve organizational needs.

Management Support and Commitment

If an information systems project has the backing and commitment of management at various levels, it is more likely to be perceived positively by both users and the technical information services staff. Both groups will believe that their participation in the development process will receive higher-level attention and priority. They will be recognized and rewarded for the time and effort they devote to implementation. Management backing also ensures that a systems project will receive sufficient funding and resources to be successful. Furthermore, all the changes in work habits and procedures and any organizational realignments associated with a new system depend on management backing to be enforced effectively. If a manager considers a new system a priority, the system will more likely be treated that way by his or her subordinates (Doll, 1985; Ein-Dor and Segev, 1978).

Level of Complexity and Risk

Systems differ dramatically in their size, scope, level of complexity, and organizational and technical components. Some systems development projects are more likely to fail or suffer delays because they carry a much higher level of risk than others. The level of project risk is influenced by project size, project structure, and the level of technical expertise of the information systems staff and project team.

Project size The larger the project—as indicated by the dollars spent, the size of the implementation staff, the time allocated for implementation, and the number of organizational units affected—the greater the risk. Very large-scale system projects have a failure rate that is 50 to 75 percent higher than for other projects because such projects are so complex and difficult to control. The behavioral characteristics of the system—who owns the system and how much it influences business processes—contribute to the complexity of large-scale system projects just as much as technical characteristics, such as the number of lines of program code, length of project, and budget (The Concours Group, 2000; Laudon, 1989; U.S. General Services Administration, 1988).

Project structure Some projects are more highly structured than others. Their requirements are clear and straightforward so the outputs and processes can be easily defined. Users know exactly what they want and what the system should do; there is almost no possibility of the users changing their minds. Such projects run a much lower risk than those with relatively undefined, fluid, and constantly changing

Figure 13-6 Consequences of poor project management. Without proper management, a systems development project will take longer to complete and most often will exceed the allocated budget. The resulting information system will most likely be technically inferior and may not be able to demonstrate any benefits to the organization.

Poor Project Management → Cost overruns
Time slippage
Technical shortfalls impairing performance
Failure to obtain anticipated benefits

requirements; with outputs that cannot be fixed easily because they are subject to users' changing ideas; or with users who cannot agree on what they want.

Experience with technology The project risk will rise if the project team and the information system staff lack the required technical expertise. If the team is unfamiliar with the hardware, system software, application software, or database management system proposed for the project, it is highly likely that the project will experience technical problems or take more time to complete because of the need to master new skills.

Management of the Implementation Process

The development of a new system must be carefully managed and orchestrated. Often basic elements of success are forgotten. Training to ensure that end users are comfortable with the new system and fully understand its potential uses is often sacrificed or forgotten in systems development projects. If the budget is strained at the very beginning, toward the end of a project there will likely be insufficient funds for training and documentation (Bikson et al., 1985).

The conflicts and uncertainties inherent in any implementation effort will be magnified when an implementation project is poorly managed and organized. As illustrated in Figure 13-6, a systems development project without proper management will most likely suffer these consequences:

- Costs that vastly exceed budgets
- Unexpected time slippage
- Technical shortfalls resulting in performance that is significantly below the estimated level
- Failure to obtain anticipated benefits

How badly are projects managed? On average, private sector projects are underestimated by one-half in terms of budget and time required to deliver the complete system promised in the system plan. A very large number of projects are delivered with missing functionality (promised for delivery in later versions). As many as 80 percent of all software projects exceed their budgets, with the "average" software project running 50 percent over budget. Between 30 and 40 percent of all software projects are "runaway" projects that far exceed the original schedule and budget projections and fail to perform as originally specified (Keil, Mann, and Rai, 2000). Why are projects managed so poorly and what can be done about it? Here we discuss some possibilities.

Ignorance and optimism The techniques for estimating the length of time required to analyze and design systems are poorly developed. Most applications are "first time" (i.e., there is no prior experience in the application area). The larger the scale of systems, the greater the role of ignorance and optimism. The net result of these factors is that estimates tend to be optimistic, "best case," and wrong. It is assumed that all will go well when in fact it rarely does.

The mythical man-month The traditional unit of measurement used by systems designers to project costs is the **man-month.** Projects are estimated in terms of how many man-months will be required. However, adding more workers to projects does not necessarily reduce the elapsed time needed to complete a systems project (Brooks, 1974). Unlike cotton picking—when tasks can be rigidly partitioned, communication between participants is not required, and training is unnecessary—building systems often involves *tasks that are sequentially linked, cannot be performed in isolation, and require extensive communications and training.* Adding labor to software projects where there are many task interdependencies can often slow down delivery as the communication, learning, and coordination costs escalate and detract from the output of participants (Andres and Zmud, 2001–2002). For comparison, imagine what would happen if five amateur spectators were added to one team in a championship professional basketball game? The team composed of five professional basketball players would probably do much better in the short run than the team with five professionals and five amateurs.

man-month

The traditional unit of measurement used by systems designers to estimate the length of time to complete a project. Refers to the amount of work a person can be expected to complete in a month.

Falling behind: bad news travels slowly upward Among projects in all fields, slippage in projects, failure, and doubts are often not reported to senior management until it is too late (Smith, Keil, and Depledge, 2001; Keil and Robey, 2001). The CON-FIRM project, a very large-scale information systems project to integrate hotel, air-line, and rental car reservations, is a classic example. It was sponsored by Hilton Hotels, Budget Rent-A-Car, and Marriott Corporation and developed by AMR Information Services, Inc., a subsidiary of American Airlines Corporation. The project was very ambitious and technically complex, employing a staff of 500. Members of the CONFIRM project management team did not immediately come forward with accurate information when the project started encountering problems coordinating various transaction processing activities. Clients continued to invest in a project that was faltering because they were not informed of its problems with database, decision-support, and integration technologies (Oz, 1994).

CHANGE MANAGEMENT CHALLENGES FOR ENTERPRISE APPLICATIONS, BUSINESS PROCESS REENGINEERING (BPR), SUPPLY CHAIN MANAGEMENT, AND CUSTOMER RELATIONSHIP MANAGEMENT

Given the challenges of innovation and implementation, it is not surprising to find a very high failure rate among enterprise system and business process reengineering (BPR) projects, which typically require extensive organizational change and which may require replacing old technologies and legacy systems that are deeply rooted in many interrelated business processes. A number of studies have indicated that 70 percent of all business process reengineering projects fail to deliver promised benefits. Likewise, a high percentage of enterprise resource planning projects fail to be fully implemented or to meet the goals of their users even after three years of work.

Many enterprise system and reengineering projects have been undermined by poor implementation and change management practices that failed to address employees' concerns about change. Dealing with fear and anxiety throughout the organization; overcoming resistance by key managers; changing job functions, career paths, and recruitment practices; and training have posed greater threats to reengineering than the difficulties companies faced visualizing and designing breakthrough changes to business processes.

Enterprise systems create myriad interconnections among various business processes and data flows to ensure that information in one part of the business can be obtained by any other unit, to help people eliminate redundant activities, and to make better management decisions. Massive organizational changes are required to make this happen. Information that was previously maintained by different systems and different departments or functional areas must be integrated and made available to the company as a whole. Business processes must be tightly integrated, jobs must be redefined, and new procedures must be created throughout the company. Employees are often unprepared for new procedures and roles (Davenport, 2000 and 1998). New organizational learning is required for organizational members to acquire complex new knowledge about new business rules and business processes and simultaneously "unlearn" what they already know (Robey, Ross, and Boudreau, 2002).

Customer relationship management (CRM) and supply chain management systems are also very difficult to implement successfully. Most firms embracing CRM need to transform their focus from a product-centric view to a customer-centric view, which requires some fundamental changes in organizational culture and business processes as well as closer cooperation between the information systems and sales and marketing groups. Between 55 percent and 75 percent of CRM projects fail to meet their objectives (McDonnell, 2001; Yu, 2001). Supply chain management also requires closer coordination among different functional groups and different organizations as well as extensive business process change.

SYSTEM IMPLICATIONS OF MERGERS AND ACQUISITIONS

Mergers and acquisitions (M&As) have been proliferating because they are major growth engines for businesses. Potentially, firms can cut costs significantly by merging with competitors, reduce risks by expanding into different industries (e.g., conglomerating), and create larger pools of competitive knowledge and expertise by joining forces with other players. There are also economies of time: A firm can gain market share and expertise very quickly through acquisition rather than building over the long term.

Although some firms, such as General Electric, are quite successful in carrying out mergers and acquisitions, research has found that more than 70 percent of all M&As result in a decline in shareholder value, and often lead to divestiture at a later time (Lipin and Deogun, 2000; Frank and Sidel, 2002). Many deals suffer from unrealistic expectations about the synergies that could result from merging companies and from poor planning.

Architects of mergers and acquisitions often fail to appreciate the difficulty of integrating the systems of different companies. Mergers and acquisitions are deeply affected by the organizational characteristics of the merging companies as well as by their information technology (IT) infrastructures. Combining the information systems of two different companies usually requires considerable organizational change and complex system projects to manage. If the integration is not properly managed, firms can emerge with a tangled hodgepodge of inherited legacy systems built by aggregating the systems of one firm after another. Without a successful systems integration, the benefits anticipated from the merger cannot be realized, or, worse, the merged entity cannot execute its business processes and loses customers.

When a company targeted for acquisition has been identified, information systems managers will need to identify the realistic costs of integration; the estimated benefits of economies in operation, scope, knowledge, and time; and any problematic systems that require major investments to integrate. In addition, IT managers can critically estimate any likely costs and organizational changes required to upgrade the IT infrastructure or make major system improvements to support the merged companies.

13.3 MANAGING IMPLEMENTATION

Not all aspects of the implementation process can be easily controlled or planned. However, the chances for system success can be increased by anticipating potential implementation problems and applying appropriate corrective strategies. Various project management, requirements gathering, and planning methodologies have been developed for specific categories of problems. Strategies have also been devised for ensuring that users play an appropriate role throughout the implementation period and for managing the organizational change process.

CONTROLLING RISK FACTORS

The first step in managing project risk is to identify the nature and level of risk confronting the project (Schmidt, Lyytinen, Keil, and Cule, 2001). Implementers can then adopt a contingency approach to project management, handling each project with the tools, project management methodologies, and organizational linkages geared to its level of risk (Barki, Rivard, and Talbot, 2001; McFarlan, 1981).

Managing Technical Complexity

internal integration tools
Project management technique that ensures that the implementation team operates as a cohesive unit.

Projects with *challenging and complex technology* to master benefit from **internal integration tools.** The success of such projects depends on how well their technical complexity can be managed. Project leaders need both heavy technical and administrative experience. They must be able to anticipate problems and develop smooth working relationships among a predominantly technical team. The team should be under the leadership of a manager with a strong technical and project management background and team members should be highly experienced. Team meetings should take place frequently. Essential technical skills or expertise not available internally should be secured from outside the organization.

Formal Planning and Control Tools

formal planning tools
Project management technique that structures and sequences tasks, budgeting time, money, and technical resources required to complete the tasks.

formal control tools
Project management technique that helps monitor the progress toward completion of a task and fulfillment of goals.

Large projects will benefit from appropriate use of **formal planning** and **formal control tools.** With project management techniques, such as Program Evaluation and Review Technique (PERT) or Gantt charts, a detailed plan can be developed. (PERT lists the specific activities that make up a project, their duration, and the activities that must be completed before a specific activity can start. A Gantt chart such as that illustrated in Figure 13-7 visu-

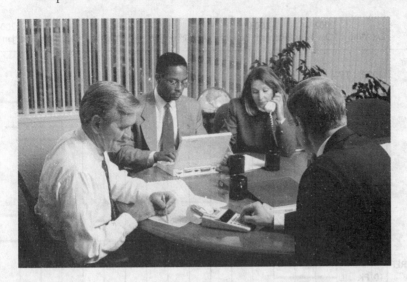

This project team of professionals is using computing tools to enhance communication, analysis, and decisionmaking.

ally represents the sequence and timing of different tasks in a development project as well as their resource requirements.) Tasks can be defined and resources budgeted.

These project management techniques can help managers identify bottlenecks and determine the impact that problems will have on project completion times. They can also help system developers partition implementation into smaller, more manageable segments with defined, measurable business results (Fichman and Moses, 1999). Standard control techniques will successfully chart the progress of the project against budgets and target dates, so deviations from the plan can be spotted.

Increasing User Involvement and Overcoming User Resistance

Projects with relatively *little structure and many undefined requirements* must involve users fully at all stages. Users must be mobilized to support one of many possible design options and to remain committed to a single design. **External integration tools** consist of ways to link the work of the implementation team to users at all organizational levels. For instance, users can become active members of the project team, take on leadership roles, and take charge of installation and training. The implementation team can demonstrate its responsiveness to users, promptly answering questions, incorporating user feedback, and showing their willingness to help (Gefen and Ridings, 2002). E-business initiatives which require rapid system responses to emerging opportunities may benefit from using special "organizational architects" with skills and expertise to bridge communication gaps between business users and technology specialists (Sauer and Willcocks, 2002).

Unfortunately, systems development is not an entirely rational process. Users leading design activities have used their positions to further private interests and to gain power rather than to promote organizational objectives (Franz and Robey, 1984). Users may not always be involved in systems projects in a productive way.

Participation in implementation activities may not be enough to overcome the problem of user resistance. The implementation process demands organizational change. Such change may be resisted because different users may be affected by the system in different ways. Whereas some users may welcome a new system because it brings changes they perceive as beneficial to them, others may resist these changes because they believe the shifts are detrimental to their interests (Joshi, 1991).

If the use of a system is voluntary, users may choose to avoid it; if use is mandatory, resistance will take the form of increased error rates, disruptions, turnover, and even sabotage. Therefore, the implementation strategy must not only encourage user participation and involvement, it must also address the issue of counterimplementation (Keen, 1981). **Counterimplementation** is a deliberate strategy to thwart the implementation of an information system or an innovation in an organization.

Strategies to overcome user resistance include user participation (to elicit commitment as well as to improve design), user education and training, management edicts and policies, and providing better incentives for users who cooperate. The new system can be made more user friendly by improving the end-user interface. Users will be more cooperative if

external integration tools
Project management technique that links the work of the implementation team to that of users at all organizational levels.

counterimplementation
A deliberate strategy to thwart the implementation of an information system or an innovation in an organization.

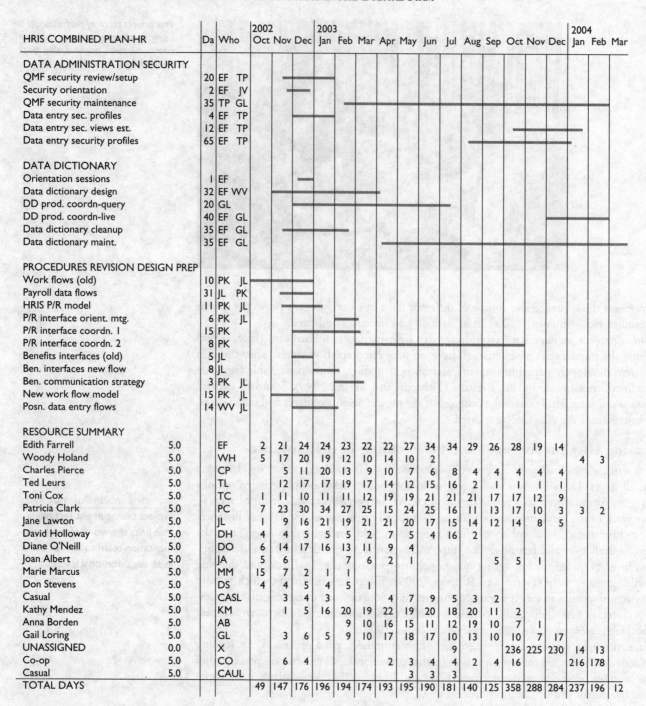

Figure 13-7 Formal planning and control tools help to manage information systems projects successfully. The Gantt chart in this figure was produced by a commercially available project management software package. It shows the task, person-days, and initials of each responsible person, as well as the start and finish dates for each task. The resource summary provides a good manager with the total person-days for each month and for each person working on the project to successfully manage the project. The project described here is a data administration project.

organizational problems are solved prior to introducing the new system. The Window on Management shows how Royal Dutch/Shell dealt with user and change management issues.

DESIGNING FOR THE ORGANIZATION

Because the purpose of a new system is to improve the organization's performance, the systems development process must explicitly address the ways in which the organization

ROYAL DUTCH/SHELL MASTERS CHANGE MANAGEMENT

In January 2000, Royal Dutch/Shell Group ordered all of its units to undertake company-wide alterations in its information systems security. The changes included requiring every computer user to change passwords every 35 days (or sooner). In addition Shell's information systems groups were ordered to make similar changes in hundreds of servers and networks. The corporate-wide mandate stated that the changes must be completed by the end of June 2000. The project, named Trust Domain, was important to Royal Dutch's ability to protect itself.

Shell Information Technology International (SITI), the company's IT services division, understood that these changes affected SITI because it meant not only ongoing password updating, but it also meant changing procedures for writing all computer code. In addition, it required making certain every desktop computer had a screen saver operating and it required changing procedures for employees who dial into SITI's computers so that the systems are secured. SITI was responsible for its 2,300 employees adhering to the new security requirements. Janet Jones, a SITI project manager, was assigned the task of managing SITI's change project.

SITI's management had learned from earlier systems projects that even managing relatively minor changes could be difficult. Jones knew that to be successful, any project had to face its organizational impact. She decided the project required a change agent, someone to be responsible for the "people" side of Trust Domain. She first brought in Christy Dillard, who was a change agent specialist Jones had worked with in an earlier project. Dillard then brought on board Anita Bettis, another experienced change agent. Dillard knew her own and Bettis's job focused on listening to the morale and reactions of the persons affected by the project while Jones would maintain responsibility for the technical and project management side. Dillard characterized her and Bettis's task this way: "Lots of people just stick their change agent in an office

and leave them there. But you have to embed yourself into the project and the team."

Bettis, Dillard, and Jones analyzed the situation and drew up a document that analyzed the impact of the change based on each employee's job. The document became a foundation for their communications plan and was used when making decisions or attending meetings. Dillard and Jones met every day so that both sides of the project (managing people and managing everything else) were both well informed on the project's progress and could air and solve their differences. They held weekly meetings with a group manager, while the change team met often with focus groups to stay in touch with employee reactions and problems. At weekly department meetings, they held project discussions, giving employees an opportunity to raise questions and objections. The team also identified unofficial leaders at these meetings (those who spoke out the most and had the most impact) so the project could involve them in helping make the changes actually happen. The project did bump into opposition from those who felt the changes were too little and/or too late and those who believed the project would fail. The change team listened to these complaints and tried to respectfully handle them.

When July 1 arrived, SITI passed an independent audit of the new security measures. However, most departments were ill prepared, and so the deadline was moved to October 1. Jones commented on SITI's success, saying "Planning a change is like a three-legged stool." The three legs, she explained, "are technology, process, and people." Her stated position was that a project must "have all three."

To Think About: Why do you think SITI management focused so strongly on the morale of its staff and their criticism of the apparently easy project? Is it important for any IT project? Explain.

Source: Simone Kaplan, "Quick Change Artists," CIO Magazine, March 15, 2002 and www.shell.com, accessed December 31, 2002.

MANAGEMENT

will change when the new system is installed, including installation of intranets, extranets, and Internet applications. In addition to procedural changes, transformations in job functions, organizational structure, power relationships, and behavior will all have to be carefully planned. When technology-induced changes produce unforeseen consequences, the organization can benefit by improvising to take advantage of new opportunities. Information systems specialists, managers, and users should remain open-minded about their roles in the change management process and not adhere to rigid, narrow perceptions (Orlikowski and Hofman, 1997; Markus and Benjamin, 1997). Table 13-4 lists the organizational dimensions that would need to be addressed for planning and implementing many systems.

Although systems analysis and design activities are supposed to include an organizational impact analysis, this area has traditionally been neglected. An **organizational impact analysis** explains how a proposed system will affect organizational structure, attitudes, decision making, and operations. To integrate information systems successfully with the organization, thorough and fully documented organizational impact assessments must be given more attention in the development effort.

organizational impact analysis

Study of the way a proposed system will affect organizational structure, attitudes, decision making, and operations.

TABLE 13-4	ORGANIZATIONAL FACTORS IN SYSTEMS PLANNING AND IMPLEMENTATION

Employee participation and involvement

Job design

Standards and performance monitoring

Ergonomics (including equipment, user interfaces, and the work environment)

Employee grievance resolution procedures

Health and safety

Government regulatory compliance

Allowing for the Human Factor

The quality of information systems should be evaluated in terms of user criteria rather than the criteria of the information systems staff. In addition to targets such as memory size, access rates, and calculation times, systems objectives should include standards for user performance. For example, an objective might be that data entry clerks learn the procedures and codes for four new online data entry screens in a half-day training session.

ergonomics

The interaction of people and machines in the work environment, including the design of jobs, health issues, and the end-user interface of information systems.

Areas where users interface with the system should be carefully designed, with sensitivity to ergonomic issues. **Ergonomics** refers to the interaction of people and machines in the work environment. It considers the design of jobs, health issues, and the end-user interface of information systems. The impact of the application system on the work environment and job dimensions must be carefully assessed.

Sociotechnical Design

Most contemporary systems-building approaches tend to treat end users as essential to the systems-building process but playing a largely passive role relative to other forces shaping the system, such as the specialist system designers and management. A different tradition rooted in the European social democratic labor movement assigns users a more active role, one that empowers them to codetermine the role of information systems in their workplace (Clement and Van den Besselaar, 1993).

sociotechnical design

Design to produce information systems that blend technical efficiency with sensitivity to organizational and human needs.

This tradition of participatory design emphasizes participation by the individuals most affected by the new system. It is closely associated with the concept of sociotechnical design. A **sociotechnical design** plan establishes human objectives for the system that lead to increased job satisfaction. Designers set forth separate sets of technical and social design solutions. The social design plans explore different work group structures, allocation of tasks, and the design of individual jobs. The proposed technical solutions are compared with the proposed social solutions. Social and technical solutions that can be combined are proposed as sociotechnical solutions. The alternative that best meets both social and technical objectives is selected for the final design. The resulting sociotechnical design is expected to produce an information system that blends technical efficiency with sensitivity to organizational and human needs, leading to high job satisfaction (Mumford and Weir, 1979). Systems with compatible technical and organizational elements are expected to raise productivity without sacrificing human and social goals.

"FOURTH-GENERATION" PROJECT MANAGEMENT

Traditional techniques for managing projects deal with problems of size and complexity by breaking large projects into subprojects; assigning teams, schedules, and milestones to each; and focusing primarily on project mechanics rather than business results. These techniques are inadequate for enterprise systems and other large-scale system projects with extremely complex problems of organizational coordination and change management, complex and sometimes unfamiliar technology, and continually changing business requirements. A new "fourth-generation" of project management techniques is emerging to address these challenges.

In this model, project planning assumes an enterprise-wide focus, driven by the firm's strategic business vision and technology architecture. Project and subproject managers focus on solving problems and meeting challenges as they arise rather than simply meeting formal project milestones. They emphasize learning as well as planning, seeking ways to adapt to

MAKE IT YOUR BUSINESS

FINANCE AND ACCOUNTING

A series of financial models are used to justify capital investments in new information systems. The finance and accounting function is responsible for supervising the financial analysis of information systems investments and for providing information on corporate cash flows used in capital budgeting calculations. You can find examples of finance and accounting applications on pages 428 and 442–443.

HUMAN RESOURCES

The human resources function can play a valuable role in system implementation by helping with change management. When a new system is proposed, human resources staff can assist with the organizational impact analysis and locate new positions for employees whose jobs would be eliminated. Human resources could also arrange for employee training in the new system. You can find examples of human resources applications on pages 414–415 and 437.

MANUFACTURING AND PRODUCTION

Supply chain management system and enterprise resource planning systems can provide significant tangible benefits such as reductions in inventory costs and intangible benefits such as faster response to customer demands. However both types of systems are among the most difficult systems to implement successfully because they require major business process changes as well as new technology.

SALES AND MARKETING

Customer relationship management systems can provide tangible benefits such as reduced direct marketing costs and intangible benefits such as better customer service and support. These systems can be difficult to implement because they may require integrating customer information from multiple sources and changes to the firm's business processes for interacting with customers and gathering customer data. User interface design is especially important for customer-facing Web applications. You can find examples of sales and marketing applications on page 428.

unforeseen uncertainties and chaos that, if properly handled, could provide additional opportunities and benefits (DeMeyer, Loch, and Pich, 2002). It may be useful for organizations to establish a separate program office to manage subprojects, coordinate the entire project effort with other ongoing projects, and coordinate the project with ongoing changes in the firm's business strategy, information technology architecture and infrastructure, and business processes (The Concours Group, 2000).

MANAGEMENT WRAP-UP

Managers must link systems development to the organization's strategy and identify precisely which systems should be changed to achieve large-scale benefits for the organization as a whole. Two principal reasons for system failure are inadequate management support and poor management of the implementation process. Managers should fully understand the level of complexity and risk in new systems projects as well as their potential business value.

Building an information system is a process of planned organizational change. Many levels of organizational change are possible. Global systems, enterprise systems, supply chain and customer relationship management systems, and business process reengineering projects are high-risk implementations because they require far-reaching organizational changes that are often resisted by members of the organization. Eliciting user support and maintaining an appropriate level of user involvement at all stages of system building are essential.

Selecting the right technology for a system solution that fits the problem's constraints and the organization's information technology infrastructure is a key business decision. Systems sometimes fail because the technology is too complex or sophisticated to be easily implemented or because system builders lack the requisite skills or experience to work with it. Managers and systems builders should be fully aware of the risks and rewards of various technologies as they make their technology selections.

For Discussion

1. It has been said that when we design an information system we are redesigning the organization. What are the ramifications of this statement?

2. It has been said that most systems fail because system builders ignore organizational behavior problems. Why?

SUMMARY

1. *How can our company measure the business benefits of our information systems? What models should be used to measure that business value?* There are many different ways in which information systems can provide business value for a firm, including increased profitability and productivity. Some, but not all of these business benefits can be quantified and measured.

Capital budgeting models are used to determine whether an investment in information technology produces sufficient returns to justify its costs. The principal capital budgeting models are the payback method, accounting rate of return on investment (ROI), cost–benefit ratio, net present value, profitability index, and internal rate of return (IRR).

Other models for evaluating information system investments involve nonfinancial and strategic considerations. Portfolio analysis and scoring models can be used to evaluate alternative information systems projects. Real options pricing models, which apply the same techniques for valuing financial options to systems investments, can be useful when considering highly uncertain IT investments.

Although information technology has increased productivity in manufacturing, especially the manufacture of information technology products, the extent to which computers have enhanced the productivity of the service sector remains under debate. In addition to reducing costs, computers may increase the quality of products and services for consumers or may create entirely new products and revenue streams. These intangible benefits are difficult to measure and consequently are not addressed by conventional productivity measures.

2. *Why do so many system projects fail? What are the principal reasons for system failures?* A very large percentage of information systems fail to deliver benefits or solve the problems for which they were intended because the process of organizational change surrounding system-building was not properly addressed. The principal causes of information system failure are (1) insufficient or improper user participation in the systems development process, (2) lack of management support, (3) high levels of complexity and risk in the systems development process, and (4) poor management of the implementation process. There is a very high failure rate among business process reengineering and enterprise system projects because they require extensive organizational change. Customer relationship manage-

ment and supply chain management system projects as well as system changes resulting from mergers and acquisitions are also difficult to implement successfully because they usually require fundamental changes to business processes.

3. *How should the organizational change surrounding a new system be managed to ensure success?* Building an information system is a process of planned organizational change that must be carefully managed. The term implementation refers to the entire process of organizational change surrounding the introduction of a new information system. One can better understand system success and failure by examining different patterns of implementation. Especially important is the relationship between participants in the implementation process, notably the interactions between system designers and users. Conflicts between the technical orientation of system designers and the business orientation of end users must be resolved. The success of organizational change can be determined by how well information systems specialists, end users, and decision makers deal with key issues at various stages in implementation.

4. *What strategies can our organization use to manage the system implementation process more effectively?* Management support and control of the implementation process are essential, as are mechanisms for dealing with the level of risk in each new systems project. Some companies experience organizational resistance to change. Project risk factors can be brought under some control by a contingency approach to project management. The level of risk in a systems development project is determined by three key dimensions: (1) project size, (2) project structure, and (3) experience with technology. The risk level of each project will determine the appropriate mix of external integration tools, internal integration tools, formal planning tools, and formal control tools to be applied.

Appropriate strategies can be applied to ensure the correct level of user participation in the systems development process and to minimize user resistance. Information system design and the entire implementation process should be managed as planned organizational change. Participatory design emphasizes the participation of the individuals most affected by a new system. Sociotechnical design aims for an optimal blend of social and technical design solutions.

KEY TERMS

Accounting rate of return on investment (ROI), 421

Capital budgeting, 417

Change agent, 429

Cost–benefit ratio, 422

Counterimplementation, 435

Ergonomics, 438

External integration tools, 435

Formal control tools, 434

Formal planning tools, 434

Implementation, 429

Intangible benefits, 418

Internal integration tools, 434

Internal rate of return (IRR), 422

Man-month, 432

Net present value, 422

Organizational impact analysis, 437

Payback method, 420

Portfolio analysis, 423

REVIEW QUESTIONS

1. Name and describe the principal capital budgeting methods used to evaluate information system projects.

2. What are the limitations of financial models for establishing the value of information systems?

3. Describe how portfolio analysis and scoring models can be used to establish the worth of systems.

4. How can real options pricing models be used to help evaluate information technology investments?

5. Have information systems enhanced productivity in businesses? Explain your answer.

6. Why do builders of new information systems need to address change management?

7. What kinds of problems provide evidence of information system failure?

8. Why is it necessary to understand the concept of implementation when managing the organizational change surrounding a new information system?

9. What are the major causes of implementation success or failure?

10. What is the user–designer communications gap? What kinds of implementation problems can it create?

11. Why is there such a high failure rate among enterprise resource planning (ERP) and business process reengineering (BPR) projects? Why are customer relationship management and supply chain management systems often difficult to implement?

12. What role do information systems play in the success or failure of mergers and acquisitions?

13. What dimensions influence the level of risk in each systems development project?

14. What project management techniques can be used to control project risk?

15. What strategies can be used to overcome user resistance to systems development projects?

16. What organizational considerations should be addressed by information system design?

APPLICATION SOFTWARE EXERCISE:

SPREADSHEET EXERCISE: CAPITAL BUDGETING FOR A NEW CAD SYSTEM

Your company would like to invest in a new computer-aided-design (CAD) system, requiring purchases of hardware, software, and networking technology as well as expenditures for installation, training, and support. The Laudon Web site for Chapter 13 contains tables showing each cost component for the new system as well as annual maintenance costs over a five-year period. You believe the new system will produce annual savings by reducing the amount of labor required to generate designs and design specifications and thus increase your firm's annual cash flow. Using the data provided and instructions on the Laudon Web site for Chapter 13, create a worksheet that calculates the costs and benefits of the investment over a five-year period and analyzes the investment using the six capital budgeting models presented in this chapter. Is this investment worthwhile? Why or why not?

GROUP PROJECT

Form a group with two or three other students. Write a description of the implementation problems you might expect to encounter for the information system you designed for the business process redesign project that follows Chapter 15. Write an analysis of the steps you would take to solve or prevent these problems. Alternatively, you could describe the implementation problems that might be expected for one of the systems described in the Window on boxes or chapter ending cases in this text. If possible, use electronic presentation software to present your findings to the class.

TOOLS FOR INTERACTIVE LEARNING

■ INTERNET CONNECTION

The Internet Connection for this chapter will direct you to a series of Web sites where you can complete an exercise to evaluate user interfaces and user–system interactions.

■ INTERACTIVE STUDY GUIDE

You can use the Interactive Study Guide to test your knowledge of the topics in this chapter and get instant feedback when you need more practice.

■ RUNNING CASE

The Running Case provides an opportunity for you to complete your analysis of the proposed new system for Dirt Bikes USA by analyzing its costs, benefits, and potential implementation problems. You can find a complete description of this project on the Laudon Web site for Chapter 13 and on the Multimedia Edition CD-ROM.

■ ELECTRONIC COMMERCE PROJECT

At the Laudon Web site for Chapter 13, you can find an Electronic Commerce project for buying and financing a home purchase.

■ MANAGEMENT DECISION PROBLEM

At the Laudon Web site for Chapter 13, you can find a Management Decision Problem on evaluating ERP Systems using a scoring model.

■ CD-ROM

If you use the Multimedia Edition CD-ROM with this chapter, you can find a video clip illustrating Manugistics' services for integrating supply chain management, enterprise, and customer relationship management systems, an audio overview of the major themes of this chapter and bullet text summarizing the key points of the chapter.

CASE STUDY—*The U.S. State Department Tries to Upgrade Its IT Infrastructure*

The purpose of modernizing an outdated information systems infrastructure is so that the organization and its plans to achieve its strategic goals will benefit. The same is true whether it is a corporation, a nonprofit organization, or a government. Movement toward modernizing the United States State Department's obsolete information technology infrastructure has been the department's goal for several years, and it has gained a higher priority since the September 11th terrorist attacks. Let us first take a look at the purpose and problems of the existing State Department's system at the end of 2001.

The State Department, with 260 posts overseas, mainly concentrates on relations with foreign governments and foreign trade and only secondarily on people issues such as protection of American citizens abroad or immigration to the United States. In issues of foreign relations and trade, confidentiality and secrecy are vital. "Fundamentally, security and communication is what the department is all about," explained Gartner electronic government analyst Christopher Baum. Also, in this information age, speed is crucial. However, the system has not only been described as obsolete, but even as "dangerously inadequate," jeopardizing the strategic missions of the United States. The problem is the department's outmoded technology infrastructure. Let us just list some basic problems:

■ Classified telecommunications systems are vital and yet 40 percent of the department's overseas posts have no system at all.

■ Another 28 percent (50 posts) have systems that are so old they are outdated Banyan products that Banyan no longer sells or supports.

■ A cable system that annually carries over 28 million electronic correspondence worldwide in the form of telegrams was installed during World War I.

■ Only some computers have Internet connections, and they must share their computers for secret communication.

■ The communications system that connects the various embassies to the department's headquarters in Washington is overloaded and often down.

■ All embassy e-mails go through Washington, even if the sender and the recipient are in the same overseas building only a few feet apart.

■ E-mail access at some posts abroad is so intermittent that foreign governments and citizens in the country find it easier to contact Washington directly rather than the local embassy.

■ E-mail is often so difficult to use that users avoid it and telephone Washington instead, even when the information is confidential or top secret and telephone communication is not as secure.

■ The e-mail system is so difficult to use that "Even when you just want to send an e-mail, you have to punch all these buttons. If you press the wrong one, you lose the whole thing," explains Frank Urbancic, U.S. consul general in Istanbul, Turkey.

■ The existing e-mail system has no way to adequately mark messages as delivered and received.

In 1998, following the two embassy bombings in Africa, a congressional committee that studied the bombings concluded that the State Department's communications were too inefficient to meet the growing terrorist threat. A modernization project began soon thereafter, although "The State Department is held in very low esteem by almost everyone in [Washington]," according to James Lindsay, a Brookings Institution scholar in Washington. Frank Carlucci, who had been a foreign service officer for 24 years before becoming secretary of defense and then national security advisor under President Reagan, believed "The Department of State has never been oriented towards information technology."

Only minimal progress had been made by early 2001 when Colin Powell became Secretary of State under the then new George W. Bush administration. Powell began to push for modernization with three technology priorities:

1. Internet access on every desk,

2. A classified connectivity program for stations abroad,

3. An information sharing system for 40 governmental agencies that operate overseas.

Even with Powell there, Fernando Burbano, the State Department CIO since 1998, said "We're trying to accelerate [the modernization], but once it's accelerated there's only so much you can do." However after the September 11th terrorist attacks, the atmosphere did change, and when the 2002 budget was passed and signed in late November 2001, allocation for the State Department included $217 million for IT modernization. Even then questions existed and observers wondered if even funds allocated in the budget can make a difference given the department's notorious reputation as bureaucratic.

Burbano knew the modernization had to be more than just installing new modern technology. He wanted the department's staff to not only be able to e-mail quickly and easily and with security, but he also wanted them to have electronic access to department action plans for all types of problems such as terrorist attacks, floods, riots, and anything else.

For the first of the three key priorities, Powell said he not only wants Internet access on every employee's desktop, but he also wants to add a secure Internet connection to 30,000 unclassified desktop computers. The 2002 budget for this part of the project is $110 million, and the pilot project was completed in April 2001. Burbano said secure access should be completed within 18 months or late 2002.

The second key project is to establish and maintain secure networks in 170 countries. This project will install access to a classified (confidential) network including e-mail in every post in the world. The goal includes a user-friendly interface of the type common in modern corporations. Burbano has said it will also include a classified intranet so that State and Defense Departments' employees will be able to communicate in a secure and efficient manner. Burbano says the project will cost about $200 million, of which $107 million is in the 2002 budget. Burbano says this project is scheduled to be completed in 2004, but he believes it can be finished in 2003. The project is beginning by replacing the outdated Banyan LANs.

The third project was actually mandated by the congressional report issued after the 1998 terrorist attacks at two African embassies. It was titled Foreign Affairs Systems Integration (FASI) and was directed to establish a collaboration system for the agencies abroad and certain nongovernmental organizations. It is to establish an electronic workplace and would allow direct exchange of e-mails for those connected to FASI. Burbano met twice in October 2001 with the office of Tom Ridge, the Homeland Security Director. The reason for the meeting was to see if he (Burbano) could build FASI in a way that would be a model for the information-sharing system Ridge needs to build for his anti-terrorist work. Burbano is planning to prototype it in Washington, D.C., and at the consulates in Mexico City and New Delhi, India, by September 2002, using the budgeted $17

million. Assuming the pilot is successful, other non–State Department agencies will pay their own costs to be part of FASI.

The question is, how successful will the State Department infrastructure project be? There are significant cultural and political hurdles to clear. Suspicions linger that the real source of the State Department's problems is its rigid bureaucracy and mismanagement, not technology. For all three projects, Burbano must establish a team of American contractors who can both pass the security requirements of the State Department and be willing to go overseas for an extended period of time to install the systems and then train the users. Another problem Burbano faces is federal agencies' well-known resistance to change. According to Craig Luigart, CIO at the U.S. Department of Education, "Developing e-government projects alone will not be sufficient to change the future look and feel of government, because at the core is people's resistance to change." Carlucci remembers the resistance he received when, in the 1950s, he was asked to correct a computer printout. He responded by asking, "Wouldn't it be easier to make sure the data going into the computer was accurate in the first place?" He then said, "I was castigated."

Sources: Sarah D. Scalet, "A Sorry State," *CIO Magazine*, January 15, 2002; and Eric Chabrow, "The Buck Stops Here," *InformationWeek*, April 15, 2002.

CASE STUDY QUESTIONS:

1. Describe the State Department's IT infrastructure. What problems ware caused by out-of-date technology?

2. What were the changes Powell and Burbano wanted to make? Explain why?

3. Summarize the problems that Powell and Burbano faced when they tried to overhaul the State Department's information systems.

4. How successful do you think the State Department's modernization effort will be? Explain your answer. What value could the new infrastructure provide? What management, organization, and technology issues does the State Department have to address?

REDESIGNING BUSINESS PROCESSES FOR HEALTHLITE YOGURT COMPANY

Healthlite Yogurt Company, a U.S. market leader in yogurt and related health products, is experiencing sharp growing pains. Healthlite's sales have tripled over the past five years. However, new local competitors, offering fast delivery from local production centers and lower prices, are challenging Healthlite for retail shelf space with a bevy of new products. Healthlite needs to justify its share of shelf space to grocers and is seeking additional shelf space for its new yogurt-based products such as frozen desserts and low-fat salad dressings. Yogurt has a very short shelf life measured in days, and must be moved very quickly.

Healthlite's corporate headquarters is in Danbury, Connecticut. Corporate headquarters has a central mainframe computer that maintains most of the major business databases. All production takes place in processing plants that are located in New Jersey, Massachusetts, Tennessee, Illinois, Colorado, Washington, and California. Each processing plant has its own minicomputer, which is connected to the corporate mainframe. Customer credit verification is maintained at corporate headquarters, where customer master files are maintained and order verification or rejection is determined. Once processed centrally, order data are then fed to the appropriate local processing plant minicomputer.

Healthlite has 20 sales regions, each with approximately 30 sales representatives and a regional sales manager. Healthlite has a 12-person marketing group at corporate headquarters. Each salesperson is able to store and retrieve data for assigned customer accounts using a terminal in the regional office linked to the corporate mainframe. Reports for individual salespeople (printouts of orders, rejection notices, customer account inquiries, etc.) and for sales offices are printed in the regional offices and mailed to them.

Sometimes, the only way to obtain up-to-date sales data is for managers to make telephone calls to subordinates and then piece the information together. Data about sales and advertising expenses, promotional campaigns, and customer shelf space devoted to Healthlite products are maintained manually at the regional offices. The central computer contains only consolidated, company-wide files for customer account data and order and billing data.

The existing order processing system requires sales representatives to write up hard-copy tickets to place orders through the mail or by fax. Each ticket lists the amount and kind of product ordered by the customer account. Approximately 20 workers at Healthlite corporate headquarters open, sort, and enter 500,000 order tickets per week into the system. Frequently orders are delayed when the fax machines break down. This order information is transmitted every evening from the mainframe to a minicomputer at each of Healthlite's processing sites. This daily order specifies the total yogurt and yogurt product demand for each processing center. The processing center then produces the amount and type of yogurt and yogurt-related products ordered and ships the orders out. Shipping managers at the processing centers assign the shipments to various transportation carriers, who deliver the product to receiving warehouses located in the regions.

A year ago, growth in new products and sales had reached a point where the firm was choking on paper. For each order, a salesperson filled out at least two forms per account. Some sales representatives have more than 80 customers. As it became bogged down in paper, Healthlite saw increased delays in the processing of its orders. Since yogurt is a fresh food product, it could not be held long in inventory. Yet Healthlite had trouble shipping the right goods to the right places in time. It was taking between 4 and 14 days to process and ship out an order, depending on mail delivery rates. Healthlite also found accounting discrepancies of $1.5 million annually between the sales force and headquarters.

Communication between sales managers and sales representatives has been primarily through the mail or by telephone. For example, regional sales managers have to send representatives letters with announcements of promotional campaigns or pricing discounts. Sales representatives have to write up their monthly reports of sales calls and then mail this information to regional headquarters.

Healthlite is considering new information system solutions. First of all, the firm would like to solve the current order entry crisis and develop immediately a new order processing system. Management would also like to make better use of information systems to support sales and marketing activities and to take advantage of new Web-based information technologies. In particular, management wants a sales-oriented Web site to help market the products but is unsure how this will fit into the sales effort. In conjunction, management wants to know how these new technologies can assist the local groceries and large chains who sell the product to the actual consumer.

Senior management is looking for a modest reduction in employee head count as new, more effective systems come online to help pay for the investment in new systems. While senior management wants the company to deploy contemporary systems, they do not want to experiment with new technologies and are only comfortable using technology that has proven itself in real-world applications.

SALES AND MARKETING INFORMATION SYSTEMS: BACKGROUND

Sales orders must be processed and related to production and inventory. Sales of products in existing markets must be monitored and new products must be developed for new markets. Firms need sales and marketing information in order to do product planning, make pricing decisions, devise advertising and other promotional campaigns, and forecast market potential for new and existing products. They must also monitor the efficiency of the distribution of their products and services. The sales function of a typical business captures and processes customer orders and produces invoices for customers and data for inventory and production. A typical invoice is illustrated here:

Healthlite Yogurt Inc.

Customer:

Highview Supermarket
223 Highland Avenue
Ossining, New York 10562

Order Number: **679940**
Customer Number: **#00395**
Date: **02/15/03**

Quantity	SKU#	Description	Unit Price	Amount
100	V3392	8 oz Vanilla	.44	44.00
50	S4456	8 oz Strawberry	.44	22.00
65	L4492	8 oz Lemon	.44	28.60
Shipping:				*10.00*
Total Invoice:				*$104.60*

Data from order entry are also used by a firm's accounts receivable system and by the firm's inventory and production systems. The production planning system, for instance, builds its daily production plans based on the prior day's sales. The number and type of product sold will determine how many units to produce and when.

Sales managers need information to plan and monitor the performance of the sales force. Management also needs information on the performance of specific products, product lines, or brands. Price, revenue, cost, and growth information can be used for pricing decisions, for evaluating the performance of current products, and for predicting the performance of future products.

From basic sales and invoice data, a firm can produce a variety of reports with valuable information to guide sales and marketing work. For weekly, monthly, or annual time periods, information

can be gathered on which outlets order the most, on what the average order amount is, on which products move slowest and fastest, on which salespersons sell the most and least, on which geographic areas purchase the most of a given product, and on how current sales of a product compare to last year's product.

THE ASSIGNMENT

Either alone, or with a group of three or four of your classmates, develop a proposal for redesigning Healthlite's business processes for sales, marketing, and order processing that would make the company more competitive. Your report should include the following:

- An overview of the organization—its structure, products, and major business processes for sales, marketing, and order processing.

- An analysis of Healthlite's problems: What are Healthlite's problems? How are these problems related to existing business processes and systems? What management, organization, and technology factors contributed to these problems?

- An overall management plan for improving Healthlite's business and system situation. This would include a list of objectives, a timeframe, major milestones, and an assessment of the costs and benefits of implementing this plan.

- Identification of the major changes in business processes required to achieve your plan.

- Identification of the major new technology components of your plan that are required to support the new business processes. If your solution requires a new system or set of systems, describe the functions of these systems, what pieces of information these systems should contain, and how this information should be captured, organized, and stored.

- A sample data entry screen or report for one of the new systems, if proposed.

- A description of the steps you would take as a manager to handle the conversion from the old system to the new.

- Quality assurance measures.

Your report should also describe the organizational impact of your solution. Consider human interface issues, the impact on jobs and interest groups, and any risks associated with implementing your solution. How will you implement your solution to take these issues into account?

It is important to establish the scope of the system project. It should be limited to order processing and related sales and marketing business processes. You do not have to redesign Healthlite's manufacturing, accounts receivable, distribution, or inventory control systems for this exercise.

PART V

MANAGING INFORMATION SYSTEMS IN THE DIGITAL FIRM

14

INFORMATION SYSTEMS SECURITY AND CONTROL

objectives

As a manager, you'll want to ensure that your firm's systems are reliable and secure. After completing this chapter, you will be able to answer the following questions:

1. *Why are information systems so vulnerable to destruction, error, abuse, and system quality problems?*

2. *What types of controls are available for information systems?*

3. *What special measures must be taken to ensure the reliability, availability, and security of electronic commerce and digital business processes?*

4. *What are the most important software quality assurance techniques?*

5. *Why are auditing information systems and safeguarding data quality so important?*

The World Trade Center Disaster: Who Was Prepared?

On the morning of September 11th, 2001, two airplanes commandeered by terrorists crashed into the World Trade Center (WTC) and a third crashed into the Pentagon, taking 3,000 lives. All WTC offices were destroyed, and some nearby buildings were badly damaged and immediately evacuated. Phones lines along the east coast of the United States were jammed, making it difficult to make and receive telephone calls. Clients of telecommunications providers, such as AT&T and Verizon, with computers and switching centers in or nearby the World Trade Center lost service altogether. Lufthansa Airlines lost telephone service for its passenger sales office in midtown Manhattan and its cargo sales office at Kennedy Airport because it had used AT&T as its primary communications provider and Verizon as the backup. Panicky customers were stalled with busy signals for three days. Lufthansa found another provider to restore phone service within a week and it is making sure that its primary and backup systems are routed from separate locations in the city.

Merrill Lynch had over 9,000 employees working at the World Trade Center and the World Financial Center nearby. Most were unharmed and were successfully relocated to other places of work. Merrill was able to resume its business

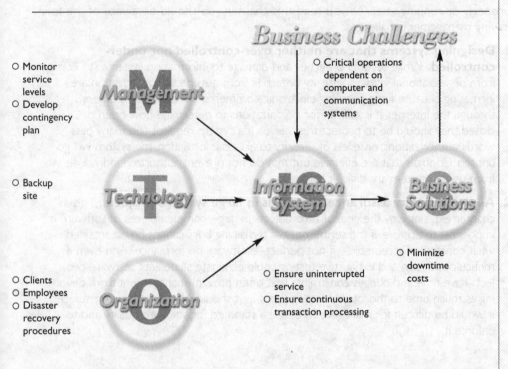

later in the day. The firm did not suffer as much as others because it had redundant telecommunications capabilities and a rock-solid disaster recovery plan.

Merrill had carried out an extensive rehearsal of this plan four months earlier, so everyone was prepared on September 11. The plan established priorities for business activities so the company knew which to revive first in the event they were disrupted. Then it "qualified" all its critical system applications and made sure the technology for restoring those applications was available in the event of a disaster. The plan included procedures for ascertaining the whereabouts of all employees, for collecting information about the damage to the firm's facilities and technology, and for selecting an appropriate response strategy. Predesignated logistics team members had assigned responsibilities for transportation, accomodations, and food. The contingency plan was designed to handle an eight-week absence from Merrill's main facilities.

Within minutes of the World Trade Center attack, Merrill's command center was operational at one of the company's other Manhattan locations. At this new backup site, the firm was able to figure out each transaction's position when business stopped on September 11. Although the equity markets were closed, Merrill's operations staff was able to settle trades that same evening.

Sources: Juliana Gruenwald, "Communications that Won't Quit," *Fortune/CNET Tech Review*, Winter 2002; John Pallatto, "Contingency Planning," *Internet World*, May 2002; Anthony Guerra, "Recent Run-Through Helps Merrill Deal with Disaster," *Wall Street and Technology*, November 2001; Dennis K. Berman and Calmetta Coleman, "Companies Test System-Backup Plans as They Struggle to Recover Lost Data," *Wall Street Journal*, September 13, 2001.

MANAGEMENT CHALLENGES

The experiences of Lufthansa Airlines and Merrill Lynch during the World Trade Center disaster illustrate the need for organizations to take special measures to protect their information systems and ensure their continued operation. Communication disruptions, use by unauthorized people, software failures, hardware failures, natural disasters, employee errors—and terrorist attacks— can prevent information systems from running properly or running at all. As you read this chapter, you should be aware of the following management challenges.

1. **Designing systems that are neither over-controlled nor under-controlled.** While security breaches and damage to information systems still come from organizational insiders, security breaches from outside the organization are increasing because firms pursuing electronic commerce are open to outsiders through the Internet. It is difficult for organizations to determine how open or closed they should be to protect themselves. If a system requires too many passwords, authorizations, or levels of security to access information, the system will go unused. Controls that are effective but that do not prevent authorized individuals from using a system are difficult to design.

2. **Applying quality assurance standards in large systems projects.** This chapter explains why the goal of zero defects in large, complex pieces of software is impossible to achieve. If the seriousness of remaining bugs cannot be ascertained, what constitutes acceptable—if not perfect—software performance? And even if meticulous design and exhaustive testing could eliminate all defects, software projects have time and budget constraints that often prevent management from devoting as much time to thoroughly testing them as it should. Under such circumstances it would be difficult for managers to define a standard for software quality and to enforce it.

Computer systems play such a critical role in business, government, and daily life that organizations must take special steps to protect their information systems and to ensure that they are accurate, reliable, and secure. This chapter describes how information systems can be controlled and made secure so that they serve the purposes for which they are intended.

14.1 SYSTEM VULNERABILITY AND ABUSE

Before computer automation, data about individuals or organizations were maintained and secured as paper records dispersed in separate business or organizational units. Information systems concentrate data in computer files that have the potential to be accessed by large numbers of people and by groups outside of the organization. Consequently, automated data are more susceptible to destruction, fraud, error, and misuse.

When computer systems fail to run or work as required, firms that depend heavily on computers experience a serious loss of business function. The longer computer systems are down, the more serious the consequences for the firm. Firms which need Web sites continuously available online for electronic commerce stand to lose millions of dollars for every business day that the sites are not working. For example, a business might lose over $10,000 for every minute of downtime for its e-commerce or supply chain management applications (The Standish Group, 2001). Some firms relying on computers to process their critical business transactions might experience a total loss of business function if they lose computer capability for more than a few days.

WHY SYSTEMS ARE VULNERABLE

When large amounts of data are stored in electronic form they are vulnerable to many more kinds of threats than when they exist in manual form. Table 14-1 lists the most common

TABLE 14-1	THREATS TO COMPUTERIZED INFORMATION SYSTEMS

Hardware failure	Fire
Software failure	Electrical problems
Personnel actions	User errors
Terminal access penetration	Program changes
Theft of data, services, equipment	Telecommunication problems

threats against computerized information systems. They can stem from technical, organizational, and environmental factors compounded by poor management decisions.

Advances in telecommunications and computer software have magnified these vulnerabilities. Through telecommunications networks, information systems in different locations can be interconnected. The potential for unauthorized access, abuse, or fraud is not limited to a single location but can occur at any access point in the network.

Additionally, more complex and diverse hardware, software, organizational, and personnel arrangements are required for telecommunications networks, creating new areas and opportunities for penetration and manipulation. Wireless networks using radio-based technology are even more vulnerable to penetration because radio frequency bands are easy to scan. LANs that use the 802.11b (Wi-Fi) standard can be easily penetrated by outsiders armed with laptops, wireless cards, external antennae, and freeware hacking software. Hackers can use these tools to detect unprotected Wi-Fi networks, monitor their traffic, and in some cases, use them to gain access to the Internet or to corporate networks. Although the range of Wi-Fi networks is only several hundred feet, it can be extended up to one-fourth mile by using external antennae. The Internet poses special problems because it was explicitly designed to be accessed easily by people on different computer systems. The vulnerabilities of telecommunications networks are illustrated in Figure 14-1.

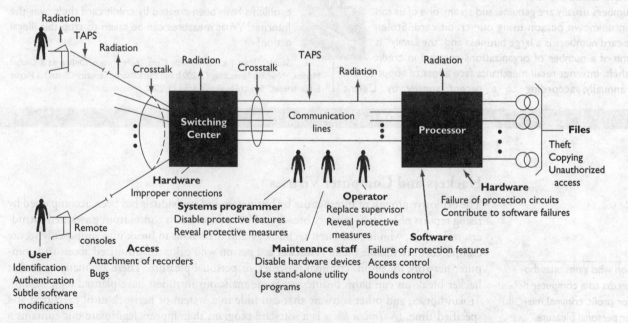

Figure 14-1 Telecommunications network vulnerabilities. Telecommunications networks are highly vulnerable to natural failure of hardware and software and to misuse by programmers, computer operators, maintenance staff, and end users. It is possible to tap communications lines and illegally intercept data. High-speed transmission over twisted wire communications channels causes interference called crosstalk. Radiation can disrupt a network at various points as well.

What Can Be Done About Internet Credit Card Theft?

Window on Organizations — MIS In Action

The former Soviet Union has spawned a number of organizations that are profiting from e-commerce. One such organization, headquartered in Odessa, Ukraine, calls itself "the family." It is a global company, buying and selling its products through both Web sites and e-mail, with payment through such online sites as <www.WebMoney.ru> ("ru" indicates Russia). While its product prices fluctuate, negotiations take place through e-mail. Management is keeping its information and its transactions secret, mainly by constantly switching its sites and e-mail addresses. It customers are global, although most of them are in the former Soviet Union, Eastern Europe, and Asia (primarily Malaysia). The organization is known for rapid, quality service, and it even advertises its products using online banners. Because its products are digital, they are delivered over the Internet. What is different about this company is that it sells stolen credit card numbers. The numbers are purchased from suppliers who are hackers capable of obtaining them by breaking in to the computer systems of online merchants.

The problem for the customers of "the family" is that the credit card numbers must be genuine because they are sold to people who will use them to steal products or funds. The seller of the numbers apparently has no way to prove that the numbers it sells are genuine. It is solely based on the seller's reputation, "The family" must rely on its customers' successful use of the numbers. The problem for the rest of us is that the numbers usually are genuine, and so any one of us can find an unknown person using our credit card. Stolen credit card numbers is a large business and "the family" is but one of a number of organizations engaged in credit card theft. Internet retail merchants face a loss of about $1 billion annually, according to a recent survey by Celent

Communications, a market research firm. Moreover, online sales using fraudulent credit cards have reached 0.25 percent of total sales using Visa and MasterCard credit cards, whereas offline the percentage is only 0.09 percent. The difference is enormous, with fraudulent online sales topping $2 billion annually versus $800 million off-line. Richard Power, editorial director of the Computer Security Institute, an association of computer security professionals, says that "the financial losses involved in this kind of theft are underestimated, underreported, and underacknowledged," and he estimates the actual cost worldwide is in the "double-digit billions."

The problem for the Federal Bureau of Investigation (FBI) and other organizations policing and trying to reduce the fraudulent use of credit cards is that the sellers of credit card numbers use very simple methods to combat detection. The sellers use chat rooms and Web sites to communicate with their customers, but they protect themselves mainly by switching Web site locations, chat rooms, and e-mail addresses very often. The decentralized Internet has become so enormous that it usually takes a huge amount of effort and time to locate an individual or organization that does not want to be found. By the time they are found, they have already moved. Moreover, with its international character, even if they are located, being able to stop and punish them is exceedingly complex and a very slow process.

Make IT Your Business

To Think About: What management and business problems have been created by credit card theft over the Internet? What measures can be taken to stop this illegal action?

Sources: Matt Richtel, "Credit Card Theft Thrives Online as a Global Market," *New York Times,* May 13, 2002; and Mark Baard, "Security Obstacles Plague E-Businesses," SearchEbusiness, April 23, 2002, <www.searchebusiness.com>.

ORGANIZATIONS

Hackers and Computer Viruses

The explosive growth of Internet use by businesses and individuals has been accompanied by rising reports of Internet security breaches. The main concern comes from unwanted intruders, or hackers, who use the latest technology and their skills to break into supposedly secure computers or to disable them. A **hacker** is a person who gains unauthorized access to a computer network for profit, criminal mischief, or personal pleasure. There are many ways that hacker break-ins can harm businesses. Some malicious intruders have planted logic bombs, Trojan horses, and other software that can hide in a system or network until executing at a specified time. (A *Trojan horse* is a software program that appears legitimate but contains a second hidden function that may cause damage.) In **denial of service attacks,** hackers flood a network server or Web server with many thousands of false communications or requests for services in order to crash the network. The network receives so many queries that it can't keep up with them and is thus unavailable to service legitimate requests. The cost of these attacks for businesses is rising at an alarming rate. The Window on Organizations describes the harm created by online theft of credit card numbers.

hacker

A person who gains unauthorized access to a computer network for profit, criminal mischief, or personal pleasure.

denial of service attack

Flooding a network server or Web server with false communications or requests for services in order to crash the network.

TABLE 14-2	EXAMPLES OF COMPUTER VIRUSES

Virus Name	Description
Concept, Melissa	Macro viruses that exist inside executable programs called macros, which provide functions within programs such as Microsoft Word. Can be spread when Word documents are attached to e-mail. Can copy from one document to another and delete files.
Code Red, Nimda	"Worm" type viruses that arrive attached to e-mail and spread from computer to computer. When launched they e-mail themselves to computers running Microsoft operating systems and software, slowing Internet traffic as they propagate and circulate.
ILOVEYOU (Love Bug)	Script virus written in script programming language such as VBScript or JavaScript. Overwrites jpg and .mp3 files. Uses Microsoft Outlook and Internet Relay Chat to spread to other systems.
Monkey	Makes the hard disk look like it has failed because Windows will not run.
Chernobyl	File infecting virus. Erases a computer's hard drive and ROM BIOS (Basic Input/Output System).
Junkie	A "multipartite" virus that can infect files as well as the boot sector of the hard drive (the section of a PC hard drive that the PC first reads when it boots up). May cause memory conflicts.
Form	Makes a clicking sound with each keystroke but only on the eighteenth day of the month. It may corrupt data on the floppy disks it infects.

Serious system disruptions have been caused by hackers propagating **computer viruses.** These are rogue software programs that spread rampantly from system to system, clogging computer memory or destroying programs or data. Many thousands of viruses are known to exist, with 200 or more new viruses created each month. Table 14-2 describes the characteristics of some common viruses.

Many viruses today are spread through the Internet, from files of downloaded software or from files attached to e-mail transmissions. Viruses can also invade computerized information systems from other computer networks as well as from "infected" diskettes from an outside source or infected machines. The potential for massive damage and loss from future computer viruses remains. The Chernobyl, Melissa, and ILOVEYOU viruses caused extensive PC damage worldwide after spreading through infected e-mail. Now viruses are spreading to wireless computing devices. Mobile device viruses could pose a serious threat to enterprise computing because so many wireless devices are now linked to corporate information systems.

Organizations can use antivirus software and screening procedures to reduce the chances of infection. **Antivirus software** is software designed to check computer systems and disks for the presence of various computer viruses. Often the software can eliminate the virus from the infected area. However, most antivirus software is only effective against viruses already known when the software is written—to protect their systems, management must continually update their antivirus software.

computer viruses
Rogue software programs that are difficult to detect, which spread rapidly through computer systems, destroying data or disrupting processing and memory systems.

antivirus software
Software designed to detect, and often eliminate, computer viruses from an information system.

CONCERNS FOR SYSTEM BUILDERS AND USERS

The heightened vulnerability of automated data has created special concerns for the builders and users of information systems. These concerns include disaster, security, and administrative error.

Disaster

Computer hardware, programs, data files, and other equipment can be destroyed by fires, power failures, or other disasters. It may take many years and millions of dollars to reconstruct destroyed data files and computer programs and some may not be able to be replaced. If an organization needs them to function on a day-to-day basis, it will no longer be able to operate. This is why companies such as Visa USA Inc. and National Trust employ elaborate emergency

Many organizations use antivirus software to check computer systems and disks for the presence of various computer viruses. Symantec's Norton Antivirus software illustrated here identifies viruses that have infected a system and provides tools for eradicating them.

backup facilities. Visa USA Inc. has duplicate mainframes, duplicate network pathways, duplicate terminals, and duplicate power supplies. Visa even uses a duplicate data center in McLean, Virginia, to handle half of its transactions and to serve as an emergency backup to its primary data center in San Mateo, California. National Trust, a large bank in Ontario, Canada, uses uninterruptable power supply technology provided by International Power Machines (IPM) because electrical power at its Mississauga location fluctuates frequently.

Rather than build their own backup facilities, many firms contract with disaster recovery firms, such as Comdisco Disaster Recovery Services in Rosemont, Illinois, and SunGard Recovery Services headquartered in Wayne, Pennsylvania. These disaster recovery firms provide hot sites housing spare computers at locations around the country where subscribing firms can run their critical applications in an emergency. Disaster recovery services offer backup for client/server systems as well as traditional mainframe applications. As firms become increasingly digital and depend on systems that must be constantly available, disaster recovery planning has taken on new importance.

Security

security
Policies, procedures, and technical measures used to prevent unauthorized access, alteration, theft, or physical damage to information systems.

Security refers to the policies, procedures, and technical measures used to prevent unauthorized access, alteration, theft, or physical damage to information systems. Security can be promoted with an array of techniques and tools to safeguard computer hardware, software, communications networks, and data. We have already discussed some disaster protection measures. Other tools and techniques for promoting security will be discussed in subsequent sections.

Errors

Computers also can serve as instruments of error, severely disrupting or destroying an organization's record keeping and operations. For instance, poor software caused the crash of a Mars Polar Lander operated by the U.S. National Aeronautics and Space Administration (NASA) in December 1999. One sensor erroneously detected that the craft's legs had popped out and shut down its rocket engines prematurely, even though another sensor designed to alert the craft when it touched ground did not show this happening. The landing system software had not been programmed to compare the feedback from both sensors (Wessel, 2001). Errors in automated systems can occur at many points in the processing cycle: through data entry, program error, computer operations, and hardware. Figure 14-2 illustrates all of the points in a typical processing cycle where errors can occur.

SYSTEM QUALITY PROBLEMS: SOFTWARE AND DATA

In addition to disasters, viruses, and security breaches, defective software and data also pose a constant threat to information systems, causing untold losses in productivity. An undiscovered error in a company's credit software or erroneous financial data can result in losses of millions of dollars. A hidden software problem in AT&T's long distance system brought down that system, bringing the New York–based financial exchanges to a halt and interfering with billions of dollars of business around the country for a number of hours. Modern passenger and commercial vehicles are increasingly dependent on computer programs for critical functions. A hidden software defect in a braking system could result in the loss of lives.

Bugs and Defects

A major problem with software is the presence of hidden **bugs** or program code defects. Studies have shown that it is virtually impossible to eliminate all bugs from large programs. The main source of bugs is the complexity of decision-making code. Even a relatively small program of several hundred lines will contain tens of decisions leading to hundreds or even thousands of different paths. Important programs within most corporations are usually much larger, containing tens of thousands or even millions of lines of code, each with many times the choices and paths of the smaller programs. Such complexity is difficult to document and design—designers document some reactions wrongly or fail to consider some possibilities. Studies show that about 60 percent of errors discovered during testing are a result of specifications in the design documentation that were missing, ambiguous, in error, or in conflict.

Zero defects, a goal of the total quality management movement, cannot be achieved in larger programs. Complete testing simply is not possible. Fully testing programs that contain thousands of choices and millions of paths would require thousands of years. Eliminating software bugs is an exercise in diminishing returns, because it would take proportionately longer testing to detect and eliminate obscure residual bugs (Littlewood and Strigini, 1993). Even with rigorous testing, one could not know for sure that a piece of software was dependable until the product proved itself after much operational use. The message? We cannot eliminate all bugs, and we cannot know with certainty the seriousness of the bugs that do remain.

The Maintenance Nightmare

Another reason that systems are unreliable is that computer software traditionally has been a nightmare to maintain. Maintenance, the process of modifying a system in production use, is the most expensive phase of the systems development process. In most organizations nearly half of information systems staff time is spent in the maintenance of existing systems.

Why are maintenance costs so high? One major reason is organizational change. The firm may experience large internal changes in structure or leadership, or change may come from its surrounding environment. These organizational changes affect information requirements. Another reason appears to be software complexity, as measured by the number and size of interrelated software programs and subprograms and the complexity of the flow of program logic between them (Banker, Datar, Kemerer, and Zweig, 1993). A third common cause of long-term maintenance problems is faulty systems analysis and design, especially analysis of information

Figure 14-2 Points in the processing cycle where errors can occur. Each of the points illustrated in this figure represents a control point where special automated or manual procedures should be established to reduce the risk of errors during processing.

bugs

Program code defects or errors.

Figure 14-3 The cost of errors over the systems development cycle. The most common, most severe, and most expensive system errors develop in the early design stages. They involve faulty requirements analysis. Errors in program logic or syntax are much less common, less severe, and less costly to repair than design errors.
Source: Alberts, 1976.

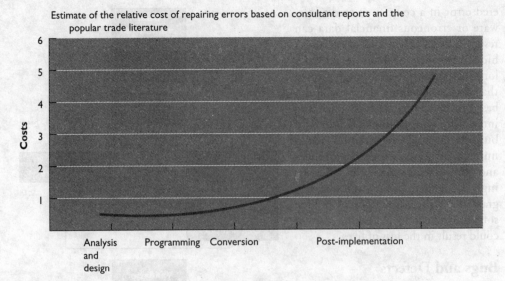

Estimate of the relative cost of repairing errors based on consultant reports and the popular trade literature

requirements. Some studies of large TPS systems by TRW, Inc., have found that a majority of system errors—64 percent—result from early analysis errors (Mazzucchelli, 1985).

Figure 14-3 illustrates the cost of correcting errors based on the experience of consultants reported in the literature. If errors are detected early, during analysis and design, the cost to the systems development effort is small. But if they are not discovered until after programming, testing, or conversion has been completed, the costs can soar astronomically. A minor logic error, for example, that could take 1 hour to correct during the analysis and design stage could take 10, 40, and 90 times as long to correct during programming, conversion, and post-implementation, respectively.

Data Quality Problems

The most common source of information system failure is poor data quality. Data that are inaccurate, untimely, or inconsistent with other sources of information can create serious operational and financial problems for businesses. When faulty data go unnoticed, they can lead to incorrect decisions, product recalls, and even financial losses (Redman, 1998). Companies cannot pursue aggressive marketing and customer relationship management strategies unless they have high-quality data about their customers. Table 14-3 describes examples of data quality problems.

TABLE 14-3   EXAMPLES OF DATA QUALITY PROBLEMS

Organization	Data Quality Problem
Royal Bank of Canada	Databases contained "garbage" characters for postal codes because employees did not have the correct client addresses to enter. When the bank tried to target a particular geographic area to promote a popular Christmas loan, a notable percentage of clients came up with the postal code HOHOHO and the bank could not obtain accurate information for mailings.
Sears Roebuck	Could not effectively pursue cross-selling among its customers because each of its businesses, including retail, home services, credit, and Web site had its own information systems with conflicting customer data. Sears needed to develop a massive data warehouse that consolidated and cleansed the data from all of these systems in order to create a single customer list.
Paint Bull	Found that nearly half the names in its purchased mailing lists of prospective customers were inaccurate or out of date. Lost $10 for every promotional package of videos and catalogs that was returned as undeliverable.
F.B.I.	A study of the FBI's computerized criminal record systems found a total of 54.1 percent of the records in the National Crime Information Center System were inaccurate, ambiguous, or incomplete. The FBI has taken some steps to correct these problems, but computerized criminal history records are used to screen employees in both the public and private sectors. Inaccurate records could unjustly deny people employment
Supermarkets	Several studies have established that 5 to 12 percent of bar-code sales at retail supermarkets are erroneous and that the average ratio of overcharges to undercharges runs 4:1.

Poor data quality may stem from errors during data input or faulty information system and database design (Wand and Wang, 1996; Strong, Lee, and Wang, 1997). In the following sections we examine how organizations can deal with data and software quality problems as well as other threats to information systems.

14.2 CREATING A CONTROL ENVIRONMENT

To minimize errors, disasters, interruptions of service, computer crimes, and breaches of security, special policies and procedures must be incorporated into the design and implementation of information systems. The combination of manual and automated measures that safeguard information systems and ensure that they perform according to management standards is termed controls. **Controls** consist of all the methods, policies, and organizational procedures that ensure the safety of the organization's assets, the accuracy and reliability of its accounting records, and operational adherence to management standards.

In the past, the control of information systems was treated as an afterthought, addressed only toward the end of implementation, just before the system was installed. Today, however, organizations are so critically dependent on information systems that vulnerabilities and control issues must be identified as early as possible. The control of an information system must be an integral part of its design. Users and builders of systems must pay close attention to controls throughout the system's life span.

GENERAL CONTROLS AND APPLICATION CONTROLS

Computer systems are controlled by a combination of general controls and application controls. **General controls** govern the design, security, and use of computer programs and the security of data files in general throughout the organization's information technology infrastructure. On the whole, general controls apply to all computerized applications and consist of a combination of hardware, software, and manual procedures that create an overall control environment. **Application controls** are specific controls unique to each computerized application, such as payroll or order processing. They consist of controls applied from the business functional area of a particular system and from programmed procedures.

General Controls and Data Security

General controls include software controls, physical hardware controls, computer operations controls, data security controls, controls over the systems implementation process, and administrative controls. Table 14-4 describes the function of each of these controls.

Although most of these general controls are designed and maintained by information systems specialists, **data security controls** and **administrative controls** require input and oversight from end users and business managers. For example, information systems specialists would be responsible for certain aspects of data security controls, such as making computer terminals available only to authorized users or using system software and application software to create a series of passwords that users would need in order to access systems. Users, however, would specify the business rules for accessing data, such as what positions in the organization have rights to view and update the data.

Figure 14-4 illustrates the security allowed for two sets of users of an online personnel database with sensitive information such as employees' salaries, benefits, and medical histories. One set of users consists of all employees who perform clerical functions such as inputting employee data into the system. All individuals with this type of profile can update the system but can neither read nor update sensitive fields such as salary, medical history, or earnings data. Another profile applies to a divisional manager, who cannot update the system but who can read all employee data fields for his or her division, including medical history and salary. These profiles would be established and maintained by a data security system based on access rules supplied by business groups. The data security system illustrated in Figure 14-4 provides very fine-grained security restrictions, such as allowing authorized personnel users to inquire about all employee information except in confidential fields such as salary or medical history.

Business users would be responsible for establishing administrative controls, which are formal organizational procedures to make sure that all of the other general and application controls are properly enforced. These controls ensure that job functions are designed to

controls
All of the methods, policies, and procedures that ensure protection of the organization's assets, accuracy and reliability of its records, and operational adherence to management standards.

general controls
Overall controls that establish a framework for controlling the design, security, and use of computer programs throughout an organization.

application controls
Specific controls unique to each computerized application.

data security controls
Controls to ensure that data files on either disk or tape are not subject to unauthorized access, change, or destruction.

administrative controls
Formalized standards, rules, procedures, and disciplines to ensure that the organization's controls are properly executed and enforced.

TABLE 14-4   GENERAL CONTROLS

Type of General Control	Description
Software controls	Monitor the use of system software and prevent unauthorized access of software programs, system software, and computer programs. System software is an important control area because it performs overall control functions for the programs that directly process data and data files.
Hardware controls	Ensure that computer hardware is physically secure, and check for equipment malfunction. Computer equipment should be specially protected against fires and extremes of temperature and humidity. Organizations that are critically dependent on their computers also must make provisions for backup or continued operation to maintain constant service.
Computer operations controls	Oversee the work of the computer department to ensure that programmed procedures are consistently and correctly applied to the storage and processing of data. They include controls over the setup of computer processing jobs and computer operations, and backup and recovery procedures for processing that ends abnormally.
Data security controls	Ensure that valuable business data files on either disk or tape are not subject to unauthorized access, change, or destruction while they are in use or in storage.
Implementation controls	Audit the systems development process at various points to ensure that the process is properly controlled and managed. The systems development audit looks for the presence of formal reviews by users and management at various stages of development; the level of user involvement at each stage of implementation; and the use of a formal cost/benefit methodology in establishing system feasibility. The audit should look for the use of controls and quality assurance techniques for program development, conversion, and testing and for complete and thorough system, user, and operations documentation.
Administrative controls	Formalized standards, rules, procedures, and control disciplines to ensure that the organization's general and application controls are properly executed and enforced.

minimize the risk of errors or fraudulent manipulation of the organization's assets. For instance, individuals responsible for operating systems (who typically belong to the information systems department) would not be the same ones who could initiate transactions that change the assets held in these systems. Administrative controls would include written policies and procedures establishing formal standards for information system operations and clearly specified accountabilities and responsibilities. Administrative controls include mechanisms for supervising personnel involved in control procedures to make sure that the controls for an information system are performing as intended.

Figure 14-4 Security profiles for a personnel system. These two examples represent two security profiles or data security patterns that might be found in a personnel system. Depending on the security profile, a user would have certain restrictions on access to various systems, locations, or data in an organization.

SECURITY PROFILE 1

User: Personnel Dept. Clerk

Location: Division 1

Employee Identification
Codes with This Profile: 00753, 27834, 37665, 44116

Data Field Restrictions	Type of Access
All employee data for Division 1 only	Read and Update
• Medical history data	None
• Salary	None
• Pensionable earnings	None

SECURITY PROFILE 2

User: Divisional Personnel Manager

Location: Division 1

Employee Identification
Codes with This Profile: 27321

Data Field Restrictions	Type of Access
All employee data for Division 1 only	Read Only

Application Controls

Application controls include both automated and manual procedures that ensure that only authorized data are completely and accurately processed by an application. Application controls can be classified as (1) input controls, (2) processing controls, and (3) output controls.

Input controls check data for accuracy and completeness when they enter the system. There are specific input controls for input authorization, data conversion, data editing, and error handling. **Processing controls** establish that data are complete and accurate during updating. Run control totals, computer matching, and programmed edit checks are used for this purpose. **Output controls** ensure that the results of computer processing are accurate, complete, and properly distributed.

Table 14-5 provides more detailed examples of each type of application control.

Not all of the application controls discussed here are used in every information system. Some systems require more of these controls than others, depending on the importance of the data and the nature of the application.

PROTECTING THE DIGITAL FIRM

As companies increasingly rely on digital networks for their revenue and operations, they need to take additional steps to ensure that their systems and applications are always available to support their digital business processes.

High-Availability Computing

In a digital firm environment, information technology infrastructures must provide a continuous level of service availability across distributed computing platforms. Many factors can disrupt the performance of a Web site, including network failure, heavy Internet traffic, and exhausted server resources. Computer failures, interruptions, and downtime can translate into disgruntled customers, millions of dollars in lost sales, and the inability to perform critical internal transactions. Firms such as those in the airline and financial service industries with critical applications requiring online transaction processing have traditionally used fault-tolerant computer systems for many years to ensure 100 percent availability. In **online transaction processing,** transactions entered online are immediately processed by the computer. Multitudinous changes to databases, reporting, or requests for information occur each instant. **Fault-tolerant computer systems** contain redundant hardware, software, and

input controls
The procedures to check data for accuracy and completeness when they enter the system.

processing controls
The routines for establishing that data are complete and accurate during updating.

output controls
Measures that ensure that the results of computer processing are accurate, complete, and properly distributed.

online transaction processing
Transaction processing mode in which transactions entered online are immediately processed by the computer.

fault-tolerant computer systems
Systems that contain extra hardware, software, and power supply components that create an environment that provides continuous uninterrupted service.

TABLE 14-5   APPLICATION CONTROLS

Name of Control	Type of Application Control	Description
Control totals	Input, Processing	Totals established beforehand for input and processing transactions. These totals can range from a simple document count to totals for quantity fields such as total sales amount (for a batch of transactions). Computer programs count the totals from transactions input or processed.
Edit checks	Input	Programmed routines that can be performed to edit input data for errors before they are processed. Transactions that do not meet edit criteria will be rejected. For example, data might be checked to make sure they were in the right format (a 9-digit Social Security numbers should not contain any alphabetic characters).
Computer matching	Input, processing	Matches input data with information held on master or suspense files, with unmatched items noted for investigation. For example, a matching program might match employee time cards with a payroll master file and report missing or duplicate time cards.
Run control totals	Processing, output	Balance the total of transactions processed with total number of transactions input or output
Report distribution logs	Output	Documentation specifying that authorized recipients have received their reports, checks, or other critical documents.

power supply components that create an environment that provides continuous, uninterrupted service. Fault-tolerant computers contain extra memory chips, processors, and disk storage devices that can back a system up and keep it running to prevent failure. They can use special software routines or self-checking logic built into their circuitry to detect hardware failures and automatically switch to a backup device. Parts from these computers can be removed and repaired without disruption to the computer system. E-Smart Direct Services, Inc., of Etobicoke, Ontario, Canada, a provider of electronic payment processing and authorization services for retailers and financial institutions, needs a technology platform with 100 percent, 24-hour system availability. The company uses fault-tolerant systems from Stratus for this purpose.

Fault tolerance should be distinguished from **high-availability computing.** Both fault tolerance and high-availability computing are designed to maximize application and system availability. Both use backup hardware resources. However, high-availability computing helps firms recover quickly from a crash, while fault tolerance promises continuous availability and the elimination of recovery time altogether. High-availability computing environments are a minimum requirement for firms with heavy electronic commerce processing or that depend on digital networks for their internal operations. High availability computing requires an assortment of tools and technologies to ensure maximum performance of computer systems and networks, including redundant servers, mirroring, load balancing, clustering, storage area networks (see Chapter 6), and a good **disaster recovery plan.** The firm's computing platform must be extremely robust with scalable processing power, storage, and bandwidth.

Disaster recovery planning devises plans for the restoration of computing and communications services after they have been disrupted by an event such as an earthquake, flood, or terrorist attack. Business managers and information technology specialists need to work together to determine what kind of plan is necessary and which systems and business functions are most critical to the company. The Manager's Toolkit describes the major elements of a disaster recovery plan.

Load balancing distributes large numbers of access requests across multiple servers. The requests are directed to the most available server so that no single device is overwhelmed. If one server starts to get swamped, requests are forwarded to another server with more capacity. **Mirroring** uses a backup server that duplicates all the processes and transactions of the primary server. If the primary server fails, the backup server can immediately take its place without any interruption in service. However, server mirroring is very expensive because each server must be mirrored by an identical server whose only purpose is to be available in the event of a failure. Clustering is a less expensive technique for ensuring continued availability. High-availability **clustering** links two computers together so that the second computer can act as a backup to the primary computer. If the primary computer fails, the second computer picks up its processing without any pause in the system. (Computers can also be clustered together as a single computing resource to speed up processing.)

Glossary (margin)

high-availability computing
Tools and technologies, including backup hardware resources, to enable a system to recover quickly from a crash.

disaster recovery plan
Plan for running the business in the event of a computer outage. Includes organizational procedures as well as backup processing, storage and database capabilities.

load balancing
Distribution of large numbers of requests for access among multiple servers so that no single device is overwhelmed.

Mirroring
Duplicating all the processes and transactions of a server on a backup server to prevent any interruption in service if the primary server fails.

clustering
Linking two computers together so that the second computer can act as a backup to the primary computer or speed up processing.

MIS IN ACTION: Manager's Toolkit

HOW TO DEVELOP A DISASTER RECOVERY PLAN

Conduct a business impact analysis to identify the firm's most critical systems and the impact a systems outage would have on the business. Managers need to determine the maximum amount of time the business can survive with its systems down and what parts of the business need to be restored first.

1. Assess the risk of particular disasters, such as floods, power outages, or terrorist attacks, occurring at your specific company. (See the discussion of risk assessment in the following section.)

2. Identify the most mission-critical applications, the files they use, and where these files and applications are located.

3. Develop an action plan for handling mission critical applications, such as using manual processes or running these applica-

tions at a disaster recovery service or backup computer system at another location.

4. Outline responsibilities of individual staff members and procedures to follow during a disaster, including how to locate and communicate with employees.

5. Test the disaster recovery plan at least once a year.

6. Use a consistent planning process and methodology so that all business groups understand the ground rules and how disaster planning will be funded.

7. Make sure you have the backing and support of senior management to ensure compliance.

Figure 14-5 Internet security challenges. There are security challenges at each of the layers of an Internet computing environment and in the communications between the client and server layers.

- Computer viruses
- Line taps
- Loss of machine

- Tapping
- Sniffing
- Message alteration
- Theft and fraud

- Hacking
- Computer viruses
- Theft and fraud
- Line taps
- Vandalism
- Denial-of-service attacks

- Theft of data
- Copying of data
- Alteration of data

Many companies lack the resources to provide a high-availability computing environment on their own. **Management service providers (MSPs),** which we introduced in Chapter 6, can handle tasks such as network, systems, storage, and security management for subscribing clients. Businesses that want to maintain their own networks, servers, desktops, and Web sites but don't have the resources to monitor them can outsource the work to MSPs.

management service provider (MSP)
Company that provides network, systems, storage, and security management for subscribing clients.

Internet Security Challenges

High-availability computing also requires a security infrastructure for electronic commerce and electronic business. Large public networks, including the Internet, are more vulnerable because they are virtually open to anyone and because they are so huge that when abuses do occur, they can have an enormously widespread impact. When the Internet becomes part of the corporate network, the organization's information systems can be vulnerable to actions from outsiders. The architecture of a Web-based application typically includes a Web client, a server, and corporate information systems linked to databases. Each of these components presents security challenges and vulnerabilities, which are illustrated in Figure 14-5 (Joshi, Aref, Ghafoor, and Spafford, 2001).

Computers that are constantly connected to the Internet via cable modem or DSL line are more open to penetration by outsiders because they use a fixed Internet address where they can be more easily identified. (With dial-up service, a temporary Internet address is assigned for each session.) A fixed Internet address creates a fixed target for hackers.

Both electronic commerce and electronic business require companies to be both more open and more closed at the same time. To benefit from electronic commerce, supply chain management, and other digital business processes, companies need to be open to outsiders such as customers, suppliers, and trading partners. Corporate systems must also be extended outside the organization so that they can be accessed by employees working with wireless and other mobile computing devices. Yet these systems also must be closed to hackers and other intruders. The new information technology infrastructure requires a new security culture and infrastructure that allows businesses to straddle this fine line. Corporations need to extend their security policies to include procedures for suppliers and other business partners.

Businesses linking to the Internet or transmitting information via intranets and extranets require special security procedures and technologies. Chapter 9 described the use of *firewalls* to prevent unauthorized users from accessing private networks. As growing numbers of businesses expose their networks to Internet traffic, firewalls are becoming a necessity.

A firewall is generally placed between internal LANs and WANs and external networks such as the Internet. The firewall controls access to the organization's internal networks by acting like a gatekeeper that examines each user's credentials before they can access the network. The firewall identifies names, Internet Protocol (IP) addresses, applications, and other characteristics of incoming traffic. It checks this information against the access rules that have been programmed into the system by the network administrator. The firewall prevents unauthorized communication into and out of the network, allowing the organization to enforce a security policy on traffic flowing between its network and the Internet (Oppliger, 1997).

There are essentially two major types of firewall technologies: proxies and stateful inspection. *Proxies* stop data originating outside the organization at the firewall, inspect them, and pass a proxy to the other side of the firewall. If a user outside the company wants to communicate with a user inside the organization, the outside user first "talks" to the proxy application and the proxy application communicates with the firm's internal computer. Likewise a computer user inside the organization goes through the proxy to "talk" with computers on the outside. Because the actual message doesn't pass through the firewall, proxies are considered more secure than stateful inspection. However, they have to do a lot of work and can consume system resources, degrading network performance.

In *stateful inspection*, the firewall scans each packet of incoming data, checking its source, destination addresses, or services. It sets up state tables to track information over multiple packets. User-defined access rules must identify every type of packet that the organization does not want to admit. Although stateful inspection consumes fewer network resources than proxies, it is theoretically not as secure because some data pass through the firewall. Cisco Systems' firewall product is an example of a stateful inspection firewall. Hybrid firewall products are being developed. For instance, Check Point is primarily a stateful inspection product but it has incorporated some proxy capabilities for communication.

To create a good firewall, someone must write and maintain the internal rules identifying the people, applications, or addresses that are allowed or rejected in very fine detail. Firewalls can deter, but not completely prevent, network penetration from outsiders and should be viewed as one element in an overall security plan. In order to deal effectively with Internet security, broader corporate policies and procedures, user responsibilities, and security awareness training may be required (Segev, Porra, and Roldan, 1998).

In addition to firewalls, commercial security vendors now provide intrusion detection tools and services to protect against suspicious network traffic. **Intrusion detection systems** feature full-time monitoring tools placed at the most vulnerable points or "hot spots" of corporate networks to continually detect and deter intruders. Scanning software looks for known problems such as bad passwords, checks to see if important files have been removed or modified, and sends warnings of vandalism or system administration errors. Monitoring software examines events as they are happening to look for security attacks in progress. The intrusion detection tool can also be customized to shut down a particularly sensitive part of a network if it receives unauthorized traffic.

intrusion detection system
Tools to monitor the most vulnerable points in a network to detect and deter unauthorized intruders.

Security and Electronic Commerce

Security of electronic communications is a major control issue for companies engaged in electronic commerce. It is essential that commerce-related data of buyers and sellers be kept private when they are transmitted electronically. The data being transmitted also must be protected against being purposefully altered by someone other than the sender, so that, for example, stock market execution orders or product orders accurately represent the wishes of the buyer and seller.

Much online commerce continues to be handled through private EDI networks usually run over VANs. VANs (value-added networks) are relatively secure and reliable. However, because they have to be privately maintained and run on high-speed private lines, VANs are expensive, easily costing a company $100,000 per month. They also are inflexible, being connected only to a limited number of sites and companies. As a result, the Internet is emerging as the network technology of choice. EDI transactions on the Internet run from one-half to one-tenth the cost of VAN-based transactions.

Many organizations rely on encryption to protect sensitive information transmitted over the Internet and other networks. **Encryption** is the coding and scrambling of messages to prevent unauthorized access to or understanding of the data being transmitted. A message can be encrypted by applying a secret numerical code called an encryption key so that it is

encryption
The coding and scrambling of messages to prevent their being read or accessed without authorization.

Figure 14-6 Public key encryption. A public key encryption system can be viewed as a series of public and private keys that lock data when they are transmitted and unlock the data when they are received. The sender locates the recipient's public key in a directory and uses it to encrypt a message. The message is sent in encrypted form over the Internet or a private network. When the encrypted message arrives, the recipient uses his or her private key to decrypt the data and read the message.

transmitted as a scrambled set of characters. (The key consists of a large group of letters, numbers, and symbols.) In order to be read, the message must be decrypted (unscrambled) with a matching key.

There are several alternative methods of encryption, but "public key" encryption is becoming popular. Public key encryption, illustrated in Figure 14-6, uses two different keys, one private and one public. The keys are mathematically related so that data encrypted with one key only can be decrypted using the other key. To send and receive messages, communicators first create separate pairs of private and public keys. The public key is kept in a directory and the private key must be kept secret. The sender encrypts a message with the recipient's public key. On receiving the message, the recipient uses his or her private key to decrypt it.

Encryption is especially useful to shield messages on the Internet and other public networks because they are less secure than private networks. Encryption helps protect transmission of payment data, such as credit card information, and addresses the problems of authentication and message integrity. **Authentication** refers to the ability of each party to know that the other parties are who they claim to be. In the nonelectronic world, we use our signatures. (Bank-by-mail systems avoid the need for signatures on checks they issue for their customers by using well-protected private networks where the source of the request for payment is recorded and can be proven. Microsoft provides an online identification service called Passport for this purpose, authenticating user identification when any Microsoft Web service is accessed.) **Message integrity** is the ability to be certain that the message being sent arrives without being copied or changed.

Digital signatures and digital certificates help with authentication. The Electronic Signatures in Global and National Commerce Act of 2000 has given digital signatures the same legal status as those written on ink or paper. A **digital signature** is a digital code attached to an electronically transmitted message that is used to verify the origins and contents of a message. It provides a way to associate a message with the sender, performing a function similar to a written signature. For an electronic signature to be legally binding in court, someone must be able to verify that the signature actually belongs to whoever sent the data and that the data were not altered after being "signed."

Digital certificates are data files used to establish the identity of people and electronic assets for protection of online transactions (see Figure 14-7). A digital certificate system uses a trusted third party known as a certificate authority (CA) to validate a user's identity. The CA system can be run as a function inside an organization or by an outside company such as VeriSign Inc. in Mountain View, California. The CA verifies a digital certificate user's identity off-line. This information is put into a CA server, which generates an encrypted digital certificate containing owner identification information and a copy of the owner's public key. The certificate authenticates that the public key belongs to the designated owner. The CA makes its own public key available publicly either in print or perhaps on the Internet. The recipient of an encrypted message uses the CA's public key to decode the digital certificate attached to the message, verifies it was issued by the CA, and then obtains the sender's public key and identification information contained in the certificate. Using this information, the recipient can send an encrypted reply. The digital certificate system would enable, for example, a credit card user and

authentication

The ability of each party in a transaction to ascertain the identity of the other party.

message integrity

The ability to ascertain that a transmitted message has not been copied or altered.

digital signature

A digital code that can be attached to an electronically transmitted message to uniquely identify its contents and the sender.

digital certificate

An attachment to an electronic message to verify the identity of the sender and to provide the receiver with the means to encode a reply.

Figure 14-7 Digital certificates. Digital certificates can be used to establish the identity of people or electronic assets. They protect online transactions by providing secure, encrypted online communication.

merchant to validate that their digital certificates were issued by an authorized and trusted third party before they exchange data.

SSL (Secure Sockets Layer) and S-HTTP (Secure Hypertext Transport Protocol) are protocols used for secure information transfer over the Internet. They allow client and server computers to manage encryption and decryption activities as they communicate with each other during a secure Web session. Some credit card payment systems use the Secure Sockets Layer (SSL) protocol for encrypting the credit card payment data.

DEVELOPING A CONTROL STRUCTURE: COSTS AND BENEFITS

Information systems can make exhaustive use of all the control mechanisms previously discussed. But they may be so expensive to build and so complicated to use that the system is economically or operationally unfeasible. Some cost/benefit analysis must be performed to determine which control mechanisms provide the most effective safeguards without sacrificing operational efficiency or cost.

One of the criteria that determines how much control is built into a system is the importance of its data. Major financial and accounting systems, for example, such as a payroll system or one that tracks purchases and sales on the stock exchange, must have higher standards of control than a tickler system to track dental patients and remind them that their six-month checkup is due. For instance, Swissair invested in additional hardware and software to increase its network reliability because it was running critical reservation and ticketing applications.

The cost-effectiveness of controls will also be influenced by the efficiency, complexity, and expense of each control technique. For example, complete one-for-one checking may be time consuming and operationally impossible for a system that processes hundreds of thousands of utilities payments daily. But it might be possible to use this technique to verify only critical data such as dollar amounts and account numbers, while ignoring names and addresses.

A third consideration is the level of risk if a specific activity or process is not properly controlled. System builders can undertake a **risk assessment,** determining points of vulnerability, the likely frequency of a problem and the potential damage if it were to occur. For example, if an event is likely to occur no more than once a year, with a maximum of $1,000

risk assessment

Determining the potential frequency of the occurrence of a problem and the potential damage if the problem were to occur. Used to determine the cost/benefit of a control.

TABLE 14-6	**ONLINE ORDER PROCESSING RISK ASSESSMENT**			

Exposure	Probability of Occurrence (%)	Loss Range/ Average ($)	Expected Annual Loss ($)
Power failure	30	5,000–200,000 (102,500)	30,750
Embezzlement	5	1,000–50,000 (25,500)	1275
User error	98	200–40,000 (20,100)	19,698

This chart shows the results of a risk assessment of three selected areas of an online order processing system. The likelihood of each exposure occurring over a one-year period is expressed as a percentage. The next column shows the highest and lowest possible loss that could be expected each time the exposure occurred and an average loss calculated by adding the highest and lowest figures together and dividing by 2. The expected annual loss for each exposure can be determined by multiplying the average loss by its probability of occurrence.

loss to the organization, it would not be feasible to spend $20,000 on the design and maintenance of a control to protect against that event. However, if that same event could occur at least once a day, with a potential loss of more than $300,000 a year, $100,000 spent on a control might be entirely appropriate.

Table 14-6 illustrates sample results of a risk assessment for an online order processing system that processes 30,000 orders per day. The probability of a power failure occurring in a one-year period is 30 percent. Loss of order transactions while power is down could range from $5,000 to $200,000 for each occurrence, depending on how long processing was halted. The probability of embezzlement occurring over a yearly period is about 5 percent, with potential losses ranging from $1,000 to $50,000 for each occurrence. User errors have a 98 percent chance of occurring over a yearly period, with losses ranging from $200 to $40,000 for each occurrence. The average loss for each event can be weighted by multiplying it by the probability of its occurrence annually to determine the expected annual loss. Once the risks have been assessed, system builders can concentrate on the control points with the greatest vulnerability and potential loss. In this case, controls should focus on ways to minimize the risk of power failures and user errors. Increasing management awareness of the full range of actions they can take to reduce risks can substantially reduce system losses (Straub and Welke, 1998).

In some situations, organizations may not know the precise probability of threats occurring to their information systems, and they may not be able to quantify the impact of such events. In these instances, management may choose to describe risks and their likely impact in a qualitative manner (Rainer, Snyder, and Carr, 1991).

To decide which controls to use, information system builders must examine various control techniques in relation to each other and to their relative cost-effectiveness. A control weakness at one point may be offset by a strong control at another. It may not be cost-effective to build tight controls at every point in the processing cycle if the areas of greatest risk are secure or if compensating controls exist elsewhere. The combination of all of the controls developed for a particular application will determine its overall control structure.

THE ROLE OF AUDITING IN THE CONTROL PROCESS

How does management know that information systems controls are effective? To answer this question, organizations must conduct comprehensive and systematic audits. An **MIS audit** identifies all of the controls that govern individual information systems and assesses their effectiveness. To accomplish this, the auditor must acquire a thorough understanding of operations, physical facilities, telecommunications, control systems,

MIS audit

Identifies all the controls that govern individual information systems and assesses their effectiveness.

Function: Personal Loans _____   Prepared by: ____ J. Ericson   Received by: _____ T. Barrow _____
Location: Peoria, Ill. _____   Preparation date: __ June 16, 2003 _____   Review date: _____ June 28, 2003 _____

Nature of Weakness and Impact	Chance for Substantial Error		Effect on Audit Procedures	Notification to Management	
	Yes/ No	Justification	Required Amendment	Date of Report	Management Response
Loan repayment records are not reconciled to borrower's records during processing.	Yes	Without a detection control, errors in individual client balances may remain undetected.	Confirm a sample of loans.	5/10/03	Interest Rate Compare Report provides this control.
There are no regular audits of computer-generated data (interest charges).	Yes	Without a regular audit or reasonableness check, widespread miscalculations could result before errors are detected.		5/10/03	Periodic audits of loans will be instituted.
Programs can be put into production libraries to meet target deadlines without final approval from the Standards and Controls group.	No	All programs require management authorization. The Standards and Controls group controls access to all production systems, and assigns such cases to a temporary production status.			

Figure 14-8 Sample auditor's list of control weaknesses. This chart is a sample page from a list of control weaknesses that an auditor might find in a loan system in a local commercial bank. This form helps auditors record and evaluate control weaknesses and shows the results of discussing those weaknesses with management, as well as any corrective actions taken by management.

data security objectives, organizational structure, personnel, manual procedures, and individual applications.

The auditor usually interviews key individuals who use and operate a specific information system concerning their activities and procedures. Application controls, overall integrity controls, and control disciplines are examined. The auditor should trace the flow of sample transactions through the system and perform tests, using, if appropriate, automated audit software.

The audit lists and ranks all control weaknesses and estimates the probability of their occurrence. It then assesses the financial and organizational impact of each threat. Figure 14-8 is a sample auditor's listing of control weaknesses for a loan system. It includes a section for notifying management of such weaknesses and for management's response. Management is expected to devise a plan for countering significant weaknesses in controls.

An auditor interviews key individuals who use and operate a specific information system concerning their activities and procedures. The auditor often traces the flow of sample transactions through the system and performs tests using automated audit software.

14.3 ENSURING SYSTEM QUALITY

Organizations can improve system quality by using software quality assurance techniques and by improving the quality of their data.

SOFTWARE QUALITY ASSURANCE METHODOLOGIES AND TOOLS

Solutions to software quality problems include using an appropriate systems development methodology, proper resource allocation during systems development, the use of metrics, and attention to testing.

Structured Methodologies

Various tools and development methodologies have been employed to help system builders document, analyze, design, and implement information systems. A **development methodology** is a collection of methods, one or more for every activity within every phase of a systems development project. The primary function of a development methodology is to provide discipline to the entire development process. A good development methodology establishes organization-wide standards for requirements gathering, design, programming, and testing. To produce quality software, organizations must select an appropriate methodology and then enforce its use. The methodology should call for systems requirement and specification documents that are complete, detailed, accurate, and documented in a format the user community can understand before they approve it. Specifications also must include agreed on measures of system quality so that the system can be evaluated objectively while it is being developed and once it is completed.

Structured methodologies have been used to document, analyze, and design information systems since the 1970s. **Structured** refers to the fact that the techniques are step-by-step, with each step building on the previous one. Structured methodologies are top-down, progressing from the highest, most abstract level to the lowest level of detail—from the general to the specific. For example, the highest level of a top-down description of a human resources system would show the main human resources functions: personnel, benefits, compensation, and Equal Employment Opportunity (EEO). Each of these would be broken down into the next layer. Benefits, for instance, might include pension, employee savings, healthcare, and insurance. Each of these layers in turn would be broken down until the lowest level of detail could be depicted.

The traditional structured methodologies are process-oriented rather than data-oriented. Although data descriptions are part of the methods, the methodologies focus on how the data are transformed rather than on the data themselves. These methodologies are largely linear; each phase must be completed before the next one can begin. Structured methodologies include structured analysis, structured design, and structured programming.

Structured Analysis

Structured analysis is widely used to define system inputs, processes, and outputs. It offers a logical graphic model of information flow, partitioning a system into modules that show manageable levels of detail. It rigorously specifies the processes or transformations that occur within each module and the interfaces that exist between them. Its primary tool is the **data flow diagram (DFD)**, a graphic representation of a system's component processes and the interfaces (flow of data) between them.

Figure 14-9 shows a simple data flow diagram for a mail-in university course registration system. The rounded boxes represent processes, which portray the transformation of data. The square box represents an external entity, which is an originator or receiver of information located outside the boundaries of the system being modeled. The open rectangles represent data stores, which are either manual or automated inventories of data. The arrows represent data flows, which show the movement between processes, external entities, and data stores. They always contain packets of data with the name or content of each data flow listed beside the arrow.

This data flow diagram shows that students submit registration forms with their name, identification number, and the numbers of the courses they wish to take. In process 1.0 the

---

development methodology
A collection of methods, one or more for every activity within every phase of a development project.

structured
Refers to the fact that techniques are carefully drawn up, step by step, with each step building on a previous one.

structured analysis
A method for defining system inputs, processes, and outputs and for partitioning systems into subsystems or modules that show a logical graphic model of information flow.

data flow diagram
Primary tool for structured analysis that graphically illustrates a system's component processes and the flow of data between them.

Figure 14-9 Data flow diagram for mail-in university registration system. The system has three processes: Verify availability (1.0), Enroll student (2.0), and Confirm registration (3.0). The name and content of each of the data flows appear adjacent to each arrow. There is one external entity in this system: the student. There are two data stores: the student master file and the course file.

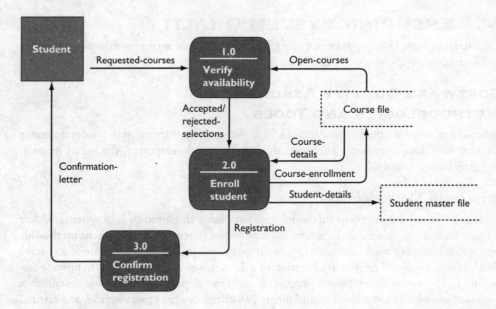

system verifies that each course selected is still open by referencing the university's course file. The file distinguishes courses that are open from those that have been canceled or filled. Process 1.0 then determines which of the student's selections can be accepted or rejected. Process 2.0 enrolls the student in the courses for which he or she has been accepted. It updates the university's course file with the student's name and identification number and recalculates the class size. If maximum enrollment has been reached, the course number is flagged as closed. Process 2.0 also updates the university's student master file with information about new students or changes in address. Process 3.0 then sends each student applicant a confirmation-of-registration letter listing the courses for which he or she is registered and noting the course selections that could not be fulfilled.

The diagrams can be used to depict higher level processes as well as lower level details. Through leveled data flow diagrams, a complex process can be broken down into successive levels of detail. An entire system can be divided into subsystems with a high-level data flow diagram. Each subsystem, in turn, can be divided into additional subsystems with second-level data flow diagrams, and the lower level subsystems can be broken down again until the lowest level of detail has been reached.

Another tool for structured analysis is a data dictionary, which contains information about individual pieces of data and data groupings within a system (see Chapter 7). The data dictionary defines the contents of data flows and data stores so that system builders understand exactly what pieces of data they contain. **Process specifications** describe the transformation occurring within the lowest level of the data flow diagrams. They express the logic for each process.

Structured Design

Structured design encompasses a set of design rules and techniques that promotes program clarity and simplicity, thereby reducing the time and effort required for coding, debugging, and maintenance. The main principle of structured design is that a system should be designed from the top down in hierarchical fashion and refined to greater levels of detail. The design should first consider the main function of a program or system, then break this function into subfunctions and decompose each subfunction until the lowest level of detail has been reached. The lowest level modules describe the actual processing that will occur. In this manner all high-level logic and the design model are developed before detailed program code is written. If structured analysis has been performed, the structured specification document can serve as input to the design process. Our earlier human resources top-down description provides a good overview example of structured design.

As the design is formulated, it is documented in a structure chart. The **structure chart** is a top-down chart, showing each level of design, its relationship to other levels, and its place in the overall design structure. Figure 14-10 shows a high-level structure chart for a payroll

---

process specifications
Describe the logic of the processes occurring within the lowest levels of a data flow diagram.

structured design
Software design discipline encompassing a set of design rules and techniques for designing systems from the top down in hierarchical fashion.

structure chart
System documentation showing each level of design, the relationship among the levels, and the overall place in the design structure; can document one program, one system, or part of one program.

Figure 14-10   High-level structure chart for a payroll system. This structure chart shows the highest or most abstract level of design for a payroll system, providing an overview of the entire system.

system. If a design has too many levels to fit onto one structure chart, it can be broken down further on more detailed structure charts. A structure chart may document one program, one system (a set of programs), or part of one program.

Structured Programming

Structured programming extends the principles governing structured design to the writing of programs to make software programs easier to understand and modify. It is based on the principle of modularization, which follows from top-down analysis and design. Each of the boxes in the structure chart represents a component **module** that is usually directly related to a bottom-level design module. It constitutes a logical unit that performs one or several functions. Ideally, modules should be independent of each other and should have only one entry and exit point. They should share data with as few other modules as possible. Each module should be kept to a manageable size. An individual should be able to read and understand the program code for the module and easily keep track of its functions.

Proponents of structured programming have shown that any program can be written using three basic control constructs, or instruction patterns: (1) simple sequence, (2) selection, and (3) iteration. These control constructs are illustrated in Figure 14-11.

The **sequence construct** executes statements in the order in which they appear, with control passing unconditionally from one statement to the next. The program will execute statement A and then statement B.

The **selection construct** tests a condition and executes one of two alternative instructions based on the results of the test. Condition R is tested. If R is true, statement C is executed. If R is false, statement D is executed. Control then passes to the next statement.

The **iteration construct** repeats a segment of code as long as a conditional test remains true. Condition S is tested. If S is true, statement E is executed and control returns to the test of S. If S is false, E is skipped and control passes to the next statement.

Limitations of Traditional Methods

Although traditional methods are valuable, they can be inflexible and time-consuming. Completion of structured analysis is required before design can begin, and programming must await the completed deliverables from design. A change in specifications requires that first the analysis documents and then the design documents must be modified before the programs can be changed to reflect the new requirement. Structured methodologies are function-oriented, focusing on the processes that transform the data. Chapter 12 described how object-oriented development addresses this problem. System builders can also use computer-aided software engineering (CASE) tools to make structured methods more flexible.

Tools and Methodologies for Object-Oriented Development

Chapters 6 and 12 have described how object-oriented development can be used to improve system quality and flexibility. A number of techniques for the analysis and design of object-oriented systems have been developed, but the **Unified Modeling Language (UML)** has become the industry standard. UML allows system builders to represent various views of an

---

structured programming
Discipline for organizing and coding programs that simplifies the control paths so that the programs can be easily understood and modified; uses the basic control structures and modules that have only one entry point and one exit point.

module
A logical unit of a program that performs one or several functions.

sequence construct
The sequential single steps or actions in the logic of a program that do not depend on the existence of any condition.

selection construct
The logic pattern in programming where a stated condition determines which of two alternative actions can be taken.

iteration construct
The logic pattern in programming where certain actions are repeated while a specified condition occurs or until a certain condition is met.

Unified Modeling Language (UML)
Industry standard methodology for analysis and design of an object-oriented software system.

Figure 14-11 Basic program control constructs. The three basic control constructs used in structured programming are sequence, selection, and iteration.

Sequence
  Action A
  Action B

Selection
  IF Condition R
    Action C
  ELSE
    Action D
  ENDIF

Iteration
  DO WHILE Condition S
    Action E
  ENDDO

object-oriented system using various types of graphical diagrams and the underlying model integrates these views to promote consistency during analysis, design, and implementation.

Table 14-7 provides an overview of UML and its components. "Things" are objects and "structural things" allow system builders to describe objects and their relationships. UML uses two principal types of diagrams: structural diagrams and behavioral diagrams.

Structural diagrams are used to describe the relationship between classes. Review Figure 6-10 in Chapter 6, which is an example of one type of structural diagram called a class diagram. It shows classes of employees and the relationships between them. The terminators at the end of the relationship lines in this diagram indicate the nature of the relationship. The relationships depicted in Figure 6-10 are examples of generalization, which is a relationship between a general kind of thing and a more specific kind of thing. This type of relationship is sometimes described as a "is a relationship." Generalization relationships are used for modeling class inheritance.

Behavioral diagrams are used to describe interactions in an object-oriented system. Figure 14-12 illustrates two types of behavioral diagrams: a use case diagram and a sequence diagram. A use case diagram shows the relationship between a actor and a system. The actor (represented in the diagram as a stick man) is an external entity that interacts with the system, and the use case represents a series of related actions initiated by the actor to accomplish a specific goal. Several interrelated use cases are represented as ovals within a box. Use case modeling is used to specify the functional requirements of a system, focusing on what the system does rather than how it does it. The system's objects and their interactions with each other and with the users of the system are derived from the use case model. A sequence diagram describes the interactions among objects during a certain period of time. The vertical axis represents time while the horizontal axis represents the participating objects and actors. Boxes along the top of the diagram represent actors and instances of objects. Lateral bars drop down from each box to the bottom of each diagram, with interactions between objects represented by arrows drawn from bar to bar. The sequence of events is displayed from top to bottom, with the first interaction at the top and the last at the bottom of the diagram. Sequence diagrams

TABLE 14-7	AN OVERALL VIEW OF UML AND ITS COMPONENTS: THINGS, RELATIONSHIPS, AND DIAGRAMS	

UML Category	UML Elements	Specific UML Details
Things	Structural Things	Classes
		Interfaces
		Collaborations
		Use Cases
		Active Classes
		Components
		Nodes
	Behavioral Things	Interactions
		State Machines
	Grouping Things	Packages
	Annotational Things	Notes
Relationships	Structural Relationships	Dependencies
		Aggregations
		Associations
		Generalizations
	Behavioral Relationships	Communicates
		Includes
		Extends
		Generalizes
Diagrams	Structural Diagrams	Class Diagrams
		Object Diagrams
		Component Diagrams
		Deployment Diagrams
	Behavioral Diagrams	Use Case Diagrams
		Sequence Diagrams
		Collaboration Diagrams
		Statechart Diagrams
		Activity Diagrams

Sources: Kenneth E. Kendall and Julie E. Kendall, *Systems Analysis and Design*, 5th ed., Upper Saddle River, NJ: Prentice Hall, 2002. Copyright © 2002. Reprinted by permission of Prentice Hall Inc.

are used in system design to derive the interactions, relationships, and operations of the objects in the system.

Computer-Aided Software Engineering (CASE)

Computer-aided software engineering (CASE)—sometimes called *computer-aided systems engineering*—is the automation of step-by-step methodologies for software and systems development to reduce the amount of repetitive work the developer needs to do. Its adoption can free the developer for more creative problem-solving tasks. CASE tools also facilitate the creation of clear documentation and the coordination of team development efforts. Team members can share their work easily by accessing each other's files to review or modify what has been done. Some studies have found that systems developed with CASE and the newer methodologies are more reliable, and they require repairs less often (Dekleva, 1992). Modest productivity benefits can also be achieved if the tools are used properly. Many CASE tools are PC-based, with powerful graphical capabilities.

CASE tools provide automated graphics facilities for producing charts and diagrams, screen and report generators, data dictionaries, extensive reporting facilities, analysis and checking tools, code generators, and documentation generators. Most CASE tools are based on one or more of the popular structured methodologies. Some, such as Visible Analyst,

computer-aided software engineering (CASE)
Automation of step-by-step methodologies for software and systems development to reduce the amounts of repetitive work the developer needs to do.

Figure 14-12 Visible Analyst is a tool for automating object-oriented analysis and design. Illustrated here are examples of use case and sequence diagrams.

illustrated in Figure 14-12, support object-oriented development. In general, CASE tools try to increase productivity and quality by doing the following:

- Enforce a standard development methodology and design discipline.
- Improve communication between users and technical specialists.
- Organize and correlate design components and provide rapid access to them via a design repository.
- Automate tedious and error-prone portions of analysis and design.
- Automate code generation, testing, and control rollout.

Many CASE tools have been classified in terms of whether they support activities at the front end or the back end of the systems development process. Front-end CASE tools focus on capturing analysis and design information in the early stages of systems development, whereas back-end CASE tools address coding, testing, and maintenance activities. Back-end tools help convert specifications automatically into program code.

CASE tools automatically tie data elements to the processes where they are used. If a data flow diagram is changed from one process to another, the elements in the data dictionary would be altered automatically to reflect the change in the diagram. CASE tools

CASE tools include capabilities for generating and validating entity-relationship diagrams and data flow diagrams. Such tools facilitate the creation of clear and accurate design specifications and the coordination of team development efforts.

also contain features for validating design diagrams and specifications. CASE tools thus support iterative design by automating revisions and changes and providing prototyping facilities.

A CASE information repository stores all the information defined by the analysts during the project. The repository includes data flow diagrams, structure charts, entity-relationship diagrams, data definitions, process specifications, screen and report formats, notes and comments, and test results. CASE tools now have features to support client/server applications, object-oriented programming, and business process redesign. Methodologies and tool sets are being created to leverage organizational knowledge of business process reengineering (Nissen, 1998).

To be used effectively, CASE tools require organizational discipline. Every member of a development project must adhere to a common set of naming conventions and standards as well as to a development methodology. The best CASE tools enforce common methods and standards, which may discourage their use in situations where organizational discipline is lacking.

Resource Allocation During Systems Development

Views on **resource allocation** during systems development have changed significantly over the years. Resource allocation determines the way the costs, time, and personnel are assigned to different phases of the project. In earlier times, developers focused on programming, with only about 1 percent of the time and costs of a project being devoted to systems analysis (determining specifications). More time should be spent in specifications and systems analysis, decreasing the proportion of programming time and reducing the need for so much maintenance time. Documenting requirements so that they can be understood from their origin through development, specification, and continuing use can also reduce errors as well as time and costs (Domges and Pohl, 1998). Current literature suggests that about one-quarter of a project's time and cost should be expended in specifications and analysis, with perhaps 50 percent of its resources being allocated to design and programming. Installation and post-implementation ideally should require only one-quarter of the project's resources. Investments in software quality initiatives early in a project are likely to provide the greatest payback (Slaughter, Harter, and Krishnan, 1998).

resource allocation
The determination of how costs, time, and personnel are assigned to different phases of a systems development project.

Software Metrics

Software metrics can play a vital role in increasing system quality. **Software metrics** are objective assessments of the system in the form of quantified measurements. Ongoing use of metrics allows the IS department and the user to jointly measure the performance of the system and identify problems as they occur. Examples of software metrics include the number of transactions that can be processed in a specified unit of time, online response time, the number of payroll checks printed per hour, and the number of known bugs per hundred lines of code.

For metrics to be successful, they must be carefully designed, formal, and objective. They must measure significant aspects of the system. In addition, metrics are of no value unless they are used consistently and users agree to the measurements in advance.

software metrics
The objective assessments of the software used in a system in the form of quantified measurements.

Testing

Chapter 12 described the stages of testing required to put an information system in operation—program testing, system testing, and acceptance testing. Early, regular, and thorough testing will contribute significantly to system quality. In general, software testing is often misunderstood. Many view testing as a way to prove the correctness of work they have done. In fact, we know that all sizable software is riddled with errors, and we must test to uncover these errors.

Testing begins at the design phase. Because no coding exists yet, the test normally used is a **walkthrough**—a review of a specification or design document by a small group of people carefully selected based on the skills needed for the particular objectives being tested. Once coding begins, coding walkthroughs also can be used to review program code. However, code must be tested by computer runs. When errors are discovered, the source is found and eliminated through a process called **debugging.**

walkthrough
A review of a specification or design document by a small group of people carefully selected based on the skills needed for the particular objectives being tested.

debugging
The process of discovering and eliminating the errors and defects—the bugs—in program code.

Electronic commerce and electronic business applications introduce new levels of complexity for testing to ensure high-quality performance and functionality. Behind each large Web site such as Amazon.com, eBay, or E*TRADE are hundreds of servers, thousands of miles of network cable, and hundreds of software programs, creating numerous points of vulnerability. These Web sites must be built and tested to make sure that they can withstand expected—and unexpected—spikes and peaks in their load. Both Web site traffic and technical components, such as hardware, software, and networks, must be taken into consideration during application development and during testing.

To test a Web site realistically, companies need to find a way to subject the Web site to the same number of concurrent users as would actually be visiting the site at one time and to devise test plans that reflect what these people would actually be doing. For example, a retail e-commerce site should create a test scenario where there are many visitors just browsing and some are making purchases.

Testing wireless applications poses additional challenges. Many wireless and conventional Web applications are linked to the same back-end systems so the total load on those systems will increase dramatically as wireless users are added. Automated load testing tools that simulate thousands of simultaneous wireless Web and conventional Web browser sessions can help companies measure the impact on system performance.

Many companies delay testing until the end of the application development phase, when design decisions have been finalized and most of the software program code has been written. Leaving Web site performance and scalability tests until the end of the application development cycle is extremely risky because such problems often stem from the fundamental workings of the system. To minimize the chance of discovering major structural problems late in the system's development process, companies should perform this testing well before the system is complete. This makes it possible to address performance bottlenecks and other issues in each application level or system component before everything is integrated.

DATA QUALITY AUDITS AND DATA CLEANSING

Information system quality can also be improved by identifying and correcting faulty data, making error detection a more explicit organizational goal (Klein, Goodhue, and Davis, 1997). The analysis of data quality often begins with a **data quality audit,** which is a structured survey of the accuracy and level of completeness of the data in an information system. Data quality audits are accomplished by the following methods:

- Surveying end users for their perceptions of data quality
- Surveying entire data files
- Surveying samples from data files

data quality audit

A survey and/or sample of files to determine accuracy and completeness of data in an information system.

Trillium provides software for data cleansing, customer identification and relationship matching. Illustrated here is its capability for putting social security numbers in disparate formats into a single standardized format.

Toyota's Data Spins Out of Control

The Lexus is Toyota's high-end luxury auto and Lexus owners expect the very best in customer service. When Toyota Motor Sales USA encountered a recurring service problem in 1998, it thought it was giving Lexus owners the gold-plated treatment. The company would contact owners, pick up their vehicles, repair them, and supply owners with loaner cars until the repairs had been completed. Toyota would return the owners' cars fixed, washed, and filled with fuel. Toyota relied on its Corporate Customer Information System to provide the information about this and other service problems. Toyota's call center in Iowa used the system to handle warranty, roadside assistance, prepaid maintenance, and other service requests.

Data from that system identified Lexus owners with troublesome tires, and Toyota began mailing them checks for $400 or more to replace troublesome tires. But some of these checks went to people who didn't even own a Lexus and one was mailed to a Toyota auditor for a vehicle he no longer owned. These mistakes pointed to a massive data quality problem because the Corporate Customer Information System used customer data stored in 15 databases in different parts of the company.

Upon learning of the problem, senior management called for a single centralized customer database that would resolve these discrepancies and shorten the amount of time call center employees spent accessing customer data. Toyota used Informatica's PowerMart and software tools for data extraction, transformation, and loading into a central data warehouse capable of storing 250 gigabytes of data.

Window on Management

MIS in Action

By April 1999, Toyota had built its central customer database and installed the Informatica software. It took an additional six months to get the system in working order. The biggest hurdle was cleansing the data. Toyota's databases had several million records that had to be checked. Some databases had wrong addresses, wrong vehicles, and wrong motors. Toyota had to use state department of motor vehicle records to check some of the data. In a few instances the company had to call customers to help them straighten their records out.

The total project cost ran over $2.5 million and Toyota believes this is money well spent. Call center employees can access customer information much more rapidly, so Toyota did not have to increase the size of its staff as the volume of calls went up. Annual vehicle sales have more than doubled from 750,000 to 1.7 million and the company trusts that the data in the central database is now accurate enough to support decision making throughout the company.

But the struggle for high data quality never ends. Toyota has continued its data cleansing work, with data from Mexico recently rolled into the system.

MAKE IT YOUR BUSINESS

To Think About: What management and organizational problems were created by poor data quality at Toyota? What management decisions had to be made to solve this problem?

Sources: Sean Gallagher, "Default Setting" *Baseline,* June 2002 and *Informatica* corporate Web site, accessed July 22, 2002, <www.informatica.com>.

MANAGEMENT

Unless regular data quality audits are undertaken, organizations have no way of knowing to what extent their information systems contain inaccurate, incomplete, or ambiguous information.

Until recently, many organizations were not giving data quality the priority it deserves (Tayi and Ballou, 1998). Now electronic commerce and electronic business are forcing more companies to pay attention to data quality because a digitally enabled firm cannot run efficiently without accurate data about customers and business partners. **Data cleansing** has become a core requirement for data warehousing, customer relationship management, and Web-based commerce.

Companies implementing data warehousing often find inconsistencies in customer or employee information as they try to integrate information from different business units. Companies are also finding mistakes in the data provided by customers or business partners through a Web site. Online Net marketplaces (see Chapter 4) are especially problematic because they use catalog data from dozens to thousands of suppliers and these data are often in different formats, with different classification schemes for product numbers, product descriptions, and other attributes. Data cleansing tools can be used to correct errors in these data and to integrate these data in a consistent company-wide format (see the Window on Management).

data cleansing
Correcting errors and inconsistencies in data to increase accuracy so that they can be used in a standard company-wide format.

MAKE IT YOUR BUSINESS

FINANCE AND ACCOUNTING

Security and reliability are absolutely critical in systems for banking and financial services because errors, fraud, and disruption of service can lead to large monetary losses and the erosion of consumer confidence in these companies and even the entire financial industry. Prevention of fraud, errors, and manipulation of assets in financial and accounting systems are key objectives of application and general controls. The accounting function is often involved in information system audits and in the design of information system controls. You can find examples of finance and accounting applications on pages 448–449, 452, and 479–481.

HUMAN RESOURCES

"People factors" are as important as technology in establishing the security and reliability of the firm's information systems. Many security breaches and system errors are caused by legitimate company "insiders." Software quality depends on the commitment to quality of the people designing the software. Establishing quality and security-consciousness among employees has become an important human resources function, because human resources data include confidential pieces of information, such as salary or illnesses, which require tight data security safeguards.

MANUFACTURING AND PRODUCTION

Manufacturing systems today are more vulnerable than in the past because they have become increasingly net-worked and integrated with each other as well as with the manufacturing systems of other firms. Supply chain management systems can be deeply affected by network outages or software quality problems because interrupted flows of information can adversely impact so many members of the supply chain. Security and reliability are thus very high priorities in the design of intranets and extranets for manufacturing and production.

SALES AND MARKETING

Electronic commerce requires secure payment systems for online purchases as well as fault-tolerant or high-availability systems that prevent interruptions of service. Encryption, digital signatures, digital certificates, and technologies for scalability and high-availability computing are important technologies for creating such systems. Data quality standards must be higher so that the company can immediately process accurate customer data. You can find examples of sales and marketing applications on pages 448–449 and 475.

MANAGEMENT WRAP-UP

Management is responsible for developing the control structure and quality standards for the organization. Key management decisions include establishing standards for systems accuracy and reliability, determining an appropriate level of control for organizational functions, and establishing a disaster recovery plan.

The characteristics of the organization play a large role in determining its approach to quality assurance and control issues. Some organizations are more quality and control conscious than others. Their cultures and business processes support high standards of quality and performance. Creating high levels of security and quality in information systems can be a process of lengthy organizational change.

A number of technologies and methodologies are available for promoting system quality and security. Technologies such as antivirus and data security software, firewalls, fault-tolerant and high-availability computing technology, and programmed procedures can be used to create a control environment, whereas software metrics, systems development methodologies, and automated tools for systems development can be used to improve software quality. Organizational discipline is required to use these technologies effectively.

For Discussion

1. It has been said that controls and security should be one of the first areas to be addressed in the design of an information system. Do you agree? Why or why not?

2. How much software testing is "enough?" What management, organization, and technology issues should you consider in answering this question?

SUMMARY

1. *Why are information systems so vulnerable to destruction, error, abuse, and system quality problems?* With data concentrated into electronic form and many procedures invisible through automation, computerized information systems are vulnerable to destruction, misuse, error, fraud, and hardware or software failures. Online systems and those utilizing the Internet are especially vulnerable because data and files can be immediately and directly accessed through computer terminals or at many points in the network. Hackers can penetrate corporate networks and cause serious system disruptions. Computer viruses can spread rampantly from system to system, clogging computer memory or destroying programs and data. Software presents problems because of the high costs of correcting errors and because software bugs may be impossible to eliminate. Data quality can also severely impact system quality and performance.

2. *What types of controls are available for information systems?* Controls consist of all the methods, policies, and organizational procedures that ensure the safety of the organization's assets, the accuracy and reliability of its accounting records, and adherence to management standards. There are two main categories of controls: general controls and application controls.

   General controls handle the overall design, security, and use of computers, programs, and files for the organization's information technology infrastructure. They include physical hardware controls, system software controls, data file security controls, computer operations controls, controls over the system implementation process, and administrative disciplines.

   Application controls are those unique to specific computerized applications. They focus on the completeness and accuracy of input, updating and maintenance, and the validity of the information in the system. Application controls consist of (1) input controls, (2) processing controls, and (3) output controls.

   To determine which controls are required, designers and users of systems must identify all of the control points and control weaknesses and perform risk assessment. They must also perform a cost/benefit analysis of controls and design controls that can effectively safeguard systems without making them unusable.

3. *What special measures must be taken to ensure the reliability, availability, and security of electronic commerce and digital business processes?* Companies require special measures to support electronic commerce and digital business processes.

They can use fault-tolerant computer systems or create high-availability computing environments to make sure that their information systems are always available and performing without interruptions. Disaster recovery plans provide procedures and facilities for restoring computing and communication services after they have been disrupted. Firewalls and intrusion detection systems help safeguard private networks from unauthorized access when organizations use intranets or link to the Internet. Encryption is a widely used technology for securing electronic transmissions over the Internet. Digital certificates provide further protection of electronic transactions by authenticating a user's identity.

4. *What are the most important software quality assurance techniques?* The quality and reliability of software can be improved by using a standard development methodology, software metrics, thorough testing procedures, and by allocating resources to put more emphasis on the analysis and design stages of systems development.

   Structured methodologies have been used to increase software quality since the 1970s. Structured analysis highlights the flow of data and the processes through which data are transformed. Its principal tool is the data flow diagram. Structured design and programming are software design disciplines that produce reliable, well-documented software with a simple, clear structure that is easy for others to understand and maintain. Unified Modeling Language (UML) provides a standard methodology for modeling an object-oriented system that promotes consistency during analysis, design, and implementation.

   Computer-aided software engineering (CASE) automates methodologies for systems development. It promotes standards and improves coordination and consistency during systems development. CASE tools help system builders construct a better model of a system and facilitate revision of design specifications to correct errors.

5. *Why are auditing information systems and safeguarding data quality so important?* Comprehensive and systematic MIS auditing can help organizations to determine the effectiveness of the controls in their information systems. Regular data quality audits should be conducted to help organizations ensure a high level of completeness and accuracy of the data stored in their systems. Data cleansing should also be performed to create consistent and accurate data for company-wide use in electronic commerce and electronic business.

KEY TERMS

Administrative controls, 457	Bugs, 455	Computer virus, 453	Data quality audit, 474
Antivirus software, 453	Clustering, 461	Controls, 457	Data security controls, 457
Application controls, 457	Computer-aided software engineering (CASE), 471	Data cleansing, 475	Debugging, 473
Authentication, 463		Data flow diagram, 467	Denial of service attack, 452

REVIEW QUESTIONS

1. Why are computer systems more vulnerable than manual systems to destruction, fraud, error, and misuse? Name some of the key areas where systems are most vulnerable.

2. Name some features of online information systems that make them difficult to control.

3. How can poor software and data quality affect system performance and reliability? Describe two software quality problems.

4. What are controls? Distinguish between general controls and application controls.

5. Name and describe the principal general and application controls for computerized systems.

6. What is security? List and describe controls that promote security for computer hardware, computer networks, computer software, and computerized data.

7. What special security measures must be taken by organizations linking to the Internet?

8. Distinguish between fault-tolerant and high-availability computing.

9. Describe the role of firewalls, intrusion detection systems, and encryption systems in promoting security.

10. Why are digital signatures and digital certificates important for electronic commerce?

11. What is the function of risk assessment?

12. How does MIS auditing enhance the control process?

13. Name and describe four software quality assurance techniques.

14. What is structured analysis? What is the role of the data flow diagram in structured analysis?

15. How is structured design related to structured programming? How can both promote software quality?

16. How does Unified Modeling Language (UML) support object-oriented analysis and design?

17. Why are data quality audits and data cleansing essential?

APPLICATION SOFTWARE EXERCISE

SPREADSHEET EXERCISE: PERFORMING A SECURITY RISK ASSESSMENT

Mercer Paints is a small but highly regarded paint manufacturing company located in Alabama. The company has a network in place, linking many of its business operations. While the firm feels that its security is adequate, the recent addition of a Web site has been an open invitation to hackers. Management requested a risk assessment. The risk assessment identified several potential exposures; these exposures, associated probabilities, and average losses are summarized in the table that can be found on the Laudon Web site for Chapter 14. In addition to the potential exposures listed, you should identify at least three other potential threats to Mercer Paints, assign probabilities, and estimate a loss range.

Using spreadsheet software and the risk assessment data provided on the Laudon Web site, calculate the expected annual loss for each exposure. Which control points have the greatest vulnerability? What recommendations would you make to Mercer Paints? Prepare a written report that summarizes your findings and recommendations.

GROUP PROJECT

Form a group with two or three other students. Select a system described in one of the chapter ending cases. Write a description of the system, its functions, and its value to the organization. Then write a description of both the general and application controls that should be used to protect the organization. If possible, use electronic presentation software to present your findings to the class.

TOOLS FOR INTERACTIVE LEARNING

■ INTERNET CONNECTION

The Internet Connection for this chapter will take you to a series of Web sites where you can complete an exercise to evaluate various secure electronic payment systems for the Internet.

■ INTERACTIVE STUDY GUIDE

You can use the Interactive Study Guide to test your knowledge of the topics in this chapter and get instant feedback where you need more practice.

■ RUNNING CASE

The Running Case provides an opportunity for you to develop a disaster recovery plan and evaluate disaster recovery services for Dirt Bikes USA. You can find a complete description of this project on the Laudon Web site for Chapter 14 and on the Multimedia Edition CD-ROM.

■ ELECTRONIC BUSINESS PROJECT

At the Laudon Web site for Chapter 14, you will find an Electronic Business Project to evaluate security outsourcing services.

■ MANAGEMENT DECISION PROBLEM

At the Laudon Web site for Chapter 14, you will find a Management Decision Problem on Analyzing Security Vulnerabilities.

■ CD-ROM

If you use the Multimedia Edition CD-ROM with this chapter, you can find a video clip illustrating Infogates' secure personalized information services, an audio overview of the major themes of this chapter, and bullet text summarizing the key points of the chapter.

CASE STUDY—*Rogue Currency Trades at Allied Irish Banks: How Could It Happen?*

On February 5, 2002, the financial world was shaken by the revelation of a $750 million foreign exchange trading loss suffered by Allfirst, a Baltimore bank providing corporate, commercial, correspondent, and retail banking services in the mid-Atlantic states. The bank had been a subsidiary of the Allied Irish Banks PLC (AIB), the largest financial institution in Ireland. The huge loss reminded many of the 1995 Barings Bank scandal where a Singapore trader named Nick Leeson had hidden $1.4 billion in losses. Those losses ended with the collapse of Barings. The history of financial market trading is replete with fraudulent traders who were not scrutinized because they were "making so much money," so an Allfirst trader only appeared to be doing the same old thing. One executive in a foreign exchange company observed, "The pressures on people to produce revenues are extraordinary."

The accused foreign exchange trader was John Rusnak, a 37 year-old man with a wife and two children who lived modestly on an $85,000 salary plus a trader's bonus that never reached $200,000. He had worked for years in the foreign exchange department of Chemical Bank, now J.P. Morgan Chase, and for the last seven years he was doing the same thing at Allfirst. The bank's management reported that his huge losses were from unauthorized trades beginning in early 2001, and they were probably from trading in Japanese yen. The yen had declined during the last few months of 2001, and Rusnak apparently expected it to turn and rise against the euro. Rusnak placed trades to benefit from the expected rise, but the yen fell 11 percent from mid-September to year-end, and Rusnak's losses kept growing. To hide his losses, Rusnak told Allfirst's Treasury Department that he had sold yen currency options to hedge his bets, but in fact he never did. Rather, he falsified trade confirmations.

In mid-January, to finance his enormous losses, Rusnak began asking for unusually large amounts of money, which triggered an investigation by senior staff members of Allfirst's Treasury department. Rusnak cooperated, and on Thursday, January 31 Allfirst confronted Rusnak with falsified options trades. The next day he

produced 12 paper confirmations to support those trades, but they appeared to be fakes. Allfirst checked on one confirmation by telephoning Bank of America (BofA) in San Francisco. BofA said it had not done that trade and proved the BofA logo on the confirmation to be a phony. Rusnak disappeared over the weekend, failed to return phone calls, and did not show up for work on Monday. That day AIB was informed of the $750 million loss and the next day AIB unwound Rusnak's yen holding, producing a huge Allfirst loss. The next day the information was released to the public, and the Federal Bureau of Investigation (FBI) moved in.

Allfirst CEO and president, Susan Keating, said, "I am greatly disappointed to learn about these events, and that policy and control procedures in place were violated." Allfirst said that Rusnak's upper limit on a trade was only $2.5 million, an impossibly low figure considering the losses he had accumulated. By Thursday February 7, it became clear that Rusnak had not fled. He hired a lawyer, David Irwin who said Rusnak had not stolen any of the bank's money and was already cooperating with the FBI. The United States attorney's office had also been called in to investigate, as were Federal Reserve bank examiners.

On Friday, AIB said it would install new trading controls as soon as possible to prevent any future trades of this type. It also said management and control of Allfirst Treasury operations would be centralized in Dublin under the direction of the head of AIB's Capital Markets Treasury. AIB also announced it would appoint an external senior expert to lead an internal investigation into the causes of the loss, including violation of internal controls, and possible internal and external collusion. The investigation report would state the facts, describe policies and controls and their effectiveness, and make recommendations for improvements. On February 10, Eugene Ludwig, the former head of the U.S. Office of the Comptroller of the Currency, was named to lead the investigation. Two days later, five Allfirst executives were suspended, and 15 executives from Dublin were sent to Baltimore to oversee Allfirst.

Federal agents reported that Rusnak stated he had taken trades, and when losses began to magnify, he began to use a secret strategy to make up for his losses. But his losses "just got deeper." The FBI said, "It isn't looking like he embezzled the $750 million," although the AIB board said the trades were not authorized by the bank. The FBI found evidence that Rusnak was not trying to steal for himself, but just to recover his immense losses when he had guessed wrong on the direction of the yen. Also the FBI pointed out that he did not flee, and he cooperated when he was discovered. On the other hand, he did not protect his currency trades with options.

On February 20, after a careful examination of the records, AIB announced that Rusnak's currency trade losses actually began five years earlier in 1997. AIB also said the total loss was now lowered to $691.2 million. AIB also reported the losses were in the bank's proprietary trading account, indicating that the bank had encouraged Rusnak to trade in order to earn profits for the bank. Allfirst was forced to resubmit five years of annual financial statements to the Securities and Exchange Commission (SEC).

On March 14, AIB released the Ludwig report. It concluded that "Mr. Rusnak circumvented the controls that were intended to prevent any such fraud by manipulating the weak control environment in Allfirst's Treasury; notably, he found ways of circumventing changes in control procedures throughout the period of his fraud." The report also said, "Mr. Rusnak took advantage of weak and inexperienced employees in the [Allfirst] Treasury control groups. These employees, by virtue of their inexperience, poor training, poor supervision and, in some cases, laziness, facilitated Mr. Rusnak in circumventing controls." The report even said Rusnak was allowed to trade during his vacation, which was against banking guidelines. However, the report concluded that no one in the bank knowingly conspired with Rusnak. Because of weak controls, six Allfirst employees were dismissed, including Rusnak, David Cronin, Allfirst's executive vice president and treasurer, Robert Ray, Rusnak's supervisor, and Jan Palmer, Allfirst's Head of Internal Audit. Keating was neither criticized nor dismissed. Allfirst's Chairman, Frank Bramble, announced his early retirement; claiming it was not related to the scandal.

What went wrong? The industry has a set of best practices for controlling such trades. When a currency trade takes place, if it is for a customer, the trader is required to hedge (buy an option in the opposite direction) to protect against a large loss. Traders normally hedge even if the trade is for the bank or for him/herself. When any trade takes place—currency or hedge—both sides must legally confirm the trade or it will not be valid. Today that is usually done through a computerized service that can automatically acknowledge and validate both sides of the trade, almost anywhere in the world, within two minutes. If a computerized service is not used, the bank must have a rigorous procedure for approving the counterparty (the other side of a trade) with whom traders are allowed to conduct business. Usually that will be done by a telephone call to the counterparty.

Workable controls in any financial transaction must include the separation of responsibilities. That is, functions must be separated so that the person making the trade cannot also control or verify the trade. In currency trading (as well as many other types of trading), the organization must separate the duties between a front office, or trading desk and the back office, which handles trade accounting and controlling, including enforcing credit limits. All trades must be approved by the back office (today that is mostly done by computer systems). Moreover, traders can neither authorize accounts nor set them up nor authorize payments to outside clients.

In 1998, AIB installed software from Misys in the United Kingdom, which could be used to control front and back office work during currency trades. The Misys suite called "Tropics" captures currency trades electronically at the front desk. It also would catch trades that were over the limit. The back office suite called Opics tracks all foreign exchange transactions. Together the two software packages provide "straight-through processing," enabling trades to be electronically fulfilled on the same day they are executed. This setup catches sham trades, trades beyond approved limits, and trades with nonapproved counterparties. Together they would automatically generate alerts to the appropriate managers if any rules were broken. AIB also used Crossmar Matching Service, which automatically electronically confirms both sides of a trade within two minutes. It is used by around 1,000 banks, corporations, and fund-management companies.

AIB installed Opics, the back office software, at Allfirst, but no Tropics front office software was installed. Therefore Allfirst did not have straight through processing, and the information on the trade was given to the back office manually. Allfirst also did not use Crossmar to validate a trade and instead was supposed to rely on telephones.

AIB used risk-management analytics software, in order to evaluate the risk of a trade being considered. Front and/or back office systems automatically feed trade data into the software. Once the risk on known trades is calculated, the company can execute countervailing trades in currency options to minimize the risk. AIB installed Askari's RiskBook, which was later acquired by State Street Corp. and renamed TruView. Allfirst did not use RiskBook (TruView), relying instead on Monte Carlo simulation software to calculate a currency trade's risk. Monte Carlo simulations are derived from statistical descriptions of data and try to simulate possible paths that underlying assets could take in the future. Once thousands of paths have been created, a firm can average the value over these paths to determine the most likely outcome. However, Allfirst's 10-K Securities and Exchange filing stated that the company did not take the average but instead chose the "tenth worst observation," which minimized the actual amount of risk to which the company was exposed. Moreover, Monte Carlo simulations are typically used for credit-risk modeling and not for currency trading. Rusnak seemed to know that Monte Carlo was inadequate and so he asked his management to purchase RiskBook. He was turned down for budgetary reasons.

According to David Atkinson, a former AIB currency trader, "The controls put in place by AIB's New York office for its own traders were very strong and I'm amazed that Allfirst didn't have similar measures. If you went a dime over any limit, [AIB's] credit officers would know that. I even got calls on trades that were within the limits, if they appeared out of the ordinary."

How did Rusnak bypass the standard safeguards? One issue is the verification of fictitious trades, which should have been found years earlier. Clearly the back office relied on Rusnak to manually give them information on each trade. Moreover, Rusnak entered his trades using Reuters software on his own computer, and the back-office staff had no access to it, enabling him to give them different information. He used other methods as well. He often gave his fake option trades a one-day expiration date, knowing no one would notice them because Allfirst reports do not list options expiring in one day. In the early days, Rusnak did produce forged confirmation documents for fake trades but ceased that practiced in September 1998 when, according to the Ludwig report, he "apparently managed to persuade an individual in the back office not to seek to confirm the purported pairs of options." It further stated "There was no need for confirmations, he apparently argued, because there was no net transfer of cash. Perhaps this practice suited the convenience of the back-office staffer."

According to the report "the bogus options were purportedly with the Tokyo or Singapore branches of major international financial institutions, and to have made confirming telephone calls would have required the employee to work in the middle of the night." In addition, Larry Smith, the back-office person responsible for verifying Rusnak's trades, told investigators his bosses had told him not to bother verifying trades with banks in Asia. Therefore the trade confirmations must have come from someone at Allfirst; probably Rusnak himself. Smith said no action was taken even after he raised his concerns about trade confirmations. Later, after Smith talked with the FBI about these events, he was fired.

To give himself cover, Rusnak sometimes implied that he had a big hedge fund for a client, or he said he was a proprietary trader (trading for his own or the bank's account, not for clients). Other times he indicated he wanted to trade with other banks that would allow him to bundle all of his trades into a single trade at the end of the day. One trader said this made it easier for him to place false trades that made it look like he was hedging against losses. To Allfirst, it would appear that he made only one trade.

As Rusnak became deeper and deeper in debt, he began to sell deep currency options to raise cash, generating a total of over $300 million in cash in 2001 (but Allfirst had to pay the client when the options expired). These were considered "synthetic loans" to Allfirst, by BofA, which consulted with AIB before approving the deal, making it clear that an AIB executive knew about Rusnak's shenanigans. AIB later denied such consultation had occurred while BofA refused comment, but Ludwig's report described the event.

The industry's Guidelines for Foreign Exchange Trading Activities were written by foreign exchange executives along with Federal Reserve Bank of New York representatives. It says "Significant book profits or losses, unusual requests, and transactions or patterns of activity inconsistent with a customer's profile should be referred to management." Buckley apparently questioned Allfirst's executive vice president and treasurer, David Cronin, about the size of Allfirst's currency trading and Cronin told Buckley to approve the trade. Ludwig's report also said that AIB group treasurer Patrick Ryan was also informed of a Rusnak position of more than $1 billion yen (around $10 million), making it clear that AIB knew Rusnak had topped his limit of $2.5 million. The banks that bought his options were BofA, Citibank, Deutsche Bank, and Bank of New York. As the options were exercised, the losses multiplied. This also raised suspicions of external collusion.

On June 6, 2002 a federal grand jury in Baltimore indicted Rusnak on seven counts, including bank fraud and false entry in bank records. He was reported to have been working on a plea agreement and may cooperate with federal prosecutors. On September 26, 2002 Allied Irish Banks announced plans to sell Allfirst Financial to M & T Bank Corporation of Buffalo for $3.1 billion in cash and stock.

Sources: Jonathan Fuerbringer, "Bank Report Says Trader Had Bold Plot," *New York Times*, March 15, 2002, "How Trail of Big Currency Losses Remained Uncovered for 5 Years," *New York Times*, March 5, 2002, "Arcane System Let Currency Trader Hide Losses," *New York Times*, February 19, 2002, "How Much Did a Bank Know About Its Currency Trader's Losses?" *New York Times*, February 16 2002, "Investigation Into Rogue Trades Finds Red Flags but Few Details," *New York Times*, February 14, 2002, and "Bank Trader's Losses Total $750 Million," *New York Times*, February 7 2002; Brian Lavery, "Irish Sells Troubled U.S. Bank but Maintain Some Influence," *New York Times*, September 27, 2002, "6 Fired as Irish Bank Acts on U.S. Trading Loss," *New York Times*, March 15, 2002, "Hidden Currency Losses Go Back 5 Years, Irish Bank Says," *New York Times*, February 21, 2002, and "Two Big Questions Await Irish Bank Inquiry," *New York Times*, February 12, 2002; Sean Gallagher, "How Allfirst Trader Fudged Data," *Baseline*, March 14, 2002, "Allfirst Financial: Out of Control," *Baseline*, March 12, 2002, and "How Allfirst Gambled on Monte Carlo," *Baseline,* March 12, 2002; Bill Atkinson and Andrew Ratner, "Amid Shareholder Threats, Allied Irish Hold Annual Meeting in Belfast Today," *Baltimore Sun*, May 29, 2002; Conal Walsh, "Fired AIB Man Seeks Cash," *The Observer*, April 28, 2002; Shawn Pogatchnik, "Allied Irish Drops Auditing Firm," *Baltimore Sun*, April 24, 2002; Richard Curran, "AIB Lends 900m to Bail Out Allfirst," *Irish Independent*, April 5, 2002; Craig Karmin and James R. Hagerty, "Allied Irish Trader Lacked Inside Help, Report Indicates," *Wall Street Journal*, March 14, 2002; Alessandra Galloni and Michael R. Sesit, "Lax Controls May Explain Loss at Allied Irish," *Wall Street Journal*, March 8, 2002; Julie Bell and William A. Patalon III, "Investors Sue Officers of Allfirst," *Baltimore Sun*, March 7, 2002; Alessandra Galloni and Michael R. Sesit, "Junior Employee Monitored Risk at Allfirst's Currency-Trading Desk," and "Controls at Allied Irish's Allfirst Likely Failed in Important Ways," *Wall Street Journal*, February 20, 2002, and "AIB Suspects Another Employee Aided Rusnak in Trading Fraud," *Wall Street Journal*, February 11, 2002; Oleg Artyukov, "John Rusnak Became Scapegoat," *Pravda*, February 9, 2002; Gary Fields, Erik Portanger, Jathon Sapsford, and Craig Karmin, "As Big Losses Grew, Trader's Solution Backfired," *Wall Street Journal*, February 8, 2002; Rupert Cocke, "Allied Irish Banks to Put in Urgent Trading Controls," *Dow Jones Newswires*, February 8, 2002; Erik Portanger, Michael R. Sesit, and Alessandra Galloni, "Allied Irish Banks Say a Rogue Trader Lost $750 Million in Unauthorized Deals," *Wall Street Journal*, February 7, 2002; Debra Marks, "Biggest Casualty From AIB Fallout Will Be Senior Mgmt," *Wall Street Journal*, February 7, 2002.

CASE STUDY QUESTIONS:

1. Briefly describe the Allied Irish and Allfirst problem that suddenly came to light early in February 2002.

2. Describe the control weaknesses at Allfirst and Allied Irish. What management, organization, and technology factors contributed to these weaknesses?

3. Who or what was responsible for the Rusnak trading losses? What role did Allied Irish and Allfirst's systems play? What role did management play?

4. Could information systems have prevented Rusnak from doing what he did? Explain.

5. If you were responsible for designing new information systems for AIB and Allfirst, what would you do to solve their control problems?

15

CHAPTER

MANAGING INTERNATIONAL INFORMATION SYSTEMS

objectives

As a manager, you'll want to know what special issues must be addressed when developing and managing international information systems. After completing this chapter, you will be able to answer the following questions:

1. *What are the major factors driving the internationalization of business?*

2. *What strategies are available for developing international businesses?*

3. *How can information systems support the various international business strategies?*

4. *What issues should manages address when developing international information systems?*

5. *What technical alternatives are available for developing global systems?*

Paul Hartmann AG Internationalizes with Global Systems

International operations now generate more than half the revenue at Paul Hartmann AG, a German surgical and hygiene products supplier with subsidiaries in over 25 countries. As the company rapidly expanded into North America and Asia, its management realized that it could lower the total cost of ownership of its technology assets if it had a centralized information systems function with common systems worldwide. It implemented SAP R/3 enterprise system modules in its subsidiaries that supported 3,000 users by the end of 2002.

The company wanted a global system that could standardize and integrate some business processes globally while allowing subsidiaries to serve the specific needs of individual countries. It had used earlier versions of SAP software in its general accounting department in its German headquarters and gradually rolled out the software to its European subsidiaries. Forty members of Paul Hartmann's information systems department worked on implementing the new SAP system. The new SAP system is operated and supported from corporate headquarters in Heidenheim, Germany.

The company needed a reliable and available communications network to achieve optimum performance from the SAP software and to facilitate global implementation of the system. A team led by Eugen Grossegesse, Paul

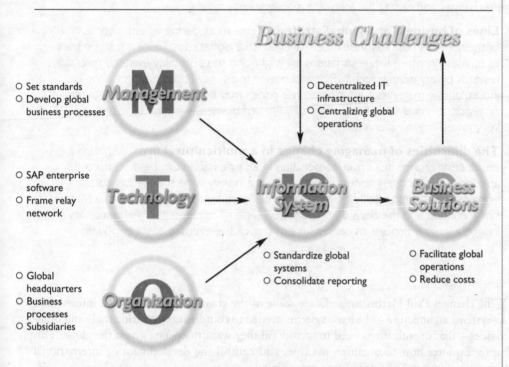

Hartmann's manager of International Networks, selected Infonet Services Corporation's international frame-relay network service. Infonet had good connections with local communications providers in various countries and was able to guarantee a response time of four hours in the event of a line problem. Paul Hartmann operates and monitors the network, which links 60 sites, from Heidenheim.

The company's next goal is to implement more SAP applications at its subsidiaries, including customer relationship management, human resources, and logistics. Long term, Paul Hartmann would like to set up regionalized systems for Central Europe, North America, and Asia to manage time zone differences using hardware and software operated in Heidenheim.

Sources: Ann Toh, "Under Control, Globally," *CIO Asia*, May 2002; Hartmann corporate Web site, accessed June 23, 2002, <www.hartmann-online.de>; and "SAP BW Takes the Leading Role at Paul Hartmann AG," IBM Corporation, 2000.

483

MANAGEMENT CHALLENGES

Paul Hartmann AG is one of many business firms moving toward global forms of organization that transcend national boundaries. Paul Hartmann could not make this move unless it reorganized its information systems and standardized some of its business processes so that the same information could be used by disparate business units in different countries. The opening vignette shows some of the issues that must be addressed when making these changes, and raising the following management challenges:

1. **Lines of business and global strategy.** Firms must decide whether some or all of their lines of business should be managed on a global basis. There are some lines of business in which locale variations are slight, and the possibility exists to reap large rewards by organizing globally. PCs and power tools may fit this pattern, as well as industrial raw materials. Other consumer goods may be quite different by country or region. It is likely that firms with many lines of business will have to maintain a very mixed organizational structure.

2. **The difficulties of managing change in a multicultural firm.** Although engineering change in a single corporation in a single nation can be difficult, costly, and long term, bringing about significant change in very large-scale global corporations can be daunting. Both the agreement on "core business processes" in a transnational context and the decision on common systems require either extraordinary insight, a lengthy process of consensus building, or the exercise of sheer power.

The changes Paul Hartmann seeks are some of the changes in international information systems architecture—the basic systems needed to coordinate worldwide trade and other activities—that organizations need to consider if they want to operate across the globe. This chapter explores how to organize, manage, and control the development of international information systems as firms become more digital.

15.1 THE GROWTH OF INTERNATIONAL INFORMATION SYSTEMS

We already have described two powerful worldwide changes driven by advances in information technology that have transformed the business environment and posed new challenges for management. One is the transformation of industrial economies and societies into knowledge- and information-based economies. The other is the emergence of a global economy and global world order.

The new world order will sweep away many national corporations, national industries, and national economies controlled by domestic politicians. Much of the Fortune 500—the 500 largest U.S. corporations—will disappear in the next 50 years, mirroring past behavior of large firms since 1900. Many firms will be replaced by fast-moving networked corporations that transcend national boundaries. The growth of international trade has radically altered domestic economies around the globe. About $1 trillion worth of goods, services, and financial instruments—one-fifth of the annual U.S. gross national product—changes hands each day in global trade.

Consider a laptop computer as an example: The CPU is likely to have been designed and built in the United States; the DRAM (or dynamic random access memory, which makes up the majority of primary storage in a computer) was designed in the United States but built in Malaysia; the screen was designed and assembled in Japan, using American patents; the keyboard is from Taiwan; and it was all assembled in Japan, where the case also was made. Management of the project, located in Silicon Valley, California, along with marketing, sales, and finance, coordinated all the activities from financing and production to shipping and sales efforts. None of this would be possible without powerful international information and telecommunication systems, an international information systems architecture.

Global Environment:
Business Drivers and Challenges

Corporate Global Strategies

Organization Structure

Management and Business
Processes

Technology Platform

↓

International Information Systems Architecture

Figure 15-1 International information systems architecture. The major dimensions for developing an international information systems architecture are the global environment, the corporate global strategies, the structure of the organization, the management and business processes, and the technology platform.

To be effective, managers need a global perspective on business and an understanding of the support systems needed to conduct business on an international scale.

DEVELOPING AN INTERNATIONAL INFORMATION SYSTEMS ARCHITECTURE

This chapter describes how to go about building an international information systems architecture suitable for your international strategy. An **international information systems architecture** consists of the basic information systems required by organizations to coordinate worldwide trade and other activities. Figure 15-1 illustrates the reasoning we will follow throughout the chapter and depicts the major dimensions of an international information systems architecture.

The basic strategy to follow when building an international system is to understand the global environment in which your firm is operating. This means understanding the overall market forces, or business drivers, that are pushing your industry toward global competition. A **business driver** is a force in the environment to which businesses must respond and that influences the direction of the business. Likewise, examine carefully the inhibitors or negative factors that create *management challenges*—factors that could scuttle the development of a global business. Once you have examined the global environment, you will need to consider a corporate strategy for competing in that environment. How will your firm respond? You could ignore the global market and focus on domestic competition only, sell to the globe from a domestic base, or organize production and distribution around the globe. There are many in-between choices.

After you have developed a strategy, it is time to consider how to structure your organization so it can pursue the strategy. How will you accomplish a division of labor across a global environment? Where will production, administration, accounting, marketing, and human resource functions be located? Who will handle the systems function?

Next, you must consider the management issues in implementing your strategy and making the organization design come alive. Key here will be the design of business procedures. How can you discover and manage user requirements? How can you induce change in local units to conform to international requirements? How can you reengineer on a global scale, and how can you coordinate systems development?

The last issue to consider is the technology platform. Although changing technology is a key driving factor leading toward global markets, you need to have a corporate strategy and structure before you can rationally choose the right technology.

After you have completed this process of reasoning, you will be well on your way toward an appropriate international information systems architecture capable of achieving your corporate goals. Let us begin by looking at the overall global environment.

international information systems architecture
The basic information systems required by organizations to coordinate worldwide trade and other activities.

business driver
A force in the environment to which businesses must respond and that influences the direction of business.

TABLE 15-1	THE GLOBAL BUSINESS DRIVERS
General Cultural Factors	**Specific Business Factors**
Global communication and transportation technologies	Global markets
Development of global culture	Global production and operations
Emergence of global social norms	Global coordination
Political stability	Global workforce
Global knowledge base	Global economies of scale

THE GLOBAL ENVIRONMENT: BUSINESS DRIVERS AND CHALLENGES

Table 15-1 illustrates the business drivers in the global environment that are leading all industries toward global markets and competition.

The global business drivers can be divided into two groups: general cultural factors and specific business factors. There are easily recognized general cultural factors driving internationalization since World War II. Information, communication, and transportation technologies have created a *global village* in which communication (by telephone, television, radio, or computer network) around the globe is no more difficult and not much more expensive than communication down the block. Moving goods and services to and from geographically dispersed locations has fallen dramatically in cost.

The development of global communications has created a global village in a second sense: There is now a **global culture** created by television and other globally shared media such as movies that permits different cultures and peoples to develop common expectations about right and wrong, desirable and undesirable, heroic and cowardly. The collapse of the Eastern bloc has speeded up the growth of a world culture enormously, increased support for capitalism and business, and reduced the level of cultural conflict considerably.

A last factor to consider is the growth of a global knowledge base. At the end of World War II, knowledge, education, science, and industrial skills were highly concentrated in North America, western Europe, and Japan, with the rest of the world euphemistically called the *Third World*. This is no longer true. Latin America, China, southern Asia, and eastern Europe have developed powerful educational, industrial, and scientific centers, resulting in a much more democratically and widely dispersed knowledge base.

These general cultural factors leading toward internationalization result in specific business globalization factors that affect most industries. The growth of powerful communications technologies and the emergence of world cultures create the condition for *global markets*—global consumers interested in consuming similar products that are culturally approved. Coca-Cola, American sneakers (made in Korea but designed in Los Angeles), and CNN Live (a television show) can now be sold in Latin America, Africa, and Asia.

global culture

The development of common expectations, shared artifacts, and social norms among different cultures and peoples.

Businesses need an international information systems architecture to coordinate the activities of their sales, manufacturing, and warehouse units worldwide.

Responding to this demand, global production and operations have emerged with precise online coordination between far-flung production facilities and central headquarters thousands of miles away. At Sealand Transportation, a major global shipping company based in Newark, New Jersey, shipping managers in Newark can watch the loading of ships in Rotterdam online, check trim and ballast, and trace packages to specific ship locations as the activity proceeds. This is all possible through an international satellite link.

The new global markets and pressure toward global production and operation have called forth whole new capabilities for global coordination of all factors of production. Not only production but also accounting, marketing and sales, human resources, and systems development (all the major business functions) can be coordinated on a global scale. Frito Lay, for instance, can develop a marketing sales force automation system in the United States and, once provided, may try the same techniques and technologies in Spain. Micromarketing—marketing to very small geographic and social units—no longer means marketing to neighborhoods in the United States, but to neighborhoods throughout the world! These new levels of global coordination permit for the first time in history the location of business activity according to comparative advantage. Design should be located where it is best accomplished, as should marketing, production, and finance.

Finally, global markets, production, and administration create the conditions for powerful, sustained global economies of scale. Production driven by worldwide global demand can be concentrated where it can be best accomplished, fixed resources can be allocated over larger production runs, and production runs in larger plants can be scheduled more efficiently and precisely estimated. Lower cost factors of production can be exploited wherever they emerge. The result is a powerful strategic advantage to firms that can organize globally. These general and specific business drivers have greatly enlarged world trade and commerce.

Not all industries are similarly affected by these trends. Clearly, manufacturing has been much more affected than services that still tend to be domestic and highly inefficient. However, the localism of services is breaking down in telecommunications, entertainment, transportation, financial services, and general business services including law. Clearly those firms within an industry that can understand the internationalization of the industry and respond appropriately will reap enormous gains in productivity and stability.

Business Challenges

Although the possibilities of globalization for business success are significant, fundamental forces are operating to inhibit a global economy and to disrupt international business. Table 15-2 lists the most common and powerful challenges to the development of global systems.

At a cultural level, **particularism,** making judgments and taking action on the basis of narrow or personal characteristics, in all its forms (religious, nationalistic, ethnic, regionalism, geopolitical position) rejects the very concept of a shared global culture and rejects the penetration of domestic markets by foreign goods and services. Differences among cultures produce differences in social expectations, politics, and ultimately legal rules. In certain countries, such as the United States, consumers expect domestic name-brand products to be

particularism
Making judgments and taking actions on the basis of narrow or personal characteristics.

TABLE 15-2	CHALLENGES AND OBSTACLES TO GLOBAL BUSINESS SYSTEMS

General

Cultural particularism: regionalism, nationalism, language differences

Social expectations: brand-name expectations; work hours

Political laws: transborder data and privacy laws, commercial regulations

Specific

Standards: different EDI, e-mail, telecommunications standards

Reliability: phone networks not uniformly reliable

Speed: different data transfer speeds differ, many slower than United States

Personnel: shortages of skilled consultants

built domestically and are disappointed to learn that much of what they thought of as domestically produced is in fact foreign made.

Different cultures produce different political regimes. Among the many different countries of the world there are different laws governing the movement of information, information privacy of their citizens, origins of software and hardware in systems, and radio and satellite telecommunications. Even the hours of business and the terms of business trade vary greatly across political cultures. These different legal regimes complicate global business and must be considered when building global systems.

For instance, European countries have very strict laws concerning transborder data flow and privacy. **Transborder data flow** is defined as the movement of information across international boundaries in any form. Some European countries prohibit the processing of financial information outside their boundaries or the movement of personal information to foreign countries. The European Directive on Data Protection, which went into effect in October 1998, restricts the flow of any information to countries (such as the United States) that do not meet strict European information laws on personal information. Financial services, travel, and health care companies could be directly affected. In response, most multinational firms develop information systems within each European country to avoid the cost and uncertainty of moving information across national boundaries.

Cultural and political differences profoundly affect organizations' standard operating procedures. A host of specific barriers arise from the general cultural differences, everything from different reliability of phone networks to the shortage of skilled consultants (see Steinbart and Nath, 1992).

National laws and traditions have created disparate accounting practices in various countries, which impact the ways profits and losses are analyzed. German companies generally do not recognize the profit from a venture until the project is completely finished and they have been paid. Conversely, British firms begin posting profits before a project is completed, when they are reasonably certain they will get the money.

These accounting practices are tightly intertwined with each country's legal system, business philosophy, and tax code. British, U.S., and Dutch firms share a predominantly Anglo-Saxon outlook that separates tax calculations from reports to shareholders to focus on showing shareholders how fast profits are growing. Continental European accounting practices are less oriented toward impressing investors, focusing rather on demonstrating compliance with strict rules and minimizing tax liabilities. These diverging accounting practices make it difficult for large international companies with units in different countries to evaluate their performance.

Cultural differences can also affect the way organizations use information technology. For example, Japanese firms fax extensively but have been reluctant to take advantage of the capabilities of e-mail. One explanation is that the Japanese view e-mail as poorly suited for much intragroup communication and for depiction of the complex symbols used in the Japanese written language (Straub, 1994).

Language remains a significant barrier. Although English has become a kind of standard business language, this is truer at higher levels of companies and not throughout the middle and lower ranks. Software may have to be built with local language interfaces before a new information system can be successfully implemented.

Currency fluctuations can play havoc with planning models and projections. A product that appears profitable in Mexico or Japan may actually produce a loss due to changes in foreign exchange rates. Some of these problems will diminish in parts of the world where the euro becomes more widely used.

These inhibiting factors must be taken into account when you are designing and building international systems for your business. For example, companies trying to implement "lean production" systems spanning national boundaries typically underestimate the time, expense, and logistical difficulties of making goods and information flow freely across different countries (Levy, 1997).

STATE OF THE ART

One might think, given the opportunities for achieving competitive advantages as outlined previously and the interest in future applications, that most international companies have rationally developed marvelous international systems architectures. Nothing could be further

---

transborder data flow

The movement of information across international boundaries in any form.

from the truth. Most companies have inherited patchwork international systems from the distant past, often based on concepts of information processing developed in the 1960s—batch-oriented reporting from independent foreign divisions to corporate headquarters, with little online control and communication. Corporations in this situation increasingly will face powerful competitive challenges in the marketplace from firms that have rationally designed truly international systems. Still other companies have recently built technology platforms for international systems but have nowhere to go because they lack global strategy.

As it turns out, there are significant difficulties in building appropriate international architectures. The difficulties involve planning a system appropriate to the firm's global strategy, structuring the organization of systems and business units, solving implementation issues, and choosing the right technical platform. Let us examine these problems in greater detail.

15.2 ORGANIZING INTERNATIONAL INFORMATION SYSTEMS

There are three organizational issues facing corporations seeking a global position: choosing a strategy, organizing the business, and organizing the systems management area. The first two are closely connected, so we will discuss them together.

GLOBAL STRATEGIES AND BUSINESS ORGANIZATION

Four main global strategies form the basis for global firms' organizational structure. These are domestic exporter, multinational, franchiser, and transnational. Each of these strategies is pursued with a specific business organizational structure (see Table 15-3). For simplicity's sake, we describe three kinds of organizational structure or governance: centralized (in the home country), decentralized (to local foreign units), and coordinated (all units participate as equals). There are other types of governance patterns observed in specific companies (e.g., authoritarian dominance by one unit, a confederacy of equals, a federal structure balancing power among strategic units, and so forth; see Keen, 1991).

The **domestic exporter** strategy is characterized by heavy centralization of corporate activities in the home country of origin. Nearly all international companies begin this way, and some move on to other forms. Production, finance/accounting, sales/marketing, human resources, and strategic management are set up to optimize resources in the home country. International sales are sometimes dispersed using agency agreements or subsidiaries, but even here foreign marketing is totally reliant on the domestic home base for marketing themes and strategies. Caterpillar Corporation and other heavy capital-equipment manufacturers fall into this category of firm.

The **multinational** strategy concentrates financial management and control out of a central home base while decentralizing production, sales, and marketing operations to units in other countries. The products and services on sale in different countries are adapted to suit local market conditions. The organization becomes a far-flung confederation of production and marketing facilities in different countries. Many financial service firms, along with a host of manufacturers, such as General Motors, Chrysler, and Intel, fit this pattern.

Franchisers are an interesting mix of old and new. On the one hand, the product is created, designed, financed, and initially produced in the home country, but for product-specific reasons must rely heavily on foreign personnel for further production, marketing, and human

domestic exporter

A strategy characterized by heavy centralization of corporate activities in the home country of origin.

multinational

A global strategy that concentrates financial management and control out of a central home base while decentralizing production, sales, and marketing operations to units in other countries.

franchiser

A firm where a product is created, designed, financed, and initially produced in the home country, but for product-specific reasons must rely heavily on foreign personnel for further production, marketing, and human resources.

TABLE 15-3   GLOBAL BUSINESS STRATEGY AND STRUCTURE

Business Function	Domestic Exporter	Multinational	Franchiser	Transnational
Production	Centralized	Dispersed	Coordinated	Coordinated
Finance/Accounting	Centralized	Centralized	Centralized	Coordinated
Sales/Marketing	Mixed	Dispersed	Coordinated	Coordinated
Human Resources	Centralized	Centralized	Coordinated	Coordinated
Strategic Management	Centralized	Centralized	Centralized	Coordinated

resources. Food franchisers such as McDonald's, Mrs. Fields Cookies, and KFC fit this pattern. McDonald's created a new form of fast-food chain in the United States and continues to rely largely on the United States for inspiration of new products, strategic management, and financing. Nevertheless, because the product must be produced locally—it is perishable—extensive coordination and dispersal of production, local marketing, and local recruitment of personnel are required. Generally, foreign franchisees are clones of the mother country units, but fully coordinated worldwide production that could optimize factors of production is not possible. For instance, potatoes and beef can generally not be bought where they are cheapest on world markets but must be produced reasonably close to the area of consumption.

Transnational firms are the stateless, truly globally managed firms that may represent a larger part of international business in the future. Transnational firms have no single national headquarters but instead have many regional headquarters and perhaps a world headquarters. In a **transnational** strategy, nearly all the value-adding activities are managed from a global perspective without reference to national borders, optimizing sources of supply and demand wherever they appear, and taking advantage of any local competitive advantages. Transnational firms take the globe, not the home country, as their management frame of reference. The governance of these firms has been likened to a federal structure in which there is a strong central management core of decision making, but considerable dispersal of power and financial muscle throughout the global divisions. Few companies have actually attained transnational status, but Citicorp, Sony, Ford, and others are attempting this transition.

Information technology and improvements in global telecommunications are giving international firms more flexibility to shape their global strategies. Protectionism and a need to serve local markets better encourage companies to disperse production facilities and at least become multinational. At the same time, the drive to achieve economies of scale and take advantage of short-term local advantage moves transnationals toward a global management perspective and a concentration of power and authority. Hence, there are forces of decentralization and dispersal, as well as forces of centralization and global coordination (Ives and Jarvenpaa, 1991).

GLOBAL SYSTEMS TO FIT THE STRATEGY

Information technology and improvements in global telecommunications are giving international firms more flexibility to shape their global strategies. The configuration, management, and development of systems tend to follow the global strategy chosen (Roche, 1992; Ives and Jarvenpaa, 1991). Figure 15-2 depicts the typical arrangements. By *systems* we mean the full range of activities involved in building information systems: conception and alignment with the strategic business plan, systems development, and ongoing operation. For the sake of simplicity, we consider four types of systems configuration. *Centralized systems* are those in which systems development and operation occur totally at the domestic home base. *Duplicated systems* are those in which development occurs at the home base but operations are handed over to autonomous units in foreign locations. *Decentralized systems* are those in which each foreign unit designs its own unique solutions and systems. *Networked systems* are those in which systems development and operations occur in an integrated and coordinated fashion across all units.

As can be seen in Figure 15-2, domestic exporters tend to have highly centralized systems in which a single domestic systems development staff develops worldwide applications. Multinationals offer a direct and striking contrast: Here foreign units devise their own systems solutions based on local needs with few if any applications in common with headquarters (the exceptions being financial reporting and some telecommunications applications). Franchisers have the simplest systems structure: Like the products they sell, franchisers

transnational

Truly globally managed firms that have no national headquarters; value-added activities are managed from a global perspective without reference to national borders, optimizing sources of supply and demand and taking advantage of any local competitive advantage.

Figure 15-2 Global strategy and systems configurations. The large Xs show the dominant patterns, and the small Xs show the emerging patterns. For instance, domestic exporters rely predominantly on centralized systems, but there is continual pressure and some development of decentralized systems in local marketing regions.

SYSTEM CONFIGURATION	Strategy			
	Domestic Exporter	Multinational	Franchiser	Transnational
Centralized	X			
Duplicated			X	
Decentralized	x	X	x	
Networked		x		X

develop a single system usually at the home base and then replicate it around the world. Each unit, no matter where it is located, has identical applications. Last, the most ambitious form of systems development is found in the transnational: Networked systems are those in which there is a solid, singular global environment for developing and operating systems. This usually presupposes a powerful telecommunications backbone, a culture of shared applications development, and a shared management culture that crosses cultural barriers. The networked systems structure is the most visible in financial services where the homogeneity of the product—money and money instruments—seems to overcome cultural barriers.

REORGANIZING THE BUSINESS

How should a firm organize itself for doing business on an international scale? To develop a global company and information systems support structure, a firm needs to follow these principles:

1. Organize value-adding activities along lines of comparative advantage. For instance, marketing/sales functions should be located where they can best be performed, for least cost and maximum impact; likewise with production, finance, human resources, and information systems.

2. Develop and operate systems units at each level of corporate activity—regional, national, and international. To serve local needs, there should be *host country systems units* of some magnitude. *Regional systems units* should handle telecommunications and systems development across national boundaries that take place within major geographic regions (European, Asian, American). *Transnational systems units* should be established to create the linkages across major regional areas and coordinate the development and operation of international telecommunications and systems development (Roche, 1992).

3. Establish at world headquarters a single office responsible for development of international systems, a global chief information officer (CIO) position.

Many successful companies have devised organizational systems structures along these principles. The success of these companies relies not only on the proper organization of activities, but also on a key ingredient—a management team that can understand the risks and benefits of international systems and that can devise strategies for overcoming the risks. We turn to these management topics next.

15.3 MANAGING GLOBAL SYSTEMS

Table 15-4 lists the principal management problems posed by developing international systems. It is interesting to note that these problems are the chief difficulties managers experience in developing ordinary domestic systems as well! But these are enormously complicated in the international environment.

A TYPICAL SCENARIO: DISORGANIZATION ON A GLOBAL SCALE

Let us look at a common scenario. A traditional multinational consumer-goods company based in the United States and operating in Europe would like to expand into Asian markets and knows that it must develop a transnational strategy and a supportive information systems

TABLE 15-4	MANAGEMENT CHALLENGES IN DEVELOPING GLOBAL SYSTEMS

Agreeing on common user requirements

Introducing changes in business processes

Coordinating applications development

Coordinating software releases

Encouraging local users to support global systems

structure. Like most multinationals it has dispersed production and marketing to regional and national centers while maintaining a world headquarters and strategic management in the United States. Historically, it has allowed each of the subsidiary foreign divisions to develop its own systems. The only centrally coordinated system is financial controls and reporting. The central systems group in the United States focuses only on domestic functions and production. The result is a hodgepodge of hardware, software, and telecommunications. The e-mail systems between Europe and the United States are incompatible. Each production facility uses a different manufacturing resources planning system (or a different version with local variations), and different marketing, sales, and human resource systems. The technology platforms are wildly different: Europe is using mostly UNIX-based file servers and IBM PC clones on desktops. Communications between different sites are poor, given the high cost and low quality of European intercountry communications. The U.S. group is moving from an IBM mainframe environment centralized at headquarters to a highly distributed network architecture, with local sites developing their own local area networks. The central systems group at headquarters recently was decimated and dispersed to the U.S. local sites in the hope of serving local needs better and reducing costs.

What do you recommend to the senior management leaders of this company, who now want to pursue a transnational strategy and develop an information systems architecture to support a highly coordinated global systems environment? Consider the problems you face by reexamining Table 15-4. The foreign divisions will resist efforts to agree on common user requirements; they have never thought about much other than their own units' needs. The systems groups in American local sites, which have been enlarged recently and told to focus on local needs, will not easily accept guidance from anyone recommending a transnational strategy. It will be difficult to convince local managers anywhere in the world that they should change their business procedures to align with other units in the world, especially if this might interfere with their local performance. After all, local managers are rewarded in this company for meeting local objectives of their division or plant. Finally, it will be difficult to coordinate development of projects around the world in the absence of a powerful telecommunications network and, therefore, difficult to encourage local users to take on ownership in the systems developed.

STRATEGY: DIVIDE, CONQUER, APPEASE

Figure 15-3 lays out the main dimensions of a solution. First, consider that not all systems should be coordinated on a transnational basis; only some core systems are truly worth sharing from a cost and feasibility point of view. **Core systems** are systems that support functions that are absolutely critical to the organization. Other systems should be partially coordinated because they share key elements, but they do not have to be totally common across national boundaries. For such systems, a good deal of local variation is possible and desirable. A final group of systems are peripheral, truly provincial, and are needed to suit local requirements only.

Define the Core Business Processes

How do you identify *core systems?* The first step is to define a short list of critical core business processes. Business processes were defined in Chapters 1 and 2, which you should review. Briefly, business processes are sets of logically related tasks such as shipping out correct orders to customers or delivering innovative products to the market. Each business process typically involves many functional areas, communicating and coordinating work, information, and knowledge.

The way to identify these core business processes is to conduct a work-flow analysis. How are customer orders taken, what happens to them once they are taken, who fills the orders, how are they shipped to the customers? What about suppliers? Do they have access to manufacturing resource planning systems so that supply is automatic? You should be able to identify and set priorities in a short list of 10 business processes that are absolutely critical for the firm.

Next, can you identify centers of excellence for these processes? Is the customer order fulfillment superior in the United States, manufacturing process control superior in Germany, and human resources superior in Asia? You should be able to identify some areas of the company, for some lines of business, where a division or unit stands out in the performance of one or several business functions.

When you understand the business processes of a firm, you can rank-order them. You then can decide which processes should be core applications, centrally coordinated, designed,

---

core systems

Systems that support functions that are absolutely critical to the organization.

Geographic Business Scope   Business Systems Scope

Figure 15-3 Agency and other coordination costs increase as the firm moves from local option systems toward regional and global systems. However, transaction costs of participating in global markets probably decrease as firms develop global systems. A sensible strategy is to reduce agency costs by developing only a few core global systems that are vital for global operations, leaving other systems in the hands of regional and local units.
Source: From *Managing Information Technology in Multinational Corporations* by Edward M. Roche,© 1992. Adapted by permission of Prentice Hall, Inc., Upper Saddle River, NJ.

and implemented around the globe, and which should be regional and local. At the same time, by identifying the critical business processes, the really important ones, you have gone a long way to defining a vision of the future that you should be working toward.

Identify the Core Systems to Coordinate Centrally

By identifying the critical core business processes, you begin to see opportunities for transnational systems. The second strategic step is to conquer the core systems and define these systems as truly transnational. The financial and political costs of defining and implementing transnational systems are extremely high. Therefore, keep the list to an absolute minimum, letting experience be the guide and erring on the side of minimalism. By dividing off a small group of systems as absolutely critical, you divide opposition to a transnational strategy. At the same time, you can appease those who oppose the central worldwide coordination implied by transnational systems by permitting peripheral systems development to progress unabated, with the exception of some technical platform requirements.

Choose an Approach: Incremental, Grand Design, Evolutionary

A third step is to choose an approach. Avoid piecemeal approaches. These surely will fail for lack of visibility, opposition from all who stand to lose from transnational development, and lack of power to convince senior management that the transnational systems are worth it. Likewise, avoid grand design approaches that try to do everything at once. These also tend to fail, due to an inability to focus resources. Nothing gets done properly, and opposition to organizational change is needlessly strengthened because the effort requires huge resources. An alternative approach is to evolve transnational applications from existing applications with a precise and clear vision of the transnational capabilities the organization should have in five years.

Make the Benefits Clear

What is in it for the company? One of the worst situations to avoid is to build global systems for the sake of building global systems. From the beginning, it is crucial that senior management at headquarters and foreign division managers clearly understand the benefits that will come to the company as well as to individual units. Although each system offers unique benefits to a particular budget, the overall contribution of global systems lies in four areas.

Global systems—truly integrated, distributed, and transnational systems—contribute to superior management and coordination. A simple price tag cannot be put on the value of this contribution, and the benefit will not show up in any capital budgeting model. It is the ability to switch suppliers on a moment's notice from one region to another in a crisis, the ability to move production in response to natural disasters, and the ability to use excess capacity in one region to meet raging demand in another.

A second major contribution is vast improvement in production, operation, and supply and distribution. Imagine a global value chain, with global suppliers and a global distribution network. For the first time, senior managers can locate value-adding activities in regions where they are most economically performed.

Third, global systems mean global customers and global marketing. Fixed costs around the world can be amortized over a much larger customer base. This will unleash new economies of scale at production facilities.

Last, global systems mean the ability to optimize the use of corporate funds over a much larger capital base. This means, for instance, that capital in a surplus region can be moved efficiently to expand production of capital-starved regions; that cash can be managed more effectively within the company and put to use more effectively.

These strategies will not by themselves create global systems. You will have to implement what you strategize and this is a whole new challenge.

IMPLEMENTATION TACTICS: COOPTATION

cooptation
Bringing the opposition into the process of designing and implementing the solution without giving up control over the direction and nature of the change.

The overall tactic for dealing with resistant local units in a transnational company is cooptation. **Cooptation** is defined as bringing the opposition into the process of designing and implementing the solution without giving up control over the direction and nature of the change. As much as possible, raw power should be avoided. Minimally, however, local units must agree on a short list of transnational systems, and raw power may be required to solidify the idea that transnational systems of some sort are truly required.

How should cooptation proceed? Several alternatives are possible. One alternative is to permit each country unit the opportunity to develop one transnational application first in its home territory, and then throughout the world. In this manner, each major country systems group is given a piece of the action in developing a transnational system, and local units feel a sense of ownership in the transnational effort. On the downside, this assumes the ability to develop high-quality systems is widely distributed, and that, say, the German team can successfully implement systems in France and Italy. This will not always be the case. Also, the transnational effort will have low visibility.

A second tactic is to develop new transnational centers of excellence, or a single center of excellence. There may be several centers around the globe that focus on specific business processes. These centers draw heavily from local national units, are based on multinational teams, and must report to worldwide management—their first line of responsibility is to the core applications. Centers of excellence perform the initial identification and specification of the business process, define the information requirements, perform the business and systems analysis, and accomplish all design and testing. Implementation, however, and pilot testing occur in World Pilot Regions where new applications are installed and tested first. Later, they are rolled out to other parts of the globe. This phased rollout strategy is precisely how national applications are successfully developed.

The Window on Management shows how GN Netcom addressed these issues as it implemented enterprise and customer relationship management systems in 24 different countries.

THE MANAGEMENT SOLUTION

We now can reconsider how to handle the most vexing problems facing managers developing the transnational information system architectures that were described in Table 15-4.

Agreeing on common user requirements: Establishing a short list of the core business processes and core support systems will begin a process of rational comparison across the many divisions of the company, develop a common language for discussing the business, and naturally lead to an understanding of common elements (as well as the unique qualities that must remain local).

Introducing changes in business processes: Your success as a change agent will depend on your legitimacy, your actual raw power, and your ability to involve users in the change design process. **Legitimacy** is defined as the extent to which your authority is accepted on grounds of competence, vision, or other qualities. The selection of a viable change strategy, which we have defined as evolutionary but with a vision, should assist you in convincing others that change is feasible and desirable. Involving people in change, assuring them that change is in the best interests of the company and their local units, is a key tactic.

legitimacy
The extent to which one's authority is accepted on grounds of competence, vision, or other qualities.

GN NETCOM'S GLOBAL SYSTEMS CHALLENGE

Denmark-based GN Netcom A/S is a leading supplier of wireless headsets for corporate call centers and of hands-free products for mobile phones. As the company expanded into 24 countries in Europe, the United States, Canada, Australia, and Asia, it faced the difficult tasks of trying to standardize its information systems while making sure that they had the flexibility to adapt to local market business requirements.

The company decided it needed centrally run production, supply chain, distribution, finance, and customer relationship management systems. One of the company's first steps was to consolidate its finished goods manufacturing and assembly operations from several plants in Europe and the United States to a plant in Xiamen, China. One obvious reason for this move was the lower cost of the Chinese workforce. But GN Netcom only made the change because of the Chinese workers' skill and willingness to learn. The move worked so well that the 170 person staff in Xiamen is now managing GN Netcom's global supply chain, inventory, and distribution logistics, none of which had been centralized in the past.

GN Netcom next began to install global enterprise resource planning (ERP) and customer relationship management (CRM) software to work with its already installed global chart of accounts. Netcom's CIO Michael Young explained that the overall system "will provide the vehicle to easily and consistently capture the critical profit and loss numbers, analyze them, and share the business metrics locally and globally." Managers at corporate headquarters will be able to view data by individual countries, or sum of countries or region.

The problems of installing these systems were complex. For example the tax structures differ greatly in the various countries, and the software had to handle such diversity. GN Netcom selected Navision Attain as the core of its CRM and ERP systems, partly because it encompasses financials, order entry, inventory management, shipping, receiving and returns, customer services, and

CRM. However, central to GN Netcom's requirements was that the software also had versions for the local languages and countries. The company also selected Hyperion Solution's data warehousing and financial reporting systems, which together enable headquarters and local offices to see sales trends and business performances.

To face the global installation problems, Young established a corporate implementation team with a development manager that spent four months just to plan the rollout for each region and country. He established a single development methodology for the whole process so that all the countries would be working the same way. Young named "a champion" in each country, and said "[I] learn from that person. I ask him [or her] how to communicate [with] and respect [her countrymen]." He continued "It's about listening, and culturally, not to be seen as an arrogant, know-it-all team." Young concluded, "As soon as we show that we respect [our co-workers] as equals, it's amazing the speed at which people move." Young made sure that managers in each country were well trained and well-informed about the details of the project.

Young points out that installing the same hardware and software environments in each country has resulted in the ability of GN Netcom to move employees anywhere in the world where they are needed. He also claims the new global systems are reducing the headcounts in finance, administration, and inventory management while keeping the sales and marketing staffs the same size despite the rapidly growing business volume.

To Think About: What were the management, technology, and organization problems that GN Netcom had to face when implementing its global systems? How well did GN Netcom deal with these problems?

Source: Ann Toh, "Attack of the Vikings," *CIO Asia*, March 2002; and GN Netcom corporate Web site, accessed June 25, 2002, <www.gnnetcom.com>.

MANAGEMENT

Coordinating applications development: Choice of change strategy is critical for this problem. At the global level there is far too much complexity to attempt a grand design strategy of change. It is far easier to coordinate change by making small incremental steps toward a larger vision. Imagine a five-year plan of action rather than a two-year plan of action, and reduce the set of transnational systems to a bare minimum to reduce coordination costs.

Coordinating software releases: Firms can institute procedures to ensure that all operating units convert to new software updates at the same time so that everyone's software is compatible.

Encouraging local users to support global systems: The key to this problem is to involve users in the creation of the design without giving up control over the development of the project to parochial interests. Recruiting a wide range of local individuals to transnational centers of excellence helps send the message that all significant groups are involved in the design and will have an influence.

Even with the proper organizational structure and appropriate management choices, it is still possible to stumble over technological issues. Choices of technology, platforms, networks, hardware, and software are the final elements in building transnational information system infrastructures.

15.4 Technology Issues and Opportunities for Global Value Chains

Information technology is itself a powerful business driver for encouraging the development of global systems and global value chains, where firms can coordinate commercial transactions and production with other firms across many different locations throughout the world. Companies pursuing electronic business on a global scale and digital integration with their customers and value partners face many challenges (Farhoomand, Tuunainen, and Yee, 2000).

MAIN TECHNICAL ISSUES

Hardware, software, and telecommunications pose special technical challenges in an international setting. The major hardware challenge is finding some way to standardize the firm's computer hardware platform when there is so much variation from operating unit to operating unit and from country to country. Managers need to think carefully about where to locate the firm's computer centers and how to select hardware suppliers. The major global software challenge is finding applications that are user friendly and that truly enhance the productivity of international work teams. The major telecommunications challenge is making data flow seamlessly across networks shaped by disparate national standards. Overcoming these challenges requires systems integration and connectivity on a global basis.

Hardware and Systems Integration

The development of global systems based on the concept of core systems raises questions about how the new core systems will fit in with the existing suite of applications developed around the globe by different divisions, different people, and for different kinds of computing hardware. The goal is to develop global, distributed, and integrated systems where business processes spanning national boundaries have become highly digital. Briefly, these are the same problems faced by any large domestic systems development effort. However, the problems are more complex because of the international environment. For instance, in the United States, IBM operating systems have played the predominant role in building core systems for large organizations, whereas in Europe, UNIX was much more commonly used for large systems. How can the two be integrated in a common transnational system?

The correct solution often will depend on the history of the company's systems and the extent of commitment to proprietary systems. For instance, finance and insurance firms typically have relied almost exclusively on IBM proprietary equipment and architectures, and it would be extremely difficult and cost ineffective to abandon that equipment and software. Newer firms and manufacturing firms generally find it much easier to adopt open UNIX systems for international systems. As pointed out in previous chapters, open UNIX-based systems are far more cost effective in the long run, provide more power at a cheaper price, and preserve options for future expansion.

After a hardware platform is chosen, the question of standards must be addressed. Just because all sites use the same hardware does not guarantee common, integrated systems. Some central authority in the firm must establish data, as well as other technical standards, with which sites are to comply. For instance, technical accounting terms such as the beginning and end of the fiscal year must be standardized (review our earlier discussion of the cultural challenges to building global businesses), as well as the acceptable interfaces between systems, communication speeds and architectures, and network software.

Connectivity

The heart of the international systems problem is telecommunications—linking together the systems and people of a global firm into a single integrated network just like the phone system but capable of voice, data, and image transmissions. However, integrated global networks are extremely difficult to create (Lai and Chung, 2002). For example, many countries cannot fulfill

TABLE 15-5	**PROBLEMS OF INTERNATIONAL NETWORKS**

Costs and tariffs

Network management

Installation delays

Poor quality of international service

Regulatory constraints

Changing user requirements

Disparate standards

Network capacity

basic business telecommunications needs such as obtaining reliable circuits, coordinating among different carriers and the regional telecommunications authority, obtaining bills in a common currency standard, and obtaining standard agreements for the level of telecommunications service provided. Table 15-5 lists the major challenges posed by international networks.

Despite moves toward economic unity, Europe remains a hodgepodge of disparate national technical standards and service levels. Although most circuits leased by multinational corporations are fault-free more than 99.8 percent of the time, line quality and service vary widely from the north to the south of Europe. Network service is much more unreliable in southern Europe.

Existing European standards for networking and EDI (electronic data interchange) are very industry specific and country specific. Most European banks use the SWIFT (Society for Worldwide Interbank Financial Telecommunications) protocol for international funds transfer, whereas automobile companies and food producers often use industry-specific or country-specific versions of standard protocols for EDI. Complicating matters further, the United States standard for EDI is ANSI (American National Standards Institute) X.12. The Open Systems Interconnect (OSI) reference model for linking networks is more popular in Europe than it is in the United States. Even standards for cellular phone systems vary from country to country.

Firms have several options for providing international connectivity: build their own international private network, rely on a network service based on the public switched networks throughout the world, or use the Internet and intranets.

One possibility is for the firm to put together its own private network based on leased lines from each country's PTT (post, telegraph, and telephone authorities). Each country, however, has different restrictions on data exchange, technical standards, and acceptable vendors of equipment. These problems magnify in certain parts of the world. Despite such limitations, in Europe and the United States, reliance on PTTs still makes sense while these public networks expand services to compete with private providers.

The second major alternative to building one's own network is to use one of several expanding network services. With deregulation of telecommunications around the globe, private providers have sprung up to service business customers' data needs, along with some voice and image communication.

Already common in the United States, IVANs (International Value-Added Network Services) are expanding in Europe and Asia. These private firms offer value-added telecommunications capacity, usually rented from local PTTs or international satellite authorities, and then resell it to corporate users. IVANs add value by providing protocol conversion, operating mailboxes and mail systems, and by offering integrated billing that permits a firm to track its data communications costs. Currently these systems are limited to data transmissions, but in the future they will expand to voice and image.

The third alternative, which is becoming increasingly attractive, is to create global intranets to use the Internet for international communication. However, the Internet is not yet a worldwide tool because many countries lack the communications infrastructure for extensive Internet use. Countries face high costs, government control, or government monitoring. Many countries also do not have the speedy and reliable postal and package delivery services that are essential for electronic commerce as well (DePalma, 2000).

Western Europe faces both high transmission costs and lack of common technology because it is not politically unified and because European telecommunications systems are still in the process of shedding their government monopolies. The lack of an infrastructure and the high costs of installing one are even more widespread in the rest of the world. The International Telecommunications Union estimated that only 500 million of the world's 1.5 billion households have basic telephone services (Wysocki, 2000). Low penetration of PCs and widespread illiteracy limit demand for Internet service in India (Burkhardt, Goodman, Mehta, and Press, 1999). Where an infrastructure exists in less-developed countries, it is often outdated, lacks digital circuits, and has very noisy lines. The purchasing power of most people in developing counties makes access to Internet services very expensive (Petrazzini and Kibati, 1999).

Many countries monitor transmissions. The governments in China and Singapore monitor Internet traffic and block access to Web sites considered morally or politically offensive . Corporations may be discouraged from using this medium. Companies planning international operations through the Internet still will have many hurdles.

Software

Compatible hardware and communications provide a platform but not the total solution. Also critical to global core infrastructure is software. The development of core systems poses unique challenges for software: How will the old systems interface with the new? Entirely new interfaces must be built and tested if old systems are kept in local areas (which is common). These interfaces can be costly and messy to build. If new software must be created, another challenge is to build software that can be realistically used by multiple business units from different countries given these business units are accustomed to their unique business processes and definitions of data.

Aside from integrating the new with the old systems, there are problems of human interface design and functionality of systems. For instance, to be truly useful for enhancing productivity of a global workforce, software interfaces must be easily understood and mastered quickly. Graphical user interfaces are ideal for this but presuppose a common language—often English. When international systems involve knowledge workers only, English may be the assumed international standard. But as international systems penetrate deeper into management and clerical groups, a common language may not be assumed and human interfaces must be built to accommodate different languages and even conventions.

What are the most important software applications? Many international systems focus on basic transaction and MIS reporting systems. Increasingly, firms such as CIBA Vision, described in the Window on Technology, are turning to supply chain management and enterprise systems to standardize their business processes on a global basis and to create coordinated global supply chains. However, these cross-functional systems are not always compatible with differences in languages, cultural heritages, and business processes in other countries (Davison, 2002; Soh, Kien, and Tay-Yap, 2000). Company units in countries that are not technically sophisticated may also encounter problems trying to manage the technical complexities of supply chain management and enterprise software.

MIS IN ACTION: MANAGER'S TOOLKIT

HOW TO DEVELOP A GLOBAL E-COMMERCE STRATEGY

Developing a successful global e-commerce strategy requires a careful assessment of costs and benefits as well as knowledge of global markets and business practices. Here are some basic questions that must be answered:

1. *What is the opportunity?* Do you have a product or service that travels well? Can your product be sold "as-is" outside your domestic market or does it require some modification for other countries?

2. *What are the impediments to sales?* What are the national laws, business regulations, tariffs, and privacy policies that might apply to your product? Is there a good infrastructure in place for transporting your product to customers?

3. *Can people actually buy what you are selling?* Is there a large enough online population in your target market? Do online consumers have enough disposable income to buy what you want to sell? Do these consumers have means of paying for purchases online?

4. *What is the nature of the competition?* Are there other companies selling a product or service that directly competes with yours abroad? Can you deliver your product or service with a better value proposition for international customers?

5. *What are the costs and benefits of selling internationally online?* How much will it cost to develop an e-commerce Web site for international sales? Are special language support, currency conversion, or personalization capabilities required? How do these costs compare to the revenue you could generate from international e-commerce sales?

This Web page from the Prentice Hall Web site for this text was translated into Spanish using AltaVista's translation tools. Web sites and software interfaces for global systems may have to be translated to accommodate users in other parts of the world.

EDI—electronic data interchange—is a common global transaction processing application used by manufacturing and distribution firms to connect units of the same company, as well as customers and suppliers on a global basis. Groupware systems, electronic mail, and videoconferencing, are especially important worldwide collaboration tools for knowledge- and data-based firms, such as advertising firms, research-based firms in medicine and engineering, and graphics and publishing firms. The Internet will be increasingly employed for such purposes.

NEW TECHNICAL OPPORTUNITIES AND THE INTERNET

Technical advances described in Chapter 8 such as wireless and Digital Subscriber Line (DSL) services, should continue to fall in price and gain in power, facilitating the creation and operation of global networks. *Communicate and compute any time, anywhere* networks based on satellite systems, digital cellphones, and personal communications services will make it even easier to coordinate work and information in many parts of the globe that cannot be reached by existing ground-based systems. Thus a salesperson in China could send an order-confirmation request to the home office in London effortlessly and expect an instant reply.

Asian Sources is a portal for promoting business in East Asia. It includes a directory of businesses and search capabilities for locating businesses and products of interest to users.

CIBA VISION BRINGS WORLDWIDE INVENTORY INTO CLEAR SIGHT

CIBA Vision, headquartered in Atlanta, Georgia, is a division of Swiss pharmaceutical giant Novartis AG and was established in 1980. While it has become one of the largest suppliers of contact lenses in the world, the growth has presented major problems. In the last ten years, the contract lens business has been transformed as contact lens users have changed from one pair of lenses each year to disposable lenses once or even twice per day. Thus, contact lens users who ten years ago bought only one or two pair per year now purchase from 365 pairs to 730 pairs annually. At the same time the company expanded into a global company and now sells massive numbers of lenses worldwide. The company currently makes and keeps track of about 120,000 different lenses because they vary in both their power and their color. Supplying and satisfying customers became a nightmare, partly because, as a global company, only 40 percent of its inventory was even visible at headquarters. Unni Makkuni, CIBA Vision's supply chain manager, claims he (and others reporting to him) "used to spend pretty much 70 percent of our time trying to chase down supply chain information." The reason, according to Makkuni, was that the company was "a highly decentralized operation in terms of supply chain . . . We didn't maximize the efficiencies of our inventories. We had excess inventories in one place and a lack of inventory in other places." CIBA Vision needed to make its item-level forecasts more accurate in every country, a very complex requirement.

The company realized it had to turn to more advanced supply chain software. CIBA Vision's goal was to achieve 99.9 percent product availability, while simultaneously reducing its inventory. Makkuni wanted to "maximize the efficiencies of our inventories," thereby reducing its inventory size and costs. After carefully assessing major supply chain vendors such as SAP and Manugistics, it settled on i2 Technologies of Dallas, Texas, because their software appeared to closely match CIBA Vision's business requirements. Implementation of the new systems was a multimillion dollar project, which began in 2000 and still was not quite fully completed as of mid-2002.

i2's Active Data Warehouse (ASW) software is a repository for all forecasting and planning data. It accepts daily data feeds from 46 systems worldwide, including the company's distribution centers and bulk warehouses. Key to CIBA Vision's needs is that the system cleans up and standardizes the data from the company's various sites around the world. The ASW is the data source for the daily planning systems. Supply chain information, including inventories, back orders, pending orders, and allocated orders is immediately available. Using these data, the Demand Planner (DP) provides item-specific forecasts based on each country-specific historical usage patterns. These software systems have raised the global inventory visibility to over 90 percent. i2's Inventory Planner (IP) models these variations in different systems around the world to determine an appropriate inventory target and calculates the optimal level in inventory at the various supply points in the supply chain. Looking at the value of i2's software, Makkuni said, "We have been able to manage global forecasting [for every country] from the central SCM [supply chain management] in Atlanta." He added, "We have been able to track forecast trends and performance-to-forecast and have significantly improved the item forecast at a country level."

The i2 system has improved coordination between manufacturing, distribution, and supply-chain management, helping CIBA Vision reduce the cycle time for introducing new products by almost 50 percent. CIBA Vision has now achieved 99.5 percent product availability worldwide while realizing a considerable reduction in inventories and inventory costs.

To Think About: How did a new supply chain management system help solve CIBA Vision's supply chain problems? What value did it provide for the company? What difficulties do you think CIBA may have encountered in implementing this system?

Sources: Peter A. Buxbaum, "Ciba Vision Keeps Eye on Supply Chain with i2 Tools," *SearchEBusiness.com*, May 28, 2002; and i2 Technologies, "Bringing Vision into the Supply Chain at CIBA Vision," 195, accessed June 19, 2002, <www.i2.com>.

TECHNOLOGY

Companies are using Internet technology to construct virtual private networks (VPNs) to reduce wide area networking costs and staffing requirements. Instead of using private, leased telephone lines or frame-relay connections, the company outsources the VPN to an Internet service provider. The VPN comprises WAN links, security products, and routers, providing a secure and encrypted connection between two points across the Internet to transmit corporate data. These VPNs from Internet service providers can provide many features of a private network to firms operating internationally.

However, VPNs may not provide the same level of quick and predictable response as private networks, especially during times of the day when Internet traffic is very congested. VPNs may not be able to support large numbers of remote users.

MAKE IT YOUR BUSINESS

FINANCE AND ACCOUNTING

The most widespread use of international systems is to allow for the flow of funds between corporate headquarters and operating units and to facilitate purchases in different countries. The core systems that firms operating internationally are most likely to build are financial reporting. You can find examples of finance and accounting applications on pages 482–483, 495, and 503–505.

HUMAN RESOURCES

Language and cultural differences can affect the successful implementation and use of international systems. Human resources specialists will need to advise system-builders on these issues and help ensure that employees receive the proper training and motivation to use international system tools. Human resources systems may be used to identify employees with the requisite language and other skills to serve as leaders in international system projects or to work on assignments outside of their home country.

MANUFACTURING AND PRODUCTION

Disparate local manufacturing and production systems make it difficult for companies to manage their inventories and supply chains as global entities. Companies aspiring to some form of global business organization are installing standard supply chain management software or enterprise software for this purpose. Extranets can also be used to develop private industrial networks for this purpose. You can find examples of manufacturing and production applications on pages 495, 500, and 503–505.

SALES AND MARKETING

Systems for selling and marketing internationally have mushroomed because of the low cost of doing business on the Web and the Internet's global reach. Companies of all sizes can set up Web sites to buy and sell on the world market instead of being limited to local markets. However, large-scale global e-commerce initiatives may require country-specific Web sites and large expenditures for customization and ongoing management. You can find examples of sales and marketing applications on pages 503–505.

Throughout this text we have shown how the Internet facilitates global coordination, communication, and electronic business. As Internet technology becomes more widespread outside the United States, it will expand opportunities for electronic commerce and international trade. The global connectivity and low cost of Internet technology will further remove obstacles of geography and time zones for companies seeking to expand operations and sell their wares abroad. Companies in Asia, Latin America, or Africa that do not have the financial or technical resources to handle EDI transactions can use Internet technology to exchange information more rapidly with business partners in their supply chains. Small companies may especially benefit from using the Internet to speed delivery of products and manage their supply chains (Chabrow, 2000; Quelch and Klein, 1996).

MANAGEMENT WRAP-UP

Managers are responsible for devising an appropriate organizational and technology infrastructure for international business. Choosing a global business strategy, identifying core business processes, organizing the firm to conduct business on an international scale, and developing an international information systems architecture are key management decisions.

Cultural, political, and language diversity magnifies differences in organizational culture and standard operating procedures when companies operate internationally in various countries. These differences create barriers to the development of global information systems that transcend national boundaries.

The main technology decision in building international systems is finding a set of workable standards in hardware, software, and networking for the firm's international information systems infrastructure and architecture. The Internet and intranets will increasingly be used to provide global connectivity and to serve as a foundation for global systems, but many companies will still need proprietary systems for certain functions, and therefore international standards.

For Discussion

1. If you were a manager in a company that operates in many countries, what criteria would you use to determine whether an application should be developed as a global application or as a local application?

2. Describe ways the Internet can be used in international information systems.

SUMMARY

1. *What are the major factors driving the internationalization of business?* There are general cultural factors and specific business factors to consider. The growth of cheap international communication and transportation has created a world culture with stable expectations or norms. Political stability and a growing global knowledge base that is widely shared contribute also to the world culture. These general factors create the conditions for global markets, global production, coordination, distribution, and global economies of scale.

2. *What strategies are available for developing international businesses?* There are four basic international strategies: domestic exporter, multinational, franchiser, and transnational. In a transnational strategy, all factors of production are coordinated on a global scale. However, the choice of strategy is a function of the type of business and product.

3. *How can information systems support the various international business strategies?* There is a connection between firm strategy and information systems design. Transnational firms must develop networked system configurations and permit considerable decentralization of development and operations. Franchisers almost always duplicate systems across many countries and use centralized financial controls. Multinationals typically rely on decentralized independence among foreign units with some movement toward development of networks. Domestic exporters typi-

cally are centralized in domestic headquarters with some decentralized operations permitted.

4. *What issues should managers address when developing international information systems?* Implementing a global system requires an implementation strategy. Typically, global systems have evolved without a conscious plan. The remedy is to define a small subset of core business processes and focus on building systems that could support these processes. Tactically, you will have to coopt widely dispersed foreign units to participate in the development and operation of these systems, being careful to maintain overall control.

5. *What technical alternatives are available for developing global systems?* The main hardware and telecommunications issues are systems integration and connectivity. The choices for integration are to go either with a proprietary architecture or with an open systems technology such as UNIX. Global networks are extremely difficult to build and operate. Some measure of connectivity may be achieved by relying on local PTT authorities to provide connections, building a system oneself, relying on private providers to supply communications capacity, or using the Internet and intranets. Companies can use Internet services to create virtual private networks (VPNs) as low-cost alternatives to global private networks. The main software issue concerns building interfaces to existing systems and providing much needed group support software.

KEY TERMS

Business driver, 485	Domestic exporter, 489	International information	Particularism, 487
Cooptation, 494	Franchiser, 489	systems architecture, 485	Transborder data flow, 488
Core systems, 492	Global culture, 486	Legitimacy, 494	Transnational, 490
		Multinational, 489	

REVIEW QUESTIONS

1. What are the five major factors to consider when building an international information systems portfolio?

2. Describe the five general cultural factors leading toward growth in global business and the four specific business factors. Describe the interconnection among these factors.

3. What is meant by a *global culture?*

4. What are the major challenges to the development of global systems?

5. Why have firms not planned for the development of international systems?

6. Describe the four main strategies for global business and organizational structure.

7. Describe the four different system configurations that can be used to support different global strategies.

8. What are the major management issues in developing international systems?

9. What are three principles to follow when organizing the firm for global business?

10. What are three steps of a management strategy for developing and implementing global systems?

11. What is meant by *cooptation,* and how can it be used in building global systems?

12. Describe the main technical issues facing global systems.

13. Describe three new technologies that can help firms develop global systems.

APPLICATION SOFTWARE EXERCISE

DATABASE AND WEB PAGE DEVELOPMENT TOOL EXERCISE: BUILDING A JOB DATABASE AND WEB PAGE FOR AN INTERNATIONAL CONSULTING FIRM

KTP Consulting operates in various locations around the world. KTP specializes in designing, developing, and implementing enterprise systems for medium to large-size companies. KTP offers its employees opportunities to travel, live, and work in various locations throughout the United States, Europe, and Asia. The firm's human resources department has a simple database that enables its staff to track job vacancies. When an employee is interested in relocating, she or he contacts the human resources department for a list of KTP job vacancies. KTP also posts its employment opportunities on the company Web site.

What type of data should be included in the KTP job vacancies database? What information should not be included in this database? Based on your answers to these questions, build a job vacancies database for KTP. Populate the database with at least 20 records. You should also build a simple Web page that incorporates job vacancy data from your newly created database. Submit a disk containing a copy of the KTP database and Web page to your professor.

GROUP PROJECT

With a group of students, identify an area of information technology and explore how this technology might be useful for supporting global business strategies. For instance, you might choose an area such as digital telecommunications (e.g., e-mail, wireless communications), enterprise systems, collaborative work group software, or the Internet. It will be necessary to choose a business scenario to discuss the technology. You might choose, for instance, an automobile parts franchise or a clothing franchise, such as the Limited Express, as example businesses. What applications would you make global, what core business processes would you choose, and how would the technology be helpful? If possible, use electronic presentation software to present your findings to the class.

TOOLS FOR INTERACTIVE LEARNING

INTERNET CONNECTION

The Internet Connection for this chapter will take you to a series of Web sites where you can complete an exercise to evaluate the capabilities of various global package tracking and delivery services.

INTERACTIVE STUDY GUIDE

You can use the Interactive Study Guide to test your knowledge of the topics in this chapter and get instant feedback where you need more practice.

RUNNING CASE

The Running Case provides an opportunity for you to use the Web to identify opportunities for global business expansion using the Web for Dirt Bikes USA. You can find a complete description of this project on the Laudon Web site for Chapter 15 and on the Multimedia Edition CD-ROM.

ELECTRONIC COMMERCE PROJECT

At the Laudon Web site for Chapter 15, you will find an Electronic Commerce Project that uses the interactive software at a series of Web sites for international marketing and pricing.

MANAGEMENT DECISION PROBLEM

At the Laudon Web site for Chapter 15, you will find a Management Decision Problem on planning a global Web site.

CD-ROM

If you use the Multimedia Edition CD-ROM with this chapter, you can find a video clip illustrating the United Parcel Service International Shipping and Processing System (ISPS), an audio overview of the major themes of this chapter, and bullet text summarizing the key points of the chapter.

CASE STUDY—*Nestlé Struggles with Enterprise Systems*

 Nestlé SA is a giant food and pharmaceuticals company that operates virtually all over the world. Headquartered in Vevey, Switzerland, the company had 1999 revenues of $46.6 billion and more than 230,000 employees at 500 facilities in 80 countries. Best known for its chocolate, coffee (it invented instant coffee), and milk products, Nestlé sells thousands of other items, most of which are adapted to fit local markets and cultures.

Traditionally this huge firm has allowed each local organization to conduct business as it saw fit, taking into account the local conditions and business cultures. To support this decentralized strategy, it has had 80 different information technology units that run nearly 900 IBM AS/400 midrange computers, 15 mainframes, and 200 UNIX systems, enabling observers to describe its infrastructure as a veritable Tower of Babel. Interestingly, despite its size, the company has had no corporate computer center.

However, Nestlé's management has found that allowing these local differences created inefficiencies and extra costs that could prevent the company from competing effectively in electronic commerce. The lack of standard business processes prevented Nestlé from, for example, leveraging its worldwide buying power to obtain lower prices for its raw materials. Even though each factory uses the same global suppliers, each negotiated its own deals and prices.

Several years ago, Nestlé embarked on a program to standardize and coordinate its information systems and business processes. The company initially installed SAP's R/3 enterprise resource planning (ERP) software to integrate material, distribution, and accounting applications in the United States, Europe, and Canada.

Nestlé is working on extending its enterprise systems to all of its facilities to make its 500 facilities act as a single-minded e-business. Once this project is completed Nestlé will be able to use sales information from retailers on a global basis to measure the effectiveness of its promotional activities and reduce overstocking and spoilage caused by having products sit around too long on grocery shelves.

The experience of Nestlé USA illustrates some of the challenges Nestlé had to face in implementing enterprise systems. Nestlé USA, an $8.1 billion subsidiary, in 2001 used to be organized as a series of brands, each operating independently. So, for example, the Stouffer's and Carnation units were separate companies, each owned by Nestlé SA, the Swiss-based parent, but reporting to Nestlé USA. In 1991, Nestlé USA reorganized itself and the different brands were brought under the parent American control. However, the Nestlé division headquarters were still dispersed, and each division was still free to make its own business decisions, although each one within the United States did report to Nestlé headquarters in Glendale, California. The situation did not really begin to change until the spring of 1997 with the arrival of Jeri Dunn as vice president and CIO of the American company.

Dunn actually knew Nestlé technology unusually well because of her long history with the company. In 1991, as associate director for application systems at Nestlé-owned Stouffer's Hotels, she was sent to Switzerland to participate in an effort to establish a common worldwide methodology for Nestlé projects. In 1995, she was promoted to assistant vice president of technology and standards for Nestlé SA, and while there came to understand and agree with the value of establishing common systems throughout global Nestlé because such a change would enable group buying which in turn would reduce costs. Dunn also realized that common systems would facilitate data sharing among subsidiaries. When she was moved to Nestlé USA in 1997 at age 42, she found that her earlier recommendations from Vevey were mostly ignored. "My team could name the standards," Dunn said, "but the implementation rollout was at the whim of the businesses."

When she arrived, Dunn found that Joe Weller, the chairman and CEO of Nestlé USA, wanted to integrate the company, although he was not an information technology specialist. Dunn joined with the executives in charge of finance, supply chain, distribution, and purchasing to create a team to study the company's strengths and weaknesses. They found many problems including the revelation that the company was paying 29 different prices for vanilla from the same vendor. Dunn's explanation was that "Every plant would buy vanilla from the vendor, and

the vendor would just get whatever it thought it could get." She also realized that every division and every factory had assigned different names to the same product, so that the company could not even check on the situation. "We had no way of comparing," she said. When their studies were completed, they were given only two hours total to present their findings to Weller and the rest of the executives. Some of those reporting were upset with the time limit, and in the end they were given the whole day. Speaking later about the meeting, Dunn said, "[The executives] didn't know how ugly it was. We had nine different general ledgers and 28 points of customer entry. We had multiple purchasing systems. We had no clue how much volume we were doing with a particular vendor because every factory set up their own vendor masters and purchased on their own."

Soon after this meeting, the members of the team offered a three- to five-year plan for the necessary improvements. Central to the plan was the recommendation that the company install SAP, an ERP (enterprise resource planning) system. The team members expected the changeover to take three to five years. Dunn knew it was more than a software change, and she later said "We made it very clear that this would be a business process reorganization and that you couldn't do it without changing the way you did business." The long time period was the result of Dunn's expectation that "There was going to be pain involved, it was going to be a slow process, and this was not a software project." By October, Nestlé had established a project team of 50 top business executives and 10 senior information systems professionals. They developed a set of best practices to become common work procedures for manufacturing, purchasing, accounting, and sales. A smaller technical team was set up that took 18 months to examine all data for every item in all divisions and set up a common data structure for the whole company.

At first the project decided not to use SAP's supply chain software because that module was brand new and appeared to be risky. It turned instead to Manugistics for its supply chain module. The team did decide to use SAP's purchasing, financials, sales, and distribution modules. All of these modules would be installed throughout every Nestlé USA division. The plan was completed by March 1998 and development work began in July 1998. The project was called Best for "business excellence through systems technology."

In June 2000, Nestlé SA followed the lead of Nestlé USA and contracted with SAP to purchase and deploy the new version of their software called mySAP.com. The new system will not only standardize and coordinate the whole company's information systems and business processes, but it also will extend SAP's enterprise software to the Web. The new system will allow each Nestlé employee to start work from a personalized Web page linked to his or her job function. The employee's job is structured to conform to the "best practices" defined by SAP for 300 work roles. According to Jean Claud Dispaux, senior Nestlé vice president for group information systems, "It is an exceptionally simple way to make sure that everyone does the same job in the same way." Nestlé will also create up to five computer centers around the world to run mySAP.com enterprise financial, accounts payable, accounts receivable, planning, production management, supply chain management, and business intelligence software. Nestlé publicity announced that the SAP contract would cost $200 million, plus Nestlé would add an additional $80 million for installing all the system for the global company. However, a year after the announcement of the project, Anne Alexandre, an HSBC Securities analyst in London who covers Nestlé, downgraded her Nestlé recommendation. Her reason was her doubts about the success of the project. "It touches the corporate culture, which is decentralized," she said, "and tries to centralize it." She added, "That's risky. It's always a risk when you touch the corporate culture." Jeri Dunn agreed after her experience with Best.

The major problem that Best faced in the United States was that both Weller and most of the key stakeholders failed to realize how much the project would change their business processes. Dunn later said, "They still thought it was just about software." The project had set a deadline for the first four modules (including Manugistics) of January 1, 2000, the date that the Year 2000 (Y2K) changes must be operating. They met this deadline, but it soon was clear that they had created as many problems as they had solved. In fact a rebellion had already taken place when the team moved to install the Manugistics module.

The problem began during the early planning stage of the project when the staffs that would be directly affected by changes were not included in the key stakeholders' team. Dunn summed up the results, saying "We were always surprising [the heads of sales and the divisions] because we would bring something up to the executive steering committee that they weren't privy to." By the beginning of 2000 it was clear that nobody wanted to learn the new processes, that nobody wanted to make the changes. The lower level workers did not understand how to use the new system and also did not understand the changes. Nobody had been prepared for the new ways of doing things, and their only hope was to call the project help desk. Dunn said the help desk reached a phenomenal 300 calls a day. They did not want to learn the changes. Even the divisional executives were confused and angry. No one seemed willing to take the extra step to learn what to do. Turnover among the employees who were to use the Manugistics software to forecast product demand reached 77 percent. Those who remained found it easier to use their familiar spreadsheets.

The simultaneous installation of the Y2K changes also caused them trouble. In the rush to be done on time, the team had failed to integrate the various modules. Therefore, for example, while the purchasing departments used the appropriate systems and data names, their systems were not integrated with the financial, planning, and sales software. As a result, when a salesperson gave a valued customer a special discount rate, it was entered in the new system, but the accounts receivable department would not know about it and would think the customer did not fully pay its bill.

The team finally called a halt to the project in June 2000. Nestlé removed the project co-leader and Dunn took over as the sole project leader. In October, Dunn held a three-day offsite retreat with the key stakeholders and the business executives. It became clear that the Y2K deadline of January 1, 2000, had put too much pressure on the project, and as a result the members of the project team had lost sight of the bigger picture. They just focused on the technology. They now needed to integrate the existing components and to complete the work on the sales and distribution modules. Dunn also decided she now wanted to switch the supply chain module to the new SAP system because it had been improved enough since her rejection of it in 1998. By the time the retreat was ended, the team decided to start the whole project over again. It would first determine the business requirements and then decide on a new completion date, abandoning the earlier date. They also agreed to educate those affected so that all employees would know not only what changes were taking place but also why, how, and when those changes would happen.

The project team created a detailed design and project road map by April 2001. Nestlé also assigned one person, Tom James, to be Best's director of process change, giving him complete responsibility for liaison between the divisions and the Best project. The team also began taking repeated surveys of the effect of the project on employees and how they were dealing with it. James and Dunn also began holding more meetings with the division heads. As a result of the information gathered in this way, James and Dunn determined the manufacturing users were not ready for the many changes, and so the rollout of that package was delayed for six months.

The new project is expected to be completed in the first quarter of 2003, late but successful. Already all of Nestlé USA are using the same software and data. The company not only has been able to produce better sales forecasts, but Dunn said the factories are following these better numbers. Altogether, the company says it has already saved $325 million by spring 2002. And Nestlé SA has learned from that project and expects to have an easier success with its project. And that, she says, is despite the fact that Dunn only had to deal with eight or nine autonomous divisions while the global headquarters was dealing with 80 autonomous countries to accomplish the same thing. She concluded by saying, "They're just taking it up a notch. If they go in with an attitude that there's not going to be resistance and pain, they're going to be disappointed."

Sources: Ben Worthen, "Nestlé's ERP Odyssey," *CIO Magazine*, May 15, 2002; William Echikson, "Nestlé: An Elephant Dances," *Business-Week Online*, December 11, 2000, <www.businessweek.com>; Steve Konicki, "Nestlé Taps SAP for E-Business," *InformationWeek*, June 26, 2000; and Candee Wilde, "SAP Customers Update Their ERP Applications," *InformationWeek*, June 12, 2000.

CASE STUDY QUESTIONS

1. Evaluate Nestlé SA and Nestlé USA by using the competitive forces and value chain models.

2. What were the problems and issues that Nestlé SA faced that caused the company to be so decentralized?

3. Do you think it was appropriate for Nestlé to distribute the decision making so widely? Explain your answer.

4. Why did Nestlé's initial enterprise system project encounter so many problems? What management, organization, and technology factors contributed to those problems?

5. If you had been in charge of the Nestlé enterprise system project, what could you have done to prevent these problems?

ASSESSING THE TOTAL COST OF OWNERSHIP (TCO) OF A WEB SITE

Your advertising company has about 65 employees and you would like to set up a Web site initially devoted to attracting new clients by advertising and showcasing your work. Most of your work consists of printed magazine advertisements and television commercials. You have not yet established a presence on the Web. You have been asked to prepare an estimate of how much it would cost to establish and operate your own Web site for two years.

At first your company will not be selling anything. Instead it will be displaying about 400 Web pages showing samples of your ads, with photographs, line art, text, and short video clips. It will also include links to customer Web sites (for those customers who agree). The site should have the capability of accepting online requests for additional information from visitors and should display information about how to contact the company by telephone, e-mail or conventional mail. You anticipate your Web site will require two gigabytes of storage to start with. You also anticipate a maximum of 50 concurrent visitors at first.

You have been instructed that your company will almost certainly want to expand usage of the site in the future, perhaps actually selling ads through the Internet, perhaps using the site for working together with existing clients. You have been asked to provide a solution that can handle other possible future uses as well.

To carry out this task, use the Web to find the information you need to complete your assignment. Use several search engines to locate a quality overview describing the process of building a Web site. Next you will need information on the most fundamental item, the Web server. After selecting and pricing Web server software, you will need to price the cost of hardware, personnel, and other software required to run your Web site. Your employees are already equipped with desktop computers running Windows XP Professional, which they use for their work. Your Web site will need its own dedicated server along with appropriate software, networking, and human resources and you would like to use hardware and software that works with your existing computing environment. Your management does not want to install content management or personalization tools at this time.

To calculate the Total Cost of Ownership (TCO) of creating and operating your Web site, you should consider the following cost components (and any others you determine will be necessary):

- Web server software
- Computer hardware to house your Web site
- Operating system software
- Web site development software for creating your Web site
- Software to analyze the performance of your Web site, including analysis of Web site traffic and analysis of links between Web pages
- Firewall and antivirus software
- Web site design and creation costs, including the following:

  a. Cost to design and set up the original Web site. (A Web site development firm has agreed to do this work for $15,000.)
  b. Initial Web page layouts, including custom graphics, photographs, line art, audio, and video elements. (Your firm can use its own staff to create these pages at cost of $200 per page.)
  c. Domain name registration fee
  d. Development of search engine keywords to direct visitors to your site and registration with search engines

- Ongoing maintenance costs: costs to update the Web site, to change existing pages, and to create new pages. Your company estimates making changes to eight pages per month. Your company does not anticipate additional hardware or software upgrades for the next two years.

- Additional personnel costs:

  a. A marketing specialist in charge of Web site content
  b. An information systems specialist to maintain the Web site
  c. Training of current and new staff, estimated at 15 people requiring 10 hours each annually

- Additional monthly telephone expenses for the cost of a leased T-1 line

INTERNATIONAL CASE STUDY

CASE STUDY 1: BIRCH POINT LODGE

V. Joseph Compeau and Professor Deborah Compeau

University of Western Ontario (Canada)

Dennis Casey sighed as he looked at the receipts and invoice for the Pattersons. It was late July 1999, and Casey, manager and former owner of the Birch Point Lodge (BPL) resort in Haliburton, Ontario, was catching up on some bookkeeping. One of his tasks was to double check that all of the extra charges (for things like motor boat rentals, tuck shop purchases, and liquor) were correctly assigned to guests during their stay and then were included on the invoice at check out. The Pattersons, longtime guests of BPL, who brought their family of four up each summer for a week, had checked out the previous day. When the final bill had been tallied, the bottle of wine they'd had at dinner the previous night had not been caught. Now Casey had to decide whether to chase the customer for payment of a $25.00 bottle of wine or eat the cost. Because of their manual system, this kind of thing happened fairly often. When the amounts were fairly small, such as this, Casey usually just covered the cost himself in the spirit of good guest relations. But the costs added up over a busy summer and it just seemed wrong to have these kinds of mistakes eating into profits. Of course the experience with Maestro, a property management system for hotels and resorts that they had purchased in 1998, had been worse. The software had been so complex that nobody could figure out how to use it effectively and besides, it was full of little bugs that the vendor was still working out. Casey figured they had spent about $9,000 installing the system and it had never been used once—they had gone back to the manual system for front desk management. But now Casey wondered again—as he had many times over the past 12 years—whether there was a better solution out there.

Company and Industry Background

Birch Point Lodge (BPL) was located about five minutes east of the town of Haliburton on Lake Kashagawigamog. Started by Casey's great-grandmother, Anne Gould, it had been in operation since 1922. Casey and his wife, Roxanne, took over ownership and management of the lodge in 1987. In 1997, the Caseys sold BPL to Eddie Hwu, a Toronto businessman, but stayed on as the day-to-day managers.

BPL was one of 12 resorts in the Haliburton region. Resorts differed from traditional hotel/motel and bed and breakfast properties, primarily in terms of number of activities and meals. Hotel/motel properties tended to have more transient guests, often dominated by business travelers. In a resort, the guests were likely to stay for longer periods and to spend more time on the resort property.

Seventy-five to 80 percent of resort businesses in Ontario were family owned businesses, like BPL, and most were small. In the Haliburton Highlands, there were only two properties of any major size: Pinestone (100 rooms) and Wigamog (80 rooms).

The early 1990s were a difficult time in the resort business. There had been substantial consolidation of properties and some bankruptcies. By 1999, BPL was one of only four resorts left out of 10 that used to exist on Lake Kashagawigamog.

BPL was an all-inclusive resort, open year-round. During the high season (May to September) they offered the full American plan, which included three full meals, as well as accommodation. The dining room was licensed and there was also a licensed patio overlooking the water. For guest use, there were canoes, paddleboats, fishing rods, rowboats, kayaks, and both touring and mountain bicycles. Fishing boats and motors were available for rent. The BPL property included several beaches plus docks and a boat ramp. In addition, there were tennis courts, shuffleboard, and playground equipment.

BPL had 29 rooms: six in the main lodge, 18 Lakeside cabins, three Hillside cabins, and two Economy cabins. All rooms and cabins accommodated a minimum of two adults. Most also accommodated two children and a few were suitable for up to six people (two adults, four children). The kitchen, main dining room, two common rooms, and the Kids' Club (a supervised craft and play area where guests could send younger children for a few hours each day) were located in the main lodge.

Casey's approach to the resort business was based on three criteria: make it clean, make it comfortable, and provide good food.

> The resort industry is a very hard one to make money in. It is seasonal, faddy, trendy, and you continually have to have the latest thing. I maintain that one of the reasons this old place has stayed here is because it doesn't do that. It passes over trends and fads, at least that's my own theory. If this year's trendy thing is purple bathtubs, all the resort operators go out and buy purple bathtubs and spend lots of money and it only lasts for a couple of years—that's the bottom line problem. With the age of us baby-boomer types, we get a lot of people not wanting phones or televisions. There seems to be a point in time right now, where simplicity is the thing.

Customers and Marketing

Birch Point Lodge, like most resorts, attracted primarily families. Their clientele was extremely loyal and often multi-generational. Guests often booked their next year's visit as they were checking out each summer, in order to ensure that they would get their preferred room or cabin.

BPL charged guests on a per person basis, depending on the type of accommodation they used, the number of nights they stayed, and the time of year. BPL's rates were less than those of neighboring properties. Exhibit 1 shows the rates for the 2000 season.

Guests were only charged based on the number of adults. Thus, families with two children paid the same rate as a couple. This was an important aspect of the resort business, but it made for a financial challenge. Casey noted:

> We're full at 80 people, but if 30 of them are kids, you're not getting paid for 30 people, even though it costs you to feed them and clean their towels, etc.

The target market was mostly Toronto and northern United States (New York, Pennsylvania, Ohio, and Michigan). BPL did very little direct advertising. Each year, they placed an ad in the *Toronto Star,* and this was successful in bringing in new guests to the lodge. In addition to the *Toronto Star* advertising, Birch Point Lodge was a member of Resorts Ontario and thus participated in their Great Escapes advertising campaign in the United States.

However, membership in Resorts Ontario was a double-edged sword. Resorts Ontario was in the process of introducing a rating system, and this was a sore point with Casey.

> It's always a controversial issue, the rating system. I always thought we would be a three star—kind of in the middle, not really elaborate, but not leather hinges and door latches either. I phoned and got the criteria. We wouldn't even be a one (star). It would cost us $20,000 to become a one—$10,000 for TVs alone.

The problem with these rating systems, from Casey's perspective, was that they were designed for hotel-type properties, and put a high value on amenities such as televisions and in-room phones. For a vacation resort, having no phones in the room and no television could be considered a benefit—an opportunity to get away from it all. Yet the criteria did not reflect this.

Birch Point Lodge also had a Web site (www.birchpointlodge.com). This was an informational site only—it described the features of the property and the activities. Guests could not book a room through the Web site, but could request information by e-mail. BPL also sent out a yearly newsletter to past customers.

Operations

In 1999, BPL had a core staff of five people. In addition to the Caseys, there was a cook, housekeeper, and a maintenance person. About 20 extra people were hired in the summer, mostly to help with housekeeping and meals. With a few exceptions, staff did not live on the premises.

A typical day for Roxanne began at about 8:00 a.m., when she arrived at the Lodge.

> Breakfast is already started. I set up the computer. I make sure the office is open. The phone will start ringing, people wanting life-jackets, boat rentals, safety kits, chocolate bars. In the afternoon, you've got the bar. I make sure the dining room is okay. Each day, the guests change. I have to make sure dining room staff has a list of changes and the cooks know how many people we have for each meal.
>
> I schedule housekeeping, they report in when finished with cottages. They have to let me know that a doorknob is off for example. Most things come through the front desk.

I do ordering for groceries. That's another thing you have to make sure of, that we have everything. You have to be running around checking so you make sure they have everything, staples in particular, after that they can be on their own to order. I set the menu with the help of the cooks.

> Scheduling of the staff is done manually. In summer, the staff get two days off, but work breakfast, lunch, dinner (three shifts per day). Most of the staff get about 40 to 44 hours per week. Summer staff gets paid minimum wage plus about 10 cents, plus gratuities. We don't like them to count on that, but you can't discount it.

At the heart of the day-to-day operation was the reservation book. This was a spiral bound ledger that the Caseys used to record guest's reservations. Each month was one page with room and cottage numbers recorded in columns and the dates as rows. The last name of the guest was recorded, as was the number of people. The last day they were staying was circled so there was a visual clue for check out. Every morning, the final bill was calculated for each guest that was checking out. The bill would include the total room charge less any deposit and all extra charges like the bar bill and motorboat rentals. At night, the check-in packages would be created for the next day's arrivals.

The Quest for a Reservations System

The Caseys had been thinking about computerized reservations since about 1988, shortly after they took over the business. At the time, Casey was a Macintosh user so he became particularly interested in a product called Mac Inn, developed for the Someplaces Different chain of resorts. However, a visit to the Hochelaga Inn in Kingston (one of the member hotels) quickly cured him of this interest.

> I started out as a Mac user. In the early years here, I wanted a reservation program. I would go flipping through the *Mac User* magazine and I came to this program called Mac Inn— designed for small properties, under 30 rooms. They listed Someplaces Different as a user. Roxanne and I were on our way to Quebec and we were going to be staying in Kingston. So I said, "We'll just play this through." So I phoned, did the whole nine yards, said I'd like a confirmation letter and so on, just to see the process.
>
> So, anyway, we did that, got our confirmation letter and it was all very nice. When we arrived at the place, I stepped up to the counter and said, "I have a reservation and my name is Casey." She walked over to the computer and started typing on it. Then she picked the book up and said "Okay Mr. Casey you're in room 104."
>
> So, they had this system, but it couldn't replace the reservation book. At this point, we decided it wasn't worth it.

Northwind's Maestro

Nothing really happened with reservations systems until 1997. After Eddie Hwu bought BPL, the topic rekindled. Hwu, who was more of a "computer guy" according to Casey, wanted to have a computerized reservations system. Hwu talked to his friend, George, who worked for a large telecommunications company in Toronto, about what they needed. George was heavily involved in long-term planning for information systems (IS) in his company and was able to offer guidance to Hwu. He looked at what was available in property management software (the generic name for software to computerize hotels, resorts, conference centers, etc.).

The major vendor, and really the only one that was identified, was a company called Northwind (www.north88.com), located in Toronto, Ontario. They marketed a product called Maestro, which included functions for the front office (check in/check out), sales and catering, accounts receivable, voice, and text messaging, Club/Spa management, work order maintenance, golf/tee times, yield management, and real-time online Web reservations.

Northwind had an impressive customer list, including the Las Vegas Sands Hotel and the Four Seasons in Florida. Northwind also felt that the software would work for resorts such as BPL. After some negotiation, Hwu decided to buy the software, at a total cost of about $8,000, including hardware upgrade costs, software, installation, training at the vendor's facility in Markham for three staff, plus some onsite training ($2,900), and one year of technical support ($1,000).

The training took place in late April of 1998. The Caseys and Cheryl (the assistant manager) went to Markham for three days of training. They knew it was going to be a problem from the very beginning. Casey recalled:

> We sat down on the first day. We were very keen. But as soon as we got into it, there would be a glitch. Something wouldn't be right and their technical people would have to stop and fix it.

Roxanne Casey added:

> It was just so intense. They would show us how to do something, but then we would realize that that doesn't work for this property, so they'd have to stop and fix it. And it would get us all confused.

After the training, Hwu took the computer down to Northwind in Markham and had the software installed. When the computer came back up to BPL, they quickly realized it just wasn't going to work. According to Roxanne Casey:

> We were never able to use it. At that time, Cheryl was doing more of the front office work. She fought with it and tried to get some help from technical support. It was so frustrating. We couldn't even figure anything out—we just couldn't do it—it was so complicated.
>
> I couldn't even get into it. We had some trouble with the passwords and I don't think I ever used it. Anyway we finally gave up because there was just no way.

With the busy summer season about to start, the Caseys felt it didn't make sense to continue with this software that just wasn't going to work. Casey talked to the vendor about getting some onsite training, but decided against it since the cost to BPL of that training would have been more than it would have cost to get another whole system.

In spite of the difficulties they had faced in trying to find reservations software that would meet their needs, Roxanne

Casey still felt that it would be very useful.

> I wanted something in the office. It just makes things a little bit more professional and it's a lot less work for you. You don't have to figure out everyone's bills, and it's all nice and neat. We avoid adding and multiplying errors. Most of the time those would be in the customer's favor and that's okay, but it's not good for us. Other times it was something that you had to credit someone for. You can also automatically generate confirmation letters. It would be much easier to send out our newsletter—right now we have a separate database for customer names and I use it to send the annual newsletter out in the winter.

RoomMaster

Another year passed. Casey continued to look for software that would meet the particular needs of a resort like BPL. About a week after the incident with the Patterson's bottle of wine, he received the latest issue of *Inn Experience*. In it was an advertisement for a software package called RoomMaster. It claimed to be designed for resorts as well as hotels and the price was right—it was only U.S.$800. Casey phoned the company, located in Montreal, and received additional information. He was impressed with what he saw and asked for the names of some customers he could talk to. It turned out that one of the customers ran a property that he and Roxanne had stayed at on one of their trips into the Eastern Townships, so Casey called. The proprietor was very satisfied with the software. He said it had only required a couple of hours of training and he had been able to work easily with the software. Another hotel operator in Thunder Bay told Casey that he had required no training at all.

When he spoke to the vendor in Montreal, Casey learned that there was a 45-day demo version of the software available on the company's Web site (www.innquest.com). Casey downloaded it so that he and Roxanne could see how it worked. Both found it fairly easy to navigate. It included features for reservations, guest ledger, billing, guest history, housekeeping and maintenance, as well as over 70 predefined reports. It looked like it would meet most of their needs.

However, there were some concerns. First, they would have to adjust some of their internal procedures to fit the software. Prices in RoomMaster had to be calculated per room night, rather than per guest package (which might be three nights or five nights). Casey and Roxanne thought that could be worked out by dividing the guest package rate by the number of room nights booked. Second, there was a problem with the handling of taxes. RoomMaster was only set up to handle three types of taxes, but BPL needed to track four: provincial sales tax (8 percent), goods and services tax (7 percent), room tax (5 percent) and liquor tax (10 percent). A possible solution was a user-defined field for liquor tax, but this would mean that liquor sales could not be calculated and entered automatically.

Another thing Casey was concerned about was technical support. Innquest charged $35 to $40 per hour for support. Although packages were available that would provide some level of free support, no support was provided on weekends or holidays.

The Decision

As Casey filed the receipt from the Pattersons' bottle of wine and recorded it under miscellaneous expenses, he thought about the benefits of a computerized system for managing BPL. He wondered whether RoomMaster could be the solution he sought. He knew that Hwu would probably buy whatever he recommended. He just wasn't sure if this was the right way to go.

Source: V. Joseph Compeau and Professor Deborah Compeau. Copyright © 2001, Ivey Management Services.

CASE STUDY QUESTIONS

1. Describe the problems Birch Point Lodge encountered with its earlier reservation and property management systems. What was the business impact of those problems?

2. How could a well-functioning computerized reservation system provide value to Birch Point Lodge's business? Explain your answer.

3. Should Birch Point Lodge adopt RoomMaster? What management, organization, and technology issues should be addressed when making this decision?

EXHIBIT 1   BIRCH POINT LODGE RATES[1]
2000 SEASON (PER ADULT, IN CANADIAN DOLLARS)

| | | Lakeside | | | Hillside | | Economy | |
		Summer	Spring/Fall	Winter[2]	Summer	Spring/Fall	Summer	Spring/Fall
Packages	Description							
14 nights	Sunday to Sunday or Friday to Friday	$1,323	$1,171		$1,217	$1,077	$926	$820
7 nights	Sunday to Sunday or Friday to Friday	698	611		624	562	489	428
6 nights	Any 6 nights	660	567		607	522	462	397
W/end 5 nights	Including w/ends	550	473		506	435	385	331
W/day 5 nights	Sunday to Thursday	499	537		459	402	349	306
W/end 4 nights	Including w/ends	460	392		423	361	322	274
W/day 4nights	Sunday to Thursday	420	364		386	335	294	255
W/end 3 nights	Including w/ends	378	317		348	292	265	222
W/day 3 nights	Sunday to Thursday	345	294		317	270	242	206
W/end 2 nights	Including w/ends	252	211		232	194	176	148
W/day 2 nights	Sunday to Thursday	220	189		202	174	154	132
W/end 1 night	According to availability	125	105	950	115	97	88	74
W/day 1 night	According to availability	115	96	750	106	90	81	69

Source: Company files.

[1]Rates include three meals during Summer season, two meals (breakfast and dinner) during Spring, Fall and Winter.

[2]Winter rates are for groups of 10 or more.

V. Joseph Compeau and Professor Deborah Compeau prepared this case solely to provide material for class discussion. The authors do not intend to illustrate either effective or ineffective handling of a managerial situation. The authors may have disguised certain names and other identifying information to protect confidentiality.

INTERNATIONAL CASE STUDY

CASE STUDY 2: JAPAN AIRLINES: IMPACT OF E-TICKETII

Amir Hoosain, Shamza Khan, Dr. Dennis Kira, and Dr. Ali Farhoomand,

The University of Hong Kong

During the 1990s, Internet usage doubled every 100 days and inspired the "e-commerce revolution," bringing changes to business fundamentals and sources of competitive advantage. Electronic commerce radically altered the way companies conducted business and provided services to customers. Firms could enter markets globally to expand their customer and supplier base by positioning businesses online. E-commerce, effectively implemented, resulted in lower costs and increased direct interaction between a business and its customers, suppliers, service providers, employees, and other parties in the value-chain.

Since privatising in 1987, Japan Airlines (JAL) faced many difficulties including image problems and intense domestic and global competition. In addition to competitive pressures and increased airport charges, fuel taxes increased while the domestic downturn affected JAL's prospects throughout the 1990s. A restructuring strategy achieved some success in JAL's cost-cutting objectives but such savings through traditional means were nearing their potential.

In the meantime, many major international carriers were making headlines with aggressive efforts to achieve the reality of electronic travel services, including electronic ticketing (e-ticketing) and smart cards. However, JAL was so busy managing its financial situation that it overlooked competing foreign carriers that were introducing e-ticketing to the Japanese market.

Airlines that had implemented e-ticketing, primarily in North America, experienced considerable savings in distribution costs through Internet sales and by automating many selling processes. The JAL management wondered, to what extent might this success be replicated by a Japanese major and what would be the best approach for pursuing e-ticketing implementation in Japan?

JAL's Growth

The precursor to Japan Airlines (JAL) was the Japan Air Transport Company, the Japanese national airline dissolved by the allies after World War II. During the U.S. occupation, Japan was not permitted to establish its own airline, but in 1951; a group of bankers founded JAL, in essence a revival of the Japan Air Transport Company. Under the Allied Peace Treaty, JAL was forbidden from using Japanese flight crew and therefore, leased pilots and a small fleet of aircraft from Northwest Airlines. By 1953, the fledgling airline had its own aircraft and crew, with government and the public sharing ownership. Under the Japan

Air Lines Company Limited Law, JAL was granted special status as the "flag carrier" and the only domestic airline allowed to operate international routes.

As the airline grew, its operations received heavy scrutiny from the government, its largest stockholder. Government involvement placed certain limitations on managerial independence and created a highly bureaucratic and complex organizational structure.[1]

In the late 1970s, deregulation revolutionised the U.S. airline industry and the movement inevitably forced the Japanese airline sector to abolish the Japan Air Lines Company Limited Law in November 1987; the government relinquished its stake in JAL and divested its shares to the public. JAL became fully privatized and acquired greater freedom to expand into new areas and to exercise autonomy in corporate decision making. In the new environment, Japanese civil aviation companies were better able to respond and adapt to changing market demands and competitor actions. Perhaps due to the legacy of government protectionism, JAL was not known for its customer orientation and when surveyed in 1986, domestic travelers rated the company's service as bureaucratic and unfriendly relative to its domestic competitors.[2] Also, as a consequence of privatization, air transport was no longer nationalized and JAL's chief domestic rival, All Nippon Airways (ANA) was permitted to enter the domain of overseas service.

During the 1990s, JAL experienced a financial downturn due to high labor costs and over expansion of its fleet and facilities, coupled with the slowing Japanese economic growth as a result of over-investments in the late 1980s. In recognition of these problems, JAL announced a U.S.$4.8 billion cost-cutting plan.

The company's restructuring agenda fell under four classifications as follows:

- Outsourcing secondary services.

- Overall staff reduction/making wages competitive within industry norms.

- Disposing of non-core assets.

- Creating lower cost subsidiary airlines such as Japan Air Charter (for short-haul international flights) and Japan Express (for short-haul domestic flights).

By 1994, passenger counts for JAL were higher, but the airline had been pressured to cut prices to match the competition's lower fares. In the same year, Osaka's new airport gave a boost to

JAL's overseas traffic, but brought intense competition by allowing more flights into Japan. In 1995, JAL and American Airlines (AA) formed an alliance, agreeing to link their computerized reservations systems (AXESS and Sabre respectively) and to serve as agents for each other's cargo businesses. This partnership was the first of several in years to come and characteristic of a rapidly evolving industry where cost-cutting and strategic alliances were critical for sustained growth.

Developments Within the Travel Industry

Throughout the 1990s, major structural changes in the airline industry were instigated through e-commerce. The use of the Internet created several advantages for airlines including direct access to customers and cost-effective methods of conducting business processes online. On the other hand, growing e-commerce activity and the Internet's globalization effect increased competitive business pressures and created a rapidly changing business landscape. The airline industry was pressured to transform organizational processes to adapt to the changing environment by becoming more competitive. The Internet provided airlines with the ability to do business on a global basis, to react quickly, differentiate services, monitor changes, and customize services with a view to winning customer loyalty. This was only attainable through the implementation of the appropriate mix of technology, process management, and corporate strategy.

Disintermediation and Reintermediation

The nature of e-commerce could reap major benefits for Japan, with its bureaucratic tangle of middlemen in a complex market distribution system. In the air travel industry, travel agents were the traditional intermediaries between airlines and travelers, and were compensated for services through commissions paid by airlines. Through the advent of e-commerce, the very survival of the traditional travel agent was threatened by disintermediation through airline direct services and travel cybermediaries.

E-commerce observers predicted the displacement of the traditional intermediary—the travel agent. This "disintermediation" process was achieved through direct access to airlines. However, cutting out the middleman caused new problems, ranging from fulfilment of single transactions from individual consumers, to setting up new customer service centres.

Travel agents needed to provide new value. Additional pressure was placed on travel agents with the airlines imposing commission caps. The emergence of e-ticketing weakened the travel agent's role in the distribution chain as their principal role of putting tickets into the travelers' hands could be eliminated by airlines and Web sites offering e-ticketing.

Most travel agents, however, demonstrated strong survival skills. According to the American Society of Travel Agents, 49 percent of travel agencies had Web sites of their own, compared with 37 percent in 1998. Studies showed that many people who surfed the Internet for deals then turned to travel agents to make their bookings.

Internet travel agents began refocusing on the leisure travel market by offering a variety of broad travel packages at competitive prices. At the same time, airlines in many cases expanded by acquiring travel sites. UA had a minority stake in GetThere.com (formerly Internet Travel Network) and Continental held a stake in Rosenbluth Interactive, owners of Biztravel.com. To some observers, however, airlines failed to fully exploit the potential of the Internet and invest continuously in their Web sites. As a result, they lagged behind online agents in innovation and the provision of integrated travel services.

Industry experts observed that while there were disintermediation forces, an equally vibrant industry of intermediaries emerged to serve the needs of airlines and customers. These new intermediaries, known as "cybermediaries", reintermediated services in the airline industry. Cybermediaries competed with the traditional travel agents and an airline's direct services. They staked territory in cyberspace between the airlines and the traveler. Cybermediaries offered several advantages over an airline's direct services:

▌ Permitting travelers to book flights on almost any airline.

▌ Providing features to assist travelers in searching for the lowest prices.

▌ Notifying travelers by e-mail when a discount fare was posted for a particular destination of interest.

The concept of e-ticketing and its impact on the ticketing process was of prime importance in enabling the development of self-service technologies and electronic travel innovations. According to a study by Jupiter Communications, travel had become the number one product purchased online, netting U.S.$911 million in 1997.[3] Online travel sales are expected to account for 35 percent of all online sales globally by 2002 and travel purchases are expected to range from U.S.$5 billion to U.S.$30 billion by 2003.[4] Much of these purchases, however, were made through innovative "virtual travel agencies."

On one hand, airlines welcomed the creation of new channels to sell and promote their products, especially those that challenged the costly travel agent system. However, these new entrants also pre-empted the airlines' own efforts to implement direct sales and minimize distribution costs. In response, some airlines imposed tighter restrictions on commissions paid through such channels, but these new industry dynamics remained a cause for concern.

Computerized Reservation Systems

With the deregulation of the U.S. airline industry in the late 1970s, American carriers had experienced similar competitive pressures and invested heavily in the innovation and development of computerized reservation systems (CRS)[5] to seek a competitive advantage. The advent of CRSs revolutionised airline business dynamics and the broader travel industry, elevating the role of information technology (IT). In 1987, JAL formed its newest subsidiary, AXESS International Network Inc., in a bid to develop its own computerized reservation system. JAL's management witnessed increased competitiveness resulting from the development of CRS (Sabre and Apollo) by its American counterparts and felt it necessary to develop a system of their own to seek a competitive advantage in the evolving CRS market.

JAL's CRS project was originally established as a marketing initiative, receiving full managerial support and huge capital and human resource investments. The resulting system—AXESS, was an integrated travel information and reservation system linked to hotel chains as well as other CRSs. The Sabre Group CRS (which had spun off from its originator, AA) bought a 25 percent stake in AXESS. AXESS became a cornerstone of JAL's strategy and was noted for its superior functionality as compared to other domestic reservation systems. This system was tightly integrated with other JAL information systems and offered enhanced services such as Japanese/English bilingual information retrieval. To ensure target users, such that travel agents and corporate inhouse travel departments would adopt AXESS, several value-adding features were incorporated, such as back office accounting and customer profile management systems. AXESS also reduced the ticket-processing time from 15 minutes to five seconds.

Introduction of E-Ticketing[6]

Airline deregulation triggered major changes including the privatization of national carriers and the proliferation of start-ups throughout the airline industry. In 1993, Valujet, an Atlanta-based no-frills carrier, pioneered a revolutionary innovation with low fares, no traditional paper tickets, and a proprietary reservation system, its comprehensive route structure and direct sales channel translated into simple accounting needs and made it especially well suited for the "e-ticketing" initiative (refer to **Appendix 1** for an illustration of the E-ticketing process).[7] In the same year, Morris Air, a small carrier based in Salt Lake City, introduced e-ticketing to increase its distribution potential; it was later acquired by Southwest Airlines. Southwest elected to implement the e-ticketing software and systems that came with the purchase, following a dispute with the Apollo/Galileo and System One systems.

Both e-ticketing pioneers, Morris Air and Valujet, gained tremendous value from the implementation. Morris Air's sales through travel agents decreased to around 33 percent and the carrier observed further benefits in check-in time and accounting labor savings; Valujet estimated that e-ticketing had cut costs by around 10 percent. Soon, major U.S. carriers were rapidly adopting e-ticketing.

Industry experts believed that e-ticketing would inevitably succeed traditional ticketing as the *de facto* standard because of the following obvious benefits for firms:[8]

- Acceptance by the airline carrier's target customers because of enhanced customer service and improved travel efficiency.

- High proportion of direct sales. By eliminating the middle-man, airlines could save on agent commission costs and agency fees.

- High proportion of business/corporate customers. Repeat business allowed airlines to monitor traveling trends and offer personalized service.

- Existence of advanced credit card payment systems. E-ticketing could be integrated easily into existing payment systems to provide "one-stop" shopping.

- Prevalence of carry-on baggage. Many customers liked to travel with minimum luggage, making e-ticketing and seamless travel attractive. Business travel was usually restricted to a short timeframe; the elimination of luggage check-in improved efficiency.

- Air travel consists primarily of point-to-point passengers. The existence of self-service check-in equipment reduced check-in times, thus improving efficiency and customer service.

- Airlines controlled the check-in environment. A simple network structure without connecting flights and multi-carrier itineraries give rise to "seamless" travel.

- Ability to adapt computer systems. Airlines preferred to use their own systems, equipment, and personnel to avoid the need to develop additional interfaces with other systems.

The earlier e-ticketing pioneers approached systems development through in-house innovation. Major U.S. and European airlines also came under pressure to respond and develop their own systems (refer to **Appendix 2** for an overview of the impact of e-ticketing on various airline functions). Other airlines adopting e-ticketing technology took a "fast follow" approach by seeking existing technology and customizing it to their requirements. Indeed, airlines opting for the "fast follow" method benefited from the standardization efforts.

Ron LeRadza, the General Manager of product distribution at Air Canada, conveyed the essence of this approach:

> We don't want to be leaders in the field. By waiting to see what problems and successes other carriers experience, we can make good progress with the introduction of our own systems.[9]

E-Ticketing in North America and Asia

Before the introduction of e-ticketing, distribution costs ranging from travel agent commissions to ticket stock, were high across the airline industry. By the mid-1990s, distribution costs represented an average of 24 percent of total costs, ranking even higher than airlines' fuel costs. Although the concept of e-ticketing emerged in 1993, it was only after initiatives by new airline entrants that major airlines overcame reservations concerning adoption and implementation. Improved value through enhanced customer service, personalized information, and other integrated travel information, was difficult to resist once e-ticketing benefits for customers and companies were clear. (Refer to **Appendix 3** for an illustration of some advantages and disadvantages of e-ticketing for the various parties in the air travel process.)

The main benefit of e-ticketing for airlines included transferring a portion of the airlines' travel agency sales, rife with commissions and segment booking fees, to direct sales channels. This opened up the potential for non-traditional channels of distribution that continued to arise with the advances of modern telecommunications.

As a result of these benefits, by early 2000, e-ticketing had become universal in North America and represented over 40 percent of total bookings for main carriers. In May 1999, UA announced that 51 percent of the seven million tickets it sold that month were e-tickets—the first time that e-ticketing use had achieved such a majority. By year's end, UA's e-ticketing service was 100 percent available to all 259 destinations in its worldwide network. Within five years, its e-ticket strategy had gone from conception to setting world standards in implementation.[10] With growing acceptance of e-ticketing, a number of basic interline e-ticketing (described later) implementations were under establishment.

Although e-ticketing was widely adopted by North American carriers, relatively few Asian carriers provided this service. E-ticketing services in Asia were first experienced in Hong Kong in 1999. By early 2000, only Singapore Airlines had introduced e-ticketing to limited destinations; Cathay Pacific offered e-ticketing to Hong Kong, Australia, Singapore and Manchester and had further plans to include Japan, the U.S., Canada, Taiwan, and London Heathrow. Airline Web sites offered features such as direct ticket sales, frequent flier program administration, flight-tracking, promotional releases, and online gift catalogs and online ticket auctions.[11]

In Japan, American carriers were pulling ahead of JAL and its domestic counterparts; UA and Delta had introduced e-ticketing and Northwest had imminent plans to follow suit. The Australian carrier, Qantas, was also set to extend its e-ticket offering to the Japanese market. A 1999 study commissioned by SITA, the leading provider of integrated telecommunications and information support to the air transport industry, revealed a possible root of this disparity—the average planned IT investment by Asia-Pacific airlines lagged far behind that of American and European carriers.

Interline e-Travel

Interline e-ticketing referred to traveling by an e-ticket with an itinerary spanning multiple carriers; this service provided great value to customers but could pose considerable complications for airlines offering the service. So far, most airlines that offered online e-ticket bookings only facilitated point-to-point tickets between certain stated destinations. Online booking facilities could not handle fares permitting stopovers and such requests had to be made at appropriate reservation offices either in person or via telephone.

In October 1996, a resolution addressing interline e-ticketing was adopted at the IATA/ATA Joint Passenger Services Conference and was made effective from January 1997.[12] These resolutions contained specifications for the eventual introduction of interline e-ticketing. However, interline e-ticketing development was progressing relatively slowly.

JAL Alliances

In January 1998, an agreement was signed between Japan and the U.S., granting JAL, Northwest Airlines, United Airlines (UA), and ANA, unlimited flying rights between the two countries. Additionally, new service opportunities were provided to Continental, American, Delta, TWA, and USAirways. The agreement was immediately criticized by JAL executives as favouring the American carriers.

However, by 1998, JAL improved profitability with proceeds from the sale of assets and managed to pay dividends for the first time in seven years; economic conditions had also improved. The number of passengers from Japan was expected to pick up, but questions still remained about JAL's ability to compete with its American and European counterparts, particularly with the opening of a new runway at Narita, which could prompt more aggressive pricing. The reduction in labor costs and the disposal of assets were nearing their limits and the airline found it difficult to make further savings in this area.

With the multitude of one-to-one code sharing and collaborative agreements JAL had accumulated, industry observers began to wonder if the airline had eventual plans to be a formal member of one of the increasing number of alliances among the international carriers. The larger American and European airlines had taken leading roles in pushing for alliances centred on code sharing and joint marketing (including shared frequent flyer programs) to benefit from the economies of scale.

Multi-carrier groups were created to address the pressures of heightened competition. Other alliances, such as UA's Star Alliance had grown to a considerable prominence. Although JAL had entered individual agreements with several Oneworld alliance members, including AA, British Airways, Cathay Pacific, and Iberia Airlines, it insisted on pursuing collaborations on a one-to-one basis. Nonetheless, by mid-1999, JAL announced the introduction of a task force to study the advantages and disadvantages of joining an alliance.

The Japan-U.S. Civil Aviation Agreement (1998)

"The purpose of the negotiations was to narrow the imbalance between Japan and the U.S., which has favored the U.S. since 1952 [when the original U.S.-Japan pact was signed]. Instead, the gap has been widened," said JAL president Akira Kondo.

To some industry observers however, the implications of the Japan-U.S. civil aviation agreement were not so bleak—Japanese carriers still had better access to the domestic corporate market and increased competition would boost overall traffic in the region, potentially to the benefit of all carriers serving Japan.

Despite the deregulation of the Japanese aviation industry, U.S. carriers did not enjoy complete freedom to undercut fares offered by Japanese airlines. While the Japanese government offered assurances that demand would determine prices on trans-Pacific routes, it was thought that JAL's fares would serve as a benchmark for other airlines. More worrisome was the threat of excess capacity across the industry and the loss of control at JAL's hubs as a result. Also on the horizon was further cause for concern—the opening of a second runway at Narita, anticipated in 2002. The new runway would dramatically increase the access that foreign carriers had to the Japanese market, with annual slots going up by as much as 70 percent.[13] Another warning came in a Standard & Poor's report on the airline, where it was suggested that with increased competition, any cost savings that would result from JAL's efforts could be offset by a necessary increase in promotional expenses.[14]

One of the more positive terms of the Japan-U.S. civil aviation agreement was the provision permitting JAL to pursue a code-sharing alliance with a major American airline. Such an alliance was formed with its marketing partner of three years, (AA). This alliance provided JAL with access to AA's extensive feeder network within the U.S., resulting in a vast increase to the booking options available for clients departing to Asia. The partnership with AA also increased JAL's appeal to passengers unfamiliar with the airline, who might otherwise prefer to make arrangements with a U.S. carrier.[15] Over the next year, JAL announced further code-sharing partnerships with Cathay Pacific, Swissair, Alitalia, and Iberia Airlines and formed an alliance with Lufthansa and Scandinavian Airlines System for a cargo route between Japan and Northern Europe.

As the competitive environment grew complicated in the area of international service, Japan's domestic market showed signs of change. By the late 1990s, JAL's domestic market share had made some headway against leaders ANA and Japan Air System (JAS). JAL benefited from the abolition of traffic thresholds on internal routes in Japan that had prohibited it from encroaching on ANA's realm of service. With internal expansion, JAL was able to provide a more extensive international feed than the other two majors and the success of its frequent flyer program contributed further to customer loyalty. This is not to say that the domestic market was devoid of developments—a number of start-up airlines, Hokkaido International Airlines (Air Do), Skymark Airlines, and Pan Asia Airways were granted operating authority by the Ministry of Transport and were making a modest emergence. While these start-ups were in their infancies, JAL and ANA implemented aggressive pricing on domestic routes in an attempt to stifle the new threat.[16]

In August 1999, JAL and JAS announced an agreement to code share certain international flights for a trial period—from October 1999 to March 2000. This was the first such plan announced by Japanese carriers and called for the use of JAL equipment and flight personnel at the JAS arrival and departure berths at Narita. Each airline maintained its own flight number and tickets continued to be sold through their separate marketing channels. At the time, JAS was also in the process of negotiating a code-sharing agreement with ANA. These developments unfolded amid some speculation that Japan's airlines may one day combine to form a "super carrier" for cost-saving and competitive purposes.[17]

Process Integration

With deregulation, JAL recognized the pressing need to advance customer service and improve profitability. To some extent, these objectives were attained through traditional modes of restructuring. Management's desire to reduce the volume of paper-based transactions led to the swift development of electronic data interchange (EDI) applications for cost reduction and logistical coordination.[18] A proprietary EDI system provided JAL with accurate and timely information to manage their complex network of relationships and to enable procurement, just-in-time delivery, and joint-venture operations. This network, developed by the Multi-Japan Network, was a JAL group member; JAL readily accepted the EDI implementation. The network's proprietary nature gave JAL confidence in information security and accuracy. EDI encouraged cost reduction by facilitating functions ranging from fuel procurement, aircraft maintenance parts delivery as well as improving the overall communication throughout the group.

For a period in 1997, JAL's Web site was the second most popular site in Japan, receiving 60,000 visitors a day, second only to *Asahi Shimbun* daily newspaper's Web site.[19] A Web site was also created to serve the American region, in conjunction with the company's efforts to expand its North American business. JAL had begun accepting reservations via the Internet in July 1996. Travel reservations were implemented through collaboration with the Travelocity system, belonging to the Sabre Group. E-ticketing

was not available, but customers could make travel arrangements through a customized version of Travelocity and traditional tickets were later sent by mail from the Travelocity service centre. Initially, this service was exclusive to domestic flights, but it was expanded to include international service in January 1997. The reservation system generated U.S.$4 million in revenue.[20]

According to JAL spokesman Akihiko Sato, most people who made reservations via the Internet were business passengers using domestic services and the proportion of repeat users was high.[21] The volume of online bookings for international travel was considerably smaller because many Japanese travelers purchased package tours for overseas travel. Direct ticket sales saved JAL the high travel agent commissions, ranging from 5 to 9 percent of ticket price.

By the late 1990s, e-ticket sales represented approximately 10 percent of all airline tickets worldwide. Many major airlines offered online booking with e-ticketing facilities. Web sites were user-friendly, self-explanatory, with step-by-step instructions on booking online. Some airlines even gave online booking rewards in the form of bonus air miles to create customer loyalty. In fact, firms realized that online Web site management should produce the ultimate goal of creating customer satisfaction and customer loyalty. During this period, there was growing popularity of the integrated front-end management process, which referred to firms creating seamless and tightly integrated management of customer order acquisition strategies. This meant that Web sites were points of entry for customers and that a customer visit online should result in the purchase of a good/service and in return, firms manage the purchase in an integrated fashion with the use of appropriate technology, process management, and strategy to execute all the functions involved.

For some, e-ticketing was seen as a source of competitive advantage, but JAL adopted a more traditional approach in their business re-engineering process rather than radically changing their business strategy. In response to the impending changes in their competitive environment, JAL formed horizontal alliances with other service providers such as car hire companies, hotels, and leisure service providers as a means of improving customer service. They also vertically integrated by establishing value-added services to core activities such as:

▌ Provision of airport transportation services.

▌ Provision of airport lounges.

▌ Provision of advance seat selection services.

▌ Provision of a baggage delivery service.

▌ Provision of priority guest services.

▌ Provision of a strong U.S. and European network by forming alliances with other major air carriers.

However, these had become commoditized services which most major airlines provided. In addition, other airline Web sites such as UA's provided customers with one-stop services for all airline booking and vacation requirements. All customers had to do was to get online, and UA would manage any requirements thereafter. It created customer satisfaction and entrenched customer loyalty. This was a management philosophy most firms were moving towards. However, JAL, while making small innovations, still had a fragmented strategy with regard to managing passengers' online bookings. Domestic passengers could only book through traditional travel agents while North American customers could book JAL seats through Travelocity.

With the expanding interconnection of customers and suppliers, e-commerce will facilitate the creation of electronic "supply Webs" surpassing the capability of a simple supply-chain. As a result, value will be added as transactions pass between participants, while costly human intervention will be kept at a minimum.

UA was one of the first among the major international airlines to implement e-commerce to enhance its value-chain. UA adopted a management philosophy with a process methodology that took into consideration every aspect of the firm and its environment. They focused on the consumer to improve interactions and streamlined operations by adding value internally to deliver superior customer service. UA carried this out by creating a new Web site that provided a new look and improved navigation. They added quick-search features that allowed customers to check schedules and flight information from the homepage as well as the ability to check their Mileage Plus account summary. To make navigation easier, the homepage was presented in four categories:

▌ *Planning Travel*—view schedules, compare fares, purchase travel, request upgrades, redeem award miles, or update customer profile.

▌ *Travel Support*—locate information about services, baggage guidelines, onboard entertainment, and airport maps.

▌ *Mileage Plus*—review frequent flyer accounts and the latest promotion updates to earn bonus points.

▌ *About United*—product information, alliances, and commitment to improving customer satisfaction.

This philosophy of integrated selling-chain management was gaining a lot of popularity among firms because it created added value for them and was touted as becoming a critical facet of conducting online business effectively. The idea was to create added value, for example, through information sharing. By sharing information along each link in an airline's process, airlines created value for customers by providing updated information on schedules and personalized customer services. Such integrated chains required firms to re-engineer their fundamental business processes to adapt their line of business to an e-commerce framework.

JAL's Future

Within a few years, online booking volumes skyrocketed and airlines scrambled with competing virtual distribution channels. Airlines offered various incentives to lure customers, and stood at fairly even market share with the online agents. Sales in 1999 were predicted to be at least U.S.$8 billion and the market was expected to go up to U.S.$20 billion in 2001.[22]

Japan's economy, however, remained largely under the influence of government ministries and *keiretsu* affiliations, resulting in a general preference for Japanese developed technology rather than the adoption of systems and technologies from abroad.[23]

In the airline industry, smart cards[24] followed on the heels of e-ticketing as a major component in companies' visions of seamless travel. With the full implementation of such technologies, customers would be able to transfer funds from a bank onto the card and make travel purchases online by transferring value from the smart card through a smart card reader installed in a personal computer. In addition, a customer's frequent flyer information, mileage record, as well as seating and meal preferences would already be stored in the card, thus expediting the online purchasing process. Once completed, an e-ticket and any necessary legal notices would then be transmitted and stored in the smart card. At the airport, the card would accelerate the check-in process, enable the use of automated kiosks, store other travel documentation, and serve as a boarding pass and baggage receipt as well as provide access to club lounges and other benefits. With potentially vast linkages to other service partners, the additional functions of the smart card were left to one's imagination.

Using technology as an enabler, airlines were rapidly adopting strategies and re-engineering their businesses to focus on adding more value to customers. Smart card technology, for example, was a vision which companies thought they could soon implement and offer as a service to customers. Airlines were experimenting with new dimensions in ticket distribution technology with the introduction of speech recognition systems capable of performing reservations, sales, and schedule and flight information functions. Some airlines viewed this as a mere supplement to the existing distribution methods, but others felt it would dramatically impact the industry when used in conjunction with e-ticketing and Internet sales.

Japan's traditionally complex bureaucratic organizational structures, coupled with heavy government regulation, seemed to hinder the development of the Japanese airline industry since its infancy and also affected its ability to innovate. JAL's strategy over the past decade focused on cost savings and efficiency improvement; however, changes remained within the realm of traditional business management practices. No major management effort was initiated to capture the opportunities offered by e-commerce and no dramatic business re-engineering processes were undertaken. At best, efforts to grow JAL's business online and seek alternative methods of growth remained fragmented; JAL's management philosophy seemed submerged by heavy cultural and regulatory influences.

JAL President and CEO Isao Kaneko could only express "cautious optimism" for a turnaround in 1999 on the recent news that Japan's economic growth was accelerating. However, JAL was under pressure despite increasing consumer spending and passenger traffic. Was this costly short-sightedness on the part of management, or was it in fact wiser in the long run for Japan's largest airline to consolidate internally and take a "fast follow" approach to e-ticketing in the light of vast implementation hurdles and uncertainties over eventual standards? Could it catch up with international airlines and compete effectively in the domestic and international market under the current management? What was the appropriate strategy to compete in the globalized and competitive environment that e-commerce posed?

CASE STUDY QUESTIONS

1. Evaluate Japan Airlines using the competitive forces and value chain models.

2. What is JAL's business strategy? How does it use information systems to support that strategy? What role do the Web and e-ticketing play in that strategy?

3. How does JAL's use of information technology differ from other major airlines?

4. How much has information technology been an enabler for Japan Airlines? Explain your answer.

Source: Amir Hoosain and Shamza Khan prepared this case under the supervision of Dr. Dennis Kira and Dr. Ali Farhoomand. Copyright © 2000 The University of Hong Kong. Ref. 00/78C

[1] A. T. Chatfield and N. Bjorn-Andersen, *Journal of Management Information Systems,* 14, No. 1 (Summer 1997) 13–40.

[2] K. Wataname, "Challenges for Japanese Airlines," *Nihon Koku no Chosen* (Tokyo: Nohon Noritsu Kyokai Management Center, 1995).

[3] "Online Travel Purchases Steadily Increase; Airlines Position to Get a Piece of the Pie," *World Airline News,* April 9, 1999.

[4] "Web@Work: E-Travel Sales on the Rise," *Asia Computer Weekly,* October 4, 1999.

[5] Computerized reservation systems facilitate online reservations with a variety of suppliers and enable prior bookings up to one year in advance.

[6] Y. Wauthy, (1997), "Business Research Project: Electronic Ticketing in the Airline Industry, History, Implementation, Consequences and Impact for the Future," Concordia University, October 1997.

[7] E-ticketing is the process when a ticket is booked either via an agent or online, the information is transmitted directly to the airline's database and once the information is sent, one can access the database to check, modify or cancel the details of the booking. After making a reservation or booking through an agent or online, the customer needs only a confirmation number and itinerary, both of which can be issued immediately over the telephone or through the airline's Web site. At the airport all that is needed is the confirmation number, photograph ID and credit card where necessary.

[8] K. Orla, "Strategic Technology Assessment: Aer Lingus and Electronic Ticketing," December 1996, www.cs.ted.ie/courses/ism/strechs/ind1/as/msg00011.html.

[9] "Electronic Ticketing Without Frontiers," Airlines International.

[10] "United Airlines' E-Ticketing (SM) Service Now Available Worldwide," *PR Newswire,* November 17, 1999.

[11] Online ticket auction is where an airline will post a travel offer on its Web site which is then open for surfers to bid against each other until the highest price is reached or bidding has closed.

[12] Resolution 722f for airlines and 722g for travel agents in neutral ticketing environments.

[13] D. Hayashi et al., *HSBC James Capel Report: Japan Airlines (*May 29, 1998).

[14] D. Jones, "From One Crisis to Another," *Air Finance Journal* (September 1998).

[15] D. Jones, (1998).

[16] "Japanese Carriers Defend Domestic Pricing Structures" *World Airlines News,* December 17, 1999.

[17] K. Laterman, "Japanese Airlines Need Restructuring to Keep Their Heads Above the Clouds," *The Street,* September 26, 1999, www.thestreet.com/int/asia/787066.html, accessed January 2000.

[18] Chatfield and Bjorn-Anderson, (1997).

[19] "JAL Internet Site Proves Popular," *Travel Trade Gazette UK & Ireland,* January 15, 1997.

[20] S. Hirao, "Japan's Electronic Commerce: Companies Learn by Trial and Error to Sell on the Net," *Japan Times Weekly International Edition,* May 11, 1998.

[21] S. Hirao, May 11, 1998.

[22] "Gomez Advisors Release First Internet Airline Scorecard," *BusinessWire,* September 8, 1999.

[23] "Smart Cards Come to Japan," *Credit Card Management,* September 1998.

[24] Smart cards are standard plastic cards containing an integrated circuit, systems and applications software, and permanent data.

APPENDIX 1

THE E-TICKETING PROCESS

*E-ticketing process diagram, e.g., Yves Wauthy, Electronic Ticketing in the airline industry.

APPENDIX 2

AN OVERVIEW OF THE IMPACT OF E-TICKETING ON VARIOUS AIRLINE FUNCTIONS

Computerized reservation systems

With the creation of an e-ticket at a CRS terminal, a record is entered into the airline's e-ticketing database according to ATA/IATA standards.

Departure control systems

This system must be adapted to allow airline check-in and gate agents access to the e-ticketing database and enable them to update the passenger's status over the course of passenger handling operations.

Accounting systems

In addition to its function as a travel document, the e-ticket serves a financial function and must be under the auspices of the accounting systems throughout the course of its use. The e-ticket is used for billing and revenue accounting purposes.

Settlement systems

Known as the Airline Reporting Corporation (ARC) in the U.S. and Bank Settlement Plan (BSP) in other countries, settlement systems are in use in travel agencies to expedite ticket and accounting functions. The systems are comprised of a neutral ticket issue to serve travel on multiple providers. The billing function is centralized by ARC/BSP, which then "settles" the transactions with the airlines. With the advent of e-ticketing, paper ticket settlement systems are no longer applicable, but new settlement systems must be implemented.

APPENDIX 3

THE ADVANTAGES AND DISADVANTAGES OF E-TICKETING FOR VARIOUS PARTIES WITHIN THE TRAVEL INDUSTRY

	Advantages	Disadvantages
Airlines	• Enables new distribution channels • Benefits direct sales over costly intermediaries • Eliminates paper ticket production • Simplifies modification and refunds • Reduction in check-in time and possibility of self-check-in • Eliminates data-entry redundancy • Accelerated revenue processing • Labor savings in terms of sales, passenger handling, and accounting functions.	• Uncertainty over acceptance by the traveling public • The matter of implementing interline e-ticketing and of similarly supporting last minute schedule changes • Display of legal information, such as the Warsaw Convention on liability • Verifying customer identification • Threat of fraud—in terms of unauthorised issuance of e-tickets and fraudulent payment via credit card
Customers	• Greater flexibility in ticket purchasing • Convenience of travelling without physical documentation that can be lost, stolen, or destroyed • Ability to modify itinerary and make cancellations without adjusting a paper ticket • Added efficiency with check-in or possibility of self-check-in • Automated access to customer profile/frequent flier information	• Complications resulting from user or system error, such as double booking, neglecting to cancel a ticket • Increased risk of letting tickets go unused, especially by corporate travelers • At the early stages of e-ticket implementation, complications might arise due to system shortcomings—particularly in making last minute changes
Travel Agents	• Higher productivity resulting from the streamlined ticketing process • Simplified modification of itineraries • Savings on ticket delivery costs • Reduced importance of geographic position of the travel agency—allowing it to cater to a broader clientele and perhaps to experience rental savings	• Large loss of agency fees due to booking by direct channels is a threat to agencies • Initial training required to become familiar with ticketing procedures • Subject to added constraints on CRS as airlines push for e-ticketing standardization across the board • E-ticketing still unsuited for complex itineraries and interlining

CASE STUDY 3: SKANDIABANKEN: DEVELOPING INFORMATION CAPABILITIES FOR AN EFFECTIVE E-BUSINESS STRATEGY (ABRIDGED)

Professor Donald A. Marchand and Katarina Paddack

International Institute for Management Development, Lausanne, Switzerland

SkandiaBanken is better than other banks in every subcategory. Its Internet service is simpler to use and easier to understand, its interest rates are better, its fees are lower, and its offering of services is immense. For people who have the opportunity to use the Internet as a tool for handling their banking business, SkandiaBanken is unbeatable.

Jury, Best Bank of the Year, *Privata Affärer* (2000)

In December 2000, SkandiaBanken heard that it had been awarded Best Bank of the Year for the third year in a row by Sweden's personal finance magazine, *Privata Affärer*. SkandiaBanken was the only bank to have been awarded the honor more than once in the competition's 10-year history. Earlier in the year, *Internetworld* magazine had also chosen SkandiaBanken as Sweden's best Internet bank, and its Norwegian operations, which had begun in April, had been recognized as Norway's Best Bank of the Year by the Norwegian computer association.

Surprised and honored that SkandiaBanken—a "niche" bank—had beaten all major competitors in both customer service satisfaction and value, CEO Göran Lenkel and CIO Kent Nilsson pondered whether the next several years would prove equally rewarding. Defying competitors' predictions that a pure direct bank could not be profitable, SkandiaBanken had been successful from the start. However, large banking competitors and other new entrants with deep pockets had begun to catch up, with improvements to their own Internet services. In addition, the opening of the European market would allow companies with similar banking models to compete on interest rates and fees—areas in which SkandiaBanken had been the most competitive in the Swedish and Norwegian markets. Which of their company's business capabilities would ensure future e-business success?

SkandiaBanken Overview

SkandiaBanken, Sweden's first "branchless" bank, was created in October 1994, marking the first successful entry of a "non-bank" into the Swedish banking market. Relying solely on Internet and telephone channels, SkandiaBanken had grown to become Sweden's fifth largest bank in personal banking by 2000 and its fourth largest bank in terms of Internet customers.[1] By the end of 2000, eight months after beginning its Norway operations, SkandiaBanken had also captured 6 percent of the Norwegian Internet banking market, surpassing expectations.

A business unit of the Skandia Group, Sweden's largest and best known insurance company, SkandiaBanken offered products and services targeted primarily at the personal banking market (*see* Figure 1). These services supplemented Skandia's existing long-term savings, asset management, and P&C insurance products. SkandiaBanken would eventually serve as an alternative distribution channel for all Skandia insurance products.

SkandiaBanken's 380 employees served over 400,000 customers from its two offices in Stockholm, Sweden, and Bergen, Norway. From 1995 to 2000, SkandiaBanken averaged yearly increases of 26 percent in new customers and anticipated a customer base of 500,000 in 2001.[2] During the same period, deposits had risen from SKr 4.3 to SKr 15.2 billion[3] (five-year annual average growth rate of 30 percent), while lending had risen from SKr 3.7 to SKr 15.3 billion (five-year annual average growth rate of 37 percent). Since 1995, in spite of competitors' predictions, SkandiaBanken had boasted six profitable years, with operating income at SKr 63 million for 2000 (*refer to* Exhibit 1), becoming one of the few profitable niche banks in Europe. By 2000, SkandiaBanken averaged 1.8 million visits per month to its Web site (www.skandiabanken.se).

SkandiaBanken's E-Business Strategy

SkandiaBanken's e-business model was based on three principles to guide value creation for the customer and the company: truthfulness, simplicity, and high interest rates.

Truthfulness

Truthfulness guided all interactions with customers and with employees. To build its reputation as the "truthful bank," SkandiaBanken set up a transparent and straightforward service fee schedule. Account interest was capitalized every month—in contrast to traditional banking accounts that calculated annual interest based on average and minimum totals.

Figure 1 SkandiaBanken Products

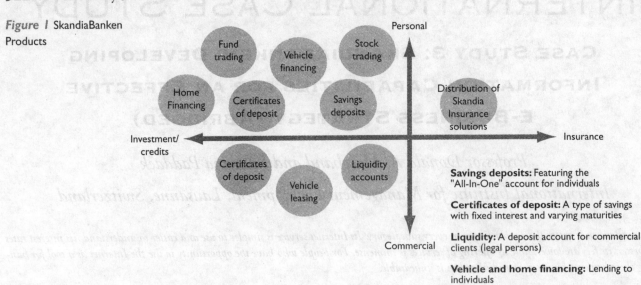

Savings deposits: Featuring the "All-In-One" account for individuals

Certificates of deposit: A type of savings with fixed interest and varying maturities

Liquidity: A deposit account for commercial clients (legal persons)

Vehicle and home financing: Lending to individuals

Stock trading: On-line stock trading service via custody account

Fund trading: Distribution and trading in funds via custody account

Vehicle Leasing: Financing of vehicle fleets

Distribution of Skandia Insurance solutions: Sales of Skandia's insurance products

In 1999, following increasingly high ATM costs, Lenkel sent customers a letter that drew media criticism. He asked customers to help SkandiaBanken keep its costs down by increasing the average ATM withdrawal amount and decreasing the frequency of withdrawals. Despite the negative press, SkandiaBanken was able to avoid charging ATM fees by telling its customers the truth and soliciting their involvement.

Simplicity

Simplicity ruled all aspects of the e-business model: customer relationships, products and services, business processes, development of IT solutions, and organizational structure.

Striving for simplicity, SkandiaBanken offered an "All-in-One" (Allt I Ett) account: savings deposits could easily be moved between funds, stock trading, and certificates of deposits. Bills could automatically be paid from the account, and salary deposited directly into the account. For the first time in Sweden's banking system, money could be easily transferred between SkandiaBanken accounts and accounts in other banks. Customers could also benefit from auto, home mortgage, or Skandia insurance products and pay for them directly from their account. By 2000, all account fees had been dropped, making SkandiaBanken the most competitive personal banking service in the market.[4]

High Interest Rates

SkandiaBanken offered the most competitive interest rates in the market, initially averaging 2 to 3 percent more than competitors' rates. To support higher-than-market interest rates, SkandiaBanken needed to cover account deposit rates in two ways. First, customers were encouraged to channel savings deposits into revenue-creating areas such as multi-investment funds and equities.

Second, SkandiaBanken focused on increasing the bank's high-interest, long-term lending avenues such as home mortgages and high-margin car financing businesses.[5] To manage deposits and lending levels, SkandiaBanken had to carefully manage three business areas that did not always share the same customer base. For example, personal banking services (including fund management and stock trading) and home mortgages were marketed both to Skandia customers and the general public, whereas auto financing worked through 500 auto dealers and included Skandia insurance products in its financing packages.

Behind the Scenes: Developing Capabilities for E-Business Success

To manage this direct model, first as a telephone bank and then as an Internet bank with telephone support, SkandiaBanken's senior managers had developed a management philosophy to guide the development of the business capabilities needed to be successful.

Nilsson described:

> We wanted to create the bank of the future—an organization that could easily change with new market trends and that would be totally responsive to customer needs. We tried to create a view of outside, looking in—from the customer's perspective.

The first part of this philosophy involved developing a company culture that supported personal responsibility and action. Lenkel explained:

> Our people are the bank. The way that we compete with information is not just through IT—we focus heavily on our

Figure 2 The Customer Viewpoint

people and their behaviors. We want our employees to have an intimate experience with our customers and establish relationships with them.

Nilsson added:

This means that our employees do not just learn *about* customers, but need to listen and learn *from* customers.

The second part of this philosophy involved getting both business and IT people to adopt a "customer viewpoint" of the organization. Nilsson explained:

I use what people at SkandiaBanken now call the "Mickey Mouse" diagram, which to me represents the customer viewpoint, to get people to think more holistically about our business [*see* Figure 2]. A customer does not just "see" the products and services being offered to him, but also evaluates us on the processes, or routines, we set up to deliver these products. The customer might not evaluate us directly on the IT that we have, but it is a necessary part of the entire model because it allows us to create the customer experience.

In the past, these three areas were separate, with people thinking only about their own area. For example, IT people would only worry about IT systems and databases, without understanding either the business processes or customer needs. Product development people would only think about what new products to develop, with no thought to delivery processes or knowledge of IT. One of the biggest problems we had was getting our well-educated, super-technical people to understand the other two circles.

I believe this is the e-business problem. People only talk about IT, without thinking of the concept more holistically in all three circles. People are looking for a technical solution. But it is not a technical solution, it is a philosophical solution, a way of business thinking. IT is not "alive"—it is not thinking, setting the rules, responding to customer needs. People are the ones who create value in the company and think of new ways to use the technology to better the customer experience.

"Our Bank Is Our People": Developing Information Behaviors and Values

Towards a Bias for Action: Information Proactiveness
Lenkel noted:

Motivating our employees to take responsibility and act on the information provided to them and gathered from our customers

is a key factor in managing this type of operation. Every time a customer calls or writes an e-mail, he or she is in direct contact with one of our employees. We have a very small call center and back office support so it is imperative that each employee knows how to get a solution for the customer.

Catrina Ingelstam, manager of Stock Brokering Services, commented:

Göran makes it clear that he wants us to act rather than stand on the sidelines. We are expected to take the initiative and are expected to inform ourselves about things that we need to know.

To emphasize the importance of individual initiative and responsibility, Lenkel refused to publish or talk about an organizational chart or formal reporting hierarchy. Nilsson explained:

When you talk about organization, people tend to get complacent and think that things can't be done in a different way. We wanted to maintain an atmosphere of creativity and action.

To stress the importance of prompt action, Lenkel discouraged formal management meetings to ensure that problems were dealt with immediately. He also instituted an open door policy, rather than an appointment-setting culture. Anyone needing to speak with him was encouraged to stop by his office at any time, and he encouraged this behavior with all members of the organization.

Developing Mature Information Behaviors to Support a Proactive Culture
Despite the informal working environment, the way information was distributed in the company was extremely formal to make sure that the information people needed to make decisions and solve customer problems was accessible, easy to understand, and complete. Lenkel noted:

We are a direct bank with very few employees. We need to make sure that people understand that it is critical that all information be made available for everyone to use.

To discourage information hoarding, Lenkel insisted that people get rid of paper sitting on their desks and enter it into the system. One employee commented:

I can find almost any type of information I need on our information system. The information is updated weekly and each unit takes responsibility for updating the information pertaining to its area. There are no written instructions about this; people just do it.

Several years later, Lenkel pushed this concept further by removing all bookcases from management offices.

Transparency was also encouraged by sharing performance information and goals throughout the organization. In addition to articulating a clear, simple business model, precise organizational, team, and personal goals were set and shared throughout the company. Organizational targets were publicized: for increases in fund distribution and worth, number of new customers, movement of customers, to the Internet, stock broking customers, fund customers and revenues. Within each business unit, additional goals were set relating to income targets, customer satisfaction, and quality. "We have no set budgets, but rely on constantly updated working plans," described one employee. Lenkel expanded on this:

> We are very transparent with setting goals for the group. Everyone knows who is doing what. Everyone knows his or her targets and calculations for revenues and costs. Employees understand this connection.

In the call center, a computer-based monitoring system tracked—in real time—service levels, average call times, down times, and customer response rates for both individuals and teams. Customer Service director Anna-Karin Laurell described:

> Anyone can check how he or she is doing at any time. We try and use the system as a tool for setting and attaining goals, rather than as a watch-dog system.

In addition, innovation and action were reinforced by a management team that expected mistakes to happen. Nilsson explained:

> We have a saying in our IT group: "Success depends on making a carefully planned series of small mistakes in order to avoid making unplanned large ones." We have one person who is in charge of keeping track of the mistakes and passing on good problem solving solutions to the rest of the group. We can't be afraid to change the path if we see that we are going the wrong way. We want to encourage people not to be afraid of making mistakes and to try to do things in different ways.

In the words of one employee:

> I think we are different from many other companies because Göran really trusts us and lets us make mistakes.

In the call center, customer representatives were hired based on their energy and their ability to listen and make quick decisions. Employees were not given telephone scripts, but were encouraged to develop their own style to deal with customers. During the first four years of operation, customer representatives were divided into teams, each with a team leader. By 2000, Lenkel had pushed the model further by eliminating all team "managers," moving to a totally self-monitoring call center system. At this time, too, service levels were among the highest in the online banking industry, with an average call pick-up of nine seconds and e-mail response rates of five minutes.[6]

"Knowing the Customer": Developing Information Management Practices

Sensing Customer Needs

Lenkel insisted on having no secretaries in the organization to ensure that information did not get filtered through a middle person:

> Our ultimate goal is to succeed in listening to our customers, and to change based on what they tell us that they want. Customer needs change constantly. If we do not know what they are thinking, what they expect from us, we will fail as a company.

Knowing the customer also meant developing simple processes to collect customer complaints and sense customer needs:

> We receive 5,000 e-mails a month with customer suggestions. And we take these suggestions very seriously. We like to think of our customers as employees that are developing the future of our bank. Unless we know them, we cannot respond to their needs.

Regular customer surveys also helped to monitor changes in customer needs and expectations. SkandiaBanken managers stressed customer sensitivity through a policy on new products or IT services: No new product or service would be introduced to customers unless they first requested it, even if the system had already been developed. Nilsson observed:

> What does this policy do? It forces our employees to constantly listen to the customer, rather than telling the customer what we think he wants or needs.

Collecting, Organizing, and Maintaining Customer Information

Responding to customers also required information to be organized in a simple, straightforward format—information not only had to be easy to access but also carefully and deliberately chosen so as not to overload the customer. Nilsson commented:

> Keeping it simple—especially in terms of providing information—is not an easy task. This is especially crucial for our business model that intends to provide customers with the information they need for self-service.

Lenkel explained:

> The key to our business is not to provide all the information, but the relevant information. You can get too much information. Part of our challenge is to decide which information to provide to the customer that makes sense to him or her. For example, based on our knowledge and expertise, we have chosen the best 80 to 90 mutual funds—out of the 1,400 available in Sweden—to offer our customers. Similarly, we filter information about equities and all other information on our Web site.

One litmus test of the information provided to customers occurred in the call center:

> If our customer representatives cannot easily explain our services and find the information they need, there is no way the customers are going to be able to do so on their own. We spend an enormous amount of time thinking about how to provide the information customers ask for in a logical, convenient, and straightforward way. This not only involves filtering information but also thinking through the entire information process and getting it down to as simple a form as possible.

To maintain the customer viewpoint of the information process and test its convenience, relevance, and quality, customer representatives in the call center worked from the same Web interface seen and used by the customer. Nilsson noted:

> I get at least one call a day from IT vendors telling me they have the CRM (customer relationship management) solution. They believe the machine, the technology, constitutes a customer relationship system. I think it is instead about the process and the people. The computer or IT system doesn't do

anything. It is the people and the information processes set up to provide the information that drive the real customer relationship.

Developing Mature Information Management Practices

When designing a new product, adding information to the Web site or developing a new information system, SkandiaBanken managers always approached the issue in the same way: first and foremost from the customer's point of view. Nilsson explained:

> Whenever the business comes up with a new product or service suggestion, we have a detailed discussion about the Mickey Mouse diagram. We get together a cross-functional group of people who will be involved—business managers, IT developers and product managers. Then we always start the conversation about the customer: What information does the customer need to have or what is the decision the customer needs to make?

Once this is clarified we move on to the specific process questions. Why do we want to add this information service? Is it based on just a "feeling" or are there facts and a business case? What are the business decision needs?

> Then we start to outline the process. Where does the information come from? What are we going to do with the information? Who needs to have access to this information—within the business unit and across the entire company? Who is going to maintain the information? What information do other departments add to the process? What format will provide the most convenient access and use?

> Next, we constantly think about the information process and how to simplify it. We want to keep the information process simple, eliminating as many sub-processes and instructions as possible to satisfy the largest number of customers.

> The last step is determining the appropriate technology application for the specific process. By the time the IT people get their hands on the project, we have already clarified customer needs, business unit needs, and clearly defined a simple information process. The one thing I have learned is that if the process is not good, forget about doing IT.

Using Information Capabilities to Save on Resources and Enhance the Customer Experience

In 1998, SkandiaBanken supported four separate call centers: for savings accounts, car leasing accounts, mortgage accounts, and equities advice. By 2000, the business units had succeeded in transferring specific knowledge and information into one call center, despite the differences in business needs and expertise.[7] Online applications and automatic approval tools for home mortgage and auto financing requests also helped to improve decisions and reduce risk in these lending areas, allowing less technical customer representatives to handle other customer issues.

A well-managed customer database also allowed SkandiaBanken to know its customers from a transaction and data point of view. Lenkel observed:

> We know from being able to link with the national database that holds salary information that we have attracted the top 10 to 15 percent of preferred banking customers in the country. From this information and from customer profiles, we are able

to offer "preferred" customers some service advantages that make their customer experience the best it could be. For example, a telephone call from a preferred customer will bump his or her call ahead of the waiting queue to a customer representative without his or her knowing the reason. Information about Web site use is also tracked and analyzed to determine the optimal way to present and organize information. Some of the most important information we get from this analysis is not what information the customer is using, but what the customer is *not* using.

Developing IT Practices

Three principles guided development of SkandiaBanken's IT systems: low cost, practicality and simplicity, and the outsourcing of non-value-adding systems.

▌ Low cost: "What does the customer want to pay for?"

One of the first principles that guided IT investment at SkandiaBanken was what the customer was willing to pay for. Nilsson explained:

> At what point will the customer be willing to pay more for the service provided by a new system? It is sometimes hard to keep enthusiastic IT developers and managers focused on this issue—they are constantly coming up with great new ideas. However, we have to always keep coming back to the question: What is the gain for the customer and at what cost?

▌ Practicality and simplicity: "Do what works"

SkandiaBanken's management team also insisted on simplicity and practicality in developing IT systems. Nilsson described:

> I am not an engineer or computer technician. My role in this was to help come up with the ideas behind the actual IT tools. A company needs to have insight into what you want to provide to the customer, independent from the technical details.

First, projects were kept small, simple, and practical. Second, "group think" excluding technical people was often used to encourage creativity, especially during the first several years of operation. Nilsson explained:

> It is *difficult* to create easy, small solutions—it is much easier to complicate things. It is the people who use the system that are the real developers. They may not know exactly how the technology works, but they know what they want to be able to do with it.

▌ Adding value: "Outsource the rest"

The last guiding principle for IT development was developing and managing value-added systems while outsourcing the rest. As a result, SkandiaBanken had only a small IT group—25 IT employees in 2000.

Building a Solid IT Operational and Process Foundation

One of the first challenges SkandiaBanken faced was to create an IT infrastructure that would be able to "talk" with any system and provide a total integrated solution. Nilsson noted:

Figure 3 Customer and Business Integration

> We were not concerned about owning all the databases we would
> need to run a low-cost operation, but instead about how to create
> an integrated interface with the customer and the business.

The outcome was the development of an IT application "switch-board" that allowed SkandiaBanken not only to link all of its databases and systems into one integrated structure but also to add new databases or remove old ones quickly and easily.

Integration of business operations at SkandiaBanken provided a unified customer interface, regardless of channel, that could be supported by a single pin number and provide information in a consistent manner (*see* Figure 3).

Pär Lundkvist, IT manager, described:

> When we were deciding how to create the bank from a
> technical standpoint, we knew we wanted it to be independent
> of the device or channel the customer was using. Today, we can
> easily integrate and operationalize a new customer channel—
> such as WAP or digital TV—within a day or two. As soon as
> the customer asks for it, we can have it up and running. The
> same applies to business systems. The new car finance system in
> Norway took us only four weeks to get up and running.

By 2000, in addition to its reputation for responsiveness, SkandiaBanken had built a reputation for system quality. That year, Microsoft wrote a case study on the reliability of SkandiaBanken's Internet site that it used in its European operations. Lundkvist noted:

> Customers need to be sure that our systems are up and running
> 24/7. We are working very hard on the quality of our systems
> and on maintaining quality service.

Business integration on the operational level also had several outcomes. In a joint venture with Ericsson and IBM, SkandiaBanken became the first bank in Europe to develop an application link for telephone-activated pop-up screens in the call center, greatly improving customer service. A call center

monitoring system helped to reduce down time, increase efficiency, and raise service levels to among the highest in the banking industry. Separating back office and administrative functions from call center activities freed customer representatives to provide better customer service. In 2000, excellence in operational systems allowed SkandiaBanken to integrate its four call centers into one, despite different customers among business units.

Developing the IT application switchboard allowed SkandiaBanken to interface directly with the existing banking industry infrastructure, eliminating the need for banking middle-men and reducing cost though streamlined information processes (*see* Figure 4).

SkandiaBanken's ability to link directly into these databases gave customers a number of service options, provided free of charge by the bank: electronic or manual bill payments either through SkandiaBanken or the national bill payment system (Post Giro); Visa card payments; foreign bill payments; and electronic transfers between accounts within SkandiaBanken or with another bank.

Developing IT Maturity: Support for Innovation and Management Decision Making

In 2001, two innovations would also have both business and customer benefits: online credit application and approval within 15 seconds for home mortgages and 4 seconds for car loans.

In the car financing business unit, IT innovation created an auto dealer portal, to be launched in late 2001. To move dealers to the Internet, SkandiaBanken began an education program—teaching them how to use the Internet and access SkandiaBanken's Web site—and often also installed software for them.

The portal, personalized for each of its 500 dealers, provided information that would help dealers perform their jobs better. Portal services and tools included: online credit application, online insurance application (Skandia), dealer news, interest rate information, online car registration, tax calculator and e-learning (financing training site for new dealer employees). The portal also provided access to three types of customized dealer information:

▌ **Sales statistics:** personalized sales statistics for each car dealer (e.g., six months sales report).

▌ **Customer reports:** personalized customer reports for follow-up business. Roger Alm, manager of Car Financing, explained:

> We provide our dealers with sales tips. For example, if we know
> that someone has only six months left on a car loan that was
> purchased three years earlier, we can provide the dealer with
> information on the customer and the car. The dealer then calls
> the customer, tells him that he has a huge demand for that type
> of used car and asks if the customer would like to come in and
> see any of his new models? We are trying to provide tools that
> make the dealer's life a little easier.

▌ **Auto auction:** gave dealers the opportunity to bid for SkandiaBanken cars for sale as a result of defaulted loans. Eventually, the site would allow dealers to buy and sell vehicles from each other.

Business analytics systems such as click-through tracking allowed SkandiaBanken to track customer use of information on the

Figure 4 SkandiaBanken Banking Infrastructure and System Linkages

Web, enabling it to test new information and decide which information to remove from the Web site and which was most useful to customers. In 2001, SkandiaBanken would give customers the ability to personalize their interface. It employed some customer datamining techniques and planned to tap this information source in the future.

Finally, excellence in IT would allow savings and lending levels across all business units to be easily monitored to maintain the needed balance in savings and lending products to remain profitable and reduce risk. Lenkel warned:

> We have to be careful not to grow too quickly in savings accounts without comparable growth levels in the higher interest lending products to offset the higher than market interest rates on savings accounts. Our business is all about balance and managed growth.

Regional Expansion: Creating a Nordic Bank

In April 2000, SkandiaBanken began its first cross-border expansion into neighboring Norway. Mimicking its development in Sweden, SkandiaBanken took over the house and car financing operations of the Norwegian insurer Vesta, which had been purchased by the Skandia Group. The new business unit in Bergen, Norway, was a copy of SkandiaBanken's Swedish operations, supporting a call center and business staff. By year-end 2000 SkandiaBanken Norge had attracted 65,000 customers, surpassing expectations, and jumped to be the leading online bank in Norway with a 6 percent market share. SkandiaBanken hoped to attain 135,000 customers by year-end 2001.

SkandiaBanken also planned to expand services into Denmark in 2001 with the acquisition of Din Bank, a pure-play Internet and telephone bank with products and services similar to those of SkandiaBanken. Din Bank, the leading niche bank in Denmark, had approximately 30,000 customers, deposits of DKr 1.7 billion[8], lending of DKr 0.6 billion and shareholders' equity of DKr 171 million.

SkandiaBanken's Competitive Advantage

Despite SkandiaBanken's current success and Nordic expansion plans, Lenkel and Nilsson were aware that it would face even greater competition in the future as traditional European banks grew better at offering Internet service and as other niche banks entered the Nordic market.

Nilsson commented:

> Even though our business model is based on e-business, our competitive advantage does not lie in the technology. Technology is extremely easy to copy. It is our philosophy, the way that we think, how we listen to customers to find out their needs and our willingness to respond quickly to the information provided by the customer that make us different from our competitors.

Lenkel added:

> Our competitive advantage? We may not have as many customers as the big four competitors in Sweden but we definitely know our customers better than they know theirs. Our competitors have a lot of baggage and legacies in terms of culture, structure, IT, and the way they have traditionally worked. It is very difficult to change that type of organization.

Nilsson explained:

> We really do not think of ourselves as a "bank." The way that we need to define ourselves is based on the financial services

EXHIBIT 1   SkandiaBanken Balance Sheet

(SKr million)	2000	1999	1998	1997	1996	1995
Interest income	1,065	857	787	654	619	501
Interest expense	(617)	(504)	(485)	(395)	(370)	(283)
Commissions (net)	150	96	128	143	97	73
Net result of financial transactions	1	0	(1)	(6)	20	2
Other operating income	49	12	12	2	7	58
Operating income total	648	461	441	398	373	351
Administrative overheads	(547)	(357)	(319)	(255)	(241)	(226)
Other operating expenses	(33)	(24)	(34)	(29)	(42)	(41)
Depreciation and write-downs of tangible fixed assets	(18)	(13)	(9)	(9)	—	—
Total expenses	(598)[9]	(394)[10]	(362)[11]	(293)	(283)	(267)
Credit loss, net	13	(4)	(3)	(1)	(4)	1
Operating income	**63**	**63**	**75**	**104**	**86**	**85**

Source: Company information

customers want and what we can deliver. Who knows where our customers will lead us? We can't predict what will happen in the next five years. But we need to be ready and willing to respond as best we can to the changes the future will bring.

Lenkel laughed:

We are definitely a small fish in a big sea with many larger fish. But we know what our customers want, and we are determined to give it to them. That is our competitive advantage.

CASE STUDY QUESTIONS

1. Analyze SkandiaBanken using the competitive forces and value chain models.

2. What is SkandiaBanken's business model and business strategy? How do information systems support this strategy?

3. Describe the relationship between SkandiaBanken's systems and its management, organizational structure, and culture.

4. Is SkandiaBanken's competitive advantage sustainable? Explain your answer.

Source: Research Associate Katarina Paddack prepared this case under the supervision of Professor Donald A. Marchand as a basis for class discussion rather than to illustrate either effective or ineffective handling of a business situation. Copyright © 2001 by **IMD** - International Institute for Management Development, Lausanne, Switzerland. Not to be used or reproduced without written permission directly from **IMD**.

---

[1] The top three banks in numbers of Internet customers included Nordea (formerly MeritaNordbanken), ForeningsSparbanken, and Skandinaviska Enskida Banken.

[2] 40 percent of SkandiaBanken's customer base were Skandia customers; the remaining 60 percent of customers came from the general public.

[3] I Swedish krona, SKr 1 = US$0.10 = ε0.11 (December 2000)

[4] In 2000, yearly fees were charged for Visa credit cards, international bank cards, and the use of Skandia Giro, a manual bill payment service.

[5] Home mortgages made up 64 percent of all lending, followed by car lending at 26 percent.

[6] Call center customer representatives were trained to respond to both telephone and Internet information requests and problems. In 2000, SkandiaBanken serviced one million calls and 60,000 e-mail requests.

[7] The call center acted as a cost center, charging each BU for services associated with its business.

[8] 1 Danish krone, DKr 1 = US$0.12 = ε0.13 (December 2001)

[9] Included investment in Norwegian operations.

[10] Included investment in Norwegian operations.

[11] Footnote to place here: Included fully expensed development costs of SKr 26 million for Internet equities trading service and a customer investment marketplace.

INTERNATIONAL CASE STUDY

CASE STUDY 4: GROWING AN APPLICATION FROM COLLABORATION TO MANAGEMENT SUPPORT— THE EXAMPLE OF CUPARLA

Gerhard Schwabe, University of Zurich

(Switzerland)

Analysis and Design

Just like in other towns, members of the Stuttgart City Council have a large workload: In addition to their primary profession (e.g., as an engineer at Daimler Benz) they devote more than 40 hours a week to local politics. This extra work has to be done under fairly unfavorable conditions. Only council sessions and party meetings take place in the city hall; the deputies of the local council do not have an office in the city hall to prepare or coordinate their work. This means, for example, that they have to read and file all official documents at home. In a city with more than 500,000 inhabitants they receive a very large number of documents. Furthermore, council members feel that they could be better informed by the administration and better use could be made of their time. Therefore Hohenheim University and partners* launched the Cuparla project to improve the information access and collaboration of council members.

A detailed analysis of their work revealed the following characteristics of council work:

- Since council members are very mobile, support has to be available to them any time and in any place.

- Council members collaborate and behave differently in different contexts: While they act informally and rather openly in the context of their own party, they behave more controlled and formal in official council sessions.

- A closer investigation of council work reveals a low degree of process structure. Every council member has the right of initiative and can inform and involve other members and members of the administration in any order.

- Council members rarely are power computer users. Computer support for them has to be very straightforward and intuitive to use.

When designing computer support we initially had to decide on the basic orientation of our software. We soon abandoned a workflow model as there are merely a few steps and there is little order in the collaboration of local politicians. Imposing a new structure into this situation would have been too restrictive for the council members. We then turned to pure document-orientation, imposing no structure at all on the council members' work. We created a single large database with all the documents any member of the city council ever needs. However, working with this database turned out to be too complex for the council members. In addition, they need to control the access to certain documents at all stages of the decision-making process. For example, a party may not want to reveal a proposal to other parties before it has officially been brought up in the city council. Controlling access to each document individually and changing the access control list was not feasible.

Therefore, the working context was chosen as a basis of our design. Each working context of a council member can be symbolized by a "room." A private office corresponds to the council member working at home; there is a party room, where he collaborates with his party colleagues, and a committee room symbolizes the place for committee meetings. In addition, there is a room for working groups, a private post office, and a library for filed information. All rooms hence have an electronic equivalent in the Cuparla software. When a council member opens the Cuparla software, he sees all the rooms from the entrance hall (Figure 1).

The council member creates a document in one room (e.g., his private office) and then shares it with other council members in other rooms. If he moves a document into the room of his party, he shares it with his party colleagues; if he hands it on to the administration, he shares it with the mayors, administration officials, and all council members.

The interface of the electronic rooms resembles the setup of the original rooms. Figure 2 shows the example of the room for a parliamentary party. On the left hand side of the screen there are document locations, whereas, on the right hand side, the documents of the selected location are presented. Documents that are currently being worked on are displayed on the "desk." These documents have the connotation that they need to be worked on without an additional outside trigger. If a document is in the files, it belongs to a topic that is still on the political agenda. However, a trigger is necessary to move it off of the shelf. If a topic is not on the political agenda any more, all documents belonging to it are moved to the archive.

The other locations support the collaboration within the party. The conference desk contains all documents for the next (weekly) party meeting. Any council member of the party can put documents there. When a council member prepares for the meeting, he or she merely has to check the conference desk for relevant information. The mailbox for the chairman contains all documents that the chairman needs to decide on. In contrast to his e-mail account all members have access to the mailbox.

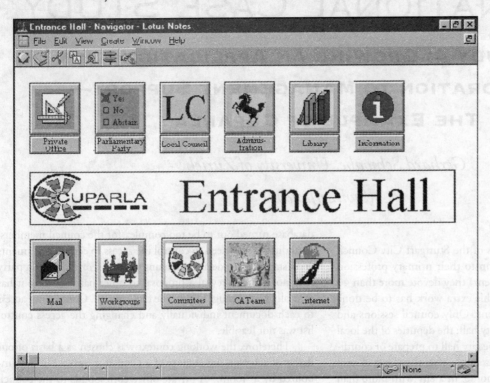

Figure 1   Entrance Hall

Double work is avoided as every council member is aware of the chairman's agenda. The mailbox of the assistant contains tasks for the party assistants; the mailbox for the secretary, assignments for the secretary (e.g., a draft for a letter). The inbox contains documents that have been moved from other rooms into this room.

Thus, in the electronic room all locations correspond to the current manual situation. Council members do not have to relearn their work. Instead, they collaborate in the shared environment they are accustomed to with shared expectations about the other peoples' behavior. Feedback from the pilot users indicates that this approach is appropriate.

Some specific design features make the software easy to use. The software on purpose does not have a fancy three-dimensional interface that has the same look as a real room. Buttons (in the entrance hall) and lists (in the rooms) are much easier to use and do not distract the user from the essential parts. Each location

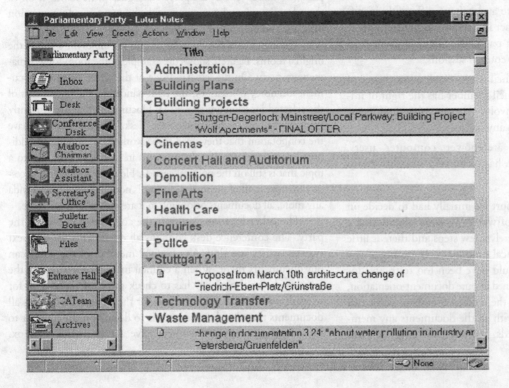

Figure 2   Parliamentary party room

(e.g., the desk) has a little arrow. If a user clicks on this arrow, a document is moved to the location. This operation is much easier for a beginner than proceeding by "drag and drop."

Furthermore, software design is not restricted to building an electronic equivalent of a manual situation. If one wants to truly benefit from the opportunities of electronic collaboration support systems, one has to include new tools that are not possible in the manual setting. For example, additional cross-location and room search features are needed to make it easy for the council member to retrieve information. The challenge of interface design is to give the user a starting point that is close to the situation he is used to. A next step is to provide the user with options to improve and adjust his working behavior to the opportunities offered by the use of a computer.

Organizational Implementation

Building the appropriate software is only one success factor for a groupware project. Organizational implementation typically is at least as difficult. Groupware often has a free rider problem: All want to gain the benefit and nobody wants to do the work. Furthermore, many features are only beneficial if all participate actively. For example, if a significant part of a council faction insists on using paper documents for their work, providing and sharing electronic documents actually means additional work for the others. This can easily lead to the situation that groupware usage never really gets started. To "bootstrap" usage we started with the (socially) simple activities and ended with the (socially) complex activities (Figure 3).

In the first step we provided the basic council information in digital form. The city council has the power to demand this initial organizational learning process from the administration. Once there is sufficient information the individual council member can already benefit from the system without relying on the usage of his fellow councillors. The usage conventions are therefore socially simple. As better information is a competitive advantage for a council member, there was an incentive for the individ-

ual effort required to learn the system. Communication support (e-mail, fax) is a more complex process, because its success depends on reliable usage patterns by all communication partners. The usage patterns are straightforward and easy to learn. We therefore implemented them in a second phase. Coordination activities (sharing to-do lists, sharing calendars) and cooperation activities (sharing documents and room locations, electronic meetings) depend on the observance of socially complex usage conventions by all group members. For example, the council member had to learn that her activities had effects on the documents and containers of all others and that "surprises" typically resulted from ill-coordinated activities of several group members. The council has to go through an intensive organizational learning process to benefit from the features. For example, the party's business processes had to be reorganized.

We offered collaboration and coordination support in the same phase to the council members. Their appropriation depended on the party's culture: A hierarchically organized party preferred to use the coordination features and requested to turn off many collaborative features. In another party most councilors had equal rights. This party preferred the collaborative features.

Economic Benefits

The ultimate success of any IS project is not only determined by the quality of the developed technology but also by its economic benefits. Thus, the economic benefit of Cuparla was evaluated in the first quarter of 1998 after about four months of use by the whole city council (pilot users had been using the system for more than a year). Evaluating the economic benefits of innovative software is notoriously difficult. Reasons for that include

1. It is difficult to attribute costs to a single project. For example, the city of Stuttgart had to wire part of their city hall for Cuparla—is this a cost of the project? And how about the servers bought for Cuparla and co-used for other purposes? And the cost for the information that was collected for the city council and is now being used in the administration's intranet?

2. Many benefits cannot be quantified in monetary terms. For instance, how much is it worth if the council members make better informed decisions? Or, how much is it worth if council membership becomes more attractive?

3. What is the appropriate level of aggregation for economic benefits? Should it be the cost and benefit for the individual council member? Or the parties? Or the whole city council? Or even the whole city of Stuttgart? Or should the improved processes be measured?

The evaluation of Cuparla was therefore not based on purely monetary terms; rather evaluation results were aggregated on five sets of criteria (cost, time, quality, flexibility, and human situation) and four levels of aggregation (individual, group, process, organization) resulting in a 4 × 5 matrix (Figure 4).

The trick is to attribute the effects only to the lowest possible level, e.g., if one can attribute the cost of an individual PC to an individual council member, it counts only there and not on the group level. On the other hand, a server probably can only be

Figure 3   Steps of groupware implementation

Figure 4 Aggregated evaluation of Cuparla (March 1998)

attributed to the group of all council members and so on. We will now briefly go through the major effects:

Costs: Both on the individual and the group level costs have gone up significantly (notebooks, ISDN, printer, server, etc.). There is a potential for cost savings if the council members forgo the delivery of paper copies of the documents. There have been some additional costs on the process level, but not as much as on the two levels below. There may have been direct cost savings by the provision of electronic documents in the council-related business processes, but we were not able to identify them. As the administration was reluctant to really reorganize its internal business processes, many potential cost savings could not be realized. As all costs could be attributed to the levels business process, group or individual, we noted a cost neutrality for the level "organization" (the costs for provisionally wiring the city hall were negligible).

Time: During the pilot phase, the system did not save time for the councilors; to the contrary, the individual councilors had to work longer in order to learn how to use the Cuparla system. However, the councilors also indicated that they used their time more productively, i.e., the overtime was well invested. Thus, we decided to summarize the effects on the individual level as "neutral." Cuparla had also not yet led to faster or more efficient decisions in the council or its subgroups. Therefore the effects are graded "unchanged." The council members see potential here, but the speed of decisions is not only a matter of work efficiency but also has a political dimension and politics does not change that fast. Some business processes were rated as being faster, particularly the processes at the interface between council and administration (e.g., the process of writing the meeting minutes). There was no effect on the organization as a whole; i.e., the city of Stuttgart was not faster at reacting to external challenges and opportunities.

Quality: The council members reported a remarkable improvement of quality of their work. The council members feel that the quality of their decisions has been improved by the much better access to information. The work of the parties has benefited from the e-mail and the collaboration features of Cuparla as well as the computer support of strategic party meetings. As the interface between different subprocesses of council work has fewer media changes and the (partially erroneous) duplication of information has been reduced, the council members and members of the administration also reported an improved quality of their business processes. The creation of an organization-wide database of council-related information even contributed to a somewhat better work in the whole administration.

Flexibility: Improved individual flexibility was the most important benefit of Cuparla. This holds true for spatial, temporal, and interpersonal flexibility. People can work and access other people any place and any time they want. On the group level Cuparla has enhanced the flexibility within parties as it has become easier to coordinate the actions of the council members. There have not been any significant changes to the flexibility on the process or organizational levels.

Human situation: Cuparla has made council membership more attractive because it has become easier to reconcile one's primary job, council work, and private life. Furthermore Cuparla is regarded as an opportunity for the council member's individual development. There were no significant changes to the human situation on the group, process, or organizational levels.

Towards a Management Support System

As mentioned above, these effects were measured after a relatively short period of usage. In 2002, the author returned to Stuttgart and investigated how Cuparla had been adopted five years after the initial implementation: Cuparla has become an indispensable part of council work. Almost all council members used Cuparla frequently. Interestingly, some original features of Cuparla were only adopted years after the original software implementation; most important, the rooms for subgroup collaboration.

Although the change slowed down after the initial organizational implementation phase, the system continued to grow due to user demand and organizational change:

1. The user population increased significantly: While in the beginning, only members of the city council and selected members from the city administration could use the system, soon other groups demanded access. Most importantly, the district councils benefited from improved information (the city of Stuttgart consists of 23 districts). Most local decisions are first prepared in the district council and on the basis of their recommendation the city council makes a final decision. Traditionally the district councils complained about lack of information both as a basis for their decisions and of the outcome of their initiatives. Many council documents are now even available on the Internet.

2. The volume of data increased significantly. By 2001, the databases were so large that older council documents were only available through online database access; only the newer documents were replicated to the notebooks of the council members (giving them the flexibility to really work any time and any place). Furthermore access to statistical data and to the city intranet increased the information basis.

3. The functionality was enhanced. Here, surprisingly simple solutions turned out to be surprisingly successful. As in most other German cities, the Stuttgart administration was sometimes lazy in working on council motions. Council members even suspected the administration would purposefully wait on difficult motions hoping that the council might forget. And indeed the council sometimes forgot, but as often council members remembered and became angry. This behavior led to distrust between council and administration and to frequent unfruitful discussions in council meetings. It was therefore decided to implement a shared "open motions" list. Any council motion was put in there and the progress of the administration's dealing with the subject was noted. Within days after implementation of this open motions list, the administration had worked through the backlog of unanswered motions. There were some subtle interface issues involved in this subsystem: the open motions list is typically too long to be inspected in detail every week. Therefore a little icon at each entry indicated if the administration had done anything at all. The council members could thus browse through the list and seek for the completely "forgotten" motions. The administration reacted quickly and soon all entries had the icon indicating work in progress. However some work just consisted of the following short notice: "This motion will be dealt with later".

Still, the open motions list was a huge success and marked the move of Cuparla from a pure Information and Cooperation Support System towards a Management Support System. In the meantime Andreas Majer, the local project manager of Cuparla, had been promoted to head the IT department. He decided to further develop the concepts of Cuparla into a Management Support System (MSS),

mainly for two reasons:

1. A MSS system could further increase the decision-making power of the local decision makers.

2. Building a MSS would give his IT department (with more than 50 IT-specialists) a shared focus and could lead the way towards the integration of applications as diverse as ERP systems, statistical information systems and geographical information systems.

Andreas Majer uses an example to describe his vision of an MSS: "Imagine a city councilor wants to analyze the success of a program providing social workers for difficult schools. Parts of the answers he will find in the official council documents dealing with the local schools. Statistical data on the schools and their neighborhoods will be provided by the statistical information system Communis and the funding for each school can be extracted from the ERP system. The existing plans for the development of the schools are explained in the yearly planning document and the geographical situation of each school can be referenced on the digital map in the Geographic Information System. Currently, each piece of information has to be retrieved from another information system. In a Management Support System one application should suffice to provide all relevant information and the information should be linked."

However, with the growth of the system, Cuparla reached its limits: Since its roots are a collaboration system, its interface and architecture are not sufficiently prepared for information and application integration. Therefore Stuttgart decided to start redesigning Cuparla in late 2002. The future interface will include some cockpit-functionality, allowing each council member to monitor significant performance indicators. Furthermore, a comprehensive search functionality will support integrated queries of several information sources. The major architectural challenge will be data integration: In order to display the relationships between data items, a data warehouse needs to be constructed. Finally, there will be several interfaces, because council members increasingly rely on PDAs and mobile phones for information access. As user needs and organizational challenges change, Cuparla will continue to grow and adapt.

ADDITIONAL READING

Schwabe, G. and Krcmar, H. "Piloting a Sociotechnical Innovation." Appears in the *Proceedings of the 8th European Conference on Information Systems ECIS 2000,* Wirtschaftsuniversität Vienna, Vienna 2000, p. 132–139.

Schwabe, G. and Krcmar, H. Digital Material in a Political Work Context—The Case of Cuparla. Appears in *Proceedings of the 8th European Conference on Information Systems ECIS 2000,* Wirtschaftsuniversität Vienna, Vienna 2000, p. 1152–1159

Schwabe, G. "Understanding and Supporting Knowledge Management and Organizational Memory in a City Council." In: Hawaii International Conference on System Sciences 1999 (HICSS99), CD-ROM, 12 pages.

Schwabe, G. and Krcmar, H. "Electronic Meeting Support for Councils." Appears in *AI and Society*, Vol. 14, 2000, p. 48–70.

CASE STUDY QUESTIONS

1. Show how organizational issues influence the software design and how the software design affects the organizational behavior.

2. Has Cuparla been effective? Describe the costs and the benefits from the point of view of a council member and from the point of view of a member of the administration.

3. Why has Cuparla been continuously changing? For what class of systems is this typical?

4. Design an interface and sketch out an architecture for a future Cuparla system. This system should both include collaboration and Management Support System functionality.

5. Where would you expect organizational barriers and facilitators for the implementation of such a future Cuparla System?

*The project partners were Hohenheim University (Coordinator), Datenzentrale Baden-Württemberg, and GroupVision Software-systeme GmbH. The project was funded as part of its R&D program by DeTeBerkom GmbH, a 100 percent subsidiary of German Telekom.

REFERENCES

CHAPTER 1

Ackoff, R. L. "Management Misinformation System." *Management Science* 14, no. 4 (December 1967): B140–B116.

Allen, Brandt R., and Andrew C. Boynton. "Information Architecture: In Search of Efficient Flexibility." *MIS Quarterly* 15, no. 4 (December 1991).

Bakos, J. Yannis. "The Emerging Role of Electronic Marketplaces on the Internet." *Communications of the ACM* 41, no. 8 (August 1998).

Barrett, Stephanie S. "Strategic Alternatives and Interorganizational System Implementations: An Overview." *Journal of Management Information Systems* (Winter 1986–1987).

Baskerville, Richard L., and Michael D. Myers. "Information Systems as a Reference Discipline." *MIS Quarterly* 26, no. 1 (March 2002).

Benjamin, Robert, and Rolf Wigand. "Electronic Markets and Virtual Value Chains on the Information Superhighway." *Sloan Management Review* (Winter 1995).

Brynjolfsson, E. T., T. W. Malone, V. Gurbaxani, and A. Kambil. "Does Information Technology Lead to Smaller Firms?" *Management Science* 40, no. 12 (1994).

Davis, Gordon B., and Margrethe H. Olson. *Management Information Systems: Conceptual Foundations, Structure, and Development,* 2nd ed. New York: McGraw-Hill (1985).

"Eastman is Keen on E-Commerce." *Information Week* (August 2, 2000).

Feeny, David E., and Leslie P. Willcocks. "Core IS Capabilities for Exploiting Information Technology." *Sloan Management Review* 39, no. 3 (Spring 1998).

Gallupe, R. Brent. "Images of Information Systems in the Early 21st Century." *Communications of the Association for Information Systems* 3, no. 3 (February 2000).

Hacki, Remo, and Julian Lighton, "The Future of the Networked Company," *McKinsey Quarterly* 3 (2001).

Hartman, Amir. "Why Tech Falls Short of Expectations." *Optimize Magazine* (July 2002).

Johnston, Russell, and Michael J. Vitale. "Creating Competitive Advantage with Interorganizational Information Systems." *MIS Quarterly* 12, no. 2 (June 1988).

Joy, Bill. "Design for the Digital Revolution." *Fortune* (March 6, 2000).

Keen, Peter G. W. *Shaping the Future: Business Design Through Information Technology.* Cambridge, MA: Harvard Business School Press (1991).

King, John. "Centralized vs. Decentralized Computing: Organizational Considerations and Management Options." *Computing Surveys* (October 1984).

Konicki, Steve. "Lockheed Martin Jet Fighter Win Ushers in New Era of Real Time Project Management." *Information Week* (November 12, 2001).

Leonard-Barton, Dorothy. *Wellsprings of Knowledge.* Boston, MA: Harvard Business School Press (1995).

Liker, Jeffrey K., David B. Roitman, and Ethel Roskies. "Changing Everything All at Once: Work Life and Technological Change." *Sloan Management Review* (Summer 1987).

Malone, Thomas W., JoAnne Yates, and Robert I. Benjamin. "Electronic Markets and Electronic Hierarchies." *Communications of the ACM* (June 1987).

———. "The Logic of Electronic Markets." *Harvard Business Review* (May–June 1989).

McFarlan, F. Warren, James L. McKenney, and Philip Pyburn. "The Information Archipelago—Plotting a Course." *Harvard Business Review* (January–February 1983).

———. "Governing the New World." *Harvard Business Review* (July–August 1983).

McKenney, James L., and F. Warren McFarlan. "The Information Archipelago—Maps and Bridges." *Harvard Business Review* (September–October 1982).

Orlikowski, Wanda J., and Stephen R. Bailey. "Technology and Institutions: What Can Research on Information Technology and Research on Organizations Learn from Each Other?" *MIS Quarterly* 25, no. 2 (June 2001)

Orlikowski, Wanda J., and Jack J. Baroudi. "Studying Information Technology in Organizations: Research Approaches and Assumptions." *Information Systems Research* 2, no. 1 (March 1991).

Quinn, James Brian. "Strategic Outsourcing: Leveraging Knowledge Capabilities." *Sloan Management Review* 40, no. 4 (Summer 1999).

Roche, Edward M. "Planning for Competitive Use of Information Technology in Multinational Corporations." AIB UK Region, Brighton Polytechnic, Brighton, UK, Conference Paper (March 1992). Edward M. Roche, W. Paul Stillman School of Business, Seton Hall University.

Rockart, John F., and James E. Short. "IT in the 1990s: Managing Organizational Interdependence." *Sloan Management Review* 30, no. 2 (Winter 1989).

Ross, Jeanne W., and Peter Weill. "Six IT Decisions Your IT People Shouldn't Make." *Harvard Business Review* (November 2002).

Sambamurthy, V., and Robert W. Zmud. "Research Commentary: The Organizing Logic for an Enterprise's IT Activities in the Digital Era-A Prognosis of Practice and a Call to Research." *Information Systems Research* 11, No. 2 (June 2000).

Scott Morton, Michael, ed. *The Corporation in the 1990s.* New York: Oxford University Press (1991).

Slywotzky, Adrian J., and David J. Morrison. *How Digital Is Your Business?* New York: Crown Business (2001).

Tornatsky, Louis G., J. D. Eveland, and David Wessel. "NASA Explores Future of Software." *The Process of Technological Innovation: Reviewing the Literature.* Washington, DC: National Science Foundation (1983).

Tuomi, Ilkka. "Data Is More Than Knowledge." *Journal of Management Information Systems* 16, no. 3 (Winter 1999–2000).

Weill, Peter, and Marianne Broadbent. *Leveraging the New Infrastructure.* Cambridge, MA: Harvard Business School Press (1998).

———. "Management by Maxim: How Business and IT Managers Can Create IT Infrastructures," *Sloan Management Review* (Spring 1997).

Zipkin, Paul. "The Limits of Mass Customization." *Sloan Management Review* (Spring 2001).

CHAPTER 2

Anthony, R. N. *Planning and Control Systems: A Framework for Analysis.* Cambridge, MA: Harvard University Press (1965).

Bensaou, M. "Portfolios of Buyer-Supplier Relationships," *Sloan Management Review* 40, no. 4 (Summer 1999).

Berry, Leonard L., and **A. Parasuraman.** "Listening to the Customer—the Concept of a Service-Quality Information System." *Sloan Management Review* (Spring 1997).

Concours Group. "ESII: Capitalizing on Interprise Systems and Infrastructure." (1999).

Culnan, Mary J. "Transaction Processing Applications as Organizational Message Systems: Implications for the Intelligent Organization." Working paper no. 88–10, Twenty-second Hawaii International Conference on Systems Sciences (January 1989).

Davenport, Tom. *Mission Critical: Realizing the Promise of Enterprise Systems.* Boston, MA: Harvard Business School Press (2000).

———. "Putting the Enterprise into Enterprise Systems." *Harvard Business Review* (July–August 1998).

Ebner, Manuel, Arthur Hu, Daniel Levitt, and **Jim McCrory.** "How to Rescue CRM." *McKinsey Quarterly* 4 (2002).

Goodhue, Dale L., Barbara H. Wixom, and **Hugh J. Watson.** "Realizing Business Benefits through CRM: Hitting the Right Target in the Right Way." *MIS Quarterly Executive* 1, no. 2 (June 2002).

Handfield, Robert B., and **Ernest L. Nichols, Jr.** *Introduction to Supply Chain Management.* Upper Saddle River, NJ: Prentice Hall (1999).

Hitt, Lorin, D.J. Wu, and **Xiaoge Zhou.** "Investment in Enterprise Resource Planning: Business Impact and Productivity Measures." *Journal of Management Information Systems* 19, no. 1 (Summer 2002).

Houdeshel, George, and **Hugh J. Watson.** "The Management Information and Decision Support (MIDS) System at Lockheed Georgia." *MIS Quarterly* 11, no. 1 (March 1987).

Huber, George P. "Organizational Information Systems: Determinants of Their Performance and Behavior." *Management Science* 28, no. 2 (1984).

Kalakota, Ravi, and **Marcia Robinson.** *E-Business2.0: Roadmap for Success.* Reading, MA: Addison-Wesley (2001).

Keen, Peter G. W. *The Process Edge.* Boston, MA: Harvard Business School Press (1997).

Keen, Peter G. W., and **M. S. Morton.** *Decision Support Systems: An Organizational Perspective.* Reading, MA: Addison-Wesley (1978).

Kumar, Kuldeep. "Technology for Supporting Supply Chain Management." *Communications of the ACM* 44, no. 6 (June 2001).

Kumar, Kuldeep, and **Jos Van Hillegersberg.** "ERP Experiences and Revolution" *Communications of the ACM* 43, no. 4 (April 2000).

Lee, Hau, L., V. Padmanabhan, and **Seugin Whang.** "The Bullwhip Effect in Supply Chains." *Sloan Management Review* (Spring 1997).

Malone, Thomas M., Kevin Crowston, Jintae Lee, and **Brian Pentland.** "Tools for Inventing Organizations: Toward a Handbook of Organizational Processes." *Management Science* 45, no. 3 (March 1999).

McDonnell, Sharon. "Putting CRM To Work." *Computerworld* (March 12, 2001).

O'Leary, Daniel E. *Enterprise Resource Planning Systems: Systems Life Cycle, Electronic Commerce, and Risk.* New York: Cambridge University Press (2000).

Palaniswamy, Rajagopal, and **Tyler Frank.** "Enhancing Manufacturing Performance with ERP Systems." *Information Systems Management* (Summer 2000).

Patton, Susannah. "The Truth About CRM." *CIO Magazine* (May 1, 2001).

Robey, Daniel, Jeanne W. Ross, and **Marie-Claude Boudreau.** "Learning to Implement Enterprise Systems: An Exploratory Study of the Dialectics of Change." *Journal of Management Information Systems* 19, no. 1 (Summer 2002).

Rockart, John F., and **Michael E. Treacy.** "The CEO Goes On-line." *Harvard Business Review* (January–February 1982).

Seybold, Patricia B. "Get Inside the Lives of Your Customers." *Harvard Business Review* (May 2001).

Soong-Yong, Choi, and **Andrew B. Whinston,** "Communities of Collaboration." *IQ Magazine.* (July/August 2001).

Sprague, Ralph H., Jr., and **Eric D. Carlson.** *Building Effective Decision Support Systems.* Englewood Cliffs, NJ: Prentice Hall (1982).

Thomke, Stefan, and **Eric von Hippel.** "Customers as Innovators." *Harvard Business Review* (April 2002).

Welty, Bill, and **Irma Becerra-Fernandez.** "Managing Trust and Commitment in Supply Chain Relationships." *Communications of the ACM* 44, no. 6 (June 2001).

Yu, Larry. "Successful Customer Relationship Management." *Sloan Management Review* 42, no. 4 (Summer 2001).

CHAPTER 3

Acona, Deborah, Henrik Breaman, and **Katrin Kaufer.** "The Comparative Advantage of X-Teams," *Sloan Management Review* 43, no. 3 (Spring 2002).

Allison, Graham T. *Essence of Decision-Explaining the Cuban Missile Crisis.* Boston: Little Brown (1971).

Alter, Steven, and **Michael Ginzberg.** "Managing Uncertainty in MIS Implementation." *Sloan Management Review* 20, no. 1 (Fall 1978).

Anthony, R. N. *Planning and Control Systems: A Framework for Analysis.* Cambridge, MA: Harvard University Press (1965).

Attewell, Paul, and **James Rule.** "Computing and Organizations: What We Know and What We Don't Know." *Communications of the ACM* 27, no. 12 (December 1984).

Beer, Michael, Russell A. Eisenstat, and **Bert Spector.** "Why Change Programs Don't Produce Change." *Harvard Business Review* (November–December 1990).

Bakos, J. Yannis, and **Michael E. Treacy.** "Information Technology and Corporate Strategy: A Research Perspective." *MIS Quarterly* (June 1986).

Bikson, T. K., and **J. D. Eveland.** "Integrating New Tools into Information Work." The Rand Corporation (1992). RAND/RP-106.

Blau, Peter, and **W. Richard Scott.** *Formal Organizations.* San Francisco: Chandler Press (1962).

Brancheau, James C., Brian D. Janz, and **James C. Wetherbe.** "Key Issues in Information Systems Management: 1994–1995 SIM Delphi Results." *MIS Quarterly* 20, no. 2 (June 1996).

Camuffo, Arnaldo, Pietro Romano, and **Andrea Vinellie.** "Benetton Transforms Its Global Network." *Sloan Management Review* 43, no. 1 (Fall 2001)

Cash, J. I., and **Benn R. Konsynski.** "IS Redraws Competitive Boundaries." *Harvard Business Review* (March–April 1985).

Chan, Yolande E. "Why Haven't We Mastered Alignment? The Importance of the IT Informal Organizational Structure." *MIS Quarterly Executive* 1, no. 2 (2002).

Chan, Yolande E., Sid L. Huff, Donald W. Barclay, and **Duncan G. Copeland.** "Business Strategic Orientation, Information Systems Strategic Orientation, and Strategic Alignment." *Information Systems Research* 8, no. 2 (June 1997).

Chen, Pei-Yu (Sharon), and **Lorin M. Hitt.** "Measuring Switching Costs and the Determinants of Customer Retention in Internet-Enabled Businesses: A Study of the Online Brokerage Industry." *Information Systems Research* 13, no.3 (September 2002).

Christensen, Clayton. "The Past and Future of Competitive Advantage." *Sloan Management Review* 42, no. 2 (Winter 2001).

Clemons, Eric K. "Evaluation of Strategic Investments in Information Technology." *Communications of the ACM* (January 1991).

Clemons, Eric K., and **Bruce W. Weber.** "Segmentation, Differentiation, and Flexible Pricing: Experience with Information Technology and Segment-Tailored Strategies." *Journal of Management Information Systems* 11, no. 2 (Fall 1994).

Clemons, Eric K., and **Michael Row.** "McKesson Drug Co.: Case Study of a Strategic Information System." *Journal of Management Information Systems* (Summer 1988).

———. "Sustaining IT Advantage: The Role of Structural Differences." *MIS Quarterly* 15, no. 3 (September 1991).

———. "Limits to Interfirm Coordination through IT." *Journal of Management Information Systems* 10, no. 1 (Summer 1993).

Coase, Ronald H. "The Nature of the Firm."(1937) in Putterman, Louis, and Randall Kroszner. *The Economic Nature of the Firm: A Reader,* Cambridge University Press, 1995.

Cohen, Michael, James March, and **Johan Olsen.** "A Garbage Can Model of Organizational Choice." *Administrative Science Quarterly* 17 (1972).

Copeland, Duncan G., and **James L. McKenney.** "Airline Reservations Systems: Lessons from History." *MIS Quarterly* 12, no. 3 (September 1988).

Davenport, Thomas H., and **Keri Pearlson.** "Two Cheers for the Virtual Office." *Sloan Management Review* 39, no. 4 (Summer 1998).

———, **Jeanne G. Harris,** and **Ajay K. Kohli,** "How Do They Know Their Customers So Well?" *Sloan Management Review* 42, no. 2 (Winter 2001).

Drucker, Peter. "The Coming of the New Organization." *Harvard Business Review* (January–February 1988).

Eardley, Alan, David Avison, and **Philip Powell.** "Developing Information Systems to Support Flexible Strategy." *Journal of Organizational Computing and Electronic Commerce* 7, no. 1 (1997).

Earl, Michael J., and **Jeffrey L. Sampler.** "Market Management to Transform the IT Organization." *Sloan Management Review* 39, no. 4 (Summer 1998).

Eisenhardt, Kathleen M. "Has Strategy Changed?" *Sloan Management Review* 43, no.2 (Winter 2002).

El Sawy, Omar A. "Implementation by Cultural Infusion: An Approach for Managing the Introduction of Information Technologies." *MIS Quarterly* (June 1985).

Etzioni, Amitai. *A Comparative Analysis of Complex Organizations.* New York: Free Press (1975).

Fayol, Henri. *Administration Industrielle et Generale.* Paris: Dunods (1950, first published in 1916).

Feeny, David E., and **Blake Ives.** "In Search of Sustainability: Reaping Long-Term Advantage from Investments in Information Technology." *Journal of Management Information Systems* (Summer 1990).

Feeny, David. "Making Business Sense of the E-Opportunity." *Sloan Management Review* 42, no. 2 (Winter 2001).

Fine, Charles H., Roger Vardan, Robert Pethick, and **Jamal E-Hout.** "Rapid-Response Capability in Value-Chain Design." *Sloan Management Review* 43, no.2 (Winter 2002).

Fisher, Marshall L., Ananth Raman, and **Anne Sheen McClelland.** "Rocket Science Retailing Is Almost Here: Are You Ready?" *Harvard Business Review* (July-August 2000).

Freeman, John, Glenn R. Carroll, and **Michael T. Hannan.** "The Liability of Newness: Age Dependence in Organizational Death Rates." *American Sociological Review* 48 (1983).

Fritz, Mary Beth Watson, Sridhar Narasimhan, and **Hyeun-Suk Rhee.** "Communication and Coordination in the Virtual Office." *Journal of Management Information Systems* 14, no. 4 (Spring 1998).

Fulk, Janet, and **Geraldine DeSanctis.** "Electronic Communication and Changing Organizational Forms." *Organization Science* 6, no. 4 (July–August 1995).

Garvin, David A. "The Processes of Organization and Management." *Sloan Management Review* 39, no. 4 (Summer 1998).

Holweg, Matthias, and **Frits K. Pil.** "Successful Build-to-Order Strategies Start with the Customer." *Sloan Management Review* 43, no. 1 (Fall 2001).

Hopper, Max. "Rattling SABRE-New Ways to Compete on Information." *Harvard Business Review* (May–June 1990).

Gilbert, Clark, and **Joseph L. Bower.** "Disruptive Change." *Harvard Business Review* (May 2002).

Gorry, G. Anthony, and **Michael S. Scott Morton.** "A Framework for Management Information Systems." *Sloan Management Review* 13, no. 1 (Fall 1971).

Gurbaxani, V., and **S. Whang.** "The Impact of Information Systems on Organizations and Markets." *Communications of the ACM* 34, no. 1 (Jan. 1991).

Hinds, Pamela, and **Sara Kiesler.** "Communication across Boundaries: Work, Structure, and Use of Communication Technologies in a Large Organization." *Organization Science* 6, no. 4 (July–August 1995).

Hitt, Lorin M. "Information Technology and Firm Boundaries: Evidence from Panel Data." *Information Systems Research* 10, no. 2 (June 1999).

Hitt, Lorin M., and **Erik Brynjolfsson.** "Information Technology and Internal Firm Organization: An Exploratory Analysis." *Journal of Management Information Systems* 14, no. 2 (Fall 1997).

Huber, George P. "Cognitive Style as a Basis for MIS and DSS Designs: Much Ado About Nothing?" *Management Science* 29 (May 1983).

Huber, George. "Organizational Learning: The Contributing Processes and Literature." *Organization Science* 2 (1991): 88–115.

———. "The Nature and Design of Post-Industrial Organizations." *Management Science* 30, no. 8 (August 1984).

Isenberg, Daniel J. "How Senior Managers Think." *Harvard Business Review* (November–December 1984).

Jensen, M. C., and **W. H. Meckling.** "Specific and General Knowledge and Organizational Science." In *Contract Economics,* edited by L. Wetin and J. Wijkander. Oxford: Basil Blackwell (1992).

Jensen, Michael C., and **William H. Meckling.** "Theory of the Firm: Managerial Behavior, Agency Costs, and Ownership Structure." *Journal of Financial Economics* 3 (1976).

Johnston, Russell, and **Michael R. Vitale.** "Creating Competitive Advantage with Interorganizational Information Systems." *MIS Quarterly* 12, no. 2 (June 1988).

Kanter, Rosabeth Moss. "The New Managerial Work." *Harvard Business Review* (November–December 1989).

Kambil, Ajit, and James E. Short. "Electronic Integration and Business Network Redesign: A Roles-Linkage Perspective." *Journal of Management Information Systems* 10, no. 4 (Spring 1994).

Kauffman, Robert J. and Yu-Ming Wang. "The Network Externalities Hypothesis and Competitive Network Growth." *Journal of Organizational Computing and Electronic Commerce* 12, no. 1 (2002).

Keen, Peter G.W. "Information Systems and Organizational Change." *Communications of the ACM* 24, no. 1 (January 1981).

Kettinger, William J., Varun Grover, Subashish Guhan, and Albert H. Segors. "Strategic Information Systems Revisited: A Study in Sustainability and Performance." *MIS Quarterly* 18, no. 1 (March 1994).

King, J. L., V. Gurbaxani, K. L. Kraemer, F. W. McFarlan, K. S. Raman, and C. S. Yap. "Institutional Factors in Information Technology Innovation." *Information Systems Research* 5, no. 2 (June 1994).

King, W. R. "Creating a Strategic Capabilities Architecture." *Information Systems Management* 12, no. 1 (Winter 1995).

Kling, Rob. "Social Analyses of Computing: Theoretical Perspectives in Recent Empirical Research." *Computing Survey* 12, no. 1 (March 1980).

Kling, Rob, and William H. Dutton. "The Computer Package: Dynamic Complexity." In *Computers and Politics,* edited by James Danziger, William Dutton, Rob Kling, and Kenneth Kraemer. New York: Columbia University Press (1982).

Kolb, D. A., and A. L. Frohman. "An Organization Development Approach to Consulting." *Sloan Management Review* 12, no. 1 (Fall 1970).

Konsynski, Benn R., and F. Warren McFarlan. "Information Partnerships—Shared Data, Shared Scale." *Harvard Business Review* (September–October 1990).

Kotter, John T. "What Effective General Managers Really Do." *Harvard Business Review* (November–December 1982).

Kraemer, Kenneth, John King, Debora Dunkle, and Joe Lane. *Managing Information Systems.* Los Angeles: Jossey-Bass (1989).

Kraut, Robert, Charles Steinfield, Alice P Chan, Brian Butler, and Anne Hoag. "Coordination and Virtualization: The Role of Electronic Networks and Personal Relationships." *Organization Science* 10, no. 6 (November–December 1999).

Laudon, Kenneth C. *Computers and Bureaucratic Reform.* New York: Wiley (1974).

———. *Dossier Society: Value Choices in the Design of National Information Systems.* New York: Columbia University Press (1986).

———. "Environmental and Institutional Models of Systems Development." *Communications of the ACM* 28, no. 7 (July 1985).

———. "A General Model of the Relationship Between Information Technology and Organizations." Center for Research on Information Systems, New York University. Working paper, National Science Foundation (1989).

———. "The Promise and Potential of Enterprise Systems and Industrial Networks." Working paper, The Concours Group. Copyright Kenneth C. Laudon (1999).

Lawrence, Paul, and Jay Lorsch. *Organization and Environment.* Cambridge, MA: Harvard University Press (1969).

Leavitt, Harold J. "Applying Organizational Change in Industry: Structural, Technological, and Humanistic Approaches." In *Handbook of Organizations,* edited by James G. March. Chicago: Rand McNally (1965).

Leavitt, Harold J., and Thomas L. Whisler. "Management in the 1980s." *Harvard Business Review* (November–December 1958).

Lee, Ho-Geun. "Do Electronic Marketplaces Lower the Price of Goods?" *Communications of the ACM* 41, no. 1 (January 1998).

Levecq, Hugues, and Bruce W. Weber. "Electronic Trading Systems: Strategic Implication of Market Design Choices." *Journal of Organizational Computing and Electronic Commerce* 12, no. 1 (2002).

Lindblom, C. E. "The Science of Muddling Through." *Public Administration Review* 19 (1959).

Machlup, Fritz. *The Production and Distribution of Knowledge in the United States.* Princeton, NJ: Princeton University Press (1962).

Main, Thomas J., and James E. Short. "Managing the Merger: Building Partnership Through IT Planning at the New Baxter." *MIS Quarterly* 13, no. 4 (December 1989).

Maier, Jerry L., R. Kelly Rainer, Jr., and Charles A. Snyder. "Environmental Scanning for Information Technology: An Empirical Investigation." *Journal of Management Information Systems* 14, no. 2 (Fall 1997).

Malone, Thomas W. "Is Empowerment Just a Fad? Control, Decision Making, and IT." *Sloan Management Review* (Winter 1997).

March, James G., and Herbert A. Simon. *Organizations.* New York: Wiley (1958).

March, James G., and G. Sevon. "Gossip, Information, and Decision Making." In *Advances in Information Processing in Organizations,* edited by Lee S. Sproull and J. P. Crecine. Vol. 1. Hillsdale, NJ: Erlbaum (1984).

Markus, M. L. "Power, Politics, and MIS Implementation." *Communications of the ACM* 26, no. 6 (June 1983).

McAfee, Andrew, and Francois-Xavier Oliveau. "Confronting the Limits of Networks." *Sloan Management Review* 43 no.4, (Summer 2002).

McFarlan, F. Warren. "Information Technology Changes the Way You Compete." *Harvard Business Review* (May–June 1984).

McFarlan, F. Warren. "Information Technology Changes the Way You Compete." *Harvard Business Review* (May–June 1984).

McKenney, James L., and Peter G. W. Keen. "How Managers' Minds Work." *Harvard Business Review* (May–June 1974).

Mendelson, Haim, and Ravindra R. Pillai. "Clock Speed and Informational Response: Evidence from the Information Technology Industry." *Information Systems Research* 9, no. 4 (December 1998).

Mintzberg, Henry. "Managerial Work: Analysis from Observation." *Management Science* 18 (October 1971).

Mintzberg, Henry. *The Structuring of Organizations.* Englewood Cliffs, NJ: Prentice Hall (1979).

———. *The Nature of Managerial Work.* New York: Harper & Row (1973).

Mintzberg, Henry, and Frances Westley. "Decision Making: It's Not What You Think." *Sloan Management Review* (Spring 2001).

Orlikowski, Wanda J., and Daniel Robey. "Information Technology and the Structuring of Organizations." *Information Systems Research* 2, no. 2 (June 1991).

Pindyck, Robert S., and Daniel L. Rubinfeld. *Microeconomics,* 5th ed. Upper Saddle River, NJ: Prentice Hall (2001).

Pinsonneault, Alain, and Kenneth L. Kraemer. "Exploring the Role of Information Technology in Organizational Downsizing: A Tale of Two American Cities." *Organization Science* 13, no. 2 (March–April 2002).

Porter, Michael. *Competitive Strategy.* New York: Free Press (1980).

———. *Competitive Advantage.* New York: Free Press (1985).

———. "How Information Can Help You Compete." *Harvard Business Review* (August–September 1985a).

_____ "Strategy and the Internet." *Harvard Business Review* (March 2001).

Porter, Michael E., and Scott Stern. "Location Matters." *Sloan Management Review* 42, no. 4 (Summer 2001).

Reich, Blaize Horner, and Izak Benbasat. "Factors that Influence the Social Dimension of Alignment between Business and Information Technology Objectives." *MIS Quarterly* 24, no. 1 (March 2000).

Reinartz, Werner, and V. Kumar. "The Mismanagement of Customer Loyalty." *Harvard Business Review* (July 2002).

Robey, Daniel, and Marie-Claude Boudreau. "Accounting for the Contradictory Organizational Consequences of Information Technology: Theoretical Directions and Methodological Implications." *Information Systems Research* 10, no. 42 (June1999).

Sauter, Vicki L. "Intuitive Decision Making." *Communications of the ACM* 42, no 6 (June 1999)

Schein, Edgar H. *Organizational Culture and Leadership.* San Francisco: Jossey-Bass (1985).

Schwenk, C. R. "Cognitive Simplification Processes in Strategic Decision Making." *Strategic Management Journal* 5 (1984).

Shapiro, Carl, and Hal R. Varian. *Information Rules.* Boston, MA: Harvard Business School Press (1999).

Shore, Edwin B. "Reshaping the IS Organization." *MIS Quarterly* (December 1983).

Short, James E., and N. Venkatraman. "Beyond Business Process Redesign: Redefining Baxter's Business Network." *Sloan Management Review* (Fall 1992).

Simon, H. A. *The New Science of Management Decision.* New York: Harper & Row (1960).

Simon, Herbert A. "Applying Information Technology to Organization Design." *Public Administration Review* (May–June 1973).

Slywotzky, Adrian J., and Richard Wise. "The Growth Crisis, and How to Escape It." *Harvard Business Review* (July 2002).

Staples, D. Sandy, John S. Hulland, and Christopher A. Higgins. "A Self-Efficacy Theory Explanation for the Management of Remote Workers in Virtual Organizations." *Organization Science* 10, no. 6 (November–December 1999).

Starbuck, William H. "Organizations as Action Generators." *American Sociological Review* 48 (1983).

Starbuck, William H., and Frances J. Milliken. "Executives' Perceptual Filters: What They Notice and How They Make Sense." In *The Executive Effect: Concepts and Methods for Studying Top Managers,* edited by D. C. Hambrick. Greenwich, CT: JAI Press (1988).

Turner, Jon A. "Computer Mediated Work: The Interplay Between Technology and Structured Jobs." *Communications of the ACM* 27, no. 12 (December 1984).

Turner, Jon A., and Robert A. Karasek, Jr. "Software Ergonomics: Effects of Computer Application Design Parameters on Operator Task Performance and Health." *Ergonomics* 27, no. 6 (1984).

Tushman, Michael L., and Philip Anderson. "Technological Discontinuities and Organizational Environments." *Administrative Science Quarterly* 31 (September 1986).

Tversky, A., and D. Kahneman. "The Framing of Decisions and the Psychology of Choice." *Science* 211 (January 1981).

Vandenbosch, Mark, and Niraj Dawar. "Beyond Better Products: Capturing Value in Customer Interactions." *Sloan Management Review* 43, no. 4 (Summer 2002).

Weber, Max. *The Theory of Social and Economic Organization.* Translated by Talcott Parsons. New York: Free Press (1947).

Williamson, Oliver E. *The Economic Institutions of Capitalism.* New York: Free Press (1985).

Wiseman, Charles. *Strategic Information Systems.* Homewood, IL: Richard D. Irwin (1988).

Wrapp, H. Edward. "Good Managers Don't Make Policy Decisions." *Harvard Business Review* (July–August 1984).

Yoffie, David B. and Michael A. Cusumano. "Judo Strategy: The Competitive Dynamics of Internet Time." *Harvard Business Review* (January 1999).

CHAPTER 4

Akcura, M. Tolga, and Kemal Altinkemer. "Diffusion Models for B2B, B2C and P2P Exchanges and E-Speak." *Journal of Organizational Computing and Electronic Commerce* 12, no. 3 (2002)

Anderson, Philip, and Erin Anderson. "The New E-Commerce Intermediaries." *Sloan Management Review* 43, no. 4 (Summer 2002)

Andrew , James P., Andy Blackburn, and Harold L. Sirkin. "The Business-to-Business Opportunity." Boston Consulting Group (October 2000).

Armstrong, Arthur, and John Hagel, III. "The Real Value of Online Communities." *Harvard Business Review* (May–June 1996).

Bakos, Yannis. "The Emerging Role of Electronic Marketplaces and the Internet." *Communications of the ACM* 41, no. 8 (August 1998).

Baron, John P., Michael J. Shaw, and Andrew D. Bailey, Jr. "Web-Based E-Catalog Systems in B2B Procurement." *Communications of the ACM* 43, no.5 (May 2000).

Barua, Anitesh, Prabhudev Konana, Andrew B. Whinston, and Fang Yin, "Driving E-Business Excellence." *Sloan Management Review* 43, no. 1 (Fall 2001).

Barua, Anitesh, Sury Ravindran, and Andrew B. Whinston. "Efficient Selection of Suppliers over the Internet." *Journal of Management Information Systems* 13, no. 4 (Spring 1997).

Bhattacherjee, Anol. "Individual Trust in Online Firms: Scale Development and Initial Test." *Journal of Management Information Systems* 19, no. 1 (Summer 2002).

Chaudhury, Abhijit, Debasish Mallick, and H. Raghav Rao. "Web Channels in E-Commerce." *Communications of the ACM* 44, No. 1 (January 2001).

Christensen, Clayton M. *The Innovator's Dilemma.* New York: HarperCollins (2000).

Coltman, Tim, Timothy M. Devinney, Alopi S. Latukefu, and David D. Midgley. "Keeping E-Business in Perspective." *Communications of the ACM* 46, no. 8 (August 2002).

Devaraj, Sarv, Ming Fan, and Rajiv Kohli. "Antecedents of B2C Channel Satisfaction and Preference: Validating E-Commerce Metrics." *Information Systems Research* 13, no.3 (September 2002).

Downes, Larry, and Chunka Mui. *Unleashing the Killer App: Digital Strategies for Market Dominance.* Boston, MA: Harvard Business School Press (1998).

Evans, Philip, and Thomas S. Wurster. *Blown to Bits: How the New Economics of Information Transforms Strategy.* Boston, MA: Harvard Business School Press (2000).

Evans, Philip and Thomas S. Wurster. "Getting Real about Virtual Commerce." *Harvard Business Review* (November–December 1999).

_____ "Strategy and the New Economics of Information." *Harvard Business Review* (September–October 1997).

Farhoomand, Ali, with Peter Lovelock. *Global E-Commerce.* Singapore: Pearson Education Asia (2001).

Gallaugher, John M. "E-Commerce and the Undulating Distribution Channel." *Communications of the ACM* 45, no. 7 (July 2002).

Ghosh, Shikhar. "Making Business Sense of the Internet." *Harvard Business Review* (March–April 1998).

Gopal, Ram D., Zhiping Walter, and Arvind K. Tripathi. "Amediation: New Horizons in Effective Email Advertising," *Communications of the ACM* 44, no. 12 (December 2001).

Grover, Varun, and Pradipkumar Ramanlal. "Six Myths of Information and Markets: Information Technology Networks, Electronic Commerce, and the Battle for Consumer Surplus." *MIS Quarterly* 23, no. 4 (December 1999).

_____ and James T.C. Teng. "E-Commerce and the Information Market." *Communications of the ACM* 44, no. 4 (April 2001).

Gulati, Ranjay, and Jason Garino. "Get the Right Mix of Bricks and Clicks." *Harvard Business Review* (May–June 2000).

Hagel, John III, and Marc Singer. *Net Worth.* Boston, MA: Harvard Business School Press (1999).

———. "Unbundling the Corporation." *Harvard Business Review* (March–April 1999).

Hui, Kai Lung, and Patrick Y.K. Chau. "Classifying Digital Products."*Communications of the ACM* 45, no.6 (June 2002).

Jones, Sara, Marc Wilikens, Philip Morris, and Marcelo Masera. "Trust Requirements in E-Business." *Communications of the ACM* 43, no. 12 (December 2000).

Kanan, P. K., Ai-Mei Chang, and Andrew B. Whinston. "Marketing Information on the I-Way." *Communications of the ACM* 41, no. 3 (March 1998).

Kaplan, Steven, and Mohanbir Sawhney. "E-Hubs: The New B2B Marketplaces." *Harvard Business Review* (May–June 2000).

Kauffman, Robert J., and Bin Wang. "New Buyers' Arrival Under Dynamic Pricing Market Microstructure: The Case of Group-Buying Discounts on the Internet, *Journal of Management Information Systems* 18, no. 2 (Fall 2001).

Kenny, David and John F. Marshall. "Contextual Marketing." *Harvard Business Review* (November–December 2000.

Koufaris, Marios. "Applying the Technology Acceptance Model and Flow Theory to Online Consumer Behavior." *Information Systems Research* 13, no. 2 (2002).

Lai, Vincent S. "Intraorganizational Communication with Intranets," *Communications of the ACM* 44, no. 7 (July 2001).

Laudon, Kenneth C. and Carol Guercio Traver. *E-Commerce: Business, Technology, Society.* Boston: Addison-Wesley (2002).

Lee, Hau L., and Seungin Whang. "Winning the Last Mile of E-Commerce." *Sloan Management Review* 42, no. 4 (Summer 2001).

Lee, Ho Geun, and Theodore H. Clark. "Market Process Reengineering through Electronic Market Systems: Opportunities and Challenges." *Journal of Management Information Systems* 13, no. 3 (Winter 1997).

Lee, Ho Geun. "Do Electronic Marketplaces Lower the Price of Goods?" *Communications of the ACM* 41, no. 1 (January 1998).

Looney, Clayton A., and Debabroto Chatterjee. "Web-Enabled Transformation of the Brokerage Industry." *Communications of the ACM* 45, no. 8 (August 2002)

Magretta, Joan. "Why Business Models Matter." *Harvard Business Review* (May 2002).

Mc Knight, D. Harrison, Vivek Choudhury, and Charlea Kacmar. "Developing and Validating Trust Measures for E-Commerce: An Integrative Typology." *Information Systems Research* 13, no.3 (September 2002).

McWilliam, Gil. "Building Stronger Brands through Online Communities." *Sloan Management Review* 41, no. 3 (Spring 2000).

Meehan, Michael. "No Pain, No Gain." *Computerworld* (March 11, 2002).

Mougayar, Walid. *Opening Digital Markets,* 2nd ed. New York: McGraw-Hill (1998).

O'Leary, Daniel E., Daniel Koukka, and Robert Plant. "Artificial Intelligence and Virtual Organizations." *Communications of the ACM* 40, no. 1 (January 1997).

Palmer, Jonathan W., and David A. Griffith. "An Emerging Model of Web Site Design for Marketing." *Communications of the ACM* 41, no. 3 (March 1998).

Pinker, Edieal, Abraham Seidmann, and Riginald C. Foster. "Strategies for Transitioning 'Old Economy' Firms to E-Business." *Communications of the ACM* 45, no. 5 (May 2002).

Prahalad, C.K., and Venkatram Ramaswamy. "Coopting Consumer Competence." *Harvard Business Review* (January–February 2000).

Rayport, J. F., and J. J. Sviokla. "Managing in the Marketspace." *Harvard Business Review* (November–December 1994).

Reichheld, Frederick E., and Phil Schefter. "E-Loyalty: Your Secret Weapon on the Web." *Harvard Business Review* (July–August 2000).

Rifkin, Glenn, and Joel Kurtzman. "Is Your E-Business Plan Radical Enough?" *Sloan Management Review* 43, no. 3 (Spring 2002).

Schoder, Detlef, and Pai-ling Yin. "Building Firm Trust Online." *Communications of the ACM* 43, no. 12 (December 2000).

Shelfer, Katherine M., and J. Drew Procaccino. "Smart Card Evolution." *Communications of the ACM* 45, no. 7 (July 2002).

Singh, Surendra N., and Nikunj P. Dalal. "Web Home Pages as Advertisements." *Communications of the ACM* 42, no. 8 (August 1999).

Smith, Michael D., Joseph Bailey, and Erik Brynjolfsson. "Understanding Digital Markets: Review and Assessment." In *Understanding the Digital Economy,* edited by Erik Brynjolfsson and Brian Kahin. Cambridge, MA: MIT Press (1999).

Subramanian, Rangan, and Ron Adner. "Profits and the Internet: Seven Misconceptions." *Sloan Management Review* 42, no. 4 (Summer 2001).

Torkzadeh, Gholamreza, and Gurpreet Dhillon. "Measuring Factors that Influence the Success of Internet Commerce." *Information Systems Research* 13, no. 2 (June 2002).

Urbaczewski, Andrew, Leonard M. Jessup, and Bradley Wheeler. "Electronic Commerce Research: A Taxonomy and Synthesis." *Journal of Organizational Computing and Electronic Commerce* 12, no. 2 (2002).

Venkatraman, N. "Five Steps to a Dot-Com Strategy: How to Find Your Footing on the Web." *Sloan Management Review* 41, no. 3 (Spring 2000).

Werbach, Kevin. "Syndication: The Emerging Model for Business in the Internet Era." *Harvard Business Review* (May–June 2000).

Westland, J. Christopher. "Preference Ordering Cash, Near-Cash and Electronic Cash." *Journal of Organizational Computing and Electronic Commerce* 12, no. 3 (2002).

Wigand, Rolf T., and Robert Benjamin. "Electronic Commerce: Effects on Electronic Markets." *JCMC* 1, no. 3 (December 1995).

Willcocks, Leslie, and Robert Plant. "Pathways to E-Business Leadership," *Sloan Management Review* (Spring 2001).

Wise, Richard, and David Morrison. "Beyond the Exchange: The Future of B2B." *Harvard Business Review* (November-December 2000).

CHAPTER 5

Associated Press. "Global Software Piracy Figures Jump for Second Straight Year." *Wall Street Journal* (June 10, 2002).

Association of Computing Machinery. "ACM's Code of Ethics and Professional Conduct." *Communications of the ACM* 36, no. 12 (December 1993).

Ball, Kirstie S. "Situating Workplace Surveillance: Ethics and Computer-based Performance Monitoring." *Ethics and Information Technology* 3, no. 3 (2001).

Bellman, Steven, Eric J. Johnson, and **Gerald L. Lohse.** "To Opt-in or Opt-out? It Depends on the Question." *Communications of the ACM* 44, no. 2 (February 2001).

Bennett, Colin J. "Cookies, Web Bugs, Webcams, and Cue Cats: Patterns of Surveillance on the World Wide Web." *Ethics and Information Technology* 3, no. 3 (2001).

Berdichevsky, Daniel, and **Erik Neunschwander.** "Toward an Ethics of Persuasive Technology." *Communications of the ACM* 42, no. 5 (May 1999).

Bowen, Jonathan. "The Ethics of Safety-Critical Systems." *Communications of the ACM* 43, no. 3 (April 2000).

Brod, Craig. *Techno Stress—The Human Cost of the Computer Revolution.* Reading MA: Addison-Wesley (1982).

Brown Bag Software vs. Symantec Corp. 960 F2D 1465 (Ninth Circuit, 1992).

Burk, Dan L. "Copyrightable Functions and Patentable Speech." *Communications of the ACM* 44, no. 2 (February 2001).

Cavazos, Edward A. "The Legal Risks of Setting up Shop in Cyberspace." *Journal of Organizational Computing* 6, no. 1 (1996).

Cheng, Hsing K., Ronald R. Sims, and **Hildy Teegen.** "To Purchase or to Pirate Software: An Empirical Study." *Journal of Management Information Systems* 13, no. 4 (Spring 1997).

Clarke, Roger. "Internet Privacy Concerns Confirm the Case for Intervention." *Communications of the ACM* 42, no. 2 (February 1999).

Collins, W. Robert, Keith W. Miller, Bethany J. Spielman, and **Phillip Wherry.** "How Good Is Good Enough? An Ethical Analysis of Software Construction and Use." *Communications of the ACM* 37, no. 1 (January 1994).

Computer Systems Policy Project. "Perspectives on the National Information Infrastructure." (January 12, 1993).

Cranor, Lorrie Faith, and **Brian A. LaMacchia.** "Spam!" *Communications of the ACM* 41, no. 8 (August 1998).

Davis, Randall. "The Digital Dilemma." *Communications of the ACM* 44, no. 2 (February 2001).

Dejoie, Roy, George Fowler, and **David Paradice,** eds. *Ethical Issues in Information Systems.* Boston: Boyd & Fraser (1991).

Denning, Dorothy E., et al. "To Tap or Not to Tap." *Communications of the ACM* 36, no. 3 (March 1993).

Friedman, Batya, Peter H. Kahn, Jr. and **Daniel C. Howek.** "Trust Online." *Communications of the ACM* 43, no. 12 (December 2000).

Froomkin, A. Michael. "The Collision of Trademarks, Domain Names, and Due Process in Cyberspace." *Communications of the ACM* 44, no. 2 (February 2001).

Fry, Jason. "The Music Man." *Wall Street Journal* (September 16, 2002).

Gattiker, Urs E., and **Helen Kelley.** "Morality and Computers: Attitudes and Differences in Judgments." *Information Systems Research* 10, no. 3 (September 1999).

Gopal, Ram D., and **G. Lawrence Sanders.** "Preventive and Deterrent Controls for Software Piracy." *Journal of Management Information Systems* 13, no. 4 (Spring 1997).

_____ "Global Software Piracy: You Can't Get Blood Out of a Turnip." *Communications of the ACM* 43, no. 9 (September 2000).

Graham, Robert L. "The Legal Protection of Computer Software." *Communications of the ACM* (May 1984).

Green, R. H. *The Ethical Manager.* New York: Macmillan (1994).

Harmon, Amy. "Software that Tracks E-Mail is Raising Privacy Concerns." *New York Times* (November 22, 2000).

Harrington, Susan J. "The Effect of Codes of Ethics and Personal Denial of Responsibility on Computer Abuse Judgments and Intentions." *MIS Quarterly* 20, no. 2 (September 1996).

Huff, Chuck, and **C. Dianne Martin.** "Computing Consequences: A Framework for Teaching Ethical Computing." *Communications of the ACM* 38, no. 12 (December 1995).

Joes, Kathryn. "EDS Set to Restore Cash-Machine Network." *New York Times* (March 26, 1993).

Johnson, Deborah G. "Ethics Online." *Communications of the ACM* 40, no. 1 (January 1997).

Johnson, Deborah G., and **John M. Mulvey.** "Accountability and Computer Decision Systems." *Communications of the ACM* 38, no. 12 (December 1995).

King, Julia. "It's CYA Time." *Computerworld* (March 30, 1992).

Kling, Rob. "When Organizations Are Perpetrators: The Conditions of Computer Abuse and Computer Crime." In *Computerization & Controversy: Value Conflicts & Social Choices,* edited by Charles Dunlop and Rob Kling. New York: Academic Press (1991).

Kreie, Jennifer, and **Timothy Paul Cronan.** "Making Ethical Decisions." *Communications of the ACM* 43, no. 12 (December 2000).

Laudon, Kenneth C. "Ethical Concepts and Information Technology." *Communications of the ACM* 38, no. 12 (December 1995).

Mariano, Gwendolyn. "Music Industry Sounds Off on CD Burning." *CNET* (June 11, 2002).

Maltz, Elliott, and **Vincent Chiappetta.** "Maximizing Value in the Digital World." *Sloan Management Review* 43, no. 3 (Spring 2002).

Martin, Jr. David M., Richard M. Smith, Michael Brittain, Ivan Fetch, and **Hailin Wu.** "The Privacy Practices of Web Browser Extensions." *Communications of the ACM* 44, no. 2 (February 2001).

Mason, Richard O. "Applying Ethics to Information Technology Issues." *Communications of the ACM* 38, no. 12 (December 1995).

Mason, Richard O. "Four Ethical Issues in the Information Age." *MIS Quarterly* 10, no. 1 (March 1986).

Memon, Nasir, and **Ping Wah Wong.** "Protecting Digital Media Content." *Communications of the ACM* 41, no. 7 (July 1998).

Milberg, Sandra J., Sandra J. Burke, H. Jeff Smith, and **Ernest A. Kallman.** "Values, Personal Information Privacy, and Regulatory Approaches." *Communications of the ACM* 38, no. 12 (December 1995).

Moores, Trevor, and **Gurpreet Dhillon.** "Software Piracy: A View from Hong Kong." *Communications of the ACM* 43, no. 12, (December 2000).

Mykytyn, Kathleen, Peter P. Mykytyn, Jr., and **Craig W. Slinkman.** "Expert Systems: A Question of Liability." *MIS Quarterly* 14, no. 1 (March 1990).

National Telecommunications & Information Administration, U.S. Department of Commerce. "Falling Through the Net: Defining the Digital Divide." July 8, 1999.

Nissenbaum, Helen. "Computing and Accountability." *Communications of the ACM* 37, no. 1 (January 1994).

Okerson, Ann. "Who Owns Digital Works?" *Scientific American* (July 1996).

O'Rourke, Maureen A. "Is Virtual Trespass an Apt Analogy?" *Communications of the ACM* 44, no. 2 (February 2001).

Oz, Effy. "Ethical Standards for Information Systems Professionals," *MIS Quarterly* 16, no. 4 (December 1992).

———. *Ethics for the Information Age.* Dubuque, Iowa: W. C. Brown (1994).

Rainie, Lee, and **Dan Packel.** "More Online, Doing More." The Pew Internet and American Life Project (Febuary 18, 2001).

Reagle, Joseph, and **Lorrie Faith Cranor.** "The Platform for Privacy Preferences." *Communications of the ACM* 42, no. 2 (February 1999).

Redman, Thomas C. "The Impact of Poor Data Quality on the Typical Enterprise." *Communications of the ACM* 41, no. 2 (February 1998).

Rifkin, Jeremy. "Watch Out for Trickle-Down Technology." *New York Times* (March 16, 1993).

Rigdon, Joan E. "Frequent Glitches in New Software Bug Users." *Wall Street Journal* (January 18, 1995).

Rotenberg, Marc. "Communications Privacy: Implications for Network Design." *Communications of the ACM* 36, no. 8 (August 1993).

Samuelson, Pamela. "Computer Programs and Copyright's Fair Use Doctrine." *Communications of the ACM* 36, no. 9 (September 1993).

———. "Copyright's Fair Use Doctrine and Digital Data." *Communications of the ACM* 37, no. 1 (January 1994).

———. "Liability for Defective Electronic Information." *Communications of the ACM* 36, no. 1 (January 1993).

———. "Self Plagiarism or Fair Use?" *Communications of the ACM* 37, no. 8 (August 1994).

———. "The Ups and Downs of Look and Feel." *Communications of the ACM* 36, no. 4 (April 1993).

Sewell, Graham, and **James R. Barker.** "Neither Good, nor Bad, but Dangerous: Surveillance as an Ethical Paradox." *Ethics and Information Technology* 3, no. 3 (2001).

Sipior, Janice C., and **Burke T. Ward.** "The Dark Side of Employee E-mail." *Communications of the ACM 42*, no.7 (July 1999).

———. "The Ethical and Legal Quandary of E-mail Privacy." *Communications of the ACM* 38, no. 12 (December 1995).

Smith, H. Jeff. "Privacy Policies and Practices: Inside the Organizational Maze." *Communications of the ACM* 36, no. 12, (December 1993).

Smith, H. Jeff, and **John Hasnas.** "Ethics and Information Systems: The Corporate Domain." *MIS Quarterly* 23, no. 1 (March 1999).

Smith, H. Jeff, Sandra J. Milberg, and **Sandra J. Burke.** "Information Privacy: Measuring Individuals' Concerns about Organizational Practices." *MIS Quarterly* 20, no. 2 (June 1996).

Straub, Detmar W., Jr., and **Rosann Webb Collins.** "Key Information Liability Issues Facing Managers: Software Piracy, Proprietary Databases, and Individual Rights to Privacy." *MIS Quarterly* 14, no. 2 (June 1990).

Straub, Detmar W., Jr., and **William D. Nance.** "Discovering and Disciplining Computer Abuse in Organizations: A Field Study." *MIS Quarterly* 14, no. 1 (March 1990).

Sullivan, Brian. "IT Worker Pleads Guilty to Sabotaging Computers." *Computerworld* (March 26, 2001).

The Telecommunications Policy Roundtable. "Renewing the Commitment to a Public Interest Telecommunications Policy." *Communications of the ACM* 37, no. 1 (January 1994).

Thong, James Y. L., and **Chee-Sing Yap.** "Testing an Ethical Decision-Making Theory." *Journal of Management Information Systems* 15, no. 1 (Summer 1998).

Tuttle, Brad, Adrian Harrell, and **Paul Harrison.** "Moral Hazard, Ethical Considerations, and the Decision to Implement an Information System." *Journal of Management Information Systems* 13, no. 4 (Spring 1997).

United States Department of Health, Education, and **Welfare.** *Records, Computers, and the Rights of Citizens.* Cambridge: MIT Press (1973).

Urbaczewski, Andrew, and **Leonard M. Jessup.** "Does Electronic Monitoring of Employee Internet Usage Work?" *Communications of the ACM* 45, no. 1 (January 2002).

Volokh, Eugene. "Personalization and Privacy." *Communications of the ACM* 43, no. 8 (August 2000).

Wang, Huaiqing, Matthew K. O. Lee, and **Chen Wang.** "Consumer Privacy Concerns About Internet Marketing." *Communications of the ACM* 41, no. 3 (March 1998).

Wellman, Barry. "Designing the Internet for a Networked Society." *Communications of the ACM* 45, no. 5 (May 2002).

Wingfield, Nick. "An eBay Merchant Disappears, Failing to Deliver the Goods." *Wall Street Journal* (February 22, 2002).

CHAPTER 6

Aries, James A., Subhankar Banerjee, Marc S. Brittan, Eric Dillon, Janusz S. Kowalik, and **John P. Lixvar.** "Capacity and Performance Analysis of Distributed Enterprise Systems." *Communications of the ACM* 45, no. 6 (June 2002).

Backus, John. "Funding the Computing Revolution's Third Wave." *Communications of the ACM* 44, no. 11 (November 2001).

Bell, Gordon, and **Jim Gray.** "What's Next in High-Performance Computing?" *Communications of the ACM* 45, no. 1 (January 2002).

Benamati, John, and **Albert L. Lederer.** "Coping with Rapid Changes in IT." *Communications of the ACM* 44, no. 8 (August 2001).

David, Julie Smith, David Schuff, and **Robert St. Louis.** "Managing Your IT Total Cost of Ownership." *Communications of the ACM* 45, no. 1 (January 2002).

Dempsey, Bert J.. Debra Weiss, Paul Jones, and **Jane Greenberg.** "What Is an Open Source Software Developer?" *Communications of the ACM* 45, no. 1 (January 2001).

Fayad, Mohamed, and **Marshall P. Cline.** "Aspects of Software Adaptability." *Communications of the ACM* 39, no. 10 (October 1996).

Fitzmaurice, George W., Rvain Balakrishnan, and **Gordon Kurtenbach.** "Sampling, Synthesis, and Input Devices." *Communications of the ACM* 42, no. 8 (August 1999).

Gerlach, James, Bruce Neumann, Edwin Moldauer, Martha Argo, and **Daniel Frisby.** "Determining the Cost of IT Services." *Communications of the ACM* 45, no. 9 (September 2002).

Gibson, Garth A., and **Rodney Van Meter.** "Network Attached Storage Architecture." *Communications of the ACM* 43, no. 11 (November 2000).

Hardaway, Don, and **Richard P. Will.** "Digital Multimedia Offers Key to Educational Reform." *Communications of the ACM* 40, no. 4 (April 1997).

Kern, Thomas, Leslie P. Willcocks, and **Mary C. Lacity.** "Application Service Provision: Risk Assessment and Mitigation." *MIS Quarterly Executive* 1, no. 2 (2002).

Kim, Yongbeom, and **Edward A. Stohr.** "Software Reuse." *Journal of Management Information Systems* 14, no. 4 (Spring 1998).

King, John. "Centralized vs. Decentralized Computing: Organizational Considerations and Management Options." *Computing Surveys* (October 1984).

Lim, Kai H., and **Izak Benbasat.** "The Influence of Multimedia on Improving the Comprehension of Organizational Information," *Journal of Management Information Systems* 19, no. 1 (Summer 2002).

Linthicum, David S. "EAI Application Integration Exposed." *Software Magazine* (February/March 2000).

Messina, Paul, David Culler, Wayne Pfeiffer, William Martin, J. Tinsley Oden, and **Gary Smith.** "Architecture." *Communications of the ACM* 41, no. 11 (November 1998).

Noffsinger, W. B., Robert Niedbalski, Michael Blanks, and Niall Emmart. "Legacy Object Modeling Speeds Software Integration." *Communications of the ACM* 41, no. 12 (December 1998).

Pancake, Cherri M., and Christian Lengauer. "High-Performance Java." *Communications of the ACM* 44, no. 10 (October 2001).

Paul, Lauren Gibbons. "What Price Ownership?" *Datamation* (December/January 1998).

Phillips, Charles. "Stemming the Software Spending Spree." *Optimize Magazine* (April 2002).

Poulin, Jeffrey S. "Reuse: Been There, Done That." *Communications of the ACM* 42, no. 5 (May 1999).

Ricadela, Aaron. "Living on the Grid." *InformationWeek* (June 17, 2002).

Robinson, Teri. "NASDAQ Is Bullish on Technology." *InformationWeek* (May 22,2000).

Schuff, David, and Robert St. Louis. "Centralization vs. Decentralization of Application Software." *Communications of the ACM* 44, no. 6 (June 2001).

Sheetz, Steven D., Gretchen Irwin, David P. Tegarden, H. James Nelson, and David E. Monarchi. "Exploring the Difficulties of Learning Object-Oriented Techniques." *Journal of Management Information Systems* 14, no. 2 (Fall 1997).

Tennenhouse, David. "Proactive Computing." *Communications of the ACM* 43, no. 5 (May 2000).

Von Hippel, Eric. "Learning from Open-Source Software." *Sloan Management Review* 42, no. 4 (Summer 2001).

CHAPTER 7

Chang, Shih-Fu, John R. Amith, Mandis Beigi, and Ana Benitez. "Visual Information Retrieval from Large Distributed Online Repositories." *Communications of the ACM* 40, no. 12 (December 1997).

Clifford, James, Albert Croker, and Alex Tuzhilin. "On Data Representation and Use in a Temporal Relational DBMS." *Information Systems Research* 7, no. 3 (September 1996).

Cooper, Brian L., Hugh J. Watson, Barbara H. Wixom, and Dale L. Goodhue. "Data Warehousing Supports Corporate Strategy at First American Corporation." *MIS Quarterly* (December 2000).

Fayyad, Usama, Ramasamy Ramakrishnan, and Ramakrisnan Srikant. "Evolving Data Mining into Solutions for Insights." *Communications of the ACM* 45, no.8 (August 2002).

Fiori, Rich. "The Information Warehouse." *Relational Database Journal* (January–February 1995).

Gardner, Stephen R. "Building the Data Warehouse." *Communications of the ACM* 41, no. 9 (September 1998).

Goldstein, R. C., and J. B. McCririck. "What Do Data Administrators Really Do?" *Datamation* 26 (August 1980).

Goodhue, Dale L., Judith A. Quillard, and John F. Rockart. "Managing the Data Resource: A Contingency Perspective." *MIS Quarterly* (September 1988).

Goodhue, Dale L., Laurie J. Kirsch, Judith A. Quillard, and Michael D. Wybo. "Strategic Data Planning: Lessons from the Field." *MIS Quarterly* 16, no. 1 (March 1992).

Goodhue, Dale L., Michael D. Wybo, and Laurie J. Kirsch. "The Impact of Data Integration on the Costs and Benefits of Information Systems." *MIS Quarterly* 16, no. 3 (September 1992).

Grosky, William I. "Managing Multimedia Information in Database Systems." *Communications of the ACM* 40, no. 12 (December 1997).

Grover, Varun, and James Teng. "How Effective Is Data Resource Management?" *Journal of Information Systems Management* (Summer 1991).

Gupta, Amarnath, and Ranesh Jain. "Visual Information Retrieval." *Communications of the ACM* 40, no. 5 (May 1997).

Hirji, Karim K. "Exploring Data Mining Implementation." *Communications of the ACM* 44, no. 7 (July 2001).

Inman, W. H. "The Data Warehouse and Data Mining." *Communications of the ACM* 39, no. 11 (November 1996).

Jukic, Boris, Nenad Jukic, and Manoj Parameswaran. "Data Models for Information Sharing in E-Partnerships: Analysis, Improvements, and Relevance." *Journal of Organizational Computing and Electronic Commerce* 12, no. 2(2002).

Kahn, Beverly K. "Some Realities of Data Administration." *Communications of the ACM* 26 (October 1983).

King, John L., and Kenneth Kraemer. "Information Resource Management Cannot Work." *Information and Management* (1988).

Kroenke, David. *Database Processing: Fundamentals, Design, and Implementation,* 8th ed. Upper Saddle River, NJ: Prentice Hall (2002).

Lange, Danny B. "An Object-Oriented Design Approach for Developing Hypermedia Information Systems." *Journal of Organizational Computing and Electronic Commerce* 6, no. 2 (1996).

March, Salvatore T., and Young-Gul Kim. "Information Resource Management: A Metadata Perspective." *Journal of Management Information Systems* 5, no. 3 (Winter 1988–1989).

McCarthy, John. "Phenomenal Data Mining." *Communications of the ACM* 43, no. 8 (August 2000).

McFadden, Fred R., Jeffrey A. Hoffer, and Mary B. Prescott. *Modern Database Management,* 6th ed. Upper Saddle River, NJ: Prentice Hall (2002).

Morrison, Mike, Joline Morrison, and Anthony Keys. "Integrating Web Sites and Databases." *Communications of the ACM* 45, no.9 (September 2002).

Rundensteiner, Elke A., Andreas Koeller, and Xin Zhang. "Maintaining Data Warehouses over Changing Information Sources." *Communications of the ACM* 43, no. 6 (June 2000).

Truman, Gregory E. "Integration in Electronic Exchange Environments." *Journal of Management Information Systems* 17, no. 1 (Summer 2000).

Watson, Hugh J., and Barbara J. Haley. "Managerial Considerations." *Communications of the ACM* 41, no. 9 (September 1998).

CHAPTER 8

Banerjee, Snehamay, and Ram L. Kumar. "Managing Electronic Interchange of Business Documents." *Communications of the ACM* 45, no. 7 (July 2002).

Boston Consulting Group. "Mobile Commerce: Winning the On-Air Consumer" (November 2000).

Brunner, Marcus, Bernhard Plattner, and Rolf Stadler. "Service Creation and Management in Active Telecom Networks." *Communications of the ACM* 44, no. 4 (April 2001).

Carr, Jim. "The Forgotten Networks." *mBusiness* (June 2001).

Chatfield, Akemi Takeoka, and Philip Yetton. "Strategic Payoff from EDI as a Function of EDI Embeddedness." *Journal of Management Information Systems* 16, no. 4 (Spring 2000).

Chatterjee, Samir, and Suzanne Pawlowski. "All-Optical Networks." *Communications of the ACM* 42, no. 6 (June 1999).

_____, and Il-Horn Hann. "Rosenbluth International: Strategic Transformation." *Journal of Management Information Systems* 16, no. 2 (Fall 1999).

Damsgaard Jan, and Kalle Lyytinen. "Building Electronic Trading Infrastructures: A Public or Private Responsibility?" *Journal of Organizational Computing and Electronic Commerce* 11, no. 2 (2001).

Duchessi, Peter, and **InduShobha Chengalur-Smith.** "Client/Server Benefits, Problems, Best Practices." *Communications of the ACM* 41, no. 5 (May 1998).

Dutta, Amitava. "Telecommunications and Economic Activity: An Analysis of Granger Causality," *Journal of Management Information Systems* 17, no. 4 (Spring 2001).

Gefen, David, and **Detmar W. Straub.** "Gender Differences in the Perception and Use of E-Mail: An Extension to the Technology Acceptance Model." *MIS Quarterly* 21, no. 4 (December 1997).

Grover, Varun, and **Martin D. Goslar.** "Initiation, Adoption, and Implementation of Telecommunications Technologies in U.S. Organizations." *Journal of Management Information Systems* 10, no. 1 (Summer 1993).

Hart, Paul J., and **Carol Stoak Saunders.** "Emerging Electronic Partnerships: Antecedents and Dimensions of EDI Use from the Supplier's Perspective." *Journal of Management Information Systems* 14, no. 4 (Spring 1998).

Housel, Tom, and **Eric Skopec.** *Global Telecommunication Revolution: The Business Perspective.* New York: McGraw-Hill (2001).

Imielinski, Tomasz, and **B. R. Badrinath.** "Mobile Wireless Computing: Challenges in Data Management." *Communications of the ACM* 37, no. 10 (October 1994).

Karahanna, Elena, and **Moez Limayem.** "E-Mail and V-Mail Usage: Generalizing Across Technologies." *Journal of Organizational Computing and Electronic Commerce* 10, no. 1 (2000).

Keen, Peter G. W. *Competing in Time: Using Telecommunications for Competitive Advantage.* Cambridge, MA: Ballinger Publishing Company (1986).

Kim, B. G., and **P. Wang.** "ATM Network: Goals and Challenges." *Communications of the ACM* 38, no. 2 (February 1995).

Lee, Ho Geun, Theodore Clark, and **Kar Yan Tam.** "Research Report: Can EDI Benefit Adopters?" *Information Systems Research* 10, no. 2 (June 1999).

Mears, Rena, and **Jason Salzetti.** "The New Wireless Enterprise." *InformationWeek* (September 18, 2000).

Meister, Frank, Jeetu Patel, and **Joe Fenner.** "E-Commerce Platforms Mature." *InformationWeek* (October 23, 2000).

Mueller, Milton. "Universal Service and the Telecommunications Act: Myth Made Law." *Communications of the ACM* 40, no. 3 (March 1997).

Nakamura, Kiyoh, Toshihiro Ide, and **Yukio Kiyokane.** "Roles of Multimedia Technology in Telework." *Journal of Organizational Computing and Electronic Commerce* 6, no. 4 (1996).

Ngwenyama, Ojelanki, and **Allen S. Lee.** "Communication Richness in Electronic Mail: Critical Social Theory and the Contextuality of Meaning." *MIS Quarterly* 21, no. 2 (June 1997).

Palen, Leysia. "Mobile Telephony in a Connected Life." *Communications of the ACM* 45, no. 3 (March 2002).

Passmore, David. "Scaling Large E-Commerce Infrastructures." *Packet Magazine* (Third Quarter 1999).

Pottie, G. J., and **W. J. Kaiser.** "Wireless Integrated Network Sensors." *Communications of the ACM* 43, no. 5 (May 2000).

Premkumar, G., K. Ramamurthy, and **Sree Nilakanta.** "Implementation of Electronic Data Interchange: An Innovation Diffusion Perspective." *Journal of Management Information Systems* 11, no. 2 (Fall 1994).

Raymond, Louis, and **Francois Bergeron.** "EDI Success in Small- and Medium-sized Enterprises: A Field Study." *Journal of Organizational Computing and Electronic Commerce* 6, no. 2 (1996).

Sharda, Nalin. "Multimedia Networks: Fundamentals and Future Directions." *Communications of the Association for Information Systems* (February 1999).

Teo, Hock-Hai, Bernard C. Y. Tan, and **Kwok-Kee Wei.** "Organizational Transformation Using Electronic Data Interchange: The Case of TradeNet in Singapore." *Journal of Management Information Systems* 13, no. 4 (Spring 1997).

Thompson, Marjorie Sarbough, and **Martha S. Feldman.** "Electronic Mail and Organizational Communication." *Organization Science* 9, no. 6 (November–December 1998).

Varshney, Upkar. "Networking Support for Mobile Computing." *Communications of the Association for Information Systems* 1 (January 1999).

_____, and **Ron Vetter.** "Emerging Mobile and Wireless Networks." *Communications of the ACM* 42, no. 6 (June 2000).

Vetter, Ronald J. "ATM Concepts, Architectures, and Protocols." *Communications of the ACM* 38, no. 2 (February 1995).

Whitman, Michael E., Anthony M. Townsend, and **Robert J. Aalberts.** "Considerations for Effective Telecommunications-Use Policy." *Communications of the ACM* 42, no. 6 (June 1999).

Wilson, E. Vance. "E-mail Winners and Losers." *Communications of the ACM* 45, no. 10 (October 2002).

CHAPTER 9

Amor, Daniel. *The E-Business Revolution,* 2nd ed. Upper Saddle River, NJ: Prentice Hall (2002).

Bhattacharjee, Yudhijit. "A Swarm of Little Notes." *Time* (September 16, 2002).

Berners-Lee, Tim, Robert Cailliau, Ari Luotonen, Henrik Frystyk Nielsen, and **Arthur Secret.** "The World Wide Web." *Communications of the ACM* 37, no. 8 (August 1994).

Bikson, Tora K., Cathleen Stasz, and **Donald A. Monkin.** "Computer-Mediated Work: Individual and Organizational Impact on One Corporate Headquarters." Rand Corporation (1985).

Billsus, Daniel, Clifford A. Brunk, Craig Evans, Brian Gladish, and **Michael Pazzani.** "Adaptive Interfaces for Ubiquitous Web Access." *Communications of the ACM* 45, no. 5 (May 2002).

Borriello, Gaetano, and **Roy Want.** "Embedded Computation Meets the World Wide Web." *Communications of the ACM* 43, no. 5 (May 2000).

Byrd, Terry Anthony. "Measuring the Flexibility of Information Technology Infrastructure: Exploratory Analysis of a Construct." *Journal of Management Information Systems* 17, no. 1 (Summer 2000).

Cheyne, Tanya L., and **Frank E. Ritter.** "Targeting Audiences on the Internet." *Communications of the ACM* 44, no. 4 (April 2001).

Concours Group. "Managing and Exploiting Corporate Intranets" (1999).

Farhoomand, Ali, Pauline S. P Ng, and **Justin K. H. Yue.** "The Building of a New Business Ecosystem: Sustaining National Competitive Advantage through Electronic Commerce." *Journal of Organizational Computing and Electronic Commerce* 11, no. 4 (2001)

Garner, Rochelle. "Internet2. . . and Counting." *CIO Magazine* (September 1, 1999).

Glezer, Chanan, and **Surya B. Yadav.** "A Conceptual Model of an Intelligent Catalog Sarch System." *Journal of Organizational Computing and Electronic Commerce* 11, no. 1 (2001).

Glover, Eric J., Steve Lawrence, Michael D. Gordon, William P. Birmingham, and **C. Lee Giles.** "Web Search-Your Way." *Communications of the ACM* 44, no. 12 (December 2001).

Grote, Brigitte, Thomas Rose, and **Gerhard Peter.** "Filter and Broker: An Integrated Architecture for Information Mediation of

Dynamic Sources." *Journal of Organizational Computing and Electronic Commerce* 12, no. 2 (2002).

Hearst, Marti, Arne Elliott, Jennifer English, Rashmi Sinha, Kirsten Swearinge, and **Ka-Ping Yee.** "Finding the Flow in Web Search." *Communications of the ACM* 45, no. 9 (Septeber 2002).

Huff, Sid, Malcolm C. Munro, and **Barbara H. Martin.** "Growth Stages of End User Computing." *Communications of the ACM* (May 1988).

Isakowitz, Tomas, Michael Bieber, and **Fabio Vitali.** "Web Information Systems." *Communications of the ACM* 41, no. 7 (July 1998).

Kanter, Rosabeth Moss. "The Ten Deadly Mistakes of Wanna-Dots." *Harvard Business Review* (January 2001).

Kautz, Henry, Bart Selman, and **Mehul Shah.** "ReferralWeb: Combining Social Networks and Collaborative Filtering." *Communications of the ACM* 40, no. 3 (March 1997).

Keen, Peter. "Ready for the 'New' B2B?" *Computerworld* (September 11, 2000).

Kendall, Kenneth E., and **Julie E. Kendall.** "Information Delivery Systems: An Exploration of Web Push and Pull Technologies." *Communications of the Association for Information Systems* 1 (April 1999).

Kontzer, Tony. "More Than an In-Box." *InformationWeek* (May 6, 2002).

Kuo, Geng-Sheng, and **Jing-Pei Lin.** "New Design Concepts for an Intelligent Internet." *Communications of the ACM* 41, no. 11 (November 1998).

Lieberman, Henry, Christopher Fry, and **Louis Weitzman.** "Exploring the Web with Reconnaissance Agents." *Communications of the ACM* 44, no. 8 (August 2001).

Papazoglou, Mike P. "Agent-Oriented Technology in Support of E-Business." *Communications of the ACM* 44, no. 4 (April 2001).

Pitkow, James, Hinrich Schutze, Todd Cass, Rob Cooley, Don Turnbull, Andy Edmonds, Eytan Adar, and **Thomas Breuel.** "Personalized Search." *Communications of the ACM* 45, no. 9 (September 2002)

Sweeney, Terry. "Voice Over IP Builds Momentum." *InformationWeek* (November 20, 2000).

Tischelle, George, and **Sandra Swanson.** "Not Just Kid Stuff." *InformationWeek* (September 3, 2001).

Valera, Francisco, Jorge E. López de Vergara, José I. Moreno, Víctor A. Villagrá, and **Julio Berrocal.** "Communication Management Experiences in E-commerce." *Communications of the ACM* 44, no. 4 (April 2001).

Varshney, Upkar, Andy Snow, Matt McGivern, and **Christi Howard.** "Voice Over IP." *Communications of the ACM* 45, no. 1 (January 2002).

Vetter, Ron. "The Wireless Web." *Communications of the ACM* 44, no. 3 (March 2001).

Wagner, Christine, and **Efraim Turban.** "Are Intelligent E-Commerce Agents Partners or Predators?" *Communications of the ACM* 45, no.5 (May 2002).

Wareham, Jonathan, and **Armando Levy.** "Who Will Be the Adopters of 3G Mobile Computing Devices? A Probit Estimation of Mobile Telecom Diffusion." *Journal of Organizational Computing and Electronic Commerce* 12, no. 2 (2002).

Weiser, Mark. "What Ever Happened to the Next-Generation Internet?" *Communications of the ACM* 44, no. 9 (September 2001).

Westin, Alan F., Heather A. Schweder, Michael A. Baker, and **Sheila Lehman.** *The Changing Workplace.* New York: Knowledge Industries (1995).

CHAPTER 10

Anandarajan, Murugan, "Profiling Web Usage in the Workplace: A Behavior-Based Artificial Intelligence Approach." *Journal of Management Information Systems* 19, no. 1 (Summer 2002).

Ackerman, Mark S., and **Christine A. Halverson.** "Reexamining Organizational Memory." *Communications of the ACM* 43, no. 1 (January 2000).

Alavi, Maryam, and **Dorothy E. Leidner.** "Knowledge Management and Knowledge Management Systems." *MIS Quarterly* 25, no. 1 (March 2001).

Alavi, Maryam, and **Dorothy Leidner.** "Knowledge Management Systems: Issues, Challenges, and Benefits." *Communications of the Association for Information Systems* 1 (February 1999).

Allen, Bradley P. "CASE-Based Reasoning: Business Applications." *Communications of the ACM* 37, no. 3 (March 1994).

Anandarajan, Murugan. "Profiling Web Usage in the Workplace: A Behavior-Based Artificial Intelligence Approach." *Journal of Management Information Systems* 19, no. 1 (Summer 2002).

Badler, Norman I., Martha S. Palmer, and **Rama Bindiganavale.** "Animation Control for Real-time Virtual Humans." *Communications of the ACM* 42, no. 8 (August 1999).

Balasubramanian, V., and **Alf Bashian.** "Document Management and Web Technologies: Alice Marries the Mad Hatter." *Communications of the ACM* 41, no. 7 (July 1998).

Bargeron, David, Jonathan Grudin, Anoop Gupta, Elizabeth Sanocki, Francis Li, and **Scott Le Tiernan.** "Asynchronous Collaboration Around Multimedia Applied to On-Demand Education." *Journal of Management Information Systems* 18, No. 4 (Spring 2002).

Barker, Virginia E., and **Dennis E. O'Connor.** "Expert Systems for Configuration at Digital: XCON and Beyond." *Communications of the ACM* (March 1989).

Becerra-Fernandez, Irma and **Rajiv Sabherwal.** "Organizational Knowledge Management: A Contingency Perspective." *Journal of Management Information Systems* 18, no. 1 (Summer 2001).

Beer, Randall D., Roger D. Quinn, Hillel J. Chiel, and **Roy E. Ritzman.** "Biologically Inspired Approaches to Robots." *Communications of the ACM* 40, no. 3 (March 1997).

Bieer, Michael, Douglas Englebart Richard Furuta, Starr Roxanne Hiltz, John Noll, Jennifer Preece, Edward A. Stohr, Murray Turoff, and **Bartel Van de Walle.** "Toward Virtual Community Knowledge Evolution." *Journal of Management Information Systems* 18, no. 4 (Spring 2002).

Birkinshaw, Julian, and **Tony Sheehan.** "Managing the Knowledge Life Cycle." *MIT Sloan Management Review* 44, no. 1 (Fall 2002).

Blanning, Robert W., David R. King, James R. Marsden, and **Ann C. Seror.** "Intelligent Models of Human Organizations: The State of the Art." *Journal of Organizational Computing* 2, no. 2 (1992).

Booth, Corey, and **Shashi Buluswar.** "The Return of Artificial Intelligence," *The McKinsey Quarterly* no. 2 (2002).

Brutzman, Don. "The Virtual Reality Modeling Language and Java." *Communications of the ACM* 41, no. 6 (June 1998).

Burtka, Michael. "Generic Algorithms." *The Stern Information Systems Review* 1, no. 1 (Spring 1993).

Busch, Elizabeth, Matti Hamalainen, Clyde W. Holsapple, Yongmoo Suh, and **Andrew B. Whinston.** "Issues and Obstacles in the Development of Team Support Systems." *Journal of Organizational Computing* 1, no. 2 (April–June 1991).

Cho, Sungzoon, Chigeun Han, Dae Hee Han, and **Hyung-Il Kim.** "Web-Based Keystroke Dynamics Identity Verification Using

Neural Network." *Journal of Organizational Computing and Electronic Commerce* 10, no. 4 (2000).

Churchland, Paul M., and Patricia Smith Churchland. "Could a Machine Think?" *Scientific American* (January 1990).

Cole, Kevin, Olivier Fischer, and Phyllis Saltzman. "Just-in-Time Knowledge Delivery." *Communications of the ACM* 40, no. 7 (July 1997).

Cross, Rob, and Lloyd Baird. "Technology is Not Enough: Improving Performance by Building Organizational Memory." *Sloan Management Review* 41, no. 3 (Spring 2000).

Cross, Rob, Nitin Nohria, and Andrew Parker. "Six Myths about Informal Networks and How to Overcome Them." *Sloan Management Review* 43, no. 3 (Spring 2002)

Davenport, Thomas H., David W. DeLong, and Michael C. Beers. "Successful Knowledge Management Projects." *Sloan Management Review* 39, no. 2 (Winter 1998).

Davenport, Thomas H., and Lawrence Prusak. *Working Knowledge: How Organizations Manage What They Know.* Boston, MA: Harvard Business School Press (1997).

Davenport, Thomas H., Robert J. Thomas and Susan Cantrell. "The Mysterious Art and Science of Knowledge-Worker Performance." *MIT Sloan Management Review* 44, no. 1 (Fall 2002).

Dhar, Vasant. "Plausibility and Scope of Expert Systems in Management." *Journal of Management Information Systems* (Summer 1987).

Dhar, Vasant, and Roger Stein. *Intelligent Decision Support Methods: The Science of Knowledge Work.* Upper Saddle River, NJ: Prentice Hall (1997).

Earl, Michael. "Knowledge Management Strategies: Toward a Taxonomy." *Journal of Management Information Systems* 18, no. 1 (Summer 2001).

Earl, Michael J., and Ian A. Scott. "What Is a Chief Knowledge Officer?" *Sloan Management Review* 40, no. 2 (Winter 1999).

El Najdawi, M. K., and Anthony C. Stylianou. "Expert Support Systems: Integrating AI Technologies." *Communications of the ACM* 36, no. 12 (December 1993).

Farhoomand, Ali, and Don H. Drury. "Managerial Information Overload." *Communications of the ACM* 45, no. 10 (October 2002).

Favela, Jesus. "Capture and Dissemination of Specialized Knowledge in Network Organizations." *Journal of Organizational Computing and Electronic Commerce* 7, nos. 2 and 3 (1997).

Fazlollahi, Bijan, and Rustam Vahidov. "A Method for Generation of Alternatives by Decision Support Systems." *Journal of Management Information Systems* 18, no. 2 (Fall 2001).

Feigenbaum, Edward A. "The Art of Artificial Intelligence: Themes and Case Studies in Knowledge Engineering." *Proceedings of the IJCAI* (1977).

Flash, Cynthia. "Who is the CKO?" *Knowledge Management* (May 2001).

Gelernter, David. "The Metamorphosis of Information Management." *Scientific American* (August 1989).

Glushko, Robert J., Jay M. Tenenbaum, and Bart Meltzer. "An XML Framework for Agent-Based E-Commerce." *Communications of the ACM* 42, no. 3 (March 1999).

Gold, Andrew H., Arvind Malhotra, and Albert H. Segars. "Knowledge Management: An Organizational Capabilities Perspective." *Journal of Management Information Systems* 18, no. 1 (Summer 2001).

Goldberg, David E. "Genetic and Evolutionary Algorithms Come of Age." *Communications of the ACM* 37, no. 3 (March 1994).

Grant, Robert M. "Prospering in Dynamically-Competitive Environments: Organizational Capability as Knowledge Integration." *Organization Science* 7, no. 4 (July–August 1996).

Gregor, Shirley, and Izak Benbasat. "Explanations from Intelligent Systems: Theoretical Foundations and Implications for Practice." *MIS Quarterly* 23, no. 4 (December 1999).

Grover, Varun, and Thomas H. Davenport. "General Perspectives on Knowledge Management: Fostering a Research Agenda." *Journal of Management Information Systems* 18, no. 1 (Summer 2001).

Guerra, Anthony. "Goldman Sachs Embraces Rules-Based Solution." *Wall Street and Technology* (May 2001).

Hansen, Morton, and Bolko von Oetinger. "Introducing T-Shaped Managers: Knowledge Management's Next Generation." *Harvard Business Review* (March 2001).

Hansen, Morton T., Nitin Nohria, and Thomas Tierney. "What's Your Strategy for Knowledge Management?" *Harvard Business Review* (March–April 1999).

Hayes-Roth, Frederick, and Neil Jacobstein. "The State of Knowledge-Based Systems." *Communications of the ACM* 37, no. 3 (March 1994).

Hinton, Gregory. "How Neural Networks Learn from Experience." *Scientific American* (September 1992).

Holland, John H. "Genetic Algorithms." *Scientific American* (July 1992).

Housel, Tom, and Arthur A. Bell. *Measuring and Managing Knowledge.* New York: McGraw-Hill (2001).

Housel, Thomas J., Omar El Sawy, Jianfang J. Zhong, and Waymond Rodgers. "Measuring the Return on E-Business Initiatives at the Process Level: The Knowledge Value-Added Approach." *ICIS* (2001).

Jarvenpaa, Sirkka L., and D. Sandy Staples. "Exploring Perceptions of Organizational Ownership of Information and Expertise." *Journal of Management Information Systems* 18, no. 1 (Summer 2001).

Lee, Soonchul. "The Impact of Office Information Systems on Power and Influence." *Journal of Management Information Systems* 8, no. 2 (Fall 1991).

Leonard-Barton, Dorothy, and John J. Sviokla. "Putting Expert Systems to Work." *Harvard Business Review* (March–April 1988).

Liu, Ziming, and David G. Stork. "Is Paperless Really More?" *Communications of the ACM* 43, no. 11 (November 2000).

Lou, Hao, and Richard W. Scannell. "Acceptance of Groupware: The Relationships Among Use, Satisfaction, and Outcomes." *Journal of Organizational Computing and Electronic Commerce* 6, no. 2 (1996).

Maes, Patti. "Agents that Reduce Work and Information Overload." *Communications of the ACM* 38, no. 7 (July 1994).

Maes, Patti, Robert H. Guttman, and Alexandros G. Moukas. "Agents that Buy and Sell." *Communications of the ACM* 42, no. 3 (March 1999).

Malhotra, Arvind, Ann Majchrzak, Robert Carman, and Vern Lott. "Radical Innovation without Collocation: A Case Study at Boeing Rocketdyne." *MIS Quarterly* 25, no. 2 (June 2001).

Markus, M. Lynne. "Toward a Theory of Knowledge Reuse: Types of Knowledge Reuse Situations and Factors in Reuse Success." *Journal of Management Information Systems* 18, no. 1 (Summer 2001).

McCarthy, John. "Generality in Artificial Intelligence." *Communications of the ACM* (December 1987).

Munakata, Toshinori, and Yashvant Jani. "Fuzzy Systems: An Overview." *Communications of the ACM* 37, no. 3 (March 1994).

Nidumolu, Sarma R., Mani Subramani, and Alan Aldrich. "Situated Learning and the Situated Knowledge Web:

Exploring the Ground Beneath Knowledge Management." *Journal of Management Information Systems* 18, no. 1 (Summer 2001).

O'Leary, Daniel, and Peter Selfridge. "Knowledge management for Best Practices." *Communications of the ACM* 43, no. 11es (November 2000).

O'Leary, Daniel, Daniel Kuokka, and Robert Plant. "Artificial Intelligence and Virtual Organizations." *Communications of the ACM* 40, no. 1 (January 1997).

Orlikowski, Wanda J. "Knowing in Practice: Enacting a Collective Capability in Distributed Organizing." *Organization Science* 13, no. 3 (May-June 2002).

Orlikowski, Wanda J. "Learning from Notes: Organizational Issues in Groupware Implementation." Sloan Working Paper, no. 3428. Cambridge, MA: Sloan School of Management, Massachusetts Institute of Technology.

Shan L. Pan, Ming-Huei Hsieh, and Helen Chen. "Knowledge Sharing through Intranet-Based Learning." *Journal of Organizational Computing and Electronic Commerce* 11, no. 3 (2001).

Piccoli, Gabriele, Rami Ahmad, and Blake Ives. "Web-Based Virtual Learning Environments: A Research Framework and a Preliminary Assessment of Effectiveness in Basic IT Skills Training." *MIS Quarterly* 25, no. 4 (December 2001).

Pomerol, Jean-Charles, Patrick Brezillon, and Laurent Pasquier. "Operational Knowledge Representation for Practical Decision Making." *Journal of Management Information Systems* 18, No. 4 (Spring 2002).

Ranft, Annette L., and Michael D. Lord. "Acquiring New Technologies and Capabilities: A Grounded Model of Acquisition Implementation." *Organization Science* 13, no. 4 (July–August 2002).

Ruhleder, Karen, and John Leslie King. "Computer Support for Work Across Space, Time, and Social Worlds." *Journal of Organizational Computing* 1, no. 4 (1991).

Rumelhart, David E., Bernard Widrow, and Michael A. Lehr. "The Basic Ideas in Neural Networks." *Communications of the ACM* 37, no. 3 (March 1994).

Salisbury, J. Kenneth, Jr. "Making Graphics Physically Tangible." *Communications of the ACM* 42, no. 8 (August 1999).

Schultze, Ulrike, and Betty Vandenbosch. "Information Overload in a Groupware Environment: Now You See It, Now You Don't." *Journal of Organizational Computing and Electronic Commerce* 8, no. 2 (1998).

Selker, Ted. "Coach: A Teaching Agent that Learns." *Communications of the ACM* 37, no. 7 (July 1994).

Sibigtroth, James M. "Implementing Fuzzy Expert Rules in Hardware." *AI Expert* (April 1992).

Sproull, Lee, and Sara Kiesler. *Connections: New Ways of Working in the Networked Organization.* Cambridge, MA: MIT Press (1992).

Starbuck, William H. "Learning by Knowledge-Intensive Firms." *Journal of Management Studies* 29, no. 6 (November 1992).

Storey, Veda C., and Robert C. Goldstein. "Knowledge-Based Approaches to Database Design," *MIS Quarterly* 17, no. 1 (March 1993).

Stylianou, Anthony C., Gregory R. Madey, and Robert D. Smith. "Selection Criteria for Expert System Shells: A Socio-Technical Framework." *Communications of the ACM* 35, no. 10 (October 1992).

Sukhatme, Gaurav S., and Maja J. Mataric. "Embedding Robots into the Internet." *Communications of the ACM* 43, no. 5 (May 2000).

Sviokla, John J. "An Examination of the Impact of Expert Systems on the Firm: The Case of XCON." *MIS Quarterly* 14, no. 5 (June 1990).

———. "Expert Systems and Their Impact on the Firm: The Effects of PlanPower Use on the Information Processing Capacity of the Financial Collaborative." *Journal of Management Information Systems* 6, no. 3 (Winter 1989–1990).

Trippi, Robert, and Efraim Turban. "The Impact of Parallel and Neural Computing on Managerial Decision Making." *Journal of Management Information Systems* 6, no. 3 (Winter 1989–1990).

Vandenbosch, Betty, and Michael J. Ginzberg. "Lotus Notes and Collaboration: Plus ca change . . . " *Journal of Management Information Systems* 13, no. 3 (Winter 1997).

Wakefield, Julie. "Complexity's Business Model." *Scientific American* (January 2001).

Walczak, Stephen. "An Empirical Analysis of Data Requirements for Financial Forecasting with Neural Networks." *Journal of Management Information Systems* 17, no. 4 (Spring 2001).

Walczak, Steven. "Gaining Competitive Advantage for Trading in Emerging Capital Markets with Neural Networks." *Journal of Management Information Systems* 16, no. 2 (Fall 1999).

Wang, Huaiqing, John Mylopoulos, and Stephen Liao. "Intelligent Agents and Financial Risk Monitoring Systems." *Communications of the ACM* 45, no. 3 (March 2002).

Weitzel, John R., and Larry Kerschberg. "Developing Knowledge Based Systems: Reorganizing the System Development Life Cycle." *Communications of the ACM* (April 1989).

Widrow, Bernard, David E. Rumelhart, and Michael A. Lehr. "Neural Networks: Applications in Industry, Business, and Science." *Communications of the ACM* 37, no. 3 (March 1994).

Wijnhoven, Fons. "Designing Organizational Memories: Concept and Method." *Journal of Organizational Computing and Electronic Commerce* 8, no. 1 (1998).

Wong, David, Noemi Paciorek, and Dana Moore. "Java-Based Mobile Agents." *Communications of the ACM* 42, no. 3 (March 1999).

Zadeh, Lotfi A. "The Calculus of Fuzzy If/Then Rules." *AI Expert* (March 1992).

Zadeh, Lotfi A. "Fuzzy Logic, Neural Networks, and Soft Computing." *Communications of the ACM* 37, no. 3 (March 1994).

Zhao, J. Leon, Akhil Kumar, and Edward W. Stohr. "Workflow-Centric Information Distribution Through E-Mail." *Journal of Management Information Systems* 17, no. 3 (Winter 2000–2001).

Zhao, J. Leon, and Vincent H. Resh. "Internet Publishing and Transformation of Knowledge Processes." *Communications of the ACM* 44, no. 12 (December 2001).

CHAPTER 11

Alavi, Maryam, and Erich A. Joachimsthaler. "Revisiting DSS Implementation Research: A Meta-Analysis of the Literature and Suggestions for Researchers." *MIS Quarterly* 16, no. 1 (March 1992).

Apte, Chidanand, Bing Liu, Edwin P. D. Pednault, and Padhraic Smuth. "Business Applications of Data Mining." *Communications of the ACM* 45, no. 8 (August 2002).

Barkhi, Reza. "The Effects of Decision Guidance and Problem Modeling on Group Decision Making." *Journal of Management Information Systems* 18, no. 3 (Winter 2001–2002).

Brachman, Ronald J., Tom Khabaza, Willi Kloesgen, Gregory Piatetsky-Shapiro, and Evangelos Simoudis. "Mining Business Databases." *Communications of the ACM* 39, no. 11 (November 1996).

Caouette, Margarette J., and Bridget N. O'Connor. "The Impact of Group Support Systems on Corporate Teams' Stages of

Development." *Journal of Organizational Computing and Electronic Commerce* 8, no. 1 (1998).

Chidambaram, Laku. "Relational Development in Computer-Supported Groups." *MIS Quarterly* 20, no. 2 (June 1996).

Del Rosario, Elise. "Logistical Nightmare." *OR/MS Today* (April 1999).

Dennis, Alan R. "Information Exchange and Use in Group Decision Making: You Can Lead a Group to Information, but You Can't Make It Think." *MIS Quarterly* 20, no. 4 (December 1996).

Dennis, Alan R., Craig K. Tyran, Douglas R. Vogel, and **Jay Nunamaker, Jr.** "Group Support Systems for Strategic Planning." *Journal of Management Information Systems* 14, no. 1 (Summer 1997).

Dennis, Alan R., Jay E. Aronson, William G. Henriger, and **Edward D. Walker III.** "Structuring Time and Task in Electronic Brainstorming." *MIS Quarterly* 23, no. 1 (March 1999).

Dennis, Alan R., Jay F. Nunamaker, Jr., and **Douglas R. Vogel.** "A Comparison of Laboratory and Field Research in the Study of Electronic Meeting Systems." *Journal of Management Information Systems* 7, no. 3 (Winter 1990–1991).

Dennis, Alan R., Joey F. George, Len M. Jessup, Jay F. Nunamaker, and **Douglas R. Vogel.** "Information Technology to Support Electronic Meetings." *MIS Quarterly* 12, no. 4 (December 1988).

Dennis, Alan R., Sridar K. Pootheri, and **Vijaya L. Natarajan.** "Lessons from Early Adopters of Web Groupware." *Journal of Management Information Systems* 14, no. 4 (Spring 1998).

Dennis, Alan R., and **Barbara H. Wixom,** "Investigating the Moderators of the Group Support Systems Use with Meta-Analysis." *Journal of Management Information Systems* 18, no. 3 (Winter 2001–2002).

Dennis, Alan R., Barbara H. Wixom, and **Robert J. Vandenberg.** "Understanding Fit and Appropriation Effects in Group Support Systems Via Meta-Analysis." *MIS Quarterly* 25, no. 2 (June 2001).

DeSanctis, Geraldine, and **R. Brent Gallupe.** "A Foundation for the Study of Group Decision Support Systems." *Management Science* 33, no. 5 (May 1987).

Dietrich, Brenda, Nick Donofrio, Grace Lin, and **Jane Snowdon.** "Big Benefits for Big Blue." *OR/MS Today* (June 2000).

Dutta, Soumitra, Berend Wierenga, and **Arco Dalebout.** "Designing Management Support Systems Using an Integrative Perspective." *Communications of the ACM* 40, no. 6 (June 1997).

Edelstein, Herb. "Technology How To: Mining Data Warehouses." *InformationWeek* (January 8, 1996).

El Sawy, Omar. "Personal Information Systems for Strategic Scanning in Turbulent Environments." *MIS Quarterly* 9, no. 1 (March 1985).

El Sherif, Hisham, and **Omar A. El Sawy.** "Issue-Based Decision Support Systems for the Egyptian Cabinet." *MIS Quarterly* 12, no. 4 (December 1988).

Fayyad, Usama, Gregory Pitatetsky-Shapiro, and **Padhraic Smyth.** "The KDD Process of Extracting Useful Knowledge from Data." *Communications of the ACM* 39, no. 11 (November 1996).

Fjermestad, Jerry. "An Integrated Framework for Group Support Systems." *Journal of Organizational Computing and Electronic Commerce* 8, no. 2 (1998).

Fjermestad, Jerry, and **Starr Roxanne Hiltz.** "An Assessment of Group Support Systems Experimental Research: Methodology, and Results." *Journal of Management Information Systems* 15, no. 3 (Winter, 1998–1999).

_____. "Group Support Systems: A Descriptive Evaluation of Case and Field Studies." *Journal of Management Information Systems* 17, no. 3 (Winter 2000–2001).

Forgionne, Guiseppe. "Management Support System Effectiveness: Further Empirical Evidence." *Journal of the Association for Information Systems* 1 (May 2000).

Gallupe, R. Brent, Geraldine DeSanctis, and **Gary W. Dickson.** "Computer-Based Support for Group Problem-Finding: An Experimental Investigation." *MIS Quarterly* 12, no. 2 (June 1988).

George, Joey. "Organizational Decision Support Systems." *Journal of Management Information Systems* 8, no. 3 (Winter 1991–1992).

Ginzberg, Michael J., W. R. Reitman, and **E. A. Stohr,** eds. *Decision Support Systems.* New York: North Holland Publishing Co. (1982).

Grobowski, Ron, Chris McGoff, Doug Vogel, Ben Martz, and **Jay Nunamaker.** "Implementing Electronic Meeting Systems at IBM: Lessons Learned and Success Factors." *MIS Quarterly* 14, no. 4 (December 1990).

Hender, Jillian M., Douglas L. Dean, Thomas L. Rodgers, and **Jay F. Nunamaker Jr.** "An Examination of the Impact of Stimuli Type and GSS Structure on Creativity." *Journal of Management Information Systems* 18, No. 4 (Spring 2002).

Henderson, John C., and **David A. Schilling.** "Design and Implementation of Decision Support Systems in the Public Sector." *MIS Quarterly* (June 1985).

Hilmer, Kelly M., and **Alan R. Dennis.** "Stimulating Thinking: Cultivating Better Decisions with Groupware Through Categorization." *Journal of Management Information Systems* 17, no. 3 (Winter 2000–2001).

Hogue, Jack T. "Decision Support Systems and the Traditional Computer Information System Function: An Examination of Relationships During DSS Application Development." *Journal of Management Information Systems* (Summer 1985).

Hogue, Jack T. "A Framework for the Examination of Management Involvement in Decision Support Systems." *Journal of Management Information Systems* 4, no. 1 (Summer 1987).

Houdeshel, George, and **Hugh J. Watson.** "The Management Information and Decision Support (MIDS) System at Lockheed, Georgia." *MIS Quarterly* 11, no. 2 (March 1987).

Kalakota, Ravi, Jan Stallaert, and **Andrew B. Whinston.** "Worldwide Real-Time Decision Support Systems for Electronic Commerce Applications." *Journal of Organizational Computing and Electronic Commerce* 6, no. 1 (1996).

Keen, Peter G. W., and **M. S. Scott Morton.** *Decision Support Systems: An Organizational Perspective.* Reading, MA: Addison-Wesley (1982).

Kohavi, Ron, Neal J. Rothleder, and **Evangelos Simoudis.** "Emerging Trends in Business Analytics." *Communications of the ACM* 45, no. 8 (August 2002).

Lais, Sami. "The Power of Location." *Computerworld* (April 15, 2002).

Leidner, Dorothy E., and **Joyce Elam.** "Executive Information Systems: Their Impact on Executive Decision Making." *Journal of Management Information Systems* (Winter 1993–1994).

Leidner, Dorothy E., and **Joyce Elam.** "The Impact of Executive Information Systems on Organizational Design, Intelligence, and Decision Making." *Organization Science* 6, no. 6 (November–December 1995).

Levinson, Meredith. "They Know What You'll Buy Next Summer (They Hope)." *CIO Magazine* (May 1, 2002).

Lewe, Henrik, and **Helmut Krcmar.** "A Computer-Supported Cooperative Work Research Laboratory." *Journal of Management Information Systems* 8, no. 3 (Winter 1991–1992).

McCune, Jenny C. "Measuring Value." *Beyond Computing* (July/August 2000).

Miranda, Shaila M., and **Robert P. Bostrum.** "The Impact of Group Support Systems on Group Conflict and Conflict Management."

Journal of Management Information Systems 10, no. 3 (Winter 1993–1994).

———. "Meeting Facilitation: Process versus Content Interventions." *Journal of Management Information Systems* 15, no. 4 (Spring 1999).

"The New Role for 'Executive Information Systems." *I/S Analyzer* (January 1992).

Nidumolu, Sarma R., Seymour E. Goodman, Douglas R. Vogel, and Ann K. Danowitz. "Information Technology for Local Administration Support: The Governorates Project in Egypt." *MIS Quarterly* 20, no. 2 (June 1996).

Niederman, Fred, Catherine M. Beise, and Peggy M. Beranek. "Issues and Concerns about Computer-Supported Meetings: The Facilitator's Perspective." *MIS Quarterly* 20, no. 1 (March 1996).

Nunamaker, J. F., Alan R. Dennis, Joseph S. Valacich, Douglas R. Vogel, and Joey F. George. "Electronic Meeting Systems to Support Group Work." *Communications of the ACM* 34, no. 7 (July 1991).

Nunamaker, Jay, Robert O. Briggs, Daniel D. Mittleman, Douglas R. Vogel, and Pierre A. Balthazard. "Lessons from a Dozen Years of Group Support Systems Research: A Discussion of Lab and Field Findings." *Journal of Management Information Systems* 13, no. 3 (Winter 1997).

O'Keefe, Robert M., and Tim McEachern. "Web-based Customer Decision Support Systems." *Communications of the ACM* 41, no. 3 (March 1998).

PeopleSoft. "Spotlight on Performance at Detroit Edison." *www.peoplesoft.com*, accessed November 3, 2002.

Pinsonneault, Alain, Henri Barki, R. Brent Gallupe, and Norberto Hoppen. "Electronic Brainstorming: The Illusion of Productivity." *Information Systems Research* 10, no. 2 (July 1999).

Radding, Alan. "Analyze Your Customers." *Datamation* (September 25, 2000).

Rockart, John F., and David W. DeLong. *Executive Support Systems: The Emergence of Top Management Computer Use.* Homewood, IL: Dow-Jones Irwin (1988).

Schwabe, Gerhard. "Providing for Organizational Memory in Computer-Supported Meetings." *Journal of Organizational Computing and Electronic Commerce* 9, no. 2 and 3 (1999).

Shand, Dawne. "Making It Up as You Go." *Knowledge Management* (April 2000).

Sharda, Ramesh, and David M. Steiger. "Inductive Model Analysis Systems: Enhancing Model Analysis in Decision Support Systems." *Information Systems Research* 7, no. 3 (September 1996).

Silver, Mark S. "Decision Support Systems: Directed and Nondirected Change." *Information Systems Research* 1, no. 1 (March 1990).

Sniezek, Janet, David C. Wilkins, Patrick L. Wadlington, and Michael R. Baumann. "Training for Crisis Decision Making: Psychological Issues and Computer-Based Solutions." *Journal of Management Information Systems* 18, No. 4 (Spring 2002).

Songini, Mark L. "Setting the Price Right." *Computerworld* (June 3, 2002).

Sprague, R. H., and E. D. Carlson. *Building Effective Decision Support Systems.* Englewood Cliffs, NJ: Prentice Hall (1982).

Todd, Peter, and Izak Benbasat. "Evaluating the Impact of DSS, Cognitive Effort, and Incentives on Strategy Selection." *Information Systems Research* 10, no. 4 (December 1999).

Turban, Efraim, and Jay E. Aronson. *Decision Support Systems and Intelligent Systems,* 6th ed. Upper Saddle River, NJ: Prentice Hall (2000).

Tyran, Craig K., Alan R. Dennis, Douglas R. Vogel, and J. F. Nunamaker, Jr. "The Application of Electronic Meeting

Technology to Support Senior Management." *MIS Quarterly* 16, no. 3 (September 1992).

Vedder, Richard G., Michael T. Vanacek, C. Stephen Guynes, and James J. Cappel. "CEO and CIO Perspectives on Competitive Intelligence." *Communications of the ACM* 42, no. 8 (August 1999).

Volonino, Linda, and Hugh J. Watson. "The Strategic Business Objectives Method for EIS Development." *Journal of Management Information Systems* 7, no. 3 (Winter 1990–1991).

Walls, Joseph G., George R. Widmeyer, and Omar A. El Sawy. "Building an Information System Design Theory for Vigilant EIS." *Information Systems Research* 3, no. 1 (March 1992).

Watson, Hugh J., Astrid Lipp, Pamela Z. Jackson, Abdelhafid Dahmani, and William B. Fredenberger. "Organizational Support for Decision Support Systems." *Journal of Management Information Systems* 5, no. 4 (Spring 1989).

Watson, Hugh J., R. Kelly Rainer, Jr., and Chang E. Koh. "Executive Information Systems: A Framework for Development and a Survey of Current Practices." *MIS Quarterly* 15, no. 1 (March 1991).

Watson, Richard T., Teck-Hua Ho, and K. S. Raman. "Culture: A Fourth Dimension of Group Support Systems." *Communications of the ACM* 37, no. 10 (October 1994).

Whiting, Rick. "Companies Boost Sales Efforts with Predictive Analysis." *Information Week* (February 25, 2002).

Wilson, Meredith. "Slices of Life." *CIO Magazine* (August 15, 2000).

Youngjin, Yoo, and Maryam Alavi. "Media and Group Cohesion: Relative Influences on Social Presence, Task Participation, and Group Consensus." *MIS Quarterly* 25, no. 3 (September 2001).

CHAPTER 12

Agarwal, Ritu, Prabudda De, Atish P. Sinha, and Mohan Tanniru. "On the Usability of OO Representations." *Comunications of the ACM* 43, no. 10 (October 2000).

Agarwal, Ritu, Jayesh Prasad, Mohan Tanniru, and John Lynch. "Risks of Rapid Application Development." *Communications of the ACM* 43, no. 11 (November 2000).

Ahituv, Niv, and Seev Neumann. "A Flexible Approach to Information System Development." *MIS Quarterly* (June 1984).

Alavi, Maryam, R. Ryan Nelson, and Ira R. Weiss. "Strategies for End-User Computing: An Integrative Framework." *Journal of Management Information Systems* 4, no. 3 (Winter 1987–1988).

Alavi, Maryam. "An Assessment of the Prototyping Approach to Information System Development." *Communications of the ACM* 27 (June 1984).

Anderson, Evan A. "Choice Models for the Evaluation and Selection of Software Packages." *Journal of Management Information Systems* 6, no. 4 (Spring 1990).

Barua, Anitesh, Sophie C. H. Lee, and Andrew B. Whinston. "The Calculus of Reengineering." *Information Systems Research* 7, no. 4 (December 1996).

Baskerville, Richard L., and Jan Stage. "Controlling Prototype Development Through Risk Analysis." *MIS Quarterly* 20, no. 4 (December 1996).

Brier, Tom, Jerry Luftman, and Raymond Papp. "Enablers and Inhibitors of Business—IT Alignment." *Communications of the Association for Information Systems* 1 (March 1999).

Broadbent, Marianne, Peter Weill, and Don St. Clair. "The Implications of Information Technology Infrastructure for Business Process Redesign." *MIS Quarterly* 23, no. 2 (June 1999).

Bullen, Christine, and John F. Rockart. "A Primer on Critical Success Factors." Cambridge, MA: Center for Information Systems Research, Sloan School of Management (1981).

Champy, James A. *X-Engineering the Corporation: Reinventing Your Business in the Digital Age.* New York: Warner Books (2002).

Cline, Marshall, and Mike Girou. "Enduring Business Themes." *Communications of the ACM* 43, no. 5 (May 2000).

Davenport, Thomas H., and James E. Short. "The New Industrial Engineering: Information Technology and Business Process Redesign." *Sloan Management Review* 31, no. 4 (Summer 1990).

Davidson, W. H. "Beyond Engineering: The Three Phases of Business Transformation." *IBM Systems Journal* 32, no. 1 (1993).

Davis, Gordon B. "Determining Management Information Needs: A Comparison of Methods." *MIS Quarterly* 1 (June 1977).

———. "Information Analysis for Information System Development." In *Systems Analysis and Design: A Foundation for the 1980's,* edited by W. W. Cotterman, J. D. Cougar, N. L. Enger, and F. Harold. New York: Wiley (1981).

———. "Strategies for Information Requirements Determination." *IBM Systems Journal* 1 (1982).

Deutsch, Claudia. "Six Sigma Enlightenment." *New York Times* (December 7, 1998).

Earl, Michael, and Bushra Khan. "E-Commerce Is Changing the Face of IT." *Sloan Management Review,* (Fall 2001)

Ein Dor, Philip, and Eli Segev. "Strategic Planning for Management Information Systems." *Management Science* 24, no. 15 (1978).

Fingar, Peter. "Component-Based Frameworks for E-Commerce." *Communications of the ACM* 43, no. 10 (October 2000).

Fuller, Mary K., and E. Burton Swanson. "Information Centers as Organizational Innovation." *Journal of Management Information Systems* 9, no. 1 (Summer 1992).

Gefen, David, and Catherine M. Ridings. "Implementation Team Responsiveness and User Evaluation of Customer Relationship Management: A Quasi-Experimental Design Study of Social Exchange Theory." *Journal of Management Information Systems* 19, no. 1 (Summer 2002).

Gill Philip. "Flower Power." *Oracle Profit Magazine* (August 1998).

Grant, Delvin. "A Wider View of Business Process Engineering." *Communications of the ACM* 45, no. 2 (February 2002).

Hagel III, John, and John Seeley Brown. "Your Next IT Strategy." *Harvard Business Review* (October, 2001).

Hammer, Michael. "Process Management and the Future of Six Sigma." *Sloan Management Review* 43, no. 2 (Winter 2002).

Hammer, Michael. "Reengineering Work: Don't Automate, Obliterate." *Harvard Business Review* (July–August 1990).

Hammer, Michael, and James Champy. *Reengineering the Corporation.* New York: HarperCollins Publishers (1993).

Hammer, Michael, and Steven A. Stanton. *The Reengineering Revolution.* New York: HarperCollins (1995).

Hirscheim, Rudy, and Mary Lacity. "The Myths and Realities of Information Technology Insourcing." *Communications of the ACM* 43, no. 2 (February 2000).

Hoffer, Jeffrey, Joey George, and Joseph Valacich. *Modern Systems Analysis and Design,* 3rd ed. Upper Saddle River, NJ: Prentice Hall (2002).

Hopkins, Jon. "Component Primer." *Communications of the ACM* 43, no. 10 (October 2000).

Huizing, Ard, Esther Koster, and Wim Bouman. "Balance in Business Process Reengineering: An Empirical Study of Fit and Performance." *Journal of Management Information Systems* 14, no. 1 (Summer 1997).

Irwin, Gretchen. "The Role of Similarity in the Reuse of Object-Oriented Analysis Models." *Journal of Management Information Systems* 19, no. 2 (Fall 2002).

Ivari, Juhani, Rudy Hirscheim, and Heinz K. Klein. "A Dynamic Framework for Classifying Information Systems Development Methodologies and Approaches." *Journal of Management Information Systems* 17, no. 3 (Winter 2000–2001).

Johnson, Richard A. "The Ups and Downs of Object-Oriented Systems Development." *Communications of the ACM* 43, no.10 (October 2000).

Keen, Peter G. W. *Shaping the Future: Business Design Through Information Technology.* Cambridge, MA: Harvard Business School Press (1991).

Kendall, Kenneth E., and Julie E. Kendall. *Systems Analysis and Design,* 5th ed. Upper Saddle River, NJ: Prentice Hall (2002).

Klein, Gary, James J. Jiang, and Debbie B. Tesch. "Wanted: Project Teams with a Blend of IS Professional Orientations." *Communications of the ACM* 45, no. 6 (June 2002).

Lee, Heeseok, and Woojong Suh. "A Workflow-Based Methodology for Developing Hypermedia Information Systems." *Journal of Organizational Computing and Electronic Commerce* 11, no. 2 (2001)

Lee, Jae Nam, and Young-Gul Kim. "Effect of Partnership Quality on IS Outsourcing Success." *Journal of Management Information Systems* 15, no. 4 (Spring 1999).

Martin, J., and C. McClure. "Buying Software Off the Rack." *Harvard Business Review* (November–December 1983).

Martin, James. *Application Development without Programmers.* Englewood Cliffs, NJ: Prentice Hall (1982).

McDougall, Paul, et al. "Decoding Web Services." *InformationWeek* (October 1, 2001).

Nerson, Jean-Marc. "Applying Object-Oriented Analysis and Design." *Communications of the ACM* 35, no. 9 (September 1992).

Nissen, Mark E. "Redesigning Reengineering through Measurement-Driven Inference," *MIS Quarterly* 22, no. 4 (December 1998).

Pancake, Cherri M. "The Promise and the Cost of Object Technology: A Five-Year Forecast." *Communications of the ACM* 38, no. 10 (October 1995).

Parker, M. M. "Enterprise Information Analysis: Cost-Benefit Analysis and the Data-Managed System." *IBM Systems Journal* 21 (1982).

Patel, Samir, and Suneel Saigal. "When Computers Learn to Talk: A Web Services Primer," *The McKinsey Quarterly* no. 1 (2002).

Phillips, James, and Dan Foody. "Building a Foundation for Web Services." *EAI Journal* (March 2002).

Prahalad, C. K., and M.S.. Krishnan. "Synchronizing Strategy and Information Technology." *Sloan Management Review* 43, no. 4 (Summer 2002).

Prahalad, C.K., and M.S. Krishnan. "The New Meaning of Quality in the Information Age." *Harvard Business Review* (September–October 1999).

Rivard, Suzanne, and Sid L. Huff. "Factors of Success for End-User Computing." *Communications of the ACM* 31, no. 5 (May 1988).

Rockart, John F. "Chief Executives Define Their Own Data Needs." *Harvard Business Review* (March–April 1979).

Rockart, John F., and Lauren S. Flannery. "The Management of End-User Computing." *Communications of the ACM* 26, no. 10 (October 1983).

Rockart, John F., and Michael E. Treacy. "The CEO Goes Online." *Harvard Business Review* (January–February 1982).

Sabherwahl, Rajiv. "The Role of Trust in IS Outsourcing Development Projects." *Communications of the ACM* 42, no. 2 (February 1999).

Schmidt, Douglas C., and Mohamed E. Fayad. "Lessons Learned Building Reusable OO Frameworks for Distributed Software." *Communications of the ACM* 40, no. 10 (October 1997).

Segars, Albert H., and Varun Grover. "Profiles of Strategic Information Systems Planning." *Information Systems Research* 10, no. 3 (September 1999).

Shank, Michael E., Andrew C. Boynton, and Robert W. Zmud. "Critical Success Factor Analysis as a Methodology for MIS Planning." *MIS Quarterly* (June 1985).

Sircar, Sumit, Sridhar P. Nerur, and Radhakanta Mahapatra. "Revolution or Evolution? A Comparison of Object-Oriented and Structured Systems Development Methods." *MIS Quarterly* 25, no. 4 (December 2001).

Swanson, E. Burton, and Enrique Dans. "System Life Expectancy and the Maintenance Effort: Exploring their Equilibration." *MIS Quarterly* 24, no. 2 (June 2000).

Tam, Kar Yan, and Kai Lung Hui. "A Choice Model for the Selection of Computer Vendors and Its Empirical Estimation" *Journal of Management Information Systems* 17, no. 4 (Spring 2001).

Thong, James Y.L., Chee-Sing Yap, and Kin-Lee Seah. "Business Process Reengineering in the Public Sector: The Case of the Housing Development Board in Singapore." *Journal of Management Information Systems* 17, no. 1 (Summer 2000).

Venkatraman, N. "Beyond Outsourcing: Managing IT Resources as a Value Center." *Sloan Management Review* (Spring 1997).

Vessey, Iris, and Sue A. Conger. "Requirements Specification: Learning Object, Process, and Data Methodologies." *Communications of the ACM* 37, no. 5 (May 1994).

Vessey, Iris, and Sue Conger. "Learning to Specify Information Requirements: The Relationship between Application and Methodology." *Journal of Management Information Systems* 10, no. 2 (Fall 1993).

Watad, Mahmoud M., and Frank J. DiSanzo. "Case Study: The Synergism of Telecommuting and Office Automation." *Sloan Management Review* 41, no. 2 (Winter 2000).

Willis, T. Hillman, and Debbie B. Tesch. "An Assessment of Systems Development Methodologies." *Journal of Information Technology Management* 2, no. 2 (1991).

Zachman, J. A. "Business Systems Planning and Business Information Control Study: A Comparison." *IBM Systems Journal* 21 (1982).

CHAPTER 13

Agarwal, Ritu, and Viswanath Venkatesnh. "Assessing a Firm's Web Presence: A Heuristic Evaluation Procedure for the Measurement of Usability." *Information Systems Research* 13, no.3 (September 2002).

Aladwani, Adel M. "An Integrated Performance Model of Information Systems Projects." *Journal of Management Information Systems* 19, no.1 (Summer 2002).

Alleman, James. "Real Options Real Opportunities." *Optimize Magazine* (January 2002).

Alter, Steven, and Michael Ginzberg. "Managing Uncertainty in MIS Implementation." *Sloan Management Review* 20 (Fall 1978).

Andres, Howard P., and Robert W. Zmud. "A Contingency Approach to Software Project Coordination." *Journal of Management Information Systems* 18, no. 3 (Winter 2001–2002).

Armstrong, Curtis P., and V. Sambamurthy. "Information Technology Assimilation in Firms: The Influence of Senior Leadership and IT Infrastructures." *Information Systems Research* 10, no. 4 (December 1999).

Attewell, Paul. "Technology Diffusion and Organizational Learning: The Case of Business Computing." *Organization Science,* no. 3 (1992).

Banker, Rajiv. "Value Implications of Relative Investments in Information Technology." Department of Information Systems and Center for Digital Economy Research, University of Texas at Dallas, January 23, 2001.

Barki, Henri, and Jon Hartwick. "Interpersonal Conflict and Its Management in Information Systems Development." *MIS Quarterly* 25, no.2 (June 2001).

Barki, Henri, Suzanne Rivard, and Jean Talbot. "An Integrative Contingency Model of Software Project Risk Management." *Journal of Management Information Systems* 17, no. 4 (Spring 2001).

Beath, Cynthia Mathis, and Wanda J. Orlikowski. "The Contradictory Structure of Systems Development Methodologies: Deconstructing the IS-User Relationship in Information Engineering." *Information Systems Research* 5, no. 4 (December 1994).

Benaroch, Michel. "Managing Information Technology Investment Risk: A Real Options Perspective." *Journal of Management Information Systems* 19, no. 2 (Fall 2002).

Benaroch, Michel, and Robert J. Kauffman. "Justifying Electronic Banking Network Expansion Using Real Options Analysis." *MIS Quarterly* 24, no. 2 (June 2000).

Bharadwaj, Anandhi. "A Resource-Based Perspective on Information Technology Capability and Firm Performance." *MIS Quarterly* 24, no. 1 (March 2000).

Bhattacherjee, Anoi. "Understanding Information Systems Continuance: An Expectation-Confirmation Model." *MIS Quarterly* 25, no.3 (September 2001).

Bhattacharjee, Sudip, and R. Ramesh. "Enterprise Computing Environments and Cost Assessment." *Communications of the ACM* 43, no. 10 (October 2000).

Boer, F. Peter. "Real Options: The IT Investment Risk Buster." *Optimize Magazine* (July 2002).

Bostrom, R. P., and J. S. Heinen. "MIS Problems and Failures: A Socio-Technical Perspective. Part I: The Causes." *MIS Quarterly* 1 (September 1977); "Part II: The Application of Socio-Technical Theory." *MIS Quarterly* 1 (December 1977).

Brooks, Frederick P. "The Mythical Man-Month." *Datamation* (December 1974).

Brynjolfsson, Erik. "The Contribution of Information Technology to Consumer Welfare." *Information Systems Research* 7, no. 3 (September 1996).

———. "The Productivity Paradox of Information Technology." *Communications of the ACM* 36, no. 12 (December 1993).

Brynjolfsson, Erik, and Lorin M. Hitt. "Beyond the Productivity Paradox." *Communications of the ACM* 41, no. 8 (August 1998).

Brynjolfsson, Erik, and Lorin M. Hitt. "Information Technology and Organizational Design: Evidence from Micro Data." (January 1998).

———. "New Evidence on the Returns to Information Systems." MIT Sloan School of Management (October 1993).

Brynjolfsson, Erik, and S. Yang. "Intangible Assets: How the Interaction of Computers and Organizational Structure Affects Stock Markets." MIT Sloan School of Management (2000).

Burkhardt, Grey E., Seymour E. Goodman, Arun Mehta, and Larry Press. "The Internet in India: Better Times Ahead?" *Communications of the ACM* 41, no. 11 (November 1998).

Buss, Martin D. J. "How to Rank Computer Projects." *Harvard Business Review* (January 1983).

Chatterjee, Debabroto, Carl Pacini, and V. Sambamurthy. "The Shareholder-Wealth and Trading Volume Effects of Information Technology Infrastructure Investments." *Journal of Management Information Systems* 19, no. 2 (Fall 2002).

Clement, Andrew, and Peter Van den Besselaar. "A Retrospective Look at PD Projects." *Communications of the ACM* 36, no. 4 (June 1993).

"Companies Struggle with ERP Implementations." *IntelligentERP News* (June 29, 2001).

Concours Group. "Delivering Large-Scale System Projects." (2000).

Cooper, Randolph B. "Information Technology Development Creativity: A Case Study of Attempted Radical Change." *MIS Quarterly* 24, no. 2 (June 2000).

Davamanirajan, Prabu, Tridas Mukhopadhyay, and Charles Kriebel. "Assessing the Business Value of Information Technology in Global Wholesale Banking: The Case of Trade Services." *Journal of Organizational Computing and Electronic Commerce* 12, no. 1 (2002).

Davenport, Thomas H. *Mission Critical: Realizing the Promise of Enterprise Systems.* Boston, MA: Harvard Business School Press, (2000).

Davern, Michael J. and Robert J. Kauffman. "Discovering Potential and Realizing Value form Information Technology Investments." *Journal of Management Information Systems* 16, no. 4 (Spring 2000).

Davis, Fred R. "Perceived Usefulness, Ease of Use, and User Acceptance of Information Technology." *MIS Quarterly* 13, no. 3 (September 1989).

De, Prabudda, and Thomas W. Ferrat. "An Information System Involving Competing Organizations." *Communications of the ACM* 41, no. 12 (December 1998).

De Berranger, Pascal, David Tucker, and Laurie Jones. "Internet Diffusion in Creative Micro-Businesses: Identifying Change Agent Characteristics as Critical Success Factors." *Journal of Organizational Computing and Electronic Commerce* 11, no. 3 (2001).

Dempsey, Jed, Robert E. Dvorak, Endre Holen, David Mark, and William F. Meehan III. "A Hard and Soft Look at IT Investments." *The McKinsey Quarterly* no. 1 (1998).

De Meyer, Arnoud, Christoph H. Loch, and Michael T. Pich. "Managing Project Uncertainty: From Variation to Chaos." *Sloan Management Review* 43, no.2 (Winter 2002).

Desmarais, Michel C., Richard Leclair, Jean-Yves Fiset, and Hichem Talbi. "Cost-Justifying Electronic Performance Support Systems." *Communications of the ACM* 40, no. 7 (July 1997).

Doll, William J. "Avenues for Top Management Involvement in Successful MIS Development." *MIS Quarterly* (March 1985).

Dos Santos, Brian. "Justifying Investments in New Information Technologies." *Journal of Management Information Systems* 7, no. 4 (Spring 1991).

Ein-Dor, Philip, and Eli Segev. "Organizational Context and the Success of Management Information Systems." *Management Science* 24 (June 1978).

El Sawy, Omar, and Burt Nanus. "Toward the Design of Robust Information Systems." *Journal of Management Information Systems* 5, no. 4 (Spring 1989).

Emery, James C. "Cost/Benefit Analysis of Information Systems." Chicago: Society for Management Information Systems Workshop Report No. 1 (1971).

Fichman, Robert G. "The Role of Aggregation in the Measurement of IT-Related Organizational Innovation." *MIS Quarterly* 25, no. 4 (December 2001).

Fichman, Robert G., and Scott A. Moses. "An Incremental Process for Software Implementation." *Sloan Management Review* 40, no. 2 (Winter 1999).

Frank, Robert, and Robin Sidel. "Firms that Lived by the Deal in '90s Now Sink by the Dozens." *Wall Street Journal* (June 6, 2002).

Franz, Charles, and Daniel Robey. "An Investigation of User-Led System Design: Rational and Political Perspectives." *Communications of the ACM* 27 (December 1984).

Gefen, David, and Catherine M. Ridings. "Implementation Team Responsiveness and User Evaluation of Customer Relationship Management: A Quasi-Experimental Design Study of Social Exchange Theory." *Journal of Management Information Systems* 19, no. 1 (Summer 2002).

Giaglis, George. "Focus Issue on Legacy Information Systems and Business Process Change: On the Integrated Design and Evaluation of Business Processes and Information Systems." *Communications of the AIS* 2, (July 1999).

Ginzberg, Michael J. "Early Diagnosis of MIS Implementation Failure: Promising Results and Unanswered Questions." *Management Science* 27 (April 1981).

Gogan, Janis L., Jane Fedorowicz, and Ashok Rao. "Assessing Risks in Two Projects: A Strategic Opportunity and a Necessary Evil." *Communications of the Association for Information Systems* 1 (May 1999).

Grover, Varun. "IS Investment Priorities in Contemporary Organizations." *Communications of the ACM* 41, no. 2 (February 1998).

Hartman, Amir. "Why Tech Falls Short of Expectations." *Optimize Magazine* (July 2002).

Hayes, Frank. "Don't Shrug Off Bugs." *Computerworld* (July 1, 2002).

Hitt, Lorin, D.J. Wu, and Xiaoge Zhou. "Investment in Enterprise Resource Planning: Business Impact and Productivity Measures." *Journal of Management Information Systems* 19, no. 1 (Summer 2002).

Housel, Thomas J., Omar El Sawy, JianfangJ. Zhong, and Waymond Rodgers. "Measuring the Return on e-Business Initiatives at the Process Level: The Knowledge Value-Added Approach." *ICIS* (2001).

Hunton, James E., and Beeler, Jesse D., "Effects of User Participation in Systems Development: A Longitudinal Field Study." *MIS Quarterly* 21, no. 4 (December 1997).

Irani, Zahir, and Peter E.D. Love. "The Propagation of Technology Management Taxonomies for Evaluating Investments in Information Systems." *Journal of Management Information Systems* 17, no.3 (Winter 2000–2001).

Johnson, Bradford C. "Retail: The Wal-Mart Effect." *The McKinsey Quarterly* (2002 no. 1).

Joshi, Kailash. "A Model of Users' Perspective on Change: The Case of Information Systems Technology Implementation." *MIS Quarterly* 15, no. 2 (June 1991).

Karat, John. "Evolving the Scope of User-Centered Design." *Communications of the ACM* 40, no. 7 (July 1997).

Keen, Peter W. "Information Systems and Organizational Change." *Communications of the ACM* 24 (January 1981).

Keil, Mark, Paul E. Cule, Kalle Lyytinen, and Roy C. Schmidt. "A Framework for Identifying Software Project Risks." *Communications of the ACM* 41, 11 (November 1998).

Keil, Mark, Joan Mann, and Arun Rai. "Why Software Projects Escalate: An Empirical Analysis and Test of Four Theoretical Models." *MIS Quarterly* 24, no. 4 (December 2000).

Keil, Mark, Richard Mixon, Timo Saarinen, and Virpi Tuunairen. "Understanding Runaway IT Projects." *Journal of Management Information Systems* 11, no. 3 (Winter 1994–95).

Keil, Mark, and Ramiro Montealegre. "Cutting Your Losses: Extricating Your Organization When a Big Project Goes Awry." *Sloan Management Review* 41, no. 3 (Spring 2000).

Keil, Mark, and Daniel Robey. "Blowing the Whistle on Troubled Software Projects." *Communications of the ACM* 44, no. 4 (April 2001).

Keil, Mark, Bernard C. Y. Tan, Kwok-Kee Wei, Timo Saarinen, Virpi Tuunainen, and Arjen Waassenaar. "A Cross-Cultural

Study on Escalation of Commitment Behavior in Software Projects." *MIS Quarterly* 24, no. 2 (June 2000).

Kelly, Sue, Nicola Gibson, Christopher P. Holland, and Ben Light. "Focus Issue on Legacy Information Systems and Business Process Change: A Business Perspective of Legacy Information Systems." *Communications of the AIS* 2 (July 1999).

Kettinger, William J., and Choong C. Lee. "Understanding the IS-User Divide in IT Innovation." *Communications of the ACM* 45, no.2 (February 2002).

Klein, Gary, James J. Jiang, and Debbie B. Tesch. "Wanted: Project Teams with a Blend of IS Professional Orientations." *Communications of the ACM* 45, no. 6 (June 2002).

Kolb, D. A., and A. L. Frohman. "An Organization Development Approach to Consulting." *Sloan Management Review* 12 (Fall 1970).

Lassila, Kathy S., and James C. Brancheau. "Adoption and Utilization of Commercial Software Packages: Exploring Utilization Equilibria, Transitions, Triggers, and Tracks." *Journal of Management Information Systems* 16, no. 2 (Fall 1999).

Laudon, Kenneth C. "CIOs Beware: Very Large Scale Systems." Center for Research on Information Systems, New York University Stern School of Business, working paper (1989).

Lientz, Bennett P., and E. Burton Swanson. *Software Maintenance Management.* Reading, MA: Addison-Wesley (1980).

Lipin, Steven, and Nikhil Deogun. "Big Mergers of 90s Prove Disappointing to Shareholders." *Wall Street Journal* (October 30, 2000).

Lohse, Gerald L., and Peter Spiller. "Internet Retail Store Design: How the User Interface Influences Traffic and Sales." *Journal of Computer-Mediated Communication* 5, no. 2 (December 1999).

Lucas, Henry C., Jr. *Implementation: The Key to Successful Information Systems.* New York: Columbia University Press (1981).

Mahmood, Mo Adam, Laura Hall, and Daniel Leonard Swanberg, "Factors Affecting Information Technology Usage: A Meta-Analysis of the Empirical Literature." *Journal of Organizational Computing and Electronic Commerce* 11, no. 2 (November 2, 2001)

Markus, M. Lynne, and Robert I. Benjamin. "The Magic Bullet Theory of IT-Enabled Transformation." *Sloan Management Review* (Winter 1997).

Markus, M. Lynne, and Robert I. Benjamin. "Change Agentry—The Next IS Frontier." *MIS Quarterly* 20, no. 4 (December 1996).

Markus, M. Lynne, and Mark Keil. "If We Build It, They Will Come: Designing Information Systems That People Want to Use." *Sloan Management Review* (Summer 1994).

Markus, M. Lynne, Conelis Tanis, and Paul C. van Fenema. "Multisite ERP Implementations." *Communications of the ACM* 43, no. 3 (April 2000).

Matlin, Gerald. "What Is the Value of Investment in Information Systems?" *MIS Quarterly* 13, no. 3 (September 1989).

McDonnell, Sharon. "Putting CRM to Work." *Computerworld* (March 12, 2001).

McFarlan, F. Warren. "Portfolio Approach to Information Systems." *Harvard Business Review* (September–October 1981).

McGrath, Rita Gunther, and Ian C.McMillan. "Assessing Technology Projects Using Real Options Reasoning." *Industrial Research Institute* (2000)

McKeen, James D., and Tor Guimaraes. "Successful Strategies for User Participation in Systems Development." *Journal of Management Information Systems* 14, no. 2 (Fall 1997).

McKinney, Vicki, Kanghyun Yoon, and Fatemeh "Mariam" Zahedi. "The Measurement of Web-Customer Satisfaction: An Expectation and Disconfirmation Approach." *Information Systems Research* 13, no.3 (September 2002).

Mumford, Enid, and Mary Weir. *Computer Systems in Work Design: The ETHICS Method.* New York: John Wiley (1979).

Nambisan, Satish, and Yu-Ming Wang. "Web Technology Adoption and Knowledge Barriers." *Journal of Organizational Computing and Electronic Commerce* 10, no. 2 (2000).

Nedda Gabriela G. Olazabal. "Banking: The IT Paradox." *The McKinsey Quarterly* no. 1 (2002).

Nolan, Richard. "Managing Information Systems by Committee." *Harvard Business Review* (July–August 1982).

Orlikowski, Wanda J., and J. Debra Hofman. "An Improvisational Change Model for Change Management: The Case of Groupware Technologies." *Sloan Management Review* (Winter 1997).

Oz, Effy. "When Professional Standards are Lax: The CONFIRM Failure and Its Lessons." *Communications of the ACM* 37, no. 10 (October 1994).

Palmer, Jonathan W. "Web Site Usability, Design and Performance Metrics." *Information Systems Research* 13, no.3 (September 2002).

Panko, Raymond R. "Is Office Productivity Stagnant?" *MIS Quarterly* 15, no. 2 (June 1991).

Peffers, Ken and Timo Saarinen. "Measuring the Business Value of IT Investments: Inferences from a Study of Senior Bank Executives." *Journal of Organizational Computing and Electronic Commerce* 12, no. 1 (2002).

Rai, Arun, Sandra S. Lang, and Robert B. Welker. "Assessing the Validity of IS Success Models: An Empirical Test and Theoretical Analysis." *Information Systems Research* 13, no. 1 (March 2002).

Rai, Arun, Ravi Patnayakuni, and Nainika Patnayakuni. "Technology Investment and Business Performance." *Communications of the ACM* 40, no. 7 (July 1997).

Randall, Dave, John Hughes, Jon O'Brien, Tom Rodden, Mark Rouncefield, Ian Sommerville, and Peter Tolmie. "Focus Issue on Legacy Information Systems and Business Process Change: Banking on the Old Technology: Understanding the Organisational Context of 'Legacy' Issues." *Communications of the AIS* 2, (July 1999).

Roach, Stephen S. "Industrialization of the Information Economy." New York: Morgan Stanley and Co. (1984).

———. "Making Technology Work." New York: Morgan Stanley and Co. (1993).

———. "Services Under Siege—The Restructuring Imperative." *Harvard Business Review* (September–October 1991).

———. "Technology and the Service Sector." *Technological Forecasting and Social Change* 34, no. 4 (December 1988).

———. "The Hollow Ring of the Productivity Revival." *Harvard Business Review* (November–December 1996).

Robey, Daniel, and M. Lynne Markus. "Rituals in Information System Design." *MIS Quarterly* (March 1984).

Robey, Daniel, Jeanne W. Ross, and Marie-Claude Boudreau. "Learning to Implement Enterprise Systems: An Exploratory Study of the Dialectics of Change." *Journal of Management Information Systems* 19, no. 1 (Summer 2002).

Ross, Jeanne W. and Cynthia M. Beath. "Beyond the Business Case: New Approaches to IT Investment." *Sloan Management Review* 43, no.2 (Winter 2002).

Ryan, Sherry D. and David A. Harrison. "Considering Social Subsystem Costs and Benefits in Information Technology Investment Decisions: A View from the Field on Anticipated Payoffs." *Journal of Management Information Systems* 16, no. 4 (Spring 2000).

Ryan, Sherry D., David A. Harrison, and Lawrence L Schkade. "Information Technology Investment Decisions: When Do Cost and Benefits in the Social Subsystem Matter?" *Journal of Management Information Systems* 19, no. 2 (Fall 2002).

Salkever, Alex. "Cybersecurity's Leaky Dikes." *Business Week* (July 2, 2002), *www.businessweek.com.*

Sarkar, Pushpak. "A Paragon of Quality." *Intelligent Enterprise* (October 2002).

Sauer, Chris, and **Leslie P. Willcocks,** "The Evolution of the Organizational Architect." *Sloan Management Review* 43, no. 3 (Spring 2002).

Scheer, August-Wilhelm, and **Frank Habermann.** "Making ERP a Success." *Communications of the ACM* 43, no. 3 (April 2000).

Schmidt, Roy, Kalle Lyytinen, Mark Keil, and **Paul Cule.** "Identifying Software Project Risks: An International Delphi Study." *Journal of Management Information Systems* 17, no. 4 (Spring 2001)

Schneiderman, Ben. "Universal Usability." *Communications of the ACM* 43, no. 5 (May 2000).

Scott, Judy E., and **Iris Vessey.** "Managing Risks in Enterprise Systems Implementations." *Communications of the ACM* 45, no. 4 (April 2002).

Sia, Siew Kien, and **Boon Siong Neo.** "Reengineering Effectiveness and the Redesign of Organizational Control: A Case Study of the Inland Revenue Authority in Singapore." *Journal of Management Information Systems* 14, no. 1 (Summer 1997).

Sircar, Sumit, Joe L. Turnbow, and **Bijoy Bordoloi.** "A Framework for Assessing the Relationship between Information Technology Investments and Firm Performance." *Journal of Management Information Systems* 16, no. 4 (Spring 2000).

Smith, H. Jeff, Mark Keil, and **Gordon Depledge.** "Keeping Mum as the Project Goes Under." *Journal of Management Information Systems* 18, no. 2 (Fall 2001).

Swanson, E. Burton. *Information System Implementation.* Homewood, IL: Richard D. Irwin (1988).

Tallon, Paul P, Kenneth L. Kraemer, and **Vijay Gurbaxani.** "Executives' Perceptions of the Business Value of Information Technology: A Process-Oriented Approach." *Journal of Management Information Systems* 16, no. 4 (Spring 2000).

Taudes, Alfred, Markus Feurstein, and **Andreas Mild.** "Options Analysis of Software Platform Decisions: A Case Study." *MIS Quarterly* 24, no. 2 (June 2000).

Teng, James T. C., Seung Ryul Jeong, and **Varun Grover.** "Profiling Successful Reengineering Projects." *Communications of the ACM* 41, no. 6 (June 1998).

Thatcher, Matt E., and **Jim R. Oliver.** "The Impact of Technology Investments on a Firm's Production Efficiency, Product Quality, and Productivity." *Journal of Management Information Systems* 18, no. 2 (Fall 2001).

Tornatsky, Louis G., J. D. Eveland, M. G. Boylan, W. A. Hetzner, E. C. Johnson, D. Roitman, and **J. Schneider.** *The Process of Technological Innovation: Reviewing the Literature.* Washington, DC: National Science Foundation (1983).

Truex, Duane P., Richard Baskerville, and **Heinz Klein.** "Growing Systems in Emergent Organizations." *Communications of the ACM* 42, no. 8 (August 1999).

Tyran, Craig K., and **Joey F. George.** "Improving Software Inspections with Group Process Support." *Communications of the ACM* 45, no. 9 (September 2002).

Wastell, David G. "Learning Dysfunctions in Information Systems Development: Overcoming the Social Defenses with Transitional Objects." *MIS Quarterly* 23, no. 1 (December 1999).

Weill, Peter, Mani Subramani, and **Marianne Broadbent.** "Building IT Infrastructure for Strategic Agility." *Sloan Management Review* 44, no. 1 (Fall 2002).

Yin, Robert K. "Life Histories of Innovations: How New Practices Become Routinized." *Public Administration Review* (January–February 1981).

Yu, Larry. "Successful Customer Relationship Management." *Sloan Management Review* 42, no.4 (Summer 2001).

Zhu, Kevin, and **Kenneth L. Kraemer.** "E-Commerce Metrics for Net-Enhanced Organizations: Assessing the Value of e-Commerce to Firm Performance in the Manufacturing Sector." *Information Systems Research* 13, no.3 (September 2002).

CHAPTER 14

Abdel-Hamid, Tarek K. Kishore Sengupta, and **Clint Swett.** "The Impact of Goals on Software Project Management: An Experimental Investigation." *MIS Quarterly* 23, no. 4 (December 1999).

Alberts, David S. "The Economics of Software Quality Assurance." Washington, DC: National Computer Conference, 1976 Proceedings.

Banker, Rajiv D., Srikant M. Datar, Chris F. Kemerer, and **Dani Zweig.** "Software Complexity and Maintenance Costs." *Communications of the ACM* 36, no. 11 (November 1993).

Banker, Rajiv D., and **Chris F. Kemerer.** "Performance Evaluation Metrics in Information Systems Development: A Principal-Agent Model." *Information Systems Research* 3, no. 4 (December 1992).

Banker, Rajiv D., Robert J. Kaufmann, and **Rachna Kumar.** "An Empirical Test of Object-Based Output Measurement Metrics in a Computer-Aided Software Engineering (CASE) Environment." *Journal of Management Information Systems* 8, no. 3 (Winter 1991–1992).

Barthelemy, Jerome. "The Hidden Costs of IT Outsourcing." *Sloan Management Review* (Spring 2001).

Bertin, Michael. "The New Security Threats." *Smart Business Magazine* (February 2001).

Bertino, Elisa, Elena Pagani, Gian Paolo Rossi, and **Pierangela Samarati.** "Protecting Information on the Web." *Communications of the ACM* 43, no.11 (Novemer 2000).

Blackburn, Joseph, Gary Scudder, and **Luk N. Van Wassenhove.** "Concurrent Software Development." *Communications of the ACM* 43, no. 11 (November 2000).

Boehm, Barry W. "Understanding and Controlling Software Costs." *IEEE Transactions on Software Engineering* 14, no. 10 (October 1988).

Chin, Shu-Kai. "High-Confidence Design for Security." *Communications of the ACM* 42, no. 7 (July 1999).

Choy, Manhoi, Hong Va Leong, and **Man Hon Wong.** "Disaster Recovery Techniques for Database Systems." *Communications of the ACM* 43, no. 11 (November 2000).

Corbato, Fernando J. "On Building Systems that Will Fail." *Communications of the ACM* 34, no. 9 (September 1991).

Dekleva, Sasa M. "The Influence of Information Systems Development Approach on Maintenance." *MIS Quarterly* 16, no. 3 (September 1992).

DeMarco, Tom. *Structured Analysis and System Specification.* New York: Yourdon Press (1978).

Dijkstra, E. "Structured Programming." In *Classics in Software Engineering,* edited by Edward Nash Yourdon. New York: Yourdon Press (1979).

Domges, Rolf, and **Klaus Pohl.** "Adapting Traceability Environments to Project-Specific Needs." *Communications of the ACM* 41, no. 12 (December 1998).

Durst, Robert, Terrence Champion, Brian Witten, Eric Miller, and **Luigi Spagnuolo.** "Testing and Evaluating Computer Intrusion Detection Systems." *Communications of the ACM* 42, no. 7 (July 1999).

Dutta, Soumitra, Luk N. Van Wassenhove, and **Selvan Kulandaiswamy.** "Benchmarking European Software Management Practices." *Communications of the ACM* 41, no. 6 (June 1998).

Forrest, Stephanie, Steven A. Hofmeyr, and **Anil Somayaji.** "Computer Immunology." *Communications of the ACM* 40, no. 10 (October 1997).

Fraser, Martin D., and **Vijay K. Vaishnavi.** "A Formal Specifications Maturity Model." *Communications of the ACM* 40, no. 12 (December 1997).

Gane, Chris, and **Trish Sarson.** *Structured Systems Analysis: Tools and Techniques.* Englewood Cliffs, NJ: Prentice Hall (1979).

Ghosh, Anup K., and **Jeffrey M. Voas.** "Inoculating Software for Survivability." *Communications of the ACM 42,* no. 7 (July 1999).

Ghosh, Anup K., and **Tara M. Swaminatha.** "Software Security and Privacy Risks in Mobile E-Commerce." *Communications of the ACM* 44, no. 2 (February 2001).

Goan, Terrance. "A Cop on the Beat: Collecting and Appraising Intrusion Evidence." *Communications of the ACM* 42, no. 7 (July 1999).

Jajoda, Sushil, Catherine D. McCollum, and **Paul Ammann.** "Trusted Recovery." *Communications of the ACM* 42, no. 7 (July 1999).

Jarzabek, Stan, and **Riri Huang.** "The Case for User-Centered CASE Tools." *Communications of the ACM* 41, no. 8 (August 1998).

Johnson, Philip M. "Reengineering Inspection." *Communications of the ACM* 41, no. 2 (February 1998).

Joshi, James B.D., Walid G. Aref, Arif Ghafoor, and **Eugene H. Spafford.** "Security Models for Web-Based Applications." *Communications of the ACM* 44, no. 2 (February 2001).

Kaplan, David, Ramayya Krishnan, Rema Padman, and **James Peters.** "Assessing Data Quality in Accounting Information Systems." *Communications of the ACM* 41, no. 2 (February 1998).

Kemerer, Chris F. "Progress, Obstacles, and Opportunities in Software Engineering Economics." *Communications of the ACM* 41, no. 8 (August 1998).

Klein, Barbara D., Dale L. Goodhue, and **Gordon B. Davis.** "Can Humans Detect Errors in Data?" *MIS Quarterly* 21, no. 2 (June 1997).

Laudon, Kenneth C. "Data Quality and Due Process in Large Interorganizational Record Systems." *Communications of the ACM* 29 (January 1986a).

———. *Dossier Society: Value Choices in the Design of National Information Systems.* New York: Columbia University Press (1986b).

Lientz, Bennett P., and **E. Burton Swanson.** *Software Maintenance Management.* Reading, MA: Addison-Wesley (1980).

Littlewood, Bev, and **Lorenzo Strigini.** "The Risks of Software." *Scientific American* 267, no. 5 (November 1992).

———. "Validation of Ultra-high Dependability for Software-Based Systems." *Communications of the ACM* 36, no. 11 (November 1993).

Marer, Eva, and **Patrick Thibodeau.** "Companies Confront Rising Network Threats." *Datamation* (July 2, 2001).

Martin, James, and **Carma McClure.** *Structured Techniques: The Basis of CASE.* Englewood Cliffs, NJ: Prentice Hall (1988).

Mazzucchelli, Louis. "Structured Analysis Can Streamline Software Design." *Computerworld* (December 9, 1985).

Needham, Roger M. "Denial of Service: An Example." *Communications of the ACM* 37, no. 11 (November 1994).

Nerson, Jean-Marc. "Applying Object-Oriented Analysis and Design." *Communications of the ACM* 35, no. 9 (September 1992).

Neumann, Peter G. "Risks Considered Global(ly)." *Communications of the ACM* 35, no. 1 (January 1993).

Oppliger, Rolf. "Internet Security, Firewalls, and Beyond." *Communications of the ACM* 40, no.7 (May 1997).

Orr, Kenneth. "Data Quality and Systems Theory." *Communications of the ACM* 41, no. 2 (February 1998).

Parsons, Jeffrey, and **Yair Wand.** "Using Objects for Systems Analysis." *Communications of the ACM* 40, no. 12 (December 1997).

Rainer, Rex Kelley, Jr., Charles A. Snyder, and **Houston H. Carr.** "Risk Analysis for Information Technology." *Journal of Management Information Systems* 8, no. 1 (Summer 1991).

Ravichandran, T., and **Arun Rai.** "Total Quality Management in Information Systems Development." *Journal of Management Information Systems* 16, no. 3 (Winter 1999–2000).

Redman, Thomas. "The Impact of Poor Data Quality on the Typical Enterprise." *Communications of the ACM* 41, no. 2 (February 1998).

Salkever, Alex. "Cybersecurity's Leaky Dikes" *BusinessWeek* (July 2, 2002), *www.businessweek.com.*

Sarkar, Pushpak. "A Paragon of Quality." *Intelligent Enterprise* (October 2002).

Scott, Louise, Levente Horvath, and **Donald Day.** "Characterizing CASE Constraints." *Communications of the ACM* 43, no. 11 (November 2000).

Segev, Arie, Janna Porra, and **Malu Roldan.** "Internet Security and the Case of Bank of America." *Communications of the ACM* 41, no. 10 (October 1998).

Sharma, Srinarayan, and **Arun Rai.** "CASE Deployment in IS Organizations." *Communications of the ACM* 43, no. 1 (January 2000).

Slaughter, Sandra A., Donald E. Harter, and **Mayuram S. Krishnan.** "Evaluating the Cost of Software Quality." *Communications of the ACM* 41, no. 8 (August 1998).

Stillerman, Matthew, Carla Marceau, and **Maureen Stillman.** "Intrusion Detection for Distributed Applications." *Communications of the ACM 42,* no. 7 (July 1999).

Straub, Detmar W., and **Richard J. Welke.** "Coping with Systems Risk: Security Planning Models for Management Decision Making." *MIS Quarterly* 22, no. 4 (December 1998).

Strong, Diane M., Yang W. Lee, and **Richard Y. Wang.** "Data Quality in Context." *Communications of the ACM* 40, no. 5 (May 1997).

Swanson, Kent, Dave McComb, Jill Smith, and **Don McCubbrey.** "The Application Software Factory: Applying Total Quality Techniques to Systems Development." *MIS Quarterly* 15, no. 4 (December 1991).

Tayi, Giri Kumar, and **Donald P. Ballou.** "Examining Data Quality." *Communications of the ACM* 41, no. 2 (February 1998).

Tyran, Craig K. and **Joey F. George.** "Improving Software Inspections with Group Process Support." *Communications of the ACM* 45, no. 9 (September 2002).

Viega, John, Tadayoshi Koho, and **Bruce Potter.** "Trust (and Mistrust) in Secure Applications." *Communications of the ACM* 44, no. 2 (February 2001).

Wand, Yair, and **Richard Y. Wang.** "Anchoring Data Quality Dimensions in Ontological Foundations." *Communications of the ACM* 39, no. 11 (November 1996).

Wang, Richard Y., Yang W. Lee, Leo L. Pipino, and **Diane M. Strong.** "Manage Your Information as a Product." *Sloan Management Review* 39, no. 4 (Summer 1998).

Wang, Richard. "A Product Perspective on Total Data Quality Management." *Communications of the ACM* 41, no. 2 (February 1998).

Weber, Ron. *Information Systems Control and Audit.* New York: McGraw-Hill (1999).

Wessel, David. "NASA Explores Future of Software." *Wall Street Journal* (April 26, 2001.)

Ye, Nong, Joseph Giordano, and **John Feldman.** "A Process Control Approach to Cyber Attack Detection." *Communications of the ACM* 44, no. 8 (August 2001).

Yourdon, Edward, and **L. L. Constantine.** *Structured Design.* New York: Yourdon Press (1978).

Zhou, Jianying. "Achieving Fair Nonrepudiation in Electronic Transactions." *Journal of Organizational Computing and Electronic Commerce* 11, no. 4 (2001).

Zviran, Moshe and **William J. Haga.** "Password Security: An Empirical Study." *Journal of Management Information Systems* 15, no. 4 (Spring 1999).

CHAPTER 15

Agarwal, P. K. "Building India's National Internet Backbone." *Communications of the ACM* 42, no. 6 (June 1999).

Blanning, Robert W. "Establishing a Corporate Presence on the Internet in Singapore." *Journal of Organizational Computing and Electronic Commerce* 9, no. 1 (1999).

Burkhardt, Grey E., Seymour E. Goodman, Arun Mehta, and **Larry Press.** "The Internet in India: Better Times Ahead?" *Communications of the ACM* 41, no. 11 (November 1998).

Chabrow, Eric. "Supply Chains Go Global." *InformationWeek* (April 3, 2000).

Chismar, William G., and **Laku Chidambaram.** "Telecommunications and the Structuring of U.S. Multinational Corporations." *International Information Systems* 1, no. 4 (October 1992).

Cox, Butler. *Globalization: The IT Challenge.* Sunnyvale, CA: Amdahl Executive Institute (1991).

Davison, Robert. "Cultural Complications of ERP." *Communications of the ACM* 45, no. 7 (July 2002).

Deans, Candace P., and **Michael J. Kane.** *International Dimensions of Information Systems and Technology.* Boston, MA: PWS-Kent (1992).

Deans, Candace P., Kirk R. Karwan, Martin D. Goslar, David A. Ricks, and **Brian Toyne.** "Key International Issues in U.S.-Based Multinational Corporations." *Journal of Management Information Systems* 7, no. 4 (Spring 1991).

DePalma, Anthony. "Getting There is Challenge for Latin American E-Tailing." *New York Times* (August 17, 2000).

Dutta, Amitava. "Telecommunications Infrastructure in Developing Nations." *International Information Systems* 1, no. 3 (July 1992).

Ein-Dor, Philip, Seymour E. Goodman, and **Peter Wolcott.** "From Via Maris to Electronic Highway: The Internet in Canaan." *Communications of the ACM* 43, no. 7 (July 2000).

Eckholm, Erik. ". . . And Click Here for China." *New York Times* (August 4, 2002).

Farhoomand, Ali, Virpi Kristiina Tuunainen, and **Lester W. Yee.** "Barrier to Global Electronic Commerce: A Cross-Country Study of Hong Kong and Finland." *Journal of Organizational Computing and Electronic Commerce* 10, no. 1 (2000).

Ives, Blake, and **Sirkka Jarvenpaa.** "Applications of Global Information Technology: Key Issues for Management." *MIS Quarterly* 15, no. 1 (March 1991).

———. "Global Business Drivers: Aligning Information Technology to Global Business Strategy." *IBM Systems Journal* 32, no. 1 (1993).

———. "Global Information Technology: Some Lessons from Practice." *International Information Systems* 1, no. 3 (July 1992).

Jarvenpaa, Sirkka L., Kathleen Knoll, and **Dorothy Leidner.** "Is Anybody Out There? Antecedents of Trust in Global Virtual Teams." *Journal of Management Information Systems* 14, no. 4 (Spring 1998).

Karin, Jahangir, and **Benn R. Konsynski.** "Globalization and Information Management Strategies." *Journal of Management Information Systems* 7 (Spring 1991).

Keen, Peter. *Shaping the Future.* Cambridge, MA: Harvard Business School Press (1991).

Kibati, Mugo, and **Donyaprueth Krairit.** "Building India's National Internet Backbone." *Communications of the ACM* 42, no. 6 (June 1999).

King, William R., and **Vikram Sethi.** "An Empirical Analysis of the Organization of Transnational Information Systems." *Journal of Management Information Systems* 15, no. 4 (Spring 1999).

Lai, Vincent S., and **Wingyan Chung.** "Managing International Data Communication." *Communications of the ACM* 45, no.3 (March 2002).

Levy, David. "Lean Production in an International Supply Chain." *Sloan Management Review* (Winter 1997).

Mannheim, Marvin L. "Global Information Technology: Issues and Strategic Opportunities." *International Information Systems* 1, no. 1 (January 1992).

Neumann, Seev. "Issues and Opportunities in International Information Systems." *International Information Systems* 1, no. 4 (October 1992).

Palvia, Shailendra, Prashant Palvia, and **Ronald Zigli,** eds. *The Global Issues of Information Technology Management.* Harrisburg, PA: Idea Group Publishing (1992).

Petrazzini, Ben, and **Mugo Kibati.** "The Internet in Developing Countries." *Communications of the ACM* 42, no. 6 (June 1999).

Quelch, John A., and **Lisa R. Klein.** "The Internet and International Marketing." *Sloan Management Review* (Spring 1996).

Roche, Edward M. *Managing Information Technology in Multinational Corporations.* New York: Macmillan (1992).

Smith, Craig S. "Ambivalence in China on Expanding Net Access." *New York Times* (August 11, 2000).

Soh, Christina, Sia Siew Kien, and **Joanne Tay-Yap.** "Cultural Fits and Misfits: Is ERP a Universal Solution?" *Communications of the ACM* 43, no. 3 (April 2000).

Steinbart, Paul John, and **Ravinder Nath.** "Problems and Issues in the Management of International Data Networks." *MIS Quarterly* 16, no. 1 (March 1992).

Straub, Detmar W. "The Effect of Culture on IT Diffusion: E-Mail and FAX in Japan and the U.S." *Information Systems Research* 5, no. 1 (March 1994).

Tan, Zixiang (Alex), Milton Mueller, and **Will Foster.** "China's New Internet Regulations: Two Steps Forward, One Step Backward." *Communications of the ACM* 40, no. 12 (December 1997).

Tan, Zixiang, William Foster, and **Seymour Goodman.** "China's State-Coordinated Internet Infrastructure." *Communications of the ACM* 42, no. 6 (June 1999).

Tractinsky, Noam, and **Sirkka L. Jarvenpaa.** "Information Systems Design Decisions in a Global Versus Domestic Context." *MIS Quarterly* 19, no. 4 (December 1995).

Walsham, Geoffrey, and **Sundeys Sahay.** "GIS and District Level Administration in India: Problems and Opportunities." *MIS Quarterly* 23, no. 1 (March 1999).

Watson, Richard T., Gigi G. Kelly, Robert D. Galliers, and **James C. Brancheau.** "Key Issues in Information Systems Management: An International Perspective." *Journal of Management Information Systems* 13, no. 4 (Spring 1997).

Wong, Poh-Kam. "Leveraging the Global Information Revolution for Economic Development: Singapore's Evolving Information Industry Strategy." *Information Systems Research* 9, no. 4 (December 1998).

Wysocki, Bernard. "The Big Bang." *Wall Street Journal* (January 1, 2000).

INDEXES

ORGANIZATIONS INDEX

INTERNATIONAL ORGANIZATIONS INDEX

SUBJECT INDEX

PHOTO AND SCREEN SHOT CREDITS

CHAPTER 11

351 "Cargo Optimization At Continental Airlines" graphic from "Setting the Price Right" by Marc L. Songini from COMPUTERWORLD, June 3, 2002. Copyright © 2002. Reprinted by permission of Reprint Management Services.

361 Courtesy of Cathy Spahn

CHAPTER 12

388 Spencer Grant/Photo Edit

390 Royalty Free/Corbis

398 From APPLICATION DEVELOPMENT WITH-OUT PROGRAMMERS by James Martin. Copyright © 1982 by James Martin. Reprinted by permission of Prentice Hall, Inc., Upper Saddle River, NJ.

404 Reprinted by permission of HARVARD BUSINESS REVIEW. From "Your Next IT Strategy" by John Hagel III and John Steeley Brown, October 2001, p. 107. Copyright © 2001 by the Harvard Business School Publishing Corporation; all rights reserved.

CHAPTER 13

435 © John Henley/Corbis

CHAPTER 14

464 From "Digital Certificates" Technology Quick Study by Ann Harrison in COMPUTERWORLD, August 14, 2000. Copyright © 2000. Reprinted by permission of Reprint Management Services.

466 © Chuck Savage/Corbis

CHAPTER 15

486 Charles Thatcher/Stone/Getty Images

493 From Managing Information Technology in Multinational Corporations by Edward M. Roche, © 1993. Reprinted by permission of Pearson Education, Inc., Upper Saddle River, NJ.

CONTRIBUTORS

CANADA
Deborah Compeau, *University of Western Ontario*
V. Joseph Compeau, *University of Western Ontario*

HONG KONG
Ali Farhoomand, *University of Hong Kong*
Amir Hoosain, *University of Hong Kong*
Shamza Khan, *University of Hong Kong*
Dennis Kira, *University of Hong Kong*

SWITZERLAND
Donald A. Marchand, *International Institute for Management Development*
Katarina Paddack, International Institute for *Management Development*
Gerhard Schwabe, *University of Zurich*

CONSULTANTS

AUSTRALIA
Robert MacGregor, *University of Wollongong*
Alan Underwood, *Queensland University of Technology*

CANADA
Wynne W. Chin, *University of Calgary*
Len Fertuck, *University of Toronto*
Robert C. Goldstein, *University of British Columbia*
Rebecca Grant, *University of Victoria*
Kevin Leonard, *Wilfrid Laurier University*
Anne B. Pidduck, *University of Waterloo*

GREECE
Anastasios V. Katos, *University of Macedonia*

HONG KONG
Enoch Tse, *Hong Kong Baptist University*

INDIA
Sanjiv D. Vaidya, *Indian Institute of Management, Calcutta*

ISRAEL
Phillip Ein-Dor, *Tel-Aviv University*
Peretz Shoval, *Ben Gurion University*

MEXICO
Noe Urzua Bustamante, *Universidad Tecnológica de México*

NETHERLANDS
E.O. de Brock, *University of Groningen*
Theo Thiadens, *University of Twente*
Charles Van Der Mast, *Delft University of Technology*

PUERTO RICO, Commonwealth of the United States
Brunilda Marrero, *University of Puerto Rico*

SWEDEN
Mats Daniels, *Uppsala University*

SWITZERLAND
Andrew C. Boynton, *International Institute for Management Development*

UNITED KINGDOM

ENGLAND
G.R. Hidderley, *University of Central England, Birmingham*
Christopher Kimble, *University of York*
Jonathan Liebenau, *London School of Economics and Political Science*
Kecheng Liu, *Staffordshire University*

SCOTLAND
William N. Dyer, *Falkirk College of Technology*

UNITED STATES OF AMERICA

Tom Abraham, *Kean University*
Evans Adams, *Fort Lewis College*
Roy Alvarez, *Cornell University*
Chandra S. Amaravadi, *Western Illinois University*
Beverly Amer, *Northern Arizona University*
John Anderson, *Northeastern State University*
Solomon Antony, *Oakland University*
Arben Asllani, *Faytetteville State University*
Jon W. Beard, *University of Richmond*
Michel Benaroch, *Syracuse University*
Kimberly Cass, *University of Redlands*
P.C. Chu, *Ohio State University, Columbus*
Lynn Collen, *St. Cloud State University*
John Dalphin, *SUNY Potsdam*
Frank S. Davis, Jr., *Bloomsburg University*
William DeLone, *American University*
John DiRenzo, *Cameron University*
Vasant Dhar, *New York University*
Laurie Eakins, *East Carolina University*
David Fickbohm, *Golden Gate University*
Robert A. Fleck, Jr., *Columbus College*
William B. Fredenberger, *Valdosta State University*
Bob Fulkerth, *Golden Gate University*
Mark A. Fuller, *Baylor University*
Minnie Ghent, *Florida Atlantic University*
Amita Goyal, *Virginia Commonwealth University*
Jeet Gupta, *Ball State University*
Vijay Gurbaxani, *University of California, Irvine*
Rassule Hadidi, *University of Illinois, Springfield*
William L. Harrison, *Oregon State University*
Albert M. Hayashi, *Loyola Marymount University*
Anthony Hendrickson, *Iowa State*
Rick Hicks, *Florida Atlantic University*
Marianne Hill, *Furman University*
Bart Hodge, *Virginia Commonwealth University*
Jack Hogue, *University of North Carolina, Charlotte*
Carolyn Jacobson, *Marymount University*
George Jacobson, *California State University, Los Angeles*
Murray Jennex, *University of Phoenix*
Rob Kauffman, *University of Minnesota*
Robert W. Key, *University of Phoenix*
Stephen Klein, *Ramapo College*
Virginia Kleist, *West Virginia State University*
Rob Kling, *Indiana University, Bloomington*
Cenk Kocas, *Michigan State University*
Brian Kovar, *Kansas State University*
Roger Letts, *Fairleigh Dickinson University*
Teresita Leyell, *Washburn University*
Susan K. Lippert, *George Washington University*
Carl Longnecker, *Loyola University*
Treise Lynn, *Wingate University*

Jane Mackay, *Texas Christian University*
Efrem G. Mallach, *University of Massachusetts, Lowell*
Gary Margot, *Ashland University*
Kipp Martin, *University of Chicago*
Richard O. Mason, *Southern Methodist University*
Khris McAlister, *University of Alabama, Birmingham*
Ronald E. McGaughey, *Arkansas Tech University*
Roger McHaney, *Kansas State University*
Patricia McQuaid, *California Polytechnic State Institute*
Lisa Miller, *University of Central Oklahoma*
Steve Newberry, *Tarleton College*
Denise Nitterhouse, *DePaul University*
Graham Peace, *Duquesne University*
Leah R. Pietron, *University of Nebraska*
Jack Powell, *University of South Dakota*
Leonard Presby, *William Patterson University*
Sheizaf Rafaeli, *University of Michigan*
Sasan Rahmatian, *California State University, Fresno*
Mary E. Rasley, *Lehigh Carbon Community College*
Brian Reithel, *University of Mississippi*
James Riha, *Northern Illinois University*
Stephanie Robbins, *University of North Carolina, Charlotte*
Marcel Robelis, *University of North Dakota*
Edward M. Roche *Barraclough Ltd.*
Paula Ruby, *Arkansas State University*
Joko W. Saputro, *University of Wisconsin, Madison*
Naveed Saleem, *University of Houston, Clear Lake*
David Scanlan, *California State University, Sacramento*
Werner Schenk, *University of Rochester*
Cort Schlichting, *Spring Hill College*
Ivan J. Singer, *University of Hartford*
Rod Sink, *Northern Illinois University*
Jill Y. Smith, *University of Denver*
Kathy Stevens, *Merrimack College*
Dennis Strouble, *Bowling Green State University*
E. Burton Swanson, *University of California, Los Angeles*
John L. Swearingen, *Bryant College*
Bernadette Szajna, *Texas Christian University*
John Tarjan, *California State University, Bakersfield*
Pam Taylor, *University of Tennessee at Chattanooga*
Jennifer Thomas, *Pace University*
Kranti Toraskar, *Penn State University*
Duane Truex, *Georgia State University*
B.S. Vijayaraman, *University of Akron*
Patrick J. Walsh, *State University of New York, Binghamton*
Diane Walz, *University of Texas, San Antonio*
Peter Weill, *Massachusetts Institute of Technology*
Frederick Wheeler, *University of Maryland, University College*
Kathie Wright, *Purdue University*
Erma Wood, *University of Arkansas, Little Rock*
Bee K.Yew, *Arkansas Tech University*
Yue Zhang, *Langston University*